# To the Uttermost Pa

This volume presents the key role played by law for Europe's global hegemony during 1300–1870. By connecting public sovereignty with property rights, it demonstrates how law enabled the concurrent development of political statehood and capitalism in Europe and beyond. Europe's global power has not been the power of princes or capital alone, but always a specific configuration of the two. To understand this power, the book shows how the relationship of sovereignty and property has its basis in local legal cultures – French, Spanish, British and German. The employment of law in foreign lands has not been a monopoly of lawyers, however, but has been practiced by theologians, political commentators, philosophers and economists. The specific relationship between public and private power has depended greatly on which type of expertise has been regarded as authoritative in the relevant context.

Professor Martti Koskenniemi is a leading critical scholar in the theory and history of international law. His works engage with themes discussed by lawyers, historians and international relations scholars across the world. He has held visiting professorships at many of world's leading universities. He is a Corresponding Fellow of the British Academy and a Member of American Academy of Arts and Sciences.

# To the Uttermost Parts of the Earth

## Legal Imagination and International Power, 1300–1870

MARTTI KOSKENNIEMI

CAMBRIDGE
UNIVERSITY PRESS

**CAMBRIDGE**
**UNIVERSITY PRESS**

University Printing House, Cambridge CB2 8BS, United Kingdom

One Liberty Plaza, 20th Floor, New York, NY 10006, USA

477 Williamstown Road, Port Melbourne, VIC 3207, Australia

314–321, 3rd Floor, Plot 3, Splendor Forum, Jasola District Centre, New Delhi – 110025, India

103 Penang Road, #05–06/07, Visioncrest Commercial, Singapore 238467

Cambridge University Press is part of the University of Cambridge.

It furthers the University's mission by disseminating knowledge in the pursuit of education, learning, and research at the highest international levels of excellence.

www.cambridge.org
Information on this title: www.cambridge.org/9780521768597
DOI: 10.1017/9781139019774



First published 2021

Printed in the United Kingdom by TJ Books Limited, Padstow Cornwall

*A catalogue record for this publication is available from the British Library.*

*Library of Congress Cataloging-in-Publication Data*
Names: Koskenniemi, Martti, author.
Title: To the uttermost parts of the earth : legal imagination and international power, 1300-1870 / Martti Koskenniemi, University of Helsinki.
Description: Cambridge, United Kingdom ; New York, NY : Cambridge University Press, 2021. | Includes bibliographical references and index.
Identifiers: LCCN 2020039508 (print) | LCCN 2020039509 (ebook) | ISBN 9780521768597 (hardback) | ISBN 9780521745345 (paperback) | ISBN 9781139019774 (epub)
Subjects: LCSH: International law–History. | Rule of law–History. | Religion and law–History. | Natural law–History. | Grotius, Hugo, 1583-1645.
Classification: LCC KZ1242 .K678 2021 (print) | LCC KZ1242 (ebook) | DDC 341.01–dc23
LC record available at https://lccn.loc.gov/2020039508
LC ebook record available at https://lccn.loc.gov/2020039509

ISBN 978-0-521-76859-7 Hardback
ISBN 978-0-521-74534-5 Paperback

You are to be witnesses unto me both in Jerusalem, and in all Judea, and in Samaria, and unto the uttermost parts of the earth.

John Donne, Sermon to the Virginia Company,
13 November 1622. In Donne, *Works*, VI, 241,
quoting Acts: 1:8 (King James version)

# *Contents*

# *Acknowledgements*

These chapters have travelled with me for a very long time during which I have benefited from the intellectual inspiration, assistance and criticism of a vast number of friends, colleagues and students. It is utterly impossible for me to mention all of them, or even name all the events, formal and informal, where these chapters, or parts of them, have been presented and received an unfailingly sympathetic, including critical, attention. The standard of critical legal scholarship set by David Kennedy and Anne Orford remains unsurpassed, and their writings and friendship have guided me throughout. Entering early modern political thought as an amateur, I learned enormously from discussions with Annabel Brett, while Michael Stolleis opened to me the palatial world of German public law that I still think provides the historical frame for much of international law as we know it. The respective chapters could not have been written without my coming to know them and their work.

My base in Helsinki has continued to offer a rare atmosphere of friendship and intellectual stimulation. Key interlocutors have included Jan Klabbers, Nanna Klabbers, Monica García-Salmones, Lauri Hannikainen, Ville Kari, Päivi Leino-Sandberg, Tommi Lindfors, Ketino Minashvili, Pekka Niemelä, Jarna Petman, Pamela Slotte, Ukri Soirila, Immi Tallgren and Taina Tuori. Visitors and graduate students in Helsinki have included Arnulf Becker-Lorca, Martin Björklund, Yifeng Cheng, Katja Creutz, Elisabetta Fiocchi Malaspina, Rotem Giladi, Janis Grzybowski, Miia Halme-Tuomisaari, Daniel Joyce, Katja Keinänen, Magdalena Kmak, Anne-Charlotte Martineau, Parvathi Menon, Reut Paz, Alan Tzvika Nissel, Alberto Rinaldi, Adriane Sanctis, Sahib Singh, Maria Varaki and Kangle

Zhang. I have an enormous debt of gratitude to the successive coordinators of the Erik Castrén Institute, Åsa Wallendahl, Mari Taskinen, Sanna Villikka and Anna van der Velde, for the good cheer and skill with which they have managed the institute during my long periods of absence.

In the course of these years, I was part of two large Helsinki-based research projects in history and international law. In the European Research Council-funded "Europe Between Revolution and Reaction" (EReRe, 2009–2013) I had the very good fortune of coming to know my co-director Bo Stråth and having intensive debates, conferences and seminars with Adrian Brisku, Kelly Grotke, Thomas Hopkins, Liliana Obregón, Francisco Ortega, Markus J. Prutsch and Minna Vainio as well as a great number of visitors at our many workshops in Helsinki and elsewhere. The Finnish Academy-financed "History of International Law: Religion and Empire" (2013–2017) offered an occasion to cooperate with the imaginative group of researchers that included Paolo Amorosa, Monica García-Salmones, Manuel Jimenez Fonseca and Walter Rech, again with many visitors spending more or less time with our project.

My encounter with new critical work in international law has been channelled over many years through the Institute of Global Law and Policy (IGLP), directed by David Kennedy. That association has been a centre of intellectual fireworks among friends such as Antony Anghie, Dan Danielsen, Dennis Davis, Justin Desautels-Stein, Karen Engle, Luis Eslava, Jorge Esquirol, Michael Fakhri, Günter Frankenberg, Chris Gevers, John Haskell, Janet Halley, Sheila Jasanoff, Duncan Kennedy, Andrew Lang, Vasuki Nesiah, Rose Parfitt, Ileana Porras, Balakhrisnan Rajagopal, Nikolås Rajkovic, Teemu Ruskola, Alvaro Santos, Hani Sayed, Chantal Thomas, Umut Özsu and many others. Another long-standing connection has been with New York University School of Law where I have lectured from 1997 to some of the world's most interesting students. Co-teaching with the late Thomas M. Franck was both a privilege and great pleasure. I am grateful for having come to know that most generous and warm-hearted man. With Benedict Kingsbury we have long-standing discussions on how to expand international law; in 2014 he opened his home at Salt Lake City for an intensive two-day seminar on the history of international law. NYU has been a context of ongoing conversations with Philip Alston, Gráinne de Burca, Stefanos Geroulanos, David Golove, Daniel Hulsebosch, Mattias Kumm, Karin Loevy and Joseph Weiler. Dinners with Nathaniel Berman nourished way beyond the food, and getting to know Francesca Iurlaro in 2019 redirected my understanding of Gentili. I am thankful for Noah Rosenblum for discussions and hospitality on a Thanksgiving. Many thanks to Colleen Johnson, Theresa Alison and Tafadzwa Pasipanodya for superb assistance at different stages of the project. Among NYU students turned into colleagues and friends I should mention Oliver Barsalou, Megan Donaldson, Sasha Khrebtukova, Doreen Lustig and Guy Sinclair all of whom have taught me a great deal about how to study the history of international law critically.

A Professorial Fellowship at Melbourne Law School in 2016–2019 provided another inspirational context for this book; it taught me what it was to teach a class for eight hours in a row, fortunately sharing that experience with Frédéric Mégret. Anne Orford's Laureate Project was surely the liveliest centre of critical international law in the world. Its superb group included Fabia Veçoso, Ntina Tzouvala, Luis Bogliolo, Marnie Lloyd, Sebastian Machado and Anna Saunders. Other Melbourne friends include Jenny Beard, Hilary Charlesworth, Maddie Chiam, Bruce Oswald, Sundhya Pahuja, Andrew Roberts and Margaret Young.

I began this work as Goodhart Professor of Legal Science at the University of Cambridge in 2008–2009 where my host was James Crawford, and I found myself running between the Lauterpacht Centre and the magnificent resources of the University Library. Chapter 2 received its initial form through an invitation to University of Toronto where I have continued to benefit from discussions with Karen Knop, Kerry Rittich, Robert Wai and others. In 2011 I was appointed to the Peace of Utrecht Chair at the University of Utrecht with Rosi Braidotti hosting me at her lively Centre of the Humanities. A Centennial Professorship at the London School of Economics in 2012–2015 allowed me to enjoy cooperating, once again, with Susan Marks. Nehal Bhuta invited me to the European University Institute in Florence in 2014 to discuss the early versions of some of these chapters with Annabel Brett, Regina Grafe, Pablo Kalmanowitz, Duncan Kelly, Martin Loughlin, Karuna Mantena, Anne Peters and Simone Zurbruchen. Many of their insights have found their way into this book. In Germany, the Max Planck Institute for Foreign and International Law with its duo of directors, Anne Peters and Armin von Bogdandy, has always provided an excellent forum for debates. These peaked in an intensive three-day master class in 2015. In the autumn of that same year I spent a couple of delightful months at the Centrum Geschichte des Wissens at ETH University in Zurich where Monika Domman, Svenja Goltermann and Lutz Wingert offered an intellectually stimulating environment that included a talk on law and force at the Cabaret Voltaire. Conversations with the French community of scholars over the years have involved Emmanuelle Jouannet, Julie Saada and Mikhail Xifarras; the history aspect of those debates peaked in a series of lectures in 2018 at the École Normale Supérieure where I benefited from discussions with my host Jean-Louis Halpérin as well as my former student and now friend and colleague, Anne-Charlotte Martineau.

Other places where these chapters have been presented in talks or seminars have included (in broadly chronological order) the universities of Göttingen, Zaragoza, Birzeit, Macerata, Sao Paulo (USP), Graduate Institute of International Affairs, Geneva, the universities of Madrid, Belgrade, Harvard Law School, Columbia University Law School, the universities of Oslo, McGill, Peking, Temple (Philadelphia), Glasgow, Brasilia (UnB), Queen Mary College London, the universities of Kent (Canterbury and Brussels), Ghent, Moscow (HSE University), Lisbon, Gothenburg, Université de Québec à Montréal (UQAM), the universities of Bologna, Milan, Cambridge, Chicago, Bogota, Tel Aviv, Aix-en-Provence and Wellington. Lectures and seminars were also given at the Irish Centre of Human Rights in Galway, the Ludwig Wittgenstein Society at Kirchberg, the Cluster of Excellence, "Normative Orders", at the University of Frankfurt, the Centro internazionale di studi gentiliani in San Ginesio and the Minerva Centre at Hebrew University. I am thankful for my hosts Christian Calliess, Yolanda Gamarra, Luigi Lacchè, Alberto do Amaral and Fabia Veçoso, Vincent Chetail, Jeffrey Dunoff, Akbar Rasulov and Christian Tams, Yifeng Chen, George Bandeira Galindo and Marcelo Neves, Quentin Skinner and Georgios Varouxakis, Harm Schepel, Maria Drakopoulou and Luis Eslava, Alex Lorite and Rémi Bachand, Trisha Rajput, Frderick Dhont and Tom Ruys, Vera Rusinova and Maria Issaieva, Lorenzo Gradoni and Gustavo Gozzi, Pedro de Freitas, Pedro Barbas Homem and Ana Fouto, Luigi Crema and Francesca Iurlaro, Bill Schabas, Klaus Günther, Jennifer Pitts, Eyal Benvenisti, Tomer Broude, Hanoch Dagan, Ludovic Hennebel and Mark Hickford. A special event was the launch of a book of readings of my texts edited by Marieke de Hoon, Wouter Werner and Alexis Galán at Bocconi University in 2017. Other friends and colleagues with whom these chapters have been discussed include David Armitage, Lauren Benton, Jochen von Bernstorff, Luca Bonadiman, Katherine

Brölmann, Anthony Carty, Edward Cavanagh, Florian Couveinhes Matsumoto, Matt Craven, Jean D'Aspremont, Oliver Diggelmann, Thomas Duve, Andrew Fitzmaurice, Stella Ghervas, Aeyal Gross, Peter Haggenmacher, Mamadou Hébie, Ivana Isailovic, Harri Kalimo, Liisi Keedus, Alexandra Kemmerer, Outi Korhonen, Dino Kritsiotis, Carl Landauer, Randall Lesaffer, Lauri Mälksoo, Paul McHugh, Samuel Moyn, Janne Nijman, Gregor Noll, Sarah Nouwen, Luigi Nuzzo, Heikki Pihlajamäki, Surabhi Ranganathan, Ignacio de la Rasilla del Moral, Love Rönnelid, Nahed Samour, Gerry Simpson, Benjamin Straumann, Benno Teschke, Grigory Vaypan, Milos Vec and Pål Wrange.

Despite all such (and many other) contacts, composing a work like this is a lonely affair. Therefore I am hugely grateful to Maria José Belmonte Sanchez for having assisted me with the footnotes and collecting the bibliography with skill and enthusiasm. Finola O'Sullivan at Cambridge University Press was unfailing in her faith in the project and in her patience with seeing the submission of the manuscript being delayed over again. What a privilege it has been to have had her as the editor for this as well as my previous books with CUP! Matthew Seal deserves thanks for careful copy-editing and Diana Witt for composing the index with intelligence and care.

I am happy to relieve my family of the burden of having to witness my mind and body occasionally wander to distant time–space locations during the preparation of this work. I thank my mother Anna-Maija for bearing with me as I invaded the balcony in the summer with the computer and the books, and Lauri and Aino, their partners Anna and Stefano, and the little Raffa, for constant good-humoured support, reminding me of those proverbial other things in life. For Tiina Astola, well, I continue to owe everything.

# Introduction

## The Legal Imagination

This is not a history of international law. Instead, it is a history of the legal imagination as it operates in relationship to the use of power in contexts that we would today call international. In an earlier work, I made the point that "modern" international law arose from an effort by a group of European lawyers in the last third of the nineteenth century to spread liberal legislation across Europe and to civilise the colonies. Although many readers reacted with sympathy to that account, they also remained puzzled about how to think about the earlier times – "But what about Vitoria, Grotius and Vattel, theories of the just war and the Peace of Westphalia?" This book is an extended response to that question. It is a history of the ways in which ambitious men, mostly in Europe, used the legal vocabularies available to them in order to react to important events in the surrounding world during the five earlier centuries. The book begins in France at around the year 1300 when a number of well-placed lawyers began to use the idioms of the *Corpus iuris* to consolidate the authority of their king at home and towards foreign rulers. The chapters then move on to Spain, France, Britain and Germany to expound the ways in which subsequent generations of theologians, courtiers, professors, legal and political men employed in addition to Roman law many other legal vocabularies to address the expansion of authority beyond their domestic world. These included variants of natural or customary law, royal prerogative, *lex mercatoria*, individual rights and the just war, among others. Sometimes they legalised forms of speech familiar from religious, philosophical or political texts or had recourse to biology or physics, for example, when they addressed the monarch as the "head" with respect to a "body" of the nation or contemplated the techniques of the balance of power. Often they put these idioms together in larger wholes that they addressed as *ius naturae et gentium*, *Droit public de l'Europe* or *äusseres Staatsrecht*.

This book is a history of the legal imagination as it sought to capture actions or policies with consequences outside the domestic sphere during roughly the period 1300–1870. Owing to their "international" dimension, the events often involved considerations or experiences that were felt in some respects to be new and unfamiliar. Old ways of thinking seemed inadequate, domestic laws and traditional principles inappropriate. These new matters, or their very novelty, often had great political, economic and sometimes even spiritual importance. They challenged earlier preconceptions and attitudes. Who were the inhabitants of the New World whose existence had not previously been known – were they human at all, or humans of a different species? How to think about war between rival Christian princes, each claiming to fight for the right faith? What to do with respect to the spread of the trade in luxuries that accompanied the expansion of long-distance trade and undermined old religious moralities?

To produce answers to such questions, lawyers, theologians and political writers of different description employed old legal vocabularies in new and imaginative ways. I think of this imagining as *bricolage* – a term used by Claude Lévi-Strauss to describe the use of familiar materials scattered around by the indigenous scientist for novel purposes in order to bridge the gap between what is known and tested and what is new or otherwise hard to understand.[1] In a parallel way, well-situated lawyers, political actors and intellectuals employed familiar legal vocabularies lying around to construct responses to new problems in order to justify, stabilise or critique the uses of power. Although intellectual ambition was often involved, this work did not arise predominantly out of an intellectual interest. It was intended to produce an authoritative statement that would have effects with respect to the distribution of material and spiritual values. What and whose action was to be endorsed, and what and whose action rejected as illegal or unjust?

[1] Lévi-Strauss presents *bricolage* as a type of mythical thinking employed in concrete problem-solution where the *bricoleur* is "adept at performing a large number of diverse of tasks", making do with "whatever is at hand", *The Savage Mind* (The University of Chicago Press 1966), 16–22.

That I have tried to produce close descriptions of the worlds of legal imagining in half a millennium has made this a long book. A lot of men and much detail traverse these chapters. They do so because I have wanted to give room for the variety of standpoints from which legal vocabularies and idioms emerge to address the world outside the domestic. Not all of my protagonists were lawyers. Some might even have felt insulted had anybody suggested as much. But they were united by their recourse to a legal vocabulary. Some had formal education in Roman law and acted as ministers, ambassadors or counsel to princes. Others were political men with humanist interests, theologians learning new ways to manage the sacrament of penance, colonial administrators worried about intervention from the metropolis or philosophers contemplating the external debt. Some were employed at courts or ministries, others at universities or trading companies. They may have composed their works as intellectuals at home or as merchants living abroad. Their imagination was fed by an almost limitless range of matters, from the justice of slavery to the drafting of diplomatic *acta*, from the rights of neutrality to the permissible interest rates in currency exchange.

None of this is quite as random as the previous remarks may seem to suggest. Any new imagining takes place within the frame of the possibilities offered by the vocabularies "lying around" when it commences. The frame is constituted in part of what the lawyer or political thinker learned during formal education, in part of the accumulated experience that forms the general sensibility of people in those kinds of positions, their consciousness of the world and of their place in it. Legal idioms communicate only part of that experience. Many other vocabularies – religious, scientific, political – complement them to provide the totality of materials from which a sensibility emerges and *bricolage* proceeds. These larger frames are often addressed by words such as "imperialism", "colonialism", "capitalism", "liberalism", "nationalism" and so on, words like the "universal" that aim to enlighten us about the trajectories through which the past has been turned into the present. Those words form a useful part of the lawyer's and the historian's craft. They synthesise elements of the past and make its multiple aspects stand for a limited set of ideas enabling us to orient our political intuitions and projects today. But they also act as epistemological obstacles, as Bachelard might have put it, blocking thinking and simplifying a varied and multiple reality into generalisations with unsustainable causal relations that produce a bad guide for future.[2] So I have largely (though not wholly) refrained from using such words. The world is a terribly unjust place and its injustices accumulate as parts of large historical trends. But I address those trends by staying as close as possible to the standpoints where people use legal idioms to imagine how to govern and what is just or unjust in the world outside what they think of as their everyday experience.

This is a history of the uses of the legal imagination in the past but also in the present. The ideas and events of the approximately half-millennium treated in this book are connected to the ways in which we think and act today as lawyers, activists and politicians, inhabitants of a world we imagine as ours. That continuity cannot be read as a single tradition. Different ways of imagining a law to be applied abroad or with respect to foreign peoples arose simultaneously at different places; they flourished and withered away in the manner that ways of speaking and thinking do. None of them ever enjoyed universal authority, few possessed much validity even across Europe. The salons of eighteenth-century Paris did not think highly of the thick volumes of natural law produced at German universities. Nor had Germans any sympathy towards the extension of British Admiralty jurisdiction to German property. However, many of the ways of imagining dealt with below left their mark in legal histories and continue to lie around ready for employment by subsequent generations of legal *bricoleurs*. They are part of the historical baggage that limits what it is possible to imagine in a persuasive fashion today.

## Legal Imagination in Action

Legal imagination operates in context. Five contextual considerations lay out the frame of the work of legal thinking and acting in the chapters that follow. First, legal work takes place in the context of persuasion. Law is not about the truth of this or that matter but about persuading audiences – usually audiences in authoritative positions – to act in some particular way. Legal persuasion takes place in the context of controversy: out of some number of possible ways of acting law is used to justify one against others. Imagination is needed to find the winning justification, to hit at the right vocabulary. The less routine the subject, the more widely must imagination travel to find a good argument.

2 Gaston Bachelard, *The Formation of the Scientific Mind* (Mary McAllester Jones intr. & trans., Manchester, Clinamen Press 2002), 24–32.

Persuasion may be directed towards influencing a court, a diplomatic negotiation or a parliamentary debate. But it may equally well operate as *imagined* adversity, a pedagogical lesson or a propaganda tract to consolidate the ranks of those who agree and to demonstrate the mistakes of those who do not. Law's persuasive power differs in different contexts, but it is striking to notice how widely not only lawyers but theologians, political philosophers and government advisors of various sorts have thought it important to have a legal argument available to persuade their audiences. One of the themes that pass through these chapters has to do about the way legal authority migrates between different disciplines. But whoever it is that is speaking must have regard to their audience in order to sound authoritative. What idiom should I use to defend my claim or attack that of my adversary? How does my audience expect me to argue?

Second, legal vocabularies operate in institutional environments. For Vitoria, that was the University of Salamanca where his teaching was part of the Counter-Reformation effort to strengthen the Church's hold on Christian consciences. While Grotius' early writings were about persuading the Amsterdam Admiralty Court, his later work, composed as a refugee in Paris, participated in a Europe-wide debate on just government at a violent time. Rousseau and Kant used the legal idiom to attack the political institutions of the old regime and to undermine its philosophical justifications while J. H. G. von Justi's prolific works were both a critical commentary on the teaching of natural law at German universities and prefaces to job applications with European princes. Many of the men considered below wrote as university professors to academic audiences, while others acted as courtiers, political or legal activists, philosophers or pamphleteers. Some possessed experience in domestic or colonial government, or wrote to influence it. Many had the ambition to assist those in power, but some were critical, though they had to bear in mind the narrow limits within which critique was tolerated and often veiled it in irony or sarcasm. Some were staunch advocates of pre-emptive military action against foreseeable enemies, others favoured a general turn to pacific policies, trade and diplomacy. Some combined work for trade companies with advocacy on commerce and colonialism, others wrote against large monopolies and in favour of expanding free trade, even giving up colonies as a path for prosperity. Many put their opinions in the form of pragmatic compromises and humanist models of virtuous statesmanship. It would be wrong to say that a person's position determines their views. But interest in these chapters is less in what people may have believed than how their imagination was confined within the conventions of authoritative speech and writing.

Third, imagination does not work through deductive inferences or algorithms. When Grotius wrote of law as a moral science or Pufendorf suggested that "moral entities" operate like natural facts, they were tapping into scientific vocabularies at moments when those were deemed especially powerful. Legal imagination may well present itself as having to do with *Wissenschaft* where it addresses an elite trained to appreciate what academics do. In other contexts, such an effort may seem odd or even laughable. It may often be more useful to address the moral or even spiritual worlds of one's audience. To invoke the rule of law in the colonies or the *Rechtsstaat* to deal with class conflict at home are political projects, not scientific hypotheses. As *bricolage,* they employ materials that are felt likely to help in convincing those to whom one speaks. As will become obvious, the audiences of legal argument are most receptive to language that is familiar from the domestic world even when what is being addressed is an activity taking place abroad. When the settlers in the British American colonies appealed to the ancient rights of Englishmen rather than universal rights of humanity, they knew how to address an audience in Westminster. With an audience of foreigners, this is unlikely to have the same effect. Las Casas reported that he did not know whether to laugh or cry when he learned about the *Requerimiento* that was supposed to inform the native American peoples of their legal position with respect to Spain. The materials "lying around" usually emerge from the domestic context and experience. Only with a truly international elite – for example one formed in Roman law or with experience in trade or diplomacy – may something like a *ius gentium* or "public law of Europe" appear authoritative. It is also often useful to distinguish arguments in routine problems from those that address the very frame within which routine takes place. In routine situations, legal *bricolage* may turn to formal materials such as treaties, customary laws, domestic analogies, judicial precedents. In diplomatic contacts between Europeans or within prize courts, not much imagination is needed to find the arguments that are persuasive, although how to argue still requires interpretative skill. But in non-routine situations such as colonial encounters or domestic upheavals, imagination may have to expand in space and time, inviting a return to basic notions about Christianity, *decorum*, state of nature, or civilisation to give the appropriate frame within which to set up an argumentative hierarchy for future routines.

Fourth, and relatedly, legal imagining takes place in a normatively indeterminate terrain where out of binary choices it seeks to construct a hierarchy most convincing to its intended audience. The available mass of materials needs to be interpreted in a way that avoids the most obvious pitfalls while pointing to what appears as a reasonable and realistic way to act. The success of Emer de Vattel's *Droit des gens* depended greatly on the author's ability to combine older mirror-of-princes standpoint with vocabularies from more recent natural law in a compromise he called "voluntary law", situated between law that was fully rational and abstract on the one hand and law that was merely contingent and voluntary on the other.[3] The result avoided ascending to the high heaven of humankind united by reason while not automatically subordinated to state policy either. In this way, he was following what those who had employed the idiom of *ius gentium* had always been doing. As we shall see, what unites the bewildering variety of meanings projected to that expression is that it denoted something "in between", not quite as morally rigorous as the divinely originated provisions of natural law, nor quite as dependent on the shifting priorities of princely policy as contract or treaty. While theologians might imagine it in a descending way as pragmatic modifications of the law handed to humans at creation in order to fit life among sinners, jurists might develop it into in an ascending way as a kind of proto-sociology indicating what was natural for historically developed human communities. Despite their different starting-points, Vitoria and Adam Smith might find themselves at the same terminus.

Fifth, my use of the term "legal imagination" combines elements of what have sometimes been discussed as legal culture, legal ideology or legal consciousness. But as in my previous work, I have refrained from associating it definitely with such technical terms. Contexts of legal speech are not always, perhaps only rarely, such that it would be appropriate to regard them as "legal". Theologians and merchants, poets and philosophers, medical doctors and economists may exercise legal imagination, and have often done so. From whom authoritative institutions take their legal advice reflects variations in the cultures, ideologies and forms of consciousness that legal argument enters only as a more or less welcome guest. It may then need to adapt itself so that the resulting hybrids (e.g. law in theology, law in *raison d'état*) may not at

[3] Emer de Vattel, *The Law of Nations* (Indianapolis, Liberty Fund 2008 [1758]), Preface, 15–17.

all support the priorities that lawyers in that environment typically have. Legalism is often felt inappropriate when authority is exercised abroad. One of the narrative strands woven into these chapters has to do precisely with the struggle for authority among different types of knowledge in Western societies. What Kant called the contest of the faculties was never merely about intellectual predominance but involved prioritising between values and distributive choices. As the idiom of natural law transforms in the course of the half millennium below, it will lend its support to cultures, ideologies and forms of consciousness where it is alternatively theology, history, diplomacy, philosophy, *raison d'état* or economic analysis that will frame the moment's persuasive speech. What is of interest here is the way biases emerge during such transformations, with some interests upheld, others pushed aside.

Legal imagination is a form of institutional action that takes place in the context of controversy through the authoritative use of language. Real stakes are involved to those employing such language but even more to people who are expected to yield to the authority of the one who speaks. This book is inspired by the effort, not to say an obsession, to think about law in the context of power, namely the power of law as language. Throughout this work, I will survey the twists and turns of legal language as it traverses the lives and practices of European men involved in the government of matters situated outside the purely domestic world. In fact one of the themes addressed by legal language in its search for authority is that of drawing the line between the domestic and the foreign. On which side a matter falls will then be decisive for how it is treated. Another theme has to do with boundary-drawing inside the law itself. There is no more important convention in legal speech than the separation between public and private. That conventional analysis deals almost exclusively with what it imagines as "public" power, the authority of the sovereign, while liberating that which it labels "private" to take its natural course somewhere else is one of the most consequential choices made in the course of this history. The relationship of sovereignty and property is a recurring theme in these chapters.

## Imagining Starts at Home

Persuasive legal *bricolage* is about finding a powerful justification for acting or taking decision in some particular way. The conceptual world that opens up when the need arises for addressing the world outside the domestic includes notions such as war, sovereignty, monarch, diplomat, jurisdiction, prerogative, treaty and so on, words that carry their international meaning on their sleeve. But it also includes words such as property, contract, company, slave, family, territory, succession, to which it is common that although we are familiar with them in the domestic legal order they are equally applicable and constantly applied in order to understand and operate beyond it. This book makes a lot of reference to such notions. It is assumed here that an important part of the way power is exercised internationally depends on notions whose primary reference is at home. This includes also the notion of *ius gentium* and cognate civil law or natural law expressions that are almost always understood from the perspective of the domestic legal system and domestic legal training. The frame within which a Spaniard or a Frenchman thinks of the law abroad comes from that person's training in Spain or France. What they imagine as "law of nations" is what Spaniards or Frenchmen imagine as such. The chapters in this book have therefore been organised with the assumption that *bricolage* begins at home. This is also why I will nowhere in this book engage in the interminable discussions about universalism and particularism. The two cannot be separated: we imagine the universal from our particular standpoint – but we do it by concepts and categories that define to us what we think of as "our standpoint" and are in that sense exterior to it. *Bricolage* begins at European locations and then extends to "the uttermost parts of the earth".

Here is how this book has been organised. Chapter 1 focuses on men educated in the thirteenth century in law faculties in Bologna, Montpellier or Orleans where they learned civil law expressions like *dominium* and *ius gentium* that opened the door to high positions in Paris where they supported their king against his domestic and foreign rivals. At other locations in the French capital, Thomas Aquinas employed those very same idioms to address the question of justified authority in human society generally. His texts were taken up two centuries later, as discussed in Chapter 2, by Spanish Dominican theologians who would employ them to discuss Spanish authority in the New World and to address the concerns of conscience opened up by the global expansion of the commercial ethic following the exploitation of New World resources. Chapters 3 and 4 discuss, respectively, the writings of the two Protestant lawyers, Alberico Gentili and Hugo Grotius, as they tried to detach legal speech from the hands of the theologians while opposing the expansion of a countervailing idiom of advice to rulers addressed as *raison d'état*. Explaining obedience to rules as a specifically human quality as against following one's interests would long remain a key theme for defending law as against other idioms for justifying authority.

Chapters 5–7 trace the ups and downs of legal authority in France and the French colonial world up to the Haitian Revolution in 1793–1804. Here law first integrated techniques of the reason of state in what came to be called the *Droit public de l'Europe* and then, in the run-up to the Revolution, imagined itself as a science of the natural and essential order of all political communities. There was a world of difference, however, between what was imagined by the intellectuals and how the administration of an absolutist ruler viewed the roles of the law and lawyers. From the influence law had in ending the religious wars it descended into quite a secondary aspect of royal rule in the seventeenth century. It was then reinvented in the eighteenth century as part of the call for abolishing feudal privileges and creating a world of equality and rights among Frenchmen. Through most of this time, the legal status of Caribbean slavery was untouched by developments in metropolitan France.

Chapters 8–10 begin by tracing the rivalry between the idioms of the common law and the royal prerogative during British commercial and colonial expansion. The narrative about the rise of a British Empire is a story of the cooption of royal sovereignty by the property rights of landed elites and owners of trading companies and the paradoxical creation of sovereignty out of the property claims of settlers in the Atlantic colonies. On the intellectual side, the French and the British narratives involve a partial conversion in the late eighteenth century of the language of natural law into that of political economy. That development was inspired by the crown's reliance on private wealth and private actors who expected commercial privileges and a relatively free hand in the colonial world, but also sometimes demanded extended opportunities to trade across the world. Britain's free trade empire was based on the combination of ideas about protection and the rule of law that were less argued in terms of the law of nations than as rules of a kind of civilisational propriety the contents of which were imagined by British politicians and colonial officers themselves.

A parallel development unfolds in Chapters 11 and 12, which visit the transformations of German academic vocabulary of *ius naturae et gentium* from a Protestant technique of advice to princes to a rationalist philosophy of statehood on the one hand and an empirical science of society on the other. The result was an immensely powerful public law idiom that succeeded in imposing the "German problem" – that is, the problem of fitting the sovereign equality of individual princes to the overall structure of an empire – as the principal problem of what German lawyers at the turn of the nineteenth century began to address as the modern law of nations. Academic natural law also provided the frame against which two powerful philosophical histories emerged, one pointing to an increasingly united world, another to the nation as the spiritual fulfilment of human association. Most German public lawyers continued, however, to think of the law of nations as the technique of European diplomacy, with only later in the century opening their imagination to a more expansive idea of civilisation that a new generation of European lawyers would employ as the basis for their reimagining what a modern international law could be.

The twelve chapters of this work trace the migration of legal authority between social and professional groups in various European and colonial contexts. That authority lies sometimes with jurists, at other times with theologians, courtiers, administrators, philosophers or scientists. Knowing where it lies gives some indication as to which kinds of interests it will advance. During these centuries we also witness law remodel itself into a type of domestic and international governance that is often associated with political economy: law as calculation of an optimal balance between conflicting rights and principles. But the legal idiom continues to accomplish two tasks that are independent of its instrumental role in governance. One is the elaboration of a constitutional architecture that both establishes and limits the sovereignty that the heads of political communities are assumed to exercise. Another defines and allocates the rights of property that underlie the structural hierarchies on which something like sovereignty can manifest itself. A principal objective of this work is to narrate the formation and consolidation of the immensely powerful frame that differentiates and juxtaposes sovereignty with property, that generates a realm of public authority in contradistinction to private rights and institutions. Sovereignty and property, public and private, are not only legal idioms and vocabularies, forms of professional specialisation and institutional authority, but also structure much of what all of us today can have as experience of the world and the alternatives for acting within it. For many people, that experience is deeply problematic and the space provided for doing something about it is extremely limited. Although this book ends towards the middle of the nineteenth century and even as it insists on situating its protagonists in their context, it is a history "of the present". Its principal concern and underlying motivation has been to work out how it is that we have come to have the experience of the present that we have.

## A World of White Men

More often than not, that experience has been one of injustice. An embarrassing aspect of the chapters that follow is that practically all the characters are white European men. I write "practically all" because when describing the travels of these men outside Europe, or indeed their professional lives at home, everything about what they had accomplished was premised on the presence of and interactions with women and with non-European, non-white populations. But aside from one or two exceptions, all of the proper names below belong to white European men, men with power and privilege, and sometimes with attitudes we would today call racist and misogynist. Locke's obliviousness to slavery in Carolina is as well known today as Kant's racism.[4] Almost all of these texts were disparaging of women. Medieval theologians such as Giles of Rome, for example, did not believe women were able to govern owing to their lack of prudence. They were therefore naturally ruled by men.[5] Jean Bodin was firmly of the view that a monarchy should never devolve to women, because:

> 'Gyneocracy' is strictly against the law of nature that has given men the force, the prudence, the weapons and the power of command that He has denied of women and the law of God has clearly ordered that women be subject to men not only in the government of monarchies but at every home and threatened his enemies by providing them women as their rulers [*maîtresses*] as a most terrible malediction.[6]

Such examples could be repeated endlessly.[7] They raise questions about *our* attitudes to them. Would it be anachronistic to apply our

4 See e.g. James Farr, 'Locke, Natural Law and New World Slavery', 36 *Political Theory* (2008), 495–522 and Lucy Allais, 'Kant's Racism', 45 *Philosophical Papers* (2016), 1–36.

5 "Ergo foemina viro naturaliter debet esse subiecta". Although Giles accepted that in rare cases women might be wiser than men, he did not think that deviated from the rule. Giles of Rome, *De regimine principum libri III. Ad francorum regem Philip IIII cognomento pulchrum* (Rome 1556), Part II Bk I Ch VI (40r).

6 Jean Bodin, *Six livres de la république* (Lyon, Tournes 1579) VI V (698).

7 See further, Anna Becker, *Gendering the Renaissance Commonwealth* (Cambridge University Press 2020).

present sensibilities – "other times, other manners"? What about slavery? Or the denial of rights to the infidel, the non-Christian, the barbarian, the uncivilised, the savage? How should we feel about Vattel's invitation to form alliances against "Turks and other Tartars ... for the purposes of punishing and even exterminating those nations"?[8] I find the suggestion to feel neutral about such sentiments – were anyone to make it – utterly objectionable, almost incomprehensible. Why should we feel any less loyal to our own views than prior generations have been to theirs? Surely there was room for argument even at the time when Giles, Bodin or Vattel wrote. People differed in their opinions. Why should these opinions be accepted as representative of something we imagine as "the past" merely because they belonged to a privileged elite that produced books that have survived? What do we know about what women or non-Christians thought about such matters? Not much – and not because they agreed, but because they lived in societies that did not allow them to be heard, societies in which such silences were produced and maintained precisely by these books and these men.

So I think such hierarchies and exclusions are part of the accumulation of tragedies and injustices produced by the will to power of European men in the course of the centuries covered by this book. Let me be clear. I neither suggest nor think that everything that European men have done has been productive of injustice and tragedy. But much has. A history of how law has been used to justify, support and occasionally critique power is about shifting perceptions of justice and injustice and the accumulation of experiences with which we today form our expectations for the future. This book and these stories may not appeal to someone who thinks that past injustices and tragedies do not speak to us, that although there are problems today, our new vocabularies will enable us to deal with them sufficiently well. But with what confidence can one speak of a better world if one is unmoved by the injustices of the past? I do not think making such judgements raises the present in any way "above" the past. The world today is an extraordinarily unjust place where massive tragedies are produced on a daily basis by the products of an imagination that we recognise as "modern". If there is reason to be critical about prejudice in the past, this is to learn about prejudice in the present.

[8] Vattel, *Law of Nations*, III III § 34 (487).

## A Note on Textual Conventions

This work uses many kinds of technical literatures that employ often different and not always compatible textual conventions. I have therefore had to decide on a few conventions myself. Here are some instructions regarding the text:

*Use of Quotation Marks*: Because I follow a linguistic view of law where separating meaning and form cannot be easily be accomplished, I have employed a lot of the phrases and expressions taken directly from my protagonists. According to one convention, one writes "morality" with quotation marks when the reference is to the expression but morality (without quotation marks) when it is to the meaning. Because I am concerned with linguistic expressions throughout, I found myself initially using such an exorbitant number of quotation marks that comprehension of the text became hard, not to say anything about the unappealing aesthetic impression. Therefore, I have minimised the use of quotation marks around single words or short expressions taken directly from my source, relying on the reader's understanding that it is still the source that speaks, and not myself. So when I write about somebody saying that sovereignty is this or that, I normally mean that this is the way the person wants to use the expression "sovereignty". For example, the normal (logical) convention would be to write: Rousseau used his theory of "sovereignty" in order to ... But I have lifted the quotation marks and written simply: Rousseau used his theory of sovereignty in order to ...

But like any linguistic rule, this one (enacted by myself) comes with exceptions. I have left quotation marks in place in the following situations:

(1) where I highlight a special meaning that some person wants to give to a widely used term, as in the following:

  Jean de Blanot used the term "*ad iurisdictionem*" in order to...

(2) where the technical meaning in the original language or in the English translation is being discussed, as in:

  Some would wish to avoid the word "feudalism" altogether

(3) situations where a conversation is being reported – for instance like this:

  To this the king added, "*Quant à nous, nous ne tenons notre royaume que de Dieu seul*".

(4) whenever it's a longer quotation or part of a discussion.

Finally, I have followed the usual practice of using quotation marks whenever I have directly quoted a modern writer commenting on the substance of the text. The source of the quotation will then appear in the footnote.

*Foreign Words and Italics:* There is much non-English language in this work. Again, this follows from my linguistic approach; people do things differently in different languages. I acknowledge that some readers may find this tiresome, and in my last revision I deleted a lot of foreign words. But I have left some that I thought operated as key words opening into a larger idiomatic structures specific to the language in question. I have followed the custom of putting foreign words and titles of books in the main text (but not in notes) in italics. Often when have translated a word into English, I have left the original in brackets in italics as in:

Stein lamented the absence of analyses of society (*Gesellschaft*).

**Note on Sources**

Aquinas: For the *Secunda* of the *Summa*, I use the extracts in the Cambridge University Press text *Aquinas, Political Writings* (R. W. Dyson ed., 2002). For the parts of the *Secunda* not included in that work as well as the texts for the *Prima*, I use the version available at www.newadvent.org/summa/index.html.

All translations in this work are mine, unless otherwise indicated.

Versions of some of these chapters have been published in the following journals: *European Journal of International Law*; *History of the Present*; *Theoretical Inquiries in Law*; *Toronto Law Review*, and as chapters in *The Oxford Handbook of International Legal Theory* (A Orford & F Hofmann eds., OUP 2016); *The Roots of International Law Liber Amicorum Peter Haggenmacher*, (P-M Dupuy & Vincent Chetail eds., Leiden Nijhoff, 2014); *International Law-Making: Essays in Honour of Jan Klabbers* (J Petman ed., London Routledge 2014); *Alberico Gentili. Giustizia, guerra, impero. Atti del convegno XIV giornata gentiliana* (Milano, Giuffrè 2014), *Erzählungen vom Konstitutionalismus* (H Lindeman et al. eds., Baden-Baden, Nomos 2012) and in *From Bilateralism to Community Interest. Essays in Honour of Judge Bruno Simma* (U Fastenrath et al eds., OUP 2011).

# Part I

## Towards the Rule of Law

# 1

# Legal Imagination in a Christian World

## *Ruling France c. 1300*

They arrived already before sunrise. The three men who rode into the town of Anagni some 50 kilometres southeast of Rome on Saturday, 7 September 1303 were the king's principal lawyer, Guillaume de Nogaret (1260–313), flanked by two companions, Thierry d'Hirson, a former servant of the king's cousin and Jacques de Jasseinnes, a royal clerk, as well as a small armed escort provided by the local *podestà*, Rinaldo da Supino. Nogaret had been assigned by his king, Philip IV (the Fair, 1268–314) to deliver a summons to the pope, Boniface VIII (Benedetto Caetani, 1221–303) to appear before the council of cardinals to respond to charges of misconduct and heresy.[1] As Nogaret sat down with his assistants to prepare the delivery and some townsfolk had come to greet him, he became witness and participant in a series of events the course of which is still disputed. Did he collude with the pope's old enemies from the clan of the Colonnas? Or did the latter aim to settle their accounts with the pope independently of the royal legate? In any case, Nogaret's small party was thrust aside as the Colonnas entered the town with 1,600 men and began to storm the fortifications of the pope's nephew, the Marquis Pietro Caetani. Somebody rang the town bells. By 6 am the pope had been able to negotiate a truce with the attackers that lasted until 3 pm. The conditions laid out by the fierce

[1] For the rather open-ended instructions that Nogaret had received, see Robert Holtzmann, *Wilhelm von Nogaret. Rat und Grossiegelbewahrer Philipps des Schönen von Frankreich* (Tübingen, Mohr 1898), 45–8, 215–27. Most accounts claim that Nogaret went to Anagni to present a summons to the pope to a church council. However, it is also argued that neither he nor Philip had such power but that Nogaret went there to extract the convocation from Boniface, and, in case he were to refuse, to use that refusal as proof of heresy against him. Melville Marion, 'Guillaume de Nogaret et Philippe le Bel', 36 *Revue de l'histoire de l'église de France* (1950), 58–9.

Sciarra Colonna under which the life of Boniface would be saved were so exorbitant that he may actually have wanted to get rid of the old man once and for all. Unsurprisingly, no agreement was reached and the attack began again in the afternoon. As the pope's nephew was given safe conduct with his sons to leave, Boniface realised that the game was over. The attackers burnt down the doors and entered the Caetani palace shouting insults and calling for the pope to lay down his tiara and give up the papacy. Boniface refused to cooperate and Sciarra drew his sword ready to slay the pope.

According to his own account, at this point Nogaret intervened and the old man's life was saved. The lawyer then delivered his summons orally at the last moment – the excommunication of the king would have entered into force the following morning.[2] The *fleur de lis* was hoisted over the palace to show that the area was under French protection. The pope was conducted into captivity while the attackers pursued negotiations about what to do with him. Meanwhile, the townspeople who had initially welcomed the king's lawyer had been taken aback by the unrespectful treatment of the pope whose family had, after all, such a long time formed the centre of life at Anagni. By Monday they had organised themselves, turned against the Colonnas and their party, stormed the palace and liberated the old pope. Nogaret, who had received a light wound during the skirmish, returned to Paris to explain to his king what had happened. He realised that Philip might not be altogether happy with being associated with a violent attack on the sovereign pontiff. In any case, there would probably be no need for the council of cardinals, and his sovereign would surely be rid of this problematic holder of the pontificate rather sooner than later. This turned out to be true. Boniface died only two weeks afterwards at his home in Rome.[3]

[2] Boniface had prepared a bull, the *Super Petri solis*, containing formal excommunication. Jean Favier, *Philippe le Bel* (édition revue, Paris, Fayard 1998), 382, 389. The pope regarded that a de facto excommunication had already taken place when Philip had blocked the delivery of bullion to Rome. It had had no effect, however.

[3] These events are recounted in many places. For the above I have used Robert Fawtier, 'Nogaret and the Crime of Anagni', in Charles T. Wood (ed.), *Philip the Fair and Boniface VIII* (2nd edn, New York, Holt, Rinehart & Winston 1971), 72–80; Favier, *Philippe le Bel*, 378–93; Dominique Poirel, *Philippe le Bel* (Paris, Perrin 1991), 247–54; and Guillaume de Thieulloy, *Le pape et le roi. 7 septembre 1303* (Paris, Gallimard 2010), 19–43; most of the documentation relating to the events and their aftermath is available in Pierre Dupuy, *Histoire du différend d'entre le pape Boniface VIII et Philippe le Bel, Roy de France* (Paris, Cramoisy 1655).

Nogaret was not deterred by the extraordinary nature of his assignment, or of the terms of the summons he was to deliver. On the contrary, as one of the "legists" who now populated the *curia regis*, he was totally committed to his king and determined to crush any papal challenge to royal authority. A native of Languedoc, Nogaret had acceded to the position of the king's principal lawyer only recently after the death on the battlefield of his predecessor, Pierre Flote (d. 1302). He had previously served as appellate court judge (*juge-mage*) and taught civil law at the University of Montpellier.[4] By now he had become the king's most trusted counsel, and soon his *garde des Sceaux* (1307) as well as prosecutor in that other famous trial in Philip's reign, the destruction of the Knights Templar. In his self-justifying writings after the Anagni affair, Nogaret would over and again stress his unyielding loyalty to his king and his nation (*domini Regis & regni Franciae*). If he dared to oppose the pope, this was because in acting for the *rex Christianissimus* he was defending Christendom itself.[5] It had been shocking enough that the pope had a few years earlier questioned the king's right to tax the clergy. Even more outrageous was the pope's more recent claim that the king was to exercise his temporal authority only "at the will and sufferance of the priest".[6] To show that the matter touched the very

4 For Nogaret's early biography, see Holtzmann, *Nogaret*, 8–17, 30–65. See also many of the essays in Bernard Moreau (ed.), *Guillaume de Nogaret. Un languedocien au service de la monarchie capétienne* (Nimes, Lucie 2012). As to his academic career, Nogaret was listed among the professors in Montpellier in 1292. As the university was established only in 1287, he is likely to have received his doctorate elsewhere. Maïté Lesné-Ferret, 'Guillaume de Nogaret dans les Olim et l'école juridique languadocienne', in Moreau (ed.), *Guillaume de Nogaret.*, 72–3. Nogaret was born in a modest family in Toulouse around 1260. The view that his father might have been involved in the Cathar heresy is probably wrong. See Joseph Strayer, *The Reign of Philip the Fair* (Princeton Legacy Library 2019), 52; Jean Coste (ed.), *Boniface VIII en process. Articles d'accusation et depositions des témoins (1303–1311)* (Rome, L'"Erma" di Bretschneider 1995), 87. After service to the king in Languedoc Nogaret entered the court in 1294 or 1295, received a seat in the Parlement of Paris in 1298 and attained the titles of "miles" and "chevalier" in 1299, by which time he also sat in the royal council and took his first embassy to Rome to meet Boniface. By March 1303 Nogaret had become the king's principal legal advisor. Holtzmann, *Nogaret*, 8–18. The king's close relation to Nogaret is evident from the fact that he could easily have repaired his relations with Rome after Boniface's death by sacrificing his counsel. Yet, he chose to protect and reward Nogaret and use him amply in later years. Holtzmann, *Nogaret*, 115–35.

5 See Dupuy, *Histoire du différend*, 309, 249–50. See also Ernst H. Kantorowicz, *The King's Two Bodies. A Study in Medieval Political Theology* (with a new preface by William Chester Jordan, Princeton University Press 1981), 249–58.

6 *Unam sanctam* (promulgated 18 November 1302), translation in Internet Medieval Sourcebook (fordham.edu/halsall/source/b8-unam.html).

foundations of the royal office, the legists had decided to react by the greatest publicity, convoking the estates in Paris and launching an unprecedented propaganda campaign against their clerical adversary.[7]

The conflict between Philip and Boniface had to do with two types of lawful authority – *dominium proprietatis* and *dominium iurisdictionis*, property and sovereignty in anachronistic translation. Did the king have the right to tax the clergy? Would he be entitled to exercise criminal jurisdiction over a bishop? That the king reacted by *legal* means was unsurprising. He was attached to the legal form, having surrounded himself by jurists some of whom – like Nogaret – had both academic and practical experience. Recourse to law was also in no way opposed to the theological substance of the royal attack, the accusation of papal heresy. On the contrary, Philip's law-centred *regimen* grew from and was constantly fertilised by liturgical practices and theories; civil law was understood to reflect divine inspiration and its professional interpreters liked to think of themselves as "Priests of Justice".[8] Moreover, although notions such as *dominium, proprietas* and *iurisdictio* were at home in both spiritual and temporal worlds, they were being subjected to increasingly sophisticated analyses within a growing cohort of civil lawyers both at the court and in the academy, assigned to give expression to the complex configuration of "feudal" relations at the centre of which sat the hallowed figure of the the French king.

The principles of royal government had been recently laid out by one of Boniface's future ideologists, the Augustinian friar and professor of theology at Paris, Giles of Rome (Aegidus Romanus, c. 1247–316). In a path-breaking and widely read work, *De regimine principum* (1277–9), which Giles had once written for the instruction of the young Philip, he united Christological and legal images by viewing the king as *lex animata*, "living law", whose will was the measure of justice.[9] Using Aristotelian texts that had recently become available in the Latin language, Giles had stressed the origins of the *regnum* in natural sociability that was also best governed

[7] Standard sources, alongside the above-mentioned collection by Dupuy, are Richard Scholz, *Die Publizistik zur Zeit Philipps des Schönen und Bonifaz VIII* (Stuttgart, Enke 1903) and Jean Rivière, *Le problème de l'église et de l'État au temps de Philippe le Bel* (Paris, Champion 1926).

[8] Kantorowicz, *The King's Two Bodies*, 119–20.

[9] "princeps vero est quaedam animata lex", Giles of Rome (Aegidus Romanus), *De regimine principum libri III. Ad francorum regem Philip IIII cognomento pulchrum* (Rome 1556), I 2, xii (48r). For an introduction to his political doctrine, see Roberto Lambertini, 'Political Thought', in Charles Briggs & Peter Eardley (eds), *A Companion to Giles of Rome* (Leiden, Brill 2016), 255–74. For the pedigree of the *lex animata*, see Kantorowicz, *The King's Two Bodies*, 127–35.

through a *regimen naturale*. This united two objectives: the perpetuation of the inherited regime and the common good.[10] In describing the role of the king Giles made use of the striking image of the good archer (*rex sagittator*) who with intense concentration, relying on nothing but his reason and will, was able to direct his subjects, like arrows, to the target.[11] To the classical question "whether it was better for the city to be ruled by the best laws or the best king", Giles gave the un-Aristotelian response that the "best king" was better because, as a kind of organ of just law himself (*quasi quoddam organum iuste legis*), he was able to apply reason to individual cases.[12] Positive laws cannot take into account circumstances; it was often better to judge by clemency or rigour, instead of strictly following the legal form.[13] This was to give effect to a higher natural law – one that Giles defined as *ius gentium* – that would consolidate the good of the community in the prince's will itself.[14]

No doubt, Philip was gratified to read that government was not some abstract set of principles but a predisposition to rule in the *image of God Himself*. Instead of requiring a limitation of the powers of the ruler, it called for *strengthening* them and making sure they would by used as God would use them, not by mechanically "following the law" but by embodying the law in one's will.[15] This meant, Giles explained to his royal student, working out what was "adequate and proportionate to the nature of the thing", namely "to which we have natural impetus and inclination".[16] Let things take their natural course. The world had been ordained hierarchically from the individual to the household and the *regnum*. Proper government – *ars regnandi*

[10] Giles of Rome, *De regimine principum*, Pref. (1r).

[11] "Rex igitur & quilibet et director populi, est quasi sagittator quidam, populus vero, est quasi sagitta quaedam dirigenda in finem & in bonum", ibid., III 2, viii (278v).

[12] Ibid., III 2, xxix (314r).

[13] "Nam particulares circumstantiae, quae lege determinari non possunt, aliquando alleviant delictum: & tunc iuste & secundum rationem clementer agitur cum delinquente. Aliquando tales circumstantiae aggravant: & tunc est rigidus incedendum". Ibid., III 2, xxix (315v).

[14] Being free from civil law did not mean that the prince was not bound by natural law and *ius gentium*. Otherwise he would become a tyrant and easily face rebellion by his subjects, as history had shown. Ibid., III 2, xxix (314v–315v), III 2 xxvi (310r), and III 2, xxxi & xiii (318r–319v & 277r–278r). See also Michel Senellart, *Les arts de gouverner. Du regimen médieval au concept du gouvernement* (Paris, Seuil 1995), 199.

[15] Senellart, *Les arts de gouverner*, 184, 200. This is why Giles preferred hereditary to electoral monarchy (the latter tended to be part of a *regimen politicum*) as well as why he (in a Machiavellian mode) called for the prince to govern so as to secure his position, Giles of Rome, *De regimine principum*, III 2, xv (289–91v).

[16] "ad quae habemus naturalem impetum & inclinationem", ibid., III 2, xxiv (306r). Or, as he stated in another place, ruling "est enim ars imitatrix naturae", III 2, viii (278r).

*et principandi* – was to make each perfect in its nature: "like medical science has the objective of physical health, kings and princes must naturally love and aim at the good of the *regnum* and the community".[17] That the king was to govern by *ius gentium* meant that he was to enable his subjects not only to "live" but to "live well" (*bene vivere*).[18] This encompassed buying and selling, renting and hiring, deposits and loans, which embodied a kind of contractual natural law (*quoddam ius naturale contractum*) – natural in view of human inclinations, contractual because set up through reason and agreement.[19]

In *De regimine principum* Giles had sketched a wholly temporal (natural) technique of ruling in which the church would appear to have no special authority. However, in a later work, *De ecclesiastica potestate*, written in support of Boniface at the very height of the conflict with Philip, Giles took the position that there was no lawful *dominium* at all outside baptism and that all rights of property and jurisdiction lay ultimately with the church.[20] By the time this latter work was published, however, this had become the view of only a small circle of papal extremists. By now, religious authority in France had become firmly vested in the crown. This did not free the king's hands, however. For the more his authority was understood as a function and an office, the more the king would find himself tied into the views of his counsel of what it involved within and beyond the *regnum*.

* * * * *

This chapter will proceed as follows. After an explanation of the political theology underlying the papal position in the conflict with King Philip, it will take up the legists' retort that the most Christian king was actually emperor (*princeps*) in his realm. I will then lay out the "feudal" context within which Philip would exercise his newly constructed "imperial" authority. How were the various feudal rights in the *regnum* to be understood in relation to king's *dominium iurisdictionis*? In these debates the *ius gentium* would play three roles: it would give systemic expression to the new kingship; it would provide the basis for

[17] "Cum ergo in arte regnandi et principandi principaliter et finaliter intendatur salus regni et principatus, sicut in arte medicandi principaliter intenditur sanitas corporis: naturaliter decet reges et principes intendere et amare bonum regni et commune", ibid., I 3, iv. (98r).

[18] Ibid., III 1, ii (238v); 2, viii (278v–279r); 2, xxv (307v–308v).

[19] Ibid., III 2, xxv (308r).

[20] "Ecclesia in temporalibus omnibus habet ius et dominium universale", Giles of Rome, *On Ecclesiastical Power. A Medieval Theory of World Government* (R. W. Dyson trans. & ed., Columbia University Press 2004), II X (162/163).

a political history of statehood; and it would endorse an economic system based on private property. The chapter will end with an outline of the operation of the principle of "common good" as the standard for reconciling the twin forms of Christian authority, *dominium iurisdictionis* and *dominium proprietatis* with reference to a text published in 1302 by one of the observers of the papal–royal dispute, the Dominican scholar John Quidort (John of Paris).

## *Clericos laicos* and *Unam sanctam*

No doubt, Boniface was himself part of the cause of his fall. Well practised in canon law, he was short-tempered, undiplomatic and keen to win points of principle at the expense of pragmatic accommodation.[21] Although the relations between the papacy and France had been traditionally good, and even as Boniface himself professed warm sympathy towards the Capet family (he had sanctified Philip's grandfather, Louis IX a couple of years earlier), he had proven quite unyielding in his relations with Philip.[22] The antagonism had its origins as far back as 1295 when the king had decided to raise money with the clergy to finance his attack on his most powerful vassal, King Edward I of England, regarding the latter's rule over the duchy of Aquitaine (Guyenne). Edward's father, Henry III of Plantagenet, had received Aquitaine as a fief from Louis IX (Saint-Louis, 1214–70) in 1259.[23] This had led Edward into humiliating subordination to the French king. As relations between the suzerain and his vassal deteriorated, Philip's patience ran out. But to wage war, he needed resources far beyond what the royal domain produced. The church was the wealthiest institution in his realm. And so he demanded from it a tax of one tenth (*décime*).[24] The pope responded in the famous encyclical *Clericos laicos* (24 February 1296), protesting vehemently against the

[21] Although Boniface had spent some time in Bologna, he had no degree and had learned his law through practice within the Roman curia. Peter Herde, *Bonifaz VIII* (Erster Halbband, 43.1 Päpste und Papsttum, Stuttgart, Hiersemann 2015), 20–4.

[22] For the "benevolent disregard" with which the French kings had looked upon the increasing papal ambitions in the thirteenth century, see Robert Fawtier, *The Capetian Kings of France. Monarchy & Nation (987–1328)* (L. Butler & R. J. Adam trans., London, Macmillan 1960), 88–90.

[23] Actually, Louis had refrained from confiscating the fief.

[24] The tenth brought in 189,000 livres tournois – almost the same amount as the annual revenue of the royal domain. It was still just a fraction of what he received from secular sources. See Favier, *Philippe le Bel*, 212.

violation of the immunity of the church. Laymen had always, Boniface indignantly claimed, wanted to subordinate the clergy, and exact its funds. This would not do. Any prelate who agreed to pay the tax, and any secular official, town or castle involved, would be immediately excommunicated.[25] Philip reacted no less decisively, barring any deliveries of money or gold to Rome, striking hard on papal finances. The pope was now threatened with bankruptcy.[26] Only a fraction of the French clergy sympathised with Boniface. Nor did many of the Roman cardinals support him. On the contrary, they had been antagonised by papal nepotism. Eventually Boniface capitulated, explaining in a new missive in late July 1297 that in cases of *defensio regni* the king may request from the church "any subsidy or contribution . . . and that the said prelates and persons can and must pay it, without consulting the Roman pontiff".[27]

The new clash with Philip began with the king's effort to deal with problems of the Languedoc Inquisition and the pope's challenge against Philip in a dispute over feudal rights in the bishopric of Pamiers. Boniface had appointed as bishop his friend, Bertrand Saisset, a combative proponent of ecclesiastical independence. The king had responded by sending a secret inquiry into Pamiers that reported that a plot against the king was being prepared.[28] In July 1301 Saisset was arrested and brought to appear before the king. As royal prosecutor, the king's *garde des Sceaux*, Pierre Flote, Nogaret's predecessor, chose to indict Saisset both for the temporal crime of *lesé majesté* and for acts of

[25] For the bull *Clericis laicos*, see Dupuy, *Histoire du différend*, 14–15. For the English text, see Brian Tierney, *The Crisis of Church and State 1050–1300* (University of Toronto Press 1988), 175–6. For discussion, see e.g. Charles-Victor Langlois, 'The Power Politics of France', in Charles T. Wood (ed.), *Philip the Fair and Boniface VIII* (2nd edn, New York, Holt, Rinehart & Winston 1971), 26–31.

[26] Money was badly needed to conclude a mediation intended to accentuate the papal office's international importance: Thieulloy, *Le pape et le roi*, 137.

[27] For the bull *Etsi de statu*, see Dupuy, *Histoire du différend*, 39–40. This translation is from R. W. Dyson, 'Introduction', in R. W. Dyson (ed.), *Three Royalist Tracts 1296–1302* (Bristol, Thoemmes 1999), xix.

[28] In particular, Saisset had accused the king of being a bastard and a money forger owing to his recourse in 1295 of the debasing of the value of the coinage. Cf. Marc Bompaire, 'La question monétaire. Avis et consultations à l'époque de Philippe le Bel et de ses fils', in Jean Kerhervé & Albert Rigaudière (eds), *Monnaie, fiscalité et finances au temps du Philippe le Bel* (Paris, Comité pour l'histoire économique et financière de la France 2007), 113. See further Julien Théry, 'Le pionnier dela théocratie royale. Guillaume de Nogaret et les conflits de Philippe le Bel avec la papauté', in Bernard Moreau (ed.), *Guillaume de Nogaret. Un Languedocien au service de la monarchie capétienne* (Nimes, Lucie 2012), 107–13.

heresy, including the commission of "manifest simony" (sale of church offices), and having contested the canonisation of Philip's grandfather.[29] These crimes were even more serious than treason, Flote suggested, because they had been committed against God and the Roman church and hence considered by the king to have been committed against himself.[30] Breaking the canon law rule that bishops could be tried only by the pope himself, Philip thus asserted his supreme jurisdiction over his realm. For Boniface, this was only the latest in a series of humiliations imposed on him by Philip and his legists. In a strongly worded letter, *Ausculta fili*, in December 1301 he called upon the king to return to the ways to God from whom he had been distanced by "perverse" manipulations of the royal council, consisting mostly of lawyers. The French bishops were to travel to Rome immediately to discuss the situation and decide on further action *ad reformationem regni et regis correctionem.*[31]

The royal council was outraged.[32] Surely the king could not condone the unheard-of proposal of French bishops travelling to Rome to discuss the conduct of their sovereign – this would be tantamount to recognising the superiority of the pope in France. Philip decided to expel Saisset and to allow half of the bishops to travel.[33] At the suggestion of his lawyers, however, he then organised a widely attended meeting in the Notre Dame in April 1302 to discuss the pope's behaviour. For this meeting, Flote produced a summary of *Ausculta fili* that sharpened its tone and content considerably.[34] The result was as desired – the hot-blooded Count of Artois arose first to profess readiness to defend with his blood and sword the supremacy of

[29] For the act of accusation against Saisset, see Dupuy, *Histoire de différend*, 653–6 and Théry, 'Le pionnier de la théocratie royale', 113–14.

[30] See further Julien Théry, 'Philippe le Bel, Le pape en son royaume', 289 *Revue L'histoire (Dieu et la politique. Le défi laïque)* (2004), 14–17.

[31] For *Ausculta fili*, see Dupuy, *Histoire du différend*, 48–52. See further Holtzmann, *Nogaret*, 39; Poirel, *Philippe le Bel*, 185–9; Thieulloy, *Le pape et le roi*, 199–203; Favier, *Philippe le Bel*, 343–8.

[32] The outrage was in part the result of manipulation. Instead of receiving the original bull, an amended version was prepared by Flote that included a straightforward claim about the king being inferior to the pope in temporal matters. For the English text of the original bull, see Tierney, *Crisis of Church and State*, 181, 185–6.

[33] Poirel, *Philippe le bel*, 221.

[34] For the text, which summarises *Ausculta fili* in six terse paragraphs ("*Scire te volumus*"), see Thieulloy, *Le pape et le roi*, 202 and for another fabricated text, purporting to be the king's reply ("*Sciat tua maxima fatuitas*"), see Tierney, *Crisis of Church and State*, 187; see further Dyson, 'Introduction', xxx–xxxi; Holtzmann, *Nogaret*, 42; Jo Ann McNamara, *Gilles Aycelin. The Servant of Two Masters* (Syracuse University Press 1971), 113–14, 117–19.

the French king in his realm. After a brief debate, the participants united behind their king.[35] The clergy representatives decided to contact Boniface directly while the nobles and the commons sent their missive to the cardinals instead, thus implying a doubt about the pope's legitimacy. To the delegation that arrived in Rome, Boniface gave the rejoinder that the king and his advisors simply had not understood the *Ausculta fili*, that they desired confrontation and that he was ready for it. After all, his predecessors had excommunicated three previous French kings, remarking that "as the king now had committed all the abuses that they had committed, and still more serious ones, we are prepared to go as far as to dispose of the king like a valet, even if with real pain and great sorrow".[36]

Meanwhile Giles of Rome, Philip's teacher, now Augustinian prior-general and professor of theology, had moved to the Roman curia. In the course of the summer of 1302 he had prepared a large work, *De ecclesiastica potestate* ("On Ecclesiastical Power"), which shared Boniface's view of the relations between spiritual and temporal authority. Temporal *dominium* could only be entirely inferior to the spiritual – inferior in dignity, in time and scope. It followed that all forms of *dominium* – not only political jurisdiction but also rights of property – derived from the church and were subject to its control:

> [T]he church has a universal right and lordship in all temporal things [*omnibus habet ius et dominium universale*] . . . the faithful have, or can have, no more than a particular lordship in such temporal things . . . and unbelievers can have no lordship with justice at all.[37]

Because the pope was an absolute monarch over the church, these rights were for him to dispose; everything the church could do, he could do. He was the supreme judge.[38] This view was expressed by Boniface in his famous bull *Unam sanctam*.[39] There was little that was completely

[35] Poirel, *Philippe le Bel*, 192–5; Thieulloy, *Le pape et le roi*, 204–5.

[36] Poirel, *Philippe le Bel*, 198. A good summary is also found in Favier, *Philippe le Bel*, 354–8.

[37] Giles of Rome, *On Ecclesiastical Power*, II X (162/163).

[38] This aspect is highlighted in Jürgen Miethke, *De potestate papae* (Tübingen, Mohr Siebeck 2000), 97–9. Of course, Giles was not the only person holding this position. See further Anthony Black, *Political Thought in Europe 1250–1450* (Cambridge University Press 1992), 49–52.

[39] For the text, see Dupuy, *Histoire du différend*, 54–6. For an English translation and background, see Tierney, *Crisis of Church and State*, 188–9 & 172–92. The text can also be found in *Medieval Sourcebook*, fordham.edu/halsall/source/b8-unam.html (2/3/09). Although *Unam sanctam* was registered on 18 November 1302, it was published only on

new in this document. It expounded the view according to which both of the "two swords" were originally given to the church and that the temporal sword was to administered "at the will and sufferance of the priest". The church, Boniface wrote, following Giles verbatim in places, had "one body and one head, not two heads like a monster". When Jesus said to Peter "Feed my sheep" [John 21:17] he meant "my sheep in general, not these, nor those in particular, whence we understand that he entrusted all to him". Boniface insisted on a single hierarchy of authority in a Christian world and the superiority of spiritual things over temporal ones, concluding that "whoever resists this power thus ordained by God, resists the ordinance of God" [Rom 13:2].[40]

The pope's missive took no notice at all of the factual consolidation of territorial *dominium* in the hands of kings and the great barons. Repeating themes and expressions from the old adversity with the emperor and failing to address the growth of territorial government, the bull was obsolete as soon as it was issued. It propounded a vision of universal lordship that had a long pedigree in Christian literatures, but was blissfully ignorant of the way it had been recently updated by the church itself.[41] By the end of the century, even most canon lawyers had accepted the view that nobody was entitled to challenge the way the kings ruled their *regna* in temporal matters (*rex superiorem non recognescens in temporalibus*). Moreover, the pope knew that the royal council was populated by men who had been trained in civil law – in fact he had met both Flote and Nogaret – who shared an imperial vision of kingship. True, the academic jurists of Orleans were still unclear about whether the king could be addressed as *princeps*, and whether that would be de iure or merely de facto. The imperial seat had anyway remained empty since the mid-thirteenth century and they were keen to integrate

15 August 1303. Boniface had delayed its publication owing to a last-ditch effort to find a negotiated settlement. After the charge of heresy had been raised, however, in early summer 1303, there was no reason to delay its publication. See Karl Ubl, 'Genese der Bulle Unam sanctam. Anlass, Vorlagen, Intention', in Martin Kaufhold (ed.), *Politischer Reflektion in der Welt des Späten Mittelalters / Political Thought in the Age of Scholasticism. Essays in Honour of Jürgen Miethke* (Leiden, Brill 2004), 142–5.

40 Translations are from Tierney, *Crisis of Church and State*, 188–9 and 172–92.

41 *Per venerabilem*, 1202. Text e.g. in Jean-Marie Carbasse & Guillaume Leyte, *L'état royal XIIe–XVIIIe siècles. Une anthologie* (Presses Universitaires de France 2004), 23–9 and Tierney, *Crisis of Church and State*, 133–4, 136–8 (extracts). The literature on *Per venerabilem* is enormous. For brief treatments, see Black, *Political Thought*, 113–15. Walter Ullmann, 'The Development of the Medieval Idea of Sovereignty', CCL *The English Historical Review* (1949), 3–4.

the territorial power in their laws. Philip was right to think that the pope was actually trying to change the status quo.

After the contents of *Unam sanctam* had been made known to the king, his new principal advisor Nogaret suggested a direct counter-attack, reading out to the enlarged royal council on 12 March 1303 a statement according to which the pope had not been elected correctly and was therefore "to be considered a thief". He added for good measure that the pope was also a practitioner of simony and had committed an infinity of manifest heresies. He was therefore to be forthwith disposed of his office.[42] The indictment was extraordinary not only in the length of the list of heresies it attributed to the pope but also in its suggestion that a church council was to sit in spiritual judgement of the pope, who was to be arrested and held in detention in wait for council's verdict. According to canon law, a pope could only be deposed by the council. To the question who was to convene it, Nogaret responded that this task belonged to the French king.[43] No role was to be played by the emperor or other princes. As stated in his coronation oath (*propter iuramentum*), Philip was the first defender of the church.[44]

By June, Philip had decided to act accordingly. A further meeting was then arranged in the Louvre where Nogaret's former student and close associate Guillaume de Plaisians (d. 1314) read to an audience of some seventy barons, prelates and other notables an extraordinary twenty-eight articles of accusation with much detail collected from the pope's visceral enemies the Colonnas.[45] The indictment repeated the charges of theft, simony and heresy, and culminated in the call for the pope's immediate deposition. The act ended with the signatures of the king, his barons and all but two of the bishops present. The king

[42] For the meeting of the enlarged royal council and the text of the indictment, see Coste, *Boniface VIII en procès*, 103–22. The accusation that Boniface had not been elected correctly referred to the renunciation of the tiara by Boniface's predecessor, Celestine V, on 13 December 1294. Celestine had been disillusioned in the position and felt incapable of responding to its challenges. He thus renounced the papacy against the objections that even as a pope might be dismissed by a general council, he could not renounce at his own initiative. Some even suggested that in fact Caetani had persuaded Celestine to take this (allegedly illegal) action. Most canon lawyers, however, approved of the procedure. See Poirel, *Philippe le Bel*, 230, 234–5 and Jean Leclerc, 'The Legitimacy of Boniface VIII', in Charles T. Wood (ed.), *Philip the Fair and Boniface VIII* (2nd edn, New York, Holt, Rinehart & Winston 1971), 35–9. For the very sharply worded accusation, see also Holtzmann, *Nogaret*, 48–54.

[43] See also Favier, *Philippe le Bel*, 369–70. [44] Coste, *Boniface VIII en procès*, 120.

[45] For the report of the meeting as well as the act of accusation, see ibid., 122–85.

bound the country to his policy.[46] Meanwhile, Nogaret was already on his way to deliver the summons to the pope.[47] He had to proceed rapidly because the pope was expected to excommunicate the king shortly and because, according to canon law, the acts of a pope summoned for heresy before the council of cardinals would no longer carry effect. This was the summons that Nogaret was bringing to Anagni as the events took their unexpected course.

## "*Ecclesia habet universale dominium …*"

". . . *super omnibus temporalibus rebus*".[48] Giles knew, of course, that in a Christian world, it would be inconceivable to exercise power without divine authorisation, expressed in the language of *dominium* (lordship).[49] In its Roman law-inspired meaning *dominium* covered especially the right of property, although not necessarily with the kind of absoluteness that Roman notions of ownership entailed. But it was also used to refer to the power that people at higher levels of social hierarchy exercised over those at lower levels – jurisdiction, the authority to determine what other people should *do*. The dual meaning highlighted the way relations of authority between people and between people and things were mixed in a feudal society, though both originated in God.[50]

When Boniface quoted the famous statement by St Paul in Romans 13:1 that "[t]here is no power but from God, and those that are ordained of God", he understood it to mean the subordination of the temporal power to the spiritual one. The two swords "would not be ordained unless one sword was under the other and, being inferior, was led by the other to the highest things".[51] Like much of the rest of *Unam sanctam*, this was likely to have come from Giles' pen. The principle of mediation was involved: everything at a lower level "achieves its good

46 Ibid., 125.

47 The mission was also to solicit support for the king. Thieulloy, *Le pape et le roi*, 218–19.

48 Giles of Rome, *On Ecclesiastical Power*, I X (176).

49 The literature is truly overwhelming. See especially Marie-France Renoux-Zagamé, *Origines théologiques du concept moderne de propriété* (Genève, Droz 1987) and further Annabel Brett, *Liberty, Right and Nature. Individual Rights in Later Scholastic Thought* (Cambridge University Press 1997), 10–48; Janet Coleman, 'Property and Poverty', in J. H. Burns (ed.), *The Cambridge History of Medieval Political Thought c. 350–c. 1450* (Cambridge University Press 1988), 611–25.

50 See Bruno Paradisi, *Studi sul medievo giuridico* (Rome, Instituto Palazzo Borromini 1987), 329–30.

51 'Unam sanctam', Tierney, *Crisis of the Church and State*, 189.

by serving and supporting that which is superior to it".[52] Because the temporal sword was "lower", Giles wrote, it "must be led by the spiritual as by a superior and the one must be must be ordained under the other as inferior under superior".[53] A king who had not been crowned by the church was as good as a robber. In particular, there was no divine kingship; all lawful rule was instituted by priesthood.[54] That there was no legitimate *dominium* outside the church at all meant that property, too, could be disposed of by it. For, Giles argued, nobody may possess anything with justice "unless he is also spiritually regenerated through the church".[55] And of course, "unbelievers [were] all unworthy of any possession, lordship, and power".[56] They might have de facto dominion but never de jure.

Unlike most Augustinians, Giles did not think of temporal power as in itself sinful. On the contrary, as he explained in his commentary to Peter Lombard's *Sentences*, there had been superior/inferior relations even before the fall. But Adam had exercised his power through charity and love and not through servitude. In fact, he explained, the fall was occasioned by Adam's effort to rule *per naturam*, through coercion in a way that "hardens the heart and makes it incapable of charity".[57] His sin had been to fall in love with power itself. Giles followed old Patristic theology by stressing that rulership began with one's own soul,

[52] R. W. Dyson, 'Introduction', in Giles of Rome, *On Ecclesiastical Power*, xxi.

[53] Giles of Rome, *On Ecclesiastical Power*, I IV (19).

[54] Ibid., I V, para 17 (54).

[55] Ibid., II VII (131). Or in other words, "for example, this man or that cannot with justice possess a farm or a vineyard or anything else which he has unless he holds it under the Church and through the Church", II VII (137).

[56] Ibid., II XI (181). The view that that there could be no lawful power at all outside Christendom and that the church possessed universal lordship (*universale dominium*) was extreme but logical for an Augustinian. See further Michael Wilks, *The Problem of Sovereignty in the Middle Ages* (Cambridge University Press 1963), 411–16. Because Giles had earlier taken an analogous view on the powers of the king Eric Voegelin branded him as a "totalitarian" thinker, obsessed by power and ready to support any absolutism if he could only ensure a place in it. Eric Voegelin, *History of Political Ideas*, vol. III: *The Later Middle Ages* (David Walsh ed., Missouri University Press 1998), 46–53. In fact, Voegelin writes, he "was a Fascist by temperament", 49. But like many extremists, he was also coherent in drawing what seem like inescapable conclusions from principles that many people readily accept. The idea of the world as a single hierarchically organised cosmos where the purpose of lower levels was to serve higher ones was a deep-rooted part of Christian cosmology. See Otto Gierke, *Political Theories of the Middle Ages* (F. W. Maitland trans. & ed., Cambridge University Press 1900), 7–21.

[57] Giles of Rome, *Commentary on Sentences*, as quoted in Graham McAleer, 'Giles of Rome on Political Authority', 60 *Journal of the History of Ideas* (1999), 31, and generally 21–36.

extending to one's family and realm. Notions such as "virtue", "piety" and "common good" reached from individual conscience to skill at work, pedagogy and, above all, government of souls (*regimen animarum*).[58] Obedience would be sought not for instrumental reasons, but for its own sake, to reach a state of obedience, expressed in the Christian virtue of humility. Authority would be that of a good shepherd, expressing compassionate care, not a will to dominate.[59] But original sin had made such harmony impossible. Secular government was needed to fight the sin of pride that tore individuals apart and made humans potential enemies to each other.[60] But while Augustine regarded *dominium* simply as an instrument to manage human sinfulness, without intrinsic worth, Giles reserved a place for it also in the state of innocence, and upheld the view that "*dominium* exercised in love" would, at least in some cases, be available for sinners as well.[61]

Another influential Augustinian teacher in Paris at the time, James of Viterbo (1255–308), put the hierocratic view in the context of Aristotelian views of rulership. God was the ultimate ruler of the world. He was *Dominus*. This included the power to rule over the things he had created, a power *respectu gubernationis rerum creatarum*. But God may also "govern [...] and rule [...] some created things through the mediation of others".[62] Humans could receive *dominium* in two ways, directly by divine positive law, and indirectly by the "order of the universe" where humans were situated at the top.[63] Most theologians limited direct divine institution of kings to the narratives of the Old Testament. Indeed, to suggest that present kings received their power directly from God – as suggested by the French legists – undermined church

58 The government of souls instituted a complex economy of exchange: the prince's salvation was dependent on his ability to see to the care and salvation of his flock while each flock member was to scrutinise their conscience for the presence of required humility. The prince would govern by example, by his effort at the constant perfection of himself. See famously, Michel Foucault, *Sécurité, territore, population. Cours au Collège de France 1977–1978* (Paris, Gallimard/Seuil 2004), 171–82.

59 R. A. Markus, 'The Latin Fathers', in J. H. Burns (ed.), *The Cambridge History of Medieval Political Thought* (Cambridge University Press 1988), 120. See further e.g. Cary J. Nederman, 'Conciliarism and Constitutionalism. Jean Gerson and Medieval Political Thought', 12 *History of European Ideas* (1990), 193–5.

60 See Heinrich Kipp, *Völkerordnung und Völkerrecht im Mittelalter* (Köln, Verlag Deutsche Glocke 1950), 16–23.

61 McAleer, 'Giles of Rome on Political Authority', 36.

62 James of Viterbo, *De regimine christiano* (ed. R. W. Dyson, Leiden, Brill 2009), II/2 (111).

63 Ibid., II/2 (113). See also Renoux-Zagamé, *Origines théologiques*, 65.

authority. Therefore, they argued that dominion was allocated to humans only indirectly, through natural law. Thus James, unlike Giles of Rome, suggested that just rulership was founded on an instinct of nature that humans shared with animals. It

> . . . is found among men generally and has existed in every time: that is, in the time of the law of nature and the written law and the gospel, and among men of all kinds, of whatever custom and condition.[64]

James did not limit lawful *dominium* only to Christians or make it dependent on baptism. It existed among Christians and the infidel in the same way, as a product of natural law. But it remained "imperfect and unformed unless it is formed and perfected by the spiritual".[65] From premises very different from those of Giles, James of Viterbo drew nevertheless similar conclusions. Although natural kingship may have pre-existed spiritual power, it remained imperfect without the active involvement of spiritual power, for example through the practice of anointing.[66] And because supernatural blessedness was infinitely higher than natural blessedness, it followed that "all temporal princes must obey him in whom spiritual power resides in the highest degree as they would our Lord Jesus Christ, and they must recognise him as a superior and a head, and they must revere and honour and submit to him".[67]

The works of Giles and James were composed hastily in face of pressing events. They were badly organised and repetitive. But they illustrate two perspectives from which the Roman church sought to respond to the challenge of secular *regnum* and an increasingly commercial economy. Giles depicted the church as encompassing the whole world so that no *dominium* – neither kingship nor property – could be held justly without its approval. For James, again, there was a realm of natural *dominium* that pre-existed spiritual consecration and had a residual legitimacy of its own. Pagan rule and ownership were not automatically unjust, only imperfect. Using the old principle that grace does not destroy nature "but perfects it" James sought to provide the church with the authority to consecrate but also to judge and if necessary remove dominion that was in Christian hands. In a statement with

[64] James of Viterbo, *De regimine christiano*, II/3 (131).

[65] Ibid., II/7 (211).

[66] Ibid., II/7 (213).

[67] Ibid., II/7 (219). The idea was not that the pope would actually use temporal power, only to authorise and direct it. See Wilks, *Problem of Sovereignty*, 304–5.

obvious implications regarding the conflict between Boniface and Philip, James concluded that the spiritual power:

> . . . has the task of judging [temporal power] because it can and must correct and guide it, punish it, and impose on it a penalty not only spiritual but temporal by reason of crime and fault, and proceed even to its deposition if the character of the fault so requires.[68]

## *Roi très Chrétien*

The king's lawyers agreed that temporal authority, *dominium*, needed a transcendental foundation. Hence they projected the king as the church's principal defender. Alongside the accusations of treason, simony, usury, murder (including that of his predecessor) and stealing church property, the main charges were those of heresy.[69] There were three reasons for proceeding in this way. First, only an account of heresy could move the council of cardinals to depose the pope; no other outcome would have been acceptable for the king and his lawyers. If the cardinals were unwilling to do this, then the matter could be understood as an emergency where the king, as the defender of the church, could take action.[70] Second, if the prevailing view was that the king had no superior in *temporal* matters, this still left it to the church (and the pope) to determine the temporal or spiritual character of some substance. There had been a long history of the church acting in ostensibly temporal matters if only some spiritual dimension was

[68] James of Viterbo, *De regimine christiano*, II/7 (215).

[69] "This double theme, of kingship as religious office and the special dynastic obligation to fulfil it, runs through all the justification for royal action against Boniface VIII", John A. Watt, 'Spiritual and Temporal Power', in J. H. Burns (ed.), *The Cambridge History of Medieval Political Thought* (Cambridge University Press 1988), 404–5. No doubt, it must also be why successive popes released everyone else involved in the attack apart from Nogaret from the ban of the church. The new pope, Benedict XI (1240–304), absolved the king and his family, cancelling all decrees against French universities and churches. Everyone in the affair apart from those present at Anagni was forgiven. His successor, the jurist Clement V (1264–314), was no more willing to lift the ban on Nogaret, especially as long as this was pursuing the plan of a posthumous trial that was dropped only in 1311. In the end, Clement promised absolution but only after heavy penance involving a series of pilgrimages to the Holy Land that Nogaret would never have the time to accomplish. Favier, *Philippe le Bel*, 395–7; Thieulloy, *Le pape et le roi*, 42–3.

[70] This was the situation foreseen by Nogaret. See especially Scholz, *Die Publizistik*, 364–5 and point [17] of Nogaret's act of accusation of 12 March 1303 where the king is addressed as *ecclasiarum patronus*, Coste, *Boniface VIII en procès*, 120.

involved. Giles, for instance, argued that "all crimes and moral sins can be called spiritual in that they slay our spirit and our soul". Accordingly, the pope was entitled to intervene "in disputes involving any temporal questions whatsoever if those disputes are brought forward together with an allegation of crime".[71] The occasion now presented itself to Philip and his legists to determine, once and for all, that the pope had no such – potentially boundless – power. The king would have full autonomy to decide his own jurisdiction.[72]

Third, the ideology of divine kingship was deeply embedded in Frankish history, and the popes had earlier had no problem with it.[73] The "royal sacrament" (*sacre*) that took the kings to Reims at the outset of their reign to receive the unction had given the popes occasion to dignify the princes of the Capet family with the epithet *Chrétien* or even *très Chrétien*. The pope may have believed that this subordinated the king to the church – but in France the ritual underlined the king's role as the church's principal defender.[74] As Nogaret and Plaisians stressed in one their self-justifying letters after Anagni, the French kings had long established churches and appointed clerics and held it obvious that the bishops were crown officials. Never had they recognised anybody, apart from God, as superior; they had always protected the church's liberties and rights, establishing cathedrals and providing gifts and benefices to the clergy.[75] Although the jurists did not go so far as to exalt the divinity of the king himself, there is no doubt that he was so

[71] Giles of Rome, *On ecclesiastical power*, III V (326/7). The pope "was indeed 'dominus temporalium' since he alone could decide where and when the political order ceased to be merely of temporary concern, and against such a decision there was no appeal". John A. Watt, *The Theory of Papal Monarchy in the Thirteenth Century. The Contribution of the Canonists* (London, Burns & Oates 1965), 133, 129–33.

[72] Thieulloy, *Le pape et le roi*, 253–4.

[73] See e.g. Walter Ullmann, *A History of Political Thought. The Middle Ages* (London, Penguin 1970), 53–8.

[74] Even Louis IX had allowed appeals from ecclesiastical to royal courts, thus underlining his supreme jurisdiction; assistance to the church was by way of grace and not duty. Watt, 'Spiritual and Temporal Power', 398–9. Until the Gregorian reforms at the end of the eleventh century, princes were deputies of Christ, "sacral figures who were considered to be the religious leaders of their people", Harold Berman, *Law and Revolution. The Formation of the Western Legal Tradition* (Harvard University Press 1983), 88. See also Senellart, *Les arts de gouverner*, 97–8.

[75] Dupuy, *Histoire du différend*, 317–18. See further Walter Ullmann, *Law and Politics in the Middle Ages. An Introduction to the Sources of Medieval Political Ideas* (London, Sources of History 1975), 127–8, and on the "episcopalism" by territorial rulers generally, Wilks, *Problem of Sovereignty*, 331–53.

regarded by many, including perhaps by himself.[76] After all, the Capets were celebrated for their ability to perform miracles, such as curing scrofula ("king's evil") by a mere touch.[77] As outsiders sometimes noted, Philip appeared to have two religions: a rather ritualistic Christianity as well as a religion of monarchy, the two often falling together so that "[t]o oppose such a king was not only evil, it was sacrilegious".[78]

After the Boniface affair, the most striking recourse to this political theology was the action taken – again under Nogaret's leadership – against the Knights Templar, the military–religious order that had been established in the twelfth century to guard roads and protect pilgrims to the Holy Land. In due course the order had also become a principal deliverer of arms and foodstuffs to Christian communities in the Middle East and a leading centre of finance and logistics for just wars. The order had furthermore engaged in banking and other economic services, operating directly under papal supervision and in close cooperation with European courts. By the mid-thirteenth century it had become one of the largest property owners in France, with castles and offices across the country.[79] Since 1279, the order had enjoyed rights of criminal jurisdiction at the heart of Paris and their headquarters had become a lively financial centre.[80] More recently, however, their reputation had begun to suffer from rumours about financial wrongdoings, and the loss of Acre in 1291 constituted a serious blow to the order's prestige.[81]

Philip's legists attacked the order by highlighting the "infamia" and "enormity" of their crimes, language earlier used against Saisset and Boniface. The order, Nogaret wrote, was the "substance of the Antichrist".[82] The knights were made to confess that their rituals

76 Philip's conviction that he had divine mandate to rule is discussed e.g. in Elizabeth Brown, 'Persona et gesta. The Image and Deeds of the Thirteenth-Century Capetians. The Case of Philip the Fair', 19 *Viator* (1988), 230 and generally 219–46.

77 See especially, Jacques Krynen, *L'empire du roi. Idées et croyances politiques en France, XIIIe–XVe siécle* (Paris, Gallimard 1993), 23–30.

78 Strayer, *Reign of Philip the Fair*, 13.

79 In 1190 the Knights Templar had also taken on the administration of the French royal treasury, an assignment they would hold until 1295 when Philip called the treasury back to the Louvre. Alain Demurger, *Vie et mort de l'ordre du Temple 1118–1314* (Paris, Seuil 1985), 203.

80 Jacques Heers, *La naissance du capitalisme au Moyen Age* (Paris, Perrin 2012), 227.

81 Demurger, *Vie et mort*, 221–5.

82 Ibid., 242–3. For the heresy charges, see Malcolm Barber, *The Trial of the Templars* (2nd edn, Cambridge University Press 2006), 202–16. On the political theology aspects of the trial, see Julien Théry, 'Une hérésie d'État. Philippe le Bel, le process des "perfides templiers" et la pontificalisation de la royauté française', in Maria-Anna Chevalier (ed.), *La fin de l'ordre du Temple* (Paris, Geuthner 2012), 86, 82–100.

included renouncing the divinity of Christ by spitting on the crucifix and making a pact with the devil by committing obscene acts. They were charged as having practised sodomy, venerated idols and celebrated the mass without the consecration of the host – a way to attack the body of Christ and the sacrament of Eucharist.[83] On 14 September 1307 royal officials across France took action and within a month most knights present in France, 546 in total, had been arrested. The pope, the sickly Clement V, was first angered by the intrusion in his jurisdiction. But as evidence of the Templars' confessions, exacted under torture, were presented to him, Clement approved the arrest of the rest of the members wherever they would be found.[84] Philip speeded up matters by persuading the archbishop of Sens to open the case in his province in May 1310 and have 54 knights burned to death as relapsed heretics.[85] Two years thereafter the pope finally suppressed the order. As most knights returned to their confessions, Jacques de Molay, the Grand Master of the Templars and their Preceptor, Geoffrey of Charney, insisted on their innocence and were burned at the stake in front of the Notre Dame in Paris on the king's order in March 1314.

But the king's concerns had been concrete and rather secular. The "international" character of the order, its direct submission to the pope, had been a serious obstruction to his authority. Moreover, in an increasingly grim economic situation resulting from the war in Flanders, Philip was tempted by the presence in Paris of one of the largest properties in his realm.[86] Under an arrangement that the king's lawyers concluded with the pope the Hospitaller knights would take over Templar properties with compensation of 200,000 livres tournois to Philip, followed by further cash instalments; the crown could keep the goods of the Temple situated in France and its debts to the Hospital were cancelled.[87] The result was "one of the largest transfers of wealth in the middle ages".[88] In trying to understand Philip's actions historians

[83] The charges were first explained in Nogaret's letter of 15 October 1307 and then formalised when the matter had moved into the pope's hands into 127 articles of accusation that served as the basis of the trials. Demurger, *Vie et mort*, 240.

[84] For the number of the arrested and other details, see ibid., 236–9.

[85] The archbishop, Philip de Marginy, was brother of Philip's long-standing minister of finance. Barber, *Trial of the Templars*, 175–9.

[86] The procrastination of the formal superior of the Templars, Pope Celeste VI, convinced Philip's lawyers that the only way forward was to carry the trial to a conclusion in Paris.

[87] Barber, *Trial of the Templars*, 271–2.

[88] Steven A. Epstein, *An Economic and Social History of Later Medieval Europe, 1000–1500* (Cambridge University Press 2009), 166.

have highlighted the king's financial motives as well as his genuine belief in the order's heretic nature.[89] Mixed motives take nothing away from the striking role that law and lawyers – Nogaret and Plaisians above all – had as instruments of a political theology that left no rival to royal supremacy. As they wrote in a long memorandum to the successor Boniface: "*est notorium toti mundo, quod reges Franciae, iste qui nunc est, et progenitores ipsius, superiorem, nisi Deum solum, in temporalibus non noverunt*".[90]

Philip's subjects must have looked at these developments with anxiety. If the king could set aside regular procedures on feudal tribute, clerical immunity and treason, did this not undermine the privileges of *all* his vassals? Could the king, for example, intervene in how they governed their fiefs or other properties? By now the legists were also using Roman law to argue that the king's powers extended beyond the circle of his formal vassals to *all* his subjects. In a draft treaty from 1294 with the king of England, for example, they had reserved Philip's *souveraineté royale* in Guyenne "as we have it over other French peers and their subjects".[91] Imperial powers also allowed the king to provide *lettres de cachet* on the strength of which Frenchmen could be imprisoned without legal process.[92] Moreover, at the universities of Orleans and Montpellier civil lawyers were busily contemplating the position of the king as equal to the Roman *princeps* and thus "emperor in his realm". Though they accepted that the German emperor was *Dominus mundi*, they also knew that the imperial chair had been vacant since 1245 and had the famous statement by Innocent III to rely upon to defend the view of royal powers in France as analogous to those of the emperor. The ideology of divine kingship, however popular it may have been, was no match, intellectually speaking, to the theories of the papalists. A much more powerful set of tools was found in the *Corpus iuris*, which offered a comprehensive frame for understanding the social transformations that had consolidated territorial kingship and the invigoration of economic life around urban centres. As *dominium* human authority would continue to need a religious foundation. But details of its *operation* could now be canvassed by the complex system of Roman (imperial) law.

[89] For a review of positions, see Barber, *Trial of the Templars*, 294–311.

[90] Dupuy, *Histoire du différend*, 317.

[91] Draft treaty of 1294, quoted in Pierre Chaplais, 'La souveraineté du Roi de France et le pouvoir legislatif en Guyenne au début du XIVe siècle', LXIX *Le Moyen Age* (1963), 452.

[92] See A. Esmein, 'Le maxime *Princeps legibus solutus est* dans l'ancien droit public français', in Paul Vinogradoff (ed.), *Essays in Legal History read before the International Congress of Historical Studies, London 1913* (Oxford University Press 1913), 206–8.

### *Rex Franciae in regno suo princeps est*

By the time Philip had reached adulthood, he had surrounded himself by lawyers using the *Corpus iuris* to give substance to his kingship by associating it with the power of the Roman emperor.[93] The French court had sought legal advice from the University of Paris at least from the 1160s, parallel to the commencement of civil law classes in Toulouse and Montpellier.[94] Philip II (Augustus, 1165–1223) had used lawyers to organise the administrative and judicial procedures in his realm, and Louis IX competed with the church in the employment of lawyers, many of whom possessed doctorates. As a result, the French government was soon in the hands of legists.[95] Of the six *clerici regis* who

[93] See E. M. Meijers, 'L'université d'Orléans au XIIIe siècle', in E. M. Meijers, *Etudes d'histoire de droit* (3 vols, Presse Universitaire Leyde 1959), III, 3–148; Robert Feenstra, 'L'enseignement du droit à Orléans. Etat des recherches menées depuis Meijers', in *Le droit savant au moyen âge et sa vulgarisation* (London, Variorum 1986), Essay III. Nineteenth-century historiography has depicted the legists as Gallican nationalists, ruthless servants of royal sovereignty. Some of this is surely anachronistic. No conscious plan is likely to have existed to undermine local nobility. Many (though not all) legists were nobles themselves and those who were not – Nogaret for instance – often acted as counsel to provincial magnates. Favier, *Philippe le Bel*, 35–6; Jean Favier, 'Les légistes et le gouvernement de Philippe le Bel', 2 *Journal des Savants* (1969), 102. By far most legists remained in the provinces, working privately or in royal service as local procurators or appellate judges. Only 11 of the 189 legists of the period studied by Strayer went to Paris. Joseph Strayer, *Les gens de justice du Languedoc sous Philippe le Bel* (Toulouse, Association Marc Bloch 1970), 38.

[94] Reception of civil law in southern France from the twelfth century onwards was facilitated by cultural links with Italy. The country of customary law, the north, followed a century later, but never as fully. See e.g. Albert Rigaudière, *Penser et construire l'État dans la France du Moyen-Age (XIIIe–XVe siècle)* (Paris, Comité pour l'histoire économique et financière de la France 2003), 93–116 and passim.

[95] According to customary and canon law, the king was to take his decision after consultation. This brought high-level "political" jurists into Philip's council once the old feudal *curia regis* had proven too cumbersome. For the professionalisation of the royal council, see Albert Rigaudière, *Introduction historique à l'étude de droit et des institutions* (Paris, Economica 2001), 245–9. About two-thirds of the varied membership of the council were legists. Élisabeth Lalou, 'Les légistes dans l'entourage de Philippe le Bel', in F. Attal, J. Carrigues, T. Kouamé & J-P. Vittu (eds), *Les universités en Europe du XIIIe siècle à nos jours* (Paris, Publications de la Sorbonne 2005), 106. Favier's list of the "political" legists includes, alongside Flote, Nogaret and Plaisians, Gilles Aycelin, archbishop of Narbonne, and Jacques Latilly (*garde des Sceaux* between Flote and Nogaret). Many would also add Raoul de Presles, the king's advocate, as well as Pierre de Mornay in the group. Favier, 'Les légistes', 97–9. On the transfer of the position of *chancelier*, the king's closest personal advisor, from theologians to jurists, see Ferdinand Lot & Robert Fawtier, *Histoire des institutions françaises au moyen age*, II: *Institutions royales* (Presses Universitaires de France 1958), 56–60. Legists also

were inherited to the *curia* of Philip the Fair from his father in 1285, at least four had been educated in civil law and the number of Orleans jurists increased massively during his reign.[96] The legists' royalist attitudes emerged from two sources. First, the canonist doctrine of the pope's plenitude of power spread to the administration of temporal justice, highlighting the role of the king as the source of all subordinate authority.[97] Second, civil law was accompanied by Roman imperial ideas, as visible in the edicts regulating law teaching at Orleans. Whatever laws were to be applied in the country, customary or civil, they were to be applied "not because the King was in any way forced to allow it but because he saw no need, for the moment, to change it".[98] Ideas of imperial kingship had been imbibed especially by the legists from the south, the country of written (civil) law, such as Flote and Nogaret.[99] But civil law was well known also in the French north, traditionally ruled by customary law, where royal judges such as Pierre de Fontaines (d. c. 1300) or Philippe de Beaumanoir (1250–96)

dominated the Parlement de Paris and played influential roles in the *Cour des comptes*, the realm's financial administration. The legists' influence followed their official position. The *garde des Sceaux*, for instance, was responsible for foreign policy, and both Flote and Nogaret carried out diplomatic assignments as did Pierre de Belleperche, one of the few who left a large number of written texts from his years of teaching civil law at Orleans. See further Franklin J. Pegues, *The Lawyers of the Last Capetiens* (Princeton University Press 1962), 108–9; Meijers, 'L'université d'Orléans au XIIIe siècle', 95–106.

96 The teaching of law had begun in Orleans in 1235, after Pope Honorius III, in order to dissuade students from moving from theology to law, had prohibited teaching civil law in Paris in 1219. The old view that Honorius had prohibited it at the request of Philip II owing to civil law's imperial bias seems doubtful. Chris Jones, *Eclipse of Empire? Perceptions of the Western Empire and its Rulers in Late-Medieval France* (Turnhout, Brepols 2007), 226–7. By mid-century, Orleans had become the principal centre of law study in France. For instance, collections of royal legislation and customary law, articulated and interspersed with fragments from the *Corpus iuris*, *Les Établissements de Saint Louis* (1273) and *Li Livres de justice et de Plet* (1260/1270), were all compiled at Orleans. See Meijers, 'L'université d'Orléans au XIIIe siècle', 1–26, 56–8. By the end of the century, the university had become known principally for its civil law teaching, which would influence also such foreign jurists as Cinus of Pistoia and Bartolus of Saxoferrato.

97 Olivier Guillot, Albert Rigaudière & Yves Saissier, *Pouvoirs et institutions dans la France médiévale*, 1: *Des origines à l'époque féodale* (3è éd., Paris, Armand Colin 2014), 307.

98 Jones, *Eclipse of Empire*, 228.

99 For a discussion of the "southern lawyers", see Franklin J. Pegues, *Lawyers of the Last Capetians* (Princeton University Press 1961), 87–107, and Strayer, *Les gens de justice*. Pierre Flote came from a noble family in Dauphiné. He was the uncle of the famous lawyer Aycelin, who played an important role in the Saisset affair and in the Templar trials. See Pegues, *Lawyers of the Last Capetians*, 87–98; Strayer, *The Reign of Philip the Fair*, 51–2 (on Flote).

used the *Corpus iuris* to give form to local customary laws: "Bien s'acorde nostre usage à la loi," Fontaines wrote.[100]

But could the French king arrogate to himself the role of the emperor? Philip and his predecessors had generally been on good terms with the holders of the position of the "king of the Romans" and Albert of Habsburg, elected in 1298, had been a reliable ally. But the French king's power had been growing in the thirteenth century. Normandy, Aquitaine and Languedoc had been attached to his *regnum* and few doubted that Philip was the most powerful king in Christendom. His effort to have his brother, Charles of Valois, elected emperor after Albert's death in 1308 had failed owing to lack of papal support and understandable concern among German princes about further expansion of French influence. But Philip's ambitions were modest; it was in any case clear to him that he was the church's principal defender and many Frenchmen believed that the long hereditary succession of the Capet family put the French throne far above the imperial seat.[101] Besides, he had little to fear from the new emperor-elect. Henry VII had been educated in France and held Luxembourg as a fief from the French king. To Philip's surprise, the new emperor wanted to take his role seriously by requiring homage from imperial vassals in Philip's *regnum.*[102] He also sought to strengthen imperial rule in northern Italy, hoping to have himself crowned in Rome. In a letter informing the Christian princes of the coronation plan he restated the old imperialist principle: even as the universe had been divided into separate *regnis et provinciis*, they were nevertheless subordinated to one monarchy (*uni principi monarchi subessent*).[103] Philip immediately responded by expressing his astonishment at such a view, reminding Henry that nothing of the kind could apply to the French monarchy that was subordinated only to the rule of Jesus Christ. Philip did not deny Henry's imperial status but

100 The compilation by Pierre de Fontaines was written around 1253. See *Le conseil de Pierre de Fontaines ou Traité de l'ancienne jurisprudence française* (A. J. Marnier ed., Paris, Durand 1846), 176. See further Philippe de Beaumanoir, *Les coutumes de Beauvaisis* (A. Salmon ed., Paris, Picard 1899).

101 For an excellent review of the French views see also, alongside Jones, *Eclipse of Empire*, Chris Jones, 'Understanding Political Conceptions in the Later Middle Ages. The French Imperial Candidatures and the Idea of the Nation-State', 42 *Viator* (2011), 83–114.

102 A good overview of the French relations with the empire is in Strayer, *The Reign of Philip the Fair*, 346–67.

103 'Encyclica in Forma Maiori', 29 June 1312, in *Monumenta Germaniae Historica* (MGH), *Legum Sectio IV, Part IV/2* (Hanover, 1909–11), No 801 (802).

insisted that he should have exempted Philip from any suggestion that he was under imperial power.[104]

According to the official view of the church, all kings were subordinated to the emperor. Boniface had confirmed this in his letter to Albert, stating that the emperor-to-be would become *imperatorem et monarcham omnium regum et principum terrenorum*. This would be notwithstanding what he called the *superbia Gallicana* about there being no superior to the French king. "But the French lie" [*Mentiuntur*], he insisted, for *de iure sunt et esse debent sub rege Romano et imperatore.*[105] Boniface even borrowed the exclamation of the prophet Jeremiah: "See, today I appoint you over nations and kingdoms to uproot and tear down, to destroy and overthrow, to build and to plant."[106] Perhaps the most influential of the first generation of canon lawyers, Huguccio of Pisa (d. 1210) gave the official view in 1190 as *Solus enim Romanus dicitur iure imperator, sub quo omnes regs debent esse.*[107] But a change was brewing. Already in the 1160s, Étienne de Tournai (1128–03), one of the first French canon lawyers (and godfather to Louis VII) glossed *distinctio* 2 of Gratian's *Decretum* that dealt with legislative powers with the remark that *rex in regno suo. Vel eundem vocat regem et imperatorem.*[108] Canon lawyers were also fast to notice the papal statement of 1202 – *rex ipse superiorem in temporalibus minime recognoscat.* As experts in a legal system with universal jurisdiction that looked up to the pope as the head of Christianity, they had no difficulty in accepting that secular princes might well have the same powers as the emperor "in their realm", especially if, as the French king, they could also be imagined as "très Chrétien". Hence, the French canon lawyer

[104] 'Responsio Philippi Regis Franciae', MGH IV, IV/2, No 811 (812). For the context and a discussion, see e.g. Andreas Osiander, *Before the State. Systemic Political Change in the West from the Greeks to the French Revolution* (Oxford University Press 2007), 285–96.

[105] 'Allegacio domini pape Bonifacii pro confirmando rege Romanorum Alberto', MGH *Constitutiones* IV, No 173 (139).

[106] "venit quidem tempus, ut constituamus cum super gentes et regna, ut eveillat et destruat, dissipet et dispergat et edificet et plantet", 'Allegacio domini', (140). Boniface also confirmed his authority to confer and remove the imperial power in accordance with papal will "si subveniat iusta et legitima causa".

[107] Huguccio, *Glossa in Apibus*, C7 q1 c1, cited in Sophie Petit-Renaud, *'Faire loy', au royaume de France. De Philippe VI à Charles V (1328–1380)* (Paris, De Boccard 2001), 23. See also Gaines Post, *Studies in Medieval Legal Thought. Public Law and the State 1100–1322* (Princeton University Press 1964), 459; Paradisi, *Studi*, 306–7.

[108] F. von Schulte (ed.), *Die Summa des Stephanus Tornacensis über das Decretum Gratiani* (Giessen, Roth 1891), 12. See further Paradisi, *Studi*, 305; Rigaudière, *Penser et construire*, 363–4, Mireille Chazan, *L'empire et l'histoire universelle de Sigebert de Gembloux à Jean de Saint Victor* (Paris, Honoré Champion 1999), 650–1 and Petit-Renaud, *'Faire loy', au royaume de France*, 28.

Alain wrote in 1208 that the king *tantum ius habet in regnum suo quantum imperator in imperio*. This was so, he explained, because the empire had undergone a process of *divisio rerum* the results of which had been reaffirmed by the *ius gentium*.[109]

In legal terms, the rise of independent *regna* was expressed by the law of nations. The empire might have been received through divine law that looked for Christian unity. But no such unity existed presently. In the twelfth century, Pope Gregorius VIII had written to Hungary's ruler that the latter was under no other power than of the mother church, and Alfonso VII of Spain (1126–57) described himself as *princeps et rex Hispaniae* as well as *Dei gratia totius Hispanae imperator*.[110] For obvious reasons, canon lawyers had little difficulty in using the *Decretum* to give effect to this view. The Bible treated kings as supreme rulers in their territories, and the canonist Alanus Anglicus pointed out that the territorial division had also been accepted by the pope: *Divisio enim regnorum de jure gentium introductum a papa approbatur licet in antiquo jure gentium imperator unus in orbe esse deberet*.[111] The juxtaposition between "old" and a "new" *ius gentium* would in due course be recaptured in the distinction between *ius gentium primaevum* that was part of secondary natural law – perhaps in the way of "conclusions" drawn from its primary rules as suggested by Aquinas – and *ius gentium secundarium* that reflected the positive practices in which the rulers of *regna* had engaged with some degree of uniformity. Alanus was clear that even as the empire was set up by God, individual rulers received their authority from the pope and were in this respect fully equal.[112]

The matter was a little trickier under civil law according to which the empire had been established by God and the emperor was *Dominus mundi* [D 14. 2, 9].[113] There were prerogatives that only

109 Quoted by Jean Rivière, 'Sur l'origine de la formule "Rex imperator in regno suo"', 4 *Revue des sciences religieuses* (1924), 584 and Rivière, *Le problème de l'Église et de l'État*, 425–30. Jurists who shared this view included the Frenchman Guillaume Durand of Mende and such Italians as Cinus of Pistoia, Oldradus de Ponte and Andrea d'Isernia in the early fourteenth century, Rivière, 'Sur l'origine', 581–3.

110 Paradisi, *Studi*, 303–10.

111 Alanus Anglicus, quoted in Chazan, *L'empire*, 461 n 151.

112 "Et quod dictum est de imperatore. . ., habeatur repetitum de quolibet principe, qui supra se dominum non habet," Alanus Anglicus, *Apparatus*, quoted in Post, *Studies*, 464, 464–5. By the mid-thirteenth century, this had become a canonist commonplace. Paradisi, *Studi*, 308–11.

113 According to Iustinian's *Novella* No. 73 "Quia igitur imperium propterea Deus de coelo constituit". Likewise, the law *Cunctos populos* that opens the *Code* was usually read so as to affirm that the emperor was "lord of the world". The text [C 1.1] reads

the emperor would enjoy, such as raising taxes or declaring just war.[114] However, by the twelfth century it had become obvious that the empire controlled only a very limited territory. The legitimacy of England, Spain and France as territorial *regna*, indpendent from the empire, had become largely uncontested. In the middle of the next century, Vincent of Beauvais in his great *Speculum* addressed the territorial *regnum* as *corpus reipublicae mysticum*, an organological "body" on a par with the church itself.[115] At the same time, civil lawyers began to interest themselves in the doctrines of *bonum commune* and *utilitas publica*. Even Giles of Rome's *De regimine principum* depicted ruling as common service and the king as the head of the political commonwealth analogously to how the pope had been seen within the church. Ideas about corporate legal subjects, the operation of institutional hierarchies, taxation and diplomatic practice were now applied in royal government as well.[116]

By the mid-thirteenth century century French civil lawyers had begun to use the distinction between *de iure* and *de facto* to allow creative application of the principles of civil law.[117] Influenced by canon lawyers operating with an actually living legal system to which new materials were constantly being added, they began to apply the provisions of the *Corpus iuris* that dealt with the *princeps* to the French king.[118] Here they could rely on the famous response by Pope Innocent III (1160–16), made almost incidentally to the question concerning the legitimation of bastards, according to which nobody was entitled to challenge the way the king ruled his regnum (*rex*

in English "We desire that all peoples [Cunctos populos] subject to Our benign Empire shall live under the same religion." Others pointed out, however, that the formulation accepts the presence also of peoples that are *not* "subject to" the empire. A frequent reference in this context is the statement by Emperor Antonius: "Ego quidem mundi dominus, lex autem maris." Ugo Nicolini, *La proprietà, il principe e l'espropiazione per pubblica utilità* (Milano, Giuffrè 1952), 115. Azo appears to oscillate. In his *Summa codicis* (3, 13) the emperor is said to possess "plurissima iurisdictio" and the king only "merum imperium". Elsewhere in discussing the French king's position he notes that "hodie videtur eandem potestatem habere in terra sua quam imperator; ergo potuit facere quod sibi placet". Paradisi regards the reference to Ulpian as "remarkable", *Studi*, 308–9.

114 Chazan, *L'empire*, 641.

115 Kantorowicz, *The King's Two Bodies*, 208.

116 See e.g. James Brundage, *Medieval Canon Law* (London, Longman 1995), 98–119 and generally Berman, *Law and Revolution*, 199 ff.

117 See e.g. Meijers, 'L'université d'Orléans au XIIIe siècle', III, 23–4.

118 On the influence of the canon lawyers in France, see Paradisi, *Studi*, 283–4, 294–5 and 314–15 and on Azo's oscillation, 308–9.

*superiorem non recognescens in temporalibus*).[119] The first jurist to take up this perhaps carelessly formulated view was the Burgundian lawyer Jean de Blanot (c. 1230–c. 1280), trained in Bologna and later official with the archbishop of Lyons. In his commentary on Iustinian's *Institutes* of 1256 [I 4.6,13] Jean wrote that the king *in temporalibus superiorem non recogniscit* and ascribed to him a *natural* power of jurisdiction.[120] Jean well understood that this breached the "feudal" principle that the "men" of a seigneur's vassals were not to be regarded as "men" of the seigneur, and his reading of the king as a Roman *princeps*, rather than a feudal lord, was unlikely to have been widely shared at the time.[121] In 1265 Jean came to the matter anew when commenting on the *Lex Iulia maiestatis* [C 9.8; D 48.4] where he affirmed that the vassals of a treasonous baron were freed from their vow to him.[122] This was so because the regnum was the *patria* and the king represented the *bonum publicum*.[123]

But it was only at the time of Philip the Fair that legists generally began to cite texts from the *Corpus iuris* to portray the king as a *princeps*

119 *Per venerabilem*, 1202. Text e.g. in Carbasse & Leyte, *L'état royal*, 25.

120 Jean de Blanot, *Tractatus super feudis et homagiis* (1256), reproduced in relevant part by Jean Acher, 'Notes sur le droit savant au moyen age', 30 *Nouvelle Revue Historique de Droit Français & Etranger* (1906), 161. Cited also in Petit-Renaud, *'Faire Loy', au royaume de France*, 30 and in Francesco Calasso, *I glossatori e la teoria della sovranità* (3rd edn, Milano, Giuffrè 1957), 114.

121 As Jean explained "Set quamvis in potestate regis ita quod iure homagii non sint astricti, sunt tamen in potestate regis iure naturalis iurisdictionis quam rex habet in regno. . . . Nam sicut omnia sunt imperatoris, quantum ad iurisdictionem, cum sit mundi dominus, sic omnia que sunt in regno, sunt regis quantum ad iurisdictionem." Blanot, *Tractatus*, 160. The "theoretical" nature of Jean's view is stressed in Bernd Schneidemüller, *Nomen patriae. Die Entstehung Frankreichs in der politisch-geographischen Terminologie (10.–13. Jahrhundert)* (Sigmaringen, Thorbecker 1987), 257–64. See also see Marguerite Boulet-Sautel, "Jean de Blanot et la conception du pouvoir royal au temps de Louis IX", *Septième centenaire de la mort de saint Louis (1970)* (Paris, Belles Lettres 1976), 57–68. Calasso points out that the formula had been in use among Italian glossators already more than half a century before Jean, *I glossatori*, 24, 110–23 and passim. The extensive debate has been usefully summarised in Robert Feenstra, 'Jean de Blanot et la formule "Rex Franciae in regno suo princeps est"', in *Études d'histoire du droit canonique dédiées à Gabriel le Bras*, tome II (Paris, Sirey 1965), 803–13.

122 Blanot, *Tractatus*, 160–1. Krynen, *L'empire du roi*, 386. Post doubts that Blanot actually regarded the French king as equal to the emperor. He may have possessed similar internal powers but was by no stretch of imagination "lord of the world". *Studies*, 471–2.

123 The king acted "propter bona tocius patriae sive propter bonum publicum regni gallie cuius administrationem gerit", Blanot, *Tractatus*, 162.

with general jurisdiction.[124] The Orleans jurist Jacques de Révigny (Jacopo Ravannis, c. 1230–96), one of the century's most influential French academic lawyers, was well versed in the dialectics of Dominican scholasticism and used the *de iure / de facto* distinction so as to find a compromise between the abstract position in the *Corpus iuris* and the political reality around him.[125] According to Révigny, although the French king seemed to think of himself independent of the emperor *de facto*, he was not so *de iure*.[126] This did not mean that he would not be "supreme" in his realm, however. Many aspects of imperial rule could be applied to him – Révigny was thinking of taxation, no doubt, as well as other public law powers.[127] Like Jean de Blanot, Révigny accepted that in case of an uprising against the king, the provision on treason under the *Lex Iulia maiestatis* was applicable. This was not, however, because the king was *princeps* but because he was an official of the emperor (*magistratus principis*).[128] But the main point was that the French king ruled as supreme authority analogously to the emperor.

[124] See Rigaudière, *Penser et construire*, 39–66; Petit-Renaud, *'Faire loy', au royaume de France*, 27–31; Jones, *Eclipse of Empire*, 222–9.

[125] Révigny's royalism would be taken on board by the Italian Cinus of Pistoia through whom it would influence the absolutist strands in later Italian commentators. See e.g. Ennio Cortese, *Il rinascimento giuridico medieval* (Roma, Bulzoni 1996), 85–6 and for Révigny's use of civil law sources, Kees Bezemer, *What Jacques Saw. Thirteenth Century France thorough the Eyes of Jacques de Révigny, professor of law at Orléans* (Frankfurt, Klostermann 1997), 1–12. For the later absolutist theories of Albericus de Rosate, Angelus and Baldus of Ubaldi and other Italian jurists, see Kenneth Pennington, *The Prince and the Law 1200–1600* (University of California Press 1993), 113–16; Nicolini, *La proprietà*, 132–42 and above all Jane Black, *Absolutism in Renaissance Milan. Plenitude of Power under the Visconti and the Sforza 1329–1535* (Oxford University Press 2009), 14–29, 35, 94–113.

[126] "quidam dicunt quod Francia exempta est ab imperio; hoc est impossibile de iure", Jacques de Révigny, Lectura in dig.vet. in premio, cited in Meijers, 'L'université d'Orléans au XIIIe siècle', 9 n. 13. On Révigny on kingship, see Bezemer, *What Jacques Saw*, 97–102. See also Post, *Studies*, 472–4; Krynen, *L'empire du roi*, 315.

[127] Kees Bezemer, 'The Law School of Orleans as a School of Public Administration', 66 *Tijdschrift voor Rechtsgeschiedenis* (1998), 249, 251. Schneidemüller stresses the degree to which Révigny uses the original Roman texts, writing of the "*populus Romanus*" and "*urbs Rome*", avoiding any effort to bring the texts up to date. *Nomen patriae*, 270–1.

[128] ". . . probatur quia rex princeps est quia non recognoscit superiorem. Dico: hoc est comitere in principem, non, sicunt ipsi dicunt, quod quod rex princeps est, set quia comitiur in magistratum principis", quoted in Robert Feenstra, '"Quaestiones de materia feudorum" de Jacques de Révigny', in Robert Feenstra, *Fata iuris romani* (Presse Universitaire Leyde 1972), 313. A slightly differtent version in Francesco Calasso, *I Glossatori*, 44. See also Schneidemüller, *Nomen patriae*, 271; Pennington, *The Prince and the Law*, 95–6; S. H. Cuttler, *The Law of Treason and Treason Trials in Medieval France* (Cambridge University Press 1981), 11–12.

He represented the *corona regnum* that entitled him, among other things, to reach beyond the limited circle of his vassals to defend the realm.[129]

Philip's legists had no scruples about the legal position of their king. As Nogaret's close collaborator, Guillaume de Plaisians put it in 1307:

> all that is situated within the frontiers of the kingdom belongs to the Lord King, at least as concerns protection, high justice and even with regard to the property that belongs to everyone that may be given, received and consumed by the Lord King for the public good or the defence of the kingdom.

The king was, he continued, *imperator in regno suo et imperare possit terre et mari et omnes populi regni sui eius regantur imperio.*[130] By now, many royal jurists would accept that the king had authority to intervene in noble privileges. Among them was Révigny's most well-known successor Pierre de Belleperche (Petrus de Bellapertica, 1230/47–1308) who joined the royal curia in the 1290s, carried out a number of diplomatic tasks, working as *garde des Sceaux* until replaced by Nogaret at the outset of the Templars' trial.[131] Yet others were reluctant to think of the king as *legibus solutus* in the way of the Roman emperor. These jurists – Révigny among them – would often side with the barons, situating kingship within old feudal law under which the king was simply a supreme suzerain in a network of reciprocal duties and privileges.[132]

But Roman law had irresistible appeal to the expanding bureaucracy; it gave logical form to feudal practices and responded to economic questions difficult to treat under customary law.[133] And the king appreciated the way it equalised the relations between the French crown and the emperor. Already Louis IX had confronted the issue in 1241 when, in the context of the convocation of a general council of the church that was expected to depose Emperor Frederick II, the latter

[129] But Révigny accepted that if fulfilling the duty to the emperor were harmful to one's *patria,* then one was entitled to defend the latter, Feenstra, 'Quaestiones', 314. And discussion in Schneidemüller, *Nomen patriae*, 272.

[130] See *Mémoire relatif au paréage de 1307*, tome I (Mende, 1896), 521. It is quoted (in French) in Rigaudière, *Penser et construire*, 527 n. 13. See also Joseph Strayer, *Medieval Statecraft and Perspectives of History* (Princeton University Press 1971), 57.

[131] The "regalistic tendencies" of Belleperche are discussed in Kees Bezemer, *Pierre de Belleperche. Portrait of a Legal Puritan* (Frankfurt, Klostermann 2005), highlights on 29, 127–31. See further Meijers, 'L'université d'Orléans au XIIIe siècle', 95–106; Pegues, *Lawyers of the Last Capetians*, 108–9.

[132] See Pennington, *The Prince and the Law*, 97–106; Susan Reynolds, *Fiefs and Vassals. The Medieval Evidence Reinterpreted* (Oxford, Clarendon 2001), 35–7.

[133] See especially Rigaudière, *Penser et construire*, 39–173. See also Jones, *Eclipse of Empire*, 220–9.

had arrested a group of French prelates on their way to the council.[134] In reaction, Louis sent identical letters to the emperor and the pope where he reminded them of the peaceful equality that France and the empire, both Charlemagne's inheritors, had enjoyed in the past. The argument then became part of the effort to highlight the Carolingian background of the Capet family and the equality of the different parts of the old empire: "the kingdom and the empire were one and the same thing".[135] In the pamphlet *Disputatio inter Clericum et Militem* that came out at the time of the struggle with Boniface, the "knight" responded angrily to the suggestion that kings were appointed by the emperor. Charlemagne's kingdom, the "knight" insisted, was divided equally between its successors so that "whatever privilege and dignity the name of empire retains in the one part, the kingdom of France has in the other".[136] The provincial lawyer Pierre Dubois, one of the few who actually wrote that Philip ought to take the imperial crown himself, or at least to his brother, drew a direct line of descent from Charlemagne to the present French king.[137]

An imperial view of the king was also expressed in the compilation of statements from Roman and canon law from Orleans around the 1260s, *Li livres de jostice et de plet*: "*Li rois ne doit tenir de nuil*".[138] The point of such a statement was to underline the fact, known from at least the twelfth century, that the king paid no feudal homage to anybody. Even if a king received land that was held of somebody as a fief, that relationship would end with the transfer.[139] The lands he held as fiefs would cease being so as he ascended the throne. The king's *bailli*, ambassador and close confidant, Philippe de Beaumanoir (1250–96),

[134] On the use of the event by French histories against the emperor, see Jones, *Eclipse of Empire*, 79–82.

[135] Carbasse & Leyte, *L'État royal*, 26. At the time of Philip Augustus, the theory of *reditus regni francorum ad stirpem Caroli imperatoris* assumed that, in marrying a descendant of the Carolingian family, Philip re-established the line to Charlemagne, broken at Hugues Capet's coronation in 987. Perhaps because his title to the crown had been questioned, Philip the Fair aimed to demonstrate an *unbroken* succession between the Carolingians and the Capets. See Jones, *Eclipse of Empire*, 145–69.

[136] 'A Debate between a Clerk and a Knight', in R. W. Dyson (ed.), *Three Royalist Tracts 1296–1302* (Bristol, Thoemmes 1999), 41. See also Krynen, *L'empire du roi*, 384–7.

[137] Pierre Dubois, *The Recovery of the Holy Land* (Columbia University Press 1956), II 116 (175).

[138] Quoted in Rigaudière, *Introduction historique*, 224. For an overview of similar statements in the thirteenth and early fourteenth century, see further Rigaudière, *Penser et construire*, 39–66; Petit-Renaud, *'Faire loy', au royaume de France*, 23–31.

[139] See e.g. Romain Telliez, *Les institutions de France médiévale XIe–Xve siècles* (Paris, Armand Colin 2009), 72–3.

remarked in his famous codification from the 1280s, *Coutumes de Beauvaisis* (1283), that "*Le roi est souverain par-dessus tout*".[140] That Beaumanoir held the French barons also "*souverain*" in their baronies shows at least the fluctuations of the vocabulary at the time.[141] In the mid-thirteenth century the French barons had the power to administer their baronies as they wanted, while the king's powers of legislation, though real, were strictly circumscribed by the duty to take counsel from the greatest nobles and to make laws only for common profit or public utility.[142]

Most Orleans jurists learned from Révigny the technique of distinguishing between the *de iure* position of the emperor and the *de facto* position of the king. There could hardly have been clearer expression of the ambivalence with which these jurists welcomed a changing world. Not all accepted this. Belleperche could not understand how mere facts could have legal significance; if the French king was to have the same authority as the emperor, then this could only be because he was, in legal terms, emperor in his realm.[143] But most jurists, keen to have their cake and eat it, too, employed the *de iure / de facto* distinction and its temporal transformation, the justification of present institutions, such as sovereignty and property, against the ideals of natural law by reference to *ius gentium*. This was certainly the case of the most famous followers of the Orleans jurists, the Italian commentators of the fourteenth century. Bartolus and Baldus derived the very independence of individual *regna* from *ius gentium* as an expression of a *de facto* development which, though contrary to the *de iure* status of imperial overlordship, still enjoyed full legal force.[144]

The leading role of the legists in the consolidation of Philip's territorial rule was an outcome of actions to strengthen French judicial and financial administration, to improve the collection of taxes and other revenues, to formalise the exercise of royal justice and to consolidate the

140 Beaumanoir, *Coutumes de Beauvaisis*, quoted in Georges Lagarde, *La naissance de l'esprit laïque*, tome I: *Bilan du XIIIe siècle* (Presses Universitaires de France 1934), 137–40.

141 Philippe Beaumanoir, *Coutumes de Beauvaisis* (Paris, Picard 1900), §1043 (23).

142 See e.g. Rigaudière, *Penser et construire*, 55–60.

143 See Meijers, 'L'université d'Orleans au XIIIe siècle', 95–106; Pegues, *Lawyers of the Last Capetians*, 108–9; Bezemer, *Pierre de Belleperche*.

144 The historian Bernard Guenée has pointed to the practically identical use of the *ius gentium* to justify the separation of independent *regna* in French universal histories and in the writings of Bartolus and Baldus. Bernard Guenée, 'Review of Joseph Canning, *The Political Thought of Baldus de Ubaldis*', 45 *Annales. Économies, sociétés, civilisations* (1990), 1099.

independence of the French church. Some of the action initiated or supported by the legists, such as the expulsions and confiscations directed at the Jews and the debasement of the value of coins, turned out counterproductive. No clear outcome arose of the war with England in 1294–7, and the disaster of Courtrai in 1302 where Philip lost a good number of his knights, underlined the continuing difficulties with Flanders. Both wars had to do with a conflict between the king and one of his strongest vassals, but their inconclusive ending turned them into mere preliminaries for the Hundred Years War. And even as Philip twice failed to have his candidate elected as the emperor, at his death in 1314 the government of France was more firmly established and the monarchy more widely respected than ever.

* * * * *

By the mid-thirteenth century, the independence of territorial *regna* began to be recognised by jurists across Europe. Some, like the leading canonist during the office of Innocent III, Alanus Anglicus, argued that, according to *ius gentium*, what had been applied to the emperor would now be applied to individual kings: *unusquisque [rex] tantum iuris habet in regno suo quantum imperator in Imperio.*[145] Gradually also civilians would echo the same view, especially with regard to France, England and Spain. The effort to reconcile these developments with Christian universality peaked in Bartolus' two-pronged view. On the one hand, "whoever would say that the emperor is not lord and monarch of the entire world would be a heretic".[146] On the other hand, it was possible to think not only of the king but also the *civitas* itself as a *princeps* (he was thinking of North Italian city-states) though only *de facto.*[147] This was so because imperial power was "only" *ratione protectionis vel administrationis.* It did not cancel out the dominion kings had over their *regna*: to rule universally did not mean to rule every particular as well.[148] It was

[145] Alanus Anglicus, 'Gloss to D.96 c.6', *Compilatio* I (c. 1208), quoted in Paradisi, *Studi*, 310.

[146] Bartolus on D 49.15, 24, English translation in Pennington, *The Prince and the Law*, 197. See further Cecil N. Sidney Woolf, *Bartolus of Sassoferrato. His Position in the History of Medieval Political Thought* (Cambridge University Press 1913), 23–31.

[147] See Magnus Ryan, 'Bartolus of Sassoferrato and Free Cities. The Alexander Prize Lecture', 10 *Transactions of the Royal Historical Society* (1999), 65–89, 66. Ryan points to the many unclarities and contradictions in that concept, however, and argues that it had more to do with the right of the city government to govern (internal sovereignty) than the city's customary independence from the emperor or the pope.

[148] Woolf, *Bartolus of Sassoferrato*, 23–5.

increasingly obvious that many "Roman" (i.e. Christian) peoples were ruled independently of the emperor. Whether this was explained as a grant or by the emperor's silent consent, it had taken place *iure gentium. Regna* and smaller *civitates* had emerged and could still be created as long as this was not *ad injuriam vel emulationem alterius.*[149] This was also the view of Bartolus' most famous student, Baldus of Ubaldi (1327–400), a future defender of the absolutism of Milanese rulers. The kings of France commit a sin in case they do not recognise the empire's universal authority *de iure.* But then he ingeniously added this did not mean that the emperor would also have all power over France; *aliud est dicere universale, aliud integrum.*[150] Even the Bible had recognised lawful kingship before the Roman empire. If the empire now had lost its power, this could only mean that the old customary *ius gentium* would now rise from the ashes.[151]

## Philip in Context 1: "Feudalism"

Whatever the relations between the French king and the emperor, the principal implications of the legists' imperial language appeared *inside* the country.[152] Philip had occasion to express his own view on the matter at a meeting of estates on 10 April 1302 convoked to debate the problem of the pope. At one point the king turned to the bishops, asking "from whom do you hold your bishoprics?", and then from the nobles, "from whom do you hold your fiefs?" Both groups were expected to respond "from the king". To this the king added, "*Quant à nous, nous ne tenons notre royaume que de Dieu seul.*"[153] This must have stunned the nobles and prelates present. If the king was answerable only to God, what then of the security of their rights and privileges? This was no trifling matter. At the end of the thirteenth century, French dukes and counts exercised extensive dominion in their lordships. In addition to ruling their vassals and tenants, they possessed seigneurial jurisdiction, produced moneys, provided letters of grace and exception and handed out all kinds of concessions on roads and

149 Ibid., 110, 114.

150 Petit-Renaud, *'Faire loy', au royaume de France*, 29.

151 See in detail Joseph Canning, *The Political Thought of Baldus de Ubaldis* (Cambridge University Press 1987), 104–58.

152 Telliez, *Les Institutions*, 73. Pennington, *The Prince and the Law*, 101; Jones, *Eclipse of Empire*, 221.

153 Cited in Eric Bournazel, 'La royauté féodale en France et en Angleterre Xe–XIIIe siècles', in Eric Bournazel & Jean-Pierre Poly, *Les féodalités* (Presses Universitaires de France 1998), 389.

waterways. Their bureaucracies and privileges rivalled and often offset the expansion of royal power.[154] Beaumanoir's *Coutumes de Beauvaisis* (1283) suggested even that *li rois est souverains par dessus tous et a de son droit la general garde de tout son roiaume par quoi il puet fere teus establissemens comme il li plest.*[155] "As he pleases" – yet another ominous reference to the king's imperial powers.[156] In a world of "feudal" relations, however, Philip would find his *dominium* in many ways constrained.

Feudalism is a notoriously difficult topic. The category is often seen as an invention by historians eager to forge a sharp contrast between a medieval and an early modern period, the latter associated with Renaissance culture and political statehood that have defined subsequent generations' historical self-understanding.[157] Some would wish to avoid the word "feudalism" altogether.[158] In any case, by early thirteenth century many of the interpersonal relations commonly associated with feudalism – a pyramidical structure of right–duty relationships between lords and vassals, the duty to render military service to the lord, the inalienability of clusters of right labelled "fiefs" – were either no longer present in France or their details varied so as to make generalisation impossible. On the other hand, professional lawyers such as Jean de Blanot or Guillaume Durand (the older, c. 1230–1296) used the twelfth-century collection *Libri feudorum* to create a reasonably uniform *academic* debate about the rights and powers of the king and his barons, vassals and other subjects. They would read feudal law by reference to Roman categories, understanding feudal homage as contract (or alternatively a right *in rem*), fief as public office and kingship as empire – thus transforming the sense of those Roman concepts to reflect the historical balance between the forces of the *regnum*.[159]

154 For the seigneurial powers, see Jean Brissaud, *A History of French Public Law* (New York, Kelley 1969), 205–42 and Dominique Barthélemy, *L'ordre seigneurial* (Paris, Seuil 1990), 200–18, and for a discussion of such "parcellised sovereignty", see Ellen Meiksins Wood, *Citizens to Lords. A Social History of Western Political Thought from Antiquity to the Middle Ages* (London, Verso 2008), 167–74.

155 Beaumanoir, *Coutumes de Beauvaisis*, § 1043 (23–4).

156 Krynen, *L'empire du roi*, 404–5.

157 See especially Kathleen Davis, 'Sovereign Subjects, Feudal Law, and the Writing of History', 36 *Journal of Medieval and Early Modern Studies* (2006), 223–61.

158 The difficulties in regard to French history are dealt with *in extenso* in Reynolds, *Fiefs and Vassals*, 258–322.

159 See especially Gérard Giordanengo, *Le droit feudal dans les pays de droit écrit. L'exemple de la Provence et du Dauphiné XII–début XIV siècle* (École française de Rome 1988), 127 and generally 111–52. See also Meijers, 'Les glossateurs et le droit féodal', in E. M. Meijers, *Etudes d'histoire de droit* (3 vols, Universitaire Pers, Leiden 1959), III, 261–70 and Emanuele Conte, 'Framing the Feudal Bond. A Chapter in the History of the

Under customary law the French king was certainly no Roman *princeps* but only the highest lord or suzerain of the *regnum Francorum* whose powers reached down to his vassals, the great lords. The maxim "the man of my man is not my man" meant that lower subjects would not owe homage to him. Although Jean de Blanot, for example, subscribed to this maxim as a matter of principle, he did not assume that it applied to the king – instead, *homines omni regni Francie sunt homines regis.* Even as they had never made any homage to him, all Frenchmen fell under the *potestate Regis iure naturalis iurisdictionis quam rex habet in regno.*[160] In his above-mentioned discussion of the case of the vassal of a treasonous lord Jean stressed that the subjects' ultimate loyalty must be to the king, because he defended the *corona* and acted *propter bona tocius patriae sive propter bonum publicum regni gallie cuius administrationem gerit.*[161] The association of kingship with the abstract and impersonal notion of the *corona* detached it from any lord–vassal relationship while *bonum publicum* linked royal rule to proto-nationalist appeals to fight for "Gallia" (*pugnando pro patria*). As the linkage between the subject and the king was forged through the common good, the result was a *political* instead of a contractual bond. Jean explained this as a result of kingship being an institution of the law of nations, *ad hoc tenentur ex iure gentium.*[162] Jean's position was taken up by the canon lawyer Guillaume Durand, also a student from Bologna, later bishop of Mende in the part of his widely read *Speculum iuris* (1270–1) that dealt with feudal law. Durand explained the principles of feudalism as in part natural law, in part *ius gentium*, to the extent that they were products of customary practice (*moribus & diutorno usu*).[163] He then followed Jean closely (without acknowledgement), affirming the character of the French king as *princeps.*[164] He would recognise no temporal superior and his rule would

*ius commune* in Medieval Europe', 80 *The Legal History Review* (2012), 481–95. Another good account is Anne-Marie Patault, *Introduction historique au droit des biens* (Presses Universitaires de France 1989), 83–112.

160 Blanot, *Tractatus*, 160. See also François L. Ganshof, *Qu'est-ce que la féodalité* (5th edn, Paris, Texto 1982), 163–4.

161 Blanot, *Tractatus*, 162. See also the discussion in Cuttler, *The Law of Treason*, 15–17.

162 Blanot, *Tractatus*, 162. See also Calasso, *I glossatori*, 116–19.

163 Guillaume Durand, *Speculum Iuris. Pars Tertia & Quarta* (Lyon 1577), IV III § 2 (144r).

164 "nam Rex Franciae princeps est in regno suo", ibid., IV III § 2 para 29 (146r). For a comparison of the textual passages of Jean de Blanot and Durand, see Calasso, *I glossatori*, 114–15. According to Marguerite Boulet-Sautel, Durand appears to use the notion of "princeps" as a general quality applicable to *any* ruler not recognising a superior – that is to say, the pope, the emperor and the king of France.

extend beyond the limited circle of his vassals.[165] Durand also shared Jean's view of the ultimate loyalty of the vassals of French barons to the king. It is the king "who governs the realm who calls them [i.e. the vassals] for the common good and for the defence of fatherland and the crown". Rather than from the constitutional law of this or that *regnum*, the bond between the king and his subjects arose from *ius gentium*.[166]

Whether royal powers extended to general legislation over the *regnum* was another matter.[167] Commentators inspired by Aristotle, such as Giles of Rome, did derive from the French king's possession of "natural jurisdiction" also something like the powers of legislative sovereignty (*leges condere*).[168] Jean de Blanot and Durand used civil law terms such as *edictum*, *constitutio* or *mandatum*, and maxims such as *princeps legibus solutus est* [D 1.3, 13] or *quod principi placuit legis habet vigorem* [I 1.2,6 & D 1.4,1] appeared frequently in legists' texts.[169] Sometimes the king issued large *ordonnances* or *établissements* that dealt with the administration of fiefs or private law matters such as guardianship of minors or noble widows.[170] Famously, royal justice was expanded by Philip II by sending itinerant

Marguerite Boulet-Sautel, 'Le princeps de Guillaume Durand', in *Études d'histoire du droit canonique dédiées à Gabriel le Bras, doyen honoraire de la Faculté de droit et de sciences économiques de Paris, membre de l'Institut*, tome II (Paris, Sirey 1965), 803–13. In the same volume Robert Feenstra demonstrates that the original formula 'Lex Franciae in regno suo princeps est', did, despite Calasso's contrary arguments, already exist in Blanot's work from which it was taken to that of Durand. Robert Feenstra, 'Jean de Blanot et la formule "Rex Franciae in regno suo princeps est"', in *Études d'histoire du droit canonique dédiées à Gabriel le Bras*, 885–95. See further, Guillaume Leyte, *Domaine et domanialité publique dans la France médiévale. XIIe–Xve siècle* (Presses Universitaires de Strasbourg 1996), 85–8.

165 "Omnes homines qui sunt in regno Franciae, sunt sub potestate & principatum Regis Franciae & in eis habet imperium iurisdictionis et potestatis", Durand, *Speculum Iuris*, IV III § 2 para 28 (146r).

166 "Nam Rex, qui habet administrationem regni, vocat eos pro communi bono, sclicet pro defensione patriae & coronae, unde sibi iure gentium obedire tenentur", ibid., IV III, § 2 para 32 (146r). See further Schneidemüller, *Nomen Patriae*, 262–4, 267–71.

167 For an extensive study, see Petit-Renaud, '*Faire loy*', *au royaume de France*.

168 Aquinas, too, highlighted the great utility of a legislator whom all subjects (and not just "vassals") would obey. Aquinas, 'Summa Theologiae, Prima Secundae [ST I-II], in *Aquinas. Political Writings* (R. W. Dyson ed., Cambridge University Press, 2002), ST I-II 90 2 (7–8, 78–80).

169 Recent discussions include Rigaudière, *Penser et construire*, 39–66 and Petit-Renaud, *'Faire loy', au royaume de France*, 23–30.

170 See e.g. Guillot, Rigaudière & Saissier, *Pouvoirs et institutions*, 266–8. These enactments were, however, prepared in consultation with the great vassals. James Lowth Goldsmith, *Lordship in France 500–1500* (London, Peter Lang 2003), 300.

*baillis* and *sénéchals* to the provinces as administrators and judges in local courts (*assizes*), soon to be permanently appointed and supervised by the *enquêteurs* from Paris.[171] With the establishment of the *Parlement of Paris* appeals from seigneurial jurisdictions were encouraged with the result that "[i]deas, however vague, of a law common to the realm were beginning to grow".[172] Moreover, local representatives of the crown were given authority in 1254 to state the custom and sometimes to abolish "bad customs".[173] But even in his ordinance-giving role the king was understood more as a judge than a legislator, guarantor of pre-existing customs – rights and privileges – that ideally had eternal force. And any decision regarding them was to be justifiable by the common good.[174] Even the great reforms of 1254 and 1302 were justified as "restoration" of order and hierarchy.[175]

As noted earlier, Philip's legists wrote in a draft treaty with England that the king would hold "sovereignty" over the duchy of Guyenne in the same way he exercised it "over the other peers of France and their subjects."[176] But this was hardly thought to involve the power of

171 Lot & Fawtier, *Histoire des institutions*, 144–58; Rigaudière, *Introduction historique*, 310–12, 250–65.

172 Reynolds, *Fiefs and Vassals*, 293. See also Richard Kaeuper, *War, Justice and Public Order* (Oxford University Press 1988), 160 (pointing to the uncertain hierarchy between royal and seigneurial courts), 162–70.

173 Rigaudière, *Penser et construire*, 224. The expansion of royal legislation had proceeded furthest in the fields of justice, the creation of a homogenous administrative structure and in monetary matters, 246–51. But this was by no means looked upon only favourably. Royal officials tended to extort and tyrannise local populations with the effect that reforms by Louis IX and Philip were to signify "a return, a reminder of the good habits of the past, a restoration of old privileges". Favier, *Philippe le Bel*, 99.

174 "[U]ntil the end of the fifteenth century", James B. Collins writes, "the French monarchy "might be called the *judicial* monarchy because the king's chief function remained that of judge . . . in the eyes of contemporaries, he *discovered* the law, he did not make it." *The State in Early Modern France* (Cambridge University Press 2012), 3.

175 M. de Lauriere, *Ordonnances des Roys de France de la troisième race*, vol. I (Paris 1723), 357–8. See further Gérard Giordanengo, 'La difficile interprétation des données négatives. Les ordonnances royales sur le droit féodal', in A. Gouron & A. Rigaudière (eds), *Renaissance du pouvoir législatif et genèse de l'état* (Montpellier, Publications de la société d'histoire de droit 1988), 99–109. For the general direction of the great reform "ordonnances" and problems in their implementation, see also Claude Gauvard, 'Ordonnance de reforme et pouvoir legislative en France au XIVe siècle (1303–413)', in A. Gouron & A. Rigaudière (eds), *Renaissance du pouvoir législatif et genèse de l'état* (Montpellier, Publications de la société d'histoire de droit 1988), 89–98.

176 Art XV, ". . . soverinete royal, tele come nous l'avons sur les autres peres de France e sour leurs sougies", Thomas Rymer (ed.), *Foedera, Conventiones, Litterae*, I-2 (London 1816), 795. On the fluctuating use of the term "sovereignty" ("fluide et imprécise")

legislation over the *regnum*, and even less tampering with noble privileges in a general way.[177] For example, efforts to legislate against local warfare were firmly rejected; feuding remained an important aspect of noble ethics, not at all something regarded as exceptional or immoral.[178] Declarations of king's peace such as that by Louis IX in 1250 or prohibitions of *port d'armes* lacked efficiency and even the prohibition of tournaments was widely resented. The great principalities, including the royal *apanages* remained de facto independent and even active kings such as Louis IX and Philip IV refrained from intervening in the daily government of seigneurial lands.[179] From the mid-thirteenth century onwards, French transcribers of local customs such as Pierre de Fontaines or Philippe de Beaumanoir, both known as staunch royalists, as well as the anonymous compilers of the *Livres de jostice et de Plet* (1260s), knew and cited the maxims of *legibus solutus* and *quod principi placuit.* But even they limited these powers to judgments or edicts covering particular cases while never suggesting that they would allow the French king a free hand to legislate against customary privileges. Many referred to the maxim *Digna vox* under which the prince was under an honourable duty to follow the law, perhaps because it would be right for the king to limit himself in order to present an example to his subjects.[180] The extreme voluntarist position that the king's will was

at the time and especially in view of the French king's involvement in the government of this most complex fief, see Pierre Chaplais, 'La souveraineté du roi de France et le pouvour législatif en Guyenne au début du XIVe siècle', LXIX *Le Moyen Age* (1963), 449–69.

177 See e.g. Post, *Studies*, 123.

178 See e.g. Lot & Fawtier, *Histoire des institutions françaises*, 37. The bishops' peace movement in the twelfth century and the effort to turn violence against the infidel by crusades had created a momentum for setting king's peace courts also beyond the royal domain. From the Council of Soissons (1155) onwards, peacekeeping was part of the royal function that collided, however, with the "droit de guerre" that remained codified by Beaumanoir as part of the custom of Beauvaisis in the 1280s and treated the head of family as *Dux belli* – in complete contrast to the way canon and civil lawyers reserved belligerent authority to the king. See Kaeuper, *War*, 137–50, 227–9.

179 "Apanages" were territories that that the king donated to his younger sons. They were in principle and in practice independent, and in later years frequently in open conflict with the king. See e.g. Goldsmith, *Lordship in France*, 287–8; Telliez, *Institutions*, 90–1.

180 *Digna vox* dated back to the fifth-century emperors Theodosius II and Valentianus III, and according to it, "it is a statement worthy of the majesty of the ruler for the Prince to profess himself bound by the laws". "Digna vox majestate regnantis legibus alligatum se principem profiteri". C 1.14. 4. Translation from Pennington, *The Prince and the Law*, 78. For the well-known tension between these

all that was needed for abolishing old and creating new law was sometimes received by analogy from hierocratic theory, and Accursius noted in his "Ordinary Gloss" that the king's will was *magna et iusta causa*.[181] On the other hand, in a dispute between Philip the Fair and Pope Nicholas IV (1227–92) royal legists cited *Digna vox* against the latter.[182] The sense of such references was often unclear, however, and had less to do with legislation than individual measures or *rescripts*, royal responses to petitions by subjects. In practice, few suggested that the king had absolute powers.[183] How little such language had to do with French reality is illustrated by the fact that Pierre de Fontaines might write about the "senate's" role in lawmaking in his famous *Conseils* (1250s) – although no such institution existed in thirteenth-century France.[184]

Ritual statements that law was "that which pleases the prince" were distant from a reality where lawmaking had traditionally taken place through consultation with major vassals. As the royal domain grew through acquisitions and confiscations and central administation extended to the rest of the *regnum*, the barons reacted by strengthening their judicial and administrative apparatus, enacting extraordinary taxes and expanding exclusive seigneurial jurisdiction.[185] The king sought actively to limit access to the class of lordships by charging new nobles with special duties (*franc-fiefs*) and by providing charters to municipal centres with royal privileges and protections, thereby isolating them from seigneurial control.[186] But as royal influence increased in towns and villages, the status of principalities and greater lordships was reinforced, as was the king's already considerable economic dependency on them: "essential work of government could not be performed without recognizing and using the power of the local lords".[187]

principles, see Pennington, *The Prince and the Law*, 76–118; Wilks, *Problem of Sovereignty*, 206–29. For practice in fourteenth-century France, see Petit-Renaud, '*Faire loy*', *au royaume de France*, 175–84.

181 Cited in Petit-Renaud, '*Faire loy*', *au royaume de France*, 114. 182 Ibid., 125.

183 For cases of the limited use of the "*potestas absoluta*" in France, see ibid., 220–8.

184 Rigaudière, *Penser et construire*, 44–60, 216–19, 234–9.

185 See e.g. Monique Bourin-Derruau, *Temps d'équilibres, temps de ruptures* (Paris, Seuil 1990), 203–4. The massive growth of the royal domain in the thirteenth century is described in Lot & Fawtier, *Histoire des institutions françaises*, 38–40 and especially 108–21. In 1328 the area of the royal domain consisted of two-thirds of the French *regnum*, 117.

186 Bourin-Derruau, *Temps d'équilibres*, 216–17. On the new municipal organisation, see Guillot, Rigaudière & Saissier, *Pouvoirs et institutions*, 273–9, 292–8. See also Goldsmith, *Lordship in France*, 285-6.

187 Joseph R. Strayer, 'The Development of Feudal Institutions', in Joseph R. Strayer, *Medieval Statecraft and the Perspectives of History* (Princeton University Press 1971), 78.

Moreover, although outsourcing "bureaucratic fiefs" (*fiefs de bourse*) and tax-collection privileges bound some nobles to the king, they also became hereditary and thus consolidated noble influence.[188] Whatever the language of the royal chancellery, the kings often saw it best to refrain from enforcing their domain on protected churches and towns.[189]

By the end of the century a kind of balance had emerged that integrated the great nobles in a system of consultation on most important issues, such as what to do with Boniface or the rebellious vassals of Flanders.[190] Despite the prevalence in the academy of an Aristotelian view of kingship, and the civil law rhetoric of *leges condere*, royal powers remained predominantly *judicial* powers, extending to individual cases and to be exercised in view of the common good. The *regnum* remained an amalgam of public and private interests, royal and noble privileges and rights of tenure of noble and non-noble subjects with enormous geographic and substantive variation.[191] But even more important than feudal privileges for the limitation of the king's powers was the king's economic dependence on his vassals.

## Philip in Context 2: The Economy

Much more than a mere pamphlet, Giles of Rome's *De regimine principum* was supposed to treat everything a prince should know about the government of himself (*de regimine sui*), his household and family (*suas coniuges regere*) and of the realm (*civitas et regni*). The three-step structure signalled that good kingship was the result of gradual growth from personal virtue to the learning of the economics of the household to governing the realm. Quite stunningly in view of his later engagement with Boniface, Giles wrote of the *regnum* as a *communitas perfecta* without reference to the church or the empire. The work had much to say about economic rulership. Following Aristotle closely, Giles stressed that it was important that the king see to his own wealth and splendour. He must, for example, build for himself impressive dwellings,

On the creation of the legal category of "nobility", see Goldsmith, *Lordship in France*, 205–6. See further, Perry Anderson, *Lineages of the Absolutist State* (London, Verso 1974), 19–27.

188 For the variety of rights and privileges that could be had as "fiefs", see e.g. Telliez, *Institutions*, 30.

189 Goldsmith, *Lordship in France*, 199–234. Likewise, Georges Minois, *Histoire du moyen age* (Paris, Perrin 2016), 218, 225–9.

190 See Rigaudière, *Penser et construire*, 223–30.

191 Bourin-Derruau, *Temps d'équilibres*, 199–229.

*habitationes mirabilis*, for his subjects to admire and to discourage rebellion.[192] He should also afford displays of liberality and magnificence, be generous in alms-giving and rational in exploiting the realm.[193] The wealth of the king was richness of the kingdom itself; he was to make displays of prodigality – far less a sin than avarice.[194] A poor king was an embarrassment to his people.

Giles stressed over again the Aristotelian principle that the realm was to be governed in such a fashion that the subjects were not only able to live, but to live well (*bene vivere*).[195] This required careful attention to their livelihood. It was, for example, an important part of a good ruler's disposition that he understand the benefits of the diversity of professions. If everyone were a weaver or a tanner, the city would be imperfect.[196] A single house or a single street could never produce goods and manufactures sufficient for all. That a city or a *regnum* was a perfect community did not at all mean that it would also be self-sufficient; it was often necessary to import grain or other merchandise from other countries. There might be carpenters in one village, and weavers in another who could reciprocally work to satisfy the needs in each.[197] Thus people in different villages or cities would help each other (*invicem*

192 "nam populus minus insurgit contra principem, videns ipsum sic magnificum". Giles of Rome, *De regimine principium*, II 3 iii (210r). At the same time, Giles stressed that each family should have the kind of housing that befits its status. Accordingly, Philip promulgated very strict sumptuary laws.

193 Ibid., II 3, iii (209r-211r). Reference here is to Aristotle, *Nicomachean Ethics* (D Ross ed. Oxford University Press 1980), IV 2 ("Magnificence"), 85–9. See further, Jacques le Goff, 'Aspect religieux et sacre de la monarchie française du Xe au XIIIe siècle', in Elisabeth Magnou-Nortier (ed.), *Pouvoirs et libertés au temps des premiers capétiens* (Paris, Hérault 1992), 320–1.

194 This question was debated for example in quodlibet questions in 1285 by the Paris theologian Godefroid de Fontaines who pointed out that even such a good as poverty might result from prodigality. See Alain Boureau, 'L'invention doctrinale de le souveraineté monarchique sur les biens à l époque de Philippe le Bel', in Jean Kerhervé & Albert Rigaudière (eds), *Monnaie, fiscalité et finances au temps du Philippe le Bel* (Paris, Comité pour l'histoire économique et financière de la France 2007), 5. See further Lydwine Scordia, 'Les autorités cités lors des débats sur l'impôt par les théologiens à la fin du XIIIe siècle', in Kerhervé & Rigaudière (eds), *Monnaie, fiscalité et finances*, 19–50.

195 Giles of Rome, *De regimine principum*, III 1, ii (238v); 2, viii (278v–279r). Throughout, Giles stressed that the natural objective of politics was not only that human beings survive, but that they live well and virtuously. To lead a "sufficient life" was a natural predisposition in humans. "oportet quid naturale esse quidquid secundum se deservit ad sufficientiam vitae", III 1, iv (241v).

196 "Si . . . omnes essent textores vel coriarii civitas imperfecta esset", ibid., III 1, viii (248v). See also II 3, vi (214r–v).

197 Ibid., III 1, v (243r).

*subvenire*) just like limbs of a single body collaborate to provide sufficient living to the whole.[198]

All this presupposed that the king understand the value of private property. Of course, Giles accepted that God had donated the world to humans in common. But among egoistic sinners, living well was possible only *secundum debita pacta & conventiones.*[199] Realistic observation of society demonstrated that a *regnum* organised through common property would occasion endless conflict and soon fall into shortage. Only owners of private property worked diligently and even the virtue of *liberalitas* could only be realised in conditions of private ownership.[200] Ideals of poverty and sharing might be proper for the life of clerics but in temporal society, engagement with private property was crucial to ensuring that the subjects would live well.[201] It was therefore prudent that the ruler manage property rights carefully, not so as to equalise properties but to eradicate greed.[202] Most theologians agreed. In his *quodlibet* writings James of Viterbo described the king as the guardian, procurator and distributor of property rights.[203]

But Philip was hardly in this position. Throughout his reign, he had to struggle to collect resources necessary for his wars and centralising ambitions; the cost of royal government more than doubled in the last three decades of the century.[204] Moreover, around 1300 Philip was at war with two of his most formidable vassals, the duke of Aquitaine (Guyenne), simultaneously king of England, Edward II, and the count of Flanders, Guy de Dampierre, in July 1302 losing 20,000 men, including scores of his leading lords, in an embarrassing military defeat to Flemish peasants. Although a fragile peace was attained with these internal adversaries (it would not last long), the wars were a continuous

198 Ibid., III 1, v; viii (243r–v, 247v–249r).

199 Ibid., III 2, xxv (308v–309r). See also the genealogy of private property and related institutions (contracts, gifts, exchanges) in Giles of Rome's *On Ecclesiastical Power*, II XII (194/5–198/9).

200 Giles of Rome, *De regimine principum*, II 3, vi & III 1, xi (214r–215r & 252v–254v).

201 Possessions, he wrote, were both natural and "necessary for life in a political community". Ibid., II 3, v (212v–213r).

202 Ibid., III 1, xvii & xviii (259v––262v). Here, like elsewhere, Giles' discussion closely follows Aristotle, 'The Politics', in *The Politics and The Constitution of Athens* (Cambridge University Press 1996), II (30–61).

203 Boureau, 'L'invention doctrinale', 16–17. Likewise, Alain Boureau, *La religion de l'Etat. La construction de la République étatique dans le discours théologique d'Occident médiéval* (Paris, Belles Lettres 2008), 265–77, 279–82.

204 They arose from c. 250,000 to c. 600,000 livres tournois, Kaeuper, *War*, 62–3. By comparison, Louis spent 1,500,000 livres tournois to his crusades of which two-thirds was received from the church.

drain of resources.[205] Even in Paris itself, the king had to compete with a dozen private jurisdictions exercised by institutions to many of which he was financially indebted. Most commercial activity was in the hands of the Hanse of Paris whose *prevôts* regularly clashed with royal officials. Even the formal power of the king to fix interest rates was undermined by Parisian usurers charging in secret far in excess of the official rate. Because the royal house was among their debtors, action against them was in practice impossible.[206]

As a feudal suzerain, the king was expected to live by the product of his own domain – *le Roi doit vivre des siennes.*[207] This, however, was barely sufficient to pay for the expenses of the *Hôtel du Roi*, to say nothing of the expanding work of the government. There were in principle four alternative sources of income: taxes, revaluation of moneys, lending from domestic and foreign sources and confiscation of properties. In addition, the "tenth" from the church, dependent on papal grants, had great significance.[208] There was no permanent tax on property or income in France. The very idea was culturally objectionable; the king was to provide alms, not to reach into his subjects' pockets. The effort to

205 For the financial crisis induced by the war in 1295–1305, see Favier, *Philippe le Bel*, 191–8.

206 At one point the merchant leader Etienne Marcel simply set up despotic rule over Paris. See Heers, *La naissance du capitalisme*, 142–8.

207 See e.g. Jacques le Goff, *Le Moyen Age et l'argent* (Paris, Perrin 2000), 87–95. What "belonged" to the king was not easy to assess. It is customary to distinguish between the "domain" and "mouvance", the former consisting of all the bases of the king's revenue as seigneur, the latter the sum total of his fiefs. See Bourin-Derruau, *Temps d'équilibre*, 149–50. The view of contemporaries on the relation of the "royal domain" to the "crown's" or to "public domain" was not always clear. The main point is that the "royal domain" consisted of the totality of the lands and the revenues that belonged to the king. Lot & Fawtier, *Histoire des institutions françaises*, 99–107 and Leyte, *Domaine et domanialité publique*, 93–195. The terminology "*domaine, dominium, domanium, fisc*, etc. remained fluid, converging towards the end of the thirteenth century as a power that was both direct (i.e. non-mediated through fiefs) and exclusive, Leyte, *Domaine et domanialité publique*, 100–43. The domain was directly administered by the king while the fiefs were usually ruled by a provincial lord. This applied especially to the "principalities" (territories held by the dukes of Aquitaine ["Guyenne"], Brittany and Bourgogne and the counts of Flanders, Champagne and Toulouse) where, though the counts and dukes were formally vassals of the king, royal authority was only secondary and sometimes very marginal. The "apanages" that kings had donated to their younger sons were also governed as virtually independent *regna*. See e.g. Telliez, *Les institutions*, 90–2; Leyte, *Domaine et domanialité publique*, 93–100, 153 ff. For the "domain"/ "fief" distinction, see Leyte, *Domaine et domanialité publique*, 111–16.

208 See Favier, *Philippe le Bel*, 185–6 and the very detailed account in Strayer, *The Reign of Philip the Fair*, 153–72.

introduce a sales tax in 1292–7 raised such an outcry that it had to be immediately transformed into a one-off tax on properties.[209] A tax on salt, *gabelle*, was collected to great opposition and modest results. The same may be said of the export monopolies that were regularised during Philip's reign.[210] Feudal law permitted extraordinary fundraising in only four cases: knighting of the oldest son, the marriage of the oldest daughter, crusade and ransoming the king.[211] Philip used the first two of these in 1309 and 1313 but by far the most important was the *defensio regni*.[212] Because this was originally understood as a tribute and not a tax, it could only be extracted from the king's direct vassals – gradually, however, the king would extend it to all his subjects.[213]

Royal revenue did increase in the thirteenth century by the transformation of personal services of vassalage into monetary payments so as to pay for a professional army.[214]. Maxims such as *quod omnes tangit* or *publica utilitas* were used to suggest that government was a national effort to which all should contribute.[215] But it would take until the latter half of the fourteenth century before taxes would become a routine aspect of French government.[216] Meanwhile additional funds were received from other parts of the royal domain, by issuing letters of nobility and minting coins as well as fees from royal justice. Duties and customs were also raised on French ports, rivers and roads but a great part of the proceeds was pocketed by collectors or kept within the noble families to

[209] The measure was seen as an unheard-of intervention in the relations between buyers and sellers. Much has been written about this "maltôte", which was regularised only with the consent of the Estates-General in 1355 and 1360 See e.g. Rigaudière, *Penser et construire*, 562–8; Heers, *La naissance du capitalisme*, 219; Favier, *Philippe le Bel*, 191; Telliez, *Institutions*, 123–6.

[210] Taxes on imports were set up only later in the fourteenth century. Rigaudière, *Penser et construire*, 568–72; Favier, *Philippe le Bel*, 186–8; Telliez, *Institutions*, 125.

[211] Boris Bove, *La guerre de cent ans* (Paris, Belin 2015), 78–9; Rigaudière, *Penser et construire*, 523–32; Favier, *Philippe le Bel*, 171–2.

[212] Rigaudière, *Penser et construire*, 536–61. However, the great nobles were relieved of significant contributions also in this regard.

[213] Caroline Decoster, 'La Fiscalisation des aides féodales', in Jean Kerhervé & Albert Rigaudière (eds), *Monnaie, fiscalité et finances au temps du Philippe le Bel* (Paris, Comité pour l'histoire économique et financière de la France 2007), 176–83, 190–4.

[214] Favier, *Philippe le Bel*, 185–6; Rigaudière, *Penser et construire*, 533–5. Commuting feudal service to monetary payment in 1303 raised 750,000 livres tournois, contributing decisively to victory over the Flemish rebels in 1304. Kaeuper, *War*, 64.

[215] E.g. Joseph Strayer, 'Defense of the Realm and Royal Power in France', in Joseph Strayer (ed.), *Medieval Statecraft and the Perspective of History* (Princeton University Press 1971), 292; Favier, *Philippe le Bel*, 173; Rigaudière, *Penser et construire*, 524–8, 535–6.

[216] Bove, *La guerre de cent ans*, 184; Kaeuper, *War*, 118.

whom the crown had outsourced them.[217] Even combined, however, these still did not suffice to cover the crown's peacetime expenses and remained completely insufficient at times of war.

The desperate nature of Philip's finances was reflected in his notorious recourse to monetary mutations. In 1260s royal moneys had been established as valid for all France (moneys produced by provincial nobles were only valid in their respective provinces). But the increase of royal expenses and the price of metal compelled the king to debase the value of silver and gold in his coins.[218] Although a fast way to his subjects' pockets without having to consult anybody, debasement led to inflation and protests, as subjects felt expropriated by the measure.[219] Stabilisation failed repeatedly.[220] Nor were the great bourgeois always safe. A large loan was forced on them in 1293 that raised the amount of 630,000 livres tournois – practically equal to all domanial revenue. It was never paid back.[221] Finally, Philip also borrowed profusely from Jews and "Lombard bankers" who had settled in France and had at one point even become the king's principal economic advisors.[222] Records of 1292 show that the tax from 110 Italian exchangers amounted to more than 12 percent of all the money collected from 15,200 contributors. The Italians were also

217 The different sources of revenue that were part of the royal domain are described in Lot & Fawtier, *Histoire des institutions françaises*, 159–79. In addition to the duties relative to trade and travel across or into France, the king also received payments for the exercise of professions, taxes from Jewish usurers, tributes from provincial nobles for the various privileges they enjoyed, and for the uses of forests and fishery and inheritances from foreigners and bastards etc. See e.g. Le Goff, *Le Moyen Age et l'argent*, 91–3.

218 In the thirteenth century, most of Western Christianity used two metals, silver and gold. There were two measures, one "legal" set up by the king and another "commercial", determined by the market. As the price of metals increased, the king began to diminish the weight of silver and gold in his coins. For a brief description of the technique and consequences of the "mutations", see Le Goff, *Le Moyen Age et l'argent*, 137–45.

219 For the way the food market and covert price-fixing undermined Philips effort's to rule the economic relations within his *regnum*, see e.g. Joel Kaye, *Economy and Nature in the Fourteenth Century. Money, Market Exchange, and the Emergence of Scientific Thought* (Cambridge University Press 1998), 15–28.

220 Much has been written on the monetary mutations by the French king. See e.g. Benoît Santiano, *La monnaie, le prince et le marchand. Une analyse économique des phénomènes monétaires au Moyen Age* (Paris, Classiques Garnier 2010).

221 Favier, *Philippe le Bel*, 188–9; Rigaudière, *Penser et construire*, 573–6.

222 At one point the king left the royal treasury to be administered by the brothers Albizzo and Musciato Guidi dei Franziesi ("Biche et Mouche"), who also collected taxes and other payments, negotiated loans and undertook diplomatic missions. In that process Biche and Mouche had collected a sizable property for themselves. But at the death of the brothers in 1307 Philip had all of their property confiscated.

fined with usury charges five times between 1277 and 1349.[223] But in the end all their property was confiscated. The more than 100,000 French Jews met the same fate in 1306–7. But such measures provided only a one-off relief and additional costs were engendered by the need to replace Jews as money collectors by farming or employing more officials.[224]

It was impossible to reconcile the ideals of economic governance with the resources available to the king. It is true that thirteenth-century France, especially Flanders, the Paris basin and the south of the country had experienced an unforeseen economic revolution. A lively and prosperous urban culture had emerged, facilitated by the massive increase of money in circulation and growing business at trade fairs.[225] In the countyside, the personal duties between the lord and the vassal were replaced by monetary compensation – i.e. rent – that enabled greater labour mobility and further expanded exchanges between the town and the countryside. Merchants and bankers would now rival old authorities in the control of the *regnum*'s resources. But little of this translated into revenue for the king. To the contrary, he was increasingly at the mercy of the commercial conditions that determined the value of his money and the amount of his annual revenue. A new phase in feudal relations had arisen. *A tous égards, elle est fille d'une économie monétaire et d'une société différenciée.*[226]

*****

What makes these developments significant is that they compel extending legal analysis of territorial rulership from the familiar ground of imperial prerogative to the slippery terrain of feudal rights and privileges. When now the king was said to have *dominium* in terms of jurisdiction, it met with the *dominium* of the local lords some of whom were his direct vassals while many were not. Confrontation was endemic. In Flanders, for example, one of the king's more troublesome fiefs, Philip clashed with its powerful count Guy de Dampierre over the treatment of its prosperous towns (Ghent, Bruges, Douiai, Ypres, Lille)

223 Heers, *La naissance du capitalisme*, 131, 229, 231–2; Kaeuper, *War*, 72–4.

224 Stéphane Mechoulan, 'L'expulsion des Juifs de France en 1306. Proposition d'analyse contemporaine sous l'angle fiscal', in Jean Kerhervé & Albert Rigaudière (eds), *Monnaie, fiscalité et finances au temps du Philippe le Bel* (Paris, Comité pour l'histoire économique et financière de la France 2007), 199–226.

225 But by 1285, as the territory became part of the French monarchy, trade had begun to move to maritime links between the Mediterranean and such northern ports as Bruges or Antwerp. See e.g. Epstein, *An Economic and Social History*, 81–4.

226 Barthélemy, *L'ordre seigneurial*, 215, 199–252.

whose bourgeoisie, "a thin crust of wealthy Francophiles",[227] had set up a draconic regime for exploiting cloth workers. The Count's effort to enhance his independence by taking the side of the latter against urban oligarchy and aligning with England's Edward II led to a long period of royal intervention in Flanders. Each party accused the other of having broken the feudal bond but Philip was able to prevent the matter from being adjudicated by the Court of Peers (a court composed of counts and dukes from six principalities plus a similar number of ecclesiastical barons) that would have subordinated his decisions to the judgment of elite lords.[228] Though Flanders and the count himself were eventually pacified, this did not take place without huge cost to Philip in material resources and in the lives of his nobles.[229] Moreover, the taxes he raised for the war in Flanders antagonised the French nobility generally, and even more so when revenue collectors continued their work even after the peace was concluded. This led to the formation of the noble "Leagues of 1314–1315" across the country that concluded in a series of "charters" designed to secure the privileges of local elites. If these failed to receive the status of England's *Magna Carta*, this was only owing to the nobles' inability to coordinate their negotiations with the king.[230]

## Ruling Humans and Owning Land

When civil lawyers came to examine the conflicts between royal jurisdiction and the rights of the landed nobility in the late twelfth century, they soon found out that the rather absolute Roman law concept of *dominium* seemed wholly inadequate to capture the specificity of feudal authority. When they then nevertheless applied that concept to create deceptively simple notions of "fief" and "vassalage" so as to express Roman ideas about rights *in rem* and rights *in personam*, their efforts

227 Strayer, *The Reign of Philip the Fair*, 326.

228 See especially Franck Funck-Brentano, *Philippe le Bel en Flandre* (Paris, Champion 1896), 187–9.

229 Alongside the fundamental works by Favier and Strayer, see David Nicholas, *Medieval Flanders* (New York, Routledge 1992), 181–208, who also links the conflict to troubles in the Flanders textile industry.

230 For a detailed study of the noble rebellion, see André Artonne, *Le mouvement de 1314 et les Chartes provinciales du 1315* (Paris, Alcan 1912). See also Charles-Victor Langlois, 'Le mouvement de 1314 et les chartes provinciales de 1315', 10 *Journal des savants* (1912), 167–75. The charters differ in their content but all had the form of a unilateral undertaking by the king in which he promised he would follow the right procedure in his government and not extract excessive charges. For the most elaborate of them, see *Charte aux normandes* (Caen, Le Roy 1788).

collided head-on with a much more varied reality in which customary notions such as *allod*, *beneficium*, *proprium*, or *hereditas* had existed without any assumption of absoluteness and where "nearly all land and a great many human beings were burdened at this time with a multiplicity of obligations differing in nature, but all apparently of equal importance".[231] In this process civil law intervened to support the consolidation of public authority from above by offering an imperial view of kingship while simultaneously strengthening private property rights from below.[232] Efforts to consolidate the two types of authority required adjusting the notion of kingship by customary views on lordship and vassalage in an environment where an increasingly *economic* understanding of rights over land was emerging.[233] The result was a:

> ... cooperative division of labour between the central monarchical state and the landed class whose power rested not on fragmented sovereignty but on its command of property.[234]

Consequently, two types of authority expanded over the French realm. As for the king: "all things that lie within the *regnum* come under the king's jurisdiction".[235] Jean de Blanot used the term "*ad iurisdictionem*" in order to stress the point that the king did not have unlimited power to intervene in the privileges of lordship. He reminded his readers of the old debate on whether the king as *princeps* was actually the *owner* of his subjects' property – *an princeps sit dominus rerum particuliarum*. If this were the case, then there would be nothing to say *legally* about the taxation of his subjects by Philip, his forced loans and confiscations. But he rejected this suggestion by taking up the legend of the encounter at the Diet of Roncaglia in 1158 between Frederick I Barbarossa and the Bologna jurists Martinus and Bulgarus. During that debate Martinus was supposed to have affirmed that the emperor was *dominus* over the whole world while the latter held that this was indeed true but did not mean

231 Marc Bloch, *Feudal Society*, vol. I: *The Growth of Ties of Dependence* (2nd edn, London, Routledge 1962), 116. See further e.g. Jean-Philippe Levy, *Histoire de la propriété* (Presses Universitaires de France 1972), 35–60.

232 Anderson, *Lineages of the Absolutist State*, 28.

233 This took place above all through the integration of the eleventh-century private compilation of Lombard systems – the *Libri feudorum* – as part of the *Corpus iuris* itself. See e.g. Peter Stein, *Roman Law in European History* (Cambridge University Press 1999), 61–2.

234 Ellen Meiksins Wood, *Citizens to Lords. A Social History of Western Political Thought from Antiquity to the Middle Ages* (London, Verso 2008), 175.

235 "... omnia, que sunt in regno sunt regis quantum ad iurisdictionem", Blanot, *Tractatus*, 160 and 162.

that he had the right of *property* over everything.[236] Already Seneca had distinguished between *dominium* and *imperium*, ascribing only the latter to the emperor on a world-wide basis: that he could give orders to everyone did not mean that he *owned* everything.[237] This view was adopted by most glossators as well. In his commentary to the law *Bene a Zenone* [C 7. 37. 3] Azo read the *omnia principis* statement as meaning that the prince "had" everything only in view of its protection (*quo ad protectionem*).[238] Accursius limited the provision to the imperial treasury (*fiscus*) and royal domain. The emperor, he stated, was certainly not the owner of Accursius' property.[239] Also the regular framing of imperial powers as *merum imperium* or *imperium merum et mixtum* referred to criminal and civil jurisdiction, not to property. But while Jean de Blanot and Guillaume Durand agreed with this definition, it left unclear the extent to which royal jurisdiction encroached on noble privileges.[240] Durand realistically observed that there was no single solution to this question. Practice varied between regions.[241] Seigneurial power was anyway a mixture of rights of jurisdiction, ownership, operating a judicial system, raising tributes and taxes and governing a domain. How far royal *dominium* (understood as jurisdiction) would limit baronial rights depended on how the common good or public utility would be construed in each case separately.[242]

236 Many versions of this legend and its political implications are discussed in Pennington, *The Prince and the Law*, 16–30. See also Nicolini, *La proprietà*, 110–15.

237 Nicolini, *La proprietà*, 108–9.

238 "... non intellige quod res alicuius privati sit sua, nisi quo ad protectionem", Azo, *Ad singulas leges XII librorum Codicis Iustinianei commentarius et magnus apparatus nunquam* (Paris 1577), in Lib. VII codicis. xxxvii (574).

239 Instead, he used the term "iurisdictio". Pennington, *The Prince and the Law*, 22; Nicolini, *La proprietà*, 116–17; See also Leyte, *Domaine et domanialité publique*, 83–5.

240 The Italian jurist Alberico da Rosciate (1290–360), who worked for the Visconti in Milan and derived the duke's powers from the people of the city itself, held the minority view that implied in the powers of legislation was ownership over everything; the prince could thus take subjects' private property. Nicolini, *La proprietà*, 119–20; Black, *Absolutism in Renaissance Milan*, 16–17, 57–9. Some doubted the verity of the legend from the outset. If the emperor were the owner of "everything", then the civil law provision that guaranteed for the owner the *actio* of *res vindicatio* would be only applicable to the emperor, which would be absurd. Emanuele Conte, 'Public Law before the State. Evidence from the Age of the Glossators of Roman Law', 2 *Yale Law School Legal Scholarship Reporting* (2006), 15–17.

241 "... secundum diversas consuetudines diversa iura habet dominus in homine suo", *Speculum Iuris*, IV III § 2 para 33 (146r).

242 On the expansion of the royal domain and the seigneurial response, see especially Goldsmith, *Lordship in France*, 199–234. By the end of the reign of Philip the Fair, the barons and greater lords had consolidated their political influence in the *regnum*

The rights attached to noble and peasant landholding differed with respect to the many kinds duties to superior lords and with respect to the family, tenants and to the community. Some these free properties remained after mid-twelfth century but with the widespread expansion of cultivation many were transformed into fiefs (*fiefs de reprise*) alongside non-noble copyholding (*censive*, *villainage*, *roture*) and peasant tenure. Under academic feudal law, each piece of land would be "held of" a whole chain of lord–vassal relations peaking in the role of the supreme lord, the *suzerain* at the top, and the masses of peasant tenants at the bottom, with widespread powers allocated to the lords in between.[243] In practice, however, the counts had long since ceased acting as royal officials and had begun to rule their fiefs as they wanted. With this system, "[c]entury after century an autonomous and autogenous landed aristocracy that drew revenues from lower class dependents reproduced itself over and over again".[244] When the civil lawyers then began to distinguish between rights of jurisdiction and property, they faced the twofold problem that, on the one hand, classical civil law did not accept split rights of *dominium*. Only one person could have *dominium* over a thing or a benefit, and whatever rights others would have on that object would be only rights to a thing of another, *iura in re aliena*. On the other hand, even as feudal landholding accepted many overlapping rights on land, it did not separate, in the way Roman law did, between rights *in rem* and rights *in personam*. Land was a prolongation of the person whose status in society was inextricable from the manner in which land was held.[245]

Feudal relations had always possessed both a personal (political) and a material (economic) aspect. The former was expressed by the notion of vassalage, a contractual bond created through homage expressed by an oath of fealty that the (noble) vassal paid to his lord. The lord would protect the vassal in exchange for a personal, initially military service, later the payment of a tribute, plus giving of counsel.[246] The material

while urban lordships, petty fiefs and the peasant copyholding ("*censives*") had moved towards relative independence as landed property.

243 See especially Reynolds, *Fiefs and Vassals*, 57–64. But see also Bloch, *Feudal Society*, 115–16; Barthélemy, *L'ordre seigneurial*, 216. The powers of lordship were sometimes divided into territorial (*seigneurie foncière*) and personal (*seigneurie banal*). But the two were always mixed and in practice dealt with together. Telliez, *Les Institutions*, 46. A good account of the clash between customary and Roman law is Patault, *Introduction historique*, 84–96.

244 Goldsmith, *Lordship in France*, 204.

245 Patault, *Introduction historique*, 48.

246 See e.g. Telliez, *Les institutions*, 20–7.

aspect was constituted of the vassal receiving a benefice, usually a piece of land (fief) of which the lord would remain *dominus* but the vassal would receive the product and right of use.[247] By the thirteenth century, the weight in these arrangements had shifted to the economic side so that the grant of land had come to be viewed as the *causa* of the transaction.[248] Monetary payment became the vassal's and the copyholder's principal duty, the "*cens*" was transforming into "rent" and both fiefs and copyholdings had become alienable and hereditary (often involving payment to the lord).[249] The intensity of the hierarchy between the lords (now grouped together as "nobles") increased as the great barons reorganised their principalities by engaging castellanies and villages as petty fiefs with taxation powers and seats of seigneurial justice.[250] An increasing number of fiefs were purchased by members of a urban bourgeoisie as investments, turning peasants into agricultural labourers.[251] One of the few significant pieces of royal legislation at this time sought to block merchants' access to nobility by ordering a payment (a *franc-fief*) for the grant of non-noble fiefs.[252] This improved royal finances, but did not prevent the transformation of feudal relations into predominantly economic ones. In general, non-noble copyholding (*censive*) and peasant tenure (*bail à rente*, *baux à long terme*) followed the way of

[247] The "fief" could also consist of some set of rights or powers, such as charging customs or taxes, minting coins or exercising jurisdiction. See Telliez, *Les institutions*, 29–43; Levy, *Histoire*, 41; Leyte, *Domaine et domanialité*, 111–19.

[248] See Paul Ourliac & Jehan de Malafosse, *Histoire du droit privé*, vol. II (2nd edn, Presses Universitaires de France 1971), 153. Originally, the vassal's part of the feudal contract (*auxilium et consilium*) was not seen in commercial terms (in contradistinction to peasant copyholding ["*censive*"]). The provision of the fief (whether land or some set of rights) was a *grant* to which the vassal's response was personal loyalty. Ourliac & de Malafosse, *Histoire du droit privé*, II, 152, 166.

[249] This summary of a complex and varying reality is indebted to Patault, *Introduction historique*, 41–55 and Brissaud, *A History*, 288–91. The serf's bond remained, of course, personal and inalienable. The lord might have the right to consent to the purchase or to purchase himself the land for an equivalent price. The same might apply for renting the fief or part of it. The buyer or the tenant might need to be "presented" to the lord. Selling a part was originally prohibited but later made conditional on consent that the lord could not arbitrarily withhold. Disputes between lords and fiefs would also gradually be transferred from seigneurial to royal courts. Ourliac & de Malafosse, *Histoire du droit privé*, II, 154–5. The failure of the vassal to carry out his obligation would no longer lead to immediate forfeiture but to some partial or temporary sanction. See further Telliez, *Les institutions*, 37–40.

[250] Goldsmith distinguishes a lordship from a petty fief by its "all encompassing power of governance". *Lordship in France*, 207.

[251] This would mark the practical end of feudalism. Jacques Le Goff, *Marchands et banquiers du Moyen âge* (Presses Universitaires de France 2001), 38.

[252] Goldsmith, *Lordship in France*, 205; Telliez, *Les institutions*, 42.

fiefs so that the material and commercial aspect of landholding overrode the personal one – but the process was slow and gradual so that a full separation of the material and personal aspects of landholding had to wait until the Revolution.

The legal commercialisation of land rights proceeded in a complex way. Already the glossators had noticed that Roman procedural law contained a specific type of action, *vindicatio utilis*, that was available for certain long-lease holders (*emphyteuta*) that appeared analogous to vassalage. Hence they moved that notion from procedural to substantive law, canvassing a specific type of right they would call *dominium utile* that would contrast with *dominium directum* encompassing the lord's "ultimate" but abstract ownership. Also, they noticed that in Roman law the notion of *proprietas* was sometimes applied to a bona fide possessor, and they took this to assist in the consolidation of the notion of *dominium utile.*[253] The idea of a divided *dominium* was not immediately accepted. Jurists such as Jean de Blanot, Révigny and Belleperche preferred an undivided dominium with *ius in res aliena* to other right-holders though they apparently disagreed on whether the real *dominium* would lie with the lord or the vassal.[254] However, by the fourteenth century the Bartolists had learned to speak of *dominum duplex* that involved both a "higher" but abstract right of *dominium directum* and a "lower" but a concrete right of *dominum utile.*[255] This allowed higher nobility to rule the *regnum* through their principalities and in collaboration with the king while leaving the conditions of seigneurial enfeoffment to be dictated by parties to the contract. This would allow large principalities to be held by aristocratic families whose local governmental functions were translated into political influence in Paris. On the other hand, fiefs held by lower nobility as well as non-noble types of landholding would emerge together as regular forms of rent-based tenancy. While peasants would have no access to political influence, tenure would provide some security of subsistence. From the fourteenth century, the tenant would increasingly be seen as the *owner* of his property, entitled to use, transform and sell it.[256]

253 See Rémi Faivre-Faucompré, 'Aux origines du concept moderne de propriété. *Dominium et proprietas* dans le droit romano-canonique, XIIe–XVe siècle', in N. Laurent-Bonne, N. Posé & V. Simon (eds), *Les Piliers du droit civil. Famille, propriété, contrat* (Paris, Mare & Martin 2014), 104–8.

254 Ibid., 108–11.

255 E.g. James Q. Whitman, *The Legacy of Roman Law in the German Romantic Era. Historical Visions and Legal Change* (Princeton University Press 2014), 167.

256 Ourliac & de Malafosse, *Histoire du droit privé*, II, 168; Bourin-Derruau, *Temps d'équilibres*, 98–9.

Under this arrangement, royal jurisdiction would be reduced to an administrative function. The status of Frenchmen would be determined by their position in the network of landed properties linked together by contracts of production and rent as well as their situation in alternatively agricultural or urban environments. The two forms of *dominium* – jurisdiction and property – would gradually come to express the relative separation of political and economic governance. Political stability would be still secured by royal bureaucrats and judges in cooperation with seigneurial justice. But the rights of economic exploitation would be based on transferable claims on land increasingly attained by an urban bourgeoisie entering the noble class despite the king's vigorous efforts to restrict this.[257] The central power's ability to intevene in the market in land transactions remained limited by its lack of resources and the perceived illegitimacy of such action. Philip himself caved in after the defeat at Courtrai as access to knighthood finally became a saleable commodity.[258]

## *Ius gentium* As Christian Authority 1: Systemic Aspects

By the early fourteenth century, legists in France and Italy had learned to use the idiom of *ius gentium* to address the division of things in both of its forms – the emergence of independent *regna* and the consolidation of private property.[259] This was a far cry from the original Roman *ius gentium* that had been developed by the *praetor peregrinus* in the first years of the Republic to collect together rules that would apply to legal relationships involving non-citizens.[260] Medieval *ius gentium* built on passages in the *Corpus iuris* that would serve both systemic and historical roles.[261] It would bridge the gap between Christian ideals and social reality, giving normative force to what appeared "only" *de facto*. And it

257 See Bloch, *Feudal Society*, II, 322–5.

258 Ibid., 324.

259 As the Neapolitan jurist Marinus de Caramanico (d. 1288) noted, "long before the empire and the Roman race of old, that is from the *ius gentium* which emerged with the human race itself, kingdoms were recognised and founded", *Super libro constititutionum*, quoted in Calasso, *I glossatori*, 196. Likewise, J. P. Canning, 'Law, Sovereignty and Corporation Theory, 1300–1450', in J. H. Burns (ed.), *The Cambridge History of Medieval Political Thought c. 350–c. 1450* (Cambridge University Press 1988), 465.

260 See e.g Stein, *Roman Law*, 12–13; Kipp, *Völkerordnung*, 99–100, 104–5.

261 The distinction between systemic and genetic is taken from the very useful Andreas Thier, 'Historische Semantiken von ius gentium und "Völkerrecht"', in Tilman Altwickel et al. (eds), *Völkerrechtsphilosophie der Frühaufklärung* (Tübingen, Mohr 2016), 30.

would offer an account of the past, present and future of European society to fit contemporary imagination. Although institutions such as territorial *regna*, war, commerce and private property had not been included in God's "plan", they were not worthless; they served the common good that included the growth of subjects to virtue.[262] A new theory of Christian government would situate prevailing institutions mid-way between divine design and the arbitrary exactions by ambitious rulers.

In Roman law, *ius gentium* had several meanings. Alongside laws that governed the relations of Roman citizens with foreigners, the notion referred to human reason in general as well as to the institutions produced by reason more or less uniformly everywhere. Cicero, for example, whose writings were widely admired in the twelfth and thirteenth centuries, had written of a "right reason", based on Stoic ideas about constancy and invariability that prompted him to speculate that "all nations at all times will be bound by this one eternal and unchangeable law".[263] The idea appealed to Christian writers, and Cicero himself called it a "heavenly norm" whose validity was independent of secular concerns. Medieval jurists noted the closeness of that idea to the well-known definition by Gaius:

> All peoples who are governed under laws and customs observe in part their own special law and in part a law common to all men. Now that law which each nation has set up as a law unti itself is special to that particular *civitas* and is called *jus civile*. . . . By contrast, that law which natural reason has established among all human beings is among all observed in equal measure and is called *jus gentium*, as being the law which all nations observe.[264]

This definition, like Cicero's, found the origin of *ius gentium* in natural reason that operated as a critical guardian of human law. The

[262] See e.g. Aquinas, II I 92 1 ("Whether it is an Effect of Law to Make Men Good?", 96–100).

[263] Cicero, 'On the Commonwealth', Book 3, in Cicero, *On the Commonwealth and On the Laws* (James E. G. Zetzel ed., Cambridge University Press 1999), 71.

[264] Gaius, D. 1.1.9. Translation here and elsewhere from Alan Watson (ed.), *Digest of Justinian*, vol. I (University of Pennsylvania Press 1999), 2. Abbreviations follow the system presented in Stephen L. Sass, 'Research in Roman Law. A Guide to their Sources and Their English Translations', 56 *Law Library Journal* (1963), 210–33. The *Digest* also contained a definition of natural law from Paulus that equated it with what was "always equitable and good" ("quod semper aequum et bonum est"), suggesting an understanding of it less as a system of law than a basic attitude or an interpretative guideline. Merio Scattola, *Das Naturrecht vor dem Naturrecht. Zur Geschichte des 'ius naturae' im 16. Jahrhundert* (Tübingen, Niemeyer 1999), 118–20.

statement had an ambiguity about it, however. Was the law applied everywhere because it was what "natural reason" had established – or was Gaius trying to make the point that certain widespread institutions (kingship, private property) were authoritative because they represented natural reason?[265] In any case, the definition's usefulness lay in the way it allowed interpreting widespread institutional practices as illustrations of natural reason.

Another famous vignette was provided by Ulpian's definition of natural law as "that which nature has taught all animals".[266] Because this highlighted the instinctual aspects of behaviour and failed to depict humans as free and reasoning agents, Ulpian (or the editors of the *Digest*) supplemented his *ius naturale* with a *ius gentium* applicable to human beings only.[267] Again, Tribonian's editors wished to attach this to the most widespread social practices they knew, using slavery and related institutions (such as manumissio) as their principal examples.[268] Moreover, they added a definition by Hermogenian that included in *ius gentium* a whole amount of public institutions such as wars, the separation of nations, and the basis of government as well as various aspects of commerce and private law that may have been what the *praetor peregrinus* applied:

> As a consequence of this *jus gentium*, wars were introduced, nations differentiated, kingdoms founded, properties individuated, estate boundaries settled, buildings put up, and commerce established, including contracts of buying and selling and letting and hiring (except for certain contractual elements established through *jus civile*).[269]

265 See Barry Nicholas, *Roman Law* (Oxford, Clarendon 1962), 54–9. Not being "social reformers", he writes, Romans were not too concerned over the apparent incongruence between the normative and the descriptive aspects of the definition. On the sources of this definition, see also Peter Haggenmacher, *Grotius et la doctrine de la guerre juste* (Presses Universitaires de France 1986), 314–15. These two understandings also express an "objective" and a "subjective" viewpoint to natural law, the fact of the existence of a natural obligation and the ability to recognise its existence. For a discussion of the various meanings of this passage, see Scattola, *Das Naturrecht vor dem Naturrecht*, 114–16; Kipp, *Völkerordnung*, 100–2.

266 "Ius naturale est, quod natura omnia animalia docuit" [D. 1.1.1.3].

267 "Ius gentium est, quo gentes humanae utuntur. Quod a naturali recedere facile intellegere licet, quia illud omnibus animalibus, hoc solis hominibus inter se commune sit" [D. 1.1.1.4]. For commentary, see Haggenmacher, *Grotius*, 315–18.

268 D. 1.1.4 (Ulpian); 1.5.4 (Florentinus); 1.5.5 (Marcian).

269 "Ex hoc iure gentium introducta bella, discretae gentes, regna condita, dominia distincta, agris termini positi, aedificia collocata, commercium, emptiones venditiones, locationes conductiones, obligationes institutae: exceptis quibusdam quae iure civili introductae sunt", D. 1.1.5.

Here now was a very large and fruitful fragment that would come in handy to explain the legal status of a number of institutions that could be met more or less everywhere in the world known to the medieval jurists. A much more limited notion was included in the seventh-century definition by Isidore of Seville:

*Jus gentium* is the seizing, building, and fortifying of settlements, wars, captivities, servitudes, postliminies, treaties, peaces, truces, the obligation not to violate an ambassador, the prohibition of intermarriage with aliens. And [it is called] *jus gentium* because nearly all nations observe it.[270]

All the items in this list linked to the official or formal relations the Romans entertained with other peoples. This definition also found its way into Gratian's *Decretum* where, however, perhaps owing to its limited wording, it played no significant role.[271] But Gratian had nothing against the emergence of autonomous *regna* or private property. To the contrary, he had no difficulty in accepting that "God [had] apportioned human laws to the human race through the emperors and

[270] "Ius gentium est sedium occupatio, aedificatio, munitio, bella, captivitates, servitutes, postliminia, foedera pacis, indutiae, legatorum non violandum religio, conubia inter alienegenas prohibita. Et inde jus gentium, qui eo jure omnes gentes fere utuntur". Isidore of Seville, *Etymologies* (Ernest Brehaut trans. & ed., Columbia University 1912, digital edition 2003, bestiary.ca/etexts/brehaut1912/brehaut%20-%20encyclopedist%20of%20the%20dark%20ages.pdf), II 1 (107). See further Haggenmacher, *Grotius*, 321–4. Isidore's natural law was of divine origin: "Omnes autem leges aut divinae sunt, aut humanae. Divinae natura, humanae moribus constant", and it was defined instinctually: "Jus naturale est communis omnium nationum, et quod ubique instinctu naturae, non constitutione aliqua habetur". Then followed the examples of procreation and child-rearing but also common property and the freedom to acquire things from land, sea and air, the return of loans and dispelling violence by force. *Etym.* 5. 4. In other words, this is the situation before the establishment of political institutions. See further Ernst Reibstein, *Die Anfänge des neueren Natur- und Völkerrechts. Studien zu den "Controversiae illustres" d. Fernandus Vasquius (1559)* (Berne, Haupt 1949), 47–55; Rudolf Weigand, *Die Naturrechtslehre der Legisten und Dekretisten von Irnerius bis Accursius und von Gratian bis Johannes Teutonicus* (München, Münchener Theologische Studien 1967), 126–8.

[271] Gratian, *The Treatise on Laws (Decretum DD 1–20)* (A. Thompson trans., Catholic University of America Press 1993), Dist. 1. C.9 (7). For commentary, see Ernst Nys, *Le droit international. Les principes, les théories, les faits* (Bruxelles, Castaigne 1904), 50–1; Paul Guggenheim, 'Jus gentium, jus naturae, jus civile et la communauté internationale issue de la division regnorum intervenue au cours des 12e et 13e siècles', 7 *Comunicazione e studi* (1955), 9–14. Here, however, their meaning somewhat changes. The subject of the *ius gentium* becomes "peoples" (*gentes*) while the subject of *ius civile* is the "people" (*populus*) or the "city" (*civitas*) and that of natural law are "nations" or "humankind". Guggenheim, 'Jus gentium', 15 n. 32.

kings of this world."[272] And private property as well as other institutions of private law had emerged by customary and enacted law on the strength of royal power.[273] However, *Decretum*, unlike the *Corpus iuris*, also affirmed the hierarchical superiority of natural law over the purely human forms of law, *ius civile* and *ius gentium*: "whatever has been either received in usages or set down in writing is to be held null and void if it is contrary to natural law".[274] This was significant. Romans would never have accepted that something that was merely "natural" and primitive would override such complex Roman institutions as those of slavery, taxation or private property, for example.[275] But *Decretum* was intended to serve Gregorius VII in his struggles with the emperor and it was no doubt useful to produce a hierarchy where natural law – over which the pope would be authoritative – overrode secular laws. Nevertheless, this did not lead Gratian to suggest that private property was illegal. In a significant concession to social developments, canon lawyers accepted that the division of properties was valid nevertheless, owing to the merely hortatory character of that aspect of natural law that provided for shared ownership.

Over again jurists struggled to fit the principles of Christian morality with transformations in the world around them. Sometimes they would understand natural law as only a recommendation that did not prohibit its contrary or regarded its rules as permissive so that they could be supplemented by *ius gentium*.[276] Sometimes a distinction was made between a more ideal version of natural law and one more attuned to present conditions, a *jus naturale primaevum* and *jus naturale secundarium* – a distinction eventually taken over by sixteenth-century Spaniards and the early work of Grotius.[277] Sometimes *ius gentium* was collapsed into

272 Gratian, *The Treatise on Laws*, Dist. 8 Part 1 C.1 (24).

273 "It is by the laws of kings that possessions are possessed". Ibid., Dist. 8 Part 1 C.1 (25).

274 Ibid., Dist. 8 Part 2 (25). See also Dist. 9 C.11 (32). Gratian uses four expressions for natural law – "ius divinum", "fas", "ius naturale" and "lex naturalis". Weigand, *Naturrechtlslehre*, 133.

275 But the compilers of the *Institutes* did insert there a passage that "naturalia enim jura civilis ratio peremere non postest" ("The rules of state law cannot destroy natural ties"), I .3.1.11. (Justinian's *Institutes*, 93).

276 See especially, Brian Tierney, *Liberty & Law. The Idea of Permissive Natural Law 1100–1800* (Catholic University of America Press 2014), 18–47; Thier, 'Historische Semantik', 35–8. On the uncertainties about the nature of medieval *ius gentium*, see also Jonathan William Robinson, *William of Ockham's Early Theory of Property Rights in Context* (Leiden, Brill 2012), 72, 74.

277 Scattola, *Das Naturrecht vor dem Naturrecht*, 125–30 and also 178–93.

natural law with a distinction made between a primary version that had the character of what was natural for humans in general and a secondary one that Bartolus, for example, understood simply as the practices of nations, *usu gentium.*[278] As Weigand's compilation of the writings of glossators shows, the twofold character of *ius gentium* was routinely recognised, one part falling under natural law, the other supporting or explaining the emergence of useful or necessary institutions, including, as in Placentinius, for example, commerce and warfare – "*propter utilitatem, ut iura commerciorum alias propter necessitatem, ut iura bellorum*".[279]

In an analogous fashion, recognition of the *de iure* status of the emperor as *Dominus mundi* [D. 14.2.9] would be accompanied by the acknowledgement that the national monarchies had *de facto* administration of their territories – the emperor's *auctoritas* met with the king's *potestas iure gentium.*[280] "This distinction between right and fact – the acceptance of Imperial claims in right, with the accompanying recognition of their invalidity in fact – was at the basis of all the political theories of Bartolus."[281] Rome was universal in one sense, the domestic prince authoritative in another. An imperial power conceived only *ratione protectionis vel administrationis* would not cancel out royal dominion: to rule universally did not mean to rule every particular as well.[282] Whether royal power over *regna* was explained as an express or tacit grant by the emperor, the process was rationalised *iure gentium. Regna* and smaller *civitates* could still rise as long as this was not *ad iniuriam vel emulationem alterius.*[283]

Whatever the variations of vocabulary, the distinctions invariably reaffirmed the validity of Christian ideals while simultaneously approving of present institutions. Freedom and slavery, peace and war, the relations of authority in the family and those in the *civitas*, common ownership and private ownership, *dominium iurisdictionis* and *dominium proprietatis*, *dominium directum* and *dominium utile* would all receive a hearing. In itself the distinction between the law of nature and the *ius civile* was always too great; it left unexplained where such distinction arose and why positive (human) law would be binding. From where came the authority of the prince or the community to command? Why would a

278 Bartolus, Prima super Digest ad D 1.1.5 n. 9 in Haggenmacher, *Grotius*, 326. Scattola, *Das Naturrecht vor dem Naturrecht*, 205–7.

279 Weigand, *Die Naturrechtslehre*, 44–5.

280 Or as Wilks speaks of "*Imperium*" having "both an authoritative and a territorial connotation", *Problem of Sovereignty*, 437 and generally 433–51.

281 Woolf, *Bartolus of Sassoferrato*, 22.

282 Ibid., 23–5.

283 Ibid., 110, 114.

contract or a loan be binding? These were the questions that *ius gentium* was needed to answer.[284] The difficulty jurists have experienced in classifying it either as natural or human law reflects the unstable nature of this middle ground. To be valid, it must have a connection to the divine design; but it cannot be collapsed into faith, either, without losing its applicability in the lives of actual communities.

## Example: *Ius gentium* in Aquinas

The ambiguity of *ius gentium* was an absolutely central aspect of its systemic place, its usefulness in mediating between an abstract natural law, born with creation, and civil law applicable merely by virtue of the will of the prince. This is nowhere better illustrated than in Thomas Aquinas' (1224/5–74*) Summa theologiae* (1265–74). The obvious starting-point was that all Christian authority, *dominium*, was to be derived from God.[285]. "The earth is the Lord's and the fullness thereof, the world and those who dwell therein" (Psalm 24). The world was God's because He had created it. But in creating the world, he had also ordered, or "ordained", it by natural law so that it had become possible for humans to grasp its manner of operation and to contribute to the realisation of the divine plan.[286] In the part of the *Summa* commonly addressed as *De gubernatione mundi* (ST I 103–13) Aquinas sketched in some detail how God reigned over his creation through the instrumentality of natural law.[287] First of all, there was a distinction between the "design of government" (*ordinatio*) and the "execution of government" (*executio*), suggesting that it was one thing to create the world, another to see to the implementation of the divine plan.[288] That God was *prima causa* did

[284] As suggested by Canning, *The Political Thought*, 104–6.

[285] See Renoux-Zagamé, *Origines théologiques*, 64–114.

[286] "The eternal law is the plan of government in the Supreme Governor", Aquinas, ST I-II 93 3 Resp (106). The view that the world belonged to God because He had created it followed the civil law provision that one becomes *dominus* when one produces or creates a thing (that previously belonged to no-one) through *specificatio* [D. 41.1.7]. See also Renoux-Zagamé, *Origines théologiques*, 40–1, 43.

[287] See especially Giorgio Agamben, *Le règne et la gloire. Homo Sacer II, 2* (Paris, Seuil 2008), especially 203–21.

[288] "In government there are two things to be considered; the design of government, which is providence itself; and the execution of the design. As to the design of government, God governs all things immediately; whereas in its execution, He governs some things by means of others", Aquinas, ST I 103 6 Resp. (For references to Aquinas without page number, see Note on Sources following the Introduction.) Moreover, that He withdrew from the daily exercise of government in no way

not mean that the universe was wholly determined; like the king who reigns but does not govern, God would usually stay in the background.[289] At the foreground were human beings, making free choices in a process where they derived from the abstract provisions of natural law rules and legal institutions to assist them in the search of temporal happiness.[290] For natural law was often too general to be action-guiding:

> The general principles of the natural law cannot be applied to all men in the same way because of the great variety of human circumstances; and hence arises the diversity of positive laws among various people.[291]

When God had created human beings he had also donated *dominium* to them. This was part of what it meant to be created in God's image. Animals, for example, would now be subjected to humans. Why this would be so was explained by Aquinas in a typically utilitarian fashion:

> ... man has a natural dominion over external things because, by means of his reason and will, he is able to make use of external things to his own advantage ... as if they were made for this purpose.[292]

But what about power over other humans, the *dominium* of the prince over his subjects? All theologians agreed that humans had been created free and equal. They were masters of their actions (*Est autem homo dominus suorum actuum*).[293] That they possessed *liberum arbitrium* was a condition of their responsibility before God and other

diminished him, just as when an earthly monarch uses ministers "the kingly power is brought into greater evidence", 6 ad 3.

289 "Now God is the cause not indeed only of some particular kind of being, but of the whole universal being... Wherefore, as there can be nothing which is not created by God, so there can be nothing which is not subject to His government". Aquinas, I 103 5 Resp. See further Agamben, *Le règne*, 213–15; Renoux-Zagamé, *Origines théologiques*, 67–72.

290 Aquinas, ST I-II 105 ad 1. That "freedom", as noted above, was a consequence of the *dominion in se* or the *dominium in actionum suarum* that characterised human nature. Thus is created a hierarchy of temporal authority from "low" to "high": "On the father of a family depends the order of the household; which order is contained in the order of the city; which order again depends on the ruler of the city; while this last order depends on that of the king, by whom the whole kingdom is ordered". ST I 105 6 Resp.

291 Aquinas, ST I-II 95 2 ad 3 (131).

292 Aquinas, ST II-II 61 1 Resp. (206). Note that the "as if" here points to the original act of creation where things in the state of innocence were supposed to serve creation as a whole. Renoux-Zagamé, *Origines théologiques*, 75–8.

293 See Aquinas, ST I-II 1 1 Resp: "Unde illae actiones vocantur propriae humanae, quarum homo est dominus. Est autem homo dominus suorum actuum per

humans.[294] This differentiated them from animals: "Only such actions were properly human of which the human being was *dominus*."[295] Human beings were also equal; they had all been created in God's image and shared equally in divine providence.[296] But even in the state of innocence, there was "inequality as to righteousness and knowledge".[297] Humans would still have to be directed to the common good by those whom greater ability to reason made natural leaders.[298] This was even more necessary after the Fall when temporal order was to be enforced over ambitious sinners struggling over their livelihood in conditions of scarcity. It no longer sufficed to live spontaneously under natural law.[299] A secular community needed a government.

Aquinas' views of royal dominion, written into the unfinished fragment *De regimine principum* (*De regno*), built likewise on Aristotle: "to govern is to guide what is governed in a suitable fashion to its proper end".[300] Private interests were to be coordinated so as to reach the common good.[301] But that good was not independent of the virtue of the citizens. After all, "a king governing his people is a minister of God".[302] Or as he put it in the *Summa*: "There is present in mankind a

rationem et voluntatem". Aquinas ties the dominion humans have over other things to their mastery over themselves (their will). "Man in a certain sense contains all things, and so according as he is master of what is within himself, in the same way he can have mastership over other things". Aquinas, ST I 96 2 Resp. See further, Brett, *Liberty, Right and Nature*, 12–18; Brian Tierney, 'Dominion of Self and Natural Rights before Locke and After', in Virpi Mäkinen & Petter Korkman (eds), *Transformations in Medieval and Early Modern Rights Discourse* (Berlin, Springer 2006), 179–82.

294 Aquinas, ST I-II 1 5. On "liberum arbitrium", see further Kurt Seelmann, *Die Lehre des Fernando Vasquez de Menchaca vom Dominium* (Cologne, Heymanns 1979), 76–80.

295 "quod est suorum actuum dominus", Aquinas, ST I-II 1 1 Resp. See also ST I 83 1 Resp: "Man has free-will: otherwise counsels, exhortations, commands, prohibitions, rewards, and punishments would be in vain."

296 Genesis 1:27. See further Renoux-Zagamé, *Origines théologiques*, 69, 71, 108–10, passim.

297 Aquinas, ST I 96 3 Resp.

298 Ibid., I 96 4 Resp.

299 See Andreas Thier, 'Heilsgeschichtliche und naturrechtliche Ordnung: Naturrecht vor und nach dem Sündenfall', in Matthias Armgardt & Tilman Repgen (eds), *Naturrecht im Antike und früher Neuzeit* (Tübingen, Mohr Siebeck 2014), 151–2.

300 Aquinas, 'De regimine principum,' in *Aquinas. Political Writings* (R. W. Dyson ed., Cambridge University Press, 2002), I XV (39).

301 "[A]ll the particular goods which men obtain, whether wealth or profit or health or skill or learning, were directed, as to their end, to the good of the community", ibid., I XVI (42).

302 Ibid., I IX (24).

kind of natural aptitude for virtue ... but some kind of discipline is necessary if that virtue is to reach perfection in man".[303] Because it cannot be assumed that all people become virtuous spontaneously, without fear of punishment, laws were needed to teach them to do by habit what they initially do by coercion.[304] There was no conflict between governing for the good of the community and teaching virtue, however. Good government fulfilled God's will. Its rewards went beyond secular happiness: "blessedness is the real reward of virtue".[305]

The principal instruments of government were civil law and the *ius gentium*. Both were what practical reason derived from natural law in its search of the common good, though differently. Civil law was received through a process that Aquinas called "determination", the "specific application of that which is expressed in general terms".[306] It was the *local* specification of a universal natural law. More interesting, however, was the *ius gentium*, which was derived from natural law as "conclusions" that resembled what science abstracted from its principles.[307] This had much broader validity than civil law, responding to conditions of human life everywhere. It was a kind of normative anthropology, a theory about human nature that combined an intrinsic need of sociability with the ability to reason. *Ius gentium* thus appeared as an intermediate category that differed from pure natural law but still did not turn into pure voluntary law. It did not collapse into whatever a lawmaker or judge might wish; the derivation had to be made by prudential reason that reflected an empirically oriented view of what was needed for social life, projecting human beings as seekers of "some advantage".[308] The ambivalence was obvious:

> the *ius gentium* is indeed natural to man in a sense, in so far as he is rational, because it is derived from natural law in the manner of a conclusion not greatly remote from its first principles, which is why men agree to it so readily. Nevertheless, it is distinct from the natural law, and especially so from the natural law which is "common to all animals".[309]

The choice of *law* as the applicable vocabulary ensured the effectiveness of the directives in institutional practice while the treatment of the *virtues*

[303] Aquinas, ST I-II 95 1 Resp (127).
[304] Ibid., I-II 92 2 ad 4 (100). For the relationship between private virtue and public good in the state, see John Finnis, *Aquinas. Moral, Political, and Legal Theory* (Oxford University Press 1998), 232–39.
[305] Aquinas, 'De regimine principum', I IX & X (24–7 & 28).
[306] Aquinas, ST I-II 95 2 Resp (130).
[307] Ibid., I-II 95 2 Resp (130).
[308] Ibid., II-II 57 3 ad 1–2 (164).
[309] Ibid., I-II 96 4 ad 1 (136).

*by* Aquinas linked government with the supernatural ends of human striving. Both originated in God but operated differently: law consisted of *external* directives that helped humans reach their good, virtue the *internal* conditions to attain it. Also *ius gentium* partook of this dual character: on the one hand, as law it consisted of conclusions from natural law that were promulgated by lawful authority. But it was also an aspect of the virtue of justice, understood as the commensurateness or appropriateness of something "by reason of some consequence of its being so". It was a set of practical conclusions that humans had drawn out of existing conditions and it was "observed by all equally" because of its "closeness to equity".[310] As examples Aquinas gave "just buyings and sellings and other such things ... without which men cannot live together".[311] They institutions emerged as conclusions produced by practical reasoning; these were appropriate to the human circumstances in general so that – unless the contrary was established – they should be respected in the life of every *civitas.*[312] Slavery, too, was part of *ius gentium.* After all, it could hardly be justified under a natural law of *liberum arbitrium.* The institution of slavery had been established owing to its advantages, including the benefit to the slave "that he is governed by someone wiser than he".[313]

In all of this, the hierarchical imagination related higher to lower levels of authority by complex metaphors such as *participation* (emperors and kings "participating" in the government of the world; human law "participating" in natural law) or by theologians and lawyers *deriving* things by applying reason to fit the low (e.g. human law, kingship) and high (e.g. natural law, empire as *Dominus mundi*) to each other.[314] The jurisdiction of the bishop would be an aspect of the pope's *plenitudo potestatis* and the magistrate a delegated user of the prince's *merum imperium.*[315] The power of the low respects what exists *de facto* but is derived from the high (*de iure*).[316] Transcendental and immanent are separate, but related: "there is no power but from God". The king is

[310] Ibid., II-II 57 3 ad 1–3 (164). [311] Ibid., I-II 95 4 Resp (135).

[312] For Aquinas' debt to Roman law in his underdtanding of natural law and *ius gentium,* see Jean-Marie Aubert, *Le droit Romain dans l'oeuvre de Saint Thomas* (Paris, Vrin 1955), 91–7.

[313] Aquinas, ST II-II 57 ad 2 (164).

[314] On Aquinas' "metaphysics of participation", see John F. Whippel, 'Metaphysics', in Norman Kretzmann & Eleonore Stump (eds), *The Cambridge Companion to Aquinas* (Cambridge University Press 1993), 93–9.

[315] See e.g. Watt, *The Theory of Papal Monarchy,* 85, 79–83.

[316] See Aquinas, ST I 103 6 Resp.

entitled to rule his *regnum*, but this did not cancel out the spiritual authority of the pope. And yet the undeniable limits to papal power would speak for separating the *jurisdiction* of the church (limited *de facto*) from the validity of Christian faith (universal *de iure*) – an operation that founded the legitimacy of the crusades.

## *Ius gentium* As Christian Authority 2: Universal History

The systemic role played by *ius gentium* in mediating Christian ideals with the reality of territorial *regna* also opened a new way to think about the history of human communities and the place of kings and the emperor in the divine plan. Aristotle's naturalistic account of the rise of political communities found its way into the works of theologians such as Aquinas and Giles of Rome. Both presented territorial *regna* as perfect communities, not only independent from higher powers but also as outcomes of a natural human instinct to seek protection and welfare. Aquinas was fully aware of the tensions between rival authorities, two of his brothers having been executed for rebellion against the emperor. Although he viewed the pope as the supreme ruler of *Christianitas*, he did not take an express position in the papal–imperial controversy and wrote about kingship and the *regnum* as if it did not exist. Human beings were political and social animals and territorial *regna* Aristotle's *civitates*.[317] Separate kingdoms were needed for defence, well-being and to enable people to lead fulfilling lives in communion with others. Reason told humans to join together and taught them how to plan their lives in security and happiness while eventually attaining their supernatural end.[318]

The naturalistic grounding of political authority was accompanied by a view of government that looked for secular objectives – peace, welfare and the common good – that were attainable to all.[319] No doubt, virtue and supernatural happiness existed as higher-level ends of government and the church had sometimes the power to abolish an infidel ruler's right to rule.[320] But most governmental tasks involved applying natural

317 "Aquinas, 'De regimine principum', I: I (5–8). 318 Ibid.

319 But even looking for the common good the prince was subordinated to the higher *telos* of the spiritual. Though Aquinas had called kings "vassals of the Church", he was unlikely to have meant automatic subordination to the pope. The church and the king both had their independent jurisdiction. See Miethke, *De potestate papae*, 40–2.

320 Paul E. Simon, 'Law and Politics', in Norman Kretzmann & Eleonore Stump (eds), *The Cambridge Companion to Aquinas* (Cambridge University Press 1993), 219.

reason available to Christians and infidel alike.[321] Yet the temporal order could still not be fully separated from the supernatural one. The latter had no other manner of expression, no other visibility than the human order. There was, then a certain practical virtue in human institutions (operating as "reason of state" or "economy") where peace and happiness were indications of the pious life: human government as God reigning over his world.[322] This view undermined older eschatologies. Instead of ending violently with the last days and the second coming, history now became a field in which nature would take its course by its elements striving to their natural end, with the assistance of human beings as secondary causes, possessors of *dominium*.[323] The rise and fall of *regna* were part of the natural course of history, outcomes of more or less successful government.

Such a vision of history was implied, for example, in the pamphlet "Before there were Clerics", *Antequam essent clerici*, composed by Philip's legists during the struggle with Boniface. The work began with the observation that "[b]efore there were clerics, the king of France had custody of his kingdom and he could make statutes to protect himself and the kingdom against the plots and injuries of his enemies".[324] France, in other words, was older than the church and its government had the task of protecting the *regnum*. Another tract "A Debate between a Clerk and a Knight", *Disputatio inter Clericum et Militem*, explained that the *regnum Franciae* had long ago separated itself from the Carolingian empire and now possessed authority equal to that of the emperor itself.[325] If civil law applied in France, this was because the king permitted it, not owing to the natural extent imperial jurisdiction. France had arisen independently of the church and the empire, and was now responsible for its own future.

To support this view, royal legists could also refer to the *ius gentium* under which "nations [were] differentiated and kingdoms founded, properties individuated, [and] state boundaries settled" [D.1.1.5.]. Against the view of time as a circular wheel of fortune or as decay from

321 It was clear, for example, that communities and human customs differed so that laws would vary from place to place. Aquinas, ST I-II 95 2 ad 3 and 4 (131); and 97 2 Resp (152). See also Foucault, *Sécurité, territore, population*, 238–40 and Post, *Studies*, 290–4.

322 Agamben, *Le règne et la gloire*, 138–42, 151–67.

323 This is the sense of Giles of Rome's view of proper Christian government as "*regimen naturale*", *De regimine principum*, Proemium.

324 'Before there Were Clerics', in Dyson, *Three Royalist Tracts*, 2/3.

325 'A Debate between a Clerk and a Knight', in ibid., 40/41–42/43.

a Golden Age, *ius gentium* expressed a Roman vision of an active institutional life that offered the prospect of a gradually improving *modernitas.*[326] We have seen Giles of Rome write of *ius gentium* as a kind of invitation to pay regard to social needs, consecrating practices such as "buying and selling and letting and hiriring" and other things, such as loans and deposits that humans needed for their living.[327] In contradistinction to natural law, *ius gentium* represented the variability of the human world, geared to assist government everywhere. It was impossible for the jurists to contemplate the period's commercial revolution, for example, without speculating about the rules of trade that applied all over Europe. They were not unchanging natural law but products of human history that exceeded the limits of this or that *regnum.*

This was wholly incompatible with the presumed eschatological significance of the empire, represented in the biblical narrative of Daniel's interpretation of an appearance in Nebuchadnezzar's dream.[328] In that interpretation, Rome was to play the role of the *kathekon* – that which restrained the coming of Antichrist and gave time for Christians to come together in Jerusalem to prepare for the end of the world.[329] This view had been included in the universal histories that appeared in France from the twelfth to the fourteenth centuries with the ambition of recounting the whole of human history through long lists of names and place, tables of sovereigns and popes, with explanations about the rise and fall of emperors, dynasties or individual *regna.* One of the most influential of these, the *Universal Chronicle* by Sigebert de Gembloux (1028–112), reaching from AD 381 up to the last year of the author's life, was a vigorous defence of the Roman empire as a force preparing Christianity for Christ's second coming.[330] Among *regna,*

[326] On the many medieval temporalities, see Jacques Le Goff, *La civilisation de l'occident médiéval* (Paris, Flammarion 2008), 140–69.

[327] "sine quibus societas humana non bene sufficit sibi ad vitam", Giles of Rome, *De regimine principum,* III 2, xxv (308r).

[328] The image was known also to other Eastern mythologies – a statue with a head of gold, arms of silver, belly and hips of bronze, legs of iron and feet partly of iron and partly of terra cotta, signifying the succession of four (or sometimes five) world empires, of which Rome would be the last. See James Muldoon, *Empire and Order. The Concept of Empire 800–1800* (London, St Martin's 1999), 101–13. From patristic times to the late medieval period, it was common to refer to the emperor or the king as "vicar of God". A listing of sources in this respect is given in Rivière, *Le problème de l'Église et de l'État,* 435–40.

[329] See Chazan, *L'empire,* 187–92; Kantorowicz, *The King's Two Bodies,* 291–5.

[330] The text, available in 42 Latin manuscripts, was used as a basis for information and ideas for such later works as the *Speculum historiale* of Vincent Beauvais in the 1240s, the *Gesta sancta memorie Ludovici regis Francie* and *Gesta Philippi* by Guillaume de

Rome had a special dignity and a universal mission. As a consequence of sin, Rome had been invaded in the fourth century, Sigebert wrote, and the empire had moved to the East. With Charlemagne, it was transferred back to the West in 801 but was then again split apart so that it was the task of the good emperor to restore its unity and bring peace and order again among Christians. Sigebert followed the fate of successive emperors, describing how God intervened on behalf of the good ones but revenged the bad ones by division and conflict. That Rome had eschatological significance did not mean that individual *regna*, born out of sin though they were, were necessarily evil. They also had their history, ultimately directed towards recapturing the lost unity under Rome. In fact, Sigebert believed that the recent rise of civil law might be a sign that the time of fragmentation was over and, possibly, that it would be for the French king to take over imperial leadership.[331]

The proposal that France should take over the empire was occasionally vented; one suggestion, which may not have been widely known at the time, came from the legist Pierre Dubois from Normandy, advocating an alliance of Christian princes in order to conquer and colonise the Holy Land.[332] Philip himself had attempted to seat both his brother and his eldest son on the imperial throne. But it is doubtful whether he seriously contemplated moving the empire to Paris. In any case, at the time of their struggle with Boniface, Philip and his legists also had available to them the universal history by Guillaume de Nangis (d. 1301), a member of the influential group of Benedictine monks at Saint-Denis and one of Sigebert's followers, that celebrated the sacred character and Carolingian origin of French kingship, contrasting the Christian heroism of Louis IX with the dark machinations of Emperor Frederick II.[333] As the pamphlet *Disputatio inter Clericum et Militem* made

Nangis, copied in the 1280s and 1290s, important in the process of consolidating the religion of French kingship, and the universal chronicle of Jean de Saint Victor in the 1320s. On Sigebert's work and especially the influence of his chronicle in the thirteenth and fourteenth centuries, see Chazan, *L'empire*, 24–5, 311–402.

331 Chazan, *L'empire*, 299–302. Sigebert had a negative view of the French kings, including Hugues Capet whom he held as a usurper, 251. It was for the later writers of universal history, especially Guillaume de Nangis, to use the victories of Philip II and the sanctification of Louis IX as indications of the glory of French kings.

332 Dubois, *Recovery of the Holy Land.*

333 M. Guizot (ed.), *Chronique de Guillaume de Nangis* (Paris, Brière 1825) (this version begins only where Sigebert de Gembloux ends and is continued by other monks from Guillaume's death). See further Jones, *Eclipse of Empire*, 73–93 and Chazan, *L'empire*, 379–89.

clear, perhaps with Guillaume's work as inspiration, the Franks had separated from the empire already half a millennium earlier and now lived in full equality with it so that "just as all things lying within the frontiers of the empire are acknowledged to be subject to the empire, so those things lying within the frontiers of France are subject to the kingdom".[334] The empire's territorial extent had varied, and it had been headed by more or less capable rulers. Alongside the empire, the *regna* had their place in the divine order – they had punished Rome for its sins and were now contemplating a sacred army to conquer Jerusalem.[335] Among *regna*, France stood out with a special mission. During the long vacancy in the imperial chair the French had learned to think of the French king, *roi très Chrétien*, as the first among the world's rulers, manifested by the special protection God had given the Capet family.[336] By the 1340s, the author of the royalist *Songe du Vergier* would coolly note that Rome had lost its territories, which in any case it had acquired unjustly. The full independence of *regna* such as France was provided by the *ius gentium*, as recognised in the *Digest*.[337]

Accordingly, the *Memoriale historiarum* of Jean de Saint-Victor, a collective work from the monastery of Saint Victor between 1302 and 1326, remained silent about Rome's eschatological necessity. The lengthy "*Tractatus*" on the division of kingdoms that prefaced the work made no reference to Daniel's prophecy and told the history of *regna* in perfectly secular terms of rise and fall.[338] At the beginning, Jean and his co-workers wrote, there had been four kingdoms that were eventually conquered by Rome, which in its turn underwent the *divisio imperii*. Rome re-emerged with Charlemagne, but was then subordinated to the pope whose deposition of Frederick II in 1245 finally ended the Western empire. Because the key sense of

334 'A Debate between a Clerk and Knight', 42/43.

335 According to Guillaume de Nangis, the task of the French kings from Philip Augustus onwards had been to protect the Church against imperial tyranny and work as an "arbitrator of nations". Like the even more widely read Vincent de Beauvois, Guillaume strongly suggested France as the real bearer of the imperial inheritance. Jones, *Eclipse of Empire*, 81–2; Chazan, *L'empire*, 251–3, 688–92.

336 See Krynen, *L'empire du roi*, 352–8.

337 *Le Songe du Vergier* (Marion Schnerb-Lièvre, ed., Paris, CNRS 1982), LI Ch XXXVI (852–3).

338 Jean de Saint-Victor, *Traité de la division des royaumes. Introduction à une histoire universelle* (Turnhout, Brepols 2002). See further, Isabelle Guyot-Bachy, *Le memoriale historiarum de Jean de Saint-Victor. Une historien et sa communauté au début du XIVe siècle* (Turnhout, Brepols 2000).

empire for the co-writers of Saint Victor was that of rule in peace (*pacifice*), the time of Henry VII did not qualify – there had been no universal peace.[339] The *Tractatus* presented a summary of historical notes showing how each *regnum* had emerged and which dynasties had come to rule them. The Franks had originated from groups of refugees from the destruction of Troy some of whom had eventually settled in the region of Paris, others elsewhere in France.[340] The alignment of these two groups led to the appointment of their first duke "Priam" from which moment Jean and his co-workers counted 961 years to the (present) reign of Philip the Fair, a reign of 50 kings.[341] Within such histories, individual *regna* had their origin in a past that was earlier than Rome or the Christian church; hence they could be argued, following Aristotle, as a natural way of human organisation.

## *Ius gentium* and Christian Authority 3: Property

In addition to its systemic and historical roles, *ius gentium* offered a way to understand medieval economic statecraft by explaining the emergence and use of private property and extending a way for the king to intervene in it. By the thirteenth century, the increasingly routine character of mercantile transactions had diminished old suspicions about private property. Demographic growth contributed to greater agricultural production and the increase of value of land kept accelerating pressure to raise rents and to create further sub-infeudations or substitutions. Profits were also made in commerce and manufacture where legal innovations had dramatically reduced what now would be called transaction costs – new types of commercial partnerships, deposit banking, insurance, bills of exchange, letters of credit and loans for long-distance exchanges would contribute to the change from periodic fairs to permanent markets that would enduringly change urban culture in France as elsewhere.[342] Of course, the moral sense of these developments remained disputed. Early church fathers had often presented a critical view of the "vice of property". Many admired the Franciscans but also enjoyed public displays of seigneurial and royal wealth and prodigality. No doubt,

[339] Chazan, *L'empire*, 696–9. [340] Jean de Saint-Victor, *Traité*, 247–55.
[341] Ibid., 259.
[342] See the concise account in Douglass C. North & Robert Paul Thomas, *The Rise of the Western World. A New Economic History* (Cambridge University Press 1973), 46–64.

thinking about property was a major problem. What in this world was private and what was communal, what to be shared? How was property to be shared – what were the obligations of wealth and the debts to the poor?[343]

Most theologians and jurists agreed that private property was a product of political community. According to natural law, in the state of innocence all *dominium* had been shared. But this had been a matter of a distant, perhaps glorified past; the law of nations would apply in the active civil life of the present. As the matter was put in the *Corpus iuris*, "the reality of the human condition [had] led the peoples of the world to introduce institutions such as 'sale, hire, partnership, deposit, loan and many others'" [I. 1.2. 2. & D. 1.1.5].[344] As Cicero explained, the division of things was a cultural, historical product:

> Now, no property is private by nature, but rather by long occupation (as when men moved into some empty property in the past), or by victory (when they acquired it by war), or by law, by settlement, by agreement or by lot. The result is that the land of Arpinum is said to belong to the Arpinates, and that of Tusculum to the Tusculani.[345]

Cicero did not speculate about the justice of this process. He simply recorded what had taken place; possessions had crystallised, and that was all. The *Corpus iuris* would then give legal imprimatur to that history and those properties.

Neither Augustine nor Ambrose were primitive communists. They accepted the division of properties as a peacekeeping device in a post-lapsarian world. The main thing was to prevent the corruption of the soul; avarice was to be avoided by distributing possessions to help the poor or, if necessary, by choosing a life of apostolic poverty.[346] Canon lawyers, too, were clear that private ownership had been introduced only after the Fall: "by customary and enacted law, one thing is called 'mine' and something else 'another's'".[347] But Gratian then added somewhat confusedly that "natural law . . . prevails in dignity over custom and enactment. So whatever has been either received in usages or set down in writing is to be held null and void if it is contrary to

343 Epstein, *An Economic and Social History*, 130–1.

344 See also Brian Tierney, 'Natura Id Est Deus. A Case of Juristic Pantheism?', 24 *Journal of the History of Ideas* (1963), 309–10.

345 Cicero, *On Duties* 1.21–2, as quoted and translated in Peter Garnsey, *Thinking about Property. From Antiquity to the Age of Revolution* (Cambridge University Press 2009), 114.

346 See Garnsey, *Thinking about Property*, 125–8.

347 Gratian, *The Treatise on Laws*, Dist 8 part 1 (24).

natural law."[348] But they soon found a kind of a middle view according to which, although private ownership may have been wrongly (*per inequitatem*) instituted, it had become a perfectly lawful aspect of post-lapsarian society. It was hardly surprising that this became the church's main position – vehemently defended by its Dominican faction – as the church itself had become a great landowner and much of the economic progress of the twelfth and early thirteenth century had taken place through exchanges of private property. The Franciscan idealisation of poverty was too radical. It put to question a basic aspect of the social order.[349] Eventually, in order to explain how human acts could deviate from natural law in this way, the canonists would ingeniously, and influentially, argue that the original rule on common property had only a permissive nature. It did not actually *prohibit* the division of property.[350] The gap between divinely instituted natural law and the reality of human society was overcome by the old Stoic idea of *adiaphora* – that there was an area of freedom where no law determined any conduct as compulsory. Common *dominium* was merely a counsel or a permission, a statement of an ideal rather than a prohibition to act otherwise.[351]

Thus, for exmple, the early decretist Rufinus (c. 1150–91) began his comment on Part I of the *Digest* by defining the meaning of *ius* in an unorthodox, "subjective" way as "a certain power of a human being, implanted in nature, to do good, and to avoid the opposite".[352] This opened the way for a conception of human agency that could explain the rise of various temporal institutions from natural law that Rufinus envisaged to exist in three variants: commands, prohibitions and recommendations (*demonstrationes*). While the first two categories included absolute provisions such as "you shall obey God" and "you shall not kill", institutions such as liberty and common ownership came under *demonstrationes* that were non-binding and repleacable by such manmade institutions as slavery or private property.[353] After the Fall, Rufinus

[348] Ibid., Dist 8 part 2 (25). [349] Coleman, 'Property and Poverty', 617.

[350] See Thier, 'Heilsgeschichte und naturrechtliche Ordnung', 158–62.

[351] For the canonists' expansive use of the permissive natural law construction, see Tierney, *Liberty & Law*, 15–47.

[352] "Est itaque naturale ius vis quedam humane creature a natura insita ad faciendum bonum cavendumque contrarium", Rufinus, *Summa Decretorum* (H. Singer ed., Paderborn, Schöningh 1902), 6. See further Robinson, *William of Ockham's Early Theory*, 85–9; Tierney, *Liberty & Law*, 23–5.

[353] "nunc enim iure civili hic est servus meus, ille est ager tuus", Rufinus, *Summa Decretorum*, 7.

explained, the sense of justice and the clarity of human knowledge had been obscured. In order to lead their lives as brutes, they began to congregate, agreeing on laws and customs that gradually enabled them to enter organised relations under the *ius gentium*.[354]

Tierney has further described how, alongside *demonstratio*, expressions such as *fas* or *libertas* were used, or the view would be expressed that natural law permitted or tolerated a deviating positive law alongside it.[355] A leading late twelfth-century canon lawyer, Hugh of Pisa (Huguccio, bishop of Ferrera, d. 1210), observed that even as divine law provided for common property (*omnia sunt communia*), this did not at all mean that some things could not become private. Divine law had the nature of a permission and not a prohibition to act otherwise.[356] In another place he suggested that natural law prohibited stealing – but as *fas* (a natural custom) it allowed passage through fields.[357] In the same way it must have allowed both private and common ownership. In fact, "that something is common by natural law neither prohibits nor commands [*precipiebeat*] anything but demonstrates what is good".[358]

By natural law something is mine and something is yours, but this is by permission (*permissione*) not by precept ... all things are called common by the natural law that is licit (*licitum*) or moral (*fas*) that consist in demonstrations (*demonstrationes*).[359]

By the time Aquinas would come to the subject, it had become part of the so-called mendicant poverty controversy. Radical members of the Franciscan order argued that apostolic poverty required clerics to renounce all claim of *dominium*. All they were entitled to was factual use (*simplex usus facti*) of things necessary for survival. The church had first viewed this position with sympathy, but the official view soon became that life without dominion was in fact impossible: one "owned" the things one consumed.[360] In view of its riches, the church had an

354 Nor was it the case that private property would have emerged *per inequitatem*. Having emerged as *ius gentium*, it clearly could not be inequitable. Ibid., 4. 21.

355 Tierney, *Liberty & Law*, 22–47.

356 Huguccio Pisanus, *Summa Decretorum. Tom I Distinctiones I–XX* (Biblioteca Apostolica Vaticana 2006), D VIII c-I (125).

357 Ibid., D I c-7 (36). 358 Ibid., D I c-7 (36).

359 Ibid., D I c-7 (35–6), translation by Tierney, *Liberty & Law*, 23.

360 For useful descriptions of the treatment of *dominium* in the Franciscan poverty dispute, see Virpi Mäkinen, *Property Rights in the Late Medieval Discussion on Franciscan Poverty* (Leuven, Peeters 2001); Brett, *Liberty, Right and Nature*, 11–20; Coleman, 'Property and Poverty', 629–43.

obvious stake in the matter. and Franciscans' principal adversary, Pope John XXII (1244–334) would eventually defend the view that private property was instituted already in the state of innocence.[361] But most theologians, Aquinas among them, followed a middle view. Although private property may have been wrongly instituted, it had become a perfectly lawful aspect of postlapsarian society, arising as a conclusion that practical reason drew from what was "necessary to human life".[362] Because its validity was not limited to this or that civil law, property had the nature of *ius gentium.*[363] But, Aquinas hastened to add, as if to stress the anthropological character of his standpoint, even as property was not natural law, it was nevertheless "natural to man in a sense, in so far as he is rational, because it is derived from natural law in the manner of a conclusion not greatly remote from its first principles, which is why men agree to it so readily".[364] On that basis Aquinas produced his famous utilitarian justification. Property was needed because: (1) everyone is more diligent when they procure something to themselves; (2) human affairs are more orderly with private property, and (3) there will then be a more peaceful state of things.[365]

Here as elsehere, *ius gentium* gave legal effect to *de facto* developments. How this was argued among lawyers may be illustrated by Bezemer's demonstration of the use of the Aristotelian concept of *causa* by Jacques de Révigny. To argue that mere possession gave right – a notion commonly accepted but hard to explain – Révigny pointed out that: "By a certain analogy, in every action, both personal and real, there are three concurrent things, namely a fact, a right resulting from this fact, and subsequent action."[366] Révigny then used this triplet – fact–right–action – to show how developments in the social world may in due course crystallise into rights that give rise to "actions" in available proceedings. The most significant use of this triplet had to do with the *dominium* that had emerged under *ius gentium.* All peoples had the

[361] In his encyclical *Quia vir reprobus,* John held that God had created Adam as owner of the world. See e.g. Thier, 'Heilsgeschichtliche und naturrechtliche Ordnung', 164.

[362] Aquinas, ST II-II 66 2 Resp (208).

[363] Ibid., I-II 96 4 Resp (135).

[364] Ibid., I-II 96 4 ad 1 (136).

[365] Ibid., II-II 66 2 Resp (208). A useful explanation of Aquinas' concept of property is Odd Langholm, *Economics in the Medieval Schools. Wealth, Exchange, Value, Money and Usury According to the Paris Theological Tradition, 1200–1350* (Leiden, Brill 1992), 198–222.

[366] Révigny, as quoted (and translated) by Kees Bezemer, 'Jacques de Révigny's Contribution to the Concept of Subjective Rights and the Origin of the Maxim "Ex facto ius oritur"', 81 *The Legal History Review* (2013), 201.

institution of private ownership. It had three elements: the *causa* whereby ownership was acquired (*possessio*, contract), the *right* of ownership itself, and the (real or personal) action. The first two of these Révigny classed under *ius gentium*, the third as *ius civile*. While the causes of rights and rights "themselves" were universal, the actions available to vindicate them came under domestic law.[367] In this way Révigny seems to have arrived at something like "subjective right" independent of the actions to vindicate them and limited the prince's right to extinguish *dominium* to individual cases, There was, for Révigny, thus a wider social significance in the fact (*causa*) that gave rise to the rights that were part of *ius gentium* and hence no longer within the powers of the king.

This fitted well with old Germanic laws on "seisin" that deferred to a community's general toleration of *de facto* situations.[368] In contrast to the subtle distinctions Roman law made between *proprietas*, *precarium* and *beneficium*, these laws paid much more attention to possession than formal–legal criteria so that, for example, unchallenged seisin of one year and a day would count as proof of title.[369] As a result, by the year 1000 a *de facto* system of landed power had come into existence in the Frankish realm that would be formalised with the help of the church, the rise of seigneurial courts and the spread of an expert culture of lawyers giving these facts legal meaning.[370] There was little one could do about how landed property had emerged. The weakness or absence of central government made redistribution inconceivable. It was more important to have a moral–legal vocabulary to assess the way it was *used*.[371]

367 Ibid., 201–6.

368 On "seisin" as de facto control over the product of land (in contrast to Roman *proprietas* as ownership of the land itself), see Bloch, *Feudal Society*, I, 115–16; Patault, *Introduction historique*, 20–31.

369 Patault, *Introduction historique*, 29–30.

370 The existence of a "break" between two phases of feudalism has been much disputed in French historiography. The question has to do with the intensity of the seigneurial violence that did away with the remains of Carolingian *regimen*. For a good description of the debate and the stakes, see Christian Lauranzon-Rosaz, 'La débat sur la "mutation féodale": état de la question', in Przemyslaw Urbanczyk (ed.), *Europe Around the Year 1000* (Warsaw, Polish Academy of Sciences 2001), 11–44.

371 Some twelfth-century efforts (limited accountability, "freedom charters") to attain some control on exploitative lordship are described in Thomas Bisson, *The Crisis of the Twelfth Century. Power, Lordship and the Origins of European Government* (Princeton University Press 2012), 322–69, and for France 398–415, 542–8.

## Towards Economic Justice?

But *de facto* could not be the only standard for recognising *dominium* or drawing its limits. After all, the thirteenth century "was an era of justice. Justice was the virtue par excellence of Kings."[372] In some way, the legal practices needed to pass the test of "justice" before they could become part of official legal culture. This was especially visible in the world of exchange. Like many other Dominicans, Aquinas had a lively interest in the new commercial practices. For example, he was at one point consulted by cloth buyers at the fair of Lagny in Champagne on the conditions of long-term commerce and engaged in correspondence with James of Viterbo on how to calculate the just price.[373] The moral and legal issues of a profit economy were debated through the Aristotelian prism of justice that "is properly concerned with those things which have to do with our relations with others".[374] To explain what justice might mean in commercial matters, Aquinas introduced the idea of commensurateness.[375] There was *natural* justice "when someone gives something in order to receive an equivalent amount back in return", and there was *positive or contractual* justice when something was to done in accordance with agreement.[376] Natural justice had to with the natural commensurateness of things – such as "the male is by nature commensurate with the female". Another commensurateness was not related to things "in themselves" but "by reason of some consequence of [their] being so: for example the possession of property".[377] It was this *artificial* commensurateness that lay at the heart of economic justice; Aquinas believed it coincided with what Gaius had meant: "Whatever natural reason establishes among all men is observed by all men equally, and is called the right of nations [*ius gentium*]."[378]

The search for "commensurateness" was unproblematic in ordinary exchanges. Mere buying and selling "in order to satisfy the needs of life" was routine household business.[379] By contrast, Aquinas shared Aristotle's suspicion of professional merchants. Buying cheap in order

372 Jacques Le Goff, *Your Money or Your Life. Economy and Religion in the Middle Ages* (New York, Zone Books 1990), 28.

373 The standard of just price, he held, was to be that of "common estimation". Anything beyond would be usurious. See Gérard Sivéry, 'La notion économique de l'usure selon saint Thomas d'Aquin', 3–4 *Revue du Nord* (2004), 697–708.

374 Aquinas, ST II-II 58 1 Resp (169).

375 Ibid., II-II 57 2 Resp (161).

376 Ibid., II-II 57 2 Resp (161–2).

377 Ibid., II-II 57 3 Resp (164).

378 Ibid., II-II 57 3 Resp (164).

379 Ibid., II-II 77 4 Resp. See further Aristotle, 'The Politics', I 8–10 (19–24).

to sell dear, the search for profit, "ha[d] a certain debasement attaching thereto, in so far as, by its very nature, it does not imply a virtuous or necessary end". In a spirit of compromise, Aquinas suggested that this might not necessarily breach virtue (or might even have a virtuous end) if it was for "moderate gain" such as the upkeep of the merchant's household, or "the assistance of the needy". Even long-distance trading might be acceptable if it was for "some public advantage" such as the "country lack[ing] the necessaries of life" or "as payment for [the merchant's] labor".[380] But this did not wholly remove the stigma. The justice of mercantile activity would depend on the assessment of where a just mean – commensurateness or proportionality – might lie, taking into account the context of economic activities as a whole. What was "moderate gain" or a commensurate exchange referred beyond individual transactions to the gains merchants *generally* received in comparable situations. That the just price was received from "common estimation" gave social relations an impersonal gloss: value, and hence justice, would be determined not by the motives or nature of individual transactions but by larger social forces.[381]

Consider the case where justice was to be determined where perfomances were qualitatively different. What would be a just exchange between a carpenter and a shoemaker? Aristotle was clear that commensurateness was in such case governed by proportional, and not "arithmetic", reciprocity. Houses and shoes can be compared to each other only by reference to some third item, namely money. "Money then, acting as a measure, makes goods commensurate and equates them."[382] This analysis led Aquinas to question how the monetary value of a pair of shoes or a house was to be determined. Many candidates had been offered: the labour that had gone to produce a house or a pair of shoes, the materials used or the usefulness of the items. But even as all were in some sense relevant, there was no *final* measure beyond what people were ready to pay for a pair of shoes or a house. This was also the principle of civil law, well known to Aquinas; a thing was worth as much as it could be sold for [I. 3.23]. Such market

380 Aquinas, ST II-II 77 4 Resp. On the distinction between the (necessary) art of household management andf the (unnatural) art of wealth-getting through retail trade and usury, see Aristotle, 'The Politics', I 9–10 (22–5).

381 "The just price of things is not fixed with mathematical precision but depends on common estimate". Aquinas, ST II-II 77 1 ad 1. For commentary, see especially Kaye, *Economy and Nature*, 37–47, 70–6, 87–101.

382 Aristotle, *The Nicomachean Ethics* (D Ross ed., Oxford University Press 1980), V 5 (120).

price left a large latitude, as it was based "on a kind of estimate".[383] That latitude, again, was determined typically through a legal assessment of whether the difference between the agreed price and the common price was exorbitant (usually over 50 percent), and thus that the rule of *laesio enormis* might be applicable. This, however, shifted focus from an analysis of the virtue of the individual parties into an examination of the processes of the market: how is a thing valued usually? This had a rather worrying consequence – namely that "the individual's responsibility in economic activity is effectively eliminated".[384]

Or think about the prohibition of usury. Already by the thirteenth century, commercial exchanges relied on an extensive practice of credit. The basic Aristotelian position in this respect was clear: money was "sterile", it did not produce anything; lending for interest was unnatural, it was to charge for nothing and therefore contrary to the principle of just exchange.[385] Moreover, the only thing that was sold by the lender was time, and time belonged to God and was not for anyone to sell. That certain civil laws permitted or even endorsed it for pragmatic reasons, "lest the advantage of many should be hindered", in no way exonerated it.[386] Despite these (and other) objections, it was clear that without credit, the economy would not function; hence, a sophisticated theory of legitimate interest arose that looked towards the damage that was occasioned for the lender (*damnum emergens*) or, more controversially, the loss incurred in case he had invested the money (*lucrum cessans*). And there were other arguments excluding moderate interest from the usury prohibition.[387] But what was "moderate" could not be determined by focusing only on the bilateral justice between the lender and the borrower. The risk to the lender depended on probabilities and uncertainties that had to do with the fluctuations of the value of the currency, the professional position of the two parties, success of the underlying transaction(s) and so on. Hence, in later analyses, the usurious nature of

383 Aquinas, ST II-II 77 1 ad 1. 384 Kaye, *Economy and Nature*, 98.

385 Aristotle, 'The Politics', I 10 (25); Aquinas, ST II-II 78 1 Resp (222). A good summary of the orthodox arguments against usury and Aquinas' version of it is Langholm, *Economics in the Medieval Schools*, 45–52, 237–48. Also excellent is Joel Kaye, *A History of Balance, 1250–1375. The Emergence of a New Model of Equilibrium and Its Impact on Thought* (Cambridge University Press 2014), 20–75. For the usury practices in the Italian and French contexts, see Heers, *La naissance du capitalisme*, 65–161.

386 Aquinas, ST II-II 78 1 Resp & ad 3 (222, 223–4).

387 For the theoretical justifications of usury as "interest", see Diana Wood, *Medieval Economic Thought* (Cambridge University Press 2012), 181–205.

interest was assessed from the perspective of the common good – the presence of money changers and bankers was understood to be *useful* for the community at large.[388] But assessment of such usefulness, and the determination of permissible interest rates, depended on a large number of nameless economic actions. Coming to terms with them required a kind of "social" thinking that situated myriad individual actions as parts within larger systems of *civitas* and market.[389] The moral–legal analysis of usury would link with productive uses of capital to which it was characteristic that they dealt with risks and probabilities derived from surveying long-term trends. The normative status of financial activities became inextricable from the rules of statecraft.

In his instruction-book to Philip Giles of Rome followed Aristotle in stressing the moderate "mean" as the appropriate perspective on all human relations.[390] It followed that the king should see to it that none of his subjects became overly wealthy or excessively poor: "*optimam esse citivatem & regnum, si ibi sit populus ex multis personis mediis constitutus*".[391] This was anything but an isolated position; the "idea of the mean was basic to most economic thought and was associated with notions of balance, equilibrium, or moderation".[392] But what this meant was far from clear. It certainly did not imply that everyone was entitled to an equal share. Neither Aristotle nor his followers wanted to institute widespread and constant redistribtion.[393] Instead, the mean was sought from proportional (geometrical) reciprocity, what Giles termed the justice of equality, and sometimes commutative justice, and that Aristotle regarded as nothing less than the social basis of the *civitas*: "For it is by proportionate requital that the city holds together."[394] Proportional justice ordered the relations of subjects to each other just as in a physical body the different parts were to support each other: without such ordering – for example, without those with abundant means assisting the needy – the body could not survive.[395] But it also

[388] "And so human law has permitted usury not because it deems it as being in accord with justice, but lest the benefit of many should otherwise be impeded", Aquinas, ST II-II 78 1 ad 3 (224).

[389] Kaye, *A History of Balance*, 60 and, on the development of usury doctrine at this time, 20–75.

[390] See especially Aristotle, *Nicomachean Ethics*, II 6–9 (32–47) and 'The Politics', IV 11 (106–7).

[391] Giles of Rome, *De regimine principum*, III 2, xxxiii (322r).

[392] Wood, *Medieval Economic Thought*, 13. [393] Aristotle, 'The Politics', II 7 (45).

[394] Aristotle, *Nicomachean Ethics*, V 5 (118).

[395] Giles of Rome, *De regimine principum*, I 2, xi (46v–47r).

made the justice of economic transactions dependent on assessment about how the whole operated; what was the current competitive price, what was and what was not advantageous to the *regnum* and how much moral leeway could be allowed.

Now such analyses demanded a great deal from the king. He was to respect private properties and commercial exchanges – but he would also need to intervene to prohibit excessive concentrations of wealth or poverty. In order to finance his expanding government Philip needed to work out a way to extract revenue that would not undermine the ability of his subjects "to live well". The long-term effects of debasing the coinage had weakened the economy, and the erratic efforts at taxation undermined confidence; Jews and the Lombard bankers could not be targeted indefinitely, and noble resistance was being organised in 1314–15 against growing demands. Moreover, in the last years of the thirteenth century the time of good harvests had come an end and urban centres had increasing difficulty in feeding the growing population. Inflation hit rents and prices that had long remained stable, encouraging speculation and impoverishing the rural population. The fairs of Champagne declined owing to the opening of the sea route directly to Flanders.[396] Uncertainty of landed property rights and inefficient protection of commerce across the continent meant that "thirteenth-century Europe [did] not break out of the Malthusian trap".[397] A huge gap had opened between writings on economic governance and the abilities of government.

## Common Good As the "Higher Law"

Philip the Fair never ceased looking for new ways to reach into the pockets of his subjects. Confiscations were an everyday occurrence and indirect expropriation by debasing the value of coins had become routine in 1295–305.[398] Although *quod principi placuit* suggested that confiscations and monetary mutations were part of royal prerogative, the extractions were always accompanied by an effort to justify them as necessary for the proper government of the *regnum*.[399] In 1307, for

[396] Favier, *Philippe le Bel*, 108–20. On the social unrest, see further 123–9.

[397] North & Thomas, *The Rise of the Western World*, 69.

[398] Jean-Louis Harouel, 'L'expropriation dans l'histoire de droit français', in Jean-Louis Harouel, *Histoire de l'expropriation* (Presses Universitaires de France 2000), 46–7. The question of Philip's right to undertake such debasement (or, in the event, augmentation), is discussed in Favier, *Philippe le Bel*, 142–69.

[399] See especially Rigaudière, *Penser et construire*, 51–60.

example, when Plaisians wrote that his king possessed everything within his kingdom, he added the reservation that he could intervene in his subjects' properties only "for a public cause and the defence of his *regnum*".[400] The Capet rulers knew well what was expected of them. As expressed in the testament of Philip II in 1190: "*Le devoir du roi est de veiller en toutes manières à l'intérêt de ses sujets et de placer l'utilité publique avant son utilité privée.*"[401] The trope of public utility and its analogues (common good, common utility etc.) underlined an ethos of government that had arisen against the violent mode of lordship of a century before when armed knights had treated the peasants as virtual slaves.[402]

Not much argument is needed to show the centrality of the common good in late medieval political language.[403] It marked an effort to move away from decades of purely exploitative lordship, connoting unity and order, and a stress on the protective and coordinative function of kingship. Organic metaphors began to spread across Europe. As the "head" of the community, the prince was to see to it that other parts operated in unison so that all would benefit.[404] Aquinas and Giles of Rome employed the image of the good archer: the king was to direct his subjects in such a way that they all were able to reach their own (individual) good; the common good was the good of each subject.[405] Under this view, ruling became a kind of political economy, the calculation of the usefulness to the *regnum* of specific types of individual good.[406] This theory received its most elaborate expression in the view

[400] "ex causa publice utilitatis et defensionis regni sui", Guillaume de Plaisians in 'Mémoire relatif au Parieage du 1307', cited in Leyte, *Domaine et domanialité*, 190 n. 365.

[401] Gérard Giordanengo, 'De l'usage du droit privé et du droit public au Moyen Âge', 7 *Cahiers de recherches médiévales et humanistes* (2000), 2. For the significance of addressing the king as a public figure in an official text, see Krynen, *L'empire du roi*, 41.

[402] Thomas Bisson, 'Medieval Lordship', 70 *Speculum* (1995), 752, 753, 743–59 and generally Bisson, *The Crisis of the Twelfth Century*.

[403] See e.g. Black, *Political Thought*, 24–8. The standard English-language work (which concentrates, however, on common good among *theologians*) is Matthew Kempshall, *The Common Good in Late Medieval Political Thought* (Oxford University Press 1999).

[404] The most influential uses of the metaphor came from the *Policraticus* of James of Salisbury.

[405] "Bonum enim commune resultat ex omni bone civium", Giles of Rome, *De regimine principum*, I 2, x (43v).

[406] Post sees here a first real "theory of government". *Studies*, 19. Post's work is also a principal source of the matter. Thomas Bisson has argued that the proliferation of violent lordship in the eleventh and twelfth centuries and the destruction of older ideas about power as virtuous rule began to be overcome only in the late twelfth and thirteenth centuries when ideals of nobility entered the definition of lordship. 'Medieval Lordship', 743–59.

of kingship as a continuation of divine government, the fulfilment of the divine plan. As such, it could be separated neither from the good of every individual nor from the supernatural good to which everything was ultimately directed. For Aquinas, royal *dominium* was part of an elaborate hierarchical arrangement of different levels of good:

> . . . a particular good is ordered to the common good as to an end; indeed the being of a part depends on the being a whole. So, also, the good of a nation is more godlike than the good of one man. Now the highest good which is God is the common good, since the good of all things taken together depends on Him.[407]

Under this view, royal government was to coordinate the good of the subjects in view of the good of the community as well as to ensure that the good of the community served the divine plan. The part was to be coherent with the whole. This was an important way to think in a period where individuals became increasingly attached to their communities – town, guild, province, church, university, nation. The Aristotelian approach prioritised the common good over a merely individual good but also suggested, as Giles of Rome did, that the good of the individual could only be realised within the confines of the common good.[408] Ruling was to give effect to this harmony.

The common good was understood in different ways. For some such as Aquinas and Giles of Rome, it had to do with making the subjects virtuous. Aquinas wrote of the prince's pastoral role but Giles only of temporal virtue – perhaps to avoid connoting the king's divinity.[409] More usual was to refer to the *utilitas publica* that included the security and welfare of the realm, including the "powers of authority vested in the king and crown".[410] The vocabulary of the common good was quite useful as it could be cited at once for action *against* positive law and custom as well as in order to implement a higher purpose.[411] The

407 Aquinas, *Summa Contra Gentiles*, III 17, 6, quoted in Kaye, *A History of Balance*, 246. See also ST I-II 92 1 ad 3 and ST II-II 58 7 ad 2 (98 & 182).

408 "For even if the end is the same for the single man and for a state, that of the state seems at all events something greater and more complete whether to attain or to preserve", Aristotle, *Nicomachean Ethics*, I 2 (2). On Giles' view of the relation of individual and common good, see Kempshall, *The Common Good*, 146–50.

409 ". . . it seems that the end for which a community is brought together is to live according to virtue", Aquinas, 'De regimine principum', xv (40). "Principaliter tamen est civitas constituta propter bene & virtuosa & feliciter vivere", Giles of Rome, *De regimine principum*, III 2, xxxii (321r). See the detailed discussion in Kempshall, *The Common Good*, 131–56, 268–73.

410 Post, *Studies*, 322. See also (on P. Jacobi) Rigaudière, *Penser et construire*, 413–15.

411 For that debate, see Post, *Studies*, 241–309.

maxim "necessity knows no law" was well known and widely accepted by canonists and legists who understood it as an expression of an ethic that put the safety and well-being of the *regnum* before arid legalism – while insisting that this objective could not be separated from the fulfilment of the divine plan. It is striking that Giles of Rome saw the end of *regimen naturale* in terms of the perpetuation of the regime while simultaneously understanding the king as a *minister Dei*.[412] The argument from necessity was also used repeatedly by the French kings to justify extraordinary taxation and to streamline the most varied aspects of government.[413] This was not necessarily bad faith manipulation of the conceptual arsenal.[414] Nothing was more orthodox than to think that individual good had to yield to the good of the community but that, rightly understood, the two were inextricable: a thriving community was always also in the interests of the subjects.

A good way to understanding the *legal* operation of common good is to go back to the distinction, made by Giles of Rome, between two types of government, *regimen politicum* and *regimen regale*. Giles did not offer these as constitutional alternatives but as means to reflect on the way the ruler related to the *civitas*. In a political regime, the ruler was part of the *civitas*, his government organised by law. In a royal regime, he stood outside the *civitas*, ruling it through his will.[415] This could take place in two ways. Either the king ruled tyrannically, in order to gain personal benefit. Or he ruled to attain the common good. This, Giles explained, consisted of virtue, knowledge and, as noted above, procuring things that were needed not only to survive but to live well (*bene vivere*).[416] To reach these objectives, laws were needed: *in legibus est salus civitatis*.[417] Once again Giles followed Aristotle in highlighting the forms of legal justice, *legalis justitia*, that comprised all the virtues; without it, the *regnum* would not survive.[418] Legal justice expressed the common good, in contrast to the justice of equality that looked only for the individual good, but it could

412 On the ten ways in which the king was to see to the conservation of his position, see Giles of Rome, *De regimine principum*, III 2, xv (289v–291v). On the other hand, for "rex enim ... est Dei minister", see I 1, xii (23v, 24r).

413 For a good overview, see Petit-Renaud, *'Faire loy', au royaume de France*, 98–112, and on the canon law origins of the maxim, see Franck Roumy, 'L'origine et la diffusion de l'adage canonique *Necessitas non habet legem* (VIIIe–XIIIe s.)', in W. P. Müller, M. E. Sommar & K. Pennington (eds), *Medieval Church and the Origins of the Western Legal Tradition* (The Catholic University of America Press 2012), 301–19.

414 See Kantorowicz, *The King's Two Bodies*, 253–7.

415 I follow here the very useful Senellart, *Les arts de gouverner*, 180–205.

416 Giles of Rome, *De regimine principum*, III 2, viii (278v–279r).

417 Ibid., III 2, xix (298v).

418 Ibid., I 2, xi (45v–48r).

not be separated from the private good of each subject.[419] However, such an "instrumental" view required that the king himself was not tied by the laws of the community; as Giles put it, the king was himself the law (*lex animata*).[420] This did not mean that he was free to will whatever he liked, only that if necessary, he could override positive law. As an organ of just law himself (*quasi quiddam organum iuste legis*), the king would always be entitled to surpass the legal form so as to give effect to the higher justice or necessity, of the common good.[421]

A functional notion of *dominium* could also be detected in the jurists' citations of Ulpian to the effect that "for the establishment of new laws, there must be evident utility before any old laws that have earlier applied as just could be set aside".[422] Roman law of course distinguished between public and private law. "Public law is that which respects the establishment of the Roman commonwealth, private that which respects individuals' interests, some matters being of public, and others of private interest."[423] But civil law gave no clear indication as to how evident utility was to be measured and almost nothing was done to clarify the distinction between public and private interests – in case of a conflict, Révigny for example simply suggested that effect should be given to principal utility.[424] Most of the time, civil law regulated the actions of the *princeps* in the same way it did those of the paterfamilias, dealing with succession and other aspects of the life of the royal family. Nor did the powers of the emperor, his regalia, as they were listed in the *Libri feudorum*, add up to a general theory of government but instead, marked privileges belonging to the *person* of the king, alongside those attributed to other dignitaries.[425]

However, "[b]y the second half of the twelfth century lay writers were beginning to express [the distinction between the office and the holder] in the form of a division between the *persona regis* and the *corona regni*".[426]

[419] Ibid., I 2, x (43v).

[420] "princeps vero est quaedam animata lex", ibid., I 2, xii (48r).

[421] Ibid., III 2, xxix (314v–315v).

[422] "In rebus novis constituendis evidens esse utilitas debet, ut recedatur ab eo iure, quod diu aequum visum est" [D 1.4.2.].

[423] "Publicum ius est quod ad statum rei Romanae spectat, privatum quod ad singulorum utilitatem" [D 1.1.1.2].

[424] Divisions between "law" and "equity" or between things, persons and actions were far more important. Giordanengo, 'De l'usage du droit privé', 3, 4–5.

[425] Ibid., 6.

[426] Wilks, *Problem of Sovereignty*, 362. On the use of the "crown" metaphor in France since the eleventh century, see Leyte, *Domaine et domanialité*, 197–218, Rigaudière, *Penser et construire*, 433–40 and Schneidemüller, *Nomen patriae*, 229–36 as well as

Also in France writers would use the notion of the *respublica* and such cognate expressions as *regnum*, *patria* and *status* to refer to an entity independent from the king's power and privileges.[427] A theory of corporate personality that drew upon the debates about the church as a *corpus mysticum Christi* projected the *regnum* as a real "body" that was the subject of its own interests, or a measurable utility, separate from those of the prince or his subjects.[428] This is sometimes illustrated by pointing to the way the glossators gave an independent role to the *fiscus* that lay with the *Chambre des comptes* and was managed by the king in his public person – something explained by Belleperche by an obscure metaphor of the king keeping it "in his breast".[429] When the theologians and jurists began to suggest that the king also had the power to legislate generally over the realm, they usually based this on its evident utility or necessity.[430] A "rational cause" was needed that would in one way or another refer to the needs or utility of the *regnum*. When critics attacked the king's monetary policy, they pointed to the way it was against the public good and in breach of the impersonal demands of government.[431] Similar considerations applied to the inalienability of the public domain. According to the coronation oath, a king was to expand the realm, not to diminish it.[432] Owing to the divine character of French kingship, jurists found it difficult to apply the *Lex regia* under which the Roman people had been assumed to have donated imperial powers to Augustus. Notwithstanding, in the thirteenth century they

exhaustively Kantorowicz, *The King's Two Bodies*, 336–83 (including on the "fiscal crown", 342–58).

427 Schneidemüller, *Nomen patriae*, 233–5. The connection of the idiom of *respublica* to that of reason of state in the twelfth and thirteenth centuries is dealt with in Post, *Studies*, 269–309. The respective uses of the four expressions mentioned in the text are discussed by Rigaudière, *Penser et construire*, 384–6.

428 For the development of the vocabulary of "*corpus mysticum*" from its liturgical connotation as the "mystical body of Christ", via that of the Church or the Christian community in general to denote the secular coporation of the respublica, see Kantorowicz, *The King's Two Bodies*, 193–232; Martin Loughlin, *Foundations of Public Law* (Oxford University Press 2010), 42.

429 Leyte, *Domaine et domanialité*, 61–7.

430 See exhaustively, Petit-Renaud, *'Faire loy', au royaume de France*, 61–112.

431 Rigaudière, *Penser et construire*, 439.

432 On the argument for "augmentation", see Leyte, *Domaine et domanialité*, 290–2. In a famous letter of August 1225, Pope Honorius III had criticised the donation of a part of his *regnum* by the king of Hungary as being "*in praeiudicium regni sui et contra Regis honorem*". 'Decretal of Gregorius IX', in Aemelius Friedberg (ed.), *Corpus Iuris Canonici II* (Graz, Academische Druck- und Verlagsanstalt 1959), col. 353.

invariably regarded kingship an office that bore with it the duty to protect and increase the realm.

When Azo commented on the civil law distinction between public and private, he did not see them as separating two realms of life and even less two types of law. Instead, he, and after him most glossators, used the adjectives "public" and "private" to refer to the objectives law possessed – namely the effort to manage the *regnum* so as to unite the well-being of individuals (private good) – that is to say, noble privileges – with the *bonum commune* (public utility).[433] Accursius, and later French legists such as Jean de Blanot, Guillaume Durand and Pierre de Belleperche, regarded this as quite natural; it was part of the very function of kingship to operate *ratione publicae utlitatis.*[434] In discussing the problem of double alliance – homage to the lord and jurisdiction of the king – Durand gave the main rule in favour of the latter:

> The king who sees to the administration of the realm calls upon them for the common good, and for the defence of fatherland and crown. Their obligation is to him, as provided by the law of nations.[435]

Like other French jurists, Révigny spoke freely of *patria* and was ready to authorise the king to depart from feudal rules if necessary.[436] The legists also learned to use the language of plenitude of power and to invoke *ex certa scientia* to empower the king to take action even against existing law.[437] This was unobjectionable when the purpose of the action was *defensio regni* or a situation of *necessitas*. But the legists tended to expand such arguments to practically *any* action to advance the welfare in the *regnum* (*ad statum prosperum et defensionem necessariam*).[438] The king could seek to advance economic exchanges, housing, public hygiene or to undertake the construction of towns at the expense of individual interests. In general any governmental measure that involved the

433 The distinction was not about who did what, but what the objective of the action was. Rigaudière, *Penser et construire*, 429–30. See further, Giordanengo, 'De l'usage du droit privé', 2–11.

434 Post, *Studies*, 278–9, 283–9; Schneidemüller, *Nomen patriae*, 266–7.

435 "Rex, qui habet administrationem regni vocat eos pro communi bono, pro defensione patriae & coronae, unde sibi iure gentium obedire tenentur", Durand, *Speculum iuris*, IV III, § 31 (146r).

436 See Leyte, *Domaine et domanialité*, 197.

437 On Pierre Jacobi's (1270–350) use of the latter expression, see Rigaudière, *Penser et construire*, 397–8.

438 Pierre Dupuy, as quoted in Helene Wieruszowski, *Vom Imperium zum nationalen Königtum* (München, Oldenbourg 1933), 173.

subordination of private interests could be defined as aspiring to the common good.[439] The same was true of the widely resented allocation of privileges to individuals.[440] The problem lay in the very general character of the objective. In a response to a legal question concerning action that Philip II had once taken in violation of the rights of one of his vassals, Azo explained that this was justified by reason of public utility (*publicae utilitas*) and then, sweepingly, that "many are the actions" that may be justified in this fashion.[441] As the opinion began with an affirmation of the French king's status as "emperor" in his realm and that *ergo potuit facere quod sibi placet*, the clear message was that nobody could question the king's determination.

It was a truism that the ruler was not entitled to put his own interest before the common good: "what renders government unjust is the fact that the private good of the ruler is sought at the expense of the good of the community".[442] Tyranny was as an important topos for both Aquinas and Giles of Rome, considered, following Aristotle, in view of the danger it presented for the maintenance of the *regnum* (and in Giles' case also the *regimen*).[443] But when Aquinas then called on the prince to coordinate the private interests "with respect to the common good", he provided no algorithm on how to do that.[444] When he observed that law was "a kind of reason directing acts towards an end" and that laws promulgated by kings must be "derived from the eternal law", he was frustratingly vague about how these inferences should be made.[445] What would justice mean in a world of fluctuating powers and self-regulating markets? The Aristotelian notion of the common good operated with individuals whose needs and aspirations were limited and at least in principle amenable to being organised into an optimal balance. With a commercial order receiving its dynamism from desires that were in principle *unlimited*, no such equilibrium seemed available.[446] There was no guarantee that any balance could survive beyond the moment it was constructed.

What Aquinas offered to deal with these contingent facts was a theory of prudence he had adopted from Aristotle. Assisted by

[439] Petit-Rénaud, *'Faire loy', au royaume de France*, 78–91. [440] Post, *Studies*, 279–81.
[441] "... multa autem licita sunt pro ratione utilitatis", Ernst Landesberg (ed.), *Die Questiones des Azo* (Freiburg, Mohr 1888), 86.
[442] Aquinas, 'De regimine principum', IV (12).
[443] Aristotle, 'The Politics', V.10 (139–54); Aquinas, 'De regimine principum', IV (11–15); Giles of Rome, *De regimine principum*, III 2, xii & xv (285r–291r).
[444] Aquinas 'De regimine principum', I (7). [445] Aquinas, ST I-II 93 3 Resp (106).
[446] See Kaye, *A History of Balance*, 282–98.

prudence, practical reason was to choose from available courses of action the one likeliest to bring out a good outcome.[447] Like *ius gentium*, prudence mediated between high-level objectives of justice and contingent factuality. It was a not a science of ends but an art of the means – a theory of government.[448] The practical experience of the world was that of ubiquitous conflict: conflict between the king and the church, the emperor and the pope, the king and his nobles, *dominium iurisdictionis* and *dominium proprietatis*. How could the various priorities be brought into harmony? This, Aquinas suggested, required a certain predisposition in the ruler, a virtue that enabled the ruler to seize the moment's requirements, fortified by study and contemplation. To this the legists would add the requirement of taking counsel, largely followed in fourteenth-century French practice.[449] A specific skill in legislation, legislative prudence, would link royal commands to assumptions about the purpose of government that – inevitably – left much discretion.[450] Ruling was not "demonstrating" of truths but "deliberation", reasoning about what, in the view of the complexity of the empirical world, might best secure the common good.[451] Sometimes this required accepting practices that were strictly speaking unjust – charging interest for a contract of loan, for example.[452] Sometimes it required going beyond positive law: "if a case emerges in which the observance of that law would be damaging to the common welfare, it should not be observed".[453] Positivity was not everything. Acts that failed to accord with reason were "acts of violence rather than laws". This did not mean that anyone could judge for themselves. Prudence "belongs only to princes . . . who

[447] Aquinas, ST II-II 60 2 Resp (195). The pragmatic and utilitarian character of Aquinas' *prudentia regnativa* is stressed in Wilks, *Problem of Sovereignty*, 118–22.

[448] See Senellart, *Les arts de gouverner*, 177.

[449] Petit-Reynaud, *'Faire loy', au royaume de France*, 317–41.

[450] See also the discussion in Aristotle, *Nicomachean Ethics*, VI 5 (142–3). The pragmatic and utilitarian character of Aquinas' political theory is highlighted in Wilks, *Problem of Sovereignty*, 118–22. The degree to which Aquinas' treatments of "law" and "virtue" need to be read together with focus on the way "prudence" acts as "a sort of architectonic virtue" that brings the two together is usefully discussed in Tierney, *Liberty & Law*, 77, 70–1, 74, 85–6. Likewise, on "prudentia regnativa", Senellart, *Les arts de gouverner*, 179.

[451] Aristotle, *Nicomachean Ethics*, VI 3 (140); Aquinas, ST I-II 94 4 Resp (121–2).

[452] Aquinas, ST II-II 78 1 ad 3 (224).

[453] Ibid., I-II 97 6 Resp (148). Also in the same place: "Thus every law is directed to the common welfare of men. It obtains the force and character of law in so far as this is so."

have authority to dispense from the laws when such cases arise".[454] Giles of Rome viewed prudence as a natural skill that slaves, women and animals lacked. Its point was to organise private interests in a rational fashion and help to choose among them; prudence would even help confirm that the choices were implemented in practice.[455] He agreed with Aquinas that prudential government was not an exact science but comparable to art in that its motivation was rectitude. Without it, a king was one in name only.[456]

The expectation that royal acts would have a *causa rationabilis* was another way to express the functionality of the royal office.[457] The obvious wisdom of this idea, however, met with the problem that it could easily become a kind of higher law allowing setting aside customary rights and privileges. Before royal jurists began to take proto-absolutist positions in response to the crises of the fourteenth century, the debate turned on how to balance the subjects' interests with those of the crown. The practical problem had to do with the king's administrative powers, the powers of handing out decisions, edicts and *rescripts* in specific situations.[458]

## Reconciling Jurisdiction and Property

Because private property was based on *ius gentium* academic jurists were clear that the king had no authority to simply abolish it. As Révigny put it: "*ius gentium non potest immutari per ius civile verum, et in sua totalitate, sed in casibus potest per ius civile derogare iure gentium*".[459] A distinction was made between the binding nature of the institution and its deviant application in a particular case that could be achieved by royal will. The question was always about expropriation in single instances, the very point of *rescripts* or administrative decisions by the king, usually in response to some private initiative. This made it possible to argue that the act was not directed against the *ius gentium* nature of the institution such as property or contract, but merely against its specific application. Nor would rescripts *contra ius* be directed against natural or divine law, though they could sometimes modify a right or even extinguish it in

[454] Ibid., I-II 96 6 Resp (148–9).
[455] Giles of Rome, *De regimine principum*, I 2 vi (40r). The three parts of prudence were invention, judgment and implementation. Ibid., I 2 vi (37r–38v).
[456] Ibid., I 2 vi (39r–v). [457] Black, *Political Thought*, 24.
[458] An exhaustive treatment is Nicolini, *La proprietà*, 179–216.
[459] Révigny, *Lectura super codicis* [C. 1. 19, 7], quoted in Nicolini, *La proprietà*, 210 n. 2.

as a punishment. While the prince could not marry a parent and a child, he could order the death penalty.[460] As regards natural law, the situation was basically the same. If (customary) feudal rights and privileges were understood as natural law, then they could not be easily tampered with. The matter was stated quite clearly in *Decretum*:

Now natural law similarly prevails by dignity over custom and enactments. So whatever has been either received in usages or set down in writing is to be held null and void if it is contrary to natural law.[461]

However, as we have seen, the view that natural law provided for common property had not prevented *divisio rerum*. Indeed, everywhere people were trading and concluding contracts without the legitimacy of private property ever being questioned. Such realities were accommodated by arguing that natural law was general in formulation, or its content merely hortatory or permissive, and that it was to be applied, modified or supplemented by the needs of practice. Aquinas rationalised this by arguing that natural law was immutable only "with respect to its general principles" while its application may vary according to the circumstances; it was amenable to "additions" and "subtractions" by civil law and *ius gentium*.[462] While the prince may not be able to abolish private property, he could limit or modify its application or extent.

In principle, the ruler could act against a right based on civil law, a product of the prince himself.[463] However, according to the Code on *rescripts* [C 1.19.2 & 7], the prince was not to decide contrary to civil law – that is to say, he was not to violate a right or a privilege – unless the matter was of relatively minor importance and no violation of the right of a third person ensued.[464] In such case, Azo and Accursius insisted that the decision was to contain a *non obstante* clause or a statement *ex certa scientia*, or even a mention *de plenitudo potestatis*, which showed that it was the prince's express intention to decide *contra ius*.[465] Later French jurists such as Révigny and Belleperche no longer regarded this as necessary if only the intention of going against the

460 E.g. Nicolini, *La proprietà*, 188–91.
461 Gratian, *The Treatise of Laws*, D Dist 8 Part 2 (25).
462 Aquinas, ST I-II 94 4 Resp, 5 Resp, (122, 123) and I-II 95 4 Resp (135).
463 See e.g. Renoux-Zagamé, *Origines théologiques*, 247–8 and the notes therein.
464 According to C 1.19.7. "... rescripts elicited, which are contrary to [civil] law, must be ignored by all the judges, unless in a matter not hurtful to another, and advantageous to the petitioner...".
465 See Nicolini, *La proprietà*, 198–206.

law was otherwise clear enough. Again, they suggested that although the prince could not just abolish a right or a privilege *in toto*, he was entitled to overrule it in a single case, for example by transferring a property to another person, if only he had a good cause (*rationalis causa*).[466] One example is provided by an opinion by one of Philip's legists, Pierre de Mornay (d. 1306), later bishop of Orleans.[467] The king had abolished the right of appeal that had customarily existed from the baronial courts of Brittany. The barons insisted that their consent was needed for tampering with their rights of jurisdiction. In the report of his decision, Mornay accepted that while such an intervention might be tolerable in individual cases, the king did not indeed have the right to abolish a customary right of appeal *in toto*.[468]

There was no general doctrine of expropriation in thirteenth-century France. The matter was treated through the question of whether the prince may abolish (*aufferre*) the rights of his subjects. Nicolini concludes in his fundamental work on the topic that "a prince may abolish private right only by just cause".[469] None of the legists suggested that the prince would own the things of his subjects; what he possessed was jurisdiction, and so he needed a just cause to expropriate or to compel to sell (*rendita coattiva*) them.[470] The just cause, again, referred to the common good or public utility, as we have seen, a notion covering a wide margin of actions from upholding peace or security to the maintenance of common hygiene and, even the advancement of local prosperity.[471] And the prince could always also expropriate as punishment for a crime [C 1.19, 7 *in fine*].[472] But the lawyers remained unwilling to specicify the conditions in any great detail and would occasionally support an

466 Ibid., 210 n. 2, 211. See also Bezemer, *What Jacques Saw*, 23–4; Black, *Absolutism in Renaissance Milan*, 12–13. The requirement of *causa* was also stressed by the theologians, Renoux-Zagamé, *Origines théologiques*, 248.

467 See Francis Guessard, 'Pierre de Mornay, Chancellier de France', 5 *Bibliothèque de l'école des chartes* (1844), 143–77 [reprinted in *Persée*]. See also Pegues, *Lawyers of the Last Capetians*, 121.

468 Pennington, *The Prince and the Law*, 99–101.

469 Nicolini, *La proprietà*, 232, 244.

470 The jurists relied on civil law doctrines that appear as exceptions to D. 50. 17.11: "Il quod nostrum est sine facto nostro ad alienum transferri non potest." Even as Roman law spoke usually of an absolute liberty of the owner to use or dispose of his property, medieval jurists added a proviso concerning the conditions set by law to the exercise of ownership. Thus, for example, the famous definition of *dominium proprietatis* by Bartolus read: "ius de re corporali perfecte disponendi, nisi lege prohibetur". See Nicolini, *La Proprietà*, 53–9, 265.

471 Eg. Leyte, *Domaine et domanialité*, 83–90.

472 Nicolini, *La proprietà*, 210–12.

outlook that would later be termed "absolutist".[473] Even Accursius once wrote that the prince's will was actually sufficient cause: *Magna et iusta causa est eius voluntas.*[474] Cinus of Pistoia, who in many matters transmitted the French jurists' views to Italy, assumed that any apparent violation was to be accompanied by a presumption that it was also intended.[475] Legists were understandably reluctant to impose binding conditions on the prince's decision-making and concentrated on supporting the use of formulas such as *non obstante* or *ex certa scientia* to make sure that the will to go against a *dominum*-right was absolutely clear. They did agree on compensation to be paid, however.[476] And in practice, when Philip undertook public works, for example to expand the royal palace in Paris, he did pay at least some compensation.[477] This did not of course apply to expropriation conceived as punishment for a crime such as the confiscation of the English fiefs of Aquitaine and Normandy and the Templar properties. But when undertaking public works to build roads, expand waterways or construct mines, a royal commission was usually set up to measure the amount of compensation.[478] The more civil lawyers debated the question of *iusta causa*, the more they were inclined to give up the search for standards to bind the prince. Again, this did not quite mean that the prince was free. Even as there was no secular tribunal to try him, constraints on conscience were

[473] In the fourteenth century, there emerged a group of increasingly "absolutist" legists keen to attach the presumption of *causa* to anything the prince did. Writing under the formidable Giangaleazzo Visconti in Milan, Baldus of Ubaldi noted dryly that "whatever cause [*quelibet ratio*] motivates the emperor [*principis*] is considered cause enough". Nicolini, *La proprietà*, 214. For the debate on this passage, see Joseph Canning, 'Italian Juristic Thought and the Realities of Power in the Fourteenth Century', in Joseph Canning & Otto Gerhard Oxle (eds), *Political Thought and Realities of Power in the Middle Ages* (Göttingen, Vandenhoeck & Ruprecht 1998), 234–7. See also Black, *Absolutism in Renaissance Milan*, 22.

[474] Accursius, Gl. Ex aliqua causa [D. 48. 19. 4], quoted in Nicolini, *La proprietà*, 214.

[475] See Nicolini, *La proprietà*, 213–15.

[476] Ibid., 252–5.

[477] References to "public utility" seem to have begun with Philip Augustus who in 1212 decided to build a wall around Paris "propter publicum regni commodium". Susan Reynolds, *Before Eminent Domain. Toward a History of Expropriation of Land for the Common Good* (University of North Carolina Press 2010), 55. The reference became standard during the time of Philip the Fair, Leyte, *Domaine et domanialité*, 191–4; Harouel, 'L'expropriation', 46.

[478] Reynolds, *Before Eminent Domain*, 56–62. The basis for compensation was received from Christian ethics, Roman law and Italian practice. Harouel, 'L'expropriation', 49–52. In cases where lords expropriated their vassals, market price was to be paid. Beaumanoir, *Coutumes de Beauvaisis*, § 1511, 1666 (262, 353).

normally real.[479] As Révigny reminded his readers, in carrying out his activities, including in judging on the property of others, the prince was to remember that he himself would become judged as well.[480]

## A Human *Dominium*: John of Paris

During the spring of 1302, at the time when *Deum time*, the abbreviated and sharpened version of Boniface's *Ausculta fili* was being debated in Paris, a Dominican theologian, Jean Quidort (John of Paris, c. 1250–306) joined this conversation by his *De potestate regia et papali*, in sharp defence of his king.[481] In 25 dense chapters John discussed the respective powers of priests and kings in ecclesiastical and temporal matters, the universal but limited roles of the pope and the emperor as well as the rights of property enjoyed by individuals. John also took issue with the question of how to depose a heretic king or a pope.[482] In the flow of pamphlets and other literature produced at the time, John's treatise enjoyed a justified reputation as "much the ablest of [the royalist tracts] in its comprehensiveness of treatment and its overall intellectual force".[483] It was more than an occasional pamphlet, its parts written with many years' distance, and much of it was designed to defend Dominican views against certain Franciscan extremists.[484]

Appropriately, as a student and a defender of Aquinas in the Parisian milieu, John began by restating the Aristotelian point that it was natural for human beings to live in society. But he then contrasted the universal society of all Christians, of which the pope was the spiritual head, with

[479] The prince was always entitled to deny any legal action against the *fisc*. Nicolini, *La proprietà*, 240 and 244.

[480] "Sua enim potentia non est limitata, de plenitude potestatis sue potest hoc facere. Caveat sibi minister Dei est, aut. de fide instrum … cum non minus iudicabitur quam ipse iudicat", cited in Pennington, *The Prince and the Law*, 115 n. 156.

[481] The exact dating of publication is unclear. The most plausible one differentiates between three versions of the tract, each in the context of the dispute between Philip and Boniface, and situates the final version between the publication of a papalist tract *De potestate papae* by Henry of Cremona, which came out as a reaction to Flote's abbreviation of *Ausculta fili*, and an anonymous tract *Quaestio in utramquem partem*, which defended the royal position in the same matter but already made reference to John's work. See Karl Ubl, 'Johannes Quidorts weg zur Sozialphilosophie', 30 *Francia* (2003), 49–71.

[482] John of Paris, *On Royal and Papal Power* (Columbia University Press 1974).

[483] J. A. Watt, 'Introduction', John of Paris, *On Royal and Papal Power*, 11.

[484] Janet Coleman, 'The Intellectual Milieu of John of Paris OP', in J. Miethke & A. Bühler (eds), *Das Publikum politischer Theorie im 14. Jahrhundert* (Munich, Oldenbourg 1992), 173–206.

the secular societies that had sprung up around the world. While it was natural that Christianity would be ruled under one monarch – the pope – this was not at all the case with the temporal world. Instead, humans instinctively set up separate societies in accordance with their circumstances. "Accordingly, they choose different types of rulers to oversee the well-being of their communities to correspond to the diversity of these communities."[485]

Human diversity prompted legal and political diversity. "There can be different ways of living, and different kinds of state conforming to differences in climate, language and the conditions of men, with what is suitable for one nation is not so to another."[486] John regarded this diversity as perfectly natural, something that was not at all the case of a purportedly universal empire.[487] Following Aristotle, John believed that these separate secular communities were to be self-sufficient and governed "under one man called a king, who rules for the sake of the common good". This kind of system where each political community is ruled by its "specific laws" was "derived from the natural law and the law of nations".[488]

The view of the world as composed of independent *regna* was an obvious outcome of the view that the human world is governed by something like a natural sociability.[489] It also served as a powerful defence of Philip's authority as not merely a French exception, something envisaged in *per venerabilem*, but as an element in a general political theory.[490] Although priests were higher in dignity than secular officials, kings were earlier in time and nothing about temporal power was in any way (causally) received from them.[491] In fact, John explained, the power of the priests had nothing to do with *dominium*; it was not about coercion or ownership but about "dispens[ing] to the faithful the sacraments".[492] *Sacerdotium* and *regnum* were wholly separate, each received directly from God, each with its own internal hierarchy.[493] Yet as a theologian John was ready to concede that the pope might have incidental power to act against incorrigibly heretical princes. But even then it would be for the people – or the nobles representing them – to depose the ruler if necessary.[494]

[485] John of Paris, *On Royal and Papal Power*, 3 (14). [486] Ibid., 3 (15).
[487] Ibid., 3 (15). [488] Ibid., 1 (9).
[489] Ibid., 1 (8). John never used that expression, however
[490] Jones, *Eclipse of Empire*, 238–41.
[491] John of Paris, *On Royal and Papal Power*, 4–6 (16–27). [492] Ibid., 12 (56).
[493] Ibid., 5 (19–21). [494] Ibid., 13 (67).

Having separated the spiritual unity of Christianity from the plurality of secular kingdoms, and having discarded the view that the latter ought to be ruled under the emperor, John came to another topic that related to an earlier phase of the dispute, namely the question of taxation rights. The pope, he argued, had no right to church property, but was merely an administrator of them.[495] As to lay property, he did not even possess the right to administer them because Christ had never claimed any such right.[496] In a surprising move, John then denied also the king's right in the properties of his subjects. For property was "acquired by individual persons through art, labor, or their own industry; and individual persons, as individuals, exercise right, power and true dominion over such goods".[497] John then made an all-important distinction:

> Now having property rights and dominion over external goods is not the same as having jurisdiction, that is the right of determining what is just and unjust with respect to them. Accordingly, ... a ruler has the power of judging and ascertaining with respect to the goods of those under his authority without, however, having dominion over them.[498]

In other words, John distinguished between the king's *jurisdiction* over the *regnum* and the rights of *property* of his subjects, the latter having acquired it through their labour and as domestic law provided. Like other theologians, John believed that God had originally given the world to humans in common and that they had first undertaken the division of properties and then set up political communities for their better administration. This had been necessary because individual possessions "have no order and relation among themselves, nor are they ordered or related to any common head ... [and] everyone can do with his own possessions as he sees fit". Such a state of things only led to the "disturbance of the general peace".[499] Hence the members of

[495] Janet Coleman has emphasised Jean as a specifically *Dominican* scholar attacking the Franciscan view according to which members of ecclesiastical communities did not have individual ownership but only use-right in properties ultimately held by the pope. The distinction between papal "administration" and the ownership of ecclesiastical communities of things they used was analogous to the distinction Jean made in secular communities between the way the ruler had "jurisdiction" and individual subjects' "property" over things. See her *A History of Political Thought from the Middle Ages to the Renaissance* (Oxford, Blackwell 2000), 118–30; Janet Coleman, 'Dominium in Thirteenth and Fourteenth-Century Political Thought and Its Seventeenth-Century Heirs. John of Paris and Locke', 33 *Political Studies* (1985), 76–85.

[496] John of Paris, *On Royal and Papal Power*, 8 (30–3).

[497] Ibid., 7 (28).

[498] Ibid., 8 (30).

[499] Ibid., 7 (28).

society, owners of property, appointed a ruler whose task it is to "govern, to act as a judge of what is just and unjust in such matters", including the determination of "a just proportion for the needs and use of the community".[500] As a theologian, John accepted that the "final end" of temporal government was supernatural beatitude. The pope was "to formulate the guiding principles of Christian faith by legislation". But he was not to act *quantum ad executionem.*[501] This was the task of the king to whom the owners of property had given the task to preserve the peace and realise the common good and individual rights, now seen as inextricably interdependent.[502]

## Conclusion: Legal Imagination in the King's Service

It did not take long for the first French graduates from Bologna, Orleans and Montpellier after leaving their alma mater to find themselves with an office in the French king's *regimen.* Nogaret for example moved directly from teaching at Montpellier to the position of a high magistrate in Nîmes to see to the king's interests in the region's land disputes.[503] Having then carried out assignments for Philip in Normandy and elsewhere he was ennobled and joined in the *curia Regis* in 1298 to rise nine years later to the position of keeper of the seals – in practice, Philip's first minister – in which postion he would take over prosecution of the Templars.[504] As someone trained in civil law Nogaret was well placed to begin the work of imagining the feudal suzerain's power as those of a Roman *princeps*, and thus to rearrange his legal position with respect to the pope and the emperor as well as the nobility at home. Together with Plaisians, Flote, Révigny, Belleperche and others, he connected materials

500 Ibid., 7 (29).

501 Wilks, *Problem of Sovereignty*, 310, 318, 322–7 and generally 288–327.

502 Janet Coleman regards the inalienability of property rights as John's most striking achievement, in 'Dominium in Thirteenth and Fourteenth-Century Political Thought', 82. The heart of the problem was the king's right of taxation. Cary Nederman writes that Aquinas "and nearly every other schoolman" held the view that what God had donated was an interlocking system of (private) rights and that John differed from them in seeing the basis of rights in the will and labour of each individual, 'Confronting Market Freedom. Economic Foundations of Liberty at the End of the Middle Ages', in Robert Bast & Andrew Gow (eds), *Continuity and Change. The Harvest of Late Medieval and Reformation History* (Leiden, Brill 2000), 10. But this seems odd: John's view about will and labour as the origin of property fitted well with a widely shared understanding of how the *ius gentium* operated.

503 Holtzmann, *Nogaret*, 13–15.

504 For the character of the position of *garde des Sceaux* at this time, see ibid., 142–5.

from Roman law with local customary principles and institutional practices articulated in canon law to begin the work historians have addressed in teleological terms as "state-building".

Roman law also not only spoke of the *princeps* but possessed materials on land ownership and commercial dealings that could be imaginatively used to begin to think about how to manage and expand the realm. This meant organising the administration of the royal domain, managing the privileges of towns and provinces, regulating trade fairs and intervening, when necessary, in the administration of noble fiefs. The almost constant warfare with domestic and foreign enemies necessitated the expansion of royal jurisdiction and the extraction of resources at home in a way that began to consolidate a new, territorial system of rule. Although natural law and the *ius gentium* were of Roman origin, they proved important for thinking about the relations of domestic and international actors in a legal frame. How to explain that God had donated the world to free human beings in common but that everywhere one looked, Christians were claiming to exercise power over other Christians (and non-Christians) and excluding others from resources they had come to possess? Making the *de iure / de facto* distinction was one way to understanding the relations between moral ideals and present facts. But a more elaborate and a less problematic way to achieve this result was to distinguish between a natural law that glanced backwards into a moral world uncontaminated by sin and a *ius gentium* that looked forward to the wealth and power of the *regnum*, its ruler and its subjects. This made jurists the indispensable associates to the king. Philip did sometimes worry about Roman law's ideological predilection for the emperor – one reason for why he did not allow it to be taught in Paris – and insisted on the total loyalty of his jurists. As the action against Boniface and the Knights Templar showed, they were only too happy to oblige. But the king was also keen to claim to himself the position of "defender of the faith". In an utterly religious world, it was inconceivable that the justification of royal authority would make no reference to Christian theology. Here, too, the *ius gentium* proved helpful, having been compiled under the authority of a Christian emperor and long employed for the administration of the church. As we have seen, it also played an important role in the writings of the leading Christian intellectual, Thomas Aquinas, most of which were composed in Paris, Europe's emerging political and cultural capital. In these texts he employed the idioms of *dominium* and *ius gentium* in order to explain how initially free human beings could be subordinated to temporal government and how the resources of the world were to be divided and appropriated for private use without endangering the beatitude of one's soul. Biblical ideals were made to fit a transforming secular world. There was a tragic aspect to that manoeuvre with which Christians would ever since have to grapple. They would do this rarely with more ingenuity than in the context of their encounter with a wholly new world more than two centuries after the death of the Angelic Doctor.

# 2

# The Political Theology of *Ius gentium*

## *The Expansion of Spain 1526–1559*

When the Dominican theologian Francisco de Vitoria (1485–546) gave his famous *relectio* on the American Indians in Salamanca in 1539, he prefaced it with a caveat that "it is not the province of the lawyer, or not of lawyers alone, to pass sentence on this question". The Indians did not fall under Castilian laws or indeed under any *leges humanae.* "[S]ince this is a case of conscience, it is the business of the priests, that is to say of the Church, to pass sentence upon it."[1] And yet, Vitoria's lectures, especially his *relectiones theologicae*, given as a summary of his teaching every year, have always been studied with great interest by lawyers, not least because they made much use of the Roman law notion of *ius naturae et gentium.* The fact that the lectures were part of teaching young clerics on the sacrament of penance has been largely overlooked. Developments in early sixteenth-century Europe and beyond had profoundly shaken Christian societies and posed new problems for conscientious believers. How to deal with the peoples of the New World whose existence, as Vitoria readily acknowledged, had been previously ignored? What about the massive influx of riches from conquered peoples that was transforming social and economic life out of recognition?[2] War was endemic. But so were trade and new commercial practices that threatened old ideals of Christian piety. Vitoria's recourse to *ius naturae et gentium* to deal with such matters resuscitated ideas that had been

[1] Vitoria, 'On the American Indians', in *Vitoria. Political Writings* (Anthony Pagden and Jeremy Lawrance eds, Cambridge University Press 1991), § 3 238.

[2] Francisco de Vitoria, *Comentarios a la Secunda secundae de Santo Tomás* [ComST II-II] (Edición preparada por Vicente Beltrán de Heredia (Salamanca, 1934/1952). I have used volumes II (Quaestiones 23–56), III (Quaestiones 57–66) and IV (Quaestiones 67–88). Each volume has separate page numbering.

treated in Aquinas' *Summa theologiae*. It is understandable that lawyers would find this appealing, and perhaps indicative of some inner quality in law and lawyers that would contribute to justice at a moment of confusion, even crisis.

Vitoria and his followers – the "Salamanca school" – offered the language of *ius naturae et gentium* to alleviate the concerns of conscience felt by their Christian contemporaries under the hypothesis about the fragility of human nature as the consequence of sin.[3] Natural law, they held, had its origins in creation but had become largely inapplicable. It needed to be supplemented or modified by another type of law that would combine secular happiness with the more fundamental objective of supernatural *felicitas*. *Ius gentium* – the law of nations – would indicate to Christians what kind of social institutions they were to set up for this purpose. The most important of these were civil power and private ownership – *dominium iurisdictionis* and *dominium proprietatis*.

## The Court of Conscience

The sacrament of penance, the subject of Vitoria's Salamanca teaching, was part of "a struggle of unparalleled dimensions for the heart, mind and soul of the Spanish populace".[4] The spiritual anxiety of the people, high officials and of the emperor himself opened the door for significant political influence for theology and the theologians.[5] Since the early thirteenth century, Christians had been instructed to give annual confession. With the Council of Trent (1545–63), penance became a principal technique of Counter-Reformation Catholicism for dealing with new religious ideas and social practices.[6] Priests who had been ordained to manage penance held the absolution from sin, and thus access to heaven in their hands, and doctrines of "fraternal correction"

[3] Juan Cruz Cruz, 'La soportable fragilidad de la ley natural: consignación transitiva del *ius gentium* en Vitoria', in Juan Cruz Cruz, *Ley y dominio en Francisco de Vitoria* (Pamplona, Eunsa 2008), 13–15.

[4] Patrick J. O'Banion, *The Sacrament of Penance and Religious Life in Golden Age Spain* (Penn State University Press 2012), 43.

[5] Vitoria readily recognised this in opening his lectures. See Vitoria, 'On Civil Power', in *Political Writings*, Prologue (3–4) and 'On American Indians', Prologue (235–8). According to Vitoria, Christians should prepare for confession by trying to remember every evening the sins they had committed during the day. O'Banion, *Sacrament of Penance*, 48.

[6] The techniques peaked in the "brainwash model" of the Inquision. See Jean-Pierre Dedieu, *L'administration de la foi. L'inquisition de Tolède XVIe–XVIIIe siècle* (Madrid, Velásquez 1989), 75–94.

and "evangelical denunciation" extended the church's moral control throughout the world of the faithful. For example, according to Innocent IV, a friar could denounce a debtor and refuse to allow confession before the debt was redeemed.[7] Simultaneously, manuals of confessors – including one by Vitoria himself – spread the orthodox view among the reading public, orienting the attitudes and behaviours of laymen at home and at work.[8]

The fact that subjects were bound in conscience to the royal policies underlined the political role of the church. The "Catholic Monarchs", Isabella and Ferdinand, had not earned their title for nothing. Inspired by a reforming religiosity, they encouraged "active participation of clergy in political life and a close cooperation between Church and state at all levels".[9] In practice that control was exercised by members of the clergy, often bishops or professors of theology. A particularly important role was played by the royal confessor whose infuence on Charles V (1500–58), for example, was pervasive. It extended from the administation of penance to the many practical aspects of government that had a spiritual dimension – and for Charles hardly any matter lacked such a dimension. The first two of the confessors of Charles, the Franciscan Jean Glapion (1460–522) and the Dominican Francisco García de Loaysa (1478–546), not only saw to the emperor's spiritual needs but were normally present when politial issues involving spiritual matters (such as the conduct of the conquest) were being debated.[10] Glapion, for example, followed Charles to Spain, became in 1522 member of the emperor's first Council of State and was sometimes regarded as equally influential as the emperor's famous Italian

[7] Wim Decock, *Theologians and Contract Law. The Moral Transformation of the Ius Commune (ca. 1500–1650)* (Leiden, Nijhoff 2013), 92 and generally 88–101.

[8] See especially Patrick J. O'Banion, '"A Priest Who Appears Good": Manuals of Confession and the Construction of Clerical Identity in Early Modern Spain', 85 *Dutch Church History* (2005), 333–48.

[9] Henry Kamen, *Spain 1469–1714. A Society of Conflict* (2nd edn, London, Longman 1991), 46. Most importantly, they would secure the power to appoint bishops first in America and in Spain itself, 45–8, 115–21. For the construction of an "*iglesias de estado*" (in contrast to "*iglesias nacional*") in late fifteenth- and early sixteenth-century Spain, see Antonio-Miguel Berna, *Monarquia e imperio. Volumen 3, Historia de España* (2nd edn, Barcelona, Critica 2007), 174, 169–230; for theologians in leading positioins in Spanish government and the role of the Inquisition, 201–4.

[10] See Alonso Getino, 'Domincos españoles confesores de los reyes', 14 *Ciencía Tomista* (1916), 415–21; Leandro Martínez Peñas, *El confesor del rey en el antiquo régimen* (Madrid, Editorial Complutense 2007), 200–38. See also Nicole Reinhardt, *Voices of Conscience: Royal Confessors and Political Counsel in Seventeenth-Century Spain and France* (Oxford University Press 2016), 28–34 (especially on the period of Philip II).

chancellor, Mercurio Gattinara.[11] While Glapion's reign remained brief, Garcia de Loaysa turned into one of the most powerful men in the empror's entourage. President of the Council of the Indies, he participated in most other councils as well, intervening in practice in all of Charles' politics. His influence appears to have been decisive in the redaction of the "new laws" of 1542 that sought better control over the activities of the settlers.[12] Among the theologians consulted by Charles was Vitoria's student and later colleague Domingo de Soto (1494–560) who travelled to Trent as the emperor's representative and eventually became his confessor.[13] But nobody reached higher than Cardinal Francisco Jiménez de Cisneros (1436–517) who rose from the position of Queen Isabella's confessor to become the regent of Castile after Ferdinand's death.[14]

Already the *Siete partidas*, the thirteenth-century Castilian code, had instructed the ruler to confess regularly to his chaplain, who was expected to give him loyal and frequent advice. By Vitoria's time, the confessor had become the most important of the royal counsellors, sitting in the councils and *juntas* to provide his opinion on decisions involving issues of conscience. One of the most famous of such *juntas* was the one set up in Valladolid in 1550–1 to debate the question of Indian slavery where Soto acted as a member and rapporteur. In the mid-seventeenth century, the Salamanca-trained diplomat and *letrado* Diego Saavedra Fajardo (1584–648) summarised the situation by observing that:

> in Spain one has recognized how important it is to have confessor assist at Council of State *to qualify and justify decisions, and to enable government by correcting the Prince if he fails his obligation.*[15]

From ordinary subjects to high nobility, sixteenth-century Spaniards interpreted the world around them through cases to be adjudicated in

11 Martínez Peñas, *El confesor,* 201–2.

12 Ibid., 214, 230. For example, his influence appears to have been decisive in the emperor's decison to free France's King François I who had been taken prisoner at the battle of Pavia in 1525. He was also appointed to the Council of State in 1526. With his friend, the influential secretary Francisco de los Cobos, he directed the emperor's financial dealings and dominated many of the commissions and *juntas.*

13 On Soto's eighteen-month span as Charles' confessor in 1549–50, see especially ibid., 255–70.

14 On Cisneros and Loaysa as royal confessors and a summary assessment of the influence of the confessors on policy in Spain in the sixteenth century, see ibid., 106–33, 207–38, 708–15, 836–9.

15 Saavedra Fajardo, as quoted in Reinhardt, *Voices of Conscience*, 67.

the "court of conscience" in accordance with argumentative rules developed in the confessional literature. Having learned about the facts of the *conquista*, about the conflicts with other Christian rulers and about the new commercial practices during confession theologians could foresee that to direct penance appropriately they needed a much more detailed casuistic than existed so far. This led towards the end of the century to the development of "probabilism", which allowed a much wider frame of manoeuvre in the moral sphere than earlier techniques.[16] Although it began as a rival to Counter-Reformation *ragion di stato*, probabilism gradually merged with "good" reason of state, geared to instructing the Christian prince on how to preserve and expand his *regnum*.[17]

In his search for the right approach to a changing world Vitoria embraced the inward turn in late fifteenth-century theology that he adopted from the nominalism of his Paris teachers.[18] This meant keeping distance to biblical positivism that relied wholly on sacred texts as well as to a rationalism that assumed that everything about the world had been decided at creation. Theologians such as Duns Scotus (1266–308), Tommaso de Vio Cajetan (1469–534) and John Mair (1467–550) had stressed the freedom of individuals to choose their path in a world whose elements were in constant flux.[19] Everybody agreed on the importance of reason (*recta ratio*), but the new generation stressed the need to undertake further work to apply it in practice. Attention was turned from behavioural categories to the *intentions* of Christians as they navigated a world of moral hazards. This allowed providing answers to problems of which tradition remained silent. Vitoria's teacher, the Scotsman Mair, for example, was perfectly open to new experiences:

[16] See further ibid., 73–82 and on the "minimalist morality" links with probabilism, Decock, *Theologians and Contract Law*, 73–82.

[17] For an extensive discussion, see Robert Bireley, *The Counter-Reformation Prince. Anti-Machiavellianism or Catholic Statecraft in Early Modern Europe* (University of North Carolina Press, 1990).

[18] Juan Belda Plans, *La escuela de Salamanca y la renovación de la teologia en el siglo XVI* (Madrid, Biblioteca de autores cristianos 2000), 359–65; Dionisio Borobio Garciá, *El sacramento de la penitencia en la escuela de Salamanca. Francisco de Vitoria, Melchior Cano, Domingo Soto* (Publicaciones Universidad Pontifica Salamanca 2006), 14–16.

[19] The Salamanca scholars are usually said to have aimed at a "throughout original combination of the rationalist optimism of Aquinas and Scotist normativity". Kurt Seelmann, *Theologie und Jurisprudenz an der Schwelle zur Moderne* (Baden-Baden, Nomos 1997), 25. The precise manner in which they sought to navigate between orthodox Thomism and the nominalism of the "moderns" remains a subject of unending historiographical debate.

"Has not Amerigo Vespucci discovered lands unknown to Ptolemy, Pliny and other geographers of the present? Why cannot the same happen in other spheres?"[20]

The urgency to find a new direction for moral reflection arose partly as a product of debates on reform internal to the church, partly as a response to the Protestant rebellion. Martin Luther's slogan of *sola fide* struck an important chord. Already fifteenth-entury Parisian theology had highlighted individual conscience as the locus of true faith, and the Counter-Reformation agenda would turn its attention from external compliance to the *forum internum.*[21] This led to a juridification of consciences in which arguments pro and contra would be used not so much to find essential truths as probable reasons for directing the will in one way or another.[22] Future confessors were taught to act in part as judges to evaluate the daily choices of Christians, in part as doctors treating sin as a sickness to be cured by appropriate acts of contrition.[23] Casuistry was oriented towards a pragmatic middle ground where the church would seek to maintain its control on Christian souls by navigating between moral rigour and social reality. This is where *ius gentium* became useful.

The legalistic orientation of the Salamanca theologians' moral casuistry extended their influence to the law faculty. One of the jurists inspired by Vitoria was the Augustinian Martin de Azpilcueta (1492–586) who had studied canon and civil law at the University of Toulouse. Azpilcueta arrived in Salamanca in 1525 – a year before Vitoria – and was appointed *Prima* Professor of Canon Law in 1537.[24]

20 Mair quoted in James F. Keenan, 'The Casuistry of John Mair, Nominalist Professor of Paris', in James F. Keenan & Thomas A. Shannon (eds), *The Context of Casuistry* (Georgetown University Press 1995), 87.

21 For the internal development of Catholic views on penance and absolution, see e.g. Thomas N. Tentler, *Sin and Confession on the Eve of the Reformation* (Princeton University Press 1977).

22 On the "juridification" of the church and confession practices from the twelfth century, see Seelmann, *Theologie und Jurisprudenz*, 10–14. For the proceduralisation of moral argument in the "court of conscience", see Decock, *Theologians and Contract Law*, 69–73.

23 The standard *summas* and manuals for confessors described the confessor both as a judge and a medical doctor, invited to assess the moral quality of an action (is it sin or not, and what kind of sin it is) as a judge would but also to take action to soothe consciences in preparation for absolution. The two roles related to the two principal functions of penance: to discipline and console. Tentler, *Sin and Confession*, esp. 12–15, 345–9.

24 After a few years between Salamanca and Coimbra, Azpilcueta took on the defence in the case of the bishop of Toledo, Bartolome de Carranza, accused of Lutheran heresy before the Holy See, moving to Rome for the last two decades of his life. For

In an autobiographic text Azpilcueta boasted of having imported from France a "useful and solid science of canon law" with a practical orientation that could be compared to the contribution made by Vitoria in theology.[25] The best-known of his works is the *Manual of Confessors* (*Manual de confessores y penitentes*, 1552, *Enchiridion confessariorum*, 1573), which inaugurated the period of High Casuistry in the church (c. 1556–656).[26] By the beginning of the seventeenth century the manual had been produced in 81 editions and innumerable revisions and compendiums. In 1576 alone, more than 1,100 copies were delivered from Seville to Mexico City.[27] The late Spanish edition contained two annexes commenting on the moral hazards relating to the economic practices of the day, the *Comentario resolutorio de cambios* and *Comentario resolutorio de usuras*.[28]

Azpilcueta's *Manual* opened the door to the otherwise secretive world of the royal confessor. It contained a list of sins that kings and noble lords might commit, covering some of the most controversial aspects of royal government. A principal concern was to avoid tyranny. Azplicueta referenced Aquinas' *De regimine principum* and noted the many ways in which the king might break divine or human laws by intervening in the properties of his subjects, for example by unjustly expropriating them. A king would sin gravely if he were negligent in procuring the welfare or security of the realm. Nor should he seek glory or riches for himself or mix private with the public interest.[29] Excessive taxation was prohibited. The king

biographies, see Ramón Martínez Tapia, *Filosofía política y derecho en el pensamiento español del s. XVI. El canonista Martín de Azpilcueta* (Notarial de Granada 1997), 24–35; Rodrigo Muñoz de Juana, *Moral y economía en la obra de Martín de Azplicueta* (Pamplona, Eunsa 1998), 92–102; Perez Zagorin, *Ways of Lying. Dissimulation, Persecution, and Conformity in Early Modern Europe* (Harvard University Press 1990), 164–7.

25 Martínez Tapia, *Filosofía política*, 29 n 14. However, Martínez Tapia accepts the comparison and holds Vitoria and Azpilcueta as the principal proponents of the reform of academic study in Salamanca, 62.

26 That period ended with the publication of Blaise Pascal's devastating *Provincial Letters*. See Albert R. Jonsen & Stephen Toulmin, *The Abuse of Casuistry. A History of Moral Reasoning* (University of California Press 1988) and e.g. Keenan, 'Casuistry of John Mair', 95.

27 O'Banion, "A Priest Who Appears Good", 336–7. For Azpilcueta's works in general, see Rodrigo Muños de Juana, *Moral y economia en la obra de Martín de Azpilcueta* (Pamplona, Eunsa 1998), 103–10.

28 Moreover, Chapter VII of the *Manual* dealt with a number of contemporary commercial practices in relation to the seventh commandment, avarice as a mortal sin.

29 Martin de Azpilcueta Navarro, *Manual de confessores y penitentes*, (Toledo, Ferrer 1554), XXV (358). See further Reinhardt, *Voices of Conscience*, 90–121.

should honour his obligations towards his creditors (a particularly important admonition in sixteenth-century Spain), and not engage in excessive sale of offices. Nobody was to be condemned for crime without being heard. The king would sin if he did not take action to prohibit usury or games endangering the soul. Any deviation from divine or natural law without a just cause was prohibited.[30] A king who had commenced an unjust war was obliged to pay restitution for all the damage caused.[31] All this might equally well have been in a treatise on natural law and the law of nations. But the fact that the theme was "sin" highlighted the authority of the church in royal government and the role of the royal confessor as its representative.

For the Salamanca scholars, to act against natural law was to sin. But the same was true of breaching civil law and *ius gentium*. After all, even "the directives of human law are to ensure the observance of divine laws".[32] Vitoria often quoted St Paul to the effect that "[w]hosoever therefore resisteth the power resisteth the ordinance of God, and they that resist shall receive themselves to damnation". God was no less a cause of human than of natural law.[33] This applied also to the customary law of nations, for example the inviolability of ambassadors, to the extent that it had the purpose of serving peace – and peace was a rule of natural law.[34] By this means a theological sanction was added to human law and government.

That Azpilcueta's *Manual* became the most widely used work for the instructions to confessors was in great part owing to its moderate tone. Even as a judge, the confessor was to utilise the benign supposition that in dubious cases took the less stringent view. For example, as he groped his way towards understanding Spain's spiralling inflation, Azpilcueta would allow merchants to charge more than the legal price (*tasa*) in response to the market's demands, in this context hitting upon what

30 Azpilcueta, *Manual*, XXV (358–62).

31 Ibid., XXV (360).

32 Vitoria, 'On Law', *Political Writings*, I-II 93 § 122bis (168). Likewise, 'On Civil Power', 3 1 § 17 (35–6). As he explained to his students, to violate *ius gentium* was to sin: "facere contra illud sit peccatum", Vitoria, ComST II-II 57 3 n 3 (15). See further Daniel Deckers, *Gerechtigkeit und Recht. Eine Historisch-kritische Untersuchung der Gerechtigkeitslehre des Francisco de Vitoria* (Freiburg: Universitätsverlag 1991), 303–5, 334–5; J. A. Fernández-Santamaría, *The State, War and Peace. Spanish Political Thought in the Renaissance 1516–1559* (Cambridge University Press 1977), 99.

33 More specifically, he was its "secondary cause". Vitoria, 'On Civil Power', 3 1 (32–6) and 'On Law', I-II 96 4 § 124 (174–5). Vitoria granted that there may be differences between divine and human laws as to whether their breach involves mortal or merely venial sins, 178–9.

34 Vitoria, ComST II-II 57 3 n 3 (15–16).

later came to be called the "quantity theory of value".[35] Focusing on intent enabled condoning practices such as professional profit-making if they were useful for the community. This also made it possible for Azpilcueta to explain the emergence of new customary law. Only if the new practice was inspired by a laudable motive, such as responding to a public need, was it justified. In this way, the focus of the law shifted from the external character of the act (permitted/prohibited) to the process whereby conscience justified it in reaction to the external world.[36] This also explains why, after having defined the most widely practised political and economic institutions as *ius gentium* and as such "human law", they, like Aquinas, conceded that they were nevertheless natural law of sorts, namely the outcome of "natural" human reactions.

This point was made expressly by the most famous of Azpilcueta's students, Diego de Covarrubias (1512–77), professor of canon law in Salamanca (1540–59), one of Spain's representatives at the Council of Trent and later president of the Council of Castile.[37] A legal humanist, Covarrubias, too, employed the *ius gentium* to find a way between scriptural morality and the economic and political demands of the day. In a *Relectio* from 1548 he restated the principle that God had donated liberty to all humans – *omnes homines natura liberos nasci.*[38] This requred him to explain how the Spaniards could employ thousands of slaves in Iberia and the New World. Like Vitoria, Covarrubias rejected the Aristotelian view about natural slavery. Slavery was established *against nature* by *ius gentium.*[39]

35 Following Joseph Schumpeter's works from the 1940s and 1950s, economic historians have attributed the first formulation of the quantity theory of money to Azpilcueta, twelve years before Jean Bodin's more famous treatment on the same theme. For a useful assessment of post-Schumpeter literature on the Spanish contribution to monetary theory, see Muñoz de Juana, *Moral y economia*, 33–69.

36 See e.g. Eduardo Fernández-Bollo, 'Consciencia y valor en Martín de Azpilcueta: ¿un agustinismo práctico en la España del siglo XVI?', 118 *Criticón* (2013), 65–6.

37 For biographies, see Luciano Pereña Vicente, *Diego Covarrubias y Leyva. Maestro de derecho internacional* (Madrid 1957), 16–22; Manuel Fraga Iribarne, 'Presentación', in Diego Covarrubias y Leyva (ed.), *Textos Jurídico-Políticos* (Madrid: Instituto de estudios políticos 1957), i–xxxi.

38 This did not mean, he added, that all would be free today. For everyone was subordinated to laws designed to provide for the good of the republic. Diego Covarrubias y Leyva, *Regulae peccatum. Iur. Lib. VI* (Leyden, Honoratum 1560), II XI (269).

39 "[C]ontra naturam iure gentium est servitus personarum inducta", ibid., II XI (265). He did accept that there was a kind of natural servitude that subordinated the immature or the debile to the wiser. But this was not the same as slavery set up as punishment; its point was to realise the interest of the subordinated party. Ibid. II XI (277–81).

But how could merely human law take away natural liberty? Covarrubias was unimpressed by Accursius' effort to explain this by differentiating between the *whole* of natural law (that could not be dispensed with) and its *parts* (that could sometimes be so dispensed). Nor did he accept Bartolus' distinction between primary and secondary natural law.[40] Instead, he introduced a distinction between positive and negative regulation by natural law. Liberty did not emerge from a positive command or prohibition. It was given by natural law negatively, by not prohibiting the contrary.[41] Hence additions to it could be made by means of a positive law of nations to which "almost all nations had consented" (*sint fere omnium hominum consensu*).[42] Slavery, he explained, had been introduced with the objective to prevent unjust wars and rebellions and as punishment for evils in civil society.[43] Natural liberty was thus made compatible with soothing the consciences of Spanish slave-owners. Most Spanish scholars, including Vitoria, approved of black slavery if only enslavement had been carried out by Africans themselves and there was no apparent reason to believe it had been undertaken illegally.[44]

Covarrubias justified private property by applying canon law as well as the writings of Vitoria and Soto. God had donated the world to humans in common. But it had then been divided by agreement among nearly all peoples because it was very useful for the republic (*valde util Reipublicae*).[45] Perhaps not quite satisfied with such a sharp contrast between the order of creation and the practices of the day, Covarrubias explained that private property – as *ius gentium* – was nevertheless consistent with what he called the *secondary intentions* of natural law. Primary intentions aimed at perfection, but this was no longer available in a world of sinners. Secondary intentions aimed

[40] Ibid., II XI (266–7). [41] Ibid., II XI (268–9).

[42] Ibid., II XI (273). For the long, winding discussion of *ius gentium* as human law in the context of slavery, see *Regulae peccatum* generally. See also Pereña, *Covarrubias*, 155–68.

[43] It is true that in the state of nature, human liberty was unlimited and nothing but common property existed, but in civil societies, many kinds of limits to it had been set "ad reprimendam hominum maliciam". Both servitude and private property were reactions to the real nature of human societies. Covarrubias, *Regulae peccatum*, II XI 3 (269, 267–9).

[44] In a response letter to fray Bernardino de Vique in 1546, Vitoria dismissed the view that Africans were unjustly tricked into slavery by the Portuguese, as this would surely not be allowed or tolerated by the faithful king of Portugal. "At any rate," he wrote, "without further information, I see no reason why the gentlemen who purchased the slaves here in Spain should have any scruples. It is sufficient that they should be prepared to fulfil their obligation should it be proven to them that these goings-on are commonplace." Vitoria, *Political Writings*, 334.

[45] Covarrubias, *Regulae peccatum*, II XI (268).

simply at punishing evil. If the Spanish owned slaves or imposed servitude on others, they were merely realising an intention *already inscribed* in natural law.[46] More generally, drawing on Aquinas, Covarrubias accepted the contrast between an instinctual natural law common to all animals and a *ius gentium* useful for human coexistence (*ut est conveniens et utile humano convictui*).[47] Of course some principles were absolute, such as "do not do evil", which emerged from reason and not from utility. But many arose from utility and convenience. The fact that they were sometimes classed under natural sometimes under human law shows that they were, in a way, "natural for humans" in the contexts of their practical lives.[48]

It is not difficult to understand the attraction of such a pragmatic conception of legality. If a person engaged in the slave trade or waged war against the Indians, the moral, and hence legal, status of their acts was not determined by their intrinsic character but the *intentions* that motivated them. Was the person acting *bona fide*? Did the action have a useful purpose? By the time Covarrubias had come to the slavery question, both the court and the Council of the Indies had yielded to the demands of the *encomenderos* (the settlers) to use captured Indians in forced labour in the mines. Never mind that the *audiencias* sent by the Council in the late 1520s and early 1530s had been under instructions to prohibit most Indian slavery. By stressing that without forced labour the colony's economy would collapse, colonists would return to Castile and the Indians would revert to their pagan ways, even the most enlightened of the *oidores*, high judges of the *audiencias*, were ready to allow deviations from Royal *cedulas*.[49] Enslavement was always, somehow, not only in the interests of the Spanish but for Indians' own good.

Although royal confessors officially rejected all kinds of "Machiavellism", their focus on the intentions behind policy allowed all kinds of mental reservations.[50] There was a difference between heart and mouth, or inner and outer speech, Azpilcueta explained.[51] It was sometimes necessary even

[46] Ibid., II XI (270). Covarrubias also accepts that slavery is just according to the Bible – even as slaves must then be justly treated.

[47] Ibid., II XI (274). [48] Ibid., II XI (277).

[49] The story of the two *audiencias*, despatched to see to the implementation of the royal orders regarding the prohibition of enslavement of peaceful "free" Indians, is well told in Lesley Byrd Simpson, *The Encomienda in New Spain. The Beginning of Spanish Mexico* (University of California Press 1950), 74–111.

[50] See Fernández-Bollo, 'Consciencia y valor en Martín de Azpilcueta', 61–2.

[51] Azpilcueta, 'Commentarius in cap. Humanae Aures, XXII. qu. V. De Veritate Responsi', as in Zagorin, *Ways of Lying*, 168–73.

for Christians to breach the moral code with impunity. A violation of the law, in contrast to a religious precept, would not automatically signal a sin if only there was no intent or plan to deceive. Although homicide or breaking one's oath were categorically prohibited by natural law, it was still possible for the prince to make exceptions when that was required "for the conservation of the republic".[52] And according to Azpilcueta, "dissimulation" against adversaries was perfectly permissible, if only there was a just cause. In fact, he noted, *qui nescit dissimulare nescit regnare* – who cannot dissimulate, cannot rule.[53]

* * * * *

The linkage between the views of the early Salamancans on law and justice and the sacrament of penance followed the Counter-Reformation effort to turn confession into "a potent means of reaching out and converting the laity".[54] Moral casuistry presumed the full authority of theology over the lives of subjects, nobles and the king, but it operated differently in respect of these groups. It was way too difficult, according to the theologians, for laymen to separate right from wrong in matters such as just war, for example. Following "wise men", the prince and his counsel, would therefore always constitute relief, even if the action were in itself sinful. On the one hand, it never sufficed for an ordinary subject to act only on the basis of their own beliefs, however honest. Ignoring official authority would always be sinful.[55] The keys to heaven had, after all, been given to Peter and through him to the officials of the church. There

[52] "Ut facere contra votum et occidere, malum est ex objecto, id est per se et absolute de jure naturale; sed tamen in multis casibus est bonum facere contra illud et occidere, quia posito quod est necessarium ad conservationem reipublicae, licet occidere." Vitoria, ComST II-II 100 2 n 16, quoted in Deckers, *Gerechtigkeit*, 136.

[53] Zagorin, *Ways of Lying*, 174.

[54] Margaret Sampson, 'Laxity and Liberty in Seventeenth-Century English Political Thought', in Edmund Leites (ed.), *Conscience and Casuistry in Early Modern Europe* (Cambridge University Press 1988), 77.

[55] The opinion "must be an opinion formed according to the judgment of a wise man", Vitoria, 'On the Law of War', 2 1 § 20 (306). It follows that "a person who does not consult a wise man in case of doubt can have no excuse", Vitoria, 'On the American Indians', Introduction (235). And further: "If the upshot of the consultation with wise men is a verdict that the action is unlawful, their opinion must be respected; and anyone who disregards it has no defense in law, even if the action is in fact lawful in itself," 'ibid., § 2 (237).

was no doubt about who were those wise men whose advice would allow certainty in one's conscience.[56]

The prince and the nobles, however, were entitled to follow "probabilistic" reasoning – a useful method to alleviate the concerns of "unduly scrupulous or overbearing conscience(s)".[57] Recognised authorities were to be heard and the matter was to be seriously reflected from all sides. As Vitoria put it, "[t]hese things which have both good and bad on both sides are like many kinds of contracts, sales and transactions; if undertaken without due deliberation, on the mere assumption that they are lawful, they may lead a man to unpardonable wrongdoing".[58] After cautious deliberation, one was free to choose any one of the probable arguments that at least some of the wise men had supported.[59] The method was later developed by one of Vitoria's followers, Bartolomé de Medina (1527–80) whose *Brief instruction on the management of the Sacrament of Penance* (1604) was widely read by state authorities and ordinary subjects. The main point was to give up the rigorism of the one right solution. If there were two or more "probable" solutions for which appropriate authority could be cited, no objection attached to choosing any one of them.[60]

Vitoria himself had written a short manual on the sacrament of penance. and this was also the object of his course in 1529–31.[61] Following the decisions of the Tridentine council, he divided penance into three parts – contrition, confession and satisfaction.[62] The confessor was to determine the form of satisfaction as a kind of punishment – typically fasting, prayer or good works as well as, normally, suffering the eventual punishment ordrered by the secular arm. The purpose of satisfaction was to restore the equilibrium and "friendship with God"

[56] Borobio García, *El sacramento de la penitencia en la escuela de Salamanca. Francisco de Vitoria, Melchior Cano, Domingo de Soto* (Universidad Pontificia de Sala 2006), 115–18, 161–8.

[57] M. W. F. Stone, 'Scrupulosity and Conscience. Probabilism in Early Modern Societies', in Harald E. Brown & Edward Vallance (eds), *Contexts of Conscience in Early Modern Europe 1500–1700* (London, Macmillan 2004), 3.

[58] Vitoria, 'On the American Indians', Introduction (235).

[59] Vitoria, 'On the Law of War', 2 § 20–33 (306–14).

[60] Bartolomé de Medina, *Breve instruction de como de ha de administrar el Sacramento de la Penitencia* (Barcelona, Graels & Dotil 1604). On Medina, see e.g. Belda Plans, *La escuela de Salamanca*, 771–8 and Stone, 'Scrupulosity and Conscience', 6–10. Of course, such "laxness" was later furiously challenged from within and outside the church itself.

[61] Francisco de Vitoria, *Confessionario muy util y provechoso* (Antwerp, Tylenio 1570).

[62] Vitoria's *Summa sacramentum ecclesiae* was published in Valladolid in 1560. See Borobio García, *El sacramento*, 11, 18–20.

disturbed by sin.[63] The fact that it was realised by penal works (*opus poenale*) highlighted its judicial character. Although penance was not strictly speaking part of natural law, Soto stressed their mutual links. It built on the natural inclination to relieve one's conscience and to seek reconciliation. Penance was also a virtue and involved accepting a punishment whose purpose was to seek the justice of equivalence.[64] As a virtue of justice, it expressed a relationship to those who had suffered and must be reconciled by restitution.[65] Although restitution was not in itself part of the sacrament, it was nevertheless a necessary prelude for it, and also a precondition for absolution, which, too, was not a part of the sacrament but its consequence. Moreover, justice required that the punishment and the satisfaction must fit the crime/sin in a way that highlighted the close relationship between secular and divine law and the need for a moral casuistry to bridge the gap between them.[66]

## The View from Salamanca

The early years of the sixteenth century saw the recently united Castile–Aragon witness unprecedented cultural flourishing, swings of economic fortune and a sense of political danger and opportunity. The conquest of the "Indies" had brought about the awkward mixture of imperatives of enrichment and evangelisation that was not easy to compress within old moral and theological categories. Scholars also worried about the Franco-Spanish wars of 1526–59 that divided the Catholic realm and undermined Christian unity. While the position of Catholics in Protestant lands – Netherlands, parts of Germany and England – raised the question of resistance to tyranny, the same question emerged from an opposite angle in the *comuneros* rebellion against Habsburg rule in Castile in 1519–21. Alongside all this hovered the expanding intellectual conflict between old theological

[63] Aquinas makes this relationship clear: "Satisfactio est compensatio offensae praeteritae ad aequilitatem iustitiae", ST III, Suppl. 12 3 Resp. ("compensation for an inflicted injury according to the equality of justice").

[64] Soto, *In quartum Sententiarum, Tomus Primus, De sacramentum poenitentiae* (Salamanticae 1570), quoted in Borobio García, *El sacramento*, 109; see also 127–8, 188–92, 235.

[65] "illa aequalitas dicitur in rebus redditio et restitutio", Soto, *De sacramentum poenitentiae*, 862, quoted in Borobio García, *El sacramento*, 190.

[66] "Non remittur peccatum, nisi ablatum" and "[i]ustum est, ut peccator tanto sibi majora inferat lamenta per poenitentiam, quanto majora intulit damna per culpam", Soto, *De Sacramentum poenitentiae*, 826–7, quoted in Borobio García, *El sacramento*, 191, 196 n 180. See further ibid., 198–9.

vocabularies and the principles and practices of an increasingly international economy and an expanding commercial ethic to which the resources of tradition were ill prepared to respond.[67]

Teaching and writing at the outset of the Catholic revival, both Dominican theologians Vitoria and Soto had studied in Paris under the guidance of leading nominalists such as the Belgian Pierre Crockaert (1465–514) and the Scotsman Mair. There they learned a legally articulated teleology that, even as it was assumed to possess divine origin, opened itself to humans everywhere.[68] Natural law and the law of nations existed as contiguous aspects of the divine plan so that there was no gap at all between teaching natural law, providing governmental counsel and relieving doubts of conscience arising from the Indies experience, constant war and the expansion of a profit economy.[69] As Vitoria pointed out, theology had "a broad and mighty field ... whose acres are infinite".[70] And Soto began his *De iustitia et iure* by reminding his readers about theology's superior jurisdiction with

[67] For an overview, see Giovanni Ambrosetti, *Il diritto naturale della riforma catolica* (Milano, Giuffre 1951), 10–22, 55–9 and passim. That the Spanish and American thinkers sought to deal with difficulties emerging with humanism, Protestantism, scepticism and the New World is usefully discussed in Jorge E. Garcia, 'Hispanic Philosophy. Its Beginning and Golden Age', in Kevin White (ed.), *Hispanic Philosophy in the Age of Discovery* (Catholic University of America Press 1997), 13–23.

[68] The political and ideological context of the first generation of the second scholastic has been described in many places. For summary treatments see e.g. Ambrosetti, *Il diritto naturale*, 22–54; Franco Buzzi, 'Il tema de *iure belli* nella seconda scolastica', in Fausto Arici & Franco Todescan (eds), *Iustus ordo e ordine della natura. Sacra doctrina e saperi politici fra XVI e XVIII secolo* (Padova, CEDAM 2007), 81–7; Rainer Specht, 'Die Spanische Spätscholastik im Kontext ihrer Zeit', in Frank Grunert & Kurt Seelmann (eds), *Die Ordnung der Praxis. Neue Studien zur spanischen Spätscholastik* (Tuebingen, Niemeyer 2001), 3–17; Deckers, *Gerecthigkeit*, 1–15; Fernández-Santamaría, *The State, War and Peace*, 58–63 and passim. Good overviews of the Thomist revival are Quentin Skinner, *The Foundations of Modern Political Thought*, vol. II: *The Age of Reformation* (Cambridge University Press 1978), 135–73 and Richard Tuck, The *Rights of War and Peace. Political Thought and the International Order from Grotius to Kant* (Oxford University Press 2001), 68–77. See also Seelmann, *Theologie und Jurisprudenz*, 15–19.

[69] The aspect of continuity is especially highlighted in Franco Todescan, *Lex, natura, beatitudo. Il problema della legge nella scolastica spagnola del sec. XVI* (Padova, CEDAM 1973), 48–55 and Buzzi, 'Il tema de *iure belli* nella seconda scolastica', 120–6. See also Ernst Reibstein, *Die Anfänge des neueren Natur- und Völkerrechts. Studien zu den "Contrioversiae illustres" des Fernandus Vasquius (1559)* (Bern, Haupt 1949), 194–6 and Luis Frayle Delgado, *Pensamiento humanista de Francisco Vitoria* (Salamanca, San Esteban 2004), 63–6.

[70] Vitoria, 'On Civil Power, in *Political Writings*, Prologue (3).

respect to law by quoting Cicero; in this way, positive law traced its validity to philosophy itself.[71]

Vitoria had joined the Dominican order in 1504 and had begun his studies at the Collège de Saint-Jacques, a part of the Sorbonne, in Paris in 1510–11. There he familiarised himself with the teachings of the masters of the conciliar age and prepared with Crockaert a new edition of the *Summa*.[72] In 1526, after three years of teaching at Valladolid, he was appointed *Prima* professor of theology in Salamanca where he went on to teach for twenty years.[73] That his teaching was based on Aquinas allowed him to present a systematic ethics consisting of a theory of law as derived from the first part (*Prima*) of the second part of the *Summa* (Q 90–108) as well as a theory of justice from the *Secunda secundae* (Q 57–122), nothing of the kind having been available in older confessional works.[74] His lectures were woven into this tapestry but also reflected Vitoria's debates with his humanist contemporaries, Erasmus and Juan Luis Vives.[75] Vitoria would apply the *ius gentium* to the *conquista*, to the wars with the French and the Saracens as well as the expansion of commerce. He utterly rejected the Lutheran heresy that relegated law to God's unfathomable grace. The right principles of jurisdiction, ownership and warfare could be found through the employment of reason and were equally applicable to Christians and unbelievers.[76] The light of reason itself was from God.[77]

[71] Domingo de Soto, *De iustitia et iure Libri decem / De la justicia y el derecho en diez Libros* (P. V. Diego Carro intro., P. M. Gonzalez Spanish trans., Madrid, Ordonez 1967 [1559]), Prologo (5).

[72] For Vitoria's early years in Paris (1508–23) and the Convent of San Gregorio in Valladolid (1523–6), see e.g. Belda Plans, *La escuela de Salamanca,* 319–26; Delgado, *Pensamiento humanista*, 21–5; Annabel Brett, *Liberty, Right and Nature. Individual Rights in Later Scholastic Thought* (Cambridge University Press 1997), 124–5.

[73] The standard (and very tendentious) biography is Luis G. Alonso Getino, *El maestro Francisco de Vitoria. Sa vida, su doctrina e influencia* (Madrid, Imprinta catolica 1930). Of the many recent biographies, see e.g. Ramón Hernandez Martín, *Francisco de Vitoria. Vida y pensamiento internacionalista* (Madrid, Biblioteca de autores cristianos 1995), 5–153; Luis Frayle Urbano, *El pensamiento humanista de Francisco Vitoria* (Salamanca, San Esteban 2004), 21–51.

[74] Belda Plans, *La escuela de Salamanca*, 487.

[75] Ambrosetti, *Il diritto naturale*, 23–5; Deckers, *Gerechtigkeit*, 34–42. Erasmus and Vitoria never met but knew and appreciated each other's work – even if Vitoria participated in a *junta* in 1527 that condemned certain passages in Erasmus' work as heretical. Delgado, *Pensamiento humanista*, 26–32 and Fernández-Santamaría, *The State, War and Peace*, 63 and 130–50.

[76] "Homo per peccatum non perdidit illud dominium", Vitoria, ComST II-II 62 1 n 17 (74) and 'On the American Indians', 2 5 (272–5).

[77] Belda Plans, *La escuela de Salamanca*, 359–65.

A few years after his death Vitoria was followed in the *Prima* chair by fellow Dominican Domingo (Francisco) de Soto. Soto had a background in arts studies but had turned to theology and spent a brief period in Paris between 1516 and 1519 where he, too, familiarised himself with the teachings of the "moderns". He then taught at Alcalá and the Dominican convent of San Esteban at Salamanca before being appointed to a *Visperas* professorship of theology from which he ascended to Vitoria's chair in 1552. Already in 1545, as Vitoria had stepped down on the basis of ill health, Soto had became a delegate of the emperor in the Council of Trent from which he would later join that "elite corps of political-cum-spiritual advisors" who would serve as confessors for Charles V and take part in *juntas* set to examine problems relating to Spanish presence in the Indies.[78] By 1535, four years before Vitoria's public lecture on the American Indians, Soto had given a *Relectio* that had included an extended discussion of Spanish imperial activities and laid out many of the arguments about public and private power later reproduced and extended in Book IV of his main work, *De iustitia et iure Libri decem.* This book, first published in 1553–4 and in a second edition in Soto's own hand in 1556–7, consisted of a comprehensive restatement of the contents of the 'Treatise on Law' and 'Treatise on Justice' of the *Summa,* rearranged so as to amount to something like an autonomous jurisprudence.[79]

Vitoria and Soto shared the humanist concern to write clearly and concretely, avoiding the abstractions of medieval scholasticism, using historical examples and commenting on contemporary problems. Vitoria's famous public lecture on civil power of 1528, for example, was targeted against arguments put forward by the *comunero* rebels and with an eye to the complex symbolism of the sack of Rome in 1527 by

[78] For Soto's biography, see briefly Brett, *Liberty, Right and Nature*, 139–41; P. V. Diego Carro, 'Introduction', in Domingo de Soto, *De la justicia y el derecho en diez Libros* (Madrid, Ordoñez 1967), XIX–XXVI. Soto was an active participant in the Council of Trent where he became known for his defence of the traditional doctrine of justification. See Belda Plans, *La escuela de Salamanca*, 405–6, and on Soto's biography generally, 399–412. For Soto's teaching and publishing activity, see Jaime Brufau Prats, *El pensamiento político de Domingo de Soto y su concepción del poder* (Salamanca, Ediciones Universidad 1960), 12–17.

[79] As a commentary to the *Summa* Soto's work presented law as an enfolding of divine reason. The ten books of *De iustitia et iure* loyally repeated the *exitus–reditus* scheme in which natural law and *ius gentium* provided a frame for royal legislation. An important aspect of this was a view of the human being as an image of God that highlighted both reason and freedom, with human beings having *dominium* over themselves. See especially Brett, *Liberty, Right and Nature*, 158–64 and Merio Scattola, 'Naturrecht als Rechtsheorie. Die Systematisierung der "res scolastica" in der Naturrechtslehre des Domingo Soto', in Grunert & Seelmann, *Die Ordnung der Praxis*, 21–47.

the imperial army.[80] In the Prologue to *De iustitia et iure*, Soto wrote that it was not at all his intention to depart from tradition but that the "evil of the times" had introduced new practices such as "unjust contracts and exchanges and the many recent forms of usury and simony", which required a new treatise that would assess their theological – and thus moral–legal – status.[81] War was a constant feature of Spanish life between the Treaty of Madrid of 1526 and the peace of Cateau-Cambrésis (1559), and the need of a united Christian front against the Turks was omnipresent in both Dominicans' texts.[82] Both also discussed at length the problems of conscience relating to expanding forms of commerce and the rise of an economy geared towards accumulation of profit rather than consumption. And both lectured to wide audiences on the conquest of the Indies – Soto in 1535 even confessing to uncertainty about its lawfulness: "*Re vera ego nescio.*"[83]

The annual public lectures by Vitoria and Soto were not just accidental commentaries on current affairs but theological contemplations within a moral–legal casuistic that was expounded at much greater length in Vitoria's regular lectures on the *Summa.*[84] Both scholars appreciated and made much use of the resources of civil and canon law that one their followers, the Dominican Melchior Cano (c. 1509–1560), regarded as "sacred" and a "temple of wisdom".[85] But they never forgot that the laws

[80] Vitoria, 'On Civil Power', 1–44. Fernández-Santamaría highlights the more general significance of the revolt of the Castilian towns for the development of political and legal theory in Spain in the sixteenth century, J. A. Fernández-Santamaría, *Natural Law, Constitutionalism, Reason of State and War*, vol. I (New York, Peter Lang 2005), 49–66.

[81] Soto, *De iustitia et iure*, Proemium, 5a–6a. This is not to encroach on the competence of jurisprudence, he wrote, but to direct the work of canon and civil law by reference to the gospel and philosophy.

[82] See further, Luciano Pereña, 'Estudio preliminaria. La tesis de la paz dinámica', in Luciano Pereña (ed.), *Francisco de Vitoria, Relectio de jure belli o paz dinámica. Escuela Española de la paz. Primera generación 1526–1560* (Madrid, Corpus Hispanorum de Pace, vol. IV, 1981), 56–63, 69–72.

[83] Domingo de Soto, *Releccion 'De dominio'. Edicion critica y Traducción, con Introducción, Apendices e Indices, por Jaime Prufau Prats* (Universidad de Granada 1964), para 34 (162).

[84] Vitoria's lectures were very famous and sometimes attended by over a thousand listeners, Specht, 'Die spanishce Spätscholastik', 11. The *relectio* was a public lecture that a professor was expected to give annually on a topic related to the year's course. It was often held on public holidays and in front of representatives from all the faculties. For the list of thirteen *relectiones* given by Vitoria during the period 1528–40 and preserved (he gave altogether fifteen *relectiones*) and the eleven given by Soto in 1533–54, see Belda Plans, *La escuela de Salamanca*, 338–41 and 415–16; see also Delgado, *Pensamiento humanista*, 55–8; Hernández Martín, *Francisco de Vitoria*, 113–26.

[85] Melchior Cano, *De locis theologicis*, quoted in Decock, *Theologians and Contract Law*, 39.

were directed to a supernatural end and that their students would use them in their practice as priests and confessors. Both shared the popular critique of lawyers as unprincipled cynics or pedantic bureaucrats, and emphasised the necessity to situate problems about the conquest of the Indies or the justice of contracts in an ethical, biblical frame.[86] As Vitoria told his students, two questions always had to be asked about the justice of contracts, one *foro contentioso* and another on *foro conscientiae*. Breaching a contract was both a breach of the law and a sin. But if a contract was invalidated by a formal defect, this did not necessarily mean it would no longer bind on the conscience.[87] The jurisdiction of jurists and theologians overlapped but did not coalesce. Theology was to supplement the law so as to open the prospect of supernatural happiness.[88]

The "School of Salamanca" is a shorthand for the group of theologians and lawyers that had been taught or inspired by the work of Vitoria in the sixteenth and early seventeenth centuries. They were not a homogenous group.[89] Alongside Dominicans such as Vitoria and Soto, and the former's students Melchior Cano and Bartolomé de Carranza (1503–76), both influential theologians serving as bishops of Canaries and Toledo respectively and counsel to the Habsburg court, it included canon lawyers such as Azpilcueta and Covarrubias and civil lawyers such as Vázquez de Menchaca (1512–69) who, alongside Soto, Cano and Carranza, acted at one point as delegate at the Council of Trent. The work of the School is conventionally divided into three periods – first, that of the "founders", Vitoria and Soto; second, "expansion", whose representative figures are the two Dominicans, Pedro de Sotomayor (1500–64) and Bartolomé de Medina (1527–81), the former also professor at Valladolid, authors of a large work on the Indies and on the theory of law and justice, the latter conventionally regarded as the founder of probabilism. Third was a period of "synthesis" consisted of men such as the Dominican Domingo de Bañez (1528–1604) and the Jesuit Francisco Suárez (1548–1617). Counting the active period of the School from the accession of Vitoria to his Salamanca chair (1526) to the death of Suárez (1617), one of the school's leading students, Luciano Pereña identifies

[86] See especially Francisco Castilla Urbano, *El pensamiento de Francisco de Vitoria. Filosofía, política e indio américano* (Barcelona, Anthropos 1992), 38–59.

[87] Vitoria, ComST II-II 62 1 n 38 (92).

[88] Belda Plans, *La escuela de Salamanca*, 354–6.

[89] For a listing of 57 members of the School, see Luciano Pereña, *La idea de justicia en la conquista de América* (Madrid, Mapfre 1992), 255–61.

altogether 125 larger synthetic works to have emerged from this intellectual circle, usually in the Thomistic genres of *De legibus*, *De iustitia et iure* or their derivatives.[90]

Towards the end of the sixteenth century, the place of the Dominicans was taken over by Jesuits who continued to write so as to combine the vocabularies of *De iustitia et iure* with governmental prudence and an open-ended moral casuistry integrating aspect of "good" reason of state, thus helping "the energetic pursuit by princes of those objectives to which Jesuits attached importance".[91] These included Luis Molina (1535–1600), Professor at the University of Evora, the father of the controversial "Molinism" and the author of an extensive treatise on justice with detailed commentary on the economic practices of the day; José de Acosta (1539–1600), missionary in Peru and Professor at the University of Lima, the author of the first synthetic and comparative work on Indian cultures, and, like Vitoria, a staunch opponent of the theory of natural slavery;[92] and Juan de Salas (1553–1612), Professor at Segovia, Barcelona and Rome whose *Tractatus de legibus* took up themes more famously dealt in the work of Francisco Suárez.[93]

The Salamanca scholars were regularly consulted by the court and sat in various governmental bodies to discuss matters of political and

[90] For this way of presenting the School, see Luciano Pereña, 'La tesis de la paz dinámica', 65 and *La idea de justicia*, 125–34. A more limited definition that concentrates on the School's theologians is given by Juan Belda Plans who begins with Vitoria (1526) and ends with the death of Bañez (1604). This list uses three criteria: (1) linkage to both Salamanca and Vitoria; (2) focus on renovation of theology, and (3) working in the tradition of the *Summa* of Aquinas. From this, two phases may be distinguished: a period of innovation leading from Vitoria to Bartolomé de Medina, the "father" of probabilism; and a second period, more doctrinal and more driven to rivalry and confrontation (especially with Jesuits), with less attention to humanist styles or themes, ranging from Medina to Pedro de Herrera (1548–630) and Bañez, the last occupant of the *Prima* chair. This excludes both jurists and Suárez (who never taught at Salamanca). Belda Plans, *La escuela de Salamanca*, 155–69. The first phase is then dominated by the "three greats" – Vitoria, Soto and Cano, 170, 178–82.

[91] Harro Höpfl, *Jesuit Political Thought. The Society of Jesus and the State c. 1540–1630* (Cambridge University Press, 2004), 182.

[92] See José de Acosta, *Natural and Moral History of the Indies* (J. E. Mangan ed., W. D. Mignolo intro. and F. M. López-Morillas trans., Duke University Press, 2002).

[93] Short biographies on all these and a huge number of other "scholastics" may be found in the Index of "Scholasticon" by Jacob Schmutz, at www.scholasticon.fr/Database/Scholastiques. On Acosta's significance, see Anthony Pagden, *The Fall of Natural Man. The American Indian and the Origins of Comparative Ethnology* (Cambridge University Press 1982), 146–200. De Salas appears frequently in Annabel Brett, *Changes of State* (Princeton University Press 2010).

theological significance. They were members of the country's intelligentsia, relatively free to engage in debates over controversial topics.[94] For example, the Dominicans attacked the notorious *limpieza* statutes that prohibited converted Jews or their descendants from taking jobs in government or other public institutions.[95] The intervention by Charles to prohibit discussion of the Indies problem in 1539 made no noticeable difference, and written versions of lectures critical of official policy circulated relatively freely.[96] On the other hand, the theologians had no real objection to royal policy or, for example, to the work of the Inquisition, set up in Spain in 1478. Some such as Cano or the influential Jesuit Juan de Mariana (1536–1624) actually collaborated in compiling and updating the *Index* in 1551 and 1559.[97] But Spain was a religiously repressive society and from the 1530s onwards, the Inquisition moved from targeting mainly *conversos* and *moriscos* to generally ensuring Catholic orthodoxy. Vitoria's *relectiones* found their way into the *Index* in 1590 and famous theologians like Carranza spent long years in prison for suspicions about *illuminati* tendencies.[98]

The genres of *De legibus* and *De iustitia et iure* – commentary on the *Summa* or parts of it – offered a rigorous though an intellectually overwrought scheme to deal with principles of Christian government. The format of the *quaestio* or the *disputatio*, the reproduction of proofs from reason, experience, the Bible and various theological authorities behind the winning proposition, as well as the meticulous statement of the contrary case – all these scholastic techniques tend to obscure the fact that the chain of arguments always juxtaposed something assumed to be

94 This is not to say there were no limits. Especially after the 1530s, professors were sometimes called upon to abjure prior opinions or retract things they had written. The bishop of Toledo, Bartolome de Carranza, a student of Vitoria's and a widely respected scholar, ambassador, counsellor and one-time confessor of Mary Tudor, was the most famous of the Inquisition's victims, having been accused of heresy and imprisoned for nearly eighteen years without charges. He was released after a final verdict in April 1576 and died a week later. For biography, see Luciano Pereña, *Misión de España en América 1540–1560* (Madrid, Instituto 'Francisco de Vitoria' 1956), 27–37.

95 Henry Kamen, *The Spanish Inquisition. An Historical Revision* (London, Phoenix 2000), 230–54, 247.

96 On the imperial reaction, see e.g. Hernandez Martín, *Francisco de Vitoria*, 132–6.

97 Kamen, *Spanish Inquisition*, 109–15.

98 Belda Plans, *La escuela de Salamanca*, 408. Even efforts by Count Olivares, the king's principal minister, to prevent putting the *relectiones* in the *Index* remained fruitless. Hernández Martín, *Francisco de Vitoria*, 125. On the religious uniformity in Spain in the period, see e.g. Antonio-Miguel Bernal, *Monarquía e imperio. Volumen 3: Historia de España* (Barcelona, Marcial Pons, Critica 2007), 163–230.

evident by revelation with an appeal to a casuistic appreciation of the context. The Salamancans used this frame for the compromises they needed for a realistic discussion of the power of the king, rights of subjects and foreigners, the moral–legal status of slavery and private property, the justice of war and expansion. Although canon lawyers such as Azpilcueta or Covarrubias, unlike the civil lawyer Vázquez de Menchaca, invariably presumed theology's authority even in the most *Realpolitik* analyses of royal power, their tendency was nonetheless to look for a middle way that allowed freedom of action in ways that seemed socially useful. This is what *ius gentium* offered to the Salamanca scholars, as it had done to Aquinas over two centuries before. The continuing ambivalence about its character (was it natural or positive law?) became the secret of its success and a fertile source for later interpretations.

## The Salamanca Concept of "Law"

Closely following Aquinas, Vitoria dealt with law in two places of his lectures on the *Summa*. In the commentary to the *Treatise on Law* in the *Prima secundae* he discussed the nature and the kinds of law, their emanation and binding force in the spirit of objective rationalism. "Law", he wrote there, "is not an act of will."[99] He then came to law a second time in the commentary to the *Secunda secundae* that dealt with the virtue of "justice". Here, too, Vitoria started with a Thomist view of law as what is rationally necessary even for God who "cannot make a triangle that would not have three sides".[100] But his discussion then developed into a long elaboration of liberty and subjective rights that took on board reflections on *ius gentium* and *dominium* inspired by what he had learned in Paris.[101]

[99] Vitoria, 'On Law', I-II 90 1, § 121 (156). Vitoria denied that God possessed a *potestas absoluta* that enabled Him to change natural necessities. No science, including theology and law, could exist without them. God did possess supernatural powers but they had been used up in the act of creation. In the *relectio* on homicide Vitoria stated his position categorically. God created humans with the qualities they had because he could not make otherwise: "Hoc ergo supposito, quod Deus non potest naturas rerum mutare, dico quod Deus fecit hominem, cum hac naturali inclinatione appetitus sensitivi. Quia aliter fieri non poterat", quoted in Deckers, *Gerechtigkeit*, 94. On the targets of the programmatic rationalism of the second scholastic, see also Ambrosetti, *Il diritto naturale*, 35–44 and Skinner, *Foundations II*, 135–43.

[100] Vitoria, ComST II-II 57 2 n 3 (8): "jus naturale est necessarium . . . Deus enim non potest facere quod triangulus non habeat tres angulos."

[101] Vitoria, 'De justitia', ComST II-II 62 ("De restitutione"), 61–221.

The commentary to the *Treatise on Law* situated natural law as part of human nature. Reflecting our *inclinations* it was always already "within us".[102] Many of its principles were quite evident – "such as that good should be done". Everyone knew – so Vitoria – that cannibalism was against natural law because "all men have held this practice to be disgusting and base".[103] To this category also belonged prohibitions such as "do not steal", "do not kill the innocent" and "do not do to others what you would not want to be done to yourself".[104] Not all principles were equally obvious. Following Aquinas, Vitoria distinguished between first principles that may never be changed and their more flexible consequences that took some account of the context as well.[105] And sometimes he mentioned a third set of natural law rules that were only very probable (*valde apparentem*). These were proved by way of showing that their contrary cannot be accepted, including maxims such as "fathers should educate their sons", for it could not be stated that fathers should not educate their sons. Because this maxim was not received from anybody's will, it must be a rule of natural law.[106]

Much of this natural law remained quite open-ended. For example, our inclinations may have little to say about the practice of government – relations between a prince and his subjects, rights of colonisation or the new commercial transactions in which Europeans were engaging across the world. Human law was needed for such situations. Though they may never deviate from natural law's first principles they may nevertheless "add" things to natural law as well as change its secondary or tertiary conclusions.[107] Unlike Aquinas, Vitoria did not mention *ius gentium* in his commentary to the 'Treatise on Law'. He reserved his extensive treatment of the matter wholly to the 'Treatise on Justice', where it played quite an important role in mediating between the imperatives of natural law and practical government.[108] But Soto did arrive at the law of nations in the discussion of "Law", where he gave it a purely objective

[102] Hence, unlike human laws, there is no need to promulgate it. It is binding immediately. Vitoria, 'On Law' in *Political Writings*, I-II 90 4, § 122 (160).

[103] Vitoria, 'On Dietary Laws', 1 3 § 5 (210).

[104] Vitoria, ComST II-II 57 2 n 4 (8).

[105] Vitoria, 'On Law', I-II 94 2 and 5 § 123 (170, 171–2).

[106] Vitoria, ComST II-II 57 2 n 4 (10). On these three types of natural law, see also Deckers, *Gerechtigkeit*, 83–97, 113–14, 126–43; Urbano, *El pensamiento*, 159–60; Cruz Cruz, 'La soportable fragilidad', 22–3.

[107] Vitoria, 'On Law', I-II 94 5 § 123 (171).

[108] On this dichotomy, see also Peter Haggenmacher, *Grotius et la doctrine de la guerre juste* (Presses Universitaires de France 1986), 334–41.

definition as "a universal proposition and command of practical reason that is innate as *habitus*".[109] Soto even attacked some "recent authors of no small notoriety" who had depicted reason as the slave of the will.[110] The legislator, whether God or prince, apprehended the object not by will but by intellect and then proclaimed it as law (*ordinatio & praeceptio*). Law was a determination by practical reason of what was needed for the common good.[111] But law was more than an instrument of secular ends: its ultimate objective was supernatural happiness.[112] The church's control was assured.[113] Through promulgation, citizens were informed not only of what the legislator, as "wise man", has regarded as just but what they ought to do to secure their consciences.[114]

Soto was also clearer than Vitoria about the role of natural law as "inclination". As the inclination became a *habitus* it coalesced with the search of virtue.[115] It proceeded first by apprehending what one was naturally inclined to do and then subordinated this to critical reason. The resulting "inclinations of reason" were precisely about how to live together in society.[116] By this two-step process natural law, as both

[109] "lex est universalis propositio ac dictamen rationis practicae quae per modum habitus inest", Soto, *De iustitia et iure*, I 1 1 (9a) and the whole argument therein (6b–10b).

[110] Ibid., I I 1 (7a).

[111] "Lex enim . . . nihil aliud est quam regula et praeceptio prudentiae per quam qui curam gerit rei publicae illam gubernat et administrat", ibid., I 3 1 (21b–22a). On Soto's (objectivist) view of prudence, see Fausto Arici, 'Il principe tra mediazione e supplenza', in Fausto Arici & Franco Todescan (eds), *Iustus ordo e ordine della natura. Sacra doctrina e saperi politici fra XVI e XVIII secolo* (Padova, CEDAM 2007), 230–5. See also Todescan, *Lex, natura, beatitudo*, 97.

[112] "lex est regula humanorum actuum. . . . Ultimus autem finis est beatitudo: ergo omnis lex ordinatur in beatitudinem." Soto, 'Commentarius Qq. 90–97 Summae theologiae Sancti Thomae', quoted in Arici, 'Il principle tra mediazione e supplenza', 231 n 38. See also Soto, *De iustitia et iure*, I 2 1 (17a–19b) and I 4 1 (29a).

[113] "Effectus legis quem potissimem aspicere habet legislator est bonos facere homines sibi subditos, per quam bonitatem finem humanum adipiscantur", Soto, *De iustitia et iure*, I 2 1 (17a). Furthermore, ". . . ambae eundem [i.e secular and spiritual power] suis legibus debeant scopum supernae salutis praefigere, spiritualis supereminet saeculari: nempe ut factorum leges instituat & si saecularis Princeps leges a vera foelicitate deflexerit, eas emendet & corrigat". Ibid., I 2 1 (18b).

[114] Ibid., I 1 4 (13b–16b). Natural law, however, required no positive act of proclamation but was instead known by all through "natural light" ("naturae luce"). Ibid. (16b).

[115] "Lex naturalis inest nobis per modum habitus." This *habitus* works through "synderesis", which captures the right mode in acting in particular situations. Ibid., I 4 1 (28a–30a).

[116] Ibid., I 4 2 (31a–b). On the way natural law collects all human virtues, see ibid., I 4 3 ("Utrus omnes virtutis actus sint de lege nature", 32b).

inclination and reason, respected the distinction between people and animals and, for example, explained the basis of human liberty.[117] The result applied to all humans, as St Paul had written, and even non-believers carried it in their hearts.[118] It was therefore a proper instrument to govern the whole human world.

The Salamanca scholars followed Aquinas in making the important distinction between principles of natural law that remain unchanged and conclusions that practical reason drew from them in view of historical conditions. The latter had the character of *ius gentium*. Thus, for example, although natural law compelled humans to live in peace, under *ius gentium* they were entitled to take up arms to defend themselves.[119] Worried about such modifications, Soto took up the old distinction between variation *in the law* and in the *material reality* surrounding the law. The duty to return a sword to its owner (the law) remained even if we should avoid executing it in view of the owner's madness (material reality).[120] The ethical force of the law was preserved, even if its precepts were not always applicable as such. This allowed using *ius gentium* to justify institutions such as kingship. slavery and private property, among others, in a way that presewed the ideals of equality, freedom and common property while recognising their inapplicability in a sinful world.[121] Such an Augustinian justifiction was blended by most Salamancans with a more optimistic view that highlighted the sociability of human inclinations. But the main point remained that whatever moral doubts may have been held regarding human institutions, once created, they

[117] See further Brett, *Liberty, Right and Nature*, 143–5.

[118] Soto, *De iustitia et iure*, I 4 1 (29a).

[119] Ibid., I 4 4 (35a). Covarrubias explains that while natural law in its first principles ("prima ius naturalis principia") was applicable to all living beings, *ius gentium* too involves natural justice, though not in an absolute manner but in relation to utility ("secundum utilitatem"), Covarrubias, *Regulae peccatum*, II XI (275). Soto followed Aquinas by making the distinction between the two types of derivation from natural law – "conclusion" that led into universally applicable *ius gentium* and "determination" that led into the domestic (civil) law of the specific *civitas*. See Cruz Cruz, 'La soportable fragilidad', 26–9.

[120] Soto, *De iustitia et iure*, I 4 5 (36a–37a).

[121] "Vita humana in pace & tranquillitate sustentanda est & consovenda. Inde, subsumpta altera praemissa quod natura corrupta in communi vivens neq; agros coleret diligenter, neque in pace viveret, gentes intulerunt dividendas esse possessiones. Ex eodem itidem principio elicuerunt servitutis legem [and]... intulerunt leges omnes venditionis, locationis, impignorationis, aliarumque; commutationum, pactorum & conventorum." Ibid., I 5 4 (44b–45a).

were binding on conscience.[122] The importance of confession as a means of social control remained undiminished.

It was clear to the Salamanca scholars that the prince was not *legibus solutus*: "although the prince is over the whole commonwealth he is nevertheless part of the commonwealth".[123] He was bound by the directive, though not the coercive, force of his laws.[124] Royal authority was *public* authority, not that of a paterfamilias or a property owner.[125] As Soto made clear, there were some who had suggested that the emperor was Lord of the World "as if he could use the things of this world like he uses his horse or his clothes".[126] But kingship was not at all of this type. The goods in France were not those *of* the king of France. The ruler may dispose of them for the common good, but only as ruler, not as owner. An owner uses things in his *own* interests, the king works in the interest of the *civitas*.[127]

Vitoria and Soto were intellectually committed to the unity and intelligibility of God's created world and its being ordained to supernatural ends. But they were also conscious that the government of consciences required cooperation with secular power. Hence their concern to integrate natural and human law into a view of territorial authority and prudential reason that would collapse neither into Lutheran voluntarism nor Machiavellian amoralism.[128] But the more refined this system of governance became, the further it moved from the divine–natural law in Aquinas' 'Treatise on Law'. As the theologians confronted the immutability of natural law with the varying facts of the

122 Ibid., I 6 4 (50b). But sometimes we may be called upon to obey unjust laws for pragmatic reasons, to avoid a greater "scandal" (51a).

123 Vitoria, 'On Law', 96 5 § 126 (181). See further Deckers, *Gerechtigkeit*, 309–19.

124 Vitoria, 'On Law', 96 5 § 126 (182).

125 For Azpilcueta's discussion of the analogy between public power and the power of the paterfamilias, see 'Notabile III in Relectio Cap. Novit. De Iudic', § 95 (139–40) and Martínez Tapia, *Filosofía política*, 146–9.

126 ". . . itaque possit uti rebus orbis sicut utitur equo suo vel veste". Soto, *Relección 'De dominio'*, § 28 (138).

127 In a work on the powers of the emperor and the king, Las Casas himself repeated the old distinction between ownership and jurisdiction, insisting that "Imperator et rex non est dominus super rebus singulorum, sed tantum quoad iurisdictionem", 'De rege potestate', in *Obras Completas* 12 (Madrid, Alianza 1990), III.1 (46 and generally 46–58).

128 See e.g. Massimo Meccarelli, 'Ein Rechtsformat für die Moderne. *Lex* und *iurisdictio* in der spanishen Spätscholastik', in Christop Strohm & Heinrich de Wall (eds), *Konfessionalität und Jurisprudenz in der frühen Neuzeit* (Berlin, Duncker & Humblot 2009), 285–311.

world, they were caught in a middle terrain, which for Vitoria and Soto crystallised as *ius gentium*, a universal law that was neither fully natural nor fully voluntary, a law groping towards something like a "sociological" reason that would be responsive to contemporary conditions of human existence.

## ***Ius gentium* As Justice**

But law of nations was not just a kind of naturalisation of contemporary practices. It also penetrated the scholastic discussion of *Quaestiones* 57–122 of the *Secunda secundae* dealing with "justice" as a specifically social virtue[129] The turn from law as external behavioural directives to the internal world of virtue was quite important for the purposes of opening up the forum of conscience as the locus of Christian government. Here Vitoria and his followers would be able to compensate for the rigidity of natural law by the much more flexible notion of *ius gentium*. Their discussion of law and justice was underlain by the hypothesis of sinfulness that intervened to make it impossible to apply natural law in its pristine form in human society.[130] The divine plan needed to be modified by teaching humans what they would need in order to attain the ultimate objective of supernatural beatitude. For this purpose, they would need to develop the *habitus* of virtue.[131] Only once they internalised that *habitus* – once they had become "just" – people would be able to understand how a general precept ought to be applied in a particular situation so as to produce the right result.[132]

The discussion began from *Quaestio* 57 of the *Secunda secundae*, interrogating the meaning of the notion of "*ius*" as the "object of justice", analogous with Ulpian's definition of giving each one their due.[133] This was fully in accordance with the objective understanding that linked natural law firmly to the pre-existing divine plan. Vitoria then explained that law's necessity was still not the same as that of mathematics. Natural law was not only what was immediately

[129] "Justitia est in ordine ad alterum, et non in ordine ad se". Vitoria, ComST II-II 57 1 n 3 (1). Soto, *De iustitia et iure*, III 1 1 (191a).
[130] Cruz Cruz, 'La soportable fragilidad', 13–40.
[131] Soto, *De iustitia et iure*, I 4 1 (29b).
[132] See Vitoria, ComST II-II 57 1 n 6 (4) and Soto, *De iustitia et iure*, III, 1 1 (193a).
[133] Vitoria, ComST II-II 57 1 n 6 (4). See also Brett, *Liberty, Right and Nature*, 125–6 and generally Deckers, *Gerechtigkeit*, 28–50.

evident (such as "do not steal" or "do not kill the innocent") but also all kinds of inferences from those.[134] Here justice operated by directing *ius gentium* to apply or modify natural law so as to attain a good outcome, such as *utilitas reipublicae*.[135] Or, as Soto explained, that fields needed to be divided was not an absolute necessity but a rational conclusion about how they can be turned into effective use.[136] The argument was not about natural law but nevertheless universally compelling.[137] That *ius gentium* now operated as a virtue (of justice) meant that it could not be reduced to application of a rule. Instead, it involved a close assessment of what was best, and in this sense necessary, for a situation. Drawing directly from Aquinas, Covarrubias expressed this by suggesting that where the justice of natural law expressed what was naturally adequate or commensurate with another (*ex sui natura adequatum & commensuratum alteri*), *ius gentium* only had to do with justice in accordance with utility and convenience (*secundum utilitatem, quae ex eo deducitur, ut alteri conveniens*).[138]

In this way, the Salamanca scholars found themselves moving from objective demands of natural law to speculations about just behaviour in the complex thicket of prevailing social relations. Instead of insisting on the absolute requirements unfolding from the divine plan, they sought to answer the question how those requirements ought to be applied in a world of sinners so as to attain security and happiness. But how would that "application" take place? How, in other words, did *ius gentium* operate? Vitoria sometimes characterised it as a kind of global consensus. For example, when he suggested that the natural law of non-aggression could be modified by the right of just war to prevent harm to the innocent, he claimed that "this is [the prince's] right by the law of nations and the authority of the whole world" ["*Totius Orbis*"]. But he then added that this right was also something more:

> the world could not exist unless some men had the power and authority to deter the wicked by force from doing harm to the good and the innocent. Yet those things which are necessary for the governance and conservation of the world belong to natural law.[139]

[134] "Illa quae inferuntur per consequentiam bonam moralem moraliter notam, id est valde apparentem esse juris naturalis…", Vitoria, ComST II-II 57 2 n 4 (9).

[135] Deckers, *Gerechtigkeit*, 133–43.

[136] Soto, *De iustitia et iure*, III, 1 1 (195b).

[137] "id est ius quod gentes universae, qua tenus rationales sunt, sibi constituerunt", ibid., III 1 3 (197a).

[138] Covarrubias, *Regulae peccatum*, II XI (275).

[139] Vitoria, 'On the Law of War', 1 4 § 19 (305).

Was *ius gentium* something that nations had "approved"? Or something that was "necessary"? It seemed pointless to separate these two approaches, one subjective, another objective. Decisive were the necessities of "governance and conservation".[140] What was "just and convenient for the whole world" provided that ambassadors were protected, ships may sail freely on the open seas, peaceful travellers had right of access to foreign lands and property that belonged to no-one came to the first good faith taker.[141] All of this reasoning moved from the rigid principles of natural law to a more contextual type of justice as good government. In this way, *ius gentium* would also offer the casuistry through which to treat the massive expansion of commerce. Usury was prohibited by natural law, but professional profit-making would be just only if it was motivated by the honest intention to provide livelihood to one's family or the good of the community.[142]

How the relations of property and contract moved from the requirements of law to the internal world of justice may also be illustrated by Azpilcueta's discussion of theft in his *Manual for confessors*, written as a gloss on the seventh commandment ('Thou shalt not steal').[143] Azpilcueta first defined "theft" very broadly as all action that caused damage to an object. But most important was the intention: without the *animus* to steal or destroy, whatever damage was caused no sin of theft was committed, although there might still remain the duty to restore.[144] The binding force of contracts, too, would now be measured by party consent. Formal requirements were secondary; even if legal

140 For a good analysis of the relations of *ius gentium* and natural law in Vitoria, see Juan Cruz Cruz, '*Ius gentium* bei Vitoria. Ein eindeutig internationalistischer Ansatz', in Alexander Fidora, Matthias Lutz-Bachmann & Andreas Wagner (eds), *Law and ius. Essays on the Foundation of Law in Medieval and Early Modern Philosophy* (Stuttgart, Fromman-Holzbook 2010), 301–32.

141 Vitoria, 'On Civil Power', 3 4 § 21 (40); 'On the American Indians', 3 1 § 3, 4 and 5 (279, 280, 281). For a full list of Vitoria's references to *ius gentium* in the various texts, see Deckers, *Gerechtigkeit*, 344–59.

142 "Negotiatio quae ordinatur ad finem honestum, ut ad sustentiationem familiae, licita est", Vitoria, ComST 77 4 n 1(146). See also the discussion of the practice of buying grain in the spring and selling it at a greater price in the fall. If this took place with an intent only to honest benefit ("solum honestum lucrum"), it was all right but if the only intention was to profit ("mala intentione"), then it was sinful. Ibid., n 9 (151).

143 Azpilcueta, *Manual de confessores*, 126–211.

144 For example, ignorance and necessity are valid excuses and the presence of good faith would mostly do away with the duty to restore. Ibid., 126–8. This was followed by an extremely detailed casuistic of the duty to restore – a primary concern in the confessional relation – in different situations.

justice voided a contract owing to a formal defect, the court of conscience might still hold it binding if that was just and equitable. This internal view would also endorse the freedom of contract, releasing the parties from any major formal conditions: a genuine offer and a genuine acceptance would suffice.[145] The older view of *ius* as the object of virtuous action remained in the form of limitations to the freedom of contract in cases of immoral purpose or unjust enrichment.[146] But the view of right as an emanation of the virtue of *justice* in inter-individual relationships turned attention to the intentions of the parties and underlined the significance of confession as a dialogue about how to adapt to the political and economic changes in society. It offered an interpretative scheme that would condone otherwise morally dubious behaviour only if the motives were pure.

Like the whole tradition in which he wrote, Vitoria had notable difficulty in explaining the nature of *ius gentium* – was it natural or human law? In one place he suggested that "dominion and supremacy (*praelatio*) were introduced by human law, not natural law".[147] But he also quoted Gaius' definition of the law of nations as "what natural reason has established among all nations".[148] Moreover, at one point he foresaw the possibility of *ius gentium* being derived from "the consent of the greater part of the world ... especially when it is for the common good of all men".[149] But in another passage from the 1528 lecture he denied that *ius gentium* would have been simply "pacts or agreements between men" but instead possessed "the validity of specific enactment (*lex*)".[150] That passage continued with Vitoria affirming that the "whole world" was "in a sense a commonwealth [that] has the power to enact

145 On the "victory of consensualism" in the Salamanca School, see Decock, *Theologians and Contract Law*, 142–214.

146 See e.g. Soto, *De iustitia et iure*, IV 5 1 (307b–308b). On moral limits of contractual freedom among the scholastics, see especially Decock, *Theologians and Contract Law*, 419–505.

147 Vitoria, 'On the American Indians', 2 1 § 25 (254).

148 Ibid., 3 1 § 2 (278). Vitoria has here supplemented "gentes" in the original by Gaius with "homines". ("Quod vero naturalis ratio inter omnes gentes constituit vocatur [] ius gentium," D 1 .1. 9.) It is unlikely, however, that this would allow the inference that he is here canvassing a "modern" international law of "nations". See e.g. Jean-Francois Courtine, 'Vitoria, Suarez et la naissance du droit de nature moderne', in Alain Renaut (ed.), *Naissances de modernité. 2 Histoire de la philosophie politique* (Paris, Calmann-Lévy 1999), 152 and Dieter Janssen, 'Die Theorie der gerechten Krieges im Denken des Francisco de Vitoria', in Grunert & Seelmann, *Die Ordnung der Praxis*, 211 n 20.

149 Vitoria, 'On the American Indians', 3 1 § 4 (281).

150 Vitoria, 'On Civil Power', 3 4 § 21 (40).

laws which are just and convenient to all men; and these make up the law of nations". No kingdom may choose to ignore it, "because it has the sanction of the whole world".[151]

Vitoria's most elaborate discussion of *ius gentium* took place in his lecture on *Quaestio* 57 within the frame of the virtue of justice. Here he rejected the old view of *ius gentium* as that part of natural law that was applicable to human beings. All natural law had to do with humans. Instead, the distinction was between that which was good or equitable *in itself* and independently of the situation and that which lacked such necessary character.[152] Situated in the latter category, the law of nations was that which was social, contingent and historical. Aquinas, as we have seen, struggled to distinguish the *ius gentium* from natural law while still maintaining its universal character. It dealt with things "without which men cannot live together" – such as private ownership (*proprietate rerum*) and political commonwealths (*conservatio regni*).[153] Its necessity was not timeless but dependent on the historical context. Vitoria agreed but added that the issue of whether *ius gentium* was natural or human law was largely terminological.[154] The important point was that it dealt with man-made, artificial equivalences between things. It was not necessary in an absolute sense; it was what was useful – what people had *agreed* to be useful – given what was known of how they lived. It did not contradict natural law but implemented it. For example, diplomacy came under *ius gentium* because it was useful, though not necessary, as a servant of a natural law that aimed for peace.[155] Theologians were the authoritative interpreters of *ius gentium* precisely because it preserved its link to natural and divine law, and breaching it was therefore a sin.[156]

151 Ibid., 3 4 § 21 (40).

152 "id est jus gentium dicitur quod non habet in se aequitatem ex natura sua, sed ex condicto hominum sancitum est", Vitoria, ComST II-II 57 3 n 2 (14).

153 *Aquinas. Political Writings* (R. W. Dyson ed., Cambridge University Press 2002), ST I-II 95 4 Resp (135). It thus exists, Courtine writes, as an intermediary between natural and positive law. Its function is to see to "la sociabilité fondamentale de l'être humain", in 'Vitoria, Suárez et la naissance du droit naturel', 135. See however also the somewhat different definition in ST II-II 57 3 ad 3 (164).

154 Vitoria identifies here a wide notion used by the jurists and a narrower one used by theologians. In the end, however, he regards it as merely a matter of taste as to which one is being used. Vitoria, ComST II-II 57 3 n 2 (14).

155 Ibid., II-II 57 3 n 4 (15–16). For further discussion of the systematic place of *ius gentium* in Vitoria, see Deckers, *Gerechtigkeit*, 359–69.

156 Vitoria, ComST II-II 57 3 n 3 (14–15).

It was this intermediate character of *ius gentium*, the way it oscillated between a law of timeless necessity and practical judgment in a particular place and time that made it both appealing and frustrating simultaneously.[157] It was neither pure reason nor pure will but a single process of normative elaboration (*naturalis ratiocinatio*). That it was situated as part of a treatise of *justice* meant that it was not so much external requirements imposed on communities as a governmental *habitus* that was sensitive to the good of the commonwealth – within the limits, Vitoria added, of what was also good for Christianity as a whole.[158] Confession and penance were a natural part of this. To be a good and successful ruler was to abide by *ius gentium*. To attempt to conquer territories without a just cause or to govern only for riches and glory and in violation of the rights of the subjects – in all such ways the king would fail in his task of representing God on earth.[159]

## Justice As *Dominium*

The distance between the ideals of creation and the institutions and practices in Castile, Europe and the New World was enormous. Like their predecessors, Vitoria and Soto accepted that originally all humans had been free and equal and shared ownership in common: *a principio mundi omnia erant communia*.[160] And yet they wrote at a moment when a thriving business of human slavery was emerging, rules of private ownership were laying the basis for worldwide commerce and princes were beginning to

[157] See also Haggenmacher's discussion of Vitoria's *ius gentium*, *Grotius*, 334–41. A similar ambivalence has to do with Vitoria's derivation of the civil commonwealth. On the one hand, in the *relectio* 'On Civil Power' it seems completely naturalistic: "the primitive origin of human cities and commonwealths was not human invention or contrivance to be numbered . . . but a device implanted in nature in man for his own safety and survival". Vitoria, 'On Civil Power', in *Political Writings*, 1 2 § 5 (9). On the other hand, in his consideration of *dominium* in his commentary on Questions 62 (on restitution) and 64 (on homicide) in the ST II-II, Vitoria sketched a single sphere of natural liberty that founded the power of the people to elect the prince and endow him with the authority to rule. As Brett concludes, "[t]here is no political organisation given in nature". Brett, *Liberty, Right and Nature*, 132, 135–6.

[158] Vitoria, 'On Civil Power', 1 9 § 12 (21–2). Here Vitoria had in mind the many controversies Charles was having both with François I and the pope, and the way they threatened to undermine the need for a united front against the Turk. Deckers, *Gerechtigkeit*, 323.

[159] Azpilcueta, *Manual de confessores*, xxv (358).

[160] Vitoria, ComST II-II 62 1 n 9 (67); Soto, *Relección 'De dominio'*, § 29 (140); *De iustitia et iure*, IV 3 1 (295a–b).

exert absolute rule over their territories. Judged by the ideals of the Christian tradition, the first half of the sixteenth century – to say nothing of what lay ahead – was a moral abomination. In fact, some of the later Spaniards such as the Jesuit Mariana put forward an extremely pessimistic view of human nature and social institutions. Humans could be ruled only through force, and nothing but the threat of tyrannicide kept rulers from oppressing their subjects.[161] Many Spanish political thinkers would share his skepticism, and influential writers such as the humanist scholar Baltasar Alamos de Barrientos (1556–1634/44) or the former Italian Jesuit Giovanni Botero (1544–1617) turned to Machiavelli and Tacitus for a more realistic portrayal of European government in the vocabulary of *raison d'état.*[162]

But theologians like Vitoria and Soto could not go down that way; instruction on the practices of confession required finding a balance between Christian ethics and the conditions of the world. This was offered to them by the casuistry of justice in the *Secunda secundae.* The most important aspect of justice was *dominium* – a notion to which Vitoria came in the context of *Quaestio* 62 on restitution. To restore someone was to bring that person to his or her original state of *dominium* and to recreate the equality that had been disturbed. To possess *dominium* was to have a *ius*. *Dominium* was not just a fact (of possession, say) but included the aspect of rightfulness. It belonged to the way in which God had organised the world.[163] By reference to the writings of the German theologian Konrad Summenhart (c. 1450–1503) Vitoria produced a subjective definition: *ius* was *facultas utendi res secundum jura vel leges*, a faculty to use a thing in accordance with law.[164] From the earlier definition of *ius* as an object of justice, *dominium* turned into something a person rightfully *had* to themselves.[165] To explain this, Vitoria began

[161] Juan de Mariana, *The King and the Education of the King (De Rege et Regis Institutione)* (G. A. Moore trans. & intro., Georgetown University 1947). For an analysis of Mariana's pessimism, see Harold E. Brown, *Juan de Mariana and Early Modern Spanish Political Thought* (Aldershot, Ashgate 2007).

[162] See J. A. Fernández-Santamaría, *Natural Law, Constitutionalism, Reason of State, and War. Counter-Reformation Spanish Political Thought*, vol. II (New York, Peter Lang 2006).

[163] On the consequent "sacralisation" of the human domain, see the very useful Marie-France Renoux-Zagamé, *Origines théologiques du concept moderne de propriété* (Geneva, Droz 1987), 115–59.

[164] Vitoria, ComST II-II 62 1 n 8 (67).

[165] Vitoria did canvass three senses of "dominium": (1) superior power ("eminentiam quamdam et superioritatem"), or the "dominium" of the prince; (2) the sense "property" ("tantum valet sicut proprietas"), and (3) the right or faculty to use something ("facultatem, quamdam ad utendum re aliqua secundum jura") , Vitoria, ComST II-II 62 1 n 6, 7, 8 (65–7).

by making the old point that originally, as the creator of the world, God had *dominium* over everything.[166] He could thus use the world as he wished (*ut voluerit*).[167] One of the ways in which God used his *dominium* was to donate it to human beings. Wary of suggesting anything heretical, Vitoria denied the status of the donation as positive divine law, an act of grace. Instead, it was inscribed in the order of creation. That humans had been created in the image of God meant that they, unlike animals, were "free", they had *dominium* over their actions: *sola creatura rationalis habet dominium sui actus.*[168] Animals and people related to things differently. Animals lived in a world of instinctual factuality in which they were not masters of things they used. Human *dominium* was inextricable from the rational mastery people had over their actions. And this presupposed liberty. Only liberty allowed the imputation of something to a person and thus to speak of a "right".[169] Soto agreed. Animals could never have dominion: *solus homo inter creaturas habet hanc potestatem per liberum arbitrium.*[170] And Azpilcueta explained that liberty had been donated to human beings "so that they would govern themselves in accordance with natural reason".[171] This gave the Salamancans the normative basis for the most important human institutions, jurisdiction over a political community and the right of property.[172]

The *topos* of *dominium* was of great theological momentum, connecting on the one hand to the question of supreme authority in a *civitas* and the problems of usury and avarice in an increasingly commercial

166 "Deus omnia creavit: ergo est dominus omnium", Vitoria, ComST II-II 62 1 n 9 (68).

167 Ibid., II-II 62 1 n 9 (68).

168 Ibid., II-II 62 1 n 11 (70). Similarly Soto, *De iustitia et iure*, IV 1 2 (284a); *Relección 'De dominio'*, § 10 (100) ("soli homini convenit esse dominum, quia habet liberum arbitrium per quod agat movendo se"). For the way Vitoria and Soto based *dominium* on human superiority, rationality and nature as "imago Dei", see further Renoux-Zagamé, *Origines théologiques*, 97–114.

169 Renoux-Zagamé, *Origines théologiques*, 135.

170 Soto, *Relección 'De dominio'*, § 10 (100).

171 "ad gubernandum illud secundum rationem naturalem", Martín de Azpilcueta Navarro, 'Notabile III in Relectio Cap. Novit. De Iudic', in Martín de Azpilcueta Navarro, *Commentarius utilis in rubricam de iudiciis* (Rome, Tornerii & Bericchia 1585), n 41 (120).

172 The question of the origin of "subjective" right has been the object of an enormous recent literature. For the way that notion arose with the Parisian "moderns" and was received by Vitoria, alongside the fundamental work of Renoux-Zagamé, see Brett, *Liberty, Right and Nature*, 126–32; Brian Tierney, *The Idea of Natural Rights* (Cambridge, Eerdmans 1997), 236–54 and (on Vitoria's notion of subjective right in relation to American Indians) 256–72; Richard Tuck, *Natural Rights Theories. Their Origin and Development* (Cambridge University Press 1979), 46–50.

economy. The universality of the institutions of sovereignty (*dominium iurisdictionis*) and property (*dominium proprietatis*) would now be developed and argued under it.[173] Both would be viewed from the perspective of "*facultas*", the (subjective) right and freedom of the subject. Soto, not unnaturally, regarded property as the original and the more important aspect of the theory.[174] But the basic problem was the same: how to justify the subordination of one human being over another? The theory of *dominium* offered a single answer to that question: whether understood as a public or private power, its source was always the right and freedom of the individual.

But natural law provided for *dominium* in common: *Deus fecit omnia communia omnibus.*[175] As we have seen, medieval theologians and lawyers had already taken pains to argue how this could coexist with private property and slavery. Like Aquinas, they held that private *dominium*, including slavery, had been introduced by "human agreement, which belongs to positive [law]".[176] Even as natural law was in principle immutable, many things could be added to it if only some advantage would follow. For instance, slavery could coexist with the natural law of human freedom inasmuch as "it is beneficial for a slave to be governed by someone wiser than he".[177] And humans could agree to give up common property because "a more peaceful state of things is preserved for mankind if each is contented with his own".[178] The Spaniards repeated these arguments over again. An early example is provided by the famous discussion of Indian property and Spanish rights of jurisdiction of 1513 by the Professor of Canon Law at Valladolid and Salamanca, member of the Council of Castile, and long-time legal advisor to the Spanish rulers, Juan Lopez Palacios Rubios (c. 1450–1524). Nature had created "all humans equal and free", he argued; "they did not have a prince and only nature governed man before there existed written

[173] Hence Soto, for instance: "duplex distinguitur dominium: alterum quod est ius seu proprietas rerum, de quo dictum est hactenus; alterum quod est potestas iurisdictionis quod est dominatio seu dominatus, sicut est dominium principum in subditos", Soto, *Relección 'De dominio'*, § 28 (138). See also Soto's discussion of the Franciscan position in *De iustitia et iure* IV 1 1 (281b–283b) and the claim of emperor as *Dominus mundi*, in ibid., IV 4 2 (303a–307b). See also Vitoria, ComST II-II 62 1 nn 6–7 (65–6).

[174] Brufau Prats, *El pensamiento politico de Domingo de Soto*, 21–2.

[175] Vitoria, ComST II-II 62 1 n 18 (74). On the myth of common dominion in Christian and communitarian thought, see Renoux-Zagamé, *Origines théologiques.*

[176] Aquinas, ST II-II 66 2 ad 1 (208).

[177] Ibid., II-II 57 3 ad 2 (164).

[178] Ibid., II-II 66 2 Resp (208).

laws".[179] But after the Fall "[w]ars, the separation of peoples, foundation of regimes and the distinction of dominions were introduced by *ius gentium*".[180] The rights of government, too, were received as a donation from God and an aspect of human nature, not of grace – but only to the time of Christ at which point they were given to Peter and his followers.[181] It was on that last point that Vitoria and Soto wholly differed from the official early view of the crown.

Vitoria's discussion of *dominium* likewise began with the assumption that *a principio mundi omnia erant communia.*[182] He was conscious of the ensuing problem:

> But if it is the case that God had created everything to be owned in common, and humans are owners of everything by natural law, how and from which facts can the division of things have come? It is not made by natural law. For natural law is always the same and never varies.[183]

How, in other words, to justify the power of kings over their subjects and the practices of ownership, contract and labour, including slave labour, that underwrote Castile's hegemony? Like the French legists of the fourteenth century, the Italian commentators and the Sorbonne theologians of the fifteenth century, Vitoria found the explanation in *ius gentium.* Original sin had dramatically altered conditions of social life. Things could no longer be shared in harmony.[184] "It was understood that without a division of things they could not live commodiously or in peace with each other."[185] Kingdoms and provinces were to be set up, fields and properties to be divided. The division could not be made by natural law that provided for equality so that what belonged to one,

179 Juan Lopez de Palacios Rubios, *De las Islas del Mar Océano* (México, Fondo de cultura económica 1954), 27.

180 Ibid., 28. 181 Ibid., 82–93.

182 Vitoria, ComST II-II 62 1 n 9 (67). See also Kurt Seelmann, *Die Lehre des Fernando Vázquez de Menchaca vom Dominum* (Cologne, Heymanns 1979), 113.

183 "Sed si ita est quod Deus fecit omnia communia omnibus, et homo est omnium dominus iure naturali, quomodo et unde facta est ista rerum divisio? [This division] non est facta de iure naturali. Patet, quia ius naturale semper est idem et non variatur", Vitoria, ComST II-II 6 1 n 18 (74).

184 For a discussion of the common *dominium* in the state of innocence, see Renoux-Zagamé, *Origines théologiques*, 254–68.

185 "non esset commoda et pacifica habitatio inter illos nisi facta divisione rerum", Vitoria, ComST II-II 62 n 24 (80). Or according to Soto, "necessitas huius divisionis fuit duplex, scilicet ne orientur discordiae et ut melius colerentur agri", *Relección 'De dominio'*, § 19 (116). The point of the division was to realise the common good. Ibid.

belonged also to another.[186] Instead, the division was made by human law.[187] That it took place through *ius gentium* meant that the division was both universal and still not "necessary" in the way of natural law. Duns Scotus had argued that original sin had prompted God to withdraw natural law. Political communities, slavery and private property had then filled the ensuing vacuum. But Vitoria and Soto could not accept such a (voluntarist) view. Natural law expressed God's eternal reason and was not subject to withdrawal: humans must be able to trust God.[188] So Vitoria argued instead that while natural law remained unchanged, it did not have the character of a command (*praeceptio*) but only of a permission (*concessio*). From the fact that natural law provided for common ownership it did not follow that it prohibited the contrary.[189] By spontaneously occupying lands and conceding to others doing likewise, it had been agreed to leave everyone in possession of what they could use.[190] Drawing on Summenhart and the Parisian Jean Gerson, Vitoria speculated that the division of things could have taken place in three alternative ways: through Adam's (or Noah's) use of paternal powers; by a ruler elected and delegated to carry it out, or through an informal consensus among peoples in the course of time. He preferred the third solution.[191] The most important European political institutions – public power in the commonwealth, private power over property – had arisen as the result of a gradual process among the greater part of European peoples.[192] The agreement had not been

[186] "Non cognoscit jus naturale differentiam inter homines, quia quidquid habet unus, est alterius de jure naturali", Vitoria, ComST II-II 62 1 n 18 (75).

[187] "divisio rerum jure humano facta est", ibid., II-II 62 1 n 20 (77).

[188] "[N]am ius naturae est immutabile; quod ergo semel est ius naturae semper est ius naturae", Soto, *Relección 'De dominio'*, § 22 (124). Also Vitoria: "ius naturale semper est idem, et non variatur", ComST II-II 62 1 n 18 (74).

[189] "Concedimus ergo quod nullus fuit praeceptum quod omnia essent communia, sed solum fuit concessio", Vitoria, ComST II-II 62 1 n 20 (77). For the early canon law origins of this argument, see Brian Tierney, 'Permissive Natural Law and Property. Gratian to Kant', 62 *Journal of the History of Ideas* (2001), 384–8.

[190] "Et forte sic facta fuit, non consensu certo et formali, sed quodam consensu interpretativo, ita quod incoeperint aliqui colere certas terras et alius alias; et ex usu illarum rerum factum est ut ille esset contentus terris quas occupaverat, et alius aliis, ita quod unus non occupabat terras alterius". Vitoria, ComST II-II 62 1 n 23 (79). See also Seelmann, *Die Lehre des Vázquez de Menchaca*, 122; Decock, *Theologians and Contract Law*, 355–7.

[191] Vitoria, ComST II-II 62 1 n 21 (78).

[192] The lack of need of universal agreement, Delgado writes, may have come to Vitoria from the necessity to distance himself from the position of François I in the matter of the election of Charles V as emperor in 1519 and to argue that, as in this case, the opposition of one would not suffice to prevent such election, 'Die Zustimmung

express but tacit, taking place so that some went east and others west and took possession of lands in a manner that remained uncontested for some time. This informal consensus sufficed under *ius gentium* to create lawful *dominium.*[193]

Soto agreed. The conditions of life had degenerated during common ownership to the extent that without dividing up their properties, communities could not survive for long. The division took place through a human act under *ius gentium.*[194] To explain how mere utility could override natural law, Soto conceived part of natural law as regulating matters merely "negatively" – by not prohibiting their contrary when this might contribute to more expedient government.[195] The rule of *omnia sunt communia* would yield to the needs of peace and efficient production. The division, and hence *ius gentium*, did express a "necessity", but of a conditional kind, efficient cultivation of the fields having become possible only by first dividing them up.[196]

The argument from *ius gentium* historicised and made concrete the way natural law was applied by turning it into a justification of the institutions of contract and property without which societies could not survive.[197] Although these institutions lacked the kind of absolute necessity embodied in natural law, they had become practically imperative owing to the transformations of social life introduced by original sin: human beings could not live, or live well, without them. Soto even claimed that private property had become so obviously

des Volkes', in Grunert & Seelmann, *Die Ordnung der Praxis*, 165. On majority rule in Vitoria, see also John P. Doyle, 'Vitoria on Choosing to Replace a King', in Kevin White (ed.), *Hispanic Philosophy in the Age of Discovery* (The Catholic University of America Press 1997), 50–1.

193 "Et iste consensus sufficit ad jus gentium, quod [quia?] jus gentium certe ut plurimum constat solo isto consensu, scilicet virtuali", Vitoria, ComST II-II 62 1 n 23 (79). From here, writes Seelmann, the way to Suárez's *pactum unionis* and to the seventeenth century's (conservative) social contract constructions is short, *Theologie und Jurisprudenz*, 33–4.

194 "Prima rerum externarum divisio facta fuit iure gentium", Soto, *De iustitia et iure*, IV 3 1 (297b).

195 "Et quantum ad dominium, ius naturae nunquam praecepto inhibuit rerum divisionem, quod per contrariam legem fuerit derogatum: sed eo sensu negativo dicitur communis possessio de iure naturae, quod nunquam lex naturalis eandem praecipit divisionem, sed permisit hoc vel illo modo possideri, quo pacto diversis hominum statibus commodius esset & expeditius", ibid., IV, 3 1 (299b). See also Soto, *Relección 'De dominio'*, § 21–2 (118–26). See further Venancio D. Carro, *Domingo de Soto y el derecho de gentes* (Madrid, Del Amo 1930), 186–200.

196 Soto, *De iustitia et iure*, III, 1 3 (196–7).

197 'De iure autem gentium omnes pene contractus introducti sunt, ut emptio & venditio, locatio etc. sine quibus humana societas constare non potest", ibid., III 1 3 (197b).

necessary that to deny it was heretical.[198] This view was accepted, sometimes by minor modifications, by subsequent theologians as well. They all viewed *ius gentium* as a human law that did not possess the necessity of natural law but was nonetheless universal as it embodied the imperatives of the human condition.

## *Dominium* in the Indies

In discussing the rights of *dominium*, Salamanca scholars were greatly inspired by concerns of conscience relating to the Spanish penetration in the New World. Two events were of particular importance: the destruction by Cortés of the Aztec empire on the Yucatan in 1519–21 and Pizarro's killing of the Inca ruler Atahualpa and the consequent plundering of the Inca riches during 1531–4. These events raised the question of the justice of Spanish violence and the basis of their title over the resources of the native peoples. The Aristotelian view of the Indians as natural slaves, espoused by such high authorities as Vitoria's Paris teacher John Mair, was contradicted by the evidence of the highly organised empires of the Aztec and the Inca.[199] By that time, many Dominicans had returned from the Indies with accounts of destruction, enslavement and plunder impossible to defend under Christian ethics. The emperor himself felt pangs of conscience and his leading theologians could hardly bypass questions about the moral and legal status of the Spanish behaviour. What kind of a sin was it to kill an Indian, or to take his property?

The instructions for Columbus from the Castilian court said nothing about such matters. No serious debate had been waged on the legal basis of his voyage. Potential problems had been resolved in the Treaty of Alcáçovas and Toledo of 1479–80 where Portugal had abandoned its claims to the Canaries in exchange for Spanish consent to Portuguese trade in Africa.[200] Columbus' first voyage was intended to make contact

198 Ibid., IV 3 1 (297b).

199 See Pagden, *The Fall of Natural Man*, 38–52; Urbano, *El pensamiento*, 212–18; Dieter Janssen, 'Die Theorie der gerechten Krieges im Denken des Francisco de Vitoria', in Grunert & Seelmann, *Die Ordnung der Praxis*, 207–8.

200 For the treaty, see John Parry & Robert Keith (eds), *New Iberian World. A Documentary History of the Discovery and Settlement of Latin America to the Early 17th Century*, 5 vols (vol. I, New York, Times Books 1984), 266–71. A useful collection of documents relating to the conquest from these early treaties and papal bulls down to the Spanish legislative acts and correspondence can be found in Francisco Morales Padrón, *Teoria y leyes de la conquista* (Madrid, Ediciones cultura hispánica 1979).

with the Eastern empires and Japan for trade purposes so as to bring valuable metals to Seville.[201] As Columbus returned, Castile's title over Hispanola was derived from the *Siete partidas* that embodied the Roman law notion of islands belonging to their first occupant.[202] The famous mediation by the pope that resulted in the five letters that include the *Inter caetera* of 5 May 1493 was prompted by the Portuguese claim on the islands as part of the Azores. The line was then affirmed and adjusted by the Treaty of Tordesillas in June 1494.[203] Here territorial allocation was justified by the pope for the purpose of preaching Christianity. It was only now that conversions entered the plan and "discovery" began to be presented as continuation of the Iberian *Reconquista*. Cortés and Pizarro would make much of the crusading rhetoric, and Isabella's famous testament of November 1504 spoke of the civilisation and salvation of the Indians.[204]

Despite the idyllic depiction of native life in Columbus' first letters from Hispanola, by the time he returned to the island in 1495 his men were already enslaving natives who had rebelled against the Spanish extractions. Columbus was likely to have thought of commencing slave trade on the mode of the Portuguese when Queen Isabella put a temporary stop to it. In 1503 the first royal governor Nicolas de Ovando received the famous instructions that laid the foundations for the labour regime on the island and in subsequent mainland colonies.[205] The Indians were to be regarded as "free and not servile".

201 David Abulafia, *The Discovery of Mankind. Atlantic Encounters in the Age of Columbus* (Yale University Press 2008), 27–30.

202 Third Part, Title 28, Law 29, see e.g. Samuel Parsons Scott & Robert J. Burns (eds), *La Siete Partidas* (University of Pennsylvania Press 2012), vol. III, 828. See also Michèle Escamilla-Colin, 'La question des justes titres: repères juridiques. Des bulles Alexandrines aux Lois de Burgos', in Carmen Val Julian (ed.), *La conquète de l'Amérique espagnole et la question du droit* (Fontenay-aux-Roses, ENS 1996), 86–7. "Spain" was here to mean Castile. After Isabella's death it became largely accepted that the New World became part of Castile's *dominium*, ruled economically and politically from Castile and in its favour. See Bernal, *Monarquía e imperio*, 300–5.

203 For these documents, see Parry & Keith, *New Iberian World*, 271–80.

204 See e.g. Harald Kleinschmidt, *Charles V. The World Emperor* (Stroud, Sutton 2004), 56–60. Escamilla-Colin, 'La question des justes titres', 92–3.

205 According to the instructions Indians were to be settled in towns under supervision of "trustworthy" settlers. They were to be ruled by their caciques, subject to check by a Spanish judge. The laws were a mixture of Indian customs acceptable to Christians and Castilian laws. A new set of instructions from 1509 corrected some abuses, and the 1512 Laws of Burgos provided for inspectors (*visitadores*) to check on the treatment of the Indians. A further set of instructions from 1516 gave more detail on the Indian settlements and the jurisdiction of native chiefs and Spanish judges. However, by that time there were so few Indians left on Hispanola that

If they did not voluntarily help the Spanish, "but wander about idle", Isabella instructed her governor to:

> compel and force the Indians to associate with the Christians on the island and to work on their buildings, and to gather and mine the gold and other minerals, and to till the fields and produce food for the Christian inhabitants ... and you are to have each one paid on the day he works and the wages and maintenance which you think he should have.[206]

By the time of the queen's death (1504), forced labour had been legitimised and slavery was available at least as punishment. Although on paper this resembled European serfdom in practice it was much more severe as it was implemented far from the control of central government across what was seen as a racial and religious boundary. As the number of Indians kept decreasing, Ferdinand, who anyway had much less scruples about the matter than the deceased queen, authorised the kidnapping of "idle" Indians from Bahamas to fill the workforce in the mines. By this time, a series of *cedulas* set up the notorious *encomienda* system of government and tribute-raising reserved for peaceful Indians. Under it, the power to collect the tribute that the king expected of his new vassals – the Indians – was delegated to the *encomenderos* by distributing (*repartimiento*) to them Indians on large stretches of land, including towns and villages. Much of the tribute/tax was converted into work service in accordance with ratios decided by the royal representative – the local judge (*corregidor*), mayor, governor or the viceroy.[207] The Indians would be granted initially for two to three-year periods but eventually for a whole lifetime of the *encomendero* and even for a second generation.[208] Under Castilian laws,

these instructions remained practically insignificant. Woodrow Borah, *Justice by Insurance. The General Indian Court of Colonial Mexico and the Legal Aides of the Half-Real* (University of California Press 1983), 19–24.

206 Lesley Byrd Simpson, *The Encomienda in New Spain. The Beginning of Spanish Mexico* (University of California Press 1982), 8.

207 The numbers to be received by each *encomendero* would depend on his rank. At one point Diego Columbus was to allocate "a hundred to royal officers and alcaldes, sixty to the married hidalgo who should bring his wife to the Indies, thirty to the simple farmer. Any surplus or deficit of Indians was to apportioned among the colonists at the same rate. The *encomenderos* were to pay the Crown a gold peso a head per annum for all the Indians in their service, and they were to be held responsible for their religious instruction." Simpson, *Encomienda*, 22. Nothing caused as much dispute and discontent as the distribution of the Indians, those having received less invariably feeling having been wrongly treated.

208 The question of succession rights to *encomiendas* was a matter of constant pleading. Because it was understood as a personal grant of the king, it was initially not

assumed applicable also in the Indies, this was a feudal arrangement establishing a personal relation between the Spaniard and the Indian: the *encomendero* was to see to the welfare of those in his charge and the latter were to work for him.[209] The *encomienda* was inalienable; it could not be bought, sold or rented. The land would belong to the king and its product to the conquistador–coloniser invited to use it to procure the tribute to the king and to see to his own profit.[210] This turned nearly all Spaniards into *hidalgos* to whom the Indians were obliged to pay personal service. Efforts at the Castilian end to control the implementation of its detailed instructions proved useless, no doubt because if they *had* been implemented, that would have destroyed the colonies' economic base and forced the Spaniards to return to Castile – an argument that over again persuaded the viceroys to give in to the demands of the *encomenderos*.

The urgency with the matter felt by the Dominicans was reflected in the rapidity and explicit nature of their reaction to depopulation in the Caribbean.[211] Father Montesinos produced his famous vindictive against the treatment of the native inhabitants from the pulpit in Santo Domingo to shocked members of his congregation on Advent Sunday in 1511 – well before Cortés had travelled to the mainland – and participated with other members of his order in the preparation of

understood as hereditary. But as *encomiendas* continued in practice, this was rationalised as a royal grant as if it had been received directly from the king. Marta Herrera Ortiz, 'La encomienda Indiana y sus repercusiones', in *Derechos contemporáneos de los pueblos indios. Justicia y derechos étnicos en México* (Universidad Nacional Autónoma de México 1992), 133.

209 See e.g. Simpson, *Encomienda*, xiii; Ortiz, 'La encomienda Indiana y sus repercusiones', 132–7; Borah, *Justice by Insurance*, 18–20 and passim; Hugh Thomas, *The Golden Empire. Spain, Charles V and the Creation of America* (New York, Random House 2010), 12–13.

210 Ortiz, 'La encomienda Indiana y sus repercusiones', 135.

211 Las Casas estimated that approximately 3 million Indians died in the first twenty years after 1492, while the conquest was still almost completely confined within the Caribbean. These numbers have been the subject of wide debate. David M. Traboulay gives the decline of population on Hispanola between 1496 and 1570 as having been from 3,770,000 to 125, while "a similar human catastrophe occurred in Puerto Rico, Jamaica and Cuba". The decline in Mexico in the sixteenth century would have been from 25 million to 1 million and in Peru from 32 million in 1520 to 5 million in 1548. See *Columbus and Las Casas. The Conquest and Christianization of America 1492–1566* (University Press of America, 1994), 55–7. The use of these and other numbers as part of the polemic over the "Leyenda negra" is discussed in Joseph Pérez, *La leyenda negra* (Madrid, Gadir 2009), 104–17. See also Pereña, *La idea de justicia*, 15–30.

the Laws of Burgos a year later.[212] Initially, Ferdinand had reacted to the sermon by writing to the provincial of the order, Alonso García de Loaysa, to end such sedition and referred to the papal donation as the legal basis for Spanish right. He also began the preparation of the first laws on the New World and the formal instructions to direct the *conquistadores*.[213] This was based on the Palacios Rubios study of 1513 that actually gave a rather sympathetic depiction of Indian life and society, pointing out the rationality of the Indians and their ability to adopt a monotheistic religion.[214] The study was written as a legal examination of *dominium* in its form as private property and jurisdiction. Palacios Rubios made three points. First, there was no right to wage war on peaceful Indians, to take their property or to enslave them without a lawful cause. The fact that the Indians were infidels did not deprive them of their right of property, given by God to all rational beings. If the Spanish tried without a cause to deprive the Indians of their goods, then the Indians had the right to wage just war against them and even enslave the Spaniards that they had caught.[215] Second, as for the right of jurisdiction of the Indian caciques, Palacios Rubios accepted the old view that even the power of temporal princes derived from a grant by the church.[216] Up to the time of the Spanish arrival, however, the church had consented "tacitly and weakly" to the government of infidel princes. If evangelisation required it, the church could withdraw this consent either wholly or in part.[217] This is what the pope

[212] See e.g. Lewis Hanke, *The Spanish Struggle for Justice in the Conquest of America* (with a new Introduction by Susan Scafidi & Peter Bakewell, Southern Methodist University Press 2002), 23–30; Pereña, *La idea de justicia*, 32–5; Simpson, *Encomienda*, 29–38.

[213] The *junta* that prepared the laws was divided between two interpretations of the situation: the Dominicans argued for the independence of Indian communities under *ius gentium*, while the legalist–royalist faction favoured a biblical view in which supreme power would lie with the Spanish king. The *junta* concluded that Spain ought to rule over them owing to their idolatrous practices, if necessary by waging war. Escamilla-Colin, 'La question des justes titres', 97.

[214] Palacios Rubios, *De las Islas del mar Océano*, 9–11. For their salvation, however, baptism was of course needed. Ibid., 12.

[215] Ibid., 45.

[216] Government over humans was originally transferred from God to Noah and his descendants. With the birth of Christ, all power was concentrated in him, and he transferred this to his representative, Peter and his successors, "From which it follows that the Pope holds supreme power over the whole universe and that every creature is subject to his as the source of law and the vicar of the Creator", ibid., 70–107, 100.

[217] Ibid., 111.

had done by the grant of 1493. Ergo, the king of Spain had *dominium iurisdictionis* over the Indians. Third, this did not mean that the Spanish could immediately wage war on Indians. They had first to explain the bases of the Christian faith, and the power of the church over the whole world. If the Indians then converted, the powers of the caciques would be reinstated. But if they refused to listen and did not, after having been given a reasonable time to reflect, allow the Spanish to enter their lands (only for the purpose of preaching), then just war could be waged on them, they could be enslaved and their property taken.[218]

This was the basis for the infamous *Requerimiento* that was to be read to the Indians before any violence could be exercised against them. It founded Spanish title on the view propounded by Innocent IV and the canon lawyer Hostiensis, to whom Palacios Rubios made constant reference.[219]It began by stating that as the creator of the world God had granted the right of ruling humans to the pope who, again, had duly passed these rights on to the rulers of Castile and Aragon in order to convert the Indians.[220] All kinds of benefits would flow to the Indians once they would permit the Spanish to enter their territories. Against eventual resistance, however, severe consequences were threatened:

> But if you do not do this, and maliciously make delay in it, I certify to you that, with the help of God, we shall powerfully enter into your country, and we shall make war against you in all ways and manners that we can, and subject you to the yoke and obedience of the Church and of their Highnesses; we shall take you and your wives and your children and make slaves of them, and as such shall sell and dispose of them as their Highnesses may command; and we shall take away your goods, and shall do you all the mischief and damage that we can, as to vassals who do not obey.[221]

[218] Ibid., 36, 37.

[219] Jörg Fisch, *Europäische Expansion und das Völkerrecht. Die Auseinandersetzungen um den Status der überseeischen Gebiete vom 15. Jahrhundert bis zur Gegenwart* (Stuttgart, Steiner 1984), 187–93.

[220] The story of the composition and use of the *Requerimiento* has been told in many places. See Patricia Seed, *Ceremonies of Possession in Europe's Conquest of the New World 1492–1640* (Cambridge University Press 1995), 69–99; Hanke, *Spanish Struggle for Justice*, 31–41; Pereña, *La idea de justicia*, 31–44; Urbano, *El pensamiento*, 208–32 (on all the debates from 1492 to the *Requerimiento*).

[221] The Requirement, reproduced in Padron, *Teoria y leyes de la conquista*, 338–40 and in English in Parry & Keith, *New Iberian World*, 290. The Spanish text is available also in Pereña, *La idea de justicia*, 237–9. Neither the *Requerimiento* nor the study by Palacios Rubios accepted the theory of natural slavery (instead, they threatened slavery as a sanction for refusing to hear evangelisation). The *Requerimiento* resembled the ritual demand of submission in Islamic *jihad* and had been adopted by the Spaniards and used already in the *reconquista*. All of these events (as well as the

The 35 articles of the Laws of Burgos (1512) were prefaced by a text highlighting the idleness of the Indians and the need to separate them from their pagan ways. The result of imposing forced labour on the Indians in the gold mines was veiled by abstract exhortations about teaching the gospel and Spanish mores (monogamy, clothing. . .) to the Indians.[222] Indians were to be relocated close to the Spanish to whom they were granted as a labour force. Whatever concerns may have motivated the laws, in practice they turned into "a cold-bloodied sanctioning of current methods of exploitation of the Indians".[223] No amount of effort from Castile helped to prevent the paid (though compulsory) work from degenerating into actual enslavement. On the contrary, as long as the system had an aspect of temporariness, the settlers had a strong interest to extract everything they could from the native population.

Throughout the early sixteenth century, the legal situation remained unclear. Most crown jurists held that Castilian laws were to be applied in full while the Dominicans favoured respecting native institutions. The official view opted for a mixture under which "the good usages and customs of the Indians [were to be respected] insofar as they are not contrary to Christian religion". In practice, this led to the disappearence of indigenous political structures but opened some avenues to challenge settler actions in Spanish *audiencas*.[224] When Las Casas produced in 1542 a long list of *Remedios*, Charles finally decided to abolish the *encomiendas*.[225] The argument was presented in a cleverly royalist garb, making the analogy to the experience of noble lords' oppression of free peasants, the king's free subjects.[226] The "new laws" (*Nuevas leyes*) of 1542–3 reorganised the Council of the Indies and declared the Indians free owners of their property, masters of their communities. They were to choose freely their place of residence and their political leaders. The *encomienda* system was to be gradually

expulsion of the Jews of 1492) were discussed to support Palacios Rubios' view on Spanish *dominium*. See further, Seed, *Ceremonies of Possession*, 69–99.

222 For the content of the 1512 Laws, see Padron, *Teoria y leyes de la conquista*, 311–26.

223 Simpson, *Encomienda*, 31.

224 For a useful review of the treatment of civil, criminal and administrative cases from New Spain in 1519–85, leading up to a sense of failure in integrating the indigenous population in Spanish laws and widescale reforms in the early seventeenth century, see Borah, *Justice by Insurance*, 37–78.

225 Simpson, *Encomienda*, 54, 128.

226 See Silvio Zavala, 'La encomienda indiana', 2 *El trimestre económico* (1935), 423–31; Ortiz, 'La encomienda Indiana y sus repercusiones', 135–7.

extinguished.[227] Public representatives of the crown, *corregidores*, would supervise this process.[228]

The settlers reacted immediately and violently, and the laws were never put into effect. As the debate continued, the emperor invited a group of fourteen theologians and lawyers, including Soto and Vitoria's successor Melchior Cano, to participate in the famous *junta* of 1550–1 that was supposed to "discuss the most convenient way in which the conquests, discoveries and settlements are to be made in an orderly way and in accordance with justice and reason".[229] For this pupose, it was to hear Las Casas and the humanist scholar and imperial cartographer Juan Gines de Sepúlveda (1489–1573) who had adopted the thesis of the Indians' natural slavery to defend colonisation in his *Democrates secundus sive de justis causis bellis apud Indos* (1541).[230] That question was

227 Zavala, 'El encomienda indiana', 434. For the content of the 1542 laws and the related imperial order of 1543, including an analysis of their amendments before the laws of 1573 prohibited further conquests, see Luciano Pereña, 'La intervención de España en America', in Juan de la Peña, *De bello contra insulanos. Intervencion de España en America* (Madrid, Consejo superior de investigaciones cientificas 1982), 33–41 and 104–27 (where he reads these "utopian" laws as a real "Declaración doctrinal de los derechos humanos") and Pereña, *La idea de justicia*, 163–77. The laws are also available in Padron, *Teoria y leyes de la conquista*, 428–46. For an English version, see Parry & Keith, *New Iberian World*, 348–59. For a history and analysis of the laws and their (marginal) effect, see Simpson, *Encomienda*, 123–44.

228 These had already been appointed during the first *Audiencia* in the 1530s but had remained largely ineffectual. Simpson, *Encomienda*, 85–8.

229 Translation from Nestor Capdevila, 'Impérialisme, empire et destruction', in Bartolomé de Las Casas, *La controverse entre Las Casas et Sepúlveda* (Paris, Vrin 2007), 133. The *junta* was composed of members of the Council of the Indies, a representative from the Council of Castile and the Council of Orders plus four theologians (Dominicans Soto, Cano and Carranza and the Franciscan Arévalo). Ibid., 134 n 1.

230 Sepúlveda's work built on the theory of natural slavery discussed in Aristotle, 'The Politics', in S. Everton (ed.), *The Politics and The Constitution of Athens* (Cambridge University Press 1996) § 5–7 (16–18). Sepúlveda made four arguments to defend the submission of Indians by war if necessary: (1) they are natural slaves; (2) they engage in abominable sins; (3) natural law provides for a duty to protect the innocent victims of cannibalism and human sacrifice, and (4) this is necessitated to prepare evangelisation. See Pagden, *The Fall of Natural Man*, 109–18; Michael Sievernich, 'Toleranz und Kommunikation. Das Recht auf Mission bei Francisco de Vitoria', in Grunert & Seelmann, *Die Ordnung der Praxis*, 186–9; Pereña, *Misión de España en América*, 10–19. Soto was the chairman–rapporteur of the committee and his report of the debate – the only source we have of it – is included e.g. in Juan de la Peña, *De bello contra insulanos*, 509–37. For a good account of the background of the 1550 debate, and the texts of the report by Soto, the "Objections" by Sepúlveda and the "Apologia" by Las Casas, see Bartolomé de Las Casas, *La controverse entre Las Casas et Sepúlveda* (Paris, Vrin 2007 [1552]). For the discussion of the concerns of conscience in 1548–50 that led to the Valladolid debate, see Pereña, 'La intervención', 44–59.

left formally unresolved but the weight of the opinion rejected the theory of natural slavery, and Las Casas succeeded in preventing the publication of the treatise. The *junta* failed to provide clear instruction on how colonisation would be "conveniently" carried out, and the Council of Castile continued its efforts to regulate the actions of the settlers, eventually in 1573 prohibiting the use of the term "conquest" by which time there was anyway little left to conquer. The euphoria was over.[231] Eldorado had not been found and the experience of evangelisation had not been encouraging. Spain's attention was increasingly taken up by events in Europe and the colonists, and the church were left relatively free to pursue their mixed objectives in the New World.

## The Salamanca Reaction

Neither Vitoria nor Soto ever visited the Indies. Their information was received from Dominican clergymen – Montesinos among them – who had been present in Hispanola since 1510 and from soldiers and clerics who returned to Spain sometimes heavily burdened in their conscience about the events they had witnessed.[232] These men flocked to the Convent of St Esteban in Salamanca and in confession narrated facts to which existing instructions on penance and absolution had little to say. Vitoria's first public reaction to the conquest appears in the letter to his friend Miguel de Arcos of 8 November 1534.[233] He then included a discussion of the Indian question in his lectures on the *Summa* of 1534–5.[234] In two famous *relectiones* in 1538[9] and 1539 Vitoria vigorously disagreed with the view of Indians as natural slaves, arguing that they enjoyed rightful *dominium* both in the sense of jurisdiction and property. War against them could be waged only in case they caused injury to Spaniards.[235] Soto had addressed that issue already in 1535,

231 Padron, *Teoria y leyes de la conquista*, 489–518. For the 1573 *Ordenanzas*, including a discussion of the significance of giving up the expression "conquest", see Capdevila, 'Impérialisme, empire, destruction', 139–43.

232 Delgado, *Pensamiento humanista*, 43–4.

233 Pereña, *La idea de justicia*, 87–9 and Vitoria, *Political Writings*, 331–3. See also Belda Plans, *La escuela de Salamanca*, 381–2.

234 Vitoria, ComST II-II 62 1 n 28 (81).

235 Vitoria, 'On the American Indians', 1 § 4–24 (239–51). Vitoria was encouraged to give his lectures of 1538 and 1539 by the dispatch by Pope Paul III of his *Sublimis deus* in 1537, which defended the freedom of the Indians and their right of property. See Sievernich, 'Toleranz und Kommunikation', 184. According to Deckers, Vitoria refrained from treating the issue earlier because he feared engaging in heresy. *Gerechtigkeit*, 227–8.

even before Pizarro's ships had arrived in Seville. He, too, argued that Indian communities should be treated like any other human communities. Neither one of the Dominicans was adopting a position that by any stretch of imagination could be called radical. It had already underlain Isabella's testament and was authoritatively reaffirmed in the bull *Sublimis Deus* by Pope Paul III in 1537.[236] It is true, Soto wrote, that the Spanish had received from the pope the authority to preach the gospel – but he could see no justification for subordinating the Indians or depriving them of their possessions.[237] The denial of the pope's and the emperor's universal lordship resulted from the Salamanca scholars' view of the political community as a creation of human beings who came together using their freedom, their *dominium in se*, to attain earthly happiness under organised government. Because they received this view from natural law it was available to defend both the political jurisdiction of pagan rulers as well as the rights of ownership of the infidel. The view of dominium as a result of grace was uniformly rejected as heretical. After all, "[o]therwise David would have lost his excellent kingship on the basis of his well-known adultery and killing of Uriah".[238]

But the theologians never regarded non-believers as equal to Christians. They divided pagans into three classes. There were those who were *de jure* but not *de facto* under Christian rule, especially the "Saracens" occupying lands thought to have belonged to Christians. Then there were those who were under such rule both *de jure* and *de facto*, and that included the Moors and Jews still in Spain. And finally there were those who were nether *de jure* nor *de facto* under Christian

[236] The latter begins by affirming that the faith should be brought to the Indians and continues that "the … Indians and all other people who may later be discovered by Christians, are by no means to be deprived of their liberty and the possession of their property; nor should they be in any way enslaved, should the contrary happen, it shall be null and of no effect". *Sublimis Deus*, reproduced in Parry & Keith, *New Iberian World*, 387.

[237] "… sed accipere ultra hoc bona illorum aut subiicere imperio nostro, non video unde habeamus tale ius". Soto, *Relección 'De dominio'*, § 34 (165). On these early reactions, including a discussion of the lecture by Vitoria's eventual successor, Melchior Cano of 1546, see also David A. Lupher, *Romans in a New World. Classical Models in Sixteenth-Century Spanish America* (University of Michigan Press 2016), 43–102; Luciano Pereña, 'La intervención de Espana en America', in Juan de la Peña, *De bello contra insulanos. Intervencion de España en America* (L. Pereña et al. eds, Madrid, Consejo superior de investigaciones cientificas 1982), 21–33.

[238] Azpilcueta, 'Notabile III in Relectio Cap. Novit. De Iudic', § 60 (126); Vitoria, 'On the American Indians', 1 2 § 5–6 (240–3). The view of *dominium* as a result of grace had already been condemned by the Council of Constance (1414–16) and led to the execution as heretics of John Wyclif and Johan Hus.

jurisdiction, including the Turks living in the Ottoman empire and the Indians of the New World. All agreed that there was a clear right to wage war in relation to the first group.[239] No such right existed towards the Indians in the third group, however: they had never been under Spanish jurisdiction and had done no harm to the Spanish. As human beings, they had been created by God and enjoyed *dominium* just like the Spanish. This did not imply cultural equality, however, and in practice the vocabulary of barbarism took away much that was granted by the denial of Indians' natural slavery.[240]

In his lectures on the *Secunda secundae* in 1534–5 Vitoria had drawn the unequivocal consequence from the natural law of *dominium* that "Christians may not occupy infidel lands inasmuch as it is the infidel, and not Christians, who are their true owners".[241] Because infidels were, by natural law, legitimate rulers over their territories, there was no other basis on which Christians may deprive them of such than by agreement or by command of the (infidel) prince.[242] As he provocatively put it, the Spanish have no better right over Indian *dominium* than Saracens had over Christian lands in Africa.[243] In the *Relectio* on the Indians Vitoria expanded on this point. Neither sin nor unbelief destroyed the right of *dominium*. After all, the Bible treated evil sinners like Solomon, Ahab and unbelievers such as Sennacherib, Pharaoh and others as "kings".[244] An admirer of the cultures of Greece and Rome, Vitoria could hardly argue that mere paganism was an obstacle to lawful authority.[245] He then went through five arguments that had been made to deny Indian *dominium*. It had been claimed that they were

239 This threefold distinction was included in Cajetan's Commentary to the *Summa* (ST II-II 66 8) to which Vitoria refers in 'On the American Indians', 1 3 § 19 (246). See also Dominique de Courcelles, 'Pensée théologique et événement. Droit de conquête et droit des gens de l'Empire espagnole du XVIe siècle', in Carmen Val Julian, *La conquête de l'Amérique espagnole et la question du droit* (Lyon, ENS-LSH Editions 2002), 22; Deckers, *Gerechtigkeit*, 220–1.

240 The term "barbarian", with its classical roots, was not part of the initial vocabulary of the conquest but emerged slowly and in response to the demise of the theory of natural slavery. Its usefulness lay in connoting cultural hierarchy that could not be pinned down to any specific elements and was handy whenever a justificatory language was needed. See Urbano, *Francisco de Vitoria*, 232–43 and Pagden, *The Fall of Natural Man*, 15–26 and 97–106 (Vitoria), 126–45 (Las Casas).

241 "christiani non possunt occupare terras infideliorum, si illi infidels sint veri domini illarum, et non sint christianorum", Vitoria, ComST II-II 62 1 n 28 (81).

242 "vel voluntate possidentis, vel auctoritate principis", ibid., II-II 62 1 n 27 (81).

243 Ibid., II-II 62 1 n 27 (81).

244 Vitoria, 'On the American Indians', 1 2 and 3 § 5 and § 7 (242, 244).

245 Urbano, *El pensamiento*, 139–40.

slaves by nature, or that they could not have *dominium* because they were "either sinners (*peccatores*), unbelievers (infidels), madmen (*amentes*) or insensate (*insensate*)".[246] On each point, Vitoria gave a negative answer, either because the presumption of the argument was wrong (sinners and infidels may in fact have *dominium*) or because they did not apply to the Indians (they were neither madmen, insensate nor slaves).[247] In an important passage, Vitoria reminded his audience what it meant to be human, namely to have mastery, *dominium*, over one's actions, to decide freely what to do or how to behave in regard to an object, including whether or not to use it.[248]

It was clear then, according to Vitoria, "that the Spaniards, when they first sailed to the land of the barbarians, carried with them no right at all to occupy their countries".[249] But this was not the end of the matter. The right of *dominium* reflected the virtue of justice between equals that was administered through the *ius gentium*. This entitled the Spanish to travel to the New World, to "trade among the barbarians, so long as they do no harm to their homeland", to use things held in common and to take things that did not belong to anybody (*res nullius*).[250] Most importantly, relations of justice, unlike relations of charity, were accompanied by means of coercion so that "if the barbarians attempt to deny the Spaniards in these matters [i.e. if they violate the rights that under *ius gentium* belong to the Spaniards], then the latter may ultimately wage just war against them".[251] Just retaliation was available also if native inhabitants prevented the Spanish from preaching, if converted Indians were under threat or if it seemed expedient for the Christian faith to give the Indians a Christian ruler.[252] The theologians and jurists also accepted that just war was available in defence of the innocent, especially to uproot human sacrifice, as well as to ally with a barbarian community waging a just war.[253] In practice, both reasons had been amply used by Cortés in his attacks on the native communities on the mainland. Not least of the incentives was that just war was accompanied by a right to punish the defeated party not only by

246 Vitoria, 'On the American Indians', 1 1 § 5 (240).
247 See also Tierney, *The Idea of Natural Rights*, 266–71.
248 Vitoria, 'On the American Indians', 1, 4 § 19 (248). On the latter point, see Seelmann, *Die Lehre des Vázquez de Menchaca*, 76–7.
249 Vitoria, 'On the American Indians', 2 2 § 30 (264).
250 Ibid., 3 1 § 3 (279).
251 Ibid., 3 1 § 6 (281).
252 Ibid., 3 1 § 14 (287).
253 Ibid., 2 3 § 15 and 17 (287–90).

depriving it from *dominium* but also by enslaving its fighters – a practice especially appreciated by the *encomenderos*.[254]

The determination with which Vitoria and his followers rejected the view that either the pope or the emperor would have universal *dominium* accounts for the nationalist cult of Vitoria.[255] It contrasts sharply with the breadth of their acceptance of Spanish violence in retaliation for Indian efforts to prevent preaching of the gospel or obstruct Spanish trade or travel. Moreover, to critique imperial claims was rather pointless – the imperial theme in the court of Charles was marginal and concerned the resuscitation of "Rome", not power over the Indians. Even as the view of Indians as natural slaves was predominantly, though never uniformly, given up, paternalist attitudes upheld the absolute intellectual and cultural supremacy of the Spanish. Vitoria, too, accepted that Indians may be "foolish and slow-witted" and although they cannot be counted as slaves, he nevertheless speculated on a possible title the Spanish might have because the Indians were "so close to being mad, that they are unsuited to setting up or administering a commonwealth".[256] The ambivalence was reflected in the contrast between Spanish legislation in books and on the ground. An important role was played by the Dominicans and the Jesuits in drafting legislation to relieve the plight of the Indians. But much of this remained hostage to the administrative practice of "*obedezco pero non cumplo*" ("I obey but do not comply").[257] There may not have been an intent to exterminate the Indians, but the conditions of labour, coupled with the European diseases, destroyed the native communities no less surely.

No doubt, it took some courage to engage critically with the policy of the emperor. Charles once wrote to the prior of the Convent of St Esteban, Soto at the time, ordering him to prohibit the members of the order from dealing with the conquest and to destroy any texts where they had done so.[258] This neither significantly tempered the Dominicans' campaign nor occasioned a serious breach between them

[254] For the standard point about the right to enslave the vanquished (infidel) in just war, see e.g. Soto, *Relección 'De dominio'*, § 25 (132–4).

[255] See now extensively, Ignacio de la Rasilla del Moral, *In the Shadow of Vitoria. A History of International Law in Spain (1770–1953)* (Leiden, Brill 2017).

[256] Vitoria, 'On the American Indians', 1 6 § 23 (250) and 3 8 § 18 (290).

[257] Henry Kamen, *Spain 1469–1714. A Society of Conflict* (2nd edn, London, Longman 1996), 160.

[258] Jean-Francois Courtine, 'Vitoria, Suarez et la naissance du droit de nature moderne', in Alain Renaut (ed.), *Naissances de modernité. 2 Histoire de la philosophie politique* (Paris, Calmann-Lévy 1999), 128; Delgado, *Pensamiento humanista*, 42–3.

and their emperor. Two years later Vitoria was again advising Charles on Indian conversions in Mexico, a matter that had been raised by the archbishop of Mexico, the Franciscan Juan de Zumárraga (1468–1548), known like Las Casas as a protector of the Indians.[259] Vitoria never expressed any real doubt about the justice of Spanish presence in the Indies and fully accepted the pope's authority to grant them monopoly rights for preaching the gospel.[260] His arguments were also ideologically useful for the crown. Covering native peoples within a universal system of law of which the Spanish were the authoritative interpreters automatically subordinated them to the imperatives of colonisation.[261] Nor was there any reciprocity. It would have been impossible for Vitoria to suggest that the Indians could propagate their religious or cultural practices on the same basis as the Christians. The Laws of Burgos and subsequent legislation foresaw a system of trusteeship or a protectorate without slavery whose objective was nevertheless uprooting Indian "barbarism".[262] Much was made of the mostly mythical tales of Indian cannibalism.[263] Even Las Casas, who refused to being scandalised over such practices, never doubted the justice of converting the Indians into the Christian faith.

The open-endedness of Vitoria's argumentation about *ius gentium*, especially as it related to the definition of injury to Spanish *dominium*-rights, and hence his theory of just war, did not escape the attention of later Spaniards. Soto, for example, narrowed the criteria for just appropriation by excluding property held in common by Indian tribes, and Cano, Covarrubias and Molina pointed to the dangers in a wide understanding of the *ius gentium*-based right of travel. There would be increasing insistence that conversions had to take place by Indian consent.[264] Some writers, such as the Dominican Juan de La Peña (1513–65), advocated the view that the Spanish ought simply leave the Indies and compensate any damage caused, leaving only priests to carry out evangelisation and small numbers of soldiers to protect

[259] Pereña, *La idea de justicia*, 90–2; Pereña, *La escuela de Salamanca. Proceso a la conquista de América* (Salamanca, Caja de Ahorros y Monte de Piedad 1986), 29–30.

[260] Vitoria, 'On the American Indians', 3 2 § 10 (284) and Pereña, 'La tesis de paz dinámica', 50–1.

[261] Robert A. Williams, *The American Indian in Western Legal Thought. The Discourses of Conquest* (Oxford University Press 1990), 107; Antony Anghie, *Sovereignty, Imperialism and the Making of International Law* (Cambridge University Press 2005), 13–37.

[262] Pereña, *La idea de justicia*, 187–233, 279–98.

[263] But see Abulafia, *The Discovery of Mankind*, 126–30.

[264] Pereña, *La idea de justicia*, 129–31.

them.[265] This was of course out of the question, as pointed out by the jurist Juan de Matienzo, member of the *Audiencia* of Mexico in a report to the king in 1561. Even as a more Realpolitik type of justification for Spanish presence would be later received from occupation and prescription, the principal justification continued to invoke cultural and religious difference, the need of exercising jurisdiction over the Indians so as to see to their education and spiritual welfare.[266]

Towards the end of the sixteenth century voices were heard among theologians about the original illegality of the conquest. For example, the Augustinian Alonso de Veracruz (1507–84), professor of theology at the University of Mexico, claimed from 1554 onwards that the Indians had been in rightful possession of their property and the Spanish had arrived as aggressors.[267] The Dominican Domingo de Salazar (1512–94), the first bishop of Manila, took note in 1583 of the "condemnation by nearly all writers in Spain and even in the Indies, the conquests that have been committed against the Indians".[268] Together with many others, the Jesuit Molina stressed the dangers to which unfettered individual rights of travel and appropriation of things not taken into active use by the Spanish might lead and sometimes advocated the right of the (indigenous) community to decide for itself how its resources ought to be used.[269] Most Spanish publicists in the latter part of the century seemed to agree that the legality of the conquest had been vitiated by the way it had been carried out.[270] But this did not lead them to condemn the continued presence of the Spanish in the Indies. The lawyer Solórzano Pereira (1575–1655) and the Jesuit José de Acosta conceded that even though the conquest had been illegal and wrong, there was no turning back – to whom would Indian properties

265 This is well described in Anthony Pagden, 'Dispossessing the Barbarian. The Language of Spanish Thomism and the Debate over the Property Rights of the American Indians', in Anthony Pagden (ed.), The *Languages of Political Theory in Early-Modern Europe* (Cambridge University Press 1987), 79–98.

266 On the final "pacification", see Pereña, *La idea de justicia*, 221–33.

267 Alonso de Veracruz, *De iusto bello contra indios* (Edición critiqua bilingue, Madrid, Consejo superior de investigaciones cientificas 1997), VI 1 (268–73).

268 Pedro Borges, 'Proceso a las guerras de conquista', in Juan de la Peña, *De bello contra insulanois, CHP vol. X* (Madrid, Consejo superior der investigaciones cientificas 1982), 24.

269 See Frank B. Costello, *The Political Philosophy of Luis de Molina (1535–1600)* (Roma Inst. Historium 1974), 128–32.

270 For a review of positions in Spain, Mexico and Peru during 1560–85, see Borges, 'Proceso a las guerras de conquista', 17–66.

be restored?[271] It remained necessary to continue conversions, to protect the innocent and to prevent the Indians from falling back on their barbarian ways – something Carranza assumed would take between sixteen and eighteen years.[272] Having condemned the past Spanish practices, Veracruz still regarded it as a just cause of war if the Indians prevented Spanish commerce: *iure gentium ubique licita est negotiatio. Ergo nullo modo possunt hispani ab ea prohiberi.*[273] It was fine for the Spanish to extract gold and other minerals from the territory; they were common to all humans under the law of nature and equally available for the Indians and the Spanish.[274]

## No Universal *Dominium*

Conquest gave the Salamanca scholars an opportunity to specify the basis and limits of the *dominium iurisdictionis*. The ruler of Castile and king of Spain had, since 1519, been titled "emperor". It is not clear how Charles V himself understood his position. The imperial advocacy of his influential Italian chancellor Gattinara was limited to hegemony in Europe and victory over the Turks. The capture of France's François I at the battle of Pavia (1529) did inspire the chancellor to speculate, for a moment, about the restitution of empire to its former glory. But he never saw the Indies as more than a sidewhow, at best a source for resources to fight the Sultan. By contrast, some of the men involved in the conquest let their imagination run higher. Cortés, for example, wrote to Charles in 1520 that he would no longer have to trade for spices but would "own them as property while the natives of these islands would recognise him as their king and natural Lord".[275] But Cortés had acted privately and on impulse; no imperial assignment had been given to him.

It was not hard for the Salamanca scholars to condemn "empire" as a basis for Spanish rights – no such claim had officially been made.

[271] See Capdevila, 'Impérialisme, empire et destruction', 131–2.

[272] Bartolomé de Carranza, 'Ratione fidei potest Caesar debellare et tenere Indios novi orbis?', in Luciano Pereña (ed.), *Misión de España en América* (Madrid, Consejo superior de investigaciones científicas 1956), 42–3. See also Pereña, 'La intervención', 32, 130–4.

[273] Alonso de Veracruz, *De iusto bello contra indios*, Conclusion 13 (330/331). But if the merchants then turn out to be robbers or extortionists, the Indians may justly turn against them in self-defence. Ibid. (332/333).

[274] Ibid., Conclusion 14 (332/333).

[275] Cortés to Charles V on 30 October 1520, quoted in Capdevila, 'Impérialisme, empire et destruction', 50.

But imperial speculations gave them a basis on which to craft their own view of royal power as an emanation of the authority of the commonwealth. In his early lecture on *dominium*, Soto made five arguments to deny universal jurisdiction. First, no such jurisdiction could be derived from divine, natural or human law. On the contrary, by natural law nobody was *dominus* over another. Second, if such power had come from natural law, then it would have always existed – but nobody had claimed it before the Romans. Third, authority to rule existed to be used. But because nobody was in a position to rule the whole world, the very idea had no basis in reality. And "God and nature never do anything in vain".[276] Fourth, by natural law a ruler's jurisdiction was recived from the community. But there had never been a moment in which all peoples (or the best part of them) would have decided to join under a world emperor.[277] Fifth, the old view that God might have given universal lordship to the Romans was completely fictitious. The Romans had never ruled the whole world. They were only one in a series of ambitious past powers, no more and no less virtuous that those others. "No-one can doubt that their [Romans'] right relied principally on their arms and that they exercised their domination over intimidated populations more by power than by justice."[278] Finally, Soto agreed with Vitoria that the pope had no temporal power over the world. Even Christ had never claimed such power. But even if he had claimed it, it would not necessarily have devolved to the pope.[279]

The canon lawyers agreed. No universal power was derivable from divine, natural or human law. As Azpilcueta argued in a long and convoluted public lecture in 1548, the claim by Bartolus that it was heretical not to recognise the emperor as *Dominus mundi* had no religious support whatsoever.[280] Nothing of the kind could be found from Scripture and never had any emperor actually ruled over the whole world. In any case, Innocent III had recognised the independence of the

276 "Sed Deus et natura nihil faciunt frustra", Soto, *Releccion 'De dominio'*, § 29 (146).

277 Soto, *Relección 'De dominio'*, § 29 (146) and *De iustitia et iure,* IV 4 2 (304).

278 "nemo potest quin ius potissimum habuerint in armis, atq; adeo potentatu potius quam iure perterritas gentes suppeditaverunt", Soto, *De iustitia et iure,* IV 4 2 (306a).

279 Soto, *Relección 'De dominio'*, §33 (158–63) and *De iustitia et iure,* IV 4 1 (300a–301b).

280 Azpilcueta, 'Notabile III in Relectio Cap. Novit. De Iudic', nn 42–51 (122–4). Azpilcueta engaged in great detail in the demonstration of the non-existence of emperor's universal power, nn 41–79 (122–30). See also the discussion in José Corriente Córdoba, 'El derecho de gentes en la obra de Martín de Azpilcueta, "el Doctor Navarro"', in Fernando M. Mariño Menéndez (ed.), *El derecho internacional en los albores del siglo XXI. Homenaje al profesor Juan Manuel Castro-Rial Canosa* (La Rioja, Dialnet, 2002), 165–9; Martínez Tapia, *Filosofía política*, 299–325.

French king, Spain had never been a part of the empire and there were countless nations, including those in the New World, that had never been ruled by the Romans.[281] It was in theory conceivable, Vitoria and Covarrubias conceded, that the peoples of the world might come together to elect a single emperor. But nothing of the kind had taken place and the very idea seemed hard to fit with natural reason.[282] Of course, it had been common for one king to rule over more than one kingdom. But this needed to take place through mutual agreement (this perhaps implied a criticism of the annexation by Castile of Navarra in the 1520s).[283] Azpilcueta disagreed also with Vitoria's speculation that a majority of nations might legitimately force a minority to accept an emperor. Natural law allowed majority decision-making only in a single republic. Outside the territorial *regnum*, however, no majority voting would be just.[284]

The Salamanca scholars drew a sharp distinction between temporal and spiritual power. The pope, in Vitoria's crisp formulation, "*is not the civil or temporal master of the whole world*".[285] They even cited John of Paris to argue that Christ's kingdom had not been of this world.[286] When Azpilcueta attacked the view of the fourteenth-century Spanish canonist Alvarus Pelagius that pagans had no jurisdiction at all, he suspected this error had been the cause for why so many in the New World had been expropriated.[287] But in fact Christ himself had recognised pagan (i.e. Roman) jurisdiction ("Give unto Caesar..."). [288] From Vitoria onwards,

[281] Azpilcueta, 'Notabile III in Relectio Cap. Novit. De Iudic', nn 157–61 (161–3). Likewise Soto, *Relección 'De dominio'*, § 29 (144). Melchior Cano listed the "Armenians of Asia, the kings of Africa and the principal kings of Germany" as never having been under a single emperor. The claim thus had no historical basis, 'De dominio indorum', Secunda Quaestio n 2, in Pereña, *Misión de España en América*, 116/117. Covarrubias pointed to a number civil laws that presupposed that the Persian king and many other "liberos populos" were not under Roman rule. To say that they were still so in law if not in fact was utterly without foundation, *Regulae peccatum*, II 9 (226–7), *Textos* 40–1.

[282] Vitoria, 'On the American Indians', 2 1 § 25 (257). Similarly Soto, *Relección, 'De dominio'*, § 33 (160); Cano, 'De dominio indiorum', Quaestio tertia n 7 (132/133–134/135) and Covarrubias, *Regulae peccatum* II.9 (229), *Textos* 44–5.

[283] Azpilcueta, 'Notabile III in Relectio Cap. Novit. De Iudic', n 149 (158).

[284] Ibid., nn 162, 163, 165 (163–4, 165). None of this prevented, of course, viewing Christianity as a single *spiritual* community, Azpilcueta, 'Notabile III Relectio Cap. Novit. De Iudic', 164 (165).

[285] Vitoria, 'On the American Indians', 2 2 § 27 (258 and generally 258–64).

[286] Azpilcueta 'Notabile III in Relectio Cap. Novit. De Iudic', n 158 (151–2).

[287] "multi nostra aetate in orbe novo suis dominiis sint spoliati", ibid., n 58 (125).

[288] Ibid., nn 73–5 (127–8).

the Spaniards derived political dominion and civil power from divine donation to the community that then used it to set up kingdoms and elect kings without any papal mediation.[289] Although they accepted (indirect) papal intervention when the interests of Christendom were threatened, they never subscribed to general papal authority in the temporal field.[290]

In the end, however, the Salamanca scholars did accept that the Spaniards had a right to travel and trade in the Indies, preach conversion and wage war with their allies against those who obstructed such activities. These were quite sufficient to allow whatever it was that the conquistadors wanted. By contrast, Las Casas would formulate an idea of a spiritual–pluralist rule with potentially anti-imperial implications. Instead of writing in terms of a "Rome" to be resuscitated and expanded into the Indies, his *Treinta proposiciónes muy juridicas* (1552) presumed that the papal donation opened an exclusively *spiritual* power for Castile over the Indies in which the dominion of both Castile and native commonwealths would stand undiminished and equal against each other. If it was true that *dominium* was given by God to all humans, then a spiritual empire – the only legitimate empire the Spaniards could claim – had to orient itself to safeguarding and supporting the power of Indian communities. Its very legitimacy would rest on how well it was able to combine its spiritual mission with the guarantee of natural dominion.[291] Like other Dominicans, Las Casas was clear that temporal jurisdiction, like any dominion of human beings over each other, could only be founded on consent: "*nulla subiectio imposita fuit sine consensu populi*".[292] It was this principle that the Spaniards had violated.

289 Vitoria, 'On Civil Power', 1 4 § 7 (11).

290 The fullest treatment of the matter is in Azpilcueta, 'Notabile III in Relectio Cap. Novit. De Iudic', where he considers a series of altogether seventeen arguments (with many divided into subordinate arguments) pro and contra the pope's universal dominion. See nn 1–41 (105–21) (but more arguments are also presented later in the text). In the end, Azpilcueta limits papal power to ecclesiastical matters but joins Vitoria in accepting the pope's *indirect* power to intervene "when this is necessary for the realization of the supranatural ends for which the institution has been set up", n 41 (120).

291 See Capdevila, 'Impérialisme, empire, et destruction', 53–8. Caprdevila's commentary on *Treinta proposiciónes* usefully highlights the argument from the conceptual emptiness of "empire" – that it may be used both for oppressive and emancipatory purposes, including to defend a policy (with Las Casas) that is actually anti-imperialist.

292 Las Casas, 'De regia potestate', II § IV 6 (64) Or even more clearly, "[n]ulla subjectio, nulla servitus, nullum onus unquam impositum fuit, nisi populus qui subiturus illa onera erat, impositioni eiusmodi voluntarie consentiret", II § IV 1 (60).

## *Dominium Iurisdictionis*

The Salamanca scholars were committed to the view that "by natural law all people were equal; and nobody was a king under natural law".[293] But the Bible recounted kings such as Nimrod ruling over vast populations. Where had their power come from? In rejecting the emperor's universal lordship, Vitoria observed that "dominion and supremacy were introduced by human law, not natural law".[294] And how to justify departure from natural by human law? In the *Relectio on Civil Power* (1528), Vitoria attacked the "folly and madness" of those who believed that the exercise of political power was in itself un-Christian.[295] In apparent contradiction with his insistence on the absence of any original *dominium* among humans, Vitoria now claimed that "public power is founded upon natural law, and [. . .] natural law acknowledges God as its only author".[296] It was as if the original sin had separated two kinds of natural law, one that would have been valid in the state of innocence, a natural law of freedom and equality, another to govern social relations after the Fall, when every human being found themselves "naked and unarmed like a castaway from a shipwreck into the miseries of this life".[297] Following an Aristotelian–Thomist theme, he observed that humans had been vested with a desire for communication and partnership through which political institutions – cities, commonwealths and rulers – would gradually emerge as natural "devices" to help them realise their shared ends.[298] The foundation of royal *dominium*

[293] "[O]mnes homines de jure naturali erant aequales; nullus erat princeps de jure naturali", Vitoria, ComST II-II 62 1 n 21 (77); and see also 'On Civil Power', 1 5 § 8 (14). Likewise Soto: "Ius autem naturae nude consideratum nullum mortalium caeteris dominio praetulit. Omnes enim nascuntur liberi. . .", *De iustitia et iure*, IV 4 2 (304a).

[294] Vitoria, 'On the American Indians', 2 1 § 25 (254).

[295] Many commentators suggest that this lecture, given only a few years after the *comuneros* revolt in Castile, needs to be read against the popular, even democratic rhetoric used by the revolutionaries as well as forms of contemporary radicalism in Germany. See e.g. Mariano Delgado, 'Die Zustimmung des Volkes', in Frank Grunert & Kurt Seelmann (eds), *Die Ordnung der Praxis. Neue Studien zur spanischen Spätscholastik* (Tübingen, Niemeyer 2001), 158–9, 163; Deckers, *Gerechtigkeit*, 286.

[296] Vitoria, 'On Civil Power', 1 2 § 6 (10). Vitoria distinguished between the four Aristotelian causes (final, formal, efficient and material).

[297] Ibid., 1 2 § 4 (7).

[298] The whole fully naturalistic sentence reads: "the primitive origin of human cities and commonwealths was not human invention or contrivance to be numbered . . . but a device implanted in nature in man for his own safety and survival". Ibid., 1 2 § 5 (9). A fully naturalistic understanding of Vitoria's derivation of civil power is Heinz-Gerhard Justenhoven, *Francisco de Vitoria zu Krieg und Frieden* (Cologne,

lay in a natural sociability that persisted even among fallen human beings. "Here we have, then, the final cause, and the most potent, of secular power, namely utility and necessity so urgent that not even gods can resist it."[299]

Alongside these, apparently purely naturalist, even instinctual explanations of political authority, the Salamanca scholars stressed the role of liberty in the organisation of social life. God had originally donated *dominium* to humans as a single, undivided power over the rest of creation.[300] They had eventually used their liberty to agree on the division of their joint dominion into separate territories, with separate rulers.[301] This had taken place "*ex consensu omnium*".[302] Not that there had ever been any single assembly or decision. Appropriation took place through informal consensus, some occupying some territories and others other territories.[303] Although Vitoria wrote of the rise of civil power in 1528 as a matter of natural law, in the lectures in 1535–6 he spoke of it as *ius gentium*, dismissing efforts at classification as no more than of terminological interest.[304] Of course, life under civil power was different from life in the state of innocence. But the two were still not in conflict. As *ius gentium* civil institutions could still be traced back to natural sociability with a divine origin. This explained why Christian

Bachem 1991), 41–5. On the apparent contradiction between Vitoria's insistence on natural freedom and the natural origin of *dominium*, see also Deckers, *Gerechtigkeit*, 276–81 and Fernández-Santamaría, *The State, War and Peace*, 65–8.

299 Vitoria, 'On Civil Power', 1 2 § 5 (10). This was a very different view from the Augustinian one that understood political institutions as responses to original sin, man-made, violent, but necessary. Attacking that position, Soto followed Vitoria in insisting that, on the contrary, civil power originated in God and was received by humans through natural law. "Potestatem autem civilem Deus per legem naturalem, quae suae sempiternae participatio est, ordinavit", Soto *De iustitia et iure*, IV 4 2 (302a). It was God who had implanted in humans "the instinct of living communally, so that they might be sufficient each to each other", "adiecit eis instinctum gregatim vivendi, ut adunati alii aliis sufficerent", ibid., IV 4 1 (302a), translation from Brett, *Liberty, Right and Nature*, 155. See further Prats, *El pensmiento político de Domingo de Soto*, 154–5. Even as human beings may have been born free under natural law, that same natural law instilled in them the duty to be obedient to kings and princes so that "through obedience, they should live secure and happy", "quibus obtemperantes, tutius foeliciusque vivant". Soto, *De iustitia et iure*, IV 4 2 (303a).

300 See Brett, *Liberty, Right and Nature*, 129–32.

301 "Et ita si homines erant domini omnium rerum, potuerunt facere quod velint, et dividere, et appropriare", Vitoria, ComST II-II 62 1 n 20 (77).

302 Ibid., II-II 62 1 n 21 (78). Likewise, Las Casas ("imperium immediate processit a populo"), 'De regia potestate', II IV 3 (62).

303 "Et iste consensus sufficit ad jus gentium", Vitoria, ComST II-II 62 1 n 23 (79).

304 Ibid., II-II 57 3 n 2 (14) and 62 1 n 23 (79).

and non-Christian communities may both have legitimate rulers and why civil power was binding on consciences.

The narrative of the natural origin of political communities strengthened the distinction between spiritual and temporal power. In Azpilcueta's long and complex recounting, humans had received from God the power to establish political communities so that they would live well and virtuously under natural reason.[305] No mediation by the church or the empire was needed. Glossing the statement by Innocent III in 1204 where he had vowed to respect the French king's jurisdiction, Azpilcueta listed the many differences between spiritual and temporal jurisdiction.[306] The church had received its powers from divine donation that had made church institutions immediately perfect. Temporal institutions, by contrast, grew gradually to more perfect forms: first houses joined villages; then villages formed political communities (*civitates*) that elected kings to govern them. True, kingdoms might sometimes elect to join empires. But they may also decide to maintain their independent jurisdiction (*ditionem et iurisdictionem habebant*), leading their lives without external interference.[307] Covarrubias agreed; while God had gifted spiritual power to Peter and his followers, temporal power was given to the community that then granted it to the king or the emperor. This did not exclude papal intervention when the interests of the church were at stake. But the two were normally (*regulariter*) to be kept separate.[308]

A second point made by the Salamancans was that even if civil power did have a sacred *origin*, it was received "only" *mediante lege naturae per civilem republicam.*[309] In Vitoria's Aristotelian language, although the *efficient* cause of civil power lay with God, operating through natural

[305] The power of the commonwealth "esse potestas naturaliter a Deo immediate data mortalium communitati ad sese gubernandum in rebus naturalibus, ut bene beateque vivant secundum rationem naturalem", Azpilcueta, 'Notabile III in Relectio Cap. Novit. De Iudic', § 85 (135). For Azpilcueta's views on the origin and exercise of civil power, see Martínez Tapia, *Filosofía política*, 97–292.

[306] This was the decretal "Novit", which began "Let no one suppose that we wish to diminish or disturb the jurisdiction and power of the king...", English translation in Brian Tierney, *The Crisis of Church and State 1050–1300* (University of Toronto Press 1988), 134.

[307] To stress the traditional character of this conclusion, Azpilcueta defended it by referring to Aristotle, Aquinas and John of Paris. 'Notabile III in Relectio Cap. Novit. De Iudic' § 94 (139).

[308] "eius usus utilis & necessarius est ad quietem ecclesiae", Covarrubias, *Regulae peccatum*, IX 7 (242–3); *Textos* 69–70.

[309] Soto, *De iustitia et iure*, IV 4 2 (302b).

law, its *material* cause was the commonwealth itself, which "takes upon itself the task of governing and administering itself and directing all its powers to the common good".[310] This was an important point to make against the view of divine kingship that had been used by Gattinara in his effort to sideline the church from government.[311] Although people were drawn to society by nature, they could freely choose their manner of government. So if it was true that "civil power is ordained by God",[312] this was so in the sense that it was first received by the people, who then delegate it to the person they choose to rule themeselves. Royal jurisdiction was a "faculty" that the king had received from the community: "commonwealths were not made for kings, but kings for the commonwealth".[313]

This narrative united a naturalist explanation of civil power with its consensual legitimation. Humans joined together in part out of a natural insinct, in part because they were unable to sustain themselves otherwise. But every community needed authority: *nulla communitas sine potestas gubernandi, praecipiendi, leges instituendi & iudicandi.*[314] Again, this did not mean that the theologians preferred absolutism. Over and again they stressed that civil power was "none other than the commonwealth's power administered through the sovereign".[315] It was to be used for the good of the community. This did not, however, grant the subjects any kind of control on government. Because the common good was not separate from supernatural *felicitas*, the reference

310 Vitoria, 'On Civil Power', 1 4 § 7 (11). Vitoria sometimes distinguished between the *validity* of royal power and its *exercise*. Ibid., 1 5 § 8 (16). See also Anthony Pagden, *The Burdens of Empire. 1539 to the Present* (Cambridge University Press 2015), 52–3. Las Casas regarded the people as the effective cause of both kings and *regna*, "populus fuit causa effectiva regum seu principum", 'De potestate regia', II IV 3 (62).

311 On Gattinara's view of divine kingship, see Thomas, *The Golden Empire*, 34.

312 "Ecce quemadmodum publica civilis potestas, ordinatio Deus est", Soto, *De iustitia et iure*, IV 4 2 (302a).

313 "regna non esse inducta propter reges, sed reges propter regna", Azpilcueta, 'Notabile III in Relectio Cap. Novit. De Iudic', § 100 (141). On royal power as legally enshrined "facultas", see ibid., § 81 (132). See further, Martínez Tapia, *Filosofía política*, 129–35.

314 Adding, "At hominum societas sine tali potestate conservari et augeri non poterat", Azpilcueta, 'Notabile III in Relectio Cap. Novit. De Iudic', § 86 (136).

315 Vitoria, 'On Civil Power', in *Political Writings*, 1 5 § 8 (14). Or as he put in his lectures, "Praeterea, princeps est electus a populo. Sed populus dat ei istam auctoritatem ut possit disponere de bonis civium", Vitoria, ComST II-II 62 1 n 33 (86). See also Brett, *Liberty, Right and Nature*, 131–2. Azpilcueta never used the term "sovereign" but instead expressions such as "potestas suprema" and "summa potestas", Martínez Tapia, *Filosfía política*, 150–2.

grounded the authority of the church, often in practice the royal confessor, on policymaking.[316] This power was visible, for example, when the Council of the Indies, acting under the presidency of García de Loaysa, declared that the danger to the Indians "and the royal conscience" had become so great that no new conquests were to be undertaken without express permission.[317] Vitoria had no doubt that the spiritual power was entitled to intervene "in cases where it is necessary for the avoidance of disturbances in the realm, or the protection of religion against pagans, or other such matters".[318] Referring to this passage, in his long discourse on the relations of the spiritual and temporal realms, Azpilcueta, too, invoked the church's right to intervene in temporal matters when that was needed for the fulfilment of the supernatural objectives of the political order (*quatenus sunt necessaria ad consequtionem finis supernaturalis*).[319] What else could a believer really think?

A different approach was taken by the humanist jurist, one-time colleague of Soto in Salamanca, member of the Court of Castile, Fernando Vázquez de Menchaca (1512–69).[320] His most well-known work, *Controversiarum illustrium aliarumque usu frequentium libri tres* (1564) has been described as part of a "radical legal tradition the analysis of right of which is based on a preoccupation with fact".[321] The book's two main parts combine a mirror of princes with a humanist tract on the effect of time on legal relationships. The latter question had already been treated by Vázquez in an earlier work, *De successiorum creatione, progressu et resolutione* (1559) and it permeated his whole understanding of the nature of law, including *ius gentium*: no rights are permanent – every day they are created and extinguished.[322] This gave the book a

316 See especially Urbano, *El pensamiento*, 35–59.

317 Thomas, *The Golden Empire*, 481.

318 Vitoria 'On the Power of the Church', 5 9 (95–101).

319 Azpilcueta, 'Notabile III in Relectio Cap. Novit. De Iudic', § 41 (120). See also Martínez Tapia, *Filosfía política*, 365–77.

320 For the biography of Vázquez, see especially Seelmann, *Die Lehre des Fernando Vázquez de Menchaca*, 25–30. The life and (especially) fame of Vázquez is also treated in Reibstein, *Anfänge*, 19–27 and Camilo Barcia Trelles, 'Fernando Vázquez de Menchaca (1512–69). L'école espagnole de Droit International du XVIe siècle', 67 *RdC* (1939), 433–42. The best recent analysis is Brett, *Liberty, Right and Nature*, 165–204.

321 Brett, *Liberty, Right and Nature*, 166.

322 "ius in rebus huiusmodi quotidie oritur & quotidie finitur", Fernando Vázquez de Menchaca, *Controversiarum illustrium aliarumque usu frequentium libri tres* (2 vols, Latin & Spanish edn Valladolid 1931–2), Praefatio 25 (17).

strikingly realist, even dark tone: humans were the greatest threat to themselves; natural rights (*iura naturalia*) that were assumed to be inalienable were being exterminated everywhere.[323] How could it possibly be claimed that *ius gentium* allowed the enslavement of people who had been made free under natural law?[324] The main objective of ruling was to keep human beings from attacking each other and setting up tyrannical regimes.[325] Like his scholastic contemporaries, Vázquez distinguished between natural law, *ius gentum* and civil law, situating most of the universal legal institutions in a *ius gentium secundarium*, a human law that had arisen gradually in practice. This included individual *regna*, wars and private property, as well as the rest of what tradition had used to include in it.[326]

The most celebrated aspect of the work has been its recognition of the power of the people to exercise control over the ruler. This power was irrevocable; the subjects had created the commonwealth for their own utility and not that of the prince.[327] In Spain for example, if the royal line were extinguished, the right to elect a new king would fall on the subjects (in practice the Castilian nobility).[328] It is said, Vázquez wrote, that a prince was *legibus solutus*. But nothing was more unjust than to reduce the law to the will of the prince. Instead, the validity of laws depended on the extent that they were useful for the people.[329] In his long preface Vázquez explained that princes often tended to reject the just claims of their subjects – in which case the subjects had full right to

323 Ibid., I, Praefatio 3 (8). See further Reibstein, *Anfänge*, 56–7; Tuck, *Rights of War and Peace*, 70–7.

324 Vázquez, *Controversiarum*, I, Praefatio 9 (9); and IV 3 (145–7).

325 Ibid., I, I I 24–5 (106–9).

326 The 1931–2 edition does not contain the latter part of Chapter 2 dealing more extensively with *ius gentium secundarium* – as well as the famous passages on the free seas on which Grotius would later draw. They may be found in *Illustrium Controversiarum aliarumque usu frequentium libri sex in duas partes divisi* (Frankfurt, Schönwetterei 1568), II 89 24–8 (355b–356a). For the notion of *ius gentium* in Vázquez, see further Reibstein, *Anfänge*, 70–3.

327 "principatus ad subditorum duntaxat non etiam ad principum utilitatem inventus sit", Vázquez, *Controversiarum*, I, Praefatio 124 (81) and I I 25 (108–9). See further Martin van Gelderen, '"So meerly humane". Theories of Resistance in Early-Modern Europe', in Annabel Brett & James Tully, with Holly Hamilton-Bleakeley, *Rethinking the Foundations of Modern Political Thought* (Cambridge University Press 2006), 157–61 (with special reference to the influence on Grotius) and further, Brett, *Liberty, Right and Nature*, 171–6.

328 Vázquez, *Controversiarum*, II, II 22 12 (68).

329 Ibid., I I 2 10 (120) and 1–2 (111–15).

disobedience.[330] He disagreed with Soto's view that subjects had no other recourse against tyranny than praying to God. Under natural law, they not only may resist – nothing is more heroic than opposition to tyranny – but they may well be assisted by other princes.[331] It also followed that to be ruled by a *foreign* power such as pope or emperor was a violation of the law of nature.[332]

Vázquez introduced a broad range of subjective rights that could be invoked to found civil commonwealths and justify resistance against tyranny. The prince had no right to intervene in his subjects' properties without a cause; any intervention was to be based on law. The "plenitude of power" was really a misnomer as all power was designed for the utility of the people.[333] Vázquez wrote of a natural liberty which, unlike the theologians' subjective rights, remained uncontrolled by a pre-existing objective legal order.[334] The holder of *dominium* was entitled to "abuse" that *dominium* with only the (de facto) limits that counter-veiling power and the law provided.[335] Power was to be exercised in the interests of the subjects, and this required close attention to the history and conditions in particular commonwealths. For law emerged from custom and was not timeless; "civil right is merely the constantly evaporating surface of the great ocean of de facto occurrence".[336]

The united Iberian peninsula had only recently arisen from relative anarchy. Disturbances such as the *Germanías* uprising in Valencia and the *comuneros* revolt in 1519–21 reminded everyone of how fragile the situation still was. Many Castilians were attached to republicanism and admired the Italian city-states.[337] Las Casas, for example, wrote eloquently about the inalienable rights of a free people: *populus eligendo*

330 "subditi ad defectionem & inobedientiam iure festinent". Ibid., I, Praefatio, 17 (12).

331 Ibid., II, II 22 6 (66).

332 Ibid., II, II 20 (27–9). Vázquez stressed over again that owing to the original equality between humans, nobody could be subordinated to the government of another without their consent. Ibid. 25 (26).

333 Ibid., I I 15. 1–4 (295–8).

334 "libertas est naturalis facultas eius, quod cuique facere libet, nisi vi aut iure prohibeatur", ibid., I I 17 5 (321).

335 Ibid., I I 17 2 (320). This, he argued, was also the correct interpretation of the definition by Bartolus that property involved the owner's *perfect* right ("ius perfecte disponendi") – this was nothing else than "liberrime disponere", 6 (322). It went further than Soto's definition, limited to uses in one's own advantage ("in suum ipsius commodum usurpare"), 8 (323).

336 Brett, *Liberty, Right and Nature*, 168.

337 See e.g. Teofilo E Ruiz, *Spanish Society 1400–1600* (London, Longman 2001), 194–205.

*principem seu regem, libertatem suam non amisit.*[338] Some such as the Trinitarian friar Alonso de Castrillo had actually used the uprising in order to point to the lack of legitimacy enjoyed by the "foreigners" – the emperor's detested Burgundian and Italian advisors.[339] But the Salamanca scholars were no revolutionaries; they did not believe that the people should participate in government.[340] They had a strong preference for monarchy that would foreclose the quarrels and seditions that aristocracy or democracy would entail.[341] Soto insisted that once the community had transferred its authority to the ruler, the transfer was complete and irrevocable. The head of the social body was superior both to its members and that body itself.[342] Or, as Vitoria stated in a series of notoriously enigmatic passages, the prince's power came both from the commonwealth and from God. Although (as *auctoritas*, or *officium*) it was received from the people, its divine origin made it irretrievable.[343]

## An Empire of Private Rights

Theologians influenced policy not only as confessors. University men such as Vitoria, Soto, Cano, Carranza and others were frequently consulted on the most varied practical matters of government ranging from the price of corn to actions to be taken against pirates.[344] Above all, their view of *dominium* and *restitutio* provided a firm basis on which to debate the justice of the economic exchanges and eventually grounded an extensive right for individuals to appropriate, use, transfer or abandon things in accordance with their choice. The Dominicans followed the church line since the Council of Constance (1414–18) according to which neither sin nor infidelity took away *dominium*; Christians may lawfully engage in trade with pagans and the rights of ownership of the latter were valid and enforceable even against the Christians.[345] The opening of the New World created unforseeen opportunities:

338 Las Casas, 'De regia potestate', II IV 4 (62).

339 See Alberto Montoro Ballestros, 'El "Tractado de República" de Alonso de Castrillo (1521)', 188 *Revista de estudios politicos* (1973), 107–52; Fernández-Santamaría, *The State, War and Peace*, 11–34.

340 Fernández-Santamaría, *The State, War and Peace*, 72–5.

341 Vitoria, 'On Civil Power', 1 8 § 11 (20). See also Urbino, *El pensamiento*, 97–103.

342 Soto, *De justitia et de iure*, IV 4 1 (302).

343 Vitoria, 'On Civil Power', 1 5 § 7–8 and 7 § 10 (16–17, 18–19). For difficulties of interpretation, see Tierney, *The Idea of Natural Rights*, 291–301.

344 See e.g. Pagden, *The Burdens of Empire*, 46–7.

345 Vitoria, ComST II-II 62 1 28 (81–2).

> Spaniards of all ranks and conditions saw their lives transformed in America by the riches that poured out: artisans set up businesses, traders purchased ships, merchants opened shops, butchers, tailors and shoemakers found new opportunities in a land where there was effectively no competition for their services.[346]

At the time Vitoria was teaching, gold and silver imported from the Indies to Seville was spreading all over Europe and the connected financial operations began to create a global network of economic relations that would change Europe's cultural and economic milieu out of recognition. Commercial operators, including the crown itself, engaged in new types of long-distance transactions, set up monopolies and speculated about prices in a moral–legal grey zone to which theologians and canon lawyers were invariably drawn.[347] How were they to view large-scale exchanges of private property motivated not by need but by the desire for profit? What to think of financial transactions carried out by bankers, money-lenders and *cambistas* flocking to the Castilian trade fairs or the use of letters of credit for long-distance payments involving profit that would appear clearly usurous under canon law? How were they to react when Charles himself felt compelled, in 1543, to authorise Flemish merchants to charge an interest of up to 10 percent?[348] Indeed, what about the notorious *juros* and *asientos* issued by Castile that led to unprecedented expansion of interest-taking by German and Genoese banking families, pressing the crown ever deeper into debt from which it would eventually rise only through scandalous bankruptcies?[349]

Castile was a relatively underdeveloped part of the Habsburg realm, ideologically conservative and dependent on manufactures and financial expertise from Flanders and Lombardy.[350] The government was

[346] Henry Kamen, *Spain's Road to Empire. The Making of a World Power 1492–1763* (Harmondsworth, Penguin 2002), 287.

[347] For a broad overview of the authors and the principal themes, see e.g. Dominec Melé, 'Early Business Ethics in Spain. The Salamanca School (1526–1614)', 22 *Journal of Business Ethics* (1999), 177–84.

[348] Michèle & Bernard Gazier, *Or et monnaie chez Martín de Azpilcueta Navarro* (Paris, Economica 1978), Part 3.1 *in fine*.

[349] Briefly, see Fernand Braudel, *Civilization & Capitalism, 15th–18th Century*, vol. II: *The Wheels of Commerce* (University of California Press 1992), 522–5 and for much more elaborate analysis, Mauricio Drelichman & Hans-Joachim Voth, *Lending to the Borrower from Hell. Debt, Taxes and Default in the Age of Philip II* (Princeton University Press 2016).

[350] For one description of Castile's paradoxical economic "backwardness", see Abelardo del Vigo, *Cambistas, mercaderes y banqueros en el siglo de oro español* (Madrid, Biblioteca de autores cristianos 1997), 15–23.

closely allied with the church and theologians intervened constantly by providing counsel on the lawfulness and moral acceptability of particular trading practices.[351] The Salamanca scholars came to these matters in their commentaries on *Quaestiones* 62, 77 and 78 of the *Secunda secundae*, dealing respectively with property rights, the lawfulness of mercantile activities in general and the question of just price and usury. Their detailed analyses extended to all the more important legal techniques of domestic and international trade, including the monetary system that supported it. Among these was Azpilcueta's discussion of Spanish inflation that would inaugurate the quantity theory of money some years before Jean Bodin's more famous treatment of the matter.[352] By reading economic practices as *ius gentium* the theologians could consecrate the freedom of contract and guarantee the stability of the system of private exchanges that would secure the operation of an emerging global network of economic relations.[353]

For Aquinas, the move from common to private property had an originally utilitarian basis: "everyone is more diligent in procuring something for himself than something which is to belong to all or many".[354] The Salamanca scholars agreed; their relatively relaxed discussion of profit-making and usury presumed the justice of mercantile practices as long as they were motivated by concern for the livelihood of their familes or the good of the commonwealth.[355] True, many Christians were critical of private property, pointing to biblical passages

351 For example, Vitoria reports having been consulted by merchants in Flanders about to whom profit should be allocated when something was bought by money borrowed from another person. Vitoria, ComST II-II 77 4 n 11 (152). For a list of fifteen letters and memoranda by Vitoria on commercial matters, see Idoya Zorroza, 'Introducción', in Francisco de Vitoria, *Contratos y usura* (Pamplona, EUNSA 2006), 41–5; some of these are reproduced in ibid., 261–9. The contribution of the Salamanca scholars to what now would be called "economic" thought was highlighted in Joseph Schumpeter, *Histoire de l'analyse économique*, vol. I: *L'age des fondateurs* (Paris, Gallimard 1983), 114–202. For another early analysis, see also Marjorie Grice-Hutchinson, *Early Economic Thought in Spain 1177–1740* (London, Allen & Unwin 1978), 81–121. Since then, interest in the "economic" views of the Spanish scholastics has burgeoned. See further Muñoz de Juana, *Moral y economía*, 33–69 as well as S. J. Gómez Camacho & Ricardo Robledo (eds), *El pensamiento económico en la escuela de Salamanca* (Ediciones Universidad Salamanca 1998).

352 For a detailed treatment, see Gazier & Gazier, *Or et monnaie*.

353 Seelmann, *Theologie und Jurisprudenz*, 17–18; Decock, *Theologians and Contract Law*, passim.

354 Aquinas, ST II-II 66 2 Resp (208).

355 As especially stressed in Schumpeter, *Histoire de l'analyse économique I*, 141–57.

such as the statement by Jesus about the difficulty of the rich man in ascending to Paradise [Luke 18:25]. But most accepted private property as a pragmatic "addition" to natural law, instead of a sinful deviation from it.[356] Soto, for example, began his discussion of private ownership by attacking Plato's communist utopia. Effective use of resources required that each had their own property to administer. Moreover, division was necessary to attain just sharing of burdens between the members of the community. In Paradise, there may have been sufficient fruit for everyone. But since the expulsion, humans had to work to sustain themselves. Common property would only lead some to working excessively while others would lay back and enjoy the fruits of their labour. Peace, tranquillity and friendship would be thwarted.[357]

Everything the Spanish theologians wrote about the freedom of contract and inheritance, prices, money and commerce as well as about the objectives and limits of public power presumed not only the existence but the beneficial nature of private property and connected transactions.[358] Such transactions had been discussed in Roman law but no systemic view of them had emerged until the scholastics brought them under the title of commutative justice "intimately bound with the sacrament of confession".[359] Vitoria, Soto and Azpilcueta were keenly

356 Aquinas, ST II-II 66 2 Resp (208); Janet Coleman, 'Property and Poverty', in J. H. Burns (ed.), *The Cambridge History of Medieval Political Thought c. 350–c. 1450* (Cambridge University Press 1988), 621–5, and on the Franciscan poverty controversy, 631–48; Brett, *Liberty, Right and Nature*, 13–20.

357 Soto, *De iustitia et iure*, IV 3 1 (296a–297a). "Hac ergo delira communitate praetermissa ... demonstrandum [est] quam sit congruens naturae corruptae possessionum divisio ... nempe ex humana negligentia & ex cupiditate", ibid., at 296b. See also Alejandro A. Chafuen, *Faith and Liberty. The Economic Thought of the Late Scholastics* (Lanham, Lexington Books 2003), 33–4. Soto also followed Aristotle by holding that under conditions of common property it would be impossible to cultivate the virtues of hospitality and liberality. "Qui enim proprium non habet, liberalis esse non potest et qui omnia possidet, alienae liberalitatis non eget", in Soto, *De justitia et iure*, IV 3 1 (297b). See also Aristotle, 'The Politics', II (36–7).

358 In this, they departed significantly from medieval writers who were usually dubious about economic activity and accepted it only to the extent it was directed towards satisfaction of necessities or caring for offspring. See e.g. Antonio García García & Bernardo Alonso Rodríguez, 'El pensamiento económico y el mundo del derecho hasta el siglo XVI', in Gómez Camacho & Robledo, *El pensamiento económico*, 66–75. Dianne Wood observes that it was the church that put a brake on economic activity. For "to be socially ambitious, to want to be upwardly mobile, was a sin", *Medieval Economic Thought* (Cambridge University Press 2002), 3, 2–5.

359 Thomas Duve, 'La teoria de la restitución en Domingo de Soto. Su significación para la historia del derecho privado moderno', in Juan Cruz Cruz, *La ley natural como fundamento moral y jurídico en Domingo de Soto* (Pamplona, Eunsa 2007), 190, 187–90.

aware that accumulation of wealth could easily cross the threshold of the sin of avarice. Each shared Aristotle's scepticism about professional trading for profit.[360] Their glosses on questions 77 and 78 of the *Secunda secundae* were framed as of *ius gentium*, which meant that they were supposed to possess universal validity. Their objective was *justice* – mainly commutative but also distributive justice – that coalesced with a search for the appropriate attitudes to be adopted by individual Christians to fit profit-seeking in their conscience. This led into an extremely detailed casuistic of commercial practices (contract, loan, insurance, exchange etc.) discussed with respect to a very great number of potential situations.[361]

The starting-point lay in the Aristotelian–Thomist doubts about the morality of professional commerce, planning one's livelihood on the practice of buying cheap and selling dear.[362] However, Vitoria accepted that if the intention was not to cause injury to the other party, the sin was only venial, not mortal. And sometimes professional trading was not sinful at all, as when a change was introduced into the object between the purchase and the sale. In this case the profit did not emerge from "nothing" but from a distinct service rendered by the merchant. If the object was sold in another location than where it had been bought – the situation of international commerce – then a transaction might even appear outright commendable because *necessarium ad bonum et ad provisionem reipublicae.*[363] That Vitoria still entertained some moral doubts was visible in his denial that the merchant's enrichment would always benefit the state as well. It was not right to concentrate wealth in the hands of a small number of rich people. Distributing the profit among the many would be necessary.[364]

360 Following Aristotle, Vitoria distinguished between two types of trading – "natural" trade was designed to fulfil human needs, and another, "unnatural" one was for profit. While the former was fine ("honesta"), the other was morally dubious ("turpis est"). ComST II-II 77 4 n 1 (145, 146). See also Soto, *De iustitia et iure*, VI 2 2 (543b–544a).

361 Belda Plans, *La escuela de Salamanca*, 926; José Barrientos García, 'El pensamiento económico en la perspectiva filosofico-teologica', in Gómez Camacho & Robledo, *El pensamiento económico*, 94–5. To give a sense of the detailed nature of the result, it might be noted that the mere discussion by Vitoria of the question "whether it is allowed to receive for loan something else than money in exchange" is divided into 75 paragraphs that discuss 51 "doubtful cases", many of them developed in several "corollaries", all of which takes 68 pages in the modern Latin edition, ComST II-II, 68 II (167–235).

362 "negotiari est valde periculosum", Vitoria, ComST II-II 77 4 n 2 (146).

363 Ibid., II-II 77 4 n 3 (147).

364 ". . . non est bonum reipublicae quod omnia bona venant ad manus paucorum avarorum", ibid., II-II 77 4 n 8 (150).

Azpilcueta treated the moral status of mercantile activity in a condensed fashion in a commentary to Gratian's *Decretum* (1581), noting that the newer literature had come to distinguish between honest and dishonourable commerce by reference to the types of profit expected. Commerce itself was neutral, but pure profit-making intention made it sinful: "a sick tree cannot bear healthy fruit".[365] Only trading in order to receive a livelihood for one's family or to profit the community was legitimate. And merchants who travelled great distances, suffering all kinds of dangers and worries along the way, did merit some kind of reward.[366] They were not only fully legitimate but perhaps even more praiseworthy than those providing only for their own family. Anyway, merchants who had been able to satisfy their family could freely continue profit-making for the good of the republic, support of the poor or other worthy causes.[367]

The view that commerce was based neither on grace nor natural law but on utility played an important role in legitimating long-distance trading. It would provide the basis on which Catholic merchants from Spain could engage in mutually profitable transactions with Islamic or Jewish traders (as they had done for centuries), travel to Protestant markets in Germany and Flanders and exchange goods with the inhabitants of the New World. The most famous sketch of this worldwide system of *dominium* was contained in Vitoria's discussion of the right of the Spaniards to travel and trade in the Indies (*ius peregrinandi* & *ius negotiandi*). Since the beginning of times, "everyone was allowed to visit and travel through any land he wished [and t]his right was clearly not taken away by the division of property (*divisio rerum*)". Because commerce had become part of the "natural partnership and communication" between people across the world, it followed that all nations were to show hospitality to strangers and that everybody had the right to "all things which are not prohibited or otherwise to the harm and detriment of others".[368]

365 "arbor enim mala non facit fructus bonos", Martín de Azpilcueta Navarro, *Commentaria in septem distinctiones de paenitentia* (Rome, Tornentia, 1586), 428. See also Muñoz de Juana, *Moral y economía*, 151–61.

366 "ergo dignus est aliqua mercede", Azpilcueta, *Commentaria in septem distinctiones*, n 7 (429).

367 "nunc pro Reipublicae, provisione, vel pro pauperibus alendis, aut aliis operibus piis, facere pergat", ibid., n 14 (429). This presumed the existence of an upper limit to the riches that a merchant could collect for himself and his family. Muñoz de Juana, *Moral y económia*, 150–60.

368 Vitoria, 'On the American Indians', 3 1 § 2 (278).

To make sure that he was not only discussing some special (colonial) relationship, Vitoria added that the same principles would apply between Christian commonwealths. For the Spanish or the French kings to intervene against travelling merchants would be "unjust ... and contrary to Christian charity".[369] Commerce was not to be disturbed unless this was necessary for the defence and government of the nation.[370] Nor could the prince limit hunting, fishing or collecting firewood from the forest without just cause. In any case, all individuals had a natural right to use everything necessary for their conservation.[371] Nor had the ruler any right to expropriate subjects without a *causa* – a persistent reality in fifteenth-century Spain. Las Casas, for example, felt compelled to repeat the old princple *Imperator et rex non est dominus super rebus singulorum, sed tantum quoad iurisdictionem.*[372] Nothing was more contrary to natural law than to deprive someone of his property.[373] According to Azpilcueta, taxation that was carried out without a just cause constituted a mortal sin on the prince's part. It turned him into a *tyrant* and perhaps even triggered the right of resistance.[374] Expropriation was possible only so far as needed by the commonwealth – "[b]eyond that, man must not only have his own rights as an individual, but he must also have their exercise in his own control: in other words, he must be *sui iuris*, have *dominium* of himself or his liberty".[375]

Much of this was pure theory. The Castilian government used multiple means to control the Indies trade and extract funds from wherever it could. The *Casa de contratación* (House of Trade) was set up in 1503 precisely to manage the Spanish monopoly. No traffic was to pass to the Indies without formal approval by the *Casa*, which also saw to the collection of

369 Ibid., 3 1 § 3 (280).

370 See also Barrientos García, 'El pensamiento económico', 120.

371 Vitoria, ComST II-II 62 1 n 13 (72–3). See also Deckers, *Gerechtigkeit*, 210–11.

372 Las Casas, 'De regia potestate', III 8 (50) and XII 9 (104). See also Massimo Meccarelli, 'La nuova dimensione geopolitica e gli strumenti giuridici della tradizione. Approcci alla tema del ius belli e del ius communicationis nella seconda scolastica', in Luigi Lacché (ed.), *'Ius gentium, ius communicationis, ius belli'. Alberico Gentili e gli orizzonti della modernità* (Milano, Giuffrè 2009), 65. Covarrubias, however, rejected the glossators' suggestion that imperial power might be about a universal right of "protection", *Regulae peccatum*, II 9 (226), *Textos* 40.

373 Las Casas, 'De regia potestate', IV.1 (60). See further XI.1 (90) and XII.1 (98).

374 Azpilcueta, *Manual de confessores*, 359–60. The protection of private *dominium* against the extractions of the prince is particularly stressed in Vázquez, *Controversiarum*, I 17 (319–26).

375 Brett, *Liberty, Right and Nature*, 159.

the *quinto* ("fifth") for the crown. Originally set up as a private trading house, it was gradually turned into a government bureau, "licensing and supervising all ships and merchants, passengers and goods, crews and equipment, passing to and from the Indies, and enforcing the laws and ordinances related thereto".[376] The exclusion of outsiders was completed by the formation of the *Consulado* (1525), a trading-guild of Spanish merchants modelled on medieval guilds. However, none of this led to effective control by Castile of the flourishing Indies trade. Huge quantities of silver arrived without being reported. And by far the greatest part of what arrived found its way immediately to the crown's creditors, private traders and manufacturers in Italy, Germany, Flanders and elsewhere. The indebtedness of the Habsburg rulers was legendary. When Charles' grandfather Maximilian I died in 1519, his debt to the Fuggers and the Welsers of Germany amounted to eighteen times his annual income – and late in his regime Charles' son Philip II had to pay two-thirds of his income as interest for his debts.[377]

An especially significant extension of the theory of *dominium* to the commercial system was the subjective (but non-arbitrary) theory of the just price.[378] Drawing on Duns Scotus, Vitoria accepted that the goods on the market had no essential or natural value. He was familiar with the paradox under which water, though normally of no value, may be sometimes regarded as more valuable than gold. But if different people value things differently, how could a just exchange be carried out? To this he responded that the just price was relative to how a thing is generally valued (*ex communi hominum aestimatione vel condicto*).[379] That "common estimation", again, was a function of many things, including the product's relative abundance or scarcity. Though price-formation was a subjective process, this did not mean there was no just price. Instead of regarding price-formation as fully open (he was critical of

[376] C. H. Haring, *The Spanish Empire in America* (New York, Harcourt Brace 1947), 297.

[377] M. N. Pearson, 'Merchants and States', in James D. Tracy (ed.), *The Political Economy of Merchant Empires* (Cambridge University Press 1991), 80 and Thomas A. Brady. 'The Rise of Merchant Empires, 1400–1700. A European Counterpoint', in ibid., 145–6.

[378] The just price is not so much an economic category in Vitoria and Soto as a measure of commutative justice in the moral–legal order. It put into practice the need to ensure equality and reciprocity of exchanges. See Juan Antonio Widow, 'Economic Teachings of Spanish Scholastics', in Kevin White (ed.), *Hispanic Philosophy in the Age of Discovery* (Catholic University of America Press 1997), 135–6. Although the price of a commodity was determined subjectively, that determination reflected an objective assessment of the situation on the market.

[379] Vitoria, ComST II-II 77 1 n 2 (117–18).

price-manipulation as well as the so-called dry contracts that involved hidden forms of usury) they fell back on the *communis aestimatio*.[380] A regular exchange contract was lawful if it involved no fraud or deception, it was carried out voluntarily (and not through coercion), involved no monopolistic price-juggling and if there was a "legal price", it had been followed.[381]

Vitoria's "subjective theory of value" was followed with minor variations by all the Salamanca scholars. It was especially appropriate for a moral–legal outlook on the economy because it made it possible to determine the justice of the transaction by taking account of all the details of the context, including assessments of the necessity and utility of the transaction *como vale en la plaza*.[382] This allowed Vitoria to respond to price variations caused by inflation and was fitting for an increasingly financialised system where attention was no longer on the costs of production or the material economy in general, but on a complex series of transactions between a number of different operators.[383] Of course, not everything was amenable for "common estimation". An insufficient number of buyers or sellers would affect price-setting so that the standard of "honest man" (*boni viri*) might offer a better standard.[384] There were rare items (such as a single house) for which the just price could only be determined by taking into account the costs, the age of the house and other such things. For luxury items (*rebus non necessariis*), such as rare paintings, the just price would be simply what is agreed, excluding again the cases of fraud, deception and ignorance.[385] On the other hand, there were moments – threatening famine, for instance – when a "legal price" (*tasa*) was to be determined by public authority. In all cases where the transaction had been unjust, there was duty of restitution.[386]

380 Deckers, *Gerechtigkeit*, 247–8; Chafuen, *Faith and Liberty*, 82–3.

381 On Vitoria's views on value and the just price, see further Demetrio Paraguirre, *Francisco de Vitoria. Una teoria social del valor económico* (Bilbao 1957), 37–70; Ricardo F. Crespo, 'La posibilidad y justicia del intercambio. De Aristoteles a Marx, pasando por Tómas de Aquino y Francisco de Vitoria', in Juan Cruz Cruz (ed.), *Ley y Dominio en Francisco de Vitoria* (Pamplona, Eunsa 2008), 273–5; Zorroza, 'Introducción', 52–6.

382 Vitoria, ComST II-II 77 1 n 2 (118).

383 Louis Baeck, 'Monetarismo y teorías del desarollo en la Península Ibérica en los siglos dieciséis y diecisiete', in Gómez Camacho & Robledo, *El pensamiento económico*, I, 172.

384 Vitoria, ComST II-II 77 1 n 4 (121).

385 Ibid., II-II 77 1 n 6 (123).

386 Ibid., II-II 77 1 n 4 (120). Of course, Vitoria held that even if a transaction was lawful under human law, it might still involve an injustice and be condemned by divine law in the court of conscience, n 8 (126).

Some decades later, Azpilcueta expanded on these principles by accepting a wider latitude of variations to the just price in view of time, place and other contextual factors.[387] It may vary depending on whether it is set up by authorities, by common estimation or, in the absence of these, by the vendor himself. The justice of price-setting depended on a variety of factors, not least on the type of merchandise, of which Azpilcueta gave a long list of examples. The perspective, however, remained always with the seller; the assumption was that the parties to the transaction were either professional merchants or professional merchants and their customers and that the substance of the problem of just price was to be approached by comparing the merchant's intentions to the large-scale trends in the economic context.[388]

By far the most achieved of the Spanish sixteenth-century commercial texts was the *Suma de tratos y contratos* (second edition 1571) by Tomás de Mercado (1530–75), who had been trained in Mexico but spent the latter part of his career in Salamanca. Mercado had observed the intensification of mining and trade in the Indies. Commerce passing through the *Casa de contratación* had become so rich, he wrote, that it "invited and attracted some of our princes to become merchants themselves so as to attain enormous gains and establish numerous new provinces [in the Indies]".[389] In a brief history of trade, Mercado gave an altogether positive description of the services that merchants had rendered to their communities but also lamented their recent tendency to enrich only themselves. The intention behind the work, he explained, was to single out the virtues and vices of commerce, by discussing all of its aspects through the texts of Aristotle, Aquinas as well as canon and civil law.[390] Like other Spanish commentators, Mercado based the value of commercial activities on the intention of the merchant: to the extent that the point was to attain a living for one's family and to fulfil the needs of the republic, it was a perfectly acceptable service comparable to that of a medical doctor or lawyer.[391] The substantive parts of the work treated trade, monetary exchanges and usury with a close eye

387 Azpilcueta, *Manual de confessores*, XXIII (328).

388 Muñoz de Juana, *Moral y económia*, 168–76, 198–201. See also 176–85 for comments on the variations in the Latin edition.

389 Tomás de Mercado, *Suma de tratos y contratos* (Madrid, Editora nacional 1975), 124, 125.

390 Ibid., 133.

391 Ibid., 143. According to Mercado, trade had a threefold legitimate objective, in order of importance: to support the republic, to assist the poor and to provide a livelihood for the family.

to the practices and needs of Castilian merchants (the work was composed for the *Consulado* of Seville). Matters discussed included the determination of the just price, sale for cash, the uses of letters of credit, commercial companies, trade in the Indies (including slave trade), monetary exchanges, interest and usury. It was a moral treatise that sometimes took a strong view, as when its second edition devoted a whole section to defend the determination of the "legal price" (for wheat) against the cruel depredations of the merchants.[392] But it was designed to commend and support commerce, and Mercado often praised the wisdom of the merchants, for example when they had diversified and coordinated their activities while prudently warning them of the injustices this might occasion.[393]

A particular point of concern for the Spanish were the novel forms of credit that facilitated long-distance trading and helped to sustain the government's engagement in its unending wars. For the crown, the problem was that the gold and silver that it needed to pay for its expenses (especially by the costs of the military operations in the Low Countries) arrived in Seville only twice a year; meanwhile, its bankers would issue letters of exchange or credit so as to pay for its suppliers and to provide salaries to its soldiers. These letters then "became the oil that kept the wheels of the empire turning":

> The notes could travel rapidly with the mail, making credit available immediately; real payment would come later, when the relevant bullion arrived. As countries spent more money on war and foreign policy, the credit that they demanded stimulated the business of international financiers and traders, who arranged themselves into consortiums to take on the huge loans (or 'asientos') asked for by the Spanish empire.[394]

The "credit boom" that was legally organised by the instrument of the letter of exchange, as well as the *juros* and *asientos* issued by the crown, extended to private trading. This was hugely significant as almost two-thirds of the bullion came to private contractors, further contributing to the emergence of an economy based on paper money that nevertheless depended on the availability of bullion and with it, speculation about availability.[395] There were two reasons why letters of exchange became the most important instruments in private trading between merchants

[392] Ibid., Bk 3. [393] Ibid., 137. [394] Kamen, *Spain's Road to Empire*, 293.

[395] For some of these numbers, see Dennis O. Flynn & Arturo Giraldez, 'Born with a "Silver Spoon". The Origin of World Trade in 1571', 6 *Journal of World History* (1995), 209–12.

visiting trade fairs in Medina del Campo, Lisbon, Rome, Flanders and other locations. First, travelling these distances with gold and silver, the only shared currencies in Europe, was a hazardous business. It was much better to carry a paper note against which the banker or the *cambista* in the destination would pay the amount needed for trading purposes. Second, in long-standing business it was practical for traders to provide such letters to each other whereby they could credit their payments at later fairs against what they had sold at earlier ones. And they could of course also use these as independent instruments for making payments to third parties that would ultimately be guaranteed by the bank or other professional credit provider with whom the original letter had been signed and issued.[396]

With this, the Salamanca scholars began to think of money as not just a sign or an instrument of exchange but as possessing value in itself so that it could be accumulated for investment purposes and exchanged for profit, i.e. interest. Traditionally, this had raised the question of usury. Was the whole economic system based on it?[397] Vitoria's extensive treatment of usury opened with an apparently unconditional prohibition of taking interest for lending: money was "sterile" and making it produce was contrary to natural law.[398] This meant that "to engage in usury, that is to accept some fee for borrowing is to sin mortally... in the same way as killing a human being is a mortal sin".[399] Nevertheless, in the course of his discussion, he qualified that view and ended up positively endorsing a reasonable fee for professional bankers and *cambistas.*[400] Lending

396 See e.g. García García & Alonso Rodriquez, 'El pensamiento económico y el mundo del derecho', 81–90. For the operations of the Spanish *cambistas* and bankers at this time generally, see the indispensable Abelardo del Vigo, *Cambistas, mercaderes y banqueros en el siglo de oro español* (Madrid: Biblioteca de autores cristianos 1997).

397 For this section, see Raymond De Roover, *La pensée économique des scolastiques* (Montreal, Institute d'études médiévales 1971), 76–90. On the difficulties experienced by the theologians to classify the nature of the exchange contract (was it a sale, a loan [*mutuum*], a rent...?), see Vigo, *Cambistas*, 235–42.

398 Vitoria, ComST II-II 78 1 n 1, 3 (153–4, 155).

399 "... accipere aliquid pro mutuatione pecunae est peccatum mortale ... [id] est peccatum mortale sicut occidere hominem est mortale". Ibid., II-II 78 1 n 2 (154, 155).

400 Ibid., II-II 78 2 nn 64–6 (226–8). The *cambista* provides a service that is useful for the community and for which it is lawful to require a benefit. However, unlike his Dominican predecessor Cardinal Cajetan, Vitoria extends this right beyond professional bankers to routine transactions by merchants that have the objective of facilitating long-distance trade, nn 66, 69 (227–8, 229). Nevertheless, the basic view that Vitoria and such first-generation Salamancans as Soto, Cano, Medina and Villalón (with the exception of Azpilcueta) had of the *cambistas* was predominantly negative. For a review, see Vigo, *Cambistas*, 229–35.

facilitated international exchanges and created the basis for accumulation that could be useful for investment purposes. Even as usury *did* violate commutative justice, in international exchanges that involved several parties it was often difficult to determine the equilibrium commanded by it. So Vitoria and others followed Aquinas in suggesting that lending caused some damage to the lender and that interest could be understood as compensation, *damnum emergens*, in some instances even for unattained profit, *lucrum cessans*.[401]

The theologians also accepted that price fluctuations between the fairs may be justly taken into account in determining the value of money to be exchanged or of a letter of exchange issued in one place to be cashed in another. But they had difficulty in accepting interest taking for purely monetary exchanges (*ars campsoria*). If money really was "sterile", how could a mere exchange produce profit?[402] To approve this in respect of professional bankers and *cambistas*, Azpilcueta argued, was justified because they, unlike ordinary citizens, put the money to productive uses instead of hoarding it.[403] Throughout his famous text on money, Azpilcueta stressed the usefulness of publicly authorised *cambistas* but condemned private (i.e. non-authorised) lending and exchanging as sinful.[404] The same applied to profits resulting from professional exchanges of regular commodities. In case the profit/interest relationship was not unreasonable (e.g. there was no *laesio enormis*), then, owing to the general interest in professional trading, it was lawful.[405] As the Salamanca scholars began to speculate about alternative avenues of investment as well as compensation for missed business opportunities their focus could no longer remain exclusively on the *forum conscientiae*. The determination of the justice of single transactions required situating

401 Vitoria, ComST II-II 78 2 nn 2–3 (167–9); Soto, *De iustitia et iure*, VI 1 1 and 3 (508a–514b, 521b–525b).

402 For an overview of the critical positions, see Vigo, *Cambistas*, 216–35.

403 Azpilcueta, *Comentario resolutorio de usuras* (1556), quoted in Stephen J. Grabill, *Sourcebook in Late-Scholastic Monetary Theory. The Contributions of Martín de Azpilcueta Navarro, Luis de Molina, S.J., and Juan de Mariana, S.J.* (New York, Lexington 2007), 7. Azpilcueta defended the view that taking interest could be justified as a fee for taking the risk by reference to "all Christian custom ... and ... the general opinion", in 'Commentary on the Resolution of Money', ibid., 1 1 (23). In comparison with most other writers at the time, Azpilcueta's views on the *cambistas* were quite positive.

404 E.g. Azpilcueta, 'Commentary', 7 24 (51) ("exchanges that are mortally evil are those where the exchanger takes more than his fair salary").

405 García García y Rodriguez, 'El pensamiento económico y el mundo del derecho', 70; Wood, *Medieval Economic Thought*, 148–9.

them in a whole chain of economic operations, real and imagined, and attitudes commonly taken with respect to them. It was not surprising that they soon received competitors from the so-called *arbitristas* whose "technocratic" and macroeconomic analyses fitted better the *fin-de-siècle* atmosphere that closed the reign of Philip II.[406]

Steps towards a "systemic" view were taken already in Mercado's long chapter on international trade practices that required different types of credit and money-lending all around the world at all times. *Cambistas*, he suggested, emerged less out of spontaneous interest for profit-making than as parts of a universal network of economic operations.[407] As demand and supply were being organised at an international scale by bankers in Italy, Germany, Flanders and England, and as the value of the paper-moneys was determined by their credit policies, the result was that the princes started to become even theoretically unable to control the price-levels in their territories. As it was these same institutions that also lent the funds needed by the Castilian court to carry out its endless wars, the king was compelled to direct whatever domestic sources of revenue he could muster directly as payments for his debts, thus binding his hands in regard to domestic policy as well.[408]

Vitoria and Soto witnessed the unprecedented rise of prices in Spain and elsewhere as a result of the massive importation of silver from the Indies.[409] This led them to follow Azpilcueta into the theory that the value of money was relative to its quantity on the market. This departed from assessing lending activities from the perspective of individual consciences. As Soto explained:

> The more plentiful money is in Medina the more unfavourable are the terms of exchange and the higher the price that must be paid by whoever wishes to send money from Spain to Flanders, since the demand of money is smaller in Spain than in Flanders. And the scarcer money is in Medina the less he need pay there, because more people want money in Medina than are sending it to Flanders.[410]

406 Baeck, 'Monetarismo', 182–98.

407 Mercado, *Suma de tratos y contratos*, 313–18.

408 For the massive indebtedness of the Spanish crown from the ascension of Charles V to the imperial chair in 1519 (largely credited to the bribes Charles purchased from German and Genovese bankers) to the end of the reign of Philip II (1598), during which time Spain declared bankruptcy three times (1557, 1575 and 1596), see Vigo, *Cambistas*, 7–13.

409 In a short period the ratio of gold/silver changed from 1/10 to 1/15. Baeck, 'Monetarismo', 176.

410 Soto, *De iustitia et iure*, VI 12 2 (595a–b). Translation in Grice-Hutchinson, *Early Economic Thought*, 103. Likewise Molina, 'Treatise on Money (1597)', Grabill, *Sourcebook*, Arguments 406–7 (197–205).

Four hundred dinars in Spain may thus have the value of three hundred in Flanders without anybody along the way making themselves guilty of the sin of usury. The most extensive contemporary study of price fluctuations, however, was Azpilcueta's analysis of the different types of exchange and, especially, of the various factors affecting the value of money. His innovation was to treat money like any other good; its value was dependent, among other things, on the quantity of it that was available when the quantity of commodities as well as buyers and sellers remained unchanged. And because those quantities varied between countries, it was natural that the prices of things likewise varied and that professional merchants would try to buy where their money was strongest and sell where they would get the best price.[411]

The notions of *dominium*, price-formation and debt on which the emerging commercial world was based were largely accepted by subsequent generations of Spanish scholastics with whom "the idea of the market was increasingly 'objectivized' and 'depersonalized'".[412] The Jesuit Molina, for example, expanded the utilitarian justification of private property by arguing that the move from natural law-based common ownership into private property had been illuminated by a natural light (*lumen naturale*) that God had inserted in all humans and that made it possible to understand that among sinners, to avoid worse evils, properties needed to be divided. This was not about what was necessary, but what was expeditious (*expediens*) for the common welfare.[413] Molina accepted the quantity theory of money and the formation of the just price – for money as for other goods – through the impersonal process of common estimation. If monetary exchanges depended on where they were carried out, "we should not consider the commonly accepted price for exchanges from one place to another unjust, but rather just and a standard to judge whether the [exchanges] that greatly move away from it because of excess or insufficiency, exceed what is just".[414]

The theory of *dominium* as the sphere of commercial freedom opened a wholly new way to speak of human authority beyond dubious claims

411 Azpilcueta, 'Commentary', 12 (69–76). For the "quantity theory of money" in Azpilcueta, see Muñoz de Juana, *Moral y económia*, 323–32.

412 Decock, *Theologians and Contract Law*, 4 and further Grice-Hutchinson, *Early Economic Thought*, 98–102.

413 Ludovici Molinae, *De iustitia et iure. Tomi sex* (Antverpiae, Keerberginum 1615), II 20 (43b).

414 Luis Molina, 'Treatise on Money (1597)', in Grabill, *Sourcebook*, Argument 410 (227).

about papal or imperial power.[415] The contacts it opened across the world were understood to give expression to the rights and liberties of individual merchants, freedom of contract especially.[416] Perhaps the most striking example is Vázquez, whom we saw earlier insisting on the inability of the prince to intervene with the liberty of his subjects without a just cause. Vázquez operated with very extensive notion of private property. The owner was entitled to use his or her property even in ways that were useless, lavish or wasteful, as long as no injury was caused to others (*rei suae liberrimum usum habere . . . ea etiam possit abuti*).[417] This very extensive notion was underlain by a definition of liberty as the natural faculty to do what one wants in ways that were not physically prevented or prohibited by law.[418] Princes, for example, were not entitled to order merchants to use their properties in particular ways, even if they constantly acted as if it they had such power.[419]

The universal structure of private rights that emerged from Vitoria, Soto and their followers spoke to popular views about the republican ideals behind the Spanish monarchy and bound the ruler – at least in principle – to rule for the common good, understood as the free operation of *dominium*-rights.[420] It set up a universal field of economic liberty that could be invoked against the holders of public power. Las Casas could not have been clearer when he denied the king any power on the properties of his subjects, *nec quoad utile, nec quoad directum*. All the prince was entitled to do was to exercise the rights of jurisdiction and protection.[421] Later in the century, the Jesuit Juan de Mariana applied this argument with great force against the practice of monetary mutations: "if the king is the director – not the master – of the private possessions of his subjects, he will not be able to take away arbitrarily any part of their possessions. . . . Such seizure occurs whenever money

415 For Vázquez, the rejection of universal authority opened a way to a full-bodied consensualism in *Controversiarum*, II II 20 24–6 (26–7).

416 For the rise of the freedom of contract in this context, see Decock, *Theologians and Contract Law*.

417 Vázquez, *Controversiarum*, I I 17 2 (320).

418 "libertas est naturalis facultas eius, quod cuique facere libet, nisi quid vi aut iure prohibeatur", ibid., I 17 5 (321). The reference to "force" ("vi") illustrates the author's (realist) wish to set *de facto* limits alongside formal–legal ones. To justify this, he distinguished between "potentia" and "actu" in a way that left the liberty as a "potentiality" untouched even when subjected to *de facto* limitation ("in actu"). See further Seelmann, *Die Lehre des Fernando Vázquez*, 92–8.

419 Vázquez, *Controversiarum*, I I 17 3, 8 (against Soto), (320–1, 323).

420 Ambrosetti, *Il diritto naturale*, 60–1.

421 Las Casas, 'De regia potestate', XII 9 (104).

is debased."[422] It also followed from this for Mariana and many others, including Vázquez, that the ruler was not entitled to raise tribute or taxes without the subjects' permission.

Wherever authority was now being exercised, it could be assessed by universal rights of property, self-defence, travel, trade, taking of possession of ownerless things and so on. This was an inevitable consequence of the fact that *dominium* was treated predominantly in the context of commutative and not distributive justice, that is, relationships between subjects themselves, excluding intervention of public power by any other motives than the realisation of the common good. Chafuen summarises the resulting economic views of the Spanish scholastics as follows:

> Late-scholastic theory analyzed profits, wages and rent as matters of commutative justice and applied rules similar to those used to analyze the prices of goods. The Schoolmen determined that wages, profits and rents are not for the government to decide. Since they are beyond the pale of distributive justice, they should be determined though common estimation of the market.[423]

In their confrontation with the intensifying economic activities on the Iberian peninsula, in the New World and beyond, Spanish theologians would gradually shed their suspicion of merchants, *cambistas* and bankers and focus on the motives for which they carried out their activities. They would learn to believe that trading and lending, banking and exchange, letters of credit and insurance, among a host of other commercial techniques, operated as a "system" that would eventually be to the benefit of Christian families and communities. The principal concern of the theologians was to prevent this process from undermining the religious basis of society. Hence the church's insistence on confession and penance. Hence also recourse to the vocabulary of "justice" that was expected to instruct on how to maintain that equality that was to pertain between Christians within economic transactions. Separating usurious transactions from normal trading practices had become overwhelmingly difficult, however. Most things had no fixed price, and long-distance commerce operated in a world where supply and demand varied greatly between different locations and at different times. By the end of the sixteenth century, theologians such as Luis Molina began to accept that the value of money "does not originate in

422 Juan de Mariana, 'A Treatise on the Alteration of Money (1609)', in Grabill, *Sourcebook*, 260.
423 Chafuen, *Faith and Liberty*, 102–3 (footnote omitted).

the currency itself, but in the circumstances, and is a very inconstant value".[424] If economic actors benefited from these differences, they were also bringing goods from places of abundance to places of scarcity, providing an indispensable service. He was ready to accept that:

> [it] is the practice of merchants who are more familiar with the estimation of goods than the scholastic doctors, and whose judgment we should abide by in these matters, especially when applied to the dealings they carry out with one another in which none of them can complain or object . . . [T]here cannot be a better rule than to pay attention to the current price in the exchange market, and to accept that price as just and accepted by the merchants' common estimation.[425]

Recourse to common estimation complicated immensely the provision of counsel of conscience. It detached the justice of forms of behaviour from the intentions of the subjects. The confessor was expected to know a great deal about various economic techniques and the fluctuations of price-levels at different markets. And could one really separate a single transaction from the system of which it was a part? This was attempted by the extremely detailed moral casuistry developed by Vitoria, Soto and their followers. In the end, however, the vocabulary of justice that focused on the relations of equality between parties to *single* transactions had to yield to a more systemic view that would treat whole classes of transactions from the perspective of the welfare of the community. For making such assessments, however, theologians would have no particular competence.

## War and *Dominium*

Something similar took place with respect to that other institution with ubiquitous presence in the lives of sixteenth-century Spaniards, war. The reign of Charles V was characterised by almost constant warfare on several fronts – to support hereditary claims in Northern Italy, to affirm superiority over the kings of France, to challenge a reluctant pope, to fight heresy in Germany and the Low Countries, to react to Turkish incursions on the Mediterranean, not to say anything about the conduct of the *conquista*. It is striking how little concerned the Salamanca theologians were about Christian belligerency. After all, the state of nature had been not only one of freedom, equality and common

424 Luis Molina, 'Treatise on Money (1597)', Argument 410, in Grabill, *Sourcebook*, 221.
425 Ibid., Argument 407, in Grabill, *Sourcebook*, 203, 205.

ownership, but also of peace: *Est de jure naturali pax.*[426] There was no lack of Christian writers who pointed to the glaring gap between the peaceful message of the Gospel and the reality of sixteenth-century Europe some of whom, like Erasmus, or indeed Luther, linked that perception to a more general critique of the culture of the period.[427] But there had also been a long Christian tradition justifying warfare on the basis of the original sin.[428] Vitoria and Soto both viewed fighting as sometimes needed for the good of the community, and ascribed to the duty of Christians to follow their sovereign to just war.[429] Abraham, Moses and David had often waged just wars and Jesus had never instructed soldiers to lay down their arms. The right to go to war had been frequently affirmed by Augustine, and many Christian princes had waged war with "saintly and learned bishops as their advisers".[430] Soto affirmed that war was sometimes necessary to prepare peace and that full pacifism by contrast was plainly heretical.[431] The same conclusion was reached by one of the later leaders of the school, Juan de La Peña (1513–65), Professor at Salamanca from 1561, defending the orthodox Catholic view.[432] Self-defence was a basic principle of natural law and applied to

426 Vitoria, ComST II-II 57 3 n 3 (15).

427 See e.g. Buzzi, 'Il tema de *iure belli* nella seconda scolastica', 74–7; Delgado, *El pensamiento humanista*, 139–40.

428 For the Augustinian tradition that saw just war as an act of charity in that it prevented the evildoer from doing more harm, see e.g. Frederick H. Russell, *The Just War in the Middle Ages* (Cambridge University Press 1975), 16–39. This reading was also reflected in the way Aquinas in the *Summa* situated war within the theological virtue of charity.

429 The situation they had in mind was the recent advance of Suleiman the Magnificent through the Balkans and towards Vienna. As Vitoria often agonised, the first objective among Christians should be to reconcile Charles V with his French enemy so as to ensure a united Christian front, an "armed peace" against the Turks. See especially Pereña, 'La tesis de la paz dinámica', 46–8, 56–63. See also the letter by Vitoria to Pedro Fernández de Velasco of 19 January 1536, in *Political Writings*, 337–8.

430 Vitoria, 'On the Law of War', 1 1 § 1 (297–8).

431 Domingo de Soto, 'Quaestio 40 De bello, A 1', in Luciano Pereña et al. (eds), *Francisco de Vitoria, Relectio de iure bello o paz dinámica. Escuela Española de la paz. Primera generación 1526–1560* (Madrid, Consejo superior de investigaciones cientificas 1981), 300, 301. Soto lectured on *De bello* in 1540 and 1556, and the text was published as part of his commentary on St Paul to the Romans and in *De iustitia et iure*. I here use the text of the lecture as published in ibid., 299–321.

432 Juan de La Peña, 'Quaestio 40 De Bello', in Luciano Pereña et al. (eds), *Juan de la Peña. De bello contra insulanos, CHP* vol. *IX* (Madrid, Consejo superior de investigaciones cientificas 1982), § 3 (406) ("sic est conclusio catholica, videlicet, bellum, servatis conditionibus iusti belli, est et fuit semper licitum, et contrarium est haeresis").

anyone unjustly attacked. Offensive war was an instrument of the prince who in undertaking it acted as a judge in order to avenge an injury.[433] In a gloss to the passage in the Gospel where Christ criticised the use of the sword, Peña argued that war was not an evil *per se*, but when just, had peace as its objective. Like medicine, it may be strong but when prescribed by right authority would bring about health (*ordinatur ad sanitatem*).[434] But as the theory of the just war encountered the conditions of the world, it expanded into such a complex moral casuistry where moral certainty could no longer be gained without consulting religious authority.

The Salamanca scholars set aside earlier texts composed by military experts that had dealt with war as a contest of forces between adversaries. Such writings had emerged in the late Middle Ages to treat the nature of the military profession and the good conduct and discipline among soldiers, with some discussion of military strategy and little serious attention to moral issues. Recent syntheses of these literatures had been composed by two military judges at the service of the Spanish armies, Pierino Belli (1502–75) and Balthasar de Ayala (c. 1548–1584). Both were engaged in the justification of Spanish wars and paid most attention to the practical matters of military law in the context of large operations abroad.[435] For Vitoria and Soto, however, the most important questions about war had to do with its justice (*ius ad bellum*) – a question they treated as a problem of conscience that was differently resolved with respect to the sovereign and his close advisors on the one hand, and regular subjects on the other.[436] This discussion usually began with the view of the just war as an aspect of the theological virtue of *charity* that Aquinas had discussed in *Quaestio* 40 of the *Secunda secundae*. From this it followed that alongside the protection of the commonwealth, war was also sometimes needed "for the purpose and good of the whole world", including the protection of the innocent, wherever they might find themselves. Just war was an act of neighbourly

433 Ibid., 1 § 4 (408), § 9 (428). "Qui potest indicere bellum iudex est", ibid., § 4 (430).

434 Ibid., § 6 (422, 418–22).

435 Pierino Belli, *A Treatise on Military Matters and Warfare* (H. C. Nutting trans., Oxford University Press 1936); Balthasar de Ayala, *De jure et officiis bellicis et disciplina militarii libri tres* (Oxford University Press 1912).

436 For a brief comparison of the two literatures, see Peter Haggenmacher, 'Just War and Regular War in Sixteenth Century Spanish Doctrine', 32 *International Review of the Red Cross* (1992), 434–45.

love and part of the mechanism whereby God ordained human beings to their supernatural ends.[437]

Three elements in the discussion of war in Vitoria and Soto are striking for a modern reader. These have to do with the systemic placing of war in their view of law and justice. A first is the brief, almost offhand treatment of war in self-defence. The right to wage defensive war was obvious and belonged not only to the prince or to the commonwealth but to all individuals and communities, so that, Vitoria pointed out, if Toledo were to attack Salamanca, then Salamanca would have the right to defend itself by force if necessary.[438] As a law of nature, the right of self-defence did not at all come under the commutative justice of *ius gentium* and, for example, did not turn the private person into a judge over the attacker.[439]

The second significant aspect of the discussion was the reversal of the traditional order of the "three criteria" so that the discussion now began with the question of the right authority (of the prince) while the subject of the just cause was relegated to the secondary place, treated with relative brevity by pointing to the presence of a wrong (*iniuria*) and excluding any general power to enforce natural law. A "wrong" was simply a violation of the right of *dominium*.

This definition opened into the third and the most important element in the scholastic theory, namely the treatment of doubt or ignorance about the war's justice. This concern emerged with element of the "right intention" (*recta ratio*) that assessed war from the perspective of personal virtue, raising the question of the state of the conscience of the prince, his ministers, generals and ordinary soldiers. The theologians' war was never *only* about its material objectives (peace and tranquillity, restitution and punishment) but also about faith and beatitude. As Azpilcueta pointed out, when the war was conducted with lack of authority or lack of a just cause, it was sinful as it violated commutative justice and could therefore be accompanied by restoration. But if it was conducted in the absence of right intention, it breached not only justice

437 Vitoria, 'On the Law of War', 1 1 § 1 (298) and 1 4 § 19 (305). See further, Haggenmacher, *Grotius*, 402–3; Buzzi, 'Il tema de *iure belli* nella seconda scolastica', 109–13.

438 "Si Toletani invadant Salmanticenses, isti possunt sua auctoritate defendere se", Vitoria, ComST II-II 40 1 n 3 (280). Likewise e.g. Soto, *De iustitia et iure*, III 1 3 (197b–198a) and Azpilcueta, *Commentarius utilis in rubricam de iudiciis*, n 55 (34).

439 It did not involve the right to punish or to forcibly capture stolen goods. Melchior Cano, 'Quaestio 40 De bello', in Pereña (ed.), *Francisco de Vitoria. Relectio de iure belli o paz dinamica*, Prima Quaestio (325).

but also *charity*, for the breach was not between the parties but between one of them and God. In that case, reparation would play no role.[440]

The Salamanca scholars took from Aquinas the view of just war as an act of public authority that the prince was to carry out in the mode of the judge. Only the lawful prince, head of an independent commonwealth, may wage it, and he did so on behalf of the whole world. Just war was the continuation of divine government.[441] Neither subjects nor minor officials or magistrates (such as the duke of Alba or the count of Benavente) had competence to wage it without authorisation.[442] Private persons may defend themselves under natural law but they may not restore property or avenge the wrong. A just *offensive* war, the only situation of real concern for Vitoria and his followers, involved an exercise of public authority in the same way as punishment of criminals did, highlighting the parallel between *ius gentium* and domestic law: "it is necessary for the proper administration of human affairs that this authority [i.e. enforcement] should be granted to the commonwealth".[443]

There were three types of permissible *causa*: to vindicate the rights of the republic and its members; to restore what has been unlawfully taken, and to punish the wrong-doers (*ad vindicandum se de hostibus, ad recuperandum sua bona et ad puniendum hostes*).[444] The language varied somewhat in the different places where Vitoria came to this matter. In the early *relectio* 'On Civil Power' Vitoria stated that "[t]he commonwealth has no power to wage war except for the protection of itself and its affairs".[445] This seemed quite limited, almost collapsing just war to

[440] "Lex iustitiae obligat restituere, non lex charitatis", Azpilcueta, *Commentarius utilis in rubricam de iudiciis*, n 105 (78–9).

[441] "What is a prince?", Vitoria asks, following Cajetan, responding that for the purposes of the just war as "princes" those qualify who have no superior. Vitoria, ComST II-II, 40 I n 3 (280). See further Urbano, *El pensamiento de Francisco de Vitoria*, 177–8; Justenhoven, *Francisco de Vitoria*, 89–94. Vitoria makes an exception, however, for the situation where a prince of a non-fully independent entity has the authority to make war under *ius gentium* or customary law, 'On the Law of War', 1 2 § 9 (302). For the practical regulation of this matter, however, Vitoria accepts that human law – including *ius gentium* – and custom may regulate this matter differently too, ibid., § 9 (302).

[442] Vitoria, 'On the Law of War', 1 2 § 6–7 (301).

[443] Ibid., 1 2 § 5 (300).

[444] Vitoria, ComST II-II 40 1 n 3 (281). Haggenmacher distinguishes five more specific objectives: defence of public good; recovery of goods stolen or their value; seizure of enemy property as reparation; measures to strengthen future peace, and punishment of the guilty, *Grotius*, 172.

[445] Vitoria, 'On Civil Power', 1 10 § 13 (21).

self-defence. Even for Soto, the just war had to do more extensively with guaranteeing the peace and security of the commonwealth (*finis belli est pax et tranquillitas et securitas reipublicae*).[446] A decade later, Vitoria suggested that the "only just cause for waging war" was that "harm has been inflicted".[447] What this left open was what might count as "harm" and what might be an appropriate reaction. In fact, the rights whose protection was to be ensured by just war were quite extensive, including rights of travel, trade and the uses of common resources.[448] Vitoria also extended the notion of "harm" to allies. But it soon became a general doctrine among the Salamancans that just war could be waged in order to defend the innocent and to punish those who had harmed them.[449]

Although there of course is a difference between war as an instrument of peace and security and war as a means for vindicating rights, whether in a narrower or wider sense, in practice these considerations tended to coalesce – preservation of *dominium* (in either of its forms) was both about order and rights (of property and jurisdiction).[450] For the theologians, war *itself* was not punishment. It was a mere technical

[446] Soto, 'Quaestio 40 De bello', in Pereña (ed.), *Francisco de Vitoria, Relectio de belli o paz dinamica*, 1 (305–6).

[447] Vitoria, 'On the Law of War', 1 3 § 13 (303).

[448] Vitoria, 'On the American Indians', 3 1 § 2 (to interfere with the right to travel "is an act of war", 278); § 3 (the Indians "cannot prevent their subjects from trading with the Spanish", 279); § 4 ("if there are any things among the barbarians that are held in common . . . it is not for the barbarians to prohibit the Spanish sharing and enjoying them", 280) and 3 2 § 12 (on evangelisation, 285). Vitoria's language was equivocal, however. In one place he said that "if the barbarians attempt to deny the Spanish in these matters which I have described as belonging to them by the law of nations (*ius gentium*) . . . [and] . . . insist on replying with violence, the Spaniards may defend themselves and do everything needful for their safety", 'On the American Indians', 3 1 § 6 (281–2). Although Vitoria is clear that the Indians may not be immediately attacked if they deny for example the right to use common resources, he accepts that this right may be ultimately enforced by means of ("defensive") war. For a fuller discussion, see Justenhoven, *Francisco de Vitoria*, 96–108.

[449] Vitoria, 'On the Law of War', 1 2 § 5 (300); 'On Dietary Laws', 1 5 *fifth conclusion* (225) and 'On the American Indians', 3 5 § 15 (287–8); 'On the Law of War', 1 4 § 19 (305–6). See also Soto, 'De bello', 1 306 ("Causa autem iusti belli est defendere innocentes a tyranno") and Cano, 'Quaestio 40 de bello', in Pereña (ed.), *Francisco de Vitoria, Relectio de belli o paz dinamica*, I, *septima conclusio* (327). See also Dieter Janssen, 'Die Theorie des gerechten Krieges im Denken des Francisco de Vitoria', in Grunert & Seelmann, *Die Ordnung der Praxis*, 216–18.

[450] For example, both Urbano and Justenhoven emphasise that for Vitoria, war is an instrument of peace and not of justice. Urbano, *El pensamiento*, 179–82; Justenhoven, *Francisco de Vitoria*, 71–5, 175. Although this is true to the extent that war is not an instrument to enforce abstract moral principles, the two miss the closeness (indeed perhaps identity) of Vitoria's view of "peace" and of the good order of "dominium".

preliminary that should be followed by a *separate act* of punishment after victory. Fighting was a kind of police action, an aspect of just government to maintain or restore order that in itself did not realise retributive justice. If the just war does express the *iustitia vindicativa*, it does this owing to its close relationship to the sacrament of penance: the "wrong" that triggered the war was also a sin, and to be absolved from sin it was necessary to suffer a penalty.[451] From this perspective, just war was indeed an act of charity that removed the obstacles to (just) peace and allowed the absolution of the sinner. Hence there was no conflict between the vindictive and the pacifying objectives of war: a just order was one where the rights of *dominium* were being enjoyed in peace.

It was not always clear how this theory fitted the wars in the New World. Enlargement of empire or the advancement of personal glory constituted prohibited causes of violence.[452] Nor was war permitted merely because the customs of foreigners might violate the laws of nature. It was not an instrument of divine judgment for sin or infidelity.[453] The sins of the Indians, Vitoria claimed, resulted from ignorance and lack of understanding, and it was not for Christian nations to avenge sin but for God.[454] Nor was it allowed to use force in order to convert the Indians – "for belief is an act of will".[455] God did not send his missionaries out as lions, Soto wrote, but as sheep in the middle of wolves, not only without weapons but without sticks, bags, bread and money.[456] On the other hand, prohibition of Catholic missionary activity or the prevention by an infidel prince of his subjects from hearing the Christians did constitute just causes of war. But violence could be used only to remove the obstacle, not to compel the unbelievers to convert or to cause damage and to put further obstacles to conversions.[457] That only voluntary

451 Haggenmacher, *Grotius*, 409–10.

452 Vitoria, 'On the Law of War', 1 3 § 10–12 (302–3). See also Soto, 'De bello', A 1 ("non potest aliquis indicere bellum sola causa amplificandi nationes et augendi rempublicam"), 305.

453 Vitoria, 'On Dietary Laws', I 5 (224–5); 'On the American Indians', 2 § 4–5 (265–75).

454 Vitoria, 'On the American Indians', 2 5 § 39, 40 (273). See further, Dieter Janssen, 'Die Theorie des gerechten Krieges', 210.

455 Aquinas, ST II-II 10 8 Resp (268).

456 Soto, *Relección 'De dominio'*, § 34 (162/163). Molina regarded any attempt to force conversion as almost tyrannical (*quasi tyrannis*). Luis de Molina, 'Utrum infideles sint compellendi ad fidem', in Pereña et al., *Juan de la Peña. De bello contra insulanos*, 356.

457 See e.g. Vitoria, 'On the American Indians', 3 2 § 12 (285–6); Molina, 'Utrum infideles sint compellendi ad fidem', 361–2 and e.g. Justenhoven, *Francisco de Vitoria*, 103–8.

conversion had the appropriate theological meaning would lead Vitoria's successors such as the Jesuit José de Acosta to argue for the invalidity of the original baptisms and for a programme of reconversion throughout the Indies.[458] The situation of Indian heretics and apostates, however, was quite different. Here it was a question of enforcing the original promise to convert; to enforce that promise was amply justified – just like heresy and apostasy at home justified handing the person over to the secular arm.[459]

Nevertheless, force might be used in order to defend the innocent – that is to say, in defence of the *dominium* that the innocent have over their lives and liberty.[460] The theologians had obviously in mind the gruesome stories they had heard of involuntary human sacrifice. That such permission could nevertheless be easily misused was stressed by Francisco de Toledo (1516–82), Viceroy of Peru, who accepted the principle, but stressed that such war could be waged only once the Indians had first been peacefully counselled to end those practices, and in any case, it was never to be done if this were to cause greater harm to the relations with the Indians.[461] In principle, it was a thin line that separated the rejection of the right to enforce natural law from the power to protect the innocent. Eventually, for Vitoria, it expanded into a rather extraordinary policing power:

> Surely it would be impossible for the world to be happy – indeed it would be the worst of all possible worlds – if tyrants and thieves and robbers were able to injure and oppress the good and the innocent without punishment, whereas the innocent were not allowed to teach the guilty a lesson in return.[462]

No doubt, such view went quite far in underwriting contemporary Spanish violence.[463] But scholastic teleology hardly gave an alternative:

458 See e.g. Pereña, *La idea de la justicia*, 135–60.

459 See e.g. Molina, 'Utrum infideles sint compellendi ad fidem', 363–6. In addition to punishing the heretics for their breach of promise, Molina justified their persecution on Realpolitik grounds: the crime of heresy destroyed the peace and tranquillity of the Christian republic, 366.

460 "the reason why the barbarians can be conquered is not that their anthropophagy and human sacrifices are against natural law, but because they involve injustice (*iniuria*) to other men", Vitoria, 'On Dietary Laws', 1 5 (225). For a discussion of the specifically *theological* basis of the Dominican defence of the "dominion over themselves" of even the infidel, see William Bain, 'Saving the Innocent, Then and Now. Vitoria, Dominion and World Order', 34 *History of Political Thought* (2013), 588–613.

461 Nor could war be justly waged if the sacrifice took place as punishment for crime or was voluntarily accepted. Francisco de Toledo, 'An ritus insularum sint tolerandi', in Pereña et al., *Juan de la Peña. De bello contra insulanos*, Quarta conclusio (380–1).

462 Vitoria, 'On the Law of War', 1 1, § 1 (298).

463 Urbano, *El pensamiento*, 184–5.

the power to prevent injustice flowed from *caritas*, an ethic of neighbourly love theologians could hardly ignore.[464] They had some awareness of the dangers. War was not to be commenced for mere trifles, they stressed, for it put the republic in peril and caused immense destruction. Misusing the justice of restitution by making exorbitant claims was in itself sinful and involved the duty to restore what has been excessively obtained.[465] The foreseeable benefits of war must be calculated against its costs. War was always to remain *ultima ratio*, available only once all other means had been exhausted.[466] A complex economy was introduced into the justice of fighting itself. Wanton violence was always prohibited. The only acts permitted were those that contributed to the objective of the war: peace and tranquillity, restoration and the punishment of the guilty.[467] The prohibition against the killing of the innocent was balanced against the need sometimes to avoid a greater evil (e.g. the death of even more innocents).[468]

But because the writings were oriented to instruct young clerics on the practice of confession, most attention was given to a third criterion – *recta intentio*, the "purity of heart".[469] This was an especially grave concern at a time of rudimentary discipline and indiscriminate violence by mercenary troops. All theologians believed that full certainty of a war's injustice constituted an absolute bar to participating in it.[470] Such a situation was a rare occurrence so that perhaps only the wars against the Turk would obviously qualify. Even for conscientious political and military leaders, matters were usually complicated by the fact that there would be something to be said for justice on both sides, especially in

464 Janssen, 'Theorie der gerechten Krieges', 234.

465 "... non licet usque ad extremum persequi inimicos in justo bello sed solum usque ad completam satisfactionem", Vitoria, ComST II-II 66 8 n 2 (342). Note also that the kings may not transfer the properties of their subjects or merchants as restitution to each other, n 4 (344). See also Soto, *De iustitia et iure*, V 3 5 (430b).

466 Vitoria, 'On Civil Power', 1 10 § 13 (21) and 'On the Law of War', 1 3 § 14 (304). And see Justenhoven, *Francisco de Vitoria*, 87–95.

467 See Vitoria, 'On the Law of War', 1 4 § 15 and 18 (304, 305). And for discussion, Justenhoven, *Francisco de Vitoria*, 127–63. "Dubitato an liceat interficere in bello. Respondeo quod si est necessarium ad victoriam", Vitoria, ComST II-II 40 1 n 9 (288) and generally nn 11–15 (284–8). Vitoria specifically condemns the destruction of French towns when no military necessity dictates it – "hoc facere est diabolicum", n 19 (287).

468 Vitoria, ComST II-II 64 6 n 2 (299); Justenhoven, *Francisco de Vitoria*, 139–40.

469 Vitoria, 'On the Law of War', 2, 1–4 § 20–32 (306–13). See also Rudolf Schlüssler 'Hadrian VI und das Recht auf Verweigerung zweifelhaft rechtmässige Befehle', in Brieskorn & Reichenauer, *Suche nach Frieden*, 43–5.

470 Vitoria, ComST II-II 40 1 n 8 (282); Soto, 'De bello', 1 304.

wars over territorial possessions among Europeans but, as Vitoria pointed out, also in wars against Indians who frequently had good reason not to trust invading Spaniards. For most people, carrying out a meticulous examination of the matter on their own would be hard or impossible. The theologians therefore distinguished between the prince and his closest counsel on the one hand, and soldiers and ordinary subjects on the other.

If regular subjects were convinced of the war's injustice, they ought not to serve in it.[471] But in dubious cases they should follow the prince.[472] Soto stressed that even in case of a "ordinary" doubt, that is to say, not a determined conviction, they were bound to follow the prince at the risk of otherwise committing a mortal sin.[473] On this basis, eventually, the whole commonwealth might be held to account for the acts of the prince. The prince, on the other hand, was in a more complex situation. First, "it [was] necessary [for him] to examine the justice and causes of war with great care, and also to listen to the arguments of the opponents if they are prepared to negotiate genuinely and fairly".[474] If after all such examination doubt still remained, war was not – in principle – to be commenced.[475] The prince was a judge, and a judge may not condemn the accused if he has any doubt about his guilt. There were also procedures and rules of thumb for dubious cases. The prince was to respect peaceful possession, for example (the Spanish made it clear that this presumption applied to the disputed Spanish rule over Milan and Burgundy). A just judge would never dispossess the one holding the property in dubious cases.[476] If nobody had effective

[471] The case of the killing of the Inca leader Atahualpa may appear precisely to be a case where the soldiers ought to have been convinced of the injustice of the act. See Vitoria's letter to Miguel de Arcos of 8 November 1535, in *Political Writings*, 331–3 and Justenhoven, *Francisco de Vitoria*, 112–13.

[472] "plebei ... non tenentur scire causam belli justam, sed possunt sequi regem", ComST II-II 40 1 n 8 (282). 'On the Law of War, 2 2 § 26 (308–9) and especially 2 3 § 31 (311–12) The same view was taken by Soto. See further Schüssler, 'Hadrian VI', *Suche nach Frieden*, 52–6.

[473] "homines de plebe et republica non debent examinare causam belli iustam, si non vocantur ad consilium, sed tenentur credere esse iustum, nisi contrarium appareat ... subditi principis tenentur credere principi", Soto, 'De bello', 1 (307).

[474] Vitoria, 'On the Law of War', 2 1 § 21 (307). Likewise Soto, 'De bello', 1(304) ("tenetur princeps diligentissime examinare et ius belli et causas belli. Immo vero tenetur primo audire accusationes et excusationes et defensiones adversariorum").

[475] "non suffit probabilitas sed certitudo in principe etiam iustissimo et christianissimo", Soto, 'De bello', 1 (304).

[476] Vitoria, 'On the Law of War', 2 3 § 27 (309–10); Soto, 'De bello', 1 (305). As one of Vitoria's followers in Salamanca, the Augustinian Juan de Guevara (1518–1600)

possession, a solution was to be reached by negotiation with the proviso that war could be waged against the one who refused to negotiate.[477] A similar duty to scrutinise the justice of the war carefully fell upon the "senators and territorial magnates".

But the most important instruction was that the prince must form his judgment "according to the opinion of a wise man".[478] It was practice that the king would set up *juntas* and *ad hoc consejos* in wartime, and those bodies would normally include theologians. Azpilcueta stressed that the king was obliged to study the causes carefully, without hurry, and that he could act only once he had consulted wise men (*viris probis & sapientibus*) and heard the adverse party (*audiendo rationes adversarii*). The royal confessor was to be involved, and he may not absolve a prince who had acted out of ignorance. It was the very point of the deliberations to dispose of that defence.[479] So important was this consultation that even if the king were finally to decide wrongly, he would be excused if only he had fulfilled the duty to consult. And conversely, the fact that the war was just would not save the king had he decided to wage it without recourse to church authority.[480] The main thing was always to act following one's concience, as enlightened by religious authority; otherwise the prince would "run the risk of betraying the commonwealth in the hands of the enemy which is worse than fighting the enemy, doubt notwithstanding".[481]

By far the largest part of Peña's later discussion also dealt with doubtful cases. Like Vitoria and Azpilcueta, he highlighted the obligation to examine the causes of war diligently. The prince may not go to war with doubt in his mind, for both belligerents might be doubtful and the war would then be equally just on both sides – *Hoc autem est*

pointed out in his long casuistic of doubtful cases, a just judge would never deprive a peaceful possessor of his possessions. If he acts in good faith, he is entitled to keep it all. But if he acts in bad faith, either as regards a part or whole of the disputed possession, then the judge ought to seek a middle way and, if possible, divide the property between the contestants. Juan de Guevara, 'Quaestio 40 De bello', in Pereña et al., eds, *Juan de la Peña, De bello contra insulanos*, 265–9.

477 Vitoria, 'On the Law of War', 2 3 § 28 (310) and generally Haggenmacher, *Grotius*, 209–16.

478 Vitoria, 'On the Law of War', 2 2 § 20 (306).

479 Azpilcueta, *Commentarius utilis in rubricam de iudiciis*, n 106 (79–80). In his *Manual*, Azpilcueta listed unjust war among the sins to which princes were especially prone, 360.

480 Vitoria, 'On the American Indians', Introduction, 234–8.

481 Vitoria, 'On the Law of War', 2, 3 § 31 (312). Likewise, Molina, *De justitia et jure* II, 113 (452), quoted in Costello, *Luis de Molina*, 144.

*impossibile.*[482] The just prince is a judge, and a judge who pronounces a guilty sentence while doubtful commits a mortal sin. The evidence of guilt must be clear as the light of day.[483] But instead of showing his readers how such clarity may be attained Peña's detailed casuistic about the various cases ended up only further muddying the waters. Proposing arbitration might help to prove that one party has justice on its side, especially if the adversary rejects the offer, but even this might not always be the case; in practice, the matter turns on casuistic assessment.[484] Like Vitoria, Peña assumed that if an ordinary subject was convinced of the war's injustice, he or she should not serve in it. For other situations, he distinguished between subjects who ought to follow their prince and those who are not subjects, and must be more discerning. Another distinction was drawn between soldiers receiving payment (who may participate in war even in doubtful cases) and soldiers who do not receive money (and ought to listen to their conscience).[485]

The difficulty of imagining one of the adversaries as a judge over the other is evident. In the end, Peña conceded that there might be ignorance on the part of the unjust belligerent, whether prince or a common soldier, and that ignorance might be either culpable or innocent in a way that must have an impact on the nature of the punishment as well as the quantity of possible restitution.[486] But the more a belligerent party's invincible ignorance became the standard case, as arguably happened in European territorial disputes, the more this highlighted the *bilateral* aspects of the war (Charles did not even propose to judge François after having captured him in 1525). Often it was sufficient that the territory was returned to its rightful owner; no other punishment was needed.[487] The application of commutative justice undermined the theory of war as enforcement; just war turns into a balancing of bilateral equities.[488]

The enforcement of *dominium* through just war capped the scholastic system of *ius gentium*. That the just prince acted as a judge over his adversary was a necessary part of this construction, however tenuous it became at a time of the fragmentation of the Christian religious world. The complex casuistic that underlay the discussion of invincible ignorance showed that

482 de La Peña,'Quaestio 40 De Bello', *Juan de la Peña*, § 14 (442).

483 "... probationes maximis in causis criminalibus debent esse luce meridiana clariores", ibid., § 12 (440).

484 Ibid., § 15 (444/445).

485 Ibid., § 16 (444/446).

486 Ibid., § 25–6 (468–74).

487 Ibid., § 22 (460–3).

488 For this slide among the scholastics, see Haggenmacher, *Grotius*, 421–37.

the whole system was already breaking apart. The difficulty of fitting a heterogenous experience within a universal reason where questions about justice and injustice would have been always *already* resolved led into probabilistic reasoning and the application of procedures and rules of thumb with which anything could be proven. Outsiders were quick to conclude that all this complex verbiage was simply "a Neoscholastic way of phrasing Machiavelli's dictum: war is an instrument of policy".[489]

## Conclusion

Vitoria and his colleagues were teachers of theology at a time when the Catholic church was employing the sacraments for the consolidation of a threatened orthodoxy. Confession was particularly important owing to the intimate access it offered to the conscience. According to Thomas Mercado:

> The confessor in Christianity is like the prince in the city to whom it belongs to see to it that all live in an orderly way and that laws are being made and executed. The confessors work, in cooperation with the penitent, to keep the law that was given at baptism, because they are judges of conscience.[490]

The confessor is so much more powerful than the priest; for the priest may counsel and persuade, "but the confessor may compel and force the penitent to obey on pain of death". One of the most important tasks of the confessor was "to make the vassals obey, in accordance the the gospel, to their lords", pay their tributes and taxes, and "keep their statutes, orders, legal prices and other commands [*posturas*]".[491] The confessors were to be "fathers of the republic, and its principal governors as well as principal guardians of what is good for it".[492] The religious aspect of Domincan teaching constantly crossed the boundary between the spiritual and the temporal, with the scholastic project involving a double move of supporting the centralised state on the one hand, and the liberties of its subjects on the other.

Vitoria and his successors used the vocabulary of natural law and *ius gentium* as instruments for the government of Christian consciences both within and outside confession. Those notions helped the prince to rule his community and the subjects to assess their duty of allegiance. The "law" that the Salamanca scholars received from Aquinas situated the Christian prince as an administrator and executor of the divine

[489] Fernández-Santamaría, *Natural Law, Constitutionalism, Reason of State, and War*, II, 165.
[490] Mercado, *Suma de tratos y contratos*, § 173 (172). [491] Ibid., § 174, 176 (172, 173).
[492] Ibid., § 177 (174).

plan, and the language of "justice" aimed to show how this was to be done in practice. The heart of justice was *dominium. Dominium* expressed the freedom that humans had received from God and that entitled them to organise their temporal existence so as to enable them to attain earthly happiness and supernatural beatitude. Pauline theology consolididated the power of the ruler and accompanied his acts with divine sanction. To fail in obedience was not only to commit a wrong but to sin. Law and faith were inextricable – a view that both liberated the ruler and bound him tightly to the church's ideological programme. This created some sense of reciprocal obligation, some search of justice and equality among Christians, as especially visible in the proliferating doctrines about just commerce. But the non-Christian world found itself over again as either the eternally alien object of Christian violence, or then disciplined by its always insufficient assimilation into an imposed hierarchy. The Salamanca scholars tried hard to compromise between received doctrine and a world undergoing rapid economic and cultural transformation. But the more daunting the challenges they faced, the more complex their accommodations became and the less control their proliferating casuistries could have on what was going on, namely a hardening of the practice of government.

Charles would soon learn to appreciate the power of the Inquisition at the service of the church and the crown.[493] Even as most of the Inquisition's activity before mid-century was directed at Protestants, *moriscos* and Jewish *conversos*, the expanding control it exercised over the Spanish reign efficiently stunned any effort at reforming the religious foundations of policy. In 1559 Philip II would tighten the controls further by ordering all Spaniards studying abroad to return home and prohibiting such study except in a handful or orthodox locations. Everything about Spanish policy would be based on king's view of Castile "as the Lord's chosen nation and the champion of His cause".[494] What this "cause" was and how it was to be implemented in policy remained subject to differing understandings even among the faithful, and the expansion of casuistry did nothing to make people return to the orthodoxies they had learned to put to question. It was therefore pointless for the Office of the Inquisition when, in 1590, it finally included Vitoria's *relectiones* in the *Index*.

[493] Thomas, *The Golden Empire*, 37.

[494] J. H. Elliott, Spain, *Europe & the Wider World 1500–1800* (Yale University Press 2009), 245.

# 3

# Italian Lessons

## Ius gentium *and Reason of States*

The setting was familiar. It was a meeting of four men in Florence at the home of the oldest of them, Bernardo del Nero, a former supporter of the recently collapsed rule of the Medici over the city. The others were Piero Capponi and Pagolantonio Soderini, two supporters of the newly established republican regime, and Piero Guicciardini, the father of the man recording the conversation. The discussion concerned the question of the government of Florence turning, at one point, to what should be done to the city's old vassal, Pisa, that had used the confusion of the intervention by France's Charles VIII to detach itself from Florentine lordship. In this matter as well as throughout the dialogue it was Bernardo, acting as the alter ago of the author, Francisco Guicciardini (1484–1540), who stressed that action needed to be decided not by reference to what was right but so as to solve the problem most efficiently. "Concerning Pisa", Bernardo began,

> this sickness is difficult to cure and has need of strong medicines and, to speak plainly, cruelty . . . one would need always to murder all the Pisans captured in the war, to decrease the number of our enemies and make the rest more timid, and if they did the same to you with yours, it would be little loss, since you would acquire others with money.[1]

Now Bernardo was not at all a man inclined to cruelty by character.[2] He readily admitted that "when I talked of murdering or keeping the

[1] Francisco Guicciardini, *Dialogue on the Government of Florence* (Alison Brown ed., Cambridge University Press 1994), II (157).

[2] As Guicciardini himself reflected towards the end of his career, "In my administrations I never liked cruelty or excessive punishments. Nor are they necessary. Except for certain cases that must serve as an example, you can sufficiently maintain fear if you punish crimes with three quarters of the penalty, provided you make it a

Pisans imprisoned, I didn't perhaps talk as a Christian: I talked according to the reason and practice of states". It was true, he said that "doing this one would acquire a name for cruelty and also of lack of conscience". But "anyone who wants to hold dominion and states in the day and age should show mercy and kindness where possible, and where there is no other alternative, one must use cruelty and unscrupulousness". Cutting through the hypocrisies of the moment, Bernardo turned to his friends, requesting them to reflect on their own lands:

> if you think carefully about it, perhaps nothing that belongs to you, since you have occupied it all, or at least most of it, by force of arms, or by buying it from someone who had no right to it?[3]

This famous moment in Guicciardini's *Dialogue on the Government of Florence* not only introduced the term "reason [and practice] of states" to the political vocabulary of what has come to be called "renaissance humanism" but constituted a full repudiation of the scholastic view of politics as a matter of Christian conscience, a point expressly made by the author. Here the issue was the traumatic experience, for the Florentine government, of the successful resistance by Pisa against efforts to retake the town it had ruled since 1406.[4] Eventually in 1509 Pisa would open its gates to the representatives of Florence, among whom was Guicciardini's friend, Niccolò Machiavelli (1469–1527), at that point second secretary in the chancellery of the Florentine republic. No massive punishment of the city's inhabitants ensued. Instead, foodstuffs were distributed to the famished population in a manner that seemed to realise one of the maxims of the famous Florentine secretary, that it was better to be feared than loved, but that it was worst of all to be hated.[5]

To "speak not as a Christian" meant that Bernardo knew well that the Pisans had no obligation to submit but were simply expected to yield to Florence's greater power. That power, then, and the readiness to use it, would guarantee the maintenance of Florentine rule over Pisa.

rule to punish all crimes." Francesco Guicciardini, *Maxims and Reflections (Ricordi)* (University of Pennsylvania Press 1965), 46 (53).

3 Guicciardini, *Dialogue*, II (158).

4 The question of retaking Pisa was one of the first of the many vexing questions that Guicciardini's friend, Machiavelli, had to deal with as he entered the Florentine chancellery in 1498. The latter, again, used the negative experiences he had of the employment of foreign *condottieri* in these efforts as inspiration for his famous advocacy for a citizen army.

5 Niccolò Machiavelli, *The Prince* (London, Penguin 1999), 54.

The radical nature of Bernardo's discourse had to do with the complete absence of any effort to appeal to the better nature of the Pisans. As we saw in the previous chapter, the Spanish scholastics based their views on legal and political authority on the famous lines in chapter XIII of St Paul's letter to the Romans: "Let everyone be subject to the governing authorities, for there is no authority except that which God has established" and that "[t]herefore, it is necessary to submit to the authorities, not only because of possible punishment but also as a matter of conscience." In Bernardo's monologue, no such obligation is heard. Only power speaks.

That the Protestant rebellion in sixteenth-century Europe would also create a political crisis had to do with the erosion of the religious justifications invoked by traditional authorities, especially theologians. The internal compulsion of obedience was dissipating. The rhetorical power of Bernardo's argument was devoid of any appeal to a sense of obedience. Factual submission was all that would be needed. The same point appeared from a different angle in another, larger work composed by Guicciardini after retiring from papal service, *La storia d'Italia* (*The History of Italy* or the *History of the Wars of Italy*, 1537). At the heart of this massive work were reflections on the north Italian diplomatic system that had maintained peace for half a century before the French aggression. Guicciardini praised Lorenzo de' Medici's management of the balance of power that had maintained conditions of peace and prosperity.[6] This had resulted from skilful use of persuasion and threats, including bribes, deception and limited violence. Nothing about Christian morality had been responsible for the peace. On the contrary, the secular ambitions of the church had been among the worst causes of instability.[7] Instead of reflecting religious inspiration, the virtue of the diplomacy of Lorenzo "the Magnificent" lay in his skilful employment of secular techniques of power and persuasion that were single-mindedly oriented to the desired goals, the *effettività fattuale*: "it is by their results that governments have to be judged".[8]

[6] Francisco Guicciardini, *The History of Italy* (Princeton University Press 1984), 3–6.

[7] Guicciardini had a long and distinguished career in the service of Medici popes, at one point as lieutenant-general of the army of the League of Cognac against the Emperor Charles V. In his *Ricordi*, he summarised this experience by noting that "I know of no one who loathes the ambition, the avarice, and the sensuality of the clergy more than I," *Ricordi*, C 28 (48).

[8] Guicciardini, *Dialogue*, I, 39.

**An Italian Lesson**

Then there was the catastrophic chain of events following the French intervention of 1494. Within half a century, the events triggered by the aggression had laid waste to the old political system. Once again, Italians felt, barbarians had put an end to the spectacular flourishing of their lands and liberties. No surprise then that as he was composing a work on the laws of war in the fragile safety of Elizabethan England nearly a century after these events, the Protestant refugee from Italy, Alberico Gentili (1552–1608) had the experience of his home country in mind. Gentili had arrived in England in 1580 to escape the intensifying activity of the Holy Inquisition in his native March of Ancona, at the time part of the Papal States.[9] In England he was rapidly integrated among other Italian refugees and intellectuals. His arrival coincided with a moment when interest in Italian humanism had been spreading among Elizabethan noblemen. Dante, Petrarca, Machiavelli and Tasso were being translated and accompanied by travel narratives about the flourishing intellectual and cultural life across Italy.[10] Elizabeth herself was fluent in Italian and through the help of her Italian teacher and friend, Giovanni Battista Castiglioni, kept contact with the Italian community around London.[11] It was through Castiglioni, too, that Gentili was able to meet publishers and translators of Italian literatures and especially the controversial publisher John Wolfe, through whom Englishmen would eventually be introduced to the works of Machiavelli and Guicciardini.[12]

[9] For the Protestant background of the Gentili family, see Diego Panizza, *Alberico Gentili, giurista ideologo nell'Inghilterra elisabettiana* (Padova 1981), 16–31. For a good account of the persecutions suffered by the family – in addition to Alberico and his brother Scipio, his father Matteo and his uncle Pancrazio as well as, after their departure into exile, his younger brother Manilio – at the hands of the Inquisition, see Vincenzo Lavinia, 'Alberico Gentili. I processi, le fedi, la guerra', in *Alberico Gentili e gli orizzonti della modernità. Atti del convegno di Macerata (2007)* (Milan, Giuffrè 2009), 173–82, and Lavinia, 'Giudici, eretici, infedeli. Per una storia dell'Inquisizione nella Marca nella prima età moderna', www.giornaledihistoria.net. A brief account of the family background, the shared Protestantism and the flight into exile is also found in Gesina van der Molen, *Alberico Gentili and the Development of International Law* (Leiden, Sijthoff 1968), 36–43.

[10] See e.g. Stefano Colavecchia, 'Alberico Gentili oltre lo ius belli. Tra guerra giusta e repubblicanesimo. Proposte per l'Europa tra Cinque e Seicento', PhD thesis, Università degli studi del Molise (2013–14), 52–77.

[11] Michael Wyatt, *The Italian Encounter with Tudor England. A Cultural Politics of Translation* (Cambridge University Press 2009), 125–6.

[12] Machiavelli's works had circulated in England in manuscript before the first volume that contained the (Italian) texts of *Il Principe* and *I Discorsi* was surreptitiously

Many things aligned Gentili to Elizabethan noblemen.[13] They were equally apprehensive about the spread of Counter-Reformation, including the prospect of a Catholic conspiracy against the queen. They worried about the growth of Spanish influence in the colonies and on the continent. Many feared the influence of foreign and home-grown religious activism; the growth of French power through the prospect of marriage with the Duke of Anjou had been a special cause of concern. The economy of the English state was weak and massive poverty, vagrancy and crime spread insecurity across the country. Towards the end of the regime succession emerged as a further worry. Elizabeth had been reasonably tolerant of confessional variety but there was no guarantee that this would also be the case with her successor. Leading politicians such as Elizabeth's principal secretary Sir Francis Walsingham and Lord Burghley (William Cecil) as well as her confidant Leicester (Robert Dudley) were united in their effort to strengthen central power against real or imagined enemies at home and abroad. In this process, "law was inevitably turned to a source of stability".[14] Writings by Jean Bodin about a firm sovereignty uniting the country over the heads of rival religious and political formations were read with the greatest interest, including by Gentili who frequently referenced Bodin in his work on the laws of war as well as in support of monarchic absolutism.[15]

published by Wolfe in 1584. Gentili had been associated in this project and may have been the "very wise man" referred to in its preface. Colavecchia, 'Alberico Gentili', 74–5; Alessandra Petrina & Michele Marrapodi, *Machiavelli in the British Isles. Two Early Modern Translations of The Prince* (London, Routledge 2009), 25–27. On Wolfe as "rebel printer" and his contacts with Gentili and other Italians, see Peter S. Donaldson, *Machiavelli and Mystery of State* (Cambridge University Press 1988), 86–110 and further Diego Pirillo, 'Republicanism and Religious Dissent. Machiavelli and the Italian Protestant Reformers', in Allessandro Arienzo et al. (eds), *Machiavellian Encounters in Tudor and Stuart England. Literary and Political Influences from the Reformation to the Restoration* (London, Routledge 2013), 121–40.

13 For a brief overview of the patronage received by Gentili from Philip Sidney and Robert Devereux and their group of "Forward Protestants", see Christopher N. Warren, *Literature and the Law of Nations 1580–1650* (Oxford University Press 2015), 35–6.

14 Christopher W. Brooks, *Law, Politics and Society in Early Modern England* (Cambridge University Press 2008), 52.

15 For the complex debt that Gentili had to Bodin, see Diego Quaglioni, 'The Italian "Readers" of Bodin, 17th–18th Centuries. The Italian "Readers" out of Italy – Alberico Gentili (1552–1608)', in Howell A. Lloyd (ed.), *The Reception of Bodin* (Leiden, Brill 2013), 371–86.

Their shared humanist interests inspired in Gentili and leading English politicians ideals of honour, virtue and civilisation that, apart from stressing vigorous resistance to Spanish power, also supported expansive designs under a strong monarchy.[16] Many of these men possessed a civil law background that lent support to Roman ideologies of imperial glory and military virtue. Walsingham, for example, initially trained in Gray's Inn, had studied civil law Padua while Sir Thomas Smith (1513–77), the first Regius Professor of Civil Law at Cambridge (1543), also a student from Padua, became Elizabeth's ambassador in Paris and secretary of state. Smith's interests varied between poetry and diplomacy and it was Smith who, with his son, began the process of colonisation of Ireland that would serve as the ideological and practical training-ground for eventual imperial venturing across the Atlantic.[17] Smith was also keen to find ways to strengthen the economic base of the English state in a way that would eventually buttress the country's position in the world. "Yea, among all the nations in the world they that be politique and civil, do master the rest though their [forces] be inferior."[18] Gentili, too, had accepted the conquest of the "Indies" and was a wholehearted supporter of war against "brutes and brutish men". Nor did he object to war in order to spread civilisation, and openly endorsed the right of foreign princes to intervene in support of the subjects of a tyrant – views that aligned him with Roman republican ideals that were widespread among the Italian refugees.[19] In a famous passage in his early *De legationibus* (1585) Gentili confessed his admiration of Machiavelli as an "eulogist of democracy, and its most spirited champion" and explained *Il Principe* not as a book of instruction for tyrants but for the people, which "by revealing [the tyrant's] secret counsels [would] strip him bare and expose him to the suffering nations".[20]

[16] For the combination of the ideal of active life and the fear of "corruption" as basic elements of the moral philosophy of Tudor colonisation, see Andrew Fitzmaurice, *Humanism and America. An Intellectual History of English Colonisation 1500–1625* (Cambridge University Press 2003), 21–5 and more widely, 20–57.

[17] See David Armitage, *The Ideological Origins of the British Empire* (Cambridge University Press 2000), 45–60.

[18] Thomas Smith, *Discourse of the Commonweal of this Realm of England* (Elizabeth Lamond ed., Cambridge University Press 1929), 23. On Smith's efforts at a colony in Ireland, see also Fitzmaurice, *Humanism and America*, 39.

[19] Pirillo, 'Republicanism and Religious Dissent', 129–30.

[20] For war against "brutes and brutish men", see Alberico Gentili, *De iure belli libri tres, Volume II, The Translation of the Edition of 1612* (John Rolfe trans., Coleman Phillipson ed., Carnegie Endowment for International Peace, Oxford, Clarendon 1933), I XXI (122), and for the Machiavelli reference, Alberico Gentili, *De legationibus Libri Tres* (Gordon J. Lain ed., Oxford University Press 1924), III IX (156).

Although Gentili would later suffer from those early references, they were quite consistent with the rest of his early work and aligned him ideologically with Elizabethan civil lawyers who saw themselves as a leading force in the transformation of England into a civilised, orderly governed "empire" in accordance with Tudor ideology.[21] Although English translations of Machiavelli's *Il Principe* and *I Discorsi* would be published only in 1640, French and Latin versions had been circulating among Tudor courtiers already from the late 1530s and the reputation of the Florentine secretary had in any case spread widely thanks to manuscript translations as well as anti-Machiavellian works openly available.[22] Gentili's outlook fit well with English civil lawyers who were the acknowledged experts of the foreign policy of the realm and regularly charged with diplomatic assignments. They also had a monopoly of cases coming to the High Court of Admiralty where Gentili, too, had most of his official business late in his career.[23] By virtue of their very training, civil lawyers were professionally inclined to support strong royal power. Gentili and his colleagues would regard it as obvious that the king was *legibus solutus* and, in most cases, entitled to intervene in his subjects' *dominium* even without a *causa*.[24]

A particularly important early contact was Sir Philip Sidney (1554–86), a prominent courtier, soldier and humanist, author of a *Defence of Poetry* as well as the epic poem *Arcadia*, whose many interests

21 Brooks, *Law, Politics and Society*, 59.

22 The general reading of Machiavelli at this time had been the one of the dark manipulator and assistant to tyrants proposed by the Protestant jurist Innocent Gentillet in his widely read *Anti-Machiavel* (1576). In England, the best known anti-Machiavellian work was Reginald Pole's *Apologia ad Carolum Quintum* (1539), which described the views of the Florentine secretary as utterly incompatible with the ethics of Christian rulership, linking them to Thomas Cromwell's support for the policy of Henry VIII. The Machiavellian legacy in England, as elsewhere, was complex but the anti-tyrannical position by Gentili was also adopted a century later in Harrington's *Oceana* (1656). See Donaldson, *Machiavelli and Mystery of State*, 7–11; Colavecchia, 'Alberico Gentili', 78–81; Alessandra Petrina, 'Reginald Pole and the Reception of *Il Principe* in Henrician England', in Alessandro Arienzo & Alessandra Petrina (eds), *Machiavellian Encounters in Tudor and Stuart England* (London, Routledge 2013), 13–27 and, with special reference to the earliest reception, Alessandra Petrina, 'Machiavelli's *Principe* and its Early Appearance in the British Isles', in Alessandra Petrina, *Machiavelli in the British Isles* (Ashgate 2009), 1–45.

23 Gentili's experience is summarised in the posthumously published collection of his opinions by his brother Scipio. See Alberico Gentili, *Hispanicae advocationis Libri Duo* (Oxford University Press 1921).

24 On this latter point, see Alberico Gentili, 'Utrum possit princeps de regno suo, suorumque subditorum rebus pro arbitratu statuere', Disputatio II, in *Disputationum Dicas Prima* (London, Wolfe 1587), 27–51.

included supporting exploratory voyages across the Atlantic. A man of first-rate contacts, Sidney was married to Frances Walsingham, the daughter of Elizabeth's secretary of state and his father, Sir Henry Sidney, had been lord deputy of Ireland. Together with Walsingham and his uncle, Leicester, he was one of the leading "Forward Protestants", advocating early action to curtail Spanish expansion in the rebellious Netherlands. He died a hero's death on the battlefield near Zutphen in 1586 as one of the leaders of the English expeditionary force. Sidney's ideals of manly virtue and active life in the service of the state inspired Gentili to depict him as a model ambassador in *De legationibus* and to dedicate the work to him.[25] Sidney knew well the works of Machiavelli, and the two versions of *Arcadia* constituted an elaborate display of precisely the kind of political and military virtues that had inspired Gentili's *De iure belli.*[26] It is therefore right to say that "the laws of war and diplomacy [presented by Gentili] both originat [ed] from common sources in Renaissance humanist practices around epic".[27] Both Gentili and Sidney were also preoccupied with the question of resistance to tyranny. They both rejected the subjects' right of rebellion and at least Sidney aligned himself with the position in *Vindiciae contra Tyrannos* by the Huguenots Hubert Languet and Philippe Duplessis-Mornay, both of whom he corresponded with, that reserved the right to resist to nobles and magistrates, men to whom the community had allocated public power.[28] Gentili's views on the matter were more complex. Though he was quite firmly against resistance by subjects in general, perhaps owing to the predominant fear in the 1580s and 1590s of a Catholic plot, he also believed that in a conflict between the call of his conscience ("obligations to God") and the instructions of his prince, the ambassador was rather to follow the former.[29] And he

[25] The work was based on an oral presentation given in 1584 at Oxford in the presence of both Sidney and Leicester who, apparently, had reacted positively to it and, as a consequence, opened the doors to Gentili in their circles. Van der Molen, *Gentili*, 50. Sidney and Gentili's brother Scipio also knew each other as poets.

[26] Sidney had recommended Machiavelli's works to his brother, and it has been assumed that his views about the mixed constitution in the *Arcadia* drew from the Florentine secretary. Petrina, *Machiavelli in the British Isles*, 16–17.

[27] Warren, *Literature and the Law of Nations*, 34 and generally 31–61.

[28] George Garnett (ed.), *Vindiciae contra Tyrannos* (Cambridge University Press 1994), 'The Third Question' (156–72). On Sidney's views on this work and on resistance, see Blair Worden, *The Sound of Virtue. Philip Sidney's Arcadia and Elizabethan Politics* (Yale University Press 1996), 281–94.

[29] Gentili, *De legationibus*, III XV (195). In *De iure belli*, Gentili ruled out resistance by ordinary subjects of an absolute ruler, but allowed it for lower magistrates in case the

did support the right of foreign princes to assist oppressed subjects. But it was very different to support independent action by ambassadors and foreign princes than the right of regular subjects to rebel against their prince. There were definite limits to his admiration of the "democratic" Machiavelli.

With the help of an introductory letter from Leicester to vice-chancellor Toby Matthew, Gentili was able to receive a teaching position at Oxford in 1580–1 and to take up counselling in diplomatic matters. His first publication in England, *De iuris intepretationi. Libri Sex* (1582), was a spirited defence of the older "Italian" style of reading civil law, directed against those who mixed all kinds of alien subjects, such as literature and history with it – a position from which he himself departed almost as soon as the work had been published. The most famous of his early counselling assignments was his involvement in the so-called Mendoza affair where the Spanish ambassador had been alleged to have been party of a conspiracy against Elizabeth's life, together with his then friend, Jean Hotman, a Protestant refugee from France, the son of François Hotman, author of the humanist–constitutionalist work *Franco-Gallia* (1574). The Privy Council eventually accepted their advice that a foreign ambassador was immune from the domestic law and instead of facing execution was to be expelled. It was this assignment that inspired him to give a public talk on the affair at Oxford, attended by Leicester and his nephew Sidney, and eventually led to his publication of the larger work *De legationibus. Libri tres* (1585).[30]

But not everything proceeded smoothly for Gentili in his new home. His friendship with Hotman was eventually broken owing to the latter's violent reaction against Gentili's criticisms of the *mos gallicus*. At Oxford, Gentili also found himself attacked by a group of Puritan theologians opposing the "*levitas*" and "Machiavellism" of the Italian immigrant, both qualities allegedly in extensive display in the work on embassies. At one point, as the prospect of a permanent position at the university seemed lost, Gentili decided to leave England for good, accepting for that purpose a diplomatic mission with the Elector of Saxony. The assignment was to enquire into the Elector's willingness to raise troops for possible intervention on the Protestant side in the French civil war.

ruler's powers had been divided with them – the situation in the German lands. As a result, in case a ruler tries forcibly to convert a private subject, that subject "has no other recourse save to follow the order of Christ and flee", I XI (52, 50–1).

30 See Van der Molen, *Gentili*, 44, 50; Panizza, *Alberico Gentili, giurista ideologo*, 44–7. For Gentili's treatment of the affair, see *De legationibus*, II XVIII (111–14).

However, urged by Leicester and Walsingham, the university eventually set aside the Puritan objections and, on 8 June 1587, Gentili was appointed to the Regius Chair of Civil Law at Oxford.[31]

## The Lawyer As Humanist Warrior

It was from his position as a leading civil lawyer in England that Gentili would appeal to his readers to be alert against the expansive designs of Catholic Spain.[32] "Do not all men with complete justice oppose on the one side the Turks and on the other the Spaniards, who are plotting and planning universal dominion?" "Shall we wait until they actually take up arms?" Gentili referred his readers over again to Guicciardini's *History* to draw lessons for contemporary England, especially threatened by the Spaniards who "when they have once crept in, [...] always secure the supreme control by every kind of artifice".[33] Such sentiments abounded in Gentili's most famous work, *De iure belli libri tres*, the first version of which was published in 1588 – the very year of the Spanish Armada. It was in thinking about the Spanish threat in light of Guicciardini's *History* that Gentili proposed a novel concept of the just war, "war on grounds of expediency" that would be based on something else than "avenging an injury" in the old scholastic sense. What would now count was "fear" – not only of a forthcoming attack but fear that if present developments were allowed to continue, security would be lost: "a defence is justified which anticipates dangers that are already meditated and prepared, and also those which are not meditated, but are probable and possible".[34] As Gentili would now teach his readers,

31 Van der Molen, *Gentili*, 51–2; Panizza, *Alberico Gentili, giurista ideologo*, 50–3.

32 For the "*levitas*" accusation, see Giovanni Minnucci, *"Silete theologi in munere alieno". Alberico Gentili tra diritto, teologia e religione* (Milan, Monduzzi 2016), 83–5. For the controversy surrounding the appointment of the "foreigner" at Oxford, see Panizza, *Alberico Gentili, giurista ideologo*, 51–3. Gentili had graduated from the University of Perugia (1572). In 1579 he was forced to escape the Inquisition with his father Matteo and brother Scipio. After having failed to receive a university position in Tübingen he landed in England in 1580 on the strength of an invitation by Queen Elizabeth's Italian teacher Giovanni Castiglione and the vice-chancellor of the University of Oxford, Toby Matthew. See Panizza, *Alberico Gentili, giurista ideologo*, 40–2; Minnucci, *"Silete theologi"*, 28–33. For more on Gentili's life, see Van der Molen, *Gentili*.

33 Gentili, *De iure belli*, I XIV (64).

34 Ibid., I XIV (66). This is read as a legal translation of Guicciardini's idea of balance of power in Pärtel Piirimäe, 'Alberico Gentili's Doctrine of Defensive War and Its Impact on Seventeenth-Century Normative Views', in Benedict Kingsbury & Benjamin Straumann (eds), *The Roman Foundations of the Law of Nations* (Oxford University Press 2010), 199.

"those who desire to live without danger ought to meet impending evils and anticipate them".[35]

In advocating an extensive right to offensive war even in the absence of a forthcoming attack, Gentili was endorsing the kind of readiness to action that was well in line with the virtues extolled by humanist admirers of Roman virtue. This was more than merely preventive self-defence.[36] There were no rules to measure when a pre-emptive war could be launched. Following his habitual way of proceeding, instead of attempting to define lawful pre-emption, Gentili gave a long list of historical examples and statements by classical authorities to show that "it is better to provide that men should not acquire too great power".[37] Indeed, for a prince not to take action if there was some reason to fear a forthcoming attack would be to fail as a leader of his people: "no-one ought to surrender his right without a struggle".[38] Of course, such fear should not be unreasonable. But people feared different things and "one must not dictate to anyone what he is to fear ... there is more than one justifiable cause for fear and no general rule can be laid down with regard to the matter".[39] This, too, sounded like Guicciardini for whom it was clear that "writing discourses about the future was ... misleading. For the affairs of this world ... must be judged day by day."[40]

In advocating early action, Gentili was aligning himself with the more belligerent faction with Elizabeth's counsel, anxious about the regime's ability to withstand a possible Spanish attack. The Spaniards, he reminded his readers, were "lawless and greedy for power", like the Turks, always seeking to attain total control of the places they had conquered.

> We must therefore oppose them; and it is better to provide that men should not acquire too great power, than to be obliged to seek a remedy later, when they have already become too powerful.[41]

But preventing the increase of adversaries' power was not the only just cause for taking action. According to the law of nations, Gentili explained, following Vitoria and others, war was sometimes necessary to protect trade routes or commercial practices – an argument directed against the Spanish–Portuguese claim of commercial monopoly in the

[35] Gentili, *De iure belli*, I XIV (61).
[36] For "necessary defence" in case the enemy "has been making preparations", see ibid., I XIII (58).
[37] Ibid., I XIV (65). [38] Ibid., I VI (32). [39] Ibid., I XIV (63–4).
[40] Guicciardini, *Ricordi*, C 114 (70). [41] Gentili, *De iure belli*, I XIV (64, 65).

Indies.[42] It was never right to suffer wrong; one had the duty to protect one's name and one's reputation. Romans had even commenced war, Gentili remembered, to react to "the vice of ingratitude".[43] Presenting a danger to one's security, obstructing commerce or navigation, preventing access to harbours or passage when it was needed to fight an enemy – none of this could be apprehended as a judicial process. In assessing the imperatives of action not only facts but *appearances* of facts counted – impressions, assumptions, preconceptions, were all relevant. For this was justice, as Gentili repeatedly told his readers, not as it might seem an omniscient God but "as it appears from man's standpoint".[44] People saw things differently, and there was nothing else than one's own appreciation on the basis of which one could act. To conclude, Gentili quoted Guicciardini's analysis of the causes of north Italian flourishing in the late fifteenth century, namely:

> the constant care of Lorenzo de' Medici, that wise man, friend of peace, and father of peace, namely, that the balance of power should be maintained among the princes of Italy. This he believed would give peace to Italy, as indeed it did so long as he lived and preserved that condition of affairs. But both the peace and the balance of power ended with him, great scion of the Medici and mighty bulwark of his native city and the rest of Italy. Is not this even to-day our problem, that one man may not have supreme power and that all Europe may not submit to the domination of one single man?[45]

Gentili's celebration of Lorenzo's political wisdom and through it, the nature of the Italian political and diplomatic system, was only one of the places where he used Guicciardini's work to think about the political and legal situation of England at the end of the sixteenth century.[46] In particular, Gentili shared the aversion, almost outrage, felt by the Florentine jurist–diplomat against religion as a pretence for political designs, quoting Guicciardini in his attack on Spain's king Ferdinand "the Catholic", who "covered almost all of his excesses with a respectable mantle of religion".[47] Guicciardini had had much experience of the

[42] Ibid., I XIX (86–92); Panizza, *Alberico Gentili, giurista ideologo*, 112–13.
[43] Gentili, *De iure belli*, I XX (96–7). [44] Ibid., I VI (31).
[45] Ibid., I XIV (65). Using historians such as Guicciardini and Paolo Giovio in the way Gentili did was common among sixteenth-century English writers and was often done in order to hide what was regarded as a 'Machiavellian' argument. Pirillo, 'Republicanism and Religious Dissent', 129–40.
[46] For a full discussion, see Paolo Carta, 'Dalle guerre d'Italia del Guicciardini al diritto di Guerra di Alberico Gentili', 10 *Laboratoire italien. Politique et société* (2010), 85–102.
[47] Gentili, *De iure belli*, I IX (40) and X (43).

politics of the clergy, having at one point acted as a general in the pope's armies. He concluded his reflection on the politics of the church by agreeing with Martin Luther in his wish to "see this bunch of rascals get their just deserts, that is to be either without vices or without authority".[48] Religion was constantly used as a pretext for worldly ambitions: "Each man declares his own war a holy one. Each one insists that his enemies are godless men. Each names his own cause righteous."[49]

Behind this opinion was a view of the nature of relations between princes that was mediated by the historical works not only by Guicciardini but also Tacitus, Machiavelli, Paolo Giovio and Jean Bodin, a view that highlighted the uncertainty of worldly affairs, the degree to which the future was ruled by *fortuna* so that it was impossible to prepare for everything that would lie ahead.[50] "Although cleverness and care may accomplish many things, they are nevertheless not enough. Man also needs good Fortune."[51] The limits of reason and experience in political action highlighted the personal qualities of the decision-maker, a favourite Renaissance subject. Those qualities applied to the good ambassador, Gentili argued, as they did to a good statesman.[52] Machiavelli had famously stressed impetuosity over circumspection in political matters, and Gentili's endorsement of readiness for anticipatory and determinate action arose from similar considerations. A good ambassador–statesman possessed a "faculty of rapid decision which in a moment improvises plans to meet a situation, and determines the degree of elaboration and the order in which clever ideas shall be expressed".[53]

Another Italian lesson called for an understanding of the darker passions of humanity, the ambition and greed that motivated human

[48] Guicciardini, *Ricordi*, C 28 (48). [49] Gentili, *De iure belli*, I IX (40).

[50] For Machiavelli, the nucleus of statecraft lay in the juxtaposition of "*virtù*" and *fortuna*, technical notions that connote succession of unpredictable events that cannot be brought under institutional control but to which it is still possible to prepare by adopting the right attitude or frame of mind. In a famous metaphor Machiavelli compared *fortuna* with "violent rivers" that tear down everything from their way and which cannot be stopped but can still be diverted or controlled. In the end, he writes, "it is probably true that fortune is the arbiter of half the things we do, leaving the other half or so to be controlled by ourselves", Machiavelli, *The Prince*, 79.

[51] Guicciardini, *Ricordi*, C 30 (49). See also Gentili, *De legationibus*, III IV ("The Ambassador should Be a Man Favoured by Fortune", 155).

[52] Gentili, *De legationibus*, III IV (158); Diego Panizza, 'Il pensiero politico di Alberico Gentili. Religione, virtù e ragion di stato', in Diego Panizza (ed.), *Alberico Gentili. Politica e religione nell'età delle guerre di religioni* (Milan, Giuffrè, 2002), 63, 120.

[53] Gentili, *De legationibus*, III V (146).

action and was the principal cause of wars. There was nothing natural in war. History had made humans "uneasy and untamed, and always engaged in a struggle for freedom or glory or domination". There were no natural enemies. Animosity was a result of the "ambition and injustice of men", the way people had learned to seek satisfaction to their "boundless desires".[54] Sallust or Tacitus had been right to observe that there was "but one cause for making war . . . namely an unbounded thirst for power and riches". Even as princes gave all kinds of excuses for their wars, in truth "frequently they have no reason at all".[55] It was this description of the political world that justified fear and prompted the necessity of rapid anticipatory action and made it sometimes impossible to fight with honourable methods. It was all right to lie to the enemy, for example. After all, if it was acceptable to deceive the enemy by actions, why should it be prohibited to do the same with words?[56]

In his instructions to the new prince, Machiavelli had emphasised the external world of performance, simulation, sometimes dissimulation.[57] The famous discussion of whether it was better to be feared or loved had nothing to do with possessing a fearful of loveable character but everything about the respective impression one was able to give. "A prince . . . need not necessarily have all the good qualities . . . but he should certainly appear to have them".[58] In Gentili's discussion of the good ambassador–statesman, too, it was the quality of the performance, the impression that was given, that was important, not the content of the assignment.[59] The view of an ambassador as a man of peace was wrong. Sometimes the ambassador's mission was peace, sometimes war, and the fulfilment of that mission was the only objective he should strive

[54] Gentili, *De iure belli*, I XII (54).

[55] Ibid., I VII (34).

[56] Ibid., II V (149–50, 153).

[57] This, too, is a moral position in which the values of *virtù* only sometimes justify recourse to means that Christian morality rejects.

[58] Machiavelli, *The Prince*, XVIII (57).

[59] "For if the sovereign is properly impressed by his first view of the embassy, the ambassador will find it much easier to proceed with the negotiations," Gentili, *De legationibus*, III II (139). Panizza reads this work as typical for "Renaissance humanism" (especially by reference to the wide use of classical sources and its orientation towards instruction of the prince) but reserves Gentili's "Machiavellian moment" to the later *De iure belli*. Panizza, *Alberico Gentili, giurista ideologo*, 114–46. The "Machiavellian" orientation is stressed (perhaps excessively) in Peter Schröder, *Trust in Early Modern Political Thought* (Cambridge University Press 2017); Schröder reads both of Gentili's "international" works from the perspective of what was needed by political leaders and ambassadors to receive or maintain the confidence of their foreign interlocutors so as to attain stability in a volatile confessional moment, 14–44.

to attain.[60] To create the desired impression required that the person possessed "certain external advantages, as well as blessings of fortune and nature".[61] They should usually come from a noble family or at least possess the qualities of a courtier. The nature of the required performance also depended on its intended audience: with the barbarians, "physical beauty" was especially venerated while sometimes it was useful to send as negotiator a person of lowly origin.[62] Good linguistic skills were always useful. The ambassador–statesman should be good orator – not in the sense of speaking with flowery ornamentation or at great length but to be "compact and clear", to use the kind of speech with which friendships can be won.[63] Insulting words and abusive language should not be tolerated.[64] It was surely not accidental that Gentili believed that academic "stage-plays" – which he defended against Puritan attacks on the Elizabethan theatre – constituted good preparation for virtuous citizenship (*nam per poetas, et poemata mores civium bones facit*).[65] Politics was performance, designed to impress and persuade. Truthfulness was not necessarily a part of it. A deceptive appearance might sometimes be used to attain a good purpose or to teach a valuable lesson.[66]

None of this meant that the ambassador–statesman should be a morally dubious character. The ambassador was not a spy.[67] Gentili summarised the *virtù* of the ambassador in a list of qualities of good Renaissance statesmanship – "fidelity, fortitude, temperance and prudence".[68] Trust was important, and much of the discussion was about

60 Gentili, *De legationibus*, I VI (17).

61 Ibid., III I (136). With the barbarians, Gentili believed, "physical beauty" was especially venerated, ibid., III III (141). But in any case, sending a "barber" or a "worthless journeyman" were grave errors, ibid., III IV (155).

62 Ibid., III III (141) and III IV (155).

63 Ibid., III VI (147–8).

64 Ibid., II XX (119).

65 Quoted in Panizza, *Alberico Gentili, giurista ideologo*, 61 n. 11.

66 The question of lying for a good purpose ("*mendacium officiosum*") came up in the debate Gentili had with Rainolds on cross-dressing in "stage-plays". In two essays, published in 1599, Gentili defended this kind of "deception" as part of the innocent pleasures of play-acting, Alberico Gentili, *Disputationes duae*. Only tyrants wanted to prohibit theatre, he wrote there, defending the venial sin of lying – for example the dissimulation that was part of acting – as sometimes advancing the public good. See Vincenzo Lavenia, '"Mendacium officiosum". Alberico Gentili's Ways of Lying', in Miriam Eliav-Feldon (ed.), *Dissimulation and Deceit in Early Modern Europe* (Berlin, Springer 2015), 35. One was never to lie against God. But the objective of society was, according to Gentili, that humans would be useful for each other, and for that purpose lying could not always be excluded.

67 Gentili, *De legationibus*, II IV & III XIV (65–8; 169–70).

68 For the treatment of the virtues, see ibid., XI–IXX (162–86). "Justice" was not part of the virtues. Like many other writers on diplomacy, Gentili had reservations about using (especially black-letter) lawyers as ambassadors, ibid., III X 160–1.

what it took to create trust and lose it.[69] But no overriding loyalty to any substantive value – to peace, Christianity or the community of nations – was required.[70] It made no difference if the ambassador represented a tyrant or an infidel prince. Both were entitled to the right of embassy, and the qualities of the good ambassador were independent of religious considerations.[71]

By making the distinction between surface appearance and inner objective Gentili was alert towards the way religious performances or the recitation of principles of the just war often amounted to mere superficial rationalisations. It was important to penetrate the true motives of those one dealt with. "[T]hose are our enemies who have cause for hostility, even though they pretend the contrary."[72] The Machiavellian question of whether it was better to be feared or loved came up in the context of what one should do with those one had vanquished in war. Should one attempt to be just, or aim to incite fear? It all depended on "the various characters of victor and vanquished", a matter about which it was impossible to formulate a general rule.[73] A just peace was often useful. But if "the evil inclination cannot be removed", then – as Guicciardini recommended with respect to Pisa – it was necessary to aim at the utter subordination of the vanquished side. In any case, "half-way measures [were] for the most part foolish".[74]

The deeply "Italian" quality of Gentili's works had to do with his doubts about the authority of moral claims in the world of politics and government. Those works were not "immoral" in the way Gentili's Puritan adversaries claimed but obsessed with the effort to align that which was useful in a world of often hostile and untrustworthy princes with what was right in accordance with a philosophical literature inherited from Western antiquity.[75] It was important to cultivate a historically informed sensibility that would combine careful reflection

[69] See e.g. the complex discussion of when advice ought to be regarded as credible, in ibid., III XXI (192–7).

[70] Outright lying or "disgraceful" action was not permitted, ibid., III XV (174).

[71] Gentili's emphatic insistence on treating Turkey on a basis of equality here may, at least so Francesca Cantù, reflect the Protestant foreign policy preference of using Turkey to counterbalance Habsburg hegemony, 'Alberico Gentili e li ius legationis', in Stephano Andretta, Stéphane Péquignot & Jean-Claude Wacquet (eds), *De l'ambassadeur. Les écrits relatifs à l'ambassadeur et à l'art de négocier du Moyen Âge au début du XIXe siècle* (l'École française de Rome 2015), books.openedition.org/efr/2914#text para21.

[72] Gentili, *De iure belli*, III XIII (358).

[73] Ibid., III XIII (354).

[74] Ibid., III XIII (357).

[75] See especially the discussion in ibid., III XII (349).

with bold readiness to take action.[76] After the collapse of the universal pretensions of the church and the empire, what was left was a world of sovereign princes, fearful, greedy, ambitious. Of course, they would be united by natural law – that was the very point of the methodological reflections in *De iure belli.* But what natural law *said* at any moment was up to those princes to determine.[77] This was a view that had been developed above all among north Italian thinkers contemplating on the chaos that followed foreign intervention. But it was a view that so far had received no clear juridical articulation.

## A New Jurisprudence

Gentili's writing on the justice of war, together with his earlier work on embassies and the later essays on the absolute power of the King (*De potestate Regis absoluta*, 1605), consolidated and translated in the language of natural law themes that had been debated among Italian political thinkers for a century since the French intervention. This had taken place in the secular vocabularies of diplomacy and techniques of maintaining *lo stato* ("the reason and practice of states"), peppered with references to Stoic writers, Cicero, Seneca and Lucretius as well as the histories of Tacitus and Livy.[78] Although his arguments sometimes resembled a scholastic *disputatio* and even as he continued to reference Vitoria and his principal followers with respect, Gentili insisted on the silence of theologians over secular matters such as war and diplomacy, directing his invectives over again against hypocritical religious justifications of political action.[79] His work abounds in references to older civil lawyers, the "Italian school" of Bartolus and Baldus, Roman republican practices and examples of prudent statecraft as well as the more recent strands of the "elegant" writers (*mos gallicus*, Bodin, Budé,

[76] See e.g. the discussion of the prudence of the ambassador–statesman in ibid., III XIV (169–72).

[77] Schröder has suggested that Gentili was "perhaps the first political thinker to recognize the fundamental problem of the relationship between sovereign states: the very nature of their sovereignty precluded pacification of what was in effect an anarchical society", *Trust in Early Modern Political Thought*, 17. But this may downplay the significance of Catholic moral casuistry that did operate with a flexible notion of commutative justice applicable between states (or their sovereign rulers).

[78] For a useful overview, see Richard Tuck, *Philosophy and Government 1572–1651* (Cambridge University Press 1993), 31–64.

[79] Gentili, *De iure belli*, I IX (38–41). Soon after the final publication of the three-volume work (1598), it was placed on the Index together with all other works of this impious heretic (1603).

Cujas, Hotman etc.).[80] However, whether he dealt with the justice of warfare, the rights and immunities of ambassadors or the nature of sovereignty in England, his most frequent reference-point, alongside historical examples, was civil law the relevant parts of which he depicted as declaratory of a universal science of natural law and the law of nations. This, he insisted at the beginning of *De iure belli*, would not take the standpoint of a single nation, as *Iustinian* and later civil lawyers had done, but represented written reason that would "belong[] to that great community formed by the entire world and the whole human race".[81]

80 Political historians such as Richard Tuck have read Gentili as a representative of "humanism", so as to contrast his writings with those of the scholastics. Richard Tuck, *The Rights of War and Peace. Political Thought and the International Order from Grotius to Kant* (Oxford University Press 2001), 16–50. In his *Literature and the Law of Nations* Warren also suggested that Gentili may be usefully discussed as a "humanist", using classical literature as a "complement to the law, aiding legal tasks with philological information about usage and, through its plots, providing cases that were common and accessible to all of literate Renaissance society", 42. The humanist reading is, however, challenged in Benjamin Straumann, 'The *Corpus iuris* as a Source of Law Between Sovereigns in Alberico Gentili's Thought', in Benedict Kingsbury & Benjamin Straumann (eds), *The Roman Foundations of the Law of Nations* (Oxford University Press 2010), 101–23. Among *legal* historians, Gentili used to be classed among the adherents of the *mos italicus* rather than the more "modern" school of legal humanists (*mos gallicus*) but more recent legal historians have drawn attention to the eclectic nature of his writings and the extensive use of history and philology in his later work. See Alain Wijffels, 'Antiqui et Recentiores. Alberico Gentili – Beyond Mos Italicus and Legal Humanism', in Paul J. du Plessis & John W. Cairns (eds), *Reassessing Legal Humanism and Its Claims. Petere Fontes* (Edinburgh University Press 2017), especially 12–23. Likewise, Alain Wijffels, 'Alberico Gentili e il rinnovamento del diritto pubblico nella tradizione dello *ius commune*', in *Alberico Gentili. Atti dei convegni nel quarto centenario della morte* (vol. II) (Milan, Giuffrè 2010), 520–3. Claire Vergerio provides a useful table of references in *De iure belli* to "Italian" and humanist writers in her 'Alberico Gentili's *De iure belli*. An Absolutist's Attempt to Reconcile the *jus gentium* and the Reason of State Tradition', 19 *Journal of the History of International Law* (2017), 10–12. The degree to which Gentili in his later career in England distanced himself from the *mos italicus* is also stressed in Panizza, *Alberico Gentili, giurista ideologo*, 43–7 and Giovanni Minnucci, *Alberico Gentili tra mos italicus e mos gallicus. L'inedito Commentario ad legem Iuliam de adulteriis* (Milan, Monduzzi 2002). The development of Gentili's views about interpretation and the value of legal humanism have been meticulously detailed in Giovanni Minnucci, *Alberico Gentili iuris interpres della prima età moderna* (Milan, Monduzzi 2011). But it is above all Panizza's work that has been responsible for the more eclectic image of Gentili produced in the last thirty years. For an update, see Italo Birocchi, 'Il de iure belli e "l'invenzione" del diritto internationale', Luigi Lacchè (ed.), *"Ius gentium, ius communicationis, ius belli". Alberico Gentili e gli orizzonti della modernità: atti del convegno di Macerata in occasione delle celebrazioni del quarto centenario della morte di Alberico Gentili (1552–1608)* (Milan, Giuffrè 2009), 103–7.

81 Gentili, *De iure belli*, I I (3). On Gentili's debts to Roman law, see further Straumann, 'The *Corpus iuris* as a Source of Law', 101–23.

It is not easy to deduce a clear methodological statement from the brief introduction to *De iure belli*. Because the laws of war, like the rest of *ius gentium*, applied between independent sovereigns, they could not be derived from the laws of this or that state. There had never been, nor was there at the time, any human legislator and thus no positive law over the princes. Instead, "questions of war ought to be settled in accordance with the law of nations, which is the law of nature" – a statement that Gentili immediately turned into epistemological direction by putting "the intricate question, what that law is and how we shall prove that it is this or that".[82] Neither theology nor philosophy were helpful. Gentili's natural law was not to be proven by abstract demonstrations but by "the appeal of the senses", or if these were defective with "an appeal to the mind which is in sound condition".[83] Instead of deriving his natural law from God or human nature, he directed his readers to seek it from "that which is in use among all the nations of men".[84]

This was to break new ground. Taking his cue from the brief sections on just war and the *jus fetiale* in Jean Bodin's *Six livres*, Gentili decided that the laws governing belligerent as well as peaceful relations between sovereigns could only be constructed by extrapolating them from history.[85] History demonstrated what "native reason has established among all human beings, and which is equally observed by all mankind".[86] Its content could also be found by examining the laws of all the nations – not literally, but by "the aggregation of the greater part of the world".[87] Such examinations would be greatly assisted by perusing

[82] Gentili, *De iure belli*, I I (5). [83] Ibid., I I (3, 7). [84] Ibid., I I (8).

[85] See Jean Bodin, *Les six livres de république* (Lyons, Tournes 1579), especially Bk V Chapter 5 (on practices of warfare from the Romans to Charles V) and 6 (on keeping faith with allies and enemies). For a very useful review of Bodin's construction of a law among nations, see further Merio Scattola, 'Jean Bodin and International Law', in Stefan Kadelbach, Thomas Kleinlein & David Roth-Isigkeit (eds), *System, Order and International Law* (Oxford University Press 2017), 78–91. Quaglioni traces the massive influence of the Latin edition of the *Six livres* on Gentili to the defensive notion of war therein. Diego Quaglioni, 'Pour une histoire de droit de guerre au début de l'âge moderne. Bodin, Gentili, Grotius', 10 *Laboratoire italien* (2010), 36–40. See further, Quaglioni, 'The Italian "Readers" of Bodin', 371–86 and Peter Schröder, 'Vitoria, Gentili, Bodin. Sovereignty and the Law of Nations', in Benedict Kingsbury & Benjamin Straumann (eds), *The Roman Foundations of the Law of Nations* (Oxford University Press 2010), 169–86.

[86] Gentili, *De iure belli*, I I (8).

[87] Ibid., I I (9): "if the Romans, Greeks, Jews, and barbarians, in short, all known peoples, have made use of a certain code of laws, it may be assumed that all men have made use of that same code".

reports on recently expanding contacts with foreign lands through trade and imperial expansion.[88] It was also "supported in many cases by the utterances of great authorities", and of course, "[t]here will be not a few things from the civil law of Iustinian which it will be possible to adapt" in order to elucidate it.[89]

In the end, Gentili's references in *De iure belli* became so eclectic that it is hard to class him under such conventional categories as "Bartolist" or "legal humanist". Two impressions strike a reader immediately when comparing Gentili to the Spanish theologians. One is the author's often blunt realism and his choice of historical examples of good and bad statecraft in an effort to speak directly, and with authority, to men in government. He accepted that the choices they faced were often difficult and suggested that "in cases of doubt one is obliged to judge from examples, and also when anything has become a custom".[90] In this respect, Gentili's writing appeared less a kind of philosophical jurisprudence (as suggested by Panizza)[91] than pragmatic counselling for the English government.[92] On the other hand, Gentili comes to resemble the theologians in the open-endedness of his discourse, the difficulty one has in extracting the author's own views from the huge number of quotations and examples he lays before the reader. Instead of seeking to lay out hard and fast rules, he ends up with elements of wise statecraft that is not too distant from the casuistry of his theological adversaries. But Gentili's Italian casuistic operates in a radically different way from that of the theologians. It does not assume that true answers to questions of the political right could be produced simply by operating the correct method – that is to say, right reason, *recta ratio* – and that any remaining uncertainty can be disposed of by recourse to external (church) authority. The decision of the good ambassador–statesman looks to history and philosophy not to find there a solution to apply more or less mechanically but to seek guidance on how to combine contrasting

88 Ibid., I I (9). 89 Ibid., I I (9, 11). 90 Ibid., I I (11).

91 See especially Diego Panizza, 'Political Theory and Jurisprudence in Gentili's *De Iure Belli*. The Great Debate between "Theological" and "Humanist" Perspectives from Vitoria to Grotius', in Pierre-Marie Dupuy & Vicent Chetail (eds), *The Roots of International Law – Liber Amicorum Peter Haggenmacher* (Leiden, Brill 2014), and Panizza, 'Alberico Gentli's *De Iure Belli*. The Humanist Foundations of a Project of International Order', in *Alberico Gentili. Atti dei convegni nel quarto centenario della morte* (vol. II) (Milan, Giuffrè 2010), 559–69.

92 Had Gentili been merely a representative of "philosophical jurisprudence", he would hardly have been in such wide demand as a legal counsel and received the mentorship of influential politicians.

considerations of *honestum* and *utile* in the appropriate situation-specific way.[93] There are no "wise men" to whom to defer, but one must act alone, and in a determinate way.

Commentators have often noted that Gentili's writings are difficult to fit into a coherent jurisprudence. It has seemed especially puzzling that Gentili defined his law of nations both as apparently immutable natural law and as an aspect (constantly changing) of custom.[94] But the argument is not that complex and follows quite coherently from the methodological scepticism with which Gentili opens *De iure belli.* The "nature" in Gentili's jurisprudence meant human nature, more specifically human nature as it always fell short of having access to knowledge about the world it confronted.[95] His whole theory of the just war was built on rejection of the ability to know the truth about "justice" – hence, for example, the very practical turn from any effort to define what natural law was into what might count as *evidence* of it. It was common, Gentili pointed out, "for both sides to maintain that they are supporting a just cause".[96] But although logically speaking, both sides contending on the same issue cannot be right, it was usually impossible to decide the matter in an authoritative way. This was so owing to the

> weakness of our human nature, because of which we see everything dimly, and are not cognizant of that purest and truest form of justice, which cannot conceive of both parties to a dispute being in the right.[97]

[93] This, I take it, is also what Panizza suggests in his many analyses of Gentili as an "ideological jurist", respectful of the conflicting values of "republicanism" and "absolutism", "cosmopolitanism" and the nation, *honestum* and *utile.* See especially his 'I valori fondanti della *respublica magna* nel *De Iure Belli* di Alberico Gentili', in *Alberico Gentili. Atti dei convegni nel quarto centenario della morte* (vol. II) (Milan, Giuffrè 2010), 491–513. For Panizza, the dialectical presence of opposing ideas nevertheless has consistency to the extent that they juxtapose the values of the nation ('*utilitas*') with those of the "great republic of humankind' ('*honestum*'), assuming that their appropriate balance would account for 'justice'. It seems to me, however, that these (and other) opposing concepts shift about in Gentili with greater autonomy, as I will argue in the text.

[94] According to Andreas Wagner, "[t]he combination of natural reason and historical acceptance hints at a complicated tension. In fact, we can identify motives both of natural law and of an empirical, positive law in Gentili's concept of international law." Andreas Wagner, 'Francisco de Vitoria and Alberico Gentili on the Legal Character of the Global Commonwealth', 31 *Oxford Journal of Legal Studies* (2011), 574.

[95] See the very useful Francesca Iurlaro, 'The Burden of Reason. *Ratio probabilis, consensio omnium* and the impact of *humanitas* on Alberico Gentili's Theory of Customary International law', 38 *History of Political Thought* (2017), 412.

[96] Gentili, *De iure belli,* I VI (31).

[97] Ibid., I VI (31).

It was humanly impossible to reach the final truth about natural law. Instead, if we try to reason about it, its self-evidence gradually and tragically dissipates. "These things are so well known, that if you try to prove them, you would render them obscure." For this reason, Gentili singled out his agreement with those who concluded that "things which are well known ought to be stated, but not demonstrated".[98] Instead of seeking to produce a logically or conceptually coherent argument of the content of natural law, Gentili chose instead to *illustrate* it by evidence from "examples of those who are regarded as honourable and of good repute" because they "appear to have acted in accordance with nature".[99] This was not to say that reasoning was unimportant, for"[r]eason, too, is an imitation of nature". But its powers were limited, and there was no guarantee that all would use it in the same way. It followed, for Gentili, that Europeans were to learn to live with disagreement or then fight it out in the "just and public contest of arms" that war was.[100]

None of this lead Gentili to positivism. He shared the old view that law was not a purely voluntary phenomenon but something given by God and inscribed in the structure of the world. "But truth exists, even though it be hidden in a well, and when it is diligently and faithfully sought, it can be brought forth and as a rule is brought forth."[101] The work of "bringing forth" was the very job of jurisprudence. Gentili never gave up the view that what the judge, the jurisconsult and ultimately the prince were doing when they operated with law was *iuris dictio*, not *creating* the law but *articulating* it, giving it formal expression. This was what linked Gentili to the Italian school where legal practice, in contradistinction to theology, consisted of piling interpretation upon interpretation in the Sisyphean effort to close the gap between human reason, weak and fragile as it was, and the law in its authentic meaning as justice and equity.[102] This also resolves the apparent puzzle concerning the alignment, in Gentili, of custom with nature. The distinction between the two gave expression to the human effort to reach the latter through the former, depicting custom itself as a type of *iuris dictio*, varying assessments of what justice and equity require in particular situations.[103]

[98] Ibid., I I (10). [99] Ibid., I I (11). [100] Ibid., I I (11). [101] Ibid., I I (8).
[102] Stephane Bonnet, *Droit et raison d'état* (Paris, Garnier 2012), 57–81.
[103] Gentili, *De iure belli*, I I (8). Using the expression in the D 1.1.1.9 gave final verity to the view.

## Sovereignty As the Virtue of Moral Ignorance

The most important break with the Salamanca scholars lay in the way Gentili postulated the equality of the belligerent powers.[104] The argument was in three steps. First was Gentili's altogether traditional definition of war as "a just and public contest of arms".[105] As he immediately noted, the fact that war was public excluded all kinds of private conflict from its scope. War was "waged by sovereigns ('*principes*')".[106] Brigands and pirates, or petty rulers did not qualify. Action against them was not war but policing, and the rules of *ius gentium* did not apply.[107] In a somewhat circular argument Gentili pointed out that only sovereigns had the status of public persons because "they acknowledge no judge or superior". As there was no judge above them it was "inevitable that the decision between sovereigns should be made by arms".[108] To this argument, Gentili then added, as a second move, the traditional language of the just war. Only wars between sovereigns can be just. The answer to the question of the war's justice was not something to be derived from philosophy, theology or domestic law, not even the *Corpus iuris*. In order to be binding on sovereigns, it had to be based on natural law. And what did natural law say? The third element in Gentili's system of just war emerged from a combination of his scepticism with the resulting equality of the sovereigns from which it followed that each sovereign was entitled to answer this question for itself. And because each would normally, indeed almost necessarily, regard its own war as just, and as there was no judge to decide such difference, it followed that both belligerent sides were to be regarded as just.

The anxiety with which the theologians rejected the very idea that both belligerents might have a just cause reflected, of course, their position as "wise men", experts of a certain highly valued knowledge. To give up the assumption of a world graspable by reason would, as the church's long struggles with the Franciscans had shown, have radically put to question Catholic theology and the authority of those teaching it. But for a Protestant refugee, nothing was more natural than doubt reason's capacity in matters of philosophy and theology. The reason of the scholastics was "that smart woman, Madam Jezebel", "the Devil's

[104] This is why Carl Schmitt made Gentili the father of *ius publicum Europaeum*. *Der Nomos der Erde im Völkerrecht des Jus Publicum Europaeum* (Berlin, Duncker & Humblot 1988), 91–2, 129–31.

[105] Gentili, *De iure belli*, I II (12).

[106] Ibid., I III I (15).

[107] Ibid., I IV (25).

[108] Ibid., I II I (15).

whore", Luther had written.[109] Aristotle's maxim was well-known that one "must not expect more precision than the subject-matter allows".[110] From this, Gentili derived the conclusion that because the subject-matter of war was human action on which theologians would have no special authority, and that even the knowledge of the jurists was fragile and coincided with contextual assessments of how to balance utility with honesty so as to arrive at the justice that joined legal reasoning with intelligent statecraft.[111]

For the theologians, just war had been a kind of criminal trial. The just sovereign was a victim and a judge at the same time – a double role hugely difficult to maintain in practice, as we have seen. Gentili would have none of such fiction; the parties were equal and if the unjust party sometimes gained victory, then "neither in the contention of arms nor in the strife carried out in the garb of peace is there any help for it".[112] He was thinking of war in a medieval fashion as a *duel*, a "just and public contest of arms", and accepted the wager of battle to resolve permanently the underlying dispute.[113] If, like the theologians, Gentili spoke of "just penalty" and recovery of "the expenses of the war and compensation for the losses",[114] this did not imply a hierarchical relationship. The word "*hostis*", used of the adversaries, indicated a certain levelling between them, separating them from robbers and brigands and inviting them "not to be too cruel and harsh" to each other.[115] The penalty and

109 Luther as quoted in Blanche Blanchard, *Reason and Belief* (1974), chapter V, available at www.giffordlectures.org/books/reason-and-belief.

110 The reference was what Aristotle had to say, in *The Nicomachean Ethics*, about political science and ethics, namely that "we must be content, then, in speaking of such subjects and with such premises to indicate the truth roughly and in outline, and in speaking about things which are only for the most part true", (D. Ross ed., Oxford University Press 1980), I 3 (3).

111 For his open-ended discussion on utility and honesty, see Gentili, *De iure belli*, III XII (349–52).

112 Ibid., I VI (33).

113 Ibid., I II (12). This aspect is especially highlighted in Panizza, 'Theory and Jurisprudence in Gentili's *De iure belli*', 217–18, 220–1. On medieval and early modern attitudes about the "wager of battle" as a process to resolve a dispute between princes, see James Q. Whitman, *The Verdict of Battle. The Law of Victory and the Making of Modern War* (Harvard University Press 2012), 50–94. As Randall Lesaffer puts it, "it was the *ius victoriae* which dominated Gentili's conception of peace" and entitled the victor to impose his will on the vanquished, though not wholly in abstraction of considerations is justice, 'Alberico Gentili's *ius post bellum* and Early Modern Peace Treaties', in Benedict Kingsbury & Benjamin Straumann (eds), *The Roman Foundations of the Law of Nations* (Oxford University Press 2010), 224, 222–40.

114 Gentili, *De iure belli*, III II (291), III III (298).

115 Ibid., I II (13).

the compensation were just as rewards of victory and outcomes of a calculation of how they would contribute to what Gentili saw as the principal purpose of the war, the establishment and consolidation of peace. "The past has an eye to vengeance, the future to a permanent establishment of peace; nay the past also has regard to this permanence..[116] The point was not that compensation and punishment fit the "crime", for there was none, but that they contribute to lasting peace. In this sense, peace was an eminently political matter, an objective of good statecraft.[117] Although "it is the will of the victor which settles everything", what the victor should will was to "grant a peace of such kind as to be lasting, since it is the nature of peace to be permanent".[118]

## Domestic Sovereignty: Absolute and Legally Confined

The meaning and significance of Gentili's "sovereignty" was that nobody could authoritatively compel you to do or believe otherwise than you have decided, though reasons of good statecraft and *ius gentium* might still persuade you to decide on one way rather than another. When, late in his career, Gentili published his *Regales disputationes* (1605), he was placing himself within that part of the English constitutional tradition that since Bracton had maintained that the prerogative was "absolute". But instead of drawing this conclusion from English history, he received it from general considerations about the nature of monarchic power as mediated by the *Corpus iuris*.[119] With express reference to Bodin, Gentili accepted that the monarch was subordinated to no temporal or spiritual power and that his will – *quod principem placuit* – was independent of its justice.[120] The king was not only *legibus solutus* but a *Deus in terris* with powers over his subjects greater than fathers in

[116] Ibid., III I (290).

[117] "la pace, e come il discorso giuridico fosse di fatto coincidente con quello di merito politico". Panizza, *Alberico Gentili, giurista ideologo*, 120.

[118] Gentili, *De iure belli*, III XIII (353).

[119] Gentili, Disputatio I. 'De potestate Regis absoluta', in *Regales disputationes tres* (London, Vautrolles 1605), 5–7, 10–11. On absolutist public law in England since Bracton and at Gentili's time, see e.g. C. H. McIlwain, *Constitutionalism Ancient and Modern* (Indianapolis, Liberty Fund 2007 [1947]), 120, and generally 65–8, 115–20. As Straumann has noted, the fact that Gentili "actually applies Roman constitutional legal norms taken from the Digest to the English constitution" meant that "thus has effectively the *populus Romanus* bestowed its authority on the absolute *Rex Anglorum*", Straumann, 'The *Corpus iuris* as a Source of Law', 107.

[120] Gentili, 'De potestate Regis absoluta', 8–9 and comment in Panizza, 'Il pensiero politico di Alberico Gentili', 182–3.

ancient times had over their children.[121] However, owing to his commitment to Roman law (as evidence of natural law and thus applicable in England) he could not ignore those of its parts that did put limits to monarchic powers. These included the *lex regia* and *Digna vox*, the view that the monarch had received his powers from the people and that they were therefore not to deviate from their laws unless absolutely necessary.[122] Although Gentili insisted that the people had donated their power to the king totally and irretrievably, he nevertheless noted that this could hardly include powers the people themselves did not have, such as alienating them to another ruler, and suggested that "even the freest possible power [was] for purposes not of tyranny, but of administration".[123] That Gentili made the old distinction between the king's ordained and his absolute powers presumed that the king would normally act in accordance with the law; absolute powers would be used only exceptionally.[124]

Although Gentili did regard the king *legibus solutus*, he refrained from extending this to freedom from divine or natural law, or from *ius gentium*.[125] After all, it would have been odd if, in that late work, he would have suggested that everything he had written in *De iure belli* was only recommendatory. And he agreed with Bodin that kings were bound by their words to each other, even if given under duress, as well as by contracts concluded with their subjects.[126] So even if the royal will was itself sufficient *ratio* for the validity of a law, this did not mean that the monarch himself was liberated to will whatever he or she desired.[127]

121 Gentili, 'De potestate Regis absoluta', 11.

122 However, quite strikingly, and perhaps to placate James, Gentili also wrote that "Est iuris divini potestas principis: non a solis hominibus constituta. Est iuris naturalis gentium". Alberico Gentili, 'De vi civium in regem semper iniusta', in *Regales Disputationes*, Disputatio III, 101–2.

123 Gentili, *De iure belli*, III XV (371, 373). See further, 'De potestate Regis absoluta', 9 and comments in Panizza, 'Il pensiero politico di Alberico Gentili', 180–1. The measure of a just king's "extraordinary" or tyrannical powers in a case of necessity is discussed on 188–90.

124 See Francis Oakley, 'The Absolute and Ordained Power of God in Sixteenth- and Seventeenth-Century Theology', 59 *Journal of the History of Ideas* (1998), 437–61.

125 "Princeps, inquit Baldus, supra ius, scilicet civile: infra ius, scilicet naturale & gentium. Non supra divinum ius: ut idem scribit hic, & Bartolus, & Angelus", Gentili, 'De potestate Regis absoluta', 17.

126 Gentili, *De iure belli*, III XIV (343–4); III XVI (377–8).

127 Forming a coherent view of Gentili's attitudes towards the way in which the sovereign was bound by reason or natural law in the three disputations of 1583, 1585 and 1587 and again in those of 1605 is hard owing to their character as disputations, experiments in arguing for opposite conclusions. Panizza interprets

Of course no temporal or spiritual power could challenge that will. The very point of the king's use of his absolute powers was to deny that anyone could ask him "*why do you do this*?"[128] The will of the king was always sufficient reason. That led Gentili to some difficulty in trying to distinguish between the prince and the tyrant. Sometimes it was necessary for a prince to take action that appeared tyrannical to defend the state. Nevertheless, it was the task of the prince to rule with justice. *De plenitudine potestatis intelligitur de potestate bona & laudabili.*[129]

The strong view about the inability to challenge the actions of a sovereign, repeated by Gentili throughout his career, contrasted strikingly with the rambling chapter in *De iure belli* where Gentili suddenly accepted the right of princes to defend the subjects of a foreign tyrant. This gave Gentili occasion to flag his attachment to the cosmopolitan commonplaces of classical literature. From the "generally recognized kinship of all men with their fellows" it followed that "[i]t is not lawful . . . to do to subjects whatever one wishes".[130] But the latter were never entitled to take the law into their own hands. Popular resistance was excluded.[131] The only enforcement could come from a foreign prince, a humanist warrior.[132] If this seemed awkward, incoherence was the price Gentili was ready to pay to join Sidney in support of the Dutch rebels.

Recognition of the weakness of the powers of reason simultaneously with ongoing massive civil conflict in sixteenth-century Europe convinced jurists such as Bodin and Gentili of the need for a powerful sovereign. "The sovereign has no earthly judge, for one over whom

these in terms of a "Tacitean turn" conflicting with the republican passages in *De legationibus and De iure belli.* 'Il pensiero politico de Alberico Gentili', 173–92. Nevertheless, Annabel Brett has read these texts with her customary care and concluded that evidence from them and from various passages in *De iure belli* suggest that the royal will can never be fully arbitrary; constraint is never absent, though subjects may not invoke it. Annabel Brett, 'Liberty and Absolutism. The Roman Heritage and the International Order in Alberico Gentili', in *Alberico Gentili. Giustizia, Guerra, Impero. Atti del convegno XIV Giornata Gentiliana* (San Ginesio 2010), especially 205–12.

128 Gentili, 'De potestate Regis absoluta', 11.

129 "Non est ea potestas ad malum & ad iniuriam", ibid., 27. See further, Davide Suin, 'Principi supremi e societas hominium. Il problema del potere nella riflessione di Alberico Gentili', XXIV *Scienza e politica* (2017), 113–14, 122–3; Panizza, 'Il pensiero politico di Alberico Gentili', 192–3.

130 Gentili, *De iure belli*, I XVI (78).

131 Alberico Gentili, 'De civium in regem semper iniusta', Disputatio III, in *Regales disputationes*, 99–132.

132 Suin, 'Principi supremi', 119–20.

another holds a superior position, is not a sovereign."[133] The argument would be brought to its logical conclusion half a century later in the "Mortall God" of Thomas Hobbes.[134] That Gentili referenced both Bodin and the *Corpus iuris* meant that he still understood the royal prerogative, whether based on Roman law, English history, or divine enactment as James I would eventually suggest, as the domain of law and not of theology or some untouchable *arcana*.[135] That situated him within a legal tradition that would think of its own professional vocabulary as the master science of government. It was above all an empowering vocabulary, one that would be less about how the prince ought to behave under some moral code than about how those ideals could be made compatible with the objectives of *utile*. Instead of an external constraint on royal policy, it was law binding as wise statecraft.

## Law between History and Philosophy

Gentili's turn to practice and history broke new ground as jurisprudence. But it would not have been alien to pragmatic thinkers such as Guicciardini or Machiavelli for whom the abstractions of moral discourse would never match the "unerring test of facts"; without it, as Gentili put it, a diplomat would remain a mere "dryland sailor" not knowing his way ahead in the world.[136] There was, he seemed to be saying, an obviousness in facts that, as they accumulate, provide a better basis for efficient statecraft, and thus for arguing about the *ius gentium*, than any abstract theories.[137] Accordingly, most of *De iure belli* consists of accounts of past events as well as citations of writings by authorities about them, often on both sides so that Gentili could leave his own

[133] Gentili, *De iure belli*, I III (15).

[134] Both also contained that fatal *lacuna*, identified by Carl Schmitt, that they did not have the power to rule on the subjects' consciences. Carl Schmitt, *The Leviathan in the State Theory of Thomas Hobbes. Meaning and Failure of a Political Symbol* (Westport, Greenwood 1996 [1938]).

[135] The paradoxical effort to make "absolutism" depend on *legal* arguments was part of Gentili's anti-theological project, suggests Alain Wijffels in 'Une disputation d'Alberico Gentili sur le droit du souverain de disposer de son royaume et des biens de ses sujets (1587)', in Jacques Krynen & Michael Stolleis (eds), *Science politique et droit public dans les facultés de droit européennes* (XIIIe–XVIIIe siècle) (Frankfurt, Klostermann 2008), 471–4.

[136] Gentili, *De legationibus*, III VIII (154).

[137] Thus, *De legationibus* received a firm status among seventeenth-century learned writers such as Pierre Bayle or Gabriel Naudé as the definitive work on diplomacy. Pirillo, 'Republicanism and Religious Dissent', 133.

conclusion open. It was not advisable, he seemed to indicate, to give abstract answers to concrete problems. All one could do was to indicate considerations that history demonstrated would be relevant in one way or another.[138] The long and important sections on insuring peace for the future, for example, proceeded by listing many historical examples and authorities. "But in that sort of discussion", he wrote, "we are approaching the boundaries of politics and leaving our subject." All one could conclude was that "the victor may, without violating the laws of nature, do anything which tends to make his victory firm and ensure a peace that is just to himself and those vanquished".[139]

It was necessary to know history – but it was also necessary to give the facts of the past an intelligible meaning and to show out of "the many precedents [. . .] which [the historian] is to follow".[140] Historical facts did not lend themselves to precedents automatically. What was needed was the intervention of thought that put facts in order and saw some pattern in them:

> Through all mortal affairs, through the infinity of the ages runs a certain similarity, for those who participate therein are always men of the same type, retaining the same nature and the same emotions forever. It is inevitable therefore, that the same results should appear.[141]

It was therefore necessary to "add to the knowledge of history that branch of philosophy which deals with morals and politics".[142] It had been Machiavelli's great virtue that "in reading history he [did] not play the grammarian, but assume[d] the role of philosopher".[143] He understood that history was not just a procession of random facts going in different directions. Instead, it was possible to attain a standpoint above pure factuality that allowed "weigh[ing] precedents with delicately

[138] This resembles Machiavelli's way of proceeding with history. As Bonnet notes, for him, "L'expérience porte sur des cas individuels qu'elle ordonne et compare, mais elle ne s'élève jamais jusqu'au jugement à valeur universelle", *Droit et raison d'état*, 139.

[139] Gentili, *De iure belli*, III XIII (359).

[140] Gentili, *De legationibus*, III IX (157).

[141] Ibid., III VIII (153). This is nearly identical to Machiavelli's methodological strictures: "he who would foresee what has to be, should reflect on what has been, for everything that happens in the world at any time has genuine resemblance to what happened in ancient times. This is due to the fact that the agents who bring such things are men, and that men have, and always have had, the same passions, whence it necessarily comes that the same effects are produced", Machiavelli, *The Discourses* (B. Crick ed., Penguin Classics 1983), III 43.8 (517).

[142] Gentili, *De legationibus*, III IX (156).

[143] Ibid., III IX (157).

balanced scales".[144] Facts needed to be chosen in view of their present importance and interpreted in light of larger ideas. None of this was possible without some philosophical training, which, when attached to the facts of political life not only became what jurisprudence should be but also what good statesmanship was.[145]

Jurisprudential analysis was philosophical reading of history.[146] The point of the use of examples in *De iure belli* was then not just to demonstrate what had been done in the past but to assist in elucidating present-day situations so as to help determining what would be the appropriate – *legally* appropriate – way of dealing with them now.[147] If this was jurisprudence, it was not just some set of principles that descended from heaven, but an orderly process of comparing present facts with accumulated experience. Much of this knowledge was conveniently available in the *Corpus iuris*:

> [T]he law which is written in those books of Justinian is not merely that of the state, but also that of nations and of nature; and with this last it is all so in accord, that if the empire were destroyed, the law itself, although long buried, would yet arise again and diffuse itself among all the nations of mankind.[148]

It was the rich tradition of Roman law that finally became the "supreme paradigm of reason and natural justice".[149] And what would be the philosophy to interpret the *Corpus iuris*? Here Gentili retreated to Ciceronian oratory about the unity of humankind. In the famous chapter on defence of honour, Gentili wanted to seduce his readers with the "beautiful words" that address "the whole world [as] one body" and "all men [as] members of that body". Citing Cicero, Augustine and others, he made note of the "fundamental principle that nature has established among men, kinship, love, kindliness, and a bond of fellowship".[150] To defend intervention against oppressive regimes, Gentili expressed the view that the subjects of another sovereign "do not seem to me to be outside of that kinship of nature and the society formed by the whole world".[151] He even quoted Seneca to the effect of

144 Ibid., III IX (157). Similarly, *De iure belli*, I I (4).
145 Gentili, *De legationibus*, III IX (156–8).
146 This, in Gentili's view, was the understanding communicated in the Digest. Gentili, *De iure belli*, I I (8). See further Iurlaro, 'Burden of Reason', 428–37.
147 Pirillo, 'Republicanism and Religious Dissent', 132–3.
148 Gentili, *De iure belli*, I III (17). See further Straumann, 'The *Corpus iuris* as a Source of Law', 111–23.
149 Panizza, 'Il pensiero politico di Alberico Gentili', 63.
150 Gentili, *De iure belli*, I XV (67, 68).
151 Ibid., I XVI (74).

there being a "duty to the human race [that was] prior and superior to that which I owe to any individual".[152]

But these references played only a limited role. They did not justify domestic resistance against tyranny, though they did entitle foreign princes to assist an oppressed people.[153] Above all, they operated as the rhetorical "double" in places where Gentili chose to proceed by juxtaposing the demands of honesty to those of expediency, providing some but rarely decisive weight to the former. There was no theory of an international community or of ideal statehood in his works. The nearest Gentili came to anything like a statement of abstract principles was the list of virtues that qualified the good ambassador-statesman – courage, temperance and prudence.[154] But these were "procedural" considerations that only indicated the manner in which an ambassador, and to all practical purposes, the jurist, was to proceed in their job.

Despite Gentili's overt celebration of the union of history and philosophy, his writing actually stayed quite distant from any historical factuality or philosophical contemplation. Both items were treated in a highly stylized way that supposed a specific cultural frame that the author shared with his readers. Gentili wrote to men well educated in classical literatures, Greek and Roman history, epic poetry, Aristotle, the Stoics and all the rest of humanist erudition. The evidence he presented and the intellectual moves he made seemed credible because and to the extent that the literatures from which they were taken seemed so.[155] Legal reasoning was not be about true facts or correct metaphysical derivations.[156] It was instead about remembering examples and retelling

[152] Ibid., I I (8). [153] Ibid., I VI (74–8).

[154] Gentili, *De legationibus*, Part III. On this point, see also Panizza, 'Il pensiero politico di Alberico Gentili', 61–5.

[155] The search of the proper form to treat historical *exempla* accounts for much of the methodological debate within sixteenth-century *ars historica*. Bodin's work was often the inspiration. Grafton writes that "in the 1580s in Cambridge . . . every desktop sported a copy of his *Republic*" – this must have been true of Gentili's Oxford as well. Anthony Grafton, *What Was History? The Art of History in Early Modern Europe* (Cambridge University Press 2007), 192 and 189–254. But Gentili's reading of Bodin was complex. In *De iure belli*, he not only criticised Bodin's dismissive attitude to earlier "Italian" writers but also his historical method which, Gentili suggested was "for the most part based on examples [with which] one could not easily derive . . . any system of law, and certainly not one which is regarded as natural and definite", I I (4). See further, Quaglioni, 'The Italian "Readers" of Bodin', 374–86.

[156] Gentili quoted Aristotle to the effect that he will not give "demonstrations" but instead "persuasive arguments which this kind of treatise allows", *De iure belli*, I I (11).

stories from classical authors. These were the source of right practical knowledge that helped dressing disparate facts with coherent meanings, separating good from bad statesmanship. Particularly authoritative were "our [i.e. Roman] jurists who have been able to compile this law from absolutely all nations; for if the Roman, Greek, Jews and barbarians, in short, all known peoples, have made use of certain code of laws, it will be assumed that all men have made use of that same code".[157]

The best illustration of this was the work *De armis romanis* that Gentili published only one year after the final edition of *De iure belli.* This provided him an opportunity to show how historical examples may, with some ingenuity, be interpreted to render opposite moral conclusions. It has been generally assumed that the views of the *Defender* reflected Gentili's own views. Where *De iure belli* refers approvingly to this work, it is always to these. But the evidence is mixed so that instead of reading *De armis romanis* by looking for Gentili's own opinions, it may be better to understand it as demonstration of rhetorical skill where largely undisputed facts, agreed between the *Accuser* and the *Defender*, are coloured differently by producing contrasting interpretations of them.[158] The scholastic format of *disputatio* was ideal for that purpose as it called for the presentation and comparison pro and contra for both of two opposite theses.[159] It was also particularly useful for someone like Gentili who believed that the justice of behaviour would be the product of philosophical reflection on historical analogies. Such an understanding would stress the situational constraints on efficient statecraft and the sensitivity and reasoning powers of the prince. This would also make sense of the three disputations from the 1580s where Gentili both defended monarchic absolutism and expressed his doubts about it. It may perhaps be said that these texts, meant for purely academic purposes, allowed Gentili to express and play with different juristic constructions about the nature of ruling.[160] Law was not about declaring truths. It was an interpretative craft that called upon imaginative reflection on the many meanings that could be given to facts and thus to rehearse the special service that law could offer to diplomacy and efficient statesmanship.[161]

[157] Ibid., I I (9). [158] As suggested by Brett, 'Liberty and Absolutism', 209–12.

[159] Panizza, 'Il pensiero politico di Alberico Gentili', 176.

[160] Brett, 'Liberty and Absolutism', 212.

[161] The development into a kind of "reason of state" in the sixteenth century is usefully discussed in Donald Kelley, 'Civil Science in the Renaissance. The Problem of Interpretation', in Donald Kelley, *The Writing of History and the Study of Law* (London, Routledge 1997), XIII, 72–3.

## The Work of *Ius gentium*: Equity, Utility, Necessity

In Gentili's legal world, the powers of human reason were limited. Although truth existed "even though it be hidden in a well", there were no supernatural means to ensure that it had been found in a particular case.[162] If everyone always thought of themselves as "just" and others unjust, this followed from what Gentili believed was the weakness of human reason, the way it allowed only a "dim" perception of the world.[163] At best one could approach the truth by examining past examples, real or poetic, recorded in authoritative writings. The *disputatio* format allowed Gentili to demonstrate how both opposing sides in most significant disputes would normally have something to be said for them so that the final verdict about human justice was no more powerful than the reasoning brought forward to support it. Hence the rhetorical or oratorical character of Gentili's law, vividly displayed in his citation practice. Exemplary historical narratives would speak to ideas about just and unjust behaviour in war and invite readers to reflect on analogies with the qualities of the heroes in those stories.[164] Figures from Vergil's Aeneas would be useful as familiar examples of psychological complexity that resonated with contemporary moral dilemmas.[165] The references to Guicciardini, Bodin and Montaigne tapped on literatures through which his readers would have been accustomed to reflecting on the religious conflict and their attitudes to public power.

What these literatures did not offer were clear-cut rules to be applied more or less mechanically. Instead, they invited Gentili to produce a cascade of examples and lists of quotations from ancient and modern sources, depicting contrasting attitudes and priorities, often concluding in rather open-ended and sometimes question-begging ways. The chapter that contemplated how defeated enemies were to be treated juxtaposed examples of honourable conduct to more expedient ones but resigned to concluding that the principal concern would often be the degree of danger posed "either to our persons or our fortunes".[166]

162 Gentili, *De iure belli*, I I (8). 163 Ibid., I VI (31).

164 See further, Warren, *Literature and the Law of Nations*, 31–61.

165 See, for example, the discussion of "Suppliants" in *De iure belli*, II XX (246–7), where Gentili discussed the slaying of Turnus by Aeneas and the commentary in Warren, *Literature and the Law of Nations*, 43–7; Christopher Warren, 'Gentili, the Poets and the Laws of War', in Benedict Kingsbury & Benjamin Straumann (eds), *The Roman Foundations of the Law of Nations* (Oxford University Press 2010), 152–3.

166 Gentili, *De iure belli*, III XII (351–2). At the outset of the chapter, Gentili first asked the question "But what can make the peace lasting?" and responded, "the one

In reflecting upon the English intervention on the continent Gentili stressed the importance of trying to choose a course of action that would be both morally sound *and* in the interests of England itself.[167] Over again, he sought to bring self-interest together with larger humanist principles of the general good. For example, deceiving one's enemy deviated from chivalric virtues and Christian truthfulness. But defeating one's enemy would often be the greater good.[168] To show mercy to those captured was important not only because of the honesty of such action but as it would facilitate later dealings with the enemy. If Gentili believed that honour would usually override individual interest, he defended that position quite classically by claiming that it "has regard to the common advantage".[169] One should refrain from committing wanton or dishonourable acts because it was "also in the interest of the victor that memorials for his victory should be set up for his glorification and as a testimony to his sovereignty".[170]

Yet this rule has an exception in the case of advantage, the neglect of which imperils safety. If there is danger either to our persons or our fortunes, we should prefer expediency to this honour of which we are speaking.[171]

Like Guicciardini, Gentili preferred acting honourably when this was possible. But in case honour conflicted with an important interest, it would have to yield. In making peace it was imperative to consider how to ensure it also for the future: this might entail some punishment, but

enduring principle, namely justice". In this way, he joined the legal with the instrumental, concluding, as would be obvious, that it all depended on the "actual facts" as well as the character of the victor and the vanquished so that "no general rule can be formulated" (353–4).

167 More generally on this technique, see Panizza, 'Alberico Gentili's *De Iure Belli*. The Humanist Foundations', 569–76. In assessing Gentili's "Machiavellian matrix" it may be useful to note that the work of the Florentine secretary is best seen as an update of (instead of deviation from) the medieval genre of mirror of princes, as discussed in more detail in Michel Senellart, *Les arts de gouverner. De régimen médiéval au concept de gouvernement* (Paris, Seuil 1995), 211–30. This is then true also of *De legationibus* as well as of those parts of *De iure belli* in which the subject has to do with how the prince (or his ambassador) should act so as to preserve and consolidate his rule in relation to hostile neighbours.

168 Gentili, *De iure belli*, II V (152). Gentili's views on lying, deception, falsehoods and subterfuges of various kinds are written into one of his essays where he defended theatrical cross-dressing against puritan attacks. The works *Disputatioines Duae. I De actoribus et spectatioribus fabularum non notandis; II De abusuu mendacii* (1599) are discussed in Panizza, 'Il pensiero politico di Alberico Gentili', 146–9, 167–8.

169 Gentili, *De iure belli*, III XII (349–50).

170 Ibid., III XII (350).

171 Ibid., III XII (351).

also and perhaps usually the fair treatment of the enemy – "a peace that is no less expedient for the vanquished to keep than for the victors".[172]

"I believe that justice should be preferred to the letter of the law."[173] What Gentili meant by this was displayed in his treatment of agreements between sovereigns, understood not as "strict law", but as good faith arrangements that were to be aligned with the needs of necessity and reason of state. "We do not follow here the strict law or the letter of the law, under which fatal errors have often been committed," Gentili noted, referencing Guicciardini's citation of the emphasis on good faith stated by Pietro de' Medici.[174] Necessity, when not trivial, gave good reason for leaving a treaty. "If an alliance is abandoned because of some reason of state which arises, no charge may be brought against an ally, again in the opinion of Ulpian."[175] That this was a good faith principle suggested that the treaty partners might, presumptively, understand such reasons, at least if they were given openly to the other party and as soon as the cause had emerged.[176] This was especially important in view of treaties of peace where the objective overrode such formal considerations as provision of signatures or deliveries or full powers, and in which the defence of duress would not apply.[177] In any case, the principle of *rebus sic stantibus* would apply fully, for every treaty was concluded with a mental reservation "provided affairs stay in the same condition".[178]

Gentili's Italian baggage included awareness of the paradoxical relationship between the stability of human nature and the endless variation of human affairs. Machiavelli had believed *fortuna* to be omnipresent, and that the only way to deal with it was to develop the kind of secular *virtù* that could make the best of unforeseen events. He did appreciate the security that laws brought about and wrote that the best emperors were those who "acted, like good princes, in accordance with the laws".[179] But laws were mere generalisations from the past, repeatedly undermined by *fortuna* and the evil of human nature. That is why "in

172 Ibid., III XIII (355). 173 Ibid., III XII (349-350). 174 Ibid., III XIV (361).

175 Gentili, *De legationibus*, III XXIV (428). Here is a typical argument where Gentili hides his own view behind a quote from Ulpian – leaving it open for him also to state the contrary whenever that might seem appropriate.

176 Gentili, *De iure belli,* III XXIV (427–8). For the equitable application of treaties under the good faith principle in Gentili, see Giuliano Marchetto, 'Une Guerra giusta per una giusta pace. Il diritto dei trattati nel *De iure belli*, III (1598) di Alberico Gentili', 10 *Laboratoire italien* (2010), 71–84.

177 Gentili, *De iure belli*, III XIV (362–4). 178 Ibid., III XIV (365).

179 Machiavelli, *Discourses*, I II (105) and I X (136).

order to maintain his state [the new prince] is often forced to act in defiance of good faith, of charity, of kindness, of religion".[180] Gentili avoided this type of language, but he shared that sensitivity. Of course, it was best to rule by law and to act honourably whenever possible. But this was not always the case. In the famous chapter on the conflict between honour and expediency Gentili had altogether left the world of general laws and enquired instead into how to deal with individual situations in the constantly changing world of war and peace.[181] The prince was to keep a constant eye on "the case of advantage, the neglect of which imperils safety".[182] This did not mean that safety should always override every other concern. But there were situations where it would entitle even unjust action, for example breaking an alliance if compliance would expose oneself to danger. "A just and unavoidable necessity makes anything lawful."[183]

It has become a standard of Gentili scholarship to make note of his development from the strict 'Bartolist' into someone deeply engaged with historical texts, diplomatic events and considerations of political appropriateness. In a late text on the laws of marriage, Gentili stressed that "[o]ur art is not only to recite what is included in the books of Iustinian but to explain for each situation where justice therein lies".[184] He sketched an image of the "*iurisperitus*" who was not just a competent civil lawyer but committed to elucidating the meaning of what was just and what unjust in social relations generally.[185] As "*sacerdotes iustitiae*", "priests" of human justice, they would leave theologians to contemplate the increasingly opaque relations between humans and God.

[180] Machiavelli, *The Prince*, XVIII (57). [181] Gentili, *De iure belli*, III XII (349).
[182] Ibid., III XII (351). [183] Ibid., III XII (351).
[184] "Nostra non est ars, recitare quid in libris Iustiniani est constitutum, sed definire explicate, quid in quaque questione est iuris". Alberico Gentilis, *Disputationem de nuptiis Libri VII* (1601), quoted in Minnucci, *Alberico Gentili iuris interpres*, 178. Minnucci draws attention to Gentili's own explanation of his "humanist turn" from thinking of himself as an "*interpres Iustiniani iuris*" to adopting the wider role as an "*interpres iuris*", 212–13. The development of Gentili's views about interpretation is discussed in Panizza, *Alberico Gentili, giurista ideologo*, 43–7. See also Giuliano Marchetto, 'Alberico Gentili e la tradizione. La letteratura consulente come fonte dello ius belli', in *Alberico Gentili. San Ginesio 1552–Londra 1608: atti dei convegni nel quarto centenario della norte* (San Ginesio, 11–12–13 settembre 2008, Oxford e Londra, 5–6 giugno 2008, Napoli 'L'Orientale', 6 novembre 2007), 77–82 and the extensive references therein. The "humanist turn" appears likewise in a published volume, *Disputationes tres. I De libris Iuris Canonici. II De libris Iuris Civilis. III De Latinita veterum Bibliorum versionis male accusata (*1605).
[185] Also Panizza, *Alberico Gentili, giurista ideologo*, 79 and generally 78–81.

## The Trouble with Theology

For a jurist whose most famous sentence reads "Let theologians be silent about matters that are none of their business" (*Silete theologi in munere alieno*), Gentili devoted enormous time engaging with theologians, often extensively borrowing from Scripture and other religious writings.[186] It is also not absolutely clear what he meant by that famous exclamation. If Gentili denied religious antagonism as a just cause of war, few commentators, including the Spanish theologians, had ever suggested otherwise.[187] Made in the context of the discussion of the confrontation with Ottoman Turkey Gentili may have instead wished to indicate that the fact that war was perpetual with them, did not result from religious adversity but from the fact that they were "our enemies, plot against us and threaten us".[188] There is also little critical engagement in Gentili's writings with Vitoria and his followers. Mostly Gentili referred to them respectfully and never engaged with them in the kind of polemic he had had with the legal humanists in his early works or with the puritans of the Oxford faculty. Nor did he shun away from theology itself to the extent that he was often ready to acknowledge the overriding nature of divine law, quite significantly when he demanded that a resident ambassador refuse to obey "if his sovereign should want him to do something which detracts even in the smallest degree from his obligations to God".[189]

But however the statement was meant, it was certainly compatible with Gentili's strong view that theologians had no special expertise in purely inter-human relations. Their competence was limited to the internal relationship humans had with God. They also possessed no monopoly for reading Scripture, and while they did have authority on the subjects covered by the first three of the ten commandments, the rest fell within the jurists' professional domain. Thus, for example, the

[186] Gentili, *De iure belli*, I XII (57).

[187] Noel Malcolm highlights the large convergence of opinions between Gentili and the Spanish theologians in regard to the treatment of the infidel in 'Alberico Gentili and the Ottomans', in Benedict Kingsbury & Benjamin Straumann (eds), *The Roman Foundations of the Law of Nations* (Oxford University Press 2010), 130–3.

[188] Gentili, *De iure belli*, I XII (56). For a discussion, see also Minnucci, "*Silete theologi*", 188–90. But see also III XIX (401–2) where Gentili, supporting himself by Biblical passages, denies the lawfulness of treaties of (military) alliance (such as the famous alliance between France and the Sultan of 1536) with the infidel. As Malcolm, suggests, here he (unlike Bodin) appeared to allow religious considerations to determine the content of his law. 'Alberico Gentili and the Ottomans', 138–45.

[189] Gentili, *De legationibus*, III XV (195).

knowledge needed for conducting diplomacy properly did not include theology and there was to be no discrimination between ambassadors from Christian and infidel nations.[190] Most of Gentili's expressly theological writings are to be found in private correspondence or in manuscripts that have remained unpublished, perhaps owing to the uncertainty Gentili felt about the wisdom of distributing them as an immigrant in a partly hostile environment.[191] Gentili himself represented a moderate and eclectic Protestantism.[192] Divine law set a boundary which even the absolute sovereign was not entitled to cross.[193] But this boundary remained internal to the sovereign's conscience; there was no way it could be enforced on the ruler. Gentili's most concise public treatment of the relations of law and theology appeared in the late work on the laws of marriage (*Disputationum de nuptiis libri VII*, 1601) where he summarised his view of theology as dealing with the relations of human beings with God as enshrined in *ius divinum*. Law's subject-matter was human relations and its object *ius humanum*. As this suggested, while theology's jurisdiction was limited narrowly to the internal world of faith, the authority of jurists extended to all social relations, including matters treated in the last seven commandments.[194]

Gentili's scepticism about the powers of reason went utterly against the Spanish theologians' view of politics. But nor did the English Puritans think highly of it. As part of his effort to integrate in the intellectual milieu of his new homeland Gentili prepared an anti-papal

[190] See e.g. Giovanni Minnucci, 'Bella religionis causa movenda non sunt'. La libertas religionis nel pensiero di Alberico Gentili', 102 *Nuove Rivista Storica* (2018), 997–8.

[191] He might also have tried to avoid violating the religious sentiments of his high-level English mentors.

[192] Gentili attacked the doctrines of purgatory, saints and indulgencies. His own beliefs have sometimes been associated with Luther's, sometimes Zwingli's. He rejected the various puritan sects and was tolerant of Trinitarian confessions. In his final years he reconciled to the Anglican church. See Panizza, *Alberico Gentili, giurista ideologo*, 27–8; Lavinia, 'Alberico Gentili', 182–6.

[193] Gentili, 'De potestate Regis absoluta', 17.

[194] This was hard to square with Gentili's reputation as a strict "Bartolist", based on his early *De iuris interpretibus libri VI* (1582), where he had insisted that legal interpretation was to be limited to the clarification of the *Corpus iuris* and had conducted a vigorous campaign against the "grammaticationes, graecationes, criticationes" of humanist jurisprudence. Panizza, *Alberico Gentili, giurista ideologo*, 43. The publication of this polemical work was received very negatively among such humanists as the Hotman family, residing in England, Jean Hotman for example (the son of François) allowed his early friendship with Gentili to lapse. See Minnucci, "*Silete theologi*", 33–61.

manifesto *De papatu Romano Antichristo* (1585/1587–91) that was subjected to many additions and has only recently been published.[195] The work reaffirmed the Lutheran doctrine of justification, rejected Purgatory and all but the two sacraments instituted by Christ. It shared the Protestant commonplace of the pope as Antichrist and dismissed any role for the church in political life. In particular Gentili attacked the pope's advocacy of the use of force against Protestants and heretics: no such violence could be justified by the Gospel. The real church, he wrote, was the papacy's opponents.[196] That he never published the work may have reflected his wish not to further alienate himself from his Puritan colleagues.[197]

The view that divine law had to do exclusively with the relations of humans and God was put forward by Gentili also in the early versions of what became *De iure belli.*[198] It was then reiterated many times in his polemic with the Oxford Puritans as well as in four chapters of the final text of *De iure belli* (1598) that dealt with, respectively, the question of whether religion was a just cause for war, whether a ruler or a victor in war should enforce religious uniformity and whether the subjects could oppose the ruler on the basis of religious views (Bk I Chapters IX–XI and Bk III Ch XI). Gentili's response to each question was negative: Religion was not a just cause of war and the victor had no right to extinguish the religion of the vanquished:

> In religion is man's highest good (*summum bonum*), and every man finds this in his own faith. Shall the victor then take away religion, the greatest of blessings, merely that he may hold his power more quietly?[199]

Toleration was the right attitude: "if men in another state live in a manner different from that which we follow in our own State, they

[195] Alberico Gentili, *De papatu Romano Antichristo* (Giovanni Minnucci ed. & introd., Siena, Monducci 2018). See further Panizza, *Alberico Gentili, giurista ideologo*, 19–40; Minnucci, "*Silete theologi*", 91–113 and Diego Quaglioni, 'Il "De papatu Romano Antichristo" del Gentili', in Luigi Lacchè (ed.), *"Ius gentium, ius communicationis, ius belli". Alberico Gentili e gli orizzonti della modernità: atti del convegno di Macerata in occasione delle celebrazioni del quarto centenario della morte di Alberico Gentili (1552–1608)* (Milan, Giuffrè 2009), 197–207.

[196] Panizza, *Alberico Gentili, giurista ideologo*, 33.

[197] Ibid., 37–8; Minnucci, *"Silete theologi"*, 108–13.

[198] *De iure belli commentatio prima* (1587) referred to in Minnucci, "*Silete theologi*", 86–7. The discussion of the matter in *De iure belli* ends: "the laws of religion do not properly exist between man and man, therefore, no man's rights are violated by differences in religion, nor is it lawful to make war because of religion", I IX (41).

[199] Gentili, *De iure belli*, III XI (343).

surely do us no wrong".[200] The same applied internally. Neither the ruler nor the subjects had a right to impose religion on each other. "I accept the argument of Bodin, that violence should not be employed against subjects who have embraced another religion than that of the ruler."[201] But instead of invoking Bodinian sovereignty, he explained that neutrality was called for because "religion is a matter of the mind and of the will, which is always accompanied by freedom".[202] To try to impose it was against the nature of religion and profoundly unjust. Far from pacification, such efforts were only conducive to atheism, and atheism was contrary to nature.[203]

The view of war as a human relationship provided a new interpretation of ongoing conflicts as well. All ostensibly religious blood-shedding was attributable to "robbers, assassins, adulterers, sacrilegious men, magicians and monsters".[204] Even the civil wars raging in France were actually secular in character: "Who does not know that as far back as memory goes there has been factions in Gaul?"[205] This was a political and social conflict with historical roots that only superficially concerned matters of faith. Religious justifications were "invention of the most greedy men [as] cloaks for their dishonesty".[206] Citing Guicciardini and the historian Paolo Giovio, Gentili singled out Ferdinand the Catholic and Charles V as rulers with especial inclination to veil their desire for dominion by religion. But the problem was larger:

> Each man declares his own war a holy one. Each one insists that his enemies are godless men. Each names his own cause righteous. Every one has upon his lips the words "sacred" and "pious", but in purpose, aim and intention, he is otherwise affected. The dispute is about human justice.[207]

It did not take long for the English theologians to think of Gentili as an adversary. The epithets "Italian trickster", "atheist" and "Machiavellian" stuck to his name immediately after the publication of *De legationibus* (1585). From that moment to the end of his life, Gentili would be engaged in an intellectual struggle with his religious adversaries,

200 Ibid., I IV (41). For Gentili's views on freedom of conscience, see Panizza, 'Il pensiero politico di Alberico Gentili', 73–114. Gentili gave many examples of peaceful community between adherents to different faiths to defend religious freedom, *libertas religionis*. However, he also invoked Bodin to stress that if a religious meeting or ceremony might cause "harm" to the state, it was to be suppressed. *De iure belli*, I X (44).

201 Gentili, *De iure belli*, I X (44).

202 Ibid., I IX (39, 38–41).

203 Ibid., III XI (342).

204 Ibid., III XI (341).

205 Ibid., III XI (340).

206 Ibid., I IX (40).

207 Ibid., I IX (40).

especially the professor of theology at Oxford, later Cambridge, John Rainolds (1549–1607), author of a commentary of Aristotle's *Rhetoric* and a critic of Shakespearean theatre. Rainolds not only attacked Gentili's view on the autonomy of government from faith but also his opinions on the role of humanist culture in the life of a Christian community.[208] The manner in which academic "stage-plays", for example, were being presented was one question where Rainolds and Gentili vehemently clashed. For Gentili, these were often useful for education and in any case part of the good life.[209] Rainolds, again, saw transvestism, especially the way men dressed in women's clothes, as sinful deception. In his private responses and in a text on the beneficial types of dissimulation, Gentili defended the pedagogical value of theatrical untruths – after all, even a medical doctor's lie sometimes had a therapeutic effect.[210] After Rainolds had published parts of their private correspondence Gentili took the matter up in a defence of poetry (1593) where he compared the "truths" produced by painting with the "untruths" of poetic language that actually teach us much about the human world.[211] Like Aristotle, Gentili observed that by using images that have no likeness in the world

[208] Panizza, *Alberico Gentili, giurista ideologo*, 63–8. The development of Gentili's dispute with the Oxford Puritan theologians is described in detail in Giovanni Minnucci's many publications. See especially, 'Bella religionis causa', 993–1017 and 'Un discorso inedito de Alberico Gentili in difesa della *iurisprudentia*', 44 *Quaderni fiorentini* (2015), 211–45. The dispute over acting in the 1590s had to do with men posing in women's dresses against the prohibition in Deuteronomy (22:5). It arose from academic theatrical performances (Seneca's *Hippolythus*) in Oxford in which Gentili had engaged together with another lawyer, William Gager. The result was an acrimonious private correspondence between Gentili and Rainolds that the latter made eventually public. Elizabeth had visited Oxford in September 1592 where she had seen Gager's play and afterwards affirmed her power to legislate on the matter (and not theology's), and critiqued Rainolds for his "obstinate preciseness". See Rosanna Camerlingo, 'Machiavelli a Oxford. Guerra e teatro da Gentili a Shakespeare', 56 (II) *Rinascimento* (2016), 129, 124–31. This did not make the matter go away, however, and Rainolds published some of the related texts in his *The Over-Throw of Stage-Plays* (1599). See further Minnucci, 'Bella religionis causa', 1000–4.

[209] In two essays from 1599, Gentili defended the "deception" that was part of the pleasures of play-acting, Alberico Gentili, *Disputationes duae. I. De actoribus et spectatoribus fabularum non notandis. II De abusu mendacii* (Hanau, Antonium 1599). See further Lavenia, '"Mendacium officiosum"', 27–44.

[210] Camerlingo, 'Machiavelli a Oxford', 126–7.

[211] Alberico Gentili, 'Commentatio ad L [egem] III C[odicis] de prof[esssoribus] et med[icis]', and J. W. Binns, 'Alberico Gentili in Defence of Poetry and Acting', 19 *Studies in the Renaissance* (1972), 253, 224–72. Formally, Gentili addressed the question of poets' immunity from taxation. Aristotle's evaluation of poetry over history comes from Chapter IX of his *Poetics*.

(and are in this sense untrue) poetry may express greater, universal truths. It does not tell what has happened but instructs us on what could happen or might have happened. Poetic examples may thus act as part of moral instruction or even auxiliary parts of jurisprudence – perhaps in the way Gentili himself had filled his writings, especially *De iure belli*, with examples from epic poetry.[212] By employing legends whose truth is "hidden in the darkness of Antiquity", the poet could discuss the character and actions of "the best and most industrious prince".[213] In any case, theologians such as Rainolds had no special authority to determine how morality or politics were to be discussed.[214]

The Puritan attack was part of expanding anti-Italian sentiment in the 1590s. Gentili was condemned not only for what he had done or published but as a scheming Italian (*trico italiano*). Rainolds joined theatrical "deception" and the Machiavellian dissimulations he associated with diplomacy, in which Gentili now was authority, with the immoral politics of the *ragion di stato*. In their correspondence 1592–3 Gentili responded by stressing his status as a religious refugee. He had never supported any intrigue against the authorities. On the contrary, he completely rejected the legitimacy of resistance. Gentili was no libertarian – as we have seen, he utterly rejected atheism, though less for its anti-religious content than its social destructiveness. Religion, he stressed, was a great force in uniting humanity. Alongside this, as he once put it, "[t]he task of a human being was to preserve civil society and go about their business".[215] Gentili's late commentaries on marriage and divorce opened an avenue to restate in a general form the respective spheres of competence of law and theology.[216] Even as marriage had been set up by God, it belonged to those institutions that

212 The appreciation and use of poetry by Alberico and his brother Scipione has been discussed in Francesca Iurlaro, 'Il testo poetica della giustizia. Alberico e Scipione Gentili leggono la *Repubblica* di Platone', 2 *Fons* (2017), 177–96 and Warren, 'Gentili, the Poets and the Laws of War', 146–62.

213 Gentili, 'Commentatio' [Binns trans.], 252

214 "And I indeed, as I am greatly influenced by the authority of theologians in matters of religion, so I am not greatly influenced by them in matters of morals and politics", Gentili, 'Commentatio' [Binns trans.] 269.

215 "fines hominis [est] conservationem naturae civilisque societatis, at propriarum actionum exercitium", Gentili, *De abusu mendacii* 196, quoted in Lavenia, '"Mendacium officiosum"', 43.

216 For example, he used the introductory chapter of *De nuptiis* to distance himself from the theologians' view that laws also obligated in the *forum internum*. Civil law cannot, for example, excuse one from sin ("iam non praebet se reprehendum ius civile: quod nec facit cedem a peccato immunem"), Gentili, *De nuptiis*, quoted in Minnucci, "*Silete theologi*", 207, 202–10.

came under the second table of Mosaic law. This is why civil lawyers routinely commented and interpreted it, extrapolating principles of (secular) justice to apply between spouses.[217]

After the conflict with Rainolds had become public, Gentili felt compelled to address the relations of theology and jurisprudence openly in a speech given in the spring of 1594 to an Oxford academic audience.[218] In this rather flowery performance, Gentili highlighted jurisprudence as not only the knowledge of certain texts but also the study of ancient jurists and historians, and perhaps for strategic reasons invoked the figure of *Astrea* that attached a symbol of justice to the image of the English queen (*Astrea nostra*).[219] The central part of the discourse was devoted to an elaborate review of the contributions of the classical jurists in Greece and in the *Corpus iuris* as well as of the various "*praetors, consules, pontifices maximos, imperatores*" who had engaged with law and developed virtuous practices of good government. Nothing of the kind had been developed in other disciplines.[220] None of them, and certainly not theology, enjoyed the universal authority that law had developed from Greek and Roman sources.

## Imperial Statecraft

With the Act of Restraint of Appeals and the Act of Supremacy, Henry VIII had declared that "this realm of England is an empire and so hath been accepted in the world governed by one Supreme Head and King having the dignity and royal estate of the imperial Crown".[221] Soon thereafter he established the Regius Chairs of Civil Law in Cambridge and Oxford to teach the law of a former empire with an absolutist

[217] Gentili, *De nuptiis*, cited and commented on in Giovanni Minnucci, 'Giuristi, teologi, libertas religionis nel pensiero di Alberico Gentili' (mimeo, on file with author) and Minnucci, "*Silete theologi*", 214–21. For the sharpness of the debate between Gentili and Rainolds, see also Panizza, *Alberico Gentili, giurista ideologo*, 64–81.

[218] The Latin text of the speech and Italian commentary can be found in Giovanni Minnucci, 'Un discorso inedito de Alberico Gentili in difesa della iurisprudentia', 44 *Quaderni fiorentini* (2015), 211–51. Only a part of the text contains a defence of jurisprudence against other disciplines. Part of it is a defence of Gentili against the *ad hominem* attacks on him as a foreigner, 236–41.

[219] Ibid., 227–8.

[220] "Sed dicant, doceant bona artes aliae: nostra haec est sola, quae viros efficere bonos potest, et solet", ibid., 250, 235–6.

[221] Ecclesiastical Appeals Act 1532, 24 Hen. 8 c. 12 (Eng.). For commentary, see Walter Ullmann, 'This Realm of England is An Empire', 30 *Journal of Ecclesiastical History* 175 (1979), 175.

ruler – Justinian – at its head. The ethos of civil law was imperial and the first civil lawyers were "almost natural exponents of royalist politics".[222] They were used typically as royal advisors, ambassadors and judges in the Admiralty Court and other prerogative courts (Star Chamber, Court of Chancery, Ecclesiastical Courts). And of course, "[w]hen there was a need to address political problems that were not purely English, this had to be done in terms of legal first principles, natural law, and the law of nations".[223] Gentili arrived in England during the golden era of English civilians occupying positions close to the court where they were instrumental in teaching the arts of classical statesmanship. Their university training and their humanistic interests bred among them a professional cosmopolitanism; they "represented the most important manifestation of both reformation and the renaissance in contemporary English Culture".[224]

As we have seen, Gentili was rapidly integrated among the group of Protestant noblemen with humanist ideals that included Leicester, Sidney, Walsingham and the earl of Essex (Robert Devereux) all of whom were preoccupied by Spanish expansion in the Americas, in Italy and the Netherlands, advocating determined action to defend the Dutch Protestants and to forestall the presumed invasion of England.[225] Sidney had produced the image of a heroic defence of the subjects of a tyrannical king in his *Old* and *New Arcadia*, and had elsewhere advocated the use of force for civilising the "barbaric" people of Ireland.[226] The last book of the *Old Arcadia* put forward "a charitable ideal of foreign intervention or conquest" that was very close to Gentili's advocacy for defending oppressed subjects of a foreign ruler and punishing the violations of the law of nature.[227] It was natural for Gentili to support the war party and to advocate pre-emptive action against

[222] Brian B. Levack, *The Civil Lawyers in England. A Political Study* (Oxford University Press 1973), 25, 25–7. See further, Glenn Burgess, *The Politics of the Ancient Constitution. An Introduction to English Political Thought 1604–1642* (London, Macmillan 1992).

[223] Burgess, *The Politics of the Ancient Constitution*, 126.

[224] Daniel R. Coquillette, *The Civilian Writers of Doctors' Commons, London. Three Centuries of Innovation in Comparative, Commercial and International Law* (Berlin, Duncker & Humblot 1988), 44.

[225] For the political ideas of Essex and the spread of Tacitism in sixteenth- and early seventeenth-century England, see Tuck, *Philosophy and Government*, 104–19.

[226] See Brian Lockey, *Law and Empire in English Renaissance Literature* (Cambridge University Press 2009), 47–79.

[227] Ibid., 50.

Spain.[228] But on the other hand neither he nor the group of his mentors were by any means principled anti-imperialists.[229] Sidney, for example, had met the geographer and active promoter of English Atlantic colonisation, Richard Hakluyt, during his time as student in Oxford in the 1570s and later financed and followed with interest the northern voyages by Martin Frobisher and Humphrey Gilbert. As the Spanish kept advancing on the continent and the Huguenot cause in France seemed momentarily lost Sidney even began to entertain plans for Protestant settlements in the New World. Two things that preoccupied him as he led the expeditionary force down to the Low Countries were colonisation and warfare.[230]

Early in the century Thomas More had envisaged his "Utopians" as a powerful colonising nation, which had occupied their island by conquest. Many Tudor grandees shared his ideals. As pointed out above, from his chair of civil law in Cambridge, Sir Thomas Smith had become an active propagandist for Irish colonisation. "Ireland, once inhabited with Englishe men, and policed with Englishe lawes, could be as great a commoditie to the Prince as the realme of England," he wrote. Depicting the Irish as uncivil and savage and highlighting the ease with which they could be "subdued", Smith planned a proposal to turn large territories in Ireland over into commercial agriculture, praising the virtues of colonisation – "How say you now, have I not set forth to you another Utopia [!]".[231] Smith was pushing a plan put forward earlier by Sir Henry Sidney, Philip's father and Elizabeth's lord deputy of Ireland, to undertake colonisation through private entrepreneurship. In their propaganda, Sidney and Smith mixed advocacy of commercial agriculture with the Roman image of imperial expansion and settlement.[232]

228 For a brief overview of the patronage received by Gentili from Philip Sidney and Robert Devereux and their group of "Forward Protestants", see Warren, *Literature and the Law of Nations*, 35–6.

229 Sidney, for example, had been influenced by the Spanish scholastics' views on intervention to help oppressed subjects of a tyrant. Lockey, *Law and Empire*, 64–70.

230 Roger Kuin, 'Querre-Muhau. Sir Philip Sidney and the New World', 51 *Renaissance Quarterly* (1998), 570 and generally 549–85.

231 Tract by Sir Thomas Smith on the Colonisation of Ards in County of Down, ["A Letter sent by T. B. Gentleman…"], printed as Appendix to George Hill, *An Historical Account of the Macdonnells of Antrim* (Belfast, Archer 1873), 405, 411. For the booklet and its context, see Mary Dewar, *Sir Thomas Smith. A Tudor Intellectual in Office* (London, Athlone 1964), 156–9.

232 For the "neo-Roman" and humanist intellectual background of the early proposals for the colonisation of Ireland by Smith and his contemporaries, see further, Robert A. Williams, *The American Indian in Western Legal Thought* (Oxford University Press 1990), 139–50; Armitage, *Ideological Origins*, 47–51; Fitzmaurice, *Humanism and America*, 35–9.

In 1571 Elizabeth authorised Smith and his son to send a private army into Ireland and granted them a feudal tenure of 360,000 acres in the Ardes (Ards) region in Ulster not far from Belfast. The charter, among many granted to English lords and gentry in Ireland, authorised Smith and his companions to subdue the rebels ("wicked, barbarous and uncivil people") and to distribute the grant of lands among themselves.[233]

In the end, fierce opposition by Irish clans, logistic problems and mismanagement led to the failure of the expedition. But the Irish experiences kept alive ideals of imperial glory that were eventually directed towards the New World.[234] Those ideals were shared by Gentili in whom they mixed with an Italian sensitivity to realism and the understanding of the mixed motives that lay behind grandiose plans of conquest. He did not endorse imperial expansion for the sake of dominion or glory.[235] But he also believed that no-one ought to give up their rights without a fight, and fighting was necessary also when the alternative was disgraceful accommodation.[236] The kind of active statecraft that he had sketched in *De legationibus* was not averse to imperial expansion once that seemed necessary or virtuous. In the famous passage where he celebrated Machiavelli as an "eulogist of democracy", he was referring to those parts of *I Discorsi* that dealt with the generalisation of *virtù* among Roman citizens as a condition for the flourishing of the republic.[237] A combative civil life would prepare a people to face up to internal and external enemies. "For it was the virtue of her armies that caused Rome to acquire an empire," Machiavelli had written, adding that "it is not the well-being of individuals that makes cities great, but the well-being of the community: and it is beyond question that it is only in republics that the common good is looked to properly in that all that promotes it is carried out."[238]

Whatever the tension there was between that passage and the defence of monarchic absolutism in Gentili's late writings, *De iure belli* upheld an ethos of virtuous, imperial statecraft in at least three ways. First was the very wide scope granted to pre-emptive action against

233 Indenture and Patent of 5 October 1571, reproduced in John Strype, *The Life of the Learned Sir Thomas Smith* (Oxford, Clarendon 1820), 131–2.

234 Armitage, *Ideological Origins*, 45–6, 49–51; Fitzmaurice, *Humanism and America*, 21–57.

235 E.g. Gentili, *De iure belli*, I VII, XII (34, 54). His endorsement of the *Corpus iuris* did not lead Gentili to advocate expansion in the Roman model. See Straumann, '*Corpus iuris* as a Source of Law', 123.

236 Gentili, *De iure belli*, I XIII (58–60).

237 Machiavelli, *Discourses*, I 4 (113–15).

238 Ibid., II 1 & 2 (270, 275).

potential disturbers of the peace and the connected readiness to use force to uphold the balance of power. The right of necessary defence did not require an actual attack – "making preparations" was enough.[239] Expedient defence did not require even a foreseeable injury. Fear of an impending disturbance in the balance of power sufficed.[240] Gentili did not want to make that suggestion seem too extreme, however, but stressed that every war, even wars of offence or vengeance, included a defensive aspect.[241] Second was the war against pirates, brigands and "brutes", violators of natural law that had by their actions become "common enemies of mankind". Separating themselves from what Gentili assumed were the natural principles of the human order such groups would not qualify as just enemies but could be attacked and destroyed by whatever means necessary. And third was the striking authorisation, resembling that contained in Book IV of the Protestant *Streitschrift Vindicae contra tyrannos* and taken up in Sidney's *Arcadia*, for just princes to intervene so as to defend foreigners against a tyrant. Gentili was certainly no pacifist and did not think of war as a judicial process. Although not a natural feature of human life, war was often a necessary means to discipline ambitious or unjust rulers or to check violations of natural law. It constituted a form of expression of virtuous statecraft.

## Expanding Civilisation and Protecting the Oppressed

The first of the three forms of "imperial" warfare (self-defence as well as defence against future aggression and to uphold the balance) has already been treated above. The second was that of expanding and defending civilisation against barbarism in its many forms. Much more generously than Vitoria, Gentili expressed his full approval for the Spanish war against the Indians who, in Gentili's imagination (fed, no doubt, by the fantastic travel narratives that Europeans had composed of their visits in the New World) "practised abominable lewdness even with beasts, and who ate human flesh slaying men for that purpose".[242]

239 Gentili, *De iure belli*, I XIII (58).

240 This was wider than the fear that justified pre-emption between individuals. A prince was not expected to wait in the way of private individuals. Ibid., I XIV (62–6).

241 Ibid., I V (29–30).

242 Cannibalism was a feature of indigenous American life that was present in almost all accounts, including in the most famous of them, José Acosta's *De procuranda Indorum Salute* (1588), which described the absence of any well-ordered society among the Indians, identifying some of the South American indigenous populations

But these were just examples of "sins [that] are contrary to human nature" and all those other actions into which he assumed Indians engaging and which were "recognised as [sins] by all except haply by brutes and brutish men".[243] It is hard to know exactly what kinds of actions, apart from cannibalism and various sexual practices that deviated from European mores, Gentili wanted to indict.[244] Despite his refusal to condone religious warfare, he did approve war against idolaters, at least when idolatry was connected with human sacrifice.[245] The notions of "brute" and "bruteness" covered a no doubt varying spate of things that Europeans regarded as perverse or "unnatural" and to which it was common, as Gentili put it, that they rendered subhuman those practising them. Some people, he wrote, "have the human form, but in reality they are beasts and should be reckoned in the number of beasts".[246] Whatever else such language may have achieved, at least it facilitated the removal of those so described from the *societas gentium.* With beasts, there could be no just war but only violence and destruction.[247] No peaceful dealings or undertakings could be had with them and they could hardly be understood to enjoy any kind of dominion over their dwelling-places.[248] Gentili rejected the Aristotelian view of Indians as natural slaves; "we are by nature all akin".[249] This was,

as "savages similar to wild animals . . . without law, without agreements, without governments", cited in Daragh Grant, 'Francisco de Vitoria and Alberico Gentili on the Juridical Status of Native American Polities', 72 *Renaissance Studies* (2019), note 140. For the use of the theme of cannibalism in justifying the conquest (including a discussion of Acosta's views), see Catalin Avramescu, *An Intellectual History of Cannibalism* (A. I. Blyth trans., Princeton University Press 2009), 106–24. For Acosta's importance in England and his classification of different types of "barbarians", see also Andrew Fitzmaurice, *Sovereignty, Property and Empire 1500–2000* (Cambridge University Press 2014), 75–9.

243 Gentili, *De iure belli,* XXV (122).

244 Gentili indicted the Indians as having been "in the habit of committing those crimes of beastly, foul, and abominable lust", ibid., I XXV (123). The sexual taboos included at least sodomy, incest and intercourse with animals but also other kinds of assumed sexual depravity. Some of these appeared also in those parts of Sidney's *Arcadia* that depicted the republic's gradual descent into barbarism that justified foreign intervention. Lockey, *Law and Empire,* 70–6.

245 Gentili, *De iure belli,* I IX (41) (atheists) and I XXV (123) (idolaters).

246 Ibid., I I (7). The theme of the native inhabitants as "beasts" may take up the Roman law rule of *ferae bestiae* that granted ownership of wild animals to those who caught them. See Fitzmaurice, *Sovereignty, Property and Empire,* 74–5. This is doubted by Christopher Tomlins, *Freedom Bound. Law, Labour and Civic Identity in Colonizing English America, 1580–1865* (Cambridge University Press 2010), 135.

247 A "just enemy" (*iustus hostis*) is "a person with whom war is waged and who is the equal of his opponent", Gentili, *De iure belli,* I II (12).

248 Tomlins, *Freedom Bound,* 128–31, 143–5.

249 Gentili, *De iure belli,* I XII (54).

however, qualified later in the work where Gentili did accept the justice of slavery. Liberty was in accordance with nature – though "only for good men". A secondary intention of nature provided for the right to punish by slavery those who breach the laws of nature.[250]

Gentili's period in Oxford and as a practising lawyer with Gray's Inn coincided with much excitement in England about transatlantic expansion. Colonisation of Ireland had been only a first step in voyages to the New World and beyond. The travels of Martin Frobisher and Humphrey Gilbert and Walter Raleigh's establishment of the ultimately failing Roanoke colony (1585) were accompanied by widespread pamphleteering. The grant of charters to the East India Company in 1600 and the Virginia Company in 1606 raised, in principle, all kinds of legal questions regarding the royal prerogative and sovereign rights in the new settlements, for example, but did not prompt Gentili to scholarly commentary. His writings on the theme of colonisation were scattered in only few relatively brief passages across the *De iure belli*.

"No one doubts to-day that what we call the New World is joined to our own and has always been known to the remote Indi," Gentili wrote, lamenting that "the inhabitants prohibited other men from commerce with them".[251] In a chapter dealing with "natural" reasons for making war, Gentili examined the ways in which creating obstacles to passage or to commerce in distant locations violated the natural right of intercourse among nations. To close one's ports to foreign shipping was illegal. Sailing across the world was for the benefit of the whole of humankind and realised God's providential design. It was therefore lawful to wage war on those who seek to prohibit commerce.[252] Like commerce, the seas were also free and Gentili quoted Cicero and the *Corpus iuris* to make the point that their use "is common to everyone". The Venetians' closing off of parts of the Adriatic was in breach of natural law and a just cause for violent retaliation.[253]

250 Indians thus become slaves not owing to their nature but "because of their wickedness and sins". Ibid., III IX (330). See also comments in Cassi, 'Conquista. *Dallo* ius communicationis *allo* ius belli *nel pensiero di Alberico Gentili*', 156–61.

251 Gentili, *De iure belli*, I XIX (89).

252 However, Gentili also accepted that it was possible (as the Chinese did) to limit access of merchants to certain ports only or to prohibit the import of things considered harmful. Ibid., I XIX (86–9).

253 Ibid., I XIX (91–2). Panizza suggests that these passages cast the protective jurisdiction of the prince into a ("cosmopolitan") instrument for enforcing *ius gentium* on the seas. Diego Panizza, 'The "Freedom of the Sea" and the "Modern Cosmopolis", in Alberico Gentili's *De Iure Belli*', 30 *Grotiana* (2009), 88–106.

Gentili never wrote about the laws of colonial settlement, but he did suggest that just war could be waged against those who prevented taking possession of unoccupied land. Nature "abhors a vacuum", and so it was not only natural but beneficial and praiseworthy to take uncultivated lands into production.[254] This was an altogether conventional position, based on Roman law – as was also its corollary, namely that taking possession had to do merely with private dominion so that jurisdiction would remain with the prince exercising sovereignty over land thus occupied.[255] For Gentili, as well as to the whole humanist tradition from More onwards, for a land to be "unoccupied" meant that it had not been taken into the kinds of use for which Europeans had the habit of using it, i.e. "improvement" and cultivation.[256]

Although Gentili's interest in colonisation was limited, what he wrote about the brutish practices of the uncivilised and of the freedoms of commerce and navigation reflected the universal basis of his *ius gentium*, the way it would express "common sentiments of humanity" that, he assumed, joined the world in "one body", "one commonwealth of all".[257] This language, cited especially in connection with arguments regarding "defence for the sake of honour", expressed a civilising ethic that he expounded in collaboration with his English mentors. Much has been written about Gentili's cosmopolitanism and his tolerance towards differing religious views. But the natural community of humankind that he envisaged also had definite boundaries. There was no room for the native communities of the New World whose "unnatural" practices put to question their very status of humans. Against them civilised princes were invited to engage in a "war of vengeance to avenge our common nature".[258] Gentili had a very negative view of the world into which European explorers and settlers had arrived. Before the establishment of nations, the division of properties and the commencement of trade – before starting to live like Gentili's contemporaneous Europeans – human beings were "incapable of respect for the common good, nor did they know enough to adopt customs or laws of reciprocal nature".[259]

[254] Gentili, *De iure belli*, I XVII (80–1).
[255] For the Roman law basis of this view, see e.g. Randall Lesaffer, 'Argument from Roman Law in Current International Law. Occupation and Acquisitive Prescription', 16 *European Journal of International Law* (2005), especially 38–46; Tomlins, *Freedom Bound*, 116–20, and generally, Fitzmaurice, *Sovereignty, Property and Empire*, 33–58, 74–5.
[256] Gentili, *De iure belli*, I XVII (81). [257] Ibid., I XV (67–9).
[258] Ibid., I XXV (125). [259] Gentili, *De legationibus*, I XX (51).

Equally outside the cosmopolitan community were pirates, robbers, brigands and runaway slaves who were to be treated as the "common enemies of all mankind".[260] Piracy was, of course, imagined at the time as a grave threat to the security of maritime commerce.[261] Gentili did not have sufficiently harsh words to condemn pirates, whom he associated with brigands and robbers, "malefactors" who had "broken the treaty of the human race".[262] Moreover, Gentili's brigands included not only the common criminals but also those who had revolted against domestic authority and who had, as a result, lost their citizenship and deprived themselves of the benefits of the law of nations.[263] Into the same group Gentili also cast atheists, namely those who are "wholly without religious belief".[264] Even as Gentili was ready to tolerate deviant religious views, he regarded religious faith as an essential bond among humans; its absence was a threat to peaceful order. Such views represented a firmly hierarchical view of humankind and the superior virtue of some people, such as the Romans, who were entitled to exercise their jurisdiction all over the world to eradicate practices that European humanists regarded as unnatural.

In addition to advocating pre-emptive war against potential disturbers of the peace as well as to avenge violations of natural law and the basic principles of the political order, Gentili's imperial statecraft included sympathy towards those who laboured under a tyrannical yoke. Deviating for a moment from Guicciardini's pessimism, which he did by express reference to Montaigne, he wanted to assume the presence of right (but not a duty) to take military action against tyrannical rulers on the basis of "the generally recognized kinship of all men with their fellows".[265] This applied not just to any grievance but one that had been amplified into a dispute regarding the commonwealth itself, where actual war existed between the ruler and the subjects.[266] True, he went on, such assistance may only rarely be given for fully unselfish reasons: "[I]t may be admitted that this reason of honour alone perhaps never led any one to that honourable defence." Instead, he added, "an honourable reason can hardly ever exist without its being possible to pretend another reason based upon either necessity

[260] Gentili, *De iure belli*, I IV (24).

[261] For a recent discussion of the image and the legal treatment of piracy in history, see Tor Krever, 'The Ideological Origins of Piracy in International Legal Thought' (PhD thesis, LSE 2018, on file with author), especially ch. 4–6.

[262] Gentili, *De iure belli*, I IV (22).

[263] Ibid., I IV (23–4, 25).

[264] Ibid., I IX (41).

[265] Ibid., I XV (69, 67–73).

[266] Ibid., I XVI (74–5).

or expediency", and he went on to explain what he meant by referring to the English intervention in the Low Countries.[267] A defence of the Dutch rebels was of course an honourable thing to do. But it would also be useful as it would help prevent a hostile power from emerging close to the English coasts. After all, "sovereignties are entitled to security and to a kind of unique bond of affection from a neighbour".[268] Even if it was made out of expectation of reward or reasons of utility, this did not undermine its justice but merely changed its qualification.[269]

Some of the passages regarding honourable action in defence of the subjects of a tyrant were strikingly blunt in their endorsement of the idea of just sovereigns as guardians of universal law.[270] The tension between Gentili's endorsement of intervention by foreign princes and his monarchic absolutism may perhaps be explained by the context of *De iure belli*, written at a time of grave danger to the Protestant cause, especially in the Spanish Netherlands.[271] But he was clear that the subjects themselves were never entitled to rebel.[272] Having denied in *De legationibus* the right of legation to rebellious subjects in general he did allow it in the case of a large-scale breakdown of domestic order where each side was able to lay a claim "by word and deed" to the whole state.[273] The exception is likely to have been intended to cover the situation of the rebellious provinces in the Low Countries. But normally, the subjects of a tyrant could expect no relief from his natural law, a point he made absolutely clear in the last of the three

[267] Ibid., I XV (71). See also Panizza, 'Il pensiero politico di Alberico Gentili', 163–4.

[268] Gentili, *De iure belli*, I XVI (78).

[269] Ibid., I XVI (78).

[270] "The subjects of another do not seem to me to be outside that kinship of nature and the society formed by the whole world", ibid., I, XVI (74). The just cause is not that of religion, but oppression. Panizza, 'Il pensiero politico di Alberico Gentili', 153. During the religious wars, the right of foreign intervention had been put forward in no uncertain terms by the Protestant authors of the *Vindiciae contra tyrannos*: "Without any doubt, where the glory of God and the kingdom of Christ is concerned, no limits, no frontiers, no barriers, ought to restrict the zeal of pious princes." A prince that fails to intervene is like someone watching with pleasure a show of gladiators and is more guilty than the gladiator who slays his opponent because he makes the show possible in the first place. *Vindiciae contra tyrannos*, 'The Fourth Question' (183).

[271] Panizza, *Alberico Gentili, giurista ideologo*, 109–10.

[272] As pointed out above, he regarded rebel subjects as "brigands" who were not entitled to any benefits under the law of nations. *De iure belli*, I IV (23–4). Particularly striking in this respect are the last paragraphs of the Disputation 'De vi civium in regem semper iniusta', in *Regales disputationis*, 130–2.

[273] Gentili, *De legationibus* II IX (82–3). For the denial of the right of embassy from domestic rebels generally, see ibid., II VII (76–8).

*Regales disputationes* of 1605.[274] The power of the king was from God so that subjects could not invoke whatever right based on merely natural law.[275] However bad the tyranny, the anarchy following a rebellion will always be worse. Nero may have killed many during the fourteen years of his reign, but thousands died in a few months of bloodshed during the reign of his three followers.[276] The only relief for oppressed subjects, alongside reliance on God and fleeing, was offered by the right of public officials to resist and the power of other princes to intervene.[277]

## Imperial Ambivalence

The themes of order and civil virtue resurfaced in *De armis Romanis* (1599), where instead of seeking to establish a firm truth about the past (which in any case was not available), Gentili experimented with alternative interpretations of the normative meaning of past events – how they could be taken as evidence of Roman bureaucratic and cultural corruption, or alternatively of Rome's imperial brilliance. In the first part, Gentili let the *Accusator* attack the injustice of Roman rule from the perspective of abstract moral principles, quoting amply the views of theologians whose authority in such matters he of course had elsewhere denied. In the second part, twice as long as the first, the *Defender* read those practices from the perspective of the patriotic virtues of the Romans and the liberty and peace that accompanied conquest.[278]

274 "vim omnem civium iniustam semper in principem esse", Gentili, 'De vim civium in regem semper iniusta', in *Regales disputations*, 99.

275 Gentili, 'De vim civium', 101–2. This is a striking departure by Gentili from his view of inter-human relations covered by human law, probably based on the description by James VI/I of himself in terms of divine kingship.

276 "Nerone occito? Pauculis mensibus trium secutorum principum plus sanguinis civium effessum est, quam quatuordecim totis annis Neronis", ibid., 103.

277 Ibid., 116. See also the discussion in Davide Suin, 'Principi supremi e societas hominium. Il problema del potere nella riflessione di Alberico Gentili', XXIV *Scienza e politica* (2017), 116–24 and Diego Pirillo, 'Tra obbedianza e resistenza. Alberico Gentili e George Buchanan', in Luigi Lacchè (ed.), *"Ius gentium, ius communicationis, ius belli". Alberico Gentili e gli orizzonti della modernità: atti del convegno di Macerata in occasione delle celebrazioni del quarto centenario della morte di Alberico Gentili (1552–1608)* (Milan, Giuffrè 2009), 212–13.

278 For an excellent analysis, see Diego Panizza, 'Alberico Gentili's *De Armis Romanis*. The Roman Model of Just Empire', in Benedict Kingsbury & Benjamin Straumann (eds), *The Roman Foundations of the Law of Nations* (Oxford University Press 2010), 53–84. Aspects of Panizza's categorical association of Gentili's "actual" views with those of the "Defender" in the above work are usefully challenged in David Lupher,

Where the *Accusator* saw the Roman just war doctrine as hypocritical window-dressing on imperial aggression, the *Defender* read justice together with utility in the republican fashion, holding Roman expansion (though not expansion in general) amply justified by the benefits it brought not only to Rome but to those who were brought into its fold. The Spanish empire had been corrupted because it was based simply on a desire for power (*libido imperi*) that gave no legal right. By contrast, Roman expansion had spread orderly rule through the civil law across the whole empire. Macedonia and Illyria, for example:

> were freed of royal yoke by us and yet not made subject to us either; ordered to live under their own laws and be free; freed of huge tax burdens; and made exempt from half the tribute which they used to pay when they were under their own king. . . . What a matchless commendation this is of Roman munificence, beneficence, liberality, magnificence, magnanimity.[279]

The *Defender*'s views represented ideals that had no chance of being realised at the moment Gentili wrote. On the contrary, the empires threatening England shared nothing of the virtues Gentili projected as admirable in the Romans. Instead of defending empire as an abstract proposition, Gentili used the qualities he assumed accounted for Roman greatness at the time to argue for an extensive view of royal sovereignty, along the lines of the Roman *princeps legibus solutus*. These views had been elaborated in a series of dialogues from the 1580s and the essays of 1605 where he defended the "imperial" absolutism of James VI/I against internal and external subversion. This view, together with his endorsement of pre-emptive war and balance of power in *De iure belli*, were of course utterly incompatible with universal rule by any single power.[280] But they were wholly in line with an imperial statecraft that stressed the power and the brilliance of the king as the best guarantee of both the internal and external peace. This did not mean that he lacked a vision of order between the sovereigns – on the contrary, Gentili's statecraft combined the virtues of bold commitment to the defence of the nation, readiness to assist one's friends and to attack one's enemies, with the objective of

'The *De armis Romanis* and the Exemplum of Roman Imperialism', in Benedict Kingsbury & Benjamin Straumann (eds), *The Roman Foundations of the Law of Nations* (Oxford University Press 2010), 85–100.

279 Alberico Gentili, *The Wars of the Romans. A Critical Edition and Translation of De armis Romanis* (Benedict Kingsbury & Benjamin Straumann ed., David Lupher trans., Oxford University Press 2010), 13 (337).

280 The essays are of course those in Gentili, *Regales disputationes*.

bringing peace and civilisation to the world. Gentili's *ius gentium* would encompass the rules of statecraft that were naturally fitting for a world of separate sovereigns who were ready to betray each other at first opportunity, but who were also dependent on cooperating with each other and occasionally prone to high-minded contemplation about the unity of the humankind they had been assigned to govern. This was a world of war and diplomacy but also of trade, exploration and expanding civilisation. It was a world where religious frames began to seem increasingly incapable of providing an ideological articulation for elite preoccupations such as those to which Sidney had given literary form in his epic poetry.[281]

In endorsing "honourable" war, Gentili quoted the Ciceronian rhetoric of human fellowship, the "kinship, love" and "kindliness" supposed to reign among all humans and the notion that "the whole world is one body, that all men are members of that body, that the world is a home, and that it forms a state".[282] And in defending the English intervention in the Dutch rebellion, Gentili made much of the right to defend one's friends against their falling under a foreign yoke – "no one else ought to be prevented from fostering liberty".[283] It would be facile to conclude from these sentences that Gentili put forward some sort of Stoic–humanist ideal of an organised world community This would omit consideration of the constant stress in Gentili on the gap between rhetoric and action, perception and reality, the sense in which the "weakness of human reason" leads us to perceive matters of justice only uncertainly. If natural law applies everywhere, it is not because all nations would have come together; the "world" has no institutional representative.[284] Gentili's invectives against the Spanish were in some considerable part inspired by the way he saw them as tyrannical hypocrites, dressing greed in the garb of theological liturgy. "At present there is no abominable crime which is not shielded under the name of piety."[285] If that is what Gentili believed, then there is no reason to

[281] Towards the end of the narrative of Sidney's *Arcadia*, the good king Euarchus of Macedonia conducts a military intervention in the realm of Arcadia that had fallen into chaos and civil war as a result of the weakness of king Basilius. Most readers understood the poem as a commentary on Elizabeth's alleged indecisiveness in the 1570s that came to a head in the plan of marriage with the Duke of Anjou. Protestants like Sidney abhorred the prospect of England falling under French influence. See Worden, *The Sound of Virtue*, especially 127–206.

[282] Gentili, *De iure belli*, I XV (67). Tuck discusses the way these ideas follow Roman ideals of virtuous conduct in *The Rights of War and Peace*, 36–40.

[283] Gentili, *De iure belli*, I XVI (77). [284] Ibid., I I (8). [285] Ibid., I IX (40).

remove "Stoic cosmopolitanism" from the list of pieties that were perfectly capable of shielding whatever abominable crimes ambitious princes might be inclined to commit. The view of war as just on both sides, the equal treatment of the belligerents and the view of the king as *Deus in terris* gave legal expression to that scepticism, moderated only by a romantic image of virtuous statecraft at the service of an altogether secular *ius gentium*.

## The Limits of Gentili's Jurisprudence

Gentili's writings did not have much of an influence in England at the time, although his uncompromising defence of royal absolutism, his description of it as essentially similar to the powers of the French king, "drew a number of angry responses from the House of Commons".[286] Citations from the *Corpus iuris* and continental commentary did nothing to address the constitutional ideology of the common law. Parliament, for instance, would possess for Gentili no more than consultative status, and at one point an anonymous letter during the Civil War claimed that his writings helped form the ideology of the royalist cause. Whatever attention he may have received was overshadowed by the equally absolutist but more easily available works, in English, of his Cambridge colleague John Cowell.[287] Apart from the few passages on war against brutes, occupation of vacant lands and the freedom of commerce and navigation, Gentili also mostly sidestepped the legal questions relating to English expansion. As the impact of civil law and civil lawyers had begun its decline around 1600, the laws of possession and sovereignty in the New World were left to be sketched in the context of legal counselling with the East India and Virginia companies, and laid out by the leading common lawyer Sir Edward Coke (1552–1634) (see Chapter 10 below).

Grotius acknowledged that he had found the works of Gentili more useful than any other prior writings dealing with war. But he critiqued Gentili for his use of examples that may have been "accommodated to the Interest of those that consult them, and not formed by the invariable

286 Brian B. Levack, 'Law and Ideology. The Civil Law and Theories of Legal Absolutism in Elizabethan and Jacobean England', in Heather Dubrow & Richard Strier (eds), *The Historical Renaissance. New Essays on Tudor and Stuart Literature and Culture* (The University of Chicago Press 1988), 229.

287 See e.g. Daniel Lee, *Popular Sovereignty in Early Modern Constitutional Thought* (Oxford University Press 2016), 279–81 and below, Chapter 10.

Rules of Equity and Justice".[288] To the extent that Gentili had specifically wanted to avoid listing mere examples, this may seem unjust. Perhaps Grotius was trying to say that what Gentili had put forward as the philosophy to discriminate between forms of past behaviour was altogether too weak and obscure to serve as a reliable orientation for legal policy. Alternatively, Grotius might have been suggesting that a key problem in Gentili's writings was to concentrate narrowly on diplomacy and war without trying to situate them in wider political and ideological developments.

Gentili's jurisprudence was limited in three important ways. First was the substantive narrowness of his *ius gentium*. His refusal to engage with theology and theologians while embracing unclear and often contradictory ideas about virtuous statecraft left his historical analogies and readings of civil law hanging in a vacuum. No larger understanding of the magnitude of European transformations is visible in his work. It is no wonder that having perused Gentili Grotius set himself the task of situating *ius gentium* not only within a general theory of law and legal sources but within a "comprehensive legal structuring of all domestic and international conditions of human life".[289] Gentili offered nothing of the sort. Whatever innovative effort lay behind his work, it remained distant from the experience of a confessionally and politically divided Europe.

The second, related, problem in Gentili's writings, just as in the works of his Italian predecessors, was that they put forward no firm notion of legal obligation. There was no explanation of what grounded the authority of the ruler over the subjects and the *regnum*. When the chain of legal inferences was interrupted before it ascended to God, what was left was custom as mere habit, and the thinnest of philosophy about humanist ideals of virtuous statecraft, skill in navigating between the requirements of *honestum* and *utilitas*. Where Gentili came closest to an independent concept of obligation was where he made the distinction between the sovereign and the tyrant that allowed intervention by foreign princes. What made a king a tyrant? As we have seen, however,

288 Hugo Grotius, *The Rights of War and Peace* (R. Tuck ed. & intro., Indianapolis, Liberty Fund 2005), Preliminary Discourse, XXXIX (110). See also Peter Haggenmacher, 'Grotius and Gentili. A Reassessment of Thomas E. Holland's Inaugural Lecture', in Hedley Bull, Benedict Kingsbury and Adam Roberts (eds), *Hugo Grotius and International Relations* (Oxford University Press 1992), 161–2.

289 "ein umfassende rechtliche Strukturierung aller staatlichen wie überstaatlichen Lebensverhältnisse", Frank Grunert, *Normbegründung und politische Legitimität. Zur Rechts- und Staatsphilosophie der deutschen Frühaufklärung* (Tübingen, Niemeyer 2000), 66.

the discussion turned on general exhortations about "the society formed by the whole world" that may have catered to his readers' humanist sensitivities but had nothing substantive to persuade them about law's authority.[290] It was honourable to react to "general violation of the common law of humanity and a wrong done to mankind", but what this meant beyond a prohibition of the unnatural practices by the native populations of America and the actions of pirates, brigands and brutes remained utterly unclear.[291] *Ius gentium* was not about obligation but about virtuous statecraft.

The third problem was the absence of a clear view of the state, independent of the ruler, in Gentili's works. This was of course not only a property of Gentili's writing. Neither Machiavelli nor Guicciardini had operated with a stable notion of *lo stato*, viewing it rather as the "situation" or "power" of the prince or the leading elites.[292] It might have been open for Gentili to develop a theory of statehood from Bodin's *Six livres*. But the reference to sovereignty in *De potestate Regis absoluta* only highlighted the king's non-subordination to external powers and his legislative monopoly.[293] Nor did Gentili use the writings of the Spanish theologians whose conjectural histories on the emergence of *dominium* might have been integrated in a commentary to the *lex regia*.[294] Perhaps he simply believed, with Guicciardini, that all stable commonwealths were born of violence, and that there was nothing more to be said usefully about the matter. The most developed passages in this respect were those where sovereigns were distinguished from brigands, pirates and runaway slaves. Only "[h]e is an enemy who has a state, a senate, a treasury, united and harmonious citizens, and

290 Gentili, *De iure belli*, I XVI (74).

291 Ibid., I XXV (124, 123–7).

292 A useful summary of studies on the Italian use of the terms "*status*" or "*lo stato*" is Christian Lazzeri, 'Introduction', in Henri de Rohan, *De l'intérêt des princes et des Etats de la Chrétienté* (C. Lazzeri ed., Paris, Presses Universitaires de France 1995) (stressing the novelty of its impersonal use in the *ragion di stato* literatures of the sixteenth century), 108–15, 118–19.

293 "Supremitas (inquit) est potestas absoluta et perpetua. . . . Hoc igitur supremitatis est, ut nihil supra se umquam cernat principatus, neque hominem, neque legem. Ergo et absoluta haec potestas est, et absque limitibus. *Princeps legibus solutus est*, ait lex, et eadem, quod lex est, *quodcunque* placet principi. Et haec lex non barbara, sed Romana est : id est praestantissima in legibus hominum. . . . Atque absoluta potestas est illa, quam in Anglia significamus nomine . . . regiae PRAEROGATIVAE", Alberico Gentili, 'De potestate regis absoluta disputatio', 9–10, cited and commented on in Panizza, *Alberico Gentili, giurista ideologico*, 159.

294 The only reference was a passage in *De legationibus* where he contrasted his contemporary Europeans to the indigenous people in the Americas who, according to him, possessed no laws or customs, I XX (51).

some basis for a treaty of peace".[295] But the lawful belligerent was the sovereign prince, not the nation, and the institutions that Gentili listed in this passage belonged to the sovereign prince and led no independent life.[296] Brigands and pirates did not lack the quality of just enemies owing to their insufficient or inappropriate institutional capacity but because they were "malefactors" who have "withdrawn" and "broken the treaty of the human race".[297] The law of nations was something that directed the actions of princes, ambassadors, military leaders and soldiers, not autonomous institutions. Nothing like the sovereignty of a "state" ever appeared in his writings.[298]

The lack of a concept of statehood meant that Gentili made no clear distinction between public and private power; the law of nations, after all, was largely an extraction from Roman private law. The private ownership of the subjects was subordinated to a higher, feudal-type power of the prince who could at any moment retract or cancel that ownership. What might this mean in early seventeenth-century England? The Civil War would eventually begin with the king's effort to intervene in the properties of his subjects, keen to insist what they saw as the "ancient rights of Englishmen".[299] At that time, Hobbes would provide both a clear understanding of the *obligation* that subjects had to their sovereign as well as of the notion of statehood within which the sovereign and the subjects were locked in a protection/obligation relationship. Nothing of the kind may be received from Gentili. The justice of which he believed the jurists were "priests" was an abstraction, hardly more than the cultural prejudices of a learned elite. Gentili failed to follow his Italian predecessors to where his intellectual adversaries were taking them. Gentili was familiar with recent work on Tacitus and the Stoics that, however, remained for him useful mainly as source material for reflecting about the *honestum* and *utile* of warfare. They would also have been available to think about the world of statehood

[295] Gentili, *De iure belli*, I IV (25). The expression "having a state" connotes a "Florentine" understanding of the state as belonging to somebody – "*lo stato di Medici*" – or, as Viroli notes, as a "system of private loyalties as a compensation for the benefits that the prince granted to particular citizens", Mauricio Viroli, *From Politics to Reason of State. The Acquisition and Transformation of the Language of Politics 1250–1600* (Cambridge University Press 2010), 186.

[296] They could have led such a life under a republican understanding of statehood that Gentili, despite the nod towards Machiavelli and Livy in *De legationibus*, did not share.

[297] Gentili, *De iure belli*, I IV (22).

[298] Panizza, 'Il pensiero politico di Alberico Gentili', 179–81.

[299] See further Chapter 10 below.

more generally.[300] It would not be Gentili, however, but his theological adversaries who were moving from the consideration of the duties of the prince to kingship as a profession of government, expanding Guicciardini's "reason and practice of states" into an independent and wide-ranging science of politics.[301]

## Another Italian Lesson – Botero and Counter-Reformation Statehood

Towards the end of the third of the *Regales disputations*, which prohibited subjects from ever taking arms against the ruler, Gentili silently acknowledged the limits of his jurisprudence: "Even tyranny is preferable to anarchy."[302] Looking back at the endless civil wars in France Gentili argued that rebellion was infinitely worse than simply bearing the burden of a tyrant and putting one's faith in Christ. In the last pages of the last of his political writings, Gentili reconciled himself to the priority of security over justice.[303] He finished by recording his agreement with the Italian historian and political writer Scipio Ammirato (1531–1601). Ammirato, an early representative of the *ragion di stato* literature, had also counselled his readers to show patience and obedience, stressing that no nation in the world had less reason to rebel against the prince than a Christian nation. Unfailing obedience, Ammirato wrote, "was the will of God whose hands held the hearts of kings".[304]

After decades of stressing the irrelevance of religion for relations between humans, Gentili found himself recommending withdrawal into private conscience as the proper reaction to tyranny and civil conflict. Ammirato's work was just one in a flow of literature coming from Italy, many directly from the Papal curia or interests close to the church, whose point was to react to the confessional crisis by producing new reflections on the nature of the highest temporal authority and its subordination to the interests of the church.[305] After the Protestant

[300] See e.g. Tuck, *Philosophy and Government*, especially 31–119.

[301] Michel Senellart, *Machiavélisme et raison d'état. XIIe–XVIIIe siècle* (Paris, Presses Universitaires de France 1988), 57–9.

[302] "Ipsa tyrannis tolerabilis prae anarchia", Gentili, 'De vi civium semper iniusta', 103.

[303] Ibid., 126–7 and comments in Panizza, 'Il pensiero politico di Alberico Gentili', 195–202.

[304] Gentili, 'De vi civium semper iniusta', 132 and Scipione Ammirato, *Discorsi sopra Cornelio Tacito nuovamente posti in luce* (Florence, Giunti 1594), XIX X (512).

[305] Ammirato himself had worked in Rome but spent most of his life at the service of Tuscan rulers. For brief reflections on him and his works, see Tuck, *Philosophy and Government*, 65–7.

rebellion, the church had not been just sitting there watching its earthly influence disappear as domestic monarchs began to derive their powers directly from God (as James did) or as jurists such as Bodin and Gentili were advancing secularised Roman ideologies of *plenitudo potestas*. The new monarch of the church, Paul III, no model himself of virtue or modesty, had called a general council in 1535 and set up a reform committee that produced the highly critical *Advice Concerning the Reform of the Church* two years later. The Jesuit Order was confirmed in 1540, reform of the Inquisition began two years later and the Council of Trent opened in 1545 with the programme to develop a concentrated response to the religious crisis. The council convened in twenty-five sessions until 1563, when it finally recommended to the pope a number of doctrinal decisions and reform decrees. Although nepotism and other problems persisted, by the end of the century Catholic political institutions had developed a new, self-confident Baroque sensibility.[306]

This sensibility was in evidence not only in Ammirato's discussion of Tacitus but more famously in the principal works by the Piedmontese diplomat and former Jesuit Giovanni Botero (1544–1617), *Cause della grandezza delle città* (1588), *Ragion di Stato* (1589) and *Relazioni universali* (1591–6). The works put forward a comprehensive theory on the security and conservation of political regimes, designed for the purposes of the Catholic status quo powers. Botero had had ample practice in the service of the Counter-Reformation. After having been honourably discharged from the Society of Jesus owing to a doctrinal difference, he was appointed secretary to Archbishop Carlo Borromeo of Milan (1579) and counsel to the cousin of the latter, the young Federico Borromeo (1586), whom he accompanied to Rome where he composed the three works. In Rome he became member of the congregation of the Index and further integrated in the papal administration, which used him also for a diplomatic assignment with the French Catholic League.[307] Towards the end of his career he would become preceptor to the young duke of Piedmont, Carlo Emmanuel (1599). His experience of the French religious wars had inspired in Botero a vehement opposition to the juristic theory of sovereignty that embodied a religiously neutral normative hierarchy, a danger concretised in the prospect of the

[306] On the Council of Trent and the papacy, see e.g. Robert Bireley, *The Refashioning of Catholicism 1450–1700* (London, Macmillan 1999), 45–66.

[307] The significance of Botero's bureaucratic work for his writings is stressed in Romain Descendre, 'Raison d'État, puissance et économie. Le mercantilisme de Giovanni Botero', 39 *Revue de métaphysique et morale* (2003), 313.

Protestant Henry of Navarre's ascent to the throne.[308] That opposition, however, hid a fundamental agreement between Botero and representatives of that juristic theory, including men such as Gentili and Jean Bodin, concerning the government of a political community.

As we have seen, Gentili's jurisprudential approach was limited in three respects: it was substantively narrow, concentrating only on war, diplomacy and the justification of absolute rule; it lacked a concept of obligation and it included no firm notion of the state. Botero's *ragion di stato* went deeper on each point, resulting in a much more powerful image of domestic and international order. To start with the question of obligation, Botero utterly rejected any suggestion to limit religion within the inner world of the individual's relationship with God. On the contrary, the Christian religion was absolutely central for the establishment of a firm rule over a people:

> So great is the power of religion in government that the state can have no secure foundation without it. Hence almost all those who have attempted to found new empires have introduced new faiths or changed the old ones. … But of all religions, none is more favourable to rulers than the Christian law, according to which not merely the bodies and possessions but even the souls and consciences of his people are subject to him: their affections and thoughts are bound, as well as their hands, and they are enjoined to obey wicked rulers as well as moderate ones, and to suffer all rather than disturb the peace.[309]

Botero attacked the juridical view of sovereignty head on. Efficient government could not operate without access to the subjects' internal world. "Yet even today there is no scarcity of men, as impious as they are foolish, who counsel princes that heresies have nothing to do with politics."[310] An ideological justification was needed for the government of Christian subjects. The Trent project did not insist on regular confession for nothing. But Botero did not seek a return to the scholastic world of virtue and the common good. The search for the supernatural was suspended as faith was invoked owing to its *instrumental* value, providing a "secure foundation" for what Botero would call "the state". The paradoxical fact was, according to Botero, that the powers of Christian rulers in a volatile world could only be preserved by securing the supreme political authority of the church.[311] Obedience to the ruler

[308] For Botero's biography, see Romain Descendre, *L'état du monde. Giovanni Botero entre Raison d'État et géopolitique* (Genève, Droz 2009), 23–55.
[309] Giovanni Botero, *The Reason of State* (London, Routledge 1956), II 16 (66).
[310] Ibid., X 9 (221).
[311] This paradoxical objective is well described in Descendre, 'Raison d'Etat', 312.

could not be secured by mere deference to the law or to the king. It had to be guaranteed by faith.

Like Gentili and Bodin, Ammirato and Botero were looking for a way to uphold or restore domestic and external security. The jurists believed that this required toleration. It was sufficient that people coordinated their action in accordance with the norm. Botero disagreed. The ruler had to enforce the faith. "[A] people devoted to religion and piety is much more obedient than one without a guiding principle."[312] Nothing made a rule weaker that the presence of infidel and heretic subjects. Thus, "the principal means of conciliating such subjects must be to convert them".[313] This could be done by education but also by disciplinary measures, such as depriving non-believers of noble status and privileges of birth. They should not be granted office and they must be compelled to wear a special type of "vile and wretched" clothing.[314] For his policies, the prince should always seek instruction from religion. He "should have at his side a copy of His holy law and should observe it with the utmost care". He "should never bring a matter before a Council of State without first submitting it to a spiritual Council containing doctors of theology and canon law".[315]

The power of Counter-Reformation *ragion di stato* was also accompanied by a new concept of political community and a theory of government that extended to the conditions of domestic peace and a stable international order. As we have seen, Gentili did not possess a clear notion of the state, and much of his work was written as instructions for the virtuous prince.[316] In a bold performative gesture, Botero defined "state" (*stato*) in the 1596 edition of the work on *Reason of State* as "a stable rule over a people" (*dominio fermo sopra I popoli*).[317] By defining it as a kind of power (*dominio*), Botero separated the state from its earlier adjectival or personal connotations – *status regni*, *status Regis*, *status rei publicae*, *lo stato di' Medici*, *état de la république* and so on.[318] It now became

312 Botero, *Reason of State*, II 16 (67). 313 Ibid., V 2 (98).
314 Ibid., V 2, 3 (98–100, 101). 315 Ibid., II 15 (64).
316 In this regard, too, Gentili was still continuing the works of Machiavelli and Guicciardini.
317 Botero, *Reason of State*, I 1 (3). For a useful discussion see Romain Descendre, 'Introduction', in Giovanni Botero, *De la raison d'état (1589–1598)* (Paris, Gallimard 2014), 12–16. In the 2017 Cambridge University Press edition this is translated "A State is a firm rule over people", which better conveys the sense that Botero's "state" does not presuppose the prior presence of a "people". Instead, it brings a plurality of different groups together, making it one people by virtue of subordinating it to a single system or rule. Bonnet, *Droit et raison d'État*, 209–10.
318 See Lazzeri, 'Introduction', 103–8.

a separate institution, a system of rule. In the 1596 edition he further stressed the independence of statehood: "Reason of State assumes a ruler and a State (the one as artificer, the other as material)."[319] When Guicciardini used the notion of "reason and practice of states" in the passage cited at the outset of this chapter he did that to refer to action taken in order to deviate from the normal requirements of law and morality. Botero's *ragion di stato* covered *all* types of technical knowledge assisting in the preservation of the state. In the 1596 edition, he recognised that the notion had come to be "said rather of such actions that cannot be considered in the light of ordinary reason".[320] This was a reference to Ammirato, whose tract had been produced in the meanwhile and which read *ragion di stato* as an express repudiation of ordinary reason.[321] But Botero did not want to limit the "reason of state" to the exceptional situation. He had a wider concept that embraced both ordinary government as well as exceptional action in abnormal circumstances. Neither Ammirato nor Botero advocated strictly illegal or immoral actions, such as assassinations of political adversaries, for example. For both, it was important, as Ammirato stressed over again, that *ragion di stato* was directed to public benefit and did not allow transgression of divine reason or divine law.[322] In this respect, but also as Ammirato's translation of "law" as "reason" suggested, both Italian writers were advocating a new vocabulary of ruling, with its distinct, new authorities, experts in politics.

A state was rule by somebody over somebody else (in French texts often associated with the authority of the *seigneur*).[323] The concreteness of the definition was underlined by the determination of the sphere of those being ruled (the subjects) by their being situated in a territory. The Italian *dominio* further detached statehood from such juridical concepts as jurisdiction, *regere*, *gubernare*, *administratio* or *custodia*, highlighting the empirical, effectual aspects of the rule.[324] This prompted Botero to engage in a study of different types of states – small, medium-sized

319 Botero, *Reason of State*, I 1 (3).

320 Ibid., I 1 (3).

321 Ammirato, *Discorsi sopra Cornelio Tacito*, XII I (230–1).

322 Ibid., 232. While reason of state always contravened one or several of the "ordinary" reasons (of nature or nations, of civil or military reason), being "greater and more universal" than these, it could still not breach the demands of religion, XII I (233–5).

323 Bonnet, *Droit et raison d'État*, 208.

324 Descendre argues that the choice of the word indicates a wish to break wholly with religious tradition too; but the relationship to the scholastic debates on *dominium* is striking. 'Introduction', 16–22.

and large ones – and to compare their advantages and disadvantages. Which would be easiest to rule? Which could be the most lasting?[325] Indeed, the whole point was to move beyond the world of formal legality towards an empirical notion of government that could then become the object of this new type of knowledge, the "reason of state".

Botero's intention was to dethrone law as the supreme science of government, *scientia civilis*, and to introduce a *new* type of knowledge to deal with a new type of object – the state – especially so as to help preserve and strengthen established Christian monarchies: "Might conquers but wisdom preserves."[326] While the first two chapters of the work dealt with affection (love) and admiration (respect), as well as virtues such as prudence, liberality, valour, temperance and faith, and thus resembled older works on the instruction of princes , including Gentili's *De legationibus* and much of *De iure belli*, the bulk of the work had to do with using and expanding the resources (*potenza*) of the state so as to strengthen it internally and towards external rivals.[327] Law and the activity of jurists, especially judges, was important but mainly to the extent that it contributed to the affection (love) of one's subjects.[328] Law and legality were not the principal social forces, however. Human beings were "rarely moved except by interest".[329] The task then was to operate with these interests – the interests of different classes of society, for example – so that they would be best used to support the state.

In order to make clear the distinction between juridical sovereignty and reason of state, Botero distinguished between independence in the formal–legal sense as "having no superior" and in the empirical sense of "needing no aid or support from others". The latter sense was far more important because it was "intrinsic and substantial" while the first sort of independence was "merely external and accidental".[330] The juridical view of the ruler as an "absolute and supreme lord" was limited to a formal or constitutional sense. What reason of state offered were techniques to make him "a powerful ruler with strength sufficient to maintain his rule".[331] This required focus on the material factors, the forces

325 Botero, *Reason of State*, I 6 (7–9). 326 Ibid., I 5 (6).

327 Book I of the work is divided into "Justice" (chapters 12–18) and "liberality" (chapters 19–22). Book II begins with "prudence" (chapters 1–9) and continues with "valour" (chapters 10–12) as well as a discussion of piety and temperance (chapters 14–17). The rest of the ten books then discuss various techniques of how to employ the population, how to treat a conquered people and how to govern, strengthen and extend the resources of one's state.

328 Botero, *Reason of State*, I 12–22 (16–33). 329 Ibid., VIII 13 (163).

330 Ibid., IX 2 (169). 331 Ibid., IX 2 (169).

and resources that gave the state such strength that it could always rely on itself. Although this removed reason of state beyond positive constitutional legality, it did not situate it outside a *wider* sense of legal order that, instead of being founded on positive enactments or logical derivations would operate with purely historical or empirical concepts.[332]

Gentili's natural law had been much more limited, focusing on war and diplomacy largely in terms of instructions to the prince. As the main focus of *ragion di stato* was not on the prince but on "stable rule over a people", the instruments and techniques of governing a territory, its material scope was quite a bit wider, producing something like a sketch of what would later be called the mercantilist state. At the heart of the "forces" of a state lay its ability to enlist the subjects in productive work. For as Botero put it, "the true strength of a ruler ... consists in his people".[333] It was by having "a large population" and employing it as efficiently as possible in all kinds of "industry" that the strength of the state and the interests of the ruler and the people could be best attained. "The ruler who has plenty of men will have plenty of everything which the ingenuity and industry of man can provide."[334] In the little work that preceded *Ragion di stato*, the *Causes of the Greatness of Cities*, Botero was very explicit about the role of agriculture, manufacturing and commerce as the secret of the rise and flourishing of great cities and in general the management of the economy as central to the business of governing a city. Gentili had little to say about the position or the property of the subjects, beyond the entitlement of the king to rule in an absolute manner, including the right to confiscate the subjects' property.[335] By contrast, Botero did everything to assure the subjects

[332] In Chapter 12 we shall see German eighteenth-century jurists collapsing the two together.

[333] Botero, *Reason of State*, VII 12 (144). [334] Ibid., VII 11 (144).

[335] Alberico Gentili, 'Disputatio II: Utrum possit princeps de regno suo, suorumque subditorum pro arbitratu statuere', in *Disputationum* (London, Wolf 1587), 27–51. "Sed supra principem nihil est. Merito igitur ratio facti principalis non quaeritur. In supremo principe ... voluntas pro caussa habetur & ratione; ideoque, principem posse, cuicquid velit, & ius suum cuilibet auferre", 45. However, Gentili accepted that the prince had only those powers that had been donated to him by the people, agreeing with Alciato that the theologians were "hallucinating" and the jurists "flattering" who claimed that there were no limits at all on princely powers (for example, he could never slaughter citizens at will because no such power resided in the people either), ibid., 48–9. By contrast, because the people may dispose of the property of its individual members ("sine caussa"), after they have transferred their power to the prince, so can he, 46. None of the possible limitations to his power in this respect is definite, for he can always decide to act out his absolute powers, 37, 39. See further, Alain Wijfels, 'Une disputation d'Alberico Gentili'.

that they would thrive by aligning their workforce with the state. "A prince should therefore", Botero wrote, "encourage and promote agriculture and show his appreciation of those who improve and make good use of their property and of those whose farms are well cared for."[336] In Books VII and VIII of his principal works, Botero examined the financial administration of the realm and the ways to increase the number and profitable activities of his people. The prince was not to accumulate riches to himself, and he was to tax the subjects only modestly in order to avoid disturbance and rebellion.[337] The more intensely the people were involved in agriculture, manufacture and commerce, the greater the revenue they provided. It was important that foreign commerce would not be based on the export of raw materials but on finished products.[338] Gentili, as we have seen, had little to say about colonisation. By contrast, Botero held colonies important for both military and economic reasons, referring to the way the Romans had "increased their numbers" by bringing home all kinds of new foodstuffs and raw materials as well as providing room for excess populations (even as he was worried that Portugal and Spain, by sending "useful and even necessary" subjects to the colonies were draining themselves of manpower in a way that, Botero assumed, was leading them to bankruptcy).[339] All in all, the power of the state lay in the wise management of its economic base. This required coordinating the citizens' interests with those of the state by channelling their activities towards industry and commerce. "Subjects must be won over to feel that it is in their interest to be under our rule and to fight for us."[340]

Reason of state did not wish to do away with law and legality but lay down the conditions for its application.[341] But as Ammirato's work showed, the two could easily be made to collapse into each other. He produced a hierarchical system of reasons that he labelled "natural reason", "civil reason", "reason of war" and "reason of nations" in a rather contrived effort to avoid speaking of the respective *laws*. Each reason formed an exception to a reason of a more general type. Thus civil reason deviated from natural reason and the reason of war from

[336] Botero, *Reason of State*, VIII 2 (148).

[337] Ibid., VII 2, 4 and 10 (132, 136, 140–3).

[338] Ibid., VIII 3 (153).

[339] Ibid., VI 4 VIII 5 (120–1, 156–7).

[340] Ibid., V 1 (95).

[341] Having reviewed the attitudes of seventeenth-century reason-of-state literatures to law, Catteeuw reproduced Ludovico Zuccolo's three "modalities" in that relationship. Reason of states could act as a legislative motive; it could assist in *applying* the law, and it could *conflict with* the law. *Censures*, 186–7.

the reason of nations. The "reason of state" was thus just a specific type of reason that was instrumental for the protection and preservation of the state – a set of arguments that generations of jurists from Bodin onwards have regularly dealt with by forms of constitutional exception. Ammirato's discourse replaced the idiom of law with that of reason – leaving it open for a jurist like Gentili to do exactly the contrary by including in their theory of sovereignty the distinction between *potestas ordinata* and *potestas absoluta*. In the struggle between the jurists and the *raison d'état* writers, the principal disadvantage of the former were the formalities of their craft. Gentili had nothing to offer to readers anxious to move beyond religious strife beyond a reading of the civil law according to which kingship was "absolute" and subjects should shut up and obey. That he must have realised the awkwardness of this is suggested by something he wrote in the very same paragraph where he referenced Ammirato. Of course, the rebellion of the French Huguenots was unjust, he claimed, despite everything they had suffered. Indeed, he exclaimed, "by God, what a good cause they had" – *bone Deus, quam bona causa tamen*![342] Nevertheless, he left his fellow Protestants in limbo by claiming that justice always sided with the prince, whatever the grievances of the subjects. By contrast, Botero would offer them productive work at the service of the state as well as the significant consolation of enriching themselves in the process.

342 Gentili, 'De vi civium in regem semper iniusta', in *Regales disputationis*, 130–2.

# 4

# The Rule of Law

## *Grotius*

"There can be no peace among nations without armies, no armies without pay, and no pay without tributes."[1] With those words Hugo Grotius (1583–1645) addressed James VI/I of England and Scotland on 6 April 1613 in his capacity as one of the leaders of the Dutch delegation in the first of the maritime conferences with England.[2] The context was the dispute between the United Provinces and England over the way the Dutch had excluded English traders from access to markets in the East Indies. The point Grotius was making was to justify the de facto monopoly claimed by the *Vereenigde Oostindische Compagnie* (VOC, the Dutch East India Company) in its trading ports on the Malay Peninsula by referring to the protection that the local ruler, the king of Johor, would receive from the Dutch against the Portuguese. In order for the company to be able to maintain military presence, and hence, Grotius claimed, peace, they needed privileged access to spices "for a reasonable price [and agreement that] they would not sell them to others rather than their rescuers".[3]

Although Grotius was well-known at the time as the author of the little work *Mare liberum* (1609) and an influential polemicist in the disputes among the Protestant factions in the United Provinces, he was not now performing in an advocacy role. Instead, he spoke as a

[1] Opening Address of Hugo Grotius Held before King James VI/I at the Maritime and Colonial Conference in London on 6 April 1613, in Peter Borschberg, *Hugo Grotius, The Portuguese and Free Trade in the East Indies* (National University of Singapore Press 2011), 265.

[2] On Hugo Grotius' role at the maritime conference of 1613, see Henk Nellen, *Hugo Grotius. A Lifelong Struggle for Peace in Church and State 1583–1645* (Leiden, Brill 2015), 149–64.

[3] Borschberg, *Hugo Grotius*, 265.

high official of the States of Holland whose argument was based on a comprehensive view of what was needed at a dangerous time to guarantee the peace and welfare of his country and its allies. He remained unmoved when the English cited that work against him, and responded by stressing the limited nature of the privileges claimed by the Dutch and on their being based on a contract with the king of Johor. But above all he emphasised the commonsense rationale that linked peace and stability with a legal arrangement whose point was to provide an adequate economic basis for the Dutch activities in the East Indies. In his farewell address more than a month later, Grotius appealed once more to the English king's sense of reasonableness "that the expenses made for the Indians' defence" should be compensated, or in other words, that it would be "inequitable [if] anyone should participate in the yield who would not participate in the cost".[4]

These arguments reflected pragmatic and increasingly widely accepted views about the role of law and legal obligation in the complex conflicts of interest and ideology that took place in Europe and beyond. In due course, Grotius would provide an extremely influential articulation to those views in his *De iure belli ac pacis* (*The Rights of War and Peace*, 1625, 1631, 1645). At the heart of his elaborations was the claim that beyond all religious, political and economic rivalries, every human being was related to another by an "Inclination ... to live with those of his own Kind, not in any Manner whatever, but peaceably, and in a Community regulated according to the best of his Understanding".[5] This "inclination", he suggested, was neither some primitive drive or a deep-seated feeling of benevolence, nor a cold calculation of interests. It was an aspect of human reason that sought to act "according to some general Principles".[6] One of such principles was "that if you have gained by what is mine; whilst I am forced to go without it, you are bound to refund as much as you have gained by it".[7] This was a quintessentially legal reason Grotius was employing, for there was "so much Equity in

[4] Farewell Address of Hugo Grotius Held before King James VI/I at the Close of the Maritime and Colonial Conference in London, 21 May 1613, in ibid., 271.

[5] Hugo Grotius, *The Rights of War and Peace* (*De iure belli ac pacis*), hereinafter *DIBP* (Richard Tuck ed. & intro., Indianapolis, Liberty Fund 2005 [1625/1631]), Preliminary Discourse, VI (79–81).

[6] Ibid., Preliminary Discourse, VII (85). The original and the translation use italics here and in many other places. I have removed them throughout for readability.

[7] Ibid., II X II 1 (689).

this maxim, that the Lawyers have made use of it to decide many Cases on which extant Laws have not provided any Thing".[8]

In his principal work Grotius aimed to show how the famous "sociability" that he addressed as "the fountain of Right" would provide legally articulated obligations for human beings *everywhere* to behave in certain ways not "repugnant to Society", and that these obligations could be proven by "some such certain Notions, as none can deny, without doing Violence to his Judgment".[9] In the passages cited above, Grotius was dealing with a cause of just war that, as he recognised, had often been left unmentioned, despite its common character – namely "debts arising from a contract or some similar source".[10] In his mature work he returned to legal obligations resulting from contract debts as well as from using or injuring another's property as just causes of war. This was a rule, he wrote "whose Justice is of the greatest Certainty and Evidence".[11] It was sociability itself that required that contracts be kept and property secured.

What emerged in the *oeuvre* of Grotius, albeit in complex, often tentative and sometimes self-contradicting ways, was an idea of law and especially of subjective rights as the source of an autonomous system of obligations binding everywhere irrespective of religious views or interests.[12] In the previous chapter we saw how Gentili had tried to capture the worlds of law and diplomacy within natural law using the resources of Roman law as evidence of universal principles. The influence of that effort had been thwarted by the way it isolated political decision-making about external affairs from concerns of domestic justice and provided no internal sense of obligation to its conception of royal authority. If Gentili's work had been overshadowed by Counter-Reformation *ragion di stato*, which had enlisted God in support of its prescriptions, Grotius, for his part, responded to the latter by offering a

[8] Ibid., II X II 2 (689). [9] Ibid., Preliminary Discourse, VIII, XI (85–6, 110–11).

[10] Hugo Grotius, *Commentary on the Law of Prize and Booty* (*De iure praedae Commentarius*), hereinafter *DIP* (Martine Julia van Ittersum, ed. & intro., Indianapolis, Liberty Fund 2006 [1604–6]), VII (103, 105).

[11] Grotius, *DIBP*, II X II 2 (689). The enforcement of legal obligation as a just cause of war (alongside self-defence, defence of property and punishment) emerging from contracts, property or injury is the subject of Chapters X–XVII of Book II of *DIBP* (685–879).

[12] Christoph Link writes of "ein Prozess totalen Verrechtlichung aller Bereiche des Soziallebens im gesellschaftlichen, staatlichen und überstaatlichen Raum", in 'Herrschaftsbegründung und Kirchenhoheit bei Hugo Grotius', in Christoph Strohm & Heinrich de Wall (eds), *Konfessionalität und Jurisprudenz in der frühen Neuzeit* (Berlin, Duncker & Humblot 2009), 350.

sense of legal obligation, instead of merely prudential counsel, that was to bind all people irrespective of their religious affiliations, indeed that would be binding "though we should even grant, what without the greatest Wickedness cannot be granted, that there is no God".[13]

At the time of Grotius' speeches to King James in England, a palpable need had emerged for some synthetic view about European society and politics. Ideological divisions were tearing the continent apart – the Protestant rebellion in Bohemia would soon trigger the Thirty Years' War. Political struggles expanded from the clash of constitutional principles at home – the extent of royal authority and right of resistance, for example – to imperial rivalry in America and the East Indies. Sustaining European polities in their perpetual wars and in their colonial projects "now depended, to an extent never seen before, on an essential underpinning of economic strength".[14] Each of these factors touched Grotius personally and each had a place in his effort to situate Dutch state-building within a conception of law that would organise public power and private rights in a system of principles whose binding force would be received from human nature itself and thus remain unaffected by the conflicts that pitted Europeans against each other. This was the "moral science" of natural law that, Grotius suggested, would build on nothing more than reason, the ability to distinguish and subordinate oneself to "general principles", as the irreducible core of human nature.[15] One need not accuse him of bad faith if those principles appeared to support, as if miraculously, a very specific organisation of social life:

> But Right Reason, and the Nature of Society ... does not prohibit all Manner of Violence, but only that which is repugnant to Society, that is

[13] Grotius, *DIBP*, Preliminary Discourse, XI (89). For a long discussion of the origin and sense of this famous statement, see Peter Haggenmacher, *Grotius et la doctrine de laguerre juste* (Paris, Presses universitaires de France, 1983), 466–523. In Haggenmacher's reading the difference between the two works is only relative; in both Grotius found the origin of natural law's binding force in God's will, though in the latter, owing to Jesuit influence, he would stress the way God had deprived himself of the right of self-contradiction by changing the law of nature: the infamous *etiamsi daremus* took nothing away from this, 501–7.

[14] M. S. Anderson, *The Origins of the Modern European State System 1494–1618* (London, Longman 1998), 49.

[15] Grotius, *DIBP*, Preliminary Discourse, VII (85). The profoundly conservative character of Grotius' social views is stressed in C. G. Roelofsen, 'Grotius and the Development of International Relations Theory. The "Long Seventeenth Century" and the Elaboration of a European States System', 18 *Grotiana* (1997), 108–10, 118–20.

what invades another's Right. For the Design of Society is, that every one should quietly enjoy his own, with the Help and the united Force of the whole Community.[16]

Grotius accompanied the concern for the rights of individuals, and the duty not to intervene in their "quiet enjoyment", by frequent nods towards a notion of justice that concerned benevolence to one's neighbours. But he insisted on a clear distinction between strict and enforceable law and the "Counsels and such other Precepts which, however, honest and reasonable they be, lay us under no Obligation [and] come not under this Notion of *Law*, or *Right*".[17] Through such distinctions, and by insisting that the strict law was binding everywhere, he was able to extend a Dutch model of political and economic life from the rebellion against Habsburg rule to the struggle over East Indian markets and to the conflicts over settlement in the Americas. That view was well-manifested in the economic and political success of the country whose virtues he had celebrated in his early years but which would eventually leave him sidelined and bitter as he watched those successes accumulate from imposed exile.

## Interpretative Perspectives

Where Gentili's interest was narrowly circumscribed to the relations between rulers and civil communities in war and peace, Grotius' natural law encompassed the whole field of law as an autonomous system of governing human action. From elucidating the conditions of just war, the work expanded into a comprehensive account of the rights of human beings everywhere and the principles of government and war that would protect those rights. His *oeuvre* not only foregrounded the role of law and lawyers in public life but achieved the complete "absorption of law in morality".[18] This legal morality embodied a specific understanding of reason that committed everyone to obedience to authority and respect for forms of social life that had been determined necessary for the protection of subjective rights. For "in Things of a moral Nature . . . those Means which conduce to a certain End, do assume the very Nature of that End".[19]

[16] Grotius, *DIBP*, I II I 5 (184). [17] Ibid., I I IX (148).

[18] Michel Villey, *La formation de la pensée juridique moderne* (Presses Universitaires de France 2003), 542, 544, 547–52.

[19] Grotius, *DIBP*, III I II 1 (1186). Likewise, *DIBP*, II V XXIV 2 (554).

Historians of legal and political thought have extensively debated whether Grotius should be read as the last representative of scholasticism or the originator of a distinctly "modern" natural law. No doubt, Grotius' views on *ius gentium* and *dominium* resemble those of the scholastic theologians. Vázquez's *Controversiae illustris* served him as a constant point of reference on civil government, territorial rights, and the laws of war.[20] As a scholar of theology and jurisprudence Grotius may perhaps be understood to offer "an abbreviated and simplified version of the central naturalist aspects of Aquinas and Suárez' theory of morality".[21] His work on the just war is best seen as a systematisation of that medieval genre.[22] On the other hand, Grotius was trained as a Protestant humanist and his prose was very different from, say, Suárez's dry and repetitive scholasticism.[23] Grotius experimented with (Ramist) methods and humanist sources and literary tropes, sometimes even claiming his conclusions to follow as mathematical truths from his premises.[24] The vocabulary of reason that Grotius inherited from the scholastics did not point to supernatural *felicitas* but to the ability of

[20] For Vitoria as a source to Grotius, see e.g. Peter Borschberg, *Hugo Grotius 'Commentarius in Theses XI'. An Early Treatise on Sovereignty, the Just War and the Legitimacy of the Dutch Revolt* (Berne, Peter Lang 1994), 48–52.

[21] Terence Irwin, *The Development of Ethics. A Historical and Critical Study. Vol. II: From Suárez to Rousseau* (Oxford University Press 2008), 98. Grotius' debt to Suárez and the other Spaniards is manifold and has often been highlighted. See especially Alfred Dufour, 'Les "Magni hispani" dans l'oeuvre de Grotius', in Frank Grunert & Kurt Seelmann (eds), *Die Ordnung der Praxis. Neue Studies zur Spanishen Spätscholastik* (Tübingen, Niemeyer 2001), 351–80.

[22] Haggenmacher, *Grotius*, passim, and Peter Haggenmacher, 'Grotius and Gentili. A Reappraisal of Thomas Holland's Inaugural Lecture', in Hedley Bull, Adam Roberts & Benedict Kingbury (eds), *Hugo Grotius and International Relations* (Oxford, Clarendon 1990), 163–7.

[23] For Grotius as a humanist, celebrating republican liberty see e.g. Richard Tuck, *Philosophy and Government 1572–1651* (Cambridge University Press 1993), 155–69. For some doubts about the usefulness of the scholastic/humanist distinction in respect of Grotius, see Andrew Fitzmaurice, *Sovereignty, Property and Empire, 1500–2000* (Cambridge University Press 2014), 88–9.

[24] "Just as the mathematicians customarily prefix to any concrete demonstration a preliminary statement of certain broad axioms on which all persons are easily agreed, in order that there may be some fixed point from which to trace the proof that follows, so shall we point out certain rules and laws of the most general nature, presenting them as preliminary assumptions which need to be recalled rather than learned for the first time, with the purpose of laying a foundation upon which our other conclusions may safely rest", Grotius, *DIP*, Introductory Remarks I (17–18). Twenty years later, Grotius agreed with Aristotle that "we cannot expect the same degrees of Evidence, in Moral, as in Mathematical Sciences". Grotius, *DIBP*, II XXIII I (1115). See also *DIBP*, I II I 3 (182) and Haggenmacher, *Grotius*, 561–3.

human beings to commit to principles of sociability that would be clearly known.[25] If, like Aristotle, he derived natural law from the idea of sociability, unlike Aristotle he translated most of it as natural *rights* and did not confine them to the *polis*. But if the modernity of Grotius was highlighted by the centrality he gave to rights and the secularising effects of his engagement with the sceptics, both were already present in medieval theologians and canon lawyers, a fact prompting Tierney to conclude that "Grotius did not create a new theory of natural rights and natural law; but what he achieved was equally important. He made it possible for the old theory to live in the new world."[26]

Deciding whether Grotius should be read backwards to the medieval period or forwards to modernity is hardly necessary nor even useful to the extent that his principal legal works, *De iure praedae* and *De iure belli ac pacis*, while taking up *topoi* familiar from the past were employed so as to respond to pressing events in the present – the Dutch revolt against their Habsburg rulers, the expansion of trade and settlement in the colonies, and the onset of the Thirty Years' War.[27] As natural law, it possessed a theory of internal obligation that was nevertheless independent of contested religious assumptions while avoiding the reduction of law to the mere search for utility. To the sceptical suggestion that "[l]aws ... were instituted by Men for the sake of Interest" and that "Natural Law [was] mere Chimera",[28] Grotius responded with his theory of rational sociability that would generate its own binding force and offer a vocabulary with which

[25] Hans Welzel, *Naturrecht und materiale Gerechtigkeit* (Göttingen, Vandenhoeck & Ruprecht 1990), 123–5.

[26] Brian Tierney, *The Idea of Natural Rights. Studies on Natural Rights, Natural Law, and Church Law 1150–1625* (Michigan, Eerdmans 1997), 342.

[27] The scholastic "feel" of Grotius' writing has to do with the way he produced an almost endless series of distinctions at key parts of his treatises, distinctions between "will" and "reason", "rules" and "laws", between "primary" and "secondary" natural law, natural law in a "wider" and "stricter" sense, between internal and external obligations, internal and external rights, natural law and voluntary laws, "faculties" and "aptitudes", expletive and attributive rights, between "law" and "morals", between "common" and "proper" sovereignty and so on. These distinctions often overlap in ways that make it hard to say how they relate to each other – whether, for example, they manifest some higher-level dichotomy between natural and positive or divine and human law and just what the hierarchical relationship was he wanted to establish between the opposites. It is often useful to read these dichotomies as rhetorical devices that carry Grotius to his desired conclusion while giving acknowledgement to some pertinent objection along the way.

[28] Grotius, *DIBP*, Preliminary Discourse, V (79).

individuals could claim respect for their rights and rulers for their laws that were supposed to secure their "peaceable Enjoyment".[29]

`If the latter concerns – in which we may now recognise those of sovereignty and property – would eventually emerge as perhaps the most important concerns of legal modernity, they were also concerns and concepts with a long pedigree. The notion of subjective rights and the genealogy of political community that accompanied it were already present in the Spanish scholastics and indeed the glossators and post-glossators. When Grotius wrote that God had created human beings "'free and *sui iuris'* so that the actions of each individual and the use of his possessions were made subject not to another's will but to his own", he was moving within an already familiar terrain.[30] Indeed he referenced those statements by the *Institutes* of civil law and Chapter VI of Aristotle's *Politics*. But when he then added that "liberty in regard to actions is equivalent to ownership in regard to property", the references to Vázquez and Aristotle could hardly veil the fact that he was also offering elements for a new understanding. Old words – new concepts? The eclectic if not eccentric way that Grotius treated his own as well as others' texts is well known.[31] More interesting than their chronological location is to try to understand what it was that made them offer persuasive answers to problems of state-building that for the contemporaries had to do with religion and the economy above anything else.

## A Political Theology of Moderation

In the early years of the Dutch republic, political and religious authority went hand in hand. The intense confessionalisation of European polities required that all exercise of public power be justified by the appropriate religious vocabulary. In the United Provinces, the truce with Spain of 1609 had diminished pressure on the Catholic side but intensified internecine conflicts between Protestant denominations. A representative of the moderate, Arminian (Remonstrant) faction with a reasonably tolerant attitude to the Catholicism of the country's prior rulers, Grotius followed his mentor, Johan van Oldenbarnevelt (1547–1619), and sided with the

[29] Ibid., III III II 1 (1247). [30] Grotius, *DIP*, II 33–4.

[31] See, for example, the extensive discussion of his use of biblical sources in Mark Somos, *Secularisation and the Leiden Circle* (Leiden, Brill 2011), (explaining the "unusual" and "odd" nature of Grotius' citations of the Bible in *DIP* as a secularisation strategy), 388–437.

States of Holland against the orthodox Calvinists, the heroes of the rebellion, allied with Prince Maurice (1567–1619) of the House of Orange.[32] In the very year of his diplomatic voyage to England, Grotius had published his *Ordinum pietas* to attack his opponents' pursuit of a Calvinist theocracy that went completely contrary to his youthful republican ideals.[33] In part commissioned by the States of Holland, in part at his own initiative, Grotius wanted here to state the Christian religion by concentrating on shared truths and ethical precepts and minimising the role of controversial materials ("doctrines"). This did not mean turning the state into a secular institution – an altogether impossible idea. Instead, the state was to seek neutrality between the opposed factions and if need be, take command of the administration of religious practice.[34] But unlike Bodin in France, the Remonstrant leaders – Oldenbarnevelt and Grotius among them – founded the government's mediating role in its firm commitment to the core teachings of Christianity. As Grotius expressed it in a written justification he wrote soon after the commencement of his (as it then seemed) life imprisonment at Loevestein castle:

> the authorities should scrutinize God's word so thoroughly as to be certain to impose nothing which is against it; if they act in this way, they shall in good conscience have control of the public churches and public worship.[35]

[32] For this context, see e.g. Richard Tuck, 'Grotius and Selden', in J. H. Burns (ed.), *The Cambridge History of Political Thought 1450–1700* (Cambridge University Press 2004), 509–14 and Barbara Kniepel, *Die Naturrechtslehre des Hugo Grotius als Einigungsprinzip der Christenheit, dargestellt an seiner Stellung zum Calvinism* (Kessel, Bladitsch 1971), 15–39.

[33] The religious antagonism was also a class conflict, with the Dutch oligarchy accused of contriving to sell the hard-won independence back to the Habsburgs. This was also the principal accusation that led to Oldenbarnevelt's execution and Grotius' imprisonment. For the Calvinists, religious toleration of the Catholics seemed close to treason. On *Ordinum pietas*, see Hans W. Blom & Harm-Jan van Dam, 'Dossier. *Ordinum pietas* (1613), Its Context and Seventeenth-Century Reception', 34 *Grotiana* (2013), 1–7 and the rest of that issue.

[34] For a useful summary of studies and interpretations of Grotius' religious works by reference to their background in Dutch religious history, see Florian Mühlegger, *Hugo Grotius. Ein christlicher Humanist in politischen Verantwortung* (Berlin, De Gruyter 2007), 6–83 and J. P. Heeren, *Hugo Grotius as Apologist for the Christian Religion* (Leiden, Brill 2004), esp. 64–75.

[35] Grotius, 'Memorie van mijne intentien en notabele bejegeningen', quoted in Harm-Jan van Dam, 'De imperio potestatum circa sacra', in Henk M. Nellen & Edwin Rabbie (eds), *Hugo Grotius Theologian. Essays in Honour of G. H. M. Posthumus Meyjes* (Leiden, Brill 1994), 22.

Grotius himself believed that his most important works had to do with advancing Christian unity, an effort reflected in his legal writings as well.[36] He hated the way disputed dogmas about predestination and free will had come to divide Protestant factions against each other. In principle, it might have been open to Grotius to follow Gentili and to focus on strictly external aspects of human behaviour. Something like this would also have been available through adherence to the "neo-stoic" view of political government developed in Leiden by Justus Lipsius (1547–1606). But although Grotius knew Lipsius' *Politica*, and probably used it at the time of the troubles of 1614–18, little of its inspiration was visible in *De iure belli ac pacis*. This is understandable. Lipsius' "Tacitist" views would have reduced law into prudential judgments in a world of endlessly ambitious rulers.[37] The Machiavellian wisdom that would generalise maxims of statecraft from history and philosophy had little to say about civil society relations or why subjects were to be bound also when that seemed to go against their interests. The latter were provided by Counter-Reformation *ragion di stato* that subordinated efficient statecraft to the supervisory role of the church. By contrast, the "sociability" that Grotius would offer his readers had no use for church authority. It was intrinsic to all humans.[38]

That the Dutch rebellion had been fed by religiously justified violence on the side of the Spanish not only confirmed the firmly Protestant identity of northern Netherlands but gave inordinate prevalence to its Calvinist faction, the best organised and the most devoted of the rebel groups. Whatever his personal convictions, William of Orange himself "[i]ncreasingly … felt obliged to identify with the Reformed Protestants".[39] In due course the Dutch synod began to organise religious life in the rebel provinces along the Calvinist model, and by the time of the truce with Spain (1609), the Reformed Protestants (around 10 per cent had joined the church) had been able to secure leadership of

36 See e.g. Kniepel, *Naturrechtslehre*; Hasso Hoffmann, 'Hugo Grotius', in Michael Stolleis (ed.), *Staatsdenker in der frühen Neuzeit* (Munich, Beck 1995), 59–60.

37 See Jan Waszinck, 'Lipsius and Grotius. Tacitism', 39 *History of European Ideas* (2013), 151–68.

38 See the detailed treatment of Grotius' view of the human ability to know the good in Janne E. Nijman, '"Grotius" *Imago Dei* Anthropology. Grounding *Jus Naturae et Gentium*', in Martti Koskenniemi, Mónica García-Salmones Rovira & Paolo Amorosa (eds), *International Law and Religion. Historical and Contemporary Perspectives* (Oxford University Press 2017), 87–110.

39 Auke Jelsma, *Frontiers of Reformation. Dissidence and Orthodoxy in Sixteenth-Century Europe* (Farnham, Ashgate 1998), 113.

the consistory (church council) and to begin the "second reformation" (*reformatio vitae*). The religious tension turned into a political opposition between the States General, now in the hands of the Reformed Protestants, and the States of Holland led by Oldenbarnevelt and the Remonstrant group. Grotius, too, subscribed to the "five articles" of the Remonstrants and especially to the view that predestination was not absolute and humans could lead lives of virtue without taking definite views on specific dogmas. Oldenbarnevelt and Grotius invoked the full sovereignty of the government of Holland over the organisation of confessional matters.

There is little doubt that Grotius saw his legal work as part of his overall religious view of the world. Until his arrest in 1618 Grotius kept composing religious essays from a high governmental position where he put forward a political theology consisting of two separate but connected arguments – that the essence of Christianity lay in a limited number of core propositions and that public authorities were entitled to ensure that religious factions would not disturb social peace. A first such work was an unpublished manuscript *Meletius*, written probably in 1611, that took its name from the sixteenth-century Greek Patriarch Meletius Pegas (1549–1601), an opponent of papal claims for supremacy who had, like Grotius himself, worried over the discord between Christian churches.[40] *Meletius* was written as an explanation of Christianity to outsiders and made no reference to the controversial doctrines but instead highlighted the importance of Christian ethics that was embodied in natural law and pointed to world peace and a golden age to come.[41] The tract attributed Christian disunity to the fact that "dogmas are declared to be the most essential part of the religion, whereas those ethical precepts are disregarded".[42] Attention should now be turned to the latter. For over dogmas we struggle with others – but over ethics only with ourselves.[43]

40 The tract was found among Grotius' papers only in 1984 and has been published in Hugo Grotius, *Meletius sive de iis quae inter Christianos conveniunt Epistola* (Guillaume Posthumus Meyjes ed., Leiden, Brill 1988).

41 Which is why Mühlegger, observes that is was a "Vorstufe zu Grotius' *De iure belli ac pacis*", *Grotius. Ein christlicher Humanist*, 135.

42 Grotius, *Meletius*, Epilogue, § 90 (133).

43 Ibid., Epilogue, § 90 (133). This is not to say that Grotius saw Christ only as a "teacher". One could not know the Gospel's message of Christ as saviour unless one knew its ethical content. Henk de Jonge, 'Grotius' View of the Gospels and the Evangelists', in Henk M. Nellen & Edwin Rabbie (eds), *Hugo Grotius Theologian. Essays in Honour of G. H. M. Posthumus Meyjes* (Leiden, Brill 1994), 66.

In *Meletius* Grotius depicted God as the efficient and final cause of everything. He ruled the world by His laws. In describing the nature of God's legislative action, Grotius covered some very familiar ground. Only he who was "master of his own action", *dominus actionum suarum*, was able to control things and "of all creation only man and these beings we call rational spirits have the free choice".[44] On this freedom was based the role of human beings as masters over things, *rerum alianum dominum*, put at their disposal by God. Here Grotius also displayed his irenic opinions; the love of neighbour extended to the whole of humanity; all humans had been created in God's image (but there was a special bond between Christians).[45] Good people were also the best subjects. What this meant, Grotius explained, somewhat like Botero (though in a different key), was that "[a]nyone invested with authority is sacrosanct to Christians" and "everybody is urged to be content with the polity he has received".[46] Grotius emphasised the *internal* obligation that laws created: "it is not sufficient to do what is commanded, unless it is done because it is commanded".[47]

The God of *Meletius* was the creator whose works in the world became visible in the way human beings follow their natural inclinations. As Grotius put it in *De iure praedae*, only a few years before *Meletius*, God ruled the world by His will as expressed in nature. The first thing we learn as we observe nature, he then suggested, was that "self-interest" was its first principle of operation. "He who bestows upon living creatures their very existence, bestows to them also the things necessary for existence."[48] The first two natural laws were based on this, namely the rights of self-preservation and ownership of everything necessary for that purpose. The right of ownership came from God but its use was up to human choice. "For God created human beings [. . .] "'free and *sui iuris*' so that the actions of each individual and the use of his possessions were made subject not to another's will but to his own."[49] But self-interest was not destructive; on the contrary, divine intervention would ensure their harmonious alliance for the general good. As Grotius explained at the outset of the famous Chapter XII (which was later published as *Mare liberum*),

> God has not willed that nature shall supply every region with all the necessities of life; and furthermore, He has granted pre-eminence in different arts to different

[44] Grotius, *Meletius*, III § 28 (112). [45] Ibid., III § 69 (126).
[46] Ibid., III § 74 (128). [47] Ibid., III § 86 (132). [48] Grotius, *DIP*, II 21.
[49] Ibid., II 33.

nations. Why are these things so, if not because it was His Will that human friendships should be fostered by mutual needs and resources, lest individuals, in deeming themselves self-sufficient, might be thereby rendered unsociable?[50]

Grotius was neither the first nor the last person to argue that commerce was based on a providential design.[51] But he was in especial need of it so as to defend Dutch action against the Portuguese in the East Indies whose monopoly claims, he argued, violated nothing less than God's will. Attacking and dispossessing the Portuguese received divine sanction: "the law governing spoils, like the law of war, has its origin in a natural instinct implanted by God Himself".[52]

Another polemical religious work, *Ordinum pietas* (1613), was written hastily at the instigation of Oldenbarnevelt and the States of Holland.[53] Here Grotius defended the position of the States of Holland in a disputed university appointment, claiming that in the matter of predestination and grace, the positions of both opposing sides – Arminians and Calvinists – were well within what could be tolerated.[54] Its main point, however, was to assert the supremacy of public authorities over the church. In the Church Order of 1571 the State had been mandated to see to orthodoxy but given no role in church administration. In 1610 Oldenbarnevelt and his allies came to the conclusion that things had to change.[55] Every individual was responsible for his or her own conscience. But it must be up to public authorities to "decide on the faith of the church inasmuch as it is public".[56] They should be able to appoint ministers, enact ecclesiastical legislation and conduct ecclesiastical censorship so as to ensure

[50] Ibid., XII 302–3. On the providential design of trade as it appeared in *DIP*, see Ileana Porras, 'Constructing International Law in the East Indian Seas. Property, Sovereignty, Commerce and War in Hugo Grotius' *De Iure Praedae* – The Law of Prize and Booty, or "On How to Distinguish Merchants From Pirates"', 31 *Brooklyn Journal of International Law* (2006), 741–804.

[51] Jacob Viner, *The Role of Providence in the Social Order. An Essay in Intellectual History* (Princeton University Press 1972), esp. 27–54.

[52] Grotius, *DIP*, XIV (439).

[53] Hugo Grotius, *Ordinum Hollandiae et Westfrisiae pietas* (1613) (Critical ed. with English trans. and *De iure praedae* by Edwin Rabbie, Leiden, Brill 1995). On Grotius' theological writings before his imprisonment in 1618, see Mühlegger, *Hugo Grotius. Ein christlicher Humanist*, and Kniepel, *Naturrechtslehre*, 9–12.

[54] The so-called Vorstius affair led to the appointment in Leiden of a professor of suspected Arminian or even Socinian tendencies, and to Grotius' composition of *Meletius*. Nellen, *Grotius*, 136–7.

[55] Grotius, *Ordinum pietas*, 15. In pursuing this policy, Grotius was looking for an arrangement that would resemble the one set up in England and he did initially receive the support of James VI/I during the Dutch–English talks of 1613.

[56] Grotius, *Ordinum pietas*, § 118 (189).

that dogmatic disputes do not disturb social peace.[57] Those who did not accept the role of the state, Grotius wrote:

> should leave the Churches, for they are public; they should not look for stipends from the treasury, for the treasury is public, or if they wish to enjoy these public facilities, they should accept that the law is laid down publicly for them, too.[58]

Nevertheless, *Ordinum pietas* was a political disaster for Grotius, locating him definitely in Oldenbarnevelt's Arminian camp. His hope to mitigate this by a more moderate tract *De Satisfactone Christi* in September 1617 came to nought.[59] In the unpublished work *De Imperio summarum potestatum circa sacra*, which was written just before his arrest in August 1618, but published only posthumously in 1647, he expanded on points made in the *Ordinum pietas* in a more scholarly tone. This was a general treatise on the relations of church and state in which Grotius expressed his admiration of the hierarchical order of the Anglican church and the position of the king as its head.[60] Grotius insisted that ecclesiastical authorities, popes for example, were to play no role in secular government. It was for supreme secular powers to exercise their judgment in sacred matters, whenever they concerned the commonwealth, including by exercising jurisdiction on them and by appointing pastors. Of course, secular authorities were not entitled to legislate on "internal" matters. Only God knew the hearts of human beings; only He may have authority on them.[61] But the duty of obedience arose from the fact that public authorities were doing God's work on earth. "Therefore, the king's authority is also spiritual, insofar as it concerns religion, which is a spiritual matter."[62]

57 Ibid., § 135, 175–83, 202 (201, 227–31, 239).

58 Ibid., § 118 (189).

59 Grotius had himself been suspected of socinian tendencies – that is of denying the doctrine of satisfaction, that the death of Christ on the cross constituted adequate expiation for the sins of humankind. For the followers of Socinus, this remained a matter of God's grace. Hugo Grotius, *Defensio fidei catolicae de satisfactione Christi adversus faustum socinum senensem* (edited, with an introduction and notes by Edwin Rabbie & with a translation by H. Mulder, Assen, Van Gorcum 1990).

60 See e.g. Marco Barducci, 'The Anglo-Dutch Context for the Writing and Reception of *De imperio summarum potestatum circa sacra*', 34 *Grotiana* (2013), 138–61.

61 "Internal actions but themselves are not a matter of human authority, but are subject to the authority of God", Hugo Grotius, *De imperio summarum potestatum circa sacra* (Critical edition with introduction, English translation and commentary by Harm-Jan van Dam, Leiden, Brill 2001), I 3 9 (219).

62 Ibid., I 2 7 (203).

## The Search for Obedience: From Religious to Legal Obligation

The political environment around Grotius was hardly less confusing than the religious. The United Provinces had begun life as a "series of former Habsburgian provinces haphazardly thrown together".[63] Ever since the Treaty of Utrecht (1579) where the States of Holland and Zeeland had joined forces with five other provinces to separate from the Catholic south and to oppose their former sovereign, the country had lived through a bloody rebellion and open warfare, with Spanish troops pillaging its southern parts.[64] Although the United Provinces attained de facto independence and recognition by outside powers in the course of the 1590s, formal war continued until the twelve-year truce (1609–21). Throughout this time, Grotius had shown the greatest patriotic and republican zeal. Appointed historiographer of Holland at Oldenbarnevelt's proposal in 1601, he had contributed to the myth about the ancient origins of the "Batavian nation" and in writings such as the *Parallela rerumpublicarum* that circulated among his friends in the following years he had even compared the Dutch polity favourably to Greece and Rome.[65] In 1607 he had been appointed Advocaat-Fiscal (Solicitor-General) of Holland and Zeeland and in that capacity had written legal memoranda for the peace negotiations with Spain in 1606–8.[66] After the conclusion of the truce he

[63] Arthur Eyffinger, 'In Quest of Synthesis. An Attempted Synopsis of Grotius' Works in Accordance with Their Genesis and Objective', 4 *Grotiana* (1983), 81.

[64] The Treaty of Utrecht was a response to the Union of Arras of 1579 that laid the basis for the ten southern provinces remaining Catholic and restoring Spanish rule in them.

[65] For a discussion, see Tuck, *Philosophy and Government*, 160–4. The *Parallela* remained unpublished, unlike *De Antiquitate Reipublicae Batavicae*, which Grotius dedicated to the States of Holland in 1610. In this latter work Grotius narrated the history of the "Batavians" from the era of Julius Caesar, seeking to show "that the Batavians have had the same form of government, in which sovereignty ("*summa potestas*") resided with the States, and still so resides, for more than seventeen hundred years". Though it was often combined with royal power, it "was always subjected to laws" ("*semper autem sub legibus*"). Hugo Grotius, *The Antiquity of the Batavian Republic* (Jan Waszink ed. & trans., Assen, Van Gorcum 2000), 107. The authorship of the (unpublished) *De Republica Emendanda,* written sometime between 1598 and 1602, remains disputed, see Arthur Eyffinger, '*De Republica Emendanda*. A Juvenile Tract by Hugo Grotius on the Emendation of the Dutch Polity', 5 *Grotiana* (1984). See also Peter Borschberg, 'Critical Introduction', in Peter Borschberg, *Hugo Grotius Commentarius in Theses X. An Early Treatise on Sovereignty, the Just War, and the Legitimacy of the Dutch Revolt* (Berne, Lang 1994), 18, 19 n. 31.

[66] See Martina Ittersum, *Profit and Principle. Hugo Grotius, Natural Rights Theories and the Rise of Dutch Power in the East Indies (1595–1615)* (Leiden, Brill 2006), 283–357; Nellen, *Grotius*, 94–7.

became "in fact Oldenbarnevelt's lieutenant", including his closest advisor in matters of religion in the young republic.[67]

It was in this capacity that Grotius found himself involved in the constitutional conflict over the relations of church and state, defending the independence of Holland against the Calvinists. Nor was his role in the Dutch–English maritime conferences of 1613 and 1615 only to persuade his interlocutors to take a positive view on Dutch expansion in the East Indies but also to persuade James to support Oldenbarnevelt in his struggle against the Calvinists as well as maintain the old alliance with England in view of resumption of the war. The strategy of the *Landsavocaat* to seek alliance with Valois France too was found suspect by many of those who worried that the municipal aristocracy, to which both Oldenbarnevelt and Grotius belonged, were preparing the reinstatement of Catholicism under cover of tolerance. Oldenbarnevelt's support of the French king against the Huguenots was viewed as a wholly cynical turn to *raison d'état*. His steadfast support for provincial autonomy and the supremacy of government over the church and his effort to use military force against the Calvinist-dominated States General were read as treason, leading to his downfall and execution and Grotius receiving a life sentence.[68]

Long after his death, Grotius remained more famous as the composer of *De veritate religionis christianae* (1640) than for *De iure belli ac pacis*.[69] His writings show his concern to develop a religious foundation to state power and to individual rights that would not be dependent on contested dogmas but would still engage the world of internal obligation beyond utilitarian calculations.[70] Faith was particularly important, he wrote in *De iure belli ac pacis*, to uphold obedience "in the universal Society of Mankind" where the laws were few and "derive their Force chiefly from the Fear of a Deity".[71] He was keen to provide conclusive and universally valid proof of the rightness of the Christian religion and to return to an earlier and purer truth of Christianity. The same desire operated in his

67 Roelofsen, 'Grotius and the Development of International Relations Theory', 105.

68 A good account of the crisis of 1616–18 and Grotius' role in it is in Nellen, *Grotius*, 209–93.

69 Jan Paul Heering, 'Hugo Grotius' *De veritate religionis christianae*', in Henk M. Nellen & Edwin Rabbie (eds), *Hugo Grotius Theologian. Essays in Honour of G. H. M. Posthumus Meyjes* (Leiden, Brill 1994), 41. For a thorough study of the contents and the reception (including translations) of this work, originally written as a poem in Latin, see J. P. Heering, *Hugo Grotius as an Apologist for the Christian Religion. A Study of His Work De veritate religionis christianae* (Leiden, Brill 2004), 199–241.

70 For the theological underpinnings of Grotius' legal work, see further Hoffmann, 'Grotius', 63 n. 34 and Kniepel, *Naturrechtslehre*, passim.

71 Grotius, *DIBP*, II XX XLIV 6 (1031).

effort to develop natural law into an incontrovertible technique for discovering universal rules to bind human beings across the confessional divide. It is impossible to see in his legal writings a powerful statement of a philosophical position.[72] They provide instead a clearing house for arguments to demonstrate the way human beings were bound by laws that, while they were grounded on a divine source, received their substance from self-evident natural facts. As he wrote in the famous passage in the Prolegomena to *De iure belli ac pacis*, he wanted:

> to refer the Proofs of those Things that belong to the Law of Nature to some such certain Notions, as none can deny, without doing Violence to his Judgment. For the Principles of that Law, if you rightly consider, are manifest and self-evident, almost after the same Manner as those Things are that we perceive with our outward Senses, which do not deceive us, if the Organs are rightly disposed, and if other Things necessary are not wanting.[73]

This resembled the attack on dogma in the theological works. It also led directly to the famous response to the sceptic view of "Right" as "nothing but an empty Name" that was "instituted by Men for the Sake of Interest".[74] Grotius felt the power of this attack and responded by reiterating his faith in natural human sociability that nobody in their right mind, that is to say, nobody with reason, could deny.[75] Law was neither an aspect of religious dogma nor about fitting one's behaviour to utility or self-interest. As nature pushed humans to society, it compelled them to respect the rules that made social life between predominantly (though not wholly) selfish individuals possible.[76] It was precisely the ability of live by *rules* that distinguished human beings as creatures of reason.

> But it must be owned that a Man grown up, being capable of acting in the same Manner with respect to Things that are alike, has, besides an exquisite Desire of Society, for the Satisfaction of which he alone of all Animals has received from nature a peculiar Instrument, viz. the Use of Speech; I say, that

[72] "It was never Grotius' explicit aim to develop a theory of natural law," Pauline Westerman, *The Disintegration of Natural Law Theory. Aquinas to Finnis* (Leiden, Brill 1998), 131. Likewise, Welzel, *Naturrecht und materiale Gerechtigkeit*, 125–6 and Edward Keene, *Beyond the Anarchical Society. Grotius, Colonialism and Order in World Politics* (Cambridge University Press 2002), 42–3.

[73] Grotius, *DIBP*, Preliminary Discourse, XL (110–11).

[74] Ibid., Preliminary Discourse, III, IV (76, 79).

[75] See also Tuck, *Philosophy and Government*, 172–9.

[76] The "reason" in Grotius, Annabel Brett has written, is not so much a "tamer of passions" as a "recognizer of likeness, or alterity", 'Natural Right and Civil Community. The Civil Philosophy of Hugo Grotius', 45 *The Historical Journal* (2002), 42.

he has besides that, a Faculty of knowing and acting, according to some general Principles; so that what relates to this Faculty is not common to all Animals, but peculiarly agrees to Mankind.[77]

Here was the essential difference between Gentili and Grotius, the effort by the latter to create a sense of obligation to compel humans to act even against their immediate self-interest. It was true, Grotius wrote, that obedience to the law was also often useful and that violation "saps the Foundation of [one's] own perpetual Interest". But law "has not Interest merely for its End". It embodied an impulse to uphold society, an impulse that "brings Peace to the Conscience while Injustice, Racks and Torments". We seek happiness but learn that "[t]hat is happy indeed which has Justice for its Boundaries".[78] If Grotius rejected what he saw as Gentili's indiscriminate use of examples and neglect of the "rules of Equity and Justice", this was because he wished to proceed from mere control of external behaviour to the "very Foundation upon which we build our Decisions".[79] To clarify this Grotius made a distinction between internal obligations that consisted of what was "really lawful in itself" and things that were "only lawful externally".[80] Even if it was true that only the latter were subject to public enforcement, law as "moral science" included both – which is why, for example, after having given an account of the very permissive rules of warfare under the law of nations in Book III of *De iure belli ac pacis*, he wrote long sections on moderation (*temperamenta belli*) that seemed to deprive the belligerent parties of "almost all the Rights, which [he] may seem to have granted them".[81] Inner obligation would have the final word.

In his *Introduction to Dutch Jurisprudence* Grotius stated quite firmly the separation of law from coercion and the pursuit of interests: A law has "an obligation affecting even the mind; for obedience must be given not only through fear, but for conscience sake, and this is a consequence of all laws".[82] He then explained this by noting that

77 Grotius, *DIBP*, Preliminary Discourse, VII (84–5).
78 Ibid., Preliminary Discourse, XIX, XXI, XXV (95, 96, 100).
79 Ibid., Preliminary Discourse, XL (110).
80 Ibid., III X I 3 (1414). For a discussion of the complex relations between "internal" and "external" justice in *DIBP*, see Haggenmacher, *Grotius*, 572–5, 579–88; Daniel Schwartz, 'Grotius on the Moral Standing of the Society of Nations', 14 *Journal of the History of International Law* (2012), 130–6.
81 Grotius, *DIBP*, III X I 1 (1411). On the "*temperantia*", see III, X–XVI (1411–1518).
82 Hugo Grotius, *Introduction to Dutch Jurisprudence* (C. Herbert transl. London, Voorst 1845 [1631]), II II (4).

all beings seek their common benefit, and further what is peculiarly their own, and especially self-preservation; as beasts, by the union of male and female, seek the propagation of their species and the rearing of their young offspring.

But a human being,

while thus acting, is conscious in his mind that he does what is right; but, in as much as he is a being endowed with reason, he is inclined to be further guided by religion, and the rules of social intercourse with mankind, the foundation of which is to do unto others as we would they should do unto us.[83]

If natural law was authoritative (as it of course was), this was because nature had been created by God.[84] This lifted nature's pronouncements from the realm of mere physical "inclinations" to the world of moral obligation. Despite the great scholastic controversy about divine voluntarism and rationalism that preoccupied theologians such as Suárez greatly, and of which Grotius was well aware, he never gave up this point – even as he tried to write in such a way that neither committed voluntarists nor rationalists would unduly object.[85] With some exasperation, he wrote that the acts reason dictates as obligatory or unlawful "must, consequently be understood to be either commanded or forbid by God himself".[86] They *must* be so understood because otherwise it would be inexplicable why they would be other than mere counsel of prudence. But as regards the content of that law – the point at which Carneades' sceptical arguments were at their strongest – the theological frame could be set aside. All that was needed was to examine the features of the social world itself, the ways in which "many men of different Times and Places" had in fact behaved.[87] Both *a priori* and *a posteriori* methods were available and their results could now be identified as binding because they emanated from God. But this was not the God of the Calvinists. It was not a God of predestination and theocracy. It was a God who had only decreed the general frame within which human society had been formed and who had bound Himself to his

83 Ibid., II VI (5).

84 Unlike Suárez, Grotius did not read the Ten Commandments, the Old or the New Testament as natural law. They were part of God's "voluntary law" – a law directed to a particular people at a particular time.

85 The continuity between the "voluntarism" of his early work and the rationalism of *DIBP* is discussed by Haggenmacher, *Grotius*, generally and 501–7.

86 Grotius, *DIBP*, I I X 2 (151–2).

87 Ibid., Preliminary Discourse XLI (112). For a good disçussion of the sources of the two methods in Aristotelian rhetoric and Stoicism, see Benjamin Straumann, *Hugo Grotius und die Antike* (Baden-Baden, Nomos 2007), 110–27.

creation. Within that frame, people were entrusted with liberty and subjective rights that would indicate to them the aspects of moral virtue that enabled them to live as good Christians.

## Natural Law As Frame

Grotius objected to the Calvinist doctrine of predestination and defended the freedom of the will, but regarded that issue as something on which Christians could reasonably disagree.[88] Similarly, in his legal works he constructed natural law so as to allow human beings to enjoy the rights of personal freedom and property and to construct political communities in accordance with their will. In those self-made communities they could live securely under domestic civil laws that would push them towards obedience, virtue and happiness. From the safety of their societies and with emboldened consciences, these industrious people could undertake voyages to distant lands to conduct profitable – and lawful – trade with the infidel.[89] They could purchase and deliver slaves across the oceans,[90] and work on and occupy "any waste or barren Land" because "whatever remains uncultivated is not to be esteemed a Property".[91]

Grotius gave an early formulation of this view as he sat down in his office in The Hague to produce the long advocacy tract *De iure praedae* for the VOC in the context of the *Santa Catarina* affair in 1604. Here he was invited to defend the capture by Captain Jacob van Heemskerck of

88 See e.g. Johannes Trapman, 'Grotius and Erasmus', in Henk M. Nellen & Edwin Rabbie (eds), *Hugo Grotius Theologian. Essays in Honour of G. H. M. Posthumus Meyjes* (Leiden, Brill 1994), 81–4.

89 For the (then unorthodox) point about contracting with the infidel being just, see Grotius, *DIP*, XIII (434).

90 This, it appears, applies only to prisoners of war made slaves under the law of nations (the usual justification for enslaving Africans captured in slavery raids). In that case, the owner "has the Power to transfer his Right to another, in the same manner as the Property of Goods". Grotius, *DIBP*, III VII V .2 (1364). In these and other paragraphs Grotius uses the term "*servitus*", which covers many different types of personal subordination. However, in these passages, "slavery" is what is being indicated. See Gustaaf Van Nifterik, 'Hugo Grotius on Slavery', 22 *Grotiana* (2001), 233–7 and 241. By 1605, the Dutch had only occasionally participated in slave trade, the first large transport having been in 1606. After its establishment in 1621 the West India Company (WIC) refrained from slaving operations for nearly a decade. Nevertheless, the company seems to have sold close to 3,000 slaves taken from captured vessels in the period 1621–37. See Johannes Postma, *The Dutch in the Atlantic Slave Trade 1600–1815* (Cambridge University Press 1990), 10–25.

91 Grotius, *DIBP*, II II XVII (448).

the Portuguese carrack *Santa Catarina* in the Strait of Singapore in February of the previous year.[92] The hugely valuable cargo had been brought to Amsterdam for auction and the question of its ownership and, by extension, of the lawfulness of the capture, had arisen with the Amsterdam Admiralty Court.[93] The first question Grotius needed to address concerned applicable law. The events had taken place in an area where neither the Portuguese nor any other nation could exercise *dominium*.[94] It was a "controversy arising between claimants of sovereign power [whose] sole judge is natural reason, the arbiter of good and evil".[95] Although much changed in Grotius' views of "natural reason" in the twenty years between *De iure praedae* and *De iure belli ac pacis*, the principal substance remained as he set them down here – the view of natural law as a combination of subjective rights of liberty and property with a system of reacting to violations and punishing the guilty.[96] Both works were written under the horizon of war and translated a set of Roman remedies into four just causes: self-defence, defence of property, collection of debts and punishment of injury.[97] This was the "frame" within which individuals may use their liberty and enjoy their properties – "life, liberty and estate"[98] – in the knowledge that any violation will trigger a right punishment by themselves or by a public authority they have set up.[99]

*De iure praedae* was a work of great abstraction. To outline the content of natural law, Grotius produced a list of nine legal sources he called "rules" (*regulae*) from which he derived thirteen "laws" (*leges*). Everything began with divine will: "What God has shown to be His Will, that is

92 For a description of the events, see Ittersum, *Profit and Principle*, 30–43. See also Grotius, *DIP*, XIII (420–36) and van Heemskerck's letter at Appendix II, 533–45.

93 The cargo had consisted of e.g. textiles, porcelain, sugar and gold, and its value, over three million guilders, is said to have amounted to almost as much as the English government's annual budget. Fitzmaurice, *Sovereignty, Property and Empire*, 91 and notes therein.

94 This is the heart of Chapter XII of *De iure praedae* and of the tract *Mare liberum* based on it and published in 1609. For the latter, see Hugo Grotius, *The Free Sea* (Richard Hakluyt trans., David Armitage ed. & intro., Indianapolis, Liberty Fund 2004).

95 Grotius, *DIP*, Introductory Remarks, 16.

96 The continuity between the essential jurisprudential content in the two works is the core message in Haggenmacher, *Grotius*, esp. 176–80, 549–52 and 615–27.

97 Grotius, *DIP*, VII (102–4) and *DIBP*, II I II 2 (393–5).

98 Hans W. Blom, 'Sociability and Hugo Grotius', 41 *History of European Ideas* (2015), 593.

99 The specifically permissive character of Grotius' natural law is usefully discussed in Brian Tierney, *Liberty & Law. The Idea of Permissive Natural Law, 1100–1800* (Catholic University of America Press 2014), 218–47.

Law".[100] In creating the world, God had also designed the principles of the natural order, including the first among these, self-interest. From this it followed that "expediency might perhaps be called the mother of justice and equity".[101] This gave Grotius the first two of his laws: "LAW I. It shall be permissible to defend [one's own] life and to shun that which threatens to prove injurious," and "LAW II. It shall be permissible to acquire for oneself, and to retain, those things which are useful for life."[102] But if the view of expediency as a source of right sounded too sceptical, Grotius continued by claiming that self-interest in humans (unlike in animals), was accompanied by friendliness towards others that was "a sovereign attribute of reason".[103] This led them to society that could "be kept safe from harm only by love and watchful care for its component parts".[104] This gave Grotius his second legal source (after divine will) that he associated with "the secondary law of nature, or primary law of nations", namely that "What the common consent of mankind has shown to be the will of all, that is law."[105] And this had produced another set of two "laws" that were the obverse of the first two, namely "LAW III. Let no one inflict injury upon his fellow," and "LAW IV. Let no one seize possession of that which has been taken into the possession of another."[106] Without these four laws, there would be no confidence that Grotius saw as the "origin of human society".[107] They lay the basis for the first two subjective rights, of person and property, as well as the authority to vindicate them by just private and public war. The remaining two material causes for just war (collection of debts and punishment of injury) were received from two further laws following on the first four under "compensatory justice": "LAW V. Evil deeds must be corrected" gave the basis for the right of punishment while "LAW VI. Good deeds must be recompensed" compelled the fulfilment of obligations.[108]

The six laws and the four just causes constituted the legal order of the state of nature both prior to the establishment of civil communities and

[100] Grotius, *DIP*, II (19).

[101] Ibid., II (21–2). The degree to which expediency dominated Grotius' early work, in contrast to the legal formalism of *De iure belli ac pacis*, is highlighted in Brett, 'Natural Right and Civil Community', 39–44.

[102] Grotius, *DIP*, II (23) and Appendix A (500). [103] Ibid., II (24).

[104] Ibid., II (26–7). [105] Ibid., II (25). [106] Ibid., II (27). [107] Ibid., II (28).

[108] Laws V and VI corresponded to two kinds of obligation, Grotius explained, "voluntary" (i.e. debts) and "involuntary" (i.e. *ex delicto*). Both loan and theft require repayment. Ibid., II (29–30). See also Haggenmacher, *Grotius*, 177–8.

outside such communities, specifically in the High Seas.[109] This was a world of initially selfish individuals who understood that they needed to cooperate and recognise each other's reciprocal rights, a world where those rights could also be vindicated by war as necessary. But it was also a world of *law* where behaviour would be controlled by the threat of punishment in the form of just war. In the domestic legal order, punishment lay with the magistrates; in the state of nature, everyone – and in this case the VOC – had the authority to enforce and punish.[110]It followed that the attack and the capture constituted a justified retaliation against a law-breaker.

The determination of the just four causes of war in *De iure praedae* in terms of subjective rights was no accident. Grotius chose deliberately "the standpoint of a particular individual": "What each individual has indicated to be his will, that is law with respect to him."[111] This grounded the binding force of contracts and laid the foundation for the confidence and good faith that were needed to secure the operation of a transnational system of commercial exchanges.[112] In the commonwealth, respect for property and prompt enforcement of contracts allowed the sovereign to "sleep" while the subjects were busily engaged in commercial dealings. Through contracting individuals would choose the nature of their relations – after all, law was premised on that freedom of choice[113] – while their private transactions would benefit the state as well. Even civil community would result from a contract to protect rights, while the binding force of that contract was based on "the rule of good faith" (*Fidei regula*).[114]

[109] The rest of the "laws" (VII–XIII) dealt with the civil community, after the conclusion of the "civil covenant", the relations of solidarity between citizens (VII & VIII) and the role of magistrates, legal procedure and the hierarchy between laws (IX–XIII).

[110] See also Straumann, *Hugo Grotius und die Antike*, 34–40, 48–55. The fact that the right to punish resided originally with individuals not only founded the sovereign's and the magistrates' rights to punish citizens in the civil community but also that it might, *in extremis*, return to them.

[111] This was "rule" three, *DIP*, II (34).

[112] "Good faith", Grotius wrote, was "a veritable necessity in those farthest corners of the world where persons previously unknown cannot very well make themselves known save through their virtues", ibid., XIV (453).

[113] Kniepel, *Naturrechtslehre*, 20–5, 32–4. "For what is that well-known concept of 'natural liberty', other than the power of the individual to act in accordance with his own will?" Grotius, *DIP*, II (33–4).

[114] Grotius, *DIP*, II (34). The significance of the rule of good faith or *fides* in *De iure praedae* and its transformation in the later works into the *appetitus societatis* is usefully discussed in Hans W. Blom, 'The Meaning of Trust. *Fides* between Self-Interest and

Twenty years later Grotius had left the deductive frame of this early work. The question treated in *De iure belli ac pacis* had to do again with the permissibility of something that Christians were eagerly practising – namely war – but with a different starting-point. Expediency gave way to sociability. Like Gentili, Grotius critiqued earlier efforts to provide a foundation for a law "which is common to many Nations or Rulers of Nations". These had either failed to attain universal scope or to do this methodologically.[115] He felt that there was a need to give a good response to those who, like Carneades, believed that any idea of law among nations was "a mere Chimera", something "instituted by Men for the sake of Interest [only]".[116] For this purpose, he now turned to the notion of "sociability" (*appetitus societatis*) to which he gave a specifically legal meaning.[117] It may be true, Grotius admitted, that what is closest to us is our self-love and the inclination of self-preservation. But that was in no way contrary to a system of law and order; on the contrary, it was the best guarantee of it. Grotius began by the famous argument that "the Mother of Natural Law is human Nature itself".[118] And a part of human nature was a:

> Desire of Society, that is, a certain Inclination to live with those of his own Kind, not in any way whatever, but peaceably and in a Community regulated according to the best of his Understanding.[119]

In the 1631 edition of *De iure belli ac pacis*, Grotius would expressly associate this inclination with the Stoic notion of *oikeiosis*, as mediated through Cicero.[120] This was not designed to further Aristotelian

*Appetitus Societatis*', in Pierre-Marie Dupuy & Vincent Chetail (eds), *The Roots of International Law* (Leiden, Brill 2014), 39–58. According to Blom, the lack of *fides* meant for Grotius that the civil community was being corrupted and on its way to destruction, 'Sociability', 593–6.

115 Grotius, *DIBP*, Preliminary Discourse, I (75).

116 Ibid., Preliminary Discourse, V (79). For the argument that Grotius' primary concern in taking up Carneades was to refute the sceptics who were Grotius' contemporaries, especially the views by Montaigne and Charron, see Richard Tuck, 'Grotius and Selden', in J. H. Burns, *The Cambridge History of Political Thought* 1450–1700 (Cambridge University Press 1991), 515–22; Richard Tuck, *Natural Rights Theories. Their Origin and Development* (Cambridge University Press 1979), 58 ff., 72–5; Richard Tuck, *Philosophy and Government 1572–1651* (Cambridge University Press 1993), 196–201. For a critique of Tuck's views, see Tierney, *The Idea of Natural Rights*, 321–4.

117 Grotius, *DIBP*, Preliminary Discourse, VI (79–81).

118 Ibid., Preliminary Discourse, XVII (93).

119 Ibid., Preliminary Discourse, VI (79–81).

120 This has been a matter of widespread commentary. See Welzel, *Naturrecht und materiale Gerichtigkeit*, 125–6; Benjamin Straumann, *Roman Law in the State of Nature* (Cambridge University Press 2015), 83–119; Christopher Brooke, *Philosophic Pride.*

happiness (*eudaimonia*) or the orthodox Stoic *summum bonum* of moral goodness but to account for the idea of being bound by rules in a community with others.[121] For this reason, Grotius expressly took up Cicero's distinction between sociability according to the "first impressions of nature" that accounted for the right of self-defence and sociability associated with "the Knowledge of the Conformity of Things with Reason which is a Faculty more excellent than the Body".[122] The former expressed itself in the same way as "every Animal seeks its own Preservation" while the latter – a higher-level orientation – took account of the situation of humans in society with others whose preferences were alien and opaque but who nevertheless shared parallel instincts. Human beings were beings of *reason* who were able to determine their relationships by legal rules; it ought therefore "be dearer to us than that natural Instinct".[123]

Unlike animals, humans operated under rules, or as Grotius put this, they were "capable of acting in the same Manner in respect of Things that are alike".[124] This bound human beings to directives of action they should follow even when (at least in the short term) doing so might go against their immediate interests. Above all it called upon them to "Abstain[] from that which is another's and the Restitution of what we have of another's or of the Profit we have made by it". It created the "Obligation of fulfilling Promises" and "the Reparation of a Damage done through our own Default".[125] The capacity of "Judgment" that would seek out binding rules functioned beyond mere "Fear, or the Allurements of present Pleasure".[126] It showed us "the Moral Deformity or Moral Necessity there is any Act, according to its Suitableness or Unsuitableness to a reasonable Nature".[127] Here was the legal *proprium* – obligation that was based neither on interest nor

*Stoicism in Political Thought from Lipsius to Rousseau* (Princeton University Press 2012), 37–58. For a comment highlighting the distance of Grotius' natural law from orthodox, virtue-oriented Stoicism, see René Brouwer, 'On the Ancient Background of Grotius' Notion of Natural Law', 29 *Grotiana* (2009), esp. 10–22. Grotius' Stoic sources are also treated in volumes 22/3 of *Grotiana* (2001–2).

121 See here especially Straumann, *Roman Law*, 103–19.

122 Grotius, *DIBP*, I II I 1–2 (180–1).

123 Ibid., I II I 2 (181). Already in the *Introduction to Dutch Jurisprudence*, Grotius had distinguished between human beings as beings of reason, by referring to the capacity to obey "rules of social intercourse" consisting above all of a sense of reciprocity ("do unto others as we should with they should do unto us"), I VI (5).

124 Grotius, *DIBP*, Preliminary Discourse, VII (84).

125 Ibid., Preliminary Discourse, VIII (85–6).

126 Ibid., Preliminary Discourse, IX (87).

127 Ibid., I I X (150–1).

revelation. It provided Grotius' response to *politici* such as Bodin whose arguments were based on "what it may be profitable or advantageous for us to do".[128] And it distinguished him from the Aristotelian theorists of virtue. Grotius ridiculed the view of virtue as a mean: if justice was about respecting the rights of others, there was nothing mediate about it. Temperance or fortitude may affect the way we interpret rules, but not the call for obedience: you either obey or you don't.[129] Of course, Grotius believed that the grounds of law and judgment lay in divine enactment: God had created human nature and the rules of reason and had told us to abide by them. In other ways, however, his will – and hence theology and the theologians – played no role in discerning the contents of natural law. That had become a purely human affair.[130]

The character of natural law (*ius naturae*) as a frame within which human society would develop was further specified by Grotius' three-part definition of "*ius*" that he took over practically unchanged from Suárez. The first meaning was the old objective one, "that which is just". But Grotius defined this in an astonishingly negative, almost question-begging way as "that which may be done without Injustice", supplying the explanation that "unjust is "that which is repugnant to the society of reasonable Creatures".[131] In practice, this superficially Thomistic notion of justice was subordinated to the subsequent two meanings of *ius* as a subjective right and a lawful command. It simply told its addressees that they are all right as long as they do not violate anybody's right or break the law.[132] This was quite consistent with his

128 Ibid., Preliminary Discourse, LVIII (131).

129 Ibid., Preliminary Discourse, XLIV–XLV (114–21). See also J. B. Schneewind, *The Invention of Autonomy. A History of Modern Moral Philosophy* (Cambridge University Press 1998), 75–8. Grotius did not deny the significance of virtue *alongside* (strict) law. It founded many of the *temperamenta* that sought to diminish the harshness of the law of nations in Book III.

130 There has been much debate about the role of Grotius in secularisation. The conclusion depends on what one means with that expression. At the time, many saw his natural law as a secularising vehicle where God's role had become irrelevant for the daily determination of social morality. See Frank Grunert, *Normbegründung und politische Legitimität* (Berlin, De Gryter 2011), 77–91. See also Mark Somos, *Secularization and the Leiden Circle* (Leiden, Brill 2011), 383–437 (arguing that Grotius' "revolutionary effort to secularize natural law" was particularly clear in the "conspicuous and consistent idiosyncrasy of Grotius' biblical interpretation", 435).

131 Grotius, *DIBP*, I I III 1 (136).

132 See further Haggenmacher, *Grotius*, 462–3. The strikingly permissive character of Grotius' natural law, especially as it unfolded in *De iure praedae*, has often been noticed. It is true that in the later work he did sometimes confine natural law to

strong stress on a particular understanding of sociability, defined in the famous passage in the Preliminary discourse as "the Fountain of Right, properly so called". What it would mean was:

> Abstaining from that which is another's and the restitution of what we have of another's, or of the Profit we have made by it, the Obligation of fulfilling Promises, the Reparation of Damage done through our own Default, and the Merit of Punishment among Men.[133]

Clearly, this was a society whose members were above all desirous to secure their possessions and to punish those who intervene in them. The absence of reference to the common good or public utility is striking. The standpoint remains as it was in *De iure praedae*, that of the individual, called upon to act justly not in pursuit of some moral *telos* but so as to protect everyone's *suum*. The normative substance of society emerged gradually from the operations of a horizontal network of subjective rights and liberties.

## A World of Rights

The system of "Laws" in *De iure praedae* was intended to justify the actions of the Dutch East India Company. In the High Seas, it was permissible to defend one's life and property by violent action and to punish the perpetrator. These rights were made operative through the four just causes that the VOC would be entitled to invoke. The causes were united by the notion of injury (*injuria*): it was causing injury that the laws prohibited and injury meant "whatever is done in opposition to right".[134] The right was prior to the good and a violation entitled the right-holder (the VOC) to take action both in its own name as well as in the name of the United Provinces.[135]

provisions that were either mandatory or prohibited something so that things "that [were] merely permitted by the Law of Nature [were] properly without the Bounds of the Law of Nature". Grotius, *DIBP*, I II V (190). Here what was permitted appeared to fall outside the law altogether. Yet much of the law of nations that had to do with belligerent action was formulated as specific permissions of types of behaviour of which Grotius was critical. Such variations of language reflected the way Grotius often moved invisibly between enforceable (expletive) justice and standards that merely concerned the inner life of virtue, which he sometimes did and sometimes did not integrate as part of his system of law. See further Tierney, *Liberty & Law*, 233–47.

133 Grotius, *DIBP*, Preliminary Discourse, VIII (86).

134 Grotius, *DIP*, II (50).

135 In *DIP* the two types of just war are treated in a symmetrical fashion, as equally important parts of the just war theory. In *DIBP*, again, just private war is left in the

But the strongest formulation of the primacy of the right over the good came in *De iure belli ac pacis* where Grotius concentrated on the (second) meaning that he ascribed to the expression of *ius* as "a Moral Quality annexed to the Person, *enabling him to have, or do, something justly*".[136] This right was possessed by all human beings and resembled greatly the "right" put forward by scholastic theologians, especially as it included the competences of public power. But unlike the theologians, Grotius suggested that the substance of strict justice, enforceable by public authorities, was filled by such rights.[137] These rights had emerged from relations of commutative justice, and their counterpart was the duty to abstain from what belonged to others, restore any property unjustly taken and keep promises.[138] Although Grotius did suggest that governments were also to exercise distributive justice by giving some attention to the merits or needs of subjects, this was a secondary concern that was not to disturb the enjoyment of rights properly speaking – namely those that "consist[ed] in leaving others in quiet Possession of what is already their own, or doing for them what in Strictness they may demand".[139]

The comprehensive nature of *De iure belli ac pacis* – the way it extended from a commentary on the just war into a theory of legal sources, a discussion of property, contract, sovereign power and punishment – had to do with the way Grotius made lawful punishment, and hence the justice of war, dependent on violation of rights. If a just cause was constituted of a violation of a subjective right, then a full treatment of the matter had to contain a full discussion of the number and nature of the rights we have, how those rights were acquired and lost, how they were transacted and enforced in daily business, and how, precisely, reactions to rights-violations

margin and the whole discussion of the rules of a bilateral "solemn public war" are limited to public war. See also Haggenmacher, *Grotius*, 589. This, no doubt, reflected Grotius' changing interest from defending the VOC in 1604 to taking issue with the beginnings of the Thirty Years' War.

136 Grotius, *DIBP*, I I IV (138). The primacy of (subjective) rights in Grotius' system was also highlighted in his *Introduction to Dutch Jurisprudence* where Grotius defined "law" in its "particular" sense as either a right of merit that followed by distributive justice or a right of property based on commutative justice, V–X (1–2). See also Tuck, *Natural Rights Theories*, 66–8.

137 Or as Haakonssen puts it, "*Ius naturale* in the strict sense is, then, every action which does not injure any other person's *suum*, which in effect means that it is every *suum* which does not conflict with the *sua* of others", *Natural Law and Moral Philosophy. From Grotius to the Scottish Enlightenment* (Cambridge University Press 1996), 27.

138 Grotius, *DIBP*, Preliminary Discourse, VIII (86).

139 Ibid., Preliminary Discourse, X (88–9).

were to be conducted. These latter tasks raised, over again, the question about the relationship between property and sovereignty.

Grotius came to that question by differentiating between two types of subjective right, those he called "faculty" (*facultas*) and those he termed "aptitude" (*aptitudo*). The term *facultas* covered "Right properly, and strictly taken".[140] As strict law, it was enforceable by public authorities. Grotius explained that in making the connection between *facultas* and subjective right he followed Roman law by including under that term the power that one had over oneself (personal liberty) and those under one's tutelage (wife, children or slaves) as well as the *dominium* that one had over one's property together with the claims one had to those who owed something to oneself.[141] Every human being possessed such *facultas* by virtue of merely being human. The network of relations between such *facultates*, or their holders was covered by what Grotius termed expletive justice ("commutative justice" in the Aristotelian language), the horizontal system of inter-individual relations characterised by the exercise of such subjective rights on the one hand, and the duty on others to respect them.[142] Possession of a *facultas* committed everyone else to abstaining from interference as well as "Restitution of what we have of another's, or of the Profit we have made by it". It also covered "the Obligation of fulfilling Promises, the Reparation of Damage done through our own Default, and the Merit of Punishment among Men".[143]

A *facultas* was contrasted by mere *aptitude* that Grotius received from the Aristotelian notion of distributive justice, relabelled "attributive justice", governing the vertical relations between public power and the subject.[144] Or in Grotius' own words:

> Attributive Justice, styled by Aristotle ... Distributive, respects Aptitude or imperfect Right, the attendant of those Virtues that are beneficial to others, as Liberality, Mercy, and prudent Administration of Government.[145]

[140] Ibid., I I V (138). [141] Ibid., I I V (138–9).

[142] Grotius had already made the distinction between two kinds of rights and the corresponding forms of (distributive and commutative) justice in the *Introduction of Dutch Jurisprudence*, X–XIII (2–3). Even as he later moved away from the Aristotelian vocabulary, already here he ended in the conclusion that associated the law of nature wholly with the maintenance of subjective rights. Tuck, *Natural Rights Theories*, 66–7; Schneewind, *Invention of Autonomy*, 79–81.

[143] Grotius, *DIBP*, Preliminary Discourse, VIII (86).

[144] For a discussion of the Grotian terminology here, see Emmanuelle Jouannet, *Emer de Vattel et l'émergence doctrinale du droit international classique* (Paris, Pedone 1998), 167–71.

[145] Grotius, *DIBP*, I I VIII 1 (143).

While *facultates* were "perfect" rights that may be exercised against everyone and implemented, if necessary, by just war, aptitudes consisted of rights "of larger Extent" that had to do with the human capacity "to discern Things pleasant or hurtful" and to which belonged things such as

> prudent Management in the gratuitous distribution of Things that properly belong to each particular Person or Society, so as to prefer sometimes one of greater before of lesser merit, a relation before a Stranger, a poor Man before one that is rich.[146]

While the rights of life and property as well as their derivatives, rights based on commutative inter-individual relationships, were binding as strict law, entitlements based on attributive (distributive) justice, resulting from considerations of merit, charity, liberality and other such virtues, remained legally unenforceable, thus "law" only in a large and tentative sense.[147] But although they did not have any strong claim on the state, they were part of "law" as moral science that had the objective pushing subjects to virtue.[148]

To further illustrate this distinction Grotius added to the 1631 edition of *De iure belli ac pacis* the story of the young Cyrus called upon to adjudicate between two boys fighting over two coats. Cyrus decided to give the bigger coat to a bigger boy and the smaller coat to the smaller boy. In this he was corrected by his tutor. The task was not to attribute the coats in accordance with what Cyrus might have thought each deserved under attributive – that is to say, distributive – justice but to give each the coat that belonged to him, over which he had subjective right, for example, because he had purchased it. The task of the state was not to distribute property according to some moral principle (such as need) but to give effect to relations of *dominium* as they existed in the network of contractual relations

146 Ibid., Preliminary Discourse, VIII (87–8).

147 Peter Haggenmacher, 'Droits subjectifs et système juridique chez Grotius', in Luc Foisneau (ed.), *Politique, Droit et Théologie chez Bodin, Grotius et Hobbes* (Paris, Kimé 1997), 74.

148 The role that Grotius left for virtues in a society predominantly ruled by natural rights has been much debated in recent years, especially after Tuck declared that with his system of subjective rights Grotius had conducted an "open attack on the basis of Aristotelian ethics", Tuck, *Natural Rights Theories*, 75. See also Richard Tuck, *The Rights of War and Peace. Political Thought and the International Order from Grotius to Kant* (Oxford University Press 2001), 98–9. For a review of the debate, see e.g. Jeremy Seth Gaddert, 'Beyond Strict Justice. Hugo Grotius on Punishment and Natural Rights', 76 *The Review of Politics* (2014), 559–88.

governing the relationships between *dominii*. The king may not tax in order to distribute wealth among his subjects.[149]

Grotius' famous concept of subjective rights departed from the scholastic view of law as an instrument of universal justice where every thing and person would possess its determined place.[150] From now on, as also suggested in the *Introduction to Dutch jurisprudence* (1631), the work of strict law would operate through the disposal by private individuals of their subjective rights in accordance with their inclinations; it would be for the state to see that they did this by respecting each other's coterminous rights.[151] The very point of *De iure belli ac pacis* was to offer a theory where the just causes of war were linked to violation of rights that had emerged from such transactions.[152] By contrast , the imperfect social rights remain confined in the court of conscience, so that

> if a Man owes another any Thing, not in strictness of Justice but by some other Virtue, suppose Liberality, Gratitude, Compassion, or Charity, he cannot be sued in any Court of Judicature, neither can War be made upon him on that Account.[153]

It has often been noted that contrary to first impressions, Grotius, far from being a pacifist, in this way actually endorsed "the most far-reaching set of rights to make war which were available in the contemporary repertoire".[154] If every violation of subjective right was a potential *casus belli*, then the world was a dangerous place indeed.

> Among the first Impressions of Nature, there is nothing repugnant to War; nay, all Things rather favour it: For both the End of War (being the Preservation of Life or Limbs, and either the securing or getting Things useful for Life) is very agreeable to those first Motions of Nature; and to make use of Force, in case of Necessity, is in no ways disagreeable thereunto; since Nature has given to every Animal Strength to defend and help itself.[155]

Grotius followed the Stoics by restricting an unlimited right of self-preservation to *prima natura*, tempering it by the secondary nature of *recta ratio*; this is where the just causes came in. But as these causes made

149 Grotius, *DIBP*, I I VIII 2 (146–7).

150 See Jouannet, *Vattel*, 167–76.

151 See Grotius, *Introduction to Dutch Jurisprudence*, I I & III (2–3, 15–18) and comments in Tuck, *Natural Rights Theories*, 66–77.

152 See e.g. Grotius, *DIBP*, III I II (1186). As Brett notes, this view "makes the polis, the 'city', an agent of commerce and indeed itself part of commerce", 'The Space of Politics and the Space of War in Hugo Grotius' *De iure belli ac pacis*', 1 *Global Intellectual History* (2016), 9.

153 Grotius, *DIBP*, II, XXII, XVI (1112).

154 Tuck, *Rights of War and Peace*, 108.

155 Grotius, *DIBP*, I II I 4 [paragraph number missing in original] (182–3).

reference to the authority to react to violation of rights, primitive self-preservation tended to return by the back door.[156] In *De iure praedae*, Grotius was able to justify the VOC's aggression against the Portuguese on the ground of the company's natural right of self-preservation, now described as a just cause. In *De iure belli ac pacis*, that argument was generalised into a system of just war by conceptualising international society, or indeed any society, in terms of the horizontal system of rights to which corresponded a duty on everyone not to cause injury to them.[157] It was then to the elucidation of what rights we have that the largest part of Book II of *De iure belli ac pacis* is devoted. That his work has been seen as a general treatise on natural law follows from the extraordinary exhaustiveness whereby he undertook this task.[158]

## Law As a Moral Science

In the course of *De iure belli ac pacis*, Grotius mediated his individualistic rights-notion in many ways. Already making the *facultas/aptitudo* distinction had acknowledged the virtue of taking into account the needs or the merit of others. "Liberality, mercy, and prudent Administration of Government" were important aspects of sociability – even as they did not establish any public claim-rights. They were not merely counsel or desiderata about virtuous behaviour, but equally aspects of natural law that, he wrote:

> comprehends the Acts of [such] other Virtues as of Temperance, Fortitude and Prudence; so that in certain Circumstances they are not only honest, but of an indispensable Obligation. Besides that . . . Charity does also oblige us.[159]

These virtues were not the effect of contractual arrangements between free, property-owning individuals, and could not, therefore, be enforced by public authorities. But they were nevertheless expected to direct the ways in which public authorities were to govern. "It is one Thing to have regard to the Laws and another to consider what Justice demands."[160] When the authorities deliberated on how to punish offenders, for example, they were to take into account "the Nature

156 Straumann, *Hugo Grotius und die Antike*, 151–7.
157 See, again, Haggenmacher, 'Droits subjectifs', 98–9.
158 "Ces développements de théorie juridique générale sont en fait si fouillés et semblent être tellement faits pour eux-mêmes qu'on oublierait par moments – s'il n'y avait des rappels périodiques en ce sens – qu'ils doivent servir en fin de compte à déterminer des causes de guerre possibles", ibid., 99.
159 Grotius, *DIBP*, II I IX 1 (403–4).
160 Ibid., III IV III 3 (1274).

and Circumstances of Fact" – a task that "doth often require great Diligence, and the proportioning of Punishment" as well as "much Prudence and Equity". For this reason "in all well regulated Societies" those that were "judged to be the best and most prudent" were to be appointed magistrates.[161] All ruling was to take place through prudence and equity, broad standards of "Moral Science" that did not possess the same exactitude as mathematics.[162] The exercise of good government was thus included by Grotius in the third meaning of "*ius*" as the same as "law" ("*Lex*") that was further divided into "natural" and "voluntary" law, the former comprising a wide category of judgments by "Right Reason, shewing the Moral Deformity of Moral Necessity there is in any Act, according to its Suitableness or Unsuitableness to a reasonable Nature". Something might be *morally necessary* even if it did not give rise to enforceable rights.[163]

In composing *De iure belli ac pacis*, Grotius was well aware that he was breaking new ground. Gentili, for example, had given useful examples but his choices had been "faulty in ... Stile, in Method" as they had not been based on "the invariable Rules of *Equity and Justice*".[164] Law was not only random examples from the past. Instead, "when taken in its largest Extent", law was "a Rule of Moral Actions, obliging us to that which is good and commendable".[165] What Grotius aimed to do was precisely to provide a science of *moral* action that was voluntary rather than natural and which therefore could (and should) be directed in accordance with "invariable rules" and principles of social life that Grotius articulated in terms of individual rights.[166] One of consequences of this was the imprecision of the result. Moral reasoning, which covered also legal reasoning, produced only more or less persuasive arguments, the famous *a priori* and *a posteriori* points on which Grotius dwelt in the Preliminary Discourse to his mature work, and which called for contextual balancing. As he wrote, "[i]n Things of a Moral nature ... those Means which conduce to certain Ends do

161 Ibid., II XX IX 4 (974–5). Many more examples of prudential administration of punishment are given in Gaddert, 'Beyond Strict Justice', 566–74.

162 Grotius, *DIBP*, II XXIII I (1115).

163 Ibid., I I X 1 (150–1).

164 Ibid., Preliminary Discourse, XXXIX (110).

165 Ibid., I I IX (147–8). This was a little unjust towards Gentili who, as we have seen in Chapter 3, stressed that the use of historical examples was to be read from a "philosophical" perspective.

166 Annabel Brett, 'The Subject of Sovereignty. Law, Politics and Moral Reasoning in Grotius' in 17 *Modern Intellectual History* (2020), 628–32.

assume the very Nature of that End".[167] If we have a right – that is to say, a moral quality – we are authorised by natural law to do what is necessary for its realisation sometimes even against innocent persons, though the "law of Charity" might call upon us mitigate such effect.[168] Here two sets of individual rights (mine and of that innocent person) clash so prudential adjustment is needed.

In other words, different kinds of moral necessity entailed different kinds of duty whose relationship was not always obvious, as illustrated by the famous contrast between just war that was regulated by natural law and solemn public war (*bellum solenne*) addressed under the voluntary law of nations.[169] The latter often permitted action that was prohibited by the former. How was this possible? Was not natural law "so unalterable, that God himself cannot change it"?[170] To explain this Grotius divided the law of nations into two sub-types – "that which is truly and in every Respect lawful, and that which only produces certain external Effect after the Manner of [Civil Law]".[171] The former implemented the precepts of the law of nature and to that extent shared its binding character on consciences. The latter deviated from the law of nature for reasons of prudence or pragmatism. It allowed reprisals against innocent subjects of an unjust prince. For example, it was sometimes necessary to recover public debt from private merchants, especially if the danger of loss otherwise became too great.[172] This was also the basis on which third parties were allowed to refrain from judging the war's justness; to avoid that they might otherwise be "quickly involved" themselves.[173]

But solemn public war was not entirely dissociated from justice and equity. It is true that it had been "established by Nations" that both sides were entitled to kill their enemies and destroy and appropriate enemy property.[174] They were also entitled to take action against innocent subjects when this was dictated by military necessity: a war

[167] Grotius, *DIBP*, III I II 1 (1186). Or, "in Things of a moral Nature, what is necessary to obtain the End has the Force of Law", ibid., II V XXIV 2 (554).

[168] Ibid., III I II 2 (1186–7) and II I IV 1 (389).

[169] The latter type of war was "generally called *Lawful*, or *made in Form*", ibid., Preliminary Discourse, XLII (113); I III IV (248); III X III (1416). See also Haggenmacher, *Grotius*, 526–9.

[170] Grotius, *DIBP*, I I X 5 (155).

[171] Ibid., Preliminary Discourse, XLII (113).

[172] Ibid., III II II (1233–4).

[173] Ibid., III IV IV (1275–7). A good discussion of the law of nations is Schwartz, 'Grotius on the Moral Standing', 130–6.

[174] Grotius, *DIBP*, III IV IV (1275), III VI II 1 and 4 (1316–17, 1319).

against a nation was waged against all its members, including women and children.[175] But all of this was subjected to the famous *temperamenta* – calls for moderation, extensively detailed in Chapters X–XVI of *De iure belli ac pacis*. Here Grotius took away with one hand what he had given to the belligerents with the other.[176] A belligerent may indeed enjoy impunity for killing the enemy – but this was never "entirely innocent"; whether this was right internally was to be measured by the moral necessity as determined from the perspective of the objectives of the action.[177]

The distinction between internal and external duties did not – as it may seem – signify the separation of ("mere") morality and law. Both were regimes of *law* as a system of moral action, in the one case, the action was "lawful in itself", in the other it was "only lawful externally".[178] The distinction embodied Grotius' realistic acknowledgement of the legality of certain practices of warfare that had been accepted by European sovereigns, whatever their status under ideal theory. He rejected the pacifism of Erasmus as firmly as he had rejected the scepticism of Carneades.[179] But the distinction allowed him to take a critical standpoint towards the warring parties even when they acted under the law of nations and to recommend actions "which our Reason declares to be honest, or comparatively good tho' they are not enjoined us".[180] Grotius would erect jurisprudence as the predominant science of moral action, instructing rulers and subjects not only about their formal rights but also about virtuous behaviour, good mores and the sense of equity and appropriateness, items "which [are] the foundation of social life".[181] A Dutch patriot would also be a staunch moralist.

Grotius had little to say about just war under natural law beyond the way it authorised self-defence just as it did with animals. It was mostly

175 Ibid., III IV VIII–IX (1281–4). See also Brett, 'Space of Politics', 13–14.
176 Haggenmacher, *Grotius*, 572. 177 Grotius, *DIBP*, III IV V 2 (1279).
178 Ibid., III X I 3 (1414) and the long discussion of the meanings of the verb *licere* in IV II 1–IV (1271–7). See also Haggenmacher, *Grotius*, 579–88 (pointing out Grotius' adoption of the scholastic distinction between "forum externum" and "forum internum").
179 Grotius, *DIBP*, Preliminary Discourse XXX (106–7).
180 Ibid., I I X 3 (153, 154). Likewise, Preliminary Discourse, XXXVI (distinguishing two types of "what is lawful", namely "that which is done with bare impunity" and that which is "really blameless", 108).
181 Haakonssen, *Natural Law*, 27.

relevant for private wars.[182] However, with the unequal relationship it created between the belligerents, it seemed uniquely suitable for violence outside Europe. Here the just party – invariably the European side – would act as a judge carrying out punishment *in extremis* on behalf of "all Mankind". This applied not only to pirates and cannibals and "those who are inhuman to their parents" but to "any Persons whatsoever" who had been engaged in "grievous Violations of the Law of Nature or Nations".[183] Quoting Aristotle and Seneca, Grotius explained that legitimate violence was available against "unjust men and insolent Princes" promulgating such "public Decrees, that of any City upon earth should injoin, or had injoined the like, it ought to have been, by the general Voice of Mankind laid in Ruins".[184] This was a more noble type of violence than solemn public war; it looked beyond bilateral utility towards ideals of charity and justice. Depending on how it would be understood, it was neatly available to justify practically all violence that Europeans were exercising against indigenous populations.[185] Quite strikingly, Grotius allied expressly with Pope Innocent IV against Vitoria and Vázquez by insisting that it was by no means necessary that the just belligerent had been the object of injury; violence against "Men who are like Beasts" was consecrated not by civil but by natural law.[186]

By contrast, the rules of solemn public war applied in the ordinary business of European war; its basis of validity lay in utility (to avoid greater evil) and it emerged from consent.[187] Most of Book III dealt with the many ways in which the lawfulness of this type of war, waged under the law of nations, was only "external" because it went against charity or some other virtue such as equity or justice. Killing of innocent

[182] Grotius, *DIBP*, I II I 1 (180). It "arises directly and immediately from the Care of our own Preservation which Nature recommends to every one", II I III (397). Departing from his earlier work, Grotius now argued that self-defence did not extend to punishment in private war, II I XVI (416–17).

[183] Ibid., III XXV VI (1157–8) and III XX XL 1 (1021). The first Dutch settlements in the West (Guiana and Manhattan Island) were set up in 1621.

[184] Ibid., II XX XL 3 (1024).

[185] See Tuck, *Rights of War and Peace*, 103.

[186] Grotius, *DIBP*, II XX XL 4 (1024–5). Grotius accepted, however, that the violation must be "very heinous and manifest" and not caused by "weakness of judgment" or "ill education", II XV XLIII 2–3 (1027). Grotius did not, apparently, regard Indians as persons without reason and incapable of dominion, II XX X 1–2 (1105). Nevertheless, the transformation of the non-European into a "beast" repeats Gentili's racist trope.

[187] For a good summary of the legal nature, conditions and effects of "solemn public war", see Haggenmacher, *Grotius*, 571–8.

hostages, for example, was sometimes authorised by custom and "our modern Lawyers".[188] However blameworthy such action might be, it remained unpunishable under the law of nations mostly because the authorisation may nevertheless have offered an incentive to refrain from causing even more harm, provision for war captives, rights on enemy property and postliminium being the usual examples.[189] But against the wide authorisations under the law of nations to pillage, plunder and (even) rape, Grotius insisted on "Moderation": the mere external lawfulness of something was no guarantee that it was in accordance with the internal obligations imposed by natural law or "genuine" law of nations. Although it was allowed by strict justice to kill a man who has taken our property, "yet it is far wide from the Law of Charity".[190]

In this way, the concept of "law" in Grotius – the third meaning of *ius* – collected many types of normative materials with varying obligatory force. All of it was nevertheless aimed to influence conduct, if not necessarily by threat of punishment, then by critiquing it from the perspective of what was honest or equitable, virtues included within what was "lawful in itself".[191] Enforcement remained only a secondary, mundane aspect of the law.[192] In his early writings, Grotius had often linked the absence of virtue in nations with corruption and decline, and as ambassador of Sweden he attacked Richelieu's *raison d'état*.[193] He would also insist on virtuous government and the "prudent Management in the gratuitous distribution of Things that properly belong to each particular person or Society".[194] As a Dutch patriot, extolling the virtues of the "ancient Batavian nation", he believed that the very origin of human society was based on keeping one's promises. Deceitfulness struck at a basic aspect of humanness and the very order of divine creation.[195] But Grotius did not forget to highlight the practical advantages of compliance as well: "People which violate the laws of Nature and Nations, break down the Bulwarks of their future Happiness and Tranquillity".[196] The extraordinarily broad moral

188 Grotius, *DIBP*, III XI XVIII 1–2 (1455–6).
189 See Schwartz, 'Grotius on the Moral Standing', 131–3.
190 Grotius, *DIBP*, III XI II 1 (1422).
191 Ibid., III X I 1 (1411–14).
192 Haggenmacher, *Grotius*, 579–88; Jouannet, *Vattel*, 177–83.
193 See the discussion in Blom, 'The Meaning of Trust', 48–50.
194 Grotius, *DIBP*, Preliminary Discourse, X (87). Likewise, *DIBP*, I I VIII 1 (143).
195 See further Peter Schröder, *Trust in Early Modern International Political Thought, 1598–1713* (Cambridge University Press 2017), 92–104.
196 Grotius, *DIBP*, Preliminary Discourse, XIX (95).

science that Grotius offered his readers was simultaneously a science of successful government.

No doubt Grotius saw himself providing a realistic view of how a political community could thrive in a world of expanding commerce, colonisation and continuous war.[197] Legal obligation would bind subjects in their conscience, and enforcement was delegated to a strong public authority the nature of which changed somewhat on the way from *De iure praedae* to *De iure belli ac pacis*. The pragmatic interest in the former to authorise the violence exercised by the VOC in the colonies was replaced by the effort in the later to limit religious resistance to public power at home and to deal with "Licentiousness in regard to War, which even barbarous Nations ought to be ashamed of".[198] In *De iure praedae* Grotius had authorised private actors to punish rights-violators while in the later work public authorities had primary responsibility for ensuring that everyone could enjoy their rights in peace. The fact that no stable theory of statehood emerged from these works resulted from the Janus-faced character of the result: depending on one's standpoint one could see either a system of natural subjective rights or a hierarchical system of public authority.[199]

## Sovereigns and Subjects: *De iure praedae*

Grotius' legal writings reflect the extraordinary history and organisation of the United Provinces in the late sixteenth and early seventeenth centuries.[200] *De iure praedae* was conceived at a time of active warfare with the Iberian powers as the VOC was determined to break the Portuguese trade monopoly in the East Indies. To justify the company's acts of war Grotius needed to provide answers to a number of questions. How was it conceivable that a profit-seeking private actor could take violent action against a commercial vessel? What was the company's

197 This was not lost on the near-contemporaries who sometimes read *De jure belli ac pacis* as a contribution to the literature of "Fürsten- und Rathsherren-spiegel", Johann Heinrich Boeckler (1611–1672), quoted in Günter Hoffmann-Loerzer, 'Studien zu Hugo Grotius' (diss., Munich 1971), 37, 38.

198 Grotius, *DIBP*, Preliminary Discourse, XXIX (106).

199 The characterisation "Janus-faced" is from Tuck, *Natural Rights Theories*, 79. The absence of a theory of statehood, again, is discussed in Christoph Link, *Hugo Grotius als Staatsdenker* (Tübingen, Mohr 1983), 17–22.

200 "His ostensibly abstract argument regarding the political system of the Dutch Republic ... is in fact a partisan view dressed in a guise that should convince the public", Roelofsen, 'Grotius and the Development of International Relations Theory', 106.

relationship to the United Provinces and the status of the latter's rebellion against the Habsburg monarchy? To understand the configuration of public power and private rights as it emerged in the advocacy tract written for the Amsterdam Admiralty court, it is necessary to lay out briefly the situation in 1604.

In the Treaty of Utrecht (1579) seven rebel territories (Holland, Zeeland, Utrecht, Friedland, Gelderland, Groningen and Overijssel) had formed the United Provinces as a kind of loose diplomatic conference, led by the States General.[201] The union was less than a federation but more than a confederacy; the provinces each held their theoretical sovereignty under the de facto leadership of Holland. Resistance culminated in the 1581 Act of Abjuration that ended Habsburg rule in the north. As war continued, the largely Catholic provinces in the south remained under Spanish rule, while the north was divided between orthodox Calvinists and the more reconciliatory upper classes represented in the Provincial States.[202] In the breathing space between 1587 and 1598 as Philip II shifted his military attention to England and France the administrative structures of the States General were consolidated under Holland's strong man, Oldenbarnevelt. The confessional conflict subsided for a moment and the United Provinces came to be recognised by the other principal powers, France and England.[203] But its administration remained loose, and contemporaries often wondered whether there actually existed "anything resembling a 'state' in the United Provinces".[204]

A serious source of friction existed between the two heads of the state – the office of the Governor-General (*Stadtholder*), inherited from the Spanish period and in the hands of the Orange-Nassau family, and the municipal oligarchy represented at the States General by Oldenbarnevelt as the Advocate of Holland. As a young man, Grotius had celebrated the ancient liberties of the "Batavians" and throughout

201 Ibid., 106–7.

202 At one desperate moment, the States General offered the crown of the new state to France's Henri III and to Queen Elizabeth both of whom declined in order not to be bogged down in endless warfare with Spain. With the Treaty of Nonsuch (1585) – the first international act of the United Provinces – England agreed on military intervention led by the earl of Leicester, which, however, failed to introduce a decisive change the military–political situation. Israel, *United Provinces*, 219–30.

203 Ibid., 233–40.

204 Fernand Braudel, *Civilization & Capitalism, 15th–18th Century*, vol. 3: *The Perspective of the World* (London, Collins 1984), 193.

the crisis of 1616–18 he insisted on the sovereignty of the Province of Holland against the States General.[205] The conflict with the latter, and especially the orthodox Calvinists, would end with disastrous consequences to Grotius and his mentor. At the time of the *Santa Catarina* affair, however, the political and economic interests of the United Provinces profited from the lull in fighting, and a governmental system of consultation and compromise emerged so as to produce "an orderly, efficient federal state, organised and directed from The Hague, by Oldenbarnevelt and the States of Holland".[206]

Grotius' first efforts to give an abstract account of the origins of public authority were included in the defence of the Dutch rebellion and of the activities of the VOC in *De jure praedae*. Because the "primary and supreme power to make war resides with the state ('*respublica*')", it was necessary for Grotius to demonstrate that "the domain of Holland in itself constitutes a state ("*respublica esse diximus*")".[207] When he also stated that the state was, in the Aristotelian sense, a "perfect community", he meant that the prince's power had been received from it and that "the greater and prior power to wage war lies with the state itself".[208] But Grotius also took extraordinary care not to suggest that the state was something independent from those who had set it up. Following the Spanish theologians, he claimed that initially nobody was entitled to exercise civil power on others. "For God created man … 'free and sui iuris', so that the actions of each individual and the use of his possessions were made subject not to another's will but his own."[209] But as masters of their liberty people could also trade it in exchange "for equal acquisition of the necessities of life".[210] Public authority did not, then, as in Hobbes, stand starkly juxtaposed to a lawless natural state but arose from express and tacit "pacts":

205 See especially Tuck, *Philosophy and Government*, 157–69. In *The Antiquity of the Batavian Republic*, Grotius compared the Dutch system whereby the state was ruled by the administrators of towns with the Amphictyonic League in Greece, 112/113.

206 Israel, *United Provinces*, 240. For a good description of the operation of government of the United Provinces, see further Jan Glete, *War and the State in Early Modern Europe. Spain, the Dutch Republic and Sweden as Fiscal–Military States, 1500–1660* (London, Routledge 2002), 145–55.

207 Grotius, *DIP*, XIII (392). For the Latin, see Hugonis Grotii, *De jure praedae commentarius* (Ger. Hamaker ed. Paris, Thorin 1869), 268. Grotius here uses "*respublica*" and "*civitas*" apparently interchangeably. Annabel Brett, *Changes of State. Nature and the Limits of the City in Early Modern Natural Law* (Princeton University Press 2010), 134.

208 Grotius *DIP*, XIII (393).

209 Ibid., II (33).

210 Ibid., II (36). See also Tuck, *Natural Rights Theories*, 60–1.

the lesser social units began to gather individuals together into one locality, not with the intention of abolishing the society which links all men as a whole but rather in order to fortify that universal society by a more dependable means of protection, and, at the same time, with the purpose of bringing together under a more convenient arrangement the numerous different products of many persons' labour which are required for the use of human life.[211]

And so the commonwealth emerged "by a general agreement for the sake of the common good".[212] This was not something imposed on the state from the outside but from the agreement by the signatories to the pact. In short, "*lex* rests upon the mutual agreement and the will of individuals".[213] This meant, according to Grotius, (mis) quoting the Stoic Hierocles, that "[t]hat which is public should not be separated from that which is private".[214] Here is Grotius' response to the *raison d'état* theorists. What was useful or expedient, namely setting up institutions of public power, did not override that which was right. What was right was defined on the basis of what the citizens would agree to be useful for protection and welfare.[215] This was also a response to the Aristotelians: the nature of the commonwealth did not look only to its just purpose, but was received from the consent, however tacit or presumed, of its subjects. The state (*respublica*, *civitas*) was not an independent entity, even less a legal "subject". It was a legal arrangement between those who founded it. Its laws were binding because based on their will and administered by the "magistrates" they had chosen – an excellent description of the United Provinces, ruled by the fragile alliance between religiously inspired rebel leaders and merchant elites.[216]

In Grotius' telling, political community arose simultaneously with private property and commerce, each supported by the other.[217] Everything began with the physical seizure of land, "some activity involving construction or the definition of boundaries". Things that

[211] Grotius, *DIP*, II (35). [212] Ibid., II (36). [213] Ibid., II (40).

[214] Ibid., II (38).

[215] Ibid., II (38–40). See also Brett, 'Natural Right and Civil Community', 39–41.

[216] As Grotius described the tasks of the States General in the commerce of the Indies: "As one of their chef functions ... it behoved these supreme magistrates to take pains to ensure the careful observance of the covenants handed down by our forebears and consecrated by the oaths of princes, covenants which gave continuity to our sovereign form of government", *DIP*, XIII (396). See also Haggenmacher, *Grotius*, 539–41.

[217] Grotius, *DIP*, XII (319). This was natural as state-creation had the twofold objective of physical protection and economic management, II Prolegomena, 35–6.

could not be seized remained common to all – hence the right of the VOC to travel and trade in the areas where Portugal was claiming monopoly rights: "the sea is an element common to all, since it is so vast that no one could possibly take possession of it, and since it is fit for use by all".[218] That political community originated in land seizure, and "pacts" did not mean that subject had a veto in its affairs. "For a commonwealth, even though it is composed of different parts, constitutes by virtue of its underlying purpose a unified and permanent body, and therefore the commonwealth as a whole should be regarded as subject to a single law."[219] It is true, Grotius wrote, that in the natural state, one was first to take care of that which was one's own and only then another's. The formation of political community, however, changed the situation:

> in questions involving a comparison between the good of single individuals and the good of all (both of which can correctly be described as 'one's own', since the term 'all' does in fact refer to the species of a unit), the more general concept should take precedence on the ground that it includes the good of individuals as well.[220]

In the civil community subjects' rights become subordinated to the general good, managed by the magistrates over the heads of the citizens.[221] But they did not enjoy absolute power. The "flatterers" were wrong: "the prince exists through and for the state; the latter does not exist through and for the prince".[222] The long passages in *De iure praedae* where Grotius critiqued the Spanish king's failure to prevent his soldiers from carrying out atrocities and destroying the Dutch countryside justified the rebellion. It was actually quite common, Grotius wrote, for a people to shake off the yoke of a tyrannical prince.[223]

To show that the United Provinces were engaged in a just war against their former sovereign Grotius first needed to show that the powers of the supreme magistrate belong to him "only in the sense that he is acting for the state and has received a mandate from it".[224] With the situation in the United Provinces in mind he then added that "when the prince [i.e. 'supreme magistrate'] is absent or negligent, and when no law exists expressly prohibiting this alternative course, the magistrate

218 Ibid., XII (322). 219 Ibid., II (36–7). 220 Ibid., II (38).

221 Grotius did not operate with a collective notion such as a "people". The collectivity emerged as an aggregate or a computation of the forms of private good of the individuals concluding the pact. Jouannet, *Vattel*, 263–4.

222 Grotius, *DIP*, XIII (414). 223 Ibid., XIII (414). 224 Ibid., XIII (393).

next in rank will undoubtedly have the power not only to defend the state but also to make war".[225] Or even more – "he who abuses sovereign power renders himself unworthy of sovereignty and ceases to be a prince".[226] By supporting the Spanish exactions Philip had abused his power and "cease[d] to be a prince . . . convert[ing] himself into a tyrant".[227] For all such reasons the States of Holland had, by applying "hereditary principles", the right to declare war against the Spanish king, their former ruler.[228]

Moreover, as the States of Holland began the rebellion they did this not only as some organised group of rebels but as a state (*respublica*), carriers of some of the "marks of sovereignty" that, when engaged in the defence of such marks, take on the character of the political commonwealth itself. That was what "the domain of Holland" undoubtedly was.[229] But from where then did the powers of the VOC emerge? A particularly important aspect of the consensual basis of the commonwealth was the famous doctrine that the right of the commonwealth to punish came from the natural right of individuals to punish the injuries they had suffered:

> [J]ust as every right of the magistrate comes to him from the state, so has the same right come to the state from private individuals; and similarly, the power of the state is the result of collective agreement. . . . Therefore, since no one is able to transfer a thing that he never possessed, it is evident that the right of chastisement was held by private persons before it was held by the state.[230]

In undertaking war, the States of Holland were exercising a right that had originally belonged to every individual. But in areas where no public authorities were present – the situation in the East Indies – those individuals could again exercise it on their own behalf. The Portuguese

[225] Ibid., VI (98). [226] Ibid., XIII (399).

[227] Ibid., XIII (399–400). Here Grotius' arguments greatly resemble classical views about resistance to tyranny, and he does refer to Aquinas, Bartolus and Vázquez in his defence of the Dutch rebellion. See further *DIP*, XIII (412–18).

[228] Ibid., XIII (392–5). The States General were, according to Grotius, "ensure[ing] the careful observance of the covenants which gave continuity to our sovereign form of government", 396.

[229] Grotius, *DIP*, VI (96), XIII (392).

[230] Ibid., VIII (136–7). This was a doctrine both conservative and radical. The derivation of sovereign power from the subjects was standard in scholastic writings – but not so that individual powers (such as right to punish) would also be individually derived in the same way. See Brad Hinshelwood, 'Punishment and Sovereignty in *De indis* and *De iure belli ac pacis*', 38 *Grotiana* (2017), 7 and 1–16.

monopoly violated the private rights of VOC.[231] It was therefore entitled to wage "just private war".[232]

A counterpart to the right of the VOC to exert punishment was the duty on the part of the *Santa Catarina* – a private Portuguese commercial vessel – to suffer it even for a violation committed not by it but by Portugal. This followed from the derivation of public power from private rights; that the political community was an agent of the pact-making individuals meant that the latter could also be punished for the deeds of the magistrates.[233] A subject derived not only benefits but also responsibilities from being a subject. The money and the properties of subjects may always be extracted as penalties for the doings of public power – after all, "God Himself ... not infrequently punished the people for the sins of the princes".[234] Attack on the *Santa Catarina* was lawful because "the Portuguese, both collectively and individually, are regarded as enemies by the States General".[235]

Alongside vindicating its natural right to punish, the VOC was also waging "just public war". "A war is justly waged by subjects, in so far as such warfare is ordered by a superior".[236] The VOC had been ordered by the States General to take action against Portuguese vessels; its captains acted "as if they had been in command of an army on land".[237] Although Grotius' principal argument in *De jure praedae* related to private war, the secondary argument illustrated the interpenetration of public and private authority in his thinking. The company's private interests were inextricable from those of the United Provinces. A perfect match existed between the Dutch governmental system, the legal role of the VOC and the horizontal character

[231] For a good discussion of the nature and extent of the Portuguese claims, see Anthony Pagden, *Burdens of Empire. 1539 to the Present* (Cambridge University Press 2015), 158–65.

[232] The persistence of the right of punishment was an innovation – nothing of the kind was to be found in the scholastics. It was an argument that could be almost indefinitely extended to justify private violence by colonists, for example, encountering indigenous resistance. But it had also obvious implications for domestic peace and order, which is why, although it was not given up, it received a much more limited role in *DIBP*.

[233] See especially Hinshelwood, 'Punishment and Sovereignty', 14–16.

[234] Grotius, *DIP*, VIII (156, 158–9). See also Johannes Thumfart, 'Freihandel als Religion. Zur Ökonomischen Theologie in den völkerrechtlichen Entwürfen Hugo Grotius' und Francisco de Vitorias', 46 *Archiv des Völkerrechts* (2008), 263.

[235] Grotius, *DIP*, XIII (418). See also the even stronger language on the "connivance" of the whole Portuguese nation in the matter in *DIP*, XII (376–9).

[236] Ibid., VIII (175).

[237] Ibid., XIII (428, also 392, 419–22).

of Grotius' system of rights.[238] Waging war may be a sovereign prerogative but, as Grotius would famously later argue against Bodin, there was no reason why such prerogatives could not be divided between several entities.

Grotius expanded on his views on the nature and extent of public authority in the *Commentary on Eleven Theses*, written during the same decade as *De iure praedae.* The work was designed to refute Monarchomach ideas about the popular basis of sovereign power while justifying the Dutch revolt as a just war by the States General to defend their constitutional rights. The argument illustrates Grotius' adherence to the positions of the provincial oligarchy and his concern over the instability that ideas about popular self-determination brought into public life. Against Bodin, Grotius held that the constitution might curtail the prince's authority in many ways.[239] It was for example quite plausible that the marks of sovereignty would lie with the prince or that – the case of the United Provinces – they were divided between the prince and the States.[240] Each holder of a mark of sovereignty, i.e. the rights of legislation, judgment as well as the right to appoint magistrates and to decide on taxes, had the right to defend its authority and when it did so, it would receive all the remaining "marks" as well. That is to say, it would then become the sole sovereign for the purpose of waging war.[241] The right of taxation in the United Provinces lay with the States General. When the Duke of Alba had sought to raise taxes, the States were entitled to block this injustice: "So, the just war was undertaken in respect of [ this specific] power."[242] The rebellion was a just public war to the extent that it had been waged by the States that shared sovereignty with the Habsburg prince.

[238] See further, Haggenmacher, *Grotius*, 144–5, 226–30. The VOC directors also held political office in the towns and provinces. Ittersum, *Profit and Principle*, 247–8. This is why "as far as the States of Holland were concerned, the VOC was an arm of the state", Jonathan I. Israel, *Dutch Primacy in World Trade, 1585–1740* (Oxford, Clarendon Press 2002), 70.

[239] Grotius, *Commentarius in Theses XI*, Theses 1–2, § 16–21 (214/15–220/1).

[240] Ibid., Thesis 4, § 24–25 (226/7). Grotius accepts that this view "may clash with an axiom that scholars [read: Bodin] have laid down . . . namely that sovereignty is not divisible", but he then goes on to claim that even they accept the presence of aristocracies and democracies where the (single) sovereignty is in fact divided between several (the prince and the States) so that they can act only conjointly, Thesis 4, § 26–27 (228/9–230/1).

[241] Ibid., Theses 4 and 5, § 23, 37,40, 42, 43 (224/5, 242/3, 244/5, 247). The view that an uprising against a tyrant might actually constitute foreign and not civil war was also affirmed in *DIP*, XIII (430).

[242] Grotius, *Commentarius in Theses XI*, Thesis 11, § 82 (280/1).

A few years later Grotius returned to the nature and extent of public power in its relationship to ecclesiastical authority, putting in a more organised form the anti-Calvinist polemics in *Ordinum pietas* (in vain – Grotius had already been irretrievably located in the Remonstrant camp). In *De imperio summarum potestatum circa sacra* (1614), he associated "supreme power" (*summa potestas, summo imperio*) with "the person exercising authority" that has no superior among humans ("*quia superiorem inter homines non habet*").[243] The unorthodox focus on the *holder* of sovereignty was immediately supplemented by more conventional attention to the *content* of sovereignty as "supreme authority", more particularly "the right to command, to permit and to prohibit".[244] It was in the nature of sovereignty, he argued, to extend also to religious matters; indeed, there was no essential distinction between religious and secular matters to begin with.[245] This did not mean that the secular ruler was also in possession of sacred functions. The relationship between *suprema potestas* and the magistrates of the church was like that between a prince and a doctor: the prince's power over the doctor did not make the prince an expert in medicine.[246]

That the notion of public authority in *Commentarius* and *De imperio* had become much stronger than the one in *De iure praedae* is easy to understand. Grotius' concern moved gradually from commercial expansion to religious strife and popular sedition. The latter two works sought to refute Calvinist theories of resistance and derived the duty of the subjects to obey as a logical consequence of supreme power. In *De jure praedae*, Grotius had presented a natural history of property and statehood in order to support the VOC's right to punish the Portuguese. There was very little in that work on the nature of civil obligation, apart from the duty of the subject to suffer punishment for the deeds of the community. By contrast, civil obligation became quite central in *De iure belli ac pacis* while the role of private war was now relegated to the margin.

In *De iure praedae*, Grotius had defended the VOC's private right of punishment. Twenty years later, he situated the justice of criminal law

243 Grotius, *De imperio summarum potestatum circa sacra*, I 1 1 (156/7).

244 Ibid., 1 1 (156/7).

245 To make his point Grotius used scriptural sources, points of natural law and natural reason, opinions of philosophers and views and practices of Christians and pagans. He also claimed that the superiority of the secular sovereign over religious matters had been accepted by such Catholic authorities as John of Paris and Francisco Vitoria. Ibid., 1 14 (178/9–180/1).

246 Ibid., 2 1 (186/7).

firmly in the horizontal system of legal relations between private right-holders. Against those who believed that "Punishment proceeds as it were from the Whole or the Community, to a Part or Member of that Community" and that it should therefore be regarded as an aspect of attributive (distributive) justice, Grotius retorted that the fact that some were punished more severely than others did *not* follow from considerations of "merit", as it may seem, but from seeking equality between the offence and the punishment.[247] Punishment was a matter of commutative justice. Punishment resembled contract inasmuch as the right of punish emerged from the crime "[s]o that he that commits a Crime, seems voluntarily to submit himself to Punishment".[248] In an extraordinary effort to maintain the individualistic basis of his system, Grotius understood criminal law in terms of the criminal having made a voluntary choice to commit the crime and thus an "injury" against the victim. The right to punish remained the right of the individual victim that had "in all well regulated Societies" been handed over to the "best and most prudent [that had been made] Magistrates".[249] Criminal law had the same rationale as civil law – namely to enable the holders of private (natural) rights to go about their business and to organise their relations without external interference.

## "[T]he Law (especially that of Nations), is in a State, like the Soul in the Human Body"[250]

In *De jure belli ac pacis*, by this time working in exile in France, Grotius achieved the final formulation of his "contractual theory of absolute sovereignty".[251] Instead of beginning from God's will, Grotius now started from the nature of human sociability.[252] He now associated the argument in the *Commentary* with the story about the emergence of private *dominium*, again making no distinction between the rise of property rights and public authority. Because the point of the exercise was the protection of liberty and property, the end-result was a "Community of Rights and Sovereignty".[253] Private and public authority were intermingled in two ways. First, the motive for the establishment of public power lay in the

247 Grotius, *DIBP*, II XX II 1–2 (951–2). 248 Ibid., II XX II 3 (954).
249 Ibid., II XX IX 4 (975). 250 Ibid., III III II 2 (1250).
251 Martin Loughlin, *Foundations of Public Law* (Oxford University Press 2010), 75. For the conditions of composition of *DIBP* in part at the Senlis, in part at his house in Paris and in a country house outside in 1622–4, see Nellen, *Grotius*, 367–79.
252 Grotius, *DIPB*, Preliminary Discourse, XVII (93). 253 Ibid., II IX VIII 2 (672).

effort to maintain social peace by which Grotius understood a situation where "every one should quietly enjoy his own, with the Help and by the united Force of the whole Community".[254] This was a restatement of Grotius' legalism; everyone's attachment to their liberty and property will inspire them to understand that this requires the reciprocal honouring of everybody else's freedom and property as well. Secondly, the process whereby the pact was concluded – by "Right of *Prior Occupancy*" or an act of subjection by consent – differed normally in no way from the ways in which private property was gained: "Jurisdiction and Property are usually acquired by one and the same Act."[255] The juridical nature of the process was illustrated by the way it joined both *corpus* and *animus*: "Where there is no Will, there is no Property."[256]

Grotius remained vague about whether the act of seizure or the pact was the real origin of sovereign authority – this did not really matter because both were simply evidence of the presence of right-creating will. Everything was transferred, but how the powers then would be distributed between the different "magistrates" differed on a case-by-case basis.[257]

> For those who had incorporated themselves into any Society, or subjected themselves to any one Man, or Number of Men, had either expresly [sic], or from the Nature of the Thing must be understood to have tacitly promised, that they would submit to whatever either the greater part of the Society, or those on whom the Sovereign Power had been conferred, had ordained.[258]

The extent of political sovereignty was then not derived from the pact but from the nature of political community as the "most perfect of all Societies".[259] The constitutional form or the initial distribution of the "marks of sovereignty" may vary, even greatly. Some sovereigns possessed patrimonial rights, others did not. Many were bound by promises or alliances (and even unequal treaties) with other states. But sovereignty itself was invariable, connoting supreme power "whose Acts are not subject to another's Power, so that they cannot be made void by any other human Will".[260] In the same way, the state remained juridically

254 Ibid., I II 5 (184). 255 Ibid., II III IV 2 (457). 256 Ibid., II IX I (664).

257 See Hinshelwood, 'Punishment and Sovereignty', 19–20.

258 Grotius, *DIBP*, Preliminary Discourse XVI (93).

259 Ibid., II V XXIII (552); Jean Terrel, *Les théories du pacte social* (Paris, Seuil 2001), 103–7, 128–30.

260 Grotius, *DIBP*, I III VII (259). Or as Grotius put it, "We must distinguish between the Thing itself, and the Manner of enjoying it". Ibid., I III XI (279). Sovereignty may thus be divided with other states, limited by treaties or even by promises to the

the same even when its constitutional form changed. The choice between monarchy, aristocracy and democracy was something for politics or the political scientist (*politicus*) to deliberate. By contrast, the presence of statehood and the identity of a *civitas* was a legal matter, unaffected by such transformations.[261] Finally, though sovereignty and property arose from the same acts, they were not to be confused. What was acquired as "sovereignty" was "jurisdiction" either in a territorial or personal sense. This would be in the hands of the constitutional ruler(s) who were bound to maintain and secure it. This contrasted with property, which could also be transferred to foreigners without affecting the powers of jurisdiction.[262]

Although governmental sovereignty/jurisdiction was received from the people and it may be divided (even with a foreign power), there was no sense that it would be ever held by the people. Grotius distinguished between sovereignty's "common" and "proper" subject in somewhat the same way he had earlier distinguished between the *respublica* and the magistrates. The former was the source of law and the constitution. By concluding the pact, the people constituted themselves as a body of citizens, both a *civitas* and a *populus*, and decided on how the marks of sovereignty were to be distributed. But they did not rule. Instead, it was the proper sovereign, the prince and other holders of marks of sovereignty, who had the exclusive power to govern.[263]

Although the origin of public power lay in the people, in the practice of government, what rights the people enjoyed was determined by public authorities.[264] The people may be the historical or spiritual core of the *respublica,* but "it does not … follow… that the People are superior to the King: for Guardianship was undoubtedly designed for the Benefit of the Pupil; and yet it gives to the Guardian a Power over

subjects (these latter, however, may not be enforced against the sovereign) without this diminishing the extent of the power that "sovereignty" connotes. See ibid., II III 14 (296); 16 (300–5) and 21 (318–30). See further, ibid., I III XXIV (335).

261 Ibid., II VIII 2 (672). Its "spirit", the association with "common sovereignty", remains, Brett, *Changes of State*, 137–8.

262 Grotius, *DIBP*, II III IV 1–2 (456–7).

263 See further, Richard Tuck, *The Sleeping Sovereign* (Cambridge University Press 2016), 68–86.

264 Grotius, *DIBP*, I III VIII–XXIV (260–335). As Haggenmacher observes, the "common subject" of sovereignty enjoys only a fleeting, ghostly existence and there is no sense that states would be "independent" or "equal"; sovereignty could exist even when a state was a protectorate of another state. *Grotius*, 539–47.

the Pupil".[265] In the context of the long discourse where Grotius sought to prove that the people may never take government in their own hands Grotius made his notorious parallel between consent to sovereignty and consent to slavery.[266] There were many reasons why someone might wish to renounce their freedom – why could not a people do the same? They might be "upon the Brink of Ruin" and thus subordinate themselves to a more powerful sovereign. In fact, Grotius claimed that there had been nations "who for many Ages lived happily under an arbitrary Government".[267]

Concerns of public order were even more strikingly predominant in Grotius' almost total rejection of the Protestant theory of resistance that he still seemed to endorse in *De iure praedae*.[268] Having first affirmed that "all Men have naturally a Right to secure themselves from Injuries by Resistance", he immediately continued: "But civil Society being instituted for the Preservation of Peace, there immediately arises a superior Right in the State over us and ours, so far as necessary for that End."[269] There was no end to the "Mischief" that would follow in case the people were entitled to turn against their ruler.[270] For, as he continued, "if that promiscuous Right of Resistance should be allowed, there would be *no longer a State* but a Multitude without Union such as the *Cyclops were, every one gives Law to his Wife and Children*".[271] The contrast to the tract twenty years earlier could not be more striking. There, he had described the Dutch rebellion as a just public war with the United Provinces defending their constitutional powers against the sovereign – here, all sedition was condemned by an emphatic account of the secular laws, gospel and Christian practices. Even wars of liberation were condemned because they did not seek the "preservation of peace", the overriding concern of the political community.[272] The theory of resistance by inferior magistrates was all wrong: "All the civil Power, that

265 Horst Denzer, *Absolutismus und ständische Verfassung. Ein Beitrag zu Kontinuität und Diskontinuität der politischen Theorie in der frühen Neuzeit* (Mainz, Zabern 1992), 45–6.

266 Grotius, *DIBP*, I III VIII 2 (274).

267 Ibid., I III VIII 1 (264). The presumption, however, was that this was not the normal case.

268 For Grotius' early arguments against the "detestable practice of adulation which is unworthy of freeborn men", see *DIP*, XIII (412–28). For his transformation into more absolutist views in *De Imperio*, see Tuck, *Natural Rights Theories*, 64–6.

269 Grotius, *DIBP*, I IV II (338).

270 Ibid., IV VIII I (260–1).

271 Ibid., I IV II (338–9). See further II XXII XI (1105–6).

272 Ibid., II XXII XI (1105). See also Christian Skirke, 'Cum sensu imbellicitatis. Grotius und die Wiederstandrecht', 62 *Zeitschrift für philosophische Forschung* (2008), 567.

such Magistrates have, is so subject to the Sovereign, that whatever they do against his Will is done without Authority."[273] For the subject, nothing was left but to obey: "it is every Man's apparent Duty, who is reduced to the State of Servitude, either civil or personal, to be content with his own Condition".[274] Only a small opening was allowed: in "extreme and inevitable Danger" the subject may resist, though without arms "unless first assaulted".[275] No doubt the case of the United Provinces in mind the citizenry might be entitled to oppose a sovereign turned into a *hostis totius populi*, where he had abdicated his government, alienated or forfeited his kingdom or conceived the utter destruction of his people (the case of Philip II, Grotius now writes) or where that right had been reserved to itself by the people.[276]

The political community in Grotius' mature work was utterly committed to "the peaceful Enjoyment [by subjects] of their own Rights".[277] It was not just some group of robbers or pirates. Even under a tyrannical rule, the community would still remain that manifestation of legally articulated reason under which subjects recognise each other as right-bearers committed to solving their disputes by a centralised enforcement. The law was absolutely central:

> And a State ["*civitas*"], however distempered, is still a State, as long as it has Laws and Judgments, and other Means necessary for Natives, and Strangers, to preserve or recover their just Rights. . . [t]he Law (especially that of Nations) is in a State, as the Soul in a human Body, for that being taken away, it ceases to be a State.[278]

It was the law that maintained the continued identity of a state. This was so because the "peace" that was the objective of the state was not just any kind of system of government, of terror for example. It was the ability of the subjects to enjoy their rights without disturbance, and to bring violations to be adjudicated by public authorities. The point of government and the basic limit to ruler's authority lay in the peaceful operation of civil society, property and commercial exchange. When Grotius wrote that the law of nations was the soul of a state he meant the basic structure of individual rights and the duty of the magistrate to enforce them. The substance of the laws or the character of the

[273] Grotius, *DIBP*, I IV VI (354). [274] Ibid., II XXII XI (1106).
[275] Ibid., I IV VII (360). The "covenant" could not be understood "to impose on all Citizens the hard Necessity of dying, rather than to take up Arms in any Case", ibid., I IV VII (358).
[276] Ibid., I IV VIII–XIV (372–7). [277] Ibid., III III II 1 (1247).
[278] Ibid., III III II 2 (1249–50). Latin text, *DIBP* 673.

constitution were secondary, "political" matters.[279] The important thing lay in the founding of a state by individual right-holders of a common sovereignty that, even as it normally lay dormant, nevertheless provided the natural and conceptual condition for just government.

Such legalism was visible everywhere. Because the people had bound the ruler(s) to act in accordance with the constitution, actions in violation of it would be void.[280] If rulers acted outside their public function, when engaged in commercial buying and selling for example, they were bound by the law just like their subjects.[281] Immunity for acts carried out in public capacity followed from the fact that they were "looked on as done by the whole Nation".[282] Saying that the law was "in a state like the soul in a human body" meant that it created that unity without which the pact-making individuals would remain alien to each other and their needs and interest in constant opposition. The unity of the state did not reside in religion and obedience was compulsory "though we should even grant ... that there is no God".[283] Grotius sometimes referred to common utility but gave it no independence from the aggregation of the special utilities of the subjects. Something more was needed, and in the section that dealt with the extinction of states (and property) Grotius explained what that something was. Although states (now variably associated with the "people") consisted of "separate and distant Members", he wrote, they were nevertheless "united in Name" as having a "Constitution" or a "Spirit (*spiritus*). It was "this Spirit and Constitution in the People" that made it cohere in "a full and compleat Association for a political Life (*vitae civilis consociatio plena atque perfecta*)" and provided it "the sovereign Power, the Bond that holds the State together ("*per quod respublica cohaeret*").[284]

"Spirit" – "constitution" – "sovereign power". The political community in Grotius' mature work received an ephemeral unity that, although based on the "pact", ultimately ascended to a higher level.[285]

279 Ibid., II IX VIII 2 (672). 280 Ibid., II XIV II 1 (804).

281 Ibid., II XIV V (806–7) and VI 2 (809). See also II III IV (296); II III XVI (300–5). Grotius accepts that the ruler may exempt himself just like he may exempt any of his subjects. That is not, however, to be presumed but "must be gathered from the Circumstances". Ibid., II XIV II 2 (804–5).

282 Ibid., II XIV I 2 (803). 283 Ibid., Preliminary Discourse, XI (89).

284 Ibid., II IX III 1 (665–6), Latin text *DIBP* 322.

285 Thus, the state continues even when all of its founding subjects are dead, and while generations pass. The spiritual entity of the state dissolves only either when all of its subjects are destroyed or when the "Frame and Constitution of the Body is dissolved and broken" as when they are brought into slavery or "utterly deprived of the Right of Sovereignty", ibid., II IX V–VI (670).

There the law became the "soul" of the state as a spiritual entity. The duty of obedience was to that entity, represented by sovereign power that governed through legislative action under the constitution. Because that entity existed as a *spirit*, subjects were bound not only externally but also in the forum of their conscience.[286]

## Public Power and Rights of Commerce: Celebrating the Dutch Experience

The work of Grotius is an early moment in the history of state-building as well as in the conception of a civil society that existed alongside the state as an expanding economic market in which Dutch merchants and companies played an important role. *De iure praedae* had already reflected on the separateness as well as the close relations that existed between the country's political leadership and its mercantile elite. Provincial governments and principal cities were ruled by urban magnates (the *Regenten*) for whom "civil office [was] not only... an instrument of government but ... a guarantee of private wealth and power".[287] By occupying governmental positions, the members of this elite could organise massive economic operations such as the establishment of the VOC and channel protection costs with the company, by entitling it to wage war, so as to maintain its operations at a sustainable level and free the States General to finance technological innovations in shipping and agriculture and to secure efficient military protection at home.[288] Already in his early republican tracts Grotius celebrated the political wisdom of the Dutch urban oligarchy and its interests in trade appeared everywhere in his principal legal works. The extensive view of public authority in *De iure belli ac pacis* was in no way inimical to the morality of private rights; it now lay in the hands of the Dutch proprietary class. The private and the public, property and sovereignty, fed on and delimited each other. As Villey once noted, the system "*est parfaitement appropriée à procurer la sûreté des possessions établies, la sûreté des transactions,*

286 Brett explains that Grotius adopts the notion of the "disposition" or "spirit" that maintains the unity of the state in those passages from the Stoic notion of *pneuma hektikon* that makes several parts cohere in a single "body", 'Natural Right and Civil Community', 48–50. I have used the text to give a *legal* sense to that coherence, the way contract creates a *volonté générale* capable of being imposed against individual contractors on the basis no other criterion than their original, contract-making will.

287 Ellen Meiksins Wood, *Liberty & Property. A Social History of Western Political Thought from Renaissance to Enlightenment* (London, Verso 2012), 112.

288 See Glete, *War and the State*, 140–73.

*la tranquillité nécessaire au développement économique, [et] la limitation des violences*".[289]

The "rule of law" was an important aspect of Dutch economic and political success. The United Provinces had just emerged from decades of rebellion into a loosely organised but nevertheless efficient military–fiscal state. Its power lay largely on its economic strength founded on the controlling position it had exercised in the trade between north and south Europe. It had become a kind of world entrepôt by offering a stable and efficient regime for protecting property and facilitating commercial exchanges. Already early on in *De iure praedae*, Grotius had expressed his understanding that trust and confidence were key to a country's economic success. Quoting Quintilian on the need of owners to be secure in their possessions, he underlined that "[i]n this principle of confidence, so to speak, lies the origin of human society".[290] If such confidence was not naturally present, it had to be created by law, accompanied by a strong sense of obedience to authority. Law would ground and delimit everybody's rights and legitimise the institutions of government. In this way law would preside over the marriage of statehood and commerce that had made the United Provinces "self-sufficient in war-making and state-making, and combined regional consolidation with world-wide expansion of Dutch trade and finance".[291]

Grotius frequently expressed his admiration of the Dutch merchant class, describing them as "a people surpassed by none in their eagerness for honourable gain".[292] He was particularly keen to celebrate the value of wholesale trade, of which Amsterdam was the world centre. In comparison to the "humble" business of private shopkeeping, wholesale commerce, especially by maritime routes, provided such an indispensable service to societies everywhere that it was "absolutely necessary according to nature's plan".[293] This mercantile ideology was underpinned by a faith in the providential design that commerce helped to sustain. Grotius referenced Vitoria to the effect that God had located human beings in distant places so that they could by commerce satisfy their reciprocal needs: "The internal logic of creation itself had brought

[289] Michel Villey, *La formation de la pensée juridique moderne* (Presses Universitaires de France 2003), 557, 552–8.
[290] Grotius, *DIP*, II (28).
[291] Giovanni Arrighi, *The Long Twentieth-Century. Money, Power, and the Origins of Our Times* (London, Verso 1994), 140.
[292] Grotius, *DIP*, I (9). [293] Ibid., XII (356).

the necessity of free navigation and free trade into being."[294] Freedom of navigation expressed the "sacrosanct law of hospitality", realising a "design of Divine justice, that one nation supplies the needs of another, so that in this way (as *Pliny* observes) whatever has been produced in any region is regarded as a product native to all regions".[295] Whether these arguments were intended to satisfy the Mennonite faction among the VOC shareholders or were part of a larger effort by Grotius to explain why the law of nations also obligated in conscience, something like the providential view was needed to counteract religious criticisms of activities whose sole motivation seemed to be profit-seeking. Over again, Grotius took pains to convince his readers that there was nothing worrying in profit-seeking activities per se, that they contributed to the general welfare and the interest of the state.[296] It was surely right that the "individuals taking upon themselves the labour and peril involved" would receive a "just profit" from their actions.[297] This was precisely the point of which Grotius tried persuade James I of England in his effort to gain the latter's acceptance for the Dutch trading privileges in the East Indies.

### The Primacy of Civil Society: Property and Contract

Grotius' arguments about private property in *De jure praedae* and *Mare liberum* belong in the tradition of "economic individualism" that leads from Cicero to Locke and onwards.[298] They form the basis on which the rights of navigation and commerce are derived.[299] As Grotius put it in his early work, "[u]nder the law of nations ... all men should be privileged to trade freely with one another". He meant thereby the "primary law of nations" that allowed deriving "the principle of exchange" from the way nature had organised human societies so that trade had become a necessity among and between them.[300] Grotius could not be more enthusiastic about free trade and navigation; they

[294] Thumfart, 'Freihandel als Religion', 265.

[295] Grotius, *DIP*, XII (303–4). See further Ileana Porras, 'Constructing International Law in the East Indian Seas', esp. 756–74.

[296] See especially Grotius, *DIP*, XV ("The Seizure of the Prize in Question was beneficial", 462–97).

[297] Ibid., XII (362).

[298] Straumann, *Hugo Grotius und die Antike*, 72.

[299] "Freedom of trade, then, springs from the primary law of nations, which has a natural and permanent cause, so that it cannot be abrogated", Grotius, *DIP*, XII (356).

[300] Ibid., XII (354–5).

brought together people from all over the world, enabling the distribution of goods everywhere. They were part of that right of hospitality according to which "anyone who abolishes this system of exchange, abolishes also the highly prized fellowship in which humanity is united. He destroys the opportunities for mutual benefactions. In short, he does violence to nature herself."[301]

To avoid disturbing this busy world of exchange by outside objectives or moralities, Grotius claimed to have found in human nature a combination of selfishness and natural sociability that prompted humans to organise their relations in a peaceful manner even outside the structures of the state. Indeed, people possessed rights and contracts that were binding already in the state of nature. Public power was needed only to deal with excess of human ambition, and to implement the rights of sociability. But it did not destroy that antecedent community. Grotius did not say too much about this community, the "people" or the "nation", the group that had made the "pact". It did not disappear with the rise of statehood, however, but received legal recognition as the "common subject of sovereignty" that existed as a network of commutative rights outside formal governmental structures. While those on whose behalf sovereignty was exercised played no role in government itself, they were entitled to make use of their freedom and their rights as they wanted as long as they did not commit "injustice". The point of public power, we have seen, was not to impose any concept of ideal society. It was needed only for "leaving others in quiet Possession of what is already their own, or in doing for them what in Strictness they may demand".[302] The supposition was that properties had been *already* divided and rules about legitimate entitlements ("what in Strictness they may demand") had been set. Existing social relations were, in other words, to be left as they were and then implemented by the laws.[303]

Like the Spanish theologians, Grotius argued that private ownership arose through a customary practice of taking possession of things that, once firmly established, had come to be protected by natural law. In the earliest epoch of human history, Grotius wrote, all property was shared in common, not as joint ownership, but a reflection of the subjective right of everybody to use the common stock. It was ownership "in a

[301] Ibid., XII (303). [302] Grotius, *DIBP*, Preliminary Discourse, X (88–9).
[303] See also the comment by Stephen Neff (ed.), *Hugo Grotius on the Law of War and Peace. A Student Edition* (Cambridge University Press 2012), 3 n 9.

universal and indefinite sense".[304] Grotius then turned to the argument familiar from the Franciscan poverty dispute about the uses of consumables being indistinguishable from ownership. The use of an object creates an absolute and exclusive right in it. The class of things to which this type of *dominium* applied was then gradually extended from food and drink to clothing and other movable and finally immovable things such as fields and pastures.[305] The key to this process was actual physical attachment to an object – violent imposition in fact – in the case of land, its occupation, accompanied by some sort of general recognition. This process was then codified in the laws on private property which, although not strictly speaking based on nature, were nevertheless "patterned after nature's plan".[306]

It was quite important for Grotius to base the rights of property on physical seizure, occupation and work rather than some imaginary contract in the distant past. In this way, historical privileges and hierarchies could be justified by their mere presence at the time he wrote. The same history, Grotius stressed, had led to the establishment of private and public property, ownership and sovereignty. In both, what was crucial was human activity on the thing possessed.[307] Like most of Grotius' argumentation, this sounded both vaguely natural and vaguely consensual at the same time, allowing a construction of the rise of private property as an objective, historical process – a kind of natural history of humanity – as well as consent to that process, derived from the absence of efficient contestation of the consolidation of existing property distribution.[308]

Grotius expanded his explanation of the origin and status of private property in his *Introduction to Dutch Jurisprudence*. Everything had been

304 Grotius, *DIP*, XII (317), *The Free Sea*, V (21–2). See further Stephen Buckle, *Natural Law and the Theory of Property. Grotius to Hume* (Oxford University Press 1991), 35–7.

305 Grotius, *DIP*, XII (317–18), *The Free Sea*, V (22).

306 Grotius, *DIP*, XII (318). See also the explanation Grotius gives of the origin of private property in a kind of "necessity of ownership", based on the fact that that "some things were sufficient for the uses only of a few individuals", in 'Defence of Chapter V', *The Free Sea*, 87.

307 Grotius, *DIP*, XII (319–20).

308 Grotius illustrated this by Cicero's old example of theatre seats that belong to nobody, until a person occupies one. At that point, he has a right not to be removed from the chair that all else must respect. But is that a point about natural law (for example, the nature of theatre-going as a social activity) or about the consent of all theatre-goers? See *DIP*, XII (318) and *DIBP*, II II I 2 (421). For a useful discussion, see Straumann, *Hugo Grotius und die Antike*, 69, 170–1. The non-consensual character of this process is stressed in Tuck, *Natural Rights Theories*, 61–2.

common by nature. But there were things that could not be used in common, for instance because they perish or wear by use and were not available in sufficient amounts for all. Things needed to be distributed, and the "most reasonable" way this could be achieved was by everyone grasping what they could. Of course, Grotius put this somewhat more mildly: "every person has not only retained for himself and his family what he has acquired by his labour, but nations as well as individuals have taken possession of property which has been unowned and by this possession acquired property".[309] To the question about how it was possible that unchanging natural law could be modified by practice in this way Grotius responded as Vitoria had done:

> although natural law left everything undivided, because a division could not be effected without human means, yet nevertheless it has not forbidden such division, but has in some measure given rise thereto; and when the division is effected by human means, natural law still farther teaches that every one must be content with his own.[310]

Even as natural law had originally provided for shared ownership, it had also "in some measure" allowed private appropriation. As the number of humans grew and their needs became more varied, it entitled human beings to use their liberty to appropriate things to create *faits accomplis* no longer subject to challenge. In Part Two of *De jure belli ac pacis*, Grotius came back to the emergence, extent and use of the right of property, and its relationship to the right to punish. The gist of the argument was the same as in the earlier work. Again, the account oscillated between a natural history and consensual process.[311] The story started with freedom, understood as ownership of humans over themselves and extending to things they needed, "ownership as self-realization".[312] With the increase of needs, growth of knowledge and the corruption of mores, a violent and "savage Sort of Life" began. Ambition and jealousy led from the ancient ways of collective cultivation and cattle-raising to dividing up the cattle and the lands. Moreover, increased production created a need for the storage of produced things. But the inability to agree about the division of the storage – with the loss

[309] Grotius, *Introduction to Dutch Jurisprudence*, II III II (73). [310] Ibid., II III II (74).

[311] Jurisprudential debates on Grotius' theory of property have focused – often with great subtlety – on precisely whether it is consensual or natural. See e.g. John Salter, 'Hugo Grotius. Property and Consent', 29 *Political Theory* (2001), 537–55.

[312] M. J. Schermaier, '*Res Communes Omnium*. The History of an Idea from Greek Philosophy to Grotian Jurisprudence', 30 *Grotiana* (2009), 34 and Grotius, *DIBP*, I II I 5 (184–5).

of the simplicity of primitive life – a "certain Compact and Agreement" had to be made about the matter, and this took place "either expressly, as by a Division; or else tacitly, as by Seizure".[313] Again, the nature of this agreement was left vacillating between simple imposition and silent consent. To "fail to object to a situation is tacitly to accept it".[314] Grotius expressed this with characteristic ambivalence:

> For as soon as living in common was no longer approved of, all Men were supposed, and ought to be supposed to have consented, that each should appropriate to himself, by Right of first Possession, what could not have been divided.[315]

The way the process was interpreted by Grotius as agreement demonstrates the openness and historical character of his "reason". Reason, in a sense, takes cognition of a *fait accompli* and then assents to it, not because it positively "wills" it, but because it sees no other reasonable way of acting.[316] In the natural history of humanity, private property was the outcome of power relations between increasingly needful and ambitious humans.[317] And once the division had been attained, by whatever means, natural law itself came to underwrite it. From now on, all encroachment on established possession would qualify as injury.[318] If property found its way into the hands of someone else than the owner, then that person had a natural obligation to restore it notwithstanding any provision in civil law or the law of nations to the contrary. Restoration belonged to "the Essence of Property".[319]

[313] Grotius, *DIBP*, II II II 4 (426–7).

[314] Buckle, *Natural Law and the Origin of Property*, 42.

[315] Grotius, *DIBP*, II II II 5 (427).

[316] I take this to be the gist of the argument in Buckle, *Natural Law and the Origin of Property*, 35–52.

[317] This narrative is likely to reflect the Stoic distinction between two stages of human nature – the self-preservation oriented "*prima natura*" that humans share with animals, and the effort to act with reason and *honestum* at a more elevated stage. See Straumann, *Roman Law*, 98–128.

[318] That Grotius had the practical implications well in mind is shown by his immediately adding that the seas, however, were left free from division. For evidence, Grotius mostly referred to his *Mare liberum*, adding nevertheless that freedom of the seas applied also to goods and merchandise and that "no Body has a Right to hinder one Nation from trading with another distant Nation; it being for the Interest of Society in general". Grotius, *DIBP*, II II VIII 5 3–5 (443). As in *De iure praedae* he added the point about providence having induced commerce so as to bring nations into "society" with each other – a point that extended to a criticism of exorbitant taxes and customs fees over passage, ibid., II II XIV 2 (445).

[319] Ibid., II X I 5 (688).

Even as much of the detail of Book II dealt with themes that had been commonplace in scholastic property debates, the tone of Grotius' discussion was rather different from those of Vitoria or Soto. Grotius expressly rejected the scholastic view that prohibited violent action to enforce natural law. A ruler was entitled to punish not only pirates or cannibals but all those who "offend against Nature" – a view that has been taken to justify "a great deal of European action against native peoples around the world".[320] People who needed passage over lands or rivers were to be granted such passage, including the right "to settle in some uninhabited Land" when "just Occasion" required this. This applied also to merchandise as well as, apparently, to military forces on their way "to recover, by a just war, what is their own Right and Due".[321] Finally, such travellers (in fact, colonists) may also seize any uncultivated land in a foreign territory; but the property they would receive would nevertheless come under the authority with jurisdiction over such area.[322]

Gone is the Aristotelian framework that assessed the permissibility of mercantile activity by reference to its purpose. The question of virtue made no appearance.[323] All assessment boils down to two criteria, as Grotius explains in *Introduction to Dutch Jurisprudence*: the will of the parties and the equality of their relationship – that equality being measured by the standards of commutative (expletive) and not distributive (attributive) justice.[324] No extrinsic consideration is needed for a promise to be binding: for a transfer of property, all that is needed is "the bare Will, sufficiently declared".[325] This was not just a matter of positive law but lay in "the Nature of immutable justice".[326] The point of interpretation was to find out party will: "Nothing is more natural, than that the Will

[320] Ibid., II XX XL (1020–5) and Tuck, *Rights of War and Peace* (arguing that these passages came into the work owing to the way the Dutch had recently begun to establish settlements in the East and eventually West Indies), 102–8.

[321] Such passage could be subjected to reasonable conditions but not excessive taxation or other hindrances. Grotius, *DIBP*, II II XIII–XVII (439–49).

[322] Ibid., II II XVII (448). In his editorial note, Barbeyrac disagreed with Grotius on this point, noting that even uncultivated land "belong[ed] to the Body of the People", ibid., note (1) (448).

[323] That is, no appearance as "strict law" – any altruism is commendable, but never enforceable.

[324] In the *Introduction to Dutch Jurisprudence*, Grotius divided the natural law of obligations into two parts, "contracts (or "*Promissio*)" and "inequality which profits another" and thus brings about a duty of the other party, III I IX (272 ff.). See also Franz Wieacker, *History of Private Law in Europe* (Oxford University Press 1996), 234.

[325] Grotius, *DIBP*, II XI I 3 (701).

[326] Ibid., II XI IV (705).

of the Proprietor, desiring to transfer his Title to another, should have its intended Effect."[327] Any voluntary exchange is presumed valid unless there has been fraud or error – that is to say, unless the free operation of the will has been prevented.[328]

The question of the justice of professional business activity – the morality of buying cheap and selling dear – was not even posed by Grotius. On the contrary, he assumed the existence of a "common Right of Actions" that gave everyone the right to buy and sell; anything else would mean "the cutting off from Men of Communication of the Goods of their common Mother, the refusing one of the Fruits of the Earth that grow for all".[329] Grotius also insisted on the limited powers of authorities to tamper with commerce. For example, the right of trade applied to foreigners as well as nationals; "it would be an Injustice to exclude any People".[330] Everyone had the right to buy what they need "at a reasonable Rate". Only in exceptional situations, such as famine, commerce may be limited – again without discriminating against foreigners. All these rules existed by virtue of "natural Liberty, never taken away by any Law whatever".[331] Although Grotius did not exclude monopolies in certain colonial situations,[332] his starting-point was free trade both at home and between sovereigns or "between Persons at a Distance", i.e. in the High Seas. "For such Contracts are to be regulated only by the Law of Nature as also such Agreements as pass between Sovereigns, considered as such."[333]

The famous chapters on promises and contracts surveyed prevailing business practices carefully distinguishing rules that were part of natural law from those enacted under the civil law of particular nations and the very few that belonged to the law of nations. For example, Grotius gave much attention to trade by commission, enquiring into the powers of the commissionary or "factor" to give promises or to accept performances, remarking specifically that rules concerning the delimitation of the powers of the representative and his master "are founded upon the Law of Nature".[334] Taking up an example close to Dutch interests, he remarked that the master of a ship must naturally be entitled to make contracts on behalf of the owner company. The liability of the

[327] Ibid., II XI I 4 (701–2). [328] E.g. ibid., II XII X (739).
[329] Ibid., II II XVIII (449–50).
[330] Ibid., II II XXII (451) and III IV 2 (457). See also Buckle, *Natural Law and the Theory of Property*, 48.
[331] Grotius, *DIBP*, II II XXIII (452). [332] Ibid., II II XXIV (453).
[333] Ibid., II XI V 1 (709). [334] Ibid., II XI XIII (718).

company, however, must be limited to the value of the ship and its goods. Otherwise "Men would be discouraged from sending Ships to Sea if they were afraid of being, as it were, infinitely accountable for what the Master of the Vessel did." And, as he explained, this would be especially bad for "Holland, whose Merchandize has of a long Time mightily flourished".[335]

Grotius rendered the details of different types of contract, sale and barter, labour contract, letting and hiring, contracts for society or insurance etc. to civil law. Such forms may "be as various as the Actions whereby any reciprocal Advantage may be procured".[336] The law of nature knew nothing of their differences and covered them only at a general level. Its basic rule was equality between parties. But this, too, may be deviated from by agreement as long as "there be no Lie in the Case, nor any Thing concealed which should have been discovered".[337] The pragmatic reason for this rule – one of the few rules that Grotius rendered into "voluntary law of nations" – was that if one needed to prove the equality of a transaction, this would "by reason of the uncertain Prices of Things" lead to unending disputes as parties would be tempted to go back on bargains turning out less advantageous than foreseen.[338] Grotius accepted the theory of market value that presumed the full justice of regular trade relations. Again, like the scholastics, Grotius defined the just price as what was agreed between the buyer and the seller – excepting the case of fraud, coercion or other such absence of genuine will. In this way, commercial relations emerged into an autonomous system of normativity: value is decided on the market place, not by royal decree.[339] The law of nations would intervene so as to make unpunishable something that would otherwise, under natural law, have violated natural equality. Instead of the just price, the quality of the object now emerged as the standard to assess the legality of the transaction. Much attention was given to who was to bear the burden of proof.[340] The main rule of *caveat emptor* was accompanied by provision for fraud on the part of the seller. The duty to disclose matters that might affect the price concerned, however, only

335 Ibid., II CI XIII (719).

336 Ibid., II XII III 5 (734–5). They are treated at length in the chapters on "Obligations" in the *Introduction to Dutch Jurisprudence*, III (270 ff.).

337 Grotius, *DIBP*, II XII XXVI 1 (763).

338 Ibid., II II XXVI 1, 3 (763, 766).

339 See Wieacker, *History of Private Law*, 234.

340 As pointed out in regard to Dutch law at this time generally by James Q. Whitman, 'The Moral Menace of Roman Law and the Making of Commerce. Some Dutch Evidence', *Yale Law School Legal Scholarship Repository* (1996), 1866–8.

qualities of the thing itself and not extraneous circumstances. In the old example concerning the seller's knowledge about more ships laden with corn under way – non-disclosure might be a breach of charity, but not an illegality.[341]

Prices in the market fluctuated as a function of scarcity. Grotius dismissed the labour theory of value and took note of the variety of factors that affect the market's common estimation – "Plenty or Scarcity of Money or Commodities" or "the Loss we sustain, the Profit we lose, a particular Fancy for certain Things, the Favour we do in buying or selling what we should not otherwise have bought or sold".[342] The just price was the market price, with the exception of those rare situations where price had been legally fixed.[343] The value of money was determined no differently – money was, as he cryptically summarised, "sometimes worth more, sometimes less".[344] Grotius rejected vehemently the argument about the sterility or barrenness of money – after all, the "Industry of Man has made Houses, and other Things naturally barren, to become fruitful".[345] Usurious practices were prohibited but some agreements usually regarded as usury in fact may contain provision for *damnum emergens* or *lucrum cessans* and are therefore unproblematic. "Moderate profit" was allowed, and this included the Dutch standard – eight per cent for lending between citizens and twelve per cent for "trading People".[346]

This did not mean that subjects' property in the civil community was sacrosanct. There were many situations where the government was entitled to intervene. Above all, property was subordinated to the ruler's "super-eminent Right" or "eminent Domain" (*dominium eminens*) that allowed the ruler to delimit such rights "for the further tranquillity of citizens", as Grotius explained in the *Introduction to Dutch Jurisprudence*.[347] The ruler was entitled to order subjects to participate

[341] Grotius, *DIBP*, II XII IX 2 (738). [342] Ibid., II XII XIV 2 (744–5).
[343] Ibid., II XII XIV 1 (744). Grotius remained silent as to when that might be advisable.
[344] Ibid., II XII XVII (751). [345] Ibid., II XII XX 1 (753).
[346] Ibid., II XII XXII (760). See also the discussion of profit and usury in the *Introduction to Dutch Jurisprudence* where Grotius bases the right of profit on the argument from *lucrum cessans*, with provision for situations where "poor people or greedy people . . . are in time ruined with usurious interest". In Holland, this is provided for the limit of 6–8 per cent per annum between individuals and 12 per cent between merchants, III X (326).
[347] Grotius, *DIBP*, III XIX VII (1540) and II XXI XI 3 (1084) and *Introduction to Dutch Jurisprudence* where Grotius stresses that such delimitations did not violate the original natural right that had left the limits of properties undetermined, II II (74).

in the defence of the realm as well as to tax them as necessary for the common good.[348] But the government had no distributive powers; effect was to be given to property rights and private contracts irrespective of considerations of need or merit.[349] The right to confiscate was limited to two cases – punishment and where this may be done for "publick Advantage" against "just Satisfaction".[350] All of these limitations only applied to subjects; foreigners were not under the ruler's sovereignty so that, apart from the case of criminal punishment, their rights remained inviolable.[351] Grotius also accepted the traditional doctrine of necessity. In a situation such as fire or distress at sea, it was permitted to intervene with property, or as Grotius put it, the original use-right that had existed in the natural state was reinvigorated.[352] But the power of expropriation for public good against just compensation was wider that the state of necessity: the civil community was entitled to demand that its members pay their share of its functioning.[353]

## A World Seen through Law

Grotius was extraordinarily effective in providing a sense of autonomy and normative power to law as a "moral science" based on the nature of human beings as capable of reasoning from rules and principles instead of just acting out their interests or inclinations. In a world of expanding conflict, saturated by talk about the *raison d'état*, many people must have been ready to hear this. Constructing a persuasive argument about a natural law governing both polities at home as well as in the

[348] For the latter case, see Grotius, *DIBP*, III XX VII 1 (1556).

[349] The king had not "been appointed Judge of what fitted each [of his subjects] best . . . it was his Business to . . . consider[]. . . which had a just Title", ibid., I I VIII 2 (147).

[350] Ibid., II XIV VII (810) and *Introduction to Dutch Jurisprudence*, where Grotius gives the example of "making and repairing dykes" and municipal works for "enlargement or improvement", II XXXIII VII (204). See further, Susan Reynolds, *Before Eminent Domain. Towards a History of Expropriation of Land for the Common Good* (University of North Carolina Press 2003), 94–100.

[351] Grotius, *DIBP*, II XIV VIII (810).

[352] Ibid., II II VI 2–3 (434). As Buckle explains, this is not an application of any right of charity but an independent justification resulting from the nature and natural limits of property, *Theory of Property*, 46–7. The standard in regard to individuals is, however, extremely tight and seems to require a danger to life ("if not starvation, then crime"). See also Haakonssen, *Natural Law*, 28.

[353] This right of compensation was mitigated by the duty of subjects to participate in the discharge of public debt, Grotius, *DIBP*, XX VII 2 (1556).

international world of commerce and war was a work of great complexity, however. A number of factors needed to be considered – the readers' religious attitudes, the way they would receive views on commerce and colonisation, the facts and strategies of contemporaneous trade and warfare above all. Not everyone immediately approved of the result. Grotius was attacked both as a closet atheist and a utopian dreamer. If later readers have situated his approach between Hobbes and Kant, this has reflected his eclectic style, the complex mediations between law and rights, natural law and *ius gentium*, internal and external duties, just war and solemn public war, the defence of free trade and monopoly rights. Behind everything in his main work *De iure belli ac pacis*, written in exile as its author had already left active service for the Dutch government, loomed his practical experience as a counsel for the East India Company.[354] It is pointless to ask whether Grotius "really" fell on one or the other side in such dichotomies, whether he "really" was a naturalist or a positivist, for example. The power of his texts lies in the way they resist closure in such terms. Their open-endedness reflected the needs of practice that he was so well acquainted with as well as the underlying thesis about most law being the effect of subjective rights and what people choose to make of them.

There was a distinct "rule of law" in Grotius. It emerged from his constant reiteration that law cannot be reduced to prudential or utilitarian maxims; it pointed to an autonomous "reason" that enabled all humans to grasp the rules that bring them together in civil communities and account for the sociability that underlay the routines within and between those communities. In *Mare liberum*, first, and in Chapter II of Book II of *De iure belli ac pacis*, then, Grotius recounted the emergence of private property from originally common ownership as a consequence of increasing "ambition" but also a wish to live more "commodiously" and in order to receive "innocent Profit".[355] From the right of appropriation of things for private use and for exchange emerged the right to travel and to trade freely to foreign markets as well as to make investments there and to protect those investments by monopoly arrangements with foreign potentates – with the condition, however, that the goods thus purchased are disposed of at reasonable rates to customers.[356] It was precisely these latter principles on which the Dutch and the English had clashed in the

[354] This theme has been especially highlighted in the many works of Martine van Ittersum. See e.g. her 'The Long Goodbye. Hugo Grotius' Justification of Dutch Expansion Overseas 1613–1645', 36 *History of European Ideas* (2010), 386–411.

[355] Grotius, *DIBP*, II II II & XI (425, 438).

[356] Ibid., II II XXIV (452–3).

East Indies and on which Grotius appealed to the good economic sense of his royal interlocutor during the talks in 1613.

This immensely influential sketch of a global system of ownership and exchange was underlain by divine providence.[357] It applied everywhere and with respect of every people as an expression of the "Vertue of natural Liberty, never to be taken away by any Law whatever".[358] And it was enforced by the right of just war that would lie both with the private actor not having been granted what was due to it as well as the public authorities that people had agreed to set up to safeguard the full implementation of their rights. As Grotius stressed in his famous argument against Carneades, this was not just some coercive arrangement concluded with the view of utility or profit. It was part of an internal moral world of obligation, an aspect of the *habitus* of a law-abiding people respectful of the religious beliefs and legal rights of others, expecting that its own rights would receive equal respect by those others as well.[359] These were a people who look for life in prosperity by moving between the tranquillity in their private homes and the factories and trading posts they have established abroad. They have left behind whatever republican ambitions they may once have had (though they may sometimes look back with more or less nostalgia towards the hard times of war and state-building) and desire nothing more than to be ruled by wise and mild sovereigns watching over the communities within which they raise their families, manage their properties and humbly accept the rewards that providence will continue to thrust on them.

[357] Grotius, *Introduction to Dutch Jurisprudence,* III VI III (310–11); *DIBP* II II XIII (444).
[358] Grotius, *DIBP*, II II XXIII (452).
[359] This, I believe, is the sense of the argument from *appetitus societatis*, which in its more "adult", non-instinctive form combined self-regarding with other-regarding virtues in the uniquely human ability to act under rules. See Grotius, *DIBP*, II II I (181–5) and the debate on the Stoic sources in Grotius in Brooke, *Philosophic Pride*, 48–58.

# Part II

# France: Law, Sovereignty and Revolution

# 5

# Governing Sovereignty

## *Negotiating French "Absolutism" in Europe 1625–1715*

In a famous letter of 1 May 1625 from his Paris exile to a friend back home Grotius reported having met with Jean-Armand du Plessis, Cardinal Richelieu (1585–1642), who had told him that "in matters of state, the weak will always have to yield".[1] Although Grotius did not agree, the two men met several times in the autumn of the following year when the Cardinal invited him to take up employment in French service as director of one of the trading companies he was proposing to set up as part of his new office as Grand Maître, Chef et Surintendant Général de la Navigation et la Commerce de France (October 1626). No doubt Grotius felt flattered that the powerful Cardinal would need his counsel in the effort to concentrate French naval and maritime matters in his hands. Grotius was happy to talk with the Cardinal and even provided him with French translations of the charters of the Dutch East and West India Companies. But he refrained from divulging the instructions of the Dutch Admiralty. He also eventually declined taking a position in one of Richelieu's trading companies. Having just a few years earlier fled from his Loevestein imprisonment he did not wish to ruin his chances of being invited to return home by helping a competitor.[2]

Nor was Richelieu overly impressed by his Dutch conversation partner. But it had been completely logical for him to contact the famous author of *Mare liberum* and the beneficiary of a small pension from the French king (Louis XIII) to whom Grotius had dedicated his recently

[1] In Henk Nellen, *Hugo Grotius, A Lifelong Struggle for Peace in Church and State 1583–1645* (Leiden, Brill 2014), 329 n. 79.

[2] See further, Erik Thompson, 'France's Grotian Moment. Hugo Grotius and Cardinal Richelieu's Commercial Statecraft', 21 *French History* (2007), 377–94.

published *De iure belli ac pacis*. Freedom of the seas was completely in line with Richelieu's anti-Habsburg policy. It gave elaborate legal basis to the French refusal to recognise the Spanish claim of monopoly of access to resources in America. It was also useful as an argument against English and Dutch hegemony around the oceans and gave support to the strategy of engaging French merchants and financers in a wide-ranging policy of naval renewal. Ability to conduct massive naval operations was also imperative for the final suppression of the Huguenots who were controlling maritime traffic in the North Sea and capturing French and Spanish vessels from La Rochelle with virtual impunity.[3] Above all, however, as the Cardinal would recognise in his *Testament politique,* he had recently come to understand that French power depended on its economic wealth and that wealth, again, was very largely a function of the efficiency of the organisation of France's foreign and colonial trade.[4]

Richelieu's objective was to re-establish France as a great power and the leader of Christianity after decades of religious civil war. His efforts took place in the context of intense military and commercial rivalry and against fierce domestic opposition. The murder of Henri IV by a Catholic zealot in 1610 had interrupted the consolidation of central power, and Sully and the regent, Maria de' Medici, had failed to prevent the re-emergence of noble factions and rivalries. The regency regime's Spanish policy threatened the religious equilibrium attained by the edict of Nantes (1598) and the great nobles resisted violently efforts to tamper with their rights and privileges.[5] Richelieu was determined to crush both noble and Protestant opposition. But he was also aware that it was impossible to re-establish French naval power and the conditions of commerce and colonisation without cooperation from important actors in French society. However absolute the powers of his king, they were insufficient for building a strong state without enlisting the assistance of the holders of customary privileges.

[3] Nellen, *Hugo Grotius*, 314.

[4] Richelieu, *Testament politique* (A. Teyssier ed., Paris, Perrin 2011), II 6–7 (293–332). For a still-useful discussion of Richelieu's views on economic policy, see Henri Hauser, *La pensée et l'action économiques du Cardinal de Richelieu* (Presses Universitaires de France 1944). See also Lucas Alexandre Boiteux, *Richelieu, "grand maître de la navigation et du commerce de France"* (Paris, CNRS 1955), 185–220.

[5] For the revolt led by the king's brother Gaston, duke of Orleans, and the formidable duke of Montmorency, in 1631–2, see e.g. Roland Mousnier, *L'homme rouge ou la vie du Cardinal Richelieu* (Paris, Laffont 1992), 441–2; Pierre Castagnos, *Richelieu face à la mer (De mémoire d'homme. L'histoire)* (Éditions Ouest-France 1989), 147–53.

This chapter has three parts. The first lays out the intellectual frame developed by jurists and writers of the *raison d'état*, together with ideas about "sovereignty" and "government" by the Angevin lawyer Jean Bodin (1530–1596). The view of France as a system of private ordering and a participatory enterprise was developed by the judge and *avocat* Charles Loyseau (1566–1627) and skilfully operated by the powerful controller-general of Louis XIV, Jean-Baptiste Colbert (1619–1683). The second part discusses Colbert's view of commerce as war by other means and engages the dynastic–legal arguments made by Louis XIV to support the search for military *gloire* in his European neighbourhood. The third part examines the aftermath of the failure of the Sun King's belligerent foreign policy, especially the devastation it created in France itself. At that time, widely admired and well-positioned lawyers such as Jean Domat (1625–1699) and François d'Aguesseau (1688–1751) began to think anew about the virtues to be cultivated and interests to be upheld in order to accommodate French greatness with peaceful European order. The Peace of Utrecht (1713) coincided with the end of the long reign of the Sun King and triggered diplomats such as François de Callières (1645–717) to reflect on European foreign policy practices generally, but also legal practices, for which he reserved a definite but modest role.

## Statehood

At the heart of Richelieu's political thinking lay the notion of the "state". The expression itself was not new. Since late-medieval times, it had been connected as an adjective to the *regnum* or the regent himself, describing the condition of the realm or the status of the king (*status regni*, *status Regis*, *état de France*, *état du prince*).[6] This did not mean that no notion

[6] For the use of the notion of "state" in France from the late Middle Ages into the late seventeenth century, see the very exhaustive 'Introduction' by Christian Lazzeri to Henri de Rohan, *De l'intérêt des princes et des Etats de la Chrétienté* (Christian Lazzeri ed., Presses Universitaires de France 1995), 43–52, 120–1 as well as James B. Collins, *The State in Early Modern France* (Cambridge University Press 2009), 3–5, 8–35. Howell A. Lloyd, summarises the trends in French sixteenth-century historical debates as follows: "Thus, writers of history . . . made what they termed 'the state' a principal object of their thought. They interpreted that term differently; and, taken together, their writings scarcely presented their contemporaries with a coherent view of the source of political authority. . . . Yet all of these writers . . . [saw the] political entity that was France as a unique association of the universal and the particular, enduring in its just institutions, an actualization of principles that were as old as the Greeks." *The State, France, and the Sixteenth Century* (London, Allen & Unwin 1983), 515 and

of corporate entity had existed before the seventeenth century. By the time Louis XI ascended the throne in 1461 the crown of France had, in monarchic iconography, come to represent the state as an entity with dignity independent from its ruler.[7] The same connotation arose from standard recourse to expressions such as public good or public utility.[8] After the end of the religious wars, Henri IV would preside over the warring factions, as illustrated by the imposition of the Treaty of Vervins and the Edict of Nantes, in the name of the state, his person ambiguously internalising that collective notion.[9] Bodin still referred to the corporate entity as *république* and used "state" (*estat*) as a reference for its condition (*l'estat de la république*). For obvious reasons – owing to its republican implications – that expression was soon replaced by the "state" (*état*) as the name for the entity itself.[10]

The separate identity and temporal duration of this corporate entity became concrete for the contemporaries in the first decades of the seventeenth century by the consolidation of the standing administration of justice and finances.[11] The fact that magistrates and other officers continued their office beyond the physical life of the king and that the debts of the deceased ruler devolved to his successor further highlighted the reality of an autonomous statehood. And yet there was much in the life of Frenchmen that worked against this impression. Many of the provinces had only recently become part of the realm (Guyenne 1451, Burgundy 1477, Provence 1482 and Brittany 1532) and all had deeply

further 146–68. For two in-depth discussions on this point, see e.g. Quentin Skinner, 'From the State of Princes to the Person of the State', in Quentin Skinner, *Visions of Politics*, vol. II: *Renaissance Virtues* (Cambridge University Press 2002), 368–413, 370–1, 388–9 and Marcel Gauchet, *La révolution moderne. L'avénement de la démocratie I* (Paris, Gallimard 2007), 77–98.

7 Jean-Marie Carbasse & Guillaume Leyte, *L'état royal, XIIe–XVIIIe siècle. Une anthologie* (Presses Universitaires de France 2004), 109–10.

8 Lazzeri, 'Introduction', 44–6. See further Eric Gojosso, *Le concept de république en France (xvie–xviiie siècle)* (Presses Universitaires d'Aix-Marseille 1998), 29–34 (stressing the way it denotes political community or commonwealth and included the idea of *utilitas commune* or *utilitas regni* without identifying these with the *utilitas regis*). During the religious wars the idea of the "Christian state" was put forward by members of the Catholic League, denoting a special sacredness endowed to the commonwealth itself. Marie-France Renoux-Zagamé, *Du droit de dieu au droit de l'homme* (Presses Universitaires de France 2003), 157–8.

9 Gauchet, *La révolution moderne*, 80–1.

10 See e.g. Jean Bodin, *Les six livres de la république* (Lyon, Tournes 1579), II I (175, 1579).

11 At this time, William F. Church writes, "the strength and permanence of the French government system were such that it was increasingly acquiring the character of a continuing, impersonal, administrative state", *Richelieu and the Reason of State* (Princeton University Press 1972), 16.

engrained customs and large privileges that could not be derogated simply by an order from Paris.[12] The period from the death of Henri IV to the assumption of personal rule by Louis XIV (1661) saw the country in constant rebellion against royal efforts to extract resources without the consent of provincial estates.[13] France was not organised by dictatorial lawmaking but by a system of orders and privileges enjoyed by interlocking corporations from the provinces to the towns, from guilds to religious communities, from officers and corporations of officers to *parlements* (sovereign courts). Noble families with tax-farming privileges and groups of financiers operated as intermediaries between the crown and resources available in society.[14] Most resources were held by rural *seigneurs* controlling provincial *parlements* while an urban bourgeoisie was gradually emerging in the largest towns, combining financial extractions and venal office-holding privileges with absent landholding rights. Feudalism was deeply engrained: *parlements* and seigneurial courts saw to the largest part of the administration of justice. Nobles who acted as governors of their provinces could at any moment raise thousands of men in their private armies to oppose royal policy.[15]

[12] Collins, *The State in Early Modern France*, 15–16.

[13] See e.g. Yves-Marie Bercé, 'Ordre et désordres dans la France de Louis XIV', in Jean-Christian Petitfils (ed.), *Le siècle de Louis XIV* (Paris, Perrin 2017), 207–20.

[14] In the early seventeenth century, France was organised by two overlapping structures: the "feudal" system of orders and privileges, and the gradual formation of social classes, connected with the intensification of commerce and finance. Alongside old landed nobility an urban nobility "of the robe" was emerging whose status was based on office-holding and engagement in financial activities. The groups resented each other's influence but were also dependent so that the formation of Richelieu's system of clientele relied on a network of grand families whose influence was based on their combining both land and money. William Beik, *Absolutism and Society in Seventeenth-Century France* (Princeton University Press 1985), 6–9. A detailed discussion of these relations in the 1660s is Daniel Dessert, 'Finances et société au XVIIe siècle. À propos de la chambre de justice de 1661', 29 *Annales. Économies, sociétés, civilisations* (1974), 847–82. The essentially "feudal" character of the law that organised the relations of French estates is dealt with in detail in David Parker, 'Absolutism, Feudalism and Property Rights in the France of Louis XIV', 179 *Past & Present* (2003), 60–96.

[15] Collins, *The State in Early Modern France*, 5–14, 28, 30–47. Useful summaries of the character of French society in the 1620s include Joël Cornette, 'Fiction et réalité de l'état baroque (1610–1652)', in Henry Méchoulan (ed.), *L'Etat baroque. Regards sur la pensée politique de la France du premier XVIIe siècle (1610–1652)* (Paris, Vrin 1985), especially 14–43 and Philip T. Hoffmann, 'Early Modern France 1450–1700', in Philip T. Hoffmann & Kathryn Norberg (eds), *Fiscal Crises, Liberty & Representative Government 1450–1789* (Stanford University Press 1994), 226–52. Fanny Cosandey & Robert Descimon, *L'absolutisme en France. Histoire et historiographie* (Paris, Seuil 2002) provides a good overview of the different understandings of French absolutism in the seventeenth century. Much of the ensuing discussion draws upon Beik, *Absolutism and Society*.

In theory, the French king derived his powers from God and as *roi très Chrétien* stood not only above all Frenchmen but also other monarchs. But paradoxically, that fact also constitutionalised his powers. As a judge and a "fountain of justice", he was to discover the law, not create it – a view underlined by the requirement that royal edicts were to be registered by the *parlements* that also had the right to make remonstrances to the king.[16] The king's will may be the law but "*il ne faut rien vouloir qui ne soit raisonnable et juste*", Richelieu wrote.[17] The contemporary expression *puissance absolue* referred to independence from other powers, it did not free the king from divine law, the laws of nature and of nations, reason, custom or public utility.[18] It was obvious that it was the duty of the king to work for *bonum commune* or *utilitas publica*.[19] Nor was he entitled to violate the order of succession or alienate French territory. Property was based on divine law to which the king was undoubtedly bound. As Richelieu's close collaborator, Cardin Le Bret (1558–1655), the most "absolutist" of the seventeenth-century jurists, pointed out in a

16 "A law", writes Renoux-Zagamé, "cannot become really and truly law, unless it is 'judged' to be such", *Du droit de dieu*, 219. For good discussions of the shifting importance of registration of the royal edicts by the *parlements*, see ibid., 212–43 as well as Arlette Jouanna, *Le prince absolu. Apogée et déclin de l'imaginaire monarchique* (Paris, Gallimard 2014), 140–62. The right to make *remonstrances* did not amount to a formal right veto but it sometimes did lead to the deferral of a proposed law. In the 1660s Louis XIV prohibited the *parlements* from interpreting royal edicts. In 1673 he removed the right of remonstrance to the period *after* the registration – thus making it a practically meaningless formality, ibid., 194–201. David Parker, too, stresses the extent to which judgment and judging remained at the heart of ruling France. Royal power was judicial power, delegated to the magistrates but remaining in the king's hands as *imperium merum*. 'Sovereignty, Absolutism and the Function of Law in Seventeenth-Century France', 122 *Past & Present* (1989), 45–9.

17 Richelieu, *Testament politique*, II 2 (216).

18 Arlette Jouanna, *Le pouvoir absolu. Naissance de l'imaginaire politique de la royauté* (Paris, Gallimard 2013), 46–9 and passim. See further Collins, *The State in Early Modern France*, xiv–xxv. These limits are debated at length in Julian H. Franklin, *Jean Bodin et la naissance de la théorie absolutiste* (Presses Universitaires de France 1993 [1973]) and more recently, Jean-Marie Carbasse, Guillaume Leyte & Sylvain Soleil, *La monarchie française du milieu du XVIe siècle à 1715. L'Esprit des institutions* (Paris, CDU SEDES 2001), 32–44. The expression *absolutisme* was first used in France by Chateaubriand in 1797. For the varying ways in which the limits of absolutism in France were conceived, see Richard Bonney, 'Absolutism. What's in a Name?', 1 *French History* (1987), 93–117, published also in Richard Bonney, *The Limits of Absolutism in ancien régime France* (Aldershot, Variorum 1996), essay I.

19 Lazzeri, 'Introduction', 52–4. The advocate of Charles V from the *Parlement* of Poitiers, Jean Juvénal des Ursins (1388–1473), had once remarked: "Le roi n'a [sur son royaume] qu'une manière d'administration et d'usage pour s'en jouir seulement pendant sa vie", Jean Juvénal des Ursins, *Tres crestien, tres hault, tres puissant roy*, cited in Carbasse & Leyte, *L'état royal*, 78.

perfectly classical manner, "*le Prince a bien la Jurisdiction sur tous les biens de ses subjets, mais non pas la proprieté, pour en disposer contre leur consentement*".[20] In popular debates, this meant above all prohibiting expropriation through taxation, a source of continuous conflict.[21] As a "guardian of the customs" the king was entitled to uproot bad customs and modify good ones, but not to launch a frontal assault against them.[22]

In the seventeenth century, the image of the king gradually changed from that of a judge to a legislator. But legislation remained scarce, fragmentary and unrelated to any legislative strategy. In the field of private relations, there was practically no legislation at all and much of what existed was ad hoc and often based on clientilist relations.[23] Most public law had to do with the proceedings of royal courts. True, every public authority, whether a *parlement*, a provincial lord or a seigneurial court, received its powers by delegation from the king. However, owing to the proprietary nature of lordship and office, the monarch's ability to control his subordinates was limited. Colbert's effort to increase royal control in the 1670s and 1680s by the despatch of non-proprietary *intendants* and commissioners into the provinces and colonies led to massive protests by nobles and officers who saw this as an unwarranted intrusion in their privileges. Provincial *parlements* were frequently at loggerheads with Richelieu and his followers, even refused to register decrees given to them, and seigneurial courts waged a constant jurisdictional battle against expanding the area of *cas royaux*.[24]

20 Confiscation, for instance, was allowed only in war or other necessity and against full compensation. Cardin Le Bret, *De la souveraineté du Roy* (Paris, Du Bray 1643), IV XI (317, 316–19). See further, James B. Collins, 'State-Building in Early-Modern Europe. The Case of France', 31 *Modern Asian Studies* (1997), 621–4.

21 The principles of the "ancient constitution" required the king to receive the consent of representative bodies for new taxes. Philip the Fair convened the first Estates General in 1302 for that purpose. Thereafter, consent was usually forced upon the Estates or the *parlements*, as most tax increases had to do to finance war efforts. In the seventeenth century, the formal requirement of consent was temporarily abolished by Louis XIV. See Collins, *The State in Early Modern France*, 22–7; Thomas Ertman, *Birth of the Leviathan. Building States and Regimes in Medieval and Early Modern Europe* (Cambridge University Press 1997), 71–3, 107–10, 123–39.

22 E.g. Carbasse, Leyte & Soleil, *La monarchie française*, 181–97.

23 See René Sève, 'Le discours juridique dans la première moitié du XVIIème siècle', in A. Robinet (ed.), *L'état baroque. Regards sur la pensée politique de la France du premier XVIIe siècle* (Paris, Vrin 1985), 129–35.

24 The notion of "sovereign court" highlighted the status of especially provincial *parlements*. Eventually, Louis XIV would prohibit the courts from using such labels, terming them instead "supreme courts".

A proprietary understanding of public power laid the legal groundwork for Richelieu's manoeuvrings with provincial authorities and great financiers. Cooperation was anything but assured, however; resistance was endemic until Louis XIV began his personal rule. By the end of the century, even this fragile peace had collapsed. The waste of public funds in constant warfare had bankrupted the state and impoverished its population. At the end of the War of the Spanish Succession (1713) French ambitions in Europe and the colonies lay in tatters. Louis XIV may never have actually pronounced the words *L'état c'est moi* but in practice he always spoke and acted as if everything in the realm had belonged to him – it was always "my state", "my crown", "my subjects".[25] In 1710 his confessor, father Le Tellier, informed Louis that according to a consultation with "*les plus habiles docteurs de Sorbonne*", everything in the realm belonged to him so that if he took something from his subjects, he only took what already belonged to him.[26] "The nation", Louis XIV is once reported to have said, "does not form a body in France; it resides wholly within the person of the king."[27] But such metaphors remained obscure and neither Richelieu nor any French lawyer believed they would have been detached from an essentially functional notion of kingship. As le Bret put it, in legislating, kings were to consider nothing but "*le bien et l'utilité de leurs peuples*".[28] In the memoirs he dictated to his son, Louis demonstrated a similar understanding of the old metaphor:

> For after all, my son, we have to give much more consideration to the good of our people than of ourselves. It seems to me that they belong as a part of ourselves, for we are the head of which they are the members.[29]

25 See Carbasse, Leyte & Soleil, *La monarchie française*, 25; Bonney, 'Absolutism. What's in a Name?', 95–6. The case that the majority view on the nature of kingship in early modern France was proprietary is made in Herbert H. Rowen, *The King's State. Proprietary Dynasticism in Early Modern France* (Rutgers University Press 1980). In 1547, the coronation oath was changed by Henri II in a way to suggest a marriage between the king and his kingdom – something that supported the view of kingship as *paterfamilias*. Collins, 'State-Building in Early-Modern Europe', 605.

26 Report quoted in Jouanna, *Le prince absolu*, 202.

27 Louis XIV, quoted (in French) in Colin Jones, *The Great Nation. France from Louis XV to Napoleon* (Harmondsworth, Penguin 2002), 3.

28 Le Bret, *De la souveraineté du Roy*, I IX (32).

29 Quoted (in French) in Joël Cornette, *La mort de Louis XVI. Apogée et crépuscule de la royauté 1er septembre 1715* (Paris, Gallimard 2015), 117. This and all translations in this chapter by author, unless otherwise indicated.

And on his deathbed in Versailles in August 1713, hated by his foreign adversaries for his aggressions and silently despised by his subjects, the Sun King may have glimpsed something significant as he remarked to his closest collaborators: "*Je m'en vais, mais l'Etat demeurera toujours.*"[30]

## Reasons of Statehood

In his closing speech at the rather inconsequential Estates-General of 1614–15 (the last of its kind before 1789) the young and ambitious Richelieu, as bishop of Luçon, had stressed the need for unity among the estates, and that this could only be attained under a monarch who would see to the "observation and fulfilment of the laws".[31] The need for unity was stressed over again in his *Testament politique*. The times of unhappiness that had befallen France had all been produced by the priority successive administrations had given to private over public interests.[32] This stood in stark contrast to Spain where the government had learned "*de préférer les intérêts de l'Etat à tous autres*".[33] There had been no end in France to the subordination of policy to private passions deviating from the pursuit of the public interest – that is to say, the interests of the state itself *(l'État en soi-même)*.[34] The task now was to coordinate the private interests and privileges so that they would "by the force of their nature" coincide with what is "most advantageous to the State".[35]

During the eighteen years that the Red Cardinal sat at the helm of the French government (1624–42), he devoted himself single-mindedly to crushing the internal opposition associated with high nobility and the Protestant "state within a state". This would be greatly assisted by the literatures of the *raison d'état* that had been developed by Counter-Reformation intellectuals such as Botero to support the interests of Christian rulers.[36] That literature, too, shared a specific understanding of statehood, expressed in the first sentence of the second edition of

[30] Ibid., 32.

[31] Richelieu's closing speech for the clerical estate, 3 February 1615, cited in Armand Teyssier, *Richelieu. La puissance de gouverner* (Paris, Michalon 2007), 25–6.

[32] Richelieu, *Testament politique*, II 3 (220–1).

[33] Ibid., II 3 (220).

[34] Ibid., I 5 (159).

[35] Ibid., I 3 (221).

[36] Out of the wealth of literature, see especially Marcel Gauchet, 'L'Etat au miroir de la raison d'état', in Marcel Gauchet, *La condition politique* (Paris, Gallimard 2005), 205–60 and e.g. Laurie Catteeuw, *Censures, et raisons d'état. Une histoire de la modernité politique (XVIe–XVIIe siècle)* (Paris, Albin Michel 2013). On the Counter-Reformation basis of *ragion di stato*, see especially Romain Descendre, *L'État du monde. Giovanni Botero entre raison d'État et géopolitique* (Genève, Droz 2009), 58–65.

Botero's principal work: "State is a stable rule over a people and Reason of State is the knowledge of the means whereby such dominion [*dominio*] may be founded, preserved and extended."[37] With *dominion* Botero meant *legitimate* power over a people. As an anti-Machiavellian he believed – as Richelieu of course did – that even ruthless action was ultimately to be justified by the strengthening of a Christian order.[38] *Raison d'état* was the knowledge of how this could be achieved.[39] As we saw in Chapter 3 above, although Botero did not exclude war and violence as parts of statecraft, most of his attention was directed to the productive uses of the resources of the realm. The greatest asset a ruler had was his people, and the best statecraft was the kind that employed the people productively.

> The wealth of a ruler depends on that of his individual subjects which comprises property together with the actual commerce in the fruits of the earth and of industry: import, export and transport from one place to another, either with the country or in other countries.[40]

A massive amount of new "statist" pamphlets inspired by these Italian literatures was published in France in the 1620s and 1630s, sometimes directly under the auspices of Richelieu himself.[41] These works presumed a specific realm of government – of ruling – with its own type of knowledge, its own morality and its distinct rules of operation that deviated from everyday knowledge and normal moral behaviour.[42] Charity and

37 Giovanni Botero, *The Reason of State* (London, Routledge 1956), 3.

38 The point that Botero was writing about legitimate rule and not despotism is made in great detail in Stéphane Bonnet, *Droit et raison d'État* (Paris, Garnier 2012), 205–15.

39 Botero's *raison d'état* was a conservative doctrine unlike Machiavelli's belligerent instructions to a *new* prince, geared to consolidate a rule that did not yet exist. See further Michel Senellart, *Machiavélisme et raison d'état. XIIe–XVIIIe siècle* (Presses Universitaires de France 1989), 84–7.

40 Botero, *Reason of State*, I 15 (21).

41 For this literature, see especially Etienne Thuau, *Raison d'Etat et pensée politique à l'époque de Richelieu* (Paris, Albin Michel 2000 [1966]), 166–409.

42 Again, the commentary literature is massive. With special emphasis on Botero and his Italian colleagues such as Scipione Ammirato, Federico Bonaventura, Traiano Boccalini, Fabio Albergati, Scipione Chieramonti and Lodovico Zuccolo, see Stéphane Bonnet, *Droit et raison d'État* (Paris, Garnier 2012); Catteeuw, *Censures, et raisons d'état*. For the English context, see Thomas Poole, *Reason of State. Law, Prerogative and Empire* (Cambridge University Press 2015). The principal examination of the literature in France remains Thuau, *Raison d'État et pensée politique*. A good overview of Richelieu's role in the production of that literature, alongside a new ideologically oriented press and historiography, is in Mousnier, *L'homme rouge*, 443–85.

forgiveness were important virtues among private individuals, Richelieu himself remarked, but not so in the government of the state:

> In the matter of crime of state, we must close the gate to pity, ignore the complaints of interested persons and the opinions of an ignorant population that sometimes complains about what is useful for it or otherwise completely necessary. Christians may need to forget the offences they have suffered as individuals, but judges are obliged not to forget those that interest the public. In fact, to leave them unpunished is to commit them anew, rather than pardon and forget about them.[43]

By merciless conduct towards noble opponents such as Chalais, Montmorency and Marillac, crushing all political, though not religious, rights of the Protestants as well as through his alliances with heretical powers the Cardinal realised in practice what *raison d'état* taught as theory. Catholic *dévots* were scandalised over the Cardinal's indifference to the interests of the church. But Richelieu knew how to argue to his religious base: "*ce qui se fait par l'Etat se faisant pour Dieu qui en est la base et le fondement*".[44] Owing to the religious character of the French state itself, putting its interests and its unity first would in no way undermine the interests of religion; on the contrary, focus on the state would advance the long-term interests of religion as well.[45]

Some of the political writers claimed that *raison d'état* meant derogation from the principles of law and administration, incapable as the latter were of expressing the mystique of statehood.[46] In his powerful work on the *Considérations politiques sur les coups d'État* (1639), Gabriel Naudé (1600–1653), secretary of Roman cardinals, later Mazarin's librarian, pointedly attacked efforts to integrate the high politics of "*arcana imperii*" – for example, unconstitutional dismissal of officials and assassinations of political opponents – into public law and government. Such measures could not be expressed by principles of law or made subject to parliamentary debates or scholarly reasoning. They could only be contemplated by princes and their closest advisors outside

43 Richelieu, *Testament politique*, II 5 (229).

44 Ibid., I 2 8 (119). See also Marcel Gauchet, 'L'État au miroir de la raison d'État', in Yves Charles Zarka, *Raison et déraison d'État. Théoriciens et théories de la raison d'état aux XVIe et XVIIe siècles* (Presses Universitaires de France 1994), 220.

45 William F. Church, *Richelieu and Reason of State* (Princeton University Press 1973), 8, 301–2. Likewise, Françoise Hildesheimer, *Relectures de Richelieu* (Paris, Condé-sur-Noireau 2000), interpreting Richelieu as a Thomist theologian, 72–97.

46 Nannerl Keohane, *Philosophy and the State in France. Renaissance to the Enlightenment* (Princeton University Press 1980), 168–70, 241–51.

moral or legal categories; their secrecy was the condition of their success.[47] But Naudé's development of the theme led him, as it had led Botero, to conventional examinations of the virtues of ruling (fortitude, temperance, justice and prudence) and stress on how *coups d'état* were to be used defensively, bearing in mind that "*la conservation du peuple soit la souveraine loi*".[48] In fact, *raison d'état* soon became a constant topic of lay conversations that was translated by public lawyers into prudential concerns that were part of a higher law, as they had been since Roman times. "*Necessitas omnem legem frangit*", wrote their leading voice, Cardin le Bret, in Richelieu's government.[49]

Botero's *raison d'état* was directed against juristic *politiques* such as Jean Bodin, whose notion of "sovereignty" was designed to further a type of political power that would stand as neutral against religious adversaries. This was an obvious anathema for Counter-Reformation activists. But the casuistic use of prudential judgment and the language of public or common interest were not at all unfamiliar to public law.[50] The legal theory of sovereignty could easily accommodate the view that a ruler must sometimes take extraordinary measures, the point having been familiar from the medieval distinction between ordinary and absolute powers that was every now and then employed as part of later absolutist theorising.[51] By presuming the existence of a law that demanded the protection of the state as a

[47] Gabriel Naudé, *Considérations politiques sur les coups d'État* (Louis Marin éd., Paris, Éditions de Paris 1988). For a useful discussion, see Yves Charles Zarka, 'Raison d'Etat, maximes d'Etat et coups d'Etat chez Gabriel Naudé', in Yves Charles Zarka, *Raison et déraison d'État. Théoriciens et théories de la raison d'état aux XVIe et XVIIe siècles* (Presses Universitaires de France 1994), 151–69. See also Senellart, *Machiavélisme*, 58.

[48] Naudé, *Considérations politiques*, 112, 182–90. Perhaps the most controversial of Naudé's propositions was his endorsement of the St Bartholomew massacres as an acceptable *coup d'état*, 129–32. Nevertheless, the way he generalised such action in terms of a medical metaphor (cutting off an infected member to preserve the body) and stressed that in conducting such action one needed to act "*en judge, et non comme partie*", aligned it with familiar debates, 113, 114.

[49] Cardin Le Bret, as quoted in Cosandey & Descimon, *L'absolutisme*, 45–9. But see further Le Bret, *De la souveraineté*, I I (where he points out that French kings have nevertheless always governed their realms "with softness and moderation", 3).

[50] For the emergence of the vocabulary of "interest", see Lazzeri, 'Introduction', 71–128.

[51] Cosandey & Descimon, *L'absolutisme*, 45–9. More generally, see Francis Oakley, 'Jacobean Political Theology. The Absolute and Ordinary Powers of the King', 29 *Journal of the History of Ideas* (1968), 323–46 and Francis Oakley, 'The Absolute and Ordained Power of God in Sixteenth- and Seventeenth-Century Theology', 59 *Journal of the History of Ideas* (1998), 437–61.

legitimate order (Bodin's *droit governement*), jurists could without difficulty integrate *raison d'état* into their *droit politique.*[52]

In the course of the early seventeenth century, the writers of the *raison d'état* began to replace the older notion of the common good by that of the interests of state to indicate the objective of convergence of particular interests in the public order.[53] This was not at all to seek to undermine anybody's well-understood interests, as Richelieu stressed.[54] It was simply to operate with a more complex sociological awareness about the political world than was being offered by moral abstractions or legal obligations, and hence a more effective (though perhaps indirect) way to give effect to the latter as well. One of the writers working under Richelieu, Henri de Rohan, duke of Rohan (1579–1638), began his famous instructions for the French monarch (1638) with the lapidary statement: "*Les Princes commandent aux peuples et l'intérêt commande aux Princes.*"[55] This involved the providential assumption that the proper management of the interests of important social groups would also be for the interest of the prince and his state. It lay out a programme for the conduct of policy based on a careful management of the resources of one's state – its climate, its population, its economy, its history and so on, principles on which Montesquieu would later base his sociological brand of natural law.[56] Like Montesquieu, Rohan assumed that intelligent policy required that such data were to be compared with the resources and the relative power of other states so as to produce a situational analysis of the *real interests* of the state at any one moment. Success in foreign affairs became a function of the ability of the prince to manoeuvre his state in a network of objective interests by taking advantage of its strengths while never exposing its weaknesses.[57]

[52] See Martin Loughlin, 'Droit politique', 17 *Jus politicum. Revue de droit politique* (2017), 295–335; Bonnet, *Droit et raison d'État*, 279–84.

[53] Senellart, *Machiavélisme* (making this point by reference to Botero and Montchrétien), 88–92.

[54] Richelieu, *Testament politique*, 220.

[55] Rohan, *De l'intérêt*, 161. The work was probably completed in 1634. Rohan, a strict Calvinist, had composed it in order to support Richelieu's more aggressive attitude towards Spain. Church, *Richelieu and Reason of State*, 352–3.

[56] Even Bodin had stressed the importance of analysing the environmental conditions of states in order to understand their constitutional systems. William F. Church, *Constitutional Thought in Sixteenth-Century France. A Study in the Evolution of Ideas* (Harvard University Press 1941), 216–17.

[57] In Rohan's work, the "international" does not appear as an autonomous sphere, but simply as a network of interlocking state interests and a foundation for the "maxims" of foreign policy appropriate for each state. In foreign policy, one should not be

An analogous project lay within Jean Bodin's renewal of public law. His early writings sought to turn jurisprudence into a comparative and historical science while the later work that contained the famous theory of sovereignty further integrated *raison d'état* in the government of the state.

## Jean Bodin 1: Towards Universal Jurisprudence

The direction of early sixteenth-century French jurisprudence had been towards the domestic and the historical. Humanist jurists regarded the "ancient" *lois fondamentales* as the proper source for order at home and beyond.[58] All nations had their own customs expressing the form of the people. In due course these customs had been codified and turned into the civil laws that broke the unity of Christianity, they argued. Roman law might still be used as an academic vocabulary and to express indigenous customs. But it had no independent normative force.[59] From this perspective the Savoyard jurist, theologian and diplomat Claude de Seyssel (c. 1450–1520) had summarised a lifetime of advisory work to French kings.[60] The French state was superior to its rivals because although it was composed of different social groups, each of them performed a function necessary to the whole; "its head and all its members are regulated with such good order that they can scarcely fall into great [dissension and] disharmony by any means".[61] Monarchy was the best of the three constitutional forms because it could "better

guided by arbitrary desires or violent passions that lead to overestimating one's forces but reason and interest, Rohan, *De l'intérêt*, 187.

58 For the somewhat obscure category of "fundamental laws", see e.g. Denis Richet, *La France modern. L'esprit des institutions* (Paris, Flammarion 1973), 46–54.

59 Charles Du Moulin (1500–1566) rejected even the purported origin of French customs in Roman law; no basis existed for subordinating France to the emperor or the pope. See Donald Kelley, *Foundations of Modern Historical Scholarship. Language, Law and History in the French Renaissance* (Columbia University Press 1970), 189–204; Kathleen Davis, *Periodization and Sovereignty. How Ideas of Feudalism and Secularization Govern the Politics of Time* (Penn University Press 2008), 27–9.

60 Claude de Seyssel, *The Monarchy of France* (Yale University Press 1981). Rebecca Ard Boone highlights Seyssel's pragmatic concerns in her *War, Domination and the Monarchy of France. Claude de Seyssel and the Language of Politics in the Renaissance* (Leiden, Brill 2007). Seyssel came from the noble elite of the duchy of Savoy. He received the title of doctor of canon and civil law in Pavia in 1486 where he also taught civil law and feudal law. From 1490 onwards he served at the councils and as ambassador of Louis XII, including periods in the *parlement* of Toulouse and the Senate of Milan. He later became bishop of Marseilles and archbishop of Turin.

61 Seyssel, *The Monarchy of France*, 49. See further Church, *Constitutional Thought*, 32 and Quentin Skinner, *The Foundations of Modern Political Thought* (Cambridge University Press 1978), II, 260–1.

remedy and obviate all dangers and difficulties".[62] This was especially true of the French monarchy where the king's absolute powers had been limited by the "bridles" of religion, justice and police, including the "many ordinances made by the kings of France themselves and afterwards confirmed and approved from time to time".[63] In France, he wrote, "the royal authority remains always entire, not totally absolute nor yet too much restrained".[64]

Seyssel's work had been produced before the religious conflict. A direct response to the new situation came from the pen of the Gallican nationalist and Huguenot François Hotman (1524–1590) whose *Franco-Gallia* (1573) openly attacked the Machiavellianism that popular imagination connected with the regent, Catherine de' Medici.[65] The Justinian code and the commentary tradition were useless for dealing with French problems. Like Seyssel, Hotman believed that Gallic customs – the ancient constitution – reflected a balanced view of French institutions, protecting the liberties of Frenchmen and upholding a contractual monarchy. Only recently had the royal house had been permeated by foreign influences; the sacred authority of the Estates-General had been undermined by an ambitious group of courtiers, "*cette canaille d'Interpretes et repetasseurs du Droict*".[66] The lost liberties were to be recovered: "the government of our public realm must be returned to its ancient and natural state by the grace and favour of God".[67]

62 Seyssel, *The Monarchy of France*, 46.

63 Ibid., 51. The expression "bridle" took up the metaphor of the horse to be tamed so that it would run in the desired direction. Although not part of classical political thought, the metaphor was sometimes used in a way that oscillated between external, "institutional" controls (exercised by the church and the *parlements*) and the internal controls in a virtuous prince. See Ulrich Langer, 'Le "frein" du roi est-il une vertu? Éthique et langage symbolique chez Seyssel', in Patricia Eichel-Lojkine (ed.), *Claude de Seyssel, Écrire l'histoire, penser le politique en France, à l'aube des temps modernes* (Presses Universitaires de Rennes 2010), 25–41. The reference to legislation being "confirmed" took up the role that the *parlements* played in French legislation. Seyssel is usually seen as an early constitutionalist, owing to his celebration of the way in which in France "the royal authority remains always entire, not totally absolute nor yet too much restrained", *The Monarchy of France*, 56, 49–57.

64 Seyssel, *The Monarchy of France*, 51.

65 Kelley, *Foundations of Modern Historical Scholarship*, 204–14.

66 François Hotman, *La Gaule française* (Paris, Fayard 1993 [1574]), 176–7.

67 "que le gouvernement de nostre chose public se portera bien, quand il sera remis en son ancien, et comme naturel estat par quelque singulière grace et et faveur du Dieu", ibid., 14. See further Kelley, *Foundations of Modern Historical Scholarship*, 209–11; Skinner, *Foundations*, II, 304, 310–15.

But although laws might be intensely national, the ways of studying them – jurisprudence – was not. For "in history, the best part of universal law lies hidden".[68] Accordingly, Bodin prefaced his early *Methodus ad facilem historiarum cognitionem* (*Method for the Easy Comprehension of History*, 1566) by a critique of the absurdity of trying to draw the principles of jurisprudence from the laws of just one state, i.e. Rome. What was needed was to "bring together and compare the legal framework of all states, or of the more famous states, and from them compile the best kind".[69] As "the true narration of things", history was to be studied by a specific (Ramist) technique of "distribution", proceeding from larger entities (cosmographies, topographies, the natural conditions of communities) to smaller ones (e.g. items such as citizen, magistrate, or sovereign). The latter were then to be rearranged so as to illustrate what was, for example, "base, honourable, useful or useless" in practical statecraft.[70] Legal knowledge was all about knowledge of the past, transported for use in the present in *loci communes* that helped its collective memorisation.[71]

*Methodus* developed a universal law on scientifically organised historical and comparative studies.[72] This was not simply a *ius naturale*

[68] Jean Bodin, *Method for the Easy Comprehension of History* (New York, Norton 1969 [1566]).

[69] Bodin, *Method*, 2. The critique was directed especially at Jacques Cujas (1520–90) and other academic jurists researching the original sense of aspects of Roman law. Against them, it employed a comparative method intended to create "a broader humanist curriculum aimed at producing jurisconsults skilled in the art of government". Martin Loughlin, *Foundations of Public Law* (Oxford University Press 2010), 57.

[70] Bodin, *Method*, 356. Bodin's point was not to insist on these as the necessary categories of assessment – the cardinal virtues might equally be used. The point was only that some such categories were needed for the purpose of learning the lessons of history. See further the discussion in Marie-Dominique Couzinet, *Histoire et méthode à la renaissance. Une lecture de la Methodus de Jean Bodin* (Paris, Vrin 1996), 35–58.

[71] Couzinet, *Histoire et méthode*, 59–79.

[72] Bodin had sketched a universal law in a set of tables prepared while he was still at the university of Toulouse in the 1550s but published contemporaneously with the *République*. The "exposé of universal law" (*Juris universi distributio*) was likewise an application of the ideal of "science" that sought to synthesize the basic legal categories and distinctions – distinctions between natural and human law, breach and sanction, persons and things etc. – into a kind of Platonic universe, where the four Aristotelian causes (formal, material, effective and final) organised them into a skeleton of social life everywhere. Jean Bodin, *Exposé du droit universel, Juris universi distributio* (Presses Universitaires de France 1985). The resulting universal jurisprudence employed Roman law formulas not because of their intrinsic universality but for their usefulness for his purposes. The relation between *Exposé* and *Methodus* might be seen in complementary terms: the one describing the materials that form "universal jurisprudence", the other organising it in universally valid categories. Couzinet, *Histoire et méthode*, 101–7.

*secundarium*, customary rules on diplomacy or warfare, but closer to the mixture of things in Isidorus' *Etymologies*, including the basic forms underlying all historical legal systems.[73] Studying it would begin by a discussion of the way natural conditions contributed to variations of local mentalities in something like an early sociology of nations. Different parts of this republic of the world would then be organically related – the north and south, dry and wet climates all having their distinct roles in upholding its "body".[74] The longest section illustrated the method by comparing the way in which the public institutions of different states, such as Romans, Spartans, Achaeans, Germans, Turks, Poles and Britons, had developed so as to extract from them "the rule of reason and the common law of nations".[75] It was the very point of the science (*ars*) of jurisprudence to turn the elements it found in the history of nations into something universal.[76] This did not, of course, bring about the unity of the world as an institutional reality. Instead it was for "princes, by using either their armies, or treaties, or mutual good will, [...] to obtain lawful conduct and adjudication of affairs outside the borders of the kingdom".[77] Because of the gap between the republic of the world produced in the legal scholar's imagination and historical reality, existing laws did not suffice for the purposes of wise government; what was needed was a juris-*prudentia*, a form of legal knowledge oriented towards political counsel and practical maxims about how nations were to be governed and how justice was to be distributed between them.[78] This is what Bodin would present in his *Six livres*.

## Jean Bodin 2: Not Tyranny, Sovereignty

For the law to be universal in its method and practice, it needed to be separated from faith. But how to achieve this in a world of intense

[73] See Jean Moreau-Reibel, *Jean Bodin, et le droit public comparé dans ses rapports avec la philosophie de l'histoire* (Paris, Vrin 1933), 30–3.
[74] Bodin, *Method*, 116–22. Chapter IX of the book specifically discusses the origins of the various peoples (334–64).
[75] Ibid., 168 and 153–290. For contextualisation and commentary, see Reibel, *Jean Bodin*, 46–68.
[76] For this effort, see also Couzinet, *Histoire et méthode*, 114–20.
[77] Bodin, *Method*, 168.
[78] See further Simone Goyard-Fabre, 'Commentaire philosophique de l'exposé du droit universel', in Jean Bodin, *Exposé du droit universel. Juris universi distributio* (Presses Universitaires de France 1985), 89–99. Couzinet, *Histoire et méthode*, 119–20. Bodin was famously critical of "mere" academic jurists, dabblers into past texts and grammatical forms. In his mind, the heart of law lay in the practical activity of courts, in the application of law to present facts.

confessional conflict where both sides only saw tyranny in each other? One suggestion came from the Bordeaux jurist Michel de Montaigne (1533–92) and his friend and collaborator the Parisian *avocat du Roi*, Etienne Pasquier (1529–1615), who went out of their way to explain that laws had always varied in relation to time and place and needed no universal, even less religious backing; their binding force could be accepted as a historical fact without metaphysical anxiety. "Now the laws maintain their credit not because they are just, but because they are laws. This is the mystical basis of their authority; they have no other."[79] Law and history were indeterminate as sources of good government – for every rule one could always find another contradicting it: "[s]o far as experience goes, we sometimes see it favouring one viewpoint, sometimes the other".[80] By separating the legal order from the more significant realm of private contemplation Montaigne sketched a view that had no need for transcendental support.[81] Likewise, Pasquier wrote in his private correspondence, even if natural law provided for self-preservation, how that could be realised was dependent on the context. Each nation developed its laws to fit its capacities and needs so that they came in unlimited variation. And still everyone was convinced of the justness of their own laws.[82]

Lawyer-intellectuals such as Montaigne or Pasquier were clear that religious violence would eventually destroy France unless the question of abstract or divine justice underlying the unity of the state was somehow deferred.[83] The famous definition of sovereignty as "the absolute and perpetual power of a commonwealth" in Bodin's main work sought to do precisely that. It would mean above all the power to

[79] Michel de Montaigne, *The Complete Essays* (Harmondsworth, Penguin 1993), 353. In his legal work at the Bordeaux *parlement* and elsewhere Montaigne had witnessed the deterioration of the French legal system resulting partly from the religious crisis, partly from extensive office venality. "How many condemnations have I seen more criminal than the crime." *Essays*, 351. He appreciated the legal power of local customs but refused to trace them back to some single source that it would be the task of history to illuminate. Customs not only differed but were contradictory. If custom succeeded in holding up social peace, that was sufficient. *Essays*, 362–3; Biancamaria Fontana, *Montaigne's Politics. Authority and Governance in the Essais* (Princeton University Press 2008), 35–44.

[80] Montaigne, *Essays*, 127.

[81] Keohane, *Philosophy and the State*, 103–6.

[82] Étienne Pasquier, 'Les letters de Pasquier', Liv. XIX in *Les Oeuvres d'Estienne Pasquier*, tome 2 (Amsterdam 1723), 551–4. See also Keohane, *Philosophy and the State*, 44–5.

[83] Throughout the period of religious fighting in France and Germany, jurists would take the lead in production of peace edicts and agreements; they would become the architects of the new order. See Olivier Christin, *La paix de religion. L'Autonomisation de la raison politique au XVIe siècle* (Paris, Seuil 1997), 107, 34–8, 104–8, 174–84.

produce laws that were valid and binding merely because the sovereign had enacted them.[84] An enormous amount of ink has been spilled on the meaning of "absolute" and "perpetual" and the related assumption that sovereignty must be indivisible. Even as Bodin accepted that sovereignty could exist not only in a monarchy but also in an aristocracy and a democracy, he assumed that it could never be divided, that division would always mean de facto subordination to another, perhaps alien, body. Non-subordination was as "the condition through which an efficient law can be imposed on a multitude".[85]

Among effects of this view was that it marked a clear line between the state and the world around it. As Loyseau would write some decades later, it gave the state its very form.[86] But it did nothing more than that. As independence from external powers it shunned any fixed positive content. After all, a sovereign with a pre-established sphere of authority would no longer be a sovereign at all![87] Instead of a set of definite powers, Bodin's sovereignty was characterised by its functionality that normally tied the sovereign to all the conventional supra-positive criteria.[88] To legislate was not to command whatever, but to derive the right policy of government from the historical conditions of the commonwealth. Divine and natural law as well as the law of nations, promises to foreign sovereigns and the fundamental laws were to be respected.[89] In an apparent contradiction to sovereignty's indivisibility, Bodin even held that new taxes required the consent of the estates, at least when the need for funds was not immediate and overriding.[90]

84 Jean Bodin, *On Sovereignty* (Julian H. Franklin ed., Cambridge University Press 1992), I 8, 1. "Puissance absolue et perpetuelle d'une République", Bodin, *Les six livres*, I VIII, 85.

85 Luc Foisneau, 'Sovereignty and Reason of State. Bodin, Botero, Richelieu and Hobbes', in Howell A. Lloyd (ed.), *The Reception of Bodin* (Leiden, Brill 2013), 328.

86 "la forme qui donne l'estre à l'Éstat", Charles Loyseau, *Traité des seigneuries* (Paris, L'Angelier 1608), II 5, 25.

87 On sovereignty's "negative" quality, see Thomas Berns, *Souveraineté, droit et gouvernementalité. Lectures du politique moderne à partir de Bodin* (Clamecy, Léo Scheer 2005), 21–49.

88 ". . . quant aux lois divines et naturelles, tous les Princes de la terre y sont sujets et n'est pas en leur puissance d'y contrevenir s'ils ne veulent estre coulpables de leze majesté divine ; faisant guerre à Dieu", Bodin, *Les six livres*, I VIII, 92.

89 See e.g. Jean-Fabien Spitz, *Bodin et la souverainété* (Presses Universitaires de France 1998), 11–30. On the other hand, of course, it was left for the sovereign himself to determine the content of those higher forms of law.

90 Bodin, *Les six livres*, VI II, 611–12. Zarka suggests plausibly that Bodin's work is characterised by the contrast between the absoluteness of sovereignty as theory, and the historical analysis of the French monarchy confined within definite limits, Yves Charles

Bodin made clear his preference for "Royal" (or "lawful") monarchy, a system of government where the ruler would scrupulously respect the freedoms and properties of his subjects. There had never been a well-functioning democracy, he argued. On the contrary, the push towards the equalisation of everything led to civil strife and tyranny. Its greatest inconvenience was that it preferred common property so that:

> by lifting the two words of Mine and Thine, the foundations of all Republics are ruined, because they are predominantly estalished to render each what belongs to them & to prevent theft as decreed by the law of God who has especially wanted that property over things would rest with each.[91]

In a thoroughly conventional vein, Bodin regarded the right of property as the "foundation of all commonwealths". Any intervention in the subjects' goods without special justification was illegal and destructive, or illegal because destructive. "True liberty consists of nothing else than the tranquil enjoyment of one's property."[92] The promises the prince had made to his subjects were binding, and the suggestion that he might intervene in his subjects' realm without a cause was totally against divine law and the law of nature.[93] True, circumstances sometimes made it necessary to take exceptional action and it was not always easy to separate actions of a tyrant from those of good king: "[T]ime, place, the persons and occasions that present themselves often compel princes to do something that seems tyrannical for some and commendable to others."[94]

But such cases were nevertheless the exception.[95] Once they had passed, a good monarch would return to the normal conduct of his affairs,

Zarka, *Philosophie et politique à l'âge classique* (Presses Universitaires de France 1998), 112–19. For the tension between Bodin's view of the right to levy taxes and the requirement of consent for new taxes, see also the very useful Gilbert Faccarello, *The Foundations of* Laissez-faire. *The Economics of Pierre de Boisguilbert* (London, Routledge 1999), 39–40.

91 "en ostant ces deux mots du Mien et Tien on ruine les fondements de toutes Républiques qui sont principalement establies pour rendre à chacun ce qui luy appartient, & defendre le larcin comme il est porté par la Loy de Dieu qui a difertement voulu que la propriété des biens fust gardée à chacun", Bodin, *Les six livres*, VI IV, 661.

92 Ibid., VI IV, 661.

93 Ibid., I VIII, 106–7, 109.

94 Ibid., II IV, 205. Hence his dictum "*De mechant homme, bon Roy*", 216–17. But see also IV VII where Bodin accepts that although "necessity knows no law", the prince must try his utmost to avoid succumbing to mere necessity and by all means to keep force on his side; for otherwise, the weakness he shows will lead to losing his allies" ("il ne trouvera pas beaucoup d'hommes qui suyvent son parti"), 448. See also Bonnet, *Droit et raison d'État*, 282.

95 See Helmut Quaritsch, 'Staatsräson in Bodin's "Republique"', in Roman Schnur (ed.), *Staatsräson. Studien zue Geschichte eines politischen Begriffs* (Berlin, De Gruyter 1975), 51–2, 57–60.

respecting laws and property rights as usual. Moreover, such departures did not lead the monarch into a realm beyond law. It was "in accordance with natural reason" that private interests had to yield to public ones.[96] Exceptional action was intended to protect the commonwealth and thus in accordance with the "superior law of sovereignty".[97]

## Jean Bodin 3: From Sovereignty to "Government"

Alongside the famous passages on sovereignty, the greater part of *Six books* dealt with the techniques of government in normal times: "A commonwealth (*république*) is the rightful government of many families and of that which belongs to them in common, with the power of sovereignty."[98] That formulation presumed a distinction between patriarchal rule over families – a Draconic type of power – and the rightful government of what was shared between *many* families. Sovereignty linked the many families into a single commonwealth while the idea of rightfulness inscribed ruling within a set of normative conditions in such a way that what is not "rightful" cannot be properly "government", either.[99] A fundamental distinction appears between two aspects of rulership that Bodin labelled "state" and "government", a distinction of which Bodin claimed to be the originator and which formed the great arch between the beginning and the end of the massive work. Government, he explained, was about policy and not necessarily tied to the form of the state. The manner of holding sovereignty was one thing, the way it was used, another.[100] A state with "popular"

96 "Car le temps, les lieux, les personnes, les occasions qui se présentent contraignent souvent les Princes à faire chose qui semblent tiranniques aux unes, & louables aux autres", Bodin, *Les six livres*, I VIII, 109.

97 Luc Foisneau, 'Bodin ou l'affirmation des droits de la souveraineté', in Alain Renaut (ed.), *Naissance de la modernité. Histoire de la philosophie politique* (Paris, Calmann-Lévy 1999), 241. See especially the discussion of the difference between prince and tyrant in *Les six livres*, II 4, 130–1. See further Julian Franklin, 'Sovereignty and the Mixed Constitution. Bodin and His Critics', in J. H. Burns & Mark Goldie (eds), *The Cambridge History of Political Thought 1450–1700* (Cambridge University Press 1991), 299–300.

98 "République est un droit gouvernement de plusieurs Ménages et de ce qui leur est commune avec puissance souveraine." Bodin, *Les six livres*, I I, 1. French language modernised, English translation MK.

99 Therefore, groups of robbers or pirates would not qualify. Ibid.

100 ". . . il y a bien différence de l'estat et du 'gouvernement': qui est une règle de police qui n'a point esté touchée de personne; car l'éstat peut estre un Monarchie et néanmoins il sera gouverné populairement si le Prince sera part des estats . . . il se peut faire aussi que la Monarchie sera gouverné Aristocratiquement . . . aussi la

constitution, for instance, may still be governed in an aristocratic way. After Rome expelled its kings and set up a republic it was ruled by the Senate. A monarch, likewise, might often find it useful to govern through a group of nobles – just like an aristocratic state might sometimes wish to elect a single governor, a dictator. Yet such a dictator would not be sovereign, not being "perpetual" but appointed only for a particular period or a particular task.[101] And in practice, as Bodin could attest merely by looking around himself, of the principles of sovereignty and government, the latter may often be the more important.

In the underappreciated Book IV, Bodin took up the classical question of the causes for changes and ruin of republics.[102] As if foreshadowing Botero he observed: "*ce n'est pas assez de connaitre lequel des républiques est le meilleur mais il faut savoir le moyen de maintenir chacun en son état*".[103] After noting the impossibility of deriving such instruction from astrological predictions or mathematical calculations, Bodin moved to techniques of government that, unlike the unitary and absolute principle of sovereignty, were diffuse and varying, dependent on complicated calculations of utility.[104] How to use the subjects' fear and love to strengthen the commonwealth? How to take care of the poor or to determine the rate of taxation? Unlike in the realm of sovereignty, here nothing was absolute; everything depended on casuistic reasoning. This was highlighted by the long discourse on the "census" in Book VI. In contrast to the legislator, the censor was to keep count of the resources of commonwealth, to survey its people's morals and determine their required contribution to public welfare, through taxes, typically. The censor was to instruct the habits and practices of the population especially in areas which laws would not reach. With the help of the census, one would find out the number of vagabonds and criminals, "idlers, swindlers [*pipeurs*] and ruffians who move about among good folks [*gens du bien*]" so as to drive them out of the country [*chasser des Republiques*].[105] This was not about applying rules but calculating what would be appropriate. In all well-governed commonwealths, subjects were to be directed to good behaviour by the

seigneurie Aristocratique peut gouverner son estat populairement ... ou bien Aristocratiquement", ibid., II II, 189–90.

101 Ibid., II I, 187–8. This matter has been highlighted in Richard Tuck, *The Sleeping Sovereign. The Invention of Modern Democracy* (Cambridge University Press 2016), 22–30.

102 Bodin, *Les six livres*, IV I–II, 186–205.

103 Ibid., IV III, 399.

104 Ibid., VI I, 582–95. See further Berns, *Souveraineté, droit et gouvernementalité*, 183–213.

105 Bodin, *Les six livres*, VI I, 585.

census. For laws had their limits and "there is no well-ordered republic that would not have used censors and census".[106]

The objective of government was justice that could alternatively be conceived in its distributive, commutative or harmonious versions, each appropriate for a particular constitutional form and requiring a specific type of governmental (censorial) action.[107] It was often useful to distribute resources or offices in accordance with "geometric proportion", by reference to need or merit. But this might also be unwise, as most offices would then go to the nobility, assumed to be automatically more meritorious. Justice required tempering such geometric concerns by "arithmetic" ones and allowing representatives of the third estate to fill lower administrative positions.[108] In commercial exchanges, again, it was usually necessary to seek arithmetic proportion – tit for tat. And yet it was sometimes necessary to take distributive action, and realise geometric proportion, in support of the poor or the needy. This combination of distributive and commutative concerns, and of geometric and arithmetic proportionality, was for Bodin, the way of "harmonious justice" – the type of governmental technique appropriate for a monarchy.[109] Good government was like composing or directing music where different notes and instruments would sound in harmony, each respecting the specific qualities of the others and all being coordinated ideally by the single head, the monarch.[110]

[106] "il n'y a gueres eu de Republique bien ordonnee qui, n'ayt usé de Censeurs & de censure", ibid., VI I, 583.

[107] Distributive concerns aligned with geometric proportions that fitted the aristocracy where *merit* was decisive. Arithmetic proportions were appropriate for democracy where each subject had *equal* measure, and "harmonious" proportions existed when these were appropriately combined, something best realised by in a royal monarchy. Ibid., VI, 732–4.

[108] Ibid., VI VI, 734–6. [109] Ibid., VI VI, 737.

[110] Ibid., VI IV, 670. Bodin distinguished between three forms of monarchy: "royal or "legal" monarchy (*monarchie royale*), "despotic monarchy" (*monarchie seigneuriale*) and "tyranny", differentiated by the degree to which they respected freedom and property. In "tyranny", the ruler simply treated his subjects as his slaves "and other people's property like his own". Ibid., II IV, 200. By contrast, both despotic and royal monarchs obeyed the laws and customs but differed in respect to their *content*. In a despotic monarchy, subjects enjoyed neither freedom nor property rights; the monarch was a "lord" over both. Ibid., II II, 190. This, Bodin explained, had been the case everywhere during the feudal period, but since then all Western European states had come to provide for the personal freedom of subjects and their free enjoyment of the right of property. Things were otherwise only with the Ottomans and the Muscovites and with respect to the conquests that European rulers such as Charles V had made in the new world. Ibid., II II, 190–2. Royal monarchy was defined precisely by the respect that the king there had for his subjects' liberty, lands and goods. Ibid., II III, 194,

## States in the World

Good government had implications for external relations as well. Treaties, for example were to held binding because "*la foi est le seul fondement et appui de justice sur laquelle sont fondés toutes les Républiques, alliances et societés des hommes*".[111] Without the duty to keep faith with one's promises, no treaties could ever be concluded and anarchy would reign.[112] Monarchs were also not entitled to debase the value of their currency for this would be to the detriment of foreigners and other states.[113] Bodin was able to incorporate much of the old law of nations into the prudential idea that this was useful to the prince himself. He was of course entitled to deviate from it so as to give effect to natural law – for example renouncing the right of enslaving one's prisoners of war. But most of the law of nations was positive law, an expression of governmental activity. A good government would negotiate treaties that were reasonable and did not go against the law of nature. Treaties of commerce and alliance concluded by prior monarchs were to be respected.[114] Even peace treaties were to be held, at least if they did not go against laws of God. Otherwise, no firm peace could ever be attained.[115] Only if a treaty was clearly prejudicial, was the succeeding ruler entitled to abrogate it.[116]

Bodin's interest in political economy led him to reflect on the costs and benefits of foreign trade. Speculating on commercial interdependence led him to the so-called quantitative theory of value by which he could link the massive inflation in Europe to the influx of precious metals from America.[117] But his views varied. In a brief essay in 1568 Bodin praised God's wisdom to see to it that no nation was completely self-sufficient and that wise policy would compel everyone to trade with their neighbours. Everyone was called upon to treat foreigners *en douceur et amitié* and to wage war against *voleurs et brigands* who intervened in peaceful commerce.[118] In the *Six Books*, however, his

[111] Ibid., V VI, 558. [112] Ibid., V VI, 556–62. [113] Ibid., VI III, 637–8.

[114] Ibid., I VIII, 107–8; Quaritsch, 'Staatsräson', 57.

[115] Bodin *Les six livres*, V VI, 558. [116] Ibid., I VIII, 111.

[117] Jean Bodin, 'Réponses aux paradoxes de M. Malestroit touchant l'enchérissement de toutes choses' (1568); see further Henri Denis, *Histoire de la pensée économique* (Presses Universitaires de France 1966), 116 and Lionel Rothkrug, *Opposition to Louis XIV. The Political and Social Origins of the French Enlightenment* (Princeton University Press 1965), 22–6.

[118] Responding to those who criticised trading with foreigners, Bodin responded by pointing to the "admirable prudence of God" in seeing to it that no nation can survive without commerce. Bodin, 'Réponses' (no page numbers). See further, Jean

attitude was more reserved. True, there was nothing dishonourable in commerce. The old French rule against nobles engaging in commerce was unnecessary – surely it was better to have a nobleman trade than to steal! Also the king could engage in commerce and colonisation; Bodin admired the Iberian conquests, for example.[119] But his perspective was now predominantly that of the revenues that taxation would bring to the crown, and he proposed fiscal reform to diminish imports and to prevent the export of money, raw materials and valuable minerals.[120] Nations were antagonistically poised vis-à-vis each other. Such measures were necessary so as to weaken potential rivals by making them dependent on their own agricultural surpluses.[121]

Like his predecessors Bodin dealt with war largely as a jurisdictional issue, one of the "marks of sovereignty", suggesting that the laws of war would apply in inter-sovereign wars but not in struggles with "brigands and thieves". Otherwise, his treatment of war and preparation for war was mainly about the utilitarianism of census.[122] He had no difficulty in accepting that there might be other objectives to war than peace. The *conquista,* for example, gave a much-needed boost to Castilian finances.[123] One of the undoubted benefits of war was the way it unified the country: "*Le plus beau moyen de conserver un état et le guarantir de rébellions, séditions & guerres civiles, et d'entretenir les sujets en bonne amitié est d'avoir un ennemi auquel on puisse faire tête.*"[124] Nothing, he wrote, kept the subjects on the path of honour and virtue better than fear of an external enemy. It was necessary therefore that the country be well fortified, that it employed military officials from respected warrior families and that military order would serve as a model for social discipline.[125]

In this way, sovereignty, government and property rights were "harmoniously" combined in a well-ordered commonwealth ruled by law that was never to be changed rapidly or without proper consideration.[126] In order to see to the morals of the commonwealth

Gardot, 'Jean Bodin. Sa place parmi les fondateurs du droit international', 50 *Recueil des Cours* (1934/IV), 672–4.

119 Bodin, *Les six livres*, VI II, 608.

120 Ibid., VI II, 611. On occasion, he stressed that the strength of a prince was the weakness of another. "In matters of state" it was certain that one had to be the strongest, or among the strong so as not to remain at the mercy of victors, V VI, 553.

121 See Rothkrug, *Opposition to Louis XIV*, 31.

122 On the marks of sovereignty, see Bodin *Les six livres*, 147–74. See also Gardot, 'Jean Bodin', 669–84.

123 Bodin, *Les six livres*, VI II, 603.

124 Ibid., V V, 529.

125 Ibid., V V, 530–1.

126 Ibid., IV III, 401–3.

as a whole, to combat unruly or violent behaviour, Bodin combined sovereignty with attention for good government and *policey*, highlighting the way legislation was always to be complemented by techniques of informal management. The nucleus of sovereignty was legislative power. But laws treated the subjects generally. They were to be complemented by censorial measures designed in view of subjects' moral status and contribution.[127] This was what Bodin's "royal monarchy" was all about and why it would become "arguably the first systematic presentation of *droit politique*".[128]

## Ordering Public and Private: Loyseau

We do not know if Richelieu had read Bodin. But he did not need the *Six livres* to believe it necessary to discipline the high nobility in order to attain what Bodin called "*la république bien ordonnée*". The great task of seventeenth-century French lawyers was to confront the extreme fragmentation of the country, the persistence of provincial and seigneurial privileges that obstructed the creation of a unified realm of public law and government. France was still a thoroughly feudal commonwealth. In legal doctrine, the situation was given sophisticated expression by Bodin's leading follower, Charles Loyseau (1564–1627), whose works on French public law from 1608 to 1610 gave a detailed and often critical description of the powers and privileges related to the lordships and the distortion that venality had introduced in the government of the realm. In the first volume of his trilogy on lordship, offices and orders, Loyseau defined "sovereignty" as one type of lordship (*seigneurie*) that, although "supreme", still presupposed the presence of other lordships.[129] At the top of a scale of feudal hierarchy, sovereign lordship

[127] In Rome, Bodin wrote, censors came to be regarded even more highly than magistrates as they began to know the habits and financial situation of each citizen and determine their taxes accordingly. Ibid., VI I, 588.

[128] Loughlin, *Foundations of Public Law*, 58 and 60–2, 69–73.

[129] Loyseau, *Traité des seigneuries*, II 1–10 (24–6). According to Loyseau, one can have relation to public power in one of three ways: as "lordship", as "office" or as "order". Lordship, in Loyseau's terminology has "dignity with power in property". Charles Loyseau, *A Treatise of Orders and Plain Dignities* (Howell A. Lloyd ed. & trans., Cambridge University Press 1994 [1610]), 6 (9). Unlike lordship, "office" does not have this power "as property" but only the *exercise* of it. But in practice, office venality had turned even such exercise into inheritable property – a practice strongly condemned by all public lawyers from Bodin onwards. As "order" (or as member of an "order"), one has only "aptitude" to public power. That is to say, one has the required "dignity", but not the function as either "property" or its delegated

would encompass the domain of the state so thoroughly as to be inseparable from it, "... for if it were taken away, it would no longer be a State... in the end, sovereignty is the form that gives existence to the State".[130] Against the older theory that gave independent constitutional powers to lower officers and magistrates, Loyseau put the view that all authority in the country derived from the king.[131] Whatever had been the nature of feudal kingship, under the Salic law the kings had been liberated from the power of the estates and become superior to every other office-holder, including those of the church. Loyseau tried hard to fit the centralising objectives of men like Richelieu to feudal history and practice. Sovereignty as state power was public power, the proper subject of public law.[132] But the way it was *held and exercised* by the monarch was proprietary. The distinction reflected Loyseau's effort in all of his three works to distinguish clearly the public and private aspects of state power and thus to give a new legal articulation to government in an absolutist state.

Loyseau called possession of public power "dignity", of which there were three types: office, lordship (*seigneurie*) and order.[133] Each related to public power in a specific way. To have an office was to have "the function and exercise" of public power.[134] The significance of that formulation had to do with the fact that to be an officer of the king, for example a magistrate, was not to "own" the appropriate power in one's own right. It was state power, held by the sovereign who had only delegated it downwards to the magistrate. As Loyseau admitted, this had been completely blurred owing to pervasive office venality, the practice of buying and inheriting public office that had dramatically limited the monarch's control of his administration. The second way of possessing public power – lordship – resembled office but was not identical with it. While to have an office was only to have "the function

"exercise". For an excellent discussion, see Brigitte Basdevant-Gaudement, *Aux origines de l'Etat moderne. Charles Loyseau (1564–1627). Théoricien de la puissance publique* (Paris, Economica 1977), 105–7.

130 "si elle estoit ostée, ce ne seroit plus un Estat ... Car en fin la Souveraineté est la forme qui donne l'estre à l 'Estat", Loyseau, *Traité des seigneuries*, II.4 (25).

131 Or, as Loyseau writes, sovereignty belongs to the state *in abstracto* but is "communicated" to its possessor – in aristocracies to the nobility, in democracies to the people and in monarchies to the king. Ibid., II 7 (25). For the complex relationship Loyseau sees between sovereignty as it belongs to the state and is possessed by the monarch, see further Basdevant-Gaudement, *Loyseau*, 110–13.

132 Loyseau's definition of public law varied between that which "relates to the state" and "public utility". See Basdevant-Gaudement, *Loyseau*, 90–5.

133 Loyseau, *A Treatise of Orders*, I 6 (9).

134 Ibid., I 6 (9).

and exercise" of public power, lordship was to possess public power "as property" (*puissance en propriété*).[135] Here the distinction between traditional ("feudal") nobility, nobility of the "sword" and the modern nobility "of the robe", received its legal articulation – the former possessed proprietary powers of his fief and vassals, the latter had (only) delegated power in principle limited by its function (though distorted owing to venality).

There were again two types of lordship, or rights on public power, private and public. Private lordship (*seigneurie privée*) was defined by Loyseau as "the true and actual property and enjoyment of a thing; it is called 'private' because it concerns a thing that every person has in his thing".[136] Exercised over human beings, it meant their reduction to the status of slaves. That was not the situation in France (or at least not in principle). Instead, lordship over human beings in France was public lordship (*seigneurie public*), which was "superiority or authority that one has over persons or things", the type of public power that, for example, the monarch as sovereign exercised over his subjects and the feudal lord as suzerain over his vassals.[137] These two types of public power – sovereignty and suzerainty – separated the principal forms of French lordship. Both involved a right to command that was held as property – but they did not turn their *objects* into properties. Loyseau emphatically denied that the monarch would have been the actual owner of the properties of his subjects, including his nobles and his officers. He only had the right to command. This made is possible to understand how sovereign lordship could exist as "royal Monarchy" in the Bodinian sense, both absolute and limited, and therefore, as a constitutional tradition ever since Seyssel had claimed, the best-organised monarchy that had ever existed.[138]

Loyseau's three-part *oeuvre* of 1608–10 gave the first full explication of the nature of forms of public authority in France. Loyseau insisted that this had been a legal and not a political exercise, depicting the system as it actually was, with all its imperfections, not how it ideally should be.

135 Loyseau, *Traité des seigneuries*, I 25 (6).

136 "c'est la vraye proprieté et joyssance actuelle de quelque chose, & est appelée privée pource quelle concerne le droict, que chacun particulier ha en sa chose", ibid., I 28 (7).

137 "superiorité ou auctorité qu'on a sur les personnes, ou sur les choses", ibid., I 27 (6–7). See further Basdevant-Gaudement, *Loyseau*, 119–23.

138 "[L]a puissance publique ne s'estende qu'au commendement et auctorité, & non pas à entreprendre la Seigneurie privée des biens des particuliers", Loyseau, *Traité des seigneuries*, III 42 (61) and also II 8, 14, 93 (26, 29, 43).

He did not hide his criticisms of the way office venality had blurred the distinction between proprietary and non-proprietary forms of public power. The leading point to retain was that even as it did not reduce its objects to the status of slaves, the power held by the monarch and noble lords was *proprietary* power and that the problems of French government were therefore about clash and adjustment of property rights across the realm. The good government of France – what I have above highlighted as a principal concern of Bodin and the *politiques* – would be about the coordination and balancing of claims of private right that the different social groups were able to make against each other.

## The State As a "Participatory Enterprise"[139]

Richelieu's focus on the state itself in abstraction from its various parts or justifications signified entry into an altogether new functionality of government. From now on, ruling France was to bind the estates and especially the most important of them, the nobility, with the machinery of the state so as to definitively suppress any independent privileges and the connected "duty to revolt".[140] Everyone would be enclosed within a network of interests, articulated as public powers and property rights, to be coordinated from the office of the principal minister himself. Increasing focus in public law from sovereignty to government and to the purportedly secret yet ubiquitously present principles of *raison d'état* signified a certain empirical turn in politics and law that was inspired by the memory of the "troubles" and intellectual attention to natural science as a frame of thinking about human society.[141] The objective standard that had eluded traditional, religiously inclined attitudes to ruling could now be looked for in *l'inexorable loi de l'intérêt*.[142] With this, Richelieu hoped to make the perceived self-interest of the nobility and the bourgeoisie coincide with the interests of the monarch and develop into something like the collective interest of the state. The postulate of the new thinking was that nothing was to be done in opposition to interest. The king was not simply to mediate between conflicting

139 Joël Cornette, 'La tente de Darius', in Henry Méchoulan & Joël Cornette (eds), *L'état classique. Regards sur la pensée politique de la France dans le second XVIIe siècle* (Paris, Vrin 1996), 17–18, 37.

140 See Arlette Jouanna, *Le devoir de révolte. La noblesse française et la gestation de l'État moderne 1559–1661* (Paris, Fayard 1989).

141 See e.g. Jean Rohou, *La XVIIe siècle, une révolution de la condition humaine* (Paris, Seuil 2002), 201–30.

142 Gauchet, 'L'état au miroir de la raison d'état', 251.

interests of his subjects but to align them with that of his own. "This political interest covers all the aspects of the action of the sovereign subject and all the domains of collective life where this sovereignty was to extend."[143]

It is well established that France was a predominant example of Charles Tilly's dictum that "war made states and states made war".[144] The period of almost constant warfare that began from the descent of Charles VIII across the Alps at the end of the fifteenth century enabled the French kings to feel their power inside and outside their realm and to gradually build up "a relatively united central authority, an increased apparatus of bureaucratic control, and a clearly defined set of national boundaries".[145] The religious wars instituted monarchy as the focus of national unity; the wars of the seventeenth century were expected to radiate the brilliance of a "*roi de guerre*" on his subjects and his nation.[146] But these qualities came with a cost. A warrior king would extract enormous resources from society. For example, the state budget before 1632 had been below 50 million livres, but three years later, after the onset of open conflict with Spain, it had risen to 200 million livres.[147] In 1706 of the 196 million livres expenditures of the crown 134 million went to war while the treasury capital remained only 54 million.[148] This meant that the king was in constant need of raising new taxes, direct and indirect, as well as loans and *rentes*, including forced loans, creating and selling offices, raising customs and other payments. It is a truism that "absolutism was, in

[143] Christian Laval, *L'homme économique. Essai sur les racines du néolibéralisme* (Paris, Gallimard 2007), 56.

[144] See especially Charles Tilly, *Coercion, Capital and European States AD 990–1992* (Oxford, Blackwell 1992). For a useful discussion and critique of recent work on war and European state-building that furthers the work of Tilly and his predecessor Otto Hintze, see Benno Teschke, *The Myth of 1648. Class, Geopolitics and the Making of Modern International Relations* (London, Verso 2003), 116–39. I agree with Teschke's insistence on the importance of social history in the analysis of the political order of absolutism.

[145] Skinner, *Foundations*, II, 354. The whole process is examined in Howell, *The State, France,* while its main stages are traced in Collins, 'State-Building in Early-Modern Europe', 107–61.

[146] Joël Cornette, *Le roi de guerre. Essai sur la souveraineté dans la France du Grand Siècle* (Paris, Payot 1993).

[147] Emmanuel Le Roy Ladurie, *L'ancien Régime* (Paris, Pluriel 1994), I, 119. From the beginning of the seventeenth century to the time of Richelieu, the amount of taxes tripled. The land tax, which in 1590 had been 6% of the gross national product, had grown to 13% by 1650. Cornette, 'Fiction et réalité', 49.

[148] Cornette, *La mort de Louis XIV*, 219.

great part, a child of taxation."[149] But increasing taxes and other sources of revenue could not be achieved by simple order from Paris:

> Lacking resources to maintain an extensive network of salaried administrators, the French kings continued to depend on local elites, who occupied positions generally established by charters guaranteeing provincial or municipal rights.[150]

Bodin, Loyseau and Le Bret all agreed that taxation required consent by the Estates General – though each also made provision for necessities of war or other calamity.[151] Since 1439, however, taxes had been regularly raised against the protests of the estates and a meeting of 1614–15, convened by the regency government to raise money to deal with Condé rebellion, failed to reach any conclusion.[152] No further Estates General was convoked until 1789 and tensions were exacerbated by the practice of keeping high nobility outside the royal council. Cooperation of local and provincial elites had been traditionally sought by consulting provincial *parlements*. During the first half of the century and into the *Fronde* (1648–53), however, noble resistance concentrated on *parlements* refusing to register or threatening to delay the registration of royal edicts.[153] Whenever the central government appeared to step on local privileges by new taxes or by sending new *intendants* to the provinces or expanding their powers, officers in the country's administrative districts would tap on local solidarities in protest.[154] Over again ruling France required the integration of special interests – regional, economic, religious, dynastic – into some kind of a compromise arrangement. If open resistance petered out after 1661, this was less owing to Frenchmen having finally learned to approve of the royal extractions than to attaining a stable balance of interests between the local elites and the court.[155]

[149] Denis Richet, *La France moderne. L'esprit des institutions* (Paris, Flammarion 1973), 77.

[150] Hilton L. Root, *The Fountain of Privilege. Political Foundations of Markets in Old Regime France and England* (University of California Press 1994), 15.

[151] See e.g. Bodin, *Les six livres*, I VIII, 109; VI II, 611–12; Le Bret, *De la souveraineté du Roy*, IV XI (317–18). (No Estates General had been convened in the period 1484–1560.)

[152] E.g. Le Roy Ladurie, *L'ancien Régime*, I, 50–2.

[153] See Jouanna, *Le prince absolu*, 140–62.

[154] For an account of the early popular rebellions during the reign of Louis XIII and the *Fronde*, see e.g. Alan James, *The Origins of French Absolutism 1589–1661* (London, Taylor & Francis 2006), 49–52 and 56–60.

[155] On the "contagion of obedience" that struck the country after 1661, see Cornette, 'La tente de Darius', 17–18; Jouanna, *Le prince absolu*, 193–207. According to Beik, this "contagion" was created by the agreement between the king and local grandees on common interests in the administration of the military, the organisation of the economy and the Protestant question, *Absolutism and Society*, 279–301.

To co-opt elites the monarch and the principal minister (Sully, Richelieu, Mazarin, also Colbert as controller-general) had recourse to two techniques. One was the strikingly widespread and much-critiqued practice of office venality. By the beginning of the seventeenth century, the most important posts in the government and judiciary had come to be thought of as private property to be exchanged freely or passed on as an inheritance.[156] The introduction of the annual *Paulette* tax in 1604 enabled the office-holder to keep the office in the family, thus further undermining the king's ability to control the composition or activities of his public service.[157] At that time, there were about 11,000 venal office-holders, more than twice the number of 1515 while in 1664 their number had grown to approximately 50,000 and possibly much more.[158] The share of sales of offices grew from 10 to 40–45 percent of royal revenue between the 1560s and 1660s.[159] It was especially high at times of crisis when new offices were auctioned to the public against the protests of old office-holders who saw the value of their investment erode by the practice. The annual income from the office (*gage*) was a less a salary than interest that the king frequently failed to pay in time.[160] Loyseau and others were particularly critical of the extension of the sale of offices to legal posts that tended to go the richest,

[156] As explained above, the proprietary right did not *sensu stricto* attach to the office, but to the privileges it endowed its holder. See Charles Loyseau. *Cinque livres du droicts des offices* (Paris, Sommaville 1620 [1610]), III (362–495) and commentary in Basdevant-Gaudement, *Loyseau*, 180–90 and passim. Venality had already begun in the fourteenth century through the replacement of church officials in state service by secular officials whose salary would consist of payments made by the public. Life tenure was accompanied by the principle of *resignatio in favorem* as well as the right to appoint deputies, with the result that an office-holder could secure both his and his family's livelihood for several generations. Ertman, *Birth of the Leviathan*, 78–83 and further Lloyd, *The State*, 72–3, 162–6. For the point about the autonomous power holders of judicial office, see David Parker, 'Sovereignty, Absolutism and the Function of the Law in Seventeenth-Century France', 122 *Past and Present* (1989), 36–74.

[157] Loyseau, *Cinque livres*, II X (331–59).

[158] William Doyle, *France and the Age of Revolution. Regimes Old and New from Louis XIV to Napoleon Bonaparte* (London, Tauris 2013), 15. Cornette gives the number of 80,000 in 'La tente de Darius', 31.

[159] In 1635, at the time of France's entry into the Thirty Years' War, "casual revenues", by far the most of which came from selling offices, "made up no less than 40 per cent of the king's income", Doyle, *France and the Age of Revolution*, 9. According to Françoise Hildesheimer, the revenue from offices rose to 45% of royal revenue during the first third of the seventeenth century. *Du siècle d'or au Grand Siècle* (Paris, Flammarion 2000), 161.

[160] Loyseau, *Cinque livres*, III I (363, 378); Basdevant-Gaudement, *Loyseau*, 198–9; Root, *Fountain of Privilege*, 172–5; Guy Rowlands, *The Dynastic State and the Army under Louis XIV. Royal Service and Private Interest* (Cambridge University Press 2002), 111.

but often incompetent candidates.[161] Efforts to reform the system were made impossible, however, by the need for additional funds created by the wars, compelling the king to sell additional patents and open even municipal offices for purchase. In 1695 alone, 6,000 letters of nobility were put up for sale.[162]

As a result, the bureaucracy grew in such a way that by the time of Louis XIV every third fully literate French man was in the service of the state, most of them holding their office as property.[163] Although small reforms were carried out regularly, it was impossible to abolish the practice owing to the exorbitant costs this would entail, the king being expected to return the value of the office.[164] In the seventeenth century venality upheld the widespread network of clientilism that enabled the ascendant nobility of the robe to control large parts of the state machinery.[165] The kings were simply too dependent on the funds received from the sale of offices and the co-option of potentially critical parts of society to give up the practice, which continued until 1789.[166]

But the sale of offices met only a part of the costs of war. To cover the rest the crown turned to private businesses, office-holding nobility and provincial elites for financial assistance that would rarely be unconditional. Already by the mid-sixteenth century, the value of the funds that François I had borrowed from Lyons financiers had risen to almost as much as the whole of the annual income from his domain.[167] At the end of the religious wars, Henri IV and Sully had stabilised the state "upon an alliance between the Crown, venal officeholders, and financiers", but

[161] See e.g. Gerald A. Greenberger, 'Lawyers Confront Centralized Government. Political Thought of Lawyers during the Reign of Louis XIV', 23 *American Journal of Legal History* (1979), 149.

[162] In one single edict in 1696 Louis sold five hundred noble titles. Ertman, *Birth of the Leviathan*, 103, 136.

[163] The numbers in different sources vary somewhat. See David Parker, *Class and State in Ancien Régime France. The Road to Modernity?* (London, Taylor & Frances 2003), 158; Collins, *The State in Early Modern France*, 199; Doyle, *France and the Age of Revolution*, 14–15.

[164] In theory, the "office" belonged to the ruler and what the officer purchased was its financial value. Hildesheimer, *Du siècle d'or*, 160. This was a reasonably stable investment because if the king wanted to abolish an office, he had to pay the current price, which was often far higher than its formal "valuation". This also made abolishing or even reforming the institution financially impossible. Doyle, *France and the Age of Revolution*, 11–23.

[165] Beik, *Absolutism and Society*, 13.

[166] Ertman, *Birth of the Leviathan*, 103 and generally 139–51; Bailey Stone, *The Genesis of the French Revolution* (Cambridge University Press 1994), 87.

[167] Robert J. Knecht, *French Renaissance Monarchy* (New York, Longman 1996), 58.

what had been gained was quickly lost in the regency regime.[168] The costs of administration grew steadily in the early seventeenth century and exploded with the preparation of the war with Spain (1635), which necessitated raising extraordinary revenue.[169] The practice of outsourcing revenue-collection to tax farmers meant that the crown was assured of stable (though always insufficient) income while the tax farmer would be able to move sometimes as much as two-thirds of the net tax to his own pocket – a problem ameliorated somewhat by the formation of general tax farms in certain provinces or with respect to particular sources of income.[170] The tax farmers were a tightly knit group of noble families that were linked to financial elites with a system of marriages, thus consolidating the *joyeuse collaboration*, a system of patronage and clientilism at the heart of the Sun King's regime.[171] The ad hoc nature of these relationships led to endemic legal conflicts adjudicated by courts that did what they could to accommodate financial or seigneurial powers with royal authority:

> Without [law], processes of negotiation, arbitration, mediation, and other informal mechanisms of dispute resolution could not function effectively. Law provided the frame of reference, the structure, and the aura of legitimacy needed to enable political rivals to settle the constant quarrels and jurisdictional conflicts that marked the workings of the Old Regime state.[172]

The group of tax farmers and financiers consisted in the mid-seventeenth century of perhaps 4,000 officers, specialised in managing the sources of payments to the crown, including *traitants* and *prêteurs*, collecting indirect

[168] Ertman, *Birth of the Leviathan*, 107.

[169] French state income was divided into "ordinary" and "extraordinary" revenue. While at the time of Henri IV the latter comprised 6.2% of total revenue, during Richelieu's time it peaked at 89.6% of the total. Hildesheimer, *Du siècle d'or*, 171.

[170] A thorough presentation is Roland Mousnier, *Les institutions de la France sous la monarchie absolue*, tome 2 (Presses Universitaires de France 1980), 71–8, 413–50. 51. Hildesheimer describes this system as closed vessel: the financier collects the private resources with which the king's war is paid; he also provides the munitions and other equipment the army needs, and is compensated for this with the privilege to appropriate part of the taxes he collects, *Du siècle d'or*, 205.

[171] Again, the best source to begin with is Mousnier, *Les institutions de la France*, 2, 48–60, 71–8. A good summary can be found in Joël Cornette, *Absolutisme et lumières 1652–1783* (8th edn, Paris, Hachette 2016), 114–16. The nobles were obstructed by the social prohibition of engaging in mercantile or banking activities – hence their links with urban financiers, which would in due course generate the nobility "of the robe" with its famously complex relations to older landowning nobility.

[172] Michael P. Breen, 'Patronage, Politics and the "Rule of Law" in Early Modern France', 33 *Proceedings for the Western Society of French History* (2005), 113.

taxes on the basis of a contract (*traité*) with the royal council and providing advances to the king and his allies against reimbursement from future revenues. Some were experts in finding new sources for royal revenue (*donneurs d'avis*) against a portion of the revenue in case the opinion was followed.[173] At the time of the *Chambre de Justice* of 1661, set up to deal with financial mismanagement under Colbert's predecessor Nicolas Fouquet, the crown's financiers came from elite families many of whom were royal officers and bore the title of *secrétaire du roi*, binding the state in a complex structure of dependencies.[174]

As co-proprietors of the state, venal office-holders, large tax farmers and financiers possessed significant power in the determination of policy.[175] Even as their activities were sometimes scrutinised by *Chambres de Justice*, they remained a class of untouchables exempted from payments in a way that transferred the burden of the crown's policies to small peasant families – with the predictable result of resentment and rebellion in the countryside.[176] While in Spain and in the Netherlands, the state was involved in a negotiating relationship with private property-owners to finance the wars and reap the benefits of colonial expansion, the French "were preoccupied with the state *as* private property".[177] Family solidarities mixed with duties of public office; private funds were used as loans to the crown, often with exorbitant levels of interest. In planning policy, the monarch needed to measure the balance of forces between different groups and constituencies – towns, provinces, noble families *parlements* and groups of courtiers and financiers. Notoriously, principal ministers from Richelieu onwards – Cardinal Mazarin (1602–1661) and Colbert – would channel huge amounts of public funds into their own pockets and those of their families and "creations".[178]

[173] See briefly, Le Roy Ladurie, *L'Ancien Régime, I*, 125–7.

[174] Daniel Dessert, 'Finance et société en XVIIe siècle. À propos de la Chambre de justice de 1661', 29 *Annales. Économies, Sociétés, Civilisations* (1974), 863. Of the 245 persons condemned in the 1661 trial, 214 were royal officers, ibid., 851–2.

[175] Up to the time of the *Chambre de Justice* of 1661, the "Mazarin clan", according to Dessert, "contrôlent toute la vie financière du royaume", 'Finance et société', 864.

[176] Stone, *Genesis*, 89.

[177] Ellen Meiksins Wood, *Liberty and Property. A Social History of Western Political Thought from Renaissance to Enlightenment* (London, Verso 2012), 151.

[178] See generally Henri Hauser, *Richelieu. L'argent et le pouvoir* (Paris, Nouveau Monde 2018 [1949]). The revenue from the position of the *Grand-Maître de navigation* in the last years of the 1630s provided for Richelieu more than 200,000 livres annually. Le Roy Ladurie, *L'Ancien Régime*, I, 118. In due course, Richelieu became the richest man in France with a fortune of over 20 million livres (twice as much as that of Marie de' Medici's), ibid., 121.

As a result, the state in France did not exist in *juxtaposition* to the corporate interests but was instrumentalised for their purposes; the state was thus not only a society or orders (which it was) but a family corporation.[179]

## Thinking about Commerce

Richelieu purchased the title of "*Grand-maître de la navigation*" with the intention of raising France into the status of a great maritime and commercial power.[180] The title enabled him to encroach on the jurisdiction and the privileges of the *admiral de France*, compelling the holder of the office, the duke of Montmorency, to resign against the somewhat nominal fee of 1,200,000 livres, and thereafter to abolish the office.[181] He then bought out the three provincial admirals, those of Ponant (Guyenne), Levant (Provence) and Brittany, ensuring to himself the rights and revenues from all French ports and coastal towns, consolidating these as fiefs and supplementing them by royal grants of the government of Le Havre (1626), La Rochelle (1630) and Nantes (1631), and finally joining them in 1631 with the lieutenant-generalship of Brittany while his cousin, La Meilleraye, took on the governorship of Rouen and was appointed lieutenant-general of Normandy. Through these manoeuvres, Richelieu secured full control of French commerce and colonisation to himself.[182]

Too long, Richelieu lamented, had France remained behind its principal rivals, Holland and England, in foreign trade. While Holland procured for European nations whatever they needed from abroad, England exported its cloth everywhere in the world. By contrast, France had neglected commerce even when it was fertile in so many products – fisheries, grain, wine – that could be sold abroad, and even when it could easily substitute imports from Spain, England and

[179] Collins, 'State-Building in Early-Modern Europe', 604. See further Ertman, *Birth of the Leviathan*, 126–33.

[180] During his early years in power, Joseph Burgin writes, Richelieu was "obsessed with commercial and maritime issues", *Cardinal Richelieu. Power and the Pursuit of Wealth* (Yale University Press 1985), 94.

[181] The privileges included the rights of anchoring and customs duties from the ports as well as the revenue from any prize judgments.

[182] The story is told in many places. But see especially Hauser, *La pensée et l'action économiques*, 24–33; Castagnos, *Richelieu face à la mer*, 16–23; Mousnier, *L'homme rouge*, 292–5, 299–307; Joseph Bergin, *Pouvoir et fortune de Richelieu* (Pluriel 1988), 87–91; Eric Roulet, *La Compagnie des îles de l'Amérique 1635–1651. Une entreprise coloniale au XXVIIe siècle* (Presses Universitaires de Rennes 2017), 24–6.

Holland by domestic production.[183] In constructing his commercial strategy Richelieu drew heavily on memoranda produced for a 1626–7 assembly of notables that he used as the occasion to persuade elite families to give up their customary distaste of commercial activities. For this purpose, he engaged his *garde des Sceaux*, Michel de Marillac to produce a code of over 400 articles that included provisions on the monopoly of French commerce on French vessels and opened a way for nobility to invest in commerce, shipping and colonisation without fear of loss of noble status.[184]

The reports he received on Dutch, English and Spanish activities abroad had convinced Richelieu that its competitors were humiliating France, depriving it of opportunities of enrichment to which it was entitled as the largest and most populous country in Europe. Perhaps the most influential of the pamphlets propagating a vigorous commercial policy was *Traicté de l'économie politique* (1615) by Antoine de Montchrétien (1575–1621).[185] Writing to support the glory, augmentation and enrichment of France, Montchrétien did not spare negative adjectives in describing how France's rivals had benefited at its expense. Merchants from Holland and England, those "blood-suckers" (*sang-suës*), dominated French trade fairs, leaving the country with their pockets full: "*ils amassent, pour parler ouvertement, et sans figure, tout l'or et l'argent de la France*".[186] Foreigners were impoverishing the country by taking jobs from Frenchmen. For every 60–80 Dutch ships carrying trade in France there were only 10–12 French ones.[187] This was completely against the law of nations: "Commerce, being part of the

[183] Richelieu, *Testament politique*, II 9 6 (293–301).

[184] The Code Michau was registered by the *Parlement of Paris* in 1629. See Collins, *The State in Early Modern France*, 47–55 and Lauriane Kadlec, 'Le code Michau. La réformation selon le garde des Sceaux Michel de Marillac', in Les Dossiers du Grihl (ed.), *La Vie de Michel de Marillac et les expériences politiques du garde des Sceaux* (2012). On the economic projects brought to the assembly, see Hauser, *La pensée et l'action économiques*, 48–73.

[185] Antoyne de Montchrétien, *Traicté de l'économie politique* (Paris, Plon 1889 [1615]), 11, 12–13, 19–23. Montchrétien's work contributed to the general attack on the "unproductive" nobility.

[186] Ibid., 162. At points, the text degenerated into xenophobic rant: "Your public squares are loud with barbarian accents, full of unfamiliar faces, packed with those newly arrived ... they settle in the best towns, occupy the most beautiful, the greatest and the most commodious houses, bring fine furniture from abroad (because they do not wish to pay us). ... They do not want to have us profit from them. That is not what they are after, but to take our money", 165–6.

[187] Ibid., 183.

law of nations, must be equal between equals and on similar conditions between similar actors."[188]

The dismal situation of French commerce was juxtaposed by Montchrétien with the wealth of French resources. Were they only to make an effort, the French would easily overtake their rivals. For this to happen, they had to rid themselves of their anti-commercial prejudice. True, merchants acted for their own profit and not for the general good. That was what human nature was like. But even so, they were unwittingly making a larger contribution: "*les necessitez diverses que chacun sentoit en son particulier, ont esté la première cause des communautez generalles*".[189] Montchrétien was not evoking any invisible hand. It fell upon the monarch to direct individual self-interest to the public good: "help them to find the means for their enrichment, whether by acquisitions or by conservation, and you will enrich yourself, too".[190] Following Bodin's view of the commonwealth as a composite of families, Montchrétien turned to the Aristotelian vocabulary of household management, *oeconomica*, to imagine the prince as paterfamilias, carefully seeing to the rational use of his country's resources: "the political art depends mediately from the economy; and as it seeks conformity with it, it should also follow its example".[191]

Montchrétien's work was a pragmatic intervention without pretensions regarding the European diplomatic system, very different from the "Grand Design" imagined by the former foreign minister of Henri IV, the duc de Sully (1559–1641), some twenty years after the death of his *maître*.[192] According to the plan, wars in Europe emerged from nations'

[188] "Le commerce, estant du droit des gens, doit estre égal entre égaux et sous pareilles conditions entre pareils", ibid., 218–19.

[189] Ibid., 39. See also Keohane, *Philosophy and Politics*, 164–5.

[190] "faites les trouver les moyens de s'enrichir, soit par acquisitions, soit par conservation, et vous estes vous mesmes riches", Montchrétien, *Traicté*, 226.

[191] "l'art politic depend médiatement de l'oeconomie; et comme il en tient beaucoup de conformité; il doit pareillement emprunter son example", ibid., 17. For the needs of good "police" regulations to organise domestic trade, see 257–71. For Montchrétien's work as a contribution to the advice-of-princes genre, see Henry C. Clark, *Compass of Society. Commerce and Absolutism in Old Regime France* (Lanham, Lexington 2007), 10–14.

[192] The only place where the "plan" exists is in a letter written by Sully to his king in 1593. Sully would later on elaborate this plan in his memoirs. The English text may be found in David Ogg (ed.), *Sully's Design of Henry IV* (London, Sweet & Maxwell, Grotius Society Publications 1923). A thorough discussion of the plan is in Elizabeth V. Soyleyman, *The Vision of World Peace in Seventeenth and Eighteenth Century France* (Washington, Kennikat 1941), 20–9 and F. H. Hinsley, *Power and the Pursuit of Peace. Theory and Practice in the History of Relations between States* (Cambridge University Press 1963), 24–9.

unequal size and resources. The continent was to be divided into fifteen dominions of comparable size, strength and wealth. The plan was essentially designed to undermine Habsburg power; it was limited to the Christian states of Western Europe and delegated the predominant role to France as guarantor of the new settlement – possibly only after a final war against Austria. There would be one Christian Republic that would admit the three Christian religions and set up a permanent organisation to deliberate on the administration of Europe's political, civil and religious affairs and to organise the conduct of free trade.[193] It is unlikely that Sully would have seriously debated the plan with his king, or that Henri would have communicated it to Elizabeth, as Sully claimed. The fact that it was so conspicuously designed to further French interests made it unrealistic as a basis for diplomatic action.

A work much closer to the proposals by Montchrétien that came out of Paris in 1623/4, and had been reputedly read by Grotius and Leibniz, was *Le nouveau Cynée* by the obscure cleric, Emeric Crucé (c. 1590–1648). Though the work failed to draw much attention at the time, it condensed key themes of Richelieu's policy. It contained a peace plan, based on the territorial status quo and an agreement to repress international disputes and domestic revolt. Crucé shared the view that a nation's strength was based on commerce and industries; wars were unnecessary and harmful. Only war for self-defence was justified, though sometimes it was necessary to fight against brigands, thieves, cannibals and savages.[194]An assembly of sovereigns should arbitrate disputes and take action against aggressors and rebels. Membership in the plan was to be universal: even China, Turkey and Ethiopia were to take part. Crucé was inspired by the Edict of Nantes and his relativism resembled that of Montaigne: "*ce qui est honoré en un endroit est abominé ou moqué en un autre*".[195] All religions were ways of knowing God.[196] In the proposed assembly, too, everyone's vote would have the same weight, but the right of initiative would nevertheless be allocated to the greatest, the pope and the French king.[197]

[193] There would be a joint military force and a representative assembly plus a general council assisted by six local councils and a court of arbitration whose members the general council would elect. *Sully's Design*, 42–4.

[194] Émeric Crucé, *Le nouveau Cynée ou discours d'État represenant les occasions et moyens d'établir une paix générale et liberté du commerce par tout le monde* (presenté par A. Fenet & A. Guillaume, Presses Universitaires de Rennes 2004), 69, 76.

[195] Ibid., 84. [196] Ibid., 81-82.

[197] It is striking however, that in sketching the protocol of the assembly, Crucé gave the second rank (after the pope) to the Emperor of Turkey ahead of the "Christian Emperor", ibid., 89.

Crucé insisted that his proposal was in the interests of rulers themselves. In a world of interdependent nations, only universal peace could provide security for each.[198] There was no greater danger to peace than sedition at home; it was to be suppressed by a joint effort: "It does not lie within human powers to disturb the divinely created order of monarchies."[199] With peace finally established, nations could turn to more beneficial activities – sciences and arts, but above all commerce. For "no other profession compares in utility with that of the merchant".[200] Crucé did not share Montchrétien's prejudices against foreign merchants and wanted a general system of free trade. He gave detailed instructions on how to keep taxes at moderate levels and how to manage monetary affairs with the ultimate view of achieving one European currency. He was critical of luxury and office venality and stressed the importance of rewarding meritorious subjects and protecting them against depredations by the rich.[201] He did not think much of lawyers, and spent many pages in attacking the uses of law for spurious disputes designed only to enrich the claimants and their counsel.[202]

It is not known whether Richelieu had read this work. He admitted in his *Testement politique* that he had only gradually come to realise the importance of trade to French power. But when he did, he took rapid action to construct an adequate naval force for the maritime provinces, to improve ports and provide tax and customs exemptions for merchants.[203] He created a plan for opening French trade to Levant and Russia.[204] Monopoly rights for trading in Africa were granted in 1630 to different parts of the west coast, predominantly in order to purchase slaves but also to dispose of domestic overproduction. Merchants from Rouen, St Malo, La Rochelle and Dieppe were invited to compete for monopoly rights with those from Paris until 1700 when the trade was, for a while, declared free.[205] But the international situation was not propitious. Most available resources were not

198 Ibid., 102, 107–13.

199 "Il n'est pas en la puissance des hommes de romper un ordre divinement établi, comme celui des Monarchies." Ibid., 68, 93–8.

200 "il n'ya métier comparable en utilité à celui du marchand", ibid., 73–4.

201 Ibid., 117–32.

202 In the new "policed" nations "[l]a Jurisprudence n'est plus nécessaire, & un bon jugement naturel suffit pour terminer les process, sans avoir recourse à une milliasse de lois & décisions, qui enveloppent les causes, au lieu de les démêler", ibid., 81, 132–5.

203 Castagnos, *Richelieu face à la mer*, 97–120; Mousnier, *L'homme rouge*, 331–4.

204 Hauser, *La pensée et l'action économiques*, 108–20.

205 See Abdoulaye Ly, *La Compagnie du Sénégal* (Paris, Karthala 2000), 67–86.

channelled to trade but to war; local customs were often suspended and merchants' property confiscated.[206] And then there was the miserable absence of a commercial culture in France. When another writer, Jean Eon, surveyed the state of French commerce after Richelieu's death in 1646 he saw little change in attitudes or practices. The French were still suffering from unjust exactions by foreign merchants. Instead of carrying out regular exchanges with the French, Eon complained, they start to control our commerce and determine the value of our goods, thus "reducing us into shameful dependency (*servitude honteuse*)".[207] But Eon's principal criticism was directed at "*la nonchalance des François au fait du Commerce*".[208] There was nothing dishonourable in commerce, he assured his readers; on the contrary, it contributed in greatly to the power and security of the state.[209] Moreover, French resources were much greater than those of its rivals, its situation with respect to the sea and the courage and experience of its seamen providing it with a superb basis to become a commercial leader.[210]

When Jean-Baptiste Colbert (1619–83), France's future controller-general, surveyed the state of the kingdom at the death of Cardinal Mazarin, he found it nothing short of disastrous.[211] In a memorandum of August 1664 Colbert approached the king with great circumspection, prefacing what he had to say by a brief overview of the unjust advantages France's rivals had been reaping from long-distance trade. The English and the Dutch, two heretic countries, now presided over all trade. Recognising the old objections against trade by noble grandees, Colbert nevertheless stressed the facility and rapidity with which naval reform and investment in colonies would augment the king's greatness and power.[212] As soon as France had taken over Dutch trade the flow of

[206] Clark, *Compass of Society*, 34.

[207] Jean Eon, *Le commerce honorable* (Nantes, Monnier 1646), 56–7.

[208] Ibid., 46.

[209] Ibid., 156–67 (noting that it enriched the country, gave knowledge of the conditions of other states and provided ships and manpower that could also be used to support a war effort).

[210] Ibid., e.g. 219–27.

[211] A good account of the early years of Colbert's efforts to centralise French commerce and colonisation is Philip P. Boucher, 'Comment se forme un ministère colonial. L'initiation de Colbert 1661–1664', 37 *Revue d'histoire de l'Amérique française* (1983), 431–52. Also Louis Cordier, *Les compagnies à charte et le politique coloniale sous le ministère de Colbert* (Paris, Rousseau 1906), 51–85.

[212] 'Mémoire sur le commerce de Jean-Baptiste Colbert (ministre d'état) à Louis XIV (roi de France), du 03 août 1664', in *Lettres, instructions et mémoires de Colbert, publiées par Pierre Clément*, II: 1 partie (Paris, Imprimerie impériale 1863), 267, 263–72.

money would turn towards Paris, "*autant augmenterons-nous la puissance, la grandeur et l'abondance de l'Estat*".[213]

Colbert's trade policy drew its force from the view that France had been treated unjustly by its neighbours, especially Holland. As he wrote as soon as he took office: France had to take measures "to reinstate it in the possession of that part of commerce which is proposed to it by the law of nations and nature itself".[214] The absence of reciprocity was an outright illegality to be corrected by treaty-making or war, if necessary. Colbert had completely internalised the view of a nation's wealth as a foremost aspect of its power and the possession of bullion as the measure of wealth. In a later memorandum Colbert explained that domestic finances depended on the constant availability of money, an objective that could be attained by attracting it from foreign countries, by making sure that it stays within the country and by preventing it from exiting by providing Frenchmen the means to make profitable use of it at home.[215] For such purposes, Colbert was ready to take drastic measures. Taxes and import prohibitions were accompanied by support for domestic manufacturing to substitute imports and provide employment.[216] A Council of Commerce was created to engage the elites. The government would create industrial monopolies and trade companies, subsidise exports, establish high tariffs for luxuries and amass as much bullion as possible.[217] The state would become active everywhere. For example, in 1668 Colbert formed an insurance company to keep revenue from maritime insurance at home.[218] Funds for such investments came from governmental officials and the judiciary – "members tied to Colbert through complex bonds of fidelity and clientage".[219]

[213] Ibid., 270.

[214] 'Arrest du Conseil d'Estat, pour le retablissement du commerce tant au dedans qu'au dehors du Royaume', 10 April 1661, quoted in Moritz Isenmann, 'Égalité, réciprocité, souveraineté. The Role of Commercial Treaties in Colbert's Economic Policy', in Antonella Alimento & Koen Stapelbroek (eds), *The Politics of Commercial Treaties in the Eighteenth Century* (New York, Palgrave Macmillan 2017), 83–4.

[215] "augmenter l'argent dans le commerce public en l'attirant des pays d'où il vient, en le conservant au dedans le royaume et empeschant qu'il n'en sortist, et donnant des moyens aux hommes d'en tirer profit". Colbert, 'Mémoire au roi sur les finances' (1670), quoted in Cornette, *Absolutisme et lumières*, 40.

[216] Collins, *The State in Early Modern France*, 112.

[217] For details of Colbert's reinvigorated economic policies, see e.g. Le Roy Ladurie, *L'Ancien Régime*, 240–52; Collins, *The State in Early Modern France*, 109–15; Lars Magnusson, *Mercantilism. The Shaping of an Economic Language* (London, Routledge 1994), 176–87.

[218] Charles W. Cole, *French Mercantilism 1683–1700* (New York, Octagon 1971), 7.

[219] Clark, *Compass of Society*, 37.

Colbert tried initially to correct the injustices of unbalanced trade by commercial treaties. The Dutch treaty of 1662 addressed some of the problems but did not prevent the two countries from cutting back their respective imports.[220] In the general tariffs of 1667 Colbert switched from import prohibitions to de facto prohibitive duties and non-tariff criteria, especially quality controls.[221] The Dutch retaliated by striking at the import of wines, and in the ensuing trade war both parties accused each other of treaty violations. The grievances peaked in the ill-conceived intervention by France in the Dutch provinces in 1672, ending the period of economic and financial reconstruction.[222] Colbert had of course written that "*la commerce est une guerre d'argent*".[223] Although doubts would be voiced after his death about the wisdom of thinking in such belligerent terms, these would have little effect. Economic considerations remained secondary during the remainder of the Sun King's reign.[224]

## Europe: Between Security and Dynastic Rights

Richelieu's insistence on reason of state did not at all prevent him from making use of natural law and the theory of the just war in his despatches.[225] These latter were replete with Thomistic elaborations

220 Traité d'Amitié, de Confédération, de Commerce & de Navigation, 27 avril 1662, in Jean Dumont, *Corps universel diplomatique de droit des gens* (Amsterdam, Brunel 1728), VI/2, 412–16.

221 Arguments in the intensifying trade war are reviewed usefully in Isenmann, 'Égalité, réciprocité, souveraineté', 92–101.

222 "Ill-conceived" despite initial victories and because it created the alliance against France and the king's reputation as a hopeless troublemaker. Louis himself later acknowledged the war as a mistake. Le Roy Ladurie, *L'Ancien Régime*, 252–6.

223 Quoted in Jean Jacquaret, 'Colbert', in Henry Méchoulan & Joël Cornette (eds), *L'état Classique. Regards sur la pensée politique de la France dans le second XVIIe siècle* (Paris, Vrin 1996), 187.

224 For example, the mass exodus of the Huguenots after the revocation of the Edict of Nantes in 1685 had enormous economic effects. The standard source for these years is Cole, *French Mercantilism 1683–1700*. The attacks on mercantilism by Vauban and Boisguilbert are discussed at 231–5. A useful overview of attitudes towards commerce at the beginning of the eighteenth century is the discussion of the opinions received by the Council of Commerce from provincial merchants, 235–72.

225 J. H. Elliott, *Richelieu and Olivares* (Cambridge University Press 1984), 122–5; Fritz Dickmann, *Der Westfälische Frieden* (Münster, Aschendorff 1959), 222–3. An extensive discussion of the legal arguments made in the context of the French declaration of war against Spain on 19 May 1635 is in Randall Lesaffer, 'Defensive Warfare, Prevention and Hegemony. The Justifications of the Franco-Spanish War of 1635', papers.ssrn.com/sol3/papers.cfm?abstract_id=951934 (Part I also in 8 *Journal of History of Int'l L.* (2006), 91–123). Here the French justifications alternated between defence of Christianity and of France's security.

and fitted well in the Cardinal's conceptual world.[226] Early in his reign Richelieu even sought to set up a treaty-based collective security system – *assecuratio pacis* – with reprisals and embargoes against suspected wrongdoers, in practice especially Spain.[227] The same concern also inspired him to adopt an interpretation of the nature of the German–Roman constitution that stressed the liberty of the imperial estates to ally themselves through treaties of protection with the French king.[228] Richelieu held the right to intervene in states that were not constituted as absolute monarchies – as the German–Roman empire obviously was not – perfectly in accordance with the law of nations. If the basis of a polity lay in a contract that the monarch violated, then the subjects must be obviously liberated to take action against him, if necessary, with outside help.[229]

Richelieu and the *raison d'état* writers held it natural that the king was bound by his treaties – without the capacity of binding himself, how could he possibly attain his objectives? No virtue was more important than being faithful to one's word, Le Bret stressed, which is why Philip of Macedon had treaties read to him aloud every day. Treaties with foreign rulers were no different from the law of nations, public laws and divine law – "*ils doivent être observées d'autant plus de fidélité qu'ils sont plus*

226 Many historians have opposed the view of Richelieu as a purely Machiavellian thinker – something he of course denied. No doubt, he was a serious theologian (as his books on theological topics and his friendship with the Capuchin cleric Father Joseph illustrate), and much of the interpretation depends on how his pious public statements are read. See further Antony Carty, 'Cardinal Richelieu between Vattel and Machiavelli', in Anthony Carty & Janne Nijman (eds), *Morality and Responsibility of Rulers. European and Chinese Origins of a Rule of Law as Justice of World Order* (Oxford University Press 2018), 149–66 and for summaries, David J. Study, *Richelieu and Mazarin. A Study of Statesmanship* (London, Macmillan 2004), 60–2, while Church suggests that "attention to the legal rights of the crown was an integral part of Richelieu's foreign policy", *Richelieu and Reason of State*, 370.

227 Alan James, 'The Development of French Naval Policy in the Seventeenth Century. Richelieu's Early Aims and Ambitions', 12 *French History* (1998), 384–402. On Richelieu's design for European collective security, see Fritz Dickmann, 'Rechtsgedanke und Machtpolitik bei Richelieu', in Fritz Dickmann, *Friedensrecht und Friedenssicherung. Studien zum Friedensproblem in der Geschichte* (Göttingen, Vandenhoeck-Ruprecht 1971), 36–78, esp. 70–3; Guido Braun, 'La diplomatie française à Münster et le problème des la sûreté et de la garantie des traités de Westphalie', 4 Perspectivia.net (2010) www.perspectivia.net/content/publikationen/discussions/4-2010/braun_diplomatie. See also Hermann Weber, 'Dieu, le roi et la Chrétieneté. Aspects de la politique du cardinal Richelieu', 13 *Francia* (1985), 240–2.

228 Klaus Malettke, *Les relations entre la France et le Saint-Empire au XVIIe siècle* (Paris, Champion 2001), 79–84 and passim.

229 Dickmann, 'Rechtsgedanke', 41–7; Church, *Richelieu and Reason of State*, 298–300.

*universels, qu'ils regardent le corps d'Éstat*".[230] No doubt, this is what Richelieu needed to think in order to set up the alliances in Italy and in imperial territory designed to undercut Habsburg hegemony. During the later part of the Thirty Years' War, his successor, Cardinal Mazarin, continued to press for an alliance of the imperial estates with France against the emperor himself, an objective eventually replaced by the Franco-Swedish "guarantee" in the Westphalia settlement.[231] With the peace of the Pyrenees (1659), Mazarin could congratulate himself on a treaty system that "placed France in its most advantageous international position for over a century".[232]

Alongside concern over French security, a predominant war motive was the king's search for *la gloire*, something believed to radiate from the person of the ruler to the body of the nation itself and down to the least of its subjects.[233] *La gloire* was not antithetical to law, either, for an honourable warrior would keep his word and treat his enemies with humanity. Bourbon absolutism was not in principle averse to the rule of law. On the contrary, by the beginning of personal rule by Louis XIV in 1661, the principles of sovereign kingship had been firmly grounded in French public law; so much so that in 1679 the Sun King finally allowed the latter to be taught at the University of Paris. In conducting foreign affairs, the king had a live sense of his responsibility under the *lois fondamentales*, two aspects of which directed his diplomacy throughout his reign: the inalienability of French territory, and laws governing succession to the throne.[234] The Dutch wars, the policy of "reunions" and eventually the War of the Spanish Succession all in one way or another involved the implementation of these provisions.

The three bishoprics of Metz, Toul and Verdun (*les Trois Évêchés*) had been under French suzerainty since the mid-sixteenth century. Under Richelieu, a *parlement* was established in Metz and an *intendant* appointed there in 1633. As former *avocat-général* at the *Parlement of Paris* and later member of the *Conseil d'État* and *Conseil Privé*, Le Bret enlisted his legal skills with Richelieu's legal propaganda war over these and other alleged French possessions on France's eastern frontier. In the final

[230] Le Bret, *De la souveraineté du Roy*, IV X (306).
[231] Malettke, *Les relations entre la France et le Saint-Empire*, 230–74.
[232] Study, *Richelieu and Mazarin*, 135.
[233] On the role of "glory" in Louis' wars, see John A. Lynn, *The Wars of Louis XIV 1667–1714* (London, Longman 1999), 27–43; Cornette, *La mort de Louis XIV*, 189–96.
[234] See Malettke, *Les relations entre la France et le Saint-Empire*, 188–9, 659.

chapter of his work on sovereignty, written at a time when France was increasingly intervening in the affairs of the empire, he described the French war as a procedure of divine justice under which France was fighting the usurpers who had been holding territory originally under the dominion of Gaul.[235] He was rewarded for his loyalty by being appointed first president of the Metz *parlement* as well as *intendant* of the three bishoprics.[236]

The war of devolution began in 1667 as an effort to press the dynastic claims of the Queen, Marie-Thèrese, to the Spanish Low Countries (Brabant, Namur, Artois and Cambrai). The claims had been based on old-regime dynastic legality and they referred to non-payment of the exorbitant dowry of 500,000 escudos as promised in the Treaty of the Pyrenees (1659). But it was also inspired by the effort to break the Anglo-Dutch monopoly on the world markets. The subsequent Dutch war (1672–8) was carried out in part as punishment but also to vent Colbert's grievances against Dutch trade and customs policy.[237] In the period between the Peace of Nijmegen (1678) and the War of the League of Augsburg (1688–97) France used legal arguments to support its policy of "reunions" in order to rationalise its boundary by enclosing territories left vague under existing treaties or allegedly part of crown inheritance.[238] Claims of feudal and treaty right were pressed in specially constituted courts (*chambres de réunion*) consisting of members of local *parlements* known to be favourable to the king's cause. Strasbourg and other towns on the eastern frontier and the Pyrenees were annexed by military means, sometimes with the justification of helping oppressed

235 Le Bret, *De la souveraineté du Roy*, III II (182–4). Here Le Bret extended the claims to French possessions of Navarre, Naples, Portugal and Flanders as well as parts of Savoy and Piedmont. See further IV VII (308–9) and Thuau, *Raison d'État,* 275–8; Cornette, *Le roi de guerre*, 128–34, 138–9; Ralph E. Giesey et al., 'Cardin Le Bret and Lese Majesty', in Ralph E. Giesey, *Rulership in France, 15th–17th Centuries* (Burlington, VT 2004), Essay XI, 187–218.

236 Laurent Jalabert, 'La politique territoriale française sur la rive gauche du Rhin (1679–1697). Des "réunions" à la Province de la Sarre', 313 *Revue historique* (2011), 62–3. For a detailed description of the legal wranglings to extend French authority in these territories by use of the unclear formulations in the Treaty of Münster (1648), see 68–78.

237 Lynn, *The Wars of Louis XIV*, 105–59; Heintz Duchhardt, *Gleichgewicht der Kräfte, Convenance, Europäische Konzert* (Darmstadt, Wissenschaftliche Buchgesellschaft 1976), 5–19. The fact of Dutch Protestantism was also a major factor behind the king's belligerency.

238 For a good description, see Malettke, *Les relations entre la France et le Saint-Empire*, 380–432.

populations.[239] The positions were methodologically strengthened by setting up French institutions in the occupied lands, by the appointment of French bishops and *intendants* as well as establishment of "sovereign councils" to absorb them in the French realm with a status more or less identical to that of the other provinces.[240]

Richelieu, Mazarin and eventually Louis XIV himself paid extraordinary attention to defending French military operations as efforts to secure natural boundaries and to realise dynastic rights by commissioning thick works of scholarship-advocacy from jurists keen to render service to their king.[241] One of the most elaborate of the early tracts was Pierre Dupuy's (d. 1651) over 700-page *Traitez touchant les droits du Roy Très-Chrétien sur plusieurs Estats et Seigneuries*, the first edition of which was published in 1631 and an expanded edition in 1655. Dupuy used treaty-texts, genealogical tables and historical narratives to defend the originally French dominion over, among other places, the kingdoms of Naples and Sicily, and such other territories as Nice (Provence), Milan, Aragon and Navarre. Because the king had been incapacitated under the fundamental laws to give away his dominion, these former French possessions remained French, the argument went, with their present holders nothing more than usurpers.[242] Another well-known tract, composed by the *avocat* and king's counsellor Antoine Aubery (1616–1695) made the point that the French rights were directly inherited from the Merovingian and Carolingian kings and that most of the empire was originally a French possession; Charlemagne had

[239] For useful discussions of these events and proceedings, see Lynn, *The Wars of Louis XIV*, 161–81; Cornette, *Le roi de guerre*, 144–9; Le Roy Ladurie, *L'Ancien Régime, I*, 312–21. See further Peter Sahlins, 'Natural Frontiers Revisited. France's Boundaries Since the Seventeenth Century', 95 *American Historical Review* (1990), especially 1424–35.

[240] For the creation of a "sovereign"/"supreme"/"provincial council" in occupied Alsace, first in 1657 and in its final, though short-lived, form in 1698, see Alain J. Lemaître, 'Le conseil souverain d'Alsace. Les limites de la souveraineté', 3 *Revue du Nord* (2015), 479–96.

[241] For the former strategy, see Sahlins, 'Natural Frontiers Revisited', 1423–51. The legal seriousness of these strategies is highlighted in Dickmann, 'Rechtsgedanke', 52–70. Likewise, Philip McCluskey, *Absolute Monarchy on the Frontiers. Louis XIV's Military Occupations of Lorraine and Savoy* (Manchester University Press 2016), 13–14, 37–9.

[242] Pierre Dupuy, *Traitez touchant les droits du Roy Très-Chrétien sur plusieurs Estats et Seigneuries possedés par divers princes voisins* (Nouvelle edition, Rouen, Maurry 1670). See also Markus Baumanns, *Die publizistischen Werk des kaiserlichen Diplomats Franz Paul Freiherr von Lisola (1613–1674)* (Baden-Baden, Humblot 1994), 83.

ruled it as French king and not as the emperor of Rome.[243] The work updated and expanded the claims made in Dupuy's treatise and caused great commotion around Europe as apparently irrefutable proof of the French designs for universal monarchy.[244]

Both works were based on a deeply feudal understanding of Europe's political system. The point was always to show that a member of the French ruling family had at some time given up French rights in violation of French fundamental laws or through otherwise unjust usurpation. The argument was based on French history and laws as well as medieval rules on vassalage and suzerainty. These works were accompanied by others, written by pamphleteers and members of the royal entourage, that made exorbitant claims to sustain the French designs. The anonymous work on *Les idées politiques de l'Empire français* even suggested a complete reorganisation of all government between the Near East and Gibraltar, Mediterranean and Moscow, with an imperial centre in Paris.[245]

It is not clear that Richelieu or his king had much faith in such designs. What the wars had achieved was a firm coalition of European powers against what they saw as France's ruthless and illegal pursuit of universal monarchy. In 1667, Baron François-Paul de Lisola (1613–74), a Frenchman in the service of imperial diplomacy, launched a full-scale attack on the Sun King's claims, counteracting them by a skilful exposition and analysis of traditional rights over territory and just war. Citing literature from Augustine to Grotius, he argued that the French military operations in the Habsburg lands were both formally and in substance against the well-established law of nations. In fact, he suggested, they were

[243] Antoine Aubery, *Des justes pretensions du Roi sur l'Empire* (Paris, Bertier 1667). The same claim, extending also to the Low Countries (Flanders, Brabant, Artois), Milan, Naples and Sicily, was also made by Bésian Arroy, Doctor of the Paris theology faculty in *Questions decidées sur la Justice des armes de Roi de France* (Paris, Loyson 1634). For Arroy, four types of legal sources determined the justice of French claims: French Salic law (which had allegedly often been violated), other French laws (especially regarding non-alienability of territory), the law of nations (which Arroy understood to provide for the golden rule – "de ne faire à autruy ce que on ne voudroit estre fait à soy") – and justice as such, 84–101, 95. The obvious fragility of these claims follows at least partly from the fact that the author was not a jurist. On the other hand, the fact that such a tract could have been put forward testified to the absence in the country of a well-developed culture of law of nature and of nations.

[244] Baumanns, *Lisola*, 94–100.

[245] Cited by Thuau, *Raison d'État*, 289–92.

merely a smokescreen over the real designs of Louis XIV and therefore had greater principled significance:

> The matter concerns observance of the Law of Nations that is common to all and preventing the introduction of maxims into the world that would destroy all exchange among humans and would make human society equally dangerous as that of lions and tigers; it concerns defending public faith in treaties against all kinds of tricks and chicaneries, conserving the rules and formalities in the law of arms that have been established by the universal consent of all nations.[246]

The contrast between Lisola's *Bouclier d'Estat* and the French works could not have been greater. The imperial ambassador took great care to refute the French claims by arguments from traditional law of nations practically non-existent in his adversaries' tracts. Other works, pamphlets of more or less scholarly merit, were produced on the German side and followed up on Lisola's suggestion that the French arguments only provided a smokescreen for its expansive intentions.[247] By now the theme of universal monarchy had become a commonplace of anti-French propaganda.[248] Lisola's arguments mirrored sentiments shared across the continent and strengthened by the intolerance shown by the Sun King by his revocation of the Edict of Nantes (1685).[249] Outrage was especially great when in 1688 France entered the German Habsburg territory, devastating parts of the Palatinate, including Mannheim, Speyer and Worms, in an apparently wanton scorched-earth strategy, earning the unending enmity of the countries that eventually joined in a

[246] "Il s'agit ici de maintenir le Droit des Gens, qui est commun à tous, & d'empescher que l'on ne introduise des maximes dans le Monde, qui destruiroient tout le commerce des Hommes, & rendroient la société humaine, aussi dangereuse que celle des Lyons & des Tygres, il s'agit de deffendre la foy publique des Traittez, contre les ruses de la chicane; de conserver le droit des armes dans les regles & les formalitez, que les consentement universel de toutes les Nations a etablies." Baron de Lisola, *Bouclier d'Estat et de Justice contre le dessein manifestement découvert de la Monarchie Universelle sous le vain prétexte des prétentions de la Reyne de France* (no publisher, 1667), 316–17.

[247] See Baumanns, *Lisola*, 98–113, 124–7.

[248] See Franz Bosbach, 'The European Debate on Universal Monarchy', in David Armitage (ed.), *Theories of Empire 1450–1800* (Aldershot, Ashgate 1998), 92–7.

[249] See Baumanns, *Lisola*, 114–27. Also, a secret treaty had in fact been prepared in 1665–8 between Louis and the Emperor, Leopold I, on the division of the Spanish world in case of death of the fragile Charles II. According to the plan, France would have received the Spanish Netherlands, Franche-Comté, Navarre and the Philippines, and the emperor Spain as well as its American possessions – a virtual division of the world. See Lucien Bély, *Les secrets de Louis XIV. Mystères d'État et pouvoir absolu* (Paris, Tallandier 2013), 316–38.

Grand Coalition against it.[250] In the famous satire *Mars Christianissimus* of 1684, Leibniz claimed that in these latter years the king had dropped all pretence of giving a legal justification to his claims. Feeling himself of divine origin, he had simply come to think of himself as the "true and sole vicar of the world with respect to all temporal matters".[251]

The destruction of the Palatinate signalled the end of French greatness in more ways than one. The wars had begun to eat seriously into French resources. At the beginning of the 1670s, the country fielded about 120,000 soldiers while at the onset of the Nine Years' War the size of the French army had arisen to 430,000.[252] Military defeats and the numbers of casualties arose steadily while the home front was forced to bear massively increased taxation. At a point where economic troubles had compelled severe cuts in French naval expenditures, Marshal Vauban (1633–1707) suggested bringing in private interests to assist the French war effort.[253] The united armies of the League of Augsburg could always produce a land army equalling the French, he wrote. The same applied to their navies.[254] So how best to fight them? If the strength of France's adversaries lay in their ability to obtain resources from their colonies and if they could not be successfully engaged in a *guerre d'escadre*, they could be struck by massively increased privateering. The long French coastline and its colonies were well adapted for such a strategy. Private *armateurs* could be incentivised to capture enemy vessels. Ships of the line, even with officers and crews, could be rented to enterprising privateers. Enemy ships could be ransomed without trial, the share of *armateurs* of the prize could be increased and their taxes diminished. Such public–private cooperation was nothing new. Half the ships used by the *Compagnie des indes orientales* during the Nine Years' War belonged to the king.[255] But Vauban's *grand*

[250] Lynn, *The Wars of Louis XIV*, 193–9. See also Malettke, *Les relations entre la France et le Saint-Empire*, 491–2.

[251] Leibniz, 'Mars Christianissimus', in *Leibniz. Political Writings* (Patrick Riley ed., Cambridge University Press 1988), 126.

[252] Cornette, *La mort de Louis XIV*, 199.

[253] For the cuts and their effect on the navy, and the subsequent turn to the *guerre de course*, see Geoffrey Symcox, *The Crisis of French Sea Power 1688–1697. From the* Guerre d'Escade *to the* Guerre de Course (The Hague, Nijhoff 1974), 143–220.

[254] Sébastien Le Prestre, Marquis de Vauban, 'Mémoire concernant la caprerie. La course et les privilèges dont elle a besoin pour se pouvoir établir', in Sébastien Le Prestre, Marquis de Vauban & Gabriel-Henri Gaillard, *Oisivetés de M. Vauban*, tome IV (Paris, Corréard 1842), 161.

[255] John Selwyn Bromley, 'The Loan of French Naval Vessels to Privateering Enterprises 1688–1713', in John Selwyn Bromley, *Corsairs and Navies 1660–1760* (London, Hambledon 1987), 187.

*guerre de course* would have a wholly new amplitude. With over 7,000 ransoms and prize condemnations in the War of the Spanish Succession "an offensive [was waged] against Allied trade [that was] perhaps the most intensive ever waged by the French nation".[256]

But the royal treasury could barely stand the war effort.[257] Bad harvests in 1691–2 and the prompt surge of grain prices led to massive famine that spread from rural areas to the cities, accompanied by riots across the country. In 1693 alone, France lost perhaps as much as one-fifth of its population and by the following year, four million Frenchmen had died of the famine.[258] The *rayonnement* of the king had begun to wear thin and the dirigist legacy of Colbert and his followers became the target of increasing public criticism. As the lawyer and economic thinker Pierre Le Pesant, sieur de Boisguilbert (1646–1714) wrote in 1695, the unjust tax system and the many obstacles to internal and external commerce were crushing all economic initiative: "*C'est une grand avance pour la Majesté que ses peuples soient riches*", he insisted, while no more than two or three edicts would be needed that "*rendront seulement les chemins libres et les impôts justement repartis*".[259]

Boisguilbert was one of the Jansenist critics of absolutism whom Louis XIV had attacked throughout his regime, including by persuading the pope to produce the bull *Unigentus* (1713) – one of the most controversial statements ever made by the papacy.[260] An influential group of intellectuals and theologians, followers of the Dutch cleric Cornelius Jansen at Port Royal, had in the 1640s begun to espouse a rigorous Augustinianism, stressing human sinfulness and God's grace as the key to human salvation. The contemplative and inner-worldly Jansenists preached the simple life and had little respect for court culture. Against official doctrine, they regarded kingship as a human, not divine institution, though they did accept obedience as a religious duty. Intellectuals such as Blaise Pascal and Pierre Nicole suggested that the role of political institutions was above all to turn self-love and egoism into useful service for society. Nobody could be a saint, but it was

256 John Selwyn Bromley, 'The French Privateering War 1702–1713', in Bromley, *Corsairs and Navies*, 220. He counts the number of ransoms as 2,200 and other (prize) condemnations as 4,545.

257 For the collection of the "extraordinaire de guerre" during Louis XIV, see Rowlands, *The Dynastic State*, 109–34.

258 Cornette, *La mort de Louis XIV*, 203.

259 Pierre Le Pesant sieur de Boisguilbert, *Le détail de France* (no publisher, 1695), 180.

260 The pope had already condemned Jansenism in 1653, and it has been said that *Unigentus* in fact gave a breath of life to an already moribund set of beliefs in 1713.

possible to be an *Honnête homme*.[261] Jansenism was especially widespread among French jurists – perhaps because access to the theology faculty was barred from boys who did not expressly disavow it. Later Jansenism became an important part of the *parlementaire* ideology that was opposed to the *mondain* features of court society.[262] The most powerful legal voice to emerge in France in the last decades of the seventeenth century was deeply implicated in this kind of thinking.

## Law for a Broken Humanity: Domat

Le Bret and Loyseau had been the principal inheritors of the previous century's strong tradition of juristic thinking but neither came close to the originality of Bodin. Le Bret had helped Richelieu to devise some of the legal strategies with respect to reunions, and Loyseau produced the most detailed legal description of the system of French public law in the early part of the century. But the only jurist whose work provided an intellectually forceful response to the malaise of the century's end and "shines such a solitary light that one almost assumes it having emerged from nowhere", was Jean Domat (1626–96).[263] Domat had been a practising *avocat du Roi* from Clermont, a friend of Pascal's who was, despite his Jansenism, invited by Louis XIV to stay in Paris in the 1680s to continue work for the reordering of French private and public law. In his main works, *Les lois civiles dans leur ordre naturel* (1689) and its extension, the posthumously published fragment, *Les quatre livres de droit public* (1697), Domat put forward a conservative, theologically based naturalism, which did not so much innovate as provide an articulation of the objectives of a Christian polity. Domat supported absolutism but, unlike his colleagues, did not view the king as the embodiment of divine law. A Jansenist, he was committed to a sceptical view of the human capacity for goodness without strong guidance on the part of public power. Self-interest was a ruling motive in human affairs and the task of law was to direct it to useful purposes. Unlike Grotius, Domat did not believe that self-interest grounded anything like a subjective right. Instead, proper government required the enforcement of the natural duties humans had to each other. This also explained why subjects were bound to

261 See especially Keohane, *Philosophy and the State in France*, 262–303.

262 See especially David A. Bell, *Lawyers and Citizens. The Making of Political Elite in Early Modern France* (Oxford University Press 1994), 68–73.

263 Renoux-Zagamé, *Du droit de dieu*, 117.

obey even laws that were unjust, as long as they were not contrary to divine law.[264]

In Domat, ideas about sovereignty and government were integrated in a rigorously Augustinian ascetics and disinterest in the secular values propagated by the court. His views could therefore spread among the bourgeois opposition and those with a wider disenchantment with worldly society.[265] Domat regarded the French legal system as a wholly disordered mélange of rules and jurisdictions. Everybody knew that murder and theft were wrong, but few could give a true explanation for this state of affairs. Domat wanted to prove the truth of such intuitions not only to the heart but to the mind.[266] Pascal and others from Port-Royal had presented an extremely sceptical view of the human capacity to know natural law – "*verité en deça des Pyrenées, erreur au-delà*".[267] But Domat wanted to show that local customs and ordinances were neither arbitrary nor whimsical but instruments of divine purpose. He began with the axiom that because law sought to direct human behaviour it was necessary to know what humans existed for. This, he wrote, was in order to love the "sovereign good" that was God.[268] Like the moralists, however, he had a bleak view of the human capacity in this respect. Instead of loving God, humans had begun to

264 Jean Domat, *Les Quatre livres du droit public. 1697* (Université de Caen, Centre de philosophie politique et juridique. Textes et Documents, 1989), 19.

265 Jansenism was the most important source of opposition to Louis XIV. It was particularly popular among jurists critical of courtly society. Bell, *Lawyers and Citizens*, 68–73; Keohane, *Philosophy and the State*, 262–6. Jansenist theology had originally stressed the role of grace and personal salvation and subscribed to a rigorous view of predestination. The papal condemnation may in fact have offered a platform for political discontent and a channel for spirituality otherwise absent from church and society. Criticism of papal absolutism within the church was translated by Jansenists in the eighteenth century into an attack on political absolutism so that the question of the limits of sovereignty became a leading theme of Jansenist constitutionalism. See Michael Sonenscher, *Before the Deluge. Public Debt, Inequality, and the Intellectual Origins of the French Revolution* (Princeton University Press 2007), 153–4.

266 Jean Domat, *Traité des lois* (Université de Caen, Centre de philosophie politique et juridique, 1989), Ch I (2–3). On Domat's search for "foundations" and order among the plethora of legal sources used in France, see Zarka, *Philosophie et politique*, 207–22, and also the brief but useful William F. Church, 'The Decline of the French Jurists as Political Theorists 1660–1789', 5 *French Historical Studies* (1967), 13–22.

267 For a helpful discussion, see Francesco Paolo Adorno, *Le discipline de l'amour. Pascal, Port-Royal et la politique* (Paris, Kimé 2010), 63–76.

268 ". . . car sa nature n'est autre chose que cet être créé à l'image de Dieu, et capable de posséder ce souverain-bien qui doit être sa vie est sa béatitude", Domat, *Traité des lois*, I (4).

love themselves. Even the most cherished virtues were simply disguised forms of self-love (*amour propre*). A workable social order necessitated institutional arrangements that would turn self-love to the general good. This was a widely used seventeenth-century theme – we have seen Grotius employ it, and it had been embodied in the works from Montaigne to Pascal as well.[269] Domat situated it within a theological frame to read even self-love as love of God's image in humans. Self-love "*n'est que dérèglement et injustice*",[270] unable to provide real happiness. It could nevertheless, if well-ordered, offer a satisfactory context for social life. With the increase of human needs, it would prompt engagement in all kinds of useful work. In this way, "the poison of society is used by God as an instrument to sustain it".[271]

Domat's rationalism offered a remarkably realistic image of society and a persuasive, utilitarian view of government. As humans turned to worldly things, it soon became clear that they did not suffice to everyone. This is how commerce and wage labour were born, pursuits that could not be sustained without the cultivation of honesty, fidelity, sincerity and good faith. Here the values of commercial society coincided with the objectives of Christian government. But private exchanges could not operate without guidance from the strong hand of royal power. One of Domat's great innovations was to set up public law formally on a par with private law, though materially subordinated to the latter. The character of social relations would result from private agreements, coordinated by public law. The principal aspect of Domat's public law was not sovereign power but the administration of *police*, the control and supervision of private activities with the view of maintaining the peace of Christian community.[272] Throughout, Domat presented his concepts as legal truths, deducible by reason from the objectives of social life, valid irrespective of time and place because enacted by God and directed to the consolidation of Christian faith.[273]

[269] On the discussions of the Augustinian/Epicurean stress on self-interest as the leading motivational force in the seventeenth and eighteenth centuries, see further Pierre Force, *Self-Interest before Adam Smith. A Genealogy of Economic Science* (Cambridge University Press 2003) and on Jansenism in particular, Christian Laval, *L'homme économique. Essai sur les racines du néolibéralisme* (Paris, Gallimard 2007), 79–105.

[270] Renoux-Zagamé, *Du droit de dieu*, 84. See also Goyard-Fabre, 'Domat', 150–7.

[271] Domat, *Traité des lois*, VIII, 26.

[272] See Bernardo Sordi, 'Public Law before "Public Law"', in Heikki Pihlajamäki, Markus D. Dubber & Mark Godefry (eds), *The Oxford Handbook of European Legal History* (Oxford University Press 2018), 714–17; David Gilles, 'Jean Domat et les fondements du droit public', 25–26 *Revue d'histoire des facultés de droit* (2006), 102–5.

[273] Domat, *Traité des lois*, XI, 36–44.

But no law could achieve this without the intervention of the judge: "It is in the use of judgment and in the enlightened sense of justice [. . .] in which consists the most essential part of the science of the laws; it is nothing else than the art to distinguish in accordance with justice and equity."[274] Even as legislator, the sovereign was above all a judge – a judge of what was needed to bring about the good of the state.[275] Public power was thoroughly utilitarian:

> Everyone knows that to produce and maintain the good of the state one must see to it that it possesses everything with which it can make sure that those who compose it have what they need and what is useful for them; that they live in peace and security against efforts of neighbours and enemies; that the authority of justice is absolute; that the military arts, the sciences, fine arts and commerce flourish through the multitude of people that enage in them.[276]

Domat's work was no doubt felt useful by the king because it set aside the effort of justifying sovereign rule. The king was instituted by God and that was that. The jurist could instead focus on the purposes for which God's law would be put and the practices it would regulate. With *amour propre* as his operating principle, Domat would subscribe to the mercantilist policy of his king. By engaging in trade nations were able to receive goods that they would otherwise lack. Even the pursuit of domestic agriculture necessitated tools and animals that would often have to be purchased from abroad so that through working diligently for their own good, nations would come closer to each other. It was useful to grant privileges to fairs and markets, and to encourage economic exchanges with foreigners.[277] Long sections of Domat's treatise of public law dwelt on the principles of policy regulation of towns, municipalities, provinces, universities, hospitals and so on.[278]

The interactions between sovereigns were also regulated by natural law, namely "the natural laws of humanity, of hospitality and fidelity, and all those that depend on these and that regulate the manner people from different nations should act towards each other in peace and war".[279] International trade was necessary and natural. Seas, for example, and fisheries, were to be open to all nations. Rules had been created for the enjoyment of those freedoms, as on the uses of the

274 Ibid., XI, 59 and 59–66.

275 The one who governs was a "judge of men", and in that capacity carried out God's task on earth. Domat, *Quatre livres du droit public*, I (20).

276 Ibid., I, 8–9.

277 Ibid., I VII I & III, 137–8, 141–4.

278 Ibid., I VII II, 140–1, I VIII, 152–69, I XV, 244–50.

279 Domat, *Traité des lois*, XI, 55–6.

oceans, but where nations clashed, nothing but war could sort out their differences.[280] Wars for glory and conquest were unjust – a brave statement in the last decades of reign of the Sun King. Only wars of self-defence were just, although they could be undertaken before the aggression has taken place, and they were to be conducted moderately.[281] None of this was new, of course, but now set within a rationalist frame that allowed setting aside the fundamental law-oriented approaches of Le Bret and other royal jurists. Domat's public law reached towards the universal, even the scientific. He was not interested in the histories of the Franks and the Gauls, the Salic law or principles of dynastic legitimacy. Instead he viewed public law as an instrument for coordinating the private pursuit of self-interest in view of the common good.[282] By channelling self-love in public institutions human beings were doing God's work in the only way realistically available to them.

## Law of Nations and Moral Regeneration; Fénelon and D'Aguesseau

The Peace of Ryswick (1697) was not as severe on France as might have been expected. Perhaps the most bitter concession was that Louis had to recognise his arch-enemy, William of Orange, as the king of England. France suffered territorial losses in Europe but in exchange received British recognition of the valuable possession of Saint-Domingue in the Caribbean. But no breathing space was offered to Frenchmen. The death of Charles II of Spain in 1700 threatened the union of French and Spanish crowns and prompted immediate action on the part of Austria, Britain and the Netherlands, later joined by Savoy and Portugal. At times in the War of the Spanish Succession (1701–13) France staggered on the brink as its soundings for peace went largely unheeded. Bad harvests in 1709 deepened a devastating rural famine. That and the creation of an anti-French coalition contributed to dissatisfaction at home for which there was no open channel of expression. Even a privileged observer, Archbishop Fénelon (1651–1715), the preceptor of the royal princes at Versailles, had to direct his criticisms at Louis' courtiers, their indifference to the suffering of the population, the uses of glory and vengeance as motives

280 Domat, *Quatre livres du droit public*, I VIII, 150–1, 152.
281 Ibid., I II II, 43.
282 Laval, *L'homme économique*, 99; Church, 'The Decline of the French Jurists', 16.

of war: "*une guerre injuste n'en est pas moins injuste pour être heureuse*".[283] Fénelon instructed his royal students to bear in mind the importance of "common rules of justice and humanity", faithfulness and modesty in public and private life and the moral hazards accompanying luxury trade.[284] These were also key themes in Fénelon's most famous work, *The Adventures of Telemachus, Son of Ulysses* (1699), which looked towards ancient virtues as the proper direction to govern France – moral adroitness, modesty, love of truth and justice, keeping one's word even to one's enemies and humanity in warfare.[285] As Telemachus arrived on the Island of Crete, admired for its prosperity, he found out that the only cause for unhappiness on the island arose from its inhabitant's endless desire for luxuries. Hence, Minos, the wisest of lawmakers, had decreed that children should be educated in the simple life and the excellence of virtue: "*Ici on punit trois vices qui sont impunies chez les autres peoples: l'ingratitude, la dissimulation et l'avarice.*"[286]

In a late text on political authority, Fénelon took up the assignment of sovereigns to control the passions that made people prefer the private interest to the public. Kings should always remember that public good was "the immutable and universal law of sovereigns".[287] This was annexed to a piece originally written for the instruction of the duke of Burgundy, the crown prince on whom the reformers had put their hopes. Here Fénelon had conducted a thinly veiled attack on Louis XIV. "Have you ever studied seriously that which is called the law of nations?", he asked among a series of rhetorical questions of his king.[288] "It is that law which regulates his most important functions and it expresses the most obvious principles of natural law valid for the whole humanity."[289] No sovereign was liberated from the force of natural law and the law of nations. Treaties were to be honestly kept and no sovereign was entitled to invoke his domestic laws – including the law on succession to the throne – over the law of nations.[290] The laws of war

[283] François de Salignac de la Mothe-Fénelon, 'Lettre à Louis XIV', in François de Salignac de la Mothe-Fénelon, *Lettre à Louis XIV et autres écrits politiques* (Paris, Bartillat 2011), 49.

[284] François de Salignac de la Mothe-Fénelon, 'Examen de conscience sur les devoirs de royauté. Mémoire pour le duc de Bourgogne' (c. 1708–9), in François de Salignac de la Mothe-Fénelon, *Directions pour la conscience d'un roi* (Paris, Benovard 1825), 21–4.

[285] François de Salignac de la Mothe-Fénelon, 'Les aventures de Télémaque, fils d'Ulysses', in Louis Vives (ed.), *Oeuvres de Fénelon, Archevêque de Cambrai*, tome 3 (Paris, Lefevre 1835), 101.

[286] Ibid., 26. [287] Fénelon, 'Examen de conscience', 106. [288] Ibid., 11.

[289] Ibid., 11. [290] Ibid., 59–61, 86–7.

were as binding as the laws of peace, and committed all sovereigns to refrain from wanton destruction. Faith was to be kept even with enemies and they were to be treated as we would ourselves wish to be treated. "There exists a certain law of nations that is the foundation of humanity itself [*le fonds de l'humanité même*]."[291] It was true that all sovereigns needed to be watchful of their neighbours and take action against efforts at hegemony. This was best achieved by acknowledging that none of them could be safe alone, that they were tied into a network of interdependencies. That was why, "both for their particular security, as well as for the common interest, they were to join in a kind of society and republic together".[292]

Fénelon completely rejected the separation of private and public morality that had accompanied the *raison d'état.* His proposal to think of the coming post-war order in terms of a *république universelle* of which European (Christian) nations would be members could not have been further away from the statecraft of Louis and his publicists.[293] What France needed according to Fénelon was moral leadership under a king who would educate the country in peacefulness and modesty; economic resources ought to be oriented towards a flourishing agriculture and not wasted in superfluities.[294] A state that would grow prosperous by relying on domestic resources, he argued, would also be stronger in its foreign policy and have no need for demonstrations of militarism.[295]

Fénelon was a clergyman whose appeals to the law of nature and of nations did not arise from professional engagement with such notions. By contrast, Henri-Francois d'Aguesseau (1688–1751) was an influential jurist, *avocat du Roi, procureur* of the *Parlement* of Paris, and, since 1717, chancellor of justice, at times also *garde des Sceaux.*[296] D'Aguesseau combined judicial practice and legislative work with extensive writing in Domat's footsteps, propounding a rationalist natural law that framed the monarchic order within a rigorous ideology of the rule of law. His principal legal works were contained in a series of *Mercurials* that commented on practice of French courts, as

291 Ibid., 56. 292 Fénelon, *Directions*, 87. 293 Ibid., 95.

294 István Hont, *Jealousy of Trade. International Competition and the Nation-State in Historical Perspective* (Harvard University Press 2006), 25–7.

295 For a comment, see Sonenscher, *Before the Deluge*, 110.

296 For general discussion, see Edgar Faure, 'Le Chancelier D'Aguesseau', *Revue des Deux Mondes* (1952), 577–87; Isabelle Storez, 'La philosophie politique du Chancelier D'Aguesseau', 266 *Revue historique* (1981), 381–400, and the essays in Claude Gauvard (ed.), *Penseurs de Code Civil* (Paris, Collection de Histoire de Justice 2009).

well as the posthumously published *Méditations métaphysiques sur la vraie ou le fausse idée de la justice* and *Essai d'institution au droit public.*[297] Like Domat, D'Aguesseau understood the heart of law to lie in judicial decision-making and anxiously emphasised judicial independence, viewing the magistracy as the nucleus of something like an apolitical republicanism.[298] The monarch was bound by divine and natural law as well as the law of nations, which was nothing other than natural law applied between nations and the principles that regulated life within nations universally.[299] In *Metaphysical meditations* he speculated at great length and with excessive generality about a divinely based natural law that could be known as the reason that in all people collaborated with *amour propre* to produce a much more optimistic outlook than Domat's.[300] Societies were formed out of the desire of the good and mutual affection, not the mere wish to avoid evil.[301] Quite strikingly, D'Aguesseau regarded all humans as born equal; all status was the result of positive law.[302] Like Domat, D'Aguesseau understood the nation as having been created by individuals for their perfection and happiness, but also for the allocation of status.[303]

D'Aguesseau suggested that all nations belonged to one great society ruled by laws of nature and that these laws, assumed to coincide with

[297] In M. Pardessus, *Oevures complètes du Chancelier D'Aguesseau* (nouvelle édition, Paris, Fantin 1819), tome 14 (*Méditations*), and tome 15, 164–272 ('Droit public'). (*Méditations* has been republished by Fayard in 2005.) D'Aguesseau was a widely respected, conservative jurist whose principal work in the field of legislation had to do with the preparation of series of private law codes that have been read as pointing the way to the *code civil*. For a list of those codes, see Storez, 'La philosophie politique', 399.

[298] Bell, *Lawyers and Citizens*, 63–6.

[299] D'Aguesseau, *Méditations métaphysiques*, 597–8, 601–6; D'Aguesseau, 'Droit public', 166.

[300] "Le droit naturel ne sera donc pour moi que ce que on appelle *Dictamen rectae rationis*". 'Dixième méditation', D'Aguesseau, *Méditations métaphysiques*, 596. For the Cartesian roots of D'Aguesseau's rationalism, see e.g. Storez, 'La philosophie politique', 391–3. See also Lucien Jaume, 'Raison publique et raison métaphysique chez D'Aguesseau. La place des *Méditations*', in Gauvard (ed.), *Penseurs de Code Civil*, 45–8.

[301] D'Aguesseau, 'Droit public', 270.

[302] For the importance of this, see Roland Mousnier, 'D'Aguesseau et le tournant des ordres aux classes sociales', 4 *Revue d'histoire économique et sociale* (1971), 449–64.

[303] The objective of public law was the "perfection and happiness" of the nation. D'Aguessaeu, 'Droit public', 165. D'Aguesseau speculated about the pain and pleasure that moved humans and that it was the task of the law to unite my (long-term) pleasure with that of others so as to bring about the "perfection" of all, D'Aguesseau, in *Méditations métaphysiques*, 574–5.

requirements of universal morality, were binding everywhere.[304] Like much French writing at the time and later, his theorising moved at such high levels of abstraction that it was often hard to see its practical implications. He expressly regarded nations like individuals, bound in their relations as were members of domestic society, but rejected any centralised enforcement among them.[305] Unlike the jurists inspired by *raison d'état*, he did not speak of rational government as law, though he did note that private interests needed to yield to the needs of the state.[306] A proper reading of the polity would be received from Roman law's focus on positive legislation and the exalted role of the judge. The duties to abide by the laws of war and to fulfil treaty requirements were part of *amour propre*. Enemies were to be loved and treaties merely renewed the natural pact among nations.[307]

D'Aguesseau was an influential figure in the royal council for almost three decades where, as *garde des Sceaux* most of his attention was directed at ruling over the French magistracy and preparing legislative projects on private law. Although his philosophical speculations moved within a robust natural law frame, they remained distant from his practical activities. These speculations, like his brief notes on public law, presumed a very different political culture from the one where he lived under Louis XIV. As the *deuxième personnage de la monarchie*,[308] he of course never joined any opposition though his insistence on the independence of judges and individual rights went some way towards a critique of the worst aspects of the reign.[309] As *garde des Sceaux* he had little to do with France's relations to its neighbours, as worked out in Utrecht at the close of the Sun King's long reign.

304 "Ces grands sociétés [i.e. nations] ne sont elles-mêmes que partie de société beaucoup plus étendues qui comprennent tous les peuples de la terre", and if they follow their *amour propre*, they "tendent toujours au bien commun de l'humanité comme à un bien supérieur à celui de chaque nation", D'Aguesseau, *Méditations métaphysiques*, 605–6. In his institutions of public law, D'Aguesseau confirmed that "les hommes considérés en général formant une société universelle du genre humain", D'Aguesseau, 'Droit public', 165. He also frequently quoted Cicero to this effect. See Mousnier, 'D'Aguesseau et le tournant des ordres', 458–60.

305 D'Aguesseau, *Méditations métaphysiques*, 605.

306 See D'Aguesseau, 'Mémoire pour prouver que les fiefs et les offices du criminel de lesé majesté appartiennent au roi', *Oeuvres completes*, tome 8, 95.

307 D'Aguesseau, *Méditations métaphysiques*, 605.

308 Storez, 'La philosophie politique', 385.

309 But as the *Parlement* was a principal source of criticism of royal policy in the eighteenth century, D'Aguesseau's stress on its dignity and right of remonstrance could be read as a modest effort to set limits to the king's power.

## Utrecht

Towards the end of the War of the Spanish Succession, Fénelon had composed a series of memoranda for friends in the court to speak against the war. He lamented the slowness of the peace talks and proposed to include as negotiators men of substantive reputation alien to the kinds of scheming he assumed to be taking place in regular peace talks.[310] It was not to be so. The French minister Colbert de Torcy (1665–1746, a nephew of the famous controller-general) used seasoned courtiers whom he could trust to outmanoeuvre their counterparts in the best tradition of *ancien régime* diplomacy. The negotiations lasted many years and involved precisely the kind of secret bargaining that Fénelon wished to exorcise from virtuous policymaking.[311] In the end, the Peace of Utrecht (1713) did not come a moment too early for France. Alongside settlement of the succession issue, the treaties contained provision on Anglo-French colonial settlement in North America as well as other territorial questions and on the fate of the *asiento*, the transfer of the monopoly of Atlantic slave trade to the English South Sea Company.[312]

Utrecht was not Fénelon's peace. But it did signify a change in the political consciousness of the contemporaries.[313] Even Louis himself on his deathbed expressed regrets at his belligerency. Many aspects of the *ancien régime*, including its dynastic wars, would no longer seem acceptable. Intellectuals and diplomats pressed for a way to think strategically about France's position in relation to its rivals. According to men such as Vauban and Boisguilbert, none of this needed to be thought as a zero-sum game; everyone's wealth was dependent on a stable peace and opening access to markets everywhere. This was to include access to the colonies in Spanish America, as Nicolas Mesnager, the merchant who was part of the French delegation, pointed out. After all, French wealth was largely created

310 For the Memoranda, see *Oeuvres de Fénelon, Achevêque de Cambrai*, tome 3 (Paris, Lefevre 1835), 410–11. See further, Lucien Bély, *L'art de la paix en Europe. Naissance de la diplomatie moderne XVIe–XVIII siècle* (Presses Universitaires de France 2007), 433, 452.

311 Bély, *L'art de la paix*, 503–24. A good account of the conduct of the peace talks from the French perspective is in Dale Miquelon, 'Envisioning the French Empire. Utrecht 1711–1713', 24 *French Historical Studies* (1991), 653–77.

312 The point about the centrality of the trade aspects of the treaty arrangements, especially for France, is made in Miquelon, 'Envisioning the French Empire', 654–5.

313 See Paul Hazard, *Le crise de la conscience européenne 1680–1715* (Paris, Fayard 1961), especially 225 ff.

through imports from the New World.[314] The Utrecht instruments expressed the common interests of European nations in varied ways. The letter of renunciation by the king of Spain of his claim to the French throne (1712) expressly stated that the "universal good and quiet of Europe" depended on the maxim that there was to be "equal weight of power" among the principal states of Europe.[315] The Franco-Dutch Peace Treaty (1713) within the general peace took up the theme of European public law, *Droit public de l'Europe*, a theme familiar as a concept if not as an expression, now extended to the pursuit of a joint European interest as law.[316]

Balance of power was referenced at Utrecht to mark a shared desire to work against universal monarchy.[317] It had a long pedigree from fifteenth- century northern Italy and the Westphalian peace, and it was sometimes used as a strategic basis for operations a nation needed to make so as to stave off present or foreseeable danger. Even Fénelon accepted war as just to prevent a neighbour from becoming over-mighty.[318] Richelieu had already envisaged France's role in Europe as the great arbitrator, and Fénelon's Directives expressed the hope that Europe would one day vindicate *les droits de la fraternité humaine.*[319] Defensive treaties would serve the role that laws and magistrates served

314 Lucien Bély, 'Behind the Stage. The Global Dimension of the Negotiation', in R. E de Brion et al. (eds), *Performances of Peace. Utrecht 1713* (Leiden, Brill 2015), 40–52.

315 Letters Patent by Philip V on 5 November 1712, in J. Almon, *A Collection of all the Treaties of Peace, Alliance and Commerce between Great Britain and Other Powers*, vol. I (1688-1727) (London, Almon 1772), 116. The renunciation was especially striking as it meant ostensibly violation of the sacrosanct laws of succession and thus went against the *lois fondamentales*. Cornette, *La mort de Louis XIV*, 276. But Louis was not the first king who held parts of crown domain as negotiating chips and also breached the succession laws in his testament by making his bastard sons his successors.

316 Wilhelm Grewe, *Epochs of International Law* (Berlin, De Gruyter 2000), 395.

317 See Marc Bélissa, *Fraternité universelle et intérêt national (1713–1795). Les cosmopolitiques du droit des gens* (Paris, Kimé 1998), 85–6. For the intellectual origins of balance-of-power thinking, see e.g. Michael Sheehan, *The Balance of Power. History & Theory* (London, Routledge 1996), 24–52; Bruno Bernardi, 'L'idée de l'équilibre européen dans le jus gentium des modernes. Esquisse d'histoire conceptuelle', 4 *Assecuratio Pacis. Les conceptions françaises de la sûreté et de la garantie de la paix de 1648 à 1815* (2010), www.perspectivia.net/content/publikationen/discussions/4-2010/bernardi_idee.

318 Alberico Gentili, *De iure belli libri tres, Vol. II, The Translation of the Edition of 1612* (John Rolfe trans., Coleman Phillipson ed., Carnegie Endowment for International Peace, Oxford, Clarendon 1933), I XX (60); Francis Bacon, 'Of Empire', in John Pitcher (ed.), *The Essays* (Harmondsworth, Penguin 1985), 116–17. Fénelon, *Directions*, 93–105.

319 Fénelon, *Directions*, 107.

at home, he suggested, and uphold the balance that would operate as a kind of "*loi naturelle de la sûreté de . . . nations*".[320] The notion of "equilibrium" entered the talks at Utrecht with overt reference to Newtonian principles, suggesting that the political world might be treated by a method derived from natural science. Whatever else it may have meant, "Europe" now came to be regarded as a "system" to be managed by specialist techniques alongside other fields of government. As one of the French negotiators of the Peace of Ryswick (1697), François de Callières, noted in his account of the diplomacy under Louis XIV, the states of Europe were

> . . . like members of one and the same republic; it is almost never possible for a considerable transformation to take place in one of the members that would not lead to troubling the peace of all the others.[321]

In accordance with the standpoint offered by political economy and *raison d'état*, Europe would now be imagined as a totality of interrelated parts that reacted to the changes in their respective positions in predictable ways. This system could be managed by rational policies so as to realise the interests of all. De Callières quoted Rohan's dictum about interest ruling princes but observed that, unfortunately, very often passions had overridden their better judgment. Diplomacy was to make the princes see where their true interests lay, to know exactly their strengths, their financial situation and their domestic power, and persuade them to act accordingly.[322] In other words, diplomacy had to become a knowledge and a science of a special type. Ideally, he wrote, this meant that diplomats should be recruited from men of the widest capacities and experience, worldly cosmopolitans embodying the wisdom of all disciplines. In practice, however, such geniuses were scarce and one had to content oneself with churchmen, military experts and jurists (*gens de robe*). Each had their advantages and disadvantages. As for the jurists, they were useful for the composition of "treaties of peace, alliances and other types of conventions". But the training of a magistrate comported a significant professional deformation, namely:

[320] François de Salignac de la Mothe-Fénelon, 'Sur la necessité des former des alliances, tant offensives que defensives contre une puissance étrangère qui aspire manifestement à la monarchie universelle', in *Oeuvres De Fénelon*, 3, 360–3, 361a–b.

[321] François de Callières, *L'art de négocier sous Louis XIV* (Paris, Nouveau Monde 2006), 17.

[322] Ibid., 39, 43–6.

The habit of making judgments gives him an air of gravity and superiority that usually makes him less flexible and more difficult at the outset; his actions are also less considerate than those of courtiers who are accustomed to living with their superiors and their equals.[323]

## A Profession in Dire Straits

De Callières' opinion was widely shared by Frenchmen. In Holland Grotius had been able to sketch a system of sociability with a legal form that would underwrite both a strong central power and an expansive commercial ethos. Richelieu's objectives were similar, but legalism of the Grotian type, subjective rights and mercantile freedoms, remained alien to French public law. France was a feudal society. Instead of subjective rights, it was ruled by a system of noble privileges and reciprocal right/duty relationships between guilds, towns, provinces, officers, lords and vassals. State-building was a process of constant bargaining. Lawyers such as Bodin and Loyseau had proposed to coordinate the interests of those entities under a unified sovereignty. Once that objective was attained, sovereignty could give way to censorial action under which all Frenchmen would be enlisted in the reproduction of a *république bien ordonnée.*

But although Richelieu, Mazarin, Colbert and Louis XIV himself were aware of the dependence of French public power on cooperation by privileged groups, they never succeeded in fully enlisting them to the projects of central power. On the contrary, the king's interminable wars and religious intolerance roused opposition with the *parlements* and bound the court ever more tightly to the interests of its financiers. By the end of the seventeenth century, little was left among the French of the *gloire* of their king, *Louis le Petit.*[324] The French jurists of the latter part of the seventeenth century failed to respond creatively to the situation. Whether or not involved as officers of the crown, they often resembled De Callières' critical sketch – inflexible bureaucrats interested in legal detail and without a wider view of government or policy.[325] Many reasons explain this. The notion of royal sovereignty developed by sixteenth-century

323 Ibid., 135.

324 On the attitudes of Frenchmen at the death of Louis XIV, see Cornette, *La mort de Louis XIV*, 52–70.

325 See especially Church, 'The Decline of the French Jurists', 1–40. French juridical training was completely oriented towards the profession of the *avocat.* But even those who went to universities received no training in the predominant political idiom of the age, natural law. Bell, *Lawyers and Citizens*, 33–4.

jurisprudence was incorporated practically unchanged in the writings of later jurists who then focused on the details of French administrative institutions in a way that left little room for innovation.[326] Venality degraded the juridical profession, and from 1661 onwards, the king encroached constantly on the functioning of the judicial system. The anti-Jansenist campaign struck especially at the magistrates, and in 1673 *parlements* were compelled to register laws before they could make remonstrances. Soon after having organised itself in 1660–5, the bar association (*Conférences de discipline*) went into abeyance for over thirty years.[327]

Engagement with public law at a time of absolutism was highly sensitive. There was virtually no writing on the law of nations that would not have been part of Bourbon propaganda. Domat's posthumously published chapters, for example, brought no new substance to the field. Consciousness of the problems of legal pluralism, disparate legal sources and overlapping jurisdictions and privileges prompted the king in 1679 to allow teaching of Roman and French law at all French universities.[328] Seven royal professors and twelve lecturers (*docteurs agrégés*) were appointed in Paris.[329] But the point was to enhance teaching of French law and most new work focused on "the almost endless intricacies of private law".[330] If public law was treated, this was through large works that described the functioning of French public institutions in a handbook-like manner. What made French intellectuals in the eighteenth century shun juristic training was their conservative outlook, connected with their pragmatic orientation towards usefulness in the courts and the *bureaux d'avocat*.[331]

326 The great codifications of civil, criminal and commercial laws (1667, 1670 and 1673), for example, were prepared within the administration, Church, 'The Decline of the French Jurists', 4.

327 Bell, *Lawyers and Citizens*, 50–62.

328 Edit de Saint-Germain-en-Laye, April 1679. See Alfred De Curzon, 'L'Enseignement du Droit Français les Universities de France', 43 *Nouvelle Revue Historique Droit Français et Étranger* (1919), 224–9.

329 See e.g. Philippe Sueur, *Histoire du droit public français. XVe–XVIIIe siècle*, tome II: *Affirmation et crise de l'État sous l'Ancien Régime* (4th edn, Presses Universitaires de France 2009), 147–9.

330 Church, 'The Decline of the French Jurists', 6.

331 Even those who went through the three-year university course in order to have access to *parlements* received no training in social or political ideas beyond what they may have had at school or college. No natural law training was offered. For the limited efforts in the Paris faculty to break away from traditional teachings of Roman and French law ("*étroitement positiviste et pandectiste*") by historical enquiries, see Guy Antonetti, 'Traditionalistes et novateurs à la faculté des droits de Paris au XVIIIe siècle', 2 *Annales d'histoire des Facultés de droit* (1985), 37–50.

## A First Diplomatic School

The more or less hidden forms of criticism that began to emerge during the last years of the government of Louis XIV often focused on the conduct of the Sun King's foreign policy, understood as excessively dependent on the ambition and lack of professionalism among the king's counsellors. That efforts at administrative rationalisation had not extended to foreign affairs was shown by the way France had alienated even potential allies. Accordingly, in 1711 as the Utrecht negotiations loomed large, Colbert de Torcy, as foreign minister, took heed of proposals that had been accumulating over the years concerning the establishment of a diplomatic academy devoted to the regularising of the careers of young diplomats and teaching them the skills that de Callières, among others, regarded as essential for successful foreign policy. On the basis of internal memoranda from close advisors, Torcy proposed to the king the establishment of an *académie politique* that began its activities in 1712 under the leadership of the seasoned diplomat Yves de Saint-Prest (c. 1640–1719).[332] Saint-Prest had earlier worked as the foreign ministry's archivist and its legal counsel, a background that may explain why public law was given such prominence in the school's curriculum. The annual intake varied between 6 and 12. Students would first stay in Paris, acquainting themselves with the theory of diplomacy – including public law and the law nations – after which they would accompany some of the more important ministers as secretaries with the expectation of later beginning a regular diplomatic career.

Torcy and Saint-Prest gave great importance to law in the rationalisation of French foreign policy. From the first *projet d'études*, teaching was to be given in languages, history and public law and the law of nations. Good knowledge of Grotius and Pufendorf was stressed. There was even a sense of urgency about the matter. As one of the designers of the project, Abbé Legrand, noted, although *De jure belli ac pacis* had been compiled in Paris and dedicated to Louis XIII, there still was no formal training in it in the country in contrast to the interest the work had aroused in England and Germany.[333] Moreover, the only version of the book that was available was the *très méchante* translation by Barbeyrac.

[332] Guy Thuillier, *La première école d'administration. L'académie politique de Louis XIV* (Genève, Droz 1996).

[333] Abbé Joachim Legrand, 'Le Projet d'Estude', in Thuillier, *La première école d'administration*, 44–5.

Legrand also suggested that teaching of the law nations at the *Collège royal* should begin immediately by a proposal that was only realised in 1774, at the personal request of Louis XVI. It was important to teach the interests of France in relation to other states, but hard to find competent teachers to do this. Saint-Prest's final plan divided the school's substantive curriculum into five study units devoted to the affairs of particular groups of nations in the relation to France, and one large unit to:

> Public law, the rights of ambassadors and other ministers of foreign countries, ceremonial of foreign courts, clauses to be inserted in treaties of truce, of peace, of commerce and alliance, and the principal maxims of good policy (*bonne Politique*).[334]

Students would read Grotius in Latin and French as well as Pufendorf and *L'ambassadeur et ses fonctions* by the Dutch ambassador Abraham de Wicquefort. Most of the legal training was given by Saint-Prest himself. This would consist of an explanation of the background and the content of the treaties of Utrecht on the basis of Saint-Prest's personal notes. During the early years, as classes were held once or twice a week, the foreign minister himself would sometimes be present at the lectures, encouraging active student participation.

The establishment of the school did not take place without critique. Ambassadors failed to appreciate the suggestion that they could no longer choose their assistants freely (usually from family members). Discipline in the school deteriorated after Torcy's departure in 1715 as students took on other assignments to finance their stay in Paris. The ministry's interest began to diminish, as did attention to the juridical part of the teaching. Grotius and Pufendorf were no longer taught, and training was directed to European history and practical skills: languages and preparing *acta*, with occasional discussions of treaties, and sometimes even the constitution of the German–Roman empire. Regular student attendance fell in the last two years and the academy was closed soon after Saint-Prest's death (1719/1720), in part because the students had been using the confidential knowledge they had received at the Louvre for critiquing the country's foreign policy, in part because many came from *les grandes familles* and saw no point in working – sometimes quite hard – for attaining positions to which they felt they were naturally entitled.[335]

[334] "Projet des exercises...", in ibid., 59.

[335] Ibid., 108–11.

The story of the first French political academy demonstrates how difficult it was to organise the conduct of foreign affairs through regular legal–administrative principles. But the need of rationalising foreign policy persisted, and in 1724 an informal debating society – *Entresol* – was opened in a private apartment of Charles Jean-François Hénault, president of the *chambre d'enquête* of the *Parlement of Paris* at the Place Vendôme. This was a gathering of perhaps 25 members – the numbers varied between the weekly sessions – who "were people of high standing, who had either already held office or were preparing to do so".[336] Among its regular attendees were former students of the *académie*, such as the future foreign minister, the marquis d'Argenson (1694–1757). *Entresol* joined protégés of the aging minister Fleury and at different moments men such as Torcy, Bolingbroke, the former British prime minister and Montesquieu participated in its weekly meetings to discuss foreign policy events and to hear and comment on texts read by members. Many of its attendees, Montesquieu among them, felt that the study of politics had been neglected in France. They were critical of the king's excesses and his poor choice of advisors. They were adherents to monarchy but wanted to reform it for the benefit of the nation. For this purpose, they advocated the rule of law, protection of individual rights, efficiency and administrative reform as well as the increasing application of science and technology in government.[337] The members regularly travelled around in Europe and often brought a comparative perspective to the debates. When Fleury learned in 1731 from reports of foreign embassies in Paris that the meetings discussed matters that might violate France's relations with foreign powers he finally intervened to persuade the members to end their meetings.

[336] Nick Childs, *A Political Academy in Paris, 1724–1731. The Entresol and Its Members* (Oxford, Voltaire Foundation 2000), 6, 200–2.
[337] Ibid., 139–59.

# 6

# Reason, Revolution, Restoration

## *European Public Law 1715–1804*

"Between the fall of the house of Charlemagne and the moment when Charles VIII, King of France, came to Italy to claim the rights of the House of Anjou, of which he was the inheritor, the nations of Europe had almost no relations at all among themselves."[1] With this, the Abbé Mably, Gabriel Bonnot de Mably (1709–85) put his finger on that precise time and place – northern Italy in 1494 – where it had become fashionable to situate the commencement of old regime diplomacy. With the accession of Charles V on the imperial throne in 1519, the scene was set for the most ambitious princes of Christendom – those of France and Austria – to begin the rivalry that would engulf the minor European rulers in more than two centuries of almost continuous war. This also inaugurated a certain understanding of European politics:

> Ambition, greed and fear have obliged all nations to reach out to each other and to consider, grant or refuse assistance to each other; and it is those very same passions that direct their contacts and that prompt them to send to each other ambassadors and ordinary envoys.[2]

There is no doubt about Mably's critical attitude towards the old regime he had come to know by attaining in 1742 the position as secretary to Cardinal Tencin who served as minister of state in

[1] Gabriel Bonnot de Mably, *Principes des négociations pour servir d'introduction au droit public de l'Europe (1757)* (Paris, Kimé 2001), 45.

[2] "C'est l'ambition, c'est l'avarice, c'est la crainte qui ont obligé toutes les nations à se rechercher mutuellement, et à se demander, se refuser ou s'accorder des secours; et ce sont encore les mêmes passions qui dirigent leur commerce, et qui les portent à entretenir les uns chez les autres des ambassadeurs ou des envoyés ordinaires." Ibid., 45.

Fleury's government. Until his break with Tencin five years later, Mably had followed and participated in the diplomacy of the day, reflecting on his experiences in the *Droit public de l'Europe* (1746) and especially its extended theoretical introduction a decade later.[3] For the previous 250 years, Europe had been split into warring regimes, determined to subjugate each other and to make and break whatever strategic alliances seemed necessary for that purpose. Even when all appeared calm the princes and their chancelleries planned new exploits to enlist national passions for future operations. "*On travaille à diviser ses ennemies, on fait naître des soupçons.*"[4] Whether planning aggression or merely worried about the conservation of status, European regimes had been drawn into endless diplomatic manoeuvring. Nobody could rely only on their own forces, and those who tried would soon collapse.

By highlighting the importance of the events in northern Italy at the turn of the sixteenth century, Mably was integrating his work with a current of European political and legal thinking that originated in that moment and for which it was important to reflect upon ruling as it was instead of as religion or morality might want it to be. The book became a commercial success; published in several editions, it was translated into German and Italian and used in England as a university textbook. The 1757 introduction, *Principes des négociations*, provided both a critique of the short-sighted egoism of monarchic diplomacy and a theoretical articulation of European public law in terms of the search for the fundamental interests of European rulers. Taking an idiom from the previous century and mixing it with contemporary politics, Mably insisted that each power must fit its policy with its interests, and not act in pursuit of the whims of its ruler. Whether powerful or weak, seeking expansion or content to conserve itself, each needed a realistic assessment of its interests, as determined by its relative position vis-à-vis other powers.[5] Mably would later become sceptical about the old regime's chances of survival. But his mid-century treatise still looked

[3] Gabriel Bonnot de Mably, *Le droit public de l'Europe. Fondé sur les traitez conclus jusqu'en l'année 1740* (2 vols, The Hague, Duren 1746). The introduction (see above note 1) was published in the 1757 edition of the work. Mably came from a modest provincial *noblesse de robe*. Like his brother, the philosopher Etienne Bonnot de Condillac, he had been taken into the protection of Madame de Tencin in whose *salon* he was introduced to Parisian elites. See further Johnson Kent Wright, *A Classical Republican in Eighteenth-Century France. The Political Thought of Mably* (Stanford University Press 1997), 35–8, 58–64 and Marc Belissa, 'Introduction', in Mably, *Principes des négociations*, 8–10.

[4] Mably, *Principes des négociations*, 46.

[5] Ibid., 50–4.

for a rationalist vocabulary beyond pious abstraction and belligerent excess so as to reform the monarchy itself.[6]

That long introductory essay gave voice to an understanding of Europe as a political network of monarchic interests. Lacking faith in virtuous utopias, Mably suggested that if only the princes knew how to identify their *real interests* they might be able to pursue their goals in relative security, perhaps even in cooperation. This would require a science that would reveal the proper maxims of policy for each nation based on a meticulous assessment of its position on the political map. For this purpose, he divided the nations into four classes: ruling power (now France), rival power (now England), and powers of the second and third rank. Each possessed a fundamental interest that it would ignore at its peril. By aiming higher than its forces allowed or by neglecting constant vigilance, a nation was heading for disaster. The balance of power would never provide sufficient protection. Instead, it would usually favour the rival power and might even become a predatory mechanism allowing, as in the partitions of Poland, dramatic redrawing of the political map.[7] For the powers of the second and third order Mably recommended alternating between pacifism and playing the principal powers against each other, defending – as he put it – the Machiavellian nature of his suggestions by their usefulness.[8]

That Mably labelled this science *European public law* highlighted a view of law as a rational instrument to channel everyone's regard for their own interests to the greatest benefit of all. Elsewhere in Europe, analogous arguments had been made by men such as Grotius and Pufendorf, translations of whose works together with the writings of Jean-Jacques Burlamaqui had become available in France in the 1720s and 1730s. But natural law never developed into a predominant political idiom or even a university discipline in France.[9] This was in part related to its association with Protestantism and Huguenot policy, and in part to what the society of the *salon* viewed as its pedantic scholasticism.[10] It was regarded as conservative, if not reactionary. The criticisms by Voltaire

[6] For the mid-century atmosphere in this respect, see Olaf Asbach, *Staat und Politik zwischen Absolutismus und Aufklärung* (Hildesheim, Olms 2005), 71–4.

[7] Mably, *Principes des négociations*, 75–6.

[8] "Je rougirais des maximes machiavéliques que je viens d'exposer, s'il n'était pas possible d'en tirer des conséquences utiles aux hommes", ibid., 85.

[9] See e.g. John Heilbron, *The Rise of Social Theory* (Cambridge, Polity 1995), 42, 42–6, 67–8.

[10] For the critical attitude taken by the *philosophes*, see Marc Belissa, *Fraternité universelle et intérêt national (1713–1795)* (Paris, Editions Kimé 1998), 69–84.

and Rousseau of natural law as part of the justifying rhetoric of the old regime were well-known.[11] In a later work from his republican period Mably himself would have an imaginary Englishman, "Lord Stanhope", observe that the natural law tradition had built "sophisms upon sophisms" to defend the view of monarchy as a best guarantee for security, reminding his French interlocutors that Grotius had after all published his writings with the blessings of Louis XIII.[12]

On the other hand, the idioms of "humanity", "reason" and "nature" were routinely invoked by the *philosophes*.[13] They also resuscitated ancient notions of law and morality, though less as a philosophical theme than in order to clear the way for reform.[14] When they needed a more elaborate grounding, enlightenment polemicists suggested that society, like nature, could be studied by dissolving it into its composite parts and interpreting individual behaviour empirically by reference to the sensations that guided human motivation.[15] The empirical analysis of human interests would eventually give expression to what the Physiocrats would call the natural and essential order of society. This order had broken its bond to the supernatural so that the only humanly conceivable justification for authority would now emerge from that order itself, especially the individual interests that it was the task of social thinkers – and lawyers – to aggregate into the interests of a "nation" with an almost mathematically calculable relationship to the outside world.[16]

[11] See e.g. Dan Edelstein, *The Enlightenment. A Genealogy* (The University of Chicago Press 2011), 58–9; Heilbron, *The Rise of Social Theory*, 96–100.

[12] Abbé de Mably, *Des droits et des devoirs du citoyen* (Paris, Lacombe 1789), 19–21.

[13] See Dan Edelstein, *The Terror of Natural Right. Republicanism, the Cult of Nature & the French Revolution* (The University of Chicago Press 2009).

[14] Carl Becker, *The Heavenly City of the Eighteenth-Century Philosophers* (2nd edn, Yale University Press 2003 [1932]), 33–70. See further Peter Gay, 'Voltaire and Natural Law', in Peter Gay, *Voltaire's Politics. The Poet as Realist* (Princeton University Press 1959), 343–6 and Peter Gay, *The Party of Humanity. Essays in the French Enlightenment* (New York, Norton 1959), 60–2, and (an express response to Becker), 198–202.

[15] Ernst Cassirer, *The Philosophy of the Enlightenment* (Princeton University Press, 1979 [1951]), 18–27, 234–48, 254–6. For the general theme of the "naturalization of the human" in eighteenth-century thought, see Stephen Gaukroger, *The Natural and the Human. Science and the Shaping of Modernity 1739–1842* (Oxford University Press 2016), esp. chapter 1.

[16] The view that political modernity emerged from "disenchantment" and in reaction to the religious wars and turned instead to "society" where, in the eighteenth century, the "sovereignty of the nation" would provide the ultimate source of authority is powerfully presented in Marcel Gauchet, *La révolution moderne. L'avènement de la démocratie, tome I* (Paris, Gallimard 2007), esp. 99–148. The wider intellectual context is laid out in Marcel Gauchet, *Le désenchantement du monde. Une histoire politique de la religion* (Paris, Gallimard 1985).

In due course, these literatures would be generalised as a "social science" – a term that would appear in Abbé Sieyès' *Qu'est-ce que le tiers état?* ("What is the Third Estate?") in 1789 where it sought to translate the "general will" into proposals for its rational government, an objective shared by much French revolutionary political and legal thought.[17] To situate the newly discovered nation in a larger frame eighteenth-century French thinkers had frequent reference to the idiom of European public law, understood as a science as Mably had sketched it. Old teachings on diplomacy and negotiations were only about intrigue, Mably had written. It was time to replace them by principles that would offer "certain guides in all times and all circumstances".[18]

This chapter explores the eighteenth-century French idea of law as a science of the government of European polities. Critics of absolutism began to enquire about the possibility of European peace as a rational project. Two polemicists, the Abbé de Saint-Pierre and Jean-Jacques Rousseau, had diametrically opposed views on this. A third one, Montesquieu, adopted a more nuanced, comparative and "sociological" perspective on the matter. He was not ignorant of the role of commerce for European order, either, the focus of the second part of this chapter, which highlights the Physiocrat effort to uncover the natural laws regulating economic relationships. The third part will examine the revolutionary reconceptualisation of property and sovereignty and the contradictory ways in which the revolutionaries related their project to rest of Europe. By the time of the Napeolonic interlude, legal imagination about international relations had come to be poised between political economy and a mildly reformed system of the "public law of Europe".

## Peace, Rule of Law and Political Science: Saint-Pierre

Despite his critical view of the old regime, Mably was not given to speculating about perpetual peace. His science of negotiations merely sought to orient the monarchs to act in accordance with their

[17] Emmanuel J. Sieyès, 'What Is the Third Estate?', in Michael Sonenscher (ed.), *Political Writings. Including the Debate between Sieyès and Tom Paine in 1791* (Indianapolis, Hackett 2003), 115. The term was used interchangeably with the more common "science of the social art", the analysis of legislation that elsewhere in Europe had been associated with the law of nature and of nations. See further Michael Sonenscher, 'Ideology, Social Science and General Facts in Late-Eighteenth Century French Political Thought', 35 *History of European Ideas* (2009), 24–38.

[18] Mably, *Principes des négociations*, 49, 50.

empirically demonstrable interests. The same objective inspired the otherwise very different *oeuvre* of Charles- Irenée Castel, Abbé de Saint-Pierre (1658–1743) – best known today through the descriptions by Jean-Jacques Rousseau as a well-meaning but hopelessly utopian producer of a blueprint for European peace. But Saint-Pierre's interests were much wider and extended from proposals for governmental reform to an elaboration of a science of politics.[19] He had lived at Versailles in the service of Madame de Maintenon, witnessing the highly personalistic ways of government under Louis XIV, the intrigues, secrecy and the search for short-term gratifications. He would attack this system in a great number of reform proposals on items ranging from the legal process to popular education, from an overhaul of the tax system to the replacing of hereditary nobility by an administrative meritocracy. He was especially scathing about office venality as an epitome of rule by privilege instead of merit.[20] French administration was to be oriented towards the "greatest utility of the greatest number of families".[21] In a work on the "polysynodie" set up by the regent,

[19] Saint-Pierre had been educated in Jesuit colleges but never joined the clergy. His early years were devoted to science, and he was appointed to the *Académie française* in 1695 from which, however, he was later expelled owing to his attacks on the regime. He had been appalled by the clientelism and inefficiency of the last years of the reign of the Sun King. In a number of articles and letters, Saint-Pierre proposed fiscal reforms and the introduction of proportional taxation as remedies to the crisis. See Merle J. Perkins, *The Moral and Political Philosophy of the Abbé de Saint-Pierre* (Geneva, Droz 1959), 73–81. Saint-Pierre hated hereditary privileges and wanted to turn state administration into an impersonal bureaucracy. He was no enthusiast of abstract debates on natural law. A science de government was to be based on "evidence" and "*esprit de raisonnement*"; it would need to be of practical use and an *Académie politique* was to be established to teach it. See e.g. Abbé de Saint-Pierre, *Nouveau plan de gouvernement* (Beman, Rotterdam 1762), 31–6, 78–81. See further Nannerl O. Keohane, *Philosophy and the State in France. The Renaissance to the Enlightment* (Princeton University Press 2017 [1980]), 362–3.

[20] Over and again in his prolific writings, the Abbé turned to five sets of problems: the quantity and arbitrary division of the tax burden; the inadequate education of the elites and the "*menu peuple*" (he did not mean they were to be given *similar* education – he had a very bleak view of the abilities of the peasants and the working class – but an education suitable for the tasks they were to carry out); the lack of ethics in public administration that led to priority of private over the public interest; the distorting influence of religion in public law, and the excessive and arbitrary recourse to war. He saw the last three decades of the Sun King's wars as a disaster, occasioned by the war minister's mistaken ideas about the interests and resources of the country. Charles-Irénée Castel de Saint-Pierre, *Discours sur la polysynodie* (London, Tonsson 1718), 42–8.

[21] Thomas E. Kaiser, 'The Abbé de Saint-Pierre, Public Opinion and the Reconstitution of the French Monarchy', 55 *The Journal of Modern History* (1983), 628, 618–43.

Saint-Pierre praised the replacement of single-person-led ministries by committees as a way to avoid mismanagement and corruption. Open debate on governmental proposals would greatly enhance royal legitimacy.[22] Richelieu and Colbert had been right to stress the need for rational government but had failed to implement anything of the kind. Private interests continued to dominate; corruption and waste undermined subjects' happiness and the wealth and power of the state. To attain change, the state was to be governed scientifically under the impersonal and transparent principles of the rule of law.[23]

Such principles also informed the Abbé's wider design for securing peace and order in Europe, the *Mémoire pour rendre la paix perpétuelle en Europe.*[24] This initial "memorandum" of 1712, written to Minister Torcy during the Utrecht peace negotiations, was followed up by successive editions of his much larger *Projet pour rendre la paix pérpetuelle entre les Souverains Chrétiens.*[25] It is not known whether the author himself had been present at Utrecht. But he was a friend and assistant to Cardinal de Polignac, one of the French negotiators, and the references to "the present peace" – which Saint-Pierre believed could not be lasting – were to the treaties produced at Utrecht.[26] As a literary achievement, the *Projet* was unimpressive. Its first full version consisted of three volumes of poorly organised arguments in favour of a permanent peace organisation and arbitration among European sovereigns. Perhaps for this reason, Saint-Pierre produced an *Abregé* of the plan in 1729 that became the focus of the eighteenth-century debates.[27]

Saint-Pierre did not believe that peace could be attained by preaching virtue and human goodness. Nor was he in the business of reawakening the notion of *Christianitas*. Any realistic effort to end

[22] Saint-Pierre, *Discours sur la polysynodie*. The committees would be composed of the most meritorious members of nobility but only with an advisory role. In such a knowledge-based system of governance debate and publicity would prevent problems arising from rule by one or more "vizirs" – the old system. The publication of this work led to the expulsion of Saint-Pierre from the French Academy in the same year (1718).

[23] Kaiser, 'The Abbé de Saint-Pierre', 626–7; Simone Goyard-Fabre, 'Je ne suis que l'apothécaire de l'Europe', in Carole Dornier & Claudine Poulouin (eds), *Les Projets de l'Abbé Castel de Saint Pierre (1658–1743)* (Presses Universitaires de Caen 2011), 30.

[24] Charles-Irénée Castel de Saint-Pierre, 'Mémoire du projet pour rendre la paix pérpetuelle en Europe' (pour le ministre M. de Torcy, 1 septembre 1712).

[25] *Projet pour rendre la paix perpétuelle entre les Souverains Chrétiens* (Utrecht, Schouten 1717). The version usually referred to, and on which Rousseau, for example, based his "Extract" and "Judgment", is the abbreviated *Abregé du projet de paix pérpetuelle* (Rotterdam, Beman 1729).

[26] Perkins, *Moral and Political Philosophy*, 51.

[27] *Abregé du projet de paix perpétuelle.*

constant war in Europe had to appeal to the passions that ruled human lives. Nor did he believe that peace could extend beyond Europe. In the first version of the project he included both Turkey and Russia, but later dropped Turkey and even came to advocate joint European war against it.[28] By adopting the plan, Saint-Pierre wrote, Europe's monarchies could guarantee their safety from external and internal dangers; in fact the plan was more concerned with domestic rebellion than interstate war. The point was to enable peaceful growth of trade and industry, and thus contribute to the prosperity of the ruling dynasties.[29] But this required a wholesale overhauling of present European diplomacy. Mutual promises among sovereigns, truces, commercial treaties, guarantees and alliances were easily overridden. They, like the balance of power, were dependent on princely whims and changes of national fortune:

> It is impossible for the balance of power system to achieve lasting peace in Europe; the misfortunes of war will always renew themselves and continue until there is among Christian sovereigns a permanent society that will give them sufficient guarantee that the promises given in treaties will be executed.[30]

Saint-Pierre proposed the establishment of a permanent institution, a *Union européenne* with 18 or 24 sovereign members (the number varied in different versions) all of which would be Christian, European states.[31] The draft treaty on the Union contained five principal elements.[32] First, the members would agree to preserve the European territorial and dynastic status quo. The Union was not to intervene in the affairs of its members for any other reason than for implementing the guarantees, including the suppression of any domestic dissent

28 Saint-Pierre, *Projet*, 431–8.

29 Saint-Pierre, 'Mémoire', Troisième discours, 153.

30 "Il est impossible que le Système de l'Équilibre rende la paix durable en Europe; qu'ainsi les malheurs de la Guerre se renouvelleront incessamment & dureront tant qu'il n'y aura pas entre les Souverainetez Chrétiennes une Société permanente qui leur donne sûreté suffisante de l'exécution des promesses faites dans les Traitez". Ibid., Deuxième discours, 73.

31 In making his proposal, Saint-Pierre wrote that he was following the examples of the constitution of the German–Roman Empire and the famous plan of the foreign minister of Henri IV, the duke of Sully. Both claims were dubious. Saint-Pierre believed – wrongly – that the German states had entered the empire as independent sovereigns and that Sully's proposal was unrelated to his anti-Austrian policy. In fact, the German states had never been sovereign and the hegemonic purposes of Sully's design were well-known. See Patrick Riley, 'The Abbé de St. Pierre and Voltaire on Perpetual Peace in Europe', 137 *World Affairs* (1974), 187–9.

32 Saint-Pierre, 'Mémoire', Quatrième discours, 271–366.

(*à soumettre les esprits rebelles*).[33] The plan included an undertaking (reflecting problems that the Spanish succession had occasioned) that no sovereign could rule over two or more States. Second, a permanent institution was to be set up in which the sovereigns would be represented in a Senate or a Diet, each having one vote.[34] The "fundamental" articles of the treaty to be concluded could be amended only by unanimous vote while the "important" ones required a three-quarters' majority. Third, the Senate was to organise European trade on the basis of a general most-favoured nation treatment. A chamber of commerce would be set up in each major town with alternate jurisdiction to adjudicate trade disputes. Fourth, territorial and other disputes were to be resolved through arbitration by the Senate. A member taking arms or refusing to execute an award would be declared the enemy of all.[35] Finally, there would be a joint military force to protect the Union from external dangers – particularly against the Turks – as well as internal dangers, rebellion and civil war. Costs of joint operations would be borne by members in accordance with their relative means.

Astonishingly, the various versions of the plan had nothing to say about the colonies. Elsewhere Saint-Pierre praised the wisdom of the government to take over the administration of Louisiana from the *Compagnie des Indes* because, as he believed, this would enable its rational development. He regarded the colonies of hot climates, such as the French Caribbean, as especially useful for the cultivation of cocoa, coffee and sugar, and stressed that after the creation of the Union, nobody needed to be fearful of attacks on colonies by their adversaries. At that point, the creation of free trade across the world would ensure that all products would be equally good value everywhere.[36]

The plan included no conception of Europe as a cultural or historical entity. It was purely pragmatic and utilitarian, designed to show how the states of present Europe, monarchies and republics, Catholic and Protestant, could best preserve the status quo and

33 Ibid., Quatrième discours, 273. Article 2 provided that the union could take action to see to it that the monarchic or republican form is maintained but also that the internal electoral laws and capitulations are honoured (276–7), and article 3 that during periods of regency or otherwise weakness in the ruling house, nothing threatens its security (279–81).

34 Article 1, ibid., Quatrième discours, 271.

35 Ibid., Quatrième discours.

36 'Année 1731', in Charles-Irénée Castel de Saint-Pierre, *Annales Politiques*, tome II (London 1758), 579–81.

advance their interests.[37] Like many of his contemporaries, Saint-Pierre felt the bonds of virtue loosening at the time, his experience at Versailles having convinced him of the predominance of passions in public life. They could not be tamed by appeals to reason, Christian piety or natural law. We are slaves of our passions so that the only thing that can restrain us is "fear of an evil that is more annoying and more terrible than the good that one desires so that it would no longer appear worthwhile".[38] Princes can only be influenced by appealing directly to their interests. "My plan is to demonstrate that all sovereigns have a greater interest to sign the treaty than to refuse to sign it."[39] The aim was to convince princes that they had a genuine interest in peace, that peace, rather than war, was the way to preserve their security and well-being. Were they to continue waging wars and signing peace treaties as in the past they could never be certain that their neighbours might not breach their promises as soon as they had developed the capacity for victory. And a peace they would secure for themselves might not last to their successors.[40]

Saint-Pierre had been an avid reader of Descartes and his writings often preached, but rarely displayed, the value for exactness in a political science based on mechanistic explanations and mathematical proof. He despised political orators who spoke only "*à exiter les sentimens & fortifier les passions qu'à faire naître les idées justes & précises*".[41] Having started with experiments on physics and chemistry, he moved first to morality to seek ways to the betterment of society.[42] But moral education alone was insufficient. It was not that humans did not know the distinction between right and wrong, but when virtue and self-interest conflicted, they always chose the latter. Moral principles were to be brought down from learned treatises and made effective in

37 See further Céline Spector, 'L'Europe de l'Abbé de Saint-Pierre', in Carole Dornier & Claudine Poulouin Dornier et al. (eds), *Les Projets de l'abbé Castel de Saint-Pierre (1658-1743)* (Presses Universitaires de Caen 2011), 39–49.

38 " la crainte d'un mal plus fâcheux et plus terrible que le bien qu'il désire de ne peut paraître désirable", Abbé de Saint-Pierre, as cited in Merle L. Perkins, 'Civil Theology in the Writings of the Abbé de Saint-Pierre', 18 *Journal of the History of Ideas* (1957), 245. This is the classic point in Albert O. Hirschman, *The Passions and the Interests. Political Arguments for Capitalism before its Triumph* (Princeton University Press 1997 [1977]).

39 Saint-Pierre, *Abregé*, 42.

40 Ibid., 12–13.

41 Saint-Pierre, *Discours sur la polysynodie*, Préface.

42 See e.g. Goyard-Fabre, 'Je ne suis que l'apothécaire de l'Europe', 22–5; Kaiser, 'The Abbé de Saint-Pierre', 628–35.

society. This was the task of politics, and of law.[43] Two steps were required. First, elites were to be educated in the resources of the state and how these could be employed for the general good. How, for example, was taxation to be used to coordinate private interests with the public good? Trade was absolutely crucial.[44] Increasing commercial exchanges would enhance the prosperity and happiness of the subjects and the solidity of the ruling regimes. Second, legislation was to be rationalised by increasing expert consultation in committees such as the newly established *Bureau d'examen des mémoires politiques*.[45] Once governmental projects were prepared with sufficient care, they were to be transformed into impersonal laws whose justifications would be available for public scrutiny.[46] In this way, subjects would understand that the government actually worked for them instead of the elites. This would restore governmental legitimacy and the efficiency of the laws.[47]

Similar ideas would apply to the government of Europe. As a citizen of the republic of letters, the political scientist was to persuade sovereigns of the usefulness of long-term policy planning; a binding treaty-system, for example, would normally be in their interests.[48] To prevent sovereigns from violating their treaties required supranational authority – not a universal monarchy but a federation to unite European rulers against a possible law-breaker.[49] The science of public law that would help govern the federation would not seek

[43] As a member and co-founder of the Club Entresol in Paris Saint-Pierre was in contact with many French political leaders.

[44] The 1717 version was entitled as a plan for a *Traité* not only in order to "rendre la paix perpétuelle" but also to "maintenir toujours la Commerce entre les Nations".

[45] Saint-Pierre, *Discours sur la polysynodie*, 11.

[46] The plurality of opinions was useful; it highlighted proper deliberation and the need of counsellors to educate themselves on public matters. This would also diminish the influence of private interests in government. Ibid., 4–5, 6–7, 24–33.

[47] Saint-Pierre, *Nouveau plan de gouvernement*, 302.

[48] For the "activist" view of the intellectual within in early enlightenment notions of the republic of letters, see Olaf Asbach, 'L'abbé de Saint-Pierre et les transformations de la république des letters au XVIIIe siècle', in Carole Dornier & Claudine Poulouin Dornier et al. (eds), *Les Projets de l'abbé Castel de Saint-Pierre (1658–1743)* (Presses Universitaires de Caen 2011), 51–62.

[49] He was, as Céline Spector has put it, "'hobbesien' à l'intérieur mais utopiste a l'extérieur" – while Rousseau, for his part, was "utopian" from the inside but "realist" from the outside, 'Le projet de paix perpetuelle. De Saint-Pierre à Rousseau', in Jean-Jacques Rousseau, *Principes du droit de la guerre. Ecrits sur la paix perpétuelle* (Bruno Bernardi & Gabriella Silvestrini eds, Paris, Vrin 2008), 275–6. On Saint-Pierre's Hobbesianism, see Perkins, *The Moral and Political Philosophy*, 52–62. See also Kaiser, 'The Abbé de Saint-Pierre', 626–7.

authority from the depths of national histories. It was an administrative tool justified simply by the benefits it would produce.[50] The Abbé was among the first enlightenment thinkers firmly wedded to the idea of "progress". By joining in a federation European states would "protect themselves permanently against all civil wars so as to enjoy the immense advantages of their permanent and universal exchanges (*un Commerce perpétuel et universel*).[51]

However, Saint-Pierre never succeeded in creating a workable social science. His imagination was rooted in the conditions of absolutism that gave no room for a civil society opposed to an omniscient governmental machinery.[52] A more radical criticism would take its starting-point from the natural rights of liberty and property and suggest that it was the principal task of government to remove obstacles to their fullest realisation. This would give rise to the debate about the benefits and evils of commerce, the dispute about the kind of society that was being created through the search for luxuries. In metropolitan France, there would be both "liberal" and "republican" pathways out of the old regime.[53]

## Peace and Commerce: Melon

Saint-Pierre's *Projet* was widely circulated among French elites who generally regarded it as hopelessly contradictory. According to Voltaire, it was as likely that peace could be maintained among European sovereigns "as the peace between elephants and rhinoceros, wolves and dogs. Carnivorous animals will tear each other apart at the first occasion."[54] During the War of the Polish Succession (1733–8) Saint-Pierre communicated his project to Cardinal Fleury, former preceptor of the young Louis XV and the effective ruler of France

[50] For the "renversement futuriste" carried out by Saint-Pierre as the first "prophet of progress", see Gauchet, *La révolution moderne*, 129–31.

[51] Saint-Pierre, 'Interest de chaque souverain en particulier de signer un traité de police durable', in *Projet*, annex, Preface.

[52] "On peut dire mème que quand le pouvoir est uni à la raizon il ne sauroit jamais être trop grand, & trop despotique pour la plus grande utilité de la Société", Saint-Pierre, 'Projet pour perfectionner le Gouvernement des Estats', in Charles-Irénée Castel de Saint-Pierre, *Ouvrages de politique*, tome 3 (Rotterdam, Briasson 1733), 2–3, 4.

[53] I use the notions of "liberal" and "republican" to contrast those who appreciate commercial values as part of modern liberty" with those critical of such values and identify these positions with Melon and Rousseau .

[54] Quoted in Jean-Pierre Bois, *L'Europe à l'époque moderne. Origines, utopies et réalités de l'idée d'Europe* (Paris, Armand Colin 1999), 211.

after the end of the Regency (1723–43). Fleury had given up France's belligerent foreign policy and sought stability and peace in Europe by cooperation with England. Saint-Pierre hoped to benefit from the diplomatic turn by sending Fleury memoranda on the peace talks and suggesting that the Cardinal use this opportunity to establish a Europe-wide institutional system of peace and arbitration.[55] Fleury received the Abbé's missives sympathetically, responding however that he had forgotten one essential article, namely one concerning the despatch of missionaries "to touch the hearts of princes so as persuade them of your views".[56]

Although Saint-Pierre had inserted a world-wide system of free trade in his proposal and advocated the establishment of chambers of commerce across Europe, he never engaged in deeper analyses of the role of trade or colonies. By contrast, in the most influential French contribution to the economic debate at the time, *Essai politique sur le commerce* (1734), the jurist and commentator Jean-François Melon (1675–1738) not only stressed the nation's need for colonies for the production of luxuries that kept the wheels of trade turning but advocated a more general employment of merchants in the business of the state itself. He was not blind to the dangers of economic dependency resulting from the trade of necessities but stressed that these would be offset by the advantages that would follow from specialisation. Trade policy, he suggested, was an absolutely central aspect of a nation's foreign relations and "*le plus grande de ses maximes, et le plus connu, c'est que le Commerce ne demande que liberté et protection*".[57] This meant liberty for selling the excess product a country had to offer and protection of essential industries, especially agriculture. As long as the nation could take care of its subsistence, it would have no reason to fear trading with others. On the contrary, as long as it was self-reliant on necessities and could export superfluities, the resulting favourable trade balance would keep it ahead of its rivals.[58]

55 For the correspondence between Saint-Pierre and Fleury, see also Asbach, *Staat und Politik*, 198–200.

56 "Vous avez oublié un article essentiel, celui d'envoyer des missionaries pour toucher les coeurs des princes et les persuader d'entrer dans vos vues", quoted in Frank L. Schuman, 'The Ethics and Politics of International Peace', 42 *International Journal of Ethics* (1932), 149.

57 Jean-Francois Melon, *Essai politique sur le commerce* (Presses Universitaires de Caen 2014), 30.

58 This was the lesson from the famous example of the four islands, ibid., 1–14.

Having made the commonplace distinction between subsistence goods and luxuries, Melon observed that France was especially well endowed in regard to exporting the latter. There was thus no need for the sumptuary laws. They both restrained liberty and prevented France from competing in the area where it would be the strongest.[59] Similar arguments would apply to colonial trade. Melon was fiercely critical of colonial monopolies and especially of the privileges of the Louisiana Company that prevented anyone from trading with the settlers, and the settlers with the outer world, apart from through the company. "*La liberté rendu à la Colonie en fait espérer de grands progrès.*"[60]

Melon's views were supported by various critics of absolutism. Alongside Mandeville's well-known work *Fable of the Bees* (1724) there were different ways to attack the policy that required merchants to identify their interests with those of the state. For example, a purely mundane position within the court society looked for no special justification at all for ostentatious displays of wealth. Voltaire's well-known celebrations of luxury and his libertarianism had a wide following.[61] On the other hand, a more serious commercial humanism sought to join the pursuit of classical ideals of virtue with prosperity and a reinforced emphasis on property rights.[62] Such views clashed head-on with Saint-Pierre's conservative utopianism; instead of having the bureaucratic machine churn more efficiently, the state needed to take a step backwards. Early political economists such as Melon and the Irishman Richard Cantillon pressed the point about merchants being best equipped to see what was needed to make commerce flourish. This was not only in the interests of the merchants but would contribute precisely to the objectives Saint-Pierre had to sought to accomplish: "the spirit of conquest and the spirit of commerce exclude each other in a nation."[63] It was pointless to go to war in search for new territory; better results came from taking more land into cultivation. By increasing its population, developing its manufactures and employing the colonies to the full a state would be much better able to increase its power without engaging in costly and unpredictable wars.

[59] Ibid., 140. [60] Ibid., 84.

[61] Christian Laval, *L'homme économique. Essai sur les racines du néolibéralisme* (Paris, Gallimard 2007), 122–6.

[62] For these three approaches, see John Shovlin, *The Political Economy of Virtue. Luxury, Patriotism, and the Origins of the French Revolution* (Cornell University Press 2006), 19–21.

[63] "L'esprit de Conquête et l'esprit de Commerce s'excluent mutuellement dans une Nation." Melon, *Essai politique*, 92.

## States and War: Rousseau

Melon's *Essai* went considerably further than Saint-Pierre in enlisting the resources of civil society – merchants and other economic entrepreneurs – in the construction of a stable European states-system. It also displayed a markedly relaxed attitude to the cultural and political effects of commerce. Not everyone agreed. The most famous comments on Saint-Pierre's proposals were those by Jean-Jacques Rousseau (1712–1778) who reversed the Abbé's assumptions about monarchic statehood and peace. In the *Extract of the Plan for Perpetual Peace* (1756/1761) and the *Judgment on Perpetual Peace* (1756/1782), Rousseau argued that real, lasting peace was impossible in a system of states.[64] He also rejected the path of *doux commerce*, stressing the destructive effects of the profit motive. A commercial society will be detrimental to republican virtue and leads ultimately into despotism.

The essays commenting on Saint-Pierre are part of Rousseau's effort in the 1750s to produce a treatise on *Institutions politiques* that was to deal also with the law of nations, commerce, the laws of war and conquest, alliances, negotiations and treaty-making. Nothing came of that, however, because as Rousseau put it at the end of *The Social Contract*, the plan was too vast. But his simultaneous sympathy with Saint-Pierre's plan and his utter disbelief in its realisation are understandable in view of the critique of the state system he had planned to flesh out in that larger work. In two unpublished fragments on the "Principles of the law of war", penned briefly before embarking on Saint-Pierre's texts, Rousseau had already made the point that the "books of savants and jurisconsults" knew nothing of the present way of European government.[65] The natural lawyers – Hobbes, Grotius and Pufendorf – had turned things upside down by suggesting that sovereigns were needed to respond to the violence in the state of nature.[66] In fact, humans were not naturally belligerent; even as egoists, they understood that they

[64] Both now published and commented on in Rousseau, *Principes du droit de la guerre*.

[65] Rousseau, 'Principes du droit de la guerre', in *Principes du droit de la guerre*, 69–81.

[66] In *Du contrat social* (1762) Rousseau attacked Grotius' "characteristic method of reasoning [which] is always to offer fact as proof of right. It is possible to imagine a more logical method, but not one more favourable to tyrants." Jean-Jacques Rousseau, *The Social Contract* (M. Cranston trans. & intro., Harmondsworth, Penguin 1968), I 2 (51). The target here was the weight Grotius attached to customs and treaty practices as evidence of the content of the law – his famous "a posteriori" method. In *Émile*, Rousseau drew no substantive distinction at all between Grotius and Hobbes. Jean-Jacques Rousseau, *Émile, ou l'éducation* (4 tomes, Francfort 1762), III 190.

needed each other. In producing a justification for state power, the tradition had actually created the situation from which it claimed to produce an exit: "All ran towards their chains believing that they were securing their liberty."[67] War did not end with states, but began with them. The law of nations was followed only to the extent that seemed useful.[68] The ambition of sovereigns was unlimited and their mutual suspicion the cause for cycles of mutual destruction.[69]

Of course, Rousseau wrote in the "Extract", the history of European nations had created a kind of system based on religion, the laws (including law of nations), commerce, and a shared cultural inheritance.[70] But this did not prevent dissension and conflict. A state of war existed in Europe so that even treaties created no more than temporary truces.[71] What fragile equilibrium had come to persist was thanks mostly to the balancing effect of the German empire.[72] Something like Saint-Pierre's project would doubtless be in everyone's interests. But, and here was the rub, the very suppositions underlying the project prevented its realisation. The monarchs were not the rational interest-followers Saint-Pierre had assumed. They would never sign into a federation, not even a confederation, if only that went beyond their momentary interests, however irrational or arbitrary.[73] As Rousseau wrote in his subsequent "Judgment", monarchs were driven by the very logic of state-formation – the constant jealousy and fear nations felt towards each other, their limitless search for security – to act in ways that were unjust and irrational. It was wrong to measure their gains in money, for example, and futile to refer to common goals – being common they had no reality to anybody.[74] Nor would revolution repair this state of things. The sovereignty of the people being inalienable and indivisible, it was incompatible with world federation. True, small republics might form confederations to find safety against great powers. But these would operate under the old system based on party interests instead of the general interest of

[67] Jean-Jacques Rousseau, *A Discourse on Inequality* (M Cranston transl. & intro. Harmondworth, Penguin 1984), Part II (122).

[68] Rousseau, 'Principes du droit de la guerre', 70.

[69] Ibid., 778.

[70] Rousseau, 'Extrait de paix perpétuelle', 89–92.

[71] Ibid., 92. Rousseau's use of the notion of "state of war" here differs from the very rigorously political notion of state of war in the fragments on the law of war. See further Blaise Bachofen, 'Les raisons de la guerre. La raison dans la guerre. Une lecture des Principes du droit de la guerre', in Jean-Jacques Rousseau, *Principes du droit de la guerre. Ecrits sur la paix perpetuelle* (Bruno Bernardi & Gabriella Silvestrini eds, Paris, Vrin 2008), 142–51.

[72] Rousseau, 'Extrait de paix perpétuelle', 96–7.

[73] Ibid., 112–13.

[74] Rousseau, 'Jugement sur la paix perpétuelle', in *Principes du droit de la guerre*, 120.

humanity. Saint-Pierre's proposals remained in the end "the illusions of a truly human heart", admirable but unworkable and incapable of being resuscitated in a revised form. What states were after was power – not fixed amounts of power but power greater than that of their neighbours' so that they would feel secure:

> Thus the greatness of a political body is purely relative. It is forced to compare itself with others in order to know itself; it becomes dependent on what surrounds it and must take account of everything that takes place around it.[75]

The price of internal peace was the externalisation of aggression – endemic, structurally determined warfare between nations. War was an inextricable part of the states-system: "one does not become a soldier until after one has become a citizen".[76]

This led Rousseau to suggest that like the state itself, war was a thoroughly political institution, namely "a constant and manifested will to destroy the enemy state".[77] It was an existential struggle, but at stake was the existence of states, not of individuals or communities. Victors may lay their hands on everything that is public in the vanquished adversary, but have no right on private individuals or their properties.[78] Although war may be waged with great violence, it is a relationship between states; the adversary is destroyed not by killing or plundering but by breaking the social contract and the *volonté générale* that sustained it.

> What, then, is it to make war against a sovereign? It is to attack the public convention and everything that results from it; for the state does not consist of more than this. If the social contract could be destroyed by one single blow there would be no more war; and with that blow it would be killed, without the death of one single human being.[79]

In Rousseau's view, the modern law of nations revealed itself unable to confront the political heart of the problem of war. As long as it presupposed entities resembling contemporary states, it could only offer temporary truces, breathing spaces to allow the states to collect their forces in order to strike anew. Rousseau did not believe that a general will might emerge one day to ground a world federation. The process of nation-building belongs to a particular state, generating itself against an

[75] Rousseau, 'Principes du droit de la guerre', 76–7. [76] Ibid., 74.

[77] "une disposition mutuelle constante et manifesté de détruire l'état ennemi". Ibid., 80.

[78] Rousseau, *Social Contract*, I IV (56–7).

[79] Rousseau, 'Principes du droit de la guerre', 81.

external world. He had little faith in international renewal: political communities will always exist in a state of nature with respect to each other, with the occasional treaty now and then.[80] This is not to say that Rousseau thought the situation hopeless.[81] Like Kant later, he believed that parties to a social contract embodying ideas of freedom and lawfulness might recognise those qualities in the general wills that were constitutive of other states as well. If war – that is real, political war – was not about hatred and killing but a process designed to make the enemy's general will dissolve, there might be alternative means to bring about this result more efficiently.[82]

## The Link between Statehood and Property

Rousseau's discussion of Saint-Pierre followed his interpretation of the natural law of Grotius, Hobbes and Pufendorf. The view they shared of human nature as unbounded egoism and the state of nature as a war of all against all was only an ideological justification for the *ancien régime.* It emerged from a view of human nature based on the perception of human beings as they were now: "all the scientific treatises ... teach us to consider men such as they have made themselves".[83] This was a corrupted humanity, however, for in truth humans in the state of nature "were rather wild than wicked".[84] Their natural self-love (*amour de soi*) was supplemented by compassion. As Rousseau famously argued in his *Second Discourse* (1755), the development of culture and civilisation had been a disaster. In their efforts to fit individuals to organised life, modern governments had profoundly failed, turning healthy self-love into unhealthy egoism (*amour-propre*).[85] The profit-motive had "made men

[80] Ibid., 70; Rousseau, *A Discourse on Inequality*, 122; Simone Goyard-Fabre, *La construction de la paix ou le travail de Sisyphe* (Paris, Vrin 1994), 166–7.

[81] Richard Tuck shares the traditional pessimist–realist view of Rousseau as actually closer to Hobbes than he would like to appear. *The Rights of War and Peace. Political Thought and the International Order from Grotius to Kant* (Oxford University Press 1999), 202–7.But this view is hard to reconcile with the connection Rousseau makes between perfectibility and liberty.

[82] David William Bates, *States of War. Enlightenment Origins of the Political* (Columbia University Press, 2012), 209.

[83] Rousseau, *A Discourse on Inequality*, 84.

[84] Ibid., 108.

[85] For discussion, see Bates, *States of War*, 178–84. For Bates, Rousseau's depiction of human nature leaves it substantively open – human beings are characterised "by their fundamental *lack* of nature" – thus allowing room for an autonomous realm of political decision within which humans make reality of their liberty by uniting in civil society and adopting a constitution.

greedy, ambitious and bad".[86] Principles grounded on it – that is to say, principles put forward by Grotius, Hobbes or Pufendorf – could not even begin to remedy the present ills.[87]

Rousseau's attack on statehood as a way to escape from the inconveniences of the state of nature did not signify rejection of the concept of the political state itself. In the conjectural history he offered in the *Second Discourse*, Rousseau hoped to provide exit from the "most horrible state of war" that had developed as a consequence of the introduction of riches and the unequal division of goods imposed by the strongest on the rest.[88] But however well-designed the governmental institutions, "the vices which make social institutions necessary, are the same vices which make the abuse of those institutions inevitable".[89] At the heart of the problems stood the passion for luxury, the accumulation of property beyond subsistence needs, which emerged with civilisation and which Rousseau associated with the mores of degenerated Parisian aristocracy. "Luxury", he wrote in *Social Contract*, "corrupts both the rich and the poor; it sells the country to effeminacy and vanity; it deprives the state of all its citizens by making some the slaves of others and all the slaves of opinion."[90] Already in his response to the Dijon academy's essay competition in 1750 "*Has the progress of the arts and sciences done more to corrupt mores than to improve them?*" Rousseau had made it clear that he believed that arts and sciences correlated with idleness and vanity, contributing to the demise of the republican spirit that only allowed empires to last:

> As the comforts of life increase as arts are brought to perfection and as luxury spreads, true courage flags, military virtues fade and this too is the world of the science sand all those arts that are practiced in the private of one's home.[91]

The dramatic opening lines of the Second Part of the *Second Discourse* further situated the rise of corruption and inequality at the moment when the first human being said "this is mine" – "how many crimes,

[86] Rousseau, *A Discourse on Inequality*, 120. Or, as he also put it, "plus on obtient, plus on desire", 'Principes du droit de la guerre', 73.

[87] Rousseau, *Social Contract*, I 2 (51–2). See also 'Principes du droit de la guerre', 70–5 and comments in Bachofen, 'Les raisons de la guerre. La raison dans la guerre. Une lecture des Principes du droit de la guerre', 137–42. Goyard-Fabre, *La construction de la paix*, 150–8.

[88] Rousseau, *A Discourse on Inequality*, 120, 118–24.

[89] Ibid., 131.

[90] Rousseau, *Social Contract*, III 4 (112).

[91] Jean-Jacques Rousseau, 'The First Discourse – Discourse on the Science and the Arts', in Susan Dunn (ed.), *The Social Contract and the First and the Second Discourses* (Yale University Press 2002), 60.

how many wars, how many murders, how many misfortunes and horrors" followed the introduction of property to the relations of humans![92] Civilisation and commercial refinement had brought neither liberty nor happiness, only a restless search for recognition and envy as the "social man lives always outside himself, he knows how to live only in the opinions of others".[93] The result of the overriding interest in one's private wealth and status was the lack of public virtues and descent into corruption and despotism, "the last stage of inequality".[94]

In the two early works *Discourse on Inequality* and the *Principles of Political Economy* Rousseau argued that modern statehood arose predominantly to protect the property of the wealthiest members of the society. They constituted a critique of the breathless search for riches and power that characterised a corrupt Europe that knew nothing of the republican spirit that was a precondition of political stability. The commercial spirit led to unending wars and conquests as the states were locked in a system of fear and ambition in which the steady rotation of rise and fall would endlessly repeat itself. The European law of nations was the natural law of corrupt societies. Rousseau was no more able than Saint-Pierre to canvass an international law and politics with a wider reach, apart from the sense in which colonial conquest might export European civilisation and political institutions to other continents. For like most eighteenth-century thinkers, Rousseau regarded Europe as the paradigm of the modern world, more than just a continent; its internal development would show the way for other parts of the world, too.[95]

## Montesquieu: The Natural Laws of Commerce

Not everyone was equally critical of luxury as Rousseau. The person most famously representing the contrary view, that "peace is the natural effect of trade",[96] was the Baron de la Brède, Charles de Secondat de Montesquieu (1689–1755) whose early writings sketched the demise of the spirit of conquest with the fall of the Roman empire and the end of

[92] Rousseau, *A Discourse on Inequality*, 109. [93] Ibid., 136.

[94] Ibid.,134. In due course, Rousseau speculated, tyranny will lead to insurrection, collapse and a return to the state of nature.

[95] On Rousseau's cultural, historical and economic notion of "Europe" as the "paradigm of civil society", see further Bruno Bernardi, 'Rousseau et l'Europe. Sur l'idée de société civile européenne', in Jean-Jacques Rousseau, *Principes du droit de la guerre. Ecrits de la paix perpetuelle* (Bruno Bernardi & Gabriella Silvestrini eds, Paris, Vrin 2008), 295–330, esp. 303–4.

[96] Montesquieu, *The Spirit of the Laws* (New York, Hafner 1949), XX 2 (Vol. I, 316).

designs for universal monarchy. In the *Considérations sur les causes de la grandeur des Romains et de leur décadence* and *Réflexions sur la monarchie universelle*, published originally together in 1734, Montesquieu produced the beginnings of a philosophical history that traced political modernity to the rise of constitutional systems where a commercial spirit would encourage citizen activism in domestic and international trade. The military hegemony of a nation over others had become impossible: "The Romans carried in triumph to Rome all the riches of the vanquished states. Today, victors bring home nothing but sterile laurels."[97] Even as it was customary to admire Rome's military virtues, it was ultimately the breathless search for territorial expansion that undid Rome. A nation could not exist on endless pillage; its behaviour in the peripheries corrupted Rome's centre. It was hence futile to look back nostalgically towards Rome's glories and conquests.[98] Thanks to the ever-expanding commerce European nations had become so dependent on each other that war between them had become senseless: "*L'Europe n'est plus qu'une nation composée de plusieurs.*"[99]

To understand how commerce, especially trade of necessities, would best uphold international peace it is necessary to turn to Montesquieu's main work, *L'Esprit des lois* (1748), which offered a holistic image of the political, legal, cultural and economic conditions that characterised the three forms of modern government – republican, monarchic and despotic. Montesquieu's grand synthesis sought to demonstrate how laws operated in each with respect to its "principle". The principle of republics, he wrote, was that of virtue that functioned in democracies as the search of equality and in aristocracies as their moderation. In monarchies, again, the ruling principle was honour that pushed them to glorious acts and natural hierarchies. This typology opened up into the comparative method where the constitutional system of a polity would be linked to the *esprit général* of its people, viewed through its environment and history.[100] Montesquieu was especially keen to find out whether modern governments were able to avoid the two dangers facing them, decline into

97 "Les Romains portaient à Rome dans les triomphes toutes les richesses des Nations vaincues. Aujourd'hui, les victoires ne donnent que des lauriers stériles." Montesquieu, *Réflexions sur la Monarchie universelle en Europe* (Genève, Droz 2000), I (72).

98 Of this, Montesquieu believed that the Spanish empire gave the best example. Montesquieu, *Réflexions*, XVI (97).

99 Ibid., XVIII (105).

100 For a useful discussion of Montesquieu's "holism", especially in view of its commercial aspects, see Paul Cheney, *Revolutionary Commerce. Globalization and the French Monarchy* (Harvard University Press 2010), 61–7.

despotism or the alienation of the citizens and their retreat into the world of private interests. As the previous generation of political thinkers had shown, virtue – the principle of republics – was too demanding and often led the citizens of democracies to yield to the advancement of private interests. This would not happen in monarchies, he argued, where the principle of honour and respect for privileges would be able to accommodate the commerce of luxury.[101]

Overall, Montesquieu appreciated the commercial virtues, "frugality, economy, moderation, labour, prudence, tranquillity, order and rule".[102] The free activity of citizens to pursue trade was beneficial for the state, too, and operated best through mercantile customs that states ought not to interfere with.[103] Different governmental forms were differently disposed with regard to commerce. While monarchies tended towards luxury, republics were predisposed to "economical commerce" where a large and egalitarian bourgeoisie would engage in exchanges on domestic and global markets.[104] The principal example was England, the English having "ever made their political interests give way to those of commerce".[105] This had not made it lose its independence, however. Even merchants wanted to defend their profits against a foreign conqueror. As a result, the most commercially oriented of peoples, the English, were ready to sacrifice their ease and their interest to preserve their liberty.[106] But Montesquieu did not hold commercial society as an unmitigated good or England's policies as beyond criticism. He was neither a Lockean liberal nor a republican: there were no inalienable rights in his works, and liberty to him meant the freedom left to citizens outside of legislation.[107] He was in favour of monarchy, tempered by intermediary bodies, the aristocracy, provincial *parlements*, businesses and guilds that would prevent monarchy's degeneration into despotism. Thus, for example, he joined the criticism of nobles engaging in commerce in France: such mixing up of social roles

[101] Montesquieu, *The Spirit of the Laws*, I 7; XX 1, 2 (I 25, 316–17). By positing "honour" instead of virtue as the principle of monarchies such as France, Montesquieu was able to lay aside the worry that the commercial spirit undermined public virtue. "Honour" was for him a purely outward phenomenon ("false honour") that did not depend on honourable action but on displays of respect to the privileges and ranks in society. See Céline Spector, *Montesquieu. Pouvoirs, richesses et sociétés* (Presses Universitaires de France 2004), 17–18 and passim.

[102] Montesquieu, *The Spirit of the Laws*, V 6 (I 46). See further Eric MacGilvray, *The Invention of Market Freedom* (Cambridge University Press 2011), 99–100, 104–5.

[103] Montesquieu, *The Spirit of the Laws*, XX 13 (I 323).

[104] Ibid., XX 4 (I 318–19).

[105] Ibid., XX 7 (I 321).

[106] Ibid., XIX 27 (I 310).

[107] Ibid., XXVI 20 (II 76).

would be detrimental to good order.[108] Living under laws was necessary but still insufficient. What was important was that subjects would feel themselves tranquil in their person and their properties.[109] And this "feeling" was above all a function of the moderation of the government, something that was best realised in a mixed monarchy.[110]

Montesquieu had surprisingly little to say about what this meant with respect to the new cosmopolitan, commercial world. Of course, law in general was a reflection of reason that governed "all the inhabitants of the earth" and of which the laws of particular peoples were only instances. In their mutual intercourse "different nations ought in time of peace to do one another all the good they can, and in time of war as little injury as possible, without prejudicing their real interests".[111] All the rules of the law of nations may be derived from this principle. Elsewhere he stressed the need to keep the law of nations separate from the civil laws of particular nations. It resulted from the fact that princes lived in a state of nature with each other that force was one of its principles and that "treaties made by force are as obligatory as those made by free consent".[112]

Much more important than his brief discussion of the law of nations was the systemic scheme that unfolded in the work and gave subsequent writers the basis on which to generalise about the stages of development linked with the expansion of commerce, and the softening of the manners that seemed inextricably linked with modern forms of government.[113] The beginning of political societies was familiar:

[108] Ibid., XX 21 (327) and discussion e.g. in Henry C. Clark, *Compass of Society. Commerce and Absolutism in Old-Regime France* (Lanham, Lexington Books 2007), 114–29. An interesting discussion of how the "politics of fusion" evident in the work reflects its author's roles in French society as a member of the Bordeaux *parlement* and a wine-growing agriculturalist is in Cheney, *Revolutionary Commerce*, 71–86.

[109] "Political liberty consists in security, or, at least, in the opinion that we enjoy security", Montesquieu, *The Spirit of the Laws*, XII 2 (I 183).

[110] This is especially powerfully argued in Jean Goldzink, *La solitude de Montesquieu. Le chef-oeuvre introuvable du libéralisme* (Paris, Fayard 2011), 129–53.

[111] Montesquieu, *The Spirit of the Laws*, I 3 (I 5). Nevertheless, Montesquieu assumed that in relations with despotic (in practice "Oriental") states, reciprocity could not be automatic. II 4, III 10; V 6. See also Jennifer Pitts, *Boundaries of the International. Law and Empire* (Harvard University Press 2018), 51–2.

[112] Montesquieu, *The Spirit of the Laws*, XXVI 20 (II 77).

[113] He even sketches what later among the Scottish economists came to be called the "four-stages theory", leading from "savage" hunter-gatherers to "barbarian" cattle-raising and the more civilised forms of agriculture and commerce (money). The more developed the manner of subsistence, the more complex, he wrote, the code of laws must become. Ibid., XVIII 7–15 (I 274–8). See also Céline Spector, 'Sujet de droit et sujet d'intérêt. Montesquieu lu par Foucault', 5 *Astérion* (2007), 95–8.

> As men have given up their natural independence to live with political laws, they have given in the natural community of goods to live under civil laws. By the first, they acquired liberty, by the second, property.[114]

The protection of liberty and property underlay all political societies and gave Montesquieu the standard to assess different constitutional forms. Everywhere, it seemed, the monarchic or republican forms were competing with their rival principles of honour and virtue sometimes realised in democratic, sometimes in aristocratic forms. Yet the best and most durable were mixed forms where the laws respected that principle which was true to the specific history of the state. If in England, for example, those conditions could be summarised in terms of a spirit of commerce, in France they were constituted by what Montesquieu called the *moeurs* (manners). In England people were independent-minded, even arrogant and competitive whereas in France they tended towards sociableness and respect of privilege and status. If Montesquieu clearly preferred the French paradigm to the English, this was because, he believed, it prevented the capture of public policy by private interests.[115]

The comparative method of the work allowed, like Bodin's nearly two centuries earlier, generalisations that produced something like a social-scientific orientation to government and fed the proliferation of universal histories. Although *Persian Letters* (1721) was predominantly concerned about the state of Europe, it gave a reasonably positive and nuanced, though of course Orientalist, view of the non-European world. *The Spirit of the Laws* made profuse reference to the Chinese and Japanese systems of law and was strongly positioned against ideas of uniformity that, Montesquieu wrote, "infallibly make an impression on little souls".[116] The book was nothing if not a principled statement of a relativist approach to the study of laws (and later condemned as such). There was no single ideal path of legal development. Instead Montesquieu produced a frame within which it was to become possible to examine how the laws of particular societies fitted with their dominant principle and spirit. But it was one of the complexities of Montesquieu's work that he also believed in the gradual expansion of commercial society. This would lead to levelling of the prices of luxury goods and the value of money across the world so that in due course

[114] Montesquieu, *The Spirit of the Laws*, XXVI 15 (II 73).
[115] See further, Spector, *Montesquieu*, 24–35, 182–217.
[116] Montesquieu, *The Spirit of the Laws*, XXIX 18 (II 169).

"the whole world [would become] composed of one single state, of which all the societies upon earth were members".[117]

## Towards the Brilliant Future

While Montesquieu believed that the commercial orientation of modern nations would guide their development, he refrained from perceiving their future in terms of determining historical laws. But many of his successors followed Saint-Pierre in an effort to enlist the powers of science and education for a utilitarian view that justified reform not by how it would realise a national spirit as reflected in stories about the ancients, but through its contribution to future progress.[118] Rousseau would introduce the idea (and the word) of perfectibility in the French debates but the most famous manifestation of that view was the *Preliminary Discourse* to D'Alembert's and Diderot's *Encyclopaedia* (1751) where the former recounted practically the whole of cultural progress in terms of utilitarian need-fulfilment. The development of arts and sciences emerged from "[t]he necessity of protecting our own bodies from pain and destruction", and especially from the body's effort to provide for "its endlessly multiplying needs".[119] Arts would gradually develop from the more immediately necessary, such as agriculture and medicine, into increasingly more abstract forms – physics, geometry and so on. Through this process we also discover "that natural law which we find within us, the source of the first laws which men must of necessity have created". Its origin D'Alembert attributed, as a good empiricist, to the universal experience of oppression suffered by the weak at the hands of the strong.[120] Cultural progress would also bring about a universal morality of natural law that would seek its origin not from God, but from universal experiences of injustice.[121]

The encyclopaedists were not a homogeneous group. Nevertheless, their analytical–compositive method made them invariably return to

[117] Or, as he suggested, "money, notes, bills of exchange, shares of companies . . . all merchandise, belong to the whole world in general", Montesquieu, *The Spirit of the Laws*, XX 23 (I 328).

[118] Gauchet, *La révolution moderne*, 126–31.

[119] Jean Le Rond d'Alembert, *Preliminary Discourse to the Encyclopedia of Diderot* (The University of Chicago Press 1995), 11, 14.

[120] Ibid., 14–15. For the *Encyclopaedia* as a part of a process of creating a single, hierarchical system of knowledge, see Michel Foucault, *Il faut défendre la société* (Cours au Collège de France 1976), 161–2.

[121] See d'Alembert, *Preliminary Discourse*, 12–13, 44.

individual experience, the urge to avoid pain and to seek pleasure, from which they would derive an enlightened sense of self-preservation encompassing concern for people not only at home but everywhere.[122] In their recurrent recourse to natural law and natural rights, the encyclopaedists found the simplest way to defend their programme of reform.[123] They would discard stories about the Franks and the Gauls. and derive their principles from their idea of the natural human being they assumed to exist as a rational egoist.[124] The most radical of the group, Paul-Henri Thiry, Baron d'Holbach (1723–1789), for example, produced a fully naturalistic structure of universal morality in which all rights and duties were determined in view of the search for continuous pleasure. His "social science" (*science des moeurs)* was based on "our physical sensations, the desires that animate us, on the love that we continue to feel towards ourselves, our real interests".[125] The task of law was to teach people to see "the necessity to be useful for those whose assistance is needed for our own felicity".[126] The difference between natural and positive law was erased; the legislator merely declared what was already inscribed in natural law. Only technical questions remained concerning how to reach general happiness, interpreted as always also compatible with enlightened individual interests.[127] This was the basis of the law of nations, too:

A nation is obliged, for its own interests, to share the same virtues as those each human being ought to show to those of his kind, whether foreigner or alien.[128]

[122] See further, Belissa, *Fraternité*, 23–49.

[123] Joseph Schumpeter, *Histoire de l'analyse économique. I – L'age des fondateurs* (Paris, Gallimard 1983 [1953]), 196–7.

[124] See further, Foucault, *Il faut défendre la société*, 186–7; Louis Dumont, *Homo aequalis I. Genèse et épanouissement de l'idéologie économique* (Paris, Gallimard 1977). The translation of egoism into action benefiting the community was a significant Augustinian theme in French thought from the seventeenth century onwards. In the eighteenth century it was often debated in reaction to Bernard Mandeville's *Fable of the Bees*. In Rousseau, it appeared in the distinction between healthy "love of oneself" and the (negative) self-love that was born with social distinctions and raised the self "above" others.

[125] "sur notre sensibilité physique, sur les désirs dont nous sommes constamment animés, sur l'amour continuel que chacun de nous a pour lui-même, sur nos vrais intérêts", Baron d'Holbach, *Système social ou principes naturels de la morale et de la politique* (Paris, Niogret 1822), tome I 77.

[126] Ibid., I 92. [127] Ibid., I 310–11

[128] Baron d'Holbach, *La morale universelle, ou les devoirs de l'homme, fondés sur la nature* (Paris, Masson 1820), tome II 2. This was obviously very close to Montesquieu's formulation, namely that "different nations ought in time of peace to do one another all the good they can, and in time of war as little injury as possible, without prejudicing their interests", *The Spirit of the Laws*, 5.

All nations had a duty of humanity towards each other, and none may do to others anything that is not within the boundaries of the equitable: "Such are the principles of the law of nations; it is at bottom nothing other than the morality of peoples."[129] There was no natural state of war between sovereigns; as members of their nations everyone belonged to a universal moral community; war was a relic from the vain search for glory, the avarice of tyrants. History showed that conquests were rarely useful, that large military forces were economically destructive and wars always ended in injustice.[130]

D'Holbach may have been extreme as a materialist but the logical consequences he drew from his naturalism were widely shared. There was a problem at the heart of that outlook, however. On the one hand, d'Holbach and others were relativists. Morality and law differed by time and place; each community had its own history and its own values that were reflected in the spirit of its laws and customs. On the other hand, they also persisted in arguing about a shared human nature on the basis of which it was possible to erect a structure of universal rights and duties. This ambivalence also extended into uncertainty about the nature of treaties and the positive practices of the law of nations. The first intuition of the radicals was to deny any validity to them; they were after all the products of old-regime diplomacy. On the other hand, what else than formal treaties between sovereigns could found the egalitarian Europe they advocated?[131] The jurist Antoine-Gaspard Boucher d'Argis (1708–1791) composed the essays on "natural law" and the "law of nations" in the *Encyclopaedia* as wholly conventional accounts of *ius naturae et gentium* from the Digest to Grotius, restating many of the positions the *philosophes* had vehemently opposed.[132] Probably for this

129 "Tels sont les principes du droit des gens, qui n'est au fond que la morale des peuples." D'Holbach, *Morale universelle*, II, 4.

130 Ibid., II, 2–21. On this point among the *philosophes* generally, see Belissa, *Fraternité*, 79–84.

131 See also ibid., 27–32.

132 Boucher d'Argis, 'Droit des Gens' and 'Droit de la Nature ou Droit naturel', in *Encyclopédie, ou dictionnaire raisonné des arts et des métiers etc.* (University of Chicago ARTFL Encyclopedia Project, Robert Morissey ed., encyclopedie.unchicago.edu), 5, 126 and 131. In particular, Boucher d'Argis rehearsed the themes about the relative overlap between natural law and the law of nations as a result of their confusing definitions in the Digest. His own position was that natural law was a law of reason, universally valid among humans, and that the law of nations was divided into "primary" and "secondary", the former dealing with rules of public and private law valid everywhere, the latter containing those conventional rules that nations have agreed or followed in practice. Most of the entries were written as overviews of the doctrines of Pufendorf and Burlamaqui.

reason Diderot inserted an essay on *Droit naturel* by himself in the form of a brief philosophical discourse. If the law of nature was universal, and could be found by reasoning, what was it? A person who reasons, Diderot claimed, will find reason as the same as the "general will" of humankind and the "*désir commun de l'espèce entier*". Because the general will was actually a true statement of what was useful for the human race, it was also compatible with d'Alembert's preliminary discourse. Diderot expressly rejected voluntarism: "Particular wills are suspect; they may be good or bad, but the general will is always good."[133] This was not a real, psychological will, however, but a proposition about the verifiable needs of the species constructed by humanity's assumed opposition to "nature". This was a new, scientifically oriented humanism, As Diderot wrote: "*C'est la nécessité de lutter contre l'ennemi commun, toujours subsistant, la nature, qui a rassemblé les hommes.*"[134] It was by working in, and against, nature that humanity would find its happiness.

## Commercial Statecraft

The debate on the relationship between national power, economic wealth and commerce was intensified in the 1760s owing to the military and economic disasters of the Seven Years' War (1756–63). In order to have the funds necessary to wage its hugely expensive colonial wars, France was compelled to compete in international markets in a way that posed wholly new demands on it.[135] Four alternative policies seemed available: pursuing autarchy by producing everything at home; seizing territory where goods naturally absent from home could be attained or produced; using colonial companies to seek out those goods and to carry out trade on the state's behalf, or finally, buying the goods it needed, that is, freedom of trade.[136] Each strategy would combine sovereign regulation with contract and property rights in a somewhat different

[133] Diderot, 'Droit naturel', in *Encyclopédie*, 5, 115–16.

[134] Diderot, 'Observations sur le Nakaz, para LXXI', quoted in Catherine Larrère, *L'invention de l'économie au XVIIIe siècle* (Presses Universitaires de France 1992), 91. For Diderot's utilitarianism generally, see ibid., 51–7, 67–75 and Cassirer, *Philosophy of Enlightenment*, 246–8.

[135] István Hont, *Jealousy of Trade. International Competition and the Nation-State in Historical Perspective* (Harvard University Press 2006), 187.

[136] The four alternatives, laid out by the Abbé Baudeau in the mid-1760s, are discussed in Emma Rothschild, 'Global Commerce and the Question of Sovereignty in the Eighteenth-Century Provinces', 1 *Modern Intellectual History* (2004), 10–22.

way. The first was unavailable as an exclusive solution as domestic agriculture needed tools and animals from abroad. The opportunity for colonial conquests was thinning out and experience with settlements was discouraging. The problems with colonial companies had become sufficiently clear in the previous century (and will be discussed in Chapter 7 below) so that most new thinking coupled some form of free trade with varying degree of protections, as Melon had suggested.

As we have seen, writers such as Melon emphasised both the dangers of economic dependency resulting from the commerce of necessities, but also the advantages of specialisation. If merchants were to be given a greater role, how to prevent the profit-making motive from undermining the "honour" that underwrote a well-functioning monarchic order? The debate launched by the Abbé Coyer on the *noblesse commerçante* did not convince those who, like Montesquieu, felt that the result would be overall corruption and decline.[137] The debate was soon monopolised by the "Neo-Colbertians", a group of perhaps forty men working under the new superintendant of commerce, J.-C.-M. Vincent Gournay (1715–1759). These men were critical of the waste involved in an economically passive nobility and argued that a type of honour belonged to commerce as well. But their deeper objective was to create a "science of commerce" that would enable attacking the privileges of guilds, monopoly companies, tax farmers and financiers. Domestic barriers of trade were to be lifted ("*laissez-faire et laissez passer*", Gournay's suggested) while international trade was to be strictly subordinated to *raison d'état*. Mercantile freedom was to be disciplined by wise policymaking that would seek a balance of trade as well as a fair distribution of the colonies.[138]

The Gournay group distinguished between the corrupting effects of luxury and the way it stimulated trade and increased national wealth. Good faith, loyalty and keeping to agreements were crucial for mercantile success. Commerce was underlain by a concrete *sociability* that would work best if allowed to operate without disturbance. In particular, Gournay and his associates stressed the extent to which the interests of parties to mercantile transactions were best known to those parties themselves.[139]

137 Abbé Coyer, *La noblesse commerçante* (Paris, Duchêne 1761). For the debate, see e.g. Shovlin, *The Political Economy of Virtue*, 58–65.

138 An excellent discussion of the theories of the "Gournay group" is Arnault Skornicki, *L'économiste, la cour et la patrie* (Paris, CNRS editions 2011), 87–97, 124, 139–40. See also Cheney, *Revolutionary Commerce*, 83–6, 103–4, 113–23.

139 See further, Larrère, *L'invention*, 135–50.

Unlike abstract views about state policy, the merchants would be immediately sanctioned for their mistakes. Allowing mercantile interests to take their natural course was conducive both to constancy and predictability of transactions, enabling the reliable measurement of outcomes.[140] The points of view of the merchant and the state were inextricable.

The most active of the Gournay group members was François Véron de Forbonnais (1722–1800) whom Diderot had invited to compose a number of instalments in the *Encyclopédie* (e.g. "commerce" and "grain") and who insisted on a clear distinction between domestic and foreign commerce.[141] While the former was natural and upheld social harmony, the latter was a largely artificial field of struggle in a zero-sum game. Forbonnais wholly rejected Montesquieu's speculations about the world-uniting aspects of trade. He and Saint-Pierre had been mistaken; there was no single human society and the logic of self-preservation would trump even utility-based internationalism. "Our cosmopolitans", Forbonnais wrote, "make the error of identifying the interest of the merchant with the interest of the nation." The relations between commercial rivals were analogous to those between enemies, and the object of commercial policy was to secure the power of the state vis-à-vis its neighbours.[142] The proper policy would seek autarchy by optimising agricultural production and maximising the number of populations engaged in labour and commerce.[143] Obstacles to domestic trade and the export of luxuries were to be lifted while customs and other duties were to be used to protect agriculture.[144] At the heart of the laws to manage the economy lay the right of property that the state was to protect and enhance:

> Thus, property must be used to support [state] power and [state] power must be used to protect property . . . the just relations between property and power are the basis of the strength of a nation.[145]

140 Hirschman, *The Passions and the Interests*, 48–56.

141 See especially François Véron de Forbonnais, *Elemens du commerce. Première partie* (2nd edn, Leiden, Briasson 1754), 74–7.

142 Ibid., 67, and discussion in Larrère, *L'invention*, 102; Michael Sonenscher, *Before the Deluge. Public Debt, Inequality, and the Intellectual Origins of the French Revolution* (Princeton University Press 2009), 173, 179–89.

143 François Véron de Forbonnais, *Principes et observations économiques* (tome première, Amsterdam, Michel Rey 1767), 55–7 and passim.

144 Larrère, *L'invention*, 99–107.

145 "Ainsi, la force doit être entretenue par la propriété et la propriété doit être protegé par la force . . . les rapports justes de la propriété et la force constituent la puissance d'une nation", Forbonnais, *Principes et observations*, 2.

In conceiving the proper relations between domestic and international trade, Forbonnais sometimes used hydraulic metaphors to highlight their interdependence and the character of laws as having to deal less with prohibition than channelling of natural phenomena.[146] He also stressed that a vigorous colonial policy would envisage the metropolis and the colony as a single unit: the colony was not to compete with the metropolis, and all colonial trade, including slave trade, was to be reserved for metropolitan merchants.[147] In the course of English naval operations against French colonial shipping in the 1750s Forbonnais argued in favour of using neutral parties to carry the Caribbean trade. The law of nations, he wrote, provided that when there was a dependency – as there was between the colonies and the metropolis – then the stronger party had to take action even if that meant violating private interests.[148]

## The Natural Laws of the Economy: The Physiocrats

Although the Gournay group viewed commerce in "systemic" terms, an increasingly influential group of French thinkers believed that they still did not attain the "natural and essential order" underlying all social life. Honour and virtue, for example, were merely superficial reflections of this order that also knew no distinction between domestic and international matters. Monopolies and privileges were a striking demonstration of the distorted state of the French public order. The most important representatives of the group of *les économistes*, Honoré Gabriel Riqueti, the Marquis de Mirabeau (1715–1789) and François Quesnay (1694–1774), borrowed extensively from natural law, dismissing England's commercial success merely as the temporary effect of a war-economy. Following it would lead large territorial states such as France to ruin. Quesnay and the members of his writing workshop – the Physiocrats – wanted to isolate the workings of the economy from government or policy. In accordance with their naturalism, they insisted

[146] Larrère, *L'invention*, 125–6.

[147] Forbonnais had nothing to say about the moral status of slavery. But he did highlight the need to keep the price of *nègres* low in order to avoid foreign competition. *Elemens du commerce*, 12–35.

[148] François Véron de Forbonnais, *Essai sur l'admission des navires neutres dans nos colonies* (Paris 1756 – original has neither author nor date or place of publication), 45. See also Antonella Alimento, 'Competition, True Patriotism and Colonial Interest. Forbonnais' Vision of Neutrality and Trade'. www.helsinki.fi/collegium/e-series/volumes/volume_10/010_05_Alimento_2011.pdf.

on agricultural production as the base of the economy. Commerce and industries were secondary – "sterile" in the Physiocrat jargon. By taking advantage of its large agricultural base France could outmanoeuvre its rivals, especially in conditions of free grain trade. Owing to its intrinsic laws, the economy worked best if left to its own devices. Laws were needed only to guarantee that no obstacles were introduced to the free use of property rights.[149]

The Physiocrats' world view was utterly individualistic. In Quesnay's formulation, natural law provided for "the right that every human being has on things they need for happiness" (*jouissance*).[150] This right remained only abstract and virtual in the natural state but became concrete by the way humans took things, especially land, into possession by labour. To secure their possessions humans would join "communities of interest" within which they would agree on division of labour and organise the government of their rights and duties.[151] The *form* of government – monarchical, aristocratic or popular – was unimportant. The main point was that without liberty and security of property there could be no profitable or stable society at all.[152] As Mirabeau put it in 1774, the principal task of political authority was to secure "*le respect absolu de propriété*". The monarch's sovereignty was above all his capacity to protect property rights – and the duty of the subject to obey was based on this.[153]

According to the Physiocrats, the natural and necessary order of society had been in a state of degradation and corruption and would be restored only once the rural basis of the economy would take its rightful place.[154] It was the task of government to help nature (*aider à la nature*) by seeing to it that nothing intervenes in its preordained movements (*marche préordonnée & prescrite*).[155] Unlike for republican theorists such as Mably or Rousseau, nature and society were not polar

[149] See further Yves Charbit, 'L'échec politique d'une théorie économique. La physiocratie', 57 *Cairn* (2002), 862–3. My reading of Physiocrat theory is especially influenced by David McNally, *Political Economy and the Rise of Capitalism. A Reinterpretation* (University of California Press 1990), 85–151 and Larrère, *L'invention.*

[150] François Quesnay, 'Le droit naturel', in M. Eugène Daire (ed.) *Collection des principaux économistes, tome 2, Physiocrates* (Osnabruck, Zeller 1966 [1846]), 41.

[151] Ibid., 49. [152] Ibid., 51.

[153] "La souveraineté donc est … puissance tutélaire et conservatrice des propriétés", Marquis de Mirabeau, *La science, ou les droits et devoirs de l'homme* (Lausanne, Grasset 1774), 125 and 156, 162–3.

[154] See Skornicki, *L'économiste*, 195–6.

[155] Marquis de Mirabeau, *Philosophie rurale, ou Économie générale et politique de l'agriculture* (Amsterdam, Les librairies associées 1763), XII (269).

opposites; on the contrary the proper government of the latter meant bringing it in line with the former. Positive laws were to "ensure the defence of society by guaranteeing the regular observation of natural laws".[156] The most important laws were those that provided for public instruction on the content of natural law. Legislation, too, was a kind of instruction; ignorance and evil existed as merely two aspects of the failure to ensure that society operated in the "most advantageous" manner. Once reason had understood the natural laws, it would immediately discard anything that went against them. Government was a kind of trusteeship (*autorité tutélaire*), and obedience to the laws did not signify a loss of freedom but realised it. This is why "human beings could not reasonably decline to obey these laws".[157]

The Physiocrats joined the long line of early eighteenth-century critics of the feudal system of divided domains and seigneurial privileges.[158] The distinction between *dominium directum* and *utile* was an arbitrary distortion of the possession-based natural system or ownership. Nor was there any reason to treat the domestic and the international worlds differently. Because nature was one, state government was simply a local manager of universal natural processes, especially land use, to ensure their efficiency. Boundary treaties between nations, for example, only repeated the existing legal disorder by failing to give full effect to the productive capacities of land.[159] The Gournay group had aimed to enhance national strength because it viewed the state as a bringer of peace, security and civilisation. That assumption had already been questioned by Rousseau. For him, and for the Physiocrats, state intervention merely *obstructed* society's natural development. By giving effect to natural rights and duties, the state would finally allow the necessary and essential order to take effect.

That order was based on agriculture. Quesnay's famous "*Tableau économique*" (1758) contained a graphic explanation of the relations between the three social classes, farmers, the only productive class,

156 "pour assurer la défense de la société, pour observer régulièrement les lois naturelles", Quesnay, 'Le droit naturel', 53.

157 "L'homme ne peut se refuser raisonnablement à l'obéissance qu'il doit à ces lois", ibid., 55.

158 See especially Rafe Blaufarb, *The Great Demarcation. The French Revolution and the Invention of Modern Property* (Oxford University Press 2016), 40–6.

159 Mirabeau, *La science*, 174–88. To the temptation among princes to use this "natural" principle to extend their jurisdiction indefinitely Mirabeau proposed the Physiocrats' favourite antidote – instruction, teaching princes that rights can only extend as far as protective duties may be efficient, 179–80, 187–8.

as well as artisans and merchants on the one hand and the landowners on the other. The natural order was constituted of the way the agricultural surplus would be transformed and circulated by artisans and merchants who would receive their income from trade, including with the landowners whose wealth, again, was constituted of the rents received from the farmers. Because only the latter were productive, taxation would be directed only to the agricultural surplus, carefully avoiding an adverse effect on subsistence and investment.[160] Its large rural spaces made France the potentially most powerful country in Europe. By taking full advantage of its situation, its king could become a *Roi Pasteur* guiding all of Europe to live in accordance with the natural basis of their respective economies.[161] The Physiocrats were natural advocates of free trade. If France were to open its borders for free trade, its international position would soon resemble the situation of Paris as the capital of France. By stimulating economic exchange it could have its wealth radiate across the world. It would become *ami des hommes*.[162] So far humanity had been ruled by small-minded men engaging in destructive wars. They had not understood that in trade, both parties will win because a nation's prosperity will necessarily increase the demand for commodities from others. Free trade was therefore enshrined in the law of nations and it was for the king of France to see to its implementation, if necessary by force.[163]

Physiocrat views on the colonies could not have been further away from those of the commercial patriots: "Commerce is to serve in liberty, but is never to command."[164] England's navigation laws and the French *exclusif* had been equally oppressive. Mirabeau speculated that the colonies would soon shed the yoke of the old world. Why not

[160] For a concise explanation of Physiocrat theory, see Jacques Valier, *Brève histoire de la pensée économique d'Aristote à nos jours* (Paris, Flammarion 2005), 41–54; Alessandro Roncaglia, *The Wealth of Ideas. A History of Economic Thought* (Cambridge University Press 2006), 96–103.

[161] The moral aspect of Physiocracy in the eyes of the contemporaries is highlighted by Sonenscher, *Before the Deluge*, 190–3. The idea of France as the leading state, and its king as "Shepherd King" appears repeatedly in Mirabeau, *L'ami des hommes, ou traité de la population* (Nouvelle édition, troisième partie – no place of publication, 1759), e.g. 184, 244.

[162] For the analogy France-Paris, see Mirabeau, *L'ami des hommes*, III, 6–7, 32–3.

[163] Ibid., III, 33, 73, 80. Mirabeau speculated about how that "shepherd" – "a friend of peoples" – would propose a treaty for all nations to sign on free trade and navigation as well as freedom of industries and, if needed, impose it on recalcitrant states. Ibid., 244–6.

[164] Ibid., III, 340.

therefore abolish the limitations and begin treating the colonies as the French provinces were treated, allowing them to set up their own systems of production and trade? Needless to say, this suggestion was fiercely opposed by the French merchants and nothing came of it before the Revolution.[165]

Nowhere are the universalist principles of this new science – political economy – laid out more clearly than in the brief essay by one of Quesnay's most influential protégés, Pierre Samuel Dupont de Nemours (1739–1817), later inspector general of commerce, and a tireless propagator of free trade in France and later in the United States.[166] A natural society had always existed between humans, Dupont wrote, formed out of their needs and interests and prior to any convention. "In this primitive state human beings possess reciprocal rights and duties of an absolute justice, deriving from a physical necessity and are thus absolutely necessary for their existence."[167] Good government was to put these rights and duties into harmonious relationship. Growth was part of the natural society itself and rulers were only to see that this took place in an orderly way. In Dupont's dramatic formulation, the human sovereign was incapable of legislating anything new – "*car les lois sont toutes faites par la main de celui qui créa les droits & les devoirs*".[168] All that positive laws were to achieve was to declare the content of natural laws of freedom and property and to implement them.[169]

Physiocrats believed that the economy possessed its own natural laws that were to dictate how kings should rule and legislatures legislate. Treating it as a science suggested that its business was to collect the evidence from the world of production and consumption so as to assist

165 See further, Pernille Røge, 'A Natural Order of Empire. The Physiocratic Vision of Colonial France after the Seven Years War', in Sophus A. Reinert & Pernille Røge (eds), *The Political Economy of Empire in the Early Modern World* (Basingstoke, Palgrave Macmillan 2013), 32–52.

166 For a useful discussion, see Martin Giraudeau, 'Performing Physiocracy. Pierre Samuel Dupont de Nemoirs and the Limits of Political Engineering', 3 *Journal of Cultural Economy* (2008), 225–42.

167 "Dans cet état primitive les hommes ont des droits et devoirs réciproques d'une justice absolue parce qu'ils sont d'une nécessité physique & par conséquent absolue pour leur existence." Pierre Samuel Dupont de Nemours, *De l'origine et des progrès d'une science nouvelle* (London, Desaint 1768), 17–18.

168 Ibid., 30.

169 Hence there was no reason to distinguish between legislation and enforcement; valid legislation was always also enforcement of the prior system of natural rights and obligations. Ibid., 31–2.

the monarch to set up what Quesnay and his followers addressed by the unfortunate expression of "legal despotism". This was a dominant theme with one of the most outspoken members of the group, the jurist Paul-Pierre Le Mercier de la Rivière (1719–1801) who turned to the physiocratic cause after a distinguished career as counsellor in the *parlement* of Paris.[170] On the strength of his contacts with the court he was first appointed as governor of the French Antilles in 1759–64 where he had occasion to experiment with the almost military organisation of agricultural production in Martinique's slave-economy. The failure of that experiment forced him to return to Paris, however, where he produced what became – if we are to believe Adam Smith – the most impressive literary achievement of the group, *L'Ordre naturel et essentiel des sociétés politiques* (*Natural and Essential Order of Political Societies*, 1767).[171]

Le Mercier's *magnum opus* translated Quesnay's economic theories into a political philosophy and a proposal for a wholesale legal reform. It combined a utilitarian political theory with absolute respect of private property. "Legal despotism" was to translate the requirements of natural science into positive laws and a substantial part of the work contained instructions on how this was to be done. The work also contained the pseudo-feudal view of the monarch as a "co-proprietor" of everything as well as the rather eccentric proposal for a confederation of European nations that, le Mercier assumed, would be a necessary outcome of his theories. All societies had a natural, underlying order: "*Cet ordre n'est qu'une branche de l'ordre physique.*"[172] By grasping this humans could realise the two objects of all their actions: enjoyment of pleasure and avoidance of pain.[173] Everything began with an "absolute" right of self-preservation and its concomitant, the right to acquire whatever was useful. For every right, there was a duty, and society could be articulated in terms of the absolute rights and

[170] For a brief biography, see Louis Philippe May, *Le Mercier de la Rivière. Aux origines de la science économique* (Paris, CNRS 1975), 150–3 and passim.

[171] Paul-Pierre Le Mercier de la Rivière, *L'Ordre naturel et essentiel des sociétés politiques* (London, Nourse 1767). At the time of its publication, the work received a mixed response. Voltaire disliked its pedantic tone and Grimm was hostile to its basic ideas. Owing to Diderot's praise, however, Le Mercier was invited to St Petersburg where the Empress failed to be impressed by his lecturing so that he was compelled to return to the debates at home on how to remedy France's dire financial situation. May, *Le Mercier de la Rivière*, 66, 72–4, 79–83.

[172] Le Mercier, *L'Ordre naturel*, 37.

[173] "… la nature … a voulu que [les hommes] ne connussent que deux mobiles, l'appétit des plaisirs & l'aversion de la douleur", ibid., 33.

duties of individuals towards each other.[174] All societies were based on the search of happiness, and happiness was abundance: "*le plus grand bonheur possible consiste pour nous dans la plus grande abondance possible d'objets propres à nos jouissances*".[175]

To achieve this, production had to increase. This, again, was possible only in a regime where everyone had the free use of their properties.[176] In the work of government, all available choices either pointed to increased abundance or did not; that is, everything was either required or prohibited, absolutely just or absolutely unjust.[177] Repeating over again the expression "absolute", Le Mercier underlined the necessary character of the order of relationships he laid out. Human laws had the absoluteness of physical laws. Quesnay had already written that "[t]he natural laws of the social order are themselves the physical laws of perpetual reproduction of those goods necessary to the subsistence, the conservation, and the convenience of men".[178] From this, he had developed a very rigorous notion of the rule of law. The laws "had already been written" by nature itself; all that was left for the ruler was to "dictate" them to society at large.[179] There was no basis to distinguish between legislative and executive power: one was merely the extension of the other. "*Partager l'autorité, c'est l'annuller.*"[180]

Exactly the same principles were operative at the international level. When visiting distant peoples, the same hospitality was found as at home. The expansion of commerce relied on a wholly intuitive respect for rights and duties shared all over the world. Different political societies were like branches of the same tree, parts of universal human society.[181] A federation of Europe was no chimera, but in fact already in existence "by the sole force of necessity of which it is the guarantor of every nation".[182] Nature compelled people to regard each other as brothers, possessing equal rights and duties across the world. In a later work on the grain trade, Le Mercier stressed that the advantages of freedom extended way beyond the domestic realm. Free competition was a precondition for justice, and

[174] Ibid., 11–17. [175] Ibid., 27 (emphasis in original removed). [176] Ibid., 33.
[177] Ibid., 11.
[178] Quesnay, 'Despotisme de la Chine', quoted in McNally, *Political Economy*, 123.
[179] Le Mercier, *L'Ordre naturel*, 75–8, 105, 113. [180] Ibid., 129.
[181] Ibid., 318–20.
[182] "par la seule force de nécessité dont elle est la sureté politique de chaque Nation en particulier", ibid., 323.

a just equilibrium can only be found by liberating both buyers and sellers to look for their trading partners everywhere in the world. This, he noted, was what it meant that God had created all humans as part of a great society.[183]

According to the Physiocrats, the state was not to intervene in the relations between private economic actors. Inequality was a necessary part of a world where citizens freely used the available economic opportunities.[184] The state was only to lift obstacles to free trade, and help channel human activities to profitable directions. The most influential of the new economists, Anne-Robert-Jacques Turgot (1727–1781) worked as controller-general in France in the period 1774–6 and had a fundamental mistrust of regulation. Any legislation on luxuries was arbitrary, harmful and unjust, he wrote. In fact regulation created the very problems it sought to alleviate. There were nowhere more publicly kept houses for the poor than in Spain – but perversely nowhere was the number of the poor greater. Nevertheless, Turgot still felt that a robust public power was needed for reasons of public utility, "the supreme law" of government. As the *intendant* of Limoge during the time of the scarcity in 1770–1 he had enacted various relief measures – never touching the grain prices, however. The qualified success prompted him to insist that commerce and competition be entirely free. It was never possible for a regulator, however knowledgeable and well-meaning, to set the prices in such a way as to "procure for the entire society the greatest sum of production, enjoyment, wealth, and strength".[185] Yet Turgot's later reforms nevertheless stalled. The effort to free the grain trade, to suppress the *corvée* and the guilds as well as to limit the privileges of the financiers and the tax-farmers provoked violent opposition. With the bad harvests and the uprisings in the countryside, Turgot's efforts came to an end.[186] As he was ousted in 1776, attention had to turn to more practical concerns to deal with the economic chaos.

183 Paul-Pierre Le Mercier de la Rivière, *L'intérêt général de l'Etat ou la liberté du commerce des blés* (Amsterdam, Desaint 1770), 90–2.

184 Anne-Robert-Jacques Turgot, *Reflections on the Formation and the Distribution of Riches* (New York, Macmillan [Liberty Fund], 1891 [1770]), 3–4.

185 Turgot, 'Lettres sur le commerce des grains' (1770), quoted in Emma Rothschild, *Economic Sentiments. Adam Smith, Condorcet and the Enlightenment* (Harvard University Press 2001), 76, 76–81.

186 A still-good analysis of Turgot's reform proposals and their ideational background as well as a translation of the texts of the famous "Six Edicts" is in Robert Shepherd, *Turgot and the Six Edicts* (Columbia University Press 1903).

## Natural Rights and the Legal Order: Sieyès

The financial situation of the court having become untenable, the king finally decided to convoke a meeting of the Estates-General on 1 May 1789. Even as Turgot was no longer at the helm, his views were propagated by revolutionaries such as Condorcet, and were turned from the economic into the political realm by the most influential polemicist of the early phase of the revolution, Emmanuel-Joseph Sieyès (1748–1836). He wanted to seize the opportunity to translate the rights valid in the state of nature into a constitution for France: "social order is like a follow-up, like a complement of the natural order".[187] Political order needed to be based on free agreement; this would not deprive anyone of their liberty but would, on the contrary, constitute an exercise of it.[188] A constitution would allow everyone to perfect themselves, protecting their rights and liberties against natural moral and physical inequalities.[189] The most important of the liberties was the free use of property: "The one is free who never has to worry about the exercise of their personal property."[190] Following Locke, Sieyès explained that property rights emerged from labour – "*[m]on travail était à moi*"; a thing became the object of ownership by occupying it. To this de facto situation society added a legal imprimatur (*consécration légale*).[191] The only justification for limiting my freedom was to prevent harm to others; this is what laws were for: "Outside the laws, everything is free for everyone."[192]

These principles were to be made reality by what Sieyès chose to call "the first of all arts – the social art".[193] This art lay at the foundation of the powers of legislation of the Estates-General. Because there were (supposedly) no slaves in France, it had to be assumed that Frenchmen were free. Being free, they were to rule themselves: "Only his own will can give his engagement the character of a moral obligation."[194] This

[187] "l'ordre social est comme une suite, comme un complément de l'ordre naturel", Abbé Sieyès, *Préliminaire de la constitution française & Reconnaissance et exposition raisonnée des droits de l'homme et du citoyen* (Paris, Baudoin 1789), 24.

[188] Ibid., 28. [189] Ibid., 25–6.

[190] "Celui-là est libre, qui a l'assurance de n'être pas inquiète dans l'exercice de sa propriété personnelle", ibid., 27.

[191] Ibid., 26, 27. [192] "Hors de la Loi, tout est libre pour tous", ibid., 28.

[193] Abbé Sieyès, 'Views of the Executive Means Available to the Representatives of France in 1789', in Abbé Sieyès, *Political Writings* (ed. & intro. M. Sonenscher, Indianapolis, Hackett 2003), 5.

[194] Ibid., 10.

meant that once an association of free individuals – the nation – had been formed, these individuals could be constrained only by "a *common will* to meet common needs".[195] Unlike Rousseau, Sieyès accepted that this could be the will of a majority, a pragmatic necessity to which all those having joined would need to agree. In an argument that he may have received from Kant, Sieyès explained that each member of such association would logically need to accept that the reciprocal recognition of the authority of their individual wills would produce the greatest happiness to all of them.[196] It was not an aggregate of individual wills that was authoritative, but a system of spontaneous reciprocity that became the substance of the nation.[197]

But Sieyès backed down from the democratic implications of his theory by making the distinction between "active" and "passive" citizens. Everyone would enjoy *passive* rights of citizenship, the protection of their person and property. But only some had the rights of *active* citizenship, and this did not include women, children, foreigners and "all those who contribute nothing to the maintenance of the public realm (*établissement public*)". Only those who contribute to the public order were to enjoy political rights and are "like the real shareholders (*actionnaires*) of the great social enterprise".[198] Citizenship was first and foremost the right to be protected by the state, not to be part of its government. The "people" was not a political but a social entity, an object but not a subject of government.[199] Sieyès supported what later came to be called "modern" liberty, which accepted that not all citizens had the time or the inclination for public service but rather wish to carry out their business without disturbance. Nostalgia for republican Athens or Rome was utterly displaced.[200]

195 Ibid., 11.

196 The objective of "happiness" (rather than "justice") shows the background of Sieyès' thinking in the Physiocrats rather than in Kant.

197 Ibid., 13–14.

198 Sieyès, *Préliminaire*, 37. The distinction between "people" and the "nation" would allow Sieyès to take increasingly anti-democratic positions during the Directory. Andrew J. S. Jainchill, *Reimagining Politics after the Terror. The Republican Origins of French Liberalism* (Cornell University Press 2008), 214–16.

199 See Marcel Gauchet, *La Révolution des pouvoirs. La souveraineté, le peuple et la représentation 1789–1799* (Paris, Gallimard 1995), 63; Larrère, *L'invention*, 295–307.

200 "Modern European peoples do not much resemble ancient ones. We are only concerned of commerce, agriculture, fabrics etc.; the desire for riches appears to make all European states into huge workshops; more attention is given there to consumption and production than happiness." Statement by Sieyès, at National Assembly on 9 September 1789, *Archives parlementaires de 1787 à 1860. Première série*, VIII (Paris, Librairie administrative P. Dupont 1875), 594.

Such liberty could never become a reality in a system of noble privileges and monopoly rights. A privilege or a monopoly, Sieyès wrote, placed its holder "beyond the boundaries of common right". It had no justification. If it was true that liberty and property are "paramount to everything else" and if these belonged to human beings already before their entry into political society, then it was the task of laws merely to protect them. Granting a privilege or an exemption to someone "is directly saying to those citizens 'You are permitted to do wrong'. No power on earth should be authorised to make such a concession."[201] Sieyès had nothing but scorn towards the vanity and complacency of the noble class, those "privileged beggars" obsessively fixated on the past. What a pathetic contrast they formed to the farmers, manufacturers, merchants and the providers of services that saw to every aspect of the life and growth of the nation![202] These all had "their function, their particular tasks, employments, which collectively form the general movement of society".[203] Not the contrast of the old estates but the division of labour between these workers was the "true basis of the progress in the social state [in contrast to the state of nature]".[204] It was this argument that prompted Sieyès to make his famous claim that the third estate was in fact "everything", that there was no legitimate room for a privileged class in the nation: "The Third Estate has to be understood as the totality of citizens belonging to the common order."[205] What is remarkable is the way in which Sieyès almost conflates the division of labour with political representation. It was not only that the nation acted through its economic classes but that the interests and cooperation between those classes, instead of institutional or administrative considerations, become the nation's principle of identity and growth.[206]

## Revolutions 1: Europe

Following Sieyès' dictum that a nation could not be represented by an association of estates, the Third Estate first declared itself the "universal

[201] Sieyès, 'An Essay on Privileges', in *Political Writings*, 69–70.
[202] Sieyès, 'What Is the Third Estate?', 94–5.
[203] Sieyès, 'An Essay on Privileges', 83.
[204] Sieyès, 'Lettres aux Economistes sur leur système de politique et de morale', quoted in Larrère, *L'invention*, 272–3.
[205] Sieyès, 'What is the Third Estate?', 99.
[206] As highlighted by Keith M. Baker, *Inventing the French Revolution* (Cambridge University Press 1990), 244–6. Likewise Jainchill, *Reimagining Politics*, 215–16.

estate" on 17 June, joined ten days thereafter by the nobility and the clergy. Having transformed themselves into a National Assembly, the deputies decided on 4 August 1789 to "totally destroy the feudal regime" by abolishing noble and non-noble privileges as well as the system of venal offices, in other words to do away with the whole corporate structure of society.[207] Within a week of hectic legislative activity, the Assembly had wiped away all seigneurial rights and jurisdictions, the division of rights to land into *dominium directum* and *dominium utile*, the privileges of provincial and urban elites, most court pensions and tax exemptions and transformed the royal domain into a national domain.[208] As one of the deputies, Le Guen de Kerengal, put it, *"[l]e peuple, impatient d'obtenir justice et las de l'oppression, s'empresse de détruire ces titres, monument de la barbarie de nos pères"*.[209]

After the collapse of the old regime, the Assembly needed to find its legitimacy from some new source; neither God, history nor the exalted status of the monarch would do. Instead, it aimed to found itself on principles that would be as universal as possible.[210] These were the natural rights whose number and content was fixed in the course of a few days from 20 to 26 August. The *Declaration of the Rights of Man and of Citizen* of 27 August was to be part of a new constitution but also to have universal purport. The revolutionaries were after all speaking in the name of humanity. According to article 2 *all* political association – and not only France – had the objective to "preserve the natural and imprescriptible rights of man. These rights included liberty, property,

[207] François Furet, 'Ancien régime', in François Furet & Mona Ozouf, *Dictionnaire critique de la révolution française* (Paris, Flammarion 1992), 27. For the run-up to the decision of 4 August and the immediate aftermath, see Michael Fitzsimmons, *The Night the Old Regime Ended. August 4, 1789 and the French Revolution* (Pennsylvania State University Press 2002), 12–23.

[208] The transformation of thousands of seigneurial jurisdictions into regular state courts and venal office-holding into forms of public service and magistracy took a long time and did not happen without difficulty. The feudal privileges were divided into those to be immediately abolished and those that were "*rachetable*". But as the implementation of this distinction proved impossible on 17 July 1793 all privileges were unconditionally abolished. The holders of the original documents were to bring them to the municipal offices to be burnt on 10 August. For a thorough discussion of the legislation passed between 4 and 11 August and its implementation, see Blaufarb, *The Great Demarcation*, 48–81. See also Jean-Philippe Lévy, *Histoire de la propriété* (Presses Universitaires de France 1972), 76–80; Paul Ourliac & Jehan de Malafosse, *Histoire du droit privé*, tome 2 (2éd., Presses Universitaires de France 1971), 169–79.

[209] Quoted in François Furet, 'Féodalité', in Furet & Ozouf, *Dictionnaire*, 193.

[210] Gauchet, *La Révolution des pouvoirs*, 55.

security and resistance to oppression."[211] There could be no legitimate intermediaries between the citizens and the nation – no-one's rights, status or position could be derived from their belonging to a particular social group. The deputies were conscious that their actions were being followed closely across Europe, as attested in a memorable formulation by Immanuel Kant a few years later reminiscing on the universal sympathy aroused by the Revolution.[212] In a flurry of cosmopolitan enthusiasm, the deputies even appointed eighteen writers and philosophers from across Europe and the United States as French citizens: everyone who fought for liberty was a French citizen and France itself was universal.[213]

But the relationship between the rights and the new constitution was problematic. Which was prior? Many argued that because the rights were the foundation of the constitution, their number and content had to be fixed first. Others claimed that the debates on rights involved such difficult philosophical conundrums that to leave the convention hostage to agreement on their – possibly inconsequential – formulations, would dangerously prolong the interregnum.[214] The proponents of the view that the rights were part of a universal natural law soon gained the upper hand. They shared the Physiocrat view that even constitutions were merely pale reflections of natural principles that could never encroach on or substitute for the latter. This position was especially well represented among the Jacobin party, which would later add to the declaration heading the 1793 constitution a provision on the right to rebel against a government that "violates the rights of the people".[215] For the Jacobins, natural law constituted a higher

[211] For the French text, see e.g. Jean Morange, *La déclaration des droits de l'homme et du citoyen* (Presses Universitaires de France 2004), 117–20.

[212] Immanuel Kant, 'The Contest of the Faculties', in *Kant. Political Writings* (Hans Reiss ed., H.B. Nisbet trans., Cambridge University Press 1991), 182. For this sense among the deputies in Paris, see Morange, *La déclaration*, 50–3.

[213] Suzanne Desan, 'Foreigners, Cosmopolitanism and French Revolutionary Universalism', in Suzanne Desan, Lynn Hunt & William Max Nelson (eds), *French Revolution in a Global Perspective* (Cornell University Press 2013), 86–100.

[214] See especially Marcel Gauchet, *La révolution des droits de l'homme* (Paris, Gallimard 1989).

[215] According to Article 35 of the Constitution of 1793: "Quand le gouvernement viole les droits du peuple, l'insurrection est, pour le peuple et pour chaque portion du peuple, le plus sacré des droits et le plus indispensable des devoirs." In a famous statement of 25 December 1793 Robespierre presented the theory of "terror" as a principle of revolutionary government, following the higher laws of *salut du people* and *necessité*. See *Oeuvres de Maximilien Robespierre* (Presses Universitaires de France 1958), tome X, 275, 273–82.

principle of revolutionary government that would, among other things, enable the suspension of the constitution for almost two years (1793–5) during which the country was de facto ruled by the Committee of Public Safety, dispensing revolutionary justice in the name of natural rights.[216] Quite strikingly, the trial of the king in the autumn of 1792 had already taken place not by reference to a constitution but by *ius naturae et gentium*.[217]

By that time, the revolution in sovereignty had already taken place. Having declared themselves a National Assembly, the deputies had transferred sovereignty from the monarch to the nation. From now on, in the words of the Constitution of 3 September 1791, "*La Souveraineté est une, indivisible, inaliénable et imprescriptible. Elle appartient à la Nation*" (Title III.1). In their quality as members of the nation, all French white men – including the king himself – had now become citizens, formally equal with each other. Nationhood admitted of no hierarchies whether based on birth or place, inherited or acquired. Any privilege created a separate order whose loyalty was not to the nation but "to the class into which he is adopted".[218] The nation ruled itself by legislation as the general will, which reaffirmed the equality of the citizens. As Sieyès put it:

> I like to conceive of the law as if it is at the center of an immense globe. Every citizen, without exception, is at equal distance from it on the circumference of the globe, and each individual occupies an equal place. Everyone depends equally upon the law; everyone offers to it his liberty and property to protect.[219]

The Assembly found this logic incontrovertible. During 4–11 August it ended special privileges. Public office could no longer be held as private property. From now on, there would be only citizens, forming the nation that possessed all public power, which it exercised not only by legislating but also by allocating executive and judicial tasks to magistrates all of whom were only to serve it.[220]

[216] Edelstein, *The Terror of Natural Right*, 170–214. [217] Ibid., 146–52.

[218] Sieyès, 'An Essay on Privileges', 75.

[219] Sieyès, 'What Is the Third Estate?', 156.

[220] The complaint had long been made that public officials had duties only towards the king, not the people. In Article VI of his proposed constitution of 1793, Robespierre attacked the magistrates as oppressors of the people and stressed that "La constitution ne reconnait d'autre pouvoir que celui du souverain: les diverses portions d'autorités exercées par les differens magistrats, ne sont que des fonctions publiques, qu'il leur délègue pour l'avantage commun", *Oeuvres de Maximilien Robespierre*, tome IX, 509.

This was of course not quite how Rousseau had seen it – for him the general will could not be represented.[221] But in large countries like France direct rule by the people was an impossibility and besides, as Sieyès had explained, not everyone wanted to or could spend their time debating public issues. The question of representation haunted the deputies throughout the revolutionary decade. According to absolutists such as Robespierre, the general will was a unitary whole that was completely and somewhat mystically present in the Assembly itself. Others such as Sieyès were sceptical of the Assembly's presupposed infallibility and suggested tempering its powers either by royal veto or by setting up a countervailing body or a tribunal to check against possible excesses.[222] But the revolutionary view that stressed the unity of the general will was hard to combat. Of the two powers, legislative and executive, the latter was to be wholly subordinated to the former. If nothing was outside the general will as it expressed itself in the decrees of the assembly, how could a countervailing power possibly be justified?

It was a revolution of property, too. The laws passed in August 1789 did away with the feudal notion of divided property rights, separating public administration from ownership. Venal office-holding and seigneurial justice had been only the most egregious examples of confounding public office with private property: "[A]s soon as a government becomes the property of a particular class, it swells beyond all measure, creating posts to meet the needs not of the governed but of those who govern," wrote Sieyès.[223] The destructive effect of the amalgam of public and private interests on the French economy had been known for a long time, not least by the Physiocrats who insisted on the natural basis of property entitlement. A statement of the inviolable and sacred nature of property was duly taken in the Declaration of August 1789 as well as in the first revolutionary Constitution of 1791.[224] The relentless individualism of the revolutionaries led them also to imagine the economic realm in terms of individual entrepreneurs – although 85 percent of Frenchmen lived in rural societies where

[221] Rousseau, *Social Contract*, III XV (141).

[222] These proposals are exhaustively covered in Gauchet, *La Révolution des pouvoirs*.

[223] Sieyès, 'What Is the Third Estate?', 95.

[224] See Article 17 of the Declaration: "La propriété étant un droit inviolable et sacré, nul ne peut en être privé, si ce n'est lorsque la nécessité publique, légalement constatée, l'exige évidemment, et sous la condition d'une juste et préalable indemnité."

common land ownership was quite usual. The nature of France as an agrarian society did not change; but its legal articulation did:

> the night of 4 August had, by the equality of all before the law, instituted the universal character of the agreement on property: not a new economic society, but a new juridical society.[225]

The Jacobin Constitution of June 1793 had a somewhat different tenor. Although the Assembly did not adopt Robespierre's social definition, it did situate the right of property in the context of rights to subsistence and labour and established public instruction to all citizens.[226] Moreover, under the Jacobin view, only property in its most general sense, as property over oneself, one's life and what one needed for survival, had the status of natural law. Rights over material goods were limited by the right of existence and the duty of the government to look to the welfare of the people.

Such concerns vanished from the Thermidorean Constitution of the year III (1795).[227] The view that because rights existed above the constitution they could be used to suspend it had become unacceptable. The legally binding force of the Declaration was abolished by the new government. Liberty was now defined as "the right to do what did not violate the rights of others".[228] Also the formulation of 1789 according to which humans were born equal and enjoyed equal rights was removed. They would have equal civil rights but not equal political rights.[229] The members of the new bourgeois republic did not imagine

225 François Furet, *La révolution 1770–1814* (Paris, Fayard 2010), 128.

226 For Robespierre's proposals, see *Oeuvres de Maximilien Robespierre*, tome IX, 460–1. According to the Constitution of 24 June 1793, accepted in a referendum of 4 August, "Nul ne peut être privé de la moindre portion de sa propriété sans son consentement, si ce n'est lorsque la nécessité publique légalement constatée l'exige, et sous la condition d'une juste et préalable indemnité" (Article 19). However, this was accompanied by a number of social provisions. According to Article 21, for example, "Les secours publics sont une dette sacrée. La société doit la subsistance aux citoyens malheureux, soit en leur procurant du travail, soit en assurant les moyens d'exister à ceux qui sont hors d'état de travailler."

227 See e.g. Marc Belissa & Yannick Bosc, *Le directoire. La république sans la démocratie* (Paris, Fabric 2018), 24–5, 47–8.

228 Constitution of 22 August 1795 (accepted in a plebiscite of 23 September 1795), Art 2.

229 The complex electoral system that had already been instituted in 1789 provided for a two-stage process in which all citizens would be entitled to vote for the members of electoral colleges; but candidature for membership in those colleges was limited to property owners. The required value of property was significantly raised in 1795. At the same time, the representative body was divided into two chambers (the

themselves as ancient Romans but as manufacturers and merchants, more interested in riches than ruling.[230]

## Exporting the Revolution?

The debates in the Assembly and the Convention often touched on foreign affairs but remained inconclusive. Individual deputies and polemicists on the Left argued that the law of nations and the public law of Europe had been part of the old regime and needed a complete overhaul.[231] The only thing left open was whether this would necessitate the adoption of a formal code or could be attained by unilateral actions and proclamations.[232] Conquest would be outlawed by the revolutionary–democratic principle according to which groups of citizens would in their relation to each other and the human race constitute independent "nations".[233] What was needed, deputy Constantin Volney suggested, was "*une politique vraie et généreuse, fondée sur les intérêts des nations*".[234] On the Right, *Realpolitik*-oriented deputies stressed the need to have good relations with neighbours while maintaining an efficient army and vigorous foreign policy. The debates peaked in the famous decree of 22 May 1790 on universal peace where the Assembly renounced all wars of conquest and decided by a compromise formula that matters of war and peace would henceforth be decided by the Assembly itself.[235] The deputies were initially

"Council of Five Hundred" and the "Council of Ancients") for three-year periods with provision for annual election of one-third.

230 See further, Georges Lefebvre, *La France sous le Directoire (1796–1799)* (Paris, édition sociale 1977), 31–8 and generally Belissa & Bosc, *Le directoire.*

231 Louis Antoine de Saint-Just, for example, regarded the system of permanent ambassadors as "une infraction à la liberté des peuples" and commerce as an effort only to prepare for war, *L'esprit de la révolution suivi de fragments sur les institutions républicaines* (Paris, Éditions 10/18, 2003 [1791]), 129, 130.

232 See Marc Belissa, *Repenser l'ordre européen (1795–1802). De la société des rois aux droits des nations* (Paris, Kimé 2006), 373–89.

233 Out of the wealth of literature, see E. J. Hobsbawm, *Nations and Nationalism Since 1780* (Cambridge University Press 1990), 20–2; Florence Gauthier, *Triomphe et mort du droit naturel en Révolution 1789–1795–1802 I* (Presses Universitaires de France 1992), 129–31.

234 Bélissa, *Fraternité*, 170. On Volney's proposed draft Declaration of the Rights and Duties of Nations, see further Boris Mirkine-Guetzévitch, 'L'influence de la Révolution française sur le développement du droit international dans l'Europe orientale', 22 *Receuil des Cours* (1928), 308–9.

235 According to Article 4 of the decree, "L'Assemblée nationale déclarant à cet effet que la nation française renonce à entreprendre aucune guerre dans la vue de faire des conquêtes, et qu'elle n'emploiera jamais ses forces contre la liberté d'aucun

prepared to continue old alliances, even the much-maligned "Family Pact" with Bourbon Spain. But war could hardly be avoided as revolutionary ideas, and eventually troops, spread to Francophone Switzerland, Savoy, Nice and Belgium.[236]

The deputies had a first occasion to clarify the Revolution's international consequences as a group of "patriots" from Avignon, at the time part of papal dominions and a number of small Alsatian enclaves, feudal vassals of German princes, expressed the wish to join revolutionary France. The principle of national self-determination clashed head-on with the public law of Europe; but the Assembly could hardly decline such requests. The matter was put very clearly by the jurist Philippe-Antoine Merlin de Douai (1754–1838), later a minister of justice and general policy under the Directory, in October 1790. The question was whether the decree that ended feudal privileges in France was also applicable in the departments of upper and lower Rhine that France had received in the Treaty of Münster (1648) and, if so, whether the German princes were entitled to indemnity. According to Merlin, these feudal rights were private properties as provided under Article 17 of the Declaration of the Rights of Man; thus they were subordinate to the rights of sovereignty that had been transferred from the German empire to France and now lay in the hands of the National Assembly.[237] As regards the duty to pay compensation, Merlin argued that the Münster treaty was not the true source of sovereignty – an instrument concluded between kings at a time when they regarded themselves as "shepherds of peoples". Instead, French sovereignty was now based on the will of the people. "*Le peuple alsacien s'est uni au people français parce que il l'a bien voulu. C'est donc sa volonté seule qui a ou consommé ou légitimé l'union.*"[238] Because no condition of compensation was linked to the "will of the people of Alsace", no such duty existed.[239] Merlin would repeat this view in the context of the incorporation of Avignon-Comtat

people". *Archives parlementaires de 1787 à 1860*, XV, 661–2. See further Jacques Godechot, *La Grande Nation. L'expansion révolutionnaire de la France dans le monde du 1789 à 1799* (2ème éd., Paris, Aubier 1983), 65–7. For some scepticism about the declaration's pacifist meaning, see Raymond Kubben, *Regeneration and Hegemony. Franco-Batavian Relations in the Revolutionary Era, 1795–1803* (The Hague, Martinus Nijhoff Publishers 2011), 101–2.

236 See further, Godechot, *La Grande Nation*, 67–71; Belissa, *Fraternité*, 229–42.

237 "Donc les ci-devant fiefs régaliens ne peuvent fournir en Alsace que des propriétés privées – soumises à la volonté générale qui est la véritable et unique souveraine", *Archives parlementaires de 1787 à 1860*, XX, 80.

238 Ibid., XX, 81. 239 Ibid., XX, 81–3.

into France the following year. The wish of the people would be decisive, and the only question was what would count as a legitimate expression of it. A nation, he pointed out in accordance with revolutionary orthodoxy, was formed by a social contract. To decide to join or not to join another, the nation could make that decision by a majority of its representatives.[240]

However, Merlin was also a pragmatist with a close eye to French interests. Even as he held that old-regime treaties were null and void, he acknowledged the possibility of situations – and the present was arguably such – when "*équité douce et bienfaisante*" might counsel a more nuanced treatment. And so he recommended in 1790 that the Assembly nevertheless accept some form of ex gratia payment to the German princes.[241] In fact, he would eventually join Danton in arguing in favour of the policy of natural boundaries, and his attitudes towards the annexation of Belgium in 1793 and 1795 developed in a more classically annexationist direction. As a member of the Committee of Public Safety Merlin continued to stress the will of the people but ignored the protests that had been made regarding the organisation of some of the plebiscites. When it came to annexing Luxembourg and Limbourg, where no consultations had been carried out, he justified this as a compensation for the costs of a war that had been imposed on France.[242]

The Declaration of War of 20 April 1792 on the Habsburg monarchy had been preceded by a long campaign of bellicose propaganda by the Girondist party, focusing on the way émigrés had pursued destabilising activities from across the border. To make the war seem compatible with the decree of 22 May 1790, the "enthusiasts" made the prima facie plausible point that a war to bring liberty to oppressed peoples was not at all a war for conquest. It was waged against tyrants, on behalf of peoples. The French soldiers "would be greeted by open

[240] *Le Moniteur universel*, No. 125 (5 May 1791), 314. This process applied only to nations that had already been formed. It did not grant a right of secession to just any group of people. *Archives parlementaires de 1787 à 1860*, XX, 82. For the development of Merlin's views on nationhood and self-determination, see Hervé Leuwers, *Un juriste en politique. Merlin de Douai (1758–1838)* (Artois Presses Université 1996), 218–22 and Hervé Leuwers, 'Révolution et guerre de conquête. Les origines de nouvelle raison d'état (1789–1795)', *Revue de Nord* (1993), 21–40.

[241] See the report by Merlin de Douai, 28 October 1790, in *Le Moniteur universel*, XXVI No. 11 & 13 (83–4, 111). *Archives parlementaires de 1787 à 1860*, XX, 75–84, esp. 83–4.

[242] The development of Merlin's public statements and private attitudes is discussed in Leuwers, *Un juriste*, 222–6. In 1795 Merlin became a minister of justice under the Thermidorean Directory and two years later a member of the Directory itself.

arms", as the Brissotin deputy Anacharsis Cloots put it.[243] With the establishment of the republic in September 1792, this line officially took over. Condorcet, for example, in a heated discourse later on, argued that princes who provided asylum to conspirators were equal to aggressors, but their peoples remained friends.

To oppose force, to resist oppression to forget all once there is no longer anything to fear, and to see only friends in vanquished adversaries, reconciled or disarmed, that is what the Frenchmen wish and that is the kind of war they declare on their enemies.[244]

With victories in the autumn and French entry into Belgium in October 1792, the line between liberation and conquest became exceedingly thin. The deputies had always accepted that extracting compensation from the liberated countries was acceptable under the law of nations. Now they would turn to favouring the idea of the union of the fraternal country with its larger brother. In a remarkable decree of 19 November 1792 the Assembly stated

That it will grant fraternity and aid to all peoples who wish to receive their liberty; and it charges the executive power with giving the generals the order necessary for bringing aid to such peoples and for defending citizens who have been, or who might be, harassed for the cause of liverty.[245]

This was nothing short of declaring the end of European public law, and the onset of a new order based on the universal validity of the revolutionary principles whose executive arm would be the French nation.[246] It was supplemented on 15 December by another decree on the "Revolutionary Administration of Conquered Territories" that contained a programme

243 Gauthier, *Triomphe et mort*, 133–5. For good overviews, see further Belissa, *Fraternité*, 268–88 and Mirkine-Guetzévitch, 'L'influence de la Révolution française', 305–16.

244 "Repousser la force, résister à l'oppression, tout oublier, lorsqu'il y a plus rien a redouter, et ne plus voir que les frères dans les adversaires vaincus, réconciliés ou désarmes: voilà ce que veulent tous les Français, et voilà quelle est la guerre qu'ils déclareront à leurs ennemis." 'Déclaration de l'assemblée nationale', 29 décembre 1792, in Marie Jean Nicolas de Caritat, Marquis de Condorcet, *Oeuvres de Condorcet*, tome 10 (Paris, Firmin 1847), 259.

245 "elle accordera fraternité et secours à tous les peuples qui voudront recouvrer leur liberté; et charge le pouvoir exécutif de donner aux généraux les ordres nécessaires pour porter secours à ces peuples, et défendre les citoyens qui auraient été vexés ou qui pourraient l'être pour la cause de la liberté", Decree of 19 November 1797, *Archives parlementaires de 1787 à 1860*, LIII, 474. Translation by Wilhelm Grewe, *Fontes Iuris Gentium 1493–1815*, vol. 2 (Berlin, De Gruyter 1988), 652.

246 According to Mirkine-Guetzéwitch, the decree "poses the principle of intervention as the basis of French public law', 'L'influence de la révolution française', 313.

for the transformation of conquered lands – the removal of the monarchs and confiscation of their property, abolishing nobility, holding popular elections and despatching representatives from France to create "fraternal relations" with the liberated peoples.[247]

The action in Belgium originated in an effort to halt émigré activity and establish a national convention along French lines, but turned gradually into confiscations, triggered by the catastrophic state of French finances, replacement of Belgian administrators by French ones and the extension of French laws to the territory. Some deputies voiced concern about the effects of expansion on the republic itself. Had not already Montesquieu – whose authority was invoked over again – stressed the degree to which Rome's decline had been caused by its unchecked expansion? As soon as the armies had crossed the Alps, he had written, and begun conquering other lands, their republican spirit had degenerated in a way that had eventually infected Rome itself.[248] Many others, however, refused to apply the Roman example. France was already a large country and – so the argument went – was only seeking either to establish itself on its natural and secure boundaries or aiming to help revolutionaries in other countries to divest themselves of tyrants. When the Convention voted on the annexation of Belgium on 1 October 1795, it viewed this in light of re-establishing the historic frontiers of France.[249] The debates on Savoy, Avignon-Comtat and the small principalities at the French borders proceeded in a similar way. Once the liberators had set in, the process to union would follow almost automatically. The most far-reaching effort to collapse the status quo of old Europe was the famous effort of setting up of "sister republics" on French boundaries. It would be wrong to interpret the Batavian, Neapolitan and Helvetic republics only as instruments of French expansionism. Dutch, Italian and Swiss "patriots" were in full possession of agency and acting to reconstruct

[247] *Archives parlementaires de 1787 à 1860*, LV, 76 and Grewe, *Fontes*, 652–7. See also Belissa, *Fraternité*, 333–6.

[248] Montesquieu, *Considérations sur la grandeur des Romains et de leur décadence* (Paris, Poussielgue 1907), IX (76–7). A useful discussion of the gradual overcoming of the republican doubts about expansion among the deputies is Jainchill, *Reimagining Politics*, 141–96.

[249] Belissa & Bosc, *Le directoire*, 191; Godechot, *La Grande Nation*, 80. The two strategies – natural frontiers and sister republics – in the various territories adjoining France are exhaustively discussed in Edward James Kolla, *Sovereignty, International Law and the French Revolution* (Cambridge University Press 2017). The annexation of Belgium is treated at 121–59.

the unity of their own nation.[250] Moreover, the goal of setting up a large federal-type union in central Europe to counterbalance Austrian and British influence had been debated already before the Revolution. Intensifying commercial and other links with the sister republics was economically useful and offset the pressure towards unscrupulous expansion. What republicans such as Robespierre were planning was to set up a specifically republican alliance.[251]

The actions after the collapse of terror regime in July 1794 may have followed *Realpolitik*-motivated strategies, but continued to be accompanied by revolutionary rhetoric.[252] In his report to the Convention in the following autumn, the lawyer Joseph Eschassériaux directed his attack on everything about old-regime diplomacy, its secret treaties and their dependence on the will of kings, their appetite for conquest and utter neglect of the *droits des peuples*; the continuous war that had devastated Europe for three centuries; destruction of commerce and industry and repeated breaches of *droit des gens*.[253] In relations with its enemies, the French republic would set aside all forms of old diplomacy. The principles it would inaugurate after victory would include only alliances based on friendship between peoples; its "universal monarchy" would be that of freedom of the seas; it would show respect for the territories, laws and blood of peoples; its foreign affairs would expand everywhere its industry, its arts and the products of its territory; its treaties would be made by the people and not by scheming courtiers; and its diplomacy would be based on "honesty, justice and equality". And with a hidden reference to the project of Saint-Pierre ("*un homme de bien*"), he ended by prophesying about the coming of a universal fraternity based on just laws.[254]

Eventually, France came to look upon itself as the representative of the law of nations in relation to what its saw as England's egregious

[250] For the way "patriots" in each were adapting the discourse of "unity" for their own purposes, see Godechot, *La Grande Nation*, 238–58.

[251] "We need to rethink the history of the sister republics as an interaction, which, though certainly distorted by French military power, was continually fashioned by the republican inventiveness of the countries experimenting with the foundation of new regimes", Pierre Serna, 'The Sister Republics, or the Ephemeral Invention of a French Republican Commonwealth', in Alan Forrest & Matthias Middell (eds), *The Routledge Companion to the French Revolution in World History* (London, Routledge 2016), 41 and 42–53. See also Jainchill, *Reimagining Politics*, 186–93.

[252] Godechot, *La Grande Nation*, 71–4, 79–87.

[253] Joseph Eschassériaux, 'Des droits des peuples; des principes qui doivent diriger un peuple républicain dans ses relations étrangères', 49 *Le Moniteur universel* (9 Novembre 1794), 450, 445–51.

[254] Ibid., 450–1.

aggressions. In the war of opinions, Boissy d'Anglas wrote, England had in vain sought to present kings as the ultimate guardians of peace and security. In fact republics had always been more preoccupied by internal than external questions so that "far from disturbing the peace of their neighbours, they were in fact more often attacked by the latter". Moreover, he assured his audience that "*[l]a sureté des personnes, la conservation des propriétés. Voilà les bases certaines de toute association politique.*"[255] How could these possibly be safer in the realm of tyrants such as Henry VIII or Cromwell than in prosperous republics such as Venice, Switzerland or the United States where the people as a whole (and not just one person) had committed to secure the obedience of the laws? According to Boissy, France was ready to live in peace and under the rule of law with all nations, irrespective of their internal regime.[256] Pointing to British violations of the freedom of the seas and as against Austria's alleged assassination of two French envoys at the Congress of Rastatt in 1797, deputies such as Merlin de Douai presented France itself as the protector of the law of nations:

> If universal justice may find an organ in a nation that has become the asylum for faith and honour, is not that same [nation] a majestic tribunal where judgment over peoples and posterity may be rendered in face of the universe and under the auspices of the supreme judge?[257]

But it was not only respect for *justice universelle* that contemporaries would witness in French practice. France would also disregard treaties when that was in its interests, as in requiring the Dutch to keep the Scheldt open against a treaty France had signed no later than 1785. But it would also strictly protest against host state interference with French diplomatic premises.[258] While French occupation forces would often behave just as such forces had always behaved, the military and political leaders often tried to make French actions

[255] Boissy d'Anglas, *Discours prononcé à la Convention nationale de France sur la situation politique de l'Europe* (Paris, Imprimerie nationale, l'An III), 11, 12.

[256] Ibid., 10.

[257] "si la justice universelle peut trouver un digne organe dans une nation devenue l'asile de la foi et de l'honneur, cette enceinte même n'est-elle pas un tribunal auguste où doit être publié devant l'univers, et sous les auspices du juge suprême, le jugement irrévocable des peuples et de la postérité?" Merlin de Douai, le 20 prairial an VII (8 juin 1799), n° 265, du 25 prairial an VII, *Le Moniteur*, réimpression, tome 29, 707.

[258] For a long list of such apparent inconsistencies, see Linda Frey & Marsha Frey, 'Grégoire and the Breath of Reason. The French Revolutionaries and the *Droit des gens*', 38 *Journal for the Western Society of French History* (2010), 170–3.

appear in conformity with the principles of republican fraternity, insisting that it was only kings who were their enemies. Overall, however, "the striking thing was how little, rather than how much, impact the upheavals had on the law of nations".[259]

The most significant rhetorical contribution of the Revolution was the insertion of the "nation" into the vocabulary of politics and diplomacy.[260] "The nation exists prior to everything: it is the origin of everything. Its will is always legal. It is the law itself," Sieyès had written.[261] It was the nation that was to be represented in the National Assembly. It was the nation that acted towards the external world. And it was the nation and promised, on 22 May 1790, not to commence any war of conquest or to take action against the freedom of any people. For the Girondist "enthusiasts" this did not exclude, perhaps even encouraged exporting liberty to adjoining territories – the nation had, in a familiar paradox, an expansive meaning. To this, Robespierre tried to give a revolutionary thrust by invoking a universal fatherland of liberty; humankind itself was "sovereign over the world".[262] Resuscitating the familiar notion that God had donated the world "*en commun à l'humanité*", he declared that no nation could arrogate to itself the status of its principal representative.[263] If nations

259 Stephen C. Neff, *War and the Law of Nations. A General History* (Cambridge University Press 2005), 93. Likewise, Wilhelm Grewe, *The Epochs of International Law* (Berlin, Gruyter 2000), 413–24.

260 The "nation" had already been part of medieval vocabulary, as we have seen. But, David Bell observes, it began to receive a new, autonomous power in the eighteenth century as an effect of secularisation as a novel point is spiritual identification. *The Cult of the Nation in France. Inventing Nationalism 1680–1800* (Harvard University Press 2001), 24–40. It now also grew into a "fighting word", first to support the "rights of the nation" against the monarchy, and then to support the French nation against the "perfidious" English. Ibid., 56–60, 78–106 and, on the latter question, Edmond Dzembowski, *Un nouveau patriotisme français 1750–1770. La France face à la puissance Anglaise à l'époque de la guerre de sept ans* (Oxford, Voltaire Foundation 1998).

261 Sieyès, 'What is the Third Estate?', 136.

262 "le souverain de la terre, qui est le genre humain", he wrote in the proposed draft Declaration of Rights and Duties to the (Jacobin) Constitution of 1793, see *Oeuvres de Maximilien Robespierre*, tome IX, 469 (Article 38).

263 The idea of the world having been donated to humanity "in common" was of course the old Dominican doctrine that, for Robespierre, excluded a right of property by mere occupation: nobody had an automatic right of property – because it was "*une institution sociale*". On the contrary, as he proposed in the debate for the 1793 constitution, "La propriété est le droit qu'a chaque citoyen de jouir de la portion de bien qui lui est garantie par la loi". He also proposed that it be expressly stated that property was limited by the rights of property, security, liberty and existence of others. *Oeuvres de Maximilien Robespierre*, tome IX, 461, 465.

were equal – as everyone agreed they had to be – then each had to go through their own revolutionary process.[264]

But if Robespierre cited the national principle to *oppose* the war, others such as Lazare Carnot, later Napoleon's minister of war, in February 1793, speaking on behalf of the Diplomatic Committee, cited it as a *casus belli* on the basis of self-defence and *salut de l'Etat*.[265] The nation could be equally invoked to defend pacifism and belligerency, revolution and conservatism, particularism and universalism. This highlights not only its utter open-endedness but a shift in the vocabularies of authority and the strategic orientation of the French analysts. Dynastic concerns were to give way to a systemic orientation at the level of Europe – preferably, though perhaps not necessarily a Europe of republics – where different nations could be seen as legal subjects on the analogy to citizens in domestic polities whose freedom and welfare would become the objective of the revolutionary system of the law of nations.[266]

It was in this spirit that Abbé Henri Grégoire (1750–1831) proposed the adoption of a declaration of the rights and duties of nations that had been modelled after the *Declaration of Rights of Man and Citizen* of 1789. Grégoire was a provincial clergyman who had come to be known as a defender of the Jews on the strength of a 1788 essay and an advocate of the abolition of the slave trade and in due course also slavery in French colonies. A member and an occasional president of the Assembly and the Convention, depicted in the foreground of David's *Tennis Court Oath*, Grégoire was a fervent Catholic but also a fighter in the republican cause whose cosmopolitan activism was channelled towards a view of France as the representative of oppressed nations everywhere.[267] Like most deputies, Grégoire

264 See especially Gauthier, *Triomphe et mort*, 131–43.

265 On Carnot's proposal, see *Archives parlementaires de 1787 à 1860*, LVIII, 547, 546–51.

266 For a good summary of this familiar theme, see Belissa, *Repenser l'ordre européen*, especially 371–407. At this stage, the "nation" denoted hardly more than the common interest of the people, as against the particular interests of the monarch and the nobility. Any idea that it would also have an ethnic, racial, linguistic or other such substantive identity was a later product. Hobsbawm, *Nations and Nationalism Since 1780*, 17–23. See also 'Nation', in Furet & Ozouf, *Dictionnaire*, 339–56.

267 See especially Bernard Plongeron, *L'abbé Grégoire ou l'Arché de la Fraternité* (Paris, Letouzey & Ané 1989), 347–50. Grégoire was "Pantheonised" (i.e. his remains were transferred into the Panthéon in Paris) in 1989 in which context several biographies of him were published. See e.g. Georges Hourdin, *L'abbé Grégoire. Évêque et démocrate* (Paris, Desclée de Brouwer 1989); Maurice Ezran, *L'abbé Grégoire. Défenseur des juifs et des noirs* (Paris, l'Harmattan 1992). See further Alyssa Goldstein Sepinwall, *The Abbé*

believed that France should support all nations to liberate themselves from tyrants. In the report he composed to the Assembly in 1792, recommending the acceptance of the request by the representatives of Savoy to join France, Grégoire granted that the time for a universal republic was not yet ripe. Too many peoples still belaboured under tyranny. Instead of speculating about such chimeras, the Assembly was now to accept the nearly unanimous request, made "without violence and foreign involvement" of Savoyard communes to join France as the forty-fourth department "of Mont Blanc".[268]

In the context of a debate on foreign affairs in the Constitution in the spring of 1793, Grégoire read to the Convention a proposal of 21 articles to be inserted in the text that already contained the sentence according to which "the French people are a friend and the natural ally of all free peoples". According to the proposal all peoples were independent and sovereign and connected to each other by "universal morality" (Articles 1–2). From Montesquieu was derived the rule that peoples ought to treat each other as they would wish themselves to be treated and do in peace as much good and in war as little evil as they could (Articles 3–4). Peoples were entitled to organise themselves as they wished; no intervention in each other's affairs was allowed. However, "no other government [was] in conformity with the rights of peoples than ones that [were] based on equality and liberty" (Article 8). Each people was the master of its territory while areas not subject to occupation (such as the seas) belonged to all (Articles 9–10). Foreigners were to abide by the laws of the country where they stayed, and a people had the right to refuse entry to foreigners it considered dangerous to their security (Articles 12–13) Any attack against the liberty of one people was an attack on all of them. Offensive leagues were contrary to the human family (Articles 15–16). Defensive wars were allowed but room was to be left for negotiations (Articles 17–18). There were to be no ranks among the representatives of peoples, and they were immune to the laws of their receiving countries in respect of their

*Grégoire and the French Revolution* (University of California Press 2005). The biographies concentrate on Grégoire's activities in favour of tolerance, the reform of the Church and his many proposals for reorganising education and fighting "vandalism", and deal with the draft declaration only in passing, if at all.

268 Henri Grégoire, *Convention nationale, Rapport sur la réunion de la Savoie à la France* (Paris, Imprimerie national 1792). On Grégoire's missions and his confidential correspondence concerning e.g. Savoyard resistance to being submerged in France, see Sepinwall, *Abbé Grégoire*, 116–23.

mission (Articles 19–20). Finally, treaties among nations were to be inviolable (Article 21).[269]

In view of the tense international situation in June 1793, however, the deputies held it sufficient to declare France friendship with all peoples; there was reason to be political and not to express futile philanthropic sentiments. Grégoire repeated his proposal in April 1795, after the signature of the Peace of Basle, condemning in his introductory words old diplomacy anew but also the kind of abstract cosmopolitanism that was nothing but "*vagabondage physique ou moral*". Real patriotism, he affirmed, would include love for humanity, too. Though Grégoire condemned the old traditions of natural law and diplomacy, the reception from the audience was cool, and the proposal was flatly rejected. In 1795–6, France was finally being victorious. So the Convention only decreed on the different uniforms for ambassadors and ministers, thus choosing against Grégoire's Article 19, and held the door open for further offensive war.

* * * * *

"Terror" fell in the summer of 1794 not owing to arguments from political or legal theory; the country had grown tired of the bloodshed; it had no great objection to the establishment of the Directory, splitting the Convention into two chambers and allocating rights of franchise by tax contributions. As the jurist presenting the new project for a constitution to the Convention in June 1795, Boissy d'Anglas, put it, the Terror had been a result of ignorance and ambition and its result had been what the new regime would consistently call it, an anarchy. To move onwards it was necessary to see to it that France would be governed by the best and by those most interested in the implementation of the laws:

> you do not find such men elsewhere than among those who, possessing property, have attached themselves to the land where it is situated, with laws that protect it and the calm that maintains it.[270]

[269] For the articles, see Pierre Fauchon, *L'abbé Grégoire. Le prêtre-citoyen* (Paris, Nouvelle-République 1989), 87–8. For a critical commentary highlighting the "chimerical" aspects of the articles, see Frey & Frey, 'Grégoire and the Breath of Reason', 163–77. The best discussion of the context and a full list of the 21 articles can be found in Marc Belissa, 'La déclaration du droit des gens de l'abbé Grégoire (june 1973, 4 Floréal an III)', in revolution-francaise.net/2010/10/06/399-declaration-droit-des-gens-abbe-gregoire-juin-1793.

[270] "... vous ne trouvez pareils hommes que parmi ceux qui, possédant une propriété ont attachés au pays qui la contient, aux lois qui la protègent, à la tranquillité que la conserve", Boissy d'Anglas, 'Discours préliminaire au projet de constitution', in *Réimpression de l'ancien Moniteur*, tome 25 (Paris, Bureau central, 1842), 92.

Full citizenship belonged to property owners; only they had a strong enough interest in peaceful government of the country. If the Montagnard revolution had been supported and often dictated from the streets, Thermidor instituted a government by proprietors.[271] The constitution of 1795 repeated the absolute notion of property right from 1789 that would also eventually find its way into the *Code civil* of 1804.[272] In the effort to terminate the Revolution, the declaration that preceded the text of the new constitution was deprived of legally binding force. It could no longer be invoked against the constitution. Provisions from 1793 that situated property in a social context and allowed rebellion against unjust rule were deleted.

By 18 Brumaire in the year VIII (9 November 1799), and the establishment of the Consulate, references to the brotherhood of peoples would disappear from the text of the constitution of 22 Frimaire of the year VIII (13 December 1799) as well as from public debate. The Directory had still stood with the principle of national frontiers. With Napoleon's victories in Italy, this line was crossed against initial popular suspicion of conquests.[273]

The republic still claimed that it stood for moral ideals, however, and as protector of the law of nations, would understand this in traditional terms as treaty-making, maritime neutrality, ambassadorial privileges and the proper conduct of military operations.[274] The most striking effort in this regard was the continental blockade, enacted by Napoleon's famous Berlin Decree of 21 November 1806, which justified the exclusion of British ships from continental ports as a retaliation against British naval warfare and especially the practice of intervening in neutral shipping under the "rule of the war of 1756". In the words of Article 1 of that decree: "*L'Angleterre admet point de droit des gens suivi universellement par tous les peuples polices.*"[275]

271 For further discussion of the turn to a "government of property-owners" in the constitution of 1795, see Belissa & Bosc, *Le Directoire*, 36–48.

272 Mikhail Xifaras describes the *Code civil* as a "triumph of the property dogma" and the "foundation of a new juridical morality", *La propriété. Etude de philosophie de droit* (Presses Universitaires de France 2004), 15.

273 Lefebvre, *La France sous le directoire 1796–1799*, 318–21.

274 See Hervé Leuwers, 'République et relations entre les peuples. Quelques éléments de l'idéal républicain autour de Brumaire an VII', 318 *Annales historiques de la révolution française* (1999), 677–93.

275 Decree of 21 November 1806 (published 5 December), 46 *Le Moniteur universel* No. 339 (1462). The text of the decree was prefaced by Talleyrand's explanation that the law of nations did not allow intervention in private rights in a war that was to be seen exclusively as a relationship between states.

The new constitution included no declaration of rights, viewed by Sieyès as unduly limitative of governmental powers and opening the door to popular revolt. The system of three consuls, a legislative body with three houses, i.e. conservative senate, tribunate and legislative assembly, was a largely self- elected totality with most power concentrated in the hands of the first consul, Napoleon himself. The brevity and obscurity of the text as well as practical difficulties in implementing local administration by elected notables all contributed to the of sidelining of the electorate: "The people are sovereign, but no longer consulted."[276] Napoleon envisaged French society as a pyramid: members of the council of state, judges and local officials would all be appointed by the head of state, surrounded by a group of senators sitting in official palaces with high salaries. Notables would be invited to take part in the work of the executive to the extent that the latter thought it advisable. Access to electoral colleges was tightened with the result that the electorate was composed of no more than perhaps one to two percent of the male population over 21 years old.[277]

## From Rights to Science

The Constitution of the Year VIII emanated from an effort by its principal drafters, Sieyès and his colleague Pierre-Louis Roederer (1754–1835), to end the revolutionary tumult by setting aside republican ideals of popular participation, instead endorsing "modern liberty" – civil rights and the protection of property.[278] But as the old-regime languages of royal will, justice and divine purpose could no longer be employed, it was not obvious what the revolutionaries could replace them with.[279] The *philosophes* had had an ambivalent attitude towards natural law, which had, to them, seemed conservative and abstract, more useful to legitimise tyranny and the atrocious practices

276 Georges Lefebvre, *Napoléon* (Paris, Alcan 1935), 70.

277 Thierry Lentz, *Le grand consulat 1799–1804* (Paris, Fayard 1999), 384, 386–8, 427–35.

278 A good overview of "liberal authoritarianism" with specific focus on the role of Sieyès and Roederer in the drafting of the Constitution of the Year VIII is Jainchill, *Reimagining Politics*, 197–242.

279 Keith Baker has shown that the revolutionaries grasped at several languages, especially those of reason, of national will and justice in the effort to develop a new direction for French politics. Keith M. Baker, 'Enlightenment Idioms, Old Regime Discourses, and Revolutionary Improvisation', in Thomas E. Kaiser & Dale K. van Kley (eds), *From Deficit to Deluge. The Origins of the French Revolution* (Stanford University Press 2011), 165–97.

of early modern warfare than to suppress them.[280] Even when translated into rights of man and citizen, it failed to create determinate consequences of policy, having eventually assisted in setting aside the constitution and commencing the Terror. The various formulations of the rights of man attached to the constitutions of the years 1791, 1793, III (1795), and VIII (1799) encompassed an array of understandings as wide as French politics itself. After those efforts, what began was the "long process of laying to sleep of the idea of rights within the French political tradition. It is filled with dark and painful memories of repeated disruptions and insurmountable dilemmas."[281]

And still, eighteenth-century political language had been full of affirmative references to the law of nature and of nations.[282] Taking his cue from the Physiocrats, Sieyès had translated natural law into the natural rights of liberty and property that he wanted to introduce into political society, where they would see to the proper functioning of the exchanges between economic classes. How this was to take place in the realm of politics and government was something that Sieyès and Roederer believed might be best studied by what Sieyès had originally called *science sociale*.[283] The effort to think about human action through the lenses of a "social science" had already been initiated by Saint-Pierre but the first time it was integrated in a doctrine of *law* was when Montesquieu began his search for the "general spirit" of a people.[284] The view that each nation ought to be governed by laws suitable to its history, environment and *moeurs* directed contemporaries to reflect on types of regulation appropriate to each specific type of state.

The fact that natural law was gradually being transformed into the idiom of political economy was a result of the anxious search by

280 See the review of critiques in Dan Edelstein, 'Enlightenment Rights Talk', 86 *Journal of Modern History* (2014), 530–40. The critiques, Edelstein suggests, were related to what the *philosophes* believed was the tradition's excessive reliance on "reason", 541–6.

281 Gauchet, *La Révolution des droits de l'homme*, 315–16.

282 See e.g. Henry Vyverberg, *Human Nature, Cultural Diversity, and the French Enlightenment* (Oxford University Press 1989), 20–33.

283 He later used also the terms *l'art social* and *la science de l'art social*. See Sieyès, 'Views', 5 and further Sonenscher, *Before the Deluge*, 259–60 and Sonenscher, 'Ideology, Social Science and General Facts in Late Eighteenth-century French Political Thought', 35 *History of European Ideas* (2009), 28. On Roederer, see Ingrid Rademacher, 'La science sociale républicaine de Pierre-Louis Roederer', 13 *Revue française d'histoire des idées politiques* (2001), 25–56; Jainchill, *Reimagining Politics*, 204–11.

284 See especially Louis Althusser, *Montesquieu. La politique et l'histoire* (Presses Universitaires de France 1959), 11–27.

French enlighteners of a *science sociale*.[285] The aim was to emulate the natural sciences so as to offer reliable results for legislative guidance. In his posthumously published *Sketch for the History of Human Progress* Condorcet had described how natural sciences had allowed human beings to have an increasingly firm control of nature. In an analogous way, the *art social* would aim to base all legislation "either on justice or a proven and recognised utility, instead of vague, uncertain and arbitrary views or presumed political advantages".[286] Condorcet admired mathematics and the natural sciences for the certainty they produced. So far, what had existed in society was only a "general consciousness of natural rights". A science of the social was needed "to know exactly" the rights that belonged to every individual and how they were to be limited and balanced against each other.[287] Condorcet followed a general tendency among French intellectuals to derive that certainty from empirical analysis or experiences of pain and pleasure that "determine the immutable and necessary laws of justice and injustice".[288] Earlier analyses of society had been based on superstition and error but the recent growth of liberty had everywhere depended on progress of knowledge and enlightenment. Polemicists had learned to know "*les véritables droits de l'homme*" that, unlike the "arbitrary" theories of Grotius and Pufendorf, did not subordinate humans perpetually under some hypothesised contract.[289]

Having reviewed the great advances of the natural sciences in the eighteenth century, Condorcet believed that his *art social* would help generalise sense-data into scientific hypotheses that would enable the quantitative measurement of social causalities and especially the consequences of alternative interventions in the social world.[290] The result

[285] See e.g. Heilbron, *The Rise of Social Theory*, 119–47.

[286] Marquis de Condorcet, *Esquisse d'un tableau historique des progress de l'esprit humain* (Paris, Flammarion 1988), 283. See Robert Wokler, 'Saint-Simon as the Passage from Political to Social Science', in Anthony Pagden (ed.), *The Languages of Political Theory in Early-Modern Europe* (Cambridge University Press 1987), 328; Wokler, 'Ideology and the Origins of Social Science', in Mark Goldie & Robert Wokler (eds), *The Cambridge History of Eighteenth-Century Political Thought* (Cambridge University Press 2006), 692.

[287] Condorcet, *Esquisse*, 229.

[288] Ibid., 223.

[289] Ibid., 217–18. The four basic natural rights for Condorcet were freedom, equality, property and the right to participate in legislation. Condorcet, 'De l'influence de la Révolution d'Amérique sur l'Europe', in Arthur Condorcet O'Connor & M. F. Arago (eds), *Oeuvres de Condorcet*, tome 8e (éd. Condorcet O'Connor, Paris, Didot 1847), 5–6.

[290] Condorcet, *Esquisse*, 250–1.

would be empirically based laws that would guarantee respect for natural rights, including the right of equality between men and women as well as the white and black races. These studies would assist governing complex societies by offering an "almost mathematical calculation" of the results of alternative policies.[291] If, as he assumed, human nature was everywhere the same, "one does not see why all the provinces of a state, or even all states, would not have the same criminal law, civil law, commercial law etc.".[292]

Sieyès and Condorcet had both been active in the short-lived *Société de 1789* that aimed to stabilise the Revolution but broke up as the deputies found themselves in opposite political camps. Its work was continued by the *Institut national des sciences et des arts* set up in October 1795 to replace the old-regime *Académies*.[293] One of the Institute's three classes was to deal with moral and political sciences, a label under which political economy, morality and legislation would collaborate in the search for scientific cures for the ills of France.[294] Although the *Institut* was formally independent, neither the Directory nor the members were under any illusion about this; they were expected to produce research to help "ending the revolution". How to fit efficient government with flourishing liberty and property rights? Contributions were expected to public education and public assistance, and essay contests were directed to moral issues and reforms of civil and criminal law. The studies drew inspiration from the notion of sympathy as developed among the Scottish enlighteners; from the same origin came the four-stage theory of social development that oriented the comparative work of *Institut* members.[295] Travel reports by explorers to Tahiti and Australia supported studies of human geography and the effects of climate on culture and civilisation, helping to lay the basis for an early ethnography and theories of racial hierarchy.[296] In a speech at the *Institut* on French colonial policy in July 1797, Talleyrand enthusiastically propagated

[291] Ibid., 283.

[292] Condorcet, as cited in Martin S. Staum, *Minerva's Message. Stabilizing the French Revolution* (McGill University Press 1996), 21.

[293] The background and the establishment of the second class of the *Institut* has been told in many places. See e.g. Staum, *Minerva's Message*, 12–14, 33–8.

[294] See Belissa & Bosc, *Le directoire*, 167–70. A meticulous analysis of the 144 members of *Institut* by reference to social background, profession and political allegiance is in Staum, *Minerva's Message*, 33–55.

[295] Staum, *Minerva's Message*, 64–74, 124–35.

[296] Jean-Luc Chappey, *La Société des Observateurs de l'Homme (1799–1804). Des anthropologues au temps de Bonaparte* (Paris, Société des Études Robespierristes, 2002).

turning attention to Africa and many *Institut* members were co-opted in the Napoleonic occupation of Egypt (1799–1802).[297]

The social thinking of *Institut* member was quite uniformly empiricist. This was especially true of the group of *idéologues*, men such as Antoine Destutt de Tracy, Georges Cabanis and Constantin-François Volney, who imposed their orientations across the class of moral and political sciences. Their goal was to understand the formation and operation of ideas by reference to the effect that the material world had on human "senses".[298] Destutt de Tracy sought to replace Montesquieu's "metaphysical" notion of law by a set of purely empirical propositions. Nations existed in a state of nature and the laws of war were extrapolations from cost–benefit calculations: how to fight "with the least pain and the most chance of success"? Although no international tribunals existed, nations were learning to settle their differences with the least disturbance. They had found it useful to conclude treaties and treat each other in accordance with the customary law of nations.[299] These steps, he suggested, made from purely utilitarian calculations, pointed to the formation of an international federation that would gradually subordinate all nations under a new public order.[300] Conquests were normally unacceptable, and all nations were to seek their natural boundaries, but never to transgress them. In particular, states were not to keep overseas territories in subordination; colonies were to be emancipated so that mutually beneficial trade would commence with them as soon as possible.[301]

The *idéologues* worried over the weakness of republican institutions and hoped to strengthen them by initially supporting the coup of 18 Brumaire.[302] But an end was put to their well-meaning efforts in

297 Charles-Maurice de Talleyrand-Périgord, *Essai sur les avantages à retirer des colonies dans les circonstances présentes* (Institut national, 1797). Altogether 21 mathematicians, 3 astronomers, 17 engineers, 13 naturalists and 22 printers were said to take part in the expedition. Marc Ferro, *Colonization. A Global History* (New York, Routledge 1997), 66.

298 Staum, *Minerva's Message*, 27–32, 154–71. Many *Institut* members and prize essay competitors in related topics shunned a purely empiricist approach to human action and motivation. See ibid., 95–117.

299 Antoine Destutt de Tracy, *Commentaire sur l'Esprit des lois de Montesquieu* (Université de Caen 1992 [1808]) X (137–9).

300 Ibid., XIII (247, 253–4).

301 Ibid., X (148–9).

302 Cabanis, for example, urged carrying out comparative constitutional studies so as to develop a science of society that would not only take account of human needs as they were now, but as increasing civilisation would develop them. He also wanted to move attention from individuals to the behaviour of large masses. The influence of the Physiocrats was visible in his stress on a strong executive. Even as the

1803 as Napoleon decided to close the activities of the class of moral and social sciences. The intellectual leadership of the *idéologues* collided with the Napoleonic preference for literary and natural sciences and threatened to institutionalise the influence of a bourgeois intelligentsia in state administration.[303] From 1803, the *idéologues'* disappeared from the political and the intellectual world. This had in part to do with the reorganisation of the sciences during the consular and imperial periods, in part with a general turn against enlightenment values, "reason" and science, the attack on materialism and the increasing favour to sentiment and feeling.[304] The first consul's decision to expand censorship struck at scientific societies across the board: "*Il faut imprimer peu et le moins sera le mieux.*"[305] The effort to create a "social science" or a "science of the social art" foundered at the impossibility of anything of the kind in a dictatorship of the pure will of the leader.

## European Public Law Restored: Rayneval

The first "social scientists", Sieyès, Condorcet and the *idéologues*, translated their revolutionary universalism into an effort to develop an empirical human science to help government bring forward the work of political regeneration that had been central to the revolutionary ideology.[306] With the imperial reorientation of sciences at the beginning of the nineteenth century, this objective was replaced by the development of a "positive" human science bent towards the classification and hierarchisation of human groups in line with restoration ideology.[307] The development of universal histories suggested that republican regeneration knew no boundaries, but the *idéologues* had made no effort to explore the effects of their empirical works on European public law or the discourse on the law of nature and

legislation was to be independent, it needed the experience of the executive. The judiciary was simply to be a branch of the executive. P. Cabanis, *Quelques considérations sur l'organisation sociale* (Paris, Imprimerie nationale l'An VIII), 11–13, 19–21, 34, 37–8.

303 Heilbron, *The Rise of Social Theory*, 173–82. For the fate of the political ambitions of leading *idéologues* such as Destutt de Tracy and Cabanis, see Jean-Luc Chappey, 'Les idéologues face du Coup d'État du 18 Brumaire an VIII', 14 *Politix* (2001), 55–75.

304 See Jean-Luc Chappey, 'Héritages républicains et résistances à "l'organisation impériale des savoirs"', 346 *Annales historiques de la Révolution française* (2006), esp. 97–108, 114–20.

305 Lefebvre, *Napoléon*, 387.

306 See Mona Ozouf, 'Régénération', in Furet & Ozouf, *Dictionnaire*, 373–89.

307 See further, Chappey, 'Héritages républicains', 105–8.

nations. Destutt de Tracy's speculations about a new European order attracted no serious following. During the revolutionary period Grégoire's 1795 project to replace the old law of nations with a declaration of 21 principles that would have treated the European order after the domestic analogy was sympathetically received but led nowhere, and the Directory had officially regarded the old public law of Europe as dead.[308] Nevertheless, old-regime practices of diplomatic hierarchy and secrecy were continued throughout the revolutionary years. With Talleyrand's appointment as foreign minister in July 1797 and 1799 retired diplomats were re-employed in the foreign service.[309] A hectic period of treaty-making began under the Directory and the Consulate in order to consolidate French victories and Napoleon's project of "general pacification". The treaties became shorter and to the point. Peace and tranquillity in Europe were cited as ideological justifications, reflecting the French desire to reintegrate in Europe while also transforming it to France's benefit. Provisions having to do with refugees and political prisoners as well as those involving a recognition of the sister republics catered to new French priorities. The language of the "nation" was used profusely. By inserting commercial clauses in the treaties of peace and by negotiating specifically commercial treaties, the effort was made to situate French trade in an optimally beneficial economic context.[310]

The effect of the effort to reform the European political order by that amalgam of old-regime practices with revolutionary language that came to dominate the Napoleonic era can be gleaned in an important but under-appreciated work of 1803 by Joseph-Mathias Gérard de Rayneval (1736–1812), *Institutions of the Law of Nature and of Nations*. Rayneval was an expert in German public law, an experienced diplomat and friend of the former foreign minister

308 See e.g. Thierry Lentz, 'De l'expansionnisme révolutionnaire au système continental (1789–1815)', in Françoise Autrand, Lucien Bély, Philippe Contamine & Thierry Lentz, *Histoire de la diplomatie française 1: Du Moyen Age à l'Empire* (Paris, Perron 2005), 527. "En 1795", Belissa writes, "tous les commentateurs sont donc d'accord pour dire et répéter que l'ancien droit public est mort et enterré", *Repenser l'ordre européen*, 373.

309 For the reorganisation of the ministry under Talleyrand and his successor Reinhard, and then after Talleyrand's reappointment in 1799, see Frédéric Masson, *Le département des affaires étrangères pendant la Révolution 1787–1804* (Paris, Plon 1911), 406–44.

310 Belissa, *Repenser l'ordre européen*, 348–70.

Vergennes.[311] Despite having been compelled to leave the ministry in 1792, Rayneval had internalised the methodological individualism of *les philosophes* (he quoted Rousseau profusely) and, with an eye no less sharp than Mably's, analysed the foreign policies of kings with a realistic focus on the "passions" that frequently led them to conduct policies inimical to their interests. In the opening sections of this work, which closely followed the eighteenth-century treatises on natural law and the law of nations, he wrote of the social pact that free and equal individuals had concluded to set up nations for their protection and well-being.[312]

Rayneval's law of nations was a natural law of reason (*droit des gens primitif*), supplemented by customs and treaties that applied between particular states and concerned particular situations. But the principles of reason were universal and applied in all human interactions, including with respect to the internal organisation of the state and government.[313] Although Rayneval's large treatise followed the structure laid out by Vattel and made frequent reference to Grotius, Pufendorf and all the rest, its substance, and especially the long notes, was attuned towards a new legal world designed to secure the right of property and the rest of the social pact:

311 For his biography, see the *notice biographique* in (Joseph-Mathias) Gérard de Rayneval, *Institutions du droit de la nature et des gens* (nouvelle édition, Paris, Gravier 1832 [1803]), tome I, v–xvi. The work has recently been translated into English as *The Last Waltz of the Law of Nations. A Translation of the 1803 Edition of the Institutions of Natural Law and the Law of Nations by Joseph-Mathias Gérard de Rayneval* (Jean Allain trans., Oxford University Press 2020).

312 As an expert in German public law, he was familiar with the massive production of academic treatises on natural law at German universities of the time. For his discussion of the social "pact", see Rayneval, *Institutions*, tome I, 34–5, 54. Perhaps surprisingly, he suggested that it was the sovereign's task to make reality of the pact. In case he failed to do so, his subjects were not only freed from obedience but entitled to invite foreign assistance to liberate themselves. "Si le prince viole le pacte social, s'il devient un tyran, les droits imprescriptibles de la nation n'autorisent-ils pas à regarder ce pacte comme rompu, et à se considérer comme dégagées de toute espèce d'obligation", Rayneval, *Institutions*, 62, 70–1. Moreover, with a tyrant, "il ne peut exister aucun pacte, aucun lien entre lui et ses sujets; il est l'ennemi de la nature entière qu'il outrage. Ainsi, ses sujets peuvent légitimement se soustraire à son joug, et même invoquer des secours étrangères pour y réussir", 273–4.

313 He accepted that while this aspect – the subject of Part I of the treatise – did not belong to the law of nations in its ordinary understanding it was still necessary to include it because it laid the natural foundation for all social organisation, including the rights and duties of individuals and that the "law of nations" was nothing but a "corollary" of the natural law that served as its foundation. Rayneval, *Institutions*, tome I, 1–2.

the first object, the first duty of the authority that has been instituted for the maintenance of society is the protection of property against every attack, all trouble, all encroachment, all usurpation.[314]

In fact, he wrote, subscribing to the ideology of the Directory, property-owners were the greatest patriots as they had the most concrete interest in the flourishing of the nation.[315] The work was published in 1803, at the moment when the treaties of Lunéville and Amiens were consolidating French victories and gave the author reason to celebrate "*le grandeur et la puissance prépondérante de la république française sur le continent*". "[P]osterity will, no doubt," he continued, "be struck with awe on how one man may simultaneously have, so to say, destroyed internal tyranny, prevented civil war, vanquished powerful enemies and given peace to the universe."[316] By now, republican revolutions were over and France was ready to live in peace with its neighbours. In his letters to European rulers, Bonaparte appealed to moderation and "general pacification".

A flurry of publications celebrated France's return to its old role as a stabilising power.[317] Perhaps the most well-known of these was *État de la France en l'an VIII* by Alexandre de Lanautte, the Count of Hauterive (1754–1830), Rayneval's acquaintance and Talleyrand's right hand, recently returned to the foreign ministry in the relatively low position of assistant director of consular affairs, later the director of the ministry's archives. In the course two centuries, Hauterive argued in a work commissioned by Napoleon, Westphalia had become a real, universal public law.[318] The recent wars had been occasioned by European diplomats' inability to adapt this system to the new situation – the ascent of Russia and Prussia and the growth of colonial trade. It was that last issue, in particular the Navigation Acts with which Britain was trying to exercise maritime dominance, that had been the source of the troubles. Unlike anywhere else, in Britain private and state interests had been bound together into world-wide trade operations that undermined

[314] "... le premier objet, le premier devoir de l'autorité instituée pour la conservation de la société, est de protéger la propriété contre tour atteinte, tout trouble, tout émiettement, toute usurpation." Ibid., I, 28.

[315] Ibid., I, 144–5. By contrast, he wrote, democracy and patriotism have nothing to do with each other, 146.

[316] Ibid., II, 298.

[317] See the excellent account in Belissa, *Repenser l'ordre européen*, 155–81 and further, Lefebvre, *Napoléon*, 87–109.

[318] Alexandre-Maurice Blanc de Lanautte Hauterive, *État de la France en l'an VIII* (Paris, Henrics, An 9 1799), 4.

stability, created superficial alliances and intervened in the commerce of all other countries.[319] War had been compelled on France but now that it had proven victorious, its only wish was to recreate the lost equilibrium and re-establish "the public law that monstrous alliances, dismemberments and partitions, the violation of all the laws and all the federal maxims had destroyed".[320]

Hauterive was an influential behind-the-scenes figure who had drafted most of Napoleon's commercial treaties and was now suggesting the contours of what would become the first consul's continental system, a kind of global balancing device against British maritime dominance.[321] Rayneval's *Institutions de droit de la nature* was an effective packaging of many such ideas. Now it was time for general pacification, he wrote. False philanthropy was to be set aside; no words had been recently more misused than liberty and equality. Hierarchies would always exist; they were a fact of life. Different constitutional forms distributed civil and political liberties differently while the equality of *rights* only depended on how the laws were respected in a country.[322] He noted that all regimes had their bright and dark sides – Rayneval clearly preferred constitutional monarchy – but tyranny and democracy were the worst. "It is a remarkable thing", he pointed out, "that despotism has the same source as liberty."[323] Rayneval did not accept the revolutionary doctrine of national sovereignty – the origin of sovereignty might well lie with the nation, but it was the ruler who was sovereign.[324]

[319] Ibid., 21–3. [320] Ibid., 37.

[321] For the debate initiated by the book, see Bo Stråth, *Europe's Utopias for Peace* (London, Bloomsbury 2016), 27–34. Hauterive was also instrumental in seeing to education in *droit des gens* in France by taking the leadership of the newly established *école diplomatique* within the foreign ministry's archives, a follow-up of the brief effort of a century before. Here young men, expecting appointment as secretaries of legations were trained in the composition of public law instruments (treaties, declarations, decrees). They were supposed to have acquainted themselves with the Code civil and were given supplementary teaching in Pufendorf, Barbeyrac, Wolff and Vattel. As a practical assignment, each was to write an account of the (just) causes of the Seven Years' War, beginning from the Westphalia peace. Alexandre-Maurice Blanc de Lanautte Hauterive, *Conseils à un élève du ministère des relations extérieures* (Épreuves pour le seul usage du service des archives n.d.), 16–17, 106, 107–10 and passim.

[322] Ibid., I, 49–56. [323] Ibid., I, 36.

[324] Ibid., I, 44–9. Also, being sovereign *never* involved a right of property: a ruler may intervene in private property only for public utility and against full compensation. Ibid., 65.

After a conventional discussion of laws and *moeurs*, Rayneval began to discourse on the basic principles of taxation, agriculture, industry and commerce as well as the importance of education in politics and morality..[325] Good government was about good laws, supplemented by "*l'intérêt, la prudence et la convenance politique*".[326] This was especially true in situations when action might be required against a potential disturber of the peace or when contemplating the wisdom of concluding or keeping a peace treaty. Long sections of the treatise were devoted to alliances, peppered by examples from recent practice intended to remind the reader that in the end, "no stipulation could annul the sacred maxim of *salus reipublicae*".[327] The work came with an Appendix that enlarged politics to the whole sphere of domestic and foreign affairs, occupying the terrain earlier writers addressed in terms of prudence or *ragion di stato*.

In their international relations, nations enjoyed rights corresponding to those natural laws allotted to individuals. But they had also bound themselves in all kinds of treaties and customs as "precautions" against the passions of their rulers, their tendency to dress personal ambition behind "*l'imposant dénomination d'intérêt, de gloire, de prospérité nationale*".[328] Commerce had now become a principal source of both peace and conflict. In choosing between freedom and prohibition, Rayneval wanted his readers to bear in mind that "prohibition, monopoly and fraud were almost synonymous, or at least inseparable from one another".[329] Competition was to be encouraged, especially if it could be managed under an economic council. Such a council should examine the state of agricultural production, industry and commerce in a neutral and independent way, guiding commercial policy free from *l'esprit de parti*.[330]

Rayneval's treatise was an eclectic compilation of rationalism and *raison d'état*. His style reflected the world of someone deeply read in German natural law with decades of advisory work for the French foreign minister. The marriage of formalist seriousness and detached

325 In modern times, he argued, too much stress had been given to exact sciences. But morals and politics were equally important. Ibid., I, 135, 249.

326 Ibid., I, 361.

327 Hence the precariousness of all alliances. Ibid., I, 283.

328 Ibid., I, 261.

329 Ibid., I, 267.

330 Such a council had also been planned under the aborted Franco-British commercial treaty of 1786 that was to follow and supervise the treaty's implementation. Ibid., I, 245–6.

irony might have been irritating had it not been accompanied by often interesting reflections on eighteenth-century diplomatic practices. But nothing else than the moment of its composition – 1803 – explains that it dealt almost exclusively with the policies of Europe and the United States. Not a single section or paragraph in the main body of the work addressed the colonies, French or other. While the author occasionally noted that some rule was also applicable universally, he never enquired what this might mean in regard to what Montesquieu would have called the Orient. Only two brief sections give some sense of the author's awareness of a wider world. A long note in the context of acquisition produced the standard argument about the *leyenda negra* that also, interestingly, included a long citation from a mid-seventeenth-century travel book where an indigenous inhabitant of the Cape Colony queried a Dutchman on what right they had come to take over land that had belonged to him and his relatives since time immemorial. To this the Dutchman had responded that the African and his nation had lost it in a contest or arms and that it was useless for them to try to regain it.

> This was the language of Europeans, of polished and enlightened men! This was the almost universal public law of that part of the globe where the perfectibility of the human species, as it is pretended, has made the greatest progress! This, in a word, was the law of the powerful in all its purity![331]

The only other place where the non-European world put in an appearance was in the treatment of slavery. No doubt, Rayneval admitted, if one considered nothing but "sentiments of sensibility and benevolence", the whole idea of human servitude would have to be abandoned. But God had endowed human beings with a faculty to use their freedom as they wished, including by giving it up. This, and not those sentiments, was "the basis on which any judgment on slavery must be made".[332] It seemed clear to Rayneval that nobody had the right to force anyone to slavery. But he then added, enigmatically, that "the question of the Negroes" was "more difficult to resolve". This was so because that matter belonged "to the realms of prudence and

[331] Ibid., I, 369. The work referred to was Olfert Dapper, *Description de l'Afrique* (Amsterdam, Wolfgang et al. 1686), 377–8.

[332] Rayneval, *Institutions*, I, 74–5.

political morality instead of the law of nations or the constitutive principles of government".[333]

Here, in these brief passages, one could receive a glimpse of what was the most intensely guarded secret not only of the Revolution but of the very formation of that thing we call "France".

[333] Ibid., I, 79. He nevertheless added that relevant considerations would then include whether production in the Caribbean was essential to the Europeans, whether slave labour could be compensated by white labour and "whether cultivation on the islands ought to be altogether abandoned rather than giving liberty to the blacks".

# 7

# Colonies, Companies, Slaves

## *French* Dominium *in the World 1627–1804*

> Because morality authorises [slavery] in the American colonies, it must equally authorise it among us. As soon as it is found to be useful, the political decision should be made to take it into use. Let us not think that possessing slaves would degrade humanity; the liberty that every European believes they enjoy is nothing but the power to break one's chains in order to receive another master.[1]

The suggestion to deviate from the long-standing principle that "there are no slaves in France" by the young Mably may have been unorthodox and difficult to square with his later opinions.[2] But it corresponded to a widespread view even among republican thinkers that slavery was above all an economic, not a moral issue, and that France's wealth and power depended on it. After all, France was the world's principal exporter of sugar, all of it produced by slaves in the French Caribbean colonies. In a later edition of the same work – *Le droit public de l'Europe* – Mably responded ironically to critics according to whom the proposal violated the laws of nature:

did not those sacred laws of states already violate the laws of nature according to which some citizens possess everything, while others have nothing?... Need creates slaves and they are all the more miserable if there are no laws that provide for their subsistence. What is debasing for humans is beggary and that is necessary among all the peoples that have not drawn limits to the greed and

[1] Gabriel Bonnot de Mably, *Le droit public de l'Europe fondé sur les traitez*, tome II (nouvelle éd. M. Rousset, Amsterdam, Uytwere 1748), 202–3.

[2] Since 1571, French courts had consistently liberated slaves that had found themselves in France and been able to make that claim. See Sue Peabody, *"There Are No Slaves in France". The Political Culture of Race and Slavery in the Ancien Régime* (Oxford University Press 1996).

fortune of citizens. The ancients were tyrants to their slaves: but is it impossible to establish laws to govern the relations between masters and slaves?[3]

And to make clear the target of his criticism, Mably added that

it went against reason to pretend that a human being is free in a country where citizens employ each other to serve them and thereby condemn them to the most wretched and hardest forms of human employment.[4]

Almost invisibly, Mably glided from a discussion of the colonies into a metaphoric use of the expression "slavery" to condemn the inequality and oppression at home.[5] Although Mably's acquaintance Jean-Jacques Rousseau did the same, it would be wrong to say that they approved colonial slavery or serfdom – at least Rousseau wrote a few lines in more or less express condemnation of it, but Mably did not.[6] The principal point of their criticism and the focus of their writings lay in old-regime Europe. For all of their celebrated universalism, the enlighteners' vision was limited by their domestic experience. Of course, the cultural and political turn that they represented, their critique of monarchic absolutism and their intense debates on the pros and cons of commercial society, had a bearing with respect to global injustice as well. But apart from scattered exceptions – of which the most famous was Abbé Raynal's *Histoire philosophique et politique des établissements et du commerce des deux Indes* (1770–80 plus many subsequent editions) – they failed to orient Europeans to think about the outside world in other ways than as an object of economic exploitation.

In *Le droit public de l'Europe*, the theme of slavery was treated only briefly and, as usual at the time, in the context of long-distance commerce. Mably had nothing to say about Turkey and other non-European polities apart from how they appeared as commercial partners to European nations. He admired the Dutch for their

3 Mably, *Le droit public de l'Europe*, tome II (troisième edn, Genève, Compagnie des Librairies 1764), 394–5.

4 Ibid., 395.

5 Condemnation of absolutist rule by the argument that it rendered the subjects into "slaves" was common among enlightenment polemicists. See e.g. Anoush Fraser Terjanian, *Commerce and Its Discontents in Eighteenth-Century French Political Thought* (Cambridge University Press 2013), 68–73.

6 Rousseau's most famous text on slavery is in *The Social Contract* (M. Cranston trans. & intr., Harmondsworth, Penguin 1958), I 4 (53–8). In the *Discours sur l'économie politique* (B. Bernardi dir., Paris, Vrin 2002 [1763]) Rousseau noted of slavery, "qu'il est contraire à la nature, et qu'aucun droit ne peut l'autoriser", 43. For the few express condemnations by Rousseau of European colonisation, see Sankar Muthu, *Enlightenment against Empire* (Princeton University Press 2003), 44–6.

successes in the East Indies and their predominance in carrying trade. He made note of the decline of Spain and agreed with those who had warned about the dangers of the East Indies trade as it sucked up European bullion and undermined domestic manufacturing. America was the most important trading partner, and Mably stressed the importance of prohibiting the Atlantic colonies from developing so as to threaten metropolitan production.[7] It was in this context that Mably speculated about the benefits of using slaves to work uncultivated soil in France and to take up manufacturing work too heavy for Frenchmen. He was no racist, however, and regarded Africans as "robust, straight and intelligent". Making them learn all kinds of trades would result in great benefits for France. Whatever the fate of those *malheureux*, Mably tried to assure himself and his readers that it would certainly be better in France than in the American mines and plantations.[8]

The brevity, not to say lightness, of Mably's treatment of slavery and the slave trade contrasts with its importance to France at the time. In 1750 there were 265,000 slaves in France's Caribbean colonies, with their number continuously growing such that at the outset of the Revolution their number had almost tripled.[9] In the eighteenth century as a whole, French traders had brought 1,180,300 slaves across the Atlantic (with approximately 13 percent of the human cargo lost on the voyage) so that their role in the development of French economy was anything but negligible.[10] As Mably stressed, the slaves worked especially "in the production of sugar and tobacco that form the heart of the richest commerce of Europe".[11] But neither here nor in his later writings on individual rights and republicanism did he suggest that those ideas might in some way conflict with slavery and the slave trade

[7] Mably, *Le droit public de l'Europe* (1748), 200–16. [8] Ibid., 202, 203–4.

[9] To 675,000. Robin Blackburn, *The Making of New World Slavery. From the Baroque to the Modern 1492–1800* (London, Verso 1997), 404. France was the third largest slave-trading nation at the time.

[10] Ibid., 383, 392. Slaves were brought to the Caribbean as part of the famous "triangular trade" whereby slavers coming from the African west coast to the Caribbean would then load sugar, coffee, tobacco and indigo to be brought to the principal ports of Bordeaux, Nantes and Saint-Malo, and leave again to Africa with cotton and copper utensils, pots and iron bars, knives, glass trinkets as well as gunpowder, guns and spirits. See Fernand Braudel, *Civilization & Capitalism, 15th–18th Century. Vol. III: The Perspective of the World* (California University Press 1992), 438–40.

[11] Mably, *Le droit public de l'Europe* (1748), 202.

or that they might also have some relevance for thinking about Europe's relations to its colonies.

* * * * *

In this chapter I will situate the property claims made by Frenchmen on Africans in the context of the laws of French colonial expansion. After a brief overview of the enlightenment views on black slavery I will turn to Richelieu's early efforts to enlist merchants from French coastal communities to begin the colonisation of *la Nouvelle France.* I will then discuss Colbert's more massive projects in the East and West Indies and the eventual loss of France's most lucrative overseas territories in the Caribbean during the Napoleonic wars. The period of absolutism failed to produce much of a legal debate about the status of overseas territories, and the patents and charters usually took for granted that France could settle whatever territory had not been already occupied by another Christian power. Colonisation took place in more or less the same way as the new provinces had been joined to metropolitan territory – with the exception that no rights or privileges were granted to the original inhabitants. A number of factors – lack of experience and enthusiasm with French merchants, the dictatorial role of the government ("Ministerial despotism"), constant warfare in Europe and the colonies, insufficient resources as well as rebellion by slaves themselves – contributed to the ultimate failure of early French colonisation. Its by far most successful aspect, the plantation economy on Saint-Domingue, was based on chattel slavery that was impossible to square with revolutionary principles. Compromising with those principles would ultimately lead to the loss of even that colonial foothold. It is striking how long it took for France and other European powers to accept that the establishment of the independent state of Haiti in 1804 would mark the end of "European public law".

## Slavery and the *Philosophes*

Slavery had been a continuously reiterated trope of the enlightenment.[12] It stood for everything the enlighteners were against, symbol

[12] For treatments of the slavery debates in eighteenth-century France, see Jean Ehrard, *Lumières et esclavage. L'Esclavage colonial et l'opinion publique en France au XVIIIe siècle* (Paris, Versaille 2008); Yves Benot, *La Révolution française et la fin des colonies 1789–1794* (Paris, Découverte 2004), 7–41; Jean-Paul Doguet, 'Présentation', in Condorcet, *Réflexions sur l'esclavage des nègres* (Paris, Flammarion, 2009 [1781]), 10–48; Bernard Gainot et al., 'Lumières et esclavage', 380 *Annales historiques de la Révolution française* (Juin 2015), 149–69.

of what was wrong in the Old World and should not find a place in the New. But it was overwhelmingly used in a metaphorical sense to connote the subordination of the people in the metropolis to the old regime. The reiterated call to break the "chains of serfdom" meant emancipation at home, not putting an end to colonial slavery. A rare expression of sympathy towards enslaved Africans appeared in the image of the "negro of Surinam" in Voltaire's *Candide*, lying on the ground outside the city gates with his left leg and right arm severed. "This is the price for which you eat sugar in Europe," the dying man said to Candide.[13] But Voltaire did not think the matter worth more than an occasional mention in his prolific writings, which were also scattered by numerous negative remarks on the Africans' intellectual and aesthetic qualities.[14]

Montesquieu's *The Spirit of the Laws* contained the most extensive treatment of slavery in France since Bodin and was often taken as a reference-point for later debates. Chapter XV opened with a sharp attack on the justifications, some mercantile, others anatomical or scientific, that had been made to defend the enslavement of Africans.[15] The grounds on which Romans had justified slavery were also rejected: it was not true that a captor was entitled to kill the captive and thus also to enslave them; to sell oneself into slavery was "so repugnant to all reason as can scarcely supposed in any man".[16] But Montesquieu's further treatment of the matter remained ambivalent. On the one hand, "as all men are born equal, slavery must be accounted unnatural".[17] Unnatural, but perhaps still not always wrong or illegal? For although Montesquieu was clear that slavery could not exist in Europe the matter could well fit the *moeurs* in other places.[18] And like Voltaire, he accepted many of the prejudices and stereotypes that were the common stock of European racialism. The physical, mental and moral properties of African "savages" compared in all respects unfavourably to those of whites. Life in warm climates produced weakness, despondency and total incapacity, and "[t]he inhabitants of warm countries [were], like old men, timorous [while] the people in cold countries are like young men, brave". Moreover, because the

[13] Voltaire, *Candide ou l'optimisme* (Paris, Presses Pocket 1989 [1759]), 96.

[14] For a discussion of Montesquieu's and Voltaire's image of the Africans, see Andrew S. Curran, *The Anatomy of Blackness. Science & Slavery in an Age of Enlightenment* (Johns Hopkins University Press 2011), 133–49.

[15] Montesquieu, *The Spirit of the Laws* (New York, Hafner 1949), XV 5 (I 238–9).

[16] Ibid., XV 2 (I 236). [17] Ibid., XV 7 (I 240). [18] Ibid., XV 8 (I 240).

"inclinations" of the inhabitants of warm climates were all passive, it also remained the case that slavery there was "more supportable".[19]

Having discarded the possibility of "slavery among us" (and thus allowed it elsewhere), Montesquieu went on without further ado to discuss the several kinds of slavery in existence and the abuses and dangers involved. The former pointed to the need to limit the masters' power, especially the sexual abuses of female slaves, the latter had to do with the threat that large number of slaves as "domestic enemies" posed to moderate governments.[20] For both reasons, Montesquieu stressed the importance of regulating slavery by laws. "Leniency and humane treatment" were needed to prevent the abuses and the dangers. Food and clothing were to be offered and care was to be taken of the sick and the elderly. But Montesquieu never referred to Colbert's *Code noir* or raised the question of slave trade or the fate of the slaves in the French Caribbean.[21]

Throughout the *Second Discourse*, Rousseau exalted the happiness and simple wisdom of those living in the state of nature: "how many cruel deaths would not a [Caribbean] savage prefer to . . . the horrid life" of a European "minister of state"![22] He wrote admiringly of noble savages and critiqued the superficiality with which European travellers had discussed the manners of the inhabitants of other continents.[23] Nevertheless, his political horizon was limited within Europe. The characterisation of the virtues of the savages in the *Second Discourse* was meant to highlight the corruption of civilised societies and not to suggest that humans should, or indeed could, retreat to wilderness. His critique of the turn to private property, for example, was not written as a prologue for giving it up. In the *Discourse on Political Economy* Rousseau even insisted that property was sometimes more important than liberty itself because it protected one's livelihood and acted as "the real foundation of civil society and the true guarantor of citizens'

[19] Ibid., XIV 2 (I 223–4). See also Curran, *Anatomy of Blackness*, 130–7. Montesquieu also vacillated in his discussion of Aristotle's view of natural slavery. On the one hand, he believed some people were "natural slaves", on the other he argued that because "all men are born equal, slavery must be accounted unnatural". *The Spirit of the Laws*, XV 7 (240).

[20] Montesquieu, *The Spirit of the Laws*, XV 11–12 (I 242–3).

[21] Ibid., XV 15–16 (I 244–7). On Montesquieu's treatment of slavery, see further Louis Sala-Molins, *Le Code Noir ou le calvaire de Canaan* (Presses Universitaires de France 2002), 216–31 (a particularly critical treatment); Malick W. Ghachem, *The Old Regime and the Haitian Revolution* (Cambridge University Press 2012), 63–5, 73–7.

[22] Jean-Jacques Rousseau, *A Discourse on Inequality* (transl. & intro. by M Cranston Harmondsworth, Penguin 1984), 137.

[23] See further Curran, *Anatomy of Blackness*, 70–3.

engagements".[24] The critique was only to give a tragic colouring to the predicament of his contemporaries. The savage was always sufficient unto himself while civilised humans were trapped in a world of imagination that created passions to which no satisfaction was available.[25] It is true, of course, that Rousseau rejected the policy of conquests and held that nobody was as miserable as a conquered people.[26] This applied above all to the conquest of territories occupied by the savages who only "breathe the salutary air of liberty".[27] But as long as there were states, it was impossible to depart from the search of new possessions from which new resources and properties could be extracted.

And yet, nowhere in his writings on international politics and law did Rousseau address the actuality of African chattel slavery. The famous critique of slavery in Book I of the *Social Contract*, for example, was intended to work as a conceptual basis for making a distinction "between subduing a multitude and ruling a society".[28] But in the Caribbean there were no more savages to subdue! The issue in the Caribbean was about the operation of a system of plantation slavery with an African workforce that was vital for France's foreign trade. Rousseau's critiques of luxury and the inequality of a commercial society might have extended to an indictment of the slave economy, and the language of the *Social Contract* sometimes points in that direction – for example when Rousseau writes that "[t]o renounce one's freedom is to renounce one's humanity, one's rights as a man and equally one's duties . . . such renunciation is contrary to man's very nature".[29] But like most *philosophes*, what he had in mind in writing such sentences was the situation of Europeans living under the tyranny of monarchic absolutism.[30]

[24] Rousseau, *Discours sur l'économie politique*, III (65). Property was the "real foundation" of the state in the sense that it was to protect their properties that humans in the natural state, and especially the richest of them, had set up political institutions. Rousseau, *Discourse on Inequality*, 133.

[25] See also Richard Velkley, *Being after Rousseau. Philosophy and Culture in Question* (The University of Chicago Press 2002), 53–5.

[26] Rousseau, *Discours sur l'économie politique*, III (70–1).

[27] Rousseau, *Discourse on Inequality*, 73.

[28] Rousseau, *The Social Contract*, I 5 (58).

[29] Ibid., I 4 (55). In his most famous romantic novel, Rousseau made his male protagonist feel "horror and pity" for seeing "the fourth part of humanity transformed into beasts in the service of others". *Julie ou la nouvelle Héloise.* tome II (troisième éd., Amsterdam, Rey 1772 [1761]), 180. Most references to slavery in the book, however, address the experience of being engulfed in romantic love.

[30] For the debate, see Ehrard, *Lumières et esclavage*, 161–4. Much more polemical are Sala-Molins, *Le Code Noir*, 231–48 and Susan Buck-Morss, *Hegel, Haiti and Universal History* (University of Pittsburgh Press 2009), 29–34, both highlighting the manner in which Rousseau's definition and discussion of slavery left Saint-Domingue untouched.

In 1698 the doctors of the Sorbonne had published a counsel of conscience that expressly addressed the question of chattel slavery of Africans. Having approved the old view that prisoners taken in a just war could indeed be enslaved, it addressed the standard case where the Africans had been taken in order to enslave them and sell them to Europeans:

In case the traders know, as most of them do, that the Negroes that they buy have been made slaves in this way, or that they have been stolen, they cannot be bought; for the title of their servitude is then unjust and that the seller has acquired them by fraud or violence.[31]

The prohibition applied also for those condemned to lose their freedom out of hatred and anger or under a tyrannical law and those selling themselves or their children without clear knowledge of what enslavement means – the usual case. It followed, then that one could not be secure in conscience if one engaged in buying or selling slaves "because there is injustice in this commerce".[32] By the middle of the next century, however, attitudes had changed as new writings in natural history had begun to take an interest in a physiological and anatomical analysis of blackness. The striking differences between Africans and Europeans were sometimes attributed to phylogenesis – that they were an altogether different species, a position taken by Voltaire, for example – that justified their unequal treatment. The century's leading work in the field, Buffon's 1749 *Histoire naturelle*, however, accepted that humans shared a single origin but held Africans a degenerate variety. Buffon, Linnaeus and other proponents of this latter view put forward all kinds of historical and natural factors supposedly responsible for this: climate was cited often, as were food and other habits.[33] Although not meant for those purposes, both

[31] "Quand les marchands savent, comme la plupart ne l'ignorent pas, que les Nègres qu'ils achètent ont été faits Esclaves de cette manière, ou qu'ils ont été dérobéz, ils ne peuvent point les acheter; parce que le titre de leur servitude est injuste & que le Vendeur les a acquis par fraude ou par violence", *Le Dictionnaire des cases de conscience, décidés suivant l, es principes de la morale, les usages de la discipline ecclesiastique, l'autorité des conciles et des canonistes, et la jurisprudence du Royaume*, tome 1 (Paris, Coignard 1733), 'Esclaves', 1443.

[32] Ibid., 1444. However, if there was no such "fault" either in the act of enslavement or with the knowledge of the buyer, there was no problem.

[33] See e.g. Jean-Claude Halpern, 'Entre esclavage et liberté. Les variations d'un éthnotype dans la France de la fin du XVIIIe siècle', in Marcel Dorigny (ed.), *Esclavage. Résistance et abolitions* (Paris, CTHS 1999), 130–2.

theories would come in handy to support the view that serving the white person could be seen as an African's natural occupation.[34]

Only in the essay on 'Esclavage' by Louis de Jaucourt (1704–1779), the most prolific contributor to the *Encyclopédie*, was there a ringing condemnation of chattel slavery. Freedom belonged to all, Jaucourt wrote, and slavery "shocks natural law and civil law".[35] But he also repeated the standard view that the natural laxity in Southern or Oriental countries explained why political slavery was so common there. The article 'Traite de nègres', however, captured the abolitionist credo and no longer repeated the standard facts supposedly accounting for the depravity of the Africans or their better suitability to servitude. "The buying of Negroes in order to sell them into slavery is a trade that violates religion, morality, natural laws & all the laws of human nature." Not one of these supposed slaves had lost their liberty because liberty simply cannot be sold: "Hence any concluded sale is null and void in itself." This is why, he wrote, judges must immediately declare them free regardless of any economic hardship that this might cause. "Surely humanity ought not to be horribly violated merely to enrich us or to provide us with luxuries!"[36] Yet none of the other relevant articles regarded slavery or the industries it upheld as illegal. At the same time, a widely used two-volume handbook written on "government of slaves" from 1777 answered the question of justification of the enslavement and transportation of Africans to the French colonies by the fact that they had been caught, imprisoned or condemned to death by the law of the strongest. Their indigenous kings had the power of life and death over them. While they then sometimes fell into the hands of ruthless masters, at other times they were given reasonable amounts of work by masters treating them humanely. The author ended the brief reflection by noting that be that as it may, the commerce had in any case become necessary for all the Atlantic colonies set up by Europeans who themselves were unable to undertake the labour in such conditions.[37] As usual, the moral concern was overweighed by the economic calculation.

34 See further, Curran, *Anatomy of Blackness*.

35 Jaucourt, 'Esclavage', in Denis Diderot and Jean le Rond D'Alembert (eds), *Encyclopédie, ou dictionnaire raisonné des sciences, des arts et des métiers, etc.* (University of Chicago, ARTFL Encyclopédie Project Spring 2011), Robert Morrissey (ed.), encyclopedie.uchicago.edu/ (Vol. 5: 937).

36 Jaucourt, 'Traite des negres', in Diderot and D'Alembert (eds), ibid., Vol. 16: 532–3.

37 M. Petit, *Traité sur le gouvernement des esclaves*, tome 2 (Paris, Knape 1777), 3–4.

In the 1770s and 1780s, increasing arguments began to be made against slavery and the slave trade.[38] In his widely read *Ami des hommes*, Mirabeau speculated that the omnipresence of slavery in the French Caribbean as well as its extreme brutality could only be explained by racist reasons: "our American slaves are a separate race of human beings, distinct and separated from our species by that most ineffaceable of features, I mean colour, and that therefore has received its misfortune from nature".[39] Like other Physiocrats, he attacked the economic rationale of slavery and critiqued the greed and short-sightedness of European merchants and planters and speculated that free trade, especially giving up the *exclusif*, would intensify the demand for higher-quality products, necessitating that Europeans take up plantation work themselves.[40] Dupont de Nemours and Turgot combined economic and principled arguments in their rejection of slavery. But neither they nor Condorcet in his influential 1788 tract *Réflexions sur l'esclavage des nègres* proposed immediate abolition; this, they held, would be economically senseless and only create more suffering among the blacks unaccustomed to liberty.[41]

The most influential pre-revolutionary attack on slavery and the slave trade, as well as colonialism itself, was the eleven volumes of Abbé Raynal's *Histoire des deux indes* whose three editions were published by a mixed group of authors in 1770, 1774 and 1780, with Diderot as a principal contributor to the last edition. The book was compiled largely from official documents and travel accounts, initially at the request of the minister of colonies. Its first edition, for which Raynal himself was mainly responsible, reported in a rather neutral fashion on European expansion, highlighting excesses and the miserable conditions in which the Europeans had come into contact with indigenous populations. Subsequent editions were substantially tightened by Diderot as well as the more obscure *philosophe*, Jean de Pechmeja, so that they attacked not only the practices of enslavement and slave trade but the ideology of

38 Curran, *Anatomy of Blackness*, 179–81. For an overview of the styles of criticism of slavery in French literatures of the period – "deplore, critique and combat" – see Doguet, 'Présentation', 10–30.

39 Marquis de Mirabeau, *L'ami des hommes, ou traité de la population* (3 Parts, Avignon 1756), III 147.

40 Ibid., III 148–9.

41 For Condorcet's proposal for the gradual liberation of slaves over the course of seventy years, see Condorcet, *Réflexions sur l'esclavage des nègres*, IX 88–97. Unlike most others, Condorcet, however, expressly rejected the economic arguments to support his gradualism.

colonisation itself. The work was condemned by the Paris *parlement* and burnt by the public hangman in 1781.[42] But it became enormously popular nonetheless. Book XI included a long description and critique of slave trading, including a response to its suggested justifications. Diderot wrote ironically about the "most sublime moral maxims that Europe had developed in the course of the past century":

> Even imaginary misfortunes draw tears from our eyes in the silence of our chambers and above all at the theatre. But the fatal destinies of the unfortunate negroes have no interest to us. We tyrannise and mutilate and burn and stab them; and we listen to these stories without emotion. The torments of a people to which we owe our delights never reach our hearts.[43]

Diderot also reiterated the theme of the black Spartacus who "will one day raise the flag of liberty to rally the masses of the unfortunate": "*Alors disparoîtra le code noir; & que le code blanc sera terrible, si le vainqueur ne consulte que le droit de repressailles!*"[44] But despite this rhetoric, the inconsistent and polyphonic work adopted only a gradualist view on abolition, advocating the freeing of women who had given birth to a sufficient number of children and those under twenty years old after they had worked against pay for five years for the master.[45]

The debate about slavery in the French colonies raises questions about property and sovereignty in a somewhat new light. On the one hand, slavery was precisely about selling and possessing human beings as property. Raynal's *Histoire des deux Indes* defined it as a "condition of a human being who, either by force or convention, has lost the property of his or her person and that the master may dispose like a thing".[46]

[42] For a meticulous comparison of the different editions, especially in view of identifying Diderot's contribution, see Yves Benot, *Les lumières, l'esclavage, la colonization* (Paris, Découverte 2005), 107–23, 138–53. For an overview, see also Melvin Richter, 'The Comparative Study of Regimes and Societies', in Mark Goldie & Robert Wokler (eds), *The Cambridge History of Eighteenth-Century Political Thought* (Cambridge University Press 2006), 165–9.

[43] "Des malheurs même imaginaires nous arrachent des larmes dans le silence du cabinet & sur-tout au théatre. Il n'y a que la fatale destinée des malheureux nègres qui ne nous s'intéressent pas. On les tyrannise, on les motile, on les brûle, on les poignarde; et nous l'entendons dire froidement et sans émotion. Les tourmens d'un people à qui nous devons nos délices ne vont jamais jusqu'à notre cœur", Guillaume-Thomas Raynal, *Histoire philosophique et politique des Etablissements et du Commerce des Européens dans les deux Indes*, tome VI (Genève, Pellet 1781), XI 22 (105–6).

[44] Ibid., XI 24 (139). [45] Ibid., XI 24 (135–6).

[46] "L'état d'un homme qui, par la force ou des conventions, a perdu la propriété de sa personne, & dont un maître peut disposer comme de sa chose", ibid., XI 24 (187).

Earlier French debates that had been critical of slavery associated it with the sovereignty of the master – slavery could not exist in France, for example, precisely owing to the Bodinian view that sovereignty in a state could not be divided: the master's power was a "pocket of sovereignty within the state" that threatened the comprehensiveness of royal sovereignty.[47] But when chattel slavery was framed rather in property than in sovereignty terms, it was easier to debate it as a purely economic matter. The Physiocrat jurist Le Mercier de la Rivière, former governor of Isles-de-Vent and Martinique, integrated it quite casually in the colonial economies. "Negroes", he wrote, "are the animals which Martinique needs."[48]

This view was also taken by Melon in his *Essai politique sur le commerce* (1734), which depicted colonies as absolutely necessary for the development of French power. Experience of slavery had demonstrated, he wrote, that the use of slaves "is contrary to neither religion nor morality. We may thus examine freely whether it might not be useful everywhere."[49] Melon's intention was to defend the luxury trade against traditionalists such as Fénelon in whose view expanding commerce contributed to the corruption of society and the decline of the patriotic spirit. But Melon retorted that luxury trades instead made money circulate more intensively providing wealth and an exit from idleness – the root of all crimes. What did it matter, he wrote, if it made a wealthy person sometimes spend more than he could afford if it contributed to giving work for so many others?[50] Besides, luxury was one thing for a prior generation, another for the present and yet certainly another for the future. As a purely relative notion it could not be reasonably legislated against, and in any case, the history of sumptuary legislation was a succession of failures.[51] Taking up an old Augustinian theme, Melon believed that legislation could not harness our passions but was to turn them to the best advantage of the community.[52] As for the

[47] Ghachem, *The Old Regime and the Haitian Revolution*, 51.

[48] Pierre le Mercier de la Rivière, *L'Ordre naturel et essentiel des sociétés politiques* (London, Nourse 1767), quoted in Emma Rothschild, 'Global Commerce and the Question of Sovereignty in the Eighteenth-Century Provinces', 1 *Modern Intellectual History* (2004), 12. But see also Le Mercier, *L'Ordre naturel*, 14 where he insists that everybody is owner of their person. See further Florence Gauthier, 'Le Mercier de la Rivière et les colonies de l'Amérique', 20 *Revue française d'histoire des idées politiques* (2004), 37–59.

[49] Jean-François Melon, *Essai politique sur le commerce* (Presses Universitaires de Caen 2104 [1735]), 58. The characterisation of Melon's influence is from John Shovlin, *The Political Economy of Virtue. Luxury, Patriotism, and the Origins of the French Revolution* (Cornell University Press 2006), 23.

[50] Melon, *Essai politique*, 126–7, 139. [51] Ibid., 130–8. [52] Ibid., 122.

slaves, Melon noted that Colbert's 1685 *Code noir* had regulated in detail the relations between the masters and the slaves, giving rise to "*un plus beau spectacle*" that had set the institution of slavery on the French colonies on a well-organised basis.[53]

For Melon, the young Mably as well as most Frenchmen, slavery was inextricable from the colonies, unchallengeable under the law of nature and of nations as long as the rights of other Christian nations were respected. Of course, there were humanitarian concerns. But as France had become dependent on its colonies – especially those producing sugar – it could not afford to think seriously about emancipation. The way to colonisation had been no easier for Frenchmen than accepting that national power and glory were based on commerce; the two views had developed in close relationship to each other. Because the economic resources available for the French crown were nowhere near sufficient for active colonisation, Richelieu had been meeting with Grotius to extract information from the Dutchman regarding how to enlist private commercial interests in the process.

## Colonisation As Struggle of Proprietary Rights: Early Developments

Richelieu had oriented himself to commercial and maritime matters once he had securely positioned himself as unofficial chairman of the Royal Council in the spring of 1624 and taken upon himself the position of Grand-Maître de la Navigation two years later.[54] By that time, Richelieu had been instructing himself on the relative backwardness of French commerce, especially when compared to the United Provinces, as well as the distance that separated France from its principal rivals, Spain and England, in the business of colonisation. In the *Testament politique* he already observed that while states enlarge their territory by war, they increase their wealth by engaging in peaceful commerce. Repeating almost verbatim counsel he had been receiving from his maritime experts, he stressed the great potential

[53] Ibid., 61–4.

[54] A good account of Richelieu's plans and the reorganisation of French maritime government as Grand-Maître de la Navigation is Alan James, *The Navy and Government of Early Modern France 1572–1661* (Royal Historical Society, Boydell Press 2004), 55–76. From a legal perspective, particularly important was the reorganisation of the *conseil de marine*, which would aim to encroach on the privileges and revenues of the admirals in coastal provinces.

France had in commerce and colonisation if only it were to commit itself to them with determination.[55]

Richelieu's colonial policy was inspired by a document produced by Admiral Isaac De Razilly, future lieutenant-general of *Nouvelle France*, which contained a broad, somewhat elementary discussion of Spanish, Dutch and English colonial activities, lamenting the lack of interest among the French nobility in corresponding ventures.[56] France cannot do without the gold and silver available in America, he wrote. Its rivals had understood this, and now their ships were importing untold riches from their overseas possessions.[57] Razilly's report laid out a comprehensive project of commercial and colonial expansion. It discussed the opportunities in Asia, Africa and America, and ended with a special plea to colonise the "coast of Eldorado" (Guyana) that, the author suggested, could be undertaken with an investment of no more than 100,000 ecus and with 1,500 men to keep away Christian rivals.[58] These and other ideas went into a proposal on maritime affairs that Richelieu brought to the Assembly of Nobles in early 1627. But though the Assembly endorsed the proposals generally, it gave no concrete commitments.[59]

France had always refused to accept the Iberian monopoly claims in the New World. In 1533 Pope Clement VII had conceded that the papal acts of the 1490s had applied only to territories known at the time. This liberated François I to authorise Jacques Cartier's (1491–1557) successive voyages in the 1530s and 1540s on the American coast.[60] The intention

55 Richelieu, *Testament politique* (A. Teyssier ed., Paris, Perrin 2011), II 6 (293).

56 Isaac de Razilly, 'Mémoire du chevalier de Razilly', in Léon Deschamps (ed.), *Isaac de Razilly. Un colonisateur du temps de Richelieu* (Paris, Delagrave 1887), 15–35. On the origins and influence of the Razilly memorandum, see also Henri Hauser, *La pensée et l'action économiques du Cardinal de Richelieu* (Presses Universitaires de France 1944), 38–43.

57 Razilly, 'Mémoire', 20, 24.

58 Ibid., 33. Razilly complained that merchants were not usually prepared to undertake such long-term investments. But this could be done by engaging many merchants with smaller sums for a project led by a single "*homme de qualité*" who would make all the practical decisions for the fulfilment of the plan, 32–3.

59 Hauser, *La pensée et l'action économiques*, 48–73; Erik Thomson, 'France's Grotian Moment? Hugo Grotius and Cardinal Richelieu's Commercial Statecraft', 21 *French History* (December 2007), 380–2, 385–6.

60 For French attitudes to the papal donation, and generally the (rather meagre) justifications of French colonial settlement, see Alice Bairoch de Sainte-Marie, 'Les colonies françaises et le droit. Une approche globale, 1600–1750', 82 *Études canadiennes* (2017), 94–104. A clear statement against the pope's jurisdiction to determine territorial rights of European sovereigns ("*son pouvoir est purement spirituel*") is included in the first history of French Canada by the lawyer and poet Marc Lescarbot, *Histoire de la nouvelle France* (2 vols, continuous pagination, Paris, Peier 1618), I 30.

to colonise was for the first time clearly stated in the Letters Patent of 15 January 1541 that invited Cartier's rival, the Sieur de Roberval, to travel to the lands bordering the Saint Lawrence river not already in possession of any Christian power, to "make contact with foreign peoples" and, if possible, "*habiter esdites terres et pays, y construyre et eddifiers villes et fortz, temples et eglises ... et establir loix de par nous ensemble officiers de justice pour les faire vivre en raison et police*".[61] But no stable claims were established, and only the cessation of civil war and peace with Spain (1598) opened the door for thinking anew about extra-European expansion. Henri of Navarre, Henri IV (1589/94–1610), once the admiral of Guyenne and the leader of the Huguenot corsairs, possessed a lively interest in maritime affairs.[62] In January 1598, he appointed the obscure nobleman Marquis de la Roche from Brittany his lieutenant-general to Canada, Newfoundland and adjacent territories.[63] The rights of lordship to be enjoyed by La Roche would resemble those given to Roberval in 1541, and included powers of legislation and criminal justice as well as the authority to distribute land "*en tous droits de propriété*" as fiefs or lordships or other appropriate forms.[64] Henri would provide no

[61] H. Harrisse, *Notes pour servir à l'histoire, à la bibliographie et à la cartographie de la Nouvelle-France et des pays adjacents 1545–1700* (Paris, Tross 1872), 244 and the whole commission 241–53. Also quoted in Michel Lavoie, *Le domaine du roi 1652–1859. Souveraineté, contrôle, mainmise, propriété, possession, exploitation* (Québec, Septentrion 2010), 19. The earlier commission, given to Cartier on 17 October 1540, appointed him "lieutenant-general" to direct the expedition, to live with native people in order to convert them. Nothing was said of territorial claims. See *Complement des ordinances et jugements des gouverneurs et intendants du Canada* (Québec, Fréchette 1856), 5–7. The first claims were those of the letters of 1541. Overall, in the period from Verrazano's voyage in 1523 and Cartier's first voyage in 1534 until 1598, few French claims were presented in intra-European diplomatic correspondence, though France did protest against Iberian violations of the freedom of navigation, and its exorbitant claims over the whole of the Indies. A good summary is Brian Slattery, 'French Claims in North America, 1500–59', 59 *Canadian Historical Review* (1978), 139–69.

[62] Eric Thierry, *La France de Henri IV en Amérique du Nord. De la création d'Acadie à la fondation de Québec* (Paris, Champion 2008), 41–4.

[63] Edit du Roy contenant le pouvoir et Commission donné par sa majesté au Marquise de Cottenmeal et de la Roche, 12 January 1598. Lescarbot, *Histoire*, II, 398–405. Also published in Williàm Smith, *History of Canada from its First Discovery to the Peace of 1763* (Quebec, Neilson 1815), Vol. I, Appendix 2. Roche had been a favourite of Catherine de' Medici who had received a commission from Henri III to occupy territories in Newfoundland not already in the possession of another Christian sovereign. Owing to a shipwreck the planned voyage of 1584 came to nought, however, and La Roche spent much of the early 1590s imprisoned in Nantes for his earlier military activities in the region. H. P. Biggar, *The Early Trading Companies of New France* (University of Toronto Library 1901), 38–9.

[64] Edit du Roy et Commission au Marquise de la Roche, Lescarbot, *Histoire*, II, 401.

economic assistance, but La Roche was expected to finance his venture by the trading monopoly he would enjoy over his lands. Profits would be divided in three equal parts between La Roche and his companions and for investment in fortifications for future settlement.[65]

Nothing came of the venture. Although La Roche eventually reached the mainland, he was compelled to return to France and leave a small group of prospective settlers on the Isle de Sable, south of Cap Breton. After further efforts, the king was approached in October 1603 by the Huguenot nobleman Pierre De Gua, Sieur De Monts (1558–1628) with wide-ranging plans for occupation and settlement in the Saint Lawrence valley and Acadia. De Monts eventually received two commissions, one from Charles de Montmorency, the holder of the office of admiral of France – an office involving an ill-defined jurisdiction over maritime and colonial areas – and the other from Henry IV, the commissions covering Acadia as well as an area reaching from Chesapeake to Cap Breton and leading eventually to the establishment of Quebec by his lieutenant the explorer Samuel de Champlain (1574–1635) in 1608.[66] While the king again refused to open his purse for the enterprise, its funding would be based on a ten-year fur trading monopoly. Alongside searching for valuable minerals, the idea was to establish a permanent presence in Canada for which purpose De Monts was to transport originally a hundred settlers per year (De Monts was able to argue the number down to sixty, but even this figure was never attained). He was also to take action to convert the native inhabitants, to trade with them and make treaties of peace and alliance or wage war if necessary.

The patent given to Roberval set the language of French colonial expansion on lines similar to acquisitions in Europe (Milan, Naples and Piedmont for example).[67] In addition, the commissions and letters

[65] See further the discussion by Helen Dewar, '"Y establir notre auctorité". Assertions of Imperial Sovereignty through Proprietorships and Chartered Companies in New France, 1598–1663' (PhD thesis, University of Toronto 2012), 27–9. Traditional rights in cod fishing were preserved, however.

[66] Helen Dewar, 'Souveraineté dans les colonies, souveraineté en métropole. Le rôle de la Nouvelle France dans la consolidation de l'autorité maritime en France, 1620–1628', 64 *Revue d'histoire de l'Amérique française* (2011), 70–1. Although huge, this was still considerably smaller than La Roche's patent, which covered all the coast from Florida to the Arctic. In a declaration of 1605 the king confirmed the appointment of De Monts as his lieutenant-general not only in Acadia but also in "Canada and other areas of Nouvelle France", Déclaration du roi, 8 February 1605, in Lescarbot, *Histoire*, II, 418.

[67] See the comparative report in François-Joseph Ruggiu, 'Colonies, Monarchies, Empire and the French Old Regime', in Robert Aldrich & Cindy McCreery (eds),

patent would also contain a reference to Christianisation and a commitment to transport priests for that purpose. This constituted the principal and sometimes only context in which the indigenous population was mentioned in these instruments. However, the settlers seem to have accepted that the latter did possess some rights in their lands and that, at least as long as they were a minority, Europeans would need to contract with the inhabitants before dispossession could take place. But once the settlers were in place, the king would regard himself as the feudal overlord, entitled to determine the conditions under which such transactions were to take place.[68] Accordingly, he allocated Acadia (mostly present-day Nova Scotia) as a fief to De Monts who was called upon "*d'assujettir, submettre et faire obeïr tous les peuples de ladite terre et les circonvoisins*".[69] He was to distribute lands and grant such titles, privileges and offices as he thought fit. And he was called upon to govern and to legislate in conformity with metropolitan laws.[70] In this way, the system of feudal lordships in the New World would mirror metropolitan practice.[71] As the king explained in a separate declaration in 1605, "*lesdits païs estoient par nous reconnuz de notre obeïssance, et les tenir et avouer comme dependances de nôtre Royaume et Couronne de France*".[72]

To pre-empt criticisms from French fishermen and coastal communities, De Monts invited merchants from Rouen, St Malo and St Jean-de-Luz to associate in a company with him (*Compagnie de Monts*) first in February 1604 and then, after initial disappointments and defections, as the *Compagnie de Canada ou Nouvelle-France*

*Crowns and Colonies. European Monarchies and Overseas Empires* (Manchester University Press 2016), 197–8.

68 At that point, remaining Indian lands would have the status of feudal (seigneurial) concessions by the French king. See Alain Beaulieu, 'The Acquisition of Aboriginal Land in Canada. The Genealogy of an Ambivalent System', in Saliha Belmessous (ed.), *Empire by Treaty* (Oxford University Press 2015), 105–7. The situation has been summarised as follows: "At no time was there any recognition on the part of the French crown of any aboriginal proprietary rights in the soil. The French settlers occupied the lands in Canada without any thought of compensating the native", George F. Stanley, 'The First Indian "Reservoir" in Canada', 4 *Revue d'histoire d'Amérique français* (1950), 209.

69 Commission du Roy au sieur de Monts, 8 November 1603, in Lescarbot, *Histoire*, II, 408–14.

70 Ibid., II, 411–13.

71 "[L]and should be granted and sub-granted in feudal terms", W. B. Munro, *The Seigneurs of Old Canada. A Chronicle of Old World Feudalism* (Toronto, Brood 1915), 11. Likewise, Lavoie, *Le domaine du roi*, 17–23.

72 Declaration du Roy, 8 February 1605, Lescarbot, *Histoire*, II, 418.

in December 1605.[73] Meanwhile, De Monts' primary interest turned to Quebec and part of Acadia (Port Royal) was allocated through sub-infeudation to the French nobleman Jean Biencourt de Poutrincourt and his relatives. A new commission of 1608 confirmed the territorial and monopoly trading rights of De Monts as lieutenant-general of *Nouvelle France* and invited his company to continue the settlement, providing the sum of 2,000 livres per year for missionary activities.[74] Resistance from Guyenne and Brittany led, however, to the revocation of De Monts' trading monopoly, opening up a brief period of free trade in New France (1609–12). This period ended when Henri of Bourbon, the Prince of Condé, a close relative of the young king, purchased the office of lieutenant-general and viceroy of *Nouvelle France*, receiving powers identical to those once allocated to De Monts:

> to establish our authority there, to extend and make known our name and, as far as possible, before subjecting and subordinating the lands and their surroundings and securing the obedience of their people.[75]

By this means the king established himself a feudal suzerain over both *Nouvelle France* (broadly the St Lawrence valley down to Quebec), with Condé as his viceroy, and Acadia under De Monts. As viceroy and lieutenant-general the two men possessed rights of legislation, treaty-making as well as authority to decide on peace and war, powers that closely resembled those of provincial governors or *intendants* in France.[76] Both also enjoyed trading monopolies as well as governmental

[73] "d'y establir nostre auctorité, estendre et faire cognoistre nostre nom si avant que faire se pourra, assubjectir, soubzmettre et faire obeyr tous les peuples desdites terres et leurs circonvoisins", Thierry, *La France de Henri IV*, 131–5, 230–1.

[74] Thierry, *La France de Henri IV*, 272; Leslie Choquette, 'Proprietorships in French North America', in L. H. Roper & B. van Ruymbeke (eds), *Constructing Early Modern Empires. Proprietary Ventures in the Atlantic World 1500–1750* (Leiden, Brill 2007), 118–19. For the companies' early efforts to create settlements in Acadia and St Lawrence Valley, see Gervais Carpin, 'Migrations to New France in Champlain's Time', in R. Litalien (ed.), *Champlain. The Birth of French America* (McGill University Press 2014), 164–72.

[75] Commission for lieutenant-general of New France, given by Louis XIII to the Prince de Condé in 1612, quoted in Dewar, '*Y establir nostre auctorité*', 70. From Document 234 in R. Le Blant & R. Baudry (eds), *Nouveaux documents sur Champlain et son époque*, Vol. I, *1560–1622* (Ottawa, Archives publiques du Canada 1967). See further Dewar, '*Y establir nostre auctorité*', 2–3, 60–81. Ruggiu, 'Colonies, Monarchies, Empire', stresses the significance of the removal of the colony under the government of a member of the royal family, highlighting its private–public nature, 198–9.

[76] But see Lavoie, *La domaine du roi*, 22–3; Dewar, '*Y establir nostre auctorité*', 70–1.

privileges but administered them in different ways. Condé delegated his trading privileges to a company (*société générale*), the *Compagnie de Rouen et Saint Malo* (CRSM, *Compagnie de Condé*), and his governmental authority to Champlain whom he appointed as his lieutenant – thus instituting repeated disputes about overlapping claims of authority. Further jurisdictional quarrels arose between Champlain and Condé as well as between Condé and his followers after the temporary retrieval of Condé's titles owing to his rebellious involvements. Having recovered office in 1619 Condé sold it in the following year for 30,000 livres to his brother-in-law Duke Henri II de Montmorency, governor of Languedoc and admiral of France, Richelieu's future nemesis.[77] As viceroy, Montmorency immediately took Champlain as his lieutenant and set up his own company (*Compagnie de Montmorency*, *Compagnie de Caën*) to enjoy the monopoly trading rights – with the result of a protracted legal dispute between the two companies.[78] Unlike his predecessors, Montmorency engaged actively in the government of the territory, including by commencing the allocation of seigneurial grants.[79] In 1625 Montmorency sold his viceregal office to his nephew, Henri de Lévis, duke of Ventadour for the sum of 100,000 livres; Richelieu would eventually come to replace de Lévis through his office as Grand-maître de la navigation. The legal situation was further complicated by the claims made by the vice-admiral of Brittany who regarded himself in that capacity as also vice-admiral of *Nouvelle France*.[80] Authorities of the coastal provinces and the port towns likewise invoked various customary and other privileges, sometimes confirmed by the king himself, so as to challenge the fur trading monopolies enjoyed by the various companies.

These conflicts demonstrate the haphazard nature of French Atlantic expansion. French authorities thought nothing of extending the system of feudal government to the New World. In areas where "other Christian princes" were not present, they regarded America as open

77 Henri Montmorency was one of the great nobles whose power Richelieu tried programmatically to diminish as part of his centralisation efforts.

78 His first successor was Pons de Lauzière, marquis de Thémines de Cardillac whom Champlain served alongside taking orders from imprisoned Condé. See Dewar, *'Y establir nostre auctorité'*, 96–111; Luc Huppé, 'L'établissement de la souveraineté au Canada', 50 *Les Cahiers de droit* (mars 2009), 171; David Hackett Fischer, *Champlain's Dream* (New York, Simon & Schuster 2008), Appendix, 602–3.

79 Fischer, *Champlain's Dream*, 603.

80 These conflicts have been examined in detail in Dewar, *'Y establir nostre auctorité'*, chapter 3 (68–157).

for expansion.[81] A national narrative has stressed the general absence of indigenous communities from places of early settlement and the overall friendship established between French settlers and those that were present.[82] However that may be, use of European expressions such as *terra nullius* or *res nullius*, discovery, cession, conquest, occupation etc. to characterise the legal situation may not be appropriate in this context – what does a territorial claim *mean* in a world seen through feudal categories encompassing lands and humans in overlapping right–duty relationships?[83] Besides, there was a need to argue differently in different directions.[84] The context of the metropolis required the production of charters and letters patent that were respectful to domestic practices. Relations with other European sovereigns called for diplomatic language to justify the presence of settlements or trading posts in areas of potential interest to others within a wider world of commercial rivalry. Settlers, on the other hand, were to be addressed by a specific language to give some control over what they were doing – but it is not at all clear that this was the language through which the settlers themselves addressed their situation. Least of the concerns were the indigenous peoples themselves. Instead of following abstract doctrines, occupation and dispossession took place largely by improvisation on the ground, contracting with the indigenous when necessary and in general dealing with problems as they arose. What contemporaries imagined they were doing was setting up a framework where royal overlordship was accompanied by rights of *dominium* vested in companies that would allocate seigneuries and fiefs to settlers and indigenous communities by reference to what was convenient.[85]

81 A good summary is Ruggiu, 'Colonies, Monarchy, Empire', 197.

82 For a description of that national narrative, see Edward Cavanagh, 'Possession and Dispossession in Corporate New France, 1600–1663. Debunking a "Juridical History" and Revisiting *Terra Nullius*', 32 *Law and History Review* (2014), 104–6 and a useful critique and reconstruction, 106–22.

83 As Dominique Deslandres has argued, as in metropolitan France itself, annexation was less about land than about rights over people, which is why the geographic extent of many of the claims could remain obscure, '"Et loing de France, en l'une & l'autre mer, Les Fleurs de Liz, tu as fait renommer". Quelques hypotheses touchant la religion, le genre et l'expansion de la souveraineté française en Amérique aux XVIe & XVIIIe siècles', 64 *Revue d'histoire de l'Amérique française* (2011), 103–5.

84 A sobering analysis of the various and often incoherent uses by imperial agents of the available language is Lauren Benton & Benjamin Straumann, 'Acquiring Empire by Law. From Roman Doctrine to Early Modern European Practice', 28 *Law and History Review* (2010), 1 38.

85 The best summary for the period 1600–63 is Cavanagh, 'Possession and Dispossession', 97–125. A good overview and assessment of the limited significance

Acadia and *Nouvelle France* came thus to be treated like any new French provinces, without any privileges claimed by or confirmed to the original inhabitants. As with metropolitan provinces, the relationship between overlapping authorities remained far from clear; the commissions for viceroys and lieutenants-general were formulated in broad terms and read in frequently conflicting ways.[86] Jurisdictional claims were also made by provincial admirals who often distributed monopoly trading privileges to their clients and appointed lieutenants to rule the lands on their behalf. Although the companies were set up predominantly to manage their trade monopolies, in practice they also claimed governmental powers, thus occasioning further jurisdictional overlaps. On top of this, merchants left outside the trading companies would often enlist the support of local authorities to block the registration of royal commissions and refuse cooperation. Here if anywhere, Richelieu's lament about everyone just thinking about their private profit, with the public interest being apparently supported by nobody, found its target.

## Rule by Company 1: *Nouvelle France*

Many of the large proposals and reports concerning the reform of French maritime and colonial policy presented by Richelieu and his *garde des Sceaux* Michel de Marillac to the Assembly of Notables of 1626–7 remained wholly utopian in view of the crown's limited resources. Hence, as Richelieu put it, it was time to "*ordonner les marchands françois ne traffiquerons seuls, mais par flotte et en compagnie, et contribueront au sol la livre de commerce et trafficq qu'ils feront*".[87] Private capital was needed to launch the kinds of long-term projects to which French merchants had so far shown little inclination.[88] Even Montchrétien had complained about the failure of the French to follow up their old contacts

attached to various symbolic acts performed by the French is Deslandes, '"Et loing de France"', 93–117.

[86] The powers of a viceroy and lieutenant-general were broadly similar. The offices differed mainly to the extent of the status of their holder in the order of French dignities.

[87] Pierre Grillon (ed.), *Les papiers de Richelieu*, tome 1 (*1624–1626*) (Paris, Pedone 1975), 577. Or, as he put it elsewhere, the point was to "force the merchants to enter [in the colonies] by giving them great privileges as our neighbours do", Richelieu, *Mémoires I*, quoted in G. Avenel, *Richelieu et la monarchie absolue* (Paris, Plon 1895), vol. III (210).

[88] Razilly, 'Mémoire', 32. See also Richelieu's proposal (no. XV) to this effect in Grillon, *Les papiers de Richelieu* I, 591.

with the Orient: "How is it possible that we have not wanted to take part in such easy conquests?"[89] The French king was to encourage merchants to emulate the Dutch by providing them with privileges and immunities if they were to pool their resources in companies so as to share their capital, risks and profits. It was not necessary for the king himself to participate – "French monarchs have a hand only for holding a sceptre" – though he might want to become an investor and so to join his personal profit with that of the public.[90]

There had already existed trading companies, including those for East and West Indies possessed by Henri Montmorency, admiral of France, a much-admired governor of Languedoc.[91] But Richelieu was suspicious of the admiral as a specimen of noble grandees ruling their lands as if they possessed sovereignty over them. By assuming the office of Grand maître de la Navigation Richelieu simply swept aside the admiral's privileges and his authority over French coastal areas so that no choice was left to Montmorency but to sell his office back to the king.[92] In due course, Richelieu would also purchase the title of viceroy of *Nouvelle France*, which, as we have seen, had circulated among French high nobility in the previous years and which would enable him to rule over French activities in the St Lawrence valley and Acadia.[93]

At the very moment when he was enlisting Grotius' experience, the Cardinal was already speaking to French merchants with the result that a contract was drawn up in Richelieu's name with a group of financiers to set up in Morbihan, Brittany, a company to administer all of France's domestic and foreign commerce and to establish courts and jurisdiction over maritime areas. The company was also to "take possession of the territories of *Nouvelle France* both on the continent and the islands and other spaces which the company is able to conquer and

89 Antoyne de Montchrétien, *Traicté de l'économie politique* (Paris, Plon 1889 [1615]), 251. On Montchrétien, see further Chapter 5.

90 Ibid., 256.

91 Henri had received the Company of the East Indies that his uncle Charles de Montmorency had established in 1611 together with the title of "admiral of France".

92 James, *Navy and Government*, 56–9. The jurisdiction of the admiral had involved most questions having to do with the government of French ports and coastal provinces, supervision of the local admiralty courts and the collection of revenues from port activity. In 1627 Richelieu abolished the office of admiral and although it was re-established in 1669, it did not become important again until 1695, Bernard Barbiche, *Les institutions de la monarchie française* (Presses Universitaires de France 2012), 213.

93 Dewar, 'Souveraineté dans les colonies', 76.

occupy".[94] Nothing came of this owing to fierce opposition of mercantile interests in Brittany.[95] The same fate befell Richelieu's second effort with the *Compagnie Nacelle de Saint-Pierre fleur-de-lisée*, a Franco-Dutch venture likewise conceived as a universal trading operation but colliding with firmly entrenched interests in France's maritime provinces.[96]

By limiting his ambition somewhat and setting up a company with a territorially limited though still enormous area of operations, the *Compagnie de Nouvelle-France* (or the *Compagnie de Cent-associés*) Richelieu eventually succeeded in beginning French colonisation in America. Unlike in England or Holland, the leading role in this process was taken by the French state, its monarch and his principal minister, determined to recover the maritime power that they believed belonged to France. As Richelieu would repeatedly state, "*quiconque est maître de la mer a un grand pouvoir sur terre*".[97] The organisation and (especially) financing of the operations would rest almost exclusively on private actors, engaged by the Cardinal through his extensive network of patronage, involving courtiers, financiers and provincial merchants attracted by monopoly privileges.[98] Traditionally, French nobility had not been entitled to engage in commercial activities. Following Razilly's advice and in collaboration with Marillac, Richelieu took action to abolish this restriction. The massive royal edict eventually known as the *Code Michau*, promulgated by the *Parlement de Paris* in January 1629, assured French nobility that they would retain their titles even as they engaged in long-distance trading

[94] "jouir et posséder les terres de la Nouvelle France tant le continent qu'isles et autres lieux, que ladite compagnie pourra conquérir et peupler en toute seigneurie et propriété avec tout pouvoir et autorité", Grillon, *Les papiers de Richelieu* I, 311, 305–13. Also cited in part in Dewar, 'Souveraineté dans les colonies', 83. As usual, the king reserved for himself "foi et hommage", together with "la souveraineté et une couronne d'or que ladite compagnie sera tenue de donne [sic] a chacune mutation du Roys", 311.

[95] The *Parlement* of Rennes refused to register the appropriate edict while the provincial estates did so only with extensive conditionality. Biggar, *Early Trading Companies*, 134 and further Dewar, 'Souveraineté dans les colonies', 82.

[96] The contract of 19 May 1626, published in Grillon, *Les papiers de Richelieu* I, 321–35. For both companies, see also Pierre Bonassieux, *Les grandes compagnies de commerce* (Paris, Plon 1892), 358–60 and 363; Biggar, *Early Trading Companies*, 134–5.

[97] Hauser, *La pensée et l'action économiques*, 41. See also Maurice Besson, *Histoire des colonies françaises* (Paris, Boivin 1931), 44–5.

[98] See especially, Marcel Trudel, *Histoire de la Nouvelle-France*, tome III: *La seigneurie des Cent-Associés 1. Les événements* (Montréal, Fides 1979), 7–13.

operations. They were now specifically encouraged to form companies for commerce and settlement.[99]

The *Compagnie de Nouvelle-France* was Richelieu's largest colonial venture. It ruled its possessions as a feudal seigneur and differed from the prior companies in joining governmental tasks with the trading monopoly – the two having previously been divided between the recipient of the commission (La Roche, Le Monts, Condé) and his company. Private investors would establish settlements in an area extending from Florida to the Arctic Circle and from Newfoundland to the Great Lakes. The charters of rival companies that had failed to establish settlements were cancelled. This time, merchants were invited to overcome their suspicions by being offered noble titles alongside the monopoly itself. No doubt they also yielded because they wanted to please the powerful Cardinal and perhaps to avoid detailed scrutiny of their tax-farming or other privileges.[100] Because French regulation of economic activities in France was both extremely detailed and obscure and "changed according to ministerial whim", it was not hard for the crown to pressure recalcitrant merchants by pointing to some regulation they had neglected.[101] One did not refuse the Cardinal's offer.

The rights and privileges endowed to the company in 1627 were very extensive. The principal – stated – objective was to give native inhabitants knowledge of *le vrai Dieu*. For that purpose, the company was to transport three Catholic clergymen to each settlement. But most of the charter focused on settlement and government, as well as the commercial monopoly. In the first place, the company would possess the area of *Nouvelle France* (Canada, in practice Nova Scotia, and the St Lawrence valley) "*en toute propriété, justice et seigneurie*".[102] Like much of the public

[99] For the background and contents of the code, see Chapter 5 and further Yves Charbit, 'Les colonies françaises au XVIIe siècle. Mercantilisme et enjeux impérialistes européens', 22 *Revue européenne des migrations internationales* (2006), 9–17.

[100] Leslie Choquette, 'Proprietorships in French North America', in R. H. Roper & B. van Ruymbeke (eds), *Constructing Early Modern Empires. Proprietary Ventures in the Atlantic World 1500–1750* (Leiden, Brill 2007), 123; Barbiche, *Les institutions de la monarchie française*, 225.

[101] Financiers behaving ostentatiously were often brought to trial in special chambers of justice in a manner that allowed the court to repudiate its debts and the king to receive the undivided approval of his subjects. See also Chapter 5 and Hilton Root, *The Fountain of Privilege. Political Markets in Old Regime France and England* (University of California Press 1994), 22, 7–8, 170–2.

[102] Acte pour l'établissement de la Compagnie des cent Associés pour le commerce du Canada, Article IV (29 April 1627), in *Édits, Ordonnances royaux, déclarations et arrêts du Conseil d'État du Roi* (Québec, Desbarats 1803), vol. I, 4. The expression "*en toute justice*" referred to the company having full civil and criminal jurisdiction "*haute,*

administration of the kingdom itself, this was an essentially feudal arrangement where the king's supremacy was limited to his retention of "*foi et hommage*", which was to be confirmed by the payment of one gold crown at the time of each royal succession. The company was authorised to distribute land and titles as well as "rights, powers and faculties" among the settlers as it saw fit. Any ennoblement was to be confirmed by the king, however. The company was granted a perpetual monopoly on the fur trade plus a fifteen-year monopoly on all other commerce except fisheries, which remained open to all Frenchmen.[103] Settlers were free to trade with the native inhabitants, but were to sell the furs to the company.

On 28 April 1627 some 400 settlers left France to settle in Acadia and Quebec. But the fate of the settlements was hardly better than that of their predecessors. Quebec was seized by the English in 1629 but handed back three years later. By this time the company's funds had been largely depleted and it was compelled to subcontract the economic uses, especially the fur trade, first to a Rouen-based company of merchants and some years later to the colonists themselves. Notwithstanding the monopoly, profit-making still turned out to be impossible so that the rights of trading and exportation were eventually split up to different subcontractors.[104] In 1654, the British occupied nearly all of the colony in Acadia and *Nouvelle France* entered a period of great economic difficulty.[105] The company's obligations under its charter regarding evangelisation and settlement dwindled. Finally, in 1663, as part of Colbert's centralisation efforts, Louis XIV decided to revoke the company's charter and abolish all prior rights and privileges.[106]

## Rule by Company 2: Caribbean

On 31 October 1626 an act of association for the establishment of a company was concluded between Richelieu and a group of associates in order to "*faire habiter et peupler les Iles de Saint-Christophe et Barbade et*

*moyenne et basse justice*" in the area. Trudel, *Histoire*, III, 8 and on the company's rights and privileges generally, 8–11.

103 Acte pour l'établissement de la Compagnie des cent Associés, Article VII (4–5). See further Choquette, 'Proprietorships in French North America', 120–1.

104 Trudel, *Histoire*, III, 38–60.

105 The number of French colonists at the time did not exceed 300. Choquette, 'Proprietorships in French North America', 121.

106 By 1663, New France "had barely 3,500 French inhabitants", ibid., 122.

*autres situées à l entrée du Pérou*".[107] The initiative had come from two Frenchmen, Pierre Belain d'Esnambuc and Urbain de Roissey, who had visited the island of Saint Christopher in the early 1620s where they had witnessed the beginnings of tobacco cultivation. On the date of the establishment of the company, Richelieu, himself a principal associate, forthwith issued a commission to the two explorers to settle and cultivate both St Christopher and Barbados for a period of twenty years. The lands were to be held under the authority of the king who was to receive ten percent of all revenue produced. The rest was to be divided between the thirteen associates, most of them well-connected financiers holding public office.[108] This was the first time when a mention of slaves would appear in a French document. A private agreement between the principal colonists, duly notarised, observed that they would leave for the voyage with eighty men and "approximately forty slaves".[109]

But the company did not create the benefits hoped for, in part owing to difficult conditions on the island and unwillingness of the settlers to sell their tobacco to the company, in part because of lack of sufficient investment. A new contract was concluded at Richelieu's home at Rue St Honoré between the Cardinal and the associates on 12 February 1635 that now also included the internal rules of the company.[110] The area of operations of what was now called *La Compagnie des îles de l'Amérique* was extended to the adjoining islands as

[107] Acte d'Association des Seigneurs de la Compagnie des Iles de l'Amérique, Paris le 31 octobre 1626, Jean Baptiste Du Tertre, *Histoire générale des antilles habitées par les françois* (Paris 1667), tome I, 8–11. For the history of the company, see the very thorough Éric Roulet, *La Compagnie des îles de l'Amérique 1635–1651. Une entreprise coloniale au XVIIe siècle* (Presses Universitaires de Rennes 2017). For the contract made on the same day between the two captains D'Esnambuc and Roissey and their associates and financiers on the investment to the project and the division of profits, see Contrat pour l'établissment des français à l'île Sant-Cristophe, in Pierre Margry, *Belain d'Estambuc et les normans aux Antilles* (Paris, Faure 1863), 99–102; Roulet, *La Compagnie des îles de l'Amérique*, 36.

[108] Commission 31 October 1626, Du Tertre, *Histoire générale*, I, 11–14; Roulet, *La Compagnie des îles de l'Amérique*, 32–44.

[109] Lucien Peytraud, *L'esclavage aux Antilles françaises avant 1780* (Paris, Hachette 1897), 5. Although slaves would be present in the French Caribbean from this time onwards, it would not be until after 1664 that they would be mentioned as part of a *state* operation. Yves Benot, *La modernité de l'esclavage. Essai sur la servitude au cœur du capitalisme* (Paris, Découverte 2003), 109–18.

[110] Contrat du restablissment du Compagnie des Isles d'Amérique avec les Articles accordez par sa Majesté aux Seigneurs Associez, Du Tertre, *Histoire générale*, I, 46–50 and Articles d'association, 51–5. For details of the re-establishment until the new letters patent of 1642, see Roulet, *La Compagnie des îles d'Amérique*, 57–71.

well.[111] According to the letters patent, crown involvement was needed because private individuals were incapable of conducting such large enterprises; it was hoped that some profit would ensue to the state.[112] The associates, now titled as "Lords of the Company" (in 1644 "Lords of the Islands"), were granted property rights over the islands ("*en toute Iustice et Seigneurie*", paying "*Foy et Hommage*" to the crown) as well as the right to distribute lands and titles, to fortify the islands and to have a full monopoly of trade for a period of twenty years. Religious instruction was to be given to the native population. And the islands were to be populated by transporting to them at least 4,000 French Roman Catholics.[113]

A new contract of January 1642 extended the company's area of operations to Martinique, Guadeloupe and other islands up to the 30th latitude. The king renewed the associates' privileges and invited them to populate all the islands in the company's new perimeter. Its property rights were affirmed and the right to concede fiefs was supplemented by the right to provide noble titles – baron, duke, marquess. Settlers were promised military and naval assistance to occupy also islands held by France's enemies or unauthorised Frenchmen. A twenty-year exemption of all customs duties was given to the company, equating it with the innermost French provinces.[114] The company sought to make reality of its expanded jurisdiction by providing commissions to two captains to hold new islands in the company's name. But the fall of the tobacco price in the later 1640s together with general problems in French and the overall European economy led to the company giving up part of its operations.[115] The French were not winning. In a report from 1662 it was recorded that out of the 150 vessels that serviced the French Caribbean, only two or three were French.[116]

111 Or the huge area of the 10th to the 20th parallel north on areas "not already occupied by a Christian prince", Contrat du restablissement, Article I, Du Tertre, *Histoire générale*, I, 47.

112 See letters patent, 8 March 1635, ibid., I, 57–9.

113 Contrat du restablissment, Articles II–V, ibid., I, 47–8.

114 Edict du Roy en faveur de la Compagnie des Iles de l'Amérique, March 1642, ibid., I, 209–10; Roulet, *La Compagnie des îles d'Amérique*, 72.

115 In 1649 Guadeloupe and Marie-Galande were sold for the price of 73,000 livres to sieur Jean Boisseret; Martinique, Saint-Lucie, Grenada and the Grenadines were sold to sieur Duparquet for 60,000 livres, and Saint-Martin, Saint-Croix and Tortue to the Order of Malta for 40,000. Joseph Chailley-Bert, *Les compagnies de colonisation sous l'ancien régime* (Paris, Colin 1898), 43–4.

116 Silvia Marzagalli, 'The French Atlantic and the Dutch. Late Seventeenth–Late Eighteenth Century', in Gert Oostindie & Jessica V. Roitman (eds), *Dutch Atlantic Connections 1680–1800* (Leiden, Brill 2014), 105.

## The Return of the State: Colbert

In his survey of the finances of the kingdom at the death of Cardinal Mazarin in 1661, Colbert found the colonies in a disastrous state. Their administration had been allocated by the discredited finance minister Fouquet to his "creations"; private interests ruled, and little information about the situation of *Nouvelle France* or the Caribbean was available in Paris.[117] As Louis XIV himself agreed, after many years of war, the time had come to turn attention to commerce – especially long-distance commerce – to increase consumption by bringing home riches from the colonies, something wholly "*conforme au genie et à la gloire de nostre nation*".[118] Colonial government was to be centralised and foreign merchants excluded. Direct colonisation by the crown was discontinued owing to the critical state of the treasury. Colbert began his reform of colonial policy by first ruling out the use of small companies.[119] Like Richelieu, he had closely studied the Dutch and English experience.[120] But he adapted them to the French model where enterprising financiers were chosen from within the network of clients close to the court and the controller general himself. A "superior council" was established in Quebec (at the time there were about 2,500 settlers) to act as a legislative body and an appeals court.[121]

117 A good account of the early years of Colbert's efforts to centralise French commerce and colonisation is Philip P. Boucher, 'Comment se forme un ministère colonial. L'initiation de Colbert 1661–1664', 37 *Revue d'histoire de l'Amérique française* (1983), 431–52. Also L. Cordier, *Les compagnies à charte et le politique coloniale sous le ministère de Colbert* (Paris, Rousseau 1906), 51–85.

118 *Déclarations du Roy, l'une. Portant sur l'établissement d'une Compagnie pour le Commerce des Indes Orientales* (Paris, 1664), *Proemium* (3–4).

119 The initial efforts to expand by means of small companies had failed. An example had been the company of merchants with a trading monopoly in Guyana set up by four associates in 1651. The act of association had provided for a combination of motives: evangelisation, commerce and colonisation. As usual, the company was established as feudal lordship with "vast powers of dominion and justice". Philip C. Boucher, 'A Colonial Company at the Time of the Fronde. The Compagnie de Terre ferme de l'Amérique ou France equinoxiale', 11 *Terrae ingcognitae* (1979), 48 and note 37. Its rapid failure was based upon wholly unrealistic expectations about what life would be like in Guyana (between the Orinoco and Amazon) and legal problems with a conflicting claim by the *Compagnie du Nord*. The venture's widely publicised failure was one reason for the French disinterest in later colonial plans.

120 Barbiche, *Les institutions de la monarchie française*, 220–8. For his extended correspondence with French ambassadors, see Cordier, *Les compagnies à charte*, 62–7. See also Philippe Haudrère & Gérard Le Bouëdec, *Les compagnies des Indes. XVIIe–XVIIIe siècles* (Rennes, Ouest-France 2011), 6–10.

121 Édit de Création du Conseil Supérieur du Québec in *Edits, Ordonannces royaux*, I, 21–4. See further, Serge Dauchy, 'Le conseil souverain de Québec. Une institution de l'ancienne France pour le Nouveau Monde', 3 *Revue du Nord* (2015), 513–26.

The Act on the Establishment of the *Compagnie des Indes Occidentales* of May 1664 began with a lament on the failure by the company of *Nouvelle-France* to set up permanent settlements and produce any revenue for the metropolis. The *pays du Canada* had been completely abandoned. Likewise, the possessions held by the *Compagnie des Isles de l'Amérique* had failed to create expected profits. Martinique, Guadeloupe and St Christopher had only enriched their proprietors to France's detriment. All this had to change. The new project began with the declaration "that it would be to our glory and the grandeur and advantage of the state to set up a powerful company to conduct all trade in the West Indies".[122]

It took some time for Colbert to eliminate the private monopolies and buy off the properties to be administered under the company.[123] Guadeloupe, Martinique and Grenada were purchased from their proprietors. Having first become their owner, the state then donated the properties to the new company alongside lands "it may conquer and settle for forty years". In the end the company received all the French Atlantic possessions (Canada, the Antilles, Acadia, Newfoundland and Guyana), "*à perpetuité en toute Proprieté, Seigneurie et Justice*".[124] It also received monopoly trading privileges in West Africa that included, significantly, the right to engage in slave trade – with Colbert offering a bounty of 13 livres per *pièce d'Inde*, i.e. a healthy male slave.[125] The rights of jurisdiction included authority to establish tribunals and appoint judges and other officers to deal with criminal and civil cases. The judges would apply French laws and edicts as well as the custom of Paris but the company, too, was entitled to promulgate its own laws and regulations as confirmed by the king.[126] The company also had the

[122] Acte de l'Etablissement de la Compagnie des Indes Occidentales (22 May 1664), in *Edits, Ordonnances royaux*, I, 30.

[123] Cordier, *Les compagnies à charte*, 88–91; Abdoulaye Ly, *La Compagnie du Sénégal* (Paris, Karthala 2000), 70.

[124] Edit portant l'Etablissement d'une Compagnie des Isles Occidentales (28 May and 31 July 1664), Art. XXI, in Médéric Louis Élie Moreau de Saint-Méry, *Loix et constitutions des colonies françoises*, tome 1 (Paris, Quillau 1784), 107. Of course, the king was also owed "*droit d'hommage et lige*".

[125] The offer was to continue until the Revolution. See ibid., Art. XV & XLI (105–6, 111) and Bonassieux, *Les grandes compagnies de commerce*, 370–1; Kenneth J. Banks, 'Financiers, Factors, and French Proprietary Companies in West Africa 1664–1713', in R. H. Roper & B. van Ruymbeke (eds), *Constructing Early Modern Empires. Proprietary Ventures in the Atlantic World 1500–1750* (Leiden, Brill 2007), 88–9. See also Ordonnance du Roy 13 janvier 1672, confirming the bounty of 13 livres, Saint-Méry, *Loix et constitutions*, 1, 259–60.

[126] Acte de l'Etablissement de la Compagnie des Indes Occidentales (22 May 1664), Art. XXII, XXIII, XXVI, XXXI, XXXIII, XXXIV, XXXV in *Edits, Ordonnances*

right to establish armies and navies and to make peace and alliances in the king's name. Above all, it was to have a commercial monopoly excepting only fisheries left open for all Frenchmen. Freedom from import and exports duties made *Nouvelle France* as well as the French Caribbean legally on a par with most provinces of metropolitan France.[127] The company was to rule its enormous territory as a feudal lord, with *dominium directum* allocated to the king. But contributions from Colbert's patronage network proved disappointing so that the king himself ended up investing 1,387,000 livres, increasing his share to more than half of the total capital. The whole venture was directed from Colbert's offices.[128] Still, the company's operations were hampered by interloping and lack of capital; towards the end of 1667 it owed its creditors more than a million livres in unpaid purchases and interests.[129]

In 1669 Colbert received the office of the secretary of state for the marine and chose a new direction for France's colonial policy.[130] The laws setting up the famous *l'exclusif* that prohibited all trade by foreigners with the French Caribbean colonies were enacted.[131] Five years later, all French American colonies were taken under direct crown administration. The secretariat of the marine would oversee everything. The threefold administrative structure familiar in France would be instituted in the colonies as well. There would be a "sovereign council"

*royaux*, I, 35–7. The effort to unify the laws in the colonies by applying the customs of Paris never worked well. Most colonists came from Normandy and were familiar with the laws and practices of the *parlement* of Rouen. Also, there were few competent judges and the entry of *avocats* was prohibited in order to discourage excessive litigation. The great codifications of civil and criminal law of 1667 and 1670 were often applied in a modified way. See Dauchy, 'Le conseil souverain', 516–24; David Gilles, 'Les acteurs de la norme coloniale face un droit métropolitain. De l'adaptation à l'appropriation (Canada XVIIe–XVIIIe)', 4 clio@Thémis (2011).

127 Acte de l'Etablissement de la Compagnie des Indes Occidentales (22 May 1664), in *Édits, Ordonnances royaux,* Art. XV–XVIII (33–4).

128 Philip Boucher, 'French Proprietary Colonies in the Greater Caribbean', in L. H. Roper & B. van Ruymbeke (eds), *Constructing Early Modern Empires. Propietary Ventures in the Atlantic World, 1500–1700* (Leiden, Brill 2007), 177–8. The French *Compagnie des Indes orientales* faced the same result. At its establishment 45% of the shares were bought by the royal family and only 16% by private merchants or investors, Haudrère & Le Bouëbec, *Les compagnies*, 9.

129 Bonassieux, *Les grandes compagnies de commerce*, 372.

130 Barbiche, *Les institutions de la monarchie française*, 220–8.

131 L'Ordonnance du roi, qui défend le commerce étranger aux isles (10 juin 1670), in Saint-Méry, *Loix et constitutions*, 1, 195–7. The prohibition also included the importation of slaves. See also Arrêt du conseil d'état touchant des passeports pour négocier aux Indes Occidentales, ibid., 206–7.

(later "superior council") for each colony, a number of governors with jurisdiction over parts of the territory as well as an *intendant* with his delegates in principle supervising the administration. In practice, the most important actors were the governors-general located at principal colonial centres.[132] But lack of funds and constant warfare in Europe contributed to the government's failure to bring its American colonies under effective control. Despite the partial liberation of private (French) trade with the colonies, and the effort to encourage intercolonial commerce between Canada and the Caribbean, the colonies remained under-provisioned.[133] Nor were the mainland colonies able to develop into viable economico-political units. They had been mostly established as trading posts in places with harsh physical conditions. No workforce was available to be enlisted as indentured labour after the English model.[134] Rival English claims contributed to tension and occasional violence. But even more disruptive were the many private claims that French noblemen had on Port Royal and other parts of Acadia – in themselves "contemptible squabbles among those who fancied themselves as big fish in the smallest of ponds", but with serious consequences on established patterns of the fur trade.[135] Reliance on tax farmers and private financiers led to a problem familiar from the metropolis: "rampant private enterprise prevented the proper functioning of the government".[136]

The French *Compagnie des Indes Orientales*, also established in 1664, was born out of a similar process. The king and the court were by far the most important investors, and until the end of his life Colbert took part in the shareholder meetings. To collect the capital needed – to "give satisfaction to the King" – Colbert undertook an unprecedented propaganda campaign across the country; towns and provincial nobles were

[132] See James Pritchard, *In Search of Empire. The French in the Americas, 1670–1730* (Cambridge University Press 2004), 241–9; Dauchy, 'Le conseil souverain', 518–26.

[133] See e.g. Bertie Mandelblatt, 'How Feeding Slaves Shaped the French Atlantic. Mercantilism and the Crisis of Food Provisioning in the Franco-Caribbean in the Seventeenth and Eighteenth Centuries', in Sophus Reinert & Pernille Røge (eds), *The Political Economy of Empire in the Early Modern World* (London, Palgrave 2013), 197–201.

[134] Elizabeth Mancke & John Reid, 'Elites, States and the Imperial Contest for Acadia', in J. Reid and E. Mancke, *The 'Conquest' of Acadia 1710. Imperial, Colonial and Aboriginal Constitutions* (Toronto University Press 2003), 34–5.

[135] Ibid., 38–9.

[136] J. F. Bosher, 'Government and Private Interests in New France', 10 *Canadian Public Administration* (1967), 257; Pritchard, *In Search of Empire*, 248–9.

enticed by extensive monopoly privileges. Noble titles would be safe. Even foreign powers were invited to invest and offered representation if they did.[137] But results remained disappointing. Most towns were uninterested and invested, if at all, only minimally. At the outset 45 percent of the shares were bought by the king and the royal family and only 16 percent by private investors.[138] No foreign monarch came along despite the extension of monopoly trading rights from the Cape of Good Hope to "all the Indies". The company would also receive proprietary rights over any territory it might occupy.[139] It was awarded lordship over all mines and minerals as well as rights to take slaves and other rights "*qui pourroient nous appartenir à cause de la Souveraineté esdits pays*". Despite the use of the term "sovereignty", this was again a feudal arrangement where in addition to all private rights, the company also received rights of diplomatic representation and to make war and conclude alliances. It was the only French corporation with an army of its own and with the right to set up a money-printing office in its headquarters in Pondicherry. Its civil and criminal jurisdiction applied to all Frenchmen and not just company officials in its sphere of operations.[140]

After Colbert's death in 1683, the successive secretaries of state for the navy – the first of them being his son Seignelay – no longer had new visions for a French colonial empire.[141] The administration remained unchanged until 1710 when a special bureau was created that later became the "*intendance général des colonies*". There had of course been much naval warfare in the Caribbean and northern Atlantic in the 1690s and during the War of the Spanish Succession, carried out on the French side largely as a *course royal*, a privateering war not only licensed by the king but carried out by naval vessels. Although the settlers in Canada had been left largely to their own devices, they had mostly prevailed.[142] The most formidable potential adversary, the Iroquois, had remained neutral.

137 For the campaign, see e.g. Henry C. Clark, *Compass of Society. Commerce and Absolutism in Old-Regime France* (Lanham, Lexington Books 2007), 43–5.

138 Haudrère & Le Bouëbec, *Les compagnies*, 9; Cordier, *Les compagnies à charte*, 105–9; Clark, *Compass of Society*, 36–9.

139 "Appartiendra à ladite Compagnie à perpetuité, en toute proprieté, Iustice & Seigneuries, toutes les terres, places & Isles, qu'elle pourra conquerir sur nos ennemis, ou qu'elle pourra occuper, soit qu'elles soient abandonées, desertes ou occupées par les Barbares", *Déclarations du Roy, l'une, Portant l'etablissement d'une Compagnie*, Art. XXVIII (15, 16).

140 Ibid., Art. XXXI (17–18).

141 For a brief overview, see Pritchard, *In Search of Empire*, 234–41.

142 For a succinct account of the wars in the Americas, see ibid., 301–401.

No matter – French losses in the colonies were significant: the French part of Saint Christopher, Hudson Bay, Newfoundland and Acadia ("with its ancient boundaries") were ceded to Britain and the way for British merchants to trade with the Iroquois was opened.[143]

After the Peace of Utrecht (1713), the royal government had little time or resources to think about America; the failure of John Law's infamous system for the reform of France's financial administration exhausted the attention of French officials. A council of marine in 1715–23 did pass new colonial legislation, including on commerce and slave trade. The *exclusif* was renewed and tightened with heavy penalties against interlopers.[144] This enriched the French North Sea port towns but occasioned the first serious revolt among the colonists who saw their livelihood threatened by the prohibition to trade with the British American colonies. Vessels in violation of the prohibitions could be attacked, their cargo seized and their captains sent to the galleys.[145] Return to the system of secretaries of state at the maturity of Louis XV further strengthened the policy of thinking about the colonies exclusively from the perspective of metropolitan interests, undermining any prospective for separate development along the lines of Virginia or Massachusetts. Although France lost all of its remaining North American colonies, with the exception of St Pierre and Miquelon, in the Treaty of Paris (1763), the maintenance of its Caribbean islands preserved the most lucrative part of its overseas possessions.

## Sugar, Slavery and Feudal Rights: Crozat

In the period 1599–1785, at least 75 large companies of commerce and colonisation saw the light of day in France.[146] During the reign of Louis

[143] Treaty between France and Great Britain, 31 March 1713, Articles X–XII, in *A Collection of all the Treaties of Peace, Alliance and Commerce . . . from 1688 to 1727* (2 vols, London, Almon 1777), I, 136–8.

[144] Lettres-patentes portant règlement pour le commerce des Colonies Françoises, du mois d'Avril 1717, in Saint-Méry, *Loix et constitutions*, 2, 557– 65.

[145] Lettres patentes du Roy, en forme d'Edit concernant le commerce étrangère aus Isles & Colonies d'Amérique, Octobre 1727 (Paris, imprimerie royale 1727), in ibid., 3, 225–36. Also available at eco.canadiana.ca/view/oocihm.43974/3?r=0&s=1. According to Pritchard, this was "the most savage piece of colonial legislation ever promulgated. The severity of the penalties made the letters unenforceable", *In Search of Empire*, 241.

[146] Many companies never began effective operations, and others were instituted several times to take over from their predecessors. For the list, see Chailley-Bert, *Les Compagnies de Colonisation*, 21–5.

XIV alone, 39 companies were set up.[147] The last great effort at outsourcing a French empire in North America was the grant of Louisiana in 1712 to the financier Antoine Crozat (1655–1738); this was eventually absorbed in Law's system and went down as an economic project with it. Crozat's career illustrates the nature and limits of French Atlantic colonisation. An important financier in southern France, Crozat had in 1689 bought himself the position of *receveur général* of Bordeaux, one the most lucrative of the tax districts in the country.[148] At a difficult time, and through clever dealings with the crown Crozat gradually became one of its principal creditors. His first significant investments in colonisation took place in the context of the delivery of massive amounts of African slaves to the Antilles. Crozat had his eyes especially on the production of sugar and tobacco in Saint-Domingue – the southern part of Hispanola (Haiti) that Spain had formally handed over to France in 1697.

The story began as the new secretary of state of marine, Jérome Phelypeaux, marquis de Pontchartrain (1674–1747), Crozat's acquaintance, decided to intervene in the unsuccessful operation of the *Compagnie d'Indes orientales* by setting up a new company to trade with South America's Pacific coasts in 1698.[149] This was the *Compagnie de la mer du sud* of which Crozat became one of the directors. A month thereafter, the king expressed his wish to set up for Saint-Domingue "*une Compagnie puissante et composée des personnes don't l'intelligence et les forces nous sont communes*". As the South Sea operation rapidly showed itself financially disappointing, Crozat and eleven other financiers turned their attention to sugar production in the Caribbean instead.[150] The colony was granted to them once again "*en toute proprieté, Justice et Seigneurie*", with the king reserving for himself and his successors only the rights of feudal homage.[151] A fifty-year monopoly was granted on all trade with Saint-Domingue as well as the right to sell lands or grant them through subinfeodation. The company was also authorised to occupy other territories on American coasts not already possessed by another European

147 Jeff Horn, *Economic Development of Early Modern France. The Privilege of Liberty 1650–1820* (Cambridge University Press 2015), 116.

148 See Pierre Menard, *Le français qui possédait l'Amérique. La vie extraordinaire d'Antoine Crozat, escroc millionnaire sous Louis XIV* (Paris, Le Cherche Midi 2017), 29–33.

149 For the Phelypeaux family in charge of the French marine and colonies, see Pritchard, *In Search of Empire*, 238–41.

150 Édit en forme des Lettres-Patentes pour l'Etablissement de la Compagnie Royale de Saint-Domingue (Septembre 1698), in Saint-Méry, *Loix et constitutions*, 1, 611.

151 Lettres-Patentes Septembre 1698, Art. IV (611–12).

power. In exchange, it was to build churches and import clerics, transport in the first five years at least 1,500 white settlers and 2,500 African slaves, and thereafter annually 100 settlers and 200 slaves. Five percent of valuable minerals was to be granted to the king. The company also received exceptional authority to trade directly with other European nations and their overseas possessions – thus ensuring that Saint-Domingue would be much better provisioned than most of the French Antilles.[152] The directors would each invest 100,000 livres and the king would help financing the construction of harbours and provide defensive equipment. The customs of Paris would be applied, but the company was also endowed with legislative powers.[153]

The war in Europe had given a boost to the expansion of the plantations in Saint-Domingue. The growing demand for a workforce was in part met by buccaneering; slaves were taken from English and Spanish colonies, and the Dutch provided additional numbers. But this was hardly enough.[154] After the dismantling of the *Compagnie des Indes Occidentales* in 1674, its trading posts on the African West coast were sold to three financiers forming the *Compagnie de Sénégal.*[155] This provided

[152] Lettres-Patentes Septembre 1698, Art. IX, X, XIV, XXIII (613–14, 615). The company was also authorised to set up courts and police and to give judgments "under the Company's seal". It was entitled to make alliances with local "princes", construct fortifications and wage war and keep any booty thus gathered, Art. VIII, XXII (612–13, 614). Bonassieux, *Les grandes compagnies de commerce*, 413.

[153] Lettres-Patentes Septembre 1698, Art. XII–XII, XXIII (613, 615).

[154] French ships, it has been estimated, carried less 20 percent of the approximately 5,000 slaves that were brought annually to its Caribbean colonies, Pritchard, *In Search of Empire*, 217–18.

[155] The Senegal company had been established in November 1673 and confirmed in 1679. See Lettres-Patentes portant confirmation de la Compagnie du Sénégal et de ses Privileges, June 1679, in Saint-Méry, *Loix et constitutions*, 1, 325–6. The company was granted monopoly right to transport at least 2,000 slaves per year to the American colonies – a number that it utterly failed to reach despite the bounty promised by Colbert. But the Senegal company was seized by the creditors of the defunct *Compagnie des Indes Occidentales*, its slave-trading rights being sold for four years to a private financier. Despite the territorial gains of the reorganised company after 1679, the bankruptcy of its bankers led to its demise in shady circumstances in 1681. At this point its legacy became part of a struggle between two banking syndicates over the control of the united tax-farming operation of French overseas territories, the *Domaine d'Occident.* See Banks, 'Financiers, Factors and French Proprietary Companies', 92–6. The company eventually found itself in the hands of the secretary of the king, sieur d'Appoungy, from whom the king bought it in 1696, setting it up formally as a "royal" company. According to Letters Patent, the trading posts and the connected lands and installations were transferred to the new company whether they had been attained by conquests or treaties with African rulers; the new company was also authorised to conquer new lands as it saw

additional numbers but was no more able to meet the demand of the colonists on Saint-Domingue than its predecessor.[156] Therefore, the king yielded to pressure by high-ranking courtiers in 1684 to extract from the Senegal company an area extending from the Gambia river down to the Cape of Good Hope to a new group acting under the name of *Compagnie de Guinée*, entrusted with a twenty-year privilege to transport annually 1,000 to 1,200 slaves to the French Antilles, again with a subsidy by the king of 13 livres per healthy male slave.[157] The Guinea company received the right to build fortifications and trading posts and was exempted from half of entry duties in Africa and in the Antilles. It was this company that Crozat and the other shareholders of the Saint-Domingue venture enlisted in 1701 to transport the slaves they needed.[158] But the financier's sight was ultimately set on the Spanish Asiento – the contract for delivery of slaves to Spanish America. With the failure of the previous Asiento-holder and the prospect of a Bourbon king on the Spanish throne, the transfer to France was concluded on 27 August 1701– "*en vertu de la permission [du Roi] et sur la procuration de la Compagnie royale de Guinée*".[159] The king even loaned his ships for the twelve-year monopoly that the Guinea

appropriate. Lettres-Patentes, portant établissement d'une nouvelle Compagnie Royale du Sénégal (Mars 1696), Art. I, Saint-Méry, *Loix et Constitutions*, 1, 547–8.

156 According to the contract with the Saint-Domingue company, it was to bring to the island annually at least 400 slaves. Menard, *Le français qui possédait l'Amérique*, 58.

157 The Guinea company was also to import 1,200 marks in gold per year to France. Lettres-Patentes sur l'Etablissement d'une Compagnie pour le Commerce Exclusif aux Côtes d'Afrique (Compagnie de Guinée), January 1685, Art. XVI, in Saint-Méry, *Loix et constitutions*, 1, 409. See further, Bonassieux, *Les grandes compagnies de commerce*, 381–5; Pritchard, *In Search of Empire*, 216–17; Banks, 'Financiers, Factors and French Proprietary Companies', 98. In principle, no territorial rights were conferred beyond those covering the trading posts and fortifications necessary to defend them. These were, however, granted "*en pleine proprieté*" (Art. V). In due course, the company began trading not only with coastal but inland African communities and expanded its trading posts so that together with the Senegal company it became at times a "*de facto* proprietary colonial government in West Africa", Banks, 'Financiers, Factors and French Proprietary Companies', 101.

158 Not least, Crozat's recent biographer writes, because the Guinea company could import refined sugar tax-free – and refining sugar in Saint-Domingue (instead of in France) was one of the projects of his company, Menard, *Le français qui possédait l'Amérique*, 77.

159 Bonassieux, *Les grandes compagnies de commerce*, 388. For the transfer of the Asiento from the Portuguese to the French, see Anne-Charlotte Martineau, 'A Forgotten Chapter in the History of International Commercial Arbitration. The Slave Trade's Dispute Settlement System', 31 *Leiden Journal of International Law* (2018), 233–6.

company received to bring slaves to Spanish America under the name of the *Compagnie d'Assiente*.[160]

But even the Asiento company remained unable to fulfil its promised quota of 4,000 slaves per year. A major cause was the abominable treatment of the slaves – the company routinely counted a 40 percent loss during the middle passage, and frequently more. The crown attempted to deal with this by authorising captains to sell up to 10 percent of the slaves for their own profit. But mistreatment, corruption, shipwrecks, privateers, interloping and Spanish bureaucratic practices undermined these efforts.[161] With the Peace of Utrecht, finally, France lost the Asiento to the English South Sea Company. Its shareholders claimed to have lost two years' worth of profits (the monopoly was to continue until 1715); their legal battle against Spanish authorities would last at least until the 1770s.[162] Although this left the rights of the former Guinea company intact, the slave trade was opened – to Crozat's horror – in January 1716 to all French merchants.[163] This was a short-lived solution, however. The slave trade, together with the rest of the French overseas trade and colonial administration including the Senegal, Guinea and Saint-Domingue companies, was absorbed in John Law's *Compagnie d'Occident* (later *Compagnie des Indes*), which was to transport annually 3,000 slaves to the French Antilles and Louisiana.[164] When nothing came of this, either, the slave trade was opened to private merchants in 1725 "in return of payment of 25 livres per head on all slaves landed in the colonies".[165]

Meanwhile, Crozat had begun to look elsewhere for profit and found a target in French Louisiana. Small numbers of Frenchmen had settled there in the 1660s as an offshoot of unauthorised private exploration from *Nouvelle France*, and proposals for settlement and exploitation had been presented to the court in the 1690s. But Louisiana was very difficult territory. Sickness and conflict decimated the number of settlers such that in 1711 no more than 200 of them, wholly dependent on the

160 The story is very complicated but a good account may be found in Bonassieux, *Les grandes compagnies de commerce*, 381–402.

161 Ibid., 392–6; Menard, *Le français qui possédait l'Amérique*, 103–6.

162 Bonassieux, *Les grandes compagnies de commerce*, 407.

163 Crozat had expected to transfer the slave trading privileges from the Guinea company to his Saint-Domingue company, Menard, *Le français qui possédait l'Amérique*, 221.

164 Bonassieux, *Les grandes compagnies de commerce*, 400–1.

165 Pritchard, *In Search of Empire*, 217.

crown, had survived.[166] Had a presence in Louisiana not been strategically important to block passage of the English and the Spanish to the Mississippi river basin and control of much of the continent, the king might have given up the colony altogether. But Crozat let himself to be persuaded by the exaggerated portrait of the riches available behind the sombre facade – gold, silver, and exorbitant trading opportunities with the Spanish.[167] In September 1712 Crozat received a fifteen-year monopoly to all Louisiana trade plus title to all mines and territories that he would take into production.[168] In exchange, the financier was to bring small numbers of settlers to the colony to commence production and exploration.[169]

But it soon became obvious that the territory was too poor for cultivation. Nothing came of commerce with Mexico, either, as this was jealously guarded by a Spanish monopoly company. Or, as Crozat concluded, Louisiana was "a land uncultivated, inhabited by savages and rascals without commercial prospects and administered by imbeciles".[170] All effort to make the colony profitable proved in vain.

[166] Bonassieux, *Les grandes compagnies de commerce*, 377–8; Bernard Gainot, *L'empire colonial français – de Richelieu à Napoléon* (Paris, Armand Colin 2015), 38; W. J. Eccles, *French America* (University of Michigan Press 1990), 167–8. A useful description of the Louisiana colony's early years 1699–1712 is Cécile Vidal, 'French Louisiana in the Age of the Companies', in L. H. Roper & B. van Ruymbeke (eds), *Constructing Early Modern Empires. Proprietary Ventures in the Atlantic World 1500–1750* (Leiden, Brill 2007), 133–8.

[167] Menard, *Le français qui possédait l'Amérique*, 169–75.

[168] Lettres-Patentes accordant au sieur Crozat, privilège pour le commerce au Louisiane, Isambert, *Recueil général des Anciennes loix françaises, tome XX (1687–1715)* (Paris, Bélin 1830). Art. 2–3, 6 (578, 579). No seigneuries were granted, however, and the king kept to himself the authority to grant land titles. Eccles, *French America*, 171. Again the custom of Paris was to be applied in the whole of Louisiana. Art 7. (580). Every ship to Louisiana was to contain ten boys and girls as settlers. In case of need, Crozat could furnish one vessel to carry out slave trading on the African west coast, Art. 9, 14 (580, 581–2).

[169] He was expected to bring to the colony two ships by year, each containing forty young men and women as well as twenty-five tons of merchandise – a wholly insufficient number for any cultivation. Crozat therefore presented the crown with a plan to transport annually between 400 and 600 individuals, but the proposal was rejected by the controller of finances. By 1714, Crozat renounced his obligations of settlement but continued selling merchandise to the small community at a profit from 100 to 300 percent. Efforts to reorganise the colony's administration and finances were undermined by disputes between company directors and the governor and *ordonnateur* of the colony. See Vidal, 'French Louisiana', 138–43. In January 1717 Crozat resigned from the company and the process was begun to amalgamate it into John Law's *Compagnie de l'Occident*, 145–50.

[170] Menard, *Le français qui possédait l'Amérique*, 185.

Meanwhile, Crozat had become the target of one of the *Chambres de Justice* set up to examine the illegal activities of the crown's financiers, ending up being charged an extraordinary tax of 6,600,000 livres. Eventually the tax was halved, and the crown agreed to the return of Louisiana at the value of 2 million livres, which finally helped Crozat by alleviating the humiliation the French state had aimed to impose on one of its principal creditors.[171]

## An Empire of Commerce?

With the Peace of Utrecht, the French began to think anew about European political order and law. But it is striking how marginal the colonies remained for men like Saint-Pierre, Montesquieu or Mably. This was so notwithstanding that in Utrecht itself, "commercial and colonial interests had installed themselves at the heart of diplomatic discussions".[172] In the end, French losses in the Atlantic had been significant; "French imperial ambitions lay in ruins".[173] But perhaps surprisingly, the French literati did not mind this too much. Territorial expansion had proven dangerous and expensive. The religious objectives that had played an important part early on had disappeared; experience instructed Frenchmen to become sceptical about conversions. Critiques became even more vocal after the loss of Canada in the Peace of Paris (1763) and the disastrous end to the effort to populate Guyana in 1763–5. It was much better to expand colonial trade instead.[174] Here all debate concentrated around the diametrically opposed interests of metropolitan merchants and colonists in the maintenance of the *exclusif.*

Debates over commerce in mid-eighteenth-century France took an increasingly critical attitude towards old-regime clientilism, the waste and corruption that had been part of the administration of overseas colonies. The economic situation was dire. In the 1780s, servicing debt costs, for example, took more than half the crown's budget, and naval expenses during the American War of Independence had amounted to

[171] See ibid., 229–32.

[172] Lucien Bély, 'Objectifs et la conduite de la politique exterieure', in Jean-Christian Petitfils (ed.), *Le siècle de Louis XIV* (Paris, Perrin 2017), 370.

[173] Pritchard, *In Search of Empire*, 399–400.

[174] Jean Tarrade, *Le commerce colonial de la France à la fin de l'ancien régime. L'évolution du régime de l'Exclusif de 1763 à 1789*, 2 vols. (Université de Paris 1972), I, 14–22.

over 30 percent of annual revenue.[175] In the aftermath of the Treaty of Paris, many writers, especially among the Physiocrat coterie, began to advocate free trade and dropping the colonial *exclusif*. Mirabeau, for instance, attacked wholesale the unnatural idea of European states ruling their overseas territories uniquely in the metropolitan interests.[176] "The art of colonisation", he wrote, "was only in its most ignorant beginnings."[177] Operating under a metropolitan yoke, compelled to trade only with Frenchmen, the colonists had little incentive to produce all they could and had to interlope merely to survive. It was wrong to believe that loosening the ties to the colonies would be a loss – on the contrary, by governing them mildly, allowing them to produce and trade in accordance with local knowledge and interests, a natural relationship would develop between France and its overseas territories that would be more beneficial to everyone. The only loss would be with the merchants (with whom the Physiocrats anyway had little sympathy) who were constantly pushing the court to maintain a system profitable only to themselves.[178]

In this context Mirabeau and Quesnay used the awkward description of the sovereign as a "co-proprietor" of the lands of the colonists. This feudal-looking notion was actually based on the idea that because all value was produced by land, as assumed by the Physiocrats, crown income also had its source on land. It was thus not only in the crown's interest but also its right to see to maximal production that would benefit the farmer and the sovereign, each in their capacity of co-proprietors.[179] This, it was argued, would equalise the position of colonial lands with territories back home:

> What is a colony if not a province like all the provinces of the same state? It should enjoy the same prerogatives and provide the same contributions as the

[175] Paul Cheney, *Revolutionary Commerce. Globalization and the French Monarchy* (Harvard University Press 2010), 197.

[176] "Nothing is as singular and contradictory to the natural order than the conditions under which the European powers seem to accord their protection and their sovereignty to their colonies." Marquis de Mirabeau, *Philosophie rurale ou économie générale et politique de l'agriculture* (Amsterdam, Librairies associés 1763), 223 and generally 223–51. See also Mirabeau, *L'ami des hommes*, III, 111–49.

[177] Mirabeau, *L'ami des hommes*, III, 111.

[178] To the argument that the profits of merchants remained in France, Mirabeau responded by asking rhetorically why then did we not think similarly in respect of the "redoubtable fortunes of the embezzlers, extortionists, usurers, speculators etc. that also remain in the country"? *La philosophie rurale*, 227.

[179] Ibid., 233.

others. It should, I say, enjoy the same prerogative to prosper, to increase its riches, its population & its contribution.[180]

In any case, "the new world will eventually throw away the yoke of the old one", Mirabeau prophesied.[181] Was it then not more useful to have developed good relations that would enable France to benefit from overseas production later when it no longer needed to support it?[182] Such arguments were not without their effects – after months of preparatory work, *arrêts* of 1767 and 1784 opened a number of free ports in the French Caribbean.[183]

Monopoly companies came likewise under fire from Physiocrats such as Abbé André Morellet (1727–1819), a contributor to the *Encyclopédie*, who produced a detailed argument showing that the profits of the *Compagnie des Indes* had constantly declined since 1725 and that there was no realistic reason to expect they would increase in the future.[184] The situation on the peninsula was unstable; the company was under English attacks. The state had neither the capacity nor the interest to support it.[185] The difficulties would be much more easily overcome by free trade. Had not all progress in long-distance trade in fact been privately initiated?[186] To the company's retort that the proposal violated its rights, Morellet responded that property was indeed the "unique foundation on which one can establish the facade of society".[187] But free trade was precisely an application of property rights. A privilege was only a limited derogation and as such, hardly sacred. A privilege might have its reasons, but those were neither absolute nor eternal so that in a clash with property, the privilege had to yield.[188] Finally, Morellet observed that there was no reason to think that the state could not protect private traders as it had protected the company; on the contrary, "I am not afraid to claim that it is more just to wage ten years of war in retaliation of a violation

[180] Ibid., 233. [181] Mirabeau, *L'ami des hommes*, 3, (1756) 139–40.

[182] See further, Pernille Røge, 'A Natural Order of Empire. The Physiocratic Vision of Colonial France after the Seven Years' War', in Sophus Reinert & Pernille Røge (eds), *The Political Economy of Empire in the Early Modern World* (London, Palgrave 2013), 32–52.

[183] On the 1784 legislation, and its effects, see Mandelblatt, 'Feeding Slaves', 210–11.

[184] Abbé Morellet, *Mémoire sur la situation actuelle de la Compagnie des Indes* (Paris, Desaint 1769).

[185] Ibid., 136. [186] Ibid., 153–62, 229.

[187] Abbé Morellet, *Examen de la réponse de M.N. au mémoire de M. l'abbé Morellet* (Paris, Desaint 1769), 19.

[188] Ibid., 20.

of the law of nations, suffered by a private merchant, than to use a hundred thousand francs to protect a company".[189]

Many reasons have been cited for the failure of French early colonisation.[190] Operations outsourced to private enterprises were taken over by inexperienced financiers, reluctant to undertake the required long-term investments and whose motives often lay in the tax-farming and duty-reducing incentives.[191] Land was usually given to colonists for free and not as an investment for long-term use or production; by the time the problem was understood, most land was already taken.[192] State finances were overstretched by constant war; instead of a coherent policy, its activities were based on clientilist manoeuvring and ad hoc reactions to events on the spot. The nonchalance with which French nobles and the general public viewed economic activities played a role, as did the conflicts of interest around the *exclusif.* On the other hand, the colonies themselves possessed insufficient capital or credit to become viable economic entities on their own right – nor were authorities at home likely to have permitted this. Settlers were closely surveyed to prevent them from developing interests independent from the metropolis. Even as the French companies often failed to satisfy the colonists' needs, metropolitan authorities remained intransigent, though seldom with much effect.

Outsourcing liberated the king to pursue his European priorities. But it was a contradictory strategy. The letters patent normally required that action be taken to set up permanent settlements and bring Christianity to the infidel. This required funds that investors would agree to spend only against the receipt of monopoly trading rights. The grant of such rights, again, outraged commercial rivals who did all they could to create obstacles through provincial *parlements*, and by legally challenging the monopoly-holders. In the end, the system of ad hoc bargaining could not be made compatible with the strategic or ideological motives behind official policy. Official neglect of indigenous actors and interests made matters worse by making every arrangement reached by local actors unstable and merely short-term.

The loss of Canada (minus Saint-Pierre and Miquelon), in the Peace of 1763 was compensated for France by the return of its

[189] Morellet, *Mémoire*, 206.

[190] A thorough early summary is Joseph Chailley-Bérth, *Les compagnies de colonisation sous l'ancien régime* (Paris, Colin 1898), 95–163.

[191] Banks, 'Financiers, Factors, and French Proprietary Companies', 80.

[192] Christian Schöfer, *La France moderne et le problème colonial* (Paris, Alcan 1907), 16.

West Indies islands – Martinique and Guadeloupe, Saint-Lucia and the western part of Hispanola (Saint-Domingue). What remained on the Indian peninsula were five commercial ports and in Africa the island of Gorée. Although the empire was as fragmented as before, its nature now concentrated minds in the French administration to the plantation economy on the islands. Because the plantations were wholly dependent on slave work, this made the French empire in a sense hostage to increasingly problematic justifications about the morality and legality of human servitude.[193] For most of the time, enslaving Africans seemed fully natural for Frenchmen –something that all Europeans believed was the only way to operate sugar and tobacco plantations in tropical conditions. Gradually, however, it began to dawn on Frenchmen that it would be utterly incompatible with other things they were also beginning to believe in.

## "Pearl of the Antilles"

Private colonisation of the Antilles having failed, the French government began in 1674 a project to reassert direct control on the islands "[the] minuteness and purposefulness [of which was] unequalled since the great days of imperial Spain".[194] The colonies would now become, the jurist Paul-Ulrich Dubuisson wrote in 1786, despite the role of private actors in ruling them, integral parts of the Kingdom of France and provinces just like Brittany or Normandy.[195] The most important of the islands and the most profitable economic unit of the region was Saint-Domingue, the western part of Hispanola that Spain had officially ceded to France in the Peace of Ryswick in 1697.[196] Its principal

[193] As Gainot puts it, the image of the colonist in France changed at this time from that of the "soldier-labourer" to that of the slave-owner, *L'empire*, 91–2.

[194] G. V. Scammell, *The First Imperial Age. European Overseas Expansion c. 1400–1715* (London, Unwin 1989), 157. Each of the French Caribbean islands was ruled by a military governor directly under the king, assisted by *intendants* and a council dominated by wealthy colonists. See further ibid., 157–60.

[195] Paul-Ulrich Dubuisson, *Lettres critiques et politiques sur les colonies & la commerce* (Genève & Paris, 1786), 13–15. Dubuisson stressed the immense value of the Caribbean colonies for France and pleaded for the crown to increase its investment, including in importing ever greater numbers of slaves. See also Anthony Pagden, *The Lords of All the World. Ideologies of Empire in Spain, Britain and France c. 1500–c. 1800* (Yale University Press 1995), 128, 136–7.

[196] The other principal parts of France's Atlantic empire included Martinique, Guadeloupe, Saint-Lucie, Tobago, and Guyana in the southern and Louisiana in the western mainland.

products were sugar, coffee, indigo, tobacco and cocoa that were mostly re-exported to third countries. The economic interests were huge. France was the world's principal exporter of sugar, and the value of production from Saint-Domingue in 1789 alone was 217.5 million livres – almost twice as much as the total value of produce to England from Barbados, Jamaica and the rest of its Caribbean colonies combined.[197] No wonder then that France had been ready to offer Canada instead of Saint-Domingue to Britain in 1763. But for most of the revolutionary period the matter remained "simultaneously marginalized and yet critical for France's economic prosperity".[198]

The products were collected from plantations owned by whites or by *gens de couleur*, free blacks or persons of mixed blood, and operated by slave labour. Many of the plantation owners lived in Paris and administered their estates through caretakers, a practice that contributed to the abominable condition of the slave communities. The Caribbean islands had been from the start important targets for slave importations, authorised in 1648 by Louis XIII on condition that this would be accompanied by efforts at Christianisation. After France had lost the Asiento in the Peace of Utrecht, generous subsidies from the government enabled a massive increase of the volume of French slave trading that by 1790 had become second only to Britain. The number of African captives brought to the French Caribbean in the period 1775–1800 arose to 419,500.[199] At that time, three of the colonies (Saint-Domingue, Martinique and Guadeloupe) shared between themselves a slave population of almost 700,000 (a number equalling that of slaves on the whole North American continent) as against a white population of about 55,000 and of *gens de couleur* of 36,000.[200] It was

[197] Products from its Caribbean colonies accounted for something between one-third and two-thirds of the total of France's foreign trade. Laurent Dubois, *A Colony of Citizens. Revolution and Slave Emancipation in the French Caribbean 1787–1804* (University of North Carolina Press 2004), 31–3, 47–51.

[198] Curran, *The Anatomy of Blackness*, 11; Braudel, *Civilization & Capitalism Vol. III*, 411–12.

[199] The numbers are from Kwame Nimako & Glenn Willemsen, *The Dutch Atlantic. Slavery, Abolition and Emancipation* (London, Pluto Press 2011), 22.

[200] Robin Blackburn, *The Overthrow of Colonial Slavery, 1776–1848* (London, Verso 1988), 161. For more of the statistics, see Dubois, *A Colony of Citizens*, 50–1. The increase of the gap between white and slave population in Saint-Domingue is also striking. In 1681 whites constituted 65% and blacks 31% of the population (with the rest of mixed race). But in 1700 the number of whites had fallen to 29% and by 1764 to only 7%, while the respective numbers of slaves were 66% and 90.7%. The fact that 50% of the newly imported slaves died within three years gives an indication of the total numbers of slaves being traded. Ghachem, *The Old Regime and the Haitian Revolution*, 35–6.

therefore not surprising that the settlers lived in constant fear of revolts and would retaliate with extreme severity to any resistance. But it was only with the revolution in Paris that a larger and better organised insurgency could begin.[201]

The merchants of Nantes, Bordeaux and Saint-Malo possessed an influential voice in the *ancien régime*. Through the *Parlement* of Bordeaux and direct contacts with the court they obstructed reforms and critiqued efforts to relax the *exclusif* that endowed them with monopoly trading rights.[202] By contrast, colonists on Saint-Domingue resented their dependency on the metropolitan merchants' willingness to buy wholesale and their often-delayed payments.[203] Because goods from France were often unavailable or expensive, the colonists were keen to trade with the American mainland. Many of them would in fact have preferred independence.[204] In 1789 the colonists set up a powerful lobbying group with the Assembly (The Club *Massiac*) that consistently opposed the application of metropolitan laws, including the *Déclaration des droits de l'homme et du citoyen* in the colonies, advocating something like self-government for Saint-Domingue. In his letter to Abbé Raynal in 1786 the colonist Dubuisson well expressed the pro-slavery view: of course, principles of humanity would require that the slaves be set free. In the absence of a credible alternative in the colonies (he brushed aside as unrealistic the hope to replace slaves with free labour), however, the interests of the state and of the colonies require not only that it be continued but that trade in slaves be freed to ensure sufficient importation – "*la fortune public en depend*".[205]

The legal regulation of slavery took place by a Colonial Ordinance of 1685, the so-called *Code noir* (amended in 1724 and officially in force until 1848) prepared under Colbert. Its sixty articles were intended to cover all aspects of the lives of slaves and their relations

[201] For an overview, stressing the colonial origin of those movements, see Yves Benot, *Les lumières, l'esclavage, la colonization* (Paris, Découverte 2005), 210–29.
[202] Blackburn, *Overthrow*, 164–5.
[203] Braudel, *Civilization & Capitalism, Vol. III*, 277–8.
[204] The colonists borrowed the revolutionary vocabulary of *liberté* by which they did not mean renouncing slavery, however, but their own liberty from the "despotism" of the governor and the ministry of the marine that supervised the administration of "*l'exclusif*" and other aspects of the island's economy. Benot, *La Révolution française*, 45–56.
[205] Dubuisson, *Lettres critiques et politiques*, 260 and generally 257–80. For the pro-slavery *Cathécisme des colonies, pour servir à l'instruction des habitans de la France of 1791*, widely circulated among the members of the Assembly, see further Halpern, 'Entre esclavage et liberté'', 133–5.

with their masters.[206] The objective was to set up a workable system of forced labour under which the worst abuses would be prohibited in the interests of preventing rebellions.[207] The slaves were to be baptised and educated in the Catholic faith. They were to be liberated from work on religious holidays. The masters were expected to clothe and feed their slaves and take care of them when sick or aged. On the other hand, the code established a severe regime of punishments within a system of "private justice" that in some ways resembled the charter-based government of colonial territories. Again, maintenance of public order was outsourced to private actors – in the case the slave-owners and slave-owning communities themselves. A fugitive who had escaped for a month would have both his ears cut and one shoulder branded with the *fleur de lys*. After a second escape his knee bone would be removed and the second shoulder branded. Punishment after a third escape would be death.[208] Death would also follow from many other acts if that "would seem appropriate".[209] The code prohibited slaves from owning property and selling sugar cane on their own and the masters were not to allow them to work for the own welfare. It also deprived them of legal capacity. Perhaps surprisingly, the code nowhere associated slavery with race, but that it was called "*Code noir* "of course speaks volumes.

According to Article 59 of the code, freed slaves would enjoy "the same rights, privileges and immunities that belong to persons born free". But the objective of subordinating the slave regime to a system of public oversight suffered from inadequate implementation.[210] The conditions of slaves varied from one domain to another but it was rare

[206] Saint-Méry, *Loix et constitutions*, 1, 414–24. The text is also available e.g. in Sala-Molins, *Le Code Noir*.

[207] A detailed discussion of the ways in which the code sought to regularise and temper the slave regime, not so much out of humanitarian reasons as in order to maintain and strengthen colonial society, is Ghachem, *The Old Regime and the Haitian Revolution*. Particularly interesting is his claim that the *Code noir* was "an important source of human rights law and ideology" as it allowed the prosecution of masters violating it, 210. There were few such cases, however, and in the best known (the *Lejeune* case), as Ghachem reports, led to the ultimate release of the accused after a long and protracted series of trials. That story is recounted by Ghachem himself in 'Prosecuting Torture. The Strategic Ethics of Slavery in Pre-Revolutionary Saint-Domingue (Haiti)', 29 *Law and History Review* (2011), 985–1029.

[208] *Le Code Noir*, Art. 38. Saint-Méry, *Loix et constitutions*, 1, 420.

[209] "si le cas le requiert", Le *Code Noir*, Art. 33–5.

[210] Ghachem, *The Old Regime and the Haitian Revolution* also provides a thorough overview of the code's implementation.

for a slave to survive more than ten years. In the eighteenth century, the massive increase of the number of slaves in the French Caribbean accentuated the fear of rebellion, and new racially motivated legislation was adopted against the free blacks and the *gens de couleur* both on the islands as well as in metropolitan France.[211] In 1738, for example, it became necessary to obtain prior permission to send or bring slaves into France as domestic servants or in order to learn trades or be educated in religion. Concern had arisen, it was explained, that these persons might actually not participate in such activities but would use the opportunity to remain in the country.[212] In the 1760s and 1770s new legislation was adopted so as to prevent the presence not only of slaves but of all coloured persons in France.[213] Manumissions were limited and mixed marriages outlawed. Coloured persons were prohibited from taking "white" names or dressing in the manner of whites. They were also prevented from entering many professions, including those of a medical doctor or lawyer.[214] Overall, what came to be called *le préjugé du couleur* entered as formal part of colonial legislation.[215]

## Revolutions 2: Saint-Domingue

The decision to convoke the Estates-General in April 1788 raised hope among the abolitionists that something might be done to apply enlightenment principles in the administration of the French plantation colonies. For this purpose, the *Société des Amis des Noirs* was set up with a modest programme for the cessation of the slave trade and gradual abolition of slavery itself. It was clear for the founders, such as

[211] Early in the eighteenth century, the government began to worry about the large numbers of liberated slaves, subordinating manumissions to "legitimate reason" as confirmed by the governor or commissioner. Déclaration sur affranchissemenets, 24 octobre 1713, in Petit, *Traité sur le gouvernement des esclaves*, 1, 61–4.

[212] Ordonnance sur la passage des Esclaves in France, 15 décembre 1738, ibid., 130–7.

[213] In August 1777 Louis XVI issued major new legislation, "*Police des Noirs*", formally motivated by the "inconvenience" of increased litigation by slaves for their freedom under the old adage that "there are no slaves in France", but actually in response to a racist worry about disorder and moral decay. There were about 4,000 blacks in France at the time. Neither this nor the earlier laws that demanded the registration of (black) slaves were very efficiently implemented. See Peabody, *"There Are No Slaves in France"*, 115–18.

[214] Dubois, *A Colony of Citizens*, 74.

[215] Gauthier, 'Le Mercier de la Rivière', 265–7; Dominique Roger, 'De l'origine du préjugé du couleur en Haiti', in Marcel Dorigny (ed.), *Haiti. Première république noire* (Société Française d'Histoire des Outre-Mers 2004), 84–101; Gainot, *L'empire colonial français*, 129–30.

the journalist Jacques-Pierre de Warville Brissot (1754–93), that immediate abolition would have destroyed the economy not only of the islands, but also of France itself. The realistic way ahead lay in beginning with the slave trade and allowing the planters gradually to move to the utilisation of free labour, even as the colonists had no intention to do so.[216] This was technically easy to attain by simply cancelling the bounty that the government had agreed to pay for each imported slave. It was also expected to immediately improve the situation of the slaves.[217]

*Amis* followed the example of similar societies in England and the United States with which it entered in active correspondence.[218] It operated as a lobbying channel within the Estates-General and, for example, sent an anti-slavery circular to the electoral districts as a result of which about one in ten of the *cahiers de doléances* raised the slavery issue on the Estates' agenda in 1789. The society gathered philanthropists, clerics, radical aristocrats, colonial officials and practitioners of high finance worried about the situation in the colonies and "saw themselves as the most enlightened representatives of a truly national interest".[219] Members included Condorcet, Mirabeau, la Rochefoucauld and Henri Grégoire whom we already met in the previous chapter proposing a code for the law of nations and who had quite radical views on the "regeneration" of the French nation.[220] A man of contrasting tendencies with an instinct for survival, Grégoire supported violent action against vandalism during Thermidor, wanted to purify the French language from its alien elements and critiqued women's participation in public life. He was opposed to the campaign against the clergy and saw the Catholic church as the spiritual heart around which a republican order was to be established. But he was quite consistent in his defence of the equality of blacks, celebrating their intellectual capacities in a widely read post-revolutionary tract

[216] Marcel Dorigny & Bertrand Gainot, *La société des Amis des Noirs 1788–1799. Contribution à l'histoire de l'abolition de l'esclavage* (Paris, UNESCO 1998), 32–5. Condorcet, for example, one of the most famous members of the society, had argued in 1781 that a seventy-year period would be appropriate for the gradual liberation of the slaves. *Réflexions sur l'esclavage des nègres*, 88–97. See also Benot, *La Révolution française*, 33–4.

[217] Benot, *La Révolution française*, 91–3.

[218] See Dorigny & Gainot, *La société des Amis*, 20–4.

[219] Blackburn, *Overthrow*, 170.

[220] On the revolutionary language of "regeneration" as used by Grégoire, see especially Alyssa Goldstein Sepinwall, *The Abbé Gregoire and the French Revolution. The Making of Modern Universalism* (California University Press 2005), 90–108.

on their cultural achievements.[221] Grégoire had been speaking in favour of the application of the Declaration of Rights of Man and Citizen in August 1789 and in December of the same year put his name to an initiative for the abolition of the slave trade once the question of *gens de couleur* had been disposed of. In subsequent years, as well as into the Napoleonic period, he kept insisting on human perfectibility and equality and stressing moral regeneration as the objective of republican education. The universalism that had prompted him to make the proposal for a *Déclaration de droit des gens* emerged less from his interest in natural law, however, than from the assumption of human equality in the eyes of God.[222]

But the prospect of an Estates-General had also energised the colonists on Saint-Domingue who wished to use the occasion to expand their autonomy.[223] For the purpose of representation they organised an illegal election of deputies among the white planters, raising the fury of the free coloureds who were supposed to enjoy equality under the *Code noir* but had in practice been subjected to humiliating limitations to their professional activity and personal situation.[224] A proposal for the representation of the colonies had been rejected in the previous year owing to the view that their legal status differed from the provinces. They were mere "possessions of the crown".[225] The Assembly debated the matter in June–July 1789; in the end, the colonists received six seats

[221] Abbé Grégoire, 'De la littérature des nègres ou recherches sur leurs facultés intellectuelles, leurs qualités morales et leur littérature', in Abbé Grégoire, *Écrits sur les noirs*, tome 1: *1789–1808* (Paris, L'Harmattan 2012) 103–226. For Grégoire's activities as a member of the *Société des Amis*, see Marcel Dorigny, 'The Abbé Grégoire and the Société des Amis des Noirs', in J. Popkin & R. Popkin (eds), *The Abbé Grégoire and His World* (Dordrecht, Springer 2000), 27–39.

[222] Dorigny, 'Abbé Grégoire and the Société des Amis', 33.

[223] It was a constant complaint among the colonists that Paris was exercising "ministerial tyranny". Although the *exclusif* had been partially relaxed in the 1760s, any controls from the capital were met with angry reaction by the merchants (once even leading to the governor's withdrawal). See Mitchell B. Garrett, *The French Colonial Question 1789–1791* (Cornell University 1918), 20–1.

[224] On the early colonial assemblies, see Laurent Dubois, *Avengers of the New World. The Story of the Haitian Revolution* (Harvard University Press 2005), 73–4 and Jeremy D. Popkin, *You Are All Free. The Haitian Revolution and the Abolition of Slavery* (Cambridge University Press 2010), 32–3, 70. The use of the *Code noir* by the *gens du couleur* to support their equality with the free white population and to ameliorate the situation of the slave population is discussed in great detail in Ghachem, *The Old Regime*.

[225] Carminella Biondi, 'Introduction', in *1789. Les colonies ont la parole. Anthologie*, tome 1 (Paris, L'Harmattan 2016), viii.

and six alternates against protests by men such as Mirabeau and Grégoire, pointing out the injustice of the fact that they represented only 10 percent of the colonies' population.[226] As the Assembly passed the *Déclaration des droits de l'homme et du citoyen* in August, Mirabeau still believed that it would apply in the colonies as well.[227]

The king's representative Jacques Necker opened the meeting of the Estates on 5 May 1789. He repeatedly referenced the colonial question and the plight of the slaves in such a way that the *Amis* began to expect that action would be taken. The principal aspect of the problem at this time was the status of the free persons of colour of whom there were in Saint-Domingue perhaps 22,000 – a number not far from that of white colonists – engaged in all kinds of trades, the military, and often as owners of plantations.[228] Many of the white colonists, especially of the "*petits blancs*", resented their activities, above those of free black men, many of whom had succeeded in setting up thriving businesses. These men followed the events in Paris with the greatest attention. In July, two wealthy mulattoes, Julian Raimond and Vincent Ogé, arrived in Paris to lobby for their representation.[229] In a well-received memorandum, Grégoire suggested that the *gens de couleur* ought to be recognised as citizens in the full meaning of the term and that the racist limitations on their family situation and right to professions were to be immediately lifted. "Feudalism", he wrote, "had been produced in another way in our colonies; the preservation of the abuses is still another reason to lift

[226] On the admission of the colonists to the Assembly on 4 July 1789, see further, Garrett, *French Colonial Question*, 10–18; David Geggus, 'Racial Equality, Slavery, and Colonial Secession during the Constituent Assembly', 94 *American Historical Review* (1989), 1293; Benot, *La Révolution française*, 44–5; Blackburn, *Overthrow*, 172–5; Gainot, *L'empire colonial français*, 114–18.

[227] Garrett, *French Colonial Question*, 19.

[228] The numbers given by Gainot for Saint-Domingue in 1789 are 27,717 for the whites and 21,808 for the free coloured population, *L'empire colonial français*, 94. The total number of free persons of colour in the French Caribbean approached 40,000. They included both wealthy, slave-owning families and poor labourers. All of them, however, were by existing legislation "consigned in perpetuity to a dishonoured intermediary class", Geggus, 'Racial Equality', 1297. Gordon S. Brown, *Toussaint's Clause. The Founding Fathers and the Haitian Revolution* (University Press of Mississippi 2005), 33–4.

[229] Raimond, for instance, had been received politely in Versailles in the 1780s, without this occasioning any change in metropolitan attitudes. The visits in Paris by the two men in 1789 were no more successful. Popkin, *You Are All Free*, 34–6, 71–2. On the "one-quarter mulatto" Raimond, see further Vertus Saint-Laurent, 'Relations internationales et la classe politique en Haiti (1789–1814)', in Marcel Dorigny (ed.), *Haiti. Première république noire* (Paris, Société française d'outre-mer 2007), 156–7.

it": "vice and virtue ought to be the only measures of public consideration and equality the sole measure of human rights".[230]

This argument was not related to the abolition of slavery. On the contrary, many of the free persons of colour were themselves slave-owners and supporters of the existing system. It was also argued that giving the free coloured persons equal rights would lift pressure towards more far-reaching reforms. Nevertheless, the opposition from the colonists remained strong and they won a first victory on 4 August 1789 as no mention of slavery or the slave trade was made at the famous session where status privileges were renounced.[231] By this time, the treatment of the free coloured persons had also taken an openly racist tone. In a letter from the Ministry of Marine, cited by Raimond in his petition to the Assembly, the ministry had refused to class men of mixed race with the free white colonists:

> [S]uch a favour would tend to destroy the difference that nature has established between the blacks and the whites as well as the political assumption [*préjugé Politique*] that has been careful to maintain a distance that people of colour and their descendants could never attain.[232]

In December, the Assembly set up a colonial committee, which included no abolitionists, to find a solution for the legal status of the colonies.[233] The result was a decree and a "constitutional instruction" of March 1790 that sought to keep the unity of the empire but allowed both colonists and metropolitan merchants to maintain much of their original position. External affairs would be directed to metropolitan bodies but internal affairs – in practice the regulation of slavery and the status of free men of colour – were left to the colonies themselves. French sovereignty would remain intact and the colonists and free

[230] Abbé Grégoire, 'Mémoire en faveur des gens de couleur au sang-melés de St Domingue, et des autres isles françaises de l'Amérique adressée à l'Assemblée Nationale', in Abbé Grégoire, *Écrits sur les noirs I: 1789–1808* (Paris, L'Harmattan 2012), 28.

[231] Geggus, 'Racial Equality', 1296. For the Assembly's treatment of the question of "free men of colour" in the fall of 1789, see further ibid., 1297–1303.

[232] "une pareille grâce tendrait à détruire la différence que la nature a mise entre les Blancs & les Noirs & que la préjugé Politique a eu soin d'entretenir une distance à laquelle les Gens de couleur & leurs descendants ne devaient jamais atteindre", J. Raimond et al., Supplique et Pétition des Citoyens de couleur (2 décembre 1789), cited in Claude Meillassoux, 'Préface. De classe et de couleur', in Florence Gauthier (ed.), *Périssent les colonies plutôt qu'un principe!* (Paris, Société des études robespierristes 2002), 13.

[233] Garrett, *French Colonial Question*, 22–4; Cheney, *Revolutionary Commerce*, 204–5.

coloured persons were to fight out their disagreement at home.[234] Frustrated, Ogé left Paris and began a short-lived rebellion on Saint-Domingue at the end of which he was captured and executed.[235] That no mention was made of the colonies in the Constitution of 1791 consolidated the status quo; the island was left to be ruled by the white colonists in more or less tense cooperation with the governor.[236]

The atmosphere in regard to the status of the *gens de couleur* changed in the course of spring 1791 as a result of growing resentment against wealthy aristocrats in the Jacobin club. The colonial assemblies were unable to control the increasingly volatile situation in Saint-Domingue, and the view that the *droits de l'homme* ought to play some role in the colonies was gaining ground.[237] On 15 May, a compromise decree was passed that gave civil rights to a limited number of non-whites born of free parents (a number of perhaps 400 out of the 22,000).[238] Addressing the *gens de couleur*, Grégoire was jubilant – "finally you, too, have a fatherland!"[239] He foresaw the beginning of a process that would in due course lead to the emancipation of the slaves, too – precisely what the colonists had feared.[240] Another person to welcome the decision was the young jurist Léger-Félicité Sonthonax (1763–1813) a friend of Brissot's, who had since 1790 published strongly worded articles in the *Révolutions de Paris* on the need to grant equality to free persons of colour, writing of a torrent that would sweep the old order of Europe away:

234 The instruction gave voting rights to "any person" who would enjoy this right in France – thus leaving colonists and the *gens de couleur* to battle with each other over what this might mean. Benot, *La Révolution française*, 72–4. The committee's chairman, Antoine Barnave, adopted the external vs. domestic affairs distinction from British imperial legislation and pushed it through with the colonists' help irrespective of the principled difficulty many saw in separating such affairs from each other. See Pagden, *Lords of All the World*, 144–6; Cheney, *Revolutionary Commerce*, 208–18.

235 Benot, *La Révolution française*, 71–2; Dubois, *Colony of Citizens*, 100–4; Dubois, *Avengers of the New World*, 87–8; Popkin, *You Are All Free*, 71–2.

236 David Geggus, 'The Caribbean in the Age of Revolution', in David Armitage & Sanjay Subrahmanyam (eds), *The Age of Revolution in Global Context c. 1760–1840* (London, Palgrave 2010), 92.

237 Garrett, *French Colonial Question*, 83, 92–7.

238 Ibid., 98–117; Geggus, 'Racial Equality', 1302–3; Pierre Pluchon, *Histoire de la colonisation française. Le premier empire colonial, des origines à la Restauration* (Paris, Fayard 1991), 878–82.

239 Abbé Grégoire, 'Lettre aux citoyens de couleur et nègres libres de Saint-Domingue, et les autres isles françaises de l'Amérique', in Abbé Grégoire, *Écrits sur les noirs*, tome 1:*1789–1808* (Paris, L'Harmattan 2012), 49, 51.

240 On the complex efforts of the French administration to ameliorate the situation of the slaves while disencouraging hopes for liberation, see Ghachem, *The Old Regime*, 121–66; Garrett, *French Colonial Question*, 104–5.

Yes, we dare to predict with confidence that the day will come – and the day is not too far off – when you will see a curly-haired African, relying only on his virtue and good sense, coming to participate in the legislative process in the midst of our national assemblies.[241]

The decision of 15 May came too late to turn the tide in the colonies, however, and was directed at the wrong problem anyway. An uprising of as many as 30,000 slaves began in August in the northern part of Saint-Domingue; up to a thousand white planters were massacred and whole villages put to the torch. The rebellion spread rapidly over most of the colony. Although the slaves occasionally employed the revolutionary vocabulary of liberty, their initial objective was only to relax the regime of punishments and to allow, as actually provided by the *Code noir*, one day a week to cultivate their own plots. It is not known how many of the slaves had heard about the Declaration but rumours circulated about an impending abolition by the king; this made white planters appear to be counter-revolutionary traitors.[242]

The revolt was initially assumed to remain short-lived. Apprehensions arose, however, when it appeared that the white colonists might request assistance from the British or even use the situation to press for secession. The Assembly despatched a commission in November 1791 to negotiate with the rebels. But this failed to calm the situation; fighting between the slaves and the whites continued, with the free coloureds caught in the middle. At this point, the Assembly agreed to change tactic and, influenced by the *Amis*, decided that the key to controlling the situation lay with the latter. It thus passed a Declaration on 28 March 1792, promulgated into law on 4 April, proclaiming full civil rights to all free men of colour and ordering new general elections as soon as practicable.[243] In order to see to the implementation of the law, the Assembly despatched further civil commissioners to Saint-Domingue in July 1792, among them Sonthonax as well as Etienne Polverel, also a lawyer, who shared his colleague's abolitionist views.[244]

[241] Léger-Félicité Sonthonax, quoted in Robert Louis Stein, *Léger-Félicité Sonthonax. The Lost Sentinel of the Republic* (London, Associated University Press 1985), 21, 82. For Sonthonax's articles, see Benot, *La Révolution française*, 130–2.

[242] Dubois, *A Colony of Citizens*, 85–98. For a careful assessment of the degree to which the slaves could have been aware of the protective provisions of the *Code noir* or what was happening in Paris, see Ghachem, *The Old Regime*, 255–76.

[243] Dubois, *Avengers of the New World*, 125–31; Blackburn, *Overthrow*, 195; Pluchon, *Histoire*, 890–3.

[244] A third commissioner, Jean-Antoine Ailhaud, soon returned to Paris. For the establishment and arrival in Saint-Domingue of this commission in September

The monarchy had fallen in August 1792 and Sonthonax and Polverel had no difficulty in working for a republic. They began their efforts towards a multiracial order by sending royalist officers and the governor-general back to France. The colonists were especially outraged when Sonthonax allowed the hearing of slaves' claims against their masters, enlisted black officers with his troops and declared new elections based on equality with free men of colour.[245] In addition to the slave uprising, the civil commissioners were now also faced with a white revolt. Whatever Sonthonax's own views, his commission was only to implement the decree of 4 April on the *gens de couleur,* his principal allies, who were as committed to slavery as the whites. But forcing the slaves back to the plantations proved impossible; even offers of amnesties were of no avail. Bands of slaves had been formed into an efficient fighting force and general talk of liberty was spreading wider.[246] By spring of 1793 France had declared war on England and Spain and white colonists were secretly negotiating with the English on secession. In this situation, Sonthonax turned to Toussaint Louverture (1743–1803), a black general commanding Spanish troops on the island. Toussaint had been born in Saint-Domingue but as a royalist was recruited on the Spanish side to fight the republicans whom he regarded as nothing short of treasonous. Having little faith in Sonthonax's intentions, he declined the latter's request of assistance and instead gave out a rights manifesto of his own:

> It is impossible that you would be fighting for the rights of man after all the cruelties that you have exercised on a daily basis. . . . It is with us that the real rights of man and justice reign! We treat the whole world with humanity and fraternity, even our most cruel enemies, and forgive them out of the kindness of our hearts, and it is with softness that we invite them to repent their errors.[247]

1792, see Stein, *Sonthonax*, 41–5. On the relations between the two lawyers, Sonthonax at the time 28 and Polverel 55 years old, see Jacques de Cauna, 'Polverel et Sonthonax, deux voies pour l'abolition de l'esclavage', in Marcel Dorigny (ed.), *Léger-Félicité Sonthonax. La première abolition de l'esclavage. La Révolution française et la Révolution de Saint-Domingue* (Paris, Publications de la société française d'histoire d'outre-mer 2005), 47–53.

245 Stein, *Sonthonax*, 48–60, 84–6; Pluchon, *Histoire*, 890–3.

246 Dubois, *Avengers of the New World*, 141, 145–51.

247 "Il n'est pas possible que vous combattiez où se trouve le droit de l'homme, après toutes les cruautés que vos [sic] exercé journellement. . . . C'est chez nous que règne le véritable droit de l'homme et de la justice! nous [sic] recevons tous le monde avec humanité, et fraternité, meme nos plus cruels ennemis, et les pardonnions de bon Coeur, et c'est avec la douceur que nous fésons recenir de leurs erreurs", Toussaint

Under pressure from English and Spanish troops, and with a new governor determined to get rid of him and his colleague, Sonthonax turned to the only direction from which help might be available, declaring free all the "Negro warriors" that would join him.[248] When this did not suffice, on 29 August 1793 he gave a general abolition order, drafted in the French and Creole languages, vastly exceeding his instructions. By producing a text of thirty articles with a long preamble Sonthonax put to work the legislative skills he had acquired as an official of the *Parlement* of Paris. All slaves would be immediately free and enjoy the rights of French citizenship. The Declaration of the Rights of Man and Citizen was to be printed and distributed everywhere. The decree stressed the duty to continue work on the plantations – now with salary – and called upon its addressees to demonstrate the error of the prejudice about the laziness of the blacks. Much of the detail sought to ensure that work on the plantations – now with salary – would continue. On that same day Toussaint declared he would be fighting to end slavery.[249]

Since the declaration of April 1792 to free the *gens du couleur* the only act passed by the Assembly in Paris on the colonies had been the decision to abolish the subsidies for slave trading (July 1793), without however abolishing the practice itself.[250] Even Robespierre was vacillating, attacking his arch-enemy, the abolitionist Brissot, for having "enfranchised and armed the negroes so as to destroy our colonies".[251]

Louverture à Monsieur Chanlatte jeune, 27 August 1793, in *Toussaint Louverture, De l'Esclavage au pouvoir* (Paris, l'Ecole 1979), 40.

248 On Sonthonax's conflict with General Galbaud, see Stein, *Sonthonax*, 63–77.

249 For the eight-page text of Sonthonax's proclamation, see Dorigny (ed.), *Sonthonax*, 196–205. For the process leading up to the decree, see Benot, *La Révolution française*, 176–9; Blackburn, *Overthrow*, 197–203; Popkin, *You Are All Free*, 266–71. For a discussion of the different views among historians on Sonthonax's motives, see Dannelle Gutarra, 'The Discourses of Sonthonax's Mission in Saint-Domingue. The Coda to the Abolition of Slavery', 17 *French Colonial History* (2017), 81–102. The second commissioner, Polverel, had been known as an anti-aristocrat defender of common properties. He also at times disagreed with Sonthonax, once suggesting that the white planters' properties ought to be immediately granted to the former slaves. Eventually he followed Sonthonax (whose jurisdiction had been limited to the West Province) so that after the third commissioner, Delpech, who opposed abolition, conveniently died, abolition was declared in the whole colony on 31 October 1793. Stein, *Sonthonax*, 91–4; Popkin, *You Are All Free*, 277–8.

250 For the heated debate, see Benot, *La Révolution française*, 91–4.

251 Pluchon, *Histoire*, 894. For the way in which Robespierre and his friend Camille Desmoulins tried not to antagonise the wealthy merchants of the port cities in their struggle against the "Brissotins", see Benot, *La Révolution française*, 100–2; Florence

To bring the Saint-Domingue situation to the notice of the Assembly a three-man delegation was sent to Paris – a white proprietor, a mulatto and a black officer – only to be arrested at the colonists' demand. However, they were rapidly set free and seated with the Convention in a dramatic session on 16 Pluviôse year II (4 February) 1794, which ended with the passing of the final abolition decree:

> The National Convention declares the slavery of the blacks abolished in all the colonies; consequently all men irrespective of color living in the colonies are French citizens and shall enjoy all the rights provided by the Constitution.[252]

It had taken two and half years from the insurrection on Saint-Domingue for the deputies finally to accept something that ought to have been obvious in 1789. Tactical manoeuvring by colonial property owners, including slave owners, had been effective.[253] But even among the "*amis*", a majority did not favour immediate abolition. Perhaps paradoxically, the arrest of the Girondists during the coup of 31 May–2 June 1793 also locked up many of the most outspoken abolitionists, like Brissot, in part because they had been portrayed in Jacobin propaganda as responsible for the slave rebellion. The attitude of Robespierre and his friends – especially their alignment with the merchants of the port cities – was ambivalent; the famous statement about "perish the colonies rather than a principle" did not represent all Robespierre had to say about the matter. But whatever the strategic fluctuations, the (Montagnard) Constitution of 24 June 1793 did contain an unequivocal provision to the effect that "no person could sell

Gauthier, *Triomphe et mort du droit naturel en Révolution 1789–1795–1802*, tome 1 (Presses Universitaires de Paris, 1992), 220–5.

252 *Archives Parlementaires de 1787 à 1860. Première série*, 84 (Paris, Librairie administrative P. Dupont 1875), 284 and the debate 276–85. For the events leading up to the decree, see Benot, *La Révolution française*, 181–7; Popkin, *You Are All Free*, 327–75; Robin Blackburn, *The American Crucible. Slavery, Emancipation and Human Rights* (London, Verso 2013), 190–1; Pluchon, *Histoire*, 895–7. Although not expressly mentioned in it, the decree was understood to have prohibited the slave trade as well.

253 Of the 1,100 or so members of the National Assembly of 1789 some 150 were owners of colonial property, and many more possessed interests in the colonies. The skill with which the colonial "deputies" (whose credentials were interrogated) manipulated the debate in the Assembly up until the decree of 16 Pluviôse is highlighted in Benot, *La Révolution française*. The efficient (though ultimately unsuccessful) lobbying in Paris by the colonists Page and Brulley also occupies much of Popkin's account of the path to the abolition decree, *You Are All Free*, 329–56. Their activities were ended as all colonists who had been members of the "illegal" assemblies were arrested soon after the passing of the 4 February decree, ibid., 368.

themselves or be sold; the human person is not alienable property".[254] The Constitution also made no distinction between metropolitan France and the colonies. As a result of this, and of subsequent decrees by the Convention, former slaves in France's Caribbean colonies turned in principle into citizens, though Martinique, Tobago and Saint-Lucia fell into British hands and slavery was reinstated.[255]

But abolition on Saint-Domingue did not bring fighting to an end. It left white colonists and many *gens de couleur* outraged, and few slaves trusted the assurances from Paris. After the fall of the Brissotins, colonial lobbyists achieved the recall of Sonthonax and Polverel to respond to charges of treason.[256] Although Sonthonax was eventually cleared of the charges, colonial interests remained active. The Thermidor Constitution of 5 Fructidor year III (22 August 1795) maintained the prohibition of slavery and defined the colonies as "integral parts of the republic ... subject to the same constitutional law".[257] On 1 January 1798 the colonies were organised into nine departments whose inhabitants were endowed with a status identical to that of citizens of the metropolis. Historians have been divided about the nature of this policy: was it a manifestation of France's colonial ambitions or instead meant to highlight the equality of the

254 Constitution of 1793, Article 18. But even then, the Convention was anything but clear on the issue: some continued to agree with Robespierre that the slave revolt was a counter-revolutionary, perhaps even royalist plot and that Sonthonax and Polverel were to be declared outlaws. Eventually, this view was left in a minority as the Constitution of 1793 was adopted, only to rise again in the Thermidorean period. On the debates in the spring of 1793, see Benot, *La Révolution française*, 166–75. For a somewhat different view, see Gauthier, *Triomphe et mort*, 216–20.

255 On Guadeloupe, for instance, the British were ousted in 1794 after which slavery was abolished. The former slaves were, however, expected to join the army or continue work on the plantations under the autocratic rule of the civil commissioner Victor Hugues. See especially Dubois, *A Colony of Citizens*, 189–221. See also Miranda Frances Spieler, 'The Legal Structure of Colonial Rule during the French Revolution', 66 *The William and Mary Quarterly* (2009), 367.

256 The arrest and recall of the two civil commissioners in the summer of 1794 and the complex proceedings in a "Commission of the Colonies" during the first six months of 1795 are discussed in Jeremy D. Popkin, 'Thermidor, Slavery, and the "Affaire des Colonies"', 38 *French Historical Studies* (2015), 67–71 and Yves Benot, 'Le procès Sonthonax ou les débats entre les accusateurs et les accusés dans l'affaire des colonies', in Marcel Dorigny (ed.), *Léger-Félicité Sonthonax. La première abolition de l'esclavage. La Révolution française et la Révolution de Saint-Domingue* (Paris, Publications de la société française d'histoire d'outre-mer 2005), 55–63. See also Stein, *Sonthonax*, 107–20; Marc Belissa & Yannick Bosc, *Le Directoire. La République sans la démocratie* (Paris, La fabrique 2018), 213–15. Polverel died in the course of the proceedings.

257 Constitution of 1795, Title I, Article 6. See further, Gauthier, *Triomphe et mort*, 260–9.

overseas territories within the metropolis?[258] It was both. Boissy d'Anglas, who presented the draft text to the Convention, avoided racist language. Instead, he believed that "*les productions de l'Amérique nous étant devenues nécessaires*", it was impossible to imagine the independence of the colonies; this would only make them fall under British rule. In renouncing their chains, Boissy argued, the slaves had not looked for political but physical freedom. This would be granted to them as French citizens. But they were also expected to take up salaried work at the plantations. Also, there would be no colonial assemblies but, as Boissy explained, by participating in the legislature in Paris, the inhabitants would be best integrated as Frenchmen.[259]

A majority of the Convention in the summer of 1795 supported continuing emancipation.[260] But the new constitution left many questions open and connecting voting rights with property ownership undermined former slaves' political standing. Moreover, monarchist victory in the elections of spring 1797 prompted the legislature to move against representatives from Saint-Domingue and to recall the Directory's civilian "agents" (among whom were Sonthonax and the spokesman of the *gens de couleur*, Julian Raimond). The new majority might have established military rule on Saint-Domingue and withdrawn the abolition decree had not the republican coup of 18 Fructidor (4 September 1797) led to a massive anti-royalist backlash, the arrest and deportation of monarchist and colonist leaders to Guyana and return to republican legality.[261]

But the Directory's attitude towards slavery was far from unambiguous.[262] Even a staunch abolitionist such as Condorcet advocated only gradual liberation, and Raimond held that the Convention needed to "reconcile … its principles of justice with the commercial interests of

258 Belissa & Bosc, *Le Directoire*, 214–15; Popkin, 'Thermidor, Slavery', 61–82; Gauthier, *Triomphe et mort*, 269–80.

259 Boissy d'Anglas, *Réimpression de l'ancien Moniteur*, vol. 25, séance de 23 Thermidor year III (10 August 1795), 418–20.

260 See Popkin, 'Thermidor, Slavery', 71–7.

261 See Jouda Guetata, 'Le refus d'application de la constitution de l'an III à Saint-Domingue 1795–1797', in Gauthier (ed.), *Périssent les colonies*, 81–90; Bernard Gainot, 'Métropole/Colonies. Projets constitutionnels et rapport des forces 1798–1802', in Yves Benot & Marcel Dorigny (eds), *Rétablissement de l'esclavage dans les colonies françaises 1802* (Paris, Maisonneuve & Larose 2003), 15–18.

262 Title VI, Articles 155 and 156 of the 1795 Constitution introduced a kind of special regime to the colonies by mandating the Directory to appoint administrators of the colonies and to send "*agents particuliers*" to govern them with the powers of the Directory itself.

the metropole".[263] Economic aspect dominated. Was it really the case – as the Physiocrats had argued – that free labour was also more profitable? Many doubted this and some suggested that forced labour might still be necessary, perhaps without calling it slavery.[264] Towards 1800 an increasing number of voices took up racist theories of natural hierarchy. For example, the Saint-Domingue jurist and publicist, perhaps the colonists' most highly appreciated representative, Médéric Moreau de Saint-Méry (1750–1819), produced an elaborate classification of African races with detailed descriptions of their qualities and usefulness in colonial production. All blacks to him were lazy and slow-witted, and even the ones living in Saint-Dominque as freemen were "*indolens & paresseux, querelleurs, bavards, menteurs & adonneurs au larcin*".[265] He also found more than 120 variations of species of mulatto and *gens de couleur* with different qualities and inclinations, producing in them more or less usefulness for particular tasks in the colonial economy.[266] His brother-in-law, also a colonist and a lawyer, Louis Baudry Deslozières (1764–1841), went further, arguing that the supposition of human equality had not at all improved the lot of the credulous blacks: "To give this impossibility the appearance of likelihood is to prepare them for endless ailments, it is to have them undergo in advance the torments of hell."[267] The laziness of the blacks was well known in the colonies, he wrote. So was the fact that Europeans were unable to work in tropical climates. Whoever invented the slave trade merited an altar by having devised a way in which the natural hierarchies of human beings could be put to useful service for all.[268] By the

[263] Raimond, 'Réflexions sur les véritables causes. . .' (1793), quoted in Popkin, *You Are All Free*, 335.

[264] See Baptiste Biancardini, 'L'opinion coloniale et la question de la relance de Saint-Domingue 1795–1802', 382 *Annales historiques de la Révolution française* (2015), 63–80.

[265] Médéric Moreau de Saint-Méry, *Description topographique, physique, civile, politique et historique de partie française de Saint-Domingue*, tome I (2 tomes, Paris, Dupont 1797), 35. Saint-Méry was appointed counsellor of the *Conseil superiéur* of Cap on Saint-Domingue and was elected one of the colonial deputies in the Constituent Assembly in autumn 1789.

[266] Ibid., 25–39, 71–99.

[267] "Donner cette impossibilité l'apparence de vraisemblance, c'est leur préparer des maux infinis; c'est vouloir leur faire subir en avance les supplices de l'enfer", Baudry Deslozières, *Les Egarements du nigrophilisme* (Paris, Migneret 1802), 56.

[268] Ibid., 22. Like many other defenders of slavery and the slave trade, Deslozières moved from a very negative characterisation of black individuals to stressing the just conditions of slavery as infinitely better than life in Africa among "cannibals". All this was accompanied by stress on the impossibility of colonisation without chattel slavery.

time of 18 Brumaire year VIII (9 November 1799), racist voices would ring much louder than abolitionist ones.

## Slavery or Independence?

After Toussaint's spectacular defection to the republican side in the spring of 1795 parts of Saint-Domingue were captured from the English–Spanish forces. Spain was forced to cede Santo Domingo (in the Treaty of Basle of 22 July 1795) while the British still clung to bits of occupied territory in the west. A conflict had emerged between the *gens de couleur* in charge of the southern provinces, supported by the English, and the former slaves aligned under Toussaint in the north, with close links to the United States.[269] Returning to the island at the head of another commission, despatched by the Directory in May 1796, Sonthonax joined Toussaint, who had been meanwhile appointed general in the colony's army. Their joint efforts to build a multiracial order in Saint-Domingue did not meet with success, however. Racial suspicions and the unwillingness of the former slaves to take up salaried work in the plantations upheld disorder and economic decline. Sonthonax's reports to Paris became increasingly pessimistic. He began to disagree with Toussaint, and the relations between the latter and the mulatto generals of the south grew ever worse, with both sides accusing each other of seeking outside help from England and the US.

In Paris, monarchist electoral victory in 1797 led to the filling of the ministry of marine with old-regime officials and colonists sympathetic to restoration of slavery.[270] Former plantation-owners protested vocally against the planned application of the constitution in the colonies, attacking the "tyrannical" rule that Sonthonax and Toussaint had set up. They also pressed for revoking the Directory's powers to send any commissioners to the island.[271] The Directory yielded somewhat and

[269] This division reflected at least in part the worry of the *gens de couleur* of loss of their privileged status in the event of a black takeover. Many of them would therefore eventually join the white colonists in supporting French action against Toussaint. See e.g, Saint-Louis, 'Relations internationales', 159–64.

[270] For personal details, see Thomas Pronier, 'L'implicte et l'explicite dans la politique de Napoléon', in Yves Benot & Marcel Dorigny (eds), *Rétablissement de l'esclavage dans les colonies françaises, 1802* (Paris, Maisonneuve and Larose 2003), 62–5.

[271] See, for example, the long attack on Sonthonax and his activities by deputy Vienot-Vaublanc at the Council of Five Hundred on 10 Prairial year V (29 May 1797), *Corps legislatif*, Conseil des Cinq-Cents No. 28 (Paris, Diréctoire 1797) and commentary in Georges Lefebvre, *La France sous le Directoire (1795–1799)* (Paris, Editions sociales 1977), 277–9; Belissa & Bosc, *Le Directoire*, 215–19.

Sonthonax was recalled to Paris, taking up his position in the legislature.[272] The re-establishment of republican legality on 18 Fructidor prompted the *Société des Amis des Noirs et Des Colonies* to begin its short-lived second life (1797–9), now inspired by novel ideas about colonisation without slavery. France would again become the "Great Nation", radiating its power and cultural achievements everywhere.[273] In his inaugural statement to the *Institut* of 15 Messidor year V (3 July 1797) Talleyrand deplored the state of the French colonies, which he attributed to insufficiently long-term planning and overly tight metropolitan control. Colonies were needed but they were to be based on the mutual advantage of the metropolis and the cultivators; trade could also, and perhaps better, be carried by faraway territories administering themselves. Preparing his audience for giving up the American colonies, and even as he refrained from making the point expressly (*trop annoncer est le moyen de ne le faire pas*) Talleyrand was laying the ground for Napoleon's expeditions in Egypt and Syria in the following year.[274]

Meanwhile in Saint-Domingue the internal conflict between Toussaint and the free coloured in the southern province – many of whom had joined their forces with former colonists – peaked in a ruthless civil war in 1799–1800 that ended with more than 30,000 casualties. Having subdued his last rivals and negotiated the departure of the English as well as having opened the west coast harbours to trade with them, Toussaint now ruled the colony almost as an autonomous republic.[275] Surrounding powers viewed the situation with the greatest concern, politicians from southern United States alleging that their workforce was being incited to rebellion. In the summer of 1798 relations between the US and France degenerated into a quasi-war with the consequence that the US established a trade embargo of French

[272] Pluchon, *Toussaint Louverture*, 76–87, 92–115. For Sonthonax's activities during his second commission, see also Stein, *Sonthonax*, 127–64. For the conflict that gradually emerged between him and Toussaint, see also Dubois, *Avengers of the New World*, 206–8; Gainot, *L'empire colonial français*, 147–54.

[273] Gainot, *L'empire colonial français*, 158–65.

[274] Charles-Maurice Talleyrand-Périgord, *Essai sur les avantages à retirer de colonies nouvelles dans les circonstances présentes* (Lu à la science publique de l'Institut national le 15 messidor an 5).

[275] See the Treaty of 30 August 1798. For English translation, see Rayford W. Logan, *The Diplomatic Relations of the United States with Haiti (1776–1881)* (University of North Carolina Press 1941), 65–6. See further Pluchon, *Toussaint Louverture*, 122–9. When the formal French commissioner Hédouville tried to control him, Toussaint finally put him on a ship back to France. See further Dubois, *Avengers of the New World*, 231–8; Saint-Louis, 'Relations internationales', 164.

territories, including its Caribbean colonies. This prompted Toussaint to contact US President John Adams in November 1798 as a result of which an exception clause was inserted to the US embargo law ("Toussaint's Clause") and a process was initiated that led to the signature of commercial treaties that gave the US rights equalling those received by the English.[276] Consular relations were established and American assistance decisively helped consolidate Toussaint's position. Nevertheless, slaveholding interests in the US saw to it that support to de jure independence would never become official policy.[277]

Toussaint had played the Americans and the British against each other and both against his formal French sovereign.[278] But his efforts to set up a working state remained unsuccessful. Military rule had created a kind of feudalism where the most valuable property was transferred into the hands of Toussaint's generals. Draconic laws were used to force ex-slaves not only to remain on the plantations – this time with salary – but also to control their private lives. Yet the economy failed to pick up.[279] The colonists were continuing their propaganda in Paris and after Napoleon's *coup d'état* on 18 Brumaire year VIII (9 November 1799), a new constitution broke the formal unity of the metropolis with the colonies: "The form of government of the French colonies is determined by special laws."[280] To assuage Toussaint Bonaparte addressed a Proclamation in December 1799 to the "brave blacks of Saint-Domingue", where he assured them that he would respect the Decree of 16 Pluviôse.[281] At the same time, he was surrounding himself with colonists and former slave-owners. The rumour was that as soon as the military situation allowed, he would seek to recapture the island and

[276] See Acts of 9 February 1799 and 27 February 1800 in *Public Statutes at Large of the United States*, Acts of the Fifth Congress, Sess III Ch 2, 613–16 and Sixth Congress, Sess 1 Ch 10, 7–11. See further Brown, *Toussaint's Clause*, esp. 130–43; Logan, *Diplomatic Relations*, 73–6; Pluchon, *Toussaint Louverture*, 187–91; Dubois, *Avengers of the New World*, 223–4.

[277] For the debates in Congress during the US–French "quasi-war", see Logan, *Diplomatic Relations*, 76–89.

[278] These very complicated events are examined in Saint-Louis, 'Relations internationales', 156–69.

[279] See e.g. Dubois, *Avengers of the New World*, 238–42; Pluchon, *Toussaint Louverture*, 269–303.

[280] Constitution of the Year VIII (13 December 1979), Art. 91.

[281] For an extract, see Thierry Lentz, 'L'échec colonial du régime consulaire', in Marcel Dorigny (ed.), *Haiti. Première république noire* (Paris, Société française d'outre-mer 2007), 47. See also Dubois, *A Colony of Citizens*, 352.

re-establish slavery.[282] As a countermove, Toussaint set up a small committee to prepare a constitution for the colony.[283] This was promulgated on 8 July 1801 and under it the government of the island was allocated to Toussaint as governor for life with the competence to choose his successor (Art. 30–31). *L'exclusif* was abolished and metropolitan France would play no role in the government of the island.[284] The constitution proclaimed liberty and equality but set up the Catholic religion as "the only one that is publicly professed" (Art. 6). It also enshrined plantation agriculture as the heart of the colony's economic life and directed the governor to allocate the rights and obligations of the cultivators and workers and to introduce the necessary workforce in the island – thus apparently condoning the buying of Africans.[285]

Toussaint's constitution was only a step away from full independence and its promulgation enraged the First Consul. Despite its revolutionary language, it enshrined in practice a system of military rule with little guarantee for the freedom of the inhabitants who were either left to move about in vagabondage or tied down to forced labour in plantations taken over by the military elite. The laws were implemented only partially and in many cases not at all so that French missions to Saint-Domingue (received only with the greatest reluctance), reported back to Paris on what they saw as complete anarchy.[286]

Once peace was agreed in Europe in October 1801, Bonaparte had been given a free hand to reassert control on the island.[287] Under the

282 French historians have been divided about whether Napoleon already intended to re-establish slavery at the time of his taking power. A persuasive argument to the effect that this was indeed his plan is made by Pronier, 'L'implicite et l'explicite', 51–67.

283 In February 1801 Toussaint set up a ten-member "Central Assembly" (with no black members) to prepare the text of the constitution. He ratified it on 8 July 1801.

284 The constitution was supplemented by a series of legislative ordinances in the summer and autumn of 1801 that further did away with what had been left of French regulation on the island. See Pluchon, *Toussaint Louverture*, 265–9. Formally speaking, this was not in conflict with the Constitution of Year VIII (Article 91) that provided that the colonies were to be ruled under "special laws". Toussaint's constitution could have been understood as such – but this was of course not Napoleon's intention.

285 Dubois, *Avengers of the New World*, 242–6.

286 Quoted in Pluchon, *Toussaint Louverture*, 214–15.

287 During the preliminaries to the Treaty of Amiens (25 March 1802), the British minister Henry Addington had expressed his expectation that France would now seek to recapture Saint-Domingue. Dubois, *A Colony of Citizens*, 366–7; David P. Geggus, *Haitian Revolutionary Studies* (Indiana University Press 2002), 177–8.

influence of colonial interests French legislators pleaded for "the reconstruction of the colonial edifice on the sacred principle of property".[288] By this time, a number of old-regime colonial officers had regained their earlier positions and the three chambers of the legislative body (Conservative Senate, *Tribunat* and the *Corps législatif*) contained many former colonists and supporters of the re-establishment of slavery. At first, Napoleon envisaged a rather grandiose operation encompassing the whole Caribbean, including Guyana and Louisiana, with the objective of turning the Gulf of Mexico into a kind of French lake. But as this seemed politically unwise and eventually impossible, a law of 30 Floréal year X (20 May 1802) provided that slavery would be re-established only in colonies returned in the Peace of Amiens (so formally not in Saint-Domingue, Guadeloupe or Guyana – where the law of 16 Pluviôse had been applied) but also foresaw the massive expansion of the slave trade designed to recommence activity in the plantations.[289]

In January 1802 the operation led by Napoleon's brother-in-law General Victor Leclerc disembarked at separate locations on Saint-Domingue. The operation had been prepared in secret and the instructions to Leclerc directed the general to first seek the confidence of the black officers and only then disarm and deport them. But despite reassuring despatches from Paris to Toussaint, the real objective of the expedition, conquest, was apparent from its very size of up to 30,000 troops initially, and then another 20,000, with many veterans

288 From a letter by a colonist to the French government, cited in Pluchon, *Toussaint Louverture*, 353.

289 Loi relative à la traite des noirs et au régime des colonies, 30 Floréal An X (20 May 1802). For the background, see Dubois, *Avengers of the New World*, 284–5; Pluchon, *Histoire*, 904–9; Pluchon, *Toussaint Louverture*, 307–13. See also generally Benot & Dorigny, *Rétablissement de l'esclavage*. For the utterly cynical Instructions of the Ministry of Marine of 14 June 1802, which saw to the gradual return to "old regime of the Blacks" on the basis of the "glorious victory" foreseen for General Leclerc and the immediate establishment of slave trade "more necessary than ever to fill the plantations", see Mayeul Macé & Bernard Gainot, 'Fin de campagne à Saint-Domingue, novembre 1802–novembre 1803', in Marcel Dorigny (ed.), *Haïti. Premier république noire* (Paris, Publications de la société française d'histoire d'outremer, 2007), 40. On 18 Brumaire, the situation of the French colonies was very varied. The law of 16 Pluviôse had been applied only in the three places mentioned in the text. Only half-hearted measures had been taken to implement it on Réunion or Isle de France, islands thus in a situation of illegality. Martinique, Tobago, St Lucia and the five Indian factories had all been occupied by the British, with slavery maintained. On the half-hearted efforts to apply abolition in the Indian Ocean islands, see Pronier, 'L'implicite et l'explicite', 58–9.

trained in Napoleon's European wars.[290] The atrocious war that followed left perhaps 100,000 islanders and 40,000 French soldiers dead, many of yellow fever but most as a result of the guerrilla warfare of Toussaint's generals, many of whom had originally fought with the French but defected once the real aims of the operation had become clear.[291] White and black civilians, men, women and children were subjected to unimaginable cruelties as the war turned into a race war.[292] Toussaint himself was captured by the French and brought to France in prison where he died on 7 April 1803. With the resumption of war in Europe in 1803 reinforcements that were badly needed owing to the ever-rising number of casualties on the French side were blocked by the British navy. That finally settled the military situation; the French had to leave. Toussaint's successor, the black general Dessalines declared Haiti independent on 1 January 1804, among his first tasks thereafter supervising the massacre of the remaining perhaps 4,000 white colonists.[293] The dream of a French American empire was over. It was sealed by the sale of Louisiana to the United States proceeds of which were used to prepare the invasion of England.

## Ending … and Starting Again

It may seem paradoxical that the deputies who in August 1789 had declared the universal rights of man and citizen were so slow to get rid of slavery in the French Caribbean and so ready to re-establish it as part of Napoleonic imperial hubris. But abolition was never a necessary part of the principal revolutionary idioms.[294] The language of the national will focused on the unity of the "nation" and drew a potentially sharp line between those who belonged and those who did not. Even Rousseau had written: "Every patriot hates foreigners; they are only men, and nothing to him. This defect is inevitable but of little

[290] For the composition and objectives of the Leclerc expedition, see e.g. Philippe R. Girard, '*Liberté, Égalité, Esclavage.* French Revolutionary Ideas and the Failure of the Leclerc Expedition to Saint-Domingue', 6 *French Colonial History* (2005), 55–65.

[291] See especially Macé & Gainot, 'Fin de campagne', 15–40.

[292] See e.g. Girard, '*Liberté*', 67–70. The motives for the brutality of the warfare and the French efforts to dissimulate its conduct and the eventual defeat are discussed in a balanced way by Macé & Gainot, 'Fin de campagne', 21–40.

[293] For the full story of the Leclerc operation, see Dubois, *Avengers of the New World*, 251–301.

[294] On those idioms, see Keith Michael Baker, 'Political Languages of the French Revolution', in Mark Goldie & Robert Wokler (eds), *The Cambridge History of Eighteenth-Century Political Thought* (Cambridge University Press 2006), 639, 639–47.

importance. The great thing is to be kind to our neighbours."[295] The hatred of the English propagated by Robespierre and the polemical literature that addressed the war as a war of nations fed by increasingly essentialised descriptions of racial difference.[296] Frenchmen generally sympathetic towards the Africans tended to have firm views about of their racial inferiority and even active *Amis* were reluctant to move towards immediate abolition.

Double standards, incoherence and confusion did not attach only to French attitudes towards slavery and the slave trade but underlay the almost total absence of serious debate about the legal status of the colonies. During absolutism they were simply absorbed within the realm without much reflection.[297] When Richelieu turned his attention to overseas territories, he did so prompted by his advisors and in order to emulate France's political rivals, not in response to pressure from merchants or eager colonisers. By using letters of patent that combined monopoly trading rights with an obligation to establish settlements and, at least initially, to convert native inhabitants, the central government tried to convince merchant classes that they had a shared interest in French expansion. Property rights and jurisdictional powers were thrown in for good measure. Even threats were used to force reluctant merchants and noblemen to invest in the New World.[298] But incessant warfare, motivated by older ideas about glory and hereditary rights, undermined these efforts. Lack of interest and knowledge further contributed to the haphazard nature of French Atlantic colonisation: "What is the worth of a few acres of snow?", Voltaire is reputed to have enquired when France let go of *Nouvelle France* in exchange for Saint-Domingue at the close of the Seven Years' War.[299]

From the early seventeenth century, French Atlantic colonies were administered as private fiefs with fealty and homage owed to the king as the feudal overlord. The situation changed only once they fell under royal government after 1663 and were forwarded to the *Compagie des*

295 Jean-Jacques Rousseau, *Emile* (B. Foxley trans., Project Gutenberg Version 2011), Bk I, www.gutenberg.org/files/5427/5427-h/5427-h.htm.

296 Out of a wealth of literature, see David A. Bell, *The Cult of the Nation in France. Inventing Nationalism 1600–1800* (Harvard University Press 2001), 101–6 and passim.

297 Cheney, *Revolutionary Commerce*, 202.

298 A typical late example would be the decision by the Conseil d'État in 1698 to threaten the landowners in Saint Christophe by expropriation unless they were to put their lands into effective production. See Ly, *La Compagnie du Sénégal*, 24 n. 3.

299 The quote appears in many places, e.g. Marc Ferro, *Colonization. A Global History* (London, Routledge 1994), 63.

*Indes Occidentales*. The company received property and jurisdiction while the king kept to himself suzerainty as well as the power to appoint governors-general and governors for particular locations.[300] The provision that the colonies were to be governed under the customs of Paris manifested their subordination under central government; but it involved no serious programme to develop them.[301] The most important piece of colonial law was fiscal legislation, namely *l'exclusif*, which saw to the absolute priority of French mercantile interests over colonial ones. The Revolution raised the question of whether the colonies were to be treated as integral parts of the realm or separately from it. Whatever the decisions in Paris, however, they were rapidly overtaken by events on the ground. The colonial lobby sought to free themselves from what they called "ministerial despotism" and especially from the *exclusif* against protests by metropolitan merchants. Against the *amis*, the colonial lobby insisted on the special nature of the colonies that would allow the racial order to continue as in the past.[302] In the end, the legal quarrels were overshadowed by the war; during the years 1806–10, French colonies one after the other fell into the hands of the English – Guyana, Martinique, Guadeloupe, Marie-Galante, Seychelles, Saint-Louis (on the coast of Senegal), Réunion, Java... With the Treaty of Paris of 1814, parts of its empire as it had been on 1 January 1792 were returned to France, with the exception, however, of Mauritius and its dependencies (including the Chagos islands), the Seychelles, Trinidad and Saint-Lucia.[303]

When Talleyrand gave his critical review of French colonisation to the *Institut* in 1797, the French were happy to follow his advice and turn their attention to Egypt. Six years thereafter, when Rayneval published his large treatise on the law of nations, even that spot had

[300] Ruggiu, 'Colonies, Monarchy, Empire', 203. This article provides the best summary of the legal status of French colonies until the Revolution that I have been able to find.

[301] The formula in the Edit en forme de Lettres-Patentes pour l'Établissement de la Compagnie Royale de Saint-Domingue (Septembre 1698), Art. XXIII was "Nos Edits, Ordonnances, et coutumes en usage de la Prevoté et Vicomté de Paris seront observez pour loix et coutumes dans ladite colonie". In addition, the company was entitled to make such regulations as were necessary for its commerce. See Saint-Méry, *Loix et constitutions*, 1, 615. This was the standard formula. Sainte-Marie, 'Les colonies françaises', 111.

[302] A good discussion of *l'affaire des colonies* in 1789–91 is Cheney, *Revolutionary Commerce*, 195–228.

[303] Definitive Treaty of Paris, 30 May 1814, Articles VIII, IX and X. Edward Hertslet, *The Map of Europe by Treaty*, 4 vols. (London, Butterworths 1875), I 9–10.

been erased from the French imperial imaginary.[304] For a moment, it seemed that the last word would remain with Benjamin Constant (1767–1830). His famous indictment of the "spirit of conquest" as utterly incompatible with modern commercial society may not have been designed as an anti-colonial tract but was as relevant to campaigns outside Europe as within. His socio-psychological analysis pointed not only to the effects of conquests on the conquered but equally on the conquering nation. Conquest corrupted part of the conquering population by compelling it to serve in its extravagant enterprises and demanded from the rest "passive obedience and sacrifices, in such a way as to disturb its reason, pervert its judgment and overturn all its ideas".[305] Conquest and war were anachronistic, and they imposed a forced uniformity on the conquered nations that was no different from death and gave rise to feelings of pure universal horror.[306] "Our century", he wrote, "values everything according to its utility" and has "nothing to hope for from conquest".[307]

Constant's views on empire and civilisation were complex and largely followed those Condorcet had put forward in his "Sketch". He did not see the growth of civilisation as clearly laid out as the latter, and was more ready to reflect on its dark sides.[308] But he was equally firm in condemning slavery and what he called the system of races that "ingenious authors" had recently advocated.[309] Against them, Constant tried to demonstrate that the backwardness or lack of civilisation in nations or human groups was not an innate property but a result of their historical situation, often oppression. Everyone was perfectible and all people could flourish in the right conditions. The blacks of Saint-Domingue, for example, could not advance owing to the lack of education and being under the whip of the colonists. Since the attainment of independence, however, the Haitians had become "reasonable legislators" as well as "*aussi habiles et aussi polis que nos diplomats*".[310]

[304] An even more striking process of forgetting concerns nineteenth-century histories of the French Revolution that tended to ignore, sometimes wholly, its colonial and slavery dimensions. See Benot, *La Révolution française*, 204–17.

[305] Benjamin Constant, 'The Spirit of Conquest and Usurpation and Their Relation to European Civilization', in *Political Writings* (B. Fontana ed., Cambridge University Press 1988), 64.

[306] Ibid., 55, 73–8, 79. [307] Ibid., 55, 81.

[308] See e.g. discussion in Jennifer Pitts, *A Turn to Empire. The Rise of Imperial Liberalism in Britain and France* (Princeton University Press 2005), 173–85.

[309] Benjamin Constant, 'De M Dunoyer et quelques-uns de ses Ouvrages', in *Mélanges de littérature et de politique* (Paris, Didier 1829), 148.

[310] Ibid., 132, 149.

Did the abolition of slavery on Saint-Domingue constitute an achievement of the Declaration of 1789? Hardly. The Declaration was passed by white men engaged in social and political revolution in France. They were looking for the collapse of an old regime that had erected obstacles to their advancement and to rid the kingdom of bureaucracy and corporatism. The colonies entered those debates only late, and even then, the loudest voice was that of former planters and colonists insisting on a return to the pre-revolutionary situation. And when the Assembly in 1794 was forced to decree the end of slavery, it did everything it could to force the ex-slaves into servitude on those same plantations from which it had purportedly freed them. The end of slavery in Saint-Domingue resulted from struggle of the slaves themselves; it was "triumph of the black revolution over the French revolution".[311]

## Epilogue: A Legal Anomaly

The shock of Haitian independence to Europeans has been compared to the shock of the Great October Revolution: "Recognition of Haiti by the four principal slaveholding nations, the United States, Great Britain, France and Spain was, therefore, unimaginable."[312] But only France took active measures against it. Although no trade agreements were made with Haiti, and the country was ostracised from diplomacy, American and British merchants were busily visiting its ports and Haitians were used as middlemen in contacts with third countries. Contraband trade flourished while investment in agriculture or industry was practically nil. Foreign merchants also interfered massively in the country's fractional internal politics, often tilting the scales among domestic rivals one way or another.[313] In the absence of official contacts to the outside world the country was reduced to a kind of neo-colonial dependence on the vicissitudes of international commerce. The United States adopted the formal position of neutrality but insisted that its citizens were entitled to carry out non-contraband trade with the former colony. Slaveholding interests succeeded in pushing forward trade prohibition for the years 1806–8, and though the act was not renewed, it led to interest in trade diminishing and Haiti retreating into a kind of existential limbo. Despite repeated efforts by Haitian leaders

[311] Pluchon, *Histoire*, 899. [312] Logan, *Diplomatic Relations*, 152.

[313] Vertus Saint-Louis, 'Commerce exterieur et concept de l'indépendence', in Michel Hector & Laënnec Hurbon (eds), *Genèse de l'État haïtien (1804–1859)* (Paris, Éditions de la Maison des sciences de l'homme 2010), 294, 275–94.

to secure US recognition, none was forthcoming. As the influential republican Albert Gallatin wrote to the secretary of the treasury in 1815: "San Domingo must be considered as being neither independent nor part of the mother country."[314]

At the Congress of Vienna in 1815, other powers gave informal recognition to France's right to re-establish itself on Saint-Domingue. But the country was in no condition to undertake an extensive and uncertain military operation. By contrast, Haitian political leadership did all it could to secure French recognition. This took place in an extraordinary form by an order of the Bourbon King Charles X on 17 April 1825. The order provided that parts of the "French part of Saint-Domingue" would remain open to merchant vessels from all nations but that the taxes and duties of French ships would be reduced to half of what was required of ships carrying other flags. The order also contained provision for the compensation of damage for properties of French colonists of 150 million francs to be paid in five annual instalments of equal value. And then the ordinance contained the following provision:

> Article 3. On these conditions We concede with the present order to the inhabitants of the French part of Saint Domingue, the total and complete independence of their government (*l'indépendance pleine et entière de leur gouvernement*).[315]

The act in fact wiped away the slave rebellion and its outcome. It never mentioned the name "Haïti" that Dessalines thought had been the island's original Indian name. Independence was a royal "grant", conditional on commercial preference for France and the payment of an exorbitant compensation to former slave-owners. If many thought it outrageous, President Pétion agreed to the terms in order to end the country's diplomatic isolation.[316] The act was brought to Haiti by a convoy of fourteen military vessels moored outside Port-au-Prince in order to ensure agreement. And yet it was not accompanied by the establishment of diplomatic relations but the dispatch of a consul-

[314] Logan, *Diplomatic Relations*, 187. See also Rose-Mie Léonard, 'L'indépendence d'Haïti. Perceptions aux États-Unis, 1804–1864', in Marcel Dorigny (ed.), *Haiti. Première république noire* (Société française d'histoire des outre-mers 2004), 207–25.

[315] Ordonnance du 17 avril 1825. In Dorigny, *Haïti, Première république noire*, 249.

[316] Itazienne Eugène, 'La normalisation des relations franco-haïtiennes (1825–1838)', in Dorigny, *Haïti, Première république noire*, 141–7; François Blancpain, 'Notes sur les "dettes" d'esclavage. Le cas d'indeminté payée par Haïti (1825–1883)', in Dorigny, *Haiti, Première république noire*, 241–5. For the negotiations between 1815 and 1825, see further Liliana Obregón, 'Empire, Racial Capitalism and International Law. The Case of Manumitted Haiti and the Recognition Debt', 31 *Leiden Journal of International Law* (2018), 603–12.

general. Only with a treaty of 12 February 1838, after the first instalment of 30 million francs was paid, did France finally give up its trade preference and the sum of the debt was reduced to 60 million francs payable in thirty years. This time, recognition was granted unconditionally. Nevertheless, payments and interest charges crippled Haiti's economy for most of the nineteenth century.[317]

The newly independent Latin American republics were no less reluctant to deal with Haiti on a basis of equality, despite President Pétion's having twice offered Simon Bolivar refuge and equipment for his struggles on the continent. Haiti was not invited to the Congress of Panama in 1825–6, convoked to enhance cooperation between the newly independent Latin American countries, and no decision was made there to recognise it.[318] In the context of its fight against the slave trade Britain concluded two treaties with Haiti in 1838 and 1839 where it seems to have recognised the country.[319] US recognition was received in 1862 in the context of the Civil War. Even after recognition, most countries were content to have consular instead of diplomatic representation in Haiti. Perhaps for this reason, in his 1904 textbook of international law, the Belgian international lawyer and first historian of the newly founded profession, Ernest Nys, still failed to list Haiti among world states.[320] Also domestically, the country remained vulnerable. After the assassination of Dessalines (who had meanwhile crowned himself emperor) in 1806, the country was divided into three parts of which one was ruled as a separate kingdom in 1806–20. During those years, Haiti had five constitutions (1805, 1806, 1807, 1811, 1816) and it was ruled by oligarchies collaborating with an authoritarian leadership. Its economy was in tatters and its commerce in foreign hands.[321]

[317] Eugène, '*La normalisation*', 151–3.

[318] Logan, *Diplomatic Relations*, 222–3, 227–8.

[319] Ibid., 231.

[320] Ernest Nys, *Le droit international. Les principes, les théories, les faits* (3 vols, Bruxelles, Castaigne 1904–6), I, 117–18, 126.

[321] See e.g. Claude Moïse, 'Création de l'État haitien – constitutins, continuités, ruptures', in Michel Hector & Laënnec Hurbon (eds), *Genèse de l'État haïtien (1804–1859)* (Paris, Éditions de la Maison des sciences de l'homme 2010), 49–62.

# Part III

## Britain: Laws and Markets

# 8

# The Law and Economics of State-Building

## *England c. 1450–c. 1650*

The French revolutionaries argued from universal principles that observers across the Channel, most notably Edmund Burke, regarded as "extravagant and presumptuous speculations" without contact to the history of Frenchmen and useful only as tools of tyranny. As guides for good and lawful government they were no match at all to the centuries of experience of a people, giving true expression of its relations with its rulers. Addressing the French nation, Burke suggested that had you "resolved to resume your ancient privileges ... your ancient and your recent loyalty and honour... [and had you] looked to your neighbours in this land, who had kept alive their ancient principles and models of the old common law" – had the French done all this, then "[y]ou would have rendered the cause of liberty venerable in the eyes of every worthy mind in every nation."[1] This would also have been the way to prosperity. Had the French followed the way of the English, then "[y]ou would have had an unoppressive but a productive revenue. You would have had a flourishing commerce to feed it." Instead, "[y]ou set up your trade without a capital". And the result was disastrous. "France has bought poverty with crime!"[2]

Burke's famous veneration of the "rights of Englishmen" against the abstract and intangible rights of humanity arose from thinking about political institutions as products of accumulating adjustments by successive generations that represent a deeper wisdom than available to a legislature at any single moment. Burke's critique took up "the great

[1] Edmund Burke, 'Reflections on the Revolution in France', in Edmund Burke, *Revolutionary Writings* (Ian Hampshire-Monk ed., Cambridge University Press 2014), 37, 38.

[2] Ibid., 38.

tradition of common-law thought" where comparison with France had often acted as inspiration or pretext for celebrating the legal institutions found at home.[3] It would be wrong to view such an attitude as necessarily parochial. Burke's argument from customary law was as much reflective of ideas about universal history as Edward Coke's much-belaboured notion of the common law as "artificial reason".[4] When Sir John Fortescue (1394–1476) in his *De laudibus legum angliae* ("In Praise of the Laws of England", 1468–71) argued that "there is no gainsaying nor legitimate doubt but that the customs of the English are not only good but the best", he meant that they were the best for England and that it was a principle of universal natural law that each country should be governed by the laws that best "adapt[] to the utility of [each] realm".[5] Comparing English laws with those of his temporary place of refuge, France, Fortescue had no difficulty in conceiving of a law of nature regulating aspects of the government of individual commonwealths. All the judges in the celebrated *Calvin's case* (1607), including both Coke and his arch-enemy Sir Francis Bacon, drew upon the law of nature and of nations when discussing the nature of the allegiance that a subject owed to his sovereign. Skilfully joining his reverence of universal legal principles with his civic humanism, Bacon observed that the law of naturalisation was a "branch of the law of nature" and, as practised in England, namely by applying both *ius sanguinis* and *ius soli*, "a law of a warlike and magnanimous nation fit for empire".[6]

From the time of Fortescue to England's mastery of the seas in the eighteenth century, English lawyers made frequent, though erratic, use of the idiom of the law of nature and of nations, sometimes as part of the common law, more often as they were operating within the royal prerogative. This dual concept would eventually weave the utility of the commonwealth tightly with the rights of property of

[3] John Pocock, *The Ancient Constitution and the Common Law* (Cambridge University Press 1957), 243.

[4] E.g. Edward Coke, *The First Part of the Institutes of the Laws of England* (2 vols, London, Clarke 1823 & 1832), vol. 1, Sect 138, 97b. See also Glenn Burgess, *The Politics of the Ancient Constitution. An Introduction to English Political Thought 1603–1642* (London, Macmillan 1992), 29–48; David Chan Smith, *Sir Edward Coke and the Reformation of the Laws* (Cambridge University Press 2014).

[5] Sir John Fortescue, 'In Praise of the Laws of England', in S. Lockwood (ed.), *On the Laws and Governance of England* (Cambridge University Press 1997), XVI, XV (27, 25).

[6] Speech of Lord Bacon, as Counsel for Calvin, in The Case of the Postnati (Calvin's case), in *Cobbett's Complete Collection of State Trials* II (T.B. Howell ed., London, Hansard 1816), 595.

Englishmen. Early political economists, such as Gerard Malynes, Edward Misselden and Thomas Mun, took pains to demonstrate that the power of the English state was inextricable from the prosperity of Englishmen. A nation's merchants were its most valuable asset. Discussing the day's commercial practices as *lex mercatoria* and a branch of the law of nations, Malynes insisted in 1629 that "of the six members of all the governments of monarchies and common-weales, [the merchants] are the principal instruments to increase or decrease the wealth thereof".[7] And in 1664, Mun believed that the members of the "Noble Profession" of the merchant were "worthily called The Steward of the Kingdoms Stock" whose work, when "performed with great skill and conscience, that so the private gain may ever accompany the publique good".[8]

In later years, some Englishmen began to worry that the expansion of English power on the seas might eventually lead to the destruction of freedom at home. This did not happen because although the state operated efficiently, its jurisdiction was closely limited and "the heavy-handedness of British rule increased the farther it extended from the metropolis".[9] One could afford being autocratic abroad – a premise that Burke passionately questioned during the Warren Hastings trial in the 1790s. However, among the early representatives of "political arithmetic", it became an article of faith that not only was liberty at home compatible with empire but it was that very liberty – understood as commercial freedom – that laid the conditions for domestic prosperity.[10] This was not unrestricted freedom. Even when the much-criticised monopolies were gradually given up after 1688, the navigation laws continued to direct trade in ways that ensured domestic growth. The commercial culture that arose from the conflicts of the seventeenth century sustained Britain through the international crises of the subsequent decades because "[t]he object of national aggrandizement was not to reacquire the long-lost medieval empire on the continent nor

7 Gerard Malynes, *Consuetodo, Vel Lex mercatoria, or The Antient Law-Merchant* (London, Bourne 1629), 62.

8 Thomas Mun, 'England's Treasure by Foreign Trade', in J. R. McCulloch (ed.), *A Select Collection of Early English Tracts on Commerce* (Political Economy Club 1856), 122.

9 John Brewer, *The Sinews of Power. War, Money and the English State 1688–1783* (Harvard University Press 1988), xviii–xix.

10 David Armitage, *The Ideological Origins of the British Empire* (Cambridge University Press 2010), 142–5. For the early English political economists' arguments for a commercial empire, see 146–69.

even to dominate Europe. It was to create a prosperous nation, rich polity based on commerce."[11] As Charles Tilly summarised:

> The English, and then British, state built on a conjunction of capital and coercion that from very early on gave any monarch access to immense means of warmaking, but only at the price of large concessions to the country's merchants and bankers.[12]

* * * * *

This chapter will begin with a survey the role of law of nations in the domestic debates concerning the conflict between the royal prerogative and the right to property that laid the groundwork for England's astonishing later ability to "give law to the world". Already in the early Tudor period the common law had adopted an economic orientation that would provide the ideological foundation for subsequent developments. It was that orientation, also, that gave the idiom of the "law of nations" in England the specifically mercantile character that led it to develop in a different direction from the *ius naturae et gentium* of the continent. But it took a civil war to inspire the period's most brilliant political thinker, Thomas Hobbes, to derive from natural law a science of government that would persuade Englishmen of the wisdom of coordinating their private rights with a legally well-defined royal prerogative. Loyal obedience at home – the subject of this chapter – would guarantee to them the protection of public power as they would reap the fruit of their overseas ventures, the subject of Chapters 9 and 10.

## *Corpus mysticum economicum*

The English translation of Fortescue's *De laudibus* appeared in the midst of rising concerns in Tudor England in 1546 about the growth of poverty and social dislocation. Read later as epitomising the constitutional ideals and principles of the golden era of Henry VII (1485–1509),[13] *De laudibus* had immense significance in English constitutional theory and practice. "Not only Tudor intellectuals but also Coke, Hale, Filmer, Hobbes and

[11] Brewer, *The Sinews of Power*, 189, 186.

[12] Charles Tilly, *Coercion, Capital, and European States* (London, Blackwell 1992), 159.

[13] Fortescue had served the erratic regime of Henry VI, including as king's sergeant and chief justice of the King's Bench. As a Lancastrian he had been exiled in France and arrested on his return to England in April 1471. He was soon pardoned, however, and rose to become a member of the Council of Edward IV.

Locke had studied or read it."[14] It was accompanied by another work, *The Governance of England*, which followed Aquinas' *De regimine principum* to provide advice on good government to the weak and indebted regime of Henry VI. *De laudibus* is usually remembered for two propositions. One concerns the nature of the common law as the "ancient constitution", the claim that since the time of ancient Britons, the country "ha[d] been continuously regulated by the same customs as now".[15] The second was the suggestion that England's relatively greater prosperity vis-à-vis France resulted from the fact that while France was ruled "only royally" (that it was a *dominium regale*), England was a mixed monarchy, *dominium politicum et regale*.[16] Fortescue depicted good government as above all good *economic* governance aiming at the utility of the realm as a whole. In his view both forms of government, the one that is "only royal" and the one that is "political and royal", were established for secular purposes, but while the former was intended to advance the ruler's interests, it was the people that were to benefit from the latter.[17] France had remained poor because the law paid regard only to the king's interests, leading to excessive taxation and neglect of the subjects' welfare. As a result the French "live in the most extreme poverty and misery, and yet they dwell in one of the most fertile realms of the world".[18] By contrast, although England was poor in natural resources, it was ruled under a better law, the king's rights to tax his subjects being dependent on their consent.

Fortescue described the realm as a mystical body, *corpus mysticum*, separate from the ruler, a consensual arrangement among the people to authorise the ruler to realise their interests and to protect "the law, the subjects, and their bodies and goods".[19] As the head of the body politic the king was a trustee of his people, unable to change the laws

[14] Neal Wood, *Foundations of Political Economy. Some Early Tudor Views on State and Society* (The University of Chicago Press 1994), 44. According to Christopher W. Brooks, it was also "one of the most important examples in English history of a work written by a lawyer for a non-professional audience", in *Law, Politics and Society in Early Modern England* (Cambridge University Press 2008), 23.

[15] Fortescue, 'In Praise of the Laws of England', XVII (26).

[16] Ibid., XIII (20–3). On the sources and interpretation of these terms, see J. H. Burns, 'Fortescue and the Political Theory of *Dominium*', 28 *The Historical Journal* (1985), 777–97.

[17] Fortescue, 'In Praise of the Laws of England', XIII (21). Fortescue used a purely utilitarian criterion to compare the systems: "by their fruits you shall know them", 'The Governance of England', in S. Lockwood (ed.), *On the Laws and Governance of England* (Cambridge University Press 1997), 3 (90).

[18] Fortescue, 'The Governance of England', 3 (89).

[19] Fortescue, 'In Praise of the Laws of England', XIII (21, 22). See also Wood, *Foundations*, 49–51.

"or to deprive [the] people of their own substance uninvited or against their wills". In an earlier work, *De natura legis naturae*, written to explain the principles of succession to the throne in England, Fortescue had already defined private property as natural law and justified this by a theory of rights based on labour.[20] In *De laudibus* and *The Governance of England* he explained further that the object of ruling was to provide adequate material life for the people so that they would "possess safer than before both themselves and their own".[21] The wealth and happiness of the subjects would become the wealth and power of the realm itself. A poor king was a great inconvenience, a hostage to his creditors and mighty nobles, unable to govern the country in the general interest. The subjects hence had an interest to provide the royal house with sufficient funds.[22] The king's council was to be composed of men of independent means, but not so powerful as to become dominant. With adequate wages they would best manage the kingdom's affairs, that is to say, to decide:

> how the export of money may be restrained, how bullion may be brought into the land, how also plate, jewels, and money recently borne out, may be recovered ... and also how the prices of merchandise grown in this land may be sustained and increased and the prices of merchandise brought in this land abated.[23]

According to Fortescue "it is the king's honour, and also his duty, to make his realm rich, and it is dishonour when he has but a poor realm, of which men will say he reigns only among beggars".[24] Not only of the royal treasury but the polity as a whole was to be subjected to careful management. The test of the justice of laws was their economic effect – did they help conducing to welfare?[25] In an extraordinary passage Fortescue related crime and popular uprisings to their social causes – "men who have lost their goods, and fallen into poverty, soon become robbers and thieves".[26] If there had not been a rebellion in France this was only because of the "cowardice and lack of heart" among Frenchmen.[27]

[20] "Property in the bread so gained accrued only to the men who had toiled for it", Sir John Fortescue, 'Concerning the Nature of the Law of Nature', in *The Works of Sir John Fortescue* (2 vols, London 1869), I 291–2.

[21] Fortescue, 'In Praise of the Laws of England', XIV (24).

[22] Fortescue, 'The Governance of England', 6–7 (94–9).

[23] Ibid., 15 (116).

[24] Ibid., 12 (109).

[25] Wood, *Foundations*, 60.

[26] Fortescue, 'The Governance of England', 12 (110).

[27] Ibid., 13 (111).

Now all of this was read as conclusions of natural law that applied equally everywhere.[28] But his experience of the contrast between France and England pushed Fortescue to focus on the specific needs of government, prompting his sixteenth-century Tudor readers to use legislation for the kinds of social engineering he had sketched.[29] These included Sir Thomas More (1477/8–1535), justice of the King's Bench and one of most eminent of English humanists, whose "Utopians" gave active attention to economic reform but also regarded the whole universe as brothers. They despised war and military glory and even refrained from treaty-making because "human nature constitutes a treaty in itself, and human beings are far more efficiently united by kindness than by contracts, by feeling than by words".[30] Utopians did go to war in self-defence, when they needed to assist friends or to liberate oppressed peoples, but they were also prepared to "take even stronger action to protect the rights of traders who are subjected to any kind of legal injustice in foreign countries, either as a result of unfair laws, or of fair ones deliberately misinterpreted".[31]

More's *Utopia* (1516) gave expression to a widely shared unease about the greed and injustice of European society, specifically targeting the "enclosures" whereby large landowners had turned arable land to grazing, evicting thousands of small farmers and throwing whole families on the road as vagabonds and beggars.[32] He hated the way some "who either do no work at all, or do work that's really not essential, are rewarded for their laziness or their unnecessary activities by a splendid life of luxury" while others get only "so little to eat, and have such a wretched time, that they'd be almost better off if they were cart-horses".[33] To this, the life of the Utopians presented a diametrical opposite. Although they were no Christians, they aimed at prosperity and justice that, they believed, would grow from the innocent pleasures of mind and body that they regarded as synonymous with a life of virtue.[34] Utopia's legal system was completely

[28] See further Fortescue, 'Concerning the Nature of the Law of Nature'.

[29] Brooks, *Law, Politics and Society*, 41.

[30] Thomas More, *Utopia* (London, Penguin 1965 [1516]), 90.

[31] Ibid., 90.

[32] Ibid., 25–8.

[33] Ibid., 110. More himself was unlikely to share the Utopians' communist ideals that were rather presented as logical (though extreme) outcomes of the contemporary humanist trope of true virtue – "the most radical critique of humanism written by a humanist". Quentin Skinner, *The Foundations of Modern Political Thought*, vol. I (Cambridge University Press 1977), 256.

[34] More, *Utopia*, 73–81.

utilitarian, its laws, as More put it, "raw-materials of pleasure".[35] They scorned traditional ideas about majesty and regarded capital punishment as immoral and wasteful, arguing, like Fortescue, that it did not take into account the causes of criminality: "you create thieves, and then punish them for stealing".[36] Criminals were to be made useful by working for the community. Utopians accepted slavery, but rejected traditional notions of class and the injustice of a world where some led a life of luxury while others toiled in hard labour. This, too, More derived from the principle of pleasure. For altruism – giving to those who did not have enough, putting the public good ahead of the private – resulted in spiritual satisfaction that far outweighed whatever losses one had to endure: "[I]n the final analysis, pleasure is the ultimate happiness which all human beings have in view, even when they are acting most virtuously."[37]

An economic notion of statehood penetrated the work. In Utopia "everything is in public ownership, no one has any fear of going short, as long as the public storehouses are full. Everyone gets a fair share, so there are never any poor men or beggars."[38] Agricultural products were distributed from common reservoirs to the provinces. No money was needed because everyone would produce sufficient amounts of necessities that would be freely available in shops and warehouses.[39] Excess products were used for export and to build a reservoir of bullion that, because the Utopians themselves had no need for it, could be used for emergencies, to lend money to other countries, or to pay the foreign mercenaries that made up their armies.[40] Utopia was also a colonising nation. After the Utopians had annexed their island, they invited the natives to join them. If the latter failed to agree, then Utopians declared war on them:

> For they consider war perfectly justifiable, when one country denies another its natural right to derive nourishment from any soil which the original owners are not using themselves, but are merely holding on to as a worthless piece of property.[41]

More's view of the role of law in organising productive work and supporting Utopia's relations with neighbours was a significant part of his humanist concern for improvement. The present legal order was suspect, the underlying social system a "conspiracy of the rich to advance their own interests under the pretext of organizing society".[42]

[35] Ibid., 73. [36] Ibid., 27. [37] Ibid., 73. [38] Ibid., 110. [39] Ibid., 60–1.
[40] Ibid., 66. [41] Ibid., 60. [42] Ibid., 111.

There was thus practically no public or constitutional law in Utopia at all. Like treaties with foreign powers, such laws were suspect – why not rely on spontaneous solidarity? One of the main complaints the Utopians had against other nations was they had too many laws; those laws were too complex for citizens to understand; and hence they had too many lawyers "over-ingenious about individual cases and points of law". By contrast, in Utopia, laws were only declarative of natural duties and "everyone's a legal expert".[43] But the Utopians were strict about enforcing commercial dealings, using the payments they received for importing goods to be distributed equitably among the inhabitants.[44]

## The Economics of Law and Government: Thomas Smith

In the Tudor social order, everyone was expected to live content with their divinely pre-ordained place in the social hierarchy that the laws were intended to express.[45] However, More wrote at a moment when that consensus had become endangered by economic and social problems as well as the heightening of religious and political tensions resulting from the break with Rome. The governmental revolution ushered in during the Tudor era was one expression of a change to come; laws would now be used as instruments of secular improvement. A lawyer representing the new spirit, with a background resembling More's, and whose concerns were akin to Fortescue's, was Sir Thomas Smith (1513–77), the first regius professor of civil law at the University of Cambridge whom we met briefly in Chapter 3. Smith worked as Elizabeth's ambassador in Paris (1562–6), privy councillor and secretary of state. His *Discourse of the Commonweal of this Realm of England* (1549, published 1581) emerged from profound concern over the state of the realm, especially the problems of "dearth" or scarcity, resulting from what many people viewed as an artificially produced undervaluation of the English currency.[46] A ruler's wealth and power depended on not

[43] Ibid., 87. [44] Ibid., 87

[45] See e.g. Stephen L. Collins, *From Divine Cosmos to the Sovereign State. An Intellectual History of Consciousness and the Idea of Order in Renaissance England* (Oxford University Press 1989), 14–28.

[46] This work has been regarded as one of the first important "economic" tracts. See Mary Dewar, 'The Authorship of the "Discourse of the Commonweal"', 19 *Economic History Review* (1966), 388. According to Wood, "[n]othing like it in either substance or form had appeared before", *Foundations*, 204. See also Enfred M. Chalk, 'Natural Law and the Rise of Economic Individualism in England', 59 *Journal of Political Economy* (1951), 333–8.

impoverishing his subjects (especially by currency manipulations).[47] Using the vocabularies of "commonwealth", "*res publica*" and even "civil society", Smith sketched a realm of governmental action that operated through its own intrinsic laws instead of those established by the state. By inventing a dialogue between the "knight", the "husbandman", the "capper" and the "doctor" (the learned expert in government) Smith deconstructed England into a system of classes completely dependent on the adequate functioning of their daily transactions. To drive the lesson home he depicted the systemic nature of these transactions through a familiar metaphor: "as in a clock there be many wheels yet the first wheel being stirred it drives the next, and that the third, till the last moves the instruments that strikes the clock".[48]

The dialogue took its inspiration from its participants' concern over the enclosures and the way each initially accused the others for the resulting "dearth".[49] In the course of the conversation, the "doctor" demonstrated the interdependence of the interests of his interlocutors; it was wrong to point an accusing finger at any one of them. The problem did not lie with the rents charged by landowners or increased prices of food or manufactures. Instead, it resulted from the debasing of the value of the coin that had made foreign goods increasingly expensive.[50] The domestic economy did not operate in isolation, Smith's "doctor" argued. It was impossible simply to legislate to bring prices down. Foreign commodities were needed and foreign merchants remained untouched by domestic laws. If the English could not offer them the price they charge, they will simply go elsewhere.[51]

Smith completely accepted the profit motive and insisted that inflation was not an evil but a problem of governance. Law was not the answer. With law you could not compel humans to work harder or invest better. The issue of enclosures, for example, was to be dealt with by working out how to make the cultivation of arable land profitable so that there would be no interest to turn it over for grazing.[52] The government was to balance and mediate between the different interests. "What makes men to multiply pastures and enclosures gladly?", the "doctor" asked. As the "knight" responded that this was "the profit that

[47] Thomas Smith, *Discourse of the Commonweal of This Realm of England* (Elizabeth Lamond ed., Cambridge University Press 1929), 34–5. Lamond attributed this work to Sir John Hales but the attribution to Smith, nowadays widely accepted, is from Dewar, 'Authorship'.

[48] Smith, *Commonweal*, 98. [49] Ibid., 18–20. [50] Ibid., 69, 104.

[51] Ibid., 42–7, 80. [52] Ibid., 54–6.

grows thereby", the doctor's emphatic conclusion was "[i]t is very true, and no other thing".[53] Enlightened governance was about creating avenues of profit-making in areas where this would be best for society as a whole. New industries could deal with idleness and broaden the tax base. For, as the doctor added, "True it is that that thing which is profitable to each man by him self, (so it be not prejudicial to any other) is profitable to the whole commonweal."[54] A prosperous nation will also be a formidable international actor. "Yea, among all the nations in the world," Smith wrote, "they that be politique and civil, do master the rest though their [forces] be inferior."[55]

More regarded it a natural part of Utopia's enlightened civilisation that it was a colonising nation. Smith brought this view into practice by enthusiastic advocacy of the colonisation of Ireland. England, Smith contended, had become overpopulated. In Ireland, the younger sons of the gentry would gain productive lands and labour would be provided for the masses of the poor. "Ireland, once inhabited with Englishe men, and policed with Englishe lawes, could be as great a commoditie to the Prince as the realme of England." Depicting the Irish as uncivil and savage but also highlighting the ease with which they could be subdued, Smith planned to turn large territories in Ireland over to commercial agriculture, his protagonist exclaiming at the end of his listing of the virtues of colonisation – "How say you now, have I not set forth to you another Eutopia [!]"[56] Smith was pushing a plan put forward earlier by Sir Henry Sidney, Elizabeth's lord deputy of Ireland, to undertake colonisation through private entrepreneurship, the only way that the notoriously conservative and parsimonious queen could be made to assent to the plan.[57]

53 Ibid., 54.

54 Ibid., 51 and further 57–60, 127–31 and comments in Henry S. Turner, 'Corporations. Humanism and Elizabethan Political Economy', in Philip J. Stern & Carl Wennerlind (eds), *Mercantilism Reimagined. Political Economy in Early Modern Britain and Its Empire* (Oxford University Press 2014), 157–8; Wood, *Foundations*, 207–10.

55 Smith, *Commonweal*, 23.

56 Tract by Sir Thomas Smith on the Colonisation of Ards in County of Down ["A Letter sent by T. B. Gentleman…"], printed as Appendix to George Hill, *An Historical Account of the Macdonnells of Antrim* (Belfast, Archer 1873), 405, 411. For the booklet and its context, see Mary Dewar, *Sir Thomas Smith. A Tudor Intellectual in Office* (London, Athlone 1964), 156–9.

57 Hiram Morgan, 'The Colonial Venture of Sir Thomas Smith in Ulster, 1571–1575', 28 *The Historical Journal* (1985), 265.

> Under Sidney's plan, private entrepreneurs and grandees would provide the financial resources . . . in exchange for royal recognition of feudal rights in any Irish territory they conquered.[58]

The idea of colonisation through private initiative lingered on even after the failure of the Irish expeditions in 1572–5. In perhaps the most widely read commentary on the Tudor constitution, *De republica anglorum* (1565, first published in 1583), Smith followed Fortescue in arguing that each nation was to have a constitution that was proper to it. In explaining the English constitution, Smith made it appear almost like a private arrangement between its classes.[59] The citizenry were divided into those who rule, the king, major and minor nobility, esquires, gentlemen, citizens, burgesses and yeomen, and "the fourth sort of men which do not rule".[60] For Smith, high official with the court, the English nation joined the interests of the crown, gentry and large merchants in an interdependent economic system led by the enlightened elite and followed passively by the rest: "only the rich could be sufficiently educated and disinterested to govern".[61] The corporate form of Smith's Irish venture was similar: half-public to the extent that it was carried out by the state's leading elites, and half-private to the extent that it would be led by and its profits directed to its initiators. As a joint-stock enterprise, it reflected Smith's principles of good government in microcosm, later followed in the colonisation of America.[62]

Irish colonisation in the sixteenth century illustrated the ubiquitous interpenetration of private interests with those of the crown that was a distinguishing feature of English statehood. Poor in natural resources, England's taxation base was narrow and its agriculture only beginning to engage with commercial production. The crown had to be attentive to the landed and commercial interests to secure a stable source of financing. The administrative machinery of the state was much smaller than in Castile or France. But like in the latter, it consisted of personal fiefdoms where

58 Robert A. Williams Jr., *The American Indian in Western Legal Thought. The Discourses of Conquest* (Oxford University Press 1990), 137.

59 Thomas Smith, *De republica anglorum* (L. Alston ed., Cambridge University Press 1906), I 16–24 (29–46).

60 Ibid., I 24 (46). For more detail on the work, see W. S. Holdsworth, 'The Prerogative in the Sixteenth Century', 21 *Columbia Law Review* (1921), 563–5.

61 Michael J. Braddick, 'Civility and Authority', in David Armitage & Michael J. Braddick (eds), *The British Atlantic World 1500–1800* (London, Macmillan 2002), 94. See e.g. Smith, *Commonweal*, 22–3; Wood, *Foundations*, 194–203.

62 See Turner, 'Corporations', 165.

> [n]early all the significant administrative positions, with the exception of the great offices of state, were now held by lay proprietary officeholders who collected the bulk of their income in the form of fees and gratuities. Pluralism, the appointment of deputies, and the granting of reversions were all common, as was the traffic in offices among private individuals.[63]

Another example of the way in which the English state coordinated its foreign policy interests with those of its nobles and merchants was the ingenious legal system that underlay Elizabeth's privateering war against Spain over the years 1585–1604: only 34 of the 197 ships that were sent to meet the Armada in 1588 were crown ships.[64] By that time, privateering had already become an industry. A private merchant or a shipper would receive a letter of reprisal from the High Court of Admiralty or the Queen herself in case that person had suffered from Spanish confiscations. Initially such practice presupposed turning first to the Spanish king to request an impartial trial; if this failed, the letter or commission may be granted in England. Providing evidence for loss soon became a mere formality, however, and letters of reprisal were issued automatically. Although some of the participants were looking for excitement and glory, "for the most part the promoters were merchants and seamen, people already in the shipping world, usually working in joint stock syndicates".[65] Of the few avenues of getting rich quickly or at least dispensing with a life of poverty at the time, joining Elizabeth's war was among the more attractive ones, despite the hazards. The roster of prize cases with the High Court of Admiralty soon filled up, and as many as one hundred private vessels participated at any one time in the Queen's war effort, contributing to the motivational combination of profit and nationalism that would lie at the origin of British naval hegemony.[66]

[63] Thomas Ertman, *The Birth of the Leviathan. Building States and Regimes in Medieval and Early Modern Europe* (Cambridge University Press 1997), 180. The importance of the practices of venality for the limited state bureaucracy in Britain in the sixteenth and seventeenth centuries is highlighted in Brewer, *The Sinews of Power*, 14–21.

[64] Brewer, *The Sinews of Power*, 10–11.

[65] Kenneth R. Andrews, *Trade, Plunder and Settlement. Maritime Enterprise and the Genesis of the British Empire, 1480–1630* (Cambridge University Press 1984), 246.

[66] Kenneth R. Andrews, *English Privateering Voyages to the West Indies 1588–1595* (Cambridge University Press 1959), 16–28. Not all of the voyages were profitable. But the value of annual prizes sometimes rose to 100,000 pounds or more, of which the Queen's formal share was between 5 and 10% (though in fact often much less). The greatest part went to large merchant-shipowners from London whose powerful fleet counted for about a half of the vessels engaged. These vessels and many of the captains trained in privateering would later form the core of the commercial fleet at

Men enriched by privateering would eventually initiate the founding of the large trading companies, including the Virginia and East India companies; they would also provide the ships and manpower to seize maritime superiority from the Dutch.[67]

Tudor rulers were keen to use patents and monopoly charters to allow themselves to be enlisted for projects of private enrichment if only that might make something trickle down the public treasury as well. In addition, Elizabeth's concern for administrative and financial rationality led to some very fruitful innovations. The stabilisation of the pound sterling and the establishment of the Royal Exchange (1560–1) laid the foundation for the gradual migration of high finance and entrepôt trade from Amsterdam to London, creating a lasting bond between the court and the merchant bankers. For example, her 42,000-pound investment in the Levant Company in 1580 produced returns that not only financed the East India Company's initial capital but, according to Maynard Keynes, generated the value of the entire capital of the principal trading companies around 1700, "and something close to £4000 million that constituted the entire stock of British investments in 1913".[68]

## Two Concepts of the Law of Nations

The role that private merchants and trading companies had in England led to two parallel ways of thinking about the law applicable outside the realm. In the first place, as the legal historian William Holdsworth has observed, in England, the "rules of international law were regarded as matters which concerned the Crown, and fell within its prerogative in relations to foreign affairs".[69] These rules were administered by civil lawyers such as Gentili or Sir Thomas Smith who were regularly

the service of the English Levant and East India companies. For the early history of English privateering, see further Grover Clark, 'The English Practice with Regard to Reprisals by Private Persons', 27 *American Journal of International Law* (1933), 694–723.

67 See especially Robert Brenner, *Merchants and Revolution. Commercial Change, Political Conflict, and London's Overseas Traders 1550–1653* (London, Verso 2003), 19, 45–50 and passim; David Scott, *Leviathan. The Rise of Britain as a World Power* (London, Collins 2013), 77–80.

68 Giovanni Arrighi, *The Long Twentieth Century. Money, Power and the Origins of Our Times* (London, Verso 2010), 191–2 and on the British strategy of flexibly combining territorial with commercial power, 200–18.

69 William Holdsworth, 'The Relation of English Law to International Law', 21 *Minnesota Law Review* (1942), 141.

consulted by the Privy Council on treaty issues and such matters as diplomatic immunities, the status of Hanseatic towns or the implications of asylum. They were in particular demand as diplomats and foreign policy advisors owing to their facility to communicate with colleagues across the continent. They were trained at the universities and became members of the "Doctors' Commons" in contrast to common lawyers who were trained in the Inns of Court.[70] Most civil law business was conducted with the High Court of Admiralty whose jurisdiction in each of its main areas of expertise – prize law, overseas mercantile and maritime matters and crimes at sea (above all piracy) – involved routine applications of the law of nations.

However, alongside rules of inter-sovereign interaction in peace and war, *ius gentium* was also understood to govern the conduct of trade and settlement by private actors, merchants and companies that had to do with private rights under the common law. In part jealous of the professional opportunities enjoyed by civil lawyers, in part genuinely opposed to the latter's royalism, common lawyers argued for the ancient nature of the common law and the way it defined and limited the powers of the king, but also "held that its purpose was the maintenance of individual rights, particularly the right to property".[71] As a result, two types of law of nations came to be employed in the English debates, one supporting the sovereignty of the king, the other the universal character of the private rights of Englishmen. While the former regulated Britain's relations with foreign powers and gave the justification to its expansion, the latter began to be associated with the commercial laws that assisted the entry of mercantile interests into the heart of English statecraft.

The middle of the sixteenth century was a golden era for English civilians who tended to look down on the archaic and disorganised nature of the common law.[72] In a passionate plea for the increased study of the civil law, Sir Robert Wiseman (1609/10–1684) highlighted its role in the organisation of the relations of nations in peace and war

[70] The numbers of civil lawyers and common lawyers in the period 1603–40 were roughly 200 and 2,000 respectively. Brian B. Levack, *The Civil Lawyers in England. A Political Study* (Oxford University Press 1973), 3; Daniel R. Coquillette, *The Civilian Writers of Doctors' Commons, London. Three Centuries of Innovation in Comparative, Commercial and International Law* (Berlin, Duncker & Humblot 1988), 31.

[71] J. P. Sommerville, *Royalists and Patriots. Politics and Ideology in England 1603–1640* (2nd edn, London, Longman 1999), 84.

[72] Harold J. Berman, 'The Origins of Historical Jurisprudence. Coke, Selden, Hale', 103 *Yale Law Journal* (1993–4), 1670.

and its great usefulness in England's dealings with other countries; while state law varied and often erred, civil law embodied what all nations had agreed as being in accordance with reason and equity.[73] Like Gentili, they argued for expansive royal powers.[74] For example, John Cowell (1554–1611), Gentili's Cambridge colleague, supported such a wide interpretation of the prerogative that it led him into conflict with parliament and ultimately also with King James.[75] Another civilian with royalist leanings was William Fulbeck (1560–1603) whose *The Pandectes of the Law of Nations* (1602) read into the law of nations the sovereign powers of kings, the laws of war and diplomacy, but also basic constitutional principles, general rules on prescription, marriage, property, contract, commercial law as well as the conventional ways of measuring time. A bencher of Gray's Inn like Gentili, Fulbeck had been trained at Oxford and published a widely read guide for law students as well as diverse plays and histories. He was known as an opponent of the conventional division between common law, civil law and canon law, arguing in a series of dialogues between representatives of the three legal disciplines in favour of a unified legal consciousness.[76] In *Pandectes*, Fulbeck wrote that hereditary monarchy was favoured by the law of nations and rejected any idea of democracy as a lawful system of government.[77] But he also made the usual point that the monarch was not to rule arbitrarily, through "voluntary conceits or unsatiable desires".[78] Fulbeck believed that in democracies "wicked and lewd persons do more flourish than good men and innocent" – ignorant and easily aroused for whatever cause, "[t]hey are like the winds, which Neptune trussed up, and delivered in bag to Ulysses".[79] Fulbeck derived both kingship and rights of property from an original state but, in an interesting twist, also affirmed that the present "degrees & callings of men" were decreed by the law of nations.[80] Once properties had been distributed, the prince would have no right to intervene in them unless

73 Sir Robert Wiseman, *The Law of Laws, or the Excellency of the Civil Law above all other Humane Laws Whatsoever* (London, Royston 1686), 50.

74 Glen Burgess, *Absolute Monarchy and the Stuart Constitution* (Yale University Press 1996), 75–8; Sommerville, *Royalists and Patriots*, 51.

75 See Sommerville, *Royalists and Patriots*, 113–19.

76 See e.g. William Fulbeck, *A Parallele or Conference of the Civil Law, Canon Law, and the Common Law of this Realme of England* (London, Company of Stationers 1618).

77 William Fulbeck, *The Pandectes of the Law of Nations, containing Several Discourses of the Questions, Points and Matters of Law wherein the Nations of the World do Consent and Accord* (London, Wight 1602), 11 [orthography modernised by MK], 13, 28–33.

78 Ibid.

79 Ibid., 29, 31.

80 Ibid., 60–5.

there were special causes, as determined by domestic laws.[81] This did not, naturally, apply to wars of conquest: "without all doubt the places, and the things of these places which the conquering army doth possess, do justly belong unto the conqueror".[82] A profoundly conservative representative of a class society, Fulbeck expressed a dislike of merchants that the succeeding generation would try its best to dilute.[83] At the same time, however, he had a live sense of the law as an instrument of government and lawyers as assisting in the work of the court in that respect – a perspective rarely apparent in the writings of the common lawyers.

Although Gentili's successor and protégé Richard Zouche (1589–1660) may have shared his royalist leanings (he was dismissed from official positions after the execution of the king), he never put them in equally uncompromising terms. Zouche's *Juris et judicii Fecialis* (1650) has sometimes been credited as the first full treatment of "public international law" in England. But the work is seldom read and there is little evidence of its influence at the time. Zouche was regius professor of civil law at Oxford, member of the Doctors' Commons and judge in the High Court of Admiralty. *Fecial Law* was the last instalment in a seven-volume work designed as a complete exposition of jurisprudence in a Roman law idiom. Zouche is remembered above all for his limitation, in Part I of the work, of the law of nations to "the law which is observed in common between princes or peoples of different nations", including matters such as how "nations are separated, kingdoms founded, commerce instituted and, lastly, wars introduced". Subjects such as property, contract or family relations, "the common element in the law which the peoples of single nations use among themselves", were excluded from that definition.[84] But whether the distinction, well known from the Digest and also employed by Suárez, had any sense beyond the taxonomic one, remains unclear. Part II proceeded to practical applications and controversial questions of the substance introduced in the first part, offering illustrations from Antiquity and recent times, interspersed with references to Roman and modern writers, often leaving its author's own view of the matter open – an approach he termed "Socratic".[85] Only in matters where a clear

[81] Ibid., 12–14. [82] Ibid., 51, also 11. [83] See ibid., 65–6.

[84] Richard Zouche, *An Exposition of Fecial Law and Procedure, or of Law between Nations, and Questions Concerning the Same...* (translation of *Juris et judicii Fecialis sive, iuris inter gentes et questionum de eodem explixation*, trans. J. L. Brierly, Washington 1911), I I (1).

[85] Ibid., 63, 74–5. See also Coquillette, *Civilian Writers*, 174–80.

English position could be discerned, such as rejection of the Spanish claim of monopoly in the Indies or the withdrawal of the privileges of the Hanseatic States, did he loyally express an opinion.[86]

Zouche presented the substance of fecial law, following the larger work of which it was a part, under four headings: relations of sovereign and subject (*status*), ownership and territorial rights (*dominium*), diplomatic and treaty relations (*debitum*) and war (*delictum*). Instead of organising his rules – such as *dominium* or citizenship, for instance – under naturalist principles, they were illuminated by practical examples. Basic constitutional forms were laid out without express preference. The same technique was followed in the treatment of such inter-state matters as territory, rank and procedure, treaty-making, as well as *ius ad bellum* and *ius in bello*. Like Gentili's *Hispanio Advocatis*, the work was best seen as a handbook for practitioners in the diplomatic part of European law of nations. Later generations have, however, assessed it without mercy as – boring.[87]

Zouche's work provided up-to-date legal advice in the form of accounts of incidents from sometimes very recent diplomatic and military practice. He did not engage in abstract discussion of the place of the law of nations in the government of England or more widely, but although like Gentili, he seemed uninterested in economics, he stressed the importance of the right to trade to the general conduct of the affairs of nations.[88] Treaties of commerce could, for example, be concluded with infidel nations and uncultivated territories could be occupied by those ready to make use of them.[89] In his work on admiralty law, Zouche frequently stressed the importance of commerce and the role of merchants for England. Like other civilians, he felt that matters of "navigation and trade" were best treated within the courts of admiralty as the courts of common law failed to give recognition to many of the rules under which they were conducted.[90] Zouche's *ius inter gentes* as well as his admiralty law were both conceived in a thoroughly practical way – one an aspect of diplomacy and belligerent ethics, the other a part of trade and navigation. Both were treated under principles of civil law and conceived as parts of the way

[86] Zouche, *Exposition*, 80, 102.

[87] Coquillette, *Civilian Writers*, 175. Likewise Arthur Nussbaum, *A Concise History of the Law of Nations* (2nd rev. edn, New York, Macmillan 1954), 165–7.

[88] Zouche, *Exposition*, 109–10. [89] Ibid., 101, 110.

[90] Richard Zouche, *The Jurisdiction of the Admiralty in England Asserted* (London, Basset 1686), 127–30.

princes, ambassadors and merchants went about their business with foreign nations and nationals.

## Common Law Views

Reading Fulbeck and Zouche, it is easy to understand why common lawyers had some difficulty with the abstractions of the civil law. In the course of the late sixteenth and early seventeenth century, the business of civil lawyers diminished dramatically owing to the attack conducted on them by the most prominent of the common lawyers, the formidable Edward Coke (1552–1634), solicitor-general and attorney-general during Elizabeth, chief justice of Common Pleas and a member of the Privy Council until his fall from grace under King James. The common law courts expanded the use of writs of *assumpsit*, established prohibitions and created fictions that enabled them to encroach on the often-lucrative work of civil law jurisdictions, including in mercantile matters of the High Court of Admiralty.[91] Efforts were made under the auspices of the Privy Council to solve these conflicts, but largely unsuccessfully. As the number of instance cases with the Admiralty Court diminished, civilians began to publish tracts and make speeches about the great utility in dealing with commercial and maritime cases under principles applicable across Europe.[92] Zouche, for example, argued that the "Wisdom and Equity of the Roman Civil Law" had made it applicable in maritime and commercial cases that were everywhere decided by special courts, applying universal laws. Moreover, the jurisdiction of such courts was not determined only by attention to the place where the events had taken place or the contracts had been concluded but by their commercial substance. It was because mercantile matters were inherently cosmopolitan that applying domestic laws to them was such a profound error.[93] "Causes concerning Merchants are not now to be

[91] For the struggle by the common lawyers to limit the jurisdiction of the civil law courts, see Coquillette, *Civilian Writers*, 103–15 and passim; Louis A. Knafla, *Law and Politics in Jacobean England. The Tracts of Lord Chancellor Ellesmere* (Cambridge University Press 1977), 134–8 (on conflict with ecclesiastical courts) and especially Levack, *Civil Lawyers*. For the struggle against ecclesiastical jurisdictions especially, see Brooks, *Law, Politics and Society*, 97–123.

[92] See e.g. Wiseman, *The Law of Laws* and the discussion in Henry J. Bourguignon, *Sir William Scott, Lord Stowell. Judge of the High Court of Admiralty 1798–1828* (Cambridge University Press 1987), 20–5. See also Lionel H. Laing, 'Historic Origins of Admiralty Jurisdiction in England', 45 *Michigan Law Review* (1946–7), 179–82.

[93] Zouche, *Jurisdiction of the Admiralty*, 88, 94–7. It was also the case, he added, that these special jurisdictions could decide the matters "summarily and in a more

decided by the peculiar and ordinary laws of every Country, but by the general Laws of Nature and Nations."[94]

Sir Thomas Ridley (1549–1629) reminded his readers that chairs of civil law had been set up by the crown precisely to train young men so "that when they came abroad, they might be more ready in all matters of negotiation and commerce, that the Prince or state should have need of them when dealing with foreign nations when they were thereto called; to which the Lawes of the Land serve nothing at all".[95] When foreign rulers sent men abroad to conduct embassies or conclude treaties, they were always civil lawyers. Surely, Ridley argued, the matter should be no different in England.[96] Ridley was especially scathing towards the practice of diverting commercial and maritime matters to be decided under domestic law – this only made the law less responsive to the needs of merchants and gradually eroded the trade law competence that was vital for England's prosperity and, ultimately, peace.[97] Another civil lawyer Sir Leoline Jenkins (1623–1685) pointed to the scandal that would ensue if "Officers of small Corporations [are made] Judges upon the Law of Nations, and your Majesty's Treaties with Foreign Princes and States".[98] Admiralty courts and the law merchant served different needs than common law, namely those of international commerce, giving effects to bills of exchange that common law courts would not recognise to the great disservice to commerce and prosperity in England.[99] Regardless, King's Bench and other common law courts continued encroaching on the practices of the High Court of Admiralty, and only its wartime prize jurisdiction enabled it to survive as a living institution into the eighteenth century.[100]

Coke's opposition to civil law even in international matters was perfectly illustrated in his replies to the admiralty's objections against the prohibitions issued by common law courts; for Coke, only if a transaction had the most marginal connection to the realm, for example, if a part of it was to be executed in England, then the whole

compendious way" than common law courts, and accept evidence referring to equity more widely than the latter, 127–9.

94 Ibid., 88, 89.

95 Sir Thomas Ridley, *A View of Civil and Ecclesiastical Law* (Oxford 1676), 118.

96 Ibid., 130–1.

97 For a discussion of Ridley, see Coquillette, *Civilian Writers*, 119–22.

98 Jenkins' Report to the King, 1675, as quoted in Francis Déak & Philip C. Jessup, 'Early Prize Court Procedure', 82 *University of Pennsylvania Law Review* (1934), 680.

99 Zouche, *Jurisdiction of the Admiralty*, 128.

100 Bourguignon, *Sir William Scott*, 26–30.

transaction would come under the common law.[101] Coke was not averse to a law of nations with universal applicability. He did not object to English courts pronouncing on international or commercial matters but insisted that that they were to do this from the perspective of the common law.[102] The common law may have grown in England but it aligned with principles of a legal reason that applied everywhere. In a famous passage in his commentary to Littleton, Coke wrote:

> Reason is the life of the law, nay the common law itself is nothing else but reason, which is to be understood as an artificial perfection of reason, gotten by study, observation, and experience...[103]

Two aspects of that statement are noteworthy. First is the alignment of the common law with natural reason that enabled Coke to expand the application of the principles underlying the common law beyond the territory of England. Coke himself had ample experience in commercial law and recognised the fertility of *lex mercatoria.*[104] Already Fortescue had thought this way, and other important common lawyers such as Lord Chancellor Ellesmere (Thomas Egerton) held it obvious that "the common law of England is grounded upon the law of God and extends itselfe to the originall lawe of nature, and the universall law of nations".[105] As a common lawyer, Sir Francis Bacon was quite emphatic about the fact that English law itself law was applicable outside the realm at least where it related to "reward, privilege or benefit" receivable in England or the duties of English subjects to the crown.[106] He also wrote that there existed "a natural and tacit confederation amongst all men" that allowed for example labelling pirates "*communes humani generis hostes*", enemies of humankind, that all nations had the power to prosecute.[107]

[101] Edward Coke, *The Fourth Part of the Institutes of the Laws of England* (5th ed., London, Flesher 1671), XXII (134–6).

[102] See e.g. Edward Coke, *The First Part of the Institutes of the Laws of England* (18th ed., London, Clarke 1823), II Sect 282 182a ("and this is *per legem mercatoriam* which (as hath been said) is part of the lawes of this realm for the advancement and continuance of commerce and trade, which is *pro bono publico*").

[103] Coke, *The First Part*, I, Sect 138, 97b.

[104] Coquillette, *Civilian Writers*, 103.

[105] Lord Chancellor Ellesmere in *Calvin's Case*, 670.

[106] Speech of Lord Bacon, as counsel for Calvin in ibid., II, 585.

[107] Sir Francis Bacon, 'Of an Holy War', in *Works of Francis Bacon, Baron of Verulam in Ten Volumes* (London, Baynes and Son 1824), 487.

Secondly, the reason referred to was the specific way of thinking of judges, in case of England common law judges, honed by years of study and practice. In *Calvin's case* (1607), for example, concerning the subjects' allegiance to the crown, Coke defined natural law as part of the law of England. It was not whatever uneducated set of assumptions about a higher law, however, but the work of judges "such as by diligent study and long experience and observation are so learned in the law of this realm, as out of the reason of the same they can rule the case in question".[108] Hence the expression "artificial reason" – a reason that was developed in practice but expressed higher principles that sometimes even allowed striking down regular statutes.[109] The idea of artificial reason was widely accepted by the common lawyers because it enabled the adaptation of the otherwise custom-oriented common law to present concerns: "What is reasonable depended to a degree on circumstances, and it was precisely this act of determining exactly what is reasonable in given circumstances that custom performed."[110] More important than legal theory for Coke was his faith in justice being expressed in the judge's pragmatic reasonableness, a "professional consensus of the legal community".[111]

The most important aspect of this "artificial reason" lay in the protection it offered to rights of property and the powers of parliament. What continental lawyers addressed as "public law" came in England under the label of the royal prerogative that Coke understood as limited by common law rules on property.[112] Moreover, the purpose of the prerogative was, common lawyers agreed, protection of the commonwealth. This they interpreted as involving the protection of Englishmen's right to exercise trade and professions and limiting the crown's power to set up monopolies. Coke himself regarded the widespread Elizabethan practice of monopoly privileges as an impermissible encroachment on parliament's competences. It violated the prohibition of usury and undermined the rights of Englishmen to property, trade and employment. Monopolies were not automatically illegal – Coke

108 Coke, *Calvin's Case*, 641.

109 As in the famous Bonham's case, which has thereafter been endlessly cited as the origin of the principle of judicial review in the Anglo-American legal system. See e.g. R. H. Helmholz, 'Natural Law and Human Rights in English Law. From Bracton to Blackstone', 3 *Ave Maria Law Review* (2005), 12–19.

110 Burgess, *Ancient Constitution*, 50.

111 Allen D. Boyer, *Sir Edward Coke and the Elizabethan Age* (Stanford University Press 2003), 187, 86–8, 92, 97–100; Berman, 'Origins of Historical Jurisprudence', 1689–1694.

112 Burgess, *Absolute Monarchy*, 194–207.

himself participated in the drafting of the first charter of the Virginia Company. But they were often, perhaps in most cases, harmful: "the ruling principle at common law was freedom of enterprise".[113] In striking down the monopoly of producing playing cards in the famous *Case of Monopolies* (*Darcy* v. *Allein* 1602), Coke observed that:

> The sole trade of any mechanical artifice, or any other monopoly, is not only a prejudice to those who exercise the same trade, but also to all other subjects, for the end of all these monopolies is for the private gain of the patentees.[114]

A monopoly impoverishes others in the trade who will now "be constrained to live in idleness and beggary". Both individual traders as well as the community will suffer because "he who has the sole selling of any commodity, may and will make the price as he pleases. . . . Therefore, every grant made in grievance or prejudice of the subject is void."[115] But not only a monopoly for the *production* of playing cards was illegal. So was also a monopoly of their *importation*:

> Also such a charter of a monopoly [is] against the freedom of trade and traffic, is against diverse acts of Parliament [] which for the advancement of the freedom of trade and traffic extends to all things vendible, notwithstanding any franchise granted to the contrary.[116]

The prohibition was not absolute. Patents and charters could be granted, and parliamentary statutes passed to limit trade for the good of the commonwealth, but every such limitation was to be narrowly construed. In the case concerning the king's prerogative in *Saltpetre* (1607), Coke limited the power of the king to intervene in the right of property only "as this concerns the necessary defence of the realm". To be dependent on foreign powers in matters of gunpowder-production was a matter of public interest. This entitled the king to take saltpetre from private properties but only if they "leave the inheritance of the subject in so good plight as they found it". Anything else would amount

113 Donald O. Wagner, 'Coke and the Rise of Economic Liberalism', 6 *The Economic History Review* (1953), 44, 30–44. See also Charles Wilson, *England's Apprenticeship 1603–1763* (London, Longman 1965), 100–3 and further *The Case of the Tailors of Habits of Ipswich*, where Coke stated that "the Common Law doth abhor all Monopolies which forbid any one to work in any lawful Trade", reprinted partly in S. Shepard (ed.), *The Selected Writings and Speeches of Sir Edward Coke*, vol. I (Indianapolis, Liberty Fund 2003), 393.

114 *Case of Monopolies* (*Darcy* v. *Allein*), in *The Reports of Sir Edward Coke in Thirteen Parts. A New Edition in Six Volumes*, vol. VI (London, Butterworths 1826) [*Coke Reports*], Part XI 86a–86b (162).

115 Ibid., 86b–87a (163).

116 Ibid., 87b–88a (165).

to "disinheritance of the subject", which "the King by prerogative cannot do".[117]

After mid-sixteenth century, common lawyers and some civilians began to address European commercial practices as part of the common law, or at least of English law, either owing to their having existed "from time immemorial" or by applying a less rigorous criterion assumed to be part of the law of nations. This was frequently identified as the law merchant (*lex mercatoria*) whose application was justified alternatively by natural law or *ius gentium*.[118] It was a practical law that enshrined varying, often local codes of expedited commercial procedure that, as the role of specific mercantile courts diminished, were integrated in the common law by recourse to fiction: a foreign transaction under a bill of exchange, in itself unacknowledged in England, might be dealt with as if it referred to a contract concluded in England.[119] Through such fictions and the expansion of the *assumpsit* formula in the sixteenth and seventeenth centuries, common law courts seized also other kinds of transactions, such as insurance and partnership arrangements previously dealt with by civil lawyers in the admiralty court as mercantile practice under *ius gentium*.[120] The seizures were fiercely opposed by civil lawyers who saw in them a threat to their livelihood and a danger to international transactions. They did this largely in vain. Common law courts kept extending their jurisdiction on a widening scale of international practices. Coke himself held it fully appropriate for the courts to apply *lex mercatoria* if only this was reasonable.[121] Because it could not be classified under natural law owing to the latter's unchanging character, there was really no choice but to regard *lex mercatoria* as part of a *ius gentium*.[122]

117 The *Case of the King's Prerogative in Salpetre* (1607) in *Coke Reports* vol. VI, Part XII-12, 2 (206–10).

118 See e.g. Coquillette, *Civilian Writers*, 34–5.

119 See especially, J. H. Baker, 'The Law Merchant and the Common Law before 1700', 38 *Cambridge Law Journal* (1979), 303–6.

120 Ibid., 308–13. For the origins of law merchant jurisprudence in thirteenth- and fourteenth-century England where courts operating at key ports or trading centres were granted the power to adjudicate affairs relating to voyaging merchants, see Coquillette, *Civilian Writings*, 124–8; Dave de Ruysscher, 'La *lex mercatoria* contextualisée. Tracer son parcours intellectuel', 90 *Revue historique de droit français et étranger* (2012), 501–10.

121 Daniel J. Hulsebosch, 'The Ancient Constitution and the Expanding Empire. Sir Edward Coke's British Jurisprudence', 21 *The Law and History Review* (2003), 451.

122 The point about the gap between the practices of common law courts and the "learned treatises on the law merchant" by civil lawyers is made in Baker, 'The Law Merchant and the Common Law', 321.

## The Structure of Commercial Power: Companies and State

By the first decades of the seventeenth century it had become clear that a nation's international power depended on its wealth, and that wealth, especially if the state possessed only limited resources, depended on the intensity of commerce. At this time, the cloth trade, England's most important export, was organised around a monopoly patent issued to the company of Merchant Adventurers. Owing to the increasing criticism directed against monopolies, the director of the company, John Wheeler, published a tract in 1601 where he explained the great utility, for the state itself, of this practice. Companies like his regularly conducted diplomacy on behalf of the state, maintained navigational links and provided naval support to the state. They produced customs revenue, engaged in works of charity, and in innumerable other ways advanced the nation's welfare. They also provided loans to the royal house and spent great sums in coronation and triumphal proceedings.

> And when for the defence of the Realme, Shippes have beene to bee made out, it hath cost them notable summes of money . . . all which could not have been done but by men united into a Societie or companie.[123]

Wheeler's company, the Merchant Adventurers, originated in a thirteenth-century London Mercers' guild that had later spread to Antwerp and different localities across England.[124] Its cloth trade was conducted almost exclusively with northern Europe. This had increased until roughly the 1540s from which point until the end of the century the company controlled about half of London's total exports, operating also as a significant financer for the crown. In compensation, the company received considerable privileges in England and at its foreign headquarters in Antwerp.[125]

The practice of chartering corporations went back to the medieval guilds and regulated monopoly companies. Without formal royal assent, members ran the risk of being charged of unlawful assembly.[126]

[123] John Wheeler, *A Treatise of Commerce* (London, Harison 1601), 111.

[124] The substantial exterritorial privileges enjoyed by the corporation in Antwerp contributed significantly to the prosperity of the town, until expulsion during the Spanish occupation in 1585. See Percival Griffiths, *A Licence to Trade. A History of the English Chartered Companies* (London, Benn 1974), 9–16. That admission to the Merchant Adventurers was limited (its membership in the seventeenth century rose to 3,500) was a source of constant complaints as were its monopoly privileges. However, its revenues to the crown were substantial and it saw itself as an instrument in the good government of the realm.

[125] Brenner, *Merchants and Revolution*, 56–7.

[126] Griffiths, *A Licence to Trade*, x.

The charter would lay out the corporation's administrative structures and its relations to the king. While unchartered commercial companies did operate at home, sixteenth-century Englishmen needed an authorisation to conduct foreign trade: "the royal prerogative had an ancient and special force in the government of trade".[127] The business of the main rival of Wheeler's company, the Merchants of Staple, likewise originating in the Middle Ages, but dealing exclusively in raw materials, had been gradually overtaken by the cloth manufactures so that at the end of the century, the Merchant Adventurers were England's leading commercial operator.[128] That a company such as Merchant Adventurers was, according to Coke, a "collegium or universitas", enabled it to hold and dispose of property and to be liable for the debts it has incurred.[129] It also had wide legislative and prorogatory jurisdiction, and was authorised to punish violators by seizing their person and assets.[130] By chartering a company, the king could prevent parliamentary intervention in matters under company jurisdiction while simultaneously making those endowed with exclusive rights dependent on the crown. It was no accident that the London merchants by and large sided with the king in the tumults of the seventeenth century.[131]

Corporations were an important part of the government of early modern England, with examples extending from the church to the town, the city, the guild, the hospital and the university. The reasons for using companies in foreign trade were both practical and legal. Setting up a trading post, factory or a settlement was costly, and the risks were enormous. The scale of the operation required multiple

[127] Coke, 'Notes of Prerogative', quoted in Griffiths, *A Licence to Trade*, ix.

[128] The Staple was a grouping of wool exporters who coordinated their retail sales at various domestic and foreign locations until being set up in Calais (at the time part of England) where it stayed until the middle of the sixteenth century. It was a regulated company of twenty-four members with strict rules on prices and profit distribution, plus jurisdiction over the town and a judicial body administering the law merchant; one-third of its proceedings went to the crown to which it also provided occasional loans. See Griffith, *A Licence to Trade*, 5–9.

[129] Lawyers debated endlessly the nature of corporations as "artificial" or "fictitious" persons. They were classed as "sole" and "aggregate", the most important of the former being the king. "Aggregate" corporations such as the commercial company consisted of a multitude of members united in their pursuit of a shared objective. See F. W. Maitland, 'The Corporation Sole', 16 *Law Quarterly Review* (1900), 335–54.

[130] John P. Davis, *Corporations, A Study of the Origin and Development of Great Business Combinations and of Their Relation to the Authority of the State* (New York, Franklin 1970 [1905]), II, 74–7.

[131] See especially, Brenner, *Merchants and Revolution.*

investors who could be engaged in two legal forms. Within "regulated companies" individual traders would unite to buy and sell into their own account, while in "joint stock companies" transactions were conducted on behalf of the company itself.[132] The stock might be joint for a single voyage or for a more extended period, and some companies alternated between the two. Moreover, establishment in a foreign territory often required the consent of the other country for which the presence of a charter signalled that the activity was supported by a foreign ruler. Hence the powers were initially always based on treaty. To the extent that extraterritoriality was treated on a customary basis – as it frequently was – it became part of customary law of nations.[133] As property-owners and legislators companies were largely immune from the rival powers of the king or parliament so that "the early modern English 'state' became a composite of agents, networks and 'grids of power' that operated within, aside and sometimes in conflict with the sovereign Crown".[134]

The stagnation of the Merchant Adventurers' cloth trade in northern Europe in the mid-sixteenth century led to a new type of commerce, namely the import of silk, spices, furs, oils, food items and luxury manufactures from Russia, the Mediterranean and the East Indies. A new merchant elite arose with novel priorities in English trade and expansion.[135] Trade relations were established through Russia with Persia and all the way to the East Indies. Preparing ships for long-term voyages required investments of a wholly unprecedented scale. Hence, a monopoly charter was issued to the Muscovy (Russia) Company in 1555 for trade and discovery in the northeast and northwest. Directed by the explorer Sebastian Cabot, the company's investors included great notables such as the lord chancellor and two privy councillors.[136] The stock was set up for several voyages and the company was authorised to draw up detailed regulations for eastern trade

132 Griffith, *A Licence to Trade*, xiii.

133 For instance, a patent by Richard III from 1485 appears to be based simply on general custom. Hope Scott QC, 'Report on British Jurisdiction in Foreign Seas (1843)', reproduced in Sir Henry Jenkyns, *British Rule and Jurisdiction beyond the Seas* (Oxford, Clarendon 1902), 247.

134 Philip J. Stern, '"Bundles of Hyphens." Corporations as Legal Communities in the Early Modern British Empire', in Lauren Benton & Richard J. Ross (eds), *Legal Pluralism and Empires 1500–1850* (New York University Press 2013), 24.

135 On the growth of the new import trade, see Brenner, *Merchants and Revolution*, 24–33, 39–45.

136 Griffith, *A Licence to Trade*, 22–3.

and to punish offenders. The charter entitled the company to conquer any "infidel lands" that had not been "commonly frequented" by Englishmen.[137] Its good relations with the Czar led to the company receiving monopoly rights and immunity in Russia, too, and local authorities were instructed to assist the company in the enforcement of its regulations and arresting interlopers. In 1566 Parliament confirmed the company's privileges.[138]

Elizabeth continued to authorise regulated companies (e.g. Hamburgh Company 1564, Spanish and Venice companies in 1577 and 1583, and Morocco Company 1588) while the joint stock model was used to trade with the Levant (Turkey Company 1581) and the East Indies (1603). "In fact, so successful was the strategy that by 1580s it was only trade with France, Scotland and Ireland that was not in the hands of a company."[139] Whether the founding act was a letter patent or a charter was unimportant. The instrument contained provisions on the company's objectives, its area of operations, internal organisation, authority towards members and employees, and powers to legislate on travel and trade in extensive areas. The companies possessed diplomatic privileges and were often treated as representatives of the crown itself. They were moreover entitled to conquer foreign territory not already occupied by Europeans and, in case of settlement colonies, to exercise territorial rights with nominal metropolitan supervision.[140] Throughout, the relationship between the company and the state remained unarticulated, to the benefit of both parties; they could stress their close relations in view of distributing profits and privileges, but separateness when issues of responsibility for the conduct of either party arose.

The close relations between the merchant community and the English state were nowhere better demonstrated than in the establishment and

[137] See William Robert Scott, *The Constitution and Finance of English, Scottish and Irish Joint-Stock Companies to 1720* (3 vols, Cambridge University Press 1912), II, 36–47; Davis, *Corporations*, II, 97–103. For extracts of the charter of 6 February 1555, see Adam Anderson, *An Historical and Chronological Deduction of the Origin of Commerce* (London, Walton 1778), 98–9.

[138] The company's monopoly and its profits began to fluctuate in the late sixteenth and early seventeenth century, with the English Revolution and Dutch commercial pressure opening Russia to "interlopers" and other nations' merchants. From the 1620s onwards the company operated under the control of the East India Company. Davis, *Corporations*, II, 99–102; Brenner, *Merchants and Revolution*, 79.

[139] Michael J. Braddick, *State Formation in Early Modern England c. 1550–1700* (Cambridge University Press 2000), 398.

[140] See below, Chapter 10.

operation of the Levant (Turkey) Company. Until the mid-sixteenth century, English commercial relations with the Ottoman empire had been conducted through the intermediary of Genoa or Venice.[141] In 1570s, stagnation of Antwerp commerce, difficulties in finding a workable trade route through Russia and the threat of Spanish control of Asian trade prompted the leading London merchants to seek Elizabeth's support for opening a maritime connection to the Levant. Two London merchants with widespread commercial interests, Edward Osborne and Richard Staper, succeeded in attaining safe conduct for one of former's employees, William Harborne, to arrive in Constantinople in July 1578. Operating initially under the treaty of 1535 between Suleiman and François I of France that entitled foreigners to trade under the protection of the French flag,[142] Harborne was able to agree a treaty with Sultan Murad that gave English subjects full freedom to trade and travel in Ottoman territories. The English were also entitled to appoint consuls with jurisdiction in disputes between Englishmen; they were freed from poll taxes and from arrests on the basis of others' crimes or unpaid taxes. English wills were to be honoured and English merchants and marines assisted if found in distress.[143]

Many reasons prompted the Queen to support the initiative. Alongside the purely economic interest, naval construction would receive a boost and there was hope to enlist Turkish support against Spain. Accordingly, a charter was issued in September 1581 to a group of twelve of the richest London merchants with close connections to the court, for a seven-year trade monopoly in the whole of the Middle East.[144] Organised initially

[141] On the first voyages to the eastern Mediterranean and the establishment of consular posts in the region, see Alfred C. Wood, *A History of the Levant Company* (London, Cass 1964), 1–4.

[142] For the English text of the treaty, see Nasim Sousa, *The Capitulatory Régime of Turkey. Its History, Origin and Nature* (Johns Hopkins Press 1933), 314–20. The treaty gave wide civil and criminal jurisdiction to the French consul. Civil cases involving Ottoman subjects were to be dealt with by Ottoman courts while criminal cases were to be referred to the Porte. Ibid., 17–33, 51–3. The treaty in itself constituted no novelty. For example, Greek, Armenian and Jewish communities as well as Venetian and Genoese merchants had enjoyed privileges in Byzantium since the conquest of 1453.

[143] 'The Charter of Privileges Granted to the English...' (June 1580), in Richard Hakluyt, *The Principal Navigations Voyages, Traffiques and Discoveries of the English Nation* (16 vols., Edinburgh, Goldsmith 1887), V, 268–73.

[144] 'The Letters Patents, or Privileges Granted by her Majestie to Sir Edward Osborne...', in ibid., 275–83. See further Wood, *A History of the Levant Company*, 11; Davis, *Corporations*, 88–92. Andrews argues, however, that the English interest at this stage was exclusively commercial. *Trade, Plunder and Settlement*, 90–1.

on a joint stock basis, the company was authorised to make laws and ordinances for the government of English mercantile activities in the enormous area allocated to it on condition that they would "not be [. . .] contrary or repugnant to the laws, estates or customs of our realm".[145] In exchange the company was expected to pay the crown an annual fee of 500 pounds. The company's ships were also regularly commissioned for privateering activities against Portuguese vessels returning from Brazil, thus contributing to the war effort and ensuring "enormous quantities of sugar without having to pay for it".[146] Harborne himself was appointed ambassador but his salary and other costs, including the ostentatious presents expected by the Sultan and his principal officers, were to be paid by the company. Even as he was derided by colleagues as "only a merchant", Harborne rapidly established the company's activities on a firm footing.

In a new charter of 7 January 1592, the company's monopoly was extended to trade routes to the east. Harborne was authorised to appoint consuls across the Ottoman realm and to take action to secure the implementation of the privileges by often recalcitrant Turkish officials. The company's first years of operation were hugely successful, with profits arising up to 300 percent for some voyages.[147]

> From its inception therefore the embassy at Constantinople had a dual aspect; its holder was at once a royal representative, commissioned by the sovereign and employed in diplomatic duties, and a commercial agent paid by a company of merchants, and pledged to safeguard and promote their business interests.[148]

In a few years the company possessed a fleet with no fewer than fifteen ships that were among the heaviest and most efficiently armed in the Mediterranean.[149] In exchange for political support, the company's ships were, with due notice, to be commandeered by the navy, and regularly used in obscure privateering ventures.[150] Most of the consular

145 'The Letters Patents', 277.

146 Brenner, *Merchants and Revolution*, 19.

147 Wood, *A History of the Levant Company*, 17; Brenner, *Merchants and Revolution*, 62. The new charter joined the Turkey company with the Venice company, providing them with a twelve-year monopoly in their respective territories and enlisting them to seek out an overland mercantile route from Aleppo via Baghdad to the Indies.

148 Wood, *A History of the Levant Company*, 12–13.

149 See Ralph Davis, 'England and the Mediterranean', in F. J. Fisher (ed.), *Essays in the Economic and Social History of Tudor and Stuart England* (Cambridge University Press 1961), 130–2.

150 Andrews, *Trade, Plunder and Settlement*, 97–8.

officials in Aleppo, Greece, Morea, Cyprus, Smyrna, Chios, Tripoli and other places were appointed by the company and reported to its headquarters in London. Only in cases of special political significance, such as Venice, was the appointment made by government.[151] Under a treaty with Mohammed III in 1597 the company gained the right to extend English protection to other nations' vessels as well – an additional source of income. The company likewise gained the monopoly of the very lucrative currant trade, including the right to levy taxes for currants imported in non-company ships. After a series of quarrels with the crown over the fee to be paid for these privileges, a new charter was issued by King James on 14 December 1605.[152] In 1631 the company received the right to post an agent in the customs house to verify the source of all cargoes to and from the Levant.[153]

In the period 1580–1620 Turkey became England's most important trade partner. With rising profits, the company could increase the salary of the new ambassador, Edward Barton, up to 1,500 pounds a year – "an opulent salary in those times" that remained for the company to pay, despite its protestations.[154] By the 1630s, the Muscovy and Levantine traders had become the elite of the London merchant community with close contacts to Charles I personally and eventually "mobiliz[ed]... in the maintenance of the established order".[155] The Restoration saw the joint control of Levant trade by the king with the great London merchants further tightened while the treaty of 1675 provided the company's consuls with wide extraterritorial jurisdiction and other privileges.[156] The company was opened for all Englishmen only in 1754 when its most profitable period had already passed. It preserved the privilege of appointing the ambassador until 1803, however, and was dissolved in 1825.[157]

The Levant Company was only one among a large number of English trading ventures whose monopoly bound tightly together the interests of the crown and the merchant elite. The state acted vigorously to prevent interloping and sometimes – as for instance with the Russian

151 Wood, *A History of the Levant Company*, 64–79.
152 Ibid., 35–9; Brenner, *Merchants and Revolution*, 63–4. For the charter, see M. Epstein, *The Early History of the Levant Company* (London, Routledge 1908), 153–210.
153 Brenner, *Merchants and Revolution*, 49, 66, 283–4.
154 Wood, *A History of the Levant Company*, 24, 26.
155 Brenner, *Merchants and Revolution*, 83, 91, 282–4.
156 See Lewis Hertslet, Hertslet's Commerical Treaties, 30 vols. (London, Whitehall 1840), II, 346–69.
157 Davis, *Corporations*, 95–7.

Czar in 1623 – agreed with foreign rulers the joint implementation of the monopoly.[158] This reflected the growing sense that trade was a matter of policy and that England's wealth and power were completely tied up with those of its leading merchants. How to understand the close dependence of state power with the activities of private merchants became the task of a new genre of writing that moved freely between expositions of new commercial practices, discussion of the legal regulation of those practices and recommendations for mercantile policy.

## Commercial State: Mercantile Law

An author whose writings were situated precisely at the crossroads of law, policy and trade was Gerard Malynes (1586–1626) whose *Lex Mercatoria* (1622/29) produced an overall justification in a legal idiom of the practices of European trade:

> Right merchants are taken to be wise in the profession, for their own good and benefit of the common-wealth, for of the six members of all the government of monarchies and common-weales, they are the principal instruments to increase or decrease the wealth thereof.[159]

Where Fulbeck had celebrated law as a "princely discipline, the center of common weales and the science of government", Malynes wanted to seize the spirit of the age and turn attention to commerce instead. The civil lawyers, Bartolus and such, he wrote, produced "long discourses and books" that were far too otherworldly.[160] How much more useful were the mercantile skills, arithmetic, geometry, cosmography, weights and measures, applied across the world that a merchant needed to know in order to do his work well! Malynes drew the reader's attention to ways of comparing the principal commodities of different countries, the customs of buying and selling, the moneys and their value, forms of exchange, ways of freighting, insurance and account-keeping as well as the practices of merchant courts. All these would come under the law merchant. Like Grotius, Malynes had a providential and harmonious view of trade – its increase expressed the

158 Ibid., 101.

159 Malynes, *Lex Mercatoria*. The "six members" were the clergy, nobility, husbandsmen, magistrates, artificers and merchants, 62. For the background of the merchant Malynes, see e,g. Coquillette, *Civilian Writers*, 133–4.

160 Malynes, *Lex Mercatoria*, 5–6.

"sympathy, concordance and agreement" joining merchants everywhere.[161] As he had written in an earlier work:

> God caused nature to distribute her benefits, or his blessings, to severall climates, supplying the barreneesse of some things in our country, with the fruitfulnesse and store of other countries, to the ende that enterchangeably one common-weale should live with another.[162]

It was the task of the law merchant to give expression to customs that had been established in the course a long history of trade.[163] The three "parts" of commodities, money and the exchange of money were the "*body, soul and spirit of commerce*".[164] Because they operated as a living organism, they could not be easily regulated by domestic law.[165] It was the third of these parts – the exchange of money – that had been the object of an earlier work he had penned as a state official, wishing to draw attention to the abuses in currency exchanges. The shortage of bullion in England, he wrote, resulted from the manipulation of currency rates by banks and exchange companies. In order to prevent this, he suggested the conclusion of an international agreement on a *par pro pari* arrangement to fix the rates of different currencies.[166] Money was a *publica mensura*, a public measure, and speculation for profits violated the most basic principles of justice.[167] To cure this, "the exchange for all places ought to be kept at a certaintie in price, according to value for value" surveyed by a "vigilant eye for the observation [of] all alterations".[168] Only a fixed standard could bring about justice between buyers and sellers and uphold the trust between them without which there could be no exchanges at all, "commercial, political or human".[169]

Nothing might have happened had not England's economic prospects weakened as the sales of broadcloth suddenly fell by over 20 percent in 1618–20. Many felt that the resulting unemployment was caused by the flow of bullion abroad generated by the outbreak of the war on

161 Ibid., 3.
162 Gerard Malynes, *Treatise of the Canker of Englands Commonwealth* (London, Field 1601), 6.
163 Malynes, *Lex Mercatoria*, 1–5. 164 Ibid., 59.
165 See Coquillette, *Civilian Writers*, 135–6.
166 Malynes, *Canker of Englands Commonwealth*, 99–125. See also, Malynes, *Lex Mercatoria*, 382–5.
167 Malynes, *Canker of Englands Commonwealth*, 11. 168 Ibid., 99, 105.
169 Andrea Finkelstein, *Harmony and the Balance. An Intellectual History of Seventeenth-Century English Economic Thought* (University of Michigan Press 2000), 46.

the continent.[170] A select group set up by King James in 1622 took on Malynes' suggestion for governmental control of currencies and the king temporarily prohibited the export of bullion. This led Edward Misselden (1608–1654), deputy governor of the Company of the Merchant Adventurers and a negotiator on behalf of the East India Company, to attack the proposal and argue that free buying and selling – supply and demand – were the only reliable determinants of the value of currencies.[171] Misselden also produced a robust defence of monopolies. Like all activity in the commonwealth, trade needed government. Under "His Majesties especial Grace and Favour" trades in England "are reduced under order and Government into Corporations, Companies and Societies [so that they] doe certainly much Advance and Advantage the Commerce of this Common-wealth".[172] Monopoly signified order and competence. Only its misuse was wrong. With trading companies operating far and wide, large investment were needed. Was it not right and just to compensate those investors?[173]

A second text by Misselden, *The Circle of Commerce* (1623), further exalted the role of trade companies, suggesting that public intervention was to be limited to correct imbalances or abuses.[174] Again, he argued that "as all other Naturall things must have their course, so also must *Exchanges*, and will no more endure a forst *Par* to be put on them, then the market will endure to have all prices prefixed or set".[175] Combining metaphors from physics and geometry with complex aesthetic parallels, Misselden depicted an organic world of trade where the "circle of commerce" would naturally lean towards the centre.[176] "Politick" intervention was needed only as medicine for "malady", to help

170 See e.g. Wilson, *England's Apprenticeship*, 52–7. Roger E. Backhouse, *The Ordinary Business of Life. A History of Economics from the Ancient World to the Twenty-First century* (Princeton University Press 2002), 77.

171 Edward Misselden, *Free Trade, or the Meanes to Make Trade Flourish* (London, Legatt 1622).

172 Ibid., 53–4. 173 Ibid., 73–5.

174 For a good overview of the debate, see e.g. Finkelstein, *Harmony and the Balance*, 26–73. See also Carlos Eduardo Suprinyak, 'Merchants and Councilors. Intellectual Divergences in Early 17th Century British Economic Thought', 21 *Nova Economia* (2011), 459–82.

175 Edward Misselden, *The Circle of Commerce, or the Ballance of Trade, in Defence of Free Trade* (London, Bourne 1623), 105.

176 Ibid., 91. For the natural/politick distinction in support of interest-taking, see 97–9. The metaphor of the "circle of commerce" took a parable from a story about a perfect circle drawn freehand by Giotto – the mastery of his hand was like the mastery of the merchant carrying out trade and bringing the most valuable gifts to his commonwealth. See Epistle dedicatorie.

merchants align their private interest with that of the commonwealth.[177] The king was like a father of a family called upon to determine the correct balance between exports and imports to stabilise the state of his realm.[178]

Unlike Malynes, Misselden regarded trade as essentially competitive: one nation's gain was another's loss. Competing over scarce resources states needed to be organised as rational workhouses to prevent idleness and combat prodigality. Taxes were to be imposed on foreigners and currency manipulation was to be fought by legislation – but not through *par* values, as Malynes had suggested.[179] Imports were to be limited and exports encouraged by organising and supporting trade, including by monopoly companies where large-scale investment or special expertise was needed.

Misselden was soon joined by Thomas Mun (1571–1641), also an official with the East India Company and equally concerned over the suggestions on exchange controls and prohibitions of bullion export. He was inspired by popular belief that the company was emptying the country of wealth by paying the commodities it brought from the Indies by money. Mun believed that exchange rates were a consequence of a trade balance that resulted from decisions by commercial operators. Commerce operated under its own laws and largely independently of governmental control:

Let Princes oppress, Lawyers extort, Usurers bite, Prodigals wast, and lastly let Merchants carry out what money they shall have occasion for use in traffique. Yet all these actions can work no other effects in the course of trade than is declared in this discourse. For so much Treasure only will be brought in or carried out of a Commonwealth, as the Forraign Trade doth over or under ballance in value. And this must come to pass by a Necessity beyond all resistance.[180]

A profitable trade was a well-ordered trade, based on letting the profit-seeking drive take its course. For, as Misselden asked significantly:

And is it not lawfull for merchants to seeke their *Privatum Commodum* in the exercise of their calling? Is not gain the end of trade? Is not the publique involved in the private, and the private in the publique? What else makes

[177] On Misselden generally, see Finkelstein, *Harmony and the Balance*, 54–73.
[178] Misselden, *Circle of Commerce*, 130–1. [179] Finkelstein, *Harmony and the Balance*, 60.
[180] Thomas Mun, 'England's Treasure by Forraign Trade', in John Ramsay McCulloch (ed.), *A Select Collection of Early English Tracts on Commerce from the Originals of Mun, Roberts, North, and Others, with a Preface and Index* (London, Political Economy Club 1856 [1664]), 208. For the same effect, see Misselden, *Circle of Commerce*, 112.

a Common-Wealth but the private-wealth, if I may so say, of the members thereof in the exercise of *Commerce* amongst themselves, and with forraine Nations?[181]

Even though Malynes' harmonious view of trade lost to that of the "ballance", his ingenious suggestion to depict mercantile techniques as parts of a universal law of reason, *lex mercatoria*, gave them a solid place in English statecraft, separate from the wholly consensual law of nations. Unlike diplomatic practices, mercantile customs were "permanent and constant" and therefore of superior normative power, to be "held in reputation as the Law of Twelve Tables was amongst the Romans".[182]

The task of *lex mercatoria*, like any law, was to render each his due. Although he preferred the use of special merchants' courts, Malynes accepted that the law merchant should not be wholly separated from the domestic legal system.[183] Owing to its supranational character, however, he preferred it be adjudicated in the Court of Chancery rather than common law courts.[184] While all three writers highlighted the operation of commercial exchanges as a natural mechanism, they were not averse to embedding them in a system of political governance. To attain this was precisely the point of the idioms and metaphors Malynes borrowed from the natural sciences. All three writers moved within a Baconian universe of science, experimentation and improvement.[185] Misselden, for example, invoked scholastic forms of reasoning that emphasised the scientific seriousness of commercial knowledge. The objective was aligning mercantile wealth-creation with the public interest in a way that further contributed to an economic understanding of statehood. Trade was not just a practice of private enrichment but an instrument of statecraft.[186]

The culmination of the effort to incorporate commercial practices into English law took place through the successive editions of *De jure maritimo et navali* (first edition 1676) by Charles Molloy (1646–1690). This was the first work written by a practising common lawyer to other

[181] Misselden, *Circle of Commerce*, 17. [182] Malynes, *Lex Mercatoria*, 8.

[183] Ibid., 460–1. [184] De Ruysscher, '*Lex mercatoria* contextualisée', 509.

[185] On the Baconian roots of the early "mercantilist" writers, see e.g. Thomas Leng, 'Epistemology, Expertise and Knowledge in the World of Commerce', in Philip J. Stern & Carl Wennerlind (eds), *Mercantilism Reimagined. Political Economy in Early Modern Britain and Its Empire* (Oxford University Press 2014), 9–100, 105–7.

[186] On this, see especially Éric Marquer, *Léviathan et la loi des marchands. Commerce et civilité dans l'oeuvre de Thomas Hobbes* (Paris, Garnier 2012), 50–69.

common lawyers with a full exposition of the commercial practices discussed by Malynes, Misselden and Mun, written into a legal treatise with appropriate professional distinctions between natural law, the law of nations, civil and common law. Unlike Malynes, Molloy did not regard commerce as natural law. Instead, maritime and commercial practices were flexible and constantly changing and hence part of "the Law of Will, or Common Consent ... and yet appears every where observed [and thus part of] that which is called the *Law of Nations*".[187]

Molloy prefaced his exposition with a historical explanation of the importance of trade, borrowing from Grotius the reference to providence. "[A]ll mankind" were "either Traders by themselves or others; and the Ends designed by Trade and Commerce, and Strength, [were] Wealth and Employment for all Sorts of People."[188] He then provided a brief history of trading relations in the world, singling out Holland, Venice, Genova and Lübeck as worthy of emulation but also English explorations around the world, observing that "among all nations, there [was] a Common Law which govern the mighty Thing of Navigation and Commerce".[189] Molloy used Bodin and Grotius to sketch the developmental narrative from common to private property, the loss of "the simple and innocent way of life".[190] This was followed by a discussion of the just war, again largely following Grotius. A just war was about the defence of the end of society, and "the end of Society is, that by mutual aid everyone may enjoy his own".[191] Molloy also gave a detailed account of the laws covering privateering, the rights of neutrals and contraband, and the issuing of letters of marque and reprisal, each of great practical relevance during the third Anglo-Dutch War, just around the corner as Molloy's first edition came out.

Molloy engaged in long discussions of dominion over the British seas and the law concerning maritime warfare, alliances, diplomacy and neutrality, followed by the laws of shipping, maritime contract and insurance as well as bills of exchange, largely abbreviating from Malynes. The last section of the work bundled together items such as slavery and bondage, naturalisation and the status of aliens, planters,

[187] Charles Molloy, *De Jure Maritimo et Navali. Or a Treatise of Affairs Maritime and of Commerce in Three Books* (7th edn, London, Walthoe 1722 [1682]), xv. For Molloy's career and some speculations about the causes of the professional success of the book, see Coquillette, *Civilian Writers*, 140–6.

[188] Molloy, *De Jure maritimo*, iii. [189] Ibid., xii. [190] Ibid., 2–3. [191] Ibid., 7.

Jews, merchants and factors as a well as a brief section on the application of the law of nature and of nations in commercial matters. Like Grotius, Molloy accepted that while under organised government the right of punishment had been given up to public magistrates, in places such as "the New World or the *American* Isles" where no government existed, the private right of punishing remained.[192] He also accepted that when settlers in America found lands that were not used by Indians for cultivation or improvement, they could be occupied lawfully.[193] A long section dealt with punishment and execution of matters of international character, for example whether a debt contracted in one country may be recovered in another or a judgment given in one enforced in another. Molloy argued for the widest possible international cooperation, including the loyal execution of foreign-based claims apart from cases of *ordre public*.[194] Seemingly a mixed bag of things, this was both an introduction to international trade law and a practitioner's handbook meant for jurists at the service of important commercial interests.[195] "Foreign Trade", Molloy wrote, was "the Sheet Anchor of us Islanders":

> It is Foreign Trade that renders us rich, honourable and great, that gives us a name and Esteem of the World and makes us masters of the treasures of other Nations and Countries and begets and maintains our Ships and Seamen, the Walls and Bulwarks of our Country.[196]

The wealth and power of England depended on private actors – merchants, trade companies and privateers. This was why English law took careful "notice of the law Merchant, and leaves the Causes of Merchants in many Instances, to their own peculiar Law".[197] Molloy believed these laws to be the expression of an essentially harmonious realm of international trade. Even the sections on maritime war avoided portraying trade as an *instrument* of war. Considerations of balance of power did not enter his legal world.

[192] Ibid., 474.

[193] Molloy also made a note of the dangers of this argument to the extent that it might be used to take into possession a neighbour's land on the pretext that one could cultivate that land better than the neighbour himself. Ibid., 423.

[194] Ibid., 475–9.

[195] Hence, for example, his plea for honouring merchants as noblemen. If nobility was originally granted for men of courage, the more reason there was to honour merchants who faced "the four Elements together which is the strongest proof that can be of the resolution of Man". Ibid., 446.

[196] Ibid., 456–7. [197] Ibid., 461.

## Monopolies As Law of Nations: The East India Company and *Sandys Case*

By the end of the of seventeenth century, the view that the most important aspect of a nation's power was its wealth had become as much a truism as the axiom that such wealth was to be understood in terms of the "balance of trade", that is to say, how much the value of its exports exceeded that of its imports. The equation suggested a strong connection between the private interest of merchants, especially merchants engaged in long-distance trade, and the public interest of the state. But did the interests of a nation really align with those of its merchants? After all, merchant elites themselves were divided about the appropriate trade policies. Endless debates in parliament and the courts about the legality of monopolies likewise suggested that assuming any automatic identity between private and public interest was altogether too facile. The very notion of public interest appeared often much less like a self-evident datum to which everyone had reason to pay deference than the king's very concrete need for money for projects whose benefit for the nation was often dubious.

In 1624 parliament enacted a statute prohibiting domestic monopolies. Exception was made for the overseas companies, however, its rationale – the need for the orderly government of trade – being propagated by great force in *Sandys* v. *The East India Company* ("the Great Case of Monopolies", 1684–5).[198] In the charter it had received from Queen Elizabeth in 1600, the East India Company (EIC) had been granted exclusive right not only to trade within its area of operations (delimited in the west by the island of St Helena and in the east by the southeast Asian archipelago) but also to control all voyaging and settlement there, to govern and legislate on its various territories, as well as to exercise civil and criminal jurisdiction, tax and rule the subjects of its territories, create and uphold diplomatic relations as well as to wage war and conclude peace with native rulers. According to the letters patent of 27 March 1668, EIC was to become the "true and absolute owner" of the Port and Island of Bombay "with all the rights, profits and

[198] The case [*Sandys Case*] is published in *Cobbett's Complete Collection of State Trials, 1680–1685*, vol. X (London, Hansard 1811), 371–555. Useful recent discussions of the case are Philip J. Stern, *The Company-State. Corporate Sovereignty & the Early Modern Foundations of the British Empire in India* (Oxford University Press 2011), 46–60 and Thomas Poole, *Reason of State. Law, Prerogative and Empire* (Cambridge University Press 2015), 134–8.

territories thereof; in as a full manner as the King himself possesseth them, by virtue of the treaty with the King of Portugal, by which the Island was ceded to His Majesty".[199] The company manifested its supreme – "sovereign" – authority over the territories it ruled in a number of ways.[200] From the beginning, it viewed itself not as a mere trader but also the government of the territories under its jurisdiction from which it also raised revenue. By playing the local princes against each other, against the Mughal empire and its European rivals the company gradually became the most powerful entity on the Indian coasts, in Bengal and down to large parts of the inner peninsula.[201] Towards the end of the seventeenth century, the company increasingly cited the need of good laws and the provision of security and protection as preliminaries for its claim to tax-collecting privileges. Upholding a well-functioning system of law and administration, including some residual form of poor relief, would have to be financed from the local sources. Even if representative assemblies were not set up in the image of the Atlantic settlements, in some centres, such as Madras, charters were provided for urban incorporation of cities on the English model.[202]

By 1680, however, illegal travel and trading in areas under EIC jurisdiction had become endemic, and the court of committees of the company decided to raise a case against one interloper, the London merchant Thomas Sandys who had prepared a ship for the purpose of unauthorised voyage in the East Indies. The ship was arrested while still on the Thames and the case was brought to the Court of Chancery and then to the Court of King's Bench. Both sides understood that the case was more about the principle, the right of a commercial company to monopoly rights abroad, than about the division of profits. For Sandys, the monopoly was simply illegal. The right of Englishmen to trade could not be abolished by a royal patent – a position that had been long held by the parliament and to which Coke had given firm expression in his earlier treatment of monopolies.[203] The lawyers of the company argued that the company's rights did not at all amount to an ordinary commercial monopoly. By opening up trade in the Indies, investing in ports and factories,

199 Quoted from Margaret Eyer Wilbur, *The East India Company and the British Empire in the Far East* (New York, Russell & Russell 1945), 161.

200 See further Stern, *The Company-State*, 19–40.

201 For the process of EIC expansion in the seventeenth century, see e.g. Ramkhrishna Mukherjee, *The Rise and Fall of the East India Company* (Berlin, VEB 1955), 112–20.

202 Stern, *The Company-State*, 83–99.

203 *Case of Monopolies*, 84b.

exercising jurisdiction and legislation, by carrying out negotiations and concluding agreements with native princes, the company was performing a public service, acting "somewhat like a Board of Trade for Asia".[204] In conditions prevailing in infidel countries and in East India, no organised commerce could exist without orderly management of the trading links, something the company had undertaken for close to a century without its powers ever having been seriously questioned. All this was being destroyed by the interlopers, the company argued, irresponsibly reaping the fruit from other peoples' work and investment. Moreover, increased competition would be detrimental to the English public interest by driving up the prices of Indian merchandise. Finally, did not the Navigation Acts of 1651 and later in any case limit trade? They, just like the charters granted to the company, were motivated above all by the public interest, having nothing at all to do with prohibited types of monopoly.[205]

In his argument for the court as the case came to decision in 1685, Lord Chief Justice Jeffreys conceded that monopolies were in and for themselves usually forbidden – "yet this cannot be understood to be so universally true (as no law can ever be) that it should in no respect, and upon no occasion or emergency whatsoever, admit of any exception or limitation".[206] In finding emphatically for the company, Jeffreys made an important point about the sources he would apply. The matter, he noted, was not only regulated by the common law but also by:

> such other laws also as to be common to other nations, as well as ours, and have been used time out of mind, by the king and people of England in diverse cases . . . namely the general laws of nations, the law-merchant, the imperial or civil law; every of which laws, so far forth as the same have been recieved and used in England time out of mind.

For such laws, he added, could also "properly said to be laws of England".[207] The lord chief justice drew a distinction between domestic and foreign trade, the latter having been "introduced by the law of nations" under the *Juris regalia*, i.e. the royal prerogative. It could therefore well be restrained. Everywhere there had come to existence "societies of trade" with privileges like those enjoyed by the EIC "for reasons both public and politic". It was true that the common law provided for freedom of trade. But the "universal laws" directed the government of things belonging to nobody to "him that

[204] Stern, *The Company-State*, 50. [205] See ibid., 48–52.
[206] Jeffreys, *Sandys Case*, 538. [207] Ibid., 523.

had the sovereignty over the people". By virtue of this universal law, for example, plantations had been established and governed by exclusive charters.[208] If Grotius had argued in favour of *Mare liberum*, this only meant the freedom of trade by one nation against others. No word was said about how that trade ought to be organised, and as was well-known, Grotius had no objection to the privileges enjoyed by the VOC.[209]

Jeffreys gave a number of examples of royal licences and charters from England and cited the precedents of the Hanseatic League, Spain, Portugal and the VOC. With reference both to the law of nations and civil law he concluded that the practice of granting such charters had a long and largely uncontested history and could be understood as customary law of nations.[210] The EIC privileges were no prohibited monopoly" but [...] supported and encouraged as conducing to public benefit by the law".[211] The counsel for Sandys had argued that the EIC had been established as a kind of "republic", altering the constitution of England. Jeffreys disagreed. The wider the royal prerogative in commercial matters had been, the greater had been the kingdom's regard and the prosperity of its inhabitants.[212] The rights of the EIC enabled the conduct of flexible policy in distant regions and with infidel princes. Through the charter the king, "makes the plaintiffs as it were his ambassadors to concert a peace", Jeffreys stated, adding that "Mr Sandys murmurs because he is not one of them".[213] In conclusion, Jeffreys held that the rights of the EIC were valid because they were established "upon a good cause, and for the public advantage of the kingdom".[214]

Espousing the basic mercantilist dictum, Jeffreys argued that foreign trade could only be advantageous if "the balance be kept equal between this and other countries", something that could only be done "by keeping up to proportionable rules for the regulation thereof with other countries". This is why, he concluded, the first thing to consider was "how this question stands, as to the law of nations".[215] Quoting Cujas and Grotius among others, as well as the practice of countries such as France and United Provinces and the debates on the privileges of the Hanseatic League, Jeffreys concluded that the long toleration of this practice fulfilled the criteria of prescription, not by domestic common law, where it was required that the practice be continued

[208] Ibid., 526. [209] Ibid., 527. [210] Ibid., 539–42. [211] Ibid., 538.
[212] Ibid., 535. [213] Ibid., 545. [214] Ibid., 521, 538, 552.
[215] Ibid., 538, 539.

since time immemorial, but "by the law of nations and the practices of all other nations".[216] Nor was this practice, as far as foreign trade was concerned, against common law or any legislation. Hence, he concluded that

> since the law of this land, and the law of nature and nations, allow the power of making companies to manage traffic, exclusive to all others to be in the prince, that this is reckoned to be 'inter Jura regalia'; that no act of parliament does restrain this prerogative; that the practice of Europe been accordingly . . . that they have been thought for the public advantage of the nation . . . that East India company have solely run the hazard, and been at great expenses, in discovering places, erecting forts and keeping forces, settling factories, and making leagues and treaties abroad; it would be against natural justice and equity (which no municipal law can take away) for others to reap the benefit and advantage of all this.[217]

The *Sandys case* read the principles of political economy as part of the law of nations owing to their having been widely practised in Europe. The EIC was less a monopoly than a public service, and as such also a beneficiary of the rights and privileges that belong to public powers. This was a hugely controversial position. For it directly raised the problem regarding the relationship between the royal prerogative and the "ancient rights of Englishmen" that would eventually form the ideological background of the Civil War (1642–9).

## Prerogative vs. Property Rights

The ascent to the English throne of James VI/I in 1603 marked the end of Elizabethan parsimony on government spending, leading to perpetual clashes with parliament and a new system of royal patronage. Desperate measures were taken, including outsourcing customs collection and inviting into government wealthy individuals with an interest in financing state activities.[218] No amount of contribution seemed

[216] Ibid., 541. [217] Ibid., 552–3.

[218] Outsourcing customs collection to private grandees in return for annual rent was already widely practised during Elizabeth's reign and formalised after the model of the "Great farm" of 1604. Even as efforts were made to centralise it, financial exigencies led to custom farming expanding at the Restoration. Farming privileges were supplemented by a duty to provide loans and advances to the king. The practice was not discontinued until after 1688. See e.g. Lawrence Harper, *The English Navigation Laws. A Seventeenth-Century Experiment in Social Engineering* (Columbia University Press 1939), 77–88; Wilson, *England's Apprenticeship*, 97–8.

sufficient for meeting the crown's expanding needs.[219] Because the English monarch was not entitled to tax his subjects without their consent, and such consent was not easily received from a reluctant parliament, the king reached into his subjects' pockets under schemes of forced loans and necessity that were argued as parts of the royal prerogative. The doctrine regarding the relations between prerogative powers and property rights was exceedingly obscure, but the subordination of the church by Henry VIII clearly suggested that the prerogative was more than a bundle of semi-feudal competencies. The old distinction between the king's ordinary and his absolute powers was given a novel life, and if the common lawyers had occasional recourse to it, they limited its application to times of war and insurrection. But it directly challenged the principles of parliamentary consent.[220]

The reception of continental absolutism during the early Stuart period was always only partial.[221] King James himself regarded the boundary between ordinary and absolute powers as a matter of royal discretion. As he put it:

> [a]lthough I have said, a good king will frame all his actions to be according to the law; yet is hee [sic] not bound thereto but of his good will, and for good example-giving to his subjects.[222]

This was too much for many common lawyers. Even as they accepted that the king had absolute powers, their limits were to be legally determined and exercised for the good of the community. In a famous passage in *Calvin's case*, Sir Francis Bacon, for example, addressed the law as "the great organ by which the sovereign power doth move", observing not only that the law defined kingship and designated kings, but that even as the king "in his person" was above the law, "yet his acts and grants are limited by law, and we argue them every day".[223]

Although civil lawyers often spoke of the king's *plenitudo potestatis* and put forward maxims such as *princeps legibus solutus est* and *quod placuit principi habet vigorem legis*, it was not always obvious what they meant by them. Nobody suggested that a king could arbitrarily reach into the

219 Ertman, *The Birth of the Leviathan*, 182–5; Braddick, *State Formation*, 85–90.

220 See especially, Holdsworth, 'Prerogative', 554–70.

221 Of the very large literature, see especially Burgess, *Absolute Monarchy*, 15–123; Sommerville, *Royalists and Patriots*, 109–33.

222 James I, *The Workes of the Most High and Mighty Prince*, as quoted in Burgess, *Absolute Monarchy*, 41.

223 Bacon, in *Calvin's case*, 580.

pockets of his subjects. Even within his absolute powers, the king was still limited by the laws of God, nature and nations and he was to act for the public good. Of course, these limits could not be enforced on him. Their power was only directive, not coercive. But in an obsessively religious era, constraints on the *forum internum* did have their reality. During Charles I's reign, these controls were threatened by a political theology that regarded the king as a supernatural being and obedience to him as a religious duty.[224] As a result, disputes about the line between the royal prerogative and the rights of property ended increasingly often in courts. The monarch did sometimes take the position that courts and parliament had no competence with regard to the prerogative. Its use was part of the mysteries of government. But although many accepted this in regard to the crown's *foreign relations* powers, nearly everybody rejected it in relation to the right of property.[225] The difficult question was: what to do if those rights were being exercised outside the realm of England – if they had to do with international trade?

The question came up in the *Case of Impositions* in 1606–10. According to the Levantine merchant John Bate, the augmentation of the import and export duties by James without parliamentary assent violated "the freedom of the merchants to enter and leave the realm without restraint, and the liberty of the subject not to pay taxes without his consent in parliament".[226] As the case was dealt with in the Court of Exchequer in 1606, the Chief Baron Sir Thomas Fleming, speaking for a unanimous court, made express reference to the king's ordinary and absolute powers, arguing that while the former had to do with "the profit of particular subjects, for the execution of civil justice [and] the determining of *meum*", the latter was "not that which is converted or executed for private use, to the benefit of any private person, but is only that which is applied to the general benefit of the people, and is *salus populi*."[227] The matter, he continued, was not to be tried under the common law; it was "most properly named Policy and Government".[228] The implication was that the monarch might overstep

224 On theologians and absolute monarchy especially in the Stuart period, see Robert Eccleshall, *Order and Reason in Politics. Theories of Absolute and Limited Monarchy in Early Modern England* (Oxford University Press 1978), 76–96.

225 Burgess, *Ancient Constitution*, 140, 154–62.

226 Brooks, *Law, Politics and Society*, 137.

227 Sir Thomas Fleming's judgment, in *Case of Impositions (Bates' case* 1606), in T. B. Howell (ed.), *Cobbett's Complete Collection of State Trials*, vol. II (London, Hansard 1816), 389.

228 Ibid., 389.

property rights of his subjects if only considerations of royal *arcana* would so demand.[229] This, as contemporaries understood, was very different from Fortescue and the Tudor jurists for whom the inviolability of private rights was the backbone of the ancient constitution. The king's case was further argued by the attorney-general, Sir John Davies, in a book that grounded the king's power to tax without parliamentary assent on civil law and the law of nations:

> *Ius Gentium*, or the general Law of Nations is of equal force in all Kingdoms, for all Kingdoms had their beginning by the Law of Nations; therefore, it standeth with good reason that the Law of Nations should be of force in all Kingdoms, and for this case in the Realms subject to the Crown of England, the Law of Nations also is in force in such cases, especially wherein the King himself, or his Subjects, have correspondence or commerce with other Nations.[230]

Davies then argued that trade and traffic with foreign nations was regulated by the law of nations under the title of the law merchant (*lex mercatoria*) – "a Law universal throughout the world".[231] It followed that merchandise carried on seas were "goods of another nature" than property in England and, not being under the common law, subject to regulation by the king of England who, Davies remarked in passing, was also "Lord of the Sea".[232]

Unsurprisingly, this position was challenged in a parliamentary petition to the king in 1610 where Lord Coke, among others, held that if the king were entitled to intervene in the rights of property without parliamentary consent, "henceforth the king of England shall be a tyrant; and [. . .] the reality of the parliament shall expire here, as it has expired in almost every other country in Europe".[233] Fundamental liberties were at stake. Sir Roger Owen and Nicholas Fuler further made the point that the attack on the right of property was "contrary to reason and to the law of nations".[234] But the matter was left unsettled and in 1614 James dissolved parliament, which did not meet until again seven years later.

229 Brooks, *Law, Politics and Society*, 138; Burgess, *Absolute Monarchy*, 80–1; Sommerville, *Royalists and Patriots*, 140–4.
230 Sir John Davies, *The Question Concerning Impositions, Tonnage, Poundage, Prizage, Custom &c.* (London, Twyford 1656), 4–5.
231 Ibid., 11. 232 Ibid., 18–19.
233 Address by Lord Coke, *Case of Impositions*, 375.
234 Nicholas Fuler in 1610, cited by Sommerville, *Royalists and Patriots*, 142. The reference to Owen is in Burgess, *Ancient Constitution*, 143.

While James was reluctant to bring his dispute with parliament to a definite resolution, his son Charles I pushed the matter further by arguing that divine right entitled him to override the common law whenever that seemed necessary.[235] The necessity had now arisen, he argued, to create a navy to challenge Dutch commercial priority. That decision launched two important constitutional cases on the delimitation of the prerogative and private rights, *Forced Loans* ("Five Knights", 1627) and *Ship Money* (1640). The former had to do with the king imposing a "loan" on his subjects, ostensibly in order to finance English participation in the Thirty Years' War. Parliament was suspicious and as five knights refused to pay, they (plus almost seventy other Englishmen) were arrested under the king's absolute powers and as a matter of state.[236] According to the attorney-general, the matter touched upon *arcana imperii* and was therefore not to be discussed in public.[237] Martial law was declared in parts of England, and complex judicial proceedings were commenced in the course of which one chief justice of the King's Bench was dismissed. Despite the king's formal victory in court, the arrested grandees were finally freed and the king agreed to a "Petition of Right" (1628) in the drafting of which Coke had played an important role. Magna Carta and six other laws having to do with taxation rights and personal freedom were reaffirmed.[238]

This dispute took place at a time of massive centralisation of the English state that had earlier consisted of a loose conglomerate of feudal powers with the king simply the most powerful of the lords. As part of the arrangement, private right-holders in a sense came to own parts of the state as offices, taxation privileges and monopoly rights of production and trade. The transformation of English agriculture from direct extraction of profit by taxes and other types of coercion to a system of commercial production with lands held in tenure and its product exchanged in markets liberated the gentry from its dependence on offices and taxation rights. From now on, the state would be needed above all to protect the system of commercial production by securing to itself the monopoly of legitimate use of force that turned out to be "extraordinarily effective in guaranteeing landed-class property".[239]

[235] The Lords were hardly assured by his promise to do this only rarely and moderately, Burgess, *Ancient Constitution*, 200–2.

[236] Ibid., 192–3. [237] Ibid., 193.

[238] See e.g. J. A. Guy, 'The Origins of the Petition of Rights Reconsidered', 25 *The Historical Journal* (1982), 389–412.

[239] Brenner, *Merchants and Revolution*, 652–3.

The social contract at the heart of the English state meant that parliament was both a guarantee of local landlords' property rights and an instrument for channelling their interests into state policy. The unstable nature of this arrangement became increasingly obvious in the early Stuart regime where the monarchy's expanding need for resources pushed it repeatedly to search for independent access to income from land. The vocabulary of absolute monarchy presupposed the kind of supreme power that directly threatened the property rights of local magnates and the commercial elites. This was not to be allowed. The modernisation of English statehood took place in part through traditional constitutional argumentation, waged in courts, in part through the development of a new type of political theory that positioned sovereignty in the fictitious entity of the state, which would seek justification for the exercise of public power exclusively from its ability to protect the private interests that it was understood to represent.

## Ship Money; *Quis judicabit*?

During the prolonged depression in the 1620s the Stuart crown's economic situation had worsened significantly. Royal income was in principle limited to the products of crown lands, customary duties and fees from tenurial relations.[240] If extraordinary expenses were needed, the king was expected to turn to parliament. Because there was no guarantee that parliament would look favourably on the king's requests, Charles I resorted to extra-parliamentary levies, operating on his prerogative powers instead of under common law, defending this by the argument that the country's military forces, especially the navy, were to be modernised in view of external threat. In 1634 Charles resorted to raising so-called ship money with the ostensible intention of strengthening the preparedness of the country to fight piracy and to prepare for possible intervention from the continent.

The *Ship Money case* (*R.* v. *Hampden*, 1637) became the climactic political event of the pre-Civil War period, resurfacing the conflict between royal prerogative and property rights that was supposed to have been resolved by the Petition of Right.[241] On 4 August 1635 Charles issues a writ for the payment of the money. A case against those refusing to pay was argued at length in front of the twelve judges

[240] Braddick, *State Formation*, 246–53.

[241] See especially Sommerville, *Royalists and Patriots*, 134–53. A good discussion of *Ship Money* and the other cases in this chapter is Poole, *Reason of State*, 21–35.

of the Court of Exchequer during 1635–7.[242] The opinions focused on the relations between the prerogative and the subjects' right of property.[243] One theme had to do with the character of the prerogative: was it part of common law or instead of law of nature and of nations, standing independently *against* the common law? Another concerned the nature of emergency measures and the notion of necessity. Were these legal or political concepts, and how was one to assess their presence? A third problem was about whether parliament (or indeed a court) was entitled to examine the monarch's determination. Pleading for the defendant, Oliver St John accepted that defence of the realm was inherent in the king's prerogative. The problem was not with that principle, but with the fact that "the Forms and Rules of Law [were] not observed".[244] Any new levy could only be decided with the approval of parliament. An external threat might allow bypassing parliament but only in case of "sudden and tumultuous war, which shuts the Courts of Justice, and brings his majesty in person to the field". But "it appear[ed] not by any thing in this Writ, that any war at all was proclaimed against any prince or state".[245]

Arguing for the king, Sir Edward Littleton stressed that the prerogative to decide in case of necessity in no way affected the rights of property of the subjects – to suggest otherwise "savour[ed] more of malignity than reason".[246] When the king acted to protect the realm, he did so to protect his subjects' properties: "The public and the private are so nearly connext that they can hardly be separated; the public loss falls immediately, and by consequence, upon particular persons. . . . It is impossible to save private fortunes if the public be lost."[247] There was no doubt, he said, of the king's duty to protect the nation against external threats. But how could he possibly do this without the power

[242] *Proceedings in the Case of Ship-Money, between the King and Mr John Hampden Esq.*, *Cobbett's Complete Collection of State Trials*, vol. III (London, Hansard 1809), 825–1315.

[243] For a good summary of the case, see D. L. Keir, 'The Case of Ship-Money', 52 *Law Quarterly Review* (1936), 546–74. Much of the argumentation in the *Ship Money case* had to do with procedural detail. One of the issues was whether it was a tax at all. For the original writ of 4 August 1635 was formulated so as to concern a service that Hampden, the defendant, was due to his monarch. While there was no question at all of the subject's duty of service, including the duty to provide vessels to the navy when the king so commanded, the case now concerned a *debt* that Hampden allegedly owed to the monarch to enable the construction of the specialised naval ships for which the money was allegedly needed. Many denied that a duty of service could be transformed into a debt. See Braddick, *State Formation*, 239–43.

[244] Argument of Mr St. John, *Ship-Money*, 861, 859–61.

[245] Ibid., 903, 905.

[246] Argument of Sir Edward Littleton, *Ship-Money*, 924.

[247] Ibid., 927.

to determine when to act and what was needed for that purpose? "Sometimes dangers are fit to be communicated to the people, and sometimes not. The King should best know what is done abroad . . . and it is very fit that preparation be done before-hand."[248] Littleton discussed many prior cases where English kings had called upon their subjects to assist them urgently without prior consultation. But the thrust of his argument was not in positive laws or customs. "Necessity", he said, "is the law of the time and place of action, and things are lawful by necessity, which otherwise are not."[249] The king was the trustee of the defence of the realm, and in this capacity he needed freedom of manoeuvre. Littleton even cited the principle of the *salus populi* – a law to which "[a]ll other laws positive are subordinate" – and stressed the natural law principle that "the common-wealth is to be preferred before all private estates".[250] For Littleton, as for most of the judges, the arguments on necessity, reason and law of nature coalesced into upholding the monarch's privilege to determine, with binding force, the existence of a danger to the realm, and to take action, including deviating from positive law, for dealing with it.[251]

The case was decided in favour of the king with a narrow 7–5 majority (two judges decided for the defendant on the basis of a technicality, agreeing with the majority in substance). Many judges stressed that this was the greatest case ever presented to a court. The attorney-general, Sir John Banks, took an uncompromisingly absolutist line: "[T]he King of England, he hath an entire empire, he is an absolute monarch."[252] This meant that all dominion, i.e. property rights in land, was originally vested in the king. Kingship predated positive law; it was based on the law of nature as well as the protection/obedience nexus that was part of the law of nations.[253] The power to charge the subjects for defensive action was "innate in the person of an absolute king" and that "the king is the sole judge, both of the danger, and when and how it is to be avoided".[254] But none of the judges went quite this far. Even as the majority held that the king had

[248] Ibid., 930. [249] Ibid., 927. [250] Ibid., 926.

[251] The arguments from *salus populi* and necessity were treated on the defendant's side by Robert Holborne who did accept that there were moments of impending danger – when "fire though not burning, yet ready to burn [or] war, *furor belli*". But, he claimed, this was not at all the case here. Here it was simply "not, what we are to do by necessity, but what is the positive law of the land". Argument of Mr Holborne, *Ship-Money*, 1013, 1011.

[252] Argument of Sir John Banks, *Ship-Money*, 1022. [253] Ibid., 1019.

[254] Ibid., 1017, 1025.

the power to decide on the presence of an external danger (owing to the defendant's demurral, this factual determination, many judges noted, was no longer in dispute) and that the extralegal principles of necessity and *salus populi* were overriding, most of them still received this position from customary practice and precedent.

As the Long Parliament met in 1640, however, it resolved that the case had been wrongly decided and commenced proceedings for the impeachment of the judges having voted for it. There had been procedural irregularities – for example, Charles had already in 1635 and 1637 received from the judges extrajudicial opinions on the presence of a danger and the legality of the levy.[255] They were hardly impartial at the later stage. But the MPs' worry was with the substance. They felt that had the *Ship Money* stood, the laws would have become "instruments of taking from us, all that we have".[256]

## From "Opinion" to Authority: Hobbes

The English Civil War raised dramatically the question of the nature of England as a political community by juxtaposing the "imperial" prerogative of the king with the rights of landed property guarded by parliament. At the same time, a new actor had appeared on the scene – the impoverished classes of towns and the countryside, victims of the turn to commercial agriculture to whom it was anything but clear whom they should support in this struggle. The lines of battle between royalists, the supporters of parliament and the crowds of radical Protestants and social reformers (Levellers and Diggers) were often confusingly drawn. By the time of the Restoration (1660), it seemed clear, however, that despite the opprobrium met by the writings of Britain's most brilliant political thinker, Thomas Hobbes (1588–1679), it was his view of English statehood that had come to prevail. Despite the animosity between future Tories and Whigs, the elites united behind the position that any kind of firm central power was better than the alternative that Hobbes had instructed them to call "anarchy". Although neither party felt comfortable with the argument in *Leviathan* (1651), both realised that only by concluding a protection/obedience

[255] Michael Mendle, 'The Ship Money Case, *The Case of Shipmony*, and the Development of Henry Parker's Parliamentary Absolutism', 32 *The Historical Journal* (1989), 517.

[256] Burgess, *Ancient Constitution*, 219. See further, Keir, 'Case of Ship-Money', 546–50.

pact could they ensure their control over the distribution of English resources and the spoils of expansion.

The life of Thomas Hobbes spanned constant international and domestic conflict. He fled to France in 1640 to avoid persecution, and on his return in 1651 was still treated with suspicion by the elite. Nevertheless, from his early translation of Thucydides' *History of the Peloponnesian War* (1628) to the *Elements of Law* (1640, privately circulated until published in 1650), *On the Citizen* (*De cive*, 1642) and *Leviathan* (1651), his views remained largely unchanged. The egoistic, violent and passionate character of human nature necessitated unflinching obedience to authority. Like other adherents to natural law, Hobbes aimed to construct politics as a science with equally certain conclusions as those of mathematics or geometry.[257] This is why, he wrote, the laws of nature were only improperly called "laws" and had better be called "Conclusions or Theoremes concerning what conducteth to the conservation and defence".[258] Like Grotius, he began with philosophical anthropology. Nothing about the violent and dangerous nature of humans could be changed by preaching virtue and harmony. Instead, these facts were to be taken as the basic truths supporting the view according to which humans moved mechanically in response to feelings of pleasure and pain. The impulsion to avoid death was "no less than that whereby a stone moves downward".[259] Moral qualities such as good and evil were simply descriptions of objects of desire, pleasure and pain. It was not these qualities, but the ability to protect humans from self-destruction that founded social order and the science of politics. Three aspects of Hobbes' work are relevant for the discussion of the law of nations: self-judgment, the nature of the representative state and the kind of government that would not be dependent on the dictatorship of "opinion".

The issue of who was entitled to judge whether a danger to the commonwealth was present was central to the *Ship Money case.* According to the majority of the judges, this power lay with the monarch. Hobbes agreed but, like Littleton, aimed to show that this

[257] The scientific philosophy of Hobbes consisted of three parts: body, human nature and citizenship. The character of the political community was based on a view on human nature, the latter understood through a theory of the movement of bodies.

[258] Thomas Hobbes, *Leviathan* (C. B. Macpherson ed. & intro., Harmondsworth, Penguin 1982) I 15 (217).

[259] Thomas Hobbes, 'De cive', in *Man and Citizen (De Homine* and *De cive)* (B. Gert ed., Indianapolis, Hackett 1991), I 7 (115).

did not encroach on the subjects' rights. In judging, the sovereign actually acted on behalf of the subjects themselves. In a late critique of the common law Hobbes stressed that it was senseless to allocate judgment about the presence of a danger to the realm to parliament. It took six weeks to convoke it, and nobody could tell how long its debates would last, as there "the most ignorant and boldest Talkers rule". If levying money was necessary owing to a danger to the commonwealth, the king would actually sin if he did not take immediate action to protect his subjects.[260] Parliament saw itself as the protector of rights that had existed since time immemorial. This was nonsense. Whatever property rights existed in reality was completely dependent on the sovereign. Before the commonwealth, there had been "no *Mine* and *Thine*".[261] It was not that there was no right, there was too much of it: "in the state of nature, to have all, and do all, is lawful for all".[262] But because everybody had the same right, and all were equally powerful, the rights cancelled each other out. Each had reason to fear that others will "come prepared with forces united to dispossess and deprive him, not only the fruit of his labour but also of his life or liberty".[263] To appeal for justice was vain because "justice" was but a word, an opinion:

> For one man calleth *Wisdome*, what another calleth *fear*, and one *cruelty*, what another *justice*; one *prodigality*, what another *magnanimity*; and one *gravity*, what another *stupidity* &c. And therefore such names can never be true grounds for any ratiocination.[264]

It was that same variety of opinion that was the source of England's troubles. It led to anarchy, war and self-destruction. Hence, as the first law of nature compelled humans "to endeavour Peace", it also necessitated transferring the right of judgment to what Hobbes in *De cive* called "*supreme power*, or *chief command*, or *dominion*", a "man or council" to whom "each citizen hath conveyed all his strength and power".[265]

To exit from the realm of opinion necessitated setting up the state with a supreme leader to judge on behalf of every subject. Earlier uses

[260] Thomas Hobbes, *A Dialogue between a Philosopher and a Student of the Common Laws of England* (J. Cropsey ed., The University of Chicago Press 1971 [1681]), 62–3. Somewhat disingenuously, Hobbes argued that there was fear that the king would misuse his powers by disenfranchising his subjects. This would undermine the basis of his own power. It is, he says, in the king's own interest not to let his subject to be "destroyed, or weakened", 76.

[261] Hobbes, *Leviathan*, I 13 (188).

[262] Hobbes, 'De cive', I 10 (117).

[263] Hobbes, *Leviathan*, I 13 (184).

[264] Ibid., I 4 (109–10).

[265] Hobbes, 'De cive', I 11 (171)

of the notion of "state" in English political literature had not distinguished so clearly between the covenant-making individuals ("multitude"), the abstract entity of the state and its carrier, the sovereign. In *Leviathan*, the wills ("opinions") of the multitude – which in itself had no unity whatsoever – were "united in one person".[266]. Hobbes carefully differentiated that person, the state, *Leviathan*, from the "sovereign" who is "he that carryeth this person".[267] The "state" became the name for the unity of the people, a fiction but, like many legal fictions, with great consequence for political life.[268] It was represented by the sovereign to whom the multitude had transferred their rights: "they have authorized all his actions, and in bestowing the Soveraign Power, made them their own".[269] Whatever rights or freedoms subjects would enjoy was henceforth conclusively determined by the sovereign. This did not signify tyranny. In transferring their rights to the sovereign the multitude accepted ownership of the sovereign's acts.[270] "[E]very Subject is by this Institution Author of all the Actions, and Judgments of the Soveraigne Instituted."[271] It was easy to see why royalists and the supporters of parliament might both accept this arrangement. "And then it is also that Propriety [property] begins."[272]

The establishment of the state made property possible and ended the reign of "opinion". Private judgments would remain devoid of political significance.[273] To oppose the sovereign would be self-contradiction "voluntarily to undo that which from the beginning [they] had voluntarily done".[274] Even conquest embodied consent; the vanquished are expected to obey the victor or choose to die.[275] Laws were binding in England, "because assented to by submission made to the Conqueror here in England".[276] All significant human relations embody the element of fear; covenants are made to mitigate it. It followed also that there

[266] Hobbes, *Leviathan*, II 17 (227).

[267] Ibid., II 17 (228). The state for Hobbes is an artificial transformation of nature by way of human acts and not an organic being with the king as its "head". Instead of an organism oriented towards virtue or beatitude the state is now a causal mechanism designed to avoid violent death. The king is now more the "spirit" of the mechanism than any single part of it. Marquer, *Léviathan*, 28–32.

[268] Quentin Skinner, 'A Genealogy of the Modern State', 162 *Proceedings of the British Academy* (2008), 340–8.

[269] Hobbes, *Leviathan*, II 24 (297). [270] Ibid., I 16 (217–18).

[271] Ibid., II 18 (232). [272] Ibid., I 15 (203). [273] Ibid., II 29 (365–7).

[274] Ibid., I 14 (191). [275] Ibid., II 20 (251–3).

[276] Hobbes, *Dialogue*, 69; *Leviathan*, II 24 (297). For the significance of this, see Michel Foucault, *'Il faut défendre la société'. Cours au Collège de France 1976* (Paris, Gallimard 1997), 77–100.

could be only *one* sovereign in a commonwealth – the presence of several, e.g. king and parliament, would reopen the door for opinions that it was the point of *Leviathan* to close. Of course, the utter dependency of private right on sovereignty was not obvious for everyone. People were inclined to resist even when that was self-destructive – "as oft as reason is against man, so oft will a man be against reason".[277] This is why they were to be instructed. The long list of things the sovereign should teach the subjects in *Leviathan* was a reminder of "how many Opinions, contrary to the peace of Man-kind, upon weak and false Principles, have neverthelesse been so deeply rooted in them".[278] Hobbes was a great critic of the of schoolmen or the *dogmatici* and regarded philosophical contemplation on good and evil as dangerous to the commonwealth. He had little respect for universities and the "Schooles of Law" that preached "false Doctrines" and "contradictory Opinions". [279] In the late *Dialogue* (1681) he railed against Coke's view of the common law as artificial reason. It was not reason that made the law but authority: "That the law had been fined by Grave and Learned Men, meaning the Professors of the Law is manifestly untrue, for all the laws of England have been made by the Kings of England."[280] In the end, as Hobbes remarked drily, legal reason could not get around the fact that "our Artificiall Man the Common-Wealth, and his Command [. . .] maketh the Law". The business of a court of law was to only give effect to the will of the sovereign, and anything else was pure injustice.[281]

The result was an image of international relations as constant danger. States and sovereigns existed, in Hobbes' famous image "in the state and posture of Gladiators; having their weapons pointing, and their eyes fixed on one another".[282] Preventive wars were basic stuff of statesmanship, well known to Hobbes as a translator of Thucydides' *Peloponnesian Wars* (1628). But he did not presume constant war or glorify it. War was the worst possible state. Covenants between states were binding and diplomacy was protected by a natural duty "[t]hat all men that mediate Peace, be allowed safe Conduct".[283] But covenants lasted only as long as the situation that gave rise to them remained stable. Justified fear was a just cause of breach – or better, dissolved any

[277] Thomas Hobbes, *The Elements of Law. Human Nature and De Corpore Politico* (J. G. A. Gaskin ed., Oxford University Press 2008 [1640]), Epistle dedicatory (19).

[278] Hobbes, *Leviathan*, II 30 (383).

[279] Hobbes, *The Elements of Law*, XIII 4 (75); *Leviathan*, II 30 (384, 385).

[280] Hobbes, *Dialogue*, 55.

[281] Hobbes, *Leviathan*, II 26 (317).

[282] Ibid., I 13 (187).

[283] Ibid., I 15 (213).

countervailing duty. Nothing could override the obligation of the sovereign to see to the *salus populi*. And only the sovereign could judge what this required. When he wrote that "necessity and security" were just causes of war Hobbes incorporated aspects of *raison d'état*.[284] But he was no Machiavellian. He was critical of reliance on prudence in statecraft as he had no faith in the ability of rulers to rise above the vicissitudes of human nature, the influence of fear, vanity and desire. Instead, his effort to find in natural law a system of indubitably certain knowledge pushed him towards a kind of calculating, scientific attitude that was alien to *raison d'état*.[285]

## Natural Law As the Science of Government

This was illustrated by Hobbes' understanding of what it was to govern well.[286] Alongside doing everything necessary to preserve peace, *Leviathan* also directed the sovereign to provide for "other Contentments of life which every man by lawfull Industry, without danger, or hurt to the Commonwealth, shall acquire to himself".[287] Even if humans were drawn together predominantly by mutual fear, they also had a "Desire of such things that are necessary for commodious living; and a Hope by their Industry to obtain them".[288] Only a "Foole" would not seek to contract with others so as to receive the goods one desires, including those that "are sensual or conducing to sensuality, which may be all comprehended under the word *conveniences*".[289] The "safety", he wrote, that

[284] See Hobbes, *Dialogue*, 158–9. According to Richard Tuck, Hobbes may also have been influenced by Francis Bacon's 1624 advocacy of war against Spain on grounds of *Realpolitik*. Richard Tuck, *The Rights of War and Peace. Political Thought and the International Order from Grotius to Kant* (Oxford University Press 2001), 127–8. Two out of the three justifying reasons Bacon laid out for a preventive war had to do with just fear of Spain, namely fear of undermining the civil state of England and fear of subversion of established religion. See Francis Bacon, 'Considerations Touching a War with Spain', in *Works of Francis Bacon, Baron of Verulam in Ten Volumes* (London, Baynes and Son 1824), III, 499.

[285] An exhaustive discussion is Noel Malcolm, *Reason of State, Propaganda, and the Thirty Years' War. An Unknown Translation by Thomas Hobbes* (Oxford, Clarendon 2007), especially 118–23.

[286] See e.g. Hobbes, 'De cive', XIII 2 (258). It is true that Hobbes did not devote nearly as much attention to the *government* of the state as he did for its legal *justification*. But once the justification was in place, it called logically for a turn to how, then, the prince was to act so as to uphold the protection/obedience nexus. This would be answered by the (science of) government.

[287] Hobbes, *Leviathan*, II 30 (376).

[288] Ibid., I 13 (188).

[289] Hobbes, 'De cive', I 2 (112).

subjects desire must be understood so "that they might as much as their human condition would afford, live delightfully". For this purpose, the sovereign was "to furnish their subjects abundantly, not only with the good things belonging to life, but also those which advance to delectation".[290] Hobbes opposed luxury just as he was against the ultimately self-destructive bulimia of enlarging imperial dominion. By contrast, he regarded commercial hospitality as part of natural law, but reminded the prince, however, to keep a close eye on its merchants so as not to allow their interests go before the nation's.[291]

*Leviathan* addressed the commonwealth in metaphoric terms as an artificial body with needs of "nutrition and procreation" that were to be filled by colonial expansion and money whose circulation Hobbes, perhaps following the experiments of his friend, the physician William Harvey, associated with how blood, "circulating, nourisheth by the way, every Member of the Body of Man".[292] Hobbes did not think of wealth simply as power but an instrument of power, and was careful to insist that it depended on "the labour and industry of men".[293] To inspire his subjects to work and trade the sovereign was to tax them only modestly and allow them to be "enriched, as much as may consist with public security".[294] But the subjects, too, had a duty to labour not only for themselves but also for the commonwealth, if necessary by arms "to build with one hand, and hold the Sword in the other".[295] There was to be "all manner of Arts: as navigation, Agriculture, Fishing and all manner of Manifacture that encourages labour". The commonwealth was to prevent the idleness of those who were fit to work but also to take care of its poor by a system of public charity.[296]

But the property rights of subjects remained wholly dependent on the sovereign who was to legislate on them and on contractual rights for the common good.[297] He was to determine where and with what items foreign trade could be exercised, bearing in mind the need to avoid benefiting enemies. Under no circumstance were mercantile interests allowed to organise themselves so as to disturb internal harmony.[298] Hobbes regarded trade companies as public, and not

290 Ibid., XIII 4 (259).
291 See István Hont, *Jealousy of Trade. International Competition and the Nation-State in Historical Perspective* (Harvard University Press 2005), 17–20, 43–5.
292 Hobbes, *Leviathan*, II 24 (300).
293 Ibid., I 10, II 24 (150–1, 295–6).
294 Hobbes, 'De cive', XIII, 6 (260).
295 Hobbes, *Leviathan*, II 30 (386).
296 Ibid., II 30 (387); 'De cive', XIII 14 (267).
297 Hobbes, *Leviathan*, II 24 (296).
298 Ibid., II 22, 24 (285–8, 299).

private, associations. He accepted their monopolistic character as necessary for the collection sufficient capital for foreign ventures but he warned against excessive influence of private interests in their administration.[299] Colonisation was a useful means for the "procreation" of the commonwealth. It could be furthered by sending idle men in the English countryside with "strong bodies" to the colonies.[300] Having received one share in the Virginia Company from his mentor, Lord Cavendish, he sat at a number of meetings of the court of the company until its dissolution in 1624. Hobbes' association with the company left, however, "few traces on his later life", and whether it had inspired the few references to American Indians in *Leviathan* must remain a matter of speculation.[301]

If despite all the evils of human nature, so vividly described by Hobbes, he also believed that humans sought contact and society, this did not rise from mutual love. Even in the state of nature, there existed "a certain market-friendship . . . which hath more jealousy in it than true love".[302] Only "Fooles" would break their covenants with the view to short-term gain, thus undermining their trustworthiness and closing the door to alliances that were in any case necessary for defence in a world of equals.[303] Out of the common recognition of an equal right to self-preservation emerged a process "not unlike to that we see in stones brought together for the building of an *Aedifice*" that gave rise to a minimal morality of mutual respect, *Compleasence*.[304] Supplementing the general theory of self-interest, these arguments brought forward a special type of calculative reason that Hobbes understood as applicable to politics and resembling arithmetic. In *Elements of Law*, he had already celebrated the *mathematici* "who have taken in hand to consider nothing else but the comparison of magnitudes, numbers, times, and motions, and their proportions to one another", men who "proceed from most low and humble principles, evident even to the meanest capacity; going on slowly, and with most scrupulous ratiocination". With these men, "it was never heard of, that there was any controversy concerning any conclusion in this subject".[305] By contrast, the *dogmatici* took their authority from

299 Ibid., II 22 (281–3).
300 But this was not to lead to extermination of the native population. Ibid., II 30 (387).
301 Noel Malcolm, 'Hobbes, Sandys and the Virginia Company', in Noel Malcom, *Aspects of Hobbes* (Oxford University Press 2002), 75–6.
302 Hobbes, 'De cive', I (111).
303 Hobbes, *Leviathan*, I 15 (203–5).
304 Ibid., I 15 (209); Tuck, *Rights of War and Peace*, 132–5.
305 Hobbes, *Elements*, I XIII 3 (74).

"men, or of custom, and take the habitual discourse of the tongue for ratiocination", men who "are imperfectly learned, and with passion press to have their opinions pass everywhere for truth".[306] The latter bred controversy and discord and were responsible for most of what Hobbes thought wrong and dangerous in the surrounding world.

To govern properly, it was not sufficient to rely on tradition or experience: "The skill of making, and maintaining Common-wealths, consisteth in certain rules, as doth Arithmetique and Geometry; not (as Tennis-play) on practice onely."[307] Where the older tradition grouped the skills of government under prudence, Hobbes distinguished between prudence and reason, or natural and acquired capacities ("wits"), *both* of which were needed to govern properly.[308] Because reason for Hobbes was calculative reason, having to do with addition and subtraction, nobody possessed it naturally but it had to be "attayned by Industry".[309] This turned it into science – namely political science – that was indispensable for good government.[310] This was much more powerful than legal thought which, despite assurances of common lawyers, did not emerge from reason, but will. A statute was nothing "but dead Letter, which of it self is not able to compel a Man to do otherwise than he himself pleaseth".[311] Even Coke himself, "who whether he had more, or less use of Reason, was not thereby Judge, but because the King made him so".[312] The task of interpreting the law, or setting it aside, lay with the king, not with the judges. Successful government was not about law or interpretation; it was about calculation, adding and subtracting.[313]

The science of government proposed by Hobbes operated with transparent words in no need of interpretation, referring to simple elements of the world that could be combined into general propositions amounting to a true mirror of human nature. With true definitions corresponding to past sense-experience, and with writing that avoided words signifying nothing (such as "immaterial substance" or "free subject"), it was possible to produce propositions about the political world, about peace and war, that enabled governing it as the natural sciences helped to master the natural world: "Because when we see how any things comes about, upon what causes, and by what manner; when

306 Ibid., I XIII 4 (75).
307 Hobbes, *Leviathan*, II 21 (261). See further ibid., I 5 (111–12).
308 Ibid., I 5 and 8 (115–17, 134, 135–8). 309 Ibid., I 5 (115).
310 Ibid., I 5 (117). 311 Hobbes, *Dialogue*, 58–9. 312 Ibid., 62.
313 E.g. Hobbes, *Leviathan*, II 26 (316–17).

the like causes come into our power, we see how to produce the like effects."[314] Moving about in the circle of physicians and scientists in France, Hobbes came gradually to believe that the kind of reasoning used in the natural sciences could, with due modification, be used in the science of politics as well.

Among men whom Hobbes may have met in Paris was William Petty (1623–1687), who like Hobbes, believed that a reliable treatment of "the Interest and Affairs of England" could not take place by the deployment of "comparative and superlative words and intellectual arguments" but had to be articulated in terms of "number, weight and measure".[315] Only arguments about what is perceived by the senses and "causes that have visible foundations in nature" were to enter such study and not "Opinions, Appetites and Passions of particular Men".[316] Written for the instruction of English politicians, Petty's writings were inspired by Baconian views about quantitative measuring as an instrument of comparing the state of a nation with that of its rivals. The work for which he is best known, *Political Arithmetick* (1690), went in great detail to demonstrate a "method for computing the value of men and people" to show that a "small people" may by its situation, and especially its trade policy overtake a much larger one, as illustrated by the advances of the Dutch. By wise computation, England, too, could emerge as a leading nation, especially if it concentrated its efforts on trade and navigation.[317] Differentiating between husbandry, manufacture and trade, somewhat like Thomas Smith a century before, Petty sketched the "body politick" as system of relations between the different parts of the population, which he treated from a quantitative point of view. The greatness of a nation did not depend so much on the virtue of its people as on how efficiently they were engaged in the production and distribution of material things.[318] Because a nation's wealth was dependent on a positive balance of trade, the labour of the population

[314] Ibid., I 5 (115). Hobbes explains his view of science and true (propositional) knowledge in many places. See *Elements*, I VI 4 (41–2); *Leviathan*, I 4–5 (105–6, 112–17).

[315] On Petty as a "disciple of Hobbes", see Marquer, *Léviathan*, 185–230. For a general discussion, see Alessandro Roncaglia, *The Wealth of Ideas. A History of Economic Thought* (Cambridge University Press 2001), 53–75.

[316] William Petty, *Political Arithmetick* (London, Clavel 1690), Preface.

[317] Ibid., 31–4.

[318] Ted McCormick, 'Population. Modes of Seventeenth-Century Demographic Thought', in Philip J. Stern & Carl Wennerlind (eds), *Mercantilism Reimagined. Political Economy in Early Modern Britain and Its Empire* (Oxford University Press 2014), 33–4.

was to be directed to import-substitution and high-level export-oriented manufacture. But the heart of the productive system was the relationship between land and labour that produced the principal items for the calculation of the aggregate value of the commonwealth.[319] By showing "the true state of the people, land, stock, trade &c" political arithmetic would strengthen that "unity, industry and obedience" that would underlie England's domestic order in later years.[320] And it would provide the foundation for the country's astonishing ability to "give law" to the rest of the world.

[319] Roncaglia, *Wealth of Ideas*, 72–4.

[320] Petty, *Political Arithmetick*, 117.

# 9

# "Giving Law to the World"

## *England c. 1635–c. 1830*

Before King James VI/I sat down in London in April 1613 to listen to the long discourses Grotius would hold on Dutch rights in the Indies, and the plight of Dutch herring fisheries in the "English Seas", it must have occurred to him that the previous time he had encountered the name of this Dutch lawyer had been four years earlier on the cover of the pamphlet *Mare liberum.* The king had there run into a claim according to which his efforts to limit Dutch fishing in his realm arose from his "brainsick covetousness" (*insanae cupiditatis*).[1] Whether it had been because of that passage, because of the many disputes he had with the Dutch, or his concerns about the religious views of Dutch Remonstrants, it had not taken him long after reading that passage to take precisely the action it so firmly condemned. The Royal Proclamation of 6 May 1609 made a note of the king's toleration of the foreign fisheries but also of the fact that their continuation had caused "great encroachments upon our Regalities" as well as diminishing of the number of "our Marines" and decay of our "Coast-towns":

No person of what Nation or qualitie soever, being not our naturall born Subject be permitted to fish upon any of our coasts and seas of Great Britain,

[1] Hugo Grotius, *The Free Sea* (D. Armitage intro. & ed., R. Hakluyt trans., Indianapolis, Liberty Fund 2011 [1609]), 33. The claim that the passage "aroused the resentment of James" is reported in George Edmundson, *Anglo-Dutch Rivalry during the First Half of the Seventeenth Century* (Oxford, Clarendon 1911), 25–6 and Helen Thornton, 'John Selden's Response to Hugo Grotius. The Argument for Closed Seas', 18 *International Journal for Maritime History* (2006), 105 n. 2.

Ireland and the rest of the isles adjacent . . . until they have orderly demanded and obtained licenses.[2]

But the implementation of that action was suspended initially for two years and although it was occasionally thereafter enforced, it would lie mostly forgotten until the tide in Anglo-Dutch relations turned again as England aimed to ally with Spain against the Franco-Dutch forces during the Thirty Years' War. But despite his pro-Spanish policy, James had been reluctant to take direct action against an old ally. His son, however, had no such scruples. As we have seen, matters peaked during the *Ship Money* controversy as Charles had decided to challenge Dutch maritime hegemony. The Ship Money fleet was created partly to renew the contents of the Proclamation of 1609 and partly to enforce the obligation of all vessels to strike the flag to all English ships in the enormous area of the "English Seas" that Charles claimed, all the way from England and Ireland down to the continental coastline. To support his claim, Charles contacted the royalist parliamentarian and jurist John Selden who had in 1619 produced a work in response to the *Mare liberum* that had remained unpublished owing to James' concerns about passages that might have offended his brother-in-law, the king of Denmark. *De dominio maris* was published first in support of Charles' most extravagant claims in 1636 and then in the 1650s as an English translation in support of the Commonwealth's war against the Dutch.[3]

## *Mare Clausum*

During the economic difficulties of the 1620s, Malynes had expressed his worry about Dutch fishing in Britain's adjacent waters. Although it was true, he wrote, that the right of "hunting, hawking and fishing" was part of the law of nations, fishing was special in the sense that it was "forbidden in other men's ponds, stankes and lakes, as comparable to theft".[4] Here for once, his interlocutor Misselden agreed, noting that according to both written law and custom "the properties of the Seas

[2] T. W. Fulton, *The Sovereignty of the Sea. An Historical Account of the Claims of England to the Dominion of the British Seas, and of the Evolution of Territorial Waters* (Edinburgh & London, Blackwood 1911), Appendix F, 755, 756.

[3] Of the "four lives" of Selden's *Mare Clausum* in 1616–21, 1630–5, 1652 and 1663, see Mark Somos, 'Selden's Mare Clausum. The Secularisation of International Law and the Rise of Soft Imperialism', 14 *Journal of the History of International Law* (2012), 292–6.

[4] Gerard Malynes, *Consuetudo, Vel Lex Mercatoria, or The Antient Law-Merchant* (London, Bourne 1629), 246.

may be proved to belong to those *Princes* and *Countries*, to which they are next adjacent".[5] The works belonged to a new literature that was mapping England's resources and paving the way for deriving concrete policy-prescriptions from the ideology of "improvement" in an increasingly competitive international context.[6]

Even James had made exclusive fishery claims in the "King's Chambers" in the Channel but had not insisted on strict enforcement. Both he and his son "earnestily believed in the common opinion of the age that sea fisheries formed a principal means of developing commerce and navigation and maintaining a powerful navy".[7] Accordingly, Charles had his lawyers dig up old Plantagenet claims and, adding to them a fair bit, claimed absolute sovereignty on an enormous "Sea of England", setting up in 1632 a monopoly company – a "Fishery Society" – with the royal family among principal members, to enforce his claims.[8] The Dutch were to be driven from the British seas so that "the whole of the sea-fisheries and fish-curing industries of the country, as well the foreign exports, [could be brought] under the control of the Council of the Society".[9] Charles also began to insist on the salute to the English flag, a demand that had been raised occasionally, but never with the verve as now, as part of the royal prerogative.[10]

The Dutch and the English had been joined in the sixteenth century by their shared Protestantism and their enmity towards Spain that had prompted Elizabeth even to provide military aid to the Dutch rebels. But in subsequent years, commercial rivalry had eroded much of this sympathy. English envy towards the Dutch was endless. How could such a small republic, with practically no natural resources to speak of, be commercially so successful? Many reasons were given to explain this: Dutch shipbuilding and navigation skills, the organisation of their entrepôt trade, low interest rates and their possession of a well-developed financial and legal system geared to efficient settlement of contract debts.[11] As envy

5 Edward Misselden, *Free Trade, or the Meanes to make Trade flourish* (London, Hope 1651), 37.

6 See further Paul Slack, *Invention of Improvement. Information and Material Progress in Seventeenth-Century England* (Oxford University Press 2014), 76–90.

7 Fulton, *Sovereignty of the Sea*, 213. For the largely futile efforts by James to enforce expanded fishing rights against the Dutch, see 165–208.

8 Ibid., 11, 209–12. The detailed limits of the "Four Seas" (or sometimes "Three Seas") claimed by England were never laid down in an authoritative manner, 15–20.

9 Ibid., 240.

10 Ibid., 204–8.

11 See Joyce Appleby, *Economic Thought and Ideology in Seventeenth-Century England* (Princeton University Press 1978), 73–98. See especially Josiah Child, *A New Discourse about Trade* (5th edn, Glasgow, Foulis 1751 [1668]).

transformed into hostility it condensed in the attack against Dutch fishing in "British waters" and in graphic descriptions of Dutch violence in the East Indies. The Dutch would also eventually be accused as atheists and as hostile to kingship.

The legal debate on *Mare Clausum* was prompted by such grievances. As we have seen, Chapter XII of Grotius' *De jure praedae* was published just before James proclaimed his licensing system. The response to Grotius, written at James' request by the Scottish lawyer William Welwod, measured in no way up to *Mare liberum*, but made quite efficiently the case that a state had the right to regulate fisheries in the interest of its coastal population. In *The Abridgement of All Sea-Lawes* (1613), Welwod accepted that the oceans and sea-lanes were to remain free but that nothing in the nature of the seas made them incapable of appropriation up to a distance of 100 miles from the shore.[12] "[I]f the uses of the seas may be in any respect forbidden and stayed it should be chiefly for the fishing, as by which the fishes may be said to be exhaust and wasted."[13] As the state took measures to conserve its coastal fisheries, it needed to make sure that safe passage was guaranteed to foreign merchants. Similar views had been expressed by other English lawyers, and Malynes, for example, went so far as to entitle the state to limit free passage in coastal areas in imitation of the Venetian practices in the Adriatic Sea.[14] In his posthumous *Fourth Institute* (1644), Coke had even reproduced documents dating back to the time of Edward I according to which the king's rights of dominion (*superioritas maris Angliae*) over the adjacent sea appeared to have received international acceptance.[15]

The most important work in this debate was Selden's response to Grotius, which enjoyed practically official status.[16] Selden (1584–1654) was a leading humanist jurist whose natural law theory took on much of what the Spanish scholastics had written on *dominium* and other aspects of *ius naturae et gentium*. His authority in England "was paramount on all

[12] William Welwod, 'Of the Community and Propriety of the Seas', ch. XXVI of *The Abridgment of All Sea-Lawes*, in Hugo Grotius, *The Free Sea* (ed. & intro. David Armitage, Indianapolis, Liberty Fund 2004), 71.

[13] Ibid., 73–4.

[14] Malynes, *Lex Mercatoria*, 174–5. For the positions of Gentili, expressed as an advocate in the High Court of Admiralty, see Fulton, *Sovereignty of the Sea*, 358–60.

[15] Edward Coke, *The Fourth Part of the Institutes of the Laws of England* (5th edn, London, Streater 1671), 142–5. See also Fulton, *Sovereignty of the Seas*, 362–6.

[16] Richard Tuck, *Rights of War and Peace. Political Thought and the International Order from Grotius to Kant* (Oxford University Press 2001), 116. John Selden, *Of the Dominion or Ownership of the Sea in Two Books* (London, Du Gard with the appointment of the Council of State 1652), Epistle dedicatorie (d).

questions relating to the sovereignty of the sea".[17] As part of his Hebrew scholarship he derived natural law from God's will and the knowledge humans had of it through natural intuition assisted by grace.[18] His view of natural law was very different from that of Grotius. It focused on the national community, understood as an ideal entity that imposed itself on the world through its identity and experience.[19] England's rights did not derive from any purportedly unchanging nature of the sea, but from England's historical relations to its surrounding waters. The works' two books sought to demonstrate "the long and continued conjunction with the British Empire, of enjoyment and possession, or lawful prescription" of the maritime territory and the history of English occupation of the areas it now claimed as well as other nations' acceptance of this.[20] Selden paid especial attention to refuting the most common justifications for *mare liberum*, the nature of the sea as incapable of occupation by the testimony of "ancient writers", jurists and other publicists. Like all the world, the sea was originally received from God and owned by all human beings in common under "the universal law of Nations, or the Common Law of Mankinde".[21] This law was not, however, of the prescriptive but the permissive kind. It could thus be "subject to Repealings, Qualifications, and daily Alterations".[22] Such "repealings" may sometimes arise by agreement, sometimes through more or less accidentally shared civil law provisions. These familiar distinctions allowed Selden to argue that the originally shared world was soon divided by Noah and his sons, the divisions being reaffirmed after the Flood and continued up to the present.[23] Vacant land came under private dominion by physical occupation and tacit consent.[24]

[17] Fulton, *Sovereignty of the Sea*, 20.

[18] The work in question is *De iure naturali & gentium iuxta disciplinam Ebraeorum libri septem* ('Seven Books on the Law of Nature and Nations with the Hebrew') of 1639. For the reading in the text, see J. P. Sommerville, 'John Selden, The Law of Nature, and the Origins of Government', 27 *The Historical Journal* (1984), 437–47 and J. P. Sommerville, 'Selden, Grotius and the Seventeenth-Century Intellectual Revolution in Moral and Political Theory', in Victoria Kahn & Lorna Hutson (eds), *Rhetoric and Law in Early Modern Europe* (Yale University Press 2001), 334–9.

[19] See in detail, Ofir Haifry, *John Selden and the Western Political Tradition* (Cambridge University Press 2017), 260–321.

[20] Selden, *Of the Dominion*, 2. The first part, consequently, treated the matter of "law", the second the matter of "fact".

[21] Ibid., 13.

[22] Ibid., 13. For a discussion of Selden's notion of "permissive natural law", see Brian Tierney, *Liberty & Law. The Idea of Permissive Natural Law, 1100–1800* (Catholic University of America Press 2014), 252–72.

[23] Selden, *Of the Dominion*, 21.

[24] Ibid., 21–3.

All through history, from the west to the east, the dominion of the sea had been a reality "among the more civilized and more eminent Nations of the past and present Age".[25] This did not exclude freedom of trade and passage, rights that may be still be allowed as a charity or by the law of nations without encroaching on the owner's entitlement to limit them for reasons of public good.[26] The fluid nature of the sea made no difference. Everything in this world was in constant flux. Even houses underwent repairs so that eventually nothing might be left of the original without ownership ever being put to question.[27]

The latter part of the book focused on English activities in the four seas surrounding the British Isles that for Selden included the seas around Ireland as well as the long stretch down to the coast of Spain.[28] Evidence was brought on English possession and administration of the Channel Islands, the immemorial application of the common law as well as England's fighting capacities, in relation to the French, and the recognition of its status by other powers.[29] Passports, letters of safe passage and grants of fisheries rights had been issued by the king to foreigners who had been happy to lower their sails to salute crown ships as representatives of the sovereign.[30]

## The Dutch Problem

In his preface to the second English language edition of Selden's work, republished during the Commonwealth (1652), Marchmont Nedham wrote that the sea was English territory "no less than the Land".[31] There was reason to make this clear to the Dutch now that Cromwell's efforts to create a Dutch–English union had failed. The ambassadors sent by the "Rump" parliament to The Hague to negotiate, had returned angry and frustrated. The Dutch appeared only lukewarm in the defence of Protestantism, the Orangist faction was strong and the country had turned to material values, "irreligion and

[25] Ibid., 45. [26] Ibid., 124. [27] Ibid., 133.

[28] The definition is in ibid., 182–7 where Selden elaborated the relation of the different seas to Britain. In the south and the east, he concluded, the limits of the British sea would be "the shores of ports of Neighbour-princes beyond sea" while the external boundary of the "British Sea" in the north and the west was undefined, 459. But Selden left their closer definition open, perhaps to allow his king room for diplomatic manoeuvring.

[29] Ibid., 333–44. [30] For this last point, see ibid., 398–403. [31] Ibid.

tyranny".[32] Moreover, they were interloping in the Mediterranean and the Caribbean and monopolising the carrying trade across the Atlantic. Their commercial aggressiveness hit against the "new merchants" controlling England's long-distance trade. Something needed to be done.

The establishment of a Council of Trade in 1650 in London brought merchants to the heart of English policymaking. The Navigation Act of the following year struck hard against the Dutch as the leading middlemen in foreign trade, prohibiting the importation of goods from Asia, Africa and America in any but English vessels.[33] The Dutch, too, had their grievances, especially now that the English had attacked Dutch vessels on the high seas under the claim that they were violating neutrality rules by carrying goods to the French Caribbean.[34] Matters came to a head when in May 1652, the Dutch Admiral van Tromp, carrying the Orangist flag and suspected as a supporter of the Stuarts, refused to salute a British naval vessel off the Kentish coast. Although greater English fire power guaranteed English victory in the First Dutch War (1652–4), the peace agreement failed to give satisfaction to English commercial claims.

The Navigation Act and its successors (1660 and 1663) were the most important pieces of legislation contributing to England's naval and commercial hegemony. They resulted from mercantile influence and marked the state's readiness to adopt a more proactive, even a "legislative" ambition as part of its global policy.[35] The laws would free English shipping from its dependency on the Dutch and "create an insulated trading system which would be covered by English law, allowing

[32] Steven C. A. Pincus, *Protestantism and Patriotism. Ideologies and the Making of English Foreign Policy, 1650–1668* (Cambridge University Press 1996), 93, 27–39. The argument for the attribution of the origins of the First Dutch War (1652–4) to an ideological and religious opposition is powerfully stated in this work.

[33] See e.g. J. R. Jones, *The Anglo-Dutch Wars of the Seventeenth Century* (London, Longman 1996), 86–7.

[34] In 1651 a total of 141 Dutch ships were seized and brought to England. Jonathan I. Israel, *Dutch Primacy in World Trade 1585–1740* (Oxford, Clarendon Press 1990), 208–9.

[35] The supporters of the act included the East India and Levant companies. By contrast, the Merchant Adventurers' staple trading in Rotterdam came practically to a halt as the war began. See e.g. L. A. Harper, *The English Navigation Laws. A Seventeenth-Century Experiment in Social Engineering* (Columbia University Press 1939), 41–9; Robert Brenner, *Merchants and Revolution. Commercial Change, Political Conflict, and London's Overseas Traders, 1550–1653* (London, Verso 2003), 625–8.

commercial growth whilst retaining independence, and thus securing sovereignty over English trade".[36] The interests of the Commonwealth and the long-distance merchants largely coincided.[37] The Restoration did not transform this state of things. In order for Charles II to live in his accustomed fashion, he needed to maximise customs revenue, and this required an intensifying of foreign trade. The establishment of a new Board of Trade in 1660 and a Royal Fishery Council in 1661 confirmed mercantile influence within Restoration policy-making. For example, its low-interest loans made the City of London an indispensable partner to the government and the East India Company, constantly lobbying to put pressure on Dutch advances in India. Key members of parliament likewise had important commercial interests to protect.[38] The royal family created the Royal Africa Company to import gold, ivory, dye-wood, hides and wax as well as slaves from areas formerly dominated by the Dutch in West Guinea. Both sides continued capturing each other's vessels and claiming their opponent was doing this illegally. This led to the Second Dutch War (1665–7), a war of aggression commenced, according to the duke of Albemarle, to seize "more of the trade the Dutch now have".[39]

English "Hollandofobia" was inspired by the popular sense that the Dutch were aiming at a universal monarchy.[40] The use of that notion together with the proliferating idiom of "giving law to others" was based on the view that international power was less dependent on massive armies or occupation of wide swaths of territory than mastery of networks of vital economic supplies that made the whole world

[36] Thomas Leng, 'Commercial Conflict and Regulation in the Discourse of Trade in Seventeenth-Century England', 48 *The Historical Journal* (2005), 945. The act was accompanied by a massive increase of navy ships from 39 in 1648 to 287 at the end of the Commonwealth. Claire Priest, 'Law and Commerce 1580–1815', in Michael Grossberg & Christopher Tomlins (eds), *The Cambridge History of Law in America* (Cambridge University Press 2008), 405.

[37] See Brenner, *Merchants and Revolution*, 625–32. The merchant–statesman relationship did not work without friction. The Council of Trade and the innumerable committees under the Privy Council often got stuck quarrelling over bureaucratic points supporting this or that special interest. When the Council of Trade was temporarily abolished in 1667, decision-making on commercial policy moved de facto to the East India Company.

[38] See Gijs Rommelse, *The Second Anglo-Dutch War (1665–1667)* (Hilversum, Verloren 2006), 43–64.

[39] Quoted in Charles Wilson, *England's Apprenticeship 1603–1763* (London, Longman 1965), 165.

[40] Pincus, *Protestantism and Patriotism*, 260–3.

dependent on the Dutch.[41] The hegemonic ambition of the Dutch appeared proven by their arrogant refusal to salute the English on waters the latter regarded as theirs. This, Charles' brother, the future James II, as lord high admiral, regarded as undoubtedly *causa belli*.[42] A legal pamphleteering war began. According to Robert Codrington's widely distributed tract, property rights in the "British seas" were "inseparably concomitant" with the British Isles, extending in the south all along the French coast from Aquitania to Normandy and Picardy.[43] The English arguments were based on Saxon, Danish and Norman claims that had been widely accepted by the unchallenged British practice of providing safe-conducts on these seas and the allegedly consistent demand for permissions to fish in them.[44] Codrington listed the many benefits to the Dutch from their illegal fishing in British waters – increase of shipping, of trade, of private and public revenue and so on, all scandalously at the expense of the English. Nor did he forget to add a long section on "the cruelty and baseness of the Dutch", illustrated by the so-called Amboina massacre of British sailors in the East Indies.[45] But the peace (1667) ratified only a stalemate. England could keep New York, and the Dutch received some of the forts seized in the Caribbean. England also gave up its long-standing claims on the Banda islands and agreed to the neutrality standard of "free ships, free goods" that actually underwrote the Dutch system of wartime carrying trade.[46]

## 1688: Towards a Mercantile State

The Third Dutch war (1672–4) followed the alliance that Charles II had concluded with Louis XIV and included the king's secret promise

[41] See Sophus A. Reinert, 'Rivalry. Greatness in Early Modern Political Economy', in Philip J. Stern & Carl Wennerlind (eds), *Mercantilism Reimagined. Political Economy in Early Modern Britain and Its Empire* (Oxford University Press 2013), 351–5. Emer de Vattel, *The Law of Nations* (ed. Joseph Chitty, Philadelphia, Johnson 1883 [1758]), III 3 § 47 (496).

[42] Wilson, *England's Apprenticeship*, 184. For the run-up to the war, see Rommelse, *The Second Anglo-Dutch War*, 99–111.

[43] Robert Codrington, *His Majesties Propriety and Dominion on the British Sea Asserted* (London, Thomas 1672 [1665]), 10. On the pamphleteering and other justifying propaganda supported by the government at this time, see Tony Claydon, *Europe and the Making of England 1660–1760* (Cambridge University Press 2007), 131–2. On the claims over the narrow seas, 137–8.

[44] Codrington, *His Majesties Propriety and Dominion*, 74–8.

[45] Ibid., 150–76.

[46] Israel, *Dutch Primacy*, 279.

to convert to Catholicism at a suitable moment.[47] As Louis entered the Netherlands, Dutch propaganda began to bite on the English, forcing Charles to make a separate peace in January 1674. This time, war was above all about court intrigues; parliament never supported it and the legal–commercial claims remained "a largely fraudulent pretence".[48] The Stuarts paid for this dearly. When William III invaded England in 1688, he claimed that its liberties and its religion were threatened by the alignment with France – a view that had resonated with many Englishmen. They were scandalised by the treatment Louis had inflicted on his Huguenot subjects and devoured the English translation of Lisola's *Bucklier d'estat*, which produced powerful evidence of the French king's exorbitant ambitions. But James II had made it clear to his advisors that he would never go to war against the French.[49] There had been other grievances against the king as well. Many were affronted over the way James ignored parliament, granting religious indulgencies against the statutes and persecuting Anglican clerics. These fears sealed the fate of the Stuart dynasty. The invitation to William of Orange to intervene was finally inspired by the suspicion that unless he took over, it would be just matter of time before the country would succumb to Louis and the inevitable "popery" accompanying French rule. But although the parties by now consolidated as Whigs and Tories agreed on regime change – to protect "their religion, liberties and properties" as the letter of invitation put it – they remained utterly opposed as to its constitutional and international meaning.[50]

With what right did William III and Mary occupy the English throne? As steadfast opponents of resistance theories, Tories denied that this was based on rebellion, a view suggesting popular consent as the basis of the monarchy. By relying instead on conquest, sometimes supported by divine providence, they could accept William as a de facto ruler and leader in the struggle against popery without compromising their constitutional principles.[51] This view was taken especially by

[47] As Mark Kishlansky writes, these clauses "were so potentially damaging that they were revealed only to [the king's] Catholic ministers", *A Monarchy Transformed. Britain 1603–1714* (London, Penguin 1996), 246.

[48] Jones, *Anglo-Dutch Wars*, 9. See further, Claydon, *Europe and the Making of England*, 132–52.

[49] On James' admiration of France and his desire to divide up the world with Louis, see Steve Pincus, *1688. The First Modern Revolution* (Yale University Press 2009), 316–22.

[50] For the extract, see ibid., 228.

[51] See further, Claydon, *Europe and the Making of England*, 241–68, also describing the way they continued to be attacked as "Jacobites" secretly desiring James' return. On

lawyers, and reference was sometimes made to conquest in a just war as defined by Grotius. However, as the first historian of the Revolution, Edmund Bohun noted, conquest was also "highly injurious to the majesties Rightful Title for the Crown of the Realme".[52] Bohun was keen to refute the resistance theory but likewise uneasy about the suggestion that England had been conquered in a just war. Only a small minority would adopt the radical Whig view of the rebellion as a popular uprising. The parliamentary declaration of February 1689 used an ambiguous formulation that focused on the abdication of James. Most people were content to rely on a de facto view without spelling out clearly the legal basis of the regime change.[53]

The Revolution of 1688 consolidated a Whig bourgeois culture of politeness that shunned religious oppositions, propagated urban values and continued the economic and social transformations that had given birth to the Commonwealth. The Revolution marked a final victory of property rights against the royal prerogative. The Declaration of Rights of 1689 drew a line that no monarch was entitled to transgress: no prerogative taxation was allowed, and no laws enacted or suspended without parliamentary consent: "[R]evenue was parliamentary and there was no mileage in raising legal objections."[54] Although William III accepted the declaration under the reservation that it contained only customary rights, it did underwrite the Whig programme to shift the centre of political power to an alliance between parliament and the landowning elite. This alliance would lay the basis of England's coming hegemony.[55]

Property rights were now guaranteed while the monarch became dependent on allocations from parliament, but also from massive loans,

the various forms taken by the argument from conquest in 1688–93, see M. P. Thompson, 'The Idea of Conquest in the Controversies over the 1688 Revolution', 38 *Journal of the History of Ideas* (1977), 33–46.

52 Edmund Bohun, quoted in Mark Goldie, 'Edmund Bohun and *jus gentium* in the Revolutionary Debate 1689–1693', 20 *The Historical Journal* (1977), 574.

53 Pincus, *1688*, 441. For the use of the ambiguity of the resolution of 6 February, see also Kishlansky, *Monarchy Transformed*, 284–6.

54 Michael J. Braddick, *State-Formation in Early Modern England, c.1550–1700* (Cambridge University Press 2000), 272, 279. For the text, see 'English Bill of Right', at <avalon.law.yale.edu/17th_century/england.asp>

55 The forces behind the programme of 1688 have been characterised as "an anti-absolutist, protestant, and agrarian capitalist aristocracy, favoring a strong state for international military and commercial power and for defense against the Catholic powers, and ... a dynamic maturing entrepreneurial merchant class, oriented toward making the most of growing opportunities that could be derived from long-distance trades and expanding colonial empire, as well as from war finance". Brenner, *Merchants and Revolution*, 713. See also Pincus, *1688*, 484–5.

organised since 1694 through the Bank of England from owners of mobile property whose interests lay in the opening of the seas for free trade. With this, a new class of speculators emerged who lived off the proceeds from government credit, creating a system of parliamentary patronage that would continue throughout the eighteenth century.[56] To finance its expanding activities (for example, almost 150,000 men in arms in 1713) the state arranged lotteries, issued bonds and borrowed from large companies and private investors.[57] Complex credit instruments were introduced to offer short- and long-terms loans for the government's war efforts.[58] Many domestic and most international commercial transactions were financed by loans and letters of exchange. Perhaps two-thirds of all transactions involved credit rather than cash.[59] As the state was "organized for the more or less explicit and limited purpose of enhancing England's international power",[60] it became the platform for triangular bargaining between the old gentry, dominating parliament, the new mercantile elites interested in opening up long-distance trade as well as the bankers and investors holding both more or less in their hands.[61]

## Rule by Property: John Locke

The proper functioning of a credit economy requires a great deal of trust in the stability of governmental institutions. Hence the emergence of an abstract language of statehood accompanying financial expansion. Already during the Civil War recourse to "reason of state" had placed political institutions rather than the king or the court as objects of

56 See e.g. J. G. A. Pocock, 'Authority and Property. The Question of Liberal Origins', in J. G. A. Pocock, *Virtue, Commerce, and History. Essays on Political Thought and History, Chiefly in the Eighteenth Century* (Cambridge University Press 1985), 67–71.

57 Government expenditure tripled in the 1690s. See further, Andrea Finkelstein, *Harmony and the Balance. An Intellectual History of Seventeenth-Century English Economic Thought* (University of Michigan Press 2000), 220–2; Patrick O'Brian, 'Inseparable Connections. Trade, Economy, the Fiscal State and the Expansion of Empire 1688–1815', in P. J. Marshall (ed.), *The Oxford History of the British Empire. The Eighteenth Century* (Oxford University Press 1998), 65–7.

58 Braddick, *State-Formation*, 265–70.

59 John Brewer, *The Sinews of Power. War, Money and the English State, 1688–1783* (Harvard University Press 1990), 186.

60 Brenner, *Merchants and Revolution*, 714.

61 That the traditional gentry continued to control parliament through the eighteenth century is forcefully argued in P. J. Cain & A. G. Hopkins, 'Gentlemanly Capitalism and British Expansion Overseas I: The Old Colonial System, 1688–1850', 39 *Economic History Review* (1986), 501–25.

subjects' loyalty. Eventually, the royal debt, too, was transformed into a national one.[62] These developments received a theoretical grounding from John Locke's *Two Treatises of Government*, written in the course of the 1680s when concern over England's subordination to France was greatest (but published only in 1689).[63] Here the exiled Locke had occasion to state his famous view that "the great and chief end . . . of men uniting into commonwealths, and putting themselves under government is the preservation of their property".[64] Whatever its constitutional form, government was a kind of trust, its supreme objective the protection of rights that individuals enjoyed already in the state of nature. If government failed its trust – as James II had done – then subjects would be freed from their duty of obedience. The question was – "Who shall be the judge whether the prince or legislative act contrary to trust?"[65] This was the same question that Hobbes had asked almost forty years earlier. But Locke gave a different response:

> the community perpetually retains a supreme power of saving themselves from the attempts and designs of anybody, even of the legislators, whenever they shall be so foolish or so wicked as to lay and carry on designs against the liberties and properties of the subject.[66]

For Locke, the "body of the people" was the ultimate judge – a proposal that Hobbes would have understood as initiating precisely the rule by opinion that he abhorred. Not even the legislative was freed from control by the community of property holders. In Locke's view, because rights were natural, they would persist and provide the standard of criticism of all government. Moreover, the power of critique belonged to each individual: "every man is Judge for himself".[67]

These well-known views reconstructed statehood as an instrument to protect the totality of subjects' pre-political rights, especially the right to property. Unlike Hobbes, Locke did not imagine the state of nature as one of perpetual fear; it was possible – and Locke gave examples – for

62 See Richard Tuck, *Philosophy and Government 1572–1651* (Cambridge University Press 2011); Braddick, *State-Formation*, 272–6.

63 James Tully, 'Locke's Political Philosophy', in James Tully, *An Approach to Political Philosophy. Locke in Contexts* (Cambridge University Press 1993), 13.

64 John Locke, *Two Treatises of Government* (William S. Carpenter ed., London, Everyman's 1984 [1690]), Second Treatise, § 124 (180).

65 Ibid., § 240 (241). 66 Ibid., § 149 (192).

67 Ibid., § 241 (241). Because the economic situation had improved so markedly, Locke did not believe that such a radical view would in practice lead to rebellion. Tully, *Approach to Political Philosophy*, 317; Ian Shapiro, *The Evolution of Rights in Liberal Theory* (Cambridge University Press 1986), 82–4.

individuals to enjoy rights, to labour, contract and divide their properties in the state of nature. Even the turn to a monetary economy, an extremely important moment, could take place prior to the establishment of the commonwealth.[68] The state was needed only to get rid of the inconveniences experienced by property-holders in the natural state, to secure the enjoyment of rights and the enforcement of contracts[69] But it did not create those rights. Even as positive laws regulated and limited them, this was to take place under the general guidance and within the limits of natural law. Here the world of the international emerged in two superimposed levels.[70] On the one hand, there was natural law that joined all property-holders of the world in a "great and natural community".[71] On the other hand, there was the law of nations, the positive laws of treaty and custom upheld and regulated by professional diplomacy and statecraft that in Britain were administered under the "federative power" of the king.[72]

Already in the early essays, Locke had distinguished between natural law and the law of nations, treating the laws of diplomacy as positive law in the latter category. Natural law was universal, providing for the right of property, with which Locke understood both "life, liberty and estate" and the more narrow category of "lands and goods", the topic of the famous chapter 5 of the *Second Treatise.*[73] Unlike Hobbes, he also made room for a universal natural law under which all men were friends and enjoyed common interests that enabled them to develop a positive law of nations by agreeing on "such as the free passage of envoys, free trade, and other things of that kind". There was nothing natural about these arrangements. They were based on common expediency and not necessarily applicable "by

68 Locke, *Two Treatises*, Second Treatise § 47–8 (139–40). See also C. B. Macpherson, *The Political Theory of Possessive Individualism. Hobbes to Locke* (Oxford University Press 2011 [1962]), 209–10.

69 See Locke, *Two Treatises*, Second Treatise § 124–7 (180–1).

70 Although *Two Treatises* did not lay out a separate thesis of international law, Locke, who had once been offered a diplomatic posting by William III, was not only famously active in the colonisation of America but also interested in and knowledgeable about international matters. His role in the establishment and the early functioning of the Board of Trade in 1696–1700, for example, seems to have been central. See Peter Laslett, 'John Locke, the Great Recoinage, and the Origins of the Board of Trade. 1695–1698', 14 *William and Mary Quarterly* (1957), 370–402. On Locke's international interests, see also David Armitage, 'John Locke's International Thought', in David Armitage, *Foundations of Modern International Thought* (Cambridge University Press 2013), 75–6; Tuck, *Rights of War and Peace*, 167–8.

71 Locke, *Two Treatises*, Second Treatise, § 128 (181). 72 Ibid., § 146 (191).

73 For the narrower sense, see ibid., § 123 (179–80) and the wider, §§ 25–51 (129–41).

other peoples of Asia and America".[74] By contrast, the natural right of property was applicable everywhere, including the colonies, under which even the native peoples rightfully possess what they had occupied, though their labour only entitled them to a fraction of the lands they claimed.[75]

In the *Second Treatise*, Locke dealt with war and peace, diplomacy, alliances and treaty-making under the monarch's federative power. The legislature could not be involved because the conduct of foreign affairs was:

> much less capable to be directed by antecedent, positive laws than the executive, and so must necessarily be left to the prudence and wisdom of those whose hands it is in, to be managed to the public good.[76]

For Locke, foreign policy was a matter of governmental prudence, an aspect of the preservation and regulation of property in a constantly fluctuating world.[77] This involved decisions on foreign trade and currency; Locke was, after all, a "consistent and theoretical 'mercantilist'".[78] The struggle for wealth and power among nations was a zero sum game and the task of the government was to manage the balance to the benefit of the country. With no minerals to be found on land, commerce was for England "the only way either for riches, or subsistence".[79] Although the normative basis for foreign policy lay in the king's prerogative, he exercised it as part of the trust the community had placed in him.[80] Were the king to contemplate an alliance that might endanger this trust – the great fear in 1679–81 – the community of property owners was entitled to resist; in this sense, foreign policy, too, was subordinate to their interests.[81]

[74] Locke, 'Essays on the Law of Nature', in *Political Essays* (M. Goldie ed., Cambridge University Press 1997), 108.

[75] Locke, *Two Treatises*, Second Treatise, § 26 (129) and below, Chapter 10.

[76] Locke, *Two Treatises*, Second Treatise, § 147 (191).

[77] Ibid., § 123, 124 (179–80).

[78] Laslett, 'Recoinage', 397.

[79] John Locke, 'Some Considerations of the Consequences of the Lowering of Interest and Raising the Value of Money', in John Locke, *The Works of John Locke in Nine Volumes* (London, Rivington 1824), IV 13. See further, Tully, *Approach to Political Philosophy*, 63.

[80] Armitage claims that Locke's discussion of "federative power" was one of his "least successful" innovations with "no immediate afterlife", 'John Locke's International Thought' (84). To me it seems, instead, that this was a realistic and accurate description of much of foreign affairs decision-making at the time and thereafter. Locke, *Two Treatises*, Second Treatise, § 161, 167 (200–202–203).

[81] Ibid., § 153, 159–60, 163, 168 (194, 199–201, 203). Note also Locke's specific references to England in § 165 and 167 (201–2).

These arguments undid Hobbes' justification of firm sovereign power. In Locke, there was no single sovereignty at all, only a set of institutional relations between the legislative and the executive powers designed to help the community to coordinate its affairs. The Lockean state was "in effect a joint-stock company whose shareholders were the men of property".[82] The absence of a theory of statehood, or of statehood *tout court*, foregrounded the position of the property owners, that is to say the landed elite, entitled to direct and control the operations of the government. Locke's, "all mankind" were the property-owners of the world who had organised themselves in different territories but remained nevertheless united by natural rights and the interest to protect them.[83] In Hobbes, all rights were dependent on the sovereign and dissolved if the sovereign failed to hold his side of the of protection/obedience bargain. In Locke, natural rights persisted even if the social contract was broken.

How far natural law and natural rights would guide government can be seen from Locke's debate with the powerful director of the East India Company, Josiah Child, on the policy of interest rates. Where Child in his many pamphlets had suggested that the way to attain growth was to lower the interest from 6 to 4 percent, Locke responded that the rate was actually the *result* of economic activities: "The rate of money does not follow the standard of the law but the price of the market."[84] An attempt to regulate the matter at home would only lead to it being made available elsewhere with higher rates. Trade would suffer "with a loss to the kingdom".[85] In Locke's view, alongside positive laws of the state, there were "natural laws of trade and 'laws of value' which could be violated only to the detriment of the nation as a whole".[86] The latter became visible in the flow of money across the economy, signalling the proper relation between the income of economic actors, landowners, manufacturers and merchants.

That natural rights applied across the globe allowed Locke to reject conquest as a rightful basis for government. But it also supported Locke's famous doctrine that allowed everyone to punish those who

[82] Macpherson, *Possessive Individualism*, 195.

[83] A very strong statement of this is Hersch Lauterpacht, *International Law and Human Rights* (London, Praeger 1950).

[84] Locke, 'Some Considerations', 38. [85] Ibid., 12–13.

[86] David McNally, *Political Economy and the Rise of Capitalism. A Reinterpretation* (University of California Press 1988), 59. Locke did, however, argue that once the "natural" rate was found out, the state had a role in making it compulsory. Shapiro, *Evolution of Rights*, 135–6.

violated natural rights and produced an extremely wide-ranging authorisation of just war against the native peoples in America.[87] Properties, Locke held, were individuated in the state of nature by the way humans "mixed their labour" with land. Even as Indians had right to the animals they killed or the fish they took from the sea, most Indian lands were not worked upon by means of agriculture. As mere "waste" they could be appropriated by anyone intending to take them for production for their own use or for commerce.[88] The only limits were constituted by the requirement of not taking so much as would be "spoiled" and the duty to leave to others an equal amount of equally good land. The latter condition had relevance as long as land was available, as in America. But in Europe, most land was already occupied. The non-spoilage condition, again, led to maintenance of rough equality among property-owners: nobody had an interest to hoard more than they could use.[89]

The invention of money changed this situation dramatically. Now it was possible to store wealth in money. With money, the only limits to production and accumulation were set by the absorptive capacities of the market. In a monetary economy, "man may, rightfully and without injury, possess more than he himself can make use of by receiving gold and silver, which may continue long in man's possession without decaying".[90] The argument highlighted the importance of trade. As Locke pointed out, "supposing an island, separate from all possible commerce with the rest of the world" in which there were abundant amounts of perishable goods but no money. Nobody would have any reason to want to "hoard up" things.[91] But as soon as money was

[87] Locke, *Two Treatises*, Second Treatise, § 7, 9 (120, 121). The origin and implications of the extension of the transfer of the "right to punish" from the historical argument about the state of nature to the present relations between commonwealths and non-citizens, especially Indians, is well described in Tuck, *Rights of War and Peace*, 170–8.

[88] Locke, *Two Treatises*, Second Treatise, § 30–2 (131–2). Under Locke's divinely inspired "workmanship model" humans had a right to "as much land as a man tills plants, improves, cultivates, and can use the product of", § 32 (132). On the analogy between God and human beings under the "workmanship model", see James Tully, *A Discourse of Property. John Locke and His Adversaries* (Cambridge University Press 1980), 8–9, 35–8, 108–10; Ellen Meiksins Wood, *Liberty & Property. A Social History of Western Political Thought from Renaissance to Enlightenment* (London, Verso 2012), 277.

[89] Locke, *Two Treatises*, Second Treatise, § 31, 32 (131, 132). The content and significance of these conditions has been the object of much debate, with Macpherson and Tully representing the extremes of unlimited accumulation and communitarian constraint.

[90] Ibid., § 50 (140–1). [91] Ibid., § 48 (140).

introduced, the door to accumulation was opened by way of commerce with things superabundant at home but lacking elsewhere:

> Trade, then, is necessary to the producing of riches, and money necessary to the carrying of trade ... if this be neglected, we shall in vain by contrivances among ourselves, and shuffling the little money we have from one another's hands, endeavour to prevent our wants: decay of trade will quickly waste all the remainder.[92]

Appropriation could also take place through the labour of another. According to another famous passage, "the grass my horse has bit, the turfs my servant has cut ... where I have a right to them in common with others, become my property".[93] Whether or not the master–servant relation in this passage was meant to extend to just any kind of wage labour is unclear.[94] But the Whig grandees for whom Locke spoke understood it as an endorsement for hiring more workers to increase the product of their lands.[95] Earlier natural lawyers may have limited property rights to what was needed for subsistence. Locke, too, wrote of needs but tended to equate need with what anybody wanted, thus opening up an analysis concentrated on demand that would operate as the engine of improvement and economic governance.[96] Although Locke was critical of luxury and excess, he rejected sumptuary laws and wished the whole world to gain "the real necessities and conveniency of life ... in greater plenty than they have now".[97] The utopia of an international market uniting

[92] Locke, 'Some Considerations', 14.

[93] Locke, *Two Treatises*, Second Treatise, § 28 (130).

[94] Out of a very large literature, see e.g. John F. Henry, 'John Locke, Property Rights, and Economic Theory', 32 *Journal of Economic Issues* (1999), 617–18 and overview in Tully, *Discourse on Property*, 135–45 (who summarises his own view that it is "incorrect and anachronistic to impute the assumption of capitalist wage-labour to Locke", 142). Tully continues the debate in *An Approach to Political Philosophy*, 122–5.

[95] Meiksins Wood, *Liberty & Property*, 274. Locke expressly associated land and money as forms of capital producing income in the form of interest. Locke, 'Some Considerations', 36.

[96] Shapiro, *Evolution of Rights*, 129–35.

[97] Locke, *Political Essays*, 255. The degree to which the exclusive rights of property were limited by general subsistence rights has been a classic theme of Locke studies. Shapiro, not denying the reality of Locke's concern for the poor, argues that as a supporter of enclosures, Locke assumed that the increased productivity would result in a trickle-down effect that would ultimately be for the benefit of all. Shapiro, *Evolution of Rights*, 92–6. On Locke's writings on welfare rights and a labour regime to discipline the poor, see Tully, *Approach to Political Philosophy*, 63–6.

free property-holders looking for "improvement" across the world was implicit in Lockean natural law.

## Giving Law to the World

As revolution transferred control of trade policy to parliament, the reforms accomplished earlier were enlisted for commercial and colonial expansion. The new Council for Trade and the Plantations supervised and coordinated the enforcement of the Navigation Acts, offering a platform for Locke and economic writers such as Charles Davenant and Josiah Child to argue about coordinating trade with policy.[98] The formation of the Anglo-Scottish Union in 1707 introduced the language of the British empire into political speech as marker of a new nationalism that would be "Protestant, commercial, maritime and free".[99] Henceforth, Britain's foreign policy would be determined by the landholding oligarchy dominating parliament and representatives of monied interest that saw to the availability of credit for waging major wars while simultaneously expanding trade. The gentry's patriotic ideals and its interest in agricultural modernisation would be coordinated with the City's development of increasingly sophisticated financial mechanisms. The new gentlemanly capitalism no longer viewed international relations in terms of royal ambition but saw them "shaped by the need to service the national debt, to fund patronage and to manage the political system in ways that preserved civil peace and the constitution".[100]

In a widely read pamphlet, the economic writer Nicholas Barbon (1640–98) summarised the many advantages of expansion of trade to England, by occasioning peace, bringing employment and increasing revenue, and by providing resources for war. And what about the risks? Some felt that a commercial nation would gradually lose its national spirit, become "effeminate" and end up being absorbed into a more powerful state. Like other English writers, Barbon had carefully perused Sir William Temple's reports from 1660s Holland. How had the Dutch been able to become a commercial leader without undermining their freedoms? The answer lay in taking a positive view of luxury and

98 Wilson, *England's Apprenticeship*, 164–9.

99 David Armitage, *Ideological Origins of the British Empire* (Cambridge University Press 2010), 173.

100 For the alliance of gentry and high finance in English expansion in the post-1688 era, see P. J. Cain & A. G. Hopkins, *British Imperialism. Innovation and Expansion 1688–1914* (London, Longman 1993), 101, 102 and 53–104.

conspicuous consumption; while "covetousness" was certainly prejudicial for all, "prodigality" was "prejudicial to the Man, but not to Trade".[101] What statesmen needed to learn was how to maintain both liberty and security, especially liberty to trade and innovate, and the security of property. Even republican thinkers such as James Harrington assumed that wealth was the basis of international power and that it was right for England to emulate the Dutch so as to expand their commerce without endangering their liberties.[102]

Barbon predicted a great future for his country. Its freedoms were not at all a burden but an asset – "for men are most industrious, where they are most free, and secure to injoy [sic] the Effects of their Labours".[103] This would include freedom of trade; all prohibitions only limited employment and led to loss of profit.[104] Like most of his contemporaries, Barbon viewed a large population as the heart of success in trade, too, and concluded that:

> And if the Subjects increase, the Ships, Excise and Customs, which are the Strength and Revenue of the Kingdom, will in Proportion increase, which may be so Great in a short Time, not only to preserve its Antient Sovereignty over the Narrow Seas, but to extend its Dominion over all the Great Ocean: An Empire, not less Glorious & of a much larger Extent, than either *Alexander's* or *Caesar's*.[105]

The new English regime was immediately thrown into a war with France that called for unprecedented resources. Where would they come from? The navigation laws were dethroning the Dutch as the leading maritime nation so that by the 1690s the most important sea lanes were coming under British control. Why this was important was laid out with admirable clarity by the most influential of the economic writers, Doctor of Civil Law Charles Davenant (1676–1714), Locke's colleague in the Board of Trade and Colonies as well as inspector-general in 1705–14. Like most Englishmen, Davenant was wary of the desire of universal monarchy as an inerasable part of "the deprived manners, and wild passions of humankind". Spain was no longer in a position to aspire to it. Its metropolitan territory had been left in such bad shape that the way had been opened for the French to try their

[101] Nicholas Barbon, *A Discourse of Trade* (London, Milbourn 1690), 32.

[102] For these debates, see e.g. István Hont, *Jealousy of Trade. International Competition and the Nation-State in Historical Perspective* (Harvard University Press 2010), 185–201 and Armitage, *Ideological Origins*, 125–45.

[103] Barbon, *Discourse of Trade*, 28. [104] Ibid., 35. [105] Ibid., 31.

hand. But history had not been kind to ambitious nations: "all these great monarchies degenerate into tyranny, with which trade is incompatible".[106] It was important for the English to learn from that experience and to safeguard what they had been taught to think of as their liberty. This was not only a side-product of increasing wealth; it was the source of a nation's commercial power and if destroyed by "corruption", loss of power would automatically follow.[107] To maintain its dominance, a nation needed to respect this liberty: "Whatever country can be in the full and undisputed possession of it, will give law to all the commercial world."[108]

What type of laws those would be was clear from Davenant's critique of regulation and monopolies. Merchants were to be encouraged to find the most profitable outlets for their products. "Trade is in its nature free, finds its own channel, and best directeth its own course"; all laws intended to regulate it serve only particular and not general interests.[109] As soon as parliament had taken control of trade policy in the 1690s, it abolished the privileges of companies such as the Merchant Adventurers and more gradually the East India Company; monopoly rights could henceforth no longer be granted by the crown, only by parliament. The door was opened to "a much more liberal commercial environment".[110] But constant vigilance was needed, assisted by political arithmetic – "the art of reasoning by figures, upon things relating to government".[111] A national balance sheet and an income statement were to become the basis for policy. Hence the "commissions" established by the Board of Trade and the enquiries requested from

[106] Charles Davenant, 'An Essay upon Universal Monarchy', in Charles Davenant, *The Political and Commercial Works of Charles D'Avenant* (5 vols, London, Horsefield 1771), IV, 34, 4. Davenant received the LL.D. from Cambridge University and joined Doctors' Commons in 1675. D. Waddell, 'Charles Davenant (1656–1714) – a Biographical Sketch', 11 *Economic History Review* (1955), 279.

[107] As Bolingbroke's advisor, Davenant pushed for free trade with France. A "free state" would always be stronger than a "tyrannical" one (such as France). The plan failed, however, owing to vocal parliamentary opposition. See e.g. Doohwan Ahn, 'The Anglo-French Treaty of Commerce of 1717. Tory Trade Politics and the Question of Dutch Decline', 36 *History of European Ideas* (2010), 167–80.

[108] Davenant, 'An Essay on the East India Trade', in *The Political and Commercial Works* I, 94.

[109] Ibid., 98.

[110] David Ormond, *The Rise of Commercial Empires. England and the Netherlands in the Age of Mercantilism, 1650–1770* (Cambridge University Press 2003), 45.

[111] Davenant, ''Discourses on the Publick Revenues and on the Trade of England [1698]', in *The Political and Commercial Works*, I, 128.

consulates around the world. Even if the assembled data was not always correct, it strengthened the sense that there was a national economy that could be managed by close surveys of exports and imports.[112] Moreover, if it was true that any commercial advantage could be gained only by the disadvantage of one's neighbour, then one needed to think of war and commerce closely together. This would also go some way towards preventing the feared loss of a national spirit. But the ideological milieu was to be administered skilfully; policy was to rely on facts and calculations, it was to be centrally controlled and aggressive. The Navigation Acts would ensure that outsiders would not reap the benefits of British investment, but also that colonies would not begin to compete with the metropolis but would be kept in place as dependent markets and producers of raw materials.[113]

## The "Blue Water Strategy"

"Giving law to all the commercial world" would take place through the navigation laws that would ensure total control of English colonial trade. There would also be increasing use of privateers; neutrality laws were amended to reflect British concepts and interests. The regulations were to be administered by the Court of Exchequer, the High Court of Admiralty and colonial vice-admiralty courts under the theory of applying the law of nations. The laws eventually broke the Dutch hold on trading items such as tobacco, furs and slaves and hastened the transfer of status as world entrepôt from Amsterdam to London. The territorial gains in the Treaty of Utrecht (1713) obstructed French expansion and further enhanced British maritime hegemony by enabling the transformation of Gibraltar, Minorca, Hudson's Bay, Newfoundland and Nova Scotia into important naval bases and transferring the Asiento – the monopoly of slave transports to the Spanish colonies – to the South Sea Company.

From the 1740s onwards the British navy would oversee all traffic between Europe and America and protect British operations in the Caribbean and the Mediterranean. By the end of the Seven Years' War (1756–63), the British fleet nearly equalled that of France and Spain combined: "When George III succeeded to the throne in

[112] Laslett, 'Recoinage', 377. [113] Finkelstein, *Harmony and the Balance*, 230–2.

1760 there was no doubt that Britannia ruled the waves."[114] Many legal innovations had contributed to that achievement. One of them was the system of generalised reprisals. Privateering had earlier been conducted on the basis of letters of *marque* that allowed individual ship owners to retaliate in case they had suffered damage at foreign hands. From the Second Anglo-Dutch War (1664) onwards private ships were authorised to attack *all* enemy vessels, even in the absence of formal war – for example in anticipation of a declaration of war against Spain in 1718. By this means, the English government was able to enlist private merchants in an almost unlimited way to support its control over maritime areas.[115]

The English would learn to think of the Navigation Acts as a kind of Magna Carta of the seas. English law extended over all maritime shipping "so that from the point when they were loaded up until they finally reached foreign ports, colonial goods were legislated for".[116] Although the policy was based on domestic laws and a virtual monopoly of colonial trade, Britain characteristically understood itself as merely "upholding the maritime law of nations in American waters".[117] Around twenty vice-admiralty courts grew across the colonial world.[118] Admiralty courts had existed in England since the fourteenth century, but as a result of the attack led by Coke in the early seventeenth century, their jurisdiction had been drastically limited.[119] The Navigation Acts gave them new life in the colonies where they began to administer the complex regulatory system of the acts, often under

[114] Brewer, *The Sinews of Power*, 175.

[115] For the practice of "general reprisals", see Wilhelm Grewe, *The Epochs of International Law* (Berlin, Gruyter 2000), 368–70.

[116] Leng, 'Commercial Conflict', 952.

[117] Eliga H. Gould, *Among the Powers of the Earth. The American Revolution and the Making of a New World Empire* (Harvard University Press 2012), 82 and generally 81–108.

[118] Claire Priest, 'Law and Commerce, 1580–1815', in M. Grossberg & C. Tomlins (eds), *The Cambridge History of Law in America* (Cambridge University Press 2011), 414–15. For the proceedings in the Court of Exchequer and the colonial vice-admiralty courts, see Harper, *English Navigation Laws*, 109–23, 182–203.

[119] Admiralty jurisdiction was exercised by courts in various seaport towns from early on. Owing to the technical difficulties (including delays) with using common law courts in matters dealing with international shipping, piracy and prize, special admiralty courts were created by royal prerogative in the mid-fourteenth century. Lionel H. Laing, 'Historic Origins of Admiralty Jurisdiction in England', 45 *Michigan Law Review* (1946–7), 166–9. But see also Damien J. Cremean, 'The Early History of Admiralty Jurisdiction', 28 *The Australian and New Zealand Maritime Law Journal* (2014), arguing for a much earlier date, 16–24.

pressure by colonial administrators and companies that saw the courts encroaching on their charters.[120]

The London admiralty upheld the fiction that prize jurisdiction applied universal law and prided itself on the neutrality of British courts, despite many well-known problems.[121] English politicians refused to act on protests, referring to judicial independence. Because the prize was adjudicated as a claim about private property, government could wash its hands and simply wait aside. The Prize Law of 1708 abolished any remaining government discretion. Government would also give up its share of the booty in a fashion that further highlighted the technical aspects of prize jurisdiction (a ten percent share would continue to go to the admiralty and later to the crown). Not even sound foreign policy reasons allowed crown meddling.[122] As the matter was put in a widely read pamphlet by James Marriott, later a judge in the High Court of Admiralty itself:

> But the English Courts of Admiralty decide not by the Laws of England, with regard to Ships or Cargoes detained as prize of war, any farther than those laws co-incide with the principles of Law acknowledged by all Nations; which are the foundations of their Decrees. . . . They are therefore not less the Courts of the captured, than of the Captor.[123]

Unsurprisingly, foreign states did not always see the matter in a similar light. Although many countries had prize courts operating under analogous rules, it was usual to allow priority to foreign policy considerations. In the *Silesian Loans case*, for instance, the Prussian side was

[120] On the jurisdiction and practice of the colonial vice-admiralty courts, see Matthew P. Harrington, 'The Legacy of the Colonial Vice-Admiralty Courts, Part II', 26 *Journal of Maritime Law & Commerce* (1996), 323–39. The first vice-admiralty court in the Western hemisphere was created in Jamaica in 1662. Most American colonies received their courts in the 1690s as the colonies had failed to enforce the navigation laws. See Matthew P. Harrington, 'The Legacy of the Colonial Vice-Admiralty Courts, Part I', 26 *J. Maritime Law & Commerce* (1995), 589–600 (with description of the conflict between the vice-admiralty court of Pennsylvania and William Penn).

[121] Colonial courts were insufficiently manned, often incompetent and unable to enforce their judgments. They were suspect of favouring the local captor, admiralty instructions were regularly breached and even when the captors brought the prize to trial they had often already sold it so that in case the neutral owner won, there was nothing to recover beyond a possible bond set by the captor. See the examples in Richard Pares, *Colonial Blockade and Neutral Rights 1739–1763* (Oxford, Clarendon 1938), 81–4 and 51–64.

[122] Ibid., 64–76, 95–101; Tara Helfman, 'Neutrality, the Law of Nations, and the Natural Law Tradition. A Study of the Seven Years' War', 30 *Yale Journal of International Law* (2005), 556–7.

[123] James Marriott, *The Case of the Dutch Ships Considered* (London, Dodsley 1758), 36.

outraged by British behaviour. Negotiations were the appropriate procedure, it held, and no sovereign would bow to the courts of another. Any talk about the dispute being between private individuals was a sham; English law was being applied on German subjects for conduct outside England.[124]

Even more important was the transformation of neutrality rules to support British control of the seas. The issue arose in regard to Dutch ships carrying goods to the French Caribbean during the Seven Years' War. From the outset, the British navy prevented French and neutral vessels with contraband goods from entering the French Atlantic colonies – a crucial source of French wealth, as we have seen. This was in accordance with the old rule, agreed in an Anglo-Dutch Treaty of 1674, according to which neutral nations had the right to trade with a belligerent as long as they did this in an impartial way and did not carry contraband goods.[125] This, however, left a business opportunity for neutrals not carrying prohibited items. They would just take over the trade the French were no longer in a position to pursue. To prevent this, British prize courts began to make a distinction between neutral trade *with* France (which remained permitted) and neutral trade *for* France where neutral ships replaced those of the enemy's. From now on, the English would regard the latter as breach of neutrality. This came to be called "the Rule of War of 1756" that in effect justified British control of all Atlantic traffic.[126]

In a much-publicised tract, of 1757, translated into several languages, Charles Jenkinson, the future Lord Liverpool, explained that the basis of English claims lay in provisions of the law of nature prevailing on the open sea. It was the natural right to protection that would allow Britain to act pre-emptively against neutrals carrying French goods. If the Dutch complained, they ran the risk of turning into enemies themselves.[127]

124 'The Prussian Case, Berlin 1752', printed in Ernest Satow, *The Silesian Loan and Frederick the Great* (Oxford, Clarendon Press 1915), 66–7. See also Pares, *Colonial Blockade*, 149–52.

125 The old rule, based on the writings of Grotius and others, allowed neutral trade with a belligerent as long as this was done in an impartial way and did not involve contraband goods. Specific exceptions had, however, been agreed to this rule in bilateral treaties. See Grewe, *Epochs*, 371–84; Helfman, 'Neutrality, the Law of Nations, and the Natural Law Tradition', 559–63.

126 From the enormous literature, see Pares, *Colonial Blockade*, 180–224; Helfman, 'Neutrality, the Law of Nations, and the Natural Law Tradition', 574–84.

127 Charles Jenkinson, *Discourse on the Conduct of the Government of Great Britain in Respect of Neutral Nations* (London, Debrett 1801 [1757]), 13. See also Marriott, *Case of the Dutch Ships Considered.*

> [T]he general laws of nations again have their force: here the property even of an ally hath no other protection than what these laws allow it: being joined therefore, to the goods of an enemy, it cannot communicate its protection to these, since the same law that gives security to the first, allows you to seize and destroy the latter.[128]

In a finely crafted pleading, Jenkinson explained that the practice of seizing enemy goods even on neutral vessels had been followed by the French and the Dutch themselves and that it had been a general practice of which only certain treaties had deviated, among them the Treaty of Westminster of 1674 between Britain and the United Provinces. These provisions had now become obsolete owing to Dutch duplicity. By failing to come to Britain's assistance as provided in a friendship treaty of 1678, the Dutch could no longer rely on the rights under those treaties.[129]

In the Seven Years' War as well as the American War of Independence, the British followed the new rule ruthlessly, intervening in any non-belligerent action they tended to see as supportive of the enemy. To the inevitable protests British diplomats responded by spreading their hands and declaring themselves unable to intervene in judicial proceedings..[130] Europeans hated the new rule and the 1780 treaty of armed neutrality between Russia and the Baltic countries was largely directed against it. This only strengthened British resolve; many activities were undertaken to ensure that its navy would "give the law to the world" – expanding the powers of vice-admiralty courts, for example, and creating a naval "sea guard" to intercept merchant ships as they entered or left American harbours.[131] All this expressed a consensus in eighteenth-century Britain about the basic values of the nation, the normalisation of the relations between the state and the commercial elites so that "imperial policies . . . represented no material interest that could be plausibly separated from the concerns and aspirations of British merchants".[132]

[128] Jenkinson, *Discourse*, 14.

[129] "Treaties of alliance being nothing more than stipulations of mutual advantages between two communities in favour each other, ought to be considered in the nature of a bargain, the conditions of which are always supposed to be equal . . . therefore, who breaks his part of the contract, destroys the equality of justice of it, and forfeits all the pretense to those benefits which the other party had stipulated in its favour." Ibid., 71–2.

[130] But there was much smuggling, often by British subjects, directed to circumscribing the regulations. See e.g. Gould, *Among the Powers of the Earth*, 83–93.

[131] Ibid., 91–2.

[132] O'Brian, 'Inseparable Connections', 72.

## The Laws of a Commercial World

Eighteenth-century English jurists faced the formidable task of integrating the British legal system into the conditions of global trade that formed the foundation of their empire. British ships would sail and British merchants would buy and sell in a world that functioned by legal techniques that were not always recognised by the common law. As we have seen, since the early seventeenth century common law courts had been massively encroaching on the business of civil law jurisdictions. There was a limit to how far this could proceed. Because it had been those civil law jurisdictions – especially the High Court of Admiralty and the vice-admiralty courts – that had operated the rules governing maritime affairs and international business relations, removing their jurisdiction to the common law courts might obstruct the process of expansion. This could be prevented by accommodating the commercial practices of common law to international business practices under the law of nations.

The starting-point of the integration lay in the acceptance of the principle that the law of nations was the law of the land. In his discussion on the "Offences against the Law of Nations" Blackstone made the following observation:

> The law of nations is a system of rules, deducible by natural reason, and established by universal consent among the civilized inhabitants of the world; in order to decide all disputes, to regulate all ceremonies and civilities, and to insure the observance of justice and good faith, in that intercourse which must frequently occur between two or more independent states, and the individuals belonging to each.[133]

According to Blackstone, the law of nations governed the conduct of both states and individuals.[134] Like Montesquieu, he suggested that nations ought, in time of peace, to do another all the good they can; and, in time of war, as little harm as possible, "without prejudice to their

[133] William Blackstone, *Commentaries on the Laws of England in Four Books* (Philadelphia, Lippincott 1893 [1765–70]), IV 5 (66).

[134] Common lawyers often equated the law of nations with natural reason; to the extent they did so, they could easily extend it to private interactions. The matter was different in more "political" cases where (as in the determination of statehood), they would, at least in the nineteenth century, defer to the judgment of the executive. See Michael Lobban, 'Custom, Common Law Reasoning and the Law of Nations in the Nineteenth Century', in A. Perreau-Saussine & J. Murphy (eds), *The Nature of Customary Law. Philosophical, Historical and Legal Perspectives* (Cambridge University Press 2006), 265–78.

real interests". The combination of utilitarianism and *raison d'état* is striking. To the extent that the balance-of-trade theory suggested that one nation could only benefit by causing a loss to another, the ultimate standpoint was to be the national interest. In any case, although the sources of this law were "natural justice" and "mutual compacts and treaties", in the absence of any tribunal over the nations, it was up to each nation's courts to interpret them. No doubt by looking back to England's seventeenth-century experience with absolutism, Blackstone made the point that it was only in arbitrary states where the application of the law of nations belonged to the royal prerogative. In England (where "no royal power can introduce a new law, or suspend the execution of the old") it was "adopted in its full extent by the common law, and is held to be a part of the law of the land".[135]

Blackstone's judgment with regard to the law of nations as part of the common law has been criticised. At least until 1688, the law of nations was understood to regulate matters in the crown's prerogative and civil law courts were entitled to apply it. But the general issue had not been authoritatively decided.[136] The eighteenth-century incidents usually mentioned in this connection relate only to diplomatic immunity. In the well-known case of the arrest of the Czar's ambassador in 1708 the English government admitted that crown officials had indeed breached the law of nations. No verdict was given in the case, however, despite the Czar's insistence that capital punishment ought to be applied. So it remains inconclusive as to whether common law would apply. Up to that time, cases in which the English government had recognised diplomatic immunities had been dealt with through executive action and not by common law courts. The 1708 incident led to the passing of a statute that voided any writ to arrest a protected person or seize that person's goods. Transgressors were liable for a penalty decided by the lord chancellor. It may well have been that the statute "was specifically passed because international law was not part of the common law of England".[137]

[135] Blackstone, *Commentaries*, IV 5 (67). Among "[t]he principal offences against the law of nations", Blackstone included the violation of safe-conducts, infringements of the rights of ambassadors and piracy, 68.

[136] William Holdsworth, 'The Relation of English Law to International Law', 26 *Minnesota Law Review* (1941–2), 141. See further, William Holdsworth, *A History of English Law* (17 vols, London, Methuen 1937), 10, 370–2.

[137] See E. R. Adair, 'The Law of Nations and the Common Law of England. A Study of 7 Anne Cap 12', 2 *Cambridge Historical Journal* (1928), 295 and generally 290–7. Likewise, Roger O'Keefe, 'The Doctrine of Incorporation Revisited', 79 *British Yearbook of International Law* (2008), 12–17.

But this hardly counts as a serious critique of Blackstone's effort to provide a naturalist grounding for a practice that seemed eminently useful at the time.[138]

At the time when Blackstone wrote (1765), there was huge interest in having common law recognise those commercial rules that underlay Britain's global predominance. How was it able to wage war while simultaneously intensifying its commercial dealing across the world and preventing its enemies from doing the same? Contemporaries were likewise astonished at its ability to finance the hugely expensive war effort by a debt that it was able to service on reasonable conditions.[139] Such facts prompted the former governor of Massachusetts, one of the most influential commentators on Britain's policy, Thomas Pownall (1722–1805), to speculate in 1766 on the character of the period that was beginning:

> the spirit of commerce will become that predominant power, which will form the general policy, and rule the powers of Europe; and hence a grand commercial interest, (the basis of a great commercial dominion, under the present scite [sic] and circumstances of the world,) will be formed and arise.[140]

Debate on commercial and colonial policy had begun already before the war. Boards of Trade had made reform proposals in the 1740s and 1750s, and political thinkers had begun to speculate on the strategic role of Britain's trade and colonial policies. After the Peace of Paris of 1763, critics began to worry about imperial overreach.[141] Writers such as Josiah Tucker, James Steuart, Joseph Massie and David Hume wrote on "jealousy of trade" with a new sense of urgency, suggesting that something like "political economy" (Steuart's expression) might offer policy-guidelines based on what

[138] Blackstone hoped to bring order to the common law by linking its rules to natural law maxims organised after the model of the *Institutes*. Later jurists often saw the result as overly simplistic. Customs and statutes could hardly be explained as mere expressions of natural law. Blackstone's sovereign remained the source of the law, itself not bound by it; the laws did not receive their justification from morals but from utility. Michael Lobban, *The Common Law and English Jurisprudence 1760–1850* (Oxford University Press 1991), 29–33.

[139] The debt during the war arose to an unprecedented £132 million, with interests rising from £2.7 million in 1756 to £4.6 million in 1763. Nancy Koehn, *The Power of Commerce. Economy and Governance in the First British Empire* (Cornell University Press 1994), 165.

[140] Thomas Pownall, *The Administration of the British Colonies* (2 vols, London, Walter 1774), I 5.

[141] On the disagreements about a peace generally felt to be conciliatory towards France, see Koehn, *Power of Commerce*, 149–84.

were imagined as the laws of trade.[142] The basic algorithm was laid out by the lawyer and diplomat Sir William Mildmay (1705–71) in his *The Laws and Policy of England Relating to Trade* (1765). To gain wealth, a nation had to employ its population as fully and in as diversified a way as possible so as to outsell its rivals by the "*cheapness of materials* [and] the *cheapness of labour*".[143] Commercial treaties with most-favoured nation clauses were useful but hardly sufficient. More important was the "expediency of laws to regulate our exports and imports, in such a manner as to encourage Trades that are beneficial, and refrain from such as may be prejudicial".[144] The monopoly of colonial trade had a threefold significance. Some part of manufacturing could be undertaken in the colonies, e.g. India, while raw materials such as sugar or timber could be brought to England at reasonable cost. The pressure on domestic labour costs, again, could be mitigated by importing cheap grain from Ireland. Like most commentators, Mildmay was aware that colonies could contribute in the form of taxes and as markets for goods produced in England, but also that these policies tended to cancel each other out.[145] But he had no doubt that the colonies should above all serve metropolitan needs. Few contemporaries would have disagreed with his summary: "new materials will introduce new Manufactures; new Manufactures will introduce new Trades; and new Trades will introduce new Wealth and Power to the kingdom in general".[146]

In Mildmay's account law was to guarantee freedom of trade and enterprise and provide protection for property – "for men will be but little anxious towards the pursuit of riches, if they cannot be secure in the possession of them".[147] And it could also become a flexible instrument of regulation in the form of strategically directed taxes, duties and "bounties". This type of thinking led to intense legislative lobbying by mercantile and colonial interests, leading to frequent changes of government and unstable colonial policies. When the Stamp Act of 1765 met with American settlers boycotting British manufactures it was almost immediately rescinded; the import duties enacted soon thereafter met with a similar response while their partial withdrawal was insufficient to mend what turned out to be a fundamental breach in

[142] See generally, Hont, *Jealousy of Trade*; Koehn, *Power of Commerce*, 66–76.
[143] Sir William Mildmay, *The Laws and Policy of England Relating to Trade* (London, Harrison 1765), 27, 22–7.
[144] Ibid., 75. [145] See e.g. Koehn, *Power of Commerce*, 76–104.
[146] Mildmay, *Laws and Policy*, 35. [147] Ibid., 8.

Britain's Atlantic colonial system.[148] Parliament's effort to restate its unconditional legislative supremacy with the Declaratory of Act of 1766 merely strengthened the colonists' conviction that their interests would never be adequately represented in the mother country.[149]

It was important for the mercantile interests directing British policy that the legal instruments through which foreign trade was conducted would be duly recognised. Hence Blackstone's invitation to give full effect to what had been "established by universal consent among the civilized inhabitants of the world":

> [T]he affairs of commerce are regulated by a law of their own, called the law merchant, or *lex mercatoria*, which all nations agree in and take notice of. And in particular it is held to be part of the law of England which decides the causes of merchants by the general rules which obtain in all commercial countries [including] in matters relating to domestic trades, as for instance ... the transfer of inland bills of exchange.[150]

Blackstone was well aware that since the late seventeenth century English courts had given de facto effect to many of the instruments of credit and exchange covered under *lex mercatoria* and that medieval jurists had applied them sometimes with a writ by the king, sometimes by Chancery under natural law or equity.[151] Alongside special trade courts operating at trade fairs under crown prerogative central courts sometimes also treated such cases.[152] With the development of the "assumpsit" formula in the fifteenth and sixteenth centuries, action was taken to diminish the delays caused by the common law's procedural formulas, for example, so as to allow insurance and partnership disputes in the King's Bench.[153] Coke himself, we have seen, read the *lex mercatoria* as part of the common law.[154] The greatest difficulties

148 See e.g. Koehn, *Power of Commerce*, 105–47.

149 For the text of the Declaratory Act of 18 March 1766, see www.stamp-act-history.com/documents/1766-declaratory-act-original-text/. For the repeal of the Stamp Act and the enactment of the Declaratory Act, see Koehn, *Power of Commerce*, 185–95.

150 Blackstone, 1 *Commentaries* I 7 (273).

151 J. H. Baker, 'Law Merchant and the Common Law', 38 *The Cambridge Law Journal* (1979), 301–2.

152 For the special courts, see e.g. Dave De Ruysscher, 'La *lex mercatoria* contextualisée. Tracer son parcours intellectuel', 90 *Revue historique de droit français et étranger* (2012), 500–4. James Steven Rodgers, *The Early History of Bills and Notes. A Study of the Origins of Anglo-American Commercial Law* (Cambridge University Press 1995), discusses the central courts' involvement in early cases, 12–43.

153 Baker, 'Law Merchant and the Common Law', 309.

154 See also De Ruysscher, 'Lex mercatoria', 507–10. Malynes held that *lex mercatoria* was best adjudicated under the equitable formulas of the Chancery or through arbitration.

related to bills of exchange that kept up much of international trade but went against accepted doctrines of privity and consideration. Eventually these, too, were accepted as part of a "custom of merchants" without formal incorporation.[155] For the civil lawyers, this presented no problem, of course. We have seen John Davies define the law merchant as part of the law of nations and within the jurisdiction of prerogative courts.[156] But Davies was making a royalist point to uphold commercial regulation as a crown prerogative. It was in his interest not to notice (or pretend not to notice), the gradual integration of mercantile customs into the common law.

Notwithstanding these legal–professional quarrels and the moral doubts about contemporary market practices, it was inconceivable that common law might ignore the five-fold increase of Britain's foreign trade in the course of the eighteenth century. Two-thirds of the transactions were made in credit rather than cash so that routine acceptance of the validity of bills of exchange, promissory notes and insurance policies was vital for the country's welfare.[157] But no doctrine had emerged to express what had become accepted in practice.[158] The lawyer to seize upon this was William Murray, Lord Mansfield (1705–93), long-time chief justice of the King's Bench, "the father of English commercial law".[159] Mansfield possessed long experience in mercantile matters as an advocate and government advisor. He was known to be "sympathetic to the interests of merchants and industrialists" and "[]as a judge, steadfast in promoting commercial interests".[160] As a member of parliament he once went so far as to argue, though unsuccessfully, against legislation limiting trade with enemy.[161] In the case of *Pillans* v. *Van Mierop* (1765) he finally tackled the question regarding the validity of a bill of exchange under English law. In

[155] Baker, 'Law Merchant and the Common Law', 310–22. For the varying fashion on which the "custom of merchants" was taken into account in seventeenth-century pleadings in common law courts, see Rodgers, *Early History of the Law of Bills and Notes*, 137–69.

[156] Sir John Davies, *The Question Concerning Impositions, Tonnage, Poundage, Prizage, Customs, &C.* (London 1656), II (10–20).

[157] See e.g. Rodgers, *Early History of the Law of Bills and Notes*, 100–24.

[158] Instead, common law judges often simply instructed juries to decide commercial cases according to their individual circumstances.

[159] See e.g. S. Todd Lowry, 'Lord Mansfield and the Law Merchant. Law and Economics in the Eighteenth Century', 7 *Journal of Economic Issues* (1973), 605–22.

[160] Norman S. Poser, *Lord Mansfield. Justice in the Age of Reason* (McGill–Queen's University Press 2013), 220.

[161] Ibid., 225.

principle, this required the receipt of a "consideration". To avoid applying the doctrine, Mansfield held the requirement as merely an evidentiary rule; if the promise was in writing, no additional evidence was needed, and the transaction was not a voidable *nudum pactum.* Mansfield carefully stressed that "This is a Matter of great Consequence to Trade and Commerce, in every Light", adding that "[t]he Law of Merchants, and the Law of the land, is the same".[162] Here, as elsewhere, Mansfield went to some length to argue about the importance that courts gave effect to the needs of commerce. The engagement had been made, there was no question of it. "It would be very destructive to Trade, and to Trust in commercial Dealing" if merchants could put written promises to question on the basis of legal technicalities.[163] Mansfield made a declaration regarding commercial cases in general:

> All Nations ought to have their naws conformable to each other, in such Cases. Fides servanda est. Simplicitas Juris Gentium prevaleat. Hodierni Mores are such that the old notion about the nudum pactum is not strictly observed, as a rule.[164]

As in many other cases, Mansfield here recognised a legal logic operating in the world of mercantile interactions that was not necessarily identical with relations between ordinary individuals. This logic was universal, operating with speed and informality that were greater than in normal domestic interactions and relied on the special trust between merchants underwritten by their mutual interest in long-standing business relations. Though different from the rules of the polity itself, they received legal effect because they were supremely useful. In the case of *Miller* v. *Race* (1758), defences usually available under the common law would not apply to bills of exchange or bank notes: "The reason of all these cases is, because the usage of trade makes the law" and applies "even against express Acts of Parliament".[165] "[N]ot a tenth part of the trade in this kingdom could be carried on without them"; because general consent gave these notes the value of money – they were called "paper money" – they must be treated as such.[166] Mansfield even accepted that judicial notice was to be taken of mercantile custom.

[162] *Pillans* v. *Van Mierop*, 97 ER 1035 [1663] [1665] (1765). According to Lobban, this was uncontroversial in regard to the law merchant, *The Common Law*, 108.

[163] *Pillans* v. *Van Mierop*, [1669–70].

[164] Ibid., [1672].

[165] *Miller* v. *Race*, in *Notes of Cases Argued, and Adjudged, in the Court of King's Bench, and of Some Determined in the Other High Courts [1753–1759*] (3 vols., London, Clarke 1825), II 189–202.

[166] Ibid., 194, 199.

For that purpose, he invited into the King's Bench juries consisting of merchants that would have the required commercial knowledge.

These mercantile cases also make understandable Mansfield's famous statement regarding the law of nations as part of English law in *Triquet* v. *Bath* (1764). The case concerned the claim of immunity by a domestic servant of a foreign ambassador. In the course of the deliberation, Mansfield said that he remembered from an earlier case, *Buvot* v. *Barbuit,* Lord Talbot having affirmed that the law of nations "in its full extent was part of the Law of England". The Act of 1708, he inferred, was thus only declaratory.[167] Later research has expressed doubts about whether Mansfield remembered correctly. Moreover, from the executive's acceptance of diplomatic practices it did not follow that they were binding as common law, and no earlier cases where common law courts would have acknowledged ambassadorial privileges seem to have been found. But the common law's basis in "reason" made is possible for its practitioners to use arguments from natural law to open the courts for *lex mercatoria.*[168] Mansfield's definition of international commerce as *ius gentium* was "in accordance with the prevailing trend of legal opinion".[169]

Mansfield was not alone to give legal recognition to instruments and practices vital for the conduct of international trade, for other judges had done the same. His contribution was to produce a coherent view about the role of the legal system in advancing the interests of trade. Few Englishmen would have objected to Daniel Defoe's view that "[w]e are not only a trading country, but the greatest trading country in the world".[170] It must have seemed natural to give legal endorsement to this fact as well. In *Pillans* v. *Van Mierop*, Mansfield recognised that the forms of the common law should not obstruct the conduct of trade relations. Granting the validity of negotiable instruments irrespectively of claims relating to the original transaction was crucial to the uninterrupted operation of banking services and related transactions. Analogously, Mansfield's steadfast refusal to admit the right of labourers to form trade unions, but instead to regard them as "conspiracies under the

[167] *Triquet* v. *Bath*, 97 ER 936 (King's Bench 1764).
[168] O'Keefe, 'The Doctrine of Incorporation Revisited', 16.
[169] Sir William Searle Holdsworth, *A History of English Law* (London, Methuen 1909), 10, 373.
[170] Daniel Defoe, *The Complete English Tradesman* (1726), cited in T. C. W. Blanning, *The Culture of Power and the Power of Culture. Old Regime Europe 1660–1789* (Oxford University Press 2002), 302.

common law", was based on a conception of juridical reason closely intertwined with the needs of industrialisation.[171] If Mansfield is commonly regarded as the founder of English commercial law, this is so in the specific sense of granting validity to and supporting the actions and interests of the commercial operators, without the kinds of doubt Adam Smith was simultaneously expressing elsewhere.[172]

Recourse to natural law – principles of reason – also authorised that other "cosmopolitan" jurist William Scott, Lord Stowell, to apply the law of nations during his period as judge of the High Court of Admiralty (1798–1828). Scott had been taught civil law in Oxford where he had also acquired knowledge of the law of nations, which he always regarded as binding on England.[173] As admiralty judge, he had frequent recourse to international commercial practices in his treatment of the instance cases (cases of damage, mariners' wages, salvage, marine insurance and possession). In *Sisters* (1804), for instance, Scott dealt with a bill of sale that was invoked as proof of ownership under the common law. According to Scott, "this [was] a question of a more general nature, arising out of a system of more general law – out of the universal maritime law which constitute[d] part of the professional learning of the Court and its Practices".[174] Under the court's prize jurisdiction, Scott combined the writings of international publicists on maritime law with considerations of economic policy, as well as past precedent of the court itself. He was particularly keen to catch pretended neutrals trading not with but for the belligerent, thereby contributing to the latter's war effort.[175] Overall, he aimed to uncover the material basis of legal relationships and, without concern for formalities of domestic law, to decide cases handed out to him under something like "universal commercial practices of Europe".[176] Nevertheless, he was much more comfortable in applying the precedents of the admiralty court itself, which he thought more accurately reflected these universal principles than the writings of publicists.[177]

## Imagining Commercial Society: David Hume

Mansfield's integration of international commercial practices in the common law constituted a judicial affirmation that trade had indeed

[171] Poser, *Mansfield*, 241–3. [172] Lowry, 'Lord Mansfield', 618.
[173] See Henry Bourguignon, *Sir William Scott, Lord Stowell. Judge of the High Court of Admiralty 1798–1828* (Cambridge University Press 1987), 35–8 and 57–8.
[174] *Sisters* (1804), 5 Rob 159, cited in ibid., 261. [175] Ibid., 139–41, 153–63.
[176] Ibid., 261. [177] Ibid., 263.

become an affair of state. The most sophisticated thinking about what this might mean came from the Scottish universities which, unlike their English counterparts, engaged in advanced reflection on the changes in the economic and political world. Continental natural law was intensively studied through the works of Grotius, Heineccius and Barbeyrac, and special concern was felt about what many thought of as the egoism reflected in the works of Hobbes and Pufendorf. In response to the former's perceived inability to explain the actual flourishing of society, Scottish thinkers such as Gersom Carmichael (1672–1729) and Francis Hutcheson (1694–1746), developed the so-called moral sense approach that assumed an intrinsic sociability in humans that operated in ways that could be articulated as part of a divinely inspired natural law.[178] In this climate of intellectual fermentation and political realism, two men chose to interpret the emerging (commercial) society around them by focusing on what they suggested were the natural workings of human sentiments in their secular, historical context – David Hume and Adam Smith.

In *A Treatise on Human Nature* (1739) the young David Hume (1711–76) proposed to examine society by analysing the empirical operation of imagination, the manner in which human beings associated or dissociated things in ways they had learned from their social and historical environments.[179] Although Hume agreed with such thinkers as Hutcheson that all humans possessed a "moral sense" that contributed to the formation and maintenance of social institutions, he did not think of it as innate, even less implanted by God. Instead he derived it from habitual ways of thinking that were partly the product of human passions, partly responses to historical circumstances. For the sceptic Hume, the natural and the moral world existed in a continuum, our impressions of the external world mixing with our feelings and opinions about them, our imagination in a word.[180] This imagination was the focal point for what Hume had to say also about the justice assumed to underlie social relations and law.

Hume did not suggest that the sentiment of justice could be credited to anything like an innate "moral sense" or even simple self-love. Like

[178] The most useful work on this tradition is Knud Haakonssen, *Natural Law and Moral Philosophy. From Grotius to the Scottish Enlightenment* (Cambridge University Press 1996).

[179] On the secular and historical sense of what was "natural" for humans in Hume, see Duncan Forbes, *Hume's Philosophical Politics* (Cambridge University Press 1975), 69–74 and passim.

[180] David Hume, *A Treatise of Human Nature* (E. C. Mossner ed., Harmondsworth, Penguin 1969 [1739–40]), I II VI (114–16).

Pufendorf, he regarded justice as an artificial virtue that arose from what human beings learned about the advantage or disadvantage of particular forms of behaviour in actual social contexts – not advantage in a single case but in typical cases.[181] Such socialised feelings motivated individuals to behave in particular ways that attained in this sense binding force. Where motivation was strong, rules were strong, where it was less, binding force diminished. None of this was to say that contracts, for example, could be broken at will. Modern society developed a feeling of sympathy towards something like public interest that made parties comply with their agreements even against an immediate private advantage.[182]As sympathy gradually matured into second nature, law began to be felt as binding merely because it was law.[183] That Hume regarded this as a *natural* process meant that he could now conceive natural law as an empirical science designed to show how imagination created and upheld predictable and habitual forms of behaviour.[184]

The law of nations, too, arose from feelings about utility: "The advantage of peace, commerce, and mutual succour, make us extend to different kingdoms the same notions of justice, which take place among individuals."[185] But the feelings created by the association of ideas in the international world were not nearly as strong as between individuals. *Ergo* international law was a weak law. Princes were only weakly motivated by it and often followed the way of immediate interest. Hume did not contemplate the possibility that the same socialising process that developed sympathy towards public interest at home might also develop internationally in the way his avid reader Kant did. Considerations of law would only rarely – if ever – override more immediate economic or political interests. These considerations applied above all to the type of law of nations that had to do with matters such as the sacredness of ambassadors, declaration of war, abstention from poisoned weapons and others that "are evidently

[181] Ibid., III II II (548–52). [182] Ibid., III II II (550–1).

[183] For a useful discussion of Hume's view of the social origin of justice and "law", see Knud Haakonssen, *The Science of a Legislator. David Hume & Adam Smith* (Cambridge University Press 1981), 12–21.

[184] For Hume's debt to natural philosophy in his analysis of moral behaviour, see Margaret Schabas, *The Natural Origins of Economics* (The University of Chicago Press 2005), 60–70. As Stephen Buckle has noted, this was very close to how the older natural law tradition understood the way self-interested "reason" operated on the social circumstances. Stephen Buckle, *Natural Law and the Theory of Property. Grotius to Hume* (Oxford, Clarendon 1991), 287.

[185] Hume, *Treatise*, III II XI (618).

calculated for the commerce, that is peculiar to different societies".[186] In the absence of a general sense of an international public interest, princes will inevitably operate transactionally, by assessing the advantages of obedience in single cases. This was also understood by the public at large so that "we must necessarily give a greater indulgence to a prince or a minister, who deceives another; than to a private gentleman, who breaks his word of honour". This, he added, was taught to us by "the practice of the world".[187]

Alongside diplomatic law, there were also rules of natural law regulating private affairs, stability of possession, its transference by consent and the performance of promises. Such rules were applicable between states just as between individuals; the same interest created the same morality.[188] The most important of them was property. Once properties had been individuated, "there remains little or nothing to be done towards settling a perfect harmony and concord".[189] The realisation that stability of possessions would make everyone better off had created what Hume called a "convention" to that effect.[190] This did not have the nature of a promise or a social contract because for a promise or a contract to be binding, we should already presume the presence of a legal system that endows it with such effect. Nor was there ever a "state of nature" – this was "a mere fiction, not unlike that of the *golden age*".[191] Hume's view of the matter was remarkably pragmatic. Rights of property, like other rules of law, reflected the historical process during which the mind associated things we occupy and hold, and have held for a long time, as being "ours". "What has long lain under our eye, and has often been employ'd to our advantage, that we are always the most unwilling to part with."[192] All human affairs were governed by habit; stability of social relations was regarded as valuable everywhere. The "artifice and human conventions" that formed the social bond arose neither from reason nor from natural benevolence but reflected an historical experience that self-interest is best advanced under an agreed set of rules to which everyone pays deference under the condition of reciprocity.[193] Reflecting on the society around himself, he noted in a manner that his friend Adam Smith would later make famous "*that it is only from the selfishness and confined generosity of men, along with scanty provision nature has made for his wants, that justice derives its origin*".[194]

[186] Ibid., III II XI (618) [187] Ibid., III II XI (619). [188] Ibid., III II XI (619).
[189] Ibid., III II III (543). [190] Ibid., III II III (541). [191] Ibid., III II III (545).
[192] Ibid., III II III (554–5). [193] Ibid., III II III (549). [194] Ibid., III II III (547).

Hume tried to bring to a conclusion the project of modern natural law of speaking about human society in a purely empirical fashion, avoiding what he viewed as an invisible but fateful slide by prior thinkers from "is" to "ought".[195] To speak of the "advantage of treaties" was to bring social analysis down from rationalist heights to the psychology of real human societies in which law's "oughtness" arose from the way the mind learned to associate ideas. Natural lawyers had sought to counter the danger of scepticism by making self-interest appear consistent with the moral life. Hume turned attention to something distinct from morality, the way the human mind operated by association of experiences though imagination. With this, something could be said that Hume supposed universally true, namely that as people moved about seeking pleasure and avoiding pain, past experience could be linked with future expectations to produce results analogous to those produced by the natural sciences as they studied the process of causality. Hume often compared money with water and electricity or human with animal behaviour.[196] The calculability of the probable consequences of our actions was the secret of the universal verity of the new human science.[197]

## The Benefits of Commerce

Hume's early *Treatise* never received the kind of attention he had hoped for. It had been a youthful tract, written in a heavy and complex style that did not appeal to the Scottish literati.[198] So he reformulated its ideas in the *Enquiry Concerning the Principles of Morals* (1751) and in political essays that illustrated and expanded the theses laid out in the *Treatise* in a style accessible for a larger audience. Hume's attention shifted from the general principles of government to their actualisation in the political and economic world. Instead of moral virtues, his science of politics concentrated on the constitutional design of institutions – monarchic, aristocratic or democratic – that laid down the conditions for their success or failure.[199] Revealing himself now as a statesman, Hume made the famous quip about commerce having become a matter of state. A society's condition was determined by its attitudes to

[195] Ibid., III I I (521). [196] See Schabas, *Natural Origins*, 70–4.

[197] See the discussion of Hume in Christian Laval, *L'homme économique. Essai sur les raciness du néolibéralisme* (Paris, Gallimard 2007), 190–2.

[198] See e.g. Tom Beauchamp, 'Introduction', in David Hume, *An Enquiry Concerning Human Understanding* (Oxford University Press 1999), xii–xiii.

[199] See especially, Forbes, *Hume's Philosophical Politics*, 224–30.

commercial agents: "the public becomes powerful in proportion to the opulence and extensive commerce of private men".[200] The fame of these essays led to Hume's appointment as attaché to the British ambassador in Paris in 1763 and a few years later to the position of under-secretary of Scottish affairs.

The essays gave an influential depiction of the conditions of political economy in Britain created by the post-1688 compromise between crown prerogative and the right of property as expressed in the powers of parliament. The institutional balance offered a useful basis for pragmatism. It avoided the tyrannies of republicanism and absolutism and provided a check for imperial ambitions. Hume did worry over excessive public debt, especially debt contracted in war time and, like most Englishmen, feared the "corruption" that might result from the expanding influence of mercantile interests and colonial expansion.[201] But this did not turn him into an opponent of commercial society. On the contrary, Hume regarded the commerce of luxury as predominantly beneficial; it encouraged industry and trade and led to the spread of knowledge and civilisation.[202] Nor was this only a matter of private enrichment. The greatness of the state was inseparable from commerce so that "the public becomes powerful in proportion to the opulence and extensive commerce of private men".[203]

Hume completely rejected the tenets of the kind of mercantilism that examined commercial exchanges from the standpoint of the treasury. National wealth was not about securing the inflow of gold or money. This would only raise prices, hamper exports and make imports more profitable.[204] If the balance of power was thought of in terms of the relative wealth of the nations, as it now was, then the increase of wealth could no longer be undertaken by regulatory means. Instead, economic operators were to be liberated to seek capital gains anywhere in the world. In the essay on the 'Jealousy of Trade', Hume

[200] David Hume, 'Of Commerce', in Hume, *Political Essays* (Knud Haakonssen ed., Cambridge University Press 1994), 94.

[201] See further Poole, *Reason of State*, 122–7.

[202] David Hume, 'Of the Refinement of the Arts', in *Political Essays*, 105–14 (he did accept the presence of *vicious* luxury as well that was excessive in that it led to setting aside duty and generosity; however, he saw it as distinctly secondary in relation to luxury's benefits). See also Hume, 'Of Commerce', 95, 101 and 'Of Refinement in the Arts', 105.

[203] Hume, 'Of Commerce', 94.

[204] David Hume, 'Of the Balance of Trade', in *Political Essays*, 136–8.

argued that if everybody traded openly with their neighbours, there was no reason to fear that the richer countries would be gradually overtaken by poorer ones – the great fear in public debates at the time. The rich countries' ability to diversify allowed them to move to more profitable production as the poor countries' goods penetrated into their market. This, Hume suggested, would make free trade benefit everyone:

> the encrease of riches and commerce in any one nation, instead of hurting, commonly promotes the riches and commerce of all its neighbours; . . . a state can carry its trade and industry very far, where all the surrounding states are buried in ignorance, sloth, and barbarism.[205]

Or, as Hume argued from another direction, wealth was not about money but about productive labour. Money was merely an instrument that enabled goods produced in one place to be sold in another. The rise and fall of the amount of money might raise or lower the prices on the market. But the resulting moving of money into and out of the country would be paralleled by the movement of merchandise with the result that levels of growth would even out in due course. It was the circulation of money, and thus the work of the merchant class, that was the key to a nation's prosperity.[206]

Hume based his views on a historical, even historical-materialist view of human societies. "Justice" was something learned with socialisation, a sentiment that made existing social institutions seem natural and even beneficial. Craving for luxuries reflected the admiration of elite lifestyles and led to desire of more foreign trade and increased opportunities for wealth-creation. It may have been Smith who put the four-stage theory of human societies at the centre of his work, but already Hume was clear that as communities settled down from hunting to cultivation, they would begin to produce excess goods that could be sold as merchandise and lead gradually to the rise of cities with cultural and other benefits unavailable earlier. "Industry, knowledge and humanity are linked together by an indissoluble chain, and are found, from experience as well as reason, to be peculiar to the more polished, and what are commonly denominated, the more luxurious ages."[207]

[205] David Hume, 'Of the Jealousy of Trade', in *Political Essays*, 150.
[206] See David Hume, 'Of Interest', in *Political Essays*, 130–1.
[207] Hume, 'Of Refinement in the Arts', 107.

What appeared clearly in these arguments was that human happiness depended on economic growth and that this was a product of a single system that reacted to changes whose mastery was the secret of successful government. There was an old idea here, combined with a novel morality: "Nature, by giving a diversity of geniuses, climates and soils, to different nations, has secured their mutual intercourse and commerce, as long as they all remain industrious and civilized."[208] Of course, jurists had been debating for ages how to make human beings "industrious and civilized", and many, Hobbes among them had regarded this as altogether impossible. This time, however, the result was to be guaranteed by opening the gates of commerce so that by following the path of their own advantage, people would also work for the general good. Active employment was the most basic of human desires.[209] If it could not be directed to benevolence, operating efficiently only within the family, it might learn to appreciate justice – respect for property and the enforcement of contracts – through which selfishness could be made to service the general good.[210]

The irreducible egoism of human nature had been part of British political debate since Hobbes, and the theorists of the "moral sense", Hutcheson and Carmichael, had sought to refute it by proposing a view of benevolence as a *natural* aspect of human subjectivity. In his commentary on Pufendorf, Carmichael, for instance, stressed the rational faculty humans had received from God that would direct them to "the cultivation of the mind to *accustom ourselves to be restrained in our passions*".[211] Any such suggestion had, however, been ridiculed in Bernard de Mandeville's widely read *Fable of the Bees* (1711), and even Rousseau had adopted the view of selfishness as something beyond the capacity of reason and nature to contain. Hume, too, accepted that reason was merely the slave of the passions and that the passion for justice was not something we were born with but grew into. What he had been saying since the *Treatise*, however, was that the passion for gain and luxury might instead be turned into public service through economic industry and civilisation: "There is no passion … capable of controlling the interested affection, but the very affection itself, by an alteration of its

[208] Hume, 'Of the Jealousy of Trade', 151.

[209] Hume 'Of Interest', 130.

[210] Hume, *Treatise*, III II II (536–40).

[211] Gersom Carmichael, 'Natural Rights', in J. Moore & M. Silverthorne (eds), *Natural Rights on the Threshold of the Scottish Enlightenment. The Writings of Gersom Carmichael* (Indianapolis, Liberty Fund 2002 [1724]), 63.

direction."[212] This was achieved by commercial society. The "love of gain" made the wheels of the economy turn, created opportunities, circulated money and "encreae[sed] frugality, by giving occupation to men, and employing them in the arts of gain, which soon engage their affection, and remove all relish for pleasure and expense".[213] The benefits would expand beyond any single state. The growth of foreign trade would lead to emulation, diversification and increased industry, the betterment of life and the increase of liberty everywhere.[214]

## "Foundation of the Laws of All Nations": Adam Smith

This was practically identical with the famous fourth chapter of the *Wealth of Nations* where Adam Smith (1723–90) argued that the spontaneous pursuit of individual interests led to the advantage of the society as a whole:

> Every individual is continually exerting himself to find out the most advantageous employment for whatever capital he can command. It is his own advantage, indeed, and not that of the society, which he has in view. But the study of his own advantage naturally, or rather necessarily, leads him to prefer that employment which is most advantageous to society.[215]

The argument is quite consistent with natural jurisprudence. Indeed, Pufendorf might have written it. The work of nature operated outside the consciousness of individuals so that once artificial restraints were lifted, then "the obvious and simple system of natural liberty [would] establish itself on its own accord".[216] As a result, not only every individual but society as a whole would find itself better off. This was an important departure from the project of natural law that had still been present in the section on "police" in Smith's lectures on jurisprudence in the 1760s, namely to develop principles of government to increase the wealth of the state. Smith had now come to conclude that this was impossible. By studying how successive systems of economic production and exchange had developed the legal and political institutions proper to them he had found a broad historical process, with wide room for local variation, operated everywhere

[212] Hume, *Treatise*, III II II (543–4). [213] Hume, 'Of Interest', 103–31.
[214] Hume, 'Of the Jealousy of Trade', 150–3.
[215] Adam Smith, *An Inquiry into the Nature and Causes of the Wealth of Nations* [*WN*] (Harmondsworth, Penguin Classics 1982 [1776]) IV II (30).
[216] Ibid., IV IX (273, 274).

outside the consciousness of individuals.[217] This process peaked in "commercial society" in which wealth would be created through the natural operation of liberty. Principles of wealth production were unavoidably opaque; it was best to leave everyone to look after their wealth by following their self-interest. When everyone did that, the result would be that the market would promote the greatest wealth of all. It was not for the government to lay down conditions for the operation of the market, but the other way around.[218]

This did not mean that there was no role left for the state. In *The Theory of Moral Sentiments* (first edition 1759), Smith had, somewhat like Hume, stressed that individuals in commercial society were not linked by natural benevolence; each pursued their good separately from others. That society would still not collapse resulted from a sense of justice that had gradually grown in its members and that was expressed and administered by the state's legal system. "Justice", he wrote at the end of a decade of teaching of moral philosophy at the University of Edinburgh, "is the main pillar that upholds the great edifice. If it is removed, the great, the immense fabric of human society . . . must in a moment crumble into atoms."[219] And in the *Lectures of Jurisprudence* held in Glasgow a few years later, he insisted that:

> The first and chief design of every system of government is to maintain justice; to prevent the members of a society from incroaching on one another's property, or siezing [sic] what is not their own. The design here is to give each the secure and peaceable possession of his own property.[220]

Smith's whole *oeuvre* – his moral theory, his jurisprudence, and the analysis of commercial society in *The Wealth of Nations* (1776) – consisted of a turn away from the old doctrine of police, the scientific government

[217] A useful discussion of the partly natural, partly spontaneous and unpredictable character of historical development in Smith is Jennifer Pitts, *The Turn to Empire. The Rise of Imperial Liberalism in Britain and France* (Princeton University Press 2006), 27–34.

[218] I follow the account on the turn to the market in Michel Foucault, *Naissance de la biopolitique. Cours au Collège de France, 1978–1979* (Paris, Gallimard 2004), 29–48 and passim. See further commentary e.g. in Ryan Walter, 'Governmentality Accounts of the Economy. A Liberal Bias?', 37 *Economy and Society* (2008), 94–114.

[219] Adam Smith, *The Theory of Moral Sentiments* (P. Moloney ed. & intro., New York, Barnes & Noble Books 2004 [1759/1790]), 115. On the centrality of justice and law in Smith's commercial society, see further McNally, *Political Economy*, 187–92.

[220] Adam Smith, *Lectures on Jurisprudence* (R. L. Meek, D. D. Raphael & P. L. Stein eds, Indianapolis, Liberty Fund 1982), (A) 5.

of welfare, to justice, developed by a science of jurisprudence that, he held, was "of all sciences by far the most important, but hitherto, perhaps, the least cultivated".[221] This had both an analytical and a critical dimension. The former laid out the properties of law and legal institutions suitable for specific societies, the latter embodied Smith's normative project, which he regarded as identical with that of Grotius, namely to create "a system of principles which ought to run through, and be the foundation of the laws of all nations".[222]

Justice required the state to provide for external and internal security and to arrange for "certain public works and certain public institutions".[223] Throughout *The Wealth of Nations*, Smith returned to the duty of the state to set up and maintain a juridical framework to coordinate the subjects' liberties. The division of labour would strengthen class distinctions and subjects would no longer feel natural sympathy towards each other. In such conditions, only a legal system that was felt as just and impartial could uphold social harmony. Of such, the English constitution was a perfect example. It provided for no standing army, made the crown dependent on parliament for revenues, protected against arbitrary arrest and set up an independent judiciary, an altogether "happy mixture of all the different forms of government properly restrained and a perfect security to liberty and property".[224] In the past, happiness had been sought by political means, by regulating employment, production, imports and exports. This had been all wrong. When it was a question of how to invest capital or which produce would be of greatest value, then "every individual, it is evident, can in his local situation, judge much better than any statesman or lawgiver".[225]

Reacting to the Revolution in France in 1790, Smith wrote about a "spirit of system" that made politicians concoct ideal plans and great reforms that "by requiring too much, frequently obtain[] nothing".[226] Tampering with natural liberty only led to state capture by special interests, especially those of great merchants.[227] In the international

221 Smith, *Theory of Moral Sentiments*, 295.

222 Ibid., 465. See also Haakonssen, *Science of a Legislator*, 99–153.

223 Smith, *WN*, IV IX (274).

224 Smith, *Lectures*, (B) 421–2. See further McNally, *Political Economy*, 201–2.

225 Smith, *WN*, IV I (33).

226 Smith, *Theory of Moral Sentiments*, 315, 316.

227 There is a tension between Smith's critique of the way the great merchants only looked for their own interest and the "natural system of liberty" where the common good is produced by everyone doing precisely that. The tension may perhaps be lifted if the problem with the merchants is associated with their regard to their *collective* interests as a group, a "spirit of corporation" intrinsically in conflict with individual interests.

world, the same effect was produced by "the mean principle of national prejudice", "the most malignant jealousy and envy" that led us to live "in continual dread and suspicion of one another".[228] This was the source of all the short-sighted regulation to hoard bullion or to limit exports and imports to keep the balance of trade policies only advantageous for small factions: "To promote the little interest of one little order of men in one country, it hurts the interests of all other orders of men in that country, and of all men in all other countries."[229]

In contrast to the political, the economic realm could always be expressed in terms of calculable interests whose free realisation would in due course, outside the consciousness of individual interest-holders, lead to general good. This was the natural law that was now to determine state policy.[230] Commercial society was highest of Smith's four stages because passions there had been translated into economic interests whose free operation was guaranteed by law. The point of the critique of the mercantile system was to show how regulation positively distorted the advancement of general welfare. This was also fully applicable in the commerce between nations. It was "absurd" to regulate to maintain balance of trade:

> A trade which is forced by means of bounties and monopolies may be and commonly is disadvantageous to the country in whose favour it is meant to be established. . . . But that trade which, without force or constraint, is naturally and regularly carried on between any two places is always advantageous, though not always equally so, to both.[231]

Prudent masters of households never attempted to manufacture at home what it would cost less to buy. And "[w]hat is the prudence in the conduct of every private family can scarce be folly in that of a great kingdom".[232]

## The Unity of Morality, Law and Commerce

The system of natural liberty – here applied to international trade – arose from Smith's interest and training in natural law and his effort to follow the empirical approach of his friend David Hume. It embodied a

228 Smith, *Theory of Moral Sentiments*, 310, 311. 229 Smith, *WN*, IV VII (195).

230 Haakonssen, *Science of a Legislator*, 151. On the way Smith's arguments remove "politics" from government, see e.g. Donald Winch, *Riches and Poverty. An Intellectual History of Political Economy in Britain, 1750–1834* (Cambridge University Press 1996), 94–7.

231 Smith, *WN*, IV III II (67). 232 Ibid., IV II (33).

psychological assumption with a political jurisprudence. In the *Theory of Moral Sentiments,* Smith rejected the hypothesis of an innate moral sense. Instead, humans had internalised an "impartial spectator", a kind of secular conscience that allowed them to distinguish between just and unjust actions.[233] The sense of justice, vital for the maintenance of commercial society, arose though socialisation, as indignation over evil or though sympathy with someone who has become the object of violation. The extent of the spectator's sympathy varied with the intensity of the violation, leading to differences in the severity of laws:

> The most sacred laws of justice ... whose violation seems to call loudest for vengeance and punishment, are the laws that guard the life and person of our neighbour; the next are those which guard his property and possessions; and the last of all come those which guard what are called his personal rights, or what is due to him from the promises of others".[234]

This was precisely what Grotius had been saying. Once lives and property were secure, it was time for the strict enforcement of contracts. In the last paragraph of the *Theory of Moral Sentiments*, Smith proposed that "in another discourse" he would "give an account of the general principles of law and government", based on the ideas about human nature laid out in this work and applied to the history of jurisprudence.[235] Smith never produced that work – something he openly regretted.[236] Instead he left Edinburgh to Glasgow where, during four years (1759–63) he gave lectures on jurisprudence in which he elaborated his influential four-stages theory of human society, linking a profound "historicisation of the human personality" with an ideological defence of commerce.[237] Older natural law understood human nature as basically unchanging. For Smith, however, human nature coalesced with the expectations and opinions that developed differently in different societies, as produced by their prevailing economic organisation, especially their property regime.[238]

233 See Nicholas Phillipson, *Adam Smith. An Enlightened Life* (Yale University Press 2010), 49–55.

234 Smith, *The Theory of Moral Sentiments*, 111.

235 Ibid., 466.

236 See James Buchan, *The Authentic Adam Smith. His Life and Ideas* (New York, Norton 2006), 66.

237 J. G. A. Pocock, 'The Mobility of Property and the Rise of Eighteenth-Century Sociology', in J. G. A. Pocock, *Virtue, Commerce, and History. Essays on Political Thought and History, Chiefly in the Eighteenth Century* (Cambridge University Press 1985), 116.

238 See further, Joseph Cropsey, *Polity and Economy. With Further Thoughts on the Principles of Adam Smith* (South Bend, St Augustine's Press 2001), 69–73.

For example, "where the age of hunters subsists . . . there is almost no property amongst them. . . . But when flocks and herds come to be reared property then becomes of a very considerable extent."[239] When ownership extended beyond physical possession, some gained more than others and government was needed "to [secure] the property of the rich from the inroads of the poor".[240] Like Hume, Smith rejected the hypothesis of a social contract. No one had ever consented to being ruled; everyone found themselves always already under a sovereign.[241] Government was a result of "the natural progress which men make in society".[242] The development peaked in commercial society where "the subjects of property are greatly increased [so that] the laws must be proportionately multiplied".[243]

Multiplication of laws reflected the complexity of the market, not the increase of governmental direction. Smith had no doubt that in this respect England's post-1688 constitution was of the highest quality.[244] The division of powers between the monarch, the great landowners in parliament and the judiciary gave rise to a system of liberty without a firm sovereign centre.[245] Private and public power were completely intertwined:

> Property and civil government very much depend on one another. The preservation of property and the inequality of possession first formed it, and the state of property must always vary with the form of government.[246]

Conjectural history took a lion's share of Smith's lectures on jurisprudence. Legislation and government were creatures of specific systems of production and exchange, designed to uphold specific forms of ownership. The argument formed a natural though perhaps surprising bridge from the world of morality in *The Theory of Moral Sentiments* to the

[239] Smith, *Lectures*, (A) 16. [240] Ibid., (A) 208. [241] Ibid., (A) 317–19, 321.
[242] Ibid., (A) 207. [243] Ibid., (A) 16.
[244] See also Jerry Evensky, *Adam Smith's Moral Philosophy. A Historical and Contemporary Perspective on Markets, Law, Ethics, and Culture* (Cambridge University Press 2005), 63–72.
[245] Smith, *Lectures*, (A) 269, 326–30.
[246] Ibid., (B) 401. Interestingly, Smith suggested that the English constitutional structure lent itself to being understood in two alternative ways. One could either construct a view of government from private rights; or one could begin with government and derive from it a system of private property. His second course followed continental jurisprudence, which took the latter direction. But his first course had been constructed in the opposite way.

commercial exchanges of *The Wealth of Nations*.[247] While the former work moved in the conventional vocabulary of benevolence and sympathy, the latter highlighted the overriding importance of interest and utility. For, as Smith explained in the latter work, in the "system of liberty", "[e]very man, as long as he does not violate the laws of justice, is left perfectly free to pursue his own interest his own way, and to bring both his industry and his capital into competition with those of any other man, or order of men".[248] Justice played a different role in these works. In the former, it aimed to prevent behaviour that violated shared feelings about proper behaviour. In the latter, it saw to the protection of property and the enforcement of contracts. Nowhere was Smith's sense of injustice clearer than in his condemnation, in the latter work, of the "absurd and oppressive monopolies [that] like the laws of Draco [. . .] may be said to have been written in blood".[249]

The differences between Smith's early and his late work result from his move from a general theory of morality to rules appropriate for commercial society. *The Wealth of Nations* was a kind of handbook for legislators of such a society, what they needed to know about its operation so as to legislate best for it. The most important thing to know was that it worked best when the legislator let "the obvious and simple system of natural liberty establish[] itself of its own accord".[250] None of this cancelled the importance of the virtues and fellow feeling exposed in the earlier book. From that perspective, commercial society would often fare badly. Division of labour created labour conditions that made workers "as stupid and ignorant as it is possible for a human being to become".[251] The labouring poor would suffer from the erosion of traditional religious and other virtues.[252] The high rate of profit everyone was looking for destroyed the parsimony and sober virtue "which in other circumstances is natural".[253] Nothing in *The Wealth of Nations* suggested that people should not try to look beyond their own interests. It was only that when such benevolence was applied to economic activities, its results were usually harmful.

Whatever nostalgia Smith felt towards moral virtues, he had little doubt that the division of labour would bring about "opulence" if only

[247] For the wealth of interpretations regarding the relations of the two works, see Athol Fitzgibbons, *Adam Smith's System of Liberty, Wealth and Virtue. The Moral and Political Foundations of the Wealth of Nations* (Oxford University Press 1995), 6–10 and passim.

[248] Smith, *WN*, IV IX (273–4).

[249] Ibid., IV viii (232).

[250] Ibid., IV ix (273).

[251] Ibid., V I 3 (368–9).

[252] See also Cropsey, *Polity and Economy*, 108–10.

[253] Smith, *WN*, IV VII (196).

economic actors were liberated to follow their self-interest. Prior writers on *raison d'état*, political arithmetic and general happiness had adopted the perspective of the state, asking themselves how it could best manage economic relations, especially foreign trade, so as to prevent the outflow of money. Smith did not think this way. Even as it is dubious whether he imagined the economy as fully autonomous, he nevertheless believed it had its own natural laws, those of the market, that legislators would have to learn to deal with. The relations of justice in a commercial society did not abolish government but directed legislation to organising defence, commerce and education.[254]

## Diplomacy, War, Empire

Like Hume, Smith believed that principles of justice operated only weakly in the international realm. Everybody was attached to their nation – "its prosperity and glory seem to reflect some sort of honour upon ourselves". The national prejudice also led people to view "with most malignant jealousy and envy, the prosperity and aggrandizement of any other neighbouring nation". Despite all the rhetoric of peace and tranquillity, everyone had in mind "the interest of their respective countries". It followed, Smith thought, that

> [t]he regard for the laws of nations, or for those rules that independent states profess or pretend to think themselves bound to observe in their dealings with one another, is often very little more than mere pretence and profession.[255]

Of course Smith, like Hume, regarded himself not at all so narrowly prejudiced, and he tried to persuade his countrymen not to overlook the real improvements in cultivation of land, in manufactures and commerce in France and learn to understand that a nation's prosperity was enhanced, not threatened, by that of its neighbours.[256] He also sketched an image of the exceptional statesman free of jealousy and ready to sacrifice their special interest "to the interest of that great society of all sensible and intelligent beings, of which God himself is the administrator and director".[257]

In *Lectures*, Smith produced a conventional account of the just war, of neutrality and of diplomacy, noting that owing to the absence of a common sovereign, these laws were characterised by uncertainty and

[254] Ibid., V, I (279–406). [255] Smith, *Theory of Moral Sentiments*, 310.
[256] Ibid., 311. [257] Ibid., 320.

irregularity.[258] The only just cause of war was an injury committed in case the demand for satisfaction was refused, and war was otherwise a proportionate response.[259] He also speculated about the ease with which enemy populations can be subjected to belligerent actions owing to the fact "we do not feel for those at distance as we do for those near us" while also praising the greater degree of refinement in modernif compared to barbarian warfare.[260] Like many enlightenment intellectuals, he was suspicious of national power and aggrandisement, war and empire. Nevertheless, he paid much attention to military virtue, organisation and expenditure; he also had no faith that commerce would necessarily pacify countries.[261] But the progress of civilisation and even military technology would have some effect in diminishing the savagery of warfare: "The invention of firearms which at first sight appears to be so pernicious, is certainly favourable both to the permanency and to the extension of civilisation."[262] Treaties and alliances were fragile: "From the smallest interest, upon the slightest provocation, we see those rules every day either evaded or directly violated without shame or remorse."[263] Like Hume, he believed that national prejudice often clouded statesmen's sense of judgment but also noted that it was often hard to separate commendable patriotism from negative jealousy.[264]

It is well-known that Smith was critical of empire and that no passages in the *Wealth of Nations* were written with more outrage than those dealing with monopoly companies that had become "in the long run universally, either burdensome or useless, and have either mismanaged or confined the trade".[265] The East India Company had "wasted and destroyed" everything; it was "altogether unfit to govern its territorial possessions".[266] Only when it seemed necessary for opening trade with some "remote and barbarous nation", setting up banking services or initiating public works, might a limited monopoly be justified, though only on a temporary basis.[267] Smith extended his critique to the imperial project itself: "Great Britain derives nothing but loss from the dominion which she assumes over her colonies."[268] Its monopoly was a wholly unjust burden on American and British consumers alike. Smith admired the way the American colonies had been able to

258 Smith, *Lectures*, (B) 545. 259 Ibid., (B), 546–7. 260 Ibid., (B) 545, 547–8.
261 See further Edwin van Haar, *Classical Liberalism and International Relations Theory. Hume, Smith, Mises and Hayek* (London, Palgrave 2009), 62–6.
262 Smith, *WN*, V I I (297). 263 Smith, *Theory of Moral Sentiments*, 310.
264 Ibid., 310–11. 265 Smith, *WN*, V I III (321–2). 266 Ibid., V I III (343).
267 Ibid., V I III (343–5). 268 Ibid., IV VII (199).

administer themselves so as to bring welfare to all their inhabitants. It would be much better if Britain gave up its American colonies and instead concluded a free trade agreement with them, though he doubted whether Britain or indeed any colonial power could reconcile itself to such action.[269] He was also sceptical about the possibility of liberating all trade even in the best of conditions. For example, even if the navigation laws had helped build up English carrier trade and encouraged long-term investment, they were to remain temporary and gradually be dismantled.[270]

Smith's discussion of the natural laws of the economy portrayed the international world as a geographical extension of the domestic market. Division of labour increased productivity and production; more goods could be produced with decreasing unit costs. The only thing that limited this process was the extent of the market. If the search for opulence and improvement were part of human nature, then it was also part of natural humanity to expand the size of the market – and Smith went into some detail to show how the means of water-carriage had expanded across the centuries to bring merchandise to ever more distant places. Things were now transported from London to Calcutta so that "[t]hose two cities ... at present carry a very considerable commerce with each other, and by mutually affording a market, give a good deal of encouragement to each other's industry".[271] There was all reason to encourage this development.[272] Hume and Tucker had already concluded that foreign trade would not lead to levelling of the differences between poor and rich countries. Instead, rich countries such as Britain would be inspired to react to competition by mechanising production so as to bring to the market increasing numbers of goods with better quality and competitive prices. England would have nothing at all to lose but everything to gain from free trade.

Previous generations of natural lawyers and economic writers had urged the state to create a positive balance of trade by hoarding bullion, limiting imports, supporting exports and monopolising colonial trade. Smith rejected all this as unworkable and unjust. A government could never know what is needed to produce wealth as well as the merchant: "every individual, it is evident, can, in his local situation, judge much

[269] Ibid., IV VII (199, 200–1).

[270] Ibid., IV II (45–6). But he was sceptical: "Not only the prejudices of the public, but what is much more unconquerable, the private interests of many individuals, irresistibly oppose it", ibid., IV II and V I (48, 343–5).

[271] Ibid., I III (123). [272] Ibid., IV III (67).

better than any statesman or lawgiver can do for him".[273] The jealousy of trade had been an offshoot of the "unnatural and retrograde order" where manufacturing and commerce had given impetus for developments in agriculture. But the natural process went in the opposite direction. What was needed was a massively commercialised agriculture on which production and manufacture could then be built. This change was to take place "not [by] positive reform but freeing the actually developed unnatural European system from all restraints and preferential policies".[274] The old idea of the balance of power had been based on the assumption that the growth of a nation will always take place at the cost of others. Under the new theory, all were to benefit. Hence the assumption that under conditions of liberty, commerce will not cease expanding, and the result will be an empire of trade.[275]

## The Laws of "Utility"

The radical critique of knowledge introduced by Smith into the debate on government effectively ended any effort to link the law of nations with substantive ideas of virtue or happiness. Mercantilist reason of state had been wrong to believe it could produce techniques for ruling the state for the general interest. The general interest was only the accumulation of private interests. How this accumulation would take place, could not be known. The link between reason of state and political economy was severed.[276] The government should not prepare plans for happiness but instead provide for liberty, understood as the free pursuit by the subjects of their interests. The operation of the market would then see to it that this would lead to the general good.

As Smith had demonstrated, the division of labour would continue regardless of national boundaries; if allowed to expand, it would gradually lead into the world-wide markets where England might play a huge role. In Europe, the balance of power had constrained rivals and prevented the rise of a single hegemon. By the end of the Seven Years' War (1763), British statesmen concluded that this no long required constant intervention. The continental system would balance itself; only passive surveillance was needed.[277] Globally, England would mediate

[273] Ibid., IV II (33). [274] Hont, *Jealousy of Trade*, 377.
[275] Foucault, *Biopolitique*, 56–7.
[276] See further, Walter, 'Governmentality Accounts of the Economy', 105, 94–114.
[277] F. H. Hinsley, *Power and the Pursuit of Peace. Theory and Practice in the History of Relations between States* (Cambridge University Press 1963), 182–5.

between Europe and the colonial world, working to become what early nineteenth-century free traders would call the workshop of the world.[278] Already in the 1770s and 1780s politicians such as the earl of Shelburne and William Pitt the Younger began to think that it might be possible for Britain to form the hub around which the global economy would turn. Shelburne, the great grandson of William Petty (the founder of political arithmetic), and the sometime patron of Smith and the young Jeremy Bentham, took up Smith's arguments as his government negotiated the treaty of 1783 with Britain's former American colonies on largely free trade principles.[279] Towards a sceptical parliament Shelburne argued that:

> if there is any nation . . . which ought to be the first to reject monopoly, it is the English. Situated . . . between the old world and the new, and between southern and northern Europe, all we ought to covet upon earth is free trade.[280]

Even as the government fell and with it, the objective of a federal union, the treaty nevertheless lay the basis for an important increase of British exports to America.[281] Laissez-faire would now structure British commercial relations, with developments peaking in the free trade arrangements in the Anglo-French treaty of 1786 whose application was only frustrated by the onset of the Revolution.[282] The Napoleonic wars further interrupted commercial expansion, as did the corn laws, much maligned by the Cobdenites. Free trade's re-emergence in the 1820s and 1830s caused some to view it as the "happy time when the sentiments of cosmopolitanism, internationalism, humanitarianism, and pacifism (all that a later generation was to

[278] Foucault, *Biopolitique*, 60–3.

[279] For an excellent discussion of the 1783 treaty as the starting-point for the introduction of the "science of legislator" in international economic law, see Anne Orford, 'Theorizing Free Trade', in Anne Orford & Florian Hoffmann (eds), *The Oxford Handbook of the Theory of International Law* (Oxford University Press 2016), 711–23.

[280] Shelburne to Parliament in February 1783, as quoted in James Ashley Morrison, 'Before Hegemony. Adam Smith, American Independence, and the Origins of the First Era of Globalization', 66 *International Organization* (2012), 419.

[281] The value of its exports to America rose from 37 to 57% of Britain's foreign trade. Bernard Semmel, *The Rise of Free Trade Imperialism. Classical Political Economy and the Empire of Free Trade and Imperialism 1750–1850* (Cambridge University Press 2009 [1970]), 30.

[282] For the context of the French 1786 treaty, see W. O. Henderson, 'The Anglo-French Commercial Treaty of 1786', 10 *The Economic History Review* (New Series), 1957, 104–12. See also Semmel, *Free Trade*, 38–44.

call 'Cobdenism') held sway".[283] But for much of the population at home and in the colonies, the period was marked by deepening poverty, hardening of elite attitudes and frustrated efforts to organise domestic or international solidarity.[284]

John Austin's *The Province of Jurisprudence Determined* (1832) represents that dual inheritance. It was published as ideas about free trade as not merely a commercial principle but an instrument of peace were at their height. Richard Cobden himself argued in Smith's footsteps for a system of natural liberty in which private individuals, the middle class and civil society in general would come to contribute to general prosperity. National boundaries would become irrelevant: "As little intercourse as possible betwixt the Governments, as much connection as possible between the nations of the world."[285] Austin's famous relegation of international law to the sphere of positive morality became widely known only later in the century but fitted well with the prevailing scepticism about diplomacy and other aspects of official state policy. Because Austin defined law as command of a superior, and there was no superior among nations, international law could not be law.[286] It was mere opinion. In the previous century, Hume and Smith had tried to integrate "opinion" into a social theory of sympathy and fellow feeling, part of the socialisation process. And James Mill speculated about

[283] Semmel, *Free Trade*, 2. For a brief description of the move towards free trade at this time, see Anthony Howe, 'Restoring Free Trade, 1776–1873', in Donald Winch & Patrick K. O'Brien (eds), *The Political Economy of British Historical Experience 1688–1914* (Oxford University Press 2002), 193–200.

[284] See e.g. Eric Hobsbawm, *The Age of Revolution 1789–1848* (London, Abacus 1997 [1962]), 250–62 and more specifically Anne Orford, 'Food Security, Free Trade and the Battle for the State', 11 *Journal of International Law and International Relations* (2015), 32–48.

[285] Cobden, cited in Niels P. Petersson, 'The Promise and Threat of Free Trade in a Globalizing Economy. A European Perspective', in Thomas Hippler & Milos Vec (eds), *Paradoxes of Peace in Nineteenth Century Europe* (Oxford University Press 2015), 95. See also Semmel, *Free Trade*, 158–69.

[286] John Austin, *The Province of Jurisprudence Determined* (H. L. A. Hart intro., Indianapolis, Hackett 1998 [1832]), 123–7, 187–8; In his lectures, Austin dismissed Roman *ius gentium* as "certain inept speculations of certain Stoic philosophers", John Austin, *Lectures on Jurisprudence, of the Philosophy of Positive Law* (4th edn, by R. Campbell, London, Murray 1873), 569, 567–85. By contrast, as one of the commissioners sent to Malta in 1836 to enquire into the state of the laws there, he firmly defended the powers of the British sovereign to give law to that colony over and above local laws and rules. If imperial power was to have reality, it was to be understood as sovereign power. See Lauren Benton & Lisa Ford, *Rage for Order, The British Empire and the Origins of International Law 1800–1850* (Harvard University Press 2016), 79–80.

public opinion as the real sanction of international law. But Austin's narrow definition did not leave room for such contemplations.[287] Instead, early sections of *Province* attacked the theory of a moral sense within which opinions might play a tangible role.

Austin's effort to clear the conceptual ground around law was embedded in a thoroughly empirical moral epistemology. In the early part of *Province*, Austin denied the existence of any innate capacity to know the good. The immediacy of our sentiments was no proof of their validity; that different individuals felt differently undermined the very assumption.[288] Instead, Austin claimed, it was possible to know "the probable effects of our conduct on that general happiness or good which is the final cause or purpose of the good and wise lawgiver in all his laws and commandments".[289] The science of the legislator would thus "rest[] upon observation and induction applied to the tendencies of our actions".[290] The object of such observation was the pleasures and pains caused by specific actions. Austin agreed with Smith that what accounted for utility in such terms was best known to individuals themselves: "[E]very individual person is the best possible judge of his interests: of what will affect himself with the greatest pleasures and pains."[291] This would not lead into egoism as people had reason to think of the good in terms of rules, and the principle of utility held good whether the motives of one's actions were selfish or altruistic.[292] Austin's theory was relevant for legislation because his rule-utilitarianism applied to classes of actions instead of individual acts. It was universalist, but in the specific manner where collective expressions such as humankind, country or public were only "concise expressions for a number of individual persons considered collectively as a whole".[293]

*Province* was composed at a time of economic difficulty, popular unrest and tightening political control. It represented a "top-down, sovereign-obeyed and threat-backed theory of law".[294] It was deeply conservative

287 See James Mill, 'Law of Nations', *Supplement to the Encyclopaedia Britannica* (London, Innes 1825), 4–9.

288 Austin, *Province*, 95–9. 289 Ibid., 104.

290 Ibid., 73. Austin did claim that he does not want to treat the science of legislation specifically, and therefore not to draw specific conclusions from his utilitarianism, 53. Nevertheless, the long discussion on ethics leaves no doubt that only considerations of utility can underlie the activity of the legislator. See also W. L. Morison, *John Austin* (Stanford University Press 1982), 68–71.

291 Austin, *Province*, 106. 292 Ibid., 112–18. 293 Ibid., 105.

294 Allan C. Hutchinson, *The Province of Jurisprudence Democratized* (Oxford University Press 2009), 28.

and anti-democratic. Like Bentham, Austin had been disgusted with the disorderly state of English law, both as an intellectual system and a governing practice, but unlike Bentham, he did not believe it could be subjected to democratic reform.[295] Although he admired German jurisprudence he did not believe it could be transposed to Britain. He was interested in codification but, as is well-known, his work remained in obscurity until later in the century when his command theory, his separation of law from morality and the resulting view of law as an instrument of social control could be used to give scientific content to expanding rule-of-law talk, including in the colonies.[296] Ethics, Austin believed, had too long been captured by what his mentor Jeremy Bentham had regarded as simple prejudices used by some to impress upon others their opinions.[297] This was now changing. The "leading principles of the science of ethics, and also of the various sciences which are nearly related to ethics [of which he thought law was one], are gradually finding their way".[298] Profound knowledge of these would always be confined to the few, but leading principles could be grasped even by the masses. This was especially so if legal science were to learn from that part of ethics that had made the greatest advances recently:

> The shortest and clearest illustrations of this most cheering truth [i.e. that increasing numbers of people were able to argue in a utilitarian fashion], are furnished by the inestimable science of political economy, which is so interwoven with every consideration belonging to morals, politics, and legislation, that it is impossible to treat any one of these sciences without a continual reference to it.[299]

Political economy was the new model for jurisprudence.[300] Henceforth, Austin argued, the people would no longer attribute want and labour to

[295] This despite the fact that *The Province of Jurisprudence Determined* came out in the year of the Great Reform Bill (1832), which expanded the franchise from 500,000 to approximately 800,000, though still excluding the largest part of the population from parliamentary influence.

[296] A useful brief biography is Wilfried E. Rumble, *Doing Austin Justice. The Reception of John Austin's Philosophy of Law in Nineteenth-Century England* (London, Bloomsbury 2004), 13–27. The enthusiasm of the British legal establishment about the conceptual neatness of *Province*, the separation of law from morality and the "scientific" allure of Austin's jurisprudence is described at 102–25.

[297] See Philip Schofield, *Utility & Democracy. The Political Thought of Jeremy Bentham* (Oxford University Press 2006), 109–36 and Austin, *Province*, 63.

[298] Austin, *Province*, 65. [299] Ibid. 66.

[300] See Morison, *John Austin*, 1–2, 48–55 (especially on the influence of James Mill's economic writings).

the unequal division of property. Instead, they could now blame the "niggardliness of nature" that was "inseparable from the condition of man upon earth". Law would help the masses to learn that the "inequality which inevitably follows the beneficent institution of property" was a function of the presence of capital, and capital was "good for the many, as well as the few" as it was origin also of the labourer's "reward".[301] At a time of massive poverty and rioting, such assurances must have sounded hollow. But this did not appear so to the gentlemen-philosophers who were busily forging the principles of political economy into something they labelled "universal jurisprudence".

## "International Law": Jeremy Bentham

The vocabulary of utility proposed a bargain between public power and the individual to realise optimal gain with minimal loss of liberty.[302] Austin had adopted it from the prolific and eccentric writings by the legal reformer, economic and political essayist Jeremy Bentham (1748–1832). Bentham's writings on international matters were limited to a series of essays on peace, colonialism and an international tribunal, composed during 1786–9 and put together by the editor of Bentham's collected works, John Bowring, in 1843 under the title of "Principles of International Law".[303] In the 1780s, Bentham had attacked Pitt's engagement of Britain in support of Sweden's belligerent Eastern policy, a policy he feared would lead into an all-out European war.[304] The events inspired Bentham's interest in an international code, but nothing came of this beyond the text known as "A Plan of Universal and Perpetual Peace". Many of the topics dealt with in that text – the critique of secrecy and of the policy of alliances, interest in disarmament and peaceful settlement – were offshoots of his attacks on recent British

301 Austin, *Province*, 67, 68.

302 On the compromise between the vocabularies of individual rights and utility in early nineteenth-century debates, see Foucault, *Biopolitique*, 41–3. At that point, the (radical) vocabulary of utility mostly predominated over the (revolutionary) vocabulary of rights, 45. This was of course overturned in the late twentieth century.

303 The organisation of the essays was not from Bentham's own hand and small parts may even have been composed by his assistant. The longest of the four essays – "A Plan for a Universal and Perpetual Peace" – is actually a composition of three distinct texts in the manuscript collection – namely 'Pacification and Emancipation', 'Colonies and Navy' and 'Cabinet no Secrecy'. See Gunhild Hoogensen, *International Relations, Security and Jeremy Bentham* (Oxford, Routledge 2005), 42–9.

304 Jeremy Bentham, 'Letters of Anti-Machiavel', in John Bowring (ed.), *The Works of Jeremy Bentham* (11 vols, Edinburgh, William Tait 1838–43), XI, 2.

policy.[305] Although he clearly regarded speculating about the rights and duties of sovereigns as of only limited interest, everything about Bentham's writing on codification and the general principles of law emanated from legal thinking that was universal to its core and aimed at a science of law that would be applicable regardless of time and place.

Bentham's legal writings are usually divided into two periods: the initial works in the 1770s and 1780s targeted the system of the common law and especially its predominant representative, William Blackstone's *Commentaries*, while the works from 1809 onwards addressed constitutional issues and legal reform in England and elsewhere. Bentham regarded the common law as a confused mess of disparate ideas that could not be subjected to scientific treatment as part of universal jurisprudence.[306] His life's project was to develop a complete code of laws that would realise the utilitarian *Grundnorm*, "the greatest happiness of the greatest number".[307] He worked with a notion of law much wider than Austin's. He accepted that constitutional and international law created *duties* for sovereigns notwithstanding their weak enforcement, but vacillated in respect of whether those duties were properly legal or moral. A treaty, for instance, was not in itself "law":

> It has intimate connection however with the body of laws, in virtue of its being apt to be converted by construction into an actual law or set of laws, and at any rate from the expectation it affords of the establishment of express laws conformable to stipulations of which it is composed.[308]

In other words, a treaty may create expectations of conforming behaviour and perhaps a moral obligation of compliance. But it did not receive legal sanction before its content was transformed into domestic law. Twenty years later, he had come to conclude that any project for a universal treaty was unrealistic and that the rights and duties between sovereigns were "properly only the rights and duties of morality".[309] But he continued to advocate the production of some kind of an

[305] See further Stephen Conway, 'Bentham versus Pitt. Jeremy Bentham and British Foreign Policy 1789', 30 *The Historical Journal* (1987), 791–809.

[306] See Lobban, *The Common Law*, 128, 156–8.

[307] For Bentham's disagreement with Smith's critique of "men of projects", see Jeremy Bentham, 'Manual of Political Economy', in *The Works*, III, 49–52.

[308] Jeremy Bentham, *Of Laws in General* (H. L. A. Hart ed., London, Athlone 1970), 16, cited in Hoogensen, *International Relations*, 73.

[309] Jeremy Bentham, 'General View of a Complete Code of Laws', in *The Works*, III, 200.

international "code" as well as the establishment of an international tribunal. "If a citizen of the world had to prepare an international code", he once wrote, "what would he propose as his object? It would be the common and equal utility of all nations."[310] An international code would be no different from any other code of law. It would call upon the government to legislate for the "happiness of the individuals, of whom a community is composed".[311]

Happiness, interests, utility... The expressions evoked the famous "sovereign masters, pain and pleasure", under which Bentham assumed that nature had placed humankind. Laws that failed to express utility were either confused about their real objective – the case of the common law – or then had no meaningful reference at all – the case of natural law and natural rights.[312] The latter were altogether fabulous entities that merely expressed a person's conviction about some moral truth for which that person felt no need to give an explanation.[313] Bentham asserted this critique over and again in his attacks on the American and French declarations and in the context of the reinstatement of the constitution of Cadiz in 1820. Rights, he wrote, are not only meaningless but invite subjects to resist whatever governmental actions they dislike: "out of one foolish word may start a thousand daggers".[314] Meaningful juridical language would only refer to things perceptible by the senses or qualities parasitic on the former (Bentham's "fictitious" entities).[315] As happiness and utility were measurable entities, it followed that if governments were to follow Bentham's suggestions, their policies would need to be assessed by measuring the amounts of pleasure or pain they caused.[316]

310 Jeremy Bentham, 'Principles of International law', in ibid., III, 537.

311 Jeremy Bentham, *Introduction to the Principles of Morals and Legislation* (Buffalo, Prometheus 1988 [1781/89]), 24.

312 Jeremy Bentham, *A Fragment on Government* (J. H. Burns & H. L. A Hart eds, Cambridge University Press 1988), 113.

313 Ibid., 53–4.

314 Jeremy Bentham, 'Anarchical Fallacies', in *The Works*, II, 497, 489–534.

315 A useful discussion of this distinction is Schofield, *Utility & Democracy*, 1–27. For wholly non-existent "fabulous" entities, see 17. Absence of direct reference to such entities did not *always* make a proposition meaningless, if only it could to be translated so that its hidden references in the empirical world became visible.

316 The pain or pleasure was to be measured by four qualities: intensity, duration, certainty/uncertainty and distance. Bentham, *Introduction to Principles of Morals and Legislation*, IV (29).

The obsessive and unfinished nature of Bentham's *oeuvre* is well known. Its many idiosyncrasies – sarcastic or condescending criticisms, neologisms, often impenetrable prose and excessive detail – may suggest that the work is most useful as a warning about the intellectual pitfalls accompanying dogmatic adherence to few striking metaphors. But even as a third-rate literary performer, Bentham gave voice and coherence to ideas that had been long brewing in the English legal culture. When developed by acolytes, those ideas appear not only as respectable but even subtle occupants of one corner of legal thought.[317] They also had relevance for how to think about law outside the state. And yet, the man who coined the neologism "international law" also gave prominence to a form of legal–political thought where nothing of the kind could have an independent existence as against structures of economic thought.

## "Universal Jurisprudence" As Political Economy

As a key example of Smith's "men of project" Bentham made a distinction between merely descriptive ("expository") and normative ("censorial") jurisprudence, and declared himself predominantly interested in the latter. Censorial jurisprudence was not to be based on improvable moral exhortations or a postulated moral sense with no value beyond the speaker's opinion but on the utilitarian calculus that was valid independently of time and place. As Bentham put it, while the "Expositor" described the systems of law valid in *different* places, the law of the "Censor", namely "that which *ought to be*, is in all countries to a great degree the same... [Hence] the Censor is, or ought to be, the citizen of the world."[318]

Bentham was convinced of the universal power of his utilitarianism.[319] All human beings not only look for happiness but have an equal desire and capacity for it. Even as his views vacillated in reaction to the French Revolution, he came in 1809 to set himself firmly in favour of democratic reform.[320] For Bentham, states and nations were nothing but forms of habitual obedience that a group of people paid to a

[317] As William Twining suggests, Bentham has a "rightful place as the Father of Modern Jurisprudence in the English-speaking world", 'Reading Bentham', 75 *Proceedings of the British Academy* (1989), 129.

[318] Bentham, *Fragment*, 8.

[319] "From his first published work until his death Bentham regularly (but not invariably) purported to adopt the standpoint of a (or the) 'citizen of the world' and to be concerned with humankind as a whole", Twining, 'Reading Bentham', 133–4.

[320] See further Schofield, *Utility & Democracy*, 78–94, 137–40.

government.[321] Why or whether they should obey was a fact about the expectations they had about the government's ability to realise their happiness.[322] The search for happiness was not limited within the boundaries of a nation and the interests of nations – the aggregate interests of their citizens – did not conflict: "if they appear repugnant anywhere, it is only in proportion as they are misunderstood".[323] The resulting jurisprudence was "universal" in three regards: as to the empirical method it proposed; the commitment to methodological individualism it involved; and its understanding of good legislation on the basis of calculation of the utility of alternative courses of action, in other words, as a political economy.

First, Bentham and Austin shared the Baconian view that every true proposition addressed some aspect of the world that lent itself to sense-perception. Sovereign was the entity whose commands enjoyed habitual obedience.[324] The theory of the social contract was wholly illusory. A state was simply the empirical fact of a group of people actually subordinating themselves to a ruler.[325] A duty had no other reality than the expectation of being sanctioned if one failed to conform.[326] This linked laws firmly to the empirical world of sensory experience, operating directly with the mechanism of pain and pleasure. That it was hard to imagine how sanctions could be applied to political communities led Bentham to reject the notion of just war; "the subjects are always honest . . . there is properly no other criminal than the chief".[327] In any case, he saw war as an unmitigated "mischief", caused by a misunderstanding by a nation of its interests. Sovereigns should reason about their grievances, demarcate their territories, move to free trade, disarm, create defensive alliances and set up "a common court of judicature" to resolve remaining disputes.[328] Both writers held it conceptually impossible that the sovereign could be

[321] Bentham, *Fragment*, 40–1. There was thus no clear move from what he called "natural society" to statehood ("state of government"). Both existed side by side, the expressions denoting degrees to which habitual obedience was being paid to particular authorities.

[322] Ibid., 56, 99, 105.

[323] Jeremy Bentham, 'An Essay or Universal and Perpetual Peace', in *The Works*, II, 559.

[324] Bentham, *Fragment*, 40. In Austin's famous definition, a sovereign is such that fills two conditions: it must be object of habitual obedience in society, and it must itself not pay such obedience to anybody. *Province*, 214.

[325] Austin, *Province*, 295–301.

[326] Bentham, *Fragment*, 109.

[327] Bentham, 'Principles of International Law', 538.

[328] Ibid., 544–5, 547, 552.

bound by law.[329] Unlike Austin, however, Bentham did not think this took away the legal reality of international law and suggested that its undoubted weaknesses be corrected by codification.[330] He accepted that constitutions and treaties could limit the sovereign's powers and that the habit of obedience may direct itself only to some of the sovereign's activities, and not to others.[331]

Bentham hoped that his writings might assist states, especially England and France, to begin negotiating a universal peace.[332] In an article from 1825, James Mill, Bentham's collaborator, took the proposal further. He accepted that the command theory "cannot be applied, at least in the ordinary sense, to the laws of nations".[333] However, "the human mind is powerfully acted upon by the approbation or disapprobation, by the praise or blame, the contempt and hatred, or the love and admiration, of the rest of mankind." The actions of nations evoke such sentiments in the rest of humankind, and this, Mill wrote, "is the only power to which we can look for any considerable sanction to the law of nations".[334] But this sanction only operates in nations where the public has a say in government, "in other words in democratic countries".[335] Thinking of enlightened public opinion as the sanction of the law of nations would be widely accepted among late nineteenth-century lawyers. It is not clear that it provided a plausible argument under Benthamite premises – but those were not the premises of the later "Gentle Civilizers".[336] But it did fit with the effort to think of jurisprudence in the image of political economy where the "consumers" would decide what the international market will come to regard as lawful.

329 Bentham, *Fragment*, 98, 111; Austin, *Province*, 254. When the sovereign habitually follows some form of behaviour or some general opinion in the community, Austin accepts that it can be said to act in accordance with the "constitution", understood, like international law, as another type of positive morality or a compound of positive morality and positive law, 257–60.

330 Bentham, 'Principles of International Law', 540.

331 Bentham, *Fragment*, 98, 101–2. See also comments in H. L. A. Hart, *Essays on Bentham. Jurisprudence and Political Theory* (Oxford University Press 1982), 230–1, 239–42. Even as it is unclear whether Bentham regarded those limitations as properly "legal", he clearly assumed they had reality and force in the international world. Bentham, *Fragment*, 98–102. See Schofield, *Utility & Democracy*, 227–31.

332 Bentham, 'Principles of International Law', 546–7.

333 Mill, 'Law of Nations', 4. 334 Ibid., 7. 335 Ibid., 9.

336 See Martti Koskenniemi, *The Gentle Civilizer of Nations. The Rise and Fall of International Law 1870–1960* (Cambridge University Press 2009), 88–97.

A second universalising tendency followed from Austin's and Bentham's methodological individualism. Sensations of pain and pleasure are sensations of individuals and a nation's interests were but "the sum of the interests of the several members who compose it".[337] This left open the problem of aggregation. If it was to be only a technical exercise, then it would involve assuming that the preferences of individuals, including their other-regarding preferences, were naturally in harmony. Or then there would have to be some value or criterion that enabled putting conflicting preferences into hierarchical order. But neither man was clear about what that value or criterion, a conception of public interest, might be. Instead, Bentham, for example, simply assumed that because it was a useful thing to achieve, Britain and France would be able to agree on free trade, on disarmament and on giving up their colonies as well as to set up a collective security pact and to persuade others to join it.[338] The utility of the subjects could not be separated from universal utility so that wise statesmanship would ultimately aim for "the most extended welfare of all the nations on the earth".[339] Bentham even wrote, in a puzzlingly optimistic sense, that most disputes between states resulted from technical uncertainties about rights or boundaries, which is why there was no reason for punishments but only restitution.[340] The argument about aggregation of private utilities was indefinitely expansive; the only real limits of the political world were the limits of the market. Every actual privileging of one utility over another, that is every governmental policy, would only mean a temporary setting aside of some value with the expectation that it would be realised once the time was ripe.[341]

The third universalising aspect of these views had to do with the all-encompassing morality of calculation at the heart of utilitarian theories of legislation and government. The happiness of the political community, we have seen, consisted of the aggregate happiness of its citizens. Wealth was a principal aspect of happiness. Bentham fully accepted Smith's ignorance principle and the resulting need for *laissez-faire*: "The motto, or watchword of government ... ought to be – *Be quiet*".[342] Government was needed only to provide security in one's person, property and labour, as well as for emergencies and

337 Bentham, *Introduction*, 3.
338 Bentham, 'Principles of International Law', 546–60. 339 Ibid., 538.
340 Ibid., 538–40. 341 Laval, *L'homme économique*, 306.
342 Bentham, 'Manual of Political Economy', 33.

defence.[343] Trade was to be free, and the extent of trade was determined by the extent of capital; and capital was itself in the position to find its most lucrative objects of investment. The science of legislation was a legal translation of political economy, formulated as instructions for what the legislator should and should not do.[344]

Bentham's attitude to colonisation varied. Most, though not all, of what he wrote on colonies was critical. Colonies might sometimes be useful for resettlement of excess populations.[345] But in general he took a negative view of the colonies. Colonial policy created disputes and war, and colonies were an enormous expense for the nation, a source of misadministration and privilege.[346] In two passionate texts from 1792 and 1820, written to the French National Assembly and the members of the Spanish *Cortès*, Bentham repeated with vigour the points about the dangers of colonies:

> You choose your own government, why are not other people to choose theirs? Do you seriously mean to govern the world, and do you call that *liberty*? What is become of the rights of men? Are you the only men who have rights? Alas my fellow citizens, have you two measures?[347]

To be governed by rulers one felt as one's own, rulers not acting for distant interests, was an incident of happiness.[348] No loss would ensue from giving up the privileges of colonial trade. This would only lead to mercantile capital being directed elsewhere, especially to domestic agriculture.[349] But it was not at all certain trade would diminish. As the American experience had shown, the increasing

[343] Ibid., 40, 41–2. Bentham saw the Navigation Acts precisely in these terms. He repeated the arguments against monopolies and subsidies of all kinds in 'Principles of International Law', 540 as well as in *Emancipate your Colonies!* (London, Heyward 1830), 16–22.

[344] Bentham, 'Manual of Political Economy'. The result was not that far from reality. Between 75 and 85% of the annual expense of the state went to the military and the navy. See John Brewer, 'The Eighteenth-Century British State. Contexts and Issues', in Lawrence Stone (ed.), *An Imperial State at War. Britain from 1689 to 1815* (London, Routledge 1994), 57.

[345] Bentham, 'Manual of Political Economy', 52. Bentham's late embrace of colonialism resulted from the influence on him of the arch-Malthusian economist Edward Gibbon Wakefield. See Semmel, *Free Trade*, 93–4.

[346] Bentham, 'Manual of Political Economy', 54–62.

[347] Bentham, *Emancipate your Colonies!*, 3.

[348] See Schofield, *Utility & Democracy*, 199–204.

[349] Bentham, 'Principles of International Law', 547. For the costliness of colonial policy to taxpayers, see also Bentham, 'Manual of Political Economy', 52–4.

prosperity of the former colony will open new markets for the goods of the former metropolis.

* * * * *

The most powerful type of English jurisprudence, with the ambition of producing universally compelling conclusions, began from the image of human beings constantly adjusting their behaviour by reference to the amounts of pain and pleasure linked with alternative forms of action. It was the task of the legislator to operate these expectations so as to induce conforming behaviour. This was to think of a law as a kind of political economy and to inaugurate international law as a law of a universal commercial society. The state's role was to maintain the conditions of the global market such that individuals can plan their actions strategically with the view of maximising profits and minimising losses. Austin had already suggested that the science of ethics needed to emulate political economy to ensure its relevance. But why think in terms of "law" at all? In a brief discourse from 1824, the future holder of the chair of political economy at the University of London, John Ramsay McCulloch (1789–1864), gave expression to a feeling that must have been widely shared, namely that "[t]he principles on which the production and accumulation of wealth and the progress of civilization depend, are not the offspring of legislative enactments".[350] Instead, political economy taught us to liberate the "desire implanted in the breast of every individual of rising in the world and improving his condition". The attainment of the public good required knowledge of "the laws which regulate the movements of human society – which cause one people to advance in opulence and refinement, at the same time that one is sinking into the abyss of poverty and barbarism". These were the laws of political economy whose importance vastly overweighed other means of government – "[t]he establishment of a wise system of public economy can compensate for every other deficiency".[351]

## "Omission and Neglect of ... International Law, As a Science"

In such an atmosphere, there was little interest among British lawyers or diplomats in anything like a "law of nations". No laws had contributed to

[350] J. R. McCulloch, *A Discourse on the Rise, Progress, Peculiar Objects and Importance of Political Economy* (Edinburgh, Constable 1824), 10.
[351] Ibid., 19.

the removal of a mortal threat to Britain by Napoleon's fall. The system of dynastic legitimacy proposed by the conservative powers in 1814–15 was politically unacceptable. European peace would continue to be kept by balancing, and that required, by definition, freedom of manoeuvre that was inimical to rules. Outside Europe, Britain saw no reason to share the privilege of ruling the waves, and its only rival in the colonial world, France, was in no position to threaten the stabilisation of what in India it called its paramountcy. Despite all the talk about the rule of law in the colonies and the open seas, there was almost no effort to imagine a law of nations to govern the international world. The well-publicised efforts of the British navy to police slave trading and piracy, for example, developed "in the absence of broad-based legal principles".[352] Although the decisions of Lord Stowell with the High Court of Admiralty were widely known, Stowell himself had never theorised them as part of a larger law of nations. But there were problems elsewhere, too.

In 1846 a parliamentary Select Committee came to a famous conclusion that there existed "no legal education, worthy of the name, of a public nature, in the country". The teaching of civil law and English law at Oxford and Cambridge was useless – "Degrees in law are no more than cheaply acquired substitutes for degrees in arts." Distinction in civil law, for example, was "in many cases the distinction of idleness than attainment". In every respect, British universities fell far below those on the continent. Oxford, for example, might supply some training in a "flowering, ornate style" that may "contribute to the general education of any gentleman designed for any other profession than the bar[;] to that of a lawyer peculiarly they contribute nothing".[353] The report lamented that there were only two chairs of law at Oxford and Cambridge and proposed new ones in international and colonial law as well as in constitutional, comparative constitutional and municipal law.[354]

Britain's global dominance from the French Revolution to the mid-nineteenth century gave birth to no significant stream of thinking about a law of nations. The post-Napoleonic years were those of industrial depression and stagnation of trade. Domestic oppression intensified and parliament vigorously opposed foreign-policy spending.[355] Smithian

[352] Benton & Ford, *Rage for Order*, 119.

[353] 'Report on Legal Education', 7 *Law Magazine & Review. A Quarterly Review of Jurisprudence* (1847), 31, 33, 34.

[354] Ibid., 37, 39.

[355] Paul W. Schroeder, *The Transformation of European Politics 1763–1848* (Oxford, Clarendon 1994), 586–7.

free traders had an uphill battle until the 1830s against Malthusian pessimists, but that did not prevent British policy in those years from developing the famous imperialism of free trade.[356] This was never an articulated or even a coherent policy, however, and even less a legal one.[357] In the margins of the "increasingly hermetic character of British law talk" two hesitant literary strands addressed the international world through a legal idiom.[358] One was an effort, weak and conservative as it was, to re-employ natural law in a new world, the other an effort to emulate the treatise-writing in which German jurists had excelled since the early eighteenth century. The series of lectures on the "Study of the Law of Nature and of Nations" by the Whig jurist and politician Sir James Mackintosh (1765–1832) at Lincoln's Inn in 1796 were well received but all that has been preserved is a 89-page introduction where Mackintosh had distinguished between a natural law covering the relations of individuals across the world and another organising the intercourse of Christian nations.[359] The course included a literary history of natural law from the "barbarous philosophy of the schools" through Grotius, Pufendorf, Vattel and Heineccius to the replacement of dubious metaphysic by Lockean clarity and precision.[360] The institutions of property and marriage played a central role everywhere, accompanied by a universal public law whose point was to guarantee "liberty" by constitutional division of powers.[361] The "mild and friendly intercourse between civilised states" had given rise to advanced rules on diplomacy, commerce and war applied among Europeans.[362]

The lectures were referenced respectfully in the few British international law texts that came out in the first part of the nineteenth century. But their abstract and philosophical approach received little

356 See e.g. Semmel, *Free Trade*, 48–75. The classic on the imperialism of free trade is John Gallagher & Ronald Robinson, 'The Imperialism of Free Trade', 6 *Economic History Review* (1953), 1–15, which has given rise to an enormous secondary literature.

357 The point was, after all, to extend "informal control sufficiently to integrate as many areas as possible into her expanding economy with its need for constantly widening markets and new sources of supply", P. J. Cain, *Economic Foundations of British Overseas Expansion 1815–1915* (London, Macmillan 1980), 13. But equally, when informal control proved insufficient, Britain was not averse to intervening in the policies of smaller or weaker states, 14.

358 The quote is from Benton & Ford, *Rage for Order*, 120.

359 Sir James Mackintosh, *A Discourse on the Study of the Law of Nature and Nations* (2nd edn, London, Goode 1828), 9–11. On the context of the delivery and (favourable) reception of the lectures, see R. J. Mackintosh (ed.), *Memoirs of the Right Honourable Sir James Mackintosh* (Boston, Little & Brown 1853), I, 99–136.

360 Mackintosh, *A Discourse*, 31–2.

361 Ibid., 56–68.

362 Ibid., 81–7.

following. In parliament, in public debates and case-law it was still Emer de Vattel's *Law of Nations* that was cited especially once it had been "anglicized" in the 1834 edition by Chitty's citations of admiralty cases and other English practices.[363] Another early work was the first English-language history of the law of nations published in 1795 by the young Robert Plumer Ward (1765–1846), later solicitor-general, who had composed his text at the request of Pitt himself. This was a naturalist history that opened with a touching admission by its author that having collected all the treaties, cases and other materials, he was still unable to derive any universal law from them.[364] Although he could see how the practices of Christian nations might become binding on Christians, he found no basis to regard them as binding on others. "Natural law" meant different things to different people so that it was futile to treat it as universal, for only religion could provide universal certainty; where religions differed, unity was impossible. Accordingly, there must be "a different law of nations for different parts of the globe".[365]

Ward situated his law of nations within European history, beginning with the Greeks and the Romans, the ferocious manners of the "Scandinavians", followed by "the most cruel maxims" and "bloody and savage customs" of the Middle Ages.[366] But even as the law of nations was unknown and habits were raw, enlightened rulers and institutions such as chivalry, feudalism, and Christianity provided a civilising influence.[367] More recently, treaties and diplomatic practices had softened the customs of war and even occasionally provided channels for pacific intercourse between "sets of nations". The resulting rules had been articulated as a "science" first by Grotius, then Pufendorf,

363 On the uses and translations of Vattel in Britain from Burke onwards, see Elisebetta Fiocchi Malaspina, *L'eterno ritorno del Droit des gens de Vattel (secc. XVIII–XIX). L'impatto sulla cultura giuridica in prospettiva globale* (Frankfurt, Max Planck Institute 2017), 143–51, 205–6. See also Ian Hunter, 'Global Justice and Regional Metaphysics. On the Critical History of the Law of Nature and of Nations', in Shaunnagh Dorsett & Ian Hunter (eds), *Law and Politics in British Colonial Thought. Transpositions of Empire* (London, Palgrave Macmillan 2010), 22–3.

364 Robert Ward, *An Enquiry into the Foundation and History of the Law of Nations from the Time of the Greeks and the Romans to the Age of Grotius* (2 vols, London, Butterworth 1795). Ward's only other work in the field was his *Treatise of the Relative Rights and Duties of Belligerent and Neutral Powers in Maritime Affairs* (London, Butterworth's 1801). On Ward's later life as a conservative politician, see Diego Panizza, *Genesi di una ideologia. Il conservatismo moderno in Robert Ward* (Milan, CEDAM 1997).

365 Ward, *Enquiry*, I, xiv, xii–xv.

366 Ibid., I, 211.

367 See e.g. ibid., II, 111–14, 125–43.

Vattel and the other great jurists, the heroes of Ward's narrative.[368] In the end, the relations between "Western nations" had been brought "to a state of comparative regularity, from the frightful desolation occasioned by the barbarians".[369]

Ward's text, which Bentham owned, was written in a conservative idiom and had no more of a visible influence in England than that of Mackintosh. Rather different in tone was a second set of works consisting of three textbooks that deliberately aimed to bring the English debates up to the level of recent German works that they often referenced.[370] Each presented international law as an outgrowth from interactions between European or Christian nations but none produced anything like a criterion for "civilization" as a condition for entry into the legal world.[371] William Oke Manning (1809–78) endorsed Georg Friedrich von Martens' programmatically positivist textbook as the foremost exposition of the field.[372] But he also endorsed the happiness principle, which, he believed, was best expressed in the works of Austin and Bentham: "[T]he obligation of every law depends on its ultimate utility."[373] By far the largest part of the work dealt with warfare and more than half of the total with themes of maritime war and neutrality of special interest to British policy. Very little was seen of the author's utilitarianism in those parts and there was no effort to analyse the legal aspects of Britain's ascendant economic hegemony. The non-European world made no significant appearance in the almost 400-page volume.

The same was true of the Scotsman James Reddie's (1773–1852) short work half of which was a literary history of the law of nations that

368 Ibid., II, 606–28. 369 Ibid., II, 358.

370 The most valuable treatment of international law in nineteenth-century Britain concludes that while "until the 1830s there was little scholarly activity with regard to international law ... the subject arguably underwent a renaissance between 1835–60". "Renaissance" may be too strong, but whatever took place in the 1830s, these works were part of it, Casper Sylvest, "The Foundations of Victorian International Law", in Duncan Bell (ed.), *Victorian Visions of Global Order. Empire and International Relations in Nineteenth-Century Political Thought* (Cambridge University Press 2007), 51, 47–66.

371 See e.g. James Reddie, *Inquiries in the Science of Law* (London, Stevens & Norton 1847), 146–7. The time for speculating about a "standard of civilization" was to come later.

372 William Oke Manning, *Commentaries on the Law of Nations* (London, Sweet 1839), 39.

373 Ibid., 63. For the view that "God designed the happiness of all his creatures", see 58. Manning did not admire Bentham's convoluted writings, however, and he objected to Austin's critiques of international law, arguing that because the notion of "law of nations" was in common use in scholarship and diplomacy, there was no reason to discard it, 4–5.

likewise acknowledged its dependence on German scholarship.[374] The other half was a sketch of the sources and the "component parts of international law". The former contained a discussion of treaties, followed by some analysis of "the general juridical relations of nations, arising from their nature and situation".[375] The "component parts" again were sovereignty, equality and the right of self-preservation, with a few pages devoted to each. Much less ambitious than Ward or Manning, Reddie sought only to provide a frame for a renewed, realistic and modern study of the field for teaching purposes.[376] It was a follow-up to an earlier work that sought to set a frame for the "science of law" in general, ostensibly to fill the recognised vacuum in Britain of properly academic treatments of the law.

The publication of the condemnatory report by the Select Committee was followed in 1848–50 by a series of unattributed essays on "international law" that lamented the "omission and neglect of the English lawyers to cultivate international law, as a science".[377] The essays reviewed the field from Grotius to Vattel and identified the German science of international law as most useful today, referencing August Heffter's textbook as "the most correct, concise, truthful, and impartial".[378] The author separated the subject sharply from morality and (Benthamite) philosophy, associating it with the study of customs and treaties. But the essays moved predominantly in the world of theories and literatures, perhaps with the aim of laying out a basis for the topic's academic treatment in England.[379]

The professional position of international law in Britain at the beginning of the century was weak. It was not practised in common law courts and the Inns of Court began to provide training in it only in 1864. It had

374 At several points, Reddie acknowledged he was following Von Ompteda's well-known exposé. See e.g Reddie, *Inquiries*, 6, 9, 26, 31–2, 55, 64, 68, 83, 88.

375 Ibid., 165.

376 Reddie's text was a follow-up to an earlier work that sought to set a frame for the "science of law" to fill the vacuum in Britain on the matter. Reddie seems to have been prescribed reading at least in the University of Toronto in 1858. Ronald St John McDonald, 'An Historical Introduction to the Teaching of International Law in Canada', 14 *Canadian Yearbook of International Law* (1975), 102.

377 [Anonymous] 'International Law, No 1', 9 *Law Review and Quarterly Journal of British and Foreign Jurisprudence* (1848), 24. The articles may actually have been written by Reddie (private exchange with Michael Lobban, February 2020).

378 Ibid., 32.

379 See the treatment of custom and treaty law, in 'International Law, No 2', 9 *Law Review and Quarterly Journal of British and Foreign Jurisprudence* (1849), 260–87 and 'International Law, No 2 cont'd', 10 *Law Review and Quarterly Journal of British and Foreign Jurisprudence* (1849), 261–84.

been part of civil law education at the universities but, as the Select Committee noted, this had undergone a marked decline from the times of Gentili or Zouche. An English lawyer might encounter international law in providing diplomatic advice or participating in an admiralty suit, but the number of professionals that did this was very limited.[380] The establishment of the first university chairs in international law (the Chichele chair in Oxford 1859 and the Whewell chair in Cambridge in 1866) did not bring an immediate change to the situation. The Oxford position went first to Mountague Bernard (1820–82), a liberal politician and polemicist whose written legacy consists of a series of short lectures and a book on *A Historical Account of the Neutrality of Great Britain during the American Civil War* (1870). The Whewell chair was first occupied by William Vernon Harcourt (1827–1904), best known under the pseudonym of *Historicus* whose articles in *The Times* dealt with miscellaneous questions of international policy and law but who never showed much interest in teaching and whose written legacy consists of two compilations of often polemical texts on international matters in *The Times*. Austin's London professorship had been on jurisprudence and the law of nations, and some of his followers, most notably Travers Twiss (1809–97) and especially John Westlake (1828–1913), began to align the field with what was going on in the continent.[381]

A final note ought to be made of Richard Wildman's two-volume treatise, published virtually simultaneously with the series of articles introducing the topic to British legal audiences. No longer a work on theories or literatures, Wildman illustrated his pragmatism by observing drily that the fact that slavery and the slave trade went against natural law did not mean that they were prohibited under the law of nations. As long as states practised them, they were lawful.[382] The work used cases

380 Membership in the Doctors' Commons was no more than twenty-five by mid-century. Michael Lobban, 'English Approaches to International law in the Nineteenth Century', in Matthew Craven et al. (eds), *Time, History and International Law* (Leiden, Brill 2006), 66–70.

381 These two men belong to the first generation of British lawyers that I have dealt with in my *Gentle Civilizer*. However, recent attention on Twiss had been directed especially to his interest in colonial matters, and notably his lobbying work for Leopold II on the latter's Congo machinations. See e.g. Andrew Fitzmaurice, 'The Justification of King Leopold II's Congo Enterprise by Sir Travers Twiss', in Shaunnagh Dorsett & Ian Hunter (eds), *Law and Politics in British Colonial Thought. Transpositions of Empire* (London, Palgrave Macmillan 2010), 109–26.

382 Richard Wildman, *Institutes of International Law* (2 vols, Benning, London 1849), I, 7–14.

from Britain and diplomatic history from all over Europe to illustrate prevailing practices and attitudes operating as evidence of customary law. Wildman recognised the flexibility of international rules and the discretion of politicians, while sternly rejecting the legitimacy of *raison d'état*.[383] The sections of treaties, arbitration and offences against the law of nations were composed as reviews of the practices of European states, supplemented by a much longer treatment of the laws of war of which the rules on maritime warfare and neutrality took the lion's share. The work might have become more famous had it not been overtaken rapidly by the massive four-volume *Commentaries* by the future admiralty judge and member of the Privy Council, Sir Robert Phillimore (1810–85), a handbook with a very extensive repertory of cases and diplomatic practices that spoke directly to the technical understanding of British jurists.[384]

British lawyers had no time for federalist speculation. Referencing the proposed intervention system under the Holy Alliance Manning cited the foreign secretary Castlereagh to the effect that anything of the sort would involve the parties assuming a supremacy incompatible with the rights of other states. In any case, the alliance had so far "merely given occasion to a number of itinerant congresses . . . and its name has justly become identified, not with the furtherance of international justice, but with the forcible propagation of a particular set of political opinions".[385] All three writers were keen to discuss the rights and duties applicable in the context of war, with special attention to maritime law, blockades, neutrality and contraband of specific interest to British lawyers. But in other aspects of international law there was no "British" tradition on which to fall back. As Mansfield had noted, although the law of nations was part of the law of England, its content had to be received from foreign writers "such as Grotius, Barbeyrac, Binkershoek, Wiquefort &c. there being no English writer of eminence upon the subject".[386] The matter had not changed by the 1830s. For better or for worse, it seemed necessary to follow "Germany, *the great and parental cultivatrix of the science of international law*".[387]

383 Ibid., I, 50.

384 Robert Phillimore, *Commentaries upon International Law*, 4 vols (vol. I Philadelphia, Johnson 1854).

385 Manning, *Commentaries*, 86.

386 *Triquet* v. *Bath*, 97 ER 936 (King's Bench 1764).

387 Reddie, *Inquiries*, 88.

## Governing a Commercial World

In their discussions of the law of nations, British jurists struggled with an alien literary and legal tradition they tried, mostly without much success, to translate into the vernacular. Grotius and Vattel were dutifully cited, but their moral science did not appeal to English audiences, least of all as an articulation of a particular view of government, so alien to what Bentham and Austin had been proposing. By contrast, British jurists were intensely interested in the laws underlying the expanding commerce that Ward already had identified as "one of the most important aspects of Convention on the laws of the world".[388] The ideology and practice of free trade were actively debated in Britain by reference to the Corn Laws. No wonder, by 1830 British commerce accounted for about one-third of world trade.[389] The rights of freedom of commerce, Joseph Chitty (1785–1841) wrote in his 1824 *Treatise on the Law of Commerce*, "involve some of the greatest questions of international law", and invoked Vattel and Grotius to the effect that it was "the interest and duty of nations to encourage commercial intercourse with each other".[390] Chitty extolled the abortive Franco-British free trade agreement of 1786 and published a long extract of Pitt's reasoning that was based on ideas inherited from Adam Smith. In his notes to the 1834 edition of Vattel, Chitty attacked Iberian monopoly claims on the Atlantic and objected to Vattel's invitation for rulers to regulate trade – "every active interference of the legislature with its subjects by prohibiting or restraining any particular branch of honest labour ... has uniformly retarded the advance of public opulence".[391] True, he wrote, the right to trade was only an "imperfect right"; states were allowed to limit trading by their nationals and to exclude foreign countries from trade with (or even access to) their colonies.[392] Nevertheless, he believed that "the legislators of almost all countries" had nowadays followed more or less similar "principles in political economy" and based his

388 Ward, *Enquiry*, II, 337.

389 C. A. Bayly, *The Imperial Meridian. The British Empire and the World 1780–1830* (London, Routledge 1989), 5.

390 Joseph Chitty, *A Treatise on the Law of Commerce and Manufactures, and the Contracts Relating Thereto* (4 vols., London, Strahan 1824), I, 73, 76, 106–7.

391 Vattel, *The Law of Nations* (ed. Chitty), 42 and 37. Chitty underlined the usefulness of the work for private individuals as it contained the clearest rules on the interpretation of private contracts with respect to admiralty and insurance law, v.

392 Chitty, *Treatise on the Law of Commerce*, 78–9.

work on the exposition of those principles, applicable, as he believed, all over the world.[393]

No Anglophone jurist tried to advocate an international code such as proposed by Bentham. In the absence of such a code, might there still be a kind of "universal jurisprudence" regulating all action, public and private, that had relevance over several jurisdictions? This situation was contemplated in 1834 in Joseph Story's (1779–1845) influential work on the conflict of laws:

> Commerce is now so absolutely universal among all countries; the inhabitants of all have such a free intercourse with each other; contracts, marriages, nuptial settlements, wills and successions are so common among persons whose domiciles are in different countries having different and even opposite laws on the same subjects, that without common principles adopted by all nations in this regard there would be an utter confusion of all rights and remedies; and intolerable grievances would grow up and weaken all the domestic relations as well as to destroy the sanctity of contracts and the security of property.[394]

To deal with these dangers, the American jurist pointed to new domestic jurisprudence that had arisen to deal with all kinds jurisdictional conflict, "a most interesting and important branch of public law".[395] Story regarded the old tradition of natural law and the law of nations as virtually extinct. But it had left an important legacy, namely the view that nations possessed exclusive jurisdiction over their territories, raising the problem that Story would deal with in his pioneering work. There was no guarantee that those laws would deal with every international issue, or that they would do it in a coordinated or harmonious way. Conflicts of domestic laws might engender violations of individual rights. A merchant, say, might find their property rights respected in one jurisdiction, but not in another. How to deal with such situations? For this, Story had a ready answer.[396]

393 Ibid., vii. Accordingly, chapter I of Chitty's treatise was intended to review the principles of political economy, laid out by "Smith, Hume, Paley and Malthus" that it was the "duty of every legislator" to apply, 1, 6–7.

394 Joseph Story, *Commentaries on the Conflict of Laws* (Boston, Hilliard 1834), 5.

395 Ibid., 9.

396 Story accepted that a blanket refusal to recognise the rights of foreign nationals (extreme sovereignty-view) would undermine rights one's own nationals might claim in those other countries. The *ordre public* rule would provide sufficient protection of sovereignty while "comity" invited states to provide reasonable accommodation to each others' sovereignties. Roxana Banu, *Nineteenth-Century Perspectives on Private International Law* (Oxford University Press 2018), 29–35.

In the silence of any positive rule, affirming or denying, or restraining the operation of foreign laws, courts of justice presume the tacit adoption of them by their own government, unless they are repugnant to its policy, or prejudicial to its interests. It is not the comity of the courts, but the comity of the nation, which is administered, and ascertained in the same way, and guided by the same reasoning by which all other principles of municipal law are ascertained and guided.[397]

It was the purpose of what Story called private international law to protect the rights of individuals moving across national boundaries. This was not owing to the existence of some supranational "code". Instead, everyone would benefit from the voluntary recognition by states of each others' laws: "Mutual utility presupposes that the interest of all nations is consulted, and not that of one only."[398] Story followed the jurists of the Dutch golden age in calling this invitation to mutual recognition "comity".[399] The laws of other states were not formally binding. But all states had an interest in yielding to the utilitarian argument that commerce and other private interactions benefited from the stable expectation that they would recognise the validity of rights based on their respective domestic laws.[400]

Story had reviewed cases from both United States and Britain, and his view was accepted and cited by British courts.[401] From 1790 onwards the House of Lords would cite foreign writers on a routine basis in cases involving the application of foreign law.[402] Sometimes this was done by reference to "general principles of law" that were to apply widely across jurisdictions.[403] As a result, rules of private international law came to regulate much of the global landscape visible to British courts. They provided that a transaction validly made

397 Story, *Commentaries*, 37.

398 Ibid., 36.

399 The view of "private international law" as a matter of comity is usually traced back to the Dutch jurists Paul and John Voet and Ulrich Huber. See e.g. Alex Mills, 'The Private History of International Law', 55 *International and Comparative Law Quarterly* (2006), 24–6.

400 Story also had very strong sense of a public policy that allowed him to condemn slavery and the slave trade. For him, "private international law" – the rules of jurisdiction – was not separate from public international law, but part of the very same fabric of a single system of universal law. See further Joel Paul, 'The Isolation of Private International law', 7 *Wisconsin International Law Journal* (1988–9), 149–77.

401 William Burge, *Commentaries on Colonial and Foreign Laws Generally in their Conflict with each other and with the Laws of England* (4 vols, London, Saunders 1838), I, ix–x.

402 See A. E. Anton, 'The Introduction into English Practice of the Continental Theories of Conflict of Laws', 4 *International and Comparative Law Quarterly* (1956), 534–41.

403 S. Romilly in *Potinger* v. *Whitman*, cited in ibid., 540.

in one place ought to be regarded as valid in other places, that the law applicable to real estate would be that of the place where it was situated, that the personal status of a person would normally be decided on the basis of his or her domicile and so on, with some difference in detail and theoretical justification. Domestic sovereignty was protected by the *ordre public* clause according to which foreign law was applicable only to the extent it did not violate the public policy of the forum state.

By mid-nineteenth century, British lawyers had come to rely on their courts' ability to use natural law, admiralty law and aspects of foreign law creatively to deal with situations of international import. No legal theory or code underlay this practice. Phillimore explained that in compiling his commentaries, it had been his intention simply to give the topic "the certainty and precision of Municipal Law".[404] But one set of increasingly important legal relationships was absent. This related to what by mid-century had come to be called "colonial law". As William Burge, the author of a large 1838 specialist work on the subject, pointed out, "systems of Colonial and Foreign Jurisprudence ... constitute a considerable part of the law administered by the supreme appellate tribunal of the British Colonial Empire".[405] What were those "systems"? Perhaps the English jurists had refrained from attempting to sketch them because they knew that Sir James Stephen – the most significant jurist in the colonial service at the time – had for some years been trying to compile a manual on the topic. Stephen, however, perhaps for reasons of perfectionism, gave up the work and forwarded his drafts to barrister Charles Clark who completed it in 1834. However, the *Summary of Colonial Laws* kept infuriatingly, though perhaps characteristically, silent about the principles underlying this topic and its systemic relations to other legal idioms.[406] For a study of legal imagination and international power, however, it is necessary to try to understand the complex hierarchical relations that constituted not only the law of the "British empire" but also the first extensive articulation of a "global law".

[404] Phillimore, *Commentaries*, I, xxiii.
[405] Burge, *Commentaries on Colonial and Foreign Laws*, i.
[406] Charles Clark, *A Summary of Colonial Law* (London, Sweet & Maxwell 1834).

# 10

# Global Law

## *Ruling the British Empire*

The gradual rise of Britain as a world power took place through public–private partnerships in which the liberties at home were linked with authoritarian expansion abroad. Contributing to the heavy hand of empire was, as Edmund Burke stressed in his speeches in the trial of the former governor-general of India, Warren Hastings, in the 1790s, the special nature of the British state that either outsourced its operations to private actors such as the East India Company (EIC) or at least made sure that aggression was in line with economic statecraft. The EIC epitomised this amalgam of the private and the public, its ambivalence underlined by both sides' reluctance to spell out its legal status clearly. The EIC had no less hesitation in justifying its operations by reference to the law of nations than critics had to use it to condemn them. In the course of the prolonged trial, Burke quoted Vattel in support of his claim that the relation between the EIC and Indian princes was that of protecting and protected powers, arguing that failure in its duty to protect had actually forfeited the company's rights. For, Burke argued,

> the Law of Nations is the Law of India as well as Europe, because it is the Law of Reason and the law of nature, drawn from the pure sources of morality, drawn from the pure sources of public good, drawn from the pure sources of natural equity, and recognised and digested into order by the labour of learned Men.[1]

1 Edmund Burke, 'Speech in reply', 20 May 1794, in P. J. Marshall (ed.), *The Writings and Speeches of Edmund Burke*, vol. VII: *India. The Hastings Trial 1789–1794* (Oxford, Clarendon 2000), 291. The quote is from Emer de Vattel, *The Law of Nations* (Indianapolis, Liberty Fund 2008 [1758]), I XVI § 196 (208–9).

The previous chapter examined the uses of the legal vocabularies leading up to an ideal of commercial society that the British believed they saw when they looked in the mirror. This chapter turns to the projection of that ideal into the non-European world, first by examining the use of the vocabulary of "improvement" to justify the capture of rights of sovereignty and property over huge swaths of North America. The promoters of settlement were above all interested in establishing private property rights on lands they regarded as waste as long as they remained reserved for indigenous hunting and gathering. The role of the crown was limited to the grant of a charter or a patent to private actors – companies or individuals – and to defending them diplomatically against rival powers. The eventual effort by the crown to give substance to its prerogatives triggered a conflict with settlers' property rights, leading to the famous moment where out of the desire of property, political independence would arise. Attention will then turn to the Indian subcontinent where the military victory of the EIC in 1757 led it to rule a large part of India with results displayed in the Hastings trial. The chapter will end with a sketch of the legal vocabularies that early nineteenth-century British politicians and lawyers believed should regulate the emergence of a stable system of states with expanding commercial relations to which observers would give the name of *Pax Britannica*.

## The Laws of Improvement

In a famous sermon in November 1622 the poet John Donne addressed the members of the Virginia Company as apostles, calling upon them to continue the work of St Paul and his companions whom Christ had admonished to preach the gospel "unto the uttermost part of the earth". Building upon a passage in the Acts of the Apostles, Donne stressed the duty of the company men and settlers to "be witnesses unto Christ":

> Preach to them doctrinally, preach to them practically; enamour them with your justice, and (as far as may consist with your security), your civility; but inflame them with your godliness and your religion.[2]

Donne was not, of course, ignorant of the rather more secular ambitions of the men of the Virginia enterprise and assured them that God had in

[2] John Donne, 'A Sermon upon the Eighth verse of the First Chapter of the Acts of the Apostles', in H. Alford (ed.), *Works of John Donne* (6 vols, London, Parker 1839), VI, 225, 241.

no way denied his apostles "the riches and commodities of the world". But these should not be foremost in their minds. Once the Virginia men had done their duty, God would reward them with those earthly gifts, as indeed was visible as Donne was speaking: "[A]lready the employment breeds mariners; already the place gives essays, nay freights of merchantable commodities; already it is a mark for the envy, and for the ambition of our enemies [the papists]."[3] Although the principal justification was religious, another one followed not far behind:

In the law of nature and nations, a land never inhabited, by any, or utterly derelicted and immemorially abandoned by the former inhabitants, becomes their that will possess it. So also is it, if the inhabitants do not in some measure fill the land, so as the land may bring forth her increase for the use of men: for as a man does not become proprietary of the sea, because he hath two or three boats, fishing in it, so neither does a man become lord of a main continent, because he hath two or three cottages in the skirts thereof. That rule which passes through all municipal laws in particular states ... *The state must take order, that every man improve that which he hath, for the best advantage of that state*, passes also through the law of nations, which is to all the world, as municipal law is to a particular state.[4]

It is not clear what went on in the minds of Donne's audience when he referred to the "law of nature and nations" or suggested that the law of nations was to the world as the municipal law was to the state. Perhaps they thought about their inherent right to join the Spanish in the search for El Dorado or were seduced by the neo-Roman languages of humanist glory and commonwealth-building used in the company's promotional activities.[5] The ambition of the early Tudor explorers in the sixteenth century had certainly been to look for gold and silver, and the first Virginia charter granted by James I in 1606 licensed the London merchants who financed the company to:

dig, mine, and search for all Manner of Mines of Gold, Silver, and Copper, as well within any Part of their said several Colonies, as of the said main Lands on

[3] Ibid., 232. [4] Ibid., 234 (italics in original).

[5] For commentary that situates Donne's sermon in the humanist languages used by the company in its self-promotion, see Andrew Fitzmaurice, *Humanism and America. An Intellectual History of English Colonisation 1500–1625* (Cambridge University Press 2003), 58–92, 140–64. Especially the gentry members of the colonising elite (in contrast to the merchants) saw expansion as a patriotic and humanist duty, a way to redress England's backwardness as compared to the continental powers. For an account of the motives of one early participant in the Virginia venture, see Theodore K. Rabb, *Jacobean Gentleman. Sir Edwin Sandys 1561–1629* (Princeton University Press 1998), 321–6.

> the Backside of the same Colonies; And to HAVE and enjoy the Gold, Silver, and Copper, to be gotten thereof, to the Use and Behoof of the same Colonies, and the Plantations thereof.[6]

As in everything about English colonisation, the spoils were to be divided between the crown and the private entrepreneurs, with the principle of division reflecting the relative significance of their contributions: one-fifth would go to the crown. By 1622, however, hope of rapid enrichment through gold and silver had dissipated. A more long-term investment was needed for exploiting North America's huge open space. Donne's invocation of "the law of nature and nations" was firmly connected with the possibilities of cultivation opened up by what the settlers saw in front of them. Already in the first charter the merchants had received:

> Licence, to make Habitation, Plantation, and to deduce a colony of sundry of our People into that part of America commonly called VIRGINIA, and other parts and Territories in America, either appertaining unto us, or which are not now actually possessed by any Christian Prince or People.[7]

In two separate, partly overlapping areas the Virginia Company was to "have all the landes, woods, soile, groundes, havens, ports, rivers, mines, mineralls, marshes, waters, fishinges, commodities and hereditamentes whatsoever". Donne insisted that the moral basis of such rights was the use of the land and that the present inhabitants could not prevent the English from taking it over – just like "a man does not become proprietary of the sea, because he hath two or three boats, fishing in it". The sermon highlighted every man's (Protestant) duty "to improve that which he hath", endowing European types of agriculture with an unquestioned moral superiority over Indian wastefulness.[8]

Already the sixteenth century had produced some widely read literature that addressed colonisation as an economic project. More's *Utopia* had provided the image of an ideal commonwealth that the English could fantasise as a metaphor for their efforts. The Utopians had "transform[ed] a pack of ignorant savages into what is now, perhaps, the most civilized nation in the world".[9] More even used the language

[6] The First Charter of Virginia; 10 April 1606, para 9, available at Yale Law School, The Avalon Project, avalon.law.yale.edu/17th_century/va01.asp. Most of the Atlantic patents and charters can be found in Yale Law School's "Avalon" digital collection.

[7] Ibid., para 1.

[8] Donne, 'A Sermon', 234.

[9] Thomas More, *Utopia* (London, Penguin 2003 [1516]), 50.

of natural rights to suggest that economic progress could be imposed by force if necessary:

> If the natives won't do what they are told, they are expelled from the area marked out for annexation. If they try to resist, the Utopians declare war – for they consider war perfectly justifiable, when one country denies another its natural rights to derive nourishment from any soil which the original owners are not using themselves, but a merely holding on to as a worthless piece of property.[10]

Here there was everything the English could hope for: rights, authority and just war to improve the land so that profit could be extracted from it.[11] More had no qualms about proposing an authoritarian republic to dispose of the idleness and corruption that he saw at home. In the early years of exploration and well into the settlement of Virginia, a boom in wool prices had encouraged the transformation of arable land into pasture (enclosures) and the sale of the lands of monasteries to private farming. This had forced thousands of small farmers and users of the common lands on to the roads and into urban centres, some as wage-labourers or servants but many as vagabonds and beggars, often resorting to crime and ending their lives either as seamen or on the gallows.[12]

The theme of employing idle men from England in colonial forestry and in the mines, as well as for planting sugar, producing silk, gathering cotton and growing grapes in the fertile soil of the New World was taken up by the indefatigable propagator and chronicler of English colonisation, Richard Hakluyt the Younger (1553–1616).[13] It was true, he wrote, that of late the French, Dutch and Russian trades had suffered serious decline and that "yt behoveth us to seeke some newe and better trade of lesse daunger and more securitie, of lesse dommage and of

[10] Ibid., 60. More's ideological role is stressed in David Armitage, *The Ideological Origins of the British Empire* (Cambridge University Press 2000), 49–50. Likewise, Jörg Fisch, *Die europäische Expansion und das Völkerrecht* (Stuttgart, Steiner 1984), 278.

[11] See further Fitzmaurice, *Humanism and America*, 21–39.

[12] For the treatment of the poor and the idle in English population discourse in the sixteenth and seventeenth centuries, see Ted MacCormic, 'Population. Modes of Seventeenth-Century Demographic Thought', in Philip J. Stern & Carl Wennerlind (eds), *Mercantilism Reimagined. Political Economy in Early Modern Britain and Its Empire* (Oxford University Press 2014), 25–45. For a somewhat different view, see Peter Linebaugh & Marcus Rediker, *The Many-headed Hydra. The Hidden History of the Revolutionary Atlantic* (London, Verso 2012), 49–60 and passim.

[13] Richard Hakluyt, 'Discourse of Western Planting [1584]', in E. G. R. Taylor (ed.), *The Original Writings & Correspondence of the Two Richard Hakluyts* (2 vols, London, Hakluyt Society 1935), II, 234, 233–9. See further Paul Slack, *The Invention of Improvement. Information & Material Progress in Seventeenth-Century England* (Oxford University Press 2015), 31–43.

more advauntage".[14] Echoing Elizabeth's famous rebuke to the Spanish ambassador in 1580, Hakluyt dismissed Spanish legal justifications in a work that would produce the grammar of English colonisation.[15] The pope had no power to allocate lands to anybody. He was only "to teache without armes or force and that the same is no power to give or to take kingsdomes nor to make lawes for the politique governemente".[16] The English, by contrast, based their title to the northern American continent on its discovery by the Welsh prince Madock in the eleventh century and the voyage of the Venetian Giovanni Caboto (John Cabot) authorised by Henry VII that led to the continent while Columbus had only ended up in the islands of Hispanola and Cuba.[17] By plundering and killing Indians the Spanish had anyway forfeited any rights in their lands.[18] English exploration would be of a wholly different kind, for the English monarchs "have the name of Defendors of the Faithe" a title that obliged them "with discrecion and myldenes [to] distill into [the Indians'] purged myndes the swete and lively liquor of the gospell".[19] But references to St Matthew or the providential nature of English voyaging gave way to expounding the many strategic and economic advantages of colonisation.[20] Fortified plantations on the American east coast would offer an excellent base to disturb the operations of the Spanish navy and contribute to the safety of English navigation.[21] It would create the basis for expanding customs revenues while offering employment at home and merchandise to the local population.[22] There was apparently no end to the riches of American

[14] Hakluyt, 'Discourse of Western Planting', 220.

[15] In her audience with Ambassador Mendoza Elizabeth is reported to have denied that the pope had any such "prerogative in matters of this kind, much less authority to bind Princes who owe him no obedience, or to make that New Worlds as it were a fief for the Spaniard and clothe his with possession". Text e.g. in Julius Goebel, *The Struggle for the Falkland Islands. A Study in Legal and Diplomatic History* (Yale University Press 1927), 63. About Hakluyt's "grammar of colonization", see Peter C. Mancall, *Hakluyt's Promise. An Elizabethan's Obsession for an English America* (Yale University Press 2007), 128–55.

[16] Hakluyt, 'Discourse of Western Planting', 299.

[17] Ibid., 293, 290–7. On the tale of the Prince Madock's reputed voyage into America around 1170, see Gesa Mackenthun, *Metaphors of Dispossession. American Beginnings and the Translation of Empire, 1492–1637* (University of Oklahoma Press 1997), 24–34.

[18] Hakluyt, 'Discourse of Western Planting', 309.

[19] Ibid., 215.

[20] As David Armitage argues, Protestantism provided a useful basis for critiquing the Spanish activities, and for stressing the importance of agricultural work. But it was hardly an independent justification for the undertaking, *Ideological Origins*, 72–5.

[21] Hakluyt, 'Discourse of Western Planting', 240–2, 270–3.

[22] Ibid., 235.

nature, the variety of commodities to be found and the abundance of precious metals.[23]

This set the tone for the debates. Hakluyt's cousin, Richard Hakluyt the Elder (the lawyer), underlined the connection between labour and land-ownership in numerous memoranda where he, too, detailed the wonders of the New World, the fertility of the soil, the abundance of fruit, the variety of animals "and all other Comodyties for the lyef of men".[24] The London merchant Robert Johnson, director of the East India Company and one of the chief propagandists of the Virginia venture, likewise celebrated the vastness of the resources in the New World and the duty to cultivate and improve them. Without English presence, he wrote, "the greatest and wealthiest part of all the rest" would remain a wilderness with only wild beasts would roam along with "savage people which have no Christian, nor civill use of any thing".[25] Johnson did not mean that the native inhabitants should be dispossessed. "Our intrusion into their possessions shall tend to their great good, no way to their hurt," adding ominously, "unlesse as unbridled beastes, they procure it to themselves."[26] Two kinds of people were needed, Johnson argued: planters to build the land and bankers to finance the venture. He stressed the providential fruit of labour and warned against going the way of the Romans who had retired in idleness only to bring decay and ruin onto themselves.[27]

One of the few legally trained company apologists, William Strachey, put the venture directly in terms of the law of nations that provided for "common fellowship and community betwixt man and man".[28] The plantations, he argued, would greatly benefit the native inhabitants. How could the Indians possibly be injured by English settlement when out of all the lands available in the New World "of which not one forte

[23] Ibid., 223.

[24] Hakluyt, 'Pamphlet for the Virginia Enterprise, 1585', in E. G. R. Taylor (ed.), *The Original Writings & Correspondence of the Two Richard Hakluyts* (2 vols, London, Hakluyt Society 1935), II, 339, 339–43. See also Armitage, *Ideological Origins*, 61–99.

[25] Robert Johnson, *Nova Britannia. Offering Most Excellent Fruites by Planting in Virginia. Exciting All Such as be Well Affected to Further the Same* (Samuel Macham, and are to be sold at his shop in Pauls Church-yard, at the signe of the Bul-head 1609), B.

[26] Ibid., C. [27] Ibid., E2.

[28] William Strachey, *Historie of Travaile into Virginia Britannia* (London, Hakluyt Society 1849), 16. Strachey was educated at Gray's Inn and travelled to Virginia in the shipwrecked *Sea Venture* in 1609. With the rest of its passengers, he was "miraculously" saved. See Andrew Fitzmaurice, 'Powhatan Legal Claims', in Saliha Belmessous (ed.), *Native Claims. Indigenous Law against Empire 1500–1920* (Oxford University Press 2012), 85–106.

of a thousand do they either use, or knowe how to turne into benefit; and therefore lyes so great a circuit vayne and idle before them?"[29] Learning the superior ways of English agriculture, native inhabitants would greatly improve their lives.[30] Finally, the argument in Robert Gray's sermon of 1609, one of many commissioned by the company, assured Englishmen that there was no reason to be apprehensive about penetrating the lands of native Americans:

these savages have no particular proprietie in any part or parcel of that countrey, but onely a general residencie there, as wild beasts have in the forrest, for they range and wander up and downe the countrey without any law or government: being led only by their owne lusts and sensualitie, there is not *meum et tuum* amongst them; so that, if the whole lande should be taken from them, there is not a man that can complaine of any particular wrong done unto him.[31]

Already during the Tudor era, men with humanist leanings such as More and Sir Thomas Smith had been advocating ideals of commonwealth-building in distant plantations.[32] The civic tradition invoked in company propaganda would align itself with Puritan religiosity in the *Mayflower* compact of 1620. The Pilgrims soon found out that they had to give up their original intention to cultivate land in common; only private ownership could guarantee efficient land-use.[33] Answering potential objections against settlement in New England in 1628, the Puritan lawyer John Winthrop (1588–1649), long-term governor of the Massachusetts Bay colony, noted that "[t]hat which lies common, and has never been replenished or subdued, is free to any that possess and improve it". Like Gray, he dismissed concerns about the rights of native inhabitants:

[T]hey enclose no land, neither have they any settled habitation, nor any tame cattle to improve the land, and so have no other but a natural right to those countries. So if we leave them sufficient for their own use, we may lawfully take the rest, there being more than enough for them and for us.[34]

29 Strachey, *Historie of Travaile into Virginia*, 19.

30 See further, H. C. Porter, *The Inconsistent Savage. England and the North American Indian, 1500–1660* (London, Duckworth 1979), 336–8.

31 Robert Gray, *A Good Speed to Virginia* (London, Kyngston 1609), 23. On Gray, see Mackenthun, *Metaphors*, 194–7. On Gray and the other sermons of 1609, see Porter, *The Inconsistent Savage*, 339–59.

32 See Fitzmaurice, *Humanism and America*, 67–82, 102–11, passim.

33 See e.g. Bernard Bailyn, *The Barbarous Years. The Conflict of Civilizations 1600–1675* (New York, Vintage 2012), 352–6; Andro Linklater, *Owning the Earth. The Transforming History of Land Ownership* (New York, Bloomsbury 2013), 25.

34 John Winthrop [plus others?], 'Reasons for the Plantation in New England', c. 1628 (The Winthrop Society), available at winthropsociety.com/doc_reasons.php.

Winthrop's reference to the natives' failure to *enclose* land reveals his intention to export the English legal–economic experience to the New World. When he then surveyed the decimation of the Indians as a result of smallpox epidemic in 1634, he concluded that "[t]he Lord hath cleared our title to what we possess". The Indians had left the land "open to any that could and would improve it".[35]

"Improvement" was not only a physical phenomenon or a technique. It was a way of organising human relations by allocating rights and duties to those who engaged in activities on the land that were assumed to have a public benefit. In the seventeenth century, it came to connote the modernisation of agricultural production by enclosing the open fields "into compact holdings, which the occupier could hedge about so as to protect them from other people's cattle".[36] The attitudes towards enclosing had been mixed at the beginning of the century, and parliament tried several times unsuccessfully to prevent or limit privatisation. By the end of the century the landlord-dominated parliament turned around, however, and rejected such proposals as a threat to property.[37] By this time, the meaning of improvement was often paired with the notion of waste, used not only to mark land that is left unused but used inefficiently or in common. As Locke put this in the collated last edition of his *Two Treatises* that was widely used in the American Revolution:

> he who appropriates land to himself by his labour, does not lessen, but increase the common stock of mankind: for the provisions serving to the support of human life, produced by one acre of inclosed and cultivated land, are (to speak much within compass) ten times more than those which are yielded by an acre of land of an equal richness lying waste in common.[38]

In the course of the seventeenth century, as nobles felt threatened by Stuart centralisation, a rhetoric of rights arose that presented entitlements to land as both abstract, detached from customary burdens, and

[35] Winthrop, as quoted in Slack, *Invention of Improvement*, 68–9.

[36] Christopher Hill, *A Century of Revolution 1603–1714* (2nd edn, London, Routledge 1981), 18. A thorough description of the different processes of withdrawal of land from the commons by enclosure is R. C. K. Gonner, *Common Land and Inclosure* (London, Macmillan 1912).

[37] Jess Edwards, 'Between "Plain Wilderness" and "Goodly Corn Fields". Representing Land Use in Early Virginia', in Robert Appelbaum & John Sweet (eds), *Envisioning an English Empire. Jamestown and the Making of a North Atlantic World* (University of Pennsylvania Press 2005), 219.

[38] John Locke, *Two Treatises on Government* (6th edn, London, Millar 1764), Second Treatise, § 38 (225–6).

absolute against the crown. At the same time, waste came to be given a legal meaning. Land held in common was waste while improvement was to turn it into private property.[39] Even as the settlers were nostalgic about Indian ways of land-use that, they believed, resembled those of feudal England, by the end of the century the theory that linked improvement with private ownership had come to predominate.[40] For example, William Penn's efforts at creating interest in a common trading stock were over by the 1690s as the cultivators "were soon divided by appetites for private profit and property and improving like other plantations in the English way".[41]

Stuart England was a weak state. At a time when wealth was increasingly seen as an essential constituent of state power, the crown was desperately looking for ways to support the competitiveness of English products. It was also taken as evident in the commercial literature by Malynes, Misselden, Mun and especially William Petty that landowners were to be assisted in their efforts to improve the productivity of their lands. Above all, as we have seen, the problem was "how to determine public interest in commerce, and how to reconcile this with the privately interested actions of merchants".[42] In the colonies this meant attributing land rights to rich landowners and elite merchants capable of investing so as to turn the land to commercial uses.[43] But as metropolitan investors found profit-making through plantations excessively slow, their place was taken by settlers whose Puritan ethos stressed the virtues

[39] Edwards, 'Between "Plain Wilderness" and "Goodly Corn Fields", 224–9. "Improvement" emerged in the fourteenth century to mean "turning something to good account or profit", usually in the context of farming. In the eighteenth century it would also connote the cultivation of gentlemanly character as well as economic and technical experimentation intended to leave a lasting legacy in the world. See David Hancock, *Citizens of the World. London Merchants and the British Atlantic Community 1735–1785* (Cambridge University Press 1995), 281–5, and generally 279–319.

[40] In sixteenth- and seventeenth-century England, pre-enclosure systems of farming were often viewed nostalgically, though without greater political or economic effect. Eric Cheyfitz, *The Poetics of Imperialism. Translation and Colonization from The Tempest to Tarzan* (Oxford University Press 1991), 46–9.

[41] Slack, *Invention of Improvement*, 254.

[42] Thomas Leng, 'Epistemology. Expertise and Knowledge in the World of Commerce', in Philip J. Stern & Carl Wennerlind (eds), *Mercantilism Reimagined. Political Economy in Early Modern Britain and Its Empire* (Oxford University Press 2014), 104.

[43] Out of a wealth of literature, see e.g. Stuart Banner, *How the Indians Lost Their Land. Law and Power on the Frontier* (Harvard University Press 2005), 29–43. For the influential calculations by William Petty of land and labour as key ingredients of national wealth, see Brenna Bhandar, *Colonial Lives of Property. Law, Land, and Racial Regimes of Ownership* (Duke University Press 2018), 39–47.

of labour over privately owned lands and who often saw Indian land-use both primitive and immoral. Squatters on Indian lands, if only able to show that they had improved the productivity of the land, would be rewarded – "who would prosecute an improver?"[44]

"[T]his westerne voyage will yielde unto us all the commodities of Europe, Affrica and Asia, as farr as wee were wonte to travel, and suppluye the wantes of our decayed trades," Richard Hakluyt the Younger had written to Queen Elizabeth in 1584.[45] The prospect for a large-scale transatlantic project had to wait until peace with Spain was concluded twenty years later. A first proposal for public investment in colonisation was rejected by the Privy Council. It was followed by initiatives by private individuals such as Sir Walter Raleigh and merchants such as Sir Thomas Smith, now governor of the Levant Company, ambassador to Moscow and one of the initiators of the East India venture. Once these men had the City's support, it was only a small step to bring the crown along.[46] The first charter was given to individuals forming the Virginia Company in April 1606.[47] It produced two colonies, one financed by London merchants and large landowners, the other by a group of merchants from Bristol, Exeter and Plymouth. The crown provided no financial support but was to receive 20 percent of the value of the minerals to be found.[48]

The grave problems in the Jamestown colony struck at the company's financing prospects. A second charter of 1609 set up a joint stock enterprise with shares initially marked by 56 companies and over 600 individuals.[49] There would now be a governor with near-absolute

[44] John C. Weaver, 'Concepts of Economic Improvement and the Social Construction of Property Rights. Highlights from the English-Speaking World', in John McLaren, A. R. Buck & Nancy E. Wright (eds), *Despotic Dominion. Property Rights in Settler Societies* (University of British Columbia Press 2005), 89, 87–90.

[45] Hakluyt, 'Discourse of Western Planting', 222.

[46] Kenneth Andrews, *Trade, Plunder and Settlement. Maritime Enterprise and the Genesis of the British Empire* (Cambridge University Press 1984), 311.

[47] First Virginia Charter; 10April 1606.

[48] Andrews, *Trade, Plunder and Settlement*, 313.

[49] For a brief economic history of the company, see Robert Brenner, *Merchants and Revolution. Commercial Change, Political Conflict, and London's Overseas Traders 1550–1653* (London, Verso 2003), 93–102. Virginia's early problems had been caused by defective organisation, inadequate composition of the settler population, unrealistic expectations about precious metals and lack of preparedness for setting up self-sustaining production. In 1609, the colony survived with only about sixty out of the several hundred who had migrated. See Edmund Morgan, *American Slavery, American Freedom* (New York, Norton 1975), 71–91; Bailyn, *Barbarous Years*, 35–96.

powers and virtual military rule in the colony.[50] Simultaneously, an intensive propaganda campaign was launched to raise money and to tempt settlers.[51] News of the continuing disorder in Jamestown (by 1611, out of the 1,500 settlers that had arrived so far, only 450 were alive), as well as of the cruelties in the first Powhatan war (1609–14), however, further undermined the company's economic standing. As a result, the initiators began to direct their attention elsewhere, and a new group of small investors, colonial traders and former interlopers, led by Sir Edwin Sandys (1561–1629), began to organise a long-term enterprise by promising 50 acres of land to every individual paying his or her own voyage to the colony.[52] As the first seven-year indentures came to an end, the former servants would, as freemen, begin to cultivate their small plots. Forcible transports of convicts and children increased, production was diversified and merchant–planter partnerships were built on which the colony's future would be based.[53] The new governor, George Yardley, suggested limiting the settlements by decreeing that future land grants would need Powhatan acceptance, but he was overruled by the company's London council. The acceptance of "a sovereignty in that heathen individual" would have infringed the company's title.[54] Finally in 1622, the uncontrolled expansion of plantations led to an Indian uprising and a severe setback for the colony.[55] The company responded with a severity that permanently affected relations with the native population. Two years later, internal company disputes and continued disorder on the ground triggered a judicial process in London that led to retrieving the company charter and turning Virginia into a crown colony.[56] Soon thereafter, the crown stated its

[50] The difficulties of the early years of the Virginia colony in 1606–9 had been exacerbated by the problems of direction, and it was now thought that rule by one man with the oversight of an elected council in London would help things. It did not. See also Christopher Tomlins, *Freedom Bound. Law, Labour and Civic Identity in Colonizing English America 1480–1865* (Cambridge University Press 2010), 261–2.

[51] Andrews, *Trade, Plunder and Settlement*, 318.

[52] Bailyn, *Barbarous Years*, 69. The was the so-called headright system.

[53] Brenner, *Merchants and Revolution*, 103–12. Most of the land-owning merchants would remain back in England, Bailyn, *Barbarous Years*, 93.

[54] *Barkham's case*, 17 July 1622, cited in Robert A. Williams, *The American Indian in Western Legal Thought. The Discourses of Conquest* (Oxford University Press 1990), 215–16.

[55] Of the 840 settlers alive at the time of the Indian attack (4,000 had migrated), 347 – more than a third – were killed.

[56] Andrews, *Trade, Plunder and Settlement*, 325–6; Morgan, *American Slavery*, 92–107; Brenner, *Merchants and Revolution*, 97–9. The transformations in the colony's government in the three successive charters (1606, 1609 and 1612) are summarised by

design to provide "one uniforme Course of Government" for all of its Atlantic possessions.[57]

But the legal transformations did not change the colony's operational pattern. The state would see itself as an improver and enlist the assistance of agricultural and mercantile interests. Free trade was declared. Vessels across the Atlantic would carry, alongside settlers, also botanists, geographers and natural scientists with the mission to survey New World resources and suggest ways for their efficient use. Through strict enforcement of the navigation laws, successive governments tried to integrate the colonies in the governance of English economic and foreign policy. The alliance of "country and court", agricultural and mercantile interests, focused on trade as the place where the success of productive changes was measured:

> Through the most varied knowledge and technologies, 'improvers' would organize the best possible future, both for the expropriated and subordinated, as for themselves. The secular utopia depended on the market: the idea of 'improvement' had at its heart the theory that Nature was best used to yield commodities which might be traded widely, rather than to support local subsistence.[58]

Improvement would link enlightenment ideas with a benevolent empire. The settlers would be reassured by Vattel that the "savages of North America had no right to appropriate all the continent to themselves".[59] Quantitative studies of New World resources would further assist in the transformation of the natural environment in accordance with productive capabilities and commercial needs. But the Atlantic colonies never turned into pliant instruments of metropolitan interests. Control measures were vigorously opposed as colonists felt they

Tomlins as changes from the unincorporated exploration to a "form of partnership between the crown and incorporated investors, to enhanced company capacity to manage the colony within the framework of royal prerogative", *Freedom Bound*, 164.

57 Proclamation for Settling the Plantation of Virginia, 13 May 1625, cited in Jack P. Greene, *Negotiated Authorities. Essays in Colonial Political and Constitutional History* (University Press of Virginia 1994), 45.

58 Richard Drayton, *Nature's Government. Science, Imperial Britain and the 'Improvement' of the World* (Yale University Press 2000), 87.

59 Vattel, *The Law of Nations*, II VII § 97 (310). The earth, he wrote, "is destined to feed its inhabitants: but this it would be incapable of doing if it were uncultivated. Every nation is thus obliged by the law of nature to cultivate the land that has fallen to its share." Nations inhabiting fertile lands without cultivating them "are injurious to their neighbours", I VIII § 81 (129). See also Fisch, *Expansion*, 275–8, 280 and Antony Anghie, 'Vattel and Colonialism. Some Preliminary Observations', in Peter Haggenmacher & Vincent Chetail (eds), *Vattel's International Law in a XXIst Century Perspective* (Boston, Nijhoff 2011), 237–53.

undermined the self-rule they enjoyed as their birthright.[60] In 1619, the crown yielded to renewing the mandate of the Virginia assembly. As a result, the government of Virginia – like most colonies in the Western hemisphere – turned into constant negotiation between Westminster, represented by the governor, and the settlers, represented in the assembly.[61] How were the fruit of improvement to be distributed? The answer to that question depended on the justifications presented for the English colonisation.

## The Game of Justifications: From Conquest to Settlement

Why would the English feel entitled to occupy territory in the Americas? By the time of the first Virginia settlement, Spaniards had been present in the Americas for more than a century while their claimed monopoly had been widely challenged. It would be natural for the English to enter the rivalry also by juridical arguments. Already in the previous century the London polymath and collaborator to Sir Humphrey Gilbert, John Dee (1527–1608), had drafted a justification for English territorial claims.[62] Alongside a refutation of Spanish arguments, Dee had produced a defence of a "British empire" based on discovery and occupation of North American lands by a line descending from the Trojan soldier "Brutus" to King Arthur, the Irish traveller Saint Brendan and Prince Madock, Elizabeth's alleged Welsh ancestor. Dee drew Elizabeth's title from "Partlie Ius Gentium, partlie Ius Civilis and partlie Ius Divino", claiming that "no other prince or potentate els in the whole world would beinge able to alledge thereto and claime the like".[63] A "British" empire that included North America, all the North Atlantic, and the entire Arctic Ocean, would only have to be recovered.[64] Using Roman and canon law on discovery and occupation and highlighting the duties of evangelisation that rested on the English

[60] Already in the first Charter of 1606 the king had promised that the settlers and their children "shall HAVE and enjoy all Liberties, Franchises, and Immunities, within any of our other Dominions, to all Intents and Purposes, as if they had been abiding and born, within this our Realm of England", First Charter of Virginia; 10 April 1606, para 15.

[61] This is the theme of Greene, *Negotiated Authorities*.

[62] John Dee, *The Limits of the British Empire* (K. MacMillan & J. Abeles eds, Westport, Praeger 2004 [1577–8]).

[63] Ibid., 21 [48].

[64] Ken MacMillan, *Sovereignty and Possession in the English New World. The Legal Foundations of Empire, 1576–1640* (Cambridge University Press 2006), 59.

monarch, Dee suggested that the Spanish needed to be expelled urgently, before prescription might consolidate their position.[65] The urgency of the matter had also been stressed by Hakluyt: without speedily establishing plantations and fortifications in key places such as mouths of rivers on the American eastern seaboard, "the French that swarme with multitude of people, or other nations mighte secretely fortify and settle themselves before us".[66]

At its commencement, the initiators of the Virginia project chose to remain silent about legal justification. Peace had been concluded with Spain in 1604, but without conclusively settling the extent of Spanish rights. Both sides continued to invoke their respective claims based on discovery and prescription but neither wanted to press the conflict into open warfare.[67] The charter issued by King James in 1606 noted only in a matter-of-fact way that the men to whom it was granted were to plant themselves in Virginia or "other parts or territories in America . . . which are not now actually possessed by any Christian Prince or People".[68] An early proposal for a legal argument was expressly rejected. Instead of appeasing the Spaniards, "[i]t will rather hasten the Spaniards rage, then retard it; because he will see it, to grow every day harder for him to defeat us".[69]

Giving a legal explanation would not deter the Spaniards whose views, company executives explained, were firmly grounded in their religion. When in 1622, Donne spoke of the law of nature and of nations, this was less meant as a technical argument with respect to Spanish claims than a defence of crown involvement in a private venture and an explanation to home audiences of the potential benefits of foreign settlement. When legal arguments were cited, it was often

65 Ibid., 59–64. Dee did not advocate war, however, only seizing land not presently in the hands of a Christian prince, something he assumed could be achieved rapidly and without excessive cost, *The Limits*, 25 [52].

66 Hakluyt, 'Discourse of Western Planting', 275.

67 The right to trade was stated to continue "as before the war" – but there was no agreement what the pre-war status had been. For the London Treaty of 1604, see Frances Gardiner Davenport, *European Treaties Bearing upon the History of the United States and its Dependencies to 1648* (Washington, Carnegie 1917), 255–6. On the Anglo-Spanish negotiations during 1604–30, see further Goebel, *Struggle for the Falkland Islands*, 110–13, 125–39; Fisch, *Expansion*, 68–71; MacMillan, *Sovereignty and Possession*, 180–94.

68 First Virginia Charter; 10 April 1606, para 1. On the company's initial silence, see Williams, *American Indian*, 202–4; Banner, *How the Indians Lost Their Lands*, 13.

69 "A Justification for Planting Virginia", in S. M. Kingsbury (ed.), *Records of the Virginia Company of London* (4 vols, Washington, US Government Printing Office 1933), III, 2.

done in a sweeping manner by mixing together points about conquest, evangelisation, occupation and purchase. In fact, the effort to the find the principal justification for the English claims may be overly ambitious. The arguments were made cumulatively, sometimes towards other Christian powers, sometimes to address the wrought relations between the settlers and the metropolis.[70] Only marginal account was taken of the indigenous population with which relations would be organised contractually in accordance with practical needs.[71] It was not a monolithic sovereignty that was being claimed – at least not before the mid-eighteenth century – but property rights and some set of jurisdictional powers. Whether attention was on crown sovereignty or settler rights was often unclear, and because the charters were formulated in feudal language, the distinction was anyway obscure.[72] In the course of time, the weight of the arguments moved from conquest to settlement and labour, reflecting a shift of emphasis from inter-imperial to intra-imperial concerns giving rise to a fragmented "transatlantic constitution" as the platform over which the settlers and the metropolis would argue their opposing legal views.[73]

The first English authorisations for discoveries across the Atlantic were made in the language of conquest. The patent issued by Henry VII to John Cabot in March 1496 allowed its recipient "to find, discover, investigate whatsoever island, countries, regions or provinces of heathens and infidels in whatsoever part of the world placed, which

[70] See Banner, *How the Indians Lost Their Land*, 20–3.

[71] A good account is in Paul McHugh, *Aboriginal Societies and the Common Law. A History of Sovereignty, Status and Self-Determination* (Oxford University Press 2004), 42–5, 63–5. No need was felt to address the native inhabitants because the settlement was believed to be analogous to trading posts; instead of territorial sovereignty, the need was for jurisdiction over Englishmen, 91–3. The elusive nature of settler sovereignty is stressed in Lauren Benton & Richard J. Ross, 'Empires and Legal Pluralism. Jurisdiction, Sovereignty and Political Imagination in the Early Modern World', in Lauren Benton & Richard J. Ross, *Legal Pluralism and Empires 1500–1850* (New York University Press 2013), 9. The gradual nature of dispossession from the late eighteenth century onwards is described in Lisa Ford, *Settler Sovereignty. Jurisdiction and Indigenous People 1788–1836* (Harvard University Press 2010).

[72] For the cumulative use of legal justifications for land-taking in the New World, see Lauren Benton & Benjamin Straumann, 'Acquiring Empire by Law. From Roman Doctrine to Early Modern European Practice', 28 *Law & History Review* (2010), 1–38 and Ken MacMillan, 'Imperial Constitutions. Sovereignty and Law in the British Atlantic', in H. V. Bowen, Elizabeth Mancke & John G. Reid (eds), *Britain's Oceanic Empire. Atlantic and the Indian Ocean World c. 1550–1850* (Cambridge University Press 2012), 90–5.

[73] For the concept of "transatlantic constitution", see Mary Sarah Bilder, *The Transatlantic Constitution. Legal Culture and the Empire* (Harvard University Press 2004).

before this time were unknown to all Christians". Once discovery had been made, Cabot and his associates were authorised to:

> conquer, occupy and possess whatsoever such towns, castles, cities and islands by them thus discovered so that they may be able to conquer, occupy and possess, as our vassals and governors lieutenants and deputies therein, acquiring for us the dominion, title and jurisdiction of the same.[74]

Likewise, the patent granted to a group of English and Portuguese merchants on 19 March 1501 authorised the patent-holders, when entering any infidel land to:

> set up our banners and engines in any town, city, caste, island or mainland . . . and to enter and seize these same towns, and as our vassals and governors, lieutenants and deputies to occupy, possess and subdue these, the property, title, dignity and suzerainty of the same being always reserved to us.[75]

The reference to conquest in these early patents was less intended as a legal–technical expression than a formulation mimicking Spanish exploits, celebrating the glories of expansion by an analogy to the greatness of Rome. But the early voyages led neither to "Cathay" nor to permanent settlement, and the crown's attention soon turned to war in Scotland and colonial rule in Ireland. After mid-century, Sir Humphrey Gilbert (1539–83), leader of the suppression of Irish resistance, suggested to the court the establishment of a base on the American coast from where naval operations could be undertaken to "annoy the King of Spain". Backed by Dee's memorandum on the limits of the British Empire and money from some of the richest London merchants, Gilbert also contemplated a colony or a trading post in the Caribbean for which purpose he received from the elder Hakluyt a memorandum highlighting the economic advantages of such a project. "[T]his first seate might in time become a stapling place for the many commodities of many countries and territories, and in tyme this place

[74] 'Letters Patent Granted to John Cabot and his Sons, 5 March 1496', in James A. Williamson (ed.), *The Cabot Voyages and Bristol Discovery under Henry VII* (Cambridge University Press 1962), 204 and 49–53. For the background and the course of the Cabot voyages 1497–8, see 33–115. A slightly different translation of the Latin original is in avalon.law.yale.edu/15th_century/cabot01.asp. Bristol fishermen had been visiting what they believed to be the northeast corner of Asia (Labrador and Newfoundland) from at least the 1480s but formal claims to the New World were first made in only connection with the Cabot voyages.

[75] Letters Patent granted to Richard Warde et al., 19 March 1501, Williamson, *Cabot Voyages*, 237.

might become of all the provinces roundabout the ounly governour".[76] Accordingly, on 11 June 1578, Gilbert was invited:

> to discover, finde, search out and view such remote, heathen and barbarous lands, countryes and territories not actually possessed by any Christian prince or people ... [and to] have and hold occupy and enjoy ... all commodities, jurisdictions and royalties [therefrom].[77]

Nothing came of the plan, however, Gilbert himself being lost at sea in 1583.

Although conquest in Coke's formulation did not necessarily signify belligerent subjugation, that was its usual connotation.[78] It had been used with respect of Ireland since the twelfth century where it had been combined with the vocabularies of barbarism and civilisation. The Irish model would be used in the early American ventures.[79] But it was only cases such as the receipt of Jamaica from Spain in 1655, New Netherlands (New York) from the Dutch in 1664 and Acadia from the French in 1713 where the territory was received from a vanquished European sovereign as a result of military action. No such large-scale action had been undertaken against the native inhabitants until after the Jamestown uprising in 1622. Therefore, the early propaganda usually resorted to peaceful discovery or occupation to address plantation-building on the

[76] 'Notes on Colonisation by Richard Hakluyt, Lawyer, 1578', in E. G. R. Taylor (ed.), *The Original Writings & Correspondence of the Two Richard Hakluyts* (2 vols, London, Hakluyt Society 1935), I, 121, 116–22. The second voyage was to begin a settlement of English Catholics, organised and financed by a joint-stock company under Gilbert himself. See further Andrews, *Trade, Plunder and Settlement*, 186–99.

[77] 'Letters Patent to Sir Humphrey Gilbert', Francis Newton Thorpe (ed.), *The Federal and State Constitutions, Colonial Charters, and Other Organic Laws of the States, Territories, and Colonies Now or Heretofore Forming the United States of America* (7 vols, Washington, Government Printing Office 1909), I, 49. See further Andrews, *Trade, Plunder and Settlement*, 183–99; Williams, *American Indian*, 151–74.

[78] According to MacMillan, "conquest" for Coke meant lands that were "newly discovered and planted as opposed to anciently inherited", *Sovereignty and Possession*, 34 n. 64. However, Coke's rationale for the wide prerogative rights of the conqueror was that he had "vitae et 'necis potestatem'" – something that connoted military victory, Sir Edward Coke, 'The Case of the Postnati (*Calvin's Case*)', in *Cobbett's Complete Collection of State Trials* II (33 vols. T.H. Howell ed., London, Hansard 1816), 638. The same is indicated by later formulations such as the Privy Council memorandum of 1722 referenced at note 107 below.

[79] See *Calvin's case*, 647–9. On Ireland as the example of later colonial exploits, see Armitage, *Ideological Origin*, 24–9, 53–60, 154–7; James H. Ohlmayer, '"Civilizing of these Rude Parts". Colonization within Britain and Ireland 1580s–1640s', in Nicholas Canny (ed.), *The Oxford History of the British Empire*, vol. I: *The Origins of Empire* (Oxford University Press 1998), 124–47.

American mainland. In his remarkable early justification of the English New World settlements, written after Gilbert's death in 1583, Sir George Peckham, planning to move the whole persecuted Catholic community to America, drew from Vitoria the argument from "mutual societas and fellowshippe" prevailing among all humans that made it "lawfull for Christians to use trade and traffique with Indfidels or Savages, carrying thither such commodities as they want, and bringing from thence some part of their plentie".[80] Peckham stressed that this must begin by assuring the Indians of the settlers' good intentions by "present[ing] unto them gratis, some kindes of our prettie merchandizes and trifles: As looking glasses, Belels, Beades, Bracelets, Chaines or collers of Bewgle, Christall, Amber, Iet, or glasse et &". Only if the Indians "barbarously will goe about to practise violence eyther in repelling the Christians from their Ports and safe-landings . . . in such a case I holde no breach of equitie for the Christians to defend themselves, to pursue revenge with force, and to doe whatsoever is necessarie for attaining their safetie".[81]

Despite the early settlers' pacific language, a combination of engrained racism and images of Roman glory kept conquest as part of the legal frame. In his *De jure belli* (1598), Gentili began like Peckham, explaining that humans were born in a bond of fellowship. But then, as we saw in Chapter 3, he turned to those who fell beyond this bond. Such *hostes humani generis* included those who sinned against natural law by human sacrifice or acts of moral depravity, among whom he read native Americans.[82] Against such men, "war is made as against brutes".[83] Conquest would also be available under common law, as made clear by Sir Edward Coke in *Calvin's case* (1607). Coke distinguished two ways in which a territory may fall under the crown, conquest and descent, illustrating the former with the case of Ireland and the latter with that of Scotland.[84] Although Coke had participated in the drafting of the Virginia Charter, he did not expressly address the manner in which the American colonies had come under the crown. But it was obvious that only conquest would apply – after all, he defined "all infidel", including Indians, as "perpetual enemies" of the Christians.[85]

80 Sir George Peckham, 'True Report of the Late Discoveries', in Richard Hakluyt, *Principall Navigations, Voyages, Traffiques and Discoveries of the English Nation*, vol. 13 (Project Gutenberg Ebook 2008), 3. Peckham's text is identified as "the most important English propaganda tract of the period" by Mackenthun, *Metaphors*, 50.

81 Peckham, 'True Report', 5–6.

82 Alberico Gentili, *De jure belli libri tres* (Oxford, Clarendon 1933), vol. II: Translation, I IV and I XXV (22, 122–3).

83 Ibid., I 122. 84 See Coke, *Calvin's case*, 638. 85 Ibid., 638.

For Coke, the principal difference between conquest and descent had to do with the legal situation thus created. If a territory came to the crown by way of inheritance, i.e. through descent, this meant that the king "cannot change those laws of himself, without consent of parliament".[86] In Scotland, England, Wales and even the "distinct dominion" of Ireland, King James was bound to follow the law and legislate with the consent of parliament.[87] But if a territory came to the crown by conquest, then one of two results would follow. If this was a Christian territory – the situation at the conquest of Ireland by Henry II – then the king "may at his pleasure alter and change the laws of that kingdom", but until he does so, "the ancient laws of that kingdom remain". In case of an "infidel land" – presumably the case of America – then:

> *ipso facto* the laws of the infidel are abrogated; for that they be not only against Christianity, but against the law of God and of nature, contained in the Decalogue: and in that case, until certain laws be established among them, the king by himself, and such judges as he shall appoint, shall judge them and their causes according to natural equity.[88]

With conquest, the powers of the crown would be much wider than with descent. It would be free to legislate by a prerogative act, without having to secure parliamentary consent.[89] Nevertheless, in Christian territories, once the crown had given laws to them, the king's legislative prerogative was exhausted: "no succeeding king could alter the same without parliament".[90] But although crown prerogative appeared to remain undiminished in infidel territory, this did not necessarily mean that the infidel themselves would come under crown jurisdiction, at least not initially. *Calvin's case* was about the personal allegiance Englishmen owed to the crown, envisaging a feudal type of a lien, the "true and faithful obedience of the subject due to his sovereign".[91]

The arguments in *Calvin's case* were to play an immensely important role in the later disputes between metropolitan and colonial bodies.

[86] Ibid., 638. [87] See e.g. Tomlins, *Freedom Bound*, 86–7.

[88] Coke, *Calvin's case*, 638.

[89] Or, as Lord Chancellor Ellesmere put it, "the conqueror may impose what lawes hee will upon [the conquered]", ibid., 680. "Conquerors", a modern commentator has summarised, "could claim an unlimited legal power over their conquests", Craig Yirush, *Settlers, Liberty and Empire. The Roots of Early American Political Theory, 1675–1775* (Cambridge University Press 2011), 37.

[90] Coke, *Calvin's case*, 639.

[91] Ibid., 613. On the personal, non-territorial compass of the rule in *Calvin's case*, see further McHugh, *Aboriginal Societies*, 47–8, 69–70.

In Coke's original formulation, the common law would not apply in the colonies, whether acquired by conquest or descent. Indeed, Coke is later reported to have stated that "[t]he common law meddles with nothing that is done beyond the seas".[92] As to parliamentary legislation, the matter was more uncertain, the view consolidating itself in the seventeenth century that it would apply only if that was specifically indicated by the text of the law.[93] King James insisted that because the colonies had not been integrated into the realm but remained distinct dominions under the crown, only the prerogative would apply.[94] A contrary view was taken by parliament as it seized power in the 1640s. The Navigation Acts from 1651 onwards became the most important pieces of colonial legislation. After the Glorious Revolution in 1688 parliament routinely legislated for the trade and external affairs of the colonies, sometimes, though always controversially, intervening in their internal government as well.[95]

Nothing was said by Coke about inter-European or inter-imperial relations. Nor did he specify how the legal relations between settlers and the native inhabitants were to be organised beyond the reference to the overruling of all infidel laws. This was never the practice on the ground, however. Most of the time, settlers claimed either that the lands had been vacant as they arrived or that they had purchased them from native inhabitants – an argument that presumed the initial validity of Indian property.[96] That settlement took place by occupying uninhabited land was often implicitly assumed by the promotional tracts but could also be derived from civil law.[97] Although the relevant provision

[92] Daniel Hulsebosch, 'The Ancient Constitution and the Expanding Empire. Sir Edward Coke's British Jurisprudence', 21 *The Law and History Review* (2003), 439; MacMillan, *Sovereignty and Possession*, 33.

[93] See especially A. Berridale Keith, *Constitutional History of the First British Empire* (Oxford, Clarendon 1930), 4–9.

[94] W. S. Holdsworth, *A History of English Law* (17 vols, London, Methuen 1903–66), XI, 233.

[95] See e.g. Jack P. Greene, *Peripheries and Center. Constitutional Development in the Extended Polities of the British Empire and the United States, 1607–1788* (New York, Norton 1986), 55–76, and for later interpretations of the pre-1642 situation, MacMillan, *Sovereignty and Possession*, 38–41.

[96] For purchase as the principal argument in early colonisation, see Banner, *How the Indians Lost Their Land*, 20–9 and passim.

[97] There is an enormous literature on the Western uses of the argument from occupation of *res nullius/terra nullius* in the context of English settlement in North America. A useful treatment is Andrew Fitzmaurice, *Sovereignty, Property and Empire 1500–2000* (Cambridge University Press 2015). Fitzmaurice suggests that *res nullius* was used much less than earlier research has assumed, and that when used, it was normally

in the Digest spoke only of occupation of islands that had emerged by accretion and the capture of wildfowl, *ferae bestiae*,[98] early patents and propagandists always referred to the right to occupy vacant land wherever such was found.[99] And of course Gentili accepted that "[t]he ruling of our jurists with regard to unoccupied land is, that those who take it have a right to it, since it is the property of no one". Natural law, he added, abhorred a vacuum, which was why anyone could occupy and receive land possessed by nobody.[100]

Later cases set aside Coke's theory of the infidel as perpetual enemies with no rights.[101] Although conquest remained the most widely employed justification,[102] the radical view that it nullified all native land entitlement was never widely accepted. On the contrary, settlers with deeply held Christian convictions such as Winthrop, William Penn or Roger Williams, founder of Rhode Island, drew Indian rights precisely from their moral theology.[103] It had always been difficult to accept that conquest entitled the conqueror to replace old law by new; this made dubious the continuity of the English common law beyond 1066.[104] The problem had been usually dealt with by assuming that William the Conqueror had decreed its continued validity also post-conquest. American settlers resisted the conquest argument as it stressed crown prerogative at the expense of the settlers' competence over the organisation of their lives. Had the settlers not conquered American lands in part for the crown but at least as much for

done in the Roman law form, i.e. as reference to *ferae bestiae*. For some of the other pertinent literature, see e.g. Anthony Pagden, '"The Struggle for Legitimacy" and the Language of Empire in the Atlantic c. 1700', in Nicholas Canny (ed.), *The Oxford History of the British Empire*, vol. I: *The Origins of Empire* (Oxford University Press 1998), 41–54

98 A general doctrine of *terra nullius* is a nineteenth-century concoction. See Fitzmaurice, *Sovereignty, Property and Empire*.

99 See e.g. the patent granted by Henry VII to the Portuguese–English group of 9 December 1502, authorising discovery of all lands apart from those "in possession of which [European] princes now find themselves", Williamson, *Cabot Voyages*, 251 and Andrews, *Trade, Plunder and Settlement*, 49.

100 Gentili, *De jure belli*, I XVII (80–1).

101 E.g. in Mansfield's reference to Coke's "absurd exception as to pagans [arising from] the mad enthusiasm of the Croisades", *Campbell* v. *Hall*, 98 ER 1047–8.

102 Antony Pagden, *Burdens of Empire. 1539 to the Present* (Cambridge University Press 2015), 124.

103 On Roger Williams' views on Indian land rights, see Banner, *How Indians Lost Their Land*.

104 See e.g. the discussion of Coke and Selden in Allan Cromartie, *Sir Matthew Hale, 1609–1676. Law, Religion and Natural Philosophy* (Cambridge University Press 1995).

themselves? In a number of late seventeenth-century cases, the argument was made that when unoccupied or sparsely inhabited country was taken over to plant and improve, conquest was not the proper legal category to address it. Thus in the famous case *Blankard* v. *Galdy* (1693) in the Court of King's Bench, Chief Justice Holt explained that:

> 1st, In case of an uninhabited country newly found out by *English* subjects, all laws in force in *England* are in force there…
>
> 2dly, *Jamaica* being conquered, and not pleaded to be parcel of the kingdom of England, but part of the possessions and revenue of the Crown of *England*, the laws of *England* did not take place there, until so declared by the conqueror or his successors.[105]

Only a few months later, in *Dutton* v. *Howell* (1693), this conclusion was reaffirmed by language that largely underwrote the settler view. Where Englishmen had entered "uninhabited desert Country", they would be entitled to be ruled by the common law "as 'twas their Birthright".[106] The position was further reinforced in a well-known Privy Council memorandum of August 1722 to the Court of Chancery, according to which:

> if there be a new and uninhabited country found by *English* subjects, as the law is the birthright of every subject, so, wherever they go, they carry their laws with them, and therefore such new found country is to be governed by the laws of *England*; tho' after such country is inhabited by the *English*, acts of parliament made in *England*, without naming the foreign plantations, will not bind them.

Regarding conquest, again, the memorandum provided that the conqueror may impose on the vanquished "what laws he pleases" and that until then, the old laws will remain, "unless where these are contrary to our religion, or enact anything that is *malum in se*, or are silent; for in all such cases, the laws of the conquering country shall prevail".[107] Despite the clarity of these statements, practice tended to deviate in a way that was difficult to capture in a rule. This perpetuated the legal conflict between the colonists and the metropolis regarding the extent of the prerogative and the relations between Westminster and colonial assemblies.[108]

105 *Blankard* v. *Galdy*, in William Salkeld (ed.), *Reports of Cases Adjudged in the Court of King's Bench* (3 vols, London, Strahan 1795), II, 411–12 and 90 ER 1089.

106 *Dutton* v. *Howell* (1693), as quoted in Paul McHugh, *Aboriginal Title. The Modern Jurisprudence of Tribal Land Rights* (Oxford University Press 2011), 295. See also Keith, *Constitutional History*, 183.

107 Case 15, in William Peere Williams, *Reports of Cases Argued and Determined in the High Court of Chancery* (3 vols., Dublin, Moore 1790), II, 75–6.

108 See especially Greene, *Peripheries*, 24–42.

According to the settlers, their rights were based upon settlement of uninhabited land or purchase from the native inhabitants. They were not to be ruled at the pleasure of the crown. They had arrived in America with liberty and property as their birthright; this also included the authority to govern themselves through representative assemblies, free from metropolitan interference.[109] In one of the few express statements on the legal situation in the mid-seventeenth century, Sir Matthew Hale argued that the American colonies had been acquired by a patent issued by the king and thus became "parcel of the dominions though not of the realm of England", adding:

> But the English planters carry along with them those English liberties that are incident to their persons. But those other laws that concern the lands, and propriety, and disposal of them, are settled according to the king's pleasure, who is lord and proprietor over them, till he shall dispose of them by patent.[110]

But what would be the precise relationship between the rights of Englishmen and the powers of the crown? The turn from conquest to settlement no doubt tilted the balance in favour of the settlers who were keen to stress the peaceful establishment of their communities, the labour they had engaged in and the hardships they had sustained. They drew upon their common law inheritance but also from the very wording of the patents and charters. Already the first Virginia Charter stated that the settlers and their children "... shall HAVE and enjoy all Liberties, Franchises, and Immunities ... as if they had been abiding and born, within this our Realm of England, or any other of our said Dominions".[111]

Similar statements from many of the instruments were regularly cited in disputes over the respective jurisdictions of metropolitan and colonial institutions.[112] Responding to the danger that the charters would be simply withdrawn, many settler propagandists began to claim that the rights were only declared in those instruments but that their basis was natural law and a view of natural rights based on the history of the settlements and settler activity to improve the lands by intensive labour.

[109] Keith, *Constitutional History*, 184–5; Hulsebosch, 'Ancient Constitution', 458–79.

[110] Sir Matthew Hale, *The Prerogatives of the King* (D. E. C. Yale ed., London, Selden Society 1976), 43–4.

[111] First Charter of Virginia; 10 April 1606, para 15.

[112] See e.g. the discussion of the efforts by the (new) Board of Trade after 1696 to strengthen the review of legislation from the colonies and to revoke the charters and the response in Jeremiah Dummer, *A Defence of the New England Charters* (1721) in Yirush, *Settlers, Liberty and Empire*, 83–112.

## Locke: Government by Improvement

The most influential formulation of this argument emerged from the famous fifth chapter of Locke's *Second Treatise*, written in 1681 to address the colonial issue when there was no longer any serious contention over private property in England itself. Locke's interest in the colonies is well-known. He had invested in the Royal Africa Company and the Merchant Adventurers to trade with the Bahamas. As secretary to Lord Shaftesbury, he had worked for the Lords Proprietors of Carolina (1668–75), thereby learning about the lives of the native inhabitants to whom he referred throughout the *Two Treatises*. He also worked as secretary to the Council of Trade and Plantations (1673–4) and later became a member of the reformed Board of Trade (1695–1700).[113] Locke viewed the colonies above all as economic units. By dressing colonial government in the language of natural rights he would justify settlement of vast tracts of land as sources of "the greatest conveniences of life".[114] When Locke and the Proprietors looked around in the New World, what they saw was unused land, or land used only for hunting and gathering. To Locke and his principals, this was anathema. Land had been donated to humans by God, and "it cannot be supposed He meant it should always remain common and uncultivated. He gave it to the use of the industrious and rational (and labour was to his title to it)."[115] By configuring English ways of agriculture – engrossing, enclosing, increasing productive capacities – as the kind of rational land-use that God had intended to accompany his donation, Locke was able to combine a Puritan ethic of labour with a theory of property rights in a way that fitted perfectly the settlers' view of their situation.

[113] These facts are recorded in many places. See e.g. James Tully, 'Rediscovering America. The *Two Treatises* and Aboriginal Rights', in James Tully, *An Approach to Political Philosophy* (Cambridge University Press 1993), 140–1; David Armitage, 'John Locke, Carolina and the *Two Treatises of Government*', in David Armitage, *Foundations of Modern International Thought* (Cambridge University Press 2013), 90–113, and especially Barbara Arneil, *John Locke and America. The Defence of English Colonialism* (Oxford University Press 1996), 88–91. Locke's views on colonial government were developed in the context of a controversy between the Caroline Proprietors and the settlers, the latter seeking protection and assistance from the Proprietors, the former insisting on timely payment of the rent. The *Fundamental Constitutions of Carolina* (1669), which Locke helped to draft, were in part designed to regulate this conflict. Linklater, *Owning the Earth*, 77–85.

[114] Locke, *Two Treatises of Government* (William S. Carpenter ed., London Everyman's 1984 [1690]), Second Treatise, § 34 (132).

[115] Ibid., § 34 (132–3).

Locke believed that natural law provided for "the preservation of mankind" and that humans thus had the right "to meat and drink and such other things as Nature affords for their subsistence".[116] But if land was originally given to humans in common, how could they take parts for their own use? Locke rejected the theory of patriarchal succession associated with Robert Filmer. This conflicted with the fact that the donation had been in common and presumed a situation of subordination that, in Locke's famous words, was "the condition of slavery, which is nothing else but the state of war continued between a lawful conqueror and a captive".[117] He also rejected the contractual view, put forward by Grotius. There was no evidence of any contract; everyone was born in a world where properties had already been divided. Moreover, although settlers had often purchased lands from the Indians, they had not always done so; first settlements had grown by simply taking adjoining lands into actual use. In Europe, property emerged from contract, and Locke needed a theory that based property in America on something else.[118]

This something else was labour, which "puts the difference of value on everything".[119] Speculating about original contracts or Adamite succession was unnecessary. What created entitlement to land was the way it was taken into productive use. This argument was familiar. Everyone was born with ownership of themselves, including the work of their hands. Through such labour something was annexed to things that entitled closing them off from use by others:

> For this 'labour', being the unquestionable property of the labourer, no man but he can have a right to what that is once joined to, at least where there is enough, and as good left for others.[120]

Locke of course believed that the Indians enjoyed the right of property. But instead of having a settled concept of private property, they seemed to enjoy things in common. To limit the right of settlers against the natives required that property was somehow individuated. The criterion was received from labour. Individual natives possessed an inclusive claim-right to things that were common and an exclusive right to what they may gather or hunt, such as fruit or venison or the deer in the

[116] Ibid., § 25 (129). [117] Ibid., § 24 (128).

[118] Out of the wealth of secondary literature, see Tully, 'Rediscovering America', 137–76.

[119] Locke, *Two Treatises*, Second Treatise, § 40 (136). [120] Ibid., § 27 (130).

forests.[121] But hunting or roaming did not establish property over land. Instead, long-term cultivation was necessary: "God, when he gave the world in common to all mankind, commanded man also to labour."[122] By not using their lands productively the Indians violated God's admonition. This argument had had a long history in the transformation of the English countryside; now it would support English colonising as well. If Indians tried to prevent this, they violated the settlers' natural rights, entitling them to retaliate: "in the state of nature, everyone has executive power over the law of Nature".[123]

The right of appropriation through labour was not unlimited. Nobody was entitled to grasp more than could be put to efficient use.[124] Wastefulness was, after all, the very sin that settlers saw Indians committing. One needed to leave "enough and as good" for others.[125] In the vast spaces of America, this limitation had little significance. It allowed, for example, as it had in England, the enclosure of land to attain greater productivity.[126] The principal limiting criteria was that of non-wastefulness; excess product would only perish in a way that "offended against the common law of Nature".[127] But the introduction of money changed the situation dramatically. Now it was possible to produce beyond sustainability and for sale on the market.[128] After all, everyone was entitled to labour not only for subsistence but also "for [. . .] benefit and the greatest convenience of life".[129] Now the right of property extended beyond what people needed to what they wanted and had the ability to purchase.[130] The desire for more land for commercial agriculture, again, created a potential for conflict and the need for conflict-resolution: "Thus, by definition, a political society only comes into being on the basis of, and to govern, a regime of private property created by expanding needs and intensive agricultural production for the market."[131]

The argument that Indian ways of land-use were not only inefficient but *immoral* must have seemed profoundly satisfactory for Locke's

121 Ibid., § 30 (131). 122 Ibid., § 32 (132). 123 Ibid., § 13 (123).

124 "As much land as a man tills, plants, improves, cultivates, and can use the product of, so much is his property", ibid., § 32 (132).

125 Ibid., § 33 (132). 126 Ibid., § 32 (132). 127 Ibid., § 38 (135).

128 Ibid., § 37 (134). 129 Ibid., § 33 (132).

130 See further, Ian Shapiro, *The Evolution of Rights in Liberal Theory* (Cambridge University Press 1986), 133–5.

131 Tully, 'Rediscovering America', 164. Likewise, Richard Tuck, *Rights and War and Peace. Political Thought and the International Order from Grotius to Kant* (Oxford University Press 2001), 176.

audience, the "educated, intelligent men of property – peers and gentry, professionals, civil servants, men of letters, clergy, merchants and manufacturers" who sometimes worried over ongoing social transformations.[132] Locke's rejection of innate ideas in his *Essay on Human Understanding* (1689) provided a theoretical grounding for the view that humans were born equal in their capacities, highlighting education, the active pursuit of knowledge and useful labour – improvement of oneself and one's environment – as the foundation of personal virtue and national strength.[133] The *Two Treatises* then sketched the political and economic context that such freedom-loving, active and industrious people would find best suited for their tastes: "As much land as man tills, plants, improves, cultivates, and can use the product of, so much is his property."[134] The work set out a virtual constitution for the Atlantic colonies.

## Colonialism As Feudalism: Transformations of Proprietary Rule

The first century of North American colonisation illustrates the way in which political sovereignty followed the rights of property. The impetus for settlement came from groups of individuals close to the crown, members of the landowning elite and City merchants, organising themselves in companies necessary for large-scale overseas enterprises. Or as Edward Coke put it, "The ends of private gain are concealed under cover of planting a colony."[135] Even as these ends were often varied, and colonists and the metropolis disagreed about how their powers should be divided, they converged at least in one theme, namely that the objective was "basically transplantation of English society and English systems of law, court and representative institutions".[136] This was true not only of the settlers who insisted that they would enjoy the same rights of property and representation as the English at home, but also of the charters that gave a stylised, nostalgic–utopian image of old English land relations to be set up across the Atlantic. These relations

[132] Neal Wood, *The Politics of Locke's Philosophy* (University of California Press 1983), 46 and generally on Locke's audience, 41–64.

[133] This aspect of the propaganda is especially highlighted in Fitzmaurice, *Humanism and America*, 21–39.

[134] Locke, *Two Treatises*, Second Treatise, § 32 (132).

[135] Coke, cited in Arneil, *Locke and America*, 68.

[136] William Cronon, *Changes in the Land. Indians, Colonists, and the Ecology of New England* (New York, Hill & Wang 1983), 498.

were personal rather than territorial, involving, as Coke explained in *Calvin's case*, a reciprocal bond of rights and duties between subject and crown. The absoluteness of the rights in the charters went, however, far beyond anything provided in common law. Instead of transposing an actual legal system, they declared an ideological project.[137]

For example, Sir Thomas Smith's 1580s Ulster initiative was eventually formulated in such a way as to allocate large manors to a group of "undertakers" who would finance the settlement of groups of freeholders, copyholders, tenants and cottagers as a "microcosm of English society" and an "example of civic living to the Irish population".[138] A similar starting-point was taken for transatlantic colonisation.[139] In the period between 1578 and 1732 the crown granted roughly thirty-five patents and charters for its Atlantic settlements. The provisions varied in view of the design of the initiators, the nature of foreseen settlement and the crown's ambitions.[140] The document itself was usually prepared by the attorney-general and although it did not normally state this expressly, some supervisory authority was vested in the Privy Council.[141] The rights granted to patent-holders were very extensive, following an old language of land distribution in England that presumed the inseparability of property and personal jurisdiction.[142] The early patents to Gilbert and Raleigh, for example, provided proprietary rights for the individuals mentioned therein – "to have, hold, occupy and enjoy … for ever, all the soyle of all such lands countries & territories so to be discovered or possessed". The territories were "to be had or used with ful power to dispose thereof & of every part thereof in fee simple or otherwise, according to the order of the laws of England".[143] The patent-holders were entitled to the

137 For the contrast between early modern (ideological) notions of absolute property and the more limited notion under common law, see Robert W. Gordon, 'Paradoxical Property', in John Brewer & Susan Staves (eds), *Early Modern Conceptions of Property* (London, Routledge 1995), 95–108. Likewise, Tomlins, *Freedom Bound*, 160.

138 Nicholas Canny, *Making Ireland British, 1580–1650* (Oxford University Press 2001), 133, 130.

139 Ibid., 162.

140 MacMillan, 'Imperial Constitutions', 74–5.

141 See especially the discussion in Ken MacMillan, *The Atlantic Imperial Constitution. Center and Periphery in the English Atlantic World* (New York, Palgrave Macmillan 2011), 14–29.

142 See further MacMillan, 'Imperial Constitutions', 74–81.

143 Letters Patent to Sir Humphrey Gilbert, 1578, Thorpe, 1 *Federal and State Constitutions*, 49, 50. This was a feudal tenure creating a relationship of vassalage in which land was held directly of the crown by the vassal as tenant-in-chief. The right to dispose of land in fee simple was "the most absolute interest a subject can possess in a land", Tomlins, *Freedom Bound*, 166 n. 102.

"rites, royalties and jurisdictions" attached to the territories they received while simultaneously confirming their allegiance to the crown by the provision of one-fifth part of the gold and silver to be found.[144]

While the first ventures were designed for excavating precious metals and setting up trading posts, most seventeenth-century Atlantic charters concerned permanent plantations.[145] Royal authorisation could take place in three basic ways. A royal commission – such as that granted to Robert Harcourt in the Caribbean in 1609 – authorised travel in a more or less clearly marked direction to occupy land of which the crown would retain the rights.[146] A second, more substantive form was a charter or patent given to a company following the Muscovy, Levant and East India models. The first charter issued to the Virginia investors in 1606 set up two settlements in which the investors would enjoy authority over:

> all the lands, Tenements and Hereditaments which shall be within the Precincts limited for that Colony, as is aforesaid, to BE HOLDEN of Us, our heirs and Successors as of our Manor of East Greenwich in the County of Kent, in free and common Soccage only, and not in Capite.[147]

A manor was not a geographical but a legal entity, the "unit of authority of a particular lord".[148] To the extent that the plantations were manors, their relation to the crown was one of personal jurisdiction, not a direct relation to territory. Land held "in free and common Soccage" was an originally feudal type of tenure that involved some rent payable either in kind or in money, but was fixed and did not involve personal service. It was lighter than "in Capite" tenure, held directly of the crown and involving variable and potentially heavy personal duties. It involved full freedom to use the land and enjoy its product, including the right to administer it, to legislate for it, to alienate it in whole or in part as well

144 Letters Patent to Sir Humphrey Gilbert, 50.

145 The exception being Hudson's Bay Company, established in 1670 by a series of trading posts predominantly for fur trading with the indigenous inhabitants. It would also, however, seek to govern the enormous area delimited by the catchment area of the rivers from Hudson Bay.

146 James A. Williamson, *The Caribbee Islands under the Proprietary Patents* (Oxford University Press 1926), 26.

147 First Virginia Charter; 10 April 1606. The charter contemplated two distinct colonies, one promoted by a group of London merchants, the other by merchants from Plymouth, Bristol and other cities. There was to be a governing council for each plus a council in London for general supervision. The second colony failed after its first year and the London council was abolished in 1609, however.

148 Keith Tribe, *Land, Labour and Economic Discourse* (London, Routledge 1977), 31.

as to create sub-tenures.[149] This would eventually be the form in which most English colonies in the New World would be organised. The lands would be held "of the crown" – that is to say, the crown would have "ultimate" jurisdiction over them, and, at least in the crown's own view, also the right to allocate land rights.[150] According to the first Virginia Charter, the company's legislative acts were to be signed by the king and "pass under the Privy Seal of our Realm of England".[151] In 1609 the Virginia company was incorporated after the East India model. In addition to full legislative powers, it was given:

> full and absolute Power and Authority to correct, punish, pardon, govern, and rule all such the Subjects of Us. . . according to such Orders, Ordinances, Constitutions, Directions, and Instructions, as by our said Council as aforesaid, shall be established; And in Defect thereof in case of Necessity, according to the good Discretions of the said Governor and Officers respectively, as well in Cases capital and criminal, as civil, both Marine and other; So always as the said Statutes, Ordinances and Proceedings as near as conveniently may be, be agreeable to the Laws, Statutes, Government, and Policy of this our Realm of England.[152]

These powers were directed to English subjects and possibly other Europeans visiting or trading with the settlers, but they did not concern the native inhabitants. Instead, settlers were to conclude alliances of friendship with the latter, instructions to the company suggested.[153] Company jurisdiction over the settlers was very extensive, including the

[149] See A. W. B. Simpson, *A History of the Land Law* (2nd edn, Oxford University Press 1986), 11–14 and 47–52. B. H. McPherson, 'Revisiting the Manor of East Greenwich', 42 *American Journal of Legal History* (1999), 35–56 and further, Tomlins, *Freedom Bound*, 161 n. 87. The Virginia council did set up sub-tenures for individual proprietors which, Tomlins writes, "tended to function as self-contained communities analogous to England's manor-dominated 'closed' parishes, or the armed Irish plantations", 264.

[150] The charters usually empowered the company or the proprietor to allocate lands to the settlers. But this took time and at any moment left the status of territories open. In the case of corporate colonies, the land could be understood as corporate land, but in proprietorships it was unclear whether that was royal demesne or owned by the proprietor himself. These matters were largely unresolved, but Mancke writes that Stuart kings "asserted their prerogative to treat Crown lands in Virginia, and elsewhere in the Americas, as private preserves to grant to clients as they wished". Mancke, 'Chartered Enterprises', in Bowen, Mancke & Reid, *Britain's Oceanic Empire*, 243.

[151] First Virginia Charter; 10 April 1606, para 7.

[152] Second Virginia Charter; 23 May 1609. avalon.law.yale.edu/17th_century/va02.asp. See further Keith, *Constitutional History*, 22–4.

[153] See e.g. McHugh, *Aboriginal Societies*, 94.

power to set up martial law – used by Governor Thomas Dale with full force in order to deal with the disorder in Jamestown during 1611–19.[154] With the change of regime in 1619 Virginia received its first general assembly (House of Burgesses) with initial powers of taxation. In 1625, owing to persistent economic problems and disputes between the company's leadership, the Privy Council cancelled the charter and turned the territory into a crown colony to be ruled by a crown-appointed governor and council. After a brief interval, however, the assembly was reconstituted and, sitting together with the governor and the council, eventually became the colony's principal legislative organ.[155]

At the same time, the king declared his personal interest in Bermuda and New England and began to tighten the supervision of the government of all Atlantic colonies.[156] Action was first taken with respect to areas under the Massachusetts Bay Company operating under rigorously Puritan rule. Owing to skilful diplomacy on the company's part, however, it was entitled to keep its charter.[157] A permanent Committee of Foreign Plantations was then set up by the king in 1634, headed by the king's close associate, the controversial Archbishop Laud, vested with the right to legislate for and to revoke laws passed by the colonies themselves. Although its powers were "extensive and almost royal in character", the committee never exercised them in full and was dissolved at the outset of the Civil War.[158] Efforts to increase the control of the colonies continued during the Commonwealth through the Navigation Act of 1651 whose enforcement would eventually become the most important cause of friction between the crown and the colonies. The Barbados Assembly, for instance, bluntly declared that it was contrary to "the freedom, safety and well-being of the island".[159] Control efforts further intensified during the Restoration when they peaked in the establishment of the Lords of Trade in 1675.[160]

154 Second Virginia Charter; 23 May 1609, paras 21 and 22. The infamous "Lawes Divine, Morall and Martiall" are available at www.encyclopediavirginia.org/Lawes_Divine_Morall_and_Martiall.

155 Keith, *Constitutional History*, 25–6, 231–54.

156 See MacMillan, *Sovereignty and Possession*, 104.

157 Keith, *Constitutional History*, 28–32; John E. Pomfret & Floyd M. Shumway, *Founding the American Colonies 1583–1660* (New York, Harper 1971), 155–67.

158 Charles M. Andrews, *British Committees, Commissions, and Councils of Trade and Plantations, 1622–1675* (Baltimore, Johns Hopkins Press 1908), 16. But see also MacMillan, *Atlantic Imperial Constitution*, 151–8.

159 Quoted in Greene, *Peripheries*, 19.

160 For the committees and councils used to control colonial affairs during the Restoration, see Andrews, *British Committees*, 61–95.

Although a few companies were authorised after the Restoration (Connecticut 1662, Rhode Island 1663, Hudson's Bay Company 1679), the third and principal form of later colonisation took place by a charter or patent issued to individual proprietors, chosen from among influential merchants and courtiers who would be given jurisdiction over enormous, often abstractly designated territories linked in a quasi-feudal relationship to the crown. The grants had a conservative streak, reverting to tenurial relationships no longer practised in England, never more so than in the "palatine" proprietorships that involved vice-regal privileges under virtual sovereignty. The proprietor would hold the land as a feudal demesne, being entitled to establish manors, exercise law-making and judicial powers and the right to assign sub-grants and leases.[161] When the proprietor then granted lands to his tenants, whether a manorial lordships, freeholds or copyholds, the result was:

> a pyramid of proprietorships beginning with the king and reaching down to the lowliest tenant. Each level of hierarchy was marked by quasi-governmental privileges under which the landholder would determine the destiny of those on the land.[162]

The first of the palatine grants was a New Scotland patent granted to Sir William Alexander of Menstrie in 1621 over "Cape Sable" – a huge area of eastern Canada along the St Croix River. The patent began with an explanation that overpopulation of England rendered it expedient "that many should be led forth into new territory, which they may fill with colonies" and advertised the king's "anxiety to propagate the Christian faith" as well as, in quite an extraordinary fashion, called on Alexander to "secure the wealth, prosperity and peace of the native subjects" and to arrange "peace, alliance, friendship, mutual conferences, assistance and intercourse with the savage aborigines and their chiefs".[163] He was also given "full power, privilege and jurisdiction of free royalty, chapelry and chancery for ever", with the power to set up towns and markets and generally all the privileges of barons of Scotland.[164]

Many other lands were given as proprietary grants before the Civil War.[165] Although many of them were abrogated and granted to new

161 MacMillan, *Atlantic Imperial Constitution*, 17.

162 Hulsebosch, 'Ancient Constitution', 453.

163 New Scotland Charter, 1621, in Edmund Farwell Slafter et al., *Sir William Alexander and American Colonization* (Boston, Wilson 1873), 128.

164 New Scotland Charter, 1621, 131–2.

165 These included the patent issued by Charles I over the Caribbean region to the earl of Carlisle in 1627 and to Sir Robert Heath over the vast area of Carolina (1629),

proprietors during the Restoration, jurisdictional powers usually remained unchanged. Nothing gives a better sense of the extensive nature of palatine powers than the charter of Maryland, granted by Charles I originally to George Calvert (1569–1632), the first baron of Baltimore, member of the Privy Council and former secretary of Sir Robert Cecil in 1632. Calvert, a convert to Catholicism, received initially a palatine proprietorship to Avalon, Newfoundland but, as the conditions there appeared overly harsh for settlement, he was granted, against strong opposition of the Virginia settlers, a large territory north of the Potomac and into the western mountains. Here the baron, as "the true Lord and Proprietary of the whole Province" was invited to exercise "free, full and absolute power . . . to Enact Laws, of what Kind soever, according to their sound Discretions whether relating to the Public State of the said Province, or the private Utility of Individuals". The baron and his heirs were to set up courts to see to penal enforcement on all persons within the province or on the way in or out. Finally, it was specified that the baron would hold:

> as ample Rights, Jurisdictions, Privileges, Prerogatives, Royalties, Liberties, Immunities, and royal Rights, and temporal Franchises whatsoever, as well by Sea as by Land, within the Region, Islands, Islets, and Limits aforesaid, to be had, exercised, used, and enjoyed, as any Bishop of Durham, within the Bishoprick or County Palatine of Durham, in our Kingdom of England.[166]

The reference to the powers of the bishop of Durham designated the Calvert property analogously to the palatinate provinces that had been originally set up in English frontier areas, such as fourteenth-century Welsh and Scottish marshlands, where the lord's vice-regal prerogatives came in exchange for protecting the realm.[167] The bishop was "exempt from English political, judicial and administrative institutions", cases from Durham could not be argued in English courts, no taxes were paid to England and Durham had no representatives in parliament.[168]

which would be transferred in 1663 to the ownership of a group of eight proprietors. A board of proprietors for New England was likewise established for the area left unused in the Virginia patent and later purchased by the Massachusetts Bay Company. Patents to individual proprietors were also issued for Maine (1622, 1639) and the territory of "Avalon" (1637). See Tomlins, *Freedom Bound*, 166–77.

166 The Charter of Maryland; 20 June 1632, avalon.law.yale.edu/17th_century/ma01.asp, Art IV.

167 Ibid., Art V and Bailyn, *Barbarous Years*, 123.

168 See Tim Thornton, 'The Palatinate of Durham and the Maryland Charter', 45 *American Journal of Legal History* (2001), 242; Albert J. Martínez, 'The Palatinate

Moreover in Maryland, unlike in Durham, the writs would run in the proprietor's name. Even as the crown reserved for itself "the Faith and Allegiance and Sovereign Dominion", Privy Council lawyers objected to the grant of such wide powers. Maryland's autonomy went much further than Virginia's and might even jeopardise the rights of Englishmen.[169]

George Calvert died soon after the grant was issued and the settlement was taken over by his son, Cecilius (1605–75), managing his estate from London. More than sixty manors of 2,000 acres or more were to be set up with full manorial ownership and judicial powers. More modest settlers would receive 100 acres per adult and 50 acres per child, with servants and tenants to work the lands. Baltimore's own income would be assured through rents from the lands thus granted.[170] Initially, the Calverts prohibited appeals to courts in England and required manorial lords to promise fealty first to them, and only thereafter to the English rulers. But the manorial system did not hold out for long. Indentured servants and commoners who had paid their own trip to the New World resented the proprietary hierarchy, and relations between religious groups were tense. Although the charter had provided virtually unlimited powers to Maryland's ruler, it also invited him to exercise them "with the Advice, Assent, and Approbation of the Free-Men of the same Province, or the greater Part of them, or of their Delegates or Deputies". Conflicts between settler groups expanded into violence and indiscriminate plundering during the Civil War. With pressure from London, the Calverts could hold on to their proprietorship only with difficulty and in 1690 the new monarchs turned Maryland into a crown colony.[171] By the time the Calverts again returned as proprietors in 1715, the assembly had already established itself as an independent force, half a century later describing its powers as the "expression of inalienable rights".[172]

The Restoration crown still authorised some proprietary colonies, most notably to the duke of York, the king's brother, an area combining parts previously claimed by the New England company and parts conquered from the Dutch in 1663 (including New York), to Carolina in 1663, the Bahamas in 1670 and the area of Pennsylvania to the Quaker leader William Penn in 1681. Although not as extensive as the Maryland charter, the grants did endow absolute rights of legislation and criminal

Clause in the Maryland Charter 1632–1776. From Independent Jurisdiction to Independence', 50 *American Journal of Legal History* (2008–10), 305–25.

169 Pomfret & Shumway, *Founding*, 73.

170 Bailyn, *Barbarous Years*, 125–6.

171 Ibid., 144–61; Pomfret & Shumway, *Founding*, 91–100.

172 Martínez, 'Palatinate Clause', 325.

and civil jurisdiction as well as monopoly of trade to the proprietors. Penn and his heirs were made "the true and absolute Proprietaries of all the Lands and Dominions" in the territory, holding all the lands "as of Our Castle of Windsor in Our County of Berks, in free and common socage".[173] This time, however, the king expressly reserved sovereignty for himself, thus manifesting his ambition to move away from a personal to a territorial understanding of his powers. The grant also provided a right of appeal to the crown that had not been included in the Maryland charter, giving substance to the by then customary provision that legislation enacted for the colony was to be "the said Lawes bee consonant to reason, and bee not repugnant or contrarie, but as neare as onveniently may bee agreeable to the Lawes and Statutes, and rights of this Our Kingdome of England".[174] Nevertheless, "these legislative and judicial powers significantly exceeded those held by most landlords and royal officials in England".[175]

Another form of government was the royal colony of which Virginia (1625) had been the first.[176] From the late seventeenth century century onwards, the Board of Trade tried systematically to convert proprietary colonies into royal ownership. Because of concerns about property rights, this would take place only gradually but was ultimately successful. Instead of having charters, crown colonies were constituted and governed by commissions under the great seal, a public document issued to the governor that envisaged the territories as provinces.[177]

[173] The proprietor was to deliver annually two beaver skins to the king, in addition to the customary twenty per cent of found valuable minerals. The Charter for the Province of Pennsylvania; 28 February 1681, para 2. avalon.law.yale.edu/17th_century/pa01.asp.

[174] Ibid., para 2.

[175] MacMillan, 'Imperial Constitutions', 78. Charter holders were also tied by liege relations to the king, manifested by annual tributes that remained, however, of a purely formal character. Michael J. Braddick, 'The English Government, War, Trade, and Settlement, 1625–1688', in Nicholas Canny (ed.), *The Oxford History of the British Empire*, vol. I: *The Origins of Empire* (Oxford University Press 1998), 297.

[176] In addition to Virginia, direct crown rule was established for Jamaica (1655), Barbados (1663), the Leeward islands (1671), New Hampshire (1679–80), Bermuda (1684), Massachusetts (1691) and New Jersey (1702). In 1719 South Carolina was formed as a royal province, to be followed by North Carolina a decade later.

[177] Leonard Labaree, *Royal Government in America. A Study of the British Colonial System before 1783* (New York, Ungar 1930), 8–14. In addition, the colonies were governed by royal "instructions" that were either general or specific and usually not public and were directed to the more detailed aspects of government, 14–18. On these, as well as the rarer form of instrument, "Proclamations", see 18–36. See also Keith, *Constitutional History*, 179–82.

The exceptions were Massachusetts Bay in 1691 and Quebec, conquered from the French in 1774, which received charters operating like formal constitutions.[178] But eventually crown colonies would also develop the same type of independence from the metropolis as other colonies did.

Whatever the design of a charter, once settlement was under way, it was very hard for metropolitan authorities to assert effective control. The grant for the Massachusetts Bay Colony, for example, was given to what was supposed to be a trading company but was actually motivated by religious persecution and the desire to set up an ideally pious commonwealth, a "City upon a Hill". The colony had an insistent desire to live as independently from England as possible. For example, its council did not, as usual, reside in London, but in the colony itself. The leaders of the colony believed they could enact what laws they wanted and did not communicate them to the Privy Council.[179] After a period of confusion with families settling spontaneously around the Boston Bay area, land ownership issues were resolved by giving the General Court authority to purchase Indian land and design the physical contours of the communities and allocate entitlements based on prestige and ability to contribute to company's welfare.[180] In 1641 and 1648 the General Court passed the famous "Body of Laws and Libertyes" that prefigured the Declaration of Rights in London and was designed to support the settlers vis-à-vis the proprietors by deriving their rights from God instead of proprietor consent.[181]

The so-called non-repugnancy clause that became standard in the English charters was "notoriously ambiguous, open to interpretation, and subject to both intercolonial and transatlantic legal disputes".[182] While the colonists were to live under the basic principles of English law, local conditions could still be reasonably taken account. The charter of Rhode Island of 1663, for instance, specifically called for a balance. The laws and ordinances were to be "as neare as may bee,

178 Labaree, *Royal Government in America*, 7–8.

179 See William E. Stoebuck, 'Reception of English Common Law in the American Colonies', 10 *William & Mary* Law Review (1968), 398–404.

180 Bailyn, *Barbarous Years*, 419.

181 For the text of the Body of Liberties (1641), see history.hanover.edu/texts/masslib.html. See Daniel R. Coquillette, 'Radical Lawmakers in Colonial Massachusetts. The "Countenance of Authoritie" and the Lawes and Libertyes', 67 *New England Quarterly* (1994), 179–211. Tomlins, *Freedom Bound*, 250–4.

182 Philip J. Stern, "Bundles of Hyphens", in Richard J. Ross & Lauren Benton (eds), *Legal Pluralism and Empires, 1500–1850* (New York University Press 2013), 29.

agreeable to the lawes of this our realme of England, considering the nature and constitutions of the place and people there".[183] But many colonies ignored their duty to submit all legislation for approval by the Privy Council. Moreover, scrutiny took a lot of time and assemblies soon learned to make legislation temporary so that it would expire before metropolitan scrutiny. When appeals were launched against local laws, mostly by disgruntled settlers, the Privy Council examined them with "an inconsistency and leniency that was probably due to a practical, realistic appreciation of local conditions".[184]

## Thinking about Native Inhabitants

The majority of Englishmen saw colonisation as a pointless drain on the country's resources. Stories of Virginia's early years increased scepticism about the viability of colonies in unhealthy lands swarming with "barbarous" enemies. The usefulness of the principal import – tobacco – was questioned and the debate on the effect of luxuries on morality was constant. But also the justice of taking Indian lands was often doubted. As we have seen, the early charters were jurisdictional rather than territorial; they did not invoke an express intention to dispossess native inhabitants who were normally treated as objects of alliances or of war, or as partners for land purchases. It was only later that efforts were made to have the Indians accept English dominion. And even then the conceptual frames of the two sides differed so dramatically that drawing definite conclusions about the legal situation remains difficult to this day.[185]

Apart from the discredited reference in *Calvin's case* to Indians as "perpetual enemies", the early texts paid almost no attention to the native inhabitants. They were seen either as objects of conversion or then as peaceful peoples unjustly subjected to Spanish exactions.[186] The very first chapter of Hakluyt's *Discourse*, for example, stressed the duty to evangelise Indian "idolaters": "the people of America crye oute unto us

[183] The Charter of Rhode Island and Providence Plantations; 15 July 1663; Bilder, *The Transatlantic Constitution*, 2–3.

[184] Stoebuck, 'Reception of English Common Law', 49. See also George Adrian Washburn, *Imperial Control of the Administration of Justice in the Thirteen American Colonies, 1684–1776* (New York, Columbia 1923) (on appeals directed against laws purportedly violating English practices of the administration of justice), 46–53.

[185] See especially, McHugh, *Aboriginal Societies*, 91–8.

[186] On the use of the "black legend" in defence of the English settlements, see H. C. Parker, *The Inconstant Savage. England and the North American Indian 1500–1660* (London, Duckworth 1979), 173–4 and passim.

their nexte neighboures to come and helpe them, and bringe unto them the gladd tidinges of the gospell".[187] But having disposed of this religious point Hakluyt, like most later propagandists, moved on to more practical topics, such as nature of the voyage and the great benefits that would ensue from the plantations.

Most early grants were made by the crown abstractly, by simply indicating geographical coordinates. The London Branch of the Virginia Company received its jurisdiction in an area between latitude 34° and 41° north, the Plymouth Branch, later New England, a territory between latitude 37° and 45° north and the Newfoundland colony between 46° and 52°.[188] No question regarding occupation or dispossession arose; the grant only indicated the sphere of personal allegiance between the crown and the settlers. Only gradually would the territory itself be read into the grant. That the Indians were outside English jurisdiction was clearly expressed in the 1621 patent to Sir William Alexander to "New Scotland" that invited the patent-holder "to cultivate peace and quiet with the native inhabitants and savage aborigines of the land".[189] A most striking formulation had been included in the New England charter the year before:

> there hath by God's visitation reigned a wonderful Plague, together with many horrible Slaughters and Murthers, committed among the Savages and brutish People there, heretofore inhabiting, in a manner to the utter Destruction, Devastation, and Depopulation of the whole Territory. [This meant that] God in his Goodness and Bountie towards Us and our People, hath thought fit and determined that those goodly Territoryes deserted as it were by their natural Inhabitants, should be possessed by [the English].[190]

Whatever its connotations, the patent clearly did not foresee dispossession, only movement into lands that had been left vacant.

But attitudes changed after the Jamestown uprising of 1622 to which the English responded with extreme violence – betrayals, poisonings and massacres. To the company's plea that Indians be treated with justice the settlers responded that "wee hold nothing injuste, that may

[187] Hakluyt, 'Discourse on Western Planting', 216–17.
[188] Mencken, 'Chartered Enterprises', 241.
[189] Charter in Favor of Sir William Alexander, 1621, in Slafter et al., *Sir William Alexander and American Colonization*, 136–7.
[190] The Charter of New England, 3 November 1620. Available at: avalon.law.yale.edu/17th_century/mass01.asp.

tend to their ruine".[191] War against savages would be just retaliation for breach of natural law. In what became a standard formulation, the Maine Patent to Sir Ferdinando Gorges of 1639 authorised the patent-holders to:

> pursue and prosecute out of the Lymitts of the said Province and Premisses and then (if itt shall soe please God) to vanquishe, apprehende and take and being taken either according to the Lawe of armes to kill or to keepe and preserve [i.e. as slaves] them att their pleasure.[192]

This projected the Indians as objects of war, utter outsiders to the English legal system with which the settlers could do practically what they wished.[193] As more settlers arrived, more problems emerged. The great Puritan migration in the 1630s brought about 20,000 people to Massachusetts, and by the end of the 1670s there were in excess of 60,000 settlers in New England.[194] The result was massive dispossession and destructive conflict. The Pequot war of 1635–8 and the wars against the Algonquians in the 1670s, for example, "culminated in the devastation of indigenous societies by massacre, mass execution, and the enslavement and deportation of survivors".[195]

Eventually, as the crown sought peaceful relations, it would also extend its dominion over the Indians. The charter for Rhode Island of 1663 called upon the colonists to "transplant themselves into the middest of the Indian natives", describing them as "the most potent princes and people of the country", and observing that "the great bodie of Narragansett Indians" had agreed "to subject themselves, their people and lands, unto us".[196] Such subjection, just like the provision calling for purchase of lands, presupposed a more or less voluntary act on the Indian part.[197] But it also implied a claim of jurisdiction over the

[191] Morgan, *American Slavery*, 100. After the other uprising in 1644 the Virginia Assembly declared the Indians to be the settlers' "irremediable enemies" and promised "to forever abandon all forms of peace and familiarity with the whole Indian Nation", quoted in Williams, *American Indian*, 219; see also generally 216–21.

[192] Grant of the Province of Maine, 1639, in Thorpe, *Federal and State Constitutions*, III 1630. This formulation would be repeated in many other charters as well. See also Tomlins, *Freedom Bound*, 176.

[193] McHugh, *Aboriginal Societies*, 94–5.

[194] Tomlins, *Freedom Bound*, 23.

[195] Ibid., 24.

[196] The Charter of Rhode Island and Providence Plantation, 15 July 1663, Thorpe, *Federal and State Constitutions*, VI, 3212.

[197] See Mamadou Hebié, *Souveraineté territoriale par traité. Une étude des accords entre puissances coloniales et entités politiques locales* (Presses Universitaires de France 2015), 165, 168–72. See also the review of English charters in this regard, 161–6.

Indians. Land rights were now to be adjudicated under English law. This was clearly implied in the commissions established by Charles II in the 1660s to survey the government of the New England and to examine what treaties or contracts had been made with native inhabitants, how they had been observed and, in case of breach, whether compensations were paid.[198] A letter of 2 June 1709 from the Board of Trade to Queen Anne bluntly recorded that the five nations bordering upon (i.e. not inside) the New York colony were under "the constant subjection and dependence ... upon the government of New York".[199] Cronon reports on a Connecticut court from 1717:

> That the lands in the government are holden of the King of Great Britain as the lord of the fee; and that no title to any lands in the colony can accrue by any purchase made of Indians on pretence of their being native proprietors thereto.[200]

It was now made abundantly clear that the Indians were living on crown land and that the crown had the right to regulate the conditions of the transactions. The move from a claim to allegiance-based personal jurisdiction to territorial sovereignty also involved more detailed singling out of the geographical limits to the claimed areas. In the east the claims were naturally limited by the ocean, but in the west they remained wholly open, and as the crown in 1763 tried to extend its dominion and control across the whole continent, it famously failed to enforce this. Nothing could prevent the extension of settlements across the Appalachians.

Native inhabitants were often mentioned in the propaganda of the Virginia Company.[201] The company's own *A True Declaration of the Estate of the Colonie of Virginia* of 1610 reiterated the commitment to evangelise them, taking distance from the way the Spanish had "first destroyed, and then instructed".[202] There would be room enough for everyone, and if the Indians did go to war, the English would have the right to defend themselves. But contracting was the rule. The English had rights:

198 See John R. Brodhead, *Documents Relative to the Colonial History of the State of New-York. Procured in Holland, England, and France* (15 vols, Albany, Weed, Parsons 1853–87), III, 53, 64.

199 Ibid., vol. 5, 74.

200 Cronon, *Changes in the Land*, 70.

201 Good accounts of the 1609–22 literature are offered in Porter, *The Inconstant Savage*, 339–75; Williams, *American Indian*, 208–12; Fitzmaurice, *Humanism and America*, 58–101.

202 For the text of the declaration, see quod.lib.umich.edu/e/eebo/A14518.0001.001?rgn=main;view=fulltext.

> because *Paspehay*, one of their Kings, sold unto us for copper, land to inherit and inhabit. Powhatan, their chief King, received voluntarily a crown and a sceptre, with full acknowledgment of duty and submission.[203]

Here then was a clear statement of both property and sovereignty. The company had purchased its lands from Powhatan, the "chief King", who had simultaneously subordinated himself to the English. Whether he had done that to the company or to the English crown was, of course, left obscure, as it must have been for Powhatan himself, if indeed a ceremony of this type at all took place.[204] But even if it did, its meaning and consequences were likely to have been seen wholly differently by the two sides. The individualised European notion of "property" was not easily translatable into Native American languages.[205] The native inhabitants probably believed that the contracts concerned use-rights, not the land itself.[206] Establishing fences and drawing boundaries around unmarked lands enabled the settlers to view themselves as improvers and to strengthen the distance between their way of life and that of the barbarians.[207] It would not take long before the English systems of surveying and measurement would become authoritative determinants of marketable land rights, financial security and the criterion for membership in colonial assemblies.[208]

Moreover, the sales were often less than fully voluntary. They were conducted under veiled threats or false pretences, and the meaning of the transactions was differently understood by the parties. The native chiefs (or those whom the settlers believed were such) did not always have the right to sell and the price was often unreasonably small.[209] Treaty-making had often all the paraphernalia of inter-state bargaining – the treaties

203 Ibid. From early deals with the Powhatans in Virginia to Massachusetts, Maryland, Pennsylvania, New York and New Jersey purchasing quickly became the norm. See further, Banner, *How the Indians Lost Their Land*, 25, 20–9.

204 For interpretations of that purported ceremony, see Mackenthun, *Metaphors*, 199–207.

205 See e.g. Cronon, *Changes in the Land*, 55–70; Cheyfitz, *Poetics of Imperialism*, 44–58. From the huge literature discussing indigenous notions of what we could call "property", see e.g. Richard Overstall, 'Encountering the Spirit in the Land. "Property" in a Kinship-Based Legal Order', in John McLaren, A. R. Buck & Nancy E. Wright (eds), *Despotic Dominion. Property Rights in British Settler Societies* (University of British Columbia Press 2005), 22–49.

206 For the conflicts of understanding, see Cronon, *Changes in the Land*, 66–8.

207 See e.g. Johnson, *Nova Britannia*, C2; Drayton, *Nature's Government*, 55–6.

208 Linklater, *Owning the Earth*, 32–4, 55–62 (with emphasis on the role of William Petty's "political arithmetic").

209 For all of such considerations, see Banner, *How the Indians Lost Their Land*, 49–84.

operated as "forums in which Indians and European met to establish or renew peace, alliance and trade; settle disputes and perhaps exchange land for gifts".[210] Some of those treaties were dealt with on the English side as interactions between virtual sovereigns, though always with the reservation that the transactions take place under English law. From the late seventeenth century onwards the treaties began to express a new relationship where tribes, even as they remained outside the plantations, accepted some sort of English protection. Although each treaty needs to be scrutinised separately, they mostly did not mean loss of identity or independence.[211] But any impression of Indian sovereignty disappeared with the Proclamation of 1763 where the crown reserved all lands not already included within its colonies "under our Sovereignty, Protection, and Dominion".[212]

Throughout the eighteenth-century land boom, crown and settlers disputed over whether the colonies were to be administered by the crown or the colonies themselves. Spectacular land grants were given to such large land projectors as the Ohio or Susquehenna companies operating in the undelimited western territories where the obscurity of the constitutional situation allowed settlements to be raised on native lands and created "disparities of wealth and status even greater than those of older settlement".[213] Gradually, even Indians with good relations with the English, such as the Mohegan of Connecticut, would lose their lands. The case of *Connecticut* v. *the Mohegans* ranged through the first half of the eighteenth century, raising many of the basic themes on land rights in northern America. At the first stage of the appeal, launched with Queen Anne, the attorney-general affirmed the crown's competence in the matter. The charter issued to the colony had not dispossessed the Mohegan.[214] In its decision to

210 Colin G. Calloway, *Pen and Ink Witchcraft. Treaties and Treaty Making in American Indian History* (Oxford University Press 2013), 48.

211 McHugh, *Aboriginal Societies*, 100. The vocabulary denoting the relationship was very varied, the Indians sometimes characterised as "alien friends" or "subject nations" with the implication, however, that at least they had sufficient identity to contract with the crown, 99–102.

212 For the text of the 1763 Proclamation, see e.g. Terry Fenge & Jim Aldridge, *Keeping Promises. The Royal Proclamation of 1763, Aboriginal Rights and Treaties in Canada* (McGill–Queen's University Press 2015), 201–6.

213 Richard R. Johnson, 'Growth and Mastery. British North America, 1690–1748', in P. J. Marshall & Alaine Low (eds), *The Oxford History of the British Empire*, vol. II: *The Eighteenth Century* (Oxford University Press 1998), 284.

214 According to the attorney-general, the act of dispossessing the Mohegan by the colonial government was therefore "illegall and void". AG to the Council of Trade

set up a commission to decide the substance of the appeal, the crown used language suggesting the Mohegan were allies rather than subjects, even as they were under its dominion.[215] The commission decided in favour of the appellants. The Mohegan had "at all times served the interests of the crown of England and the colony of Connecticut [and had] *faithfully kept their leagues and treaties* with the said colony".[216] In its appeal to the Privy Council, however, the colony claimed that these lands had been attained by conquest before the charter had been granted. For years the settlers had laboured over and improved them. Theories about Indian rights, it claimed, were too varied and unclear for anything definite to be derived from them.[217] The Privy Council eventually recognised the Mohegan as a "Nation" enjoying treaty rights and "politically independent from the colony though under the dominion of the crown". Another commission was to determine the boundaries.[218] No effect was ever given to the decision on the ground, however, and in 1743 another commission determined by a narrow majority that the colony had set aside sufficient land for the Mohegan.[219]

The *Mohegan case* did not resolve the land rights questions, juxtaposing the views of the crown to those of the settlers. Indian rights were conceived in view of diplomatic needs and American land policies. The colony, again, appealed to cumulative arguments from discovery, conquest and treaty rights, as well as the alleged individual rights of the settlers derived from their labour. In practice, relations between the two sides would be determined by their actions on the ground, squatting and labour above all, to be constantly renegotiated. Although the Mohegan's right of appeal was affirmed, their substantive claims were eventually defeated.

The need to establish a more ordered relationship with the Indians arose during the Seven Years' War when it dawned on the English that they would have to fight not only against the French but against native

and Plantations, 29 February 1704, in Cecil Headlam (ed.), *Calendar of State Papers, Colonial, America and West Indies*, vol. 22, *1704-5* (London, His Majesty's Stationery Office 1916), § 146 (61).

215 Yirush, *Settlers, Liberty, and Empire*, 120.

216 The quotes are from the unpublished unanimous commission decision, as reported in ibid., 122.

217 For this argument by the Connecticut clergyman John Bulkley, see Fitzmaurice, *Sovereignty, Property and Empire*, 173–81.

218 Yirush, *Settlers, Liberty, and Empire*, 125.

219 Ibid., 140.

communities unless encroachments by settlers would cease.[220] It was also feared that further western expansion would strike at British exports owing to the distance that would now make inevitable the rise of a local manufacturing industry.[221] Accordingly, the 1763 Proclamation provided that all further purchases from the Indians were to be made by government bodies, the Indian side was to be represented by persons authorised by the tribes and all settlement west of the Ohio–Mississippi watershed would be prohibited.[222] The proclamation had little effect. The western limit was agreed at Fort Stanwix in 1768 without the presence of Cherokees and Shawnees, who had significant claims on the relevant areas.[223] Illegal sales skyrocketed and the military was needed to protect settlers who found themselves as squatters. Private interests and lobbying undermined government policy as many officials joined as shareholders in the land companies.[224] One of the speculators, George Washington, regarded the proclamation merely as a "temporary expedient to quiet the minds of the Indians".[225] As a last measure, the British government decided in 1774 to extend the boundaries of its recently acquired Quebec province into the Ohio–Mississippi hinterland to block further western expansion.[226]

The settlers were furious; they wanted to transact with the Indians as before. Their position was supported by an infamous legal opinion produced by two successive lord chancellors (the so-called Pratt [Camden] & Yorke memorandum) that explained that a grant from the crown had not been necessary for the East India Company to purchase lands from native rulers on the Indian peninsula. The circulated version omitted the East India context and was presented as proof that the crown's American policy had been *ultra vires*.[227] The proclamation was portrayed as an illegal encroachment on the colonists'

[220] See especially Jack M. Sosin, *Whitehall and the Wilderness. The Middle West in British Colonial Policy 1760–1775* (University of Nebraska Press 1991), 27–51 (stressing that the territorial provisions of the 1763 Proclamation had received de facto effect during the war so that the Board of Trade in London simply gave imprimatur to a de facto situation).

[221] Williams, *American Indian*, 234.

[222] For the process in London that led to the 1763 Proclamation, see Sosin, *Whitehall*, 52–78.

[223] See Calloway, *Pen & Ink Witchcraft*, 49–95.

[224] A good analysis is in Banner, *How the Indians Lost Their Lands*, 92–111.

[225] Quoted in Sosin, *Whitehall*, 107.

[226] Quebec Act of 22 June 1774 (14 Geo.III c. 83). See ibid., 240–55.

[227] The story of the Pratt–Yorke memorandum is told e.g. in Williams, *American Indian*, 275–80; Banner, *How the Indians Lost Their Lands*, 102–3.

liberties. The dispute was intensified by the enlargement of British military presence in the inland colonies as well as by the Stamp Act of 1764 and accompanying legislation. The most important consequence of the proclamation was, however, that it affirmed crown sovereignty over the lands east *and* west of the Appalachians – Indian rights across the continent were defined by and derived from crown grant.[228] On the other hand, the rights of occupancy that the crown now granted to the tribes present at Fort Stanwix came to be seen as something less than property because, for the first time, the Indians would not be able to sell to whom they wanted.[229] Paradoxically, it was now the settlers who appealed to the natural right of native inhabitants to own and sell their lands to the settlers independently of the crown. This was part of a larger, developing view among the settlers that they had come to America not by conquest and their life was not dependent on the vicissitudes of the prerogative – but that they had entered a kind of state of nature where they were free to determine the conditions of their lives with the Indians.[230] In the 1760s, they still agreed to allegiance to the crown as the head of the empire, though not to parliament in Westminster where they had no representation.[231] It was the apparent repudiation by the crown itself of that compromise in 1773 that pressed the colonists to follow the natural right argument to its conclusion.

### *Asserting Sovereignty: 1609–1763*

Seventeenth-century American colonies were private enterprises not established according to any comprehensive design. If Englishmen thought of them at all, they saw them as "economic units intended to contribute to the prosperity of England and to provide it with a solid claim to the vast riches of the New World".[232] Because the units were understood as metropolitan outposts, it was easy to provide them with

[228] According to Fitzmaurice, crown officials accepted that no actual sovereignty of the crown west of the Appalachians existed. *Sovereignty, Property and Empire*, 184. But the minimal presence of the crown there did not prevent it from claiming dominion and the illegality of private land activity.

[229] Williams, *American Indian*, 229.

[230] The increasing use of natural law arguments in support of the colonists is well described in Yirush, *Settlers, Liberty, and Empire*, 229–62 and Fitzmaurice, *Sovereignty, Property and Empire*, 189–93 (with especial reference to the writings of Richard Blunt).

[231] See John Pocock, 'Political Thought in the English-Speaking Atlantic 1760–1790. Part I: The Imperial Crisis', in John Pocock (ed.), *The Varieties of British Political Thought 1500–1800* (Cambridge University Press 1993), 262.

[232] Greene, *Negotiated Authorities*, 43.

loosely defined powers and to promise the settlers that they would, in the words of the Virginia Charter of 1609, enjoy "all Liberties, Franchizes, and Immunities of Free Denizens and natural Subjects within any of our other Dominions ... as if they had been abiding and born within this our Realm of England, or in any other of our Dominions". This famous clause was always referred to in order to argue that tightening metropolitan control violated the legal status of the colonists, their rights of property and self-government, including the right to be tried by a jury.[233]

Although metropolitan authorities frequently left the colonies to govern themselves, they did sometimes intervene. Before 1763 such intervention was rarely pushed to the point of open revolt. In wartime, the loyalty of settlers was attained by not insisting on too literal an implementation of metropolitan regulations. The process of reviewing colonial acts was flexible, and the system of commissions and instructions to the governors allowed the emergence of a kind of constitutional pluralism in the British Atlantic.[234] The settlements lay far away and efficient implementation of metropolitan priorities was in any case often impossible. In practice, the colonial assemblies gradually grew into the most important institutions of colonial governance. The governors sent to watch over metropolitan interests were often too dependent on local actors – they received their salary from the colony – to provide a powerful counterforce.

It was not that the Stuarts lacked interest in the colonies. The Committee of Foreign Plantations set up by Charles I in 1634 did not achieve much, however. During the Civil War and the Interregnum it was parliament's turn to assert its desire to control the colonies, especially to quell royalist rebellion.[235] But even now the internal government of the colonies also remained largely untouched. This situation changed with the Restoration as Charles II began to allocate new territories to loyal nobles. He also established a permanent Plantations Commission (1660–3), and in 1665–70 directed colonial matters to the Privy Council. In 1675 the Councils of Foreign Plantations and Trade were reconstituted as "Lords of Trade and Plantations" to supervise all colonial government. A short-lived

[233] Second Virginia Charter, 23 May 1609.

[234] This is stressed in Daniel J. Hulsebosch, 'The Origin and Nature of Colonial Grievances', in Stephen Foster (ed.), *British North America in the Seventeenth and Eighteenth Centuries* (Oxford University Press 2013), 289–316.

[235] See Keith, *Constitutional History*, 48–58.

Dominion of New England was likewise established in 1686 without any local representation at all.[236] The Navigation Act was extended to bar non-English ships from colonial ports and to prevent foreigners from trading in the colonies. Enumerated products were to be brought to England for re-exportation and offices for collectors and surveyors were created to enforce the provisions against the settlers' mounting hostility.[237] Colonial manufacture was suppressed by high duties so as to prevent competition with English products and to limit American production to raw materials. Credit was to be received only from English sources at interests determined by the latter.[238]

Nor were the colonists left in peace after the Glorious Revolution. William followed the policy of his predecessors, though he did not seek to suppress the colonial assemblies. An act of 1696 required oaths from governors of chartered colonies to implement customs regulations and created a system of vice-admiralty courts to enforce metropolitan policies, as noted in the previous Chapter.[239] Although the king might have wanted to do away with Atlantic pluralism once and for all, this was prevented by parliament eventually forcing the king to establish a Board of Trade to allow mercantile and landowning interests to influence colonial policy. Men such as Charles Davenant and Josiah Child played an important role in the board by articulating the mercantilist principles on which its work was to be based. More detailed instructions were given to the governors. The board took the initiative to withdraw private charters, as was done with Bahamas and Massachusetts Bay, and when this was not possible, to buy the territories back to the crown.[240] In a strongly worded declaration in March 1701, the board stated that the colonies had failed to respect the conditions laid down in

[236] On efforts during the Restoration to control the colonies, see especially ibid., 59–132. See also Greene, *Peripheries*, 13–15.

[237] See e.g. Keith, *Constitutional History*, 74–7; Claire Priest, 'Law and Commerce, 1580–1815', in Michael Grossberg & Christopher Tomlins (eds), *The Cambridge History of Law in America* (Cambridge University Press 2008), 406–7, 414–15.

[238] For a useful summary of the measures, see Priest, 'Law and Commerce, 1580–1815', 406–15.

[239] A limited number of such courts had existed already previously, but now new ones were created and all of them received new commissions from the crown. For the vigorous opposition to admiralty courts by the settlers, see Keith, *Constitutional History*, 137, 261–265. William Penn himself once insisted that the creation of an admiralty court in Pennsylvania violated his patent. See Matthew P. Harrington, 'The Legacy of the Colonial Vice-Admiralty Courts (Part I)', 26 *Journal of Maritime Law & Commerce* (1995), 595–600.

[240] Keith, *Constitutional History*, 133.

their charters and that their laws had sometimes been "repugnant to the Laws of England". They had failed to comply with the Navigation Acts, kept no military forces and felt no need to consider the needs of their neighbours. The charters were to be "reassumed by the Crown and these colonies be put in the same state and dependency as your Majestie's other Plantations".[241]

But the board's efforts remained largely inconsequential. During the Walpole era (1720–48), little was done to follow up the earlier measures. Customs revenue increased and trade flourished. The system of communications and grievances operated smoothly, allowing the government to concentrate on other matters.[242] Most of the statutes submitted for review by the Privy Council were accepted. But even when the council disallowed an act – such as a New York statute of 1691 enlarging the powers of the assembly – its opinion had often no practical result.[243] Governors, too, often remained passive. Without independent funds and a military force they could hardly oppose colonists determined to follow their own lights.[244] During the period of increasing activism after 1748, the colonies often found support from parliament, which refused to give royal instructions the force of law.[245] By that time, representative institutions in America were already ruled by a self-confident elite with political experience, capacity to challenge royal instructions and ability to negotiate with virtual equality with metropolitan authorities.[246]

That parliament in mid-eighteenth century lacked determination to crush the self-determination process was hardly surprising. The landowners

241 Cecil Headlam (ed.), *Calendar of State Papers Colonial, America and West Indies*, vol. 19: *1701* (London, His Majesty's Stationery Office 1910), 141, 142–3. See further the detailed overview of all the colonies in their ability to protect themselves, in their relations with the Indians and with respect to their government, suggesting that all the colonies be put under one "Lord Lieutenant or Captain General from whom all others [sic] Governors of particular provinces should receive their orders", in *Representation of the Lords Commissioners for Trade and Plantations to the King [microform]: on the state of the British colonies in North America* (1721), especially 41–2 and 35–42.

242 The beneficial nature of the "salutary neglect" has been questioned. See Keith Mason, 'Britain and the Administration of the American Colonies', in H. T. Dickinson (ed.), *Britain and the American Revolution* (London, Longman 1998), 28.

243 Hulsebosch, 'The Origin and Nature of Colonial Grievances', 295, 297–9.

244 Even where the instructions to the governors during the Restoration encouraged the latter to veto colonial legislation, they rarely did this, wishing rather to avoid open conflict with the settler elite. Labaree, *Royal Government in America*, 218–23.

245 For the efforts at tightening control by the Board of Trade in 1748–56, see Mason, 'Britain and Administration of the American Colonies', 36–9.

246 Greene, *Negotiated Authorities*.

that stood behind the coup of 1688 were aligned with the large plantation-owners in the New World.[247] The old division between colonial producers and British merchants broke down at several points.[248] Colonial ports began to be populated by an expanding local merchant class. As Britain's European trade declined from 74 to 33 percent in the course of the century, colonial trade became increasingly vital, contributing to the gradual emergence of a wholly transatlantic commercial culture. Moreover, the financial revolution turned London merchant bankers into principal investors of the transatlantic trade, the fastest-growing aspect of the British economy.[249] Planters in the Caribbean and on the mainland purchased everything by credit. The alliance between landowners and merchants transgressed the simple dichotomy between metropolis and colony and prevented its intensification to the point of breach. Increasing the colonies' tax burden, for example, would have immediately struck at the lucrative Atlantic trade – mercantile lobbies were active and colonies fast to respond with boycotts of metropolitan goods.[250] Active intervention in the colonies would also have contributed to the growth of state debt that worried a number of observers.[251] Only after the enormous expense of the Seven Years' War had made the public debt skyrocket did it finally begin to seem necessary that the Atlantic colonies share in the costs of a war that had, after all, to do with their security as well.

From the perspective of Westminster, colonies were above all corporations whose rights were based on the articles of incorporation, mere plantations and sources of raw materials to be used for enhancing the prosperity of the mother country. They could be withdrawn

[247] Up to 1867 members of the landowning elite counted for 75% of the membership of the House of Commons. Linda Colley, *Britons, Forging the Nation 1707–1837* (2nd edn, London, Pimlico 2003), 61.

[248] See P. J. Marshall, *The Making and Unmaking of Empires. Britain, India and America c. 1750–1783* (Oxford University Press 2005), 20–5.

[249] In 1700–1 British exports to America counted for 11% and in 1772–3 38% of British trade. The value of imports from North America and West Indies, in 1772–3, again was 39%. Nuala Zahedieh, 'Economy', in David Armitage & Michael Braddick (eds), *The British Atlantic World 1500–1800* (London, Palgrave 2002), 58, 60.

[250] For the special interests lobbying in the House of Commons, see John Brewer, *The Sinews of Power. War, Money and the English State 1688–1783* (Harvard University Press 1988), 231–49.

[251] Between 1700 and 1783, the national debt rose from £14 million to £245 million. Peacetime interest payments were more than half of public expenditure. Ibid., 114. See also P. J. Cain & A. G. Hopkins, *British Imperialism. Innovation and Expansion 1688–1914* (New York, Longman 1993), 74

or modified at the discretion of the crown.[252] This was not at all how the settlers viewed the matter. According to them, the charters constituted a contract under which they would improve the lands in the harsh conditions of the New World in exchange for the ancient rights of Englishmen, vested especially in the colonial assemblies. This argument was made with great force in the book by Jeremiah Dummer, "[w]idely regarded as the most brilliant Harvard scholar of his generation".[253] The *Defence of the New England Charters* (1721) constructed the charter rights of Massachusetts, Connecticut and Rhode Island as "Praemiums for Services to be perform'd, and therefore [...] as Grants upon a valuable *Consideration*".[254] The settlers had with great expense, endless disappointments and disasters taken into use lands that proved very valuable to England. If the crown were to withdraw the patents, "it will take away the Whole it gave, and deprive the Patentees of the only Recompense they were to have for all their Toils and Fatigues".[255]

In due course, the view of a contract between the crown and the settlers would be consecrated as constitutional custom.[256] Any effort by Westminster to dictate the forms of land-use or taxation would violate the contract. The settlers referred to *Calvin's case* where Coke had stated that wherever Englishmen would find themselves in conquered territory, they, unlike the indigenous inhabitants, were "capable of lands in the kingdom or country conquered ... and have the like privileges and benefits there, as they may have in England".[257] This did not mean that all rights of Englishmen would automatically follow them abroad, only the most important ones, namely those of property and representation. Settlers understood Coke's statement that no succeeding king could alter the laws "without parliament" to

[252] Greene, *Constitutional Origins*, 97, 111; Jack P. Greene, 'Empire and Identity', in P. J. Marshall & Alaine Low (eds), *The Oxford History of the British Empire,* vol. II: *The Eighteenth Century* (Oxford University Press 1998), 223–5.

[253] Stephen Foster & Evan Haefeli, 'British North America in the Empire. An Overview', in Stephen Foster (ed.), *British North America in the Seventeenth and Eighteenth Centuries* (Oxford University Press 2013), 35. On Dummer, see also Yirush, *Settlers, Liberty, and Empire*, 96–112.

[254] Jeremiah Dummer, *The Defence of the New England Charters* (London, Wilkins 1721), 7.

[255] Ibid., 15.

[256] Greene, *Constitutional Origins*, 127–9.

[257] Coke, *Calvin's case*, 639. In other words, an Englishman wherever he resided "shall be subject to all services and public charges in this realm, as any [other] Englishman", 655.

mean the colonial assemblies, not parliament in Westminster where, of course, they had no representation.[258]

The settlers frequently made the parallel between themselves and the rebellious nobles of 1688. Was the government now not behaving precisely in the manner of the Stuarts? In due course, colonial propagandists began to argue that their rights were independent of the charters, that they were inherent, based on natural law and not eliminable even by withdrawal of the charters.[259] Metropolitan bodies disagreed. For them, the assemblies' powers depended on royal favour that could always be withdrawn; the analogy with Westminster was an "intoxicated" dream.[260] Mostly, the view from Britain was that the prerogative and English laws applied without restrictions in the colonies, a position for which some support could be received from Coke as well as from Sir Matthew Hale.[261] But there was never any coherent view in London about the status of the common law in the colonies.[262] A 1720 memorandum to the Council of Trade stated that "The Common Law of England is the Common law of the Plantations, and all the Statutes in affirmance of the Common Law pass'd in England antecedent to the settlement of any Colony are in force for that Colony."[263] Such statements would buttress the the colonists' view that the only legitimate way to intervene in their properties was by securing their consent, i.e. that the colonists were either to have representation in London or be allowed to legislate for themselves.

"At every stage in the controversy to 1776 and beyond, Americans claimed to defend property rights."[264] They were inspired by the Lockean view that the security of property was the foundation of political government. But they could also look to Blackstone's famous definition of "property" as "that sole and despotic dominion which one man claims and exercises over external things of the world, in total

[258] On what has been called "Coke's Imperial Constitution", see Hulsebosch, 'The Ancient Constitution', 439, especially 458–79. For the very large literature examining the colonists' claim to enjoy the ancient rights of Englishmen, see e.g. Greene, *Peripheries*, 23–8; Greene, *Negotiated Authorities*, 59–62.

[259] Greene, *Peripheries*, 15–16, 20–3, 25, 35–7.

[260] Ibid., 35.

[261] See further, Yirush, *Settlers, Liberty, and Empire*, 40–2.

[262] Ibid., 49.

[263] Cecil Headlam (ed.), *Calendar of State Papers Colonial, America and West Indies*, vol. 32: *1720–1721* (London, His Majesty's Stationery Office 1933), 53.

[264] P. J. Marshall, 'Parliament and Property Rights in the Late Eighteenth Century British Experience', in John Brewer & Susan Staves (eds), *Early Modern Conceptions of Property* (London, Routledge 1995), 533.

exclusion of the right of any other individual in the universe".[265] Blackstone himself did not think that the common law had authority in the colonies and that even statutes applied only when specifically so intended. The result was a great variety of English laws that applied across the colonial world, but colonists felt a "near-obsessive concern for security of property".[266] They shared a core sense of property that aligned with "freedom" and that could never be taken away. If it were, then they would no longer be citizens but slaves; even the expropriation of one penny where there was no limit to that power would open the door for the expropriation of everything.

## Sovereignty from Property Rights 1763–76

Having fought alongside the English in the Seven Years' War (1756–63), the settlers felt they deserved recognition for their sufferings. To their great disappointment, however, the government now intensified its control efforts.[267] The receipt of Canada, Florida and Grenada brought into the empire large, potentially hostile populations. There were new administrative responsibilities and colonial defences needed to be improved. The victory had been attained at great cost, some of which was to be paid by the colonies. With the public debt soaring at almost £140 million parliament was determined that the least the colonies could do was to pay for the billeting of 10,000 English troops in American fortresses.[268] The resulting Stamp Act in 1764 triggered the process that led many colonists "reluctantly to conclude that protecting their economic interests and security for their liberties could never be achieved within the British Empire".[269] As it withdrew the Stamp Act in March 1766, parliament simultaneously declared:

[265] William Blackstone, *Commentaries on the Laws of England in Four Books* (2 vols., Philadelphia, Lippincott 1893), II, 2 (1).

[266] David Tomas Konig, 'Regionalism in Early American Law', in Michael Grossberg & Christopher Tomlins (eds), *The Cambridge History of Law in America* (Cambridge University Press 2008), 158, 144–77.

[267] See e.g. Stephen Conway, 'Britain and the Revolutionary Crisis, 1763–1791', in P. J. Marshall & Alaine Low (eds), *The Oxford History of the British Empire*, vol. II: *The Eighteenth Century* (Oxford University Press 1998), 325–46.

[268] On the British perception of the role of the American colonies after 1763, see e.g. John Derry, 'Government Policy and the American Colonies 1760–1776', in H. T. Dickinson (ed.), *Britain and the American Revolution* (London, Longman 1998), 44–63.

[269] Greene, *Negotiated Authorities*, 76.

That the said colonies and plantations in *America* have been, are, and of right ought to be subordinate unto, and dependent upon the imperial crown and parliament of *Great Britain*; and that the King's majesty, by and with the advice and consent of the lords spiritual and temporal, and commons of *Great Britain*, in parliament assembled, had, has had, and of right ought to have, full power and authority to make laws and statutes of sufficient force and validity to bind the colonies and people of *America*, subjects of the crown of *Great Britain*, in all cases whatsoever.[270]

But little followed from that statement. Already in the previous May Virginia's House of Burgesses had declared that the settlers enjoyed "all the liberties privileges, franchises and immunities that have at any time been held and enjoyed, and possessed by the people of Great Britain". And the many declarations of rights that had been passed by the colonial assemblies in the course of the years – e.g. the Bill of Privileges in Jamaica (1677) and the Charter of Liberties of New York (1683) – had been modelled so as to highlight that it was an *English* tradition the colonists were appealing to. In fact, "[p]olitical discourse in the thirteen colonies was almost without exception British political discourse".[271] The principle of "no taxation without representation" was repeated across the colonial assemblies.

But parliament never planned to destroy the liberties of the colonists or to reduce them to slavery. An extraordinary back-and-forth characterised British policy. New measures were withdrawn as soon as they were made, governments kept changing and few politicians understood the Americans' anxiety about their freedoms and properties. When the government threatened to make non-implementation of parliamentary statutes high treason, it breached the essentially commercial traditions of the empire and related principles of individual enterprise.[272] The colonists were unable to understand the metropolitan reaction. John Dickinson (1732–1808), the 'Penman of the Revolution' and the future president of Pennsylvania, declared that "Great Britain cannot injure us by taking away our commerce without hurting herself *immediately*."[273] The good of the empire, he believed, required that the settlers produce, trade and govern themselves freely. That had been the content of the

[270] Declaratory Act, 18 March 1766, text in avalon.law.yale.edu/18th_century/declaratory_act_1766.asp.

[271] Marshall, *Making and Unmaking of Empires*, 43.

[272] Greene, *Negotiated Authorities*, 59.

[273] John Dickinson, *Essay on the Constitutional Power of Great Britain over the Colonies in America* (With the Resolves of the Committee for the Province of Pennsylvania) (Philadelphia 1744), 412–13.

original agreement that persuaded the white settlers to begin life in America, and as they never tired of explaining. What distinguished them was their freedom.

Many believed likewise in London, too. The anxious debate on empire and freedom led Adam Smith and Edmund Burke, alongside many others, to stress the right of self-government as what distinguished the English from all other empires.[274] Without freedom, English colonies would degenerate into tyrannies and lose the valuable service they gave to the metropolis. The Stamp and Sugar Acts and the other legislative measures of the 1760s and 1770s did not emerge from a dark conspiracy but from an effort to distribute the burdens among the empire's constituent parts in a way that many regarded as more just, though views predictably differed. Parliament never seriously deliberated the expropriation of the colonial charters. After all, the landed elite owned four-fifths of the land in the British Isles: "Their political, economic, and cultural hegemony [was] exemplified by their pre-eminence in government, Parliament, the law, the Church, the civil service, and the armed forces."[275] An ideologically based attack on property rights in the colonies was inconceivable. The two sides of the Atlantic were bound together by an ideology of "liberty and trade" that prevented any drastic tampering with property rights in America.

In a strongly worded and heavily footnoted *Essay on Constitutional Power* of 1774, Dickinson enlisted the "immutable and inalienable rights of human nature" together with the settlers' charter grants as the basis for drawing the line between the powers of parliament in London and the settler assemblies.[276] The parliamentary policies of the previous decade, he thought, had been based on the view that there was no line at all – a situation that he, like many other colonists, depicted as a slippery slope to slavery. Such a position rendered the settlers themselves into property, "unworthy of freedom".[277] If the king of England was the ruler of the colonies he was so because the colonies had so contracted. They had never contracted to subject themselves to parliamentary legislation in their internal affairs; those were matters of the common law, as applicable

[274] See e.g. Greene, 'Empire and Identity', 222–3.

[275] David Sugarman & Ronnie Warrington, 'The Equity of Redemption', in John Brewer & Susan Staves (eds), *Early Modern Conceptions of Property* (London, Routledge 1995), 121.

[276] Dickinson, *Constitutional Power*, 361–3.

[277] Ibid., 330, 346.

in the colonies, and of right and custom.[278] Why should the right of property be "the solid foundation of [the British] constitution and an empty name in her colonies"?

When the Continental Congress met in 1774 and the thirteen colonies set up the economic boycott against Britain, the momentum for pacific settlement had passed. From the perspective of Westminster, the Congress was wholly illegal. The Coercive Acts, as well as the rejection by George III of the olive branch petition drafted by Dickinson in July 1775, were seen as parts of a tyrannical breach of the contract between the metropolis and the colonies. Their view was, as explained in the Declaration of Independence in July 1776, that the king himself had been the source of "repeated injuries and usurpations, all having in direct object the establishment of an absolute Tyranny over these States".[279]

## Into a New Commercial Order: Pownall

By now, increasing numbers of observers saw the whole problem as wrongly posed. If the empire's power was based on the structure of its economy, then it might be best served by setting aside its territorial ambitions. After all, expansion was originally organised by a jurisdictional and not a territorial order. Why not reimagine transatlantic empire as a jurisdictional, commercial system serving its both sides equally? Adam Smith had already suggested that the independence of the colonies, with intense commercial links with Britain, might actually prove best for everyone. This position was taken by the former governor of Massachusetts, Thomas Pownall (1722–1805) in a series of publications that commented on transatlantic relations from the perspective of a theory of natural law where liberty and trade converged as the twin forces of political society. In five successive editions of his *Administration of the Colonies* (1764–74) Pownall tried to canvass a new constitutional system for the transatlantic sphere that would take account of the interests of both sides. The liberty of the colonists, he argued, could be best guaranteed under the crown if both sides were only willing to compromise. By the time of the book's fifth edition in 1774, war had

[278] Ibid., 386–94. Like others, Dickinson accepted the extension of parliamentary powers to the colonies' trade and external affairs, however.

[279] Declaration of Independence, 4 July 1776, e.g. in www.archives.gov/founding-docs/declaration-transcript.

begun and Pownall could no longer expect a compromise. Instead, he appealed for European statesmen to:

> adopt a system whose basis thus lies in nature; and which by natural means alone (if not perverted) must lead to a general dominion, founded in the general interest and prosperity of the commercial world.[280]

Pownall contrasted heavily regulated colonial commerce with the situation where nations move naturally "by a general, common and mutual principle of attraction". This was the way of the future where the "general commercial interest which is most extensive, necessary and permanent, settles and commands the market". Universal free trade would become "the foundation of commercial dominion which, whether we attend to it or not, will be formed". This required giving up the subordinate status of the American colonies and enlisting their enormous economic potential in a comprehensive pursuit for a general "system" with Britain as its centre. Henceforth:

> Great Britain may be no more considered as the kingdom of this Isle only, with many appendages, colonies, settlements, and other extraneous parts; but as a GRAND MARINE DOMINION, CONSISTING OF OUR POSSESSIONS IN THE ATLANTIC, AND IN AMERICA, UNITED IN A ONE [sic] CENTER; WHERE THE SEAT OF GOVERNMENT IS.[281]

In 1780, as there was no longer any prospect of re-establishing Britain's American empire, Pownall suggested a complete overhaul of the old European system, associated with balance of trade, secret diplomacy, war and national interest. Addressing his new work to all European sovereigns, he noted that America had now become too great a naval power for any nation to subordinate. But the Americans possessed a "spirit of investigation" that will lead them to exclude monopolies and privilege free trade in a way to make America eventually a free port to Europe.[282] European sovereigns should seize upon the occasion and by giving up territorial ambitions accept what Pownall called "the principle of general communion, genuine spirit of life of commerce".[283] With footnotes to Adam Smith, he envisioned a new system based on "nature", namely the realisation that

[280] Thomas Pownall, *The Administration of the Colonies* (5th edn, London, Walter 1774), I 11.

[281] Ibid., 10, 5–10.

[282] Thomas Pownall, *A Memorial most Humbly Addressed to the Sovereigns of Europe on the Present State of Affairs between the Old and the New World* (2nd edn, London 1780), 92.

[283] Ibid., 103.

> if Nature has so formed Man, if policy has so formed Society, that each labouring in his destined and definite and line of labour, produces a surplus of supply, it is the Law of Nature and of Nations, it is of perfect justice as well as policy, that men and nations should be free, reciprocally to interchange, and respectively as their wants mark the course, these surpluses, that this Communion of Nations with each other ... ought to be thus enjoyed and exercised to the benefit and interest of each, and to the common good of all.[284]

Pownall proposed a Congress of the "great Trading Bodies of Europe" at the end of the present crisis, a Council of Commerce for all Europe and North America. It would be headed by a "standing perpetual Council of deliberation and advice, and a set of judicial administration common to all". Owing to the unsettled and disputed character of the law, it should also include a Great and General Court of Admiralty.[285] As soon as the present crisis ends, he wrote, the sovereigns should send their ministers to meet "with power and instructions to form some general laws and establishment on the ground of Universal Commerce". This should include three types of provisions: how to manage the system of free seas; how to organise navigational rights taking into account the present claims of maritime states; and a provision for what Pownall called "*Libertas universalis Commerciorum*, free ports and free markets, in open equal traffic".[286]

After the peace of 1783 British merchants were able to recover their markets almost immediately and colonial produce continued to arrive in Britain in nearly as great quantities as before, suggesting that territorial empire was not at all necessary for enjoying the economic benefits with which it had been defended.[287] Although no general arrangement of course followed, and the Navigation Acts continued in force until the 1820s, the bilateral treaty of 1783 contributed to new thinking about global political and legal order. The rights of property would still need protection from the sovereign. But there was an increasing push away from old diplomacy and the associated system of bounties and monopolies, as Pownall suggested. If the Americans were to take the initiative, he further speculated, this would be the beginning of a new era: "America will then be the *Arbitress* of the commercial, and perhaps ... the *Mediatrix of peace*, and of the political business of the world."[288]

[284] Ibid., 115. [285] Ibid., 121. [286] Ibid., 123–4.

[287] P. J. Marshall, 'Britain Without America – A Second Empire?', in P. J. Marshall & Alaine Low (eds), *The Oxford History of the British Empire*, vol. II: *The Eighteenth Century* (Oxford University Press 1998), 585.

[288] Pownall, *A Memorial*, 77.

## Another Kind of Property: Slaves

If the free settlers had come to rely on English ideas of liberty and the rule of law, for a large class of immigrants, law pointed in another direction. The first African slaves were bought by Virginia settlers from Dutch traders in 1619. The ratio of indentured servants in relation to African slaves decreased rapidly. In 1705 their number in Virginia remained around 2,500 while that of African slaves had risen to 16,000.[289] In the West Indies – Bahamas, Barbados, the Leeward Islands and Jamaica after its conquest from Spain – dependence on African slaves had always been greater owing to the needs of sugar production. By the end of the seventeenth century, Barbados alone already had 50,000 black slaves and the economic significance of slave-run production for the English state had become huge. Sugar and tobacco would represent something between 20 and 30 percent of the value of its annual revenue, and the planter class turned into a formidable political force: "by the middle decades of the eighteenth century, the West India interest represented the most influential colonial lobby in London, and absentee sugar planters held several dozen seats in the House of Commons".[290]

It was not easy to integrate slavery in the English ideology of liberty and the rule of law. One story was that because Christ himself had lived under Roman rule but kept silent about Roman slavery, there could be nothing unChristian in this practice.[291] But few questions were posed regarding its acceptability in the Caribbean. The islands had been received by conquest, so that under the doctrine laid out by Coke and confirmed by Blackstone, English law would not apply and the islands' labour regime could be arranged as the settlers wished. Moreover, reference could always be made to Coke's *Institutes of the Laws of England* (1628) according to which "the constitutions of nations" provided that war captives, instead of being killed, could be taken as slaves and that God had agreed for servitude also for such other crimes as

289 Tomlins, *Freedom Bound*, 271. Useful statistics are also to be found in Thomas D. Morris, *Southern Slavery and the Law 1619–1860* (University of North Carolina Press 1996), 3–6.

290 Christopher L. Brown, 'The Politics of Slavery', in David Armitage & Michael J. Braddick (eds), *The British Atlantic World 1500–1800* (London, Macmillan 2002), 216–17.

291 William Goodell, *The American Slave Code in Theory and Practice* (London, Clarke etc. 1854), 11.

dishonouring one's parents.[292] To the extent that the slaves could been seen as captives in African wars, the settlers and company men could always reason that buying enslaved humans was different from enslaving them. Charles Davenant, for example, simply noted that the slaves received from Africa came from "the perpetual wars among some or other of them; and the victors do commonly sell their vanquished neighbours, as well as their own slaves, to such European merchants as they happen to be most in friendship with at that time".[293] Astonishingly, a racialist system of plantation slavery arose in the Atlantic colonies without a clear basis either in the common law, colonial legislation or the *lex mercatoria*.[294] Even a late edition of Molloy's popular work on mercantile customs made only a fleeting reference to "Virginia and other plantations" within a general treatment of freedom and bondage under natural, Roman and English law.[295] But colonies had been set up under the royal prerogative as private realms; it was not for Westminster to intervene in the way they were ruled. Significantly, the requirement that colonists' laws should not be "repugnant" to those of England was never seriously invoked to challenge the colonial codes on slavery.[296]

The history of British transatlantic slavery begins with the settlement of uninhabited Bahamas in the 1620s for the purposes of tobacco production. The patent granted to the earl of Carlisle in 1627 gave him proprietorship over all of the English Caribbean, including Barbados, with the same palatine rights of jurisdiction and royalty as granted to the bishops of Durham.[297] This meant, according to

[292] Edward Coke, *First Part of the Institutes of the Law of England* (2 vols, London, Clarke 1823), I (116b). See also Robin Blackburn, *The Making of New World Slavery. From the Baroque to the Modern 1492–1800* (London, Verso 2010), 236–9.

[293] Charles Davenant, 'Reflections upon the Constitution and Management of the Trade to Africa', in C. Whitworth (ed.), *The Political and Commercial Works of Charles D'avenant* (5 vols, London, Horsefield 1771), V, 114.

[294] See the very useful Jonathan A. Bush, 'Free to Enslave. The Foundations of Colonial American Slave Law', 5 *Yale Journal of Law and the Humanities* (1993), 417–70.

[295] Charles Molloy, *De Iure Maritimo et Navali, or a Treatise of the Affairs Maritime and of Commerce* (7th ed., London, Walthoe 1722 [1676]), 383, 380–91. See also Bush, 'Free to Enslave', 452–6.

[296] See Alan Watson, *Slave Law in the Americas* (University of Georgia Press 1989), 636. The point about "privatization to permit unfreedom" is usefully made in Bush, 'Free to Enslave', 460, 460–5.

[297] Barbados was the object of a long legal battle between Carlisle and the earl of Pembroke and their successors, with royal favour and legal justice switching from one side to the other. Williamson, *Caribbee Islands*, 40. Force was eventually needed

Blackstone, "as fully as the king hath in his palace; regalem potestatem in omnibus."[298] The intense work regime that was required by large-scale sugar production led Barbadian planters to replace indentured servants by Africans with the result that in 1653 there were already 20,000 black slaves on the island, outnumbering the 8,000 indentured servants and 10,000 freeholders and freemen, mostly former servants.[299] With such numbers, fear of slave rebellion grew – one had already taken place on Providence island in 1638 – which seemed to call for increasingly draconic discipline. For that purpose, the new Barbadian Assembly enacted an "Act for the Better Ordering and Governing of Negroes" (1661) that drew upon sixteenth-century English statutes on policing of beggars and vagabonds.[300] The act did not regulate the status, sale or purchase of slaves. Instead, it made slave behaviour a matter of public concern beyond a private slave–master relationship. The act not only limited the freedom of movement of slaves – they needed a specific ticket from their master if found outside the estate – but allocated to all white and black members of the community the duty to enforce those limits. There would be slave patrols to catch runaway slaves and special slave courts composed of justices of the peace and laymen (usually slaveholders). That punishments meted out to the slaves would never have been allowed under English law was brought to the attention of the Lords of Trade in 1679. According to the review of the laws, however, the corporeal punishments, i.e. branding and dismembering, were reasonable in view of the blacks being a dangerous and "a brutish sort of People".[301] Unlike the

for Carlisle to take possession of the island and to begin to enjoy the duties, taxes and fees for commerce and the disposal of land. He governed the island with exclusive "executive, judicial and legislative authority", and the royal government rarely intervened, 88, 101–2. But the proprietary disputes ended only as the island was turned into a royal colony in 1662, with the inheritors of Carlisle and interested parties receiving limited rights and royalties, 211–12.

298 Blackstone, *Commentaries*, Introduction iv (115).

299 Blackburn, *Making of New World Slavery*, 231. For the rapid rise of the slave population and decline of indentured service on Barbados in the latter part of the seventeenth century, see also Herbert S. Klein, *The Atlantic Slave Trade* (Cambridge University Press 2010), 32.

300 For a comparison of the 1661 Barbados legislation with sixteenth-century English policing laws, see Bradley J. Nicholson, 'Legal Borrowing and the Origins of Slave Law in the British Colonies', 38 *The American Journal of Legal History* (1994), 38–54. For the development of Barbadian slavery and slavery laws until the comprehensive laws of 1661, see Edward B. Rugemer, *Slave Law and the Politics of Resistance in the Early Atlantic World* (Harvard University Press 2018), 11–30.

301 Opinion quoted in Morgan, *American Slavery*, 314.

*Siete partidas* or the French *Code noir*, the law in Barbados was silent about the status of the slaves or the duties of masters. Its overwhelming concern was the control of the slave population.[302]

The mainland colonies possessed incremental pieces of legislation on aspects of slavery and indentured service, not always clearly distinguished. The proprietary colony of Carolina, for example, had begun in 1669 immediately on a slave-owning basis, including with Indian slavery against the specific prohibition by the Lords Proprietors.[303] According to the infamous Article 110 of the "Fundamental Constitution" of Carolina, authoritative though never formally adopted, "[e]very freeman of Carolina shall have absolute power and authority over his negro slaves, of what opinion or religion soever".[304] Locke's role in the drafting of this provision has been the subject of much debate. It seems clear that Locke knew about the slave trade and slave regime, having started to work in 1667 for one of the Lord Proprietors of South Carolina, the earl of Shaftesbury, and having had many official assignments in the colony's administration. He was also investor in the Royal African Company and, after Shaftesbury's death, a "leading commissioner of the Board of Trade for colonial affairs".[305] He also participated actively in the review of the Fundamental Constitutions in 1670 and 1682. Yet there is no indication that he would have objected to their slavery provisions.[306] The *Two Treatises*, of course, takes a critical view of slavery, regarding it as "nothing else, but the State of War continued between a lawful Conqueror and a Captive". But Locke also allowed the enslavement of war captives with the understanding that the master's power on the

302 See further, Sally E. Hadden, 'The Fragmented Laws of Slavery in the Colonial and Revolutionary Eras', in Michael Grossberg and Christopher Tomlins (eds), *The Cambridge History of Law in America* (Cambridge University Press 2008), 260–3; Watson, *Slave Law in the Americas*, 63–7; Rugemer, *Slave Law*, 28–30.

303 See e.g. L. H. Roper, 'The 1701 "Act for the better ordering of Slaves". Reconsidering the History of Slavery in Proprietary South Carolina', 64 *William and Mary Quarterly* (2007), 397–8.

304 Art 100 of Fundamental Constitutions of Carolina, 1 March 1669, in Thorpe, *Federal and State Constitutions,* V, 2785. Under the American slave codes, slaves were normally defined as "immovables" or real estate, though they could usually be sold or hired separately as well as realised for the owner's debt. See Goodell, *American Slave Code*, 9–48 and Morris, *Southern Slavery and the Law*, 61–80; Bush, 'Free to Enslave', 427–8.

305 James Farr, 'Locke, Natural Law, and New World Slavery', 36 *Political Theory* (2008), 497–9.

306 For Locke's part in administering Carolina, see especially Armitage, 'John Locke, Carolina, and the *Two Treatises of Government*', 96–107.

enslaved would be both absolute and arbitrary.[307] The best that can be said, perhaps, is that Locke's failure to raise the matter with the Lords Proprietors reflected an assumption that his theory applied only to a white man's political community.[308]

The first full-scale mainland slave codes followed the Barbadian act. One such act was the comprehensive slave code of South Carolina, written, like the Barbadian law, in a public law idiom and from the perspective of the maintenance of the racial order the whole community was called upon to enforce. Should the master allow liberties not provided for in the code – for instance, were he to permit slaves to work for themselves, to plant corn or rice or to keep animals – or if he refused to whip or brand the slave in the required ways, the master himself would be liable for punishment.[309] The community was to keep vigilant watch over black movements and arrest runaways. There were no provisions of conversion, education or protection of slaves – on the contrary, later amendments prohibited teaching writing and reading to slaves as well. The white communities resented the presence of free negroes and subjected manumission to stringent conditions.[310] Moreover, the prospect of relapsing into slavery was a constant threat on freed blacks whose treatment differed in innumerable ways from that of the white population.

The status of slavery in England itself was anything but clear. The claim that the "air of England is too pure for a slave to breathe" had been heard in the country since the sixteenth century.[311] Against what is sometimes asserted, slavery was not abolished in England with the judgment by Lord Mansfield in *Somerset's* case (1772), which concerned only the more limited issue of whether English authorities were bound to assist a slave-master to put his servant on a ship back to Jamaica. The famous statement that "[t]he state of slavery is of such a nature, that it is incapable of being introduced on any reasons, moral or political; but

307 Locke, *Two Treatises*, Second Treatise § 24 (128).

308 This is a slightly more condemnatory conclusion than that drawn in the careful discussion by Farr, 'Locke, Natural Law, and New World Slavery', 507, 508–10, 515–16. On racist attitudes as the justifications for black slavery in America, see further, Morris, *Southern Slavery*, 17–37.

309 For a full discussion, see Watson, *Slave Law in the Americas*, 67–75.

310 See further, ibid., 75–82.

311 The saying comes reputedly from a 1560 case involving a Russian master and his serf. Daniel J. Hulsebosch, 'Somerset's Case at the Bar. Securing the "Pure Air" of English Jurisdiction within the British Empire', 13 *Texas Wesleyan Law Review* (2006–7), 699.

only positive law", and its often-quoted terminus of slavery being "so odious, that nothing can be suffered to support it, but positive law", merely noted the fact of absence in England of laws enabling the enforcement of the laws of Virginia (under which Somerset was the slave of his master, Charles Stewart). At the time of the decision and some time thereafter there were perhaps 10,000–15,000 servants in England whose condition resembled that of slaves. Mansfield had no intention to free all of those, either in England or in the colonies. Like Somerset's counsel, he was aware of the dramatic economic consequences that would have followed. Although what Mansfield actually said is subject to some controversy, it seems that he did wish *de iure* slavery to end in England in due course, and that the decision might precipitate that result.[312] But none of this meant or could have meant abolishing colonial slavery. Sitting on King's Bench, Mansfield's jurisdiction did not reach that far; his judgments were not binding outside England.[313] The matter might have been taken up in the Privy Council as an imperial conflicts-of-law case that could have determined slave codes to be "repugnant" to English law. This was never done, and the fact that colonial laws often contradicted English law by no means led to their abrogation.[314]

In fact, the English state was all too happy to assist the colonists to purchase the slaves they needed. In the early seventeenth century, most slaves were purchased from the Dutch West India Company (WIC). The earl of Warwick had set up a Guinea Company for the purpose of bringing slaves to Barbados, but this had been undermined by the costs of keeping permanent trading posts on the African coasts. In the 1660s members of the royal family (Duke of York and Prince Rupert) established the Company for Royal Adventurers to Africa which, despite substantial investment by London merchants, finally turned to the more lucrative privateering. In 1672 the Royal Africa Company (RAC) was likewise set up by the royal family together with men such as Lord Shaftesbury with an interest in developing the colonial economies.[315]

312 *Somerset v. Stewart*, 98 ER 499 (1772). For a careful reconstruction of the different reports, of Mansfield's own later statements and of the practice of English authorities after 1772, see William R. Cotter, 'The Somerset Case and the Abolition of Slavery in England', 79 *History* (1994), 31–56.

313 There is even some evidence that Mansfield actually recognised the status of Somerset as a slave under *Virginian* law. Daniel Hulsebosch, 'Nothing but Liberty. Somerset's Case and the British Empire', 24 *Law and History Review* (2006), 650–3.

314 Ibid., 654–5.

315 See K. C. Davis, *The Royal African Company* (London, Longman 1957), 64–70.

The RAC was to have the monopoly for a thousand years, including the right to wage war against any non-Christian enemies – in practice to protect its fortifications and factories – marking its allegiance to the royal family by the payment of two elephants' teeth whenever a member of the royal family set foot in Africa.[316] By the time its monopoly ended in 1713 the RAC had bought about 125,000 black slaves from Africa to the Caribbean and the English mainland colonies.[317] But the company's operations were undermined by a persistent anti-monopoly sentiment. Separate traders made use of the argument of the monopoly going against the liberty of all Englishmen to enrich themselves while the company defended itself by reference to the investments it had made and that, it claimed, serviced the whole African trade. The RAC also presented itself as a civilising force against the "plundering, stealing and sometimes killing" by the independent traders.[318] But the company waged a losing battle, and its monopoly was finally abolished in 1713.[319] At this time, the Asiento, the right to transport 144,000 black Africans to the Spanish Indies in the space of thirty years, was transferred to the newly established South Sea Company, which continued to collaborate with the RAC until 1739.[320]

During the period 1640–1700, altogether 263,000 slaves were brought to the English colonies in the New World, about half of them to Barbados. The following century would witness altogether over 6 million slaves transported across the Atlantic, of which the largest part, about 2.5 million people, to the English colonies.[321] By this time, about 80 percent of the population in the Caribbean were slaves while in the Southern mainland plantation colonies their portion arose to one-third or more. Chattel slavery of the Africans was of

[316] William Robert Scott, *The Constitution and Finance of English, Scottish, and Irish Joint-Stock Companies to 1720* (3 vols, Cambridge University Press 1912), II, 20.

[317] The approximate loss at the middle passage was one-fifth, Blackburn, *Making of New World Slavery*, 254–6. Most of the slaves were first delivered to the Caribbean but increasingly, in the early years of the eighteenth century, to Virginia where indentured service had practically disappeared. Morgan, *American Slavery*, 304–8.

[318] Charles Davenant, *Reflections upon the Constitution and Management of the African Trade*, cited in William Pettigrew, *Freedom's Debt. The Royal African Company and the Politics of the Atlantic Slave Trade 1672–1752* (University of North Carolina Press 2013), 188.

[319] Scott, *Constitution and Finance*, II, 22–5; Davis, *Royal African Company*, 122–52.

[320] More could be delivered against a small duty. See e.g. Georges Scelle, 'The Slave-Trade in the Spanish Colonies of America. The Assiento', 4 *American Journal of International Law* (1910), 650–61; Eric Williams, 'The Golden Age of the Slave System for Britain', 25 *The Journal of Negro History* (1940), 64.

[321] Blackburn, *Making of New World Slavery*, 269 and 383.

course quite essential for the maintenance and growth of the plantation economy the most important products of which, tobacco and sugar, were in increasing demand. Attitudes towards it varied in England. Stories about cruelty towards slaves in the Caribbean told by travellers contributed often to a low image of the settler population, strengthened by the common knowledge of its origins in the masses of the urban and rural poor.[322] In the next century, the image of "Creolian despotism", the expansion of trade in luxuries brought in from the colonies, and the expanding slave trade, created the fear that the liberties of England herself might be under threat.[323] That worry was eventually overcome. The British Caribbean experienced a boom in production between the collapse of Saint-Domingue and the end of slave trade in 1807.[324] Revolution in America allowed outsourcing moral anxieties to the settler communities that would integrate slavery for almost a century into their economies. By enlisting those economies into their free trade empire in 1783, and policing the seas in order to prevent others from doing the same, the English could now sleep in peace at night while leaving Washington to flip-flop on the issue for the rest of his life.[325]

## Fighting Property: The East India Company 1600–1757

The practice of chartering companies to rule over large territories was nowhere more striking than in respect of the East India Company (EIC). The first charter of December 1600 constituted the investors as "one Body Corporate and Politick" possessing liberties, privileges and jurisdictions pertaining to the government of themselves and their

322 See Jack P. Greene, *Evaluating Empire and Confronting Colonialism in Eighteenth-Century Britain* (Cambridge University Press 2013), 50–83.

323 Armitage, *Ideological Origins*, 125–45; Greene, *Evaluating Empire*, 156–99.

324 The question of slavery's contribution to British industrialisation has been the object of a wealth of studies since Eric Williams' *Capitalism and Slavery* (1944). One conclusion from that debate is that drawn by Blackburn according to whom "exchanges with the slave plantations helped British capitalism to make a breakthrough to industrialism and global hegemony ahead of its rivals", *Making of New World Slavery*, 572.

325 "The tragedy was not that Washington failed to free his slaves in his life time but that the tide was already running in the opposite direction. Nothing and no one – not even George Washington – could halt that trend." Philip D. Morgan, '"To Get Quit of Negroes". George Washington and Slavery', 39 *Journal of American Studies* (2005), 428–9, quoting from Henry Wiencek, *An Imperfect God. George Washington, His Slaves, and the Creation of America* (Baltimore, Farrar, Strauss & Giroux 2003), 359.

granted territories.[326] Henceforth, Englishmen would only be allowed to trade with company licence in the huge area from the Cape of Good Hope to the Strait of Magellan, with the exception of territories already possessed by other Christians. The monopoly was extended indefinitely in 1609. Unlike in the Atlantic realm, there was no effort to justify expansion by reference to conceptions of conquest or settlement. Lockean arguments about labour as a source of rights made no appearance.[327] The only justification, as we saw in the previous chapter, was the one received in the *Sandys* case of 1684–5 from the law of nations and the royal prerogative. Trade in potentially hostile territories required investment in factories and fortifications that might not be forthcoming unless the investors were guaranteed monopoly rights. As in the Atlantic colonies, the EIC was entitled to promulgate laws as long as they were "not contrary or repugnant to the Laws, Statutes or Customs of this Our Realm".[328] An initial stock of £68,373 from 218 investors provided the capital for the first voyage. A permanent stock was set up in 1657, allowing the shares to be valued and exchanged at the London Stock Exchange. Company leadership consisted originally of a governor and twenty-four directors (or committees) elected annually by a general court of stockholders. The separation of management and ownership, designed to allow efficient administration, would be a recipe for future problems.[329]

The company's initial ambition was to break the Portuguese spice monopoly and its first factory was set up in Bantam on Java. Conflict with the Dutch, however, compelled the English eventually to leave the area.[330] A presence on the Indian mainland began in Surat where the EIC received trading rights from the Mughal emperor in 1612.

[326] Charter granted by Queen Elizabeth, 31 December 1600, in John Shaw (ed.), *Charters relating to the East India Company from 1600 to 1761; reprinted from a former collection with some additions and a preface for the Government of Madras* (Madras, Hill 1887), 2.

[327] Partha Chatterjee, *The Black Hole of Empire. History of a Global Practice of Power* (Princeton University Press 2012), 47–8. Instead, justification for British rule was drawn from racialised grounds, especially from assumed "Indian despotism, depravity and corruption". Robert Travers, *Ideology and Empire in Eighteenth-Century India* (Cambridge University Press 2007), 43.

[328] Charter of 31 May 1609, *Charters*, 25.

[329] See e.g. John Keay, *The Honourable Company. A History of the East India Company* (London, HarperCollins 1993), 25–7; Nick Robins, *The Corporation That Changed the World. How the East India Company Shaped the Modern Multinational* (London, Pluto 2006), 23–4.

[330] Keay, *Honourable Company*, 39–51; Robins, *Corporation That Changed the World*, 43–4.

The imports of textiles, calicoes, cotton and silk was extremely lucrative, dividends to shareholders rising up to 50 percent in the 1680s.[331] The company's status as a territorial power was strengthened when Charles II received the archipelago of Bombay as dowry from Portugal in 1661 and handed it over to the company. Here the EIC would enjoy "all the Rights, Profits, Territories and Appurtenances ... whatsoever... in as large and ample Manner, to all Intents, Constructions and Purposes as We Ourselves now have and enjoy... by Virtue of the said Grant of [the King of Portugal]".[332] Under English law, the company again had the status of a manorial lord with jurisdiction over all English subjects as well as rights of legislation, adjudication and administration "as be requisite for the good Government and Safety". The crown reserved to itself the "Faith and Allegiance, to Us due and belonging, and Our Royal Power and Sovereignty, or and over our Subjects and Inhabitants there".[333] The company was also granted the powers of defence and martial law; in such cases it would possess the authority of "any Captain General of [English] Army".[334]

The Restoration charter of 1661 renewed the monopoly and extended the company's territorial rights over "all the Plantations, Forts, Fortifications, Factories or Colonies" where it operated. These included the power to appoint governors and set up courts to judge all persons living under company rule. It was also expressly entitled to make war and peace with non-Christians.[335] Authority to set up admiralty courts was granted two years later, with jurisdiction over prize and commercial and maritime cases.[336] The charter of 1686 reaffirmed these powers with specific mention of the EIC's authority to raise naval and military forces and declare martial law if necessary.[337]

During most of the last quarter of the seventeenth century, EIC directorship was in the hands of the formidable Sir Josiah Child

[331] Robins, *Corporation That Changed the World*, 46–7.

[332] Charter Granted to the EIC relating to the Island of Bombay, 26 March 1669, *Charters*, 48.

[333] Ibid., *Charters*, 49, 52. See also Keay, *Honourable Company*, 131.

[334] Charter Granted to the EIC relating to the Island of Bombay, 26 March 1669, *Charters*, 54. These rights also extended to the Island of St Helena, which operated as a port of call for the company's ships as well as a trial location for establishing a plantation regime akin to those in the Caribbean. Letters Patent Granted to the EIC relating to the Island of St Helena, 16 December 1673, *Charters*, 59–61.

[335] Letters Patents Granted to the EIC by Charles II on 3 April 1661, *Charters*, 44–5.

[336] Charter Granted to the EIC by Charles II on 9 August 1683, *Charters*, 69–73.

[337] Charter Granted to the EIC by James II on 12 April 1686, *Charters*, 74–83, 81.

(1630–99) in whose view mere trade would never suffice to keep local potentates and rival European powers in check. The company was to learn from the Dutch and operate as a sovereign, gradually seeking to eclipse its dependency on the Mughal emperor. Child had no scruples in engaging the emperor on the battlefield, in 1686 sending ten ships and six infantry companies to force concessions in Bengal. That he aimed to turn the company into "a formidable martial government in India" raised considerable concerns in England.[338] Such belligerency seemed unsuitable for a commercial enterprise, and Child's methods to attain favour with the court were deemed inappropriate.[339] After the *Sandys* case, the company's foothold in India seemed solid, however, and action was taken to expand control in Southeast Asia. A settlement was negotiated at Sumatra, and in 1686 the company could report that it was "the Sole Government in that place".[340] Further action was taken against the Dutch on Java, and interloping and anti-English activities in Siam were brought to an end by war.[341]

While the company's stock price continued to soar, its aggressive actions and concern over corruption – bribery of English and Indian officials – led to parliamentary investigations and the establishment of a rival company, the Dowgate Adventurers. Because the latter possessed neither factories nor experience in India, however, the two companies were joined together by a charter issued to a United East India Company in 1709 in exchange for an interest-free loan to the crown of £1,200,000.[342] Years of relative calm followed during which shareholders could expect a steady annual dividend of about 8 percent. Receipt of Emperor Farrukhsiyar's *firman* of 1716 gave the company "a lasting title to the most extensive commercial and territorial privileges ever granted to a foreign power".[343] The company also received the infamous *dastak*, freedom from customs duties in Mughal territory against an annual lump sum of 3,000 rupees. It gained villages and

338 Robins, *Corporation That Changed the World*, 49; Keay, *Honourable Company*, 141–4. See also Chatterjee, *Black Hole*, 36–7.

339 These included an annual gift of 10,000 guineas to the Stuarts plus loans to the government in exchange for confirmation of the monopoly. See Keay, *Honourable Company*, 178 and Letters Patents granted on 3 April 1661 by Charles II, *Charters*, 32–46 and Charter of 14 April 1686 by James II, 74–83.

340 Philip J. Stern, *Company-State. Corporate Sovereignty and the Early Modern Foundations of British Rule in India* (Oxford University Press 2011), 75.

341 Ibid., 69–72, 77–80.

342 Keay, *Honourable Company*; Robins, *Corporation That Changed the World*, 53–4.

343 Keay, *Honourable Company*, 229, 231.

townships in Bengal on which it would build its principal office of Calcutta. Its jurisdiction and its right to mint coinage were confirmed.

Throughout this period, the EIC was in principle under the sovereignty of the Mughal emperor who dealt with it in terms of unilateral *firmans.* Relations with native Indian princes were organised in part by treaties, in part by *sanads* and letters whereby the company promised to extend its protection to determined territories.[344] Interpretation was a major source of conflict as the treaties not only determined the details of company relations with native rulers but also "appropriated resources of Indian states including revenues in the form of subsidies or tribute, subjects as soldiers and commercial goods".[345] As the sovereignty of Mughal rulers gradually eroded and the independence of provinces such as Bengal and Hyderabad increased, the latter also began to resist the expansion of company privileges. These struck especially at the treasury of the nawab of Bengal, the unfortunate Siraj-ud-Daula, leading to the desperate effort by him to attempt the conquest of Calcutta in 1756 and its famous recapture by the company. Resistance finally collapsed after the battle of Plassey in the following year – less a battle than a palace coup – after which the company became the de facto ruler of all of Bengal, installing puppet nawabs to give its rule formal legitimacy.[346] The first historian of the company's military exploits, Robert Orme, dismissed doubts about the legal basis of those operations. They were, he wrote, authorised by the unreliability of the local rulers, the servility of the populations, and above all the natural right to retaliate and punish those who obstructed the company's treaty-based trading rights.[347]

## The EIC after 1765: "Farmers to the Public"

The story of later British rule over India as a "dramatic transformation of the East India Company from trader to sovereign during the mid-1760s" has to be qualified by attention to ways in which the company already operated as a sovereign during the seventeenth century.[348]

[344] Barbara Ranusack, *Indian Princes and Their States* (Cambridge University Press 2003), 51–2.

[345] Ibid., 48–9.

[346] See Keay, *Honourable Company*, 271–327.

[347] For a discussion of Robert Orme's 1767/1778 *A History of the Military Transactions of the British Nation in Indostan*, see Chatterjee, *Black Hole*, 44–9.

[348] H. V. Bowen, 'British India 1765–1813. The Metropolitan Context', in P. J. Marshall & Alaine Low (eds), *The Oxford History of the British Empire*, vol. II: *The Eighteenth Century* (Oxford University Press 1998), 530. The corrective owes especially to Stern, *Company-State*.

But consciousness of the EIC's formidable powers and their misuse began to be felt by metropolitan audiences only after the mid-eighteenth century. At the time, Bengal, the richest province of the Mughal empire, accounted for perhaps 25 percent of global manufacturing.[349] In the 1760s, Bengal's treasury was absorbed into that of the company, which also received the coveted *diwani*, the right to collect territorial revenue. French and other foreigners were expelled and local production was geared exclusively to the company's needs such that "[b]y 1765, the Company was de facto sovereign in Bengal".[350] By the end of the century, 85–90 percent of Bengali textiles went to Britain. To press prices below anything produced in England, the company reduced its Indian weavers to near-slavery.[351] Simultaneously, EIC executives routinely enriched themselves by private trading for which, they claimed, the *dastak* was as applicable as to the company's own commerce. The tenuous efforts to separate official from private commerce, the amount of which by now exceeded the company's own trade, was doomed to fail. Authorities expected to police private trade were precisely the ones who benefited from it. In 1763 the company took to war to replace a nawab who had tried to limit the misuse of the *dastak* by a more supple one ready to reaffirm old ways of business.[352] Despite doubts in London and on the ground, the company kept stocking and running up the price of rice in 1769–70 as natural disasters struck at an increasingly vulnerable Bengal population. The result was a famine in which between 1.2 and 10 million Bengalis perished.[353]

In the eighteenth century the EIC received diplomatic representatives (*vakils*) from local courts and sent residents and political officers to interact with Indian princes. Its Secret Committee directed its diplomacy under the supervision of its Court of Directors. After the Regulating Act of 1773 it was in principle expected to do this by coordinating with the government in London but the latter's interests

349 Robins, *Corporation That Changed the World*, 61.

350 H.V. Bowen, 'Investment and Empire in the Later Eighteenth Century. East India Stockholding, 1765–1791', XLII *Economic History Review* (1989), 187.

351 Robins, *Corporation That Changed the World*, 76–8.

352 On the dispute regarding the extent of the *dastak*, see Keay, *Honourable Company*, 235–7, 369–78.

353 Hastings estimated the number as a third of the population. But the numbers and estimated causes vary greatly. For one useful discussion, see John McLane, *Land and Local Kingship in Eighteenth-Century Bengal* (Cambridge University Press 2009), 194–207.

were captured by the situation in America.[354] During the period of Warren Hastings as governor-general of India (1773–85) the collection of taxes was centralised and the company's administration penetrated deep into Indian society. The Mughal emperor remained the formal sovereign but most government income was taken over by the company, including the right to collect taxes and customs revenues in the provinces of Bengal, Bihar and Orissa.[355] Although the value of company stock soared, most of the money went to upholding its military force. It was gradually realised in London that the adequate management of the revenue necessitated a transformation of the company's relationship to the crown. This brought up the question of formal sovereignty. Only few years earlier, Clive himself had stated that that "[so] large a sovereignty may possibly be an object too extensive for a mercantile company".[356] By insisting that formal sovereignty lay with the local rulers, the company could limit its investments and keep Britain's European enemies from attacking its territories – perhaps the same reason why Britain itself refrained in its treaties with foreign powers from claiming sovereignty over Bengal.[357] Nevertheless, doubts about the conquests and rumours about mismanagement and corruption led to increasing demands for a formal statement that sovereignty in India actually belonged to the crown. But the government had no wish to involve itself in another imperial skirmish. It had sufficient worries in North America and the Indian question was "neither popular nor well understood".[358]

During a parliamentary inquiry in 1767, the government's position was to attain as much of the revenue as possible to the treasury without the assumption of administrative duties. But suggestions that the *diwani* actually belonged to the crown were met by the proprietors' insistence that this would violate their charter rights. Formally, there was little doubt about crown sovereignty. In a memorandum of 1757 the attorney-general and solicitor-general affirmed that in case a territory was attained by conquest, the crown received sovereignty as well as

354 See Jeremy Black, *British Diplomats and Diplomacy 1688–1800* (University of Exeter Press 2001), 170–1; Ranusack, *Indian Princes*, 53–4.

355 H. V. Bowen, *Revenue and Reform. The India Problem in British Politics 1757–1773* (Cambridge University Press 1991), 6, 11–12.

356 Robert Clive to William Pitt, 7 January 1759, quoted in Bowen, 'India. The Metropolitan Context', 532.

357 Travers, *Ideology and Empire*, 47.

358 This was so despite the fact that almost a quarter were EIC stock-owners, Bowen, *Revenue and Reform*, 31, 38.

"actual possession of the land". However, if rights were received by treaty crown sovereignty was accompanied by property rights residing "in the grantees ... as English settlements".[359] The formulation was used to support both sides: did the company receive the *diwani* as a consequence of a military operation or in pursuit of an agreement with the emperor? The controversy continued unabated until a financial settlement provided that the company would pay the state an annual fee of £400,000 in exchange for postponing the question of formal rights.[360] And so, tensions persisted. For example, until 1763 the crown had no diplomatic presence on the Indian subcontinent. When it then despatched a representative to negotiate with local rulers, EIC directors downgraded his status into just one member of a "joint negotiation".[361]

It became gradually clear however, that the revenue would not be nearly as high as foreseen. The company was drawn deeper into financial trouble as military costs doubled and civilian expenses tripled. By the 1770s Bengal was in recession, its resources largely depleted. Close to collapse, with a debt of £1.2 million to the government in 1772, a reorganisation of the company's relationship to the crown was imperative. The preparation of what became Lord North's Regulating Act of 1773 was characterised by the government's wish to control the company's operations, the proprietors' insistence that this would violate their charter rights and parliament's utter disinterest in the matter.[362] According to the government, the company "could acquire nothing by conquest but for the state [which was why] the public has been entitled to these conquests. ... The company in this respect are farmers to the public."[363] Indian government was to be allocated to a governor-general, appointed by the crown, assisted by a council as well as a supreme court with a likewise crown-appointed chief justice. The company's general court condemned the proposals unanimously as "unconstitutional and defective". The proprietors were outraged by the suggestion that all military conquests were for the crown and that using acquisitions for private emolument was strictly illegal.[364] But the

359 George Chalmers (ed.), *Opinions of Eminent Lawyers on Various Points of English Jurisprudence* (2 vols, London, Reed & Hunter 1814), I, 195.

360 Chatterjee, *Black Hole*, 43–4; Bowen, *Revenue and Reform*, 48–66.

361 Bowen, *Revenue and Reform*, 81. His private instructions, however, directed him to act as a plenipotentiary. See also Marshall, *Making and Unmaking of Empires*, 218–19.

362 See e.g. Keay, *Honourable Company*, 378–85.

363 Lord North to parliament on 9 March 1773, as quoted in Bowen, *Revenue and Reform*, 159.

364 Ibid., 170, 176.

proposals passed both Houses with a great majority and Warren Hastings was appointed governor-general on 3 May 1773.[365]

## "The Merchant Is Become the Sovereign"

The Regulating Act affirmed crown sovereignty as well as company ownership.[366] It subordinated the presidencies of Bombay and Madras to the governor-general and provided civilian and criminal jurisdiction over all Englishmen as well as local inhabitants working for the company or otherwise willing to submit to British jurisdiction.[367] The powers of war and peace as well as legislative jurisdiction over the company's "factories and places subordinate, or to be subordinate" were granted to the governor-general.[368] But the legislation of 1773 failed to organise effective metropolitan control and further parliamentary inquiries did not lead to alternative solutions. One of the more clear-sighted observers of the debate of 1773 was again Thomas Pownall who examined the Indian issue in the general context of the British empire. Even under the experiment of the Regulating Act, Pownall concluded, with the revenue "actually in the possession of this company", it was the company that had the *exercise* of sovereignty in its hands.[369] The *diwani* had not met expectations and the company was in dire straits, its "tyranny" in Bengal having "absolutely destroyed the country itself". Unless something was done, the result will be "the ruin of the whole edifice of the British empire".[370]

To respond to the widespread criticisms of the company in the 1770s Pownall wanted to assure his readers that notwithstanding the way colonial possessions may have been received, it was in the "nature of political community" and "the spirit of our constitution" that dominion would be vested in the crown.[371] The crown did not thereby

365 For the property concerns voiced by Whig MPs against the proposals, see Jon E. Wilson, *The Domination of Strangers. Modern Governance in Eastern India, 1780–1835* (New York, Palgrave 2008), 55.

366 The East India Company Act, 1773 (13 Geo III c. 63), in P. Mukherji, *Indian Constitutional Documents 1773–1915* (Calcutta, Thacker 1915), especially 1–9.

367 The definition of the extent of the court's jurisdiction remained, however, a matter of some controversy. See B. B. Misra, *The Central Administration of the East India Company, 1773–1834* (Oxford University Press 1959), 21–2.

368 The East India Company Act, 1773, Mukherji, *Indian Constitutional Documents*, 36 (6).

369 Thomas Pownall, *The Right, Interest and Duty of the Government, as Concerned in the Affair of the East Indies* (London, Almon 1781), 1.

370 Ibid., 3, 4.

371 Ibid., 36, 17–23.

become a "grand Seigneur" with ownership of everything. Instead, it would possess "political property" while subjects acquired their lands as "personal property". In India, all this had been turned upside down – local rulers received their sovereignty from the company, often through farcical treaties. Being rights of "personal" and not "political" sovereignty, however, they cannot lead into the power of government "without some legal and constitutional interposition of the crown".[372] Pownall agreed with Smith that the experience of all times was that "the greatest evil arises 'when traders become princes and merchants sovereigns'". Hence India and the whole system of British empire was to be held "in the crown, to be executed by the crown, while the property and all the rights, privileges and franchises should be confirmed and more fully established in the company".[373] Relations between Britain and the native states were to be those between a "State-holder" and a "subject State", modelled after the kind of gratitude and attachment that Pownall suggested had characterised Rome's relationship to Macedonia. The subject state would enjoy its liberties and its productive activities, while "a commercial state . . . had the government and protection of it".[374] The system of the Regulating Act had that potential. But it equally had the potential of mixing the municipal matters of the subordinate state with that of its protector, deranging the operation of old customs. The result "*will be the most transcendent curse of Despotism*".[375]

The Regulating Act failed to do away with corruption, patronage and private trade. The company found itself in continuous war with Mughal successor states and the French. A vicious circle arose where the rising costs of military action were to be offset by new territorial revenues, which again called for enhanced military preparedness. The expenses of civilian administration soared.[376] But although increasing voices stressed the national honour at stake, the state refrained from taking on direct administration.[377] As the company neared financial collapse in the 1780s, the Whig government proposed to turn over Indian rule to the state and to redefine the company as a mere merchant. But its bill was defeated and the government fell on that very proposal. The confiscation of charter rights was inconceivable.

[372] Ibid., 27. [373] Ibid, 28–9. [374] Ibid., 33. [375] Ibid., 38.

[376] See Marshall, *Making and Unmaking*, 217–23.

[377] For the nationalist aspects of the debate at the time, see Sudipta Sen, *Distant Sovereignty. National Imperialism and the Origins of British India* (London, Routledge 2002), 6–9.

According to the company's legal counsel, Mr Hardinge, the right of monopoly trade and the right choosing officials belonged to the company "[as] the sixpence in my pocket is mine".[378] A compromise was attained by Pitt's India Act of 1784 that established a Board of Control (Commissioners for the Affairs of India) to strengthen state supervision of the company's political activities.[379] The act expressly prohibited the company from undertaking aggressive war.[380] But drawing a line between political and commercial matters was hard and the company routinely justified its military action by the objective of securing commercial advantage. When the charter came to be renewed for another twenty years in 1793 the relations between the company and the state remained as they had been.[381]

A new system of government was put in place with the so-called permanent settlement in Bengal in 1793 that the Governor-General Lord Cornwallis negotiated with the leading local landowners (*zamindars*). From now on, the company would guarantee the property rights of the *zamindars* against a fixed sum of annual revenue. The purpose was to create a landowning elite resembling the British through which Bengal could be governed indirectly but more efficiently while an incentive would be provided for investing in increased production.[382] But the new system did not bring the advantages expected. The relation between landlords and tenants was left unclear; no reliable way was found on how to determine whether rents had been paid or were excessive. A market in land was created that resulted in massive transfers of property to members of local gentry close to the company. The absence of reliable accounts of local customs made British judges and administrators imagine Indian conditions to be analogous to feudal

[378] George Hardinge, *Speech of Mr Hardinge, Counsel of the Directors of the East India Company at the bar of the House of Lords, on Tuesday the 16th of December, 1783* (London, Stockdale 1784), 10.

[379] East India Company Act 1784, 24 Geo III, c. 25, in Mukherji, *Indian Constitutional Documents*, 9–27. The act increased governmental supervision significantly, occasioning company protests when it appeared to extend also to its commercial affairs. It was a compromise that was seen as reasonably successful from the government side. Bowen, 'India. The Metropolitan Context', 543–7.

[380] East India Company Act 1784, paras 34, 35 (22, 23). Instead, it was secretly agreed with company directors to vest power of decision of possible military operations to the government, C. H. Philips, *The East India Company 1784–1834* (Manchester University Press 1961), 275.

[381] For the years of the Board of Commissioners [Board of Control] under its powerful president Henry Dundas, and the Declaratory Act of 7 March 1788, see Philips, *East India Company*, 56–9. For the renewal of the Charter in 1793, see 71–9.

[382] Wilson, *Domination of Strangers*, 57.

Europe and decide that a combination of formal rights with ideas about improvement provided the best basis to settle property disputes.[383] Efforts to ameliorate the situation of the tenants continued until the late nineteenth century while, as before, abstract legal categories about landowning and status failed to attain a workable grasp of a colonial reality to which its administration remained utterly alien.[384]

## Paramountcy

During the wars with France the board began to encourage aggressive action by the EIC, for example by annexing the powerful Mysore state. The British were to become "arbiters of India".[385] Governor-General Wellesley developed the system of flexible subordination of local rulers to the EIC. As he explained:

> The fundamental principle … is to place those states in such a degree of dependence on British power as may deprive them of the means of prosecuting any measures or of forming any confidence hazardous to the security of the British empire, and may enable us to preserve the tranquillity of India by exercising a general control over those states, calculated to prevent the operation of that restless spirit of ambition and violence which is the characteristic of every Asian government.[386]

British troops would be kept in the subordinate state's territory, at the latter's expense, and a British resident would oversee the conduct of foreign affairs.[387] Two rival vocabularies now expressed aspects of this system. The first of these, "suzerainty", cast the company as a kind of superior sovereign with important limitations to the powers of the inferior sovereign. The more overtly imperial policy was labelled "paramountcy", expressing the company's special status as an arbiter between the local rulers and gatekeeper to outsiders. Charles Metcalfe, British resident in Hyderabad, expressed it in 1825 in the following way:

> We have by degrees become the paramount State of India. Although we exercised the power of this supremacy in many instances before 1817, we have

[383] Ibid., 57–69. See also Sen, *Distant Sovereignty*, 17–22.
[384] Wilson, *Domination of Strangers*, 127–32.
[385] Philips, *East India Company*, 103–4, 111.
[386] Wellesley despatch of 4 February 1804, quoted in Ranusack, *Indian Princes*, 62.
[387] See e.g. Gunnel Cederlöf, *Founding an Empire on India's North-Eastern Frontiers, 1790–1840* (Oxford University Press 2013), 162–3.

used and asserted them more generally since the extension of our influence by the events of that and the following years. ... [O]ur duty requires that we should support the legitimate successor of the Prince while policy seems to dictate that we should as much as possible abstain from any further interference in their affairs.[388]

Throughout the eighteenth century, the EIC had been careful not to challenge the Mughal emperor's formal sovereignty and continued to pay tribute to him. With the turn to a more aggressive policy of the 1790s – something company directors in London opposed – the forms of that old system were finally set aside. But when Indian princes were encouraged to declare their independence from the emperor, only few of them agreed. That the Board of Control failed to achieve a formal declaration of crown sovereignty reinforced the view that the rights of administration and revenue in the Indian provinces belonged to the company, however difficult it was to express this in terms of legal theory.[389] In the end, however, the wars of Mysore (1790–2, 1798–9) and the Marathas (1803–6) destroyed company finances: its debts doubled within three years and continued to grow thereafter. MPs in London began to realise that the company was living on borrowed time. As a result of massive pressure from private mercantile and shipping interests, trade to India was opened in the Charter Act of 1813.[390] The act also finally included the statement that "undoubted sovereignty" over all company territories belonged to the crown.[391] The king's advocate had advised that this was in itself unnecessary – the sovereignty of the king being obvious – and meant no change in the company's formal position. However, the clause that obliged the company "to promote the interest and happiness of the native inhabitants of India" implied an ideological change at home.[392] In practice, the act completed the fall of the company from its exalted position. But the

[388] Metcalfe, quoted in Ranusack, *Indian Princes*, 55.

[389] Bowen, 'India. The Metropolitan Context', 547 and 537–46.

[390] For a review of the pressures that led from the partial to the complete dismantling of the company's monopoly of India (though not China) trade between 1793 and 1812, see Anthony Webster, *The Twilight of the East India Company. The Evolution of Anglo-Asian Commerce and Politics, 1790–1860* (Woodbridge, Boydell 2009), 39–63.

[391] Act for the Continuing in the East India Company for a Further Term, the Possession of the Territories in India, 53 Geo III c. 155 (East India Act 1813) in *The Law Relating to India and the East India Company* (2nd edn, London, Allen 1841), 167 See also Philips, *East India Company*, 191; Bowen, 'India. The Metropolitan Context', 547.

[392] East India Act 1813, XXXIII, *Law Relating to India*, 170. The wording was introduced at the insistence of a group of "saints", led by Lord Wilberforce.

discontinuation of the company's monopoly in India did not apply to its increasingly lucrative actions in China.

## The Move to Protection: China

In China, that monopoly came to an end on 1 April 1834.[393] But even thereafter, private traders found themselves constrained by Canton as the only trading post and being compelled to do their business with the Hong merchants, a group of monopoly intermediaries towards Chinese customers. The traders believed that this arrangement showed the excessive deference that the East India Company had paid to Qing authorities. They hated the dismissive treatment they received and worried over the accumulating debt owed to them by the Hong.[394] They were especially incensed by the prohibition of the importation of the most important item of British trade with China, namely opium, which was used for the payment of such British imports as tea, porcelain and silk.[395] Although the prohibition had existed since 1729, it had been rarely enforced and, according to British merchants, was used principally to extort advantages from them. Matters came to a head when in 1834 the unauthorised efforts by the new British superintendant, Lord Napier, to change the Canton system fell to naught. That Napier succumbed to illness during the voyage was alleged to have resulted from Chinese mistreatment.[396]

The criticism by the private traders of the Chinese government, the Canton system and the alleged docility of the company was

393 Act to Regulate Trade in China and India, 28 August 1833, 3 & 4 Will 4 c. 85, *Law Relating to India*, 439–42.

394 For the accumulating complaints by the British merchant community regarding the limitations of China trade at the end of the eighteenth and beginning of the nineteenth century, see Song-Chuan Chen, *Merchants of War and Peace. British Knowledge of China in the Making of the Opium War* (Hong Kong University Press 2019), 104–7.

395 There are few reliable statistics of the significance of the British–Indian opium trade. In the 1830s and 1840s, it has been estimated as annually in excess of 5 million pounds sterling, that is to say, over 40% of India's exports. D. A. Washbrook, 'India, 1818–1860. The Two Faces of Colonialism', in Andrew Porter (ed.), *The Oxford History of the British Empire*, vol. III: *The Nineteenth Century* (Oxford University Press 1999), 403. The actual numbers of opium chests brought to China more than doubled in 1842–58. Steffen Rimner, *Opium's Long Shadow. From Asian Revolt to Global Drug Control* (Harvard University Press 2018), 32.

396 For Napier's undiplomatic voyage to China and his death, see Julia Lovell, *The Opium War. Drugs, Dreams and the Making of China* (London, Picador 2011), 5–7.

forcefully laid out by James Matheson, former EIC official and now partner of Jardine & Matheson, major opium traders.[397] Having attacked company policy and the arbitrary way in which the Chinese implemented their anti-opium laws, Matheson wanted to show the illegality of Chinese behaviour under the law of nations. His main point was about tacit agreement, estoppel and customary relations. Surely, he argued,

> the Chinese are bound, by their conduct during a long series of years, while in the course of reaping the benefits of commercial intercourse, which they themselves have uniformly sanctioned by acquiescence, and even *invited* . . . *on the faith of which* we have been induced to enter into vast speculations, to construct a system of commercial dealings on a very expensive and permanent scale.[398]

Matheson produced a long quotation from Vattel defending the view that "*[m]en are . . . under an obligation to carry out that commerce with each other*", reproducing the old point about the natural commercial interdependency of nations. But mostly he wanted to stress that the Chinese had given the British to understand that they would continue to refrain from enforcing their anti-opium laws. Even though China – like any country – did have the right to prohibit the importation of particular items, with respect to opium "China *has long since surrendered such rights*, and is no longer in a position to enforce them as against the British nation".[399] Matheson concluded by requesting the British government to threaten forceful action against Qing government. It was likely, he surmised, that no action actually needed to be taken. Threatening would be enough, perhaps supported by the occupation of one island on the Chinese coast, Chusan for example. For although the Chinese often "adapt language pregnant with direful import", if challenged they will always "sink into the most ignominious submission".[400] It would now be the time to send a plenipotentiary to speak

[397] The lives and activities of James Matheson and William Jardine are the matter of legend, colourfully described in Richard J. Grace, *Opium and Empire. Lives and Careers of William Jardine and James Matheson* (McGill–Queen's University Press 2014). Their role in the Opium War is treated at 259–87.

[398] James Matheson, *Present Position and Prospects of the British Trade with China* (London, Smith 1836), 32. The point about estoppel was express: "It is a reasonable and salutary rule of our municipal law, that a party shall always be bound by his admissions when they have been such as have induced a third party to alter his conduct", 37 and further 37–44.

[399] Ibid., 35. [400] Ibid., 60, 69.

directly to the emperor, "with sufficient powers to enforce, if necessary, the assertion of our rights".[401]

The situation remained unchanged until the Qing Commissioner Lin's famous arrival in Canton in March 1839.[402] Lin blockaded the whole British merchant community there, including Superintendent Charles Elliot, and began the confiscation and destruction of over 20,000 tons of opium seized from the British factories. On 1 October the cabinet decided to take military action in what became rapidly and pejoratively called the "Opium war". The letter by the foreign secretary Lord Palmerston to the Chinese emperor of February 1840 laid out the demand for "satisfactory compensation and redress for injuries inflicted by the Chinese authorities upon British subjects resident in China, and for insults offered by those same authorities to the British Crown".[403] The letter was full of claims giving an excellent window to the kind of legal order the British government believed should govern its relations not only with China, but also in the international world generally because, as Palmerston stressed, there was no treaty in force between the countries.

Palmerston accepted that the Chinese government had the right to prohibit the importation of opium and even to confiscate illegally imported opium: "The Queen of England desires that Her Subjects who may go into Foreign Countries should obey the laws of those Countries: and her Majesty does not wish to protect them from the just consequences of any offences they may commit in foreign parts." Sovereign equality required that foreigners – wherever they came from – comply with the laws of the host country. But those laws must be impartially applied so that foreigners are not discriminated

[401] Ibid., 78. Matheson was neither the only, nor the most radical of the pamphleteers arguing for action against China. Hamilton Lindsay, a former representative of the EIC in China, also appealed to war and later justified it by the allegedly silent acceptance of opium trade by Qing authorities. The illegality of opium in China, he wrote, was only "nominal". The "highest functionaries . . . not only connive at, but participate in [its] profits". Moreover, blockading the the merchants of a country would never be condoned in Europe – "And why, I ask, should the Chinese enjoy an exemption from the rules that guide our intercourse with all other nations of the world?" H. Hamilton Lindsay, *Is the War with China a Just One?* (London, Ridgway 1840), 8, 18.

[402] A good account of Commissioner Lin's mission, compiled in great part from Lin's diary, is in Arthur Waley, *The Opium War through Chinese Eyes* (London, Routledge 2005 [1958]), 11–154. See also Hosea B. Morse, *The International Relations of the Chinese Empire* (3 vols, London, Longman 1910), I, 213–55.

[403] Lord Palmerston to the Minister of the Emperor of China, 20 February 1840, in Morse, *International Relations*, Appendix A (621). The apology was also linked with the treatment and eventual death of the previous superintendent, Lord Napier.

against.[404] Because Chinese officials had long participated in contraband trade, and no action had been taken against them, the actions against foreigners were arbitrary and unjust. Like Matheson, the foreign secretary invoked desuetude: "it is notorious that for many years past, the importation had been connived at and permitted by the Chinese authorities at Canton".[405]

The demand for compensation focused on the deprivations and damage suffered by the British inhabitants in Canton.[406] The Chinese government had decided "to seize peaceable British Merchants, instead of seizing the contraband opium; to punish the innocent for the guilty, and to make the sufferings of the former, the means of compulsion upon the latter". The arrest of Elliot, the foreign secretary's letter went on, had been "in violation of the law of Nations, and in utter disregard of the respect which is due to him to [sic] an officer of the British Crown".[407] Redress was demanded for the ransom given to release those arrested, for the property given up to Chinese authorities or destroyed as well as the costs of the naval expedition despatched to implement the demands. Satisfaction was to be received also for the "affront offered by the Crown of Great Britain" and assurance that in the future British representatives will be treated "in manner consistent with the usages of civilized Nations". Finally, future security was to be had in the form of an island or islands from which the British merchants may carry their trade without interference. To enforce the demands, Palmerston added an extraordinary passage. He will "at once set out a Naval and Military force to the Coast of China ... to blockade the principal Chinese ports [and] intercept and detain and hold in deposit all Chinese vessels which he may meet with".[408]

404 The Chinese Emperor of course had no such pretence of equality and Palmerston's despatches often insisted that British officials protest against any connotation of Chinese superiority. See e.g. Lord Palmerston to Plenipotentiaries in China, 9 January 1841, in ibid., Appendix E (632–6).

405 Lord Palmerston to the Minister of the Emperor of China, 20 February 1840, in ibid., Appendix A (622).

406 The original instructions did not mention compensation for the destroyed opium, and Palmerston granted that the Chinese government was in its rights to confiscate it. But in further despatches to Elliot and to his successor, the value of opium found its way to the demands. See e.g. Lord Palmerston to Plenipotentiaries in China, 9 January 1841, in ibid., Appendix E (634) and especially the calculation in the Letter of Lord Palmerston to Sir Henry Pottinger, Appendix K (656).

407 Lord Palmerston to the Minister of the Emperor of China, 20 February 1840, ibid., Appendix A (623).

408 Lord Palmerston to the Minister of the Emperor of China, 20 February 1840, ibid., Appendix A (625).

The British navy occupied the archipelago of Chusan and proceeded on the river Beihe close to Beijing. In early negotiations in January 1840, Elliot agreed on compensation of six million dollars and the cession of Hong Kong. But as Palmerston pointed out in series of angry despatches, the agreement fell far short of the British demands.[409] War resumed and Elliot was replaced by Sir Henry Pottinger who had much less sympathy towards the Chinese.[410] Palmerston was annoyed by the superior tone with which the Chinese addressed the English (removing that tone became one of the peace terms) and never showed much flexibility. From the first contacts, naval blockades of Chinese ports and rivers were used to support British demands. The operations themselves were characterised by crushing British naval and military superiority and both sides' inability to speak to and understand each other. The emperor had not even seen the British demands until late in the campaign as the navy had already proceeded to the gates of Nanjing itself.[411] Lord Aberdeen, Palmerston's successor in the Tory government, continued his predecessor's policy and in a despatch of November 1841 stressed that the British were not looking for permanent conquests, for these would be costly and involve too intense contacts with Chinese authorities. "A secure and well regulated trade is all we desire."[412]

The Nanjing Treaty of August 1842 included all the British demands. There was to be a compensation of 21 million dollars, five ports were to open for British trade and Hong Kong was granted "in perpetuity" to Britain. A "Chief High Officer" would be allowed to communicate directly with their Chinese counterparts "on a footing of perfect equality". The monopoly of the Hong merchants was to go

409 The compensation for opium was held inadequate and no provision was made for compensating the costs of the British expedition or the debts of bankrupt Hong merchants. But the Chinese, not quite understanding the superior force they were facing, rejected the proposed agreement.

410 For the rejection of the treaty signed between Elliot and the Chinese representative Qishen in January 1840, see Morse, *International Relations*, 271–8. On Pottinger and his appointment, see Lovell, *Opium War*, 177, 179–82.

411 The massive scale of the Chinese military defeat was greatly affected by the deceptive messages received in Beijing from the battleground, by the lack of proper understanding of British war aims, and the outdated and corrupt forms of Manchu administration. These aspects of the war are greatly stressed in Lovell, *Opium War*, as well as Peter Ward Fay, *The Opium War 1840–1842. Barbarians in the Celestial Empire in the Early Part of the Nineteenth Century and the War by Which They Forced Her Gates Ajar* (University of North Carolina Press 1975), 337–71.

412 Lord Aberdeen to Sir Henry Pottinger, 4 November 1841, Morse, *International Relations*, Appendix M (663).

and their debts were included in the compensation. A schedule for a "fair and regular tariff" of customs duties was to be adopted and kept public.[413] The negotiations themselves were a sorry affair, and it is unclear whether the emperor or his advisors felt committed to the result. The main objective was to get the red-headed devils out of Chinese soil.[414] On the British side, *The Times* and many politicians felt that the war had been less than glorious with its dubious moral background and the crushing military imbalance.[415] British diplomacy had been both utterly legalistic and utterly unbalanced from beginning to end. The treaty provisions and the port system were to be supervised by the British consuls and the British would enjoy immunity from local jurisdiction. Not a word was said in the treaty of either opium or Christian missionaries, but both would now flood freely into Chinese territory. Palmerston had always been uneasy about the opium trade and prohibited raising that issue in the treaty itself. It was the Qing authorities' task to prevent the illegal trade, he told himself; the British government could play no role in the matter. As they seemed incapable of doing so, the best result, he assumed, would be to legalise and tax opium.[416]

But the treaty did not shift the trade balance significantly and the merchants continued their complaints to London. The treaty port system was insufficient. As *The Times* put it, Britain must "enforce the right of civilized nations to free commerce and communications with every part of this vast territory".[417] This is what was achieved by the Treaty of Peace, Friendship and Commerce of 1858 (Treaty of Tianjin), concluded after the Second Opium War. Additional ports were opened and the British gained greater freedom of travel. The use of the Chinese character for "barbarian" of the British was prohibited. A permanent ambassador would survey the treaty's implementation from Beijing, a network of consular offices was opened and British consuls received jurisdiction on "[a]ll questions in regard to rights, whether of property or person, arising between British subjects". Crimes committed by British citizens would likewise be adjudicated by

413 Treaty of Peace, Friendship, Commerce, Indemnity etc. between Great Britain and China, 29 August 1842, text in *Consolidated Treaty Series*, vol. 93 (465–74).

414 On the conduct of the negotiations, see Lovell, *Opium War*, 230–40; Fay, *Opium War*, 356–71.

415 Lovell, *Opium War*, 243.

416 That objective was realised in respect of Siam.

417 *The Times*, quoted in Lovell, *Opium War*, 250.

British officers while civil disputes were to be settled equitably between the British consul and Chinese authorities.[418] Above all, opium was legalised and subjected to tax.[419]

## A Global Rule of Law

The legalistic treatment of Chino-British relations, the centrality of mercantile interests and the involvement of the British government in protecting them while presenting itself as merely enforcing the rule of law were key themes of early nineteenth-century British foreign policy. Permanent engagements and territorial commitments were to be avoided. Exception was made to non-intervention only when necessary for upholding rules that would allow British trade to flourish "The world [was to be made] safe for the monarchical, propertied, gentlemanly order that had survived, providentially, the threats of republicanism and secularism."[420] Nobody epitomised that policy more than the Whig politician Henry John Temple, Viscount Palmerston (1784–1865).[421] Once, in reference to a suggestion for occupying Ethiopia, he remarked: "I do not see any advantage in our getting land in these quarters. All we want is trade and land is not necessary for trade; we can carry on commerce on ground belonging to other people."[422] Two political ideas have been associated with his name, liberalism and constitutionalism. The former was manifested in his enthusiastic though not unqualified support for free trade and the eradication of slavery and the slave trade – objectives Britain often pursued simultaneously. By "constitutionalism" Palmerston meant support for orderly statehood, parliamentary rule and opposition to legitimist policies of European conservative powers.[423] His primary foreign policy concern in Europe was to maintain the balance of power, for which purpose he was ready to use naval force to check

[418] Treaty of Peace, Friendship and Commerce, between Great Britain and China, 26 June 1858 in *Consolidated Treaty Series*, vol. 119, (163–87).

[419] Agreement containing Rules of Trade, made in pursuance of Article XXVI of the Treaty of 26 June 1858, Rule 5, in ibid., 177.

[420] P. J. Cain & A. G. Hopkins, *British Imperialism. 1688–2000* (London, Routledge 2001), 98.

[421] He was secretary of war in 1809–28, foreign secretary 1830–41 and 1846–51, and prime minister in 1855–8 as well as 1859–65.

[422] Palmerston, quoted in Ronald Hyam, *Britain's Imperial Century, 1815–1914. A Study of Empire and Expansion* (Boston, Barnes & Noble Books 1976), 107.

[423] E. D. Steele, *Palmerston and Liberalism, 1855–1865* (Cambridge University Press 1991), 247.

the expansion of conservative influence.[424] He also presided over the consolidation of British global hegemony, something he, like most of his liberal colleagues, held to be naturally beneficial: "I may say without any vainglorious boast . . . that we stand at the head of moral, social and political civilization. Our task is to lead the way and direct the march of other nations."[425]

The empire certainly did not emerge in a fit of absence of mind. But it did not emerge from a policy of world conquest either. Gunboats and dictates were often employed but always with some reluctance and an eye to minimising costs. Instead of forcing British interests on reluctant nations, it was better to have them internalise those interests in the form of general rules about public diplomacy and private rights. Formal colonies were to be avoided, and consular jurisdiction and extraterritoriality could be used whenever necessary. "To trade with civilized men is infinitely more profitable than to govern savages," Palmerston's contemporary, the first law member of the Supreme India Council, the formidable Thomas Macaulay observed in July 1833.[426] Later as secretary of war he would fully support Palmerston's China policy, providing it with an articulation that would later become Palmerston's signature:

> Everyone in the scale of civilized nations should know that Englishmen were ever living under the protecting eye of their own country . . . although far from their native country, and then in danger in a part of the world remote from that to which they must look for protection, yet that they belonged to a state which would not suffer a hair of one of its members to be harmed with impunity.[427]

Macaulay, Palmerston and the rest of early Victorian imperialists felt themselves of a wholly different breed from their eighteenth-century

[424] For Palmerston's policy in opposition of the absolutist party (supported by the three conservative European powers) in Portugal's civil war of 1829–32, see Kenneth Bourne, *Palmerston. The Early Years 1784–1841* (London, Lane 1982), 389–406.

[425] Palmerston in 1848, as quoted by Martin Lynn, 'Policy, Trade and Informal Empire', in Andrew Porter (ed.), *The Oxford History of the British Empire*, vol. III: *The Nineteenth Century* (Oxford University Press 1999), 102.

[426] Thomas Babington Macaulay, 'Speech in Parliament on the Government of India Bill, 10 July 1833', in G. M. Young (ed.), *Macaulay, Prose and Poetry* (Harvard University Press 1957), 716–18.

[427] Macaulay, HC Deb, 7 April 1840, Hansard, 53 (1840), 719. Macaulay himself did not so much seek to differentiate himself from Clive or Hastings as interpret their actions as coming from an unyielding, somewhat myopic commitment of service to the state. See Robert E. Sullivan, *Macaulay. The Tragedy of Power* (Harvard University Press 2009), 242–51.

predecessors such as Clive or Hastings. If the trial of the latter had ended in acquittal, Burke's speeches and the stories of the predatory "nabobs" had been internalised by a later generation that felt its duty to uphold law, order, virtue and even self-sacrifice in the great task of merging the interest of a benevolent Britain with that of less fortunate peoples everywhere.[428] That idea, the *Pax Britannica*, was to be guaranteed by the unrivalled capacity of the royal navy to operate practically anywhere in the world.

An intense effort at giving order to the international and colonial world characterised early nineteenth-century British policy.[429] The objective was not to subordinate alien peoples but to support an international system of independent states, preferably governed in a constitutional fashion, ready to engage in commercial dealings with each other. In the 1820s that policy dictated British recognition of the independence of the Spanish colonies, immediately followed by the conclusion of treaties of friendship, commerce and navigation with each.[430] As George Canning noted when he made public the government's decision to recognise Mexico, Colombia and Argentina, this was done in "the General Commercial interests of the World".[431] No sooner had these entities emerged than British investors began to finance their many infrastructural projects (ports, towns, agricultural facilities). Money flowed to the mining sector and to government bonds that became the principal item traded in the London stock exchange.[432]

428 See especially Eddy Kent, *Corporate Character. Representing British Power in Imperial India 1786–1901* (University of Toronto Press 2014), 26–58.

429 See especially Lauren Benton & Lisa Ford, *Rage for Order. The British Empire and the Origins of International Law 1800–1850* (Harvard University Press 2016).

430 See e.g. the Treaty on Amity, Commerce and Navigation between Colombia and Great Britain of 18 April 1825, in *Consolidated Treaty Series*, vol. 75, 195–206. While Article I sought to establish "perpetual, sincere and firm amity" between the parties, the rest of the treaty established a reciprocal free trade and most-favoured nation treatment, plus provision for freedom of conscience, consular relations and cooperation in fighting the slave trade. For the practically identical provisions of the Treaty of Amity, Commerce and Navigation between Great Britain and Rio de la Plata (2 February 1825), see ibid. 75–84.

431 Canning, cited in Frank G. Dawson, *The First Latin American Debt Crisis. The City of London and the 1822–1825 Loan Bubble* (Yale University Press 1990), 92.

432 The first bonds traded in 1822 were those of Colombia, Chile, Peru and "Poyais" (a fictitious Latin American republic set up by the Scottish adventurer Gregor McGregor) with an approximate 6–7% yield. However, problems soon appeared. The Colombian parliament repudiated the loan because, it was alleged, its negotiator had exceeded his instructions. The Chilean, Peruvian and "Poyais" loans also experienced trouble. But confidence in the viability of the new states was not lost

Although the bubble burst at the end of 1824, and only Brazil would be able to fully service its loans, a dependency had been set up whose fruits could be collected later as Britain became the continent's principal European trading partner and its chief financial intermediary. Economic policy and political alliances in the republics were shaped "above all by the need to retain the confidence of British creditors".[433]

Men such as Palmerston, Macaulay and Sir James Stephen, who "virtually single-handedly [ran] the British Empire for more than twenty years as a colonial undersecretary", were all committed to the rule of law.[434] They believed it to be inherent in their Britishness and that its enforcement was supremely justified by its fortunate coalescence with the interests of backward territories. "The assertion of the right to rule others because their power was bound by law (and hence sanitized of self-interest) was a central justification of British elites home and abroad."[435] Rule of law was everywhere. It was invoked to govern the colonies, to control British travelers, merchants and explorers moving outside formal colonial territory, to organise British diplomacy and violence and to assist in "opening" the world to free trade. The first of these – colonial law – consisted of a mixture of British and local laws designed to increase the role of the latter as the ambition to educate the indigenous to English ways was gradually given up.[436] In white settlement colonies, such as North America, the settlers always insisted that they would enjoy the ancient rights of Englishmen and that they would have access to impartial judges ready to protect them against overly ambitious governors.[437] In colonies of mixed population, these ideas were challenged by the difficulties of implementing the abolition of slavery (1834). Racism

and in 1824 bonds (or 5% and 6% respectively) were offered in London by Mexico and Brazil. See Dawson, *The First Latin American Debt Crisis*, 47–68.

433 Cain & Hopkins, *British Imperialism. 1688–2000*, 272 and the discussion of the expansion of British influence in Argentina, Brazil and Chile at 252–71. See also Alan Knight, 'Britain and Latin America', in Andrew Porter (ed.), *The Oxford History of the British Empire*, vol. III: *The Nineteenth Century* (Oxford University Press 2001), 122–45.

434 Keally McBride, *Mr. Mothercountry. The Man Who Made the Rule of Law* (Oxford University Press 2017), 24.

435 Ibid., 15.

436 See especially Charles Clark, *A Summary of Colonial Law* (London, Sweet and Maxwell 1834) and Chapter 9 above.

437 See e.g. John McLaren, 'The Uses of the Rule of Law in British Colonial Societies in the Nineteenth Century', in Shaunnagh Dorsett & Ian Hunter (eds), *Law and Politics in British Colonial Thought. Transpositions of Empire* (London, Palgrave 2010), 75–9.

led to recurrent scandals of misrule such as the Indian mutiny of 1857 and the Morant Bay rebellion in Jamaica in 1865,[438] turning metropolitan authorities away from their civilising ambitions towards a more despotic type of rule and non-interference with native customs supposedly appropriate in backward societies.[439]

Rule of law was also invoked to deal with British citizens travelling in non-European territory who often behaved in ways that were unjust or otherwise contrary to the government's interests. Early colonial administrators such as Sir James Stephen opposed the unilateral extensions of British law to non-colonial territory because, he believed, this required formal sovereignty and firm territorial control.[440] Annexations would have been costly and involve the government in all kinds of conflicts with local authorities. Thus, in 1843 parliament enacted the "Foreign Jurisdiction Act", which enabled the crown to exercise enforcement jurisdiction over British subjects in foreign territory "in the same and as ample manner as if her Majesty had acquired that jurisdiction by the cession or conquest of territory".[441] The act allowed British officials to exercise their policing powers wherever and whenever they felt they could so, in view of agreements with foreign countries or past practices, but did not oblige them when that would be too burdensome.[442]

[438] In response to the protests of October 1865 Governor Edward Eyre had over 400 black Jamaicans shot or executed and over 600 flogged. See R. W. Kostal, *A Jurisprudence of Power. Victorian Empire and the Rule of Law* (Oxford University Press 2005). For an earlier scandal that likewise raised the rule-of-law theme among the British public, see James Epstein, *Scandal of Colonial Rule. Power and Subversion in the British Atlantic during the Age of Revolution* (Cambridge University Press 2012).

[439] For the "crisis of liberal imperialism" in the turn to more despotic views reaffirming native "difference" in the latter part of the century in the writings of men such as James Fitzjames Stephen and Henry Maine, see Karuna Mantena, *Alibis of Empire. Henry Maine and the Ends of Liberal Imperialism* (Princeton University Press 2010), 39–55. The role of imperial "scandals" in triggering reforms of imperial law is also highlighted in Benton & Ford, *Rage for Order*, 14–16.

[440] See McBride, *Mr. Mothercountry*, 66–93.

[441] W. Ross Johnston, *Sovereignty and Protection. A Study of British Jurisdictional Imperialism in the Late Nineteenth Century* (Duke University Press 1973), 36. Where the act was to be applied and the extent of the powers granted was to be determined by Orders in Council for each case separately. Such acts were made for Turkey in 1844, Siam 1856, Morocco 1857, China and Japan 1865, Zanzibar 1866, Madagascar and Muscat in 1867.

[442] See 'An Act to Remove Doubts as to the Exercise of Power and Jurisdiction by Her Majesty within Diverse Countries and Places out of Her Majesty's Dominion' (Foreign Jurisdiction Act) 6 & 7 Vict., c. 94 and the famous memorandum on which it was based by Mr Hope Scott, 'British Jurisdiction in Foreign States', in Sir Henry Jenkyns, *British Rule and Jurisdiction beyond the Seas* (Oxford, Clarendon 1902),

Although the act and its implementing legislation were sometimes used for expansionist purposes, they did not necessarily cause resistance. Many parts of the non-European world – such as China and the Ottoman empire – had been accustomed to plural legal regimes, including those that applied to European merchant communities. In Mughal India, the EIC had actively sought to accommodate the coexistence of indigenous and European legal systems.[443] Extraterritoriality could initially be seen as a brief and limited type of legal intervention that also provided a focus the organisation of resistance and indigenous statehood. It was only in the latter part of the nineteenth century that it began to appear as an intolerable affront to local sovereignty.[444]

Canning's recognition of the breakaway republics in Latin America, Britain's support to Greek independence and Ottoman unity as well as Palmerston's personal investment in the creation of Belgium each was part of the effort to stabilise a system of states governed by the law of nations. And what were stable states? The early textbooks reviewed in the former chapter assumed that the law of nations governed relations between "independent states" without presenting a definition of what that might mean or distinguishing between civilised and uncivilised entities.[445] By contrast, the period's most accomplished work, Phillimore's four-volume *International Law* (1854), put forward a flexible notion of statehood that accommodated many different entities, allocating to them varying rights and competences. Subordinate parties to unequal alliances, for example, could be treated as subjects of

242–66. See also J. R. Pennell, 'The Origins of the Foreign Jurisdiction Act and the Extension of British Sovereignty', 83 *Historical Research* (2009), 465–85.

443 See Lauren Benton, *Law and Colonial Cultures. Legal Regimes in World History, 1400–1900* (Cambridge University Press 2002), 129–66 (tracing also the effort after the "Mutiny" to absorb indigenous laws in "modern" British laws).

444 See ibid., 210–52 together with the rest of Benton's extensive writings on colonial pluralism as well as e.g. Turan Kayaoglu, *Legal Imperialism. Sovereignty and Extraterritoriality in Japan, the Ottoman Empire, and China* (Cambridge University Press 2014). Moves towards a more intrusive form of extraterritoriality took place by the creation of supreme consular courts in Constantinople (1857), the Middle East and Shanghai (1865), intended to orient local courts to apply British-style jurisprudence. David Todd, 'Beneath Sovereignty. Extraterritoriality and Imperial Internationalism in Nineteenth-Century Egypt', 36 *Law and History Review* (2018), 110–21.

445 By contrast, James Mackintosh had found three "levels" of the law of nations – the most essential rules followed "even among the most barbarian nations", rules conducive to "mutual advantage" and those that led to "mild and friendly relations between civilized states". Sir James Mackintosh, *A Discourse on the Study of the Law of Nature and Nations* (London, Goode 1799), 81–2. Yet such discourse did not penetrate the language of the English jurists until later in the century.

international law, though "in a subordinate degree". So would the Ottoman Porte, "with only such exceptions as the reason of the thing may dictate".[446] Sovereignty was one thing, sovereign rights another. Phillimore accepted that the East India Company did exercise sovereign rights to the extent they were delegated by the crown and parliament.[447] Phillimore's list of states included five Central American republics and even "Hayti", and he agreed with Lord Stowell that "the African States had long ago acquired the character of established governments, with whom we have regular treaties acknowledging and confirming to them the relations of legal communities".[448] Although dealing with them "in some points entailed [its] relaxed application . . . they are nevertheless treated as having the rights and duties of states by the civilized world".[449] Phillimore gave the impression of international law as a well-organised system that left European policymakers free to treat foreign entities in ways that seemed pragmatically advisable. For that purpose he described in some detail recent actions by Britain and other European powers in Turkey, Portugal and Latin America, approving occasional intervention for the reasons of humanity, self-defence, preservation of the balance of power and protection of co-religionists. The main rule was non-intervention, Phillimore stressed, underlining Britain's role in managing this system; he even cited, with approval, Canning's famous boast that by recognising the independence of Latin American republics "I called the New World into existence, to redress the balance of the Old".[450]

[446] Robert Phillimore, *Commentaries upon International Law* (4 vols, Philadelphia, Johnson 1854–61), I, 101. He defined a "state" as "a people permanently occupying a fixed territory (*certam sedem*), bound together by common laws, habits, and customs into one body politic, exercising, through the medium of an organized Government, independent sovereignty and control over all persons and things within its boundaries, capable of making war and peace, and of entering into all International relations with the other communities of the globe", 94. No constitutional or religious criteria were appropriate. The treatment of the Ottoman empire noted an important Palmerstonian foreign policy goal: "the preservation and safety of the Ottoman Power was necessary for the safety of the European Communities", 98.

[447] Ibid., I, 138.

[448] Ibid., I, 96–7, 137–8.

[449] Ibid., I 97. The wording was carefully chosen, and the proposition itself may follow from Phillimore's expertise in maritime and admiralty law where the functional reasons for treating non-European entities on a par with European ones were greater than in other areas. Nevertheless, his views are in striking contrast with those a mere half-century later where men like Westlake deprived uncivilised communities of all status under international law.

[450] Ibid., I, 315–29.

And finally, there was the international commercial system, partly enshrined in free trade agreements, partly in the rules for enforcing property rights. Palmerston was clear that "it is the business of the government to open and secure the roads for the merchant".[451] In the 1830s and up to 1846 ideological pressures for free trade came from the Anti-Corn Law League, which often framed commerce as an instrument of international peace and harmony.[452] The internationalism of Cobden and Peel was supplemented by jurists such as Chitty who wrote of trade liberalisation as a natural aspect of freedom: "The restrictions on trade which have been endorsed absolutely or conditionally by almost all powerful nations of the world, have been the cause of a thousand wars."[453] A series of commercial treaties were concluded by Britain after 1823 on the basis of reciprocity, but eventually that requirement was given up altogether, with the development peaking in the repeal of the Corn Laws in 1846 and the abandonment of the Navigation Acts three years later.[454]

In the British mind, modern property rights were an important aspect of a stable global order.[455] Where they were threatened, Britain might intervene, preferably in cooperation with others. No statement has come to illustrate this policy better than Palmerston's response to parliament in the *Don Pacifico* affair in June 1850:

> As the Roman, in days of old, held himself free from indignity, when he could say, *Civis romanus sum* so also a British subject, in whatever land he may be, shall feel confident that the watchful eye and the strong arm of England will protect him from injustice and wrong.

Pacifico, a naturalised British citizen, had suffered damage to his house in Athens after an anti-Semitic crowd had set it on fire. As the Greek government had failed to compensate, Palmerston ordered a naval

451 Palmerston, quoted in Cain & Hopkins, *British Imperialism. 1688–2000*, 100.

452 For the whole story, see Anne Orford, 'Theorizing Free Trade', in A. Orford & F. Hoffmann (eds), *The Oxford Handbook of the Theory of International Law* (Oxford University Press), 710–26.

453 Joseph Chitty, *A Treatise on the Laws of Commerce and Manufactures* (New Jersey, The Lawbook Exchange Ltd 2011 [1824]), 73.

454 See e.g. P. J. Cain, 'Economics and Empire. The Metropolitan Context', in Andrew Porter (ed.), *The Oxford History of the British Empire*, vol. III: *The Nineteenth Century* (Oxford University Press 2001), 38–42.

455 On the British efforts to replace the African slave trade by "legitimate" production of palm oil that required introducing property rights in land (and eventual annexation), see Anthony G. Hopkins, 'Property Rights and Empire-Building. Britain's Annexation of Lagos, 1861', 40 *Journal of Economic History* (1980), 777–98.

blockade of the Greek coast, eventually securing a payment of 4,000 pounds. The action was condemned by France and Russia, and many English MPs regarded it as excessive. But it was hailed by the British population at large and secured Palmerston's electoral victory in the following year. Its arrogant jingoism may not, however, provide a full reflection of British attitudes. Rather, mid-nineteenth-century British policy is best seen as an opportunistic effort to survey the operation of the rules and the expansion of private influence through trade and take action only occasionally to support it.[456]

Often such intervention was neither possible nor necessary. Extraterritoriality, consular jurisdiction and more subtle forms of pressure on local rulers were cheaper and often more efficient. There was no reason to limit one's choices in advance. This was well explained by Palmerston in his response to a parliamentary motion by Lord Bentinck in July 1847, for Britain to intervene for the recovery of unpaid Spanish bonds held by British investors.[457] Citing Vattel, Grotius and Blackstone, Bentinck had argued that the bondholders' property right was absolute and that Britain had the unconditional legal duty to protect it.[458] In principle, Palmerston said, he agreed with Bentinck and the bondholders. But he differed as to whether such reaction was a matter of legal duty. Instead, he believed it fell within the government's political discretion. In his response Palmerston stressed that had the government of Spain violently seized the property of British subjects, or had there been a "compact between the two governments", it would undoubtedly be the duty of the English government to demand redress. The same was true "if any act of injustice or persecution [was] committed on a British subject".

> [But w]hen a British subject suffers injustice from a subject of foreign power, his application is to the laws of that country. . . . It is for the

[456] The classic discussion of how Victorian imperialism operated by "releasing private enterprise from the dead hand of the state", based on their earlier work on the "imperialism of free trade", is Ronald Robinson and John Gallagher, with Alice Denny, *Africa and the Victorians. The Official Mind of Imperialism* (London, Macmillan 1981), 1. For a good summary of aspects of Britain's "informal influence" in the nineteenth century, see Lynn, 'Policy, Trade and Informal Empire', 101–21.

[457] It transpired, according to Lord Bentinck, that they held these loans up to a sum of 46 million pounds sterling on which no interest had been paid. John Bassett Moore, *A Digest of International Law* (8 vols, Washington, Government Printing Office 1906), VI, 285–6.

[458] The legal position of the bondholders and Lord Bentick are expounded extensively in the pamphlet *The Speech of Viscount Palmerston in reply to the Motion by Lord George Bentinck M.P.* (London, Royal Exchange 1848).

advantage of this country to encourage dealings between its subjects and those foreign powers; I do not know that it is for the advantage of this country to give any great encouragement to British subjects to invest their capital in loans to foreign states.[459]

The British government would not act as a guarantor for its investors. This would only involve it "in serious disputes with foreign powers, on matters with regard to which the government of the day might have no opportunity of being consulted, or of giving opinion one way or another". In the following year, Palmerston sent a circular to British embassies, clarifying that whether or not to react in support of British bondholders

is for the British government entirely a question of discretion, and by no means a question of International Right. ... If the question is to be considered simply as a question of International Right, there can be no doubt whatever of the perfect right which the government of every country possesses to take up [such matter].[460]

It is true that "some of the most important conversations about global order were occurring far away from law schools and halls of diplomacy, in the course of mundane jurisdictional disputes arising in and on the boundaries of empires".[461] And no doubt, British hegemony in the early nineteenth century was pluralistic and fragmentary – pragmatic in a word. But "law schools and halls of diplomacy" were nevertheless places where the frame of imperial action was made express and justified. The "rage for order" that was such a palpable aspect of the British imperial ascent emerged from the self-image of a nation that believed itself as different from its despotic neighbours. This image had been formed in Fortescue's laudation of English laws, in Gentili's attack on Spanish hypocrisy and in Burke's attack of Hastings' machinations. And it produced Palmerston's

warning [to] foreign Governments who are debtors to British subjects, that the time may come when this House will no longer sit patient under the wrongs and injustice inflicted upon the subjects of this country ... that, if they do not make proper efforts adequately to fulfil their engagements, the Government of this country, whatever men may be in office, may be compelled by the force of public opinion and by the votes of Parliament to depart from that which has hitherto been the established practice of England, and to insist upon the payment of debts due to British subjects. That we have the means of enforcing

[459] Ibid., 1–2.
[460] Foreign Office circular January 1848, reproduced in Phillimore, *Commentaries*, II, 9.
[461] Benton & Ford, *Rage for Order*, 4.

the rights of British subjects, I am not prepared to dispute . . . England, I trust, will always have the means of obtaining justice for its subjects from any country upon the earth.[462]

Only a British foreign secretary would in have been able, in the mid-nineteenth century, to make that statement truthfully. British policy was a policy of global law. "Foreigners", Phillimore wrote, "are entitled not only to freedom from injury, but to the execution of justice in respect to their transactions with the subjects of [a foreign] State." True, they would first have to exhaust the local remedies. Britain had no interest to disturb domestic stability, as long as it was not organised as "a plain violation of the substance of *natural justice*".[463] Significantly, in Phillimore's systemic presentation of the law, intervention was an incident of the rule of *equality* of states – the same rule that Palmerston saw broken by Chinese official communications that treated the British as barbarians and insisted that they petition local authorities about their complaints. In a system where everyone was formally equal – such as in reciprocal free trade – advantage lay with the one with a realistic ambition to become the workshop of the world.[464] In the 1820s and 1830s, British merchant houses proliferated everywhere and the value of British exports tripled between 1830 and 1857. London replaced Amsterdam as the world's financial centre and British investment abroad boomed. These were typically investments by London-based elite groups with a close contact to government, including merchant bankers that became leading lenders to foreign states.[465] By mid-century, Britain had become "*the* world supplier of capital".[466] That trend was strengthened in subsequent decades so that for every

462 Palmerston, July 1847, as quoted in Phillimore, *Commentaries*, II, 11–12.

463 Ibid., II, 3–4, 5. According to Phillimore, a person who had settled in foreign land "cannot require his native Government to interfere on the subject of the operation of municipal laws, or the judgment of municipal tribunals upon his rights of immovable property in this foreign land", 6.

464 Bernard Semmel, *The Rise of Free Trade Imperialism* (Cambridge University Press 2009 [1970]), 8.

465 Baring's for example, had already at the end of the Napoleonic war achieved a position such that "it was likened to the sixth Great Power in Europe", John Orbell, 'Private Banks and International Finance in the Light of the Archives of Baring Brothers', in Yussef Cassis et al. (ed.), *The World of Private Banking* (London, Routledge 2009), 143.

466 Philip L. Cottrell, 'London's First "Big Bang"? Institutional Change in the City 1855–83', in Yussef Cassis et al. (ed.), *The World of Private Banking* (London, Routledge 2009), 65 (noting especially the contribution of the liberalisation of corporate law (1855–7) to the growth of British financing).

100 pounds invested home in the period 1865–1914, 156 and 161 pounds went to foreign and imperial companies respectively.[467] There was all the reason, therefore, to insist on international law and order. If justice was denied to foreign creditors, Phillimore wrote, if a debtor state "adopt[ed] measures of domestic finances, so fraudulent and iniquitous, so evidently repugnant to the first principles of justice, with so manifest an intention of defeating the claims of its creditors [then this will] authorise the Government of the creditors in having recourse to measures of retaliation, reprisals or to open war".[468]

Mostly things did not need to go that far.[469] In his often polemical and always entertaining commentaries for *The Times,* William Harcourt, leader of the Liberal Party and the first Whewell professor of international law (1869) at Cambridge discussed the question of intervention, noting immediately that this meant leaving the "firm and beaten path which law has defined and in practice consolidated, to explore the fluctuating and trackless depths of policy". He admitted that the matter aroused strong feelings and that there were "persons who think that if France, England, and Russia could only make up their minds to do what is very safely, though somewhat indefinitely, called 'something', the whole affair would be settled 'out of hand".[470] The cases of intervention in Greece and Belgium, and the suggested intervention in the US Civil War, exemplified the difficulties, the unforeseen hostility among those interfered against and between interferers themselves as well as the dangers any commitment to the eventual solution involves, bearing in mind that "of all things, the most cruel is mistaken and useless interference".[471] Talk about the rule of law among early nineteenth-century British politicians and bureaucrats was understandable in view of achieving and maintaining a stable international order. That may sometimes require interference, as Palmerston and Phillimore noted. But it may normally be more useful to display that other Victorian virtue, sober restraint. Empires thrive in part by imposing the rules, but more efficiently by sitting back and letting others consent to them.

[467] Cain & Hopkins, *British Imperialism. 1688–2000*, 170.

[468] Phillimore, *Commentaries*, II, 12.

[469] In the years 1857–62, for example, out of the 102 private applications for using force, only a handful were granted. John Darwin, *The Empire Project. The Rise and Fall of the British World System* (Cambridge University Press 2009), 39, 661 n. 47.

[470] William Harcourt, *Letters by Historicus on Some Questions of International Law* (London, Macmillan 1863), 43.

[471] Ibid., 50.

# Part IV

## Germany: Law, Government, Freedom

# 11

# A Science of State-Machines

## Ius naturae et gentium *As a German Discipline c. 1500–1758*

In a reflection on the "Present state of the European political system" from 1738 the then 26-year-old crown prince of Brandenburg-Prussia, the future Frederick II, described the task of ruling in the following terms:

> Just like a competent mechanic would not content himself to seeing the external surface of a clock but would rather like to see its structure and moving parts; in the same way a competent politician aims to know the permanent principles followed by courts, the structure of the policies of each prince, and the origins of events; he would leave nothing to chance; his spirit would aim to predict the future and to penetrate the chains of causes leading to the most distant centuries; in a word, prudence consists of knowing everything in order to judge and foresee all.[1]

Here was a lively image of the art of governing a state as akin to operating a machine, a clock, a favourite eighteenth-century metaphor. Frederick himself was called by friends and enemies the great state-mechanic or a "virtuoso of state-science" while the machine metaphor was also extended, apprehensively or admiringly, to Frederick's Prussia, especially its military operations.[2] The image goes a long way to express the effort to rationalise public administration by the enlightened despots of whom Frederick was the most famous example; later in the century it would further express the idea of well-ordered state as an automatism that would run without the help

[1] 'Frédéric II, Considérations sur l'état présent du corps politique de l'Europe', in *Oeuvres posthumes de Frédéric II, Roi de Prusse*, tome VI (Amsterdam 1789), 62.

[2] See Barbara Sollberg-Rilinger, *Der Staat als Machine, Zur politischen Metaphorik des absolutischen Fürstenstaats* (Berlin, Duncker & Humblot 1986), 62–75.

of human intervention.[3] This was not the only metaphor that eighteenth-century legal and political thinkers borrowed from technology and the natural sciences. Another was that of the balance of power through which the relations of state-machines were compared with the relations of physical objects existing in a field of countervailing forces. In what became the most successful work on the law of nations of the period, Frederick's contemporary Emer de Vattel wrote of Europe as a system and integral body instead of a "confused heap of detached pieces" whose stability could best be attained by an equilibrium of power, a situation where "no potentate would be able absolutely to predominate, and prescribe law to the others".[4]

The images were related. Those who were most insistent on thinking about the state mechanistically were also most inclined to resort to the balance as the aptest description of international policy and law. The images came in especially handy for academic minds at Protestant universities looking for a non-confessional language of state power to impress the rulers from whom they had received their professorships. Unlike the French, the German enlightenment was an academic business. In 1700, there would be around forty universities in Germany most of which – especially Halle (established in 1694) and later Göttingen (1734) – were programmatically oriented to offering local rulers novel ideas about law and government.[5] Natural law would help explain human beings as naturally part of the *bürgerliche Gesellschaft* whose earthly happiness (*Glückseligkeit*) the state was to bring about. There would be no divine rights. Religion would have nothing to do with public power. Governing the state would be simply managing the causalities of human behaviour:

> The point was to find an order that would possess validity for Catholics as well as Protestants, for Christians as well as Heathens, an order whose binding force would be obvious [*einsehbar*] for all.[6]

[3] See Ere Nokkala, 'The Machine of the State in Germany – the Case of Johann Heinrich Gottlob von Justi (1717–1771)', 5 *Contributions to the History of Concepts* (2009), 71–93.

[4] Emer de Vattel, *The Law of Nations* (Béla Kapossy & Richard Whatmore eds, Indianapolis, Liberty Fund 2008 [1758]), III 3 § 47 (496).

[5] Twenty-two were Protestant and eighteen Catholic. Notker Hammerstein, 'Zur Geschichte und Bedeutung der Universitäten im Heiligen Römischen Reich Deutschen Nation', 241 *Historische Zeitschrift* (1985), 287. Many of these were very small, with between 100 and 300 students. Especially the Protestant universities were almost without exception established by local rulers with practical usefulness in mind, 290.

[6] Christoph Link, 'Rechtswissenschaft', in Rudolf Vierhaus (ed.), *Wissenschaften im Zeitalter der Aufklärung* (Göttingen, Vandenhoeck & Ruprecht 1985), 123.

Thinking of the state as a machine and viewing the international world as a balance turned attention away from the interminable casuistries of scholasticism and the confessional conflict. Instead of speculations about justice or the ends of human life, the metaphors pointed backwards into the causes of political phenomena that needed to be learned in order to control and manage them. Things were not moved by teleology but by causality, and mastering the latter might finally enable controlling political events in the way Frederick suggested – "knowing everything in order to judge and foresee all".

Absolutism was a response to a religious and social crisis. Its rationalising urge drew force from a natural law that would in due course lead into the modern administrative state.[7] The process began from the turn to utility in sixteenth-century Protestant Aristotelianism as a way to overcome confessional conflict. Although the subsequent Grotius-reception was not painless, by the beginning of the eighteenth century, natural law had spread to all Protestant and some Catholic universities, and by mid-century it had become the predominant vocabulary of German political thought.[8] In the law faculty, it contributed to the high quality of such subjects as *ius publicum universale* (later *Allgemeine Staatsrecht*, or general theory of law and state) and *ius gentium naturale*. The development went along two paths. One led into an empirical–utilitarian science of government, seeking to assist the realisation of the objectives of public policy (*Staatszwecke*), security and happiness. Academic jurists would lecture and publish works on imperial history and political prudence or "state-wisdom" (*Staatsklugheit*).[9] The other direction led to the laws of reason that proposed to lay out the objectives of state action. The high point of such *Vernunftrecht* was reached in the abstractions of Christian Wolff who reconstructed the whole world of law through deductive inferences from higher-level principles to detailed instructions of policy. With the Wolffians, true philosophy promised to bring

[7] Reinhart Koselleck, *Critique and Crisis. Enlightenment and the Pathogenesis of Modern Society* (MIT Press 1988).

[8] It was not only the most general part of the law – a jurisprudence – but a general propaedeutic to all discourses around the human being, including political philosophy, history and theology. Hans-Erik Bödeker and István Hont, 'Naturrecht, Politische Ökonomie und Geschichte der Menschheit. Der Diskurs über die Gesellschaft in frühen Neuzeit', in Otto Dann & Diethelm Klippel (eds), *Naturrecht – Frühaufklärung – Revolution* (Hamburg, Meiner 1995), 82.

[9] Out of the large number of materials, see e.g. Hans Erik Bödeker, 'Die Staatswissenschaftliche Fächersystem im 18. Jahrhundert', in Rudolf Vierhaus (ed.), *Wissenschaften im Zeitalter der Aufklärung* (Göttingen, Vandenhoeck & Ruprecht 1985), 145–50.

together power and wisdom, *summa potestas* and *summa sapientia*, which would mould the ruler into "an agent of a social reason".[10]

Each strand had its distinct approach to the law of nations. The *sozialrechtlich* view remained sceptical about international rules and viewed diplomacy, treaty-making and war as law only in a wide sense as the prudential maxims of good policy. The rationalists were inclined to see the international world as an ideal set of harmonious principles that it was the point of law to realise in practice. The actual policies of the two did not differ markedly. Both counselled against precipitated belligerency, supported strict mercantilist policy and held it imperative that the ruler guide everything with a strong hand. The social philosophy strand focused on history and the growth of state power while the rationalists cautioned against "Machiavellianism" and speculated about how to make the interests of everyone coincide. Both would eventually borrow so much from each other as to become virtually indistinguishable in Emer de Vattel's *Droit des Gens* (1758).[11]

International law is a specifically German discipline.[12] Not only have German jurists played a powerful role in the field and many of its rules have been developed with the greatest sense of urgency at German universities. It is the very frame – the "grammar" – of international legal argument that has been inherited from the German debates that juxtaposed an overriding imperial jurisdiction to the territorial competences of imperial estates that gradually learned to think of themselves as sovereign. How to square the circle of the simultaneous validity of imperial and territorial laws is the international law problem *par excellence*, the root from which its other quandaries arise. The narrative of the law of nations in Germany must therefore begin with a sketch of the efforts of Protestant thinkers to support the rulers of territorial estates within the constitutional struggles of the German–Roman Empire.

[10] Werner Schneiders, 'Die Philosophie der aufgeklärten Absolutismus. Zum Verhältnis von Philosophie und Politik, Nicht nur im 18. Jahrhundert', in Hans Erich Bödeker & Ulrich Hermann (eds), *Aufklärung als Politisierung – Politiserung der Aufklärung* (Hamburg, Meiner 1987), 33. For an extensive discussion of the contrast between "Thomasian" civil philosophy and the metaphysical rationalism of the Wolffians, see Ian Hunter, *Rival Enlightenments. Civil and Metaphysical Philosophy in Early Modern Germany* (Cambridge University Press 2001).

[11] See my *From Apology to Utopia. The Structure of International Legal Argument* (Reissue with a New Epilogue Cambridge University Press 2005).

[12] Martti Koskenniemi, 'Between Coordination and Constitution. International Law as a German Discipline', 15 *Redescriptions. Yearbook of Political Thought, Conceptual History and Feminist Theory* (2011), 45–70.

## The Rise of State-Science: From Piety to Utility

Spanish Dominicans translated questions about state government into the ethics of ruling. The clash between that world and Protestantism could not have been manifested more sharply than by Martin Luther's (1483–1546) assigning to the flames the books of canon law that dominated law teaching at the University of Wittenberg.[13] Yet Luther never developed an alternative, so that the content of canon law would soon re-enter, appropriately purged, in evangelical handbooks and interpretative guides for lawyers. Luther himself never ceased attacking the Aristotelian–Thomistic principle that God was accessible through reason and natural law. God was a matter of faith – *sola fide* – not of reason. However, the social unrest of the 1520s compelled Luther to take a stand on the rightful principles of secular government. He did this by separating the kingdom of God and the kingdom of the world, but stressing the subject's *religious* duty to obey the secular ruler.[14] For the Augustinian Luther, most earthly beings were unjust sinners. They belonged to the kingdom of the world. It was there that law and the prince were needed to protect the just and punish the wicked, by war if necessary. In the latter case, subjects were to follow their prince and "to kill enemies without scruple, to rob and to burn and to do whatever damages to the enemy, according to the usages of war, until he is defeated".[15] Law was not about weak and corruptible reason but about sovereign power.

Luther's suspicion of lawyers, especially those *utrusque iuris*, was not shared by his collaborator Philip Melanchthon (1497–1560), for whom legal training at its best was "practical philosophy of written and unwritten law, justice in its totality".[16] Melanchthon found in Aristotle resources

[13] For Luther, "the canon law had become the instrument of clerical arbitrariness, abuse and avarice". John Witte, 'Canon Law in Lutheran Germany: A Surprising Case of Legal Transplantation', in *Lex et Romanitas. Essays for Alan Watson* (Berkeley, University of California, The Robbins Collection 2000), 197–8. For Luther's and Calvin's attack on Thomist Aristotelianism, see e.g. Peter Harrison, 'The Natural Philosopher and the Virtues', in Conal Condren et al. (eds), *The Philosopher in Early Modern Europe. The Nature of a Contested Identity* (Cambridge University Press 2006), 213–19.

[14] See e.g Luther, 'On Secular Authority. How Far Does the Obedience Owed to it Extend?', in Harro Höpfl (ed.), *Luther and Calvin, On Secular Authority* (Cambridge University Press 1991), 8 10.

[15] Ibid., 40.

[16] Jutta Brückner, *Staatswissenschaften, Kameralismus und Naturrecht. Ein Beitrag zur Geschichte des politischen Wissenschaft im Deutschland des späten 17. und frühen 18. Jahrhunderts* (Munich, Beck 1977), 152.

for weaving a Protestant view of secular government within an all-encompassing theory of natural law (*lex naturae*) covering the whole of Christian morality. Being innate, it could, with God's help, be grasped by conscience.[17] Its predominant source was the two tables of the Decalogue that Melanchthon read to include the main tenets of Christian dogma and key principles of Roman law, including the rights of property, jurisdiction and contracts as well as the rest of *ius gentium* in the Digest.[18] This reinserted natural law in the realm of faith and enabled the reformers to put the prince in the position of a Christian paterfamilias, duty-bound to promote religion and fight heresy.[19] The theocratic nature of the Lutheran polity was further strengthened by the practice that in questions of doubt, the prince and the magistrates were to turn to university theologians for counsel (*consilia*).[20] This enabled the determination of Christian *Obrigkeit* by evangelical jurists and theologians whose cooperation at Protestant universities secured the political consolidation of the Lutheran confession.[21]

Luther and Melanchthon had no specific doctrine of law of nations. They wrote in conditions of parcellised sovereignty where local princes guarded jealously their right of taxation and access to peasant labour. When the reformers gave their support to the Protestant princes of the Schmalkaldic League in the 1530s, they invoked a federalist interpretation of the imperial constitution. *Imperium*, they held, belonged directly to the territorial rulers and their right of self-defence was derived from canon and civil law.[22] During the social conflict of the 1520s and 1530s Melanchthon first called upon subjects to bear the actions of even wicked princes with patience but later wrote that "we should obey God rather than men", even endorsing the older view that authorised resistance against a tyrant.[23] After the Protestant estates had been consolidated in

[17] See Merio Scattola, *Das Naturrecht vor dem Naturrecht. Zur Geschichte des 'ius naturae' im. 16. Jahrhundert* (Tübingen, Niemeyer 1999), 42–3; Witte, 'Canon Law in Lutheran Germany', 215–18.

[18] Scattola, *Naturrecht*, 49.

[19] See Horst Dreitzel, *Protestantisher Aristotelismus und absoluter Staat. Die 'Politica' des Henning Arnisaeus (ca. 1575–1636)* (Wiesbaden, Steiner 1970), 92.

[20] John Witte Jr., *Law and Protestantism. The Legal Teachings of the Lutheran Reformation* (Cambridge University Press 2002), 131, 180–1.

[21] Quentin Skinner, *The Foundations of Modern Political Thought* (2 vols, Cambridge University Press 1977), II, 66–9; Dreitzel, *Protestantischer Aristotelismus*, 96.

[22] Skinner, *Foundations*, II, 196–8; Robert M. Kingdon, 'Calvinism and Resistance Theory 1550–1580', in J. H. Burns and Mark Goldie (eds), *The Cambridge History of Political Thought 1450–1700* (Cambridge University Press 1991), 200–3.

[23] See Scattola, *Naturrecht*, 55–66; Skinner, *Foundations*, II, 204–6.

the Peace of Augsburg (1555), this doctrine became a cornerstone of Calvinist political theory. Evangelical lawyers also held it to be obvious that Protestant princes would conduct their relations with the external world through biblical ethics. Johannes Oldendorp (1486–1567), a leading jurist of the reformation era, derived his natural law and the law of nations wholly from God and regarded the Ten Commandments as its most important source.[24] He aimed to systematise what had in his view become a scandalously fragmented world of separate laws and confusing distinctions. Writing in a Roman law idiom, Oldendorp ascribed no independent law-creating powers to human communities at all. The law of nations was simply another form of natural law. Its origin lay with God, its defining characteristic being that, unlike civil law, it bound many nations (*Est multorum populorum authoritas*).[25] Because it was innate in the hearts of humans everywhere it could also be used to govern the external relations of separate communities.[26]

Melanchton's work on natural law supported the rise of a Protestant Aristotelianism at German universities that examined the government of political community from the perspective of the subjects' secular happiness. The principal forum was the philosophy (arts) faculty where practical philosophy was divided into politics, *oikonomia* and ethics; these dealt respectively with the government of the *polis*, the family and individual conscience. Out of these, ethics tended to dominate, pushing politics, too, into an examination of the virtues of the Christian prince.[27] Because legal training followed only after students had passed the philosophy courses, even Protestant jurists tended to think within an Aristotelian frame, integrating law with ideals of evangelical freedom and divine providence.[28] One such work was the widely read *Regentenbuch* by the

[24] Witte, *Law and Protestantism*, 154–68; Scattola, *Naturrecht*, 149–55; Carl von Kaltenborn, *Die Vorläufer des Hugo Grotius auf dem Gebiete der Ius naturae et gentium* (Leipzig, Mayer 1848), I, 233–6.

[25] Johannes Oldendorp, *Iuris naturalis gentium et civilis* (Cologne 1539), extracts in Kaltenborn, *Vorläufer*, II, 11–12, 15–17.

[26] See further Scattola, *Naturrecht*, 149–56.

[27] This gave rise to the widespread *Fürstenspiegel* literature. See especially Hans Maier, 'Die Lehre der Politik an den deutschen Universitäten, vornehmlich vom 16. bis 18. Jahrhundert', in Dieter Oberdörfer (ed.), *Wissenschaftliche Politik. Eine Einführung in Grundfragen ihrer Tradition und Theorie* (2nd edn, Freiburg, Rossbach 1966), 64–72. See also Maier, *Die ältere deutsche Staats- und Verwaltungslehre* (München, DTV 1986), 164–72.

[28] For an early – and partisan – description, see Kalternborn, *Die Vorläufer des Hugo Grotius*, 190–217. See also Michael Stolleis, *Geschichte des öffentlichen Rechts in Deutschland. Erster Band 1600–1800* (Munich, Beck 1988), 85–6.

Mansfeld jurist and diplomat Georg Lauterbeck (1505/10–78), written right after the Augsburg peace to teach territorial rulers how to combine efficient government with the demands of religious piety. The five books of the work were composed of examples from ancient and modern history on most areas of government, including some detail on the principles of warfare.[29] Manliness and mercy appeared as values not only more Christian but also as more efficient in war than cruelty and betrayal. War should not be easily commenced, the ruler should listen to more than one advisor, promises to one's enemies should be kept and alliances should not be needlessly concluded.[30] Pious and patriarchical, the work viewed law as an instrument of princely rule and contained no independent concept of a legal system.

Nor did it respond to the constitutional problem created by the increase of the prerogatives of territorial rulers at the cost of the imperial centre. Partly formalised in the reforms of 1495, they now extended to legislation, defence and foreign policy and were conceptualised as territorial supremacy (*Landeshoheit*), which nevertheless fell short of formal sovereignty.[31] Although the confessions agreed that the ends of political communities coincided with Christian virtue, they differed completely on what this might mean. Instead of alleviating the conflict, the Augsburg Peace actually sharpened it. Under the maxim *cuis regio – eius religio* the clash of territorial rulers took the form of religious opposition. While Protestant princes would argue for the equality of the confessions, Catholic rulers would insist that the common law that was to decide their disputes included canon law provisions on the treatment of heresy as well.[32] Under such terms, toleration was impossible. As a result, many legal and political thinkers would turn to secular vocabularies such as neo-Stoicism, Tacitism and *raison d'état* that would go beyond education in the virtues. Government was to operate under

[29] Georg Lauterbeck, *Regentenbuch* (Leipzig 1557), III, 86. [30] Ibid., III, 3–7.

[31] *Landeshoheit* consisted of specific ("positive") regalia and not the fullness of authority connoted by "sovereignty". See e.g. Hanns Gross, *Empire and Sovereignty. A History of the Public Law Literature in the Holy Roman Empire, 1599–1804* (The University of Chicago Press 1973), 13–14; Thomas Ertman, *Birth of the Leviathan. Building States and Regimes in Medieval and Early Modern Europe* (Cambridge University Press 1997), 238–42; Peter Preu, *Polizeibegriff und Staatszwecklehre. Die Entwicklung des Polizeibegriffs durch die Rechts- und Staatswissenschaften des 18. Jahrhunderts* (Göttingen, Schwartz 1983), 37–9.

[32] Fritz Dickmann, 'Das Problem der Gleichberechtigung der Konfessionen im Reich im 16. und 17. Jahrhundert', in *Friedensrecht und Friedenssicherung. Studien zum Friedensproblem in der neueren Geschichte* (Göttingen, Vandenhoeck & Ruprecht 1971), 17–26.

its own laws, analogous to those drawn from nature.[33] Machiavellism remained a term of opprobrium, but making the distinction between good and bad reason of states facilitated the entry of technical considerations into legal commentary.[34]

The first chairs of an independent *Politica* had been created at the end of the sixteenth century in the United Provinces from where the teachings of an experience-based "civil prudence" by the Dutch humanist Justus Lipsius (1547–1606) began to spread to universities in Germany.[35] One of the first advocates of a renewed study of politics, the Helmstedt neo-Aristotelian Henning Arnisaeus (1575–1636) used medicine as the methodological paradigm to be imitated by the *politici*. States (*reipublicae*) were the form that the civil society (*civitas*) took for itself as it emerged in response to the needs of human sociability.[36] The study of politics was a study of the "health" of statehood, understood as an order of *summa potestas*. Such study should limit itself to the real factors contributing to its maintenance. It would understand the purpose of the state as immanent to the state itself.[37] Arnisaeus, who was not a jurist, integrated large aspects of

[33] In fact, both sides had used an appeal to "German liberties" against the emperor, Protestant princes even joining with Germany's arch-enemy, France's Henri II. See further Hajo Holborn, *A History of Modern Germany. The Reformation* (Princeton University Press 1959), 231–42 and Michael Stolleis, 'Arcana imperii und Ratio Status. Bemerkungen zur politischen Theories des frühen 17. Jahrhunderts', in Michael Stolleis, *Staat und Staatsräson in der frühen Neuzeit. Studien zur Geschichte des öffentlichen Rechts* (Frankfurt, Suhrkamp 1990), 28–9.

[34] On the reception of Machiavelli in Germany around 1600, see Brückner, *Staatswissenschaften*, 159–63; Thomas Simon, *"Gute Policey". Ordnungsleitbilder und Zielverstellungen politischen Handelns in der Frühen Neuzeit* (Frankfurt, Klostermann 2004), 197–208, Stolleis, *Geschichte*, I, 90–3, 197–203; Michael Stolleis, '"Löwe und Fuchs". Eine politische Metaphere für Frühabsolutismus', in Stolleis, *Staat und Staatsräson*, 21–36. See further e.g. Harro Höpfl, 'Orthodoxy and the Reason of State', XXIII *History of Political Thought* (2002), 211–37.

[35] See Michael Stolleis, 'Lipsius-Recepzion in der politisch-juristischen Literatur 17. Jahrhunderts in Deutschland', in Stolleis, *Staat und Staatsräson*, 232–66; Stolleis, *Geschichte*, I, 97–104. See further Horst Dreitzel, 'Reason of State and the Crisis of Political Aristotelianism. An Essay on the Development of 17th Century Political Philosophy', XXVIII *History of European Ideas* (2002), 163–87.

[36] Henning Arnisaeus, *Doctrina politica in genuinam methodum qua est Aristotelis reducta* (editio nova, Amsterdam, Elsevier 1651), I I (15–19, 38–41), VII (157–8). The discussion of the internal forces threatening the stability of the *respublica* and the "remedies" in Part II Ch IV–V followed closely the *raison d' état* literature. Like Botero, Arnisaeus treated even religion instrumentally – "nothing contributes more to the stability of the *respublica* than religion", II IV (507).

[37] Ibid., I (24, 157–8). See further, Dreitzel, *Protestantischer Aristotelismus*, 116–19, 155–9, 177–83. See also Martin van Gelderen, 'The State and Its Rivals in early-Modern

natural law and *ius gentium* in his conception of government. They were to be supplemented by prudential, historical and technical idioms intended to help the state learn to govern itself.[38] The separation of the *civitas* from the *respublica*, its order of government, further highlighted the insufficiency of mere natural law; statecraft required more than deductions from rules.[39] Unlike Oldendorp, Arnisaeus did not equate *ius gentium* with natural law but regarded it as positive law, practised by advanced peoples (*cultiores gentes*) and covering all generally practised laws, from marriage and contracts to war and diplomacy. Christianity did not form a privileged realm, and the rules of inter-Christian wars did not differ from those applicable between Christians and heathens. Even as war was against natural law, pragmatic reasons suggested leaving the question of its justice aside.[40] Inspired by Bodin, Arniseus worried over protracted confessional tension. His aim was to produce a normative language that would be independent from theological ethics. By relying on experience and observation, it would engage directly with practical problems of government.[41]

Another influential work was Arnold Clapmar's (1574–1604) posthumously published *De arcanis rerumpublicarum* (1605) that combined themes of *ragion di stato* with Tacitist use of examples about good and bad statecraft from Roman history.[42] Clapmar had received his influences in Protestant Altdorf where he occupied a chair in history and politics. In order to secure the maintenance of peace in a religiously divided polity it was necessary, he wrote, to learn the secrets of effective government (*arcana*) as well as the arts of dissimulation (*simulacra*) from the ancients, especially Aristotle and Tacitus who had used them to

Europe', in Quentin Skinner and Bo Stråth (eds), *States and Citizens. History, Theory, Prospects* (Cambridge University Press 2003), 89; Brückner, *Staatswissenschaften*, 152–5. On the tasks of the "Politica" genre, see also Robert von Friedeberg, 'Persona and Office. Althusius on the Formation of Magistrates and Councillors', in Conal Condren et al. (eds), *The Philosopher in Early Modern Europe. The Nature of a Contested Identity* (Cambridge University Press 2006), 162–9.

[38] Dreitzel, *Protestantischer Aristotelismus*, 188–212.

[39] For the *civitas* (matter) vs. *respublica* (form) distinction, see Arnisaeus, *Doctrina politica* I (137) and commentary in Annabel Brett, *Changes of State. Nature and the Limits of the City in Early Modern Natural Law* (Princeton University Press 2010), 131–4.

[40] Dreitzel, *Protestantischer Aristotelismus*, 202–3.

[41] Hunter, *Rival Enlightenments*, 77–80; Heinrich Meier, '*Der Lehre der Politik*'. *Vier Kapitel zur Unterscheidung Politischer Theologie und Politischer Philosophie* (Stuttgart, J. B. Metzler Verlag 2009), 81–4. This is why he often became the target of attacks by the natural lawyers. Brückner, *Staatswissenschaften*, 153.

[42] Arnold Clapmar, *De arcanis rerum publicarum libri sex* (Amsterdam, Elzevirium 1644).

protect the city and its rulers.[43] Clapmar made a careful distinction between *arcana imperii* that were designed to uphold the form of the state (*quae presentem Reipublicae formam conservant*) and *arcana dominationis* meant to protect the rulers themselves (*eorum qui principatem in Republica obtinent*).[44] Each constitutional form would have its own *arcana* respecting the way its dominion would be most efficiently guaranteed.[45] In contrast to regular legislation, *arcana* involved hidden techniques (*actes abstrusae*) that may be designed to uphold law but are not law in themselves.[46] Behind their apparent immorality they serve a more important, long-term justice. Every profession had its informal techniques. *Arcana* were what jurists used to apply legal principles from state to state and regime to regime.[47] Such views had great influence in the German debates, opening the door for utilitarian arguments within a naturalist frame. Reason of state would become *Gute Policey*.[48] It would support public law notions such as necessity, public good and the *salus populi*, amalgamating lawful government with effective government.[49] While a purely empirical Machiavellism would remain unacceptable, normative direction could now be received from a natural law that would understand how to organise human passions into a rational system of government.[50]

## Empire vs. the Territories

Already well before Westphalia, a lively debate had begun among European jurists on the legal status of the Holy Roman Empire (of the German Nation). Famously, Bartolus had regarded the emperor as possessor of *de iure* lordship over imperial territories while *de facto* legislative powers would belong to these territories themselves. This

[43] On the techniques of dissimulation and appearance – use of honorific titles, writing patriotic poetry, celebrating heroes etc. – that underlie the different constitutional forms of government, see ibid., VI ("De simulachriis imperii"), 270 ff.

[44] Ibid., III 1 (108–9). See further Michel Senellart, *Les arts de gouverner. Du regimen médiéval au concept de gouvernement* (Paris, Seuil 1995), 267–9.

[45] Clapmar, *De arcanis*, I 8 (18–19) and also III.

[46] Senellart, *Les arts de gouverner*, 260. [47] Clapmar, *De arcanis*, I 2 (4–6).

[48] Brückner, *Staatswissenschaften*, 159–63. For the reception of reason of state in Germany after Clapmar, see further Dreitzel, 'Reason of State', 168–79.

[49] Berd Roeck, *Reichssystem und Reichsherkommen. Die Diskussion über die Staatlichkeit des Reiches in der politischen Publizistik des 17. und 18. Jahrhunderts* (Stuttgart, Steiner 1984), 80.

[50] I am much indebted for this argument to Stolleis, 'Arcana imperii und Ratio Status', 37–76.

rather paradoxical notion left conflicts to be resolved on an ad hoc basis. The growth of territorial power made it increasingly difficult to follow Justinian to understand the relations between the hundreds of lay and ecclesiastical lordships and the emperor. By the late thirteenth century, the empire had almost come to seem like a voluntary union between equals, with imperial electors operating as a kind of imperial advisory council.[51] The Diet's role had been formalised in the constitutional reform that began in 1495 and led to the system of Electoral Capitulations in which the emperor would promise to preserve the privileges of the territorial rulers.[52]

The Protestant rebellion highlighted the urgency to fix the imperial constitution more firmly. What Gierke would call the "great peace union of the estates" preserved the emperor as its formal head.[53] Alongside a system of six, later seven, imperial circles to implement the *Ewige Landfriede*, the reforms led to the establishment of the Imperial Cameral Court (*Reichskammergericht*) in Wetzlar as a supreme court with standing judiciary, accompanied by an Imperial Aulic Council (*Reichshofrat*) in Vienna with a broadly similar mandate. The overlapping jurisdiction of these two bodies, the Wetzlar court more inclined towards Protestant estates and old German laws and the Vienna Council towards the emperor and Roman law, remained an inexhaustible source of jurisdictional conflict.[54] Together with burgeoning territorial legislation, they channelled the confessional split into juridical arguments on the powers of territorial rulers and their relations to the emperor.[55] The complexity of the latter issue – the *forma imperii* – would lay the ground for almost two centuries of constitutional quarrels. Here lie the origins of the eventually massive predominance of German jurists in theorising the law of nations. How to reconcile national sovereignty with an overriding legal order is simply the "German problem" of jurisdictional delimitation between territorial estates and the empire, writ large.

51 See Gross, *Empire and Sovereignty*, 14–15. The view of the empire as a union of estates (and not of any "nation") is highlighted in Otto von Gierke, *Community in Historical Perspective* (Mary Fischer trans. & Anthony Black ed., Cambridge University Press 1990), 72–4.

52 On the system of capitulations, see Gross, *Empire and Sovereignty*, 42–7.

53 Gierke, *Community in Historical Perspective*, 73.

54 See Stolleis, *Geschichte*, I, 156–66. See further Michael Hughes, *Law and Politics in 18th Century Germany. The Imperial Aulic Council in the Reign of Charles VI* (London, Royal Historical Society 1988), 27–56.

55 Stolleis, *Geschichte*, I, 126–46.

Under the old view, supported by Roman law, the empire was a monarchy, with the emperor enjoying *imperium merum & mixtum*, supreme criminal and civil jurisdiction. Against this view, territorial legislation had expanded in the sixteenth century to the extent that it had persuaded Jean Bodin to qualify sovereignty in the Reich as actually vested in the estates. The empire would be an aristocracy of which the emperor was only "the first and chief person".[56] Protestant princes supported this view as it downplayed the importance of Roman law with its preference for the imperial court in Vienna. They relied on a mixture of competences drawn from old German laws, imperial capitulations and the Augsburg arrangements that would make it possible to understand *Landeshoheit* as a kind of quasi-sovereignty.[57]

The jurists were heavily influenced by confessional orientations, those at Calvinist universities seeking a metaphysical grounding to popular sovereignty against Lutheran deference to the prince's *maiestas*. The views of Johannes Althusius (1557–1638) may not have had great influence at the time, but offered a spiritual matrix to conceive the empire as a union with the imperial electors as representatives of the people.[58] In his early writings Althusius employed *ius gentium* like the Spanish theologians, as a mutable type of natural–positive law underlying the principal social institutions.[59] His later work concentrated on the emergence and government of the state (*regnum, respublica*) as the highest of the many layers of communities, a "*consociatio publica universalis major*".[60] Althusius propounded a rather mystical view of the state as a composite of local associations, private, such as the family, as well as public, such as the city. Even as the monarch was its soul or head, he was nevertheless dependent on the other parts of the state body.[61] Sovereignty in

56 "*chef & premier*", Jean Bodin, *Les six livres de la république* (Lyon, Tournes 1629), II V (210). See also Bodin, *Method for the Easy Comprehension of History* (B. Reynolds trans., New York, Norton 1969 [1567]), 206–8. On Bodin's influence in Germany, see also Stolleis, *Geschichte*, I, 172–82.

57 Stolleis, *Geschichte*, I, 185.

58 Johannes Althusius, *Politica* (Frederick S. Carney ed. & trans., Indianapolis, Liberty Fund 1996 [1603]), XVII § 52–9 (101–2). Althusius observed that his theory of "symbiotic association" as the foundation of all genuinely "political" community was "permitted and approved by the law of nations, '*ius gentium*'", V § 2 (39).

59 Brett, *Changes of State*, 81–2. The Spanish connection is particularly stressed in Ernst Reibstein, *Johannes Althusius als Fortsätzer der Schule von Salamanca* (Karlsruhe, Müller 1955).

60 Peter Jochen Winters, 'Johannes Althusius', in Michael Stolleis (ed.), *Staatsdenker in der frühen Neuzeit* (Munich, Beck 1995), 41.

61 Reibstein, *Johannes Althusius*, 207–8. For Althusius' changing conceptions of the commonwealth, see Brett, *Changes of State*, 213–19.

Althusius was located in the body politic and the prince was its supreme magistrate, appointed by a contract where he bound himself to rule by God, right reason and the common good.[62] The objective of government was to provide the material necessities of life and the protection of the commonwealth, including by just war "for preserving liberty, privileges, rights, peace and tranquillity, and for defending true religion".[63] Althusius' concern was to defend the autonomy of Calvinist communities, but his views could be used to present the relations between the estates and the emperor as a system of reciprocal rights and obligations.[64] Most jurists were satisfied to operate with something like a *status mixtus* under which sovereign competences were shared between imperial institutions analogously to old feudal law.[65] Even as ideas of territorial self-government and imperial rule both persisted, by the time of the Thirty Years' War, most legislation, defence and foreign policy had fallen into the hands of the territorial princes.[66] The continued disputes about the location of formal sovereignty reflected practical interests and the position of the jurists in the imperial or territorial bureaucracies.

The most widely followed debate took place between the old-Protestant imperialist Dietrich (Theodore) Reinkingk (1590–1664), representative of the duke of Bremen in the Westphalian peace talks, and Boguslaw v. Chemniz, ("Hippolyte a Lapide", 1605–1678), court historiographer of Sweden and vocal critic of Habsburg rule. Reinkingk represented a neo-medieval divine right theory, defending the absolute supremacy of the emperor over the estates, deriving the jurisdiction of the territorial powers from the emperor. As the last of the Four Empires, Germany was vested with an eschatological purpose, he argued, carrier of the Roman heritage through the *translatio imperii*. Of course, territorial estates had their competences as laid out in 1555; princes were to see to the spiritual welfare of their subjects.[67] But their jurisdiction flowed ultimately from the emperor. Reinkingk also wrote long passages on just war in defence of fatherland, religion and friends and allies. Using biblical examples and references to St Augustine but also to Grotius he stressed the extreme severity of the decision to go to

[62] Althusius, *Politica*, XIX § 7 (121). [63] Ibid., XVI § 1, 17 (88).

[64] Gross, *Empire and Sovereignty*, 146–57.

[65] See ibid., 170–9; Stolleis, *Geschichte*, I, 179–80.

[66] For a brief modern summary, see Peter H. Wilson, *The Holy Roman Empire 1495–1806* (2nd edn, London, Palgrave 2011), 11–36.

[67] Christoph Link, 'Dietrich Reinkingk', in Michael Stolleis (ed.), *Staatsdenker in der Frühen Neuzeit* (Munich, Beck 1995), 92–3.

war but also the constraints or Christian morality.[68] On the opposite side in the Thirty Years' War, Chemniz attacked the monopolisation of the imperial seat by the Habsburg family.[69] Viewing the empire as an aristocracy, based on ancient German freedoms, Chemniz employed the idiom of *ratio status* to argue that sovereignty belonged to the empire itself, as represented by the imperial Diet. Chemniz rejected the use of Roman law in imperial government and deplored the way imperial electors had arrogated to themselves the rights and liberties of the estates. His work became "a real "Cathecism of the princes".[70] To Reinkingk's horror, Chemniz felt it wholly in accordance with the *raison d'état* to confiscate Habsburg lands and to reform the imperial constitution so as to provide for the leadership of the Diet, assisted by the *Reichsregiment* left over from earlier reforms.[71]

## Westphalia in Context

The Peace of Westphalia (1648) did not bring these debates to an end. To the contrary, the fact that imperial estates were able to participate in the conference in their own name and to become parties to what was an international treaty consolidated the fragmenting tendencies in Germany.[72] The recognition of their territorial supremacy further consolidated the position of the princes as did the right accorded to them to keep military forces and to conclude alliances with outside

[68] Dietrich [Theodore] Reinkingk, *Biblische Policey* (Frankfurt, Spörlin 1653), 481 ff.

[69] For the German translation of the Latin original, see Hippolithi a Lapide, *Abriss der Staats-Verfassung, Staats-Verhältnis und Bedürfniss des Römischen Reichs Deutscher Nation* (Mainz 1761).

[70] Stolleis, *Geschichte*, I, 204.

[71] He defined *ratio status* in the conventionally neutral way as the "advancement of the general good and the welfare of the state". Lapide, *Abriss der Staats-Verfassung*, 72. He also stressed the many religious and legal limits to *raison d'état*, 77–99. For the attack on Reinkingk's view, see 129 ff. See further, Rudolf Hoke, 'Hippolitus a Lapide', in Michael Stolleis (ed.), *Staatsdenker in der frühen Neuzeit* (Munich, Beck 1995), 118–28; Stolleis, *Geschichte*, I, 203–7.

[72] See Art I & XVII §10–11, Treaty of Osnabrück, in Wilhelm Grewe, *Fontes historiae iuris gentium*, II: 1493–1815 (3 vols., Berlin, De Gruyter 1988), 188, 201. The imperial estates became parties both as estates of the empire and in their own right as allies (*Verbündeten*) to the respective principal parties (emperor and empire on the one side, France and Sweden on the other). See Heinhard Steiger, 'Der Westfälische Frieden – Grundgesetz für Europe?', in Heinz Duchhardt (ed.), *Der Westfälische Friede* (Munich, Oldenbourg 1998), 40–4. For the contrast between the old (fragmentation) and newer (flexible pluralism) interpretations, see Wilson, *Holy Roman Empire*, 47–50.

powers as long as they were not directed against the emperor or the empire itself.[73] But contemporaries persisted in thinking about the empire as a single state. After all, imperial law and the jurisdiction of imperial institutions did cover the whole territory of the empire.[74] Many of the rights received by the estates only repeated de facto concessions extracted from the emperor earlier, and nobody suggested that *Landeshoheit* amounted to full sovereignty.[75] The *forma imperii* controversy persisted well beyond Westphalia.[76] The writings of Reinkingk and Chemniz became partisan symbols for the opposition between Christian politics and reason of state, Caesarean imperialism and the "ancient" freedoms of the territorial estates. But Reinkingk's views of a unitary empire were hopelessly outdated, and Chemniz's hopes about the leading role of the Diet were undermined by the ambitions of territorial rulers. What the latter's writings achieved, however, was the banalisation of the alliance between public law and *raison d'état.*[77] The search for sovereignty would merge with the effort to advance the security and welfare of the state.

It is striking to what extent jurists were undisturbed by the way Westphalia transgressed the boundary between imperial law and the law of nations, feudal law and the laws of royal succession. Far into the mid-seventeenth century the Holy Roman Empire had stood at the centre of European political and legal imagination. The settlement extended from a constitutional law of the empire, reaffirmed by the new *Reichsabschied* of 1654, to an international treaty involving territorial changes, compensations and a pledge for permanent peace involving

[73] Art VIII.1 and VIII.2 of the Treaty of Osnabrück, Grewe, *Fontes iuris gentium*, II, 197. For a (slightly anachronistic) discussion of significance of the provisions to the constitution of Germany from the perspective of international law, see Albrecht Randelzhofer, *Völkerrechtliche Aspekte des Heiligen Römischen Reiches nach 1648* (Berlin, Duncker & Humblot 1966), 54–62. Many of the treaty's provisions on the imperial estates mostly restated old principles of feudal law (including the principle that a vassal was not entitled to ally against the lord). Karl-Heinz Ziegler, 'Die Bedeutung des Westfälischen Friedens für das europäische Völkerrecht', in his *Fata Iuris Gentium. Kleine Schriften zur Geschichte des europäischen Völkerrechts* (Baden-Baden, Nomos 2008), 312–14.

[74] See e.g. Roeck, *Reichssystem*, 60–2, 70–3; Bernd Mathias Kremer, 'Die Interpretation des Westfälischen Friedens durch den "Schulen" des IusPublicum', in Heinz Duchhardt (ed.), *Der Westfälische Friede* (Munich, Oldenbourg 1998), 766–7.

[75] Kremer, 'Die Interpretation des Westfälischen Friedens', 769; Steiner, 'Grundgesetz für Europa', 68.

[76] See Kremer, 'Die Interpretation des Westfälischen Friedens', 766–9; Stolleis *Geschichte*, I, 170–86.

[77] Stolleis, *Geschichte*, I, 207–8; Dreitzel, 'Reason of State', 168–70.

nearly all European powers. Some became guarantors of the imperial constitution, others objects of collective recognition, all as apparently equal treaty partners. The papal protest against negotiating with heretics having been swept aside, the parties could still understand themselves as concluding a Christian peace.[78] Together with the subsequent peace treaties of Nijmegen and Regensburg, Westphalia would inspire jurists to imagine a "public law of Europe" consisting of relations between formal sovereigns and a mosaic of dynastic rights adjusted by concessions to the victorious powers.[79]

Simultaneously, Germany would lose its status as the continuation of the Rome of the Caesars, a development with both eschatological and political significance. The Book of Daniel had prophesied the end of the world at the demise of Rome so that giving up thinking of Germany as a continuator of the empire opened a way from a biblical to a properly political vision of world history. The biblical story had been questioned by individual jurists, but a decisive rupture between ancient Rome and the German–Roman Empire was achieved in the works of the polymath Hermann Conring (1606–81). As a student in Leiden Conring had acquainted himself with the neo-stoic ideas of the university's most famous teacher, the recently deceased Lipsius. In 1632 he was appointed professor of natural philosophy and rhetoric at the University of Helmstedt. For long periods of time, he regarded medicine as his principal profession so that when Queen Christina invited him to Stockholm in 1650 this was as royal counsellor and court physician.[80] But Conring never left Germany for a longer period, preferring the life of a scholar, publishing translations of Tacitus and Machiavelli, presiding over countless dissertations on politics and the reason of state, and providing counsel to territorial rulers.[81] His intellectual objective was to separate the study of politics from the public law of specific states; if the jurist ought to know the

[78] This formulation would in different variants serve until the late eighteenth century to denote a more or less shared sense of European cultural and historical unity. For the intertwining of the imperial and international aspects of the treaties, see Steiger, 'Grundgesetz für Europa', 67–80.

[79] For the intermixture of the many types of law in the post-Westphalian "states-system", see Heinhard Steiger, 'Rechtliche Strukturen der europäischen Staatsordnung 1648–1792', 59 *Die Zeitschrift für ausländisches öffentliches Recht und Völkerrecht* (1999), 609–45. I agree with the interpretation by Benno Teschke, *The Myth of 1648. Class, Geopolitics and the Making of Modern International Relations* (London, Verso 2003), especially 238–46.

[80] Constant Fasolt, *The Limits of History* (The University of Chicago Press 2004), 77.

[81] Ibid., 77–88.

laws of a single state, the political expert was to be able to administer all states.[82] This would combine a historically oriented science of statehood with a utilitarian view of rulership. Although Conring supported absolutist monarchy, he did not think the sovereign's powers as unlimited but defined by the public good, articulated in an early theory of state purpose (*Staatszweck*).[83]

In 1651 Conring published a dissertation on the reason of states over which he had presided and for which he was generally held to be the author.[84] The 59 theses of the work combined old ideas of Christian rulership with new Machiavellian literatures organised under Aristotelian constitutional categories; laws should fit the form of the state, its nature and needs and there ought not to be excessive amounts of them.[85] Conring defined *ratio status* in the most general of terms, as the interest (*utilitas*) of the political community, understood ethically and oriented towards natural law.[86] Ruling was not to go against religion, morality or justice, although exceptions could be made to the laws if public utility required this. But in general, Conring's *ratio status* was a theory of good government that aimed at peace and security by lawful and morally acceptable means.[87] Because its focus was not the good of the ruler but the happiness of civil society, it opened the way from old normative–theoretical natural law to an empirical–instrumental *Staatskunst*.[88]

This was a serious effort to separate the study of statehood from the reading of positive laws and constitutions, something that Conring had long been interested in making.[89] The result was two path-breaking works – *On the Origin of German Law* ("De origine juris Germanici") and

[82] Gross, *Empire and Sovereignty*, 271–2; Notker Hammerstein, *Ius und Historie. Ein Beitrag zur Geschichte des historischen Denkens an deutschen Universitäten im späten 17. und im 18. Jahrhundert* (Göttingen, Vandenhoeck & Ruprecht 1972), 98–102.

[83] See especially Dietmar Willoweit, 'Hermann Conring', in Michael Stolleis (ed.), *Staatsdenker in der frühen Neuzeit* (Munich, Beck 1995), 132–40.

[84] Hermann Conring, *Dissertatio de ratione status* (Helmstedt, Müller 1651).

[85] Ibid., XIX–XXI.

[86] Ibid., XI. Michael Stolleis, 'Machiavellismus und Staatsräson. Ein Beitrag zu Conrings politischem Denken', in Stolleis, *Staat und Staatsräson*, 79.

[87] Conring, *Dissertatio*, XLV–XLIIX [*sic*]. See further Stolleis, 'Machiavellismus', 79–80; Michel Senellart, 'Y a-t-il un théorie allemande de la raison d'état au XVII siècle?', in Yves Zarka (ed.), *Raison et déraison d'Etat* (Presses Universitaires de France 1994), 278.

[88] See e.g. Axel Rüdiger, *Staatslehre und Staatsbildung. Die Staatswissenschaft an der Universität Halle im 18. Jahrhundert* (Tübingen, Niemeyer 2005), 134–44.

[89] Gross, *Empire and Sovereignty*, 258–66.

*On the Roman Empire of the Germans* ("De germanorum Imperio Romano"), both published in 1643. In the former, Conring demonstrated that there was no evidence at all that Emperor Lothar III would have decided in the 1130s to inaugurate the study of Roman law in Bologna and to use the Justinian code in German courts. Conring reconstructed the actual process whereby Roman law had been gradually and only in the course of the fifteenth century adopted in German courts and bureaucracies by jurists trained in Roman law. The latter work – *On the Roman Empire of the Germans* – made a decisive break between the two empires, opening the way for a novel historical–political consciousness for Germany. The Roman empire had ceased to exist by the irruption of the German tribes. Charlemagne and Otto the Great had adopted the title of Roman emperor simply as "an incidental supplement to the original title of *rex Germanorum*".[90]

Conring wrote his conclusions in a shorter work, *New Discourse on the Roman-German Emperor*, which was originally submitted as a dissertation at Helmstedt but clandestinely and against Conring's wishes published in 1641.[91] The original Roman Empire never ruled over the whole world, either in fact or in law. It "cannot have been founded on any other rights or titles than those on which possessions or acquisitions are normally founded".[92] Of the old empire, nothing was left apart from the city of Rome, its immediate vicinity and some scattered Italian territories. The imperial title gave Charlemagne nothing but "control over the city of Rome, the pope, the exarchate of Ravenna, and certain towns outside the borders of the Lombard kingdom".[93] From these historical facts it followed, Conring concluded, that Roman law was not automatically binding in Germany and even less as some kind of a universal law. The German king had no claim to rule as the alleged continuator of the line of Roman emperors. He ruled only over Germany as a separate though a large and powerful state. But as there was no longer any universal empire, "even a small independent state as, for example, the republic of Ragusa, enjoys exactly the same rights of sovereignty [*maiestas*] as a larger one."[94]

90 Ibid., 281.

91 The relationship of the two works is meticulously reconstructed in Fasolt, *Limits of History*, 92–154. The only significant difference found by Fasolt was that while the shorter work concluded that Rome as an empire was gone, the longer one insisted that it lived in the lands around Rome but had been usurped by the pope, 112–18.

92 Hermann Conring, *New Discourse on the Roman-German Emperor* (C. Fasolt ed. & trans., Tempe, AZ, Center for Medieval and Renaissance Studies 2005 [1641]), XII (11).

93 Ibid., XXVIII (37).

94 Ibid., LVI (81).

## Reception of Grotius: Setting Up the Frame

The few natural law tracts in sixteenth-century Germany did not intend to challenge Aristotelianism; the closed confessional state of post-1555 had no need for the neutral space natural law offered for conflicting beliefs.[95] A change would come after 1648 with the slow introduction of Grotius at German universities. Initially, Grotius had been known through his religious writings (especially *De veritate religionis Christianae*), which were dealt with critically by orthodox Lutherans and Calvinists.[96] Although there had been some awareness of *De jure belli ac pacis* during the Thirty Years' War, wider notice of the work began to spread only in the latter half of the century through expanding contacts with Dutch culture. Already by 1661 thirteen Latin editions were circulating in Germany and the first German commentaries came out in the 1660s and 1670s, including annotated student editions and larger analyses, both positive and critical.[97] The first chair in "natural law and the law of nations" established in the Heidelberg philosophy faculty in 1661 was designed for teaching "according to Grotius". This was soon followed by Kiel (1665), Jena (1665), Greifswald (1674), Helmstedt (1675?), Marburg (1676), Giessen (1677), Strasbourg (1694) and other, especially Protestant universities.[98] The high point of the reception was the publication of the first German translation in 1707 followed by further editions by Christian Wolff in 1734 and the Cocceji brothers in 1752. In his introduction to the

95 Horst Denzer, *Moralphilosophie und Naturrecht bei Samuel Pufendorf* (Munich, Beck 1972), 317–18; Meier, 'Die Lehre der Politik', 76–8.

96 Günter Hoffmann-Loerzer, 'Studien zu Hugo Grotius' (diss., Munich 1971), 242–4.

97 The first brief work was J. von Felden's *Annotata ad H. Grotium de iure belli ac pacis* (1653), which produced an Aristotelian critique of Grotius' conception of "justice". Then followed Georg Adam Struve's *Grotius Enucleatus Sive Controversiae de iure belli ac pacis* (1660) and the works by Jan Klenck (1662) and Jacob Thomasius (1670). The first large Grotius commentary was by the Strasbourg professor Johann Heinrich Böckler (1663), followed by Caspar Ziegler (1666) and Johann Adam Osiander (1667). See Denzer, *Moralphilosophie*, 316–17; Werner Schneiders, *Naturrecht und Liebesethik. Zur Geschichte der praktischen Philosophie im Hinblick auf Christian Thomasius* (Hildesheim, Olms 1971), 66–7. For a full list of these works, many of which supplemented the original text with large commentaries, see Hoffmann-Loertzer, 'Studien', 250–60.

98 Hoffmann-Loertzer, 'Studien', 261; Denzer, *Moralphilosophie*, 319; Stolleis, *Geschichte*, I, 195. See further Frank Grunert, 'The Reception of Hugo Grotius' *De jure belli ac pacis* in Early German Enlightenment', in Tim Hochstrasser and Peter Schröder (eds), *Early Modern Natural Law Theories* (Dordrecht, Kluwer 2003), 89–105. The first Catholic universities to set up chairs of natural law were Freiburg (1716) and Salzburg (1717). See Schröder and Pielemeyer, 'Naturrecht an den deutschen Universitäten', 257.

1707 text, Christian Thomasius celebrated the work's usefulness for princes and their advisors; it helped them to decide how to accommodate concerns of conscience with the good of one's community, justice among princes with the protection of one's subjects.[99]

The content of the reception was varied. Many objected to Grotius' haphazard choice of source-materials and the relative scarcity of Christian texts. The "impious hypothesis" seemed dubious; was Grotius a closet atheist? Jurists who would later be regarded as members of the Grotian school rejected innate moral and legal norms and embraced the focus on self-preservation as a radical departure from scholasticism.[100] By the end of the century, natural law had become such an important tool in the legitimation of statehood that even orthodox Christian jurists such as Veit Ludwig von Seckendorff (1626–92), counsellor for Saxe-Gotha and the author of the influential *Teutsche Fürsten-Staat* (1656), would in his late *Christen-Staat* of 1685 take issue with Pufendorf's separation of nature and revelation. Seckendorff stood at the beginning of a long line of German thinkers who saw the total care of the population as the objective of princely government. In that latter work, Seckendorff claimed that the normative guidance for that purpose was received from the Ten Commandments, which were also valid for pagans owing to their practical usefulness.[101] The attempt was a failure, a theological grounding of natural law lacked precisely those historical and empirical aspects that accounted for its attraction.[102]

Natural law first entered the philosophy faculty as part of practical philosophy where it contributed to the relative rise in importance of politics at the cost of ethics in the Aristotelian curriculum.[103] It also provided a descriptive frame for understanding the operation of human societies, preparing students for their study in the "higher faculties", including law. Chairs of natural law later came to be established in the law faculty, too, where they took on the role of general theory of law and government, integrating the settlement of the Thirty Years' War in a theoretical architectonic justifying the consolidation of absolutist

99 Hoffmann-Loertzer, 'Studien', 266–7.

100 Grunert, 'The Reception of Grotius', 89–102.

101 Veit Ludwig von Seckendorff, *Christen-Staat* (Leipzig, Fritschen 1716), 883–6.

102 See Frank Grunert, *Normbegründung und politische Legitimation. Zur Rechts- und Staatsphilosophie der deutschen Frühaufklärung* (Tübingen, Niemeyer 2000), 29–35.

103 Meier, 'Die Lehre der Politik', 89–90; Notker Hammerstein, 'Thomasius und die Rechtsgelehrsamkeit', in Notker Hammerstein (ed.), *Geschichte als Arsenal. Ausgewählte Aufsätze zu Recht, Hof und Universitäten der Frühen Neuzeit* (Göttingen, Wellstein 2010), 258–9.

statehood and developing in the eighteenth century into an increasingly pragmatic discipline of statecraft.[104] It also eased the religious worries emerging with confessional antagonisms in Europe and the discovery of alien cultures outside:

> So it was that the discussion of public law which had begun in the universities of the Counter-reformation Catholic Spain, slipped from the hands of catholic science and, in the 17th century, with Althusius, Grotius, and Hobbes, became the domain of Protestant jurists and political philosophers.[105]

By 1700 natural law had become the ruling ideology of the early German enlightenment.[106] Its success depended on the power of the *frame* it offered within which it was possible to combine philosophical ambition with the practical tasks of government. The most powerful and the most misunderstood aspect of that Grotian frame has to do with the distinction between natural and voluntary law, which in Germany and elsewhere came to be translated into the all-pervasive opposition between natural law and positivism – or perhaps, reason and will, *ratio* and *voluntas* – suggesting to subsequent generations that there was a deeply philosophical problem to be resolved before one's legal work could get going. These oppositions and their many permutations would enable jurists to create argumentative chains that appeared more or less abstract or concrete, more or less philosophical or practice-oriented as might be needed in view of the expectations of their changing audiences. So powerful has the frame been that most studies of German (or indeed any) law have been habitually classed as either more or less "naturalist" and "positivist".[107]

[104] See Denzer, *Moralphilosophie*, 312–22.

[105] Wilhelm Schmidt-Biggemann, 'New Structures of Knowledge', in Hilde de Ridder-Symons (ed.), *A History of the University in Europe*, vol. VII (Cambridge University Press 1996), 121.

[106] Link, 'Rechtswissenschaft', 122–9.

[107] This is fine if focus is on styles of argument, the contrast between rational principles on the one hand, and treaties and practices on the other. What counts as persuasive depends on the situation: positive law works on legal routine, naturalism on its frame. But it is essential not to lose sight of the interdependence between the two. As I have elaborated elsewhere, all natural law needs (positive) evidence to make itself known, and all positive law needs an explanation on why it should be held binding. It is this system of argumentative moves that has, ever since Grotius, made it difficult and often pointless to class particular jurists as either naturalists or positivists: *to be persuasive, a jurist needs to be both.* Law is not philosophy. See further my "Transformations of Natural Law. Germany 1648–1815", in *The Oxford Handbook of International Legal Theory* (A. Orford & F. Hoffmann eds, Oxford University Press 2016), 59–81.

## Rethinking the Empire: Pufendorf

That Grotius would have initiated a sharp new beginning in natural law "can be regarded essentially an 'invention' of Pufendorf".[108] Although he produced a powerful defence of absolutism, Grotius never suggested a general theory of political statehood. Even as the subjective rights in *De jure belli ac pacis* would form the basis of a commutative system of inter-individual relations, they never expanded into a view of a universal civil society in juxtaposition to territorially limited sovereignties. Both of these were included in Samuel Pufendorf's (1632–94) view of moral entities that would situate natural law and the law of nations in a human world of rational arguments and utilitarian pursuits. Grotius' view of innate sociability bound him closely to his Spanish predecessors while Pufendorf liberated humans to imagine social worlds based on nothing beyond their will and ability to reason. But it was Grotius who produced the frame within which reason became visible in what humans did and where those who could mould reality in accordance with their will were entitled to think this wholly right – as Rousseau would in due course indignantly point out.[109] Pufendorf, the son of a Lutheran minister in Saxony and holder in Heidelberg of the first chair in the law of nature and of nations (1661), possessed an ingenious ability to express these Grotian insights in an "eclectic" view of statehood that would finally move the debate on the constitution of the Roman–German Empire into a historically reliable, pragmatic approach to the post-confessional state.

Dismissing Pufendorf as an unoriginal mediator has long been out of fashion.[110] Although the idea of a specifically human sociability based on the ability to recognise and obey legal rules was a Grotian innovation, it was Pufendorf who linked it to the historical process of how civil

[108] István Hont, 'The Languages of Sociability and Commerce. Samuel Pufendorf and the Theoretical Foundations of the "Four Stages Theory"', in *Jealousy of Trade. International Competition and the Nation-State in Historical Perspective* (Harvard University Press 2005), 164.

[109] Jean-Jacques Rousseau, *The Social Contract* (M. Cranston trans. & intro., Harmondsworth, Penguin, 1968), 51.

[110] The old point was made in e.g. Leonard Krieger, *The Politics of Discretion. Pufendorf and the Acceptance of Natural Law* (The University of Chicago Press 1965), and Notker Hammerstein 'Samuel Pufendorf', in Michael Stolleis (ed.), *Staatsdenker im 17. und 18. Jahrhundert* (2nd edn, Frankfurt, Metzner 1987), 172. New assessments are included in Alfred Dufour, 'Pufendorf', in J. H. Burns and Mark Goldie (eds), *The Cambridge History of Political Thought 1450–1700* (Cambridge University Press 1991), 561–88 and Hunter, *Rival Enlightenments*, 148–96.

society would eventually organise itself in a firm statehood. For the old Aristotelian school, law participated in the search of the good that resided in the immutable nature of things. That view was both teleological and essentialist. By contrast, Pufendorf's law was applicable within and between communities sharing different notions of the good – the situation of Post-Westphalian Europe *par excellence* – each creating its political life from the contingencies of its culture and history. Pufendorf's contribution was to produce a civil society, anterior to the political community and ruled by principles reasonably analogous to the ones natural sciences operated to govern the physical world.[111] Pufendorf's state was to service this civil society by providing for its peace and welfare.[112]

Pufendorf's life has been recounted in many places.[113] After a few years of theology studies in Leipzig he moved in 1656 to Jena where he became interested in novel theories of the scientific method. Appointment in the service of the Swedish diplomat Peter Julius Coyet in Copenhagen provided him with the opportunity to compose his first book, *Elementorum jurisprudentia universalis*, in 1660 on the strength of which he received the chair in Heidelberg in the following year. This was supported by Conring with whom he had been corresponding on the prospect of preparing a complete treatise on the law of nature – a project leading nine years later into his principal publication, *De jure naturae et gentium* (1672).[114] Conring had just detached the constitutional history of the empire from its eschatological moorings and, with his *Notitia rerumpublicarum* opened a way for an empirical–utilitarian political science. In their correspondence Pufendorf was able to clarify his eclectic method that stressed intellectual independence and the need

[111] See e.g. Hans Medick, *Naturzustand und Naturgeschichte der bürgerlichen Gesellschaft* (Göttingen, Vandenhoeck & Ruprecht 1973), 40–63. Pufendorf did not (unlike Hobbes) think that human affairs were governed by the *same* laws as the natural world. The opening section of *On the Law of Nations* creates alongside the world of natural entities that of "moral entities" – a distinction foreshadowing that between natural and human sciences.

[112] On these two tasks, see further Simon, *"Gute Policey"*, 218 ff.

[113] See e.g. Krieger, *Politics of Discretion*, 11–38; Pierre Laurent, *Pufendorf et la loi naturelle* (Paris, Vrin 1982), 9–24; Simone Goyard-Fabre, *Pufendorf et le droit naturel* (Presses Universitaires de France 1994), 8–18.

[114] Samuel Pufendorf, *De jure naturae et gentium, libri octo*, trans. as *On the Law of Nature and Nations. Eight Books* (2 vols, W. Oldfather trans., Oxford, Clarendon 1934). This is not to say that Pufendorf would not in many ways have continued older traditions of political thought. See Goyard-Fabre, *Pufendorf*, 43–4 and passim. His "modernity" refers to his effort to explain the origin and functioning of society from principles immanent in society itself.

to extract from existing approaches those that best suited the matter to be examined.[115] This meant combining abstract principles of natural reason with (concrete) considerations of *ratio status* that Conring had recently domesticated for constitutional analysis – the Grotian frame updated, in other words.[116]

The first place where Pufendorf had occasion to experiment with this method was the 1667 commentary on the Reich constitution that he composed under the pseudonym of an Italian nobleman "Severinus de Monzambano".[117] As we have seen, the matter had earlier been treated under the three Aristotelian categories and their mixed forms but it had received new urgency owing to the incursions by Louis XIV into German territory, the rising ambitions of the Habsburgs and the establishment of the first *Rheinbund* (1658).[118] In the polemically written but largely admired work, Pufendorf adopted Conring's historical idiom, arguing that the Reich was neither monarchy, aristocracy nor "polity" but instead a historically specific, composite form of public power – *civitas composita* – a system of states that nonetheless constituted a whole.[119] The Aristotelian categories were too abstract to fit a concrete, historical entity. Neither theology nor philosophy provided an appropriate vocabulary. The nature of the constitution was an eminently legal question and "law" what reason would produce from a close historical analysis what was needed for security and welfare. There was no single, easily locatable *maiestas* anywhere in the imperial realm. The powers of Vienna had arisen from agreements, capitulations and imperial practices that expressed the interests of each estate, its *Staatsräson.* Written in support of Pufendorf's mentor, the Palatinate Elector Karl Ludwig,

115 See especially, T. J. Hochstrasser, *Natural Law Theories in the Early Enlightenment* (Cambridge University Press 2000), 42–60. On "eclectic philosophy", see further Horst Dreitzel, 'The Reception of Hobbes in the Political Philosophy of the Early German Enlightenment', 29 *History of European Ideas* (2003), 255–8.

116 Brückner, *Staatswissenschaft*, 164–8.

117 Samuel Pufendorf, "Severinus de Monzambano Veronese de Statu Imperii germanici ad Laelium Fratrem, Dominum Trezolani," *Liber unum – Über die Verfassung des Deutschen Reiches* (H. Bresslau trans., Berlin, Hobbing 1922), VI, § 9. For the English text, see now Samuel Pufendorf, *The Present State of Germany* (M. J. Seidl ed. & intro., Indianapolis, Liberty Fund 2007), 176–7. For a discussion, see Peter Schröder, "The Constitution of the Holy Roman Empire after 1648. Samuel Pufendorf's Assessment in his Monzambano", 42 *The Historical Journal* (1999), 961–83.

118 Michael Stolleis, 'Textor und Pufendorf über die Ratio Status Imperii im Jahre 1667', in Stolleis, *Staat und Staatsräson*, 110.

119 In the English translation, "System of several Independent States united by a League or a Confederacy", Pufendorf, *The Present State of Germany*, VIII § 4–5 (216, 215–20).

stress on the liberty of the estates was natural. But Pufendorf also rejected Chemnitz's radical proposal to depose the Habsburgs and to reorganise the Reich as an aristocracy. The empire, too, had its own *Staatsräson*, best expressed in the balance between its many elements. True, it was in many ways sick. Its defensive abilities were woefully inadequate and its internal administration inefficient.[120] These problems could only be dealt with by developing Germany into a system of states where the interests of all would be mixed with the tempers of the different confessions, an arrangement that would also be in the general European interest.[121]

Although Monzambano became a huge success, many worried that the expression "system of states" would contribute to further German weakness. Pufendorf followed the work by two shorter texts where he dealt specifically with irregular forms of statehood, *Disquisitio de republica irregulari* (1669) and *De systematibus civitatum* (1675), making there the distinction between simple and composite states with both regular and irregular variants. The latter work concentrated expressly on alliances between sovereign states which, although they constituted a unity, still left their members sovereign.[122] These early federalist works did not deny the statehood of the empire, but gave up the effort to defend its Roman heritage. If the result was a *monstrum*, as Pufendorf famously claimed, this was only in respect of the Aristotelian categories; its health could be improved by gradually renegotiating the relationship of its *Volk* to their territories.[123]

In the year after *Monzambano* Pufendorf followed his brother into Swedish service, first to occupy the newly established chair on natural law and the law of nations at the University of Lund, then as privy counsellor and historiographer of King Charles XI. From now on he would combine polemical exchanges with his academic antagonists with government business, including the production of a history of Sweden, the second volume of the larger work *Introduction to the History of the Great Empires and States of Contemporary Europe* (1682–5).[124] The latter work was designed to teach young men looking for a court position the arts of

[120] Ibid., VII § 8–10 (201–9). [121] Ibid., Ch VIII § 3 (213).

[122] Samuel Pufendorf, 'De systematibus civitatum', in Samuel Pufendorf, *Dissertationes Academicae Selectiores* (London, Junghans 1675), 264–330.

[123] Roeck, *Reichssystem*, 45–9.

[124] Samuel Pufendorf, *Commentarii de rebus Suecicis ab expeditione Gustavi-Adolphi usque ad abdicationem Christinae* (Utrecht, 1686); Samuel Pufendorf, *Einleitung zu der Historie der vornähmsten Reiche und Staaten von Europa* (Frankfurt, Knoch 1709).

government where the reason of state would be deduced from the nation's history and brought forth as its interest. Recent history was especially important, for it was hard to "*apprehend, what great Benefit we can expect to receive from* Cornelius Nepos, Curtius, *and the first Decad of* Livy, *as to our Modern Affairs*". Instead, "*what a considerable Advantage it is to understand the Modern History as well of our Native Country, as also its neighbouring Nations, is sufficiently known to such as are employ'd in States Affairs*".[125] History would combine the virtues of statesmanship with accurate facts about the rise and fall of nations, thus helping the aspiring courtiers to distinguish the nation's "Imaginary and Real Interests".[126]

In these works, Pufendorf emerged as a historian and a political advisor, putting into effect his utilitarian notion of statehood and public law that underlay the earlier analysis of the German constitution. In 1688 he came to Berlin at the service of Frederick William the Great Elector of Brandenburg-Prussia as counsellor and *Historiographus primarius*, producing in that capacity a 1,600–page history of the Great Elector's reign.[127] By now, events leading up to the Peace of Nijmegen had made clear the hegemonic intentions of Louis XIV; the work was compiled largely as a defence of the imperial realm where Frederick William himself appeared as an exemplary prince, always alert, in Pufendorf's telling, to the call of *Staatsräson*.[128]

## A New Science of Society

The coincidence of scepticism, confessional antagonism and civil war in seventeenth-century Europe has been famously addressed as "the crisis of European conscience".[129] As the power of old legal and moral vocabularies diminished, scholars were drawn to natural science to

[125] Samuel Pufendorf, *Introduction to the History of the Principal Kingdoms and States of Europe* (Jodocus Cull trans., Michael J. Seidler intro. & ed., Indianapolis, Liberty Fund 2013 [1682]), Preface to the Reader (5, 6).

[126] Ibid., Preface (7). In this way, late in life, Pufendorf seemed to suggest that the study of natural law would become concrete and receive applicability as *raison d'état*. Krieger, *Politics of Discretion*, 188, 187–201.

[127] The work was published posthumously. Samuel Pufendorf, *De rebus gestis Friderici-Wilhelmi Electoris Brandenburgici* (2 vols, Berlin, Schrey 1695). He also wrote a history of the first years of the Grand Elector's successor, Elector Frederick III, but this was deemed unfit for publication until the end of the eighteenth century.

[128] See Detlev Döring, 'Pufendorfs Berufung nach Brandenburg-Preussen', in Fiammetta Palladini and Gerald Hartung (eds), *Samuel Pufendorf und die europäische Frühaufklärung* (Berlin, Akademie 1996), 21–8.

[129] Paul Hazard, *La crise de la conscience européenne 1680–1715* (Paris, Fayard 1971).

speak with more confidence about human matters that otherwise seemed in tatters. Ten years after Westphalia Pufendorf had entered the University of Jena where he fell under the influence of the Cartesian ethicist Erhard Weigel (1625–99), contemplating how to substitute a more rigorously mathematical method for the scholasticism ruling German universities. Pufendorf had been disappointed in the primacy of theology and the connected notion of science for which certainty meant, as he put it, that "*habemus expressum textum in Aristotele*".[130] While he valued Aristotle, he objected to the scholastic straitjacket. A properly scientific method could only be either empirical or mathematical.[131] Under paradoxically favourable external circumstances – he was imprisoned in Copenhagen owing to his position with the Swedish ambassador at the start of the Swedish–Danish war in 1658 – he wrote his first work, *Elementorum jurisprudentiae universalis*, where he experimented with mathematical formulae within a moral language.[132] Although contemporaries were impressed, Pufendorf himself became soon dissatisfied with his youthful abstractions. In his mature work of 1672, *De jure naturae et gentium*, abbreviated in the following year as *De officio humanis et civis juxta legem naturalem*, in what became the most widely used treatise of natural law in late seventeenth- and early eighteenth-century century Europe, he turned into a new direction.[133]

Aristotle had written that "[t]he good . . . is not something common answering to one Idea".[134] It has no universal form, independent of subject or situation. It was not possible to imagine norms enjoining humankind as a whole. This had prompted scholasticism to build a complex casuistry of the different forms of good appropriate for particular situations. Pufendorf wished to challenge this scepticism. Could there not be universal moral truths as well, purged of accidental qualities? To have something of the kind, he assumed in *De jure naturae et gentium*, required paying close attention to the observable invariables of

[130] Siegfried Wollgast, 'Die deutsche Frühaufklärung und Samuel Pufendorf', in Fiammetta Palladini and Gerald Hartung (eds), *Samuel Pufendorf und die europäische Frühaufklärung* (Berlin, Akademie 1996), 56.

[131] Pufendorf made these points in the so-called Boinenburg correspondence in 1663 as he was preparing his main work. See Laurent, *Pufendorf*, 28–9.

[132] Samuel Pufendorf, *Two Books of the Elements of Universal Jurisprudence* (Thomas Behme ed. & intro., Indianapolis, Liberty Fund 2009).

[133] For the latter work, see Samuel Pufendorf, *On the Duty of Man and Citizen according to Natural Law* (James Tully ed., Michael Silverthorne trans., Cambridge University Press 1991).

[134] Aristotle, *The Nicomachean Ethics* I.6 (D. Ross ed., Oxford University Press 1980), I 6 (10).

human nature. For Aristotle and Grotius, sociability had been an innate quality, reachable through metaphysical reflection. Pufendorf was dissatisfied with this. If sociability were something innate, then it would be visible in children while we would have to assume that most adults had forgotten it. But children learn sociability as they are socialised into the world of their parents.[135] There was no natural path to our moral and political institutions. Property, contract and sovereignty rested on nothing else than a conclusion human beings had drawn from what they knew of each other, namely that they were self-loving and weak and therefore needed to leave "pure" civil society for the political state.[136] But – here was the crux – although these institutions were artificial, they were not arbitrary. Instead, they emerged from the application of reason on empirical data. To demonstrate how reason operated Pufendorf had recourse to the thought-experiment of the state of nature that he received from the analytical–composite method he had learned with Weigel in Jena.[137]

That method consisted in first analysing the complex empirical world into its anthropologically basic elements and then explaining that complexity by recomposing it from the elements thus received.[138] The most basic datum we knew about human beings was their self-love, connected with an intense drive for self-preservation in the conditions of pathetic weakness. Moreover, humans were also filled with "a great conglomeration of affections and desires unknown to beast [and a] craving for luxuries, ambition, honours, and the desire to surpass others".[139] For such creatures, reason dictated one overriding rule. It commanded sociability:

[135] Pufendorf, *On the Law of Nature and of Nations*, II 3 § 13 (20–2). See further, Hochstrasser, *Natural Law Theories*, 86–95.

[136] Pufendorf, *On the Law of Nature and of Nations*, II 2 § 12; 3 § 14–15; VII 1 § 7 (176–7, 205–7, 959). Pufendorf did not have well-defined notions of the two. His German translator used "*bürgerliche Gesellschaft*" for any relationship of community between superiors and subordinates. Manfred Riedel, 'Gesellschaft, bürgerliche', in Otto Brunner et al. (eds), *Geschichtliche Grundbegriffe*, Band 2 (8 vols., Stuttgart, Klett-Cotta 2004), 739–40. For a useful discussion of the "social" in Pufendorf, see Hochstrasser, *Natural Law Theories*, 95–106.

[137] For Pufendorf's method in its contemporaneous context, see Denzer, *Moralphilosophie und Naturrecht*, 35–58 and 279–96. See further Hunter, *Rival Enlightenments*, 169–80; Goyard-Fabre, *Pufendorf*, 63–88.

[138] See further, Theo Kobusch, 'Pufendorf's Lehre vom moralischen Sein', in Fiammetta Palladini and Gerald Hartung (eds), *Samuel Pufendorf und die europäische Frühaufklärung* (Berlin, Akademie 1996), 67–71.

[139] Samuel Pufendorf, *On the Law of Nature and of Nations*, II I § 6 (150).

Man, then, is an animal with an intense concern for his own preservation, needy by himself, incapable of protection without the help of his fellows, and very well fitted for the mutual provision of benefits.[140]

There was nothing locally specific about these features; the conclusion that humans had to behave sociably had the same universal power as the laws of geometry.[141] The state of nature was not at all as Hobbes believed, empty of substantive natural law. On the contrary, by enjoining their self-love with their weakness humans could reason and then contract into existence all the basic institutions of civil society.[142] This was how they had, for example, agreed to live in paternally ruled households and to create private property.[143] Obligation had as much reality before the conclusion of the social contract as thereafter – indeed this was the only way to explain why the social contract *itself* was binding. Because Hobbes had no concept of obligation he remained unable to distinguish natural duties from mere coercion.[144] But also the suggestion by Grotius, namely that there would be natural law even if there were no God, was absurd. For even if this could explain what was naturally good and bad, it could not explain why we should follow the former and avoid the latter. For there to be command, a superior was needed and in the natural state that could only be God.[145]

140 Pufendorf, *On the Duty*, 35. The popular use of the term "mos geometricus" signified at this time either (1) a method that strived for clarity and systemic coherence as well as the postulation and derivation of concepts and axioms, or (2) specifically the analytical–composite approach. Denzer, *Moralphilosophie*, 282–3.

141 For the Stoic influences in Pufendorf's work, see Hochstrasser, *Natural Law Theories*, 66–70.

142 Pufendorf, *On the Law of Nature and of Nations*, II II § 9 (172–3). For an extensive discussion of Pufendorf's "natural private law", valid already in the state of nature, see Goyard-Fabre, *Pufendorf*, 125–57.

143 Pufendorf's original "communism" was of the negative variant – one in which things "belonged no more to one than to another". *On the Law of Nature and of Nations*, IV IV § 5 (537). Private property was created first by taking of possession of things and then agreeing on how and when such taking might lead to exclusive right, § 6–8 (539–45). See Stephen Buckle, *Natural Law and the Theory of Property. Grotius to Hume* (Oxford, Clarendon 1991), 91–107; James Tully, *A Discourse on Property. John Locke and His Adversaries* (Cambridge University Press 1980), 86–91.

144 This notion of "obligation" creates the link between Pufendorf and earlier theological views about how to distinguish factual power from authority. In both, a command by the superior – God – is needed in order to create a creditor–debtor relationship implied in the idea of "obligation". See the especially useful Gerald Hartung, *Die Naturrechtsdebatte. Geschichte der Obligatio vom 17 bis 20 Jahrhundert* (Freiburg, Alber 1998), 17–25, 38–50.

145 See e.g. Pufendorf, *On the Law of Nature and of Nations*, II 3 § 19 (215).

Thus property and contract existed already in the state of nature, with natural law providing these with binding force:

> a quiet and decorous society cannot exist without distinct dominions of things [...] [T]herefore, such were introduced in accordance with the proper requirements of human affairs, and with the aim of natural law. After this was done, the same law enjoins the observance of whatever things work to the end of the dominion instituted.[146]

Property, contract and a market for goods would thus already exist in the state of nature. They were basic aspects of the algorithm about self-love, weakness and reason. Because the argument did not limit itself to the *polis*, it was applicable and indeed applied on an everyday basis in the relations between states. After all, "[t]here are many states to-day which seek abroad the means to supply their needs or pleasure, and yet they do not feel it necessary to combine with those with whom they trade into one state".[147] But this did not take away the precariousness of property and contract in the natural state. Though some people were always ready to keep their agreements, many more were "occupied by an insatiable desire for superfluous things and by ambition" so that no possessions would remain secure.[148] The growth of civil society institutions, and the final setting up of the state could then all be received from an argument about self-love, weakness and the ability to reason. This would also explain the necessity to have laws and taxes and a powerful sovereign able to maintain peace so that self-love could be directed to spontaneous pursuits, productive work and commerce.[149]

The empirical observation of human beings, joined with rational reflection on the conditions where they lived, opened a novel outlook on social life. There would be no need for theology, virtue or love to explain human institutions.[150] This was made plain in the first chapter of *De jure naturae et gentium*, which put forward a view of moral entities (*entia moralia*) that were comparable to physical entities and formed the basis for a moral (social) science akin to the natural

[146] Ibid., IV 4 § 14 (555). [147] Ibid., VII 1 § 4 (958). [148] Ibid., VII 1 § 4 (954).

[149] Ibid., II III § 16 (210–13). See further Hont, 'The Languages of Sociability and Commerce', 164–84.

[150] Contemporaries were fully conscious of the revolutionary nature of Pufendorf's theory. See Siegfried Wollhardt 'Die Grundregel der Naturrecht', in Frank Grunert and Siegfried Wollhardt (eds), *Aufklärung als praktische Philosophie* (Tübingen, Niemeyer 1998), 130–1. See further Laurent, *Pufendorf*, 119–21; Medick, *Naturzustand*, 40–63.

sciences.[151] Meanings, Pufendorf argued, were not intrinsic but created by the way humans gave names to things by language. But language possessed no more essential meanings than the world did. It was a tool people used to impose meanings on the raw facts they encountered. By labelling things and experiences as good or bad, useful or useless and so on, people constituted their social and cultural worlds.[152] Such radicalism earned Pufendorf life-long adversaries from representatives of Biblical natural law.[153] Though he did not cease to explain that the binding force of natural law was received from God and that the way in which humans imposed value on things accorded with providence, the chain binding humans to a supernatural being had worn dangerously thin. This was no accident. It was disingenuous of Pufendorf to point out that of course humans had duties to God, even as they were only imperfect and not enforceable by public institutions.[154] The very point, after all, had been to purge statehood, law and politics from theology and remove matters of faith into the realm of personal piety.

Pufendorf's construction of *entia moralia* produced a theory of various civil society institutions (property, family, corporation, city, state) that responded to historical experience. The members of civil society qualified to contract on political statehood were always the fathers of households, the principal economic units, to whom other household members (women, children, servants) were subordinated. The contract for statehood was intended to preserve properties and pre-existing social

[151] For discussion of Pufendorf's "moral entities", see Denzer, *Moralphilosophie*, 67–9; Dufour, 'Pufendorf', 564–7; Laurent, *Pufendorf*, 124–9; Hunter, *Rival Enlightenments*, 164–6.

[152] Pufendorf conceived "moral entities" analogically to "substances", which were either simple, such as monarchs, or composite and public, such as states, or private, such as corporations. There were also moral "modes" that may have quality and quantity and cover matters such as "authority over one's person and action" (i.e. one's freedom) or the "dominion" one has over one's things (property) or over one's subjects (sovereignty). Pufendorf, *On the Law of Nature and of Nations*, I 1 § 12, 19–20 (11–12, 18–20).

[153] For his many polemical engagements, see Detlef Döring, "Biographisches über Samuel von Pufendorf," in Bodo Geyer and Helmut Goerlich (eds), *Samuel Pufendorf und seine Wirkungen auf die heutige Zeit* (Baden-Baden, Nomos 1996), 30–2.

[154] See Pufendorf, *On the Duty*, Preface (7–8) and I 4 (39–45) as well as Schneiders, *Naturrecht*, 86–91. In a late work, written in reaction to the revocation of the Edict of Nantes, Pufendorf came back to the confessional issue by seeking to balance between freedom of conscience and the duty of the ruler to control the clergy. Samuel Pufendorf, *On the Nature and Qualification of Religion in Reference to Society* (S. Zurbruchen ed., Indianapolis, Liberty Fund 2002 [1687]).

hierarchies. *Imperium* presumed *dominium*. Family law, for example, was about the rights of the *pater familias* over the wife and the children, just as contract law was about the human being's ownership of their actions in a world where freedom was understood as a property.[155] No sharp distinction was therefore needed between civil society and statehood. In both realms the same laws of (artificial) sociability applied. By seeing to the interests of others, we benefit ourselves.

For nature has not commanded us to be sociable, to the extent that we neglect to take care of ourselves. Rather the sociable attitude is cultivated by men in order that by the mutual exchange among many of assistance and property, we may be enabled to take care of our own concerns to greater advantage.[156]

The most obvious example of this was commerce. Through commerce, self-interested individuals could attain what they needed without having to assume that they did this out of love.[157] Moreover, when they did carry out exchanges, they could determine the price of objects they exchanged freely, merely on the basis of need and availability. Price and value were after all moral entities that did not exist in goods themselves but were projected on them by humans.[158] It is true that there were duties of humanity that enjoined all humans to help each other. But these would be performed mostly by exchanging goods and by learning skills that could add to the general benefit.[159] They did not give rise to rights properly understood; the latter could only be based on contracts, guaranteed by natural law.[160]

## A Natural Law of Sovereign Will

One of the moral entities imposed by humans on the world was the state: "The whole of Pufendorf's philosophy of society, law and history is concentrated on the state."[161] True, there were relations of natural law already in civil society. Contracts were made and things exchanged, and natural law enjoined that "every man ought to do as much as he can to cultivate and preserve sociability".[162] But Pufendorf came from the family of a Lutheran priest and knew that human beings were full of

155 Reidel, 'Gesellschaft, bürgerliche', 741.
156 Of course, Pufendorf believed that the coincidence of private and public good was guaranteed by providence. *On the Law of Nature and of Nations*, II 3 § 18 (214).
157 Ibid., VII 1 § 6 (958–9). 158 Ibid., V I (675–98). 159 Ibid., III 3 (346–51).
160 Ibid., III 4 § 1–2 (379–81). 161 Dufour, 'Pufendorf', 570.
162 Pufendorf, *On the Duty*, I 3 § 9 (35).

sin: "[N]o animal is more fierce and uncontrolled than man, more prone to vices which are calculated to disturb the peace of society."[163] Even as contracts were made and properties divided, there would still remain quarrels about how to interpret or delimit them. A secular superior was needed. Although political statehood was established by human beings themselves, its necessity was dictated to them by reason itself.[164] By conceiving state power then as legislative sovereignty, reason would inaugurate positive law as the predominant technique of government.

In this way, all law would carry both a natural and positive element – the former would explain the roots of obligation, the latter made its contents known.[165] Or, in a nicely paradoxical formulation, "Pufendorf's voluntarism is rational by nature".[166] The natural law argument shows the rationality of legislative sovereignty, positive law identifies the sovereign will that determines its content and enforces it. All of this is derived from the interests of the civil society itself:

> since the greatest diversity of judgements and desires is to be observed among men, because of which an infinite number of disputes can arise, the interests of peace also require that it be publicly defined what each man should consider his own, and what another's, what should be held lawful, and what unlawful, in the state. . . . So also what a man still retains of his natural liberty, or, in other words, how every one should temper the use of his right to the tranquillity of the state.[167]

The same natural reason operated in civil society and within the state – in the former in an absolute, in the latter in a hypothetical way. Natural law made contracts absolutely binding already in the state of nature. But they became enforceable only when translated into hypothetical precepts that "presuppose a certain state or institution formed or received by men".[168] Once property has been instituted it follows from natural law that stealing is a crime. Punishment is needed as most will not obey automatically.[169] The technique was compelling

[163] Pufendorf, *On the Law of Nature and Nations*, VII 1 § 4 (954).

[164] The Pufendorfian state was created in a threefold process. The heads of households first came together to establish a political community ("contract of society"). They would then pass a "Decree" providing for its constitutional form and the location of its sovereignty. Finally, they would agree to subordinate themselves to the state thus created ("contract of subordination"). Pufendorf, *On the Law of Nature and of Nations*, VII 2 § 7–8 (974–7).

[165] See further Goyard-Fabre, *Pufendorf*, 101.

[166] Dufour, 'Pufendorf', 568.

[167] Pufendorf, *On the Law of Nature and of Nations*, VII 4 § 2 (1011).

[168] Ibid., II 3 § 24 (229–30).

[169] Ibid., VII 4 § 3 (1011–12).

for, as Pufendorf wrote, "of two evils men cannot avoid choosing what appears to be the lesser".[170] In this way, the interests of subjects coincided with state policy.

Positive law arose from sovereign command and did not bind the sovereign.[171] But natural law did. One of the most important of its precepts was that "[t]he safety of the people is the supreme law". The sovereign had a (rational) duty to see to *pax et tranquillitas* and *conservatio status*.[172] Although Pufendorf left only a very narrow margin for the subjects to be critical of the sovereign, this is not to say that he had any sympathy for tyranny.[173] The whole point of a scientific account of statehood was to bind the ruler to the principles that science, or its representatives, would produce. Thus, for example, the prince had an obligation not only to keep his own treaties but also those of his predecessors, unless they had become pernicious to the state. In the latter case, because the sovereign had a greater duty to his state than to foreigners, he must repudiate them.[174] When Pufendorf wrote that sovereign commands were obligatory when they were based on "just reasons", critics from Leibniz onwards accused him of contradiction. Either duties are born of will, or from a justice that precedes will.[175] Not so for Pufendorf. Between the utopia of scholastic justice and the apology of arbitrary will lay the *social rationality of natural law* as a science of government, a composite of techniques of peace, security and welfare. If these are lost, then social power is lost; the link between protection and obedience is broken.[176] The sovereign ceases to be such as a simple rational conclusion from his failure to govern properly.

The success of Pufendorf's natural law followed from its many, sometimes paradoxical, qualities. In the first place, it possessed universal

[170] Ibid., VII 4 § 3 (1012).

[171] Pufendorf, *On the Duty*, 146.

[172] Pufendorf, *On the Law of Nature and of Nations*, VII 9, § 3 (1118); Pufendorf, *On the Duty*, 151, 151–7.

[173] Pufendorf clearly preferred that the powers of the ruler were limited in the original contract, see *On the Law of Nature and of Nations*, VII 6 § 9–12 (1066–77). Although here he refused to condone rebellion even against a tyrant, he did endorse the Glorious Revolution in 1688 where the sovereign had "clearly with evil intention" departed from his promises, VII 8 § 7 (1111); VII 2 § 10 (979) and see further, Michael Seidl, '"Turkish Judgment" and the English Revolution. Pufendorf and the Right of Resistance', in Fiammetta Palladini and Gerald Hartung (eds), *Samuel Pufendorf und die europäische Frühaufklärung* (Berlin, Akademie 1996), 91–8.

[174] Pufendorf, *On the Law of Nature and of Nations*, VIII 9 § 8 (1337).

[175] For on overview, see e.g. Hochstrasser, *Natural Law Theories in the Early Enlightenment*, 79–83 and passim.

[176] Hunter, *Rival Enlightenments*, 156, 158–63.

validity – the transformation of civil society into the state would operate in its basic features everywhere. Yet it explained the variety of states and state forms by reference to what history had produced. Second, it "ma[de] 'society' a foundational category of modern political thought".[177] People acceded into statehood through the mediation of culture, the spontaneous cultivation of the necessities of life: "utilitarian sociability worked alongside political sovereignty, assisting it".[178] Third, it made royal absolutism coexist with a rudimentary idea of individual freedoms; the state of nature was ultimately a realm of individualism. However, like Grotius, Pufendorf found little role for individual liberties once they had been exhausted in the two initial contracts. It was for later theorists to articulate a view of the realm of a *bürgerliche Gesellschaft,* coexisting, with its own rights, alongside statehood.[179] Fourth, it provided a non-confessional basis for a society disturbed by religious controversy. The justification of coercion was no longer derived from metaphysical abstractions but "from man's chastened recognition of his rationally ungovernable and permanently flawed passional nature".[180] Fifth, it was remarkably realistic. Contemporaries could recognise the Pufendorfian state in the presence of large standing military forces on German soil whose upkeep needed an efficient system of taxation – something that again required a well-developed fiscal–military state for which Pufendorf produced an excellent justification.[181] And finally, even as it was an expressly naturalist construction its main effect of was to justify positive law.[182] If the frame came from Grotius, Pufendorf gave it the immediate obviousness it has preserved ever since.

## A New Law of Nations

Pufendorf has sometimes been dismissed from histories of international law on account of his denial of the possibility of positive law among nations. There could be none because nobody was entitled to give law

177 Hont, *Jealousy of Trade*, 45. 178 Ibid., 46.

179 Diethelm Klippel, *Politische Freiheit und Freiheitsrechten im deutschen Naturrecht des 18 Jahrhunderts* (Paderborn, Schönigh 1976), 136–41. See also Medick, *Naturzustand*, 32–5.

180 Hunter, *Rival Enlightenments*, 160.

181 Harald Kleinschmidt, *Geschichte der internationalen Beziehungen* (Stuttgart, Reklam 1998), 132–4.

182 See further, Jan Schröder, 'Politische Aspekte des Naturrechts in der zweiten Hälfte des 17 Jahrhunderts', in Diethelm Klippel (ed.), *Naturrecht und Staat. Politische Funktionen des europäischen Naturrechts* (Munich, Oldenburg 2006), 19–34.

to them "as if it proceeded from a superior".[183] However, this is to misunderstand the character of the law of nations he was proposing in which treaties and customs were aspects of growing commercial civilisation and binding in terms of the *raison d'état.* There was no clear sense of *ius gentium* at the end of the seventeenth century; Pufendorf wanted to develop that Grotian idiom into a realist view on the way the relations between the more advanced nations had developed. Long ago, when natural law had been forgotten, people had become accustomed to treating alien nations as enemies, Pufendorf wrote. To this situation treaties and customary law brought a change. Although the duties among nations were already founded on natural law, treaties and customary forms of behaviour reminded nations of its demands and added to their mutual duties in accordance with their needs – with respect to commercial matters, for example, by giving up or diminishing customs duties on a reciprocal basis.[184]

The international world was no more a sphere of absolute enmity than the state of nature had been. Between the natural sociability of Grotius and the all-engulfing enmity of Hobbes, there was the history of civil society, within which the algorithm of self-love, weakness and reason had produced a gradually deepening commercial culture where properties were delineated, contracts concluded and things exchanged.[185] Natural ambition led humans already in the natural state to learn agriculture, herd sheep, grow wine, make clothing and other arts. The refinement of habits that followed was not a product of statehood but of cities; there was a "rivalry in culture" between cities, "which is served in many places by no fewer trades than serve man's necessity". Luxury trade transgressed the limits of political communities; it was a spontaneous product of human nature; the social relations to which it gave rise existed independently of statehood.[186]

According to Pufendorf, even outside statehood, in the international realm, people could fulfil their needs only by cooperation, and were bound by their contracts. No less than at home, people came under the duty to pay for what they had bought and to respect the dominion of others.[187] Pufendorf's discussion of human neediness and price-formation

[183] Pufendorf, *On the Law of Nature and of Nations*, II 3 § 23 (226).
[184] Ibid., VIII 9 § (1330–1).
[185] For this argument in more detail, see Hont, 'The Languages of Sociability and Commerce', 168–84.
[186] Pufendorf, *On the Law of Nature and of Nations*, VII 1 § 6 (958–9).
[187] Ibid., II 3 § 24 (229–30).

reflected his close observation of domestic and international commerce: "Money is created to better aid commerce, not merely between citizens of the same state, but between those of different states."[188] In fixing the value of the money, the ruler needed to take the concerns of the merchants into account; it should be neither too high nor too low. But in most situations the value of things would be freely determined between the buyer and the seller. In primitive exchanges bartering goods might still be feasible but a nation that wanted to have "part in the advances of civilization" was compelled to enter a commercial culture operating on the basis of fluctuating currencies.[189]

In Pufendforf's mature theory, the world was divided into two types of normativity – the spontaneous realm of society and culture, and the institutions of state and sovereignty. Although Pufendorf clearly believed the one to follow the other, he also accepted that the two would operate together and that it was precisely the purpose of state power to ensure that the obligations created in social exchanges would have reality. This also applied to international treaties. They were like any laws based on the will of the sovereign to support and enforce an antecedent set of social relations, in this case the effort of two (or more) states to bring about security and welfare. They were binding as they "define the terms of reciprocal performance of some duty already enjoined by natural law".[190] They bound as the *Staatszweck* provided. That is why Pufendorf could write that even in a constitutional change, the treaty will continue to bind the state.[191]

When he then turned to the public law part of *ius gentium* Pufendorf would address the princes whose office it was to deal with foreign affairs by all the techniques of *raison d'état*: "the science of government is so difficult that it requires all of men's ability". To carry it out properly sovereigns should "make friends of wise men and such as are skilled in human affairs, and hold at distance flatterers, useless fellows, and all who have learned nothing but folly".[192] The point of such counsel – in itself quite traditional – would be to illuminate the

188 Ibid., V 1 § 14 (693).

189 Ibid., V 1 § 11 (690). See further, Arild Saether, *Natural Law and the Origin of Political Economy. Samuel Pufendorf and the History of Economics* (London, Routledge 2017), 87–106.

190 Pufendorf, *On the Duty*, II 17 § 1 (173).

191 Pufendorf, *On the Law of Nature and of Nations*, VIII 9 § 6 (1336); *On the Duty*, II 17 § 7 (174).

192 Pufendorf, *On the Law of Nature*, VII IX, § 2 (1118).

algorithms or self-love and weakness and to give a ready portrait of Europe as a set of egoistic but interdependent sovereigns whose interest was to cooperate, not to fight. The law of nations externalised the search for *salus populi* into the foundation of foreign policy.[193] As *entia moralia* states would conclude treaties in matters in which natural law already provided relevant direction; the treaty would either make express or extend that natural duty in some way.[194] It also followed that "no state is obligated more to anyone than to its own citizens".[195] Treaties of alliance, for example, would be binding (it would thus be wrong to say that Pufendorf dismissed positive law) – but their binding force would extend only to the limit where coming to the party's assistance would cause injury to itself. For every treaty, there was a *Staatsräson*-derived reservation concerning changed circumstances. It was no different with just war:

> The just causes of engaging in war come down to the preservation and protection of our lives and property against unjust attack, or the collection of what is due to us from others but has been denied, or the procurement of reparations for wrong inflicted and of assurance for the future.[196]

Perhaps owing to his family's experience in the Thirty Years' War, Pufendorf insisted on the *ultima ratio* character of war. It was allowed only for reasons similar to those given by Grotius: self-defence, including defence of property, the enforcement of debt and to gain reparation. Although mere fear of the power of a neighbour did not entitle attacking it, justified fear supported by unusual or open military preparations did.[197] No private wrong would justify an attack unless it could be shown that the ruler had been in some way complicit.[198] Unlike Grotius, Pufendorf rejected any authority on states to enforce natural law if they suffered no direct injury. War was not to be waged on the American Indians on the basis of their alleged cannibalism, for example.[199] Wars were not punishment – "since they neither proceed from a superior as such, nor have their direct object the reform of the guilty party but the defence and assertion of my safety, my property,

[193] Brückner, *Staatswissenschaften*, 171.
[194] Pufendorf, *On the Law of Nature and of Nations*, VIII 9 § 2–3 (1329–32).
[195] Ibid., VIII 6 § 14 (1306). [196] Pufendorf, *On the Duty*, II 16 § 2 (168).
[197] Pufendorf, *On the Law of Nature and of Nations*, VIII 6 § 5 (1295–7).
[198] Pufendorf, *On the Duty*, II 16 § 9 (169–70).
[199] Pufendorf *On the Law of Nature and of Nations*, VIII VI § 2 & 5 (1293 & 1297).

and my rights".[200] Pufendorf was critical of Grotian legalism; there was no reason to become fixated by rules. Obeying a treaty of alliance may be simply "absurd" if it served only to "heighten rather than diminish the state of war".[201] Customs and agreements to mitigate the violence of war had to do with gentlemanly conduct. They were like promises made to the enemy. The lawful interest of the belligerent to bring the war rapidly to a conclusion may justify breaching them.[202]

At the time of Pufendorf's writing, the theme of balance of power was expanding from bilateral relations to the European political order itself. In his analysis of the German constitution, Pufendorf had regarded Germany as the key to European peace, stressing the need to align the estates so as to counteract the much-feared ambitions of Louis XIV.[203] Throughout in his writings on statehood, federalism and alliances, Pufendorf pursued his anti-formalism; states had varying interests and could get along less by rule-following than intelligent policy. Ambitious rulers could best be kept in check by complex alliances.[204] That the law of nations was natural law meant that it was about the good government of the state in its relations with other states; it became indistinguishable from *Staatsräson*.[205] This exploded the limits of old academic disciplines and made natural law instrumental in legitimating the power of the German princes. It also produced a pragmatic view of the European order, "a shared basis for understanding for the political-legal elite ... and the standard for political argumentation".[206] It did this, however, at the cost of the sense of obligation.

200 Ibid., VIII VI, § 7 (1298). See also Richard Tuck, *The Rights of War and Peace. Political Thought and the International Order from Grotius to Kant* (Oxford University Press 1999), 159–60; Tetsuya Toyoda, *Theory and Politics of the Law of Nations. Political Bias in International Law Discourse of Seven German Court Councilors in the Seventeenth and Eighteenth Centuries* (Leiden, Nijhoff 2011), 44–9.

201 Pufendorf, *On the Law of Nature and of Nations*, VIII 7 § 2 (896).

202 Ibid., II 3 § 23 and VIII 7 § 2 (227–8, 1316–17).

203 Pufendorf, *Present State of Germany*, VII 6, VIII 8 (193–4, 2013). See also Georg Schmidt, *Geschichte des alten Reiches. Staat und Nation in der frühen Neuzeit 1495–1806* (Munich, C. H. Beck 1999), 213–16.

204 See further, Peter Schröder, 'The Concepts of Universal Monarchy and Balance of Power in the First Half of the Seventeenth Century', in Martti Koskenniemi et al. (eds), *International Law and Empire. Historical Explorations* (Oxford University Press 2017), 97–8.

205 See also Stolleis, 'Textor und Pufendorf', 106–33.

206 Barbara Stollberg-Rilinger, 'Vom Volk übertragene Recht?', in Diethelm Klippel (ed.), *Naturrecht und Staat. Politische Funktionen des europäischen Naturrechts* (Munich, Oldenburg 2006), 117. Likewise, Knud Haakonssen, 'German Natural Law', in Mark Goldie and Robert Wokler (eds), *The Cambridge History of Eighteenth-Century Political Thought* (Cambridge University Press 2006), 256–7.

## *Ius gentium* As Diplomatic Propriety: Thomasius

The close alignment of the University of Halle (*Fridericiana*) with the state of Brandenburg-Prussia was illustrated by the pomp and circumstance accompanying its inauguration on 12 July 1694, the birthday of its founder the elector, later king, Frederick III.[207] Unlike other German universities, this was not to be a private corporation but a public institution. Its *Prorector* was chosen by the faculties, but acted as the king's representative. The university's resources were completely dependent on the state.[208] But *Fridericiana* was expected to enjoy relatively great autonomy, especially from the church, and to adopt a pragmatic, even utilitarian approach to academic work – an assignment enthusiastically endorsed by Christian Thomasius (1655–1728) who had just been expelled from Leipzig owing to his unorthodox teaching methods and lecturing in the vernacular. From the outset, Thomasius stressed the scholars' *libertas philosophandi* and the separation of law from theology. Emphasis on reason and freedom highlighted the critical, self-reflective and self-determining aspects of the Thomasian project.[209] His curricular proposals stressed rhetoric, the languages and *decorum* in a way that placed the individuals in the service of their communities. "Universities", he wrote, "must become the seminars of the republic."[210] As the reforms he initiated in Halle spread in Germany, they grounded law as the pragmatic foundation of new political order.[211]

A natural lawyer in the Pufendorfian mode, Thomasius was a sharp-tongued polemicist and reformer with a keen interest in the cooperation between *doctor* and *princeps*. He was invited to Halle to see to the modernisation of the training of Prussian bureaucracy and for that purpose, he experimented with curricular reforms, eventually earning the reputation as the "uncrowned king of the learned world at the turn of the 18th century".[212] An open-minded supporter of enlightened

[207] Rüdiger, *Staatslehre*, 29. [208] Ibid., 44–5.

[209] Werner Schneiders stresses the degree to which Thomasian thinking about reason and freedom resembles Kant a century later, 'Vernunft und Freiheit. Christian Thomasius als Aufklärer', 11 *Studia Leibnitiana* (1979), 3–21, 13.

[210] Quoted in Hammerstein, 'Zur Geschicte und Bedeutung', 318.

[211] See especially Stolleis, *Geschichte*, I, 237 ff. Regarding Halle, see Rüdiger, *Staatslehre*. See also Hochstrasser, *Natural Law Theories*, 31 and on the role of the new natural law theories in university reform in north Germany generally, 30–7.

[212] Hammerstein, *Ius und Historie*, 43, 148–68.

absolutism, his journalism and public campaigns against torture and witch trials made him the most influential of Pufendorf's followers. Engaged in the modern discipline of natural law Thomasius eventually became the rector of the university on the strength of his reforms, which involved inaugurating law as predominant among the higher faculties and substituting logic, science, history and an overall utilitarian orientation for the abstract virtues of scholastic Aristotelianism.[213]

Wisdom, Thomasius insisted, was to know the useful, and jurisprudence was the study of what was useful for society: "*Rechts-Gelehrten fast allein die ganze Vorsorge vor das Gemein-Wesen aufgetragen werde[n].*"[214] There was no point in academic teaching that had lost its commitment to improving the life of the community.[215] While theologians taught wisdom in the church and medical doctors wisdom in the treatment of illness, the lawyers were to teach wisdom in general and in government. This meant moving from abstract discussions of virtue into an empirical study of emotional responses (affects) to external stimuli (*Affektenlehre*); law would become a kind of socio-psychological technique of behavioural direction.[216] Historical studies of public law were expected to inform legislative reforms. A good politician, Thomasius argued, was also a good jurist and the other way around.[217]

In his mature *Fundamenta juris naturae et gentium* (1705), Thomasius set aside his earlier view that all humankind was bound by divine positive law. The gift of revelation was not universally given. Instead, there was natural law that involved Thomasius' famous threefold distinction between the secular norms of *honestum* (*Ehrlirchkeit,* personal morality), *decorum* (*Anständigkeit,* social morality/politics) and *iustum* (*Gerechtigkeit,* law), thus demarcating sharply between internal and external norms of which only the last were a proper field of public intervention.[218] Thomasius was not

[213] The profile of Thomasius as an activist against the predominance of theology at university and the predominance of the clergy in the state is sketched in Ian Hunter, *The Secularisation of the Confessional State. The Political Thought of Christian Thomasius* (Cambridge University Press 2007).

[214] Christian Thomasius, *Kurzer Entwurff der politischen Klugheit* (Frankfurt & Leipzig, 1705), III § 51 (83).

[215] Hammerstein, *Ius und Historie,* 54–5, 82–4; Meier, 'Die Lehre der Politik', 94–5.

[216] See Christoph Bühler, *Die Naturrechtslehre und Christian Thomasius (1655–1728)* (Regensburg, Roderer 1991). I have used the German translation, *Grundlehren des Natur- und Völkerrechts* (F. Grunert ed., Hildesheim, Olms 2003 [1709]).

[217] Hammerstein, *Ius und Historie,* 62–71. See also Hammerstein, 'Thomasius und die Rechtsgelehrsamkeit', 245–68.

[218] Thomasius, *Grundlehren,* I VI § 24–43 (114–18). See further, Klaus Luig, 'Christian Thomasius', in Michael Stolleis (ed.), *Staatsdenker im 17. und 18. Jahrhundert.*

interested in otherworldly virtue but nor was he a social revolutionary. As a proponent of a Pietist ethics of obedience he neither put forward a theory of subjective rights nor suggested that private individuals should become active in politics. His patriarchalism was about the duties of public officials, conceived in a *rechtstaatlich* frame.[219]

Unlike theology, public law was for Thomasius a historical discipline. Teaching it would take the form of lectures on German history, *Reichs-Historie.*[220] If morality and natural law had no universal grounding, but were relative to human volition and desire – as Thomasius argued – then it was precisely history that offered the way to generalise about it so as to draw lessons for present government.[221] Whether as a historical study of the Roman-German Empire (*ius publicum imperii*) or of government generally (*ius publicum universale*), public law would become the flagship of the new law faculties, in the service of princely government.[222]

In the prologue to *Fundamenta* Thomasius recounted his conversion to Pufendorf's view that God had not implanted norms in humans; theology would not help in the study of law.[223] Instead, careful behavioural study demonstrated that human nature was dominated by the will to which reason was only a servant.[224] Will, again, depended on moral affects, consisting of reactions to the external world, dictated by the search for pleasure and the avoidance of pain, projected popularly as "good" and "bad" and, in Thomasius' moral theory, as the objectives of inner or external peace. In social life, it was impossible to reach these objectives without cooperation.[225] Even as the wise may cooperate spontaneously for their own good, humans in general were stupid (*narrisch*) and egoistic, engrossed in negative and harmful affects so that they had to be guided to the good path by authority. Such guidance could be of two kinds, non-binding counsel (*consilium, Rath*) or commands (*imperium, Herrschaft*). The former was given by the wise – the professor acting as the prince's counsellor – but in respect of the great

*Reichspublizistik, Politik, Naturrecht* (Frankfurt, Metzner 1987), 233; Stolleis, *Geschichte*, I, 287–8 and Bühler, *Naturrechtslehre*, 37–42. For a useful comparison of the three sets of norms – *honestum, iustum, decorum* – see further Grunert, *Normbegründung und politische Legitimität*, 217–25.

219 Hammerstein, *Ius und Historie*, 71–84.

220 See further, ibid., 109–24.

221 This point is powerfully made in Hochstrasser, *Natural Law Theories*, 4–11.

222 Stolleis, *Geschichte*, I, 300–1.

223 Thomasius, *Grundlehren*, Vorrede.

224 Ibid., I I § 37 (21).

225 Ibid., I 2 § 44–57 (67–9). Or as he put it, the happiness of one depended on the happiness of others, I 6 § 26 (115).

mass of people, commands by the prince were needed, backed by sanctions to coerce conformity.[226]

Like Pufendorf, Thomasius accepted that religion was instrumental for social discipline, though not in the sense of the Protestant confessional state. The precepts of natural religion had to do only with faith in God, love of one's neighbour and a critical attitude towards one's own affects. Beyond that, everything was a matter of indifference so that the prince could legislate as he saw best. In particular, "there is nothing in the nature of God that commands us to worship him in an external way".[227] Religion was for Thomasius analogous to natural law; both related to internal peace and *honestum* – the highest of the normative spheres in his moral theory, or his natural law in its wider sense. Internal peace would follow from being a good citizen and an obedient subject.[228] By contrast, *iustum* sought to regulate external behaviour by controlling the work of the affects through punishments. It had nothing to do with religion or morality.[229] With this, natural law was redefined as counsel, as guidelines to support legislative sovereignty, only the products of which became *iustum*, law in its narrow meaning.[230]

The historical studies carried out by Thomasius led him to support the territorial estates against the imperial centre – the estates had *summa potestas*, wide legislative and international powers.[231] Like all states, their relations were regulated by the *ius gentium*, though not within the confines of *iustum*. There was no superior–inferior relation among sovereigns.[232] Thomasius returned to the old question: was *ius gentium* natural or positive law? On the one hand, it seemed mutable and so not

226 Ibid., I 4 § 51–7 (85). For Thomasius' conception of the "wise" (*Die Weise*) and the "stupid" (*Die Narren*), see ibid. § 1–50 (76–84).

227 Christian Thomasius, 'The Right of Protestant Princes in regard to Indifferent Matters [adiaphora]', in I. Hunter, T. Ahnert and F. Grunert (eds), *Essays on Church, State and Politics* (Indianapolis, Liberty Fund 2007), 54.

228 For the distinction between a wider and narrower sense of natural law, see Thomasius, *Grundlehren*, I 5 § 4 (94–5).

229 Only scholastic theologians had confused "honestum" with "justum" in their advocacy for papal rule, ibid., Vorrede X–XII (3–4).

230 Ibid., I 5 § 30, 34 (99, 100). Bühler, *Naturrechtslehre*, 38–9.

231 Luig, 'Christian Thomasius', 241.

232 Already in his early work, Thomasius had surveyed the semantic vagueness of *ius gentium*, identifying five different meanings for the term: (1) the "faculties" that all humans are recognised as having naturally; (2) customs of many peoples (*gentes*), including property, wars and servitudes; (3) laws that obligate all people; (4) civil laws of many people, and (5) *ius gentium* "properly speaking", i.e. laws binding in relations between peoples. Christian Thomasius, *Institutionum iuris prudentiae Divinae Libri tres* (Halle, Saalfeld 1702), I 2 § 103 (84).

really part of natural law, on the other agreements under it were not based on a superior–inferior relationship and hence not really positive law either. Efforts to argue that there was an analogous (superior–inferior) relationship between moral and barbaric nations (*höfflichen und barbarischen Wölckern*) led nowhere; who can tell which nations belong in which group? The whole distinction was an anachronistic leftover from Greek and Roman times.[233] Moreover, there was no international legislator and never had nations come together to set up a law to themselves. But even if they had done this, the force of any such agreement would still be based on natural and not positive law – it would remain *consilium*.[234] There were of course many rules on embassies, treaty-making and war. Each was conceived by Thomasius as part of the public law of the state and the jurisdiction of the monarch, to be used for the peace and happiness of the community. But instead of *iustum*, they belonged to *decorum*. They were habitual forms of behaviour among nations, subject to changes typical for matters of that kind.[235]

Thinking of the law of nations as part *decorum* did not deny its reality; on the contrary, it situated nations in the historical world of speech and communication. It may not be legally enforceable but it was still "the soul of human society".[236] Like positive law, *decorum* dealt with social peace, but instead of stopping at sovereign commands, extended to all the cultural and administrative practices and the everyday interactions of *gute Policey*, giving practical sense to the general exhortation for nations to do to each other what they would wish others to do to them.[237] What this meant could not be laid out in a general rule because it depended on the historical relations in the community. Instead, *decorum* was better understood as a type of prudence (*Klugheit*), needed in the application of the law or the moral precept.[238] In the end, *decorum* produced for Thomasius exactly the effect that the Grotian frame had intended to achieve: it gave effect to the interests of the state,

233 Thomasius, *Grundlehren*, I 5 § 72–3 (106).

234 Ibid., I 5 § 76 (107). Nor can merely factual behaviour give rise to tacit agreement, § 77 (107).

235 Ibid., I 5 § 70 and generally 65–81 (105–8). See further, Luig, 'Christian Thomasius', 241; Frank-Steffen Schmidt, *Praktisches Naturrecht zwischen Tomasius und Wolff. Der Völkerrechtler Adam Friedrich Glafey (1692–1753)* (Baden-Baden, Nomos 2007) 235.

236 "Seele der menschlichen Gesellschaft", quoted from Hammerstein, 'Zur Geschichte und Bedeutung', 318.

237 Thomasius, *Grundlehren*, I 6 § 41 (118); Rüdiger, *Staatslehre*, 149–51.

238 Thomasius, *Grundlehren*, I 6 § 68, 80 (121, 124).

allowing its affects to direct its conduct in a way that brought it quite close to *ragion di stato*. And it allowed situating that interest within established rules of state conduct.[239]

Under Thomasius' leadership, the influence of the Halle law faculty would radiate everywhere in Protestant Germany.[240] Its professors were encouraged to focus on the historical and practical aspects of their craft. They had relative freedom to express religious opinions, though heresy remained forbidden. They would concentrate especially on public law, natural law, imperial history and empirical *Staatenkunde* in which they were helped by the historically oriented preliminary teaching in the philosophy (arts) faculty. To know your discipline was to know it historically, more specifically as *historia litteraria*.[241] Focus moved from Aristotelian ethics to the instrumental techniques of ruling, from "politics" to *Policey*, designed to support the material basis of efficient government. Law students received a forward-looking and pragmatic attitude that was eminently suitable for future employment with the bureaucracy in Berlin.[242]

## Law As Government of the State-Machine: Gundling

That Thomasius relegated *ius gentium* into *decorum* did not mean he thought it insignificant. In its varying understandings, it still belonged to natural law in a wide sense and its teaching became a standard part of public law. Shunning Christian metaphysics, its substance would now be construed from *Reichs-Historie* in the context of the histories of other European states. It was nowhere realised with more skill and élan than in the works of Thomasius' favourite student Nicolaus Hieronymus Gundling (1671–1729). Gundling had studied theology at Altdorf but turned to public law after having encountered Thomasius and received a position as the latter's principal student-assistant at Halle. During 1706–29 he taught there first philosophy and thereafter, as professor of

[239] In the short treatise on political wisdom, Thomasius distinguished between the wisdom that looked for the good society (*Weisheit*) and the wisdom that satisfied itself with avoiding evil (*Klugheit*), situating the ruler in the human world of instrumental reasoning. *Kurzer Entwurff*, 8.

[240] Schrader, *Geschichte*, 146–68; Hammerstein, *Ius und Historie*, 160–3; 167–8; Stolleis, *Geschichte*, I, 298–300.

[241] Notker Hammerstein, 'Innovation und Tradition. Akademien und Universitäten im Heiligen Römischen Reich deutscher Nation', 278 *Historische Zeitschrift* (2004), 606.

[242] E.g. Schrader, *Geschichte*, 168, 267–9; Rüdiger, *Staatslehre*, 144–57.

natural law and the law of nations, statecraft, imperial history, public law and *ius gentium*.[243] In a talk in 1711 he described the university as an *atrium libertatis* and stressed that nothing was more practical and useful than the freedom of science.[244]

Gundling was known as a sharp-witted and opinionated lecturer, who, like Thomasius, had no time for metaphysical speculations. The point of the study of sciences, including *ius naturae et gentium*, was utility, a point he repeated over and again at the outset of his lectures and the mostly posthumous works based on them.[245] Although much of what he wrote was addressed to princes and their advisors (*grosse Herren*), he believed that laymen ought to be interested in the skills of European statecraft.[246] Like most eighteenth-century intellectuals, he had a divided attitude towards rulers. On the one hand, their decisions had a crucial impact on the external felicity of their nations, and his large works on statecraft and the law of nature and of nations were supposed to teach them how to govern wisely. On the other hand, he was sceptical of their ability to operate the maxims of good statecraft. Like most people, princes and their advisors acted in pursuit of their passions and would not usually learn from their mistakes. Such views led Gundling to a rather straightforward political realism, tempered by his often ironical attitude to well-known dilemmas of foreign policy and law.[247]

Gundling had imbibed Pufendorf's "eclectic" lesson. The way to knowledge went always through a particular discipline, and to learn a discipline was to learn it historically, as an accumulation of knowledge. Because one needed to know at least the basics of as many disciplines as possible, Gundling produced enormous literary histories that expanded

[243] Stolleis, *Geschichte*, I, 298, 304–6. See also Annelise Bock, 'Nicolaus Hieronymus Gundling (1671–1729) und sein "Entwurf einer Teutschen Reichs-Historie"' (PhD diss., Düsseldorf, 2005).

[244] Rudolf Vierhaus, 'Göttingen Die modernste Universität im Zeitalter der Aufklärung', in Alexander Demandt (ed.), *Stätten des Geistes. Große Universitäten Europas von der Antike bis zur Gegenwart* (Cologne, Bohlau 1999), 247–8.

[245] See e.g. Nicolaus Hieronymus Gundling, *Ausführlicher Discours über die Natur- und Völcker-Recht* (2nd edn, Frankfurt & Leipzig, Springs 1734), 1–3. On Gundling's utilitarianism, see further Hammerstein, *Ius und Historie*, 206–11.

[246] Rüdiger, *Staatslehre*, 234–6.

[247] On Gundling's attitudes towards "Grosse Herren", see Daniela Fischer, 'Nicolaus Hieronymus Gundling, 1671–1729. Der Blick einer frühen Aufklärers auf die Obrigkeit, die Gesellschaft und die gebildeten seiner Zeit' (PhD diss., Trier 2002), 19–38.

into encyclopaedic compilations of knowledge.[248] His over 1,300-page *Collegium Historico-Literarum* (1738), for example, aimed to initiate law students in all the various disciplines they would need in their consulting practices. Annotated literature references from many countries were arranged in thirteen chapters dealing with topics from moral philosophy to natural and civil law, household management (*oeconomia*) and special classes of atheistic, polemical or rare books.[249] Gundling sought to teach students to read critically and combine texts from different fields so as to measure what in the present was true or false, good or bad, honest or dishonest.[250] "For a real jurist is the one who understands the connections of all sciences, including logic and morality. Only the one who rightly understands human nature is proficient as a legislator."[251]

Like Thomasius, Gundling stressed that the point of the study of natural law was to attain outer peace.[252] Internal peace was not law's business, though it could hardly be attained without the presence of outer peace as well.[253] Gundling shared Thomasius' distinction between law, ethics and politics (sometimes labelled *decorum*, sometimes *prudentia*). Although all three belonged to natural law *lato sensu*, only *iustum* – the regulation of outer peace – was the object of Gundling's large treatise on natural law. This had to do with the direction of the will and suppression of the passions through the understanding.[254] Scripture was not needed; it was sufficient to inspect the *lumen rationis*, and even an atheist could know it. Purged of controversial doctrines, however, faith might be help ensure domestic tranquillity.[255]

[248] The most impressive of these was the posthumously published five-volume *Vollständige Historie der Gelahrheit* (1734–6), which proceeded in a partly chronological, partly disciplinary structure that sought to lay out the whole "history of the republic of letters".

[249] Literary history was "Nichts anderes, als seine Beschreibung deres Schriften und Bücher deres Gelehrten", Nicolaus Hieronymus Gundling, *Collegium Historico-Literarum oder ausführliche Discourse über die Vornehmenden Wissenschaftler und besonderes der Rechtsgelahrheit* (Bremen, Saurmann 1738), 490.

[250] Ibid., 294.

[251] "Denn ein verus [Jurisconsultus] ist Der, qui connexium omnium Scientiarum habet. Dahin aber gehöret sowohl die Logic als Moral. Wer demnach der menschliche Natur Recht versteht, der ist tüchtig ad leges ferendas, um zu regieren." Ibid., 586.

[252] Gundling, *Natur- und Völcker-Recht*, II § 18–19 (55).

[253] Ibid., I § 12–18; II § 19 (13–16, 56).

[254] Ibid., I § 13, 19–22 (15, 16–20); II § 18 (55–6).

[255] On Gundling's attitudes towards religion, see Fischer, 'Gundling, 1671–1729', 70–106.

Gundling did not believe in natural sociability. In the state of nature, everyone was free to do what they willed – it was a dangerous place.[256] But *libertas* did not mean *licentia*. The freedom in the state of nature was accompanied by corresponding duties (*jura et obligatio in connatam*) that directed humans to live peacefully.[257] The great dangers were avarice and ambition. For example, as long as possessions were not clearly delineated nobody could be secure in the enjoyment of the fruit of their labour. Hence the move from the absolute to a hypothetical state of nature and the world of legal institutions.[258] The right of occupation, for example, remained a mere fact of possession until it was enshrined in a property system. Gundling had no patience with interminable academic controversies over the origins of ownership and *imperium*. In fact, we knew nothing about Adam and his descendants. Like other legal rules, property had been set up in the state of nature from which it eventually graduated into statehood.[259] At that point, several families had joined into a peace pact – "when one draws the sword, then all will draw it".[260] Were everyone wise, no positive laws would be needed. As this was not the case, the prince needed to legislate and provide sanctions to his laws; although he needed to legislate wisely, he was not to explain his laws but expect that his subjects obey because legislating for the common good was his right of majesty.[261]

Gundling combined a wide range of disciplines in a systemic understanding of the workings of the state-machine. From a discussion of the absolute natural law concepts of *dominium*, contract, damage and responsibility, the work proceeded to chapters on their development into hypothetical state of nature and positive law. By far the largest contemporary application of hypothetical state of nature was with relations between nations that, like individuals, possessed inherent rights and duties (*obligatio et jura in connatam*). By using these rights states had created the institutions

256 "Omnes enim homines externi liberi nascuntur: possunt facere quod placet", Nicolaus Hieronymus Gundling, *Ius naturae ac gentium* (2nd edn, Halle, 1728), III § 15 (40).

257 Ibid., III § 25–8 (42).

258 For his colourful description, see Gundling, *Natur- und Völcker-Recht*, III § 39–41 (67).

259 Ibid., XIX § 3–5 (231–3).

260 Ibid., XXXIV § 18–36 (418 and generally 412–21). Like most public lawyers from Brandenburg-Prussia, Gundling understood its historical origin as an arrangement between noble families, thus grounding the constitutional status of the noble estate in Prussian life.

261 Gundling regarded as ridiculous the way James I had explained his laws in long Latin discourses to parliament, thus inviting his subjects to disagree and rebel, as they then did. *Natur- und Völcker-Recht*, XXXV § 12–17 (423–4).

of international commerce, diplomacy and war.[262] Unlike Thomasius, Gundling wanted to think of the law of nations as real *iustum*. In the absence of a superior, it could be thought of analogously to contracts. Its implementation took place by *politica*, which sometimes, though perhaps not often, led to war.[263] Gundling also agreed with Thomasius that efforts to introduce subordination in the international world by distinguishing between moral and immoral nations led nowhere. It was good to remember, he noted, that the Malabarians treated Europeans as godless savages. As hypothetical natural law, the law of nations consisted of reasonable conclusions about what was needed to preserve peace. Submitting ambassadors to the jurisdiction of the receiving states, for example, would severely undermine peaceful relations. Hence the law on immunities.[264] The way to realise state responsibility was by war. States must be able to defend themselves and their rights even preventively, in order to keep aggression in check. This was wholly reasonable, and "even Christ had not commanded anything contrary to reason".[265] A breach of a treaty, too, unless accompanied by a compelling *causa*, or if concluded with a barbaric nation such as Turkey, was a breach of the peace, which is why *grosse Herren* needed to keep their word, even as they often acted otherwise, as Gundling showed in his long review of European treaty practice.[266]

In the posthumous *Introduction to Real State-Wisdom* (1751) Gundling adopted a purely instrumental view of politics designed to unite the interests and status of the monarch with that of his people.[267] The science of state-wisdom (*Staatsklugheit, Staatskunst*) was essential to the *grosse Herren* but important also for subjects seeking enlightenment about matters of state.[268] Special attention was to be given to recent events: "*Ein politischer hat nichts nöthiger als die neue Historie.*"[269] Making a distinction between "architectonic" and "administration", the creation and operation of statehood, he was critical of the jurists' excessive interest in

262 Ibid., I § 40–2 (26).
263 Ibid., I § 69–73 (36); VIII § 7 (109).
264 Ibid., I § 69–73 (35).
265 Ibid., VIII § 4 (109).
266 Ibid., XI § 1–9, 30–2 (162–7,182–3).
267 Nicolai Hieronymus Gundling, *Einleitung zu wahren Staatsklugheit, aus desselben mündlichen Vortrag* (Frankfurt & Leipzig, Springs 1751), I II (24).
268 Ibid., Vorbereitung (3–14). Gundling understood *Staatskunst* widely. A major part had to do with ruling the state ("the estate of rulers", "*Regenten*"), and it also had to do with the way domestic estates, the military, the people and the learned estates, maintained themselves as well as how individuals were to conserve their status. Gundling's domestic world was deeply hierarchical so that the "external peace" that was the object of both his natural law and his *Staatsklugheit* meant the maintenance of existing social relations. See e.g. ibid., II (49–56, 65–9).
269 Ibid., XVI XIII (699).

the former and wanted to develop a novel discipline of good administration – *politica administratoria* – that would be autonomous from Aristotelian ethics and empirical doctrines of cameralism, but also from mere law-application.[270] If politics was about strategies of maintaining one's status or post, then it had to expand beyond constitutional doctrines.[271] But Machiavellism would have no part of this. State-wisdom would not be about teaching betrayal. Only legally permissible means were available. Yet sometimes it was necessary to move from normal to extraordinary forms of action; *arcana imperii* were in the end no different from *jura imperii*. Even humanely terrible action – such as killing of enemies – might be necessary so as to prevent rebellion or even to hold the reins of power. This could be justified by the needs of peace-keeping that united natural law *largo sensu* with the strategies for maintaining the long-term happiness of the state.[272] But mostly Gundling's examples intended to show that honesty was in the end more useful than deceitfulness.[273] It was also infinitely better to learn about peacemaking, treaties and good administration than about the glories of kings and their wars. In the end, however, the student was to learn that there were no general rules. Colonies might have been useful for Holland, but not for Spain.[274]

Gundling's state-wisdom included extensive attention to the prosperity of the state. This could not be attained by the prince alone but depended on a lively commerce: "*Es muss Capitalisten im Lande sein.*"[275] A good prince would try his best to make trade flourish; by enriching themselves, merchants would also make the state prosper: "A well-directed trade policy is a marvelous instrument to raise the status of the State."[276] It was important to facilitate access to markets, to lower

270 As he wrote in his introduction to "real" State-wisdom: "die Verwaltung eines Staats zweierlei ist. Entweder geschiehet selbige nach dem Recht und nach den Gesetzen; oder aber nach der Klugheit zu regieren. Die erstere wird wir, als zum Recht des Natur gehörig, weglassen." Ibid., I VI (34).

271 See further, Rüdiger, *Staatslehre*, 234–42.

272 Gundling, *Einleitung zu wahren Staatklugheit*, II XII (82–7). There was no essential difference between "arcana dominationis" and maxims of state-wisdom. The former only seemed evil but on closer scrutiny were revealed to have the laudable objective of protecting the state – as when Emperor Ferdinand II had Wallenstein assassinated or Henri IV did the same to the Guise brothers. Only uneducated minds regarded such actions as evil when their point was to protect the security of the state. XVII (738, 740–8). On *Staats-Streichen* (*coups d'état*) that first appear illegal but in fact are not, see 783–8.

273 Ibid., Vorbereitung (10), I (24–7).

274 Ibid., I VII (38).

275 "nur nicht allzu grosse und überwichtige Capitalisten", ibid., XIII V (502).

276 Ibid., XIII I (485). See further, Rüdiger, *Staatslehre*, 245–8.

taxes and customs as well as to employ the new techniques of banking: "Merchants should be tempted by all kinds of freedoms and privileges."[277] The attention of the nobility had traditionally been on agriculture; they were to be encouraged to engage in foreign trade and the production of high-quality manufactures. With frequent reference to the examples of Holland, England and Sweden, Gundling stressed the importance of urban economies and the circulation of money.[278] Yet all this became so demanding that Gundling doubted whether the princes really were up to the job: "With princes, everything depends on state officials. It is they who normally rule; they also rule the prince. Teacher becomes minister, minister teacher."[279]

## "Nobody Trusts Alliances"

In an essay published at the outset of the Seven Years' War, Gundling defended vigorously the view that states had the right to take military action whenever a neighbour had become powerful enough to possess the capacity for victory. Grotius, he wrote, had allowed preventive war only once there was positive evidence of aggressive intent. This was too strict. A state that possessed the ability to break out of the balance of power will always do so. Neither providence nor Christian solidarity suffice to deter. Only by striking first would the balance, and the peace, be kept.[280] Rulers were not free to set themselves under the power of stronger ones. Their morality was different from that of their subjects: "One cannot rule the world with *Pater nosters* or destroy one's enemies by *Ave Marias*."[281] One should not believe in alliances, either, only raw military force helped to maintain or redress the balance. Carneades was right – a prince should never give up the right to strike.[282]

Gundling's text on the balance of power participated in a wide European debate since the Utrecht peace.[283] The metaphor of the

277 Gundling, *Einleitung zu wahren Staatklugheit*, XIII IV (499).

278 E.g. ibid., XIII VII–XIV, XVIII (507–31, 538–9).

279 Ibid., I VI (35).

280 Nicolaus Hieronymus Gundling, *Erörterung der Frage. Ob wegen der anwächsenden Macht der Nachbarn man Degen entblößen könne?* (Frankfurt & Leipzig, 1757), § 4–6, 8, 24 (4–6, 19).

281 Ibid., § 29 (23).

282 Ibid., § 16, 27–8 (10–11, 20–1). Although Christian rulers had better principles than pagans, there was little difference in their actions. On the contrary, Christians had shown extraordinary military aggressiveness, § 21–2 (15–18).

283 For some of the relevant literature, see Heinz Duchhardt, *Gleichgewicht der Kräfte, Convenance, Europäische Konzert* (Darmstadt, Wissenschaftliche Buchgesellschaft 1976), esp. 68–73.

balance, taken from physics, was sometimes discussed in terms of preemption against a powerful neighbour, sometimes as defence of an equilibrium among several powers. Gundling's interest was mostly about deterring a single power, and if in this regard he vindicated Gentili over Grotius, he did not seem overly concerned about the status of the right to strike. A natural law permission or a maxim of political statecraft? For all practical purposes, the two collapsed together, leaving, as Gundling wrote, *Catheder-Herren in der Hof-Schule* cry out in vain for justice. Only a bad ruler would put such abstractions ahead of the state-interest. France must be deterred and nothing did this better than the sight of 100,000 soldiers in the field.[284] Gundling differed wholly from the Göttingen Professor Ludewig Martin Kahle (1712–75) whose widely read 1740 essay identified the balance as a rule of natural law. Kahle, too, wrote ostensibly about the need to check French ambitions – though he generalised the point, perhaps in view of recent Prussian action, to apply to the very nature of international relations. Past practice and considerations of principle all pointed in Kahle's view to a natural obligation on princes to seek to preserve the equilibrium – the "foremost norm of the law of peace and war".[285]

While Kahle's presentation was written in the idiom of public law, Gundling's text moved freely between ethics, law and politics. He cited Tacitus and Bayle and many others to show the readiness with which Christian rulers had always privileged the state-interest, ridiculing professors discoursing on justice or morality.[286] Princes simply could not act like private persons; where the latter sin by commission, the former sin by omission. Nobody can produce full proof of the hostile plans of one's neighbour and a prince cannot simply wait.[287] "Nobody should think that acting in accordance with the laws is sufficient. Such person still lacks that which is most important."[288] Jurists, too, especially when serving as counsellors to princes needed political *Klugheit*. This could be received from historical-comparative

[284] Gundling, *Erörterung der Frage*, § 29 (23–4).

[285] "esse belli & pacis praecipuam normam", Ludewig Kahle, *Commentatio juris publici de trutina Europeae* (Göttingen, Schmidt 1740), § XIV (58). On Kahle, see Zieger, 'Die ersten hundert Jahre', 48–50.

[286] Gundling, *Erörterung der Frage*, § 17–27 (11–20).

[287] Ibid., § 25 (19)

[288] Gundling, *Einleitung zu wahren Staatsklugheit*, I (22).

studies, *Staatengeschichte* or *Staaten-Lehre*. To be an expert in public law was to know what was needed to realise the interest of the state.[289]

Gundling devoted his *Discourse on the Present Situation of European States* (1712, second edition 1733), the first German work on comparative politics, to students looking for a position with a territorial prince. There were two ways of learning politics, he wrote, either from large principles illustrated by examples or by going directly to the facts themselves. The former was difficult and time-consuming; it was better to go directly to the *politica specialis*. This expanded from the formal rules of every state's public law to their commercial relations and foreign policy attitudes.[290] It included a description of the history, the people, the land, property and climate of each state. The state's past constituted its major and its present the minor premise and the conclusion was a statement of its interest.[291] Focus was on European states, because, he wrote, it would have been too onerous to deal with all the one hundred states in existence; and what would it serve to know of Peru or Siam? They were relevant only as objects of European policies. A *monarchia universalis* was a laudably pacific idea – but no prince would ever agree to anything of the kind; even if established, it would soon collapse in a general rebellion.[292]

Gundling's, Europe had reality as a system of politics and history that was often revealed by its irreducible opposition to Turkey. Like Mably, who was engaged in a rather similar project in Paris, Gundling was sceptical of the wisdom of the ruling class and wanted to teach princes to think in terms of long-term policies. But unlike his French contemporary he favoured a strong monarchy and even recommended the use of religious forms, dissimulation and coups d'état (*Staats-Streichen*) when that was necessary to consolidate one's reign.[293] His statehood was not the effect of a social contract – he had no more faith in the subjects keeping their contracts than in princes doing this. It was a utilitarian instrument for realising what the Germans had come accustomed to calling the state-interest.[294] But he did not wish to sound like a Machiavellian; the best way to realise state-interest was normally

[289] Ibid., I VII (21–45, 234–44, 250–4). Hammerstein, *Ius und Historie*, 233–5.

[290] Nicholaus Hieronymus Gundling, *Ausführliche Discours über den ietzigen Zustand Der Europäischen Staaten*, vol. I: *Von dem Nutzen und Noth-wendigkeiten der Staaten-Notiz überhaupt* (Frankfurt & Leipzig, 1733), 2.

[291] Ibid., 8. For an overview of the sources, see 9–20.

[292] Ibid., 23–4.

[293] See especially Gundling, *Einleitung zu wahren Staatsklugheit*, XVII (783–800).

[294] Ibid., VII (234–9). See further, Fischer, *Nicolaus Hieronymus Gundling*, 107–23, 163–78.

through law, not because it stood for any moral idea but owing to the experience it condensed.[295] "I will observe the treaty of peace as long as that is required by the good of my republic; I will disdain my vows as soon as that is what the maxims of the State demand."[296]

## "In Germany, There Are No Despots"

On 16 December 1740, only a few months after having ascended the throne, Frederick II led his army across the frontier of the Austrian province of Silesia on the Oder River. In less than two weeks he had reached the provincial capital of Breslau. The troops had confronted only meagre resistance so that the whole operation had been "less a conquest than an occupation".[297] There had been much speculation about the aims of the campaign in the Prussian court after the unexpected death of Emperor Charles VI in October and the entry into force of the Pragmatic Sanction that launched his daughter Maria Theresa onto the Austrian throne. Both in a military and an economic way, the Habsburg monarchy was in a disastrous state and many adjoining states, not all of them friends with Prussia, expected to take advantage of its weakness. Frederick had always been aware of Prussia's problematic geopolitical situation. By annexing Silesia he aimed to prevent the formation of a contiguous Polish–Saxon territory at his borders. There was also a legal point. Would a new emperor respect his predecessor's promise to support Prussian claims to the duchies of Jülich and Berg on the Rhine that had conditioned Prussian consent to the Austrian succession regime? But whatever the power of such reasonings, Frederick had not been shy to reveal his sentiments: "I love war for the glory," he wrote to a friend.[298] Those who knew him realised that as a ruler, he would not waste an opportunity to prove his military prowess.

Frederick was certainly a good example of Gundling's ideal of the well-informed prince, ready to take decisive action. In the year before his ascent to the throne, Frederick had published a critical essay on political realism, *Anti Machiavel*, where he had depicted the prince as a faithful administrator of his state: "*le Souverain, bien loin d'être le maître*

[295] As highlighted by Hammerstein, *Ius und Historie*, 241.
[296] Gundling, *Erörterung der Frage*, § 16 (12), quoting from Bayle's *Dictionary*.
[297] Tim Blanning, *Frederick the Great. King of Prussia* (London, Penguin Random House 2015), 92.
[298] Letter by Frederick II to his friend Charles-Étienne Jordan, as quoted in ibid., 93.

*absolu des peoples qui sont sous sa domination, n'en est que le premier magistrat*".[299] The worst were the usurpers who breached the very law that gave sovereigns their quality as such. The future king attacked Machiavelli for presenting only one way to royal greatness, war and conquest. A better way surely was good government, encouragement of arts and sciences and the overall improvement of the organisation and resources of one's country. Advancing commerce might sometimes bring the best results, while sometimes attention was to be directed to the agricultural base.[300] But the most famous passages of *Anti Machiavel* had to do with the future king's reflection on the suffering and unpredictability that every war occasions. Princes should keenly uphold the balance of power in Europe and for that purpose "never neglect their alliances".[301] A war could be justly commenced only in self-defence, for upholding of rights or redressing a balance disrupted or threatened "by the way the excessive greatness of a power appears threatened to overflow and swallow up the universe".[302]

It has been customary to label Frederick's actions as in breach of everything that he had preached in the *Anti Machiavel.* Contemporaries had been scandalised by the action – none had been foreseen, no declaration of war, no demands or ultimatums had preceded it. Frederick himself was dubious about the legal justifications that his diplomats had produced.[303] But setting aside the king's flair for cynical utterances, it is hard to think of his action as greatly removed from what had been customary in Europe. The shock had perhaps more to do with the audacity of the young king and his effort to break out from the relatively modest status of his country. Certainly readers of Gundling's texts had no reason to feel surprised. Nor should one take at face value their moral posturing. Gundling once cited a popular work where a "Turkish spy" had written home that "the animosities of all the other princes of the world do not compare with the enmities of Europe's Christian rulers. I do not understand why these infidel [i.e. Christians] cannot live in peace – and maybe they do not understand this themselves, either."[304]

[299] [Frederick the Great], *Anti Machiavel ou Essai de critique sur le Prince de Machiavel*, publié par M. de Voltaire (La Haey, Paupie 1740), 2.
[300] Ibid., 153–5. [301] Ibid., 186–7. [302] Ibid., 188.
[303] See e.g. Blanning, *Frederick the Great*, 77–8.
[304] Gundling, *Erörterung der Frage*, § 21 (16). The work in question is *L'espion dans les cours des Princes Chrétiens,* tome I (14th edn, Cologne, Kinkius 1715), CVII Letter (41).

The empirical–utilitarian turn that led from Pufendorf to Gundling had been contentious. If sovereign rule was merely about the pragmatics of utility, who would speak for humankind as a whole? This concern was expressed in Leibniz's famous attack on Pufendorf's apparent inability to distinguish between tyrannical and just rule. To make this distinction, an external standard was needed. And in fact, Leibniz argued, Pufendorf knew this and, postulating that citizens had a duty to obey laws that the sovereign had just grounds to enact, had failed to enquire into those just grounds. Where did they come from?[305] Leibniz himself had made a career of trying to understand the underlying coherence of a superficially diverse world. His theory of monads had been designed to operate a *reductio ad unum* on the scale of creation as a whole while his legal theory aimed to demonstrate the compatibility of European sovereignty with the fact that "all Christendom forms a species of republic in which Caesar has some authority".[306] Leibniz's notion of justice as the "charity of the wise" involved a harmonious, theologically inspired notion of government that would ascend from a strict obligation not to cause injury to increasingly higher levels about (distributive) justice and, finally, personal piety.[307] Human and God's justice would be the same. Leibniz believed that the wise were to be wholly engaged in society, and he himself provided active advice to German princes.[308] In the Preface to a treaty collection from 1693, he juxtaposed universal benevolence with the cupidity and dangerousness

[305] Leibniz, 'Opinion on the Principles of Pufendorf', in Patrick Riley (ed.), *Leibniz. Political Writings* (Cambridge University Press 1988), 74.

[306] Leibniz, 'Caesarianus Fürstenerius', in ibid., 111.

[307] Leibniz, 'Codex Juris gentium' (Praefatio), in ibid., 165–76 and further Roger Berkowitz, *The Gift of Science. Leibniz and the Modern Legal Tradition* (Harvard University Press 2005), 11–66. For the idea of the "City of God", see Francis Cheneval, *La cité des peuples. Mémoires de cosmpolitisme* (Paris, Cerf 2005), 24–34 and Leibniz's famous critique of Louis XIV's foreign policy, see the ironic 'Mars Christissianimus', in Riley (ed.), *Political Writings*, 121–45. For Leibniz's notion of justice as the "charity of the wise", see especially René Sève, *Leibniz et l'école moderne de droit naturel* (Presses Universitaires de France 1989), 69–131.

[308] His most famous intervention took place when in 1670 when he defended the rights of representation of Johann-Friedrich, the duke of Hanover-Lünenburg in the negotiations for the peace of Nijmegen. Developing a notion of *dominium territorialis* (in contrast to the limited rights of imperial jurisdiction), Leibniz suggested that the right to send ambassadors to peace conferences should apply when an entity's territorial and military power was such that it should enjoy an all-European role, something he had no doubt his employer possessed. Leibniz, 'Caesarianus Fürstenerius', 111–20. See further, Tetsuya Toyoda, *Theory and Politics of the Law of Nations*, 86–98.

of international policy: "rulers play cards in private life and with treaties in public affairs". Taking prudent precautions was always necessary.[309]

But the views put forward by Leibniz pointed backwards to an era preceding the confessional split and were in stark contrast with the works of Thomasius and Gundling as well as the *innerlichkeit* of Pietist religiosity. That he recommended a reformed papacy as the foundation of European order showed how far he was from political realities.[310] Nevertheless the view that law could not just be a reflection of state-interest continued to have its attractions. As Adam Friedrich Glafey (1692–1753), *Privatdocent* in Leipzig and counsellor to the elector of Saxony in Dresden, insisted, an autonomous reason derived from the relations between nations the rules that would bind them: "*Das Jus Gentium tractiert die Pflichten so ein Volk dem andern nach dem Lichte dem Vernufft schuldig ist.*"[311] To highlight this point Glafey changed the title of his early textbook on *Vernufft- und Völcker-Recht* (1722) in the second edition to simply *Recht der Vernunfft* (1732). It was superfluous and misleading to use the conjunctive form: the law of nations was part of the law of reason, a particularly important part, no doubt, but nevertheless only a species in a genus.[312] This did not mean that jurists were to become scholastic contemplators. Nor was it true that only suspicion and war reigned among nations. On the contrary, recent history was full of practical examples of the operation of the laws of reason in state policy.[313] It was possible for princes to learn, for example, that disturbing the peace will always be against the interest of the nation. The rule of reason would direct nations to understand that they would best realise their own happiness by acting in accordance with the general interest.[314]

Glafey was, like Pufendorf and Thomasius, known as an eclectic, without strong attachment to fixed doctrine.[315] His solution to the

309 Leibniz, 'Codex juris gentium' (Praefatio), 165, 166.

310 Stolleis, *Geschichte*, I, 275.

311 Adam Friedrich Glafey, *Vernunfft- und Völcker-Recht* (Frankfurt, 1723 [1722]), II 2 § 66 (232).

312 See Frank-Steffen Schmidt, *Praktisches Naturrecht*, 215–16.

313 Glafey, *Vernunfft- und Völcker-Recht*, II 5 § 39 (307).

314 Ibid. (dealing with the famous objections by Carneades and Hobbes), II 3 § 31–4 (200–1).

315 Schmidt, *Praktisches Naturrecht*, 3, 13. For Glafey's biography, see 7–61. For his activity as counsellor, see Toyoda, *Theory and Politics*, 103–22. For Glafey's "eclectic" history of the law of nations, see his *Geschichte des Rechts der Vernunfft* (Leipzig, Riegel 1739), which contains a detailed survey of the writings and ideas of Gentili, Grotius, Hobbes, Pufendorf, Thomasius and a number of later jurists, ending the work in a celebration of the role of the Germans in maintaining and developing the (literary) tradition of *ius naturae et gentium*, III § 272 (288).

conflict between Leibnizian metaphysics and the utilitarianism of Thomasian jurists was to restate the Grotian frame. Natural and voluntary (positive) law were inseparable so that while the obligation of the rule (*formale jus gentium*) came from natural law, its content (*materiale jus gentum*) was derived from consent.[316] Agreements were binding precisely because natural law, in its concern for the general interest, provided this. Pufendorf and his followers had separated the external and internal worlds too dramatically. Aspects of the internal world, such as knowledge of natural law, had external reality in the social contract. The external stability that was attained was a function of this internal knowledge.[317] Agreements between sovereigns differed therefore in no essential way from their laws. Although they could not be enforced, they bound because they offered a rational way to uphold peace and security. Learning reason, princes would learn how to conduct lawful policy. Customary law, for example, could thus be understood as an externalisation of natural reason while its content was derived from what the nations who had participated in its formation had willed.[318] That will was not necessarily universal. For different groups of nations different laws might apply, sometimes more widely than in Europe, sometimes more narrowly.[319]

Glafey's writings constituted an exemplary demonstration of the process of how, in the course of the eighteenth century, natural law turned into increasingly detailed governmental directives. The relative emphasis on the two sides of the argument – reason and will – would vary in accordance with the context. In normal times positive laws are obeyed without question while in moments of conflict and stress, the reason that underlies them reveals itself and is challenged. It did not take long for German jurists to become bilingual in this way, learning to defend the imperial estates against the *Reich* or indeed the people of a territory against its ruler by reference to a natural reason that

316 Glafey, *Vernunfft- und Völcker-Recht*, II 2 § 310 (page number invisible).

317 Hartung, *Die Naturrechtsdebatte*, 108–9.

318 Glafey, *Vernunfft- und Völcker-Recht*, II 1 § 52 (94) and III V § 62–4 (432).

319 Ibid., II 1 § 315–17 (201–2). Glafey lamented the absence of comparative studies of European laws and admired the great compilations of the laws of the Roman–German Empire by the indefatigable Johann Jakob Moser (1701–85), expressing the hope that the latter would one day produce similar compilations of European law of nations. Moser would eventually record that wish and did produce them. See *Grund-Sätze des jetzt-üblichen Europäischen Völcker-Rechts in Friedens-Zeiten* (Hanau, 1750) and the corresponding wartime volume (Hanau, 1752) as well as the late ten volumes of *Versuch des des neuesten europäischen Völcker-Rechts in Friedens- und Kriegs-Zeiten* (10 vols., 1777–80).

founded the contractual basis of public power while at other times making impeccably positivist arguments on the binding nature of imperial law when acting as court counsellors at home or in front of imperial institutions.[320]

However, by status and inclination, German natural lawyers sided with the territorial rulers, often undermining old statutes or customs. Glafey, for example, had no regard for old ideas about popular will that he believed put the people unjustifiably before the prince.[321] The people would never be able to operate the state-machine. This aspect of natural law took several forms. One of them was the doctrine of the secularised state purpose – *Staatszwecklehre* – that originally looked for security but turned in the eighteenth century to stress the happiness of the population: "The fundamental proposition of natural law and the law of nations is: do that which prolongs the life of humans and makes them happy to the maximum while avoiding what causes unhappiness and hastens death."[322] The open-endedness of this position justified the most varied policies, from building up a standing military force to the organisation of manufacturing industries, from the establishment of schools and universities to the regulation of urban lives. Although the natural lawyers practically to a man were supporters of monarchic absolutism, they did not think it detracted at all from the happiness of the subjects. The view that the state arose out of voluntary subordination brought the legitimacy of the monarch always back to the subjects – it was *their* security and *their* happiness that the state-machine was expected to produce. When Germans looked to the west of the Rhine, they therefore felt they lived in a particularly free society: "*In Deutschland gibt es keinen Despoten.*"[323]

## Generating Welfare and Security: Wolff

On 6 June 1740, a mere week after having ascended to the throne of Brandenburg-Prussia, Frederick II invited the most famous of the eighteenth-century naturalists, Christian Wolff (1679–1754), back to Halle. Many years before, his father had expelled Wolff from Prussia

320 Barbara Stollberg-Rilinger, 'Vom Volk übertragene Recht?', in Diethelm Klippel (ed.), *Naturrecht und Staat. Politische Funktionen des europäischen Naturrechts* (München, Oldenbourg 2007), 105–7, 109–12.
321 Jan Schröder, 'Politische Aspekte', 20–7; Stolleis, *Geschichte*, I, 276–7.
322 Thomasius, *Grundlehren*, I 6 § 21 (172).
323 Schneiders, 'Die Philosophie der aufgeklärten Absolutismus', 34, 32–52.

owing to suspicions about the latter's atheism, triggered at least in part by Wolff's favourable descriptions of Chinese society and religion. Frederick William I had eventually come to regret that decision but had been unable to reverse it, and Wolff for his part had found favour in teaching in Marburg. After a festive return to Halle in December 1740, Wolff took up his ultra-rationalist work, following Leibniz in the line of thinkers convinced that it was the task of philosophy to explain to rulers how to realise the happiness of their subjects within an essential harmonious world. Natural law was to become a coherent system to assist the prince to bring about the perfection of the nation that would coincide with the perfection of its subjects.[324] That perfection, as he repeated over again in his *Deutsche Politik*, crystallised in the objectives of *Wohlfahrt und Sicherheit*, welfare and security.[325] The sovereign, Wolff explained, was to relate to his subjects in the way the paterfamilias related to his children.[326]

The eight volumes of *Jus naturae* (1740–8) expounded in excruciating detail a view of the rights and duties expected to assist in the perfection of society. There was no distinction between the legal and the moral, everything was part of a harmonious teleology.[327] Wolff's text proceeded as a cascade of analytical tautologies, rarely illustrated by examples, perhaps because they were so obvious and open-ended that it was impossible to falsify them either. This was a wholly different view of the world from the one communicated by Pufendorf and his followers. Gundling had viewed law as an instrument for restraining passions; for Wolff it was about the attainment of happiness. Pufendorf had been pragmatic and pessimistic, Wolff was philosophical and optimistic. The world's problems were always already resolved in its firmament; the task for the lawyer–philosopher was to make that resolution visible by deductive reasoning.[328] It would then be applied by the ruler over the heads of the subjects:

[324] However, where Leibniz had believed that the perfection of the individual required ultimately unity with God, for Wolff, it was sufficient for individuals to become perfect in their relation to society. Hochstrasser, *Natural Law Theories*, 164.

[325] Christian Wolff, *Vernünfftige Gedanken von dem gesellschaftlichen Leben der Menschen und in sonderheit dem gemeinen Wesen* (6th edn, Frankfurt, 1747), e.g. § 215 (163), § 229 (173), § 433 (459).

[326] "Regierende Personen verhalten sich zu Unterthanen wie Väter zu den Kindern", ibid., § 264 (200).

[327] Christian Wolff, *Ius naturae methodo scientifica pertractatum*, I–VIII (Frankfurt, Renger 1740–8). See also the shortened version, *Grundsätze der Natur- und Völkerrechts* (Halle, Renger 1769), especially (on "perfection, "*Volkommenheit*"), § 9–12 (6–8). See further, Link, 'Rechtswissenschaft', in Vierhaus, *Wissenschaften*, 125–6.

[328] See especially the Preface to Wolff, *Jus gentium* (5–8).

> [b]ecause the common man ("*der gemeine Mann*") neither can distinguish between the useful and the harmful as he does not have enough far-sightedness nor has the virtue and love for his neighbours so that he could reposition his supposed profit in particular cases to the general good.[329]

Everything must be imagined, initiated, planned and implemented by the ruler. This was not to say that the king could do whatever he wanted. The laws of peace and welfare bound him like everyone else.[330] Those laws would be known by erudite counsellors who would communicate their demands to the prince. Emerging as conclusions derived from the highest level of abstraction the laws would regulate the most minute detail of the subjects' lives, ranging "from rules of dress, through order and cleanliness in the streets, to rules on the export and import of goods".[331]

In his *Law of Nations* Wolff notoriously wrote of a supreme state (*Civitas maxima*) – a kind of ghost of the Holy Roman Empire, a rationalist construction possessing "a kind of sovereignty" over its individual members.[332] Membership in this body dictated that nations were to show solidarity with each other. But the nation's duties towards itself remained predominant and had to do with the principles of good government, already outlined in *Deutsche Politik*, principles about a suitable constitution and the best use of available resources.

329 Wolff, *Vernünfftige Gedanken*, § 253 (190).

330 The sovereign only had the power to bring about the welfare or security of his nation; if he acted otherwise, he acted outside his competence. Subjects were not entitled to judge, however, as they did not know all the details behind a decision. Ibid., § 467 (507–8). See further Frank Grunert, 'Absolutism(s). Necessary Ambivalences in the Political Theory of Christian Wolff', 73 *Legal History Journal* (2005), 143–51. The quotes are from 146.

331 Keith Tribe, *Governing Economy. The Reformation of German Economic Discourse 1750–1840* (Cambridge University Press 1988), 31.

332 Christian Wolff, *Jus gentium methodo scientifica pertractatum* (J. H. Drake trans., Clarendon, Oxford 1934), Prolegomena, § 9–20 (13–17). In *The Rights of War and Peace*, Richard Tuck claims that the supreme state provides a "mechanism for individuals to secure their desires", 188. But the relevant passage of *Jus gentium* (§ 7 [11] that speaks of a "great society which nature herself has established among men" is not the same as the "supreme state" that "all nations" have been assumed to have set up in § 9–12 (12–14). The global community of individuals lacks political representation – it is the "individual nations" that "are understood to have bound themselves to the whole", or in practice their rulers, § 12 (13) and e.g. § 285 (145). As it is those nations that are part of the supreme state, mere "groups of men dwelling together" or "separate families dwelling in the same land" that do not form "nations" do not belong to it, § 399 (157), even as they are part of the "society, which nature itself has established among men" in § 7 (11). The same construction appears in Vattel as well.

Patriotism was everyone's duty.[333] Action was needed from policing to education, from religious affairs to monetary policy. A state was rich if it had many rich inhabitants.[334] Commerce was necessary and framed here as well as in *Deutsche Politik* by financial and monetary concerns. A nation received its wealth "by combining the money of the individuals into one sum".[335] There was no better way to ensure the entry of money into the territory than commerce – at the same time, care needed to be taken that commerce did not lead into the exit of more wealth than it brought in.[336]

The supreme state did not do much work for Wolff. It framed the nation's duties towards others in terms of a call upon mutual assistance. But the rest followed as familiar points about occupation, treaties, dispute-settlement, war and the peace treaty so that the end-result resembled an idealised image of the eighteenth-century diplomatic world, close to Glafey's work. The balance of power, for example, was described as a peacekeeping mechanism. Every nation had the right to expand, but others were entitled to take action against manifest threats.[337] The only just cause of war was a wrong done. Because there was right to undertake war for the sake of expediency, permissible violence was always translatable into punishment.[338] The strangeness of Wolff's derivations is illustrated by his claim that although in war, all the subjects of the adversary, including women and infants, become enemies, that was no problem because after all "[w]e ought to love and cherish our enemy as ourselves".[339]

But reason could not remain at the level of unobjectionable truisms. Frustration with jurists had led Frederick William I in 1727 to establish chairs of cameralism in Halle and Frankfurt/Oder, hoping to generate studies to help fulfil Prussia's financial and administrative needs.[340] But what content cameralism should have in the law faculty

[333] Wolff, *Jus gentium*, § 143 (78).
[334] Wolff, *Vernünfftige Gedanken*, § 476, 485 (550, 571).
[335] Wolff, *Jus gentium*, § 66 (40).
[336] Wolff, *Vernünfftige Gedanken*, § 476–88 (570–99).
[337] Wolff, *Jus gentium*, § 646–52 (332–6).
[338] Ibid., § 617 (314).
[339] Ibid., § 723, 725, 743 (373–4, 382).
[340] The first holder of this chair in Halle, Simon Peter Gasser (1667–1745), was immediately appointed *Geheimrat* in the Prussian government. He received his salary directly from the king and did not, therefore, need to give private lectures. His teaching was mostly directed to domain administration and taxation, and was unsurprisingly condemned as "unscientific" by the rest of the law faculty. Frederick II never showed equal interest in the topic and by the 1770s, serious teaching in cameralism at Halle had come to an end. See Tribe, *Governing Economy*, 42–3; Rüdiger, *Staatslehre*, 203–6, 213–20.

remained unclear, often also to the holders of the chair themselves, and its academic career remained brief and undistinguished.[341] Frederick William also commenced the work for reform of Prussian legislation that eventually peaked as the *Allgemeines Landesrecht* (1794), which concretised natural law maxims and eventually assisted in its relegation at the university to general or theoretical legal studies. By mid-century critics had grown tired of principles such as happiness or perfection from which whatever policy guidance could be derived.[342] The view gradually consolidated that even as natural law might operate as a basic philosophy of government, its practical contribution was best limited to providing gap-filling materials in the daily application of positive laws.[343]

## Between Humankind and a System of European States: Vattel

Unlike Wolff, his most famous (self-appointed) follower, the Swiss *littérateur* Emer de Vattel (1714–67), had actual experience in foreign affairs. A Protestant republican from the principality of Neuchâtel, Vattel spent the decade leading up his 1758 treatise *Le droit des gens* as advisor to the elector of Saxony, also the king of Poland. The treatise was composed in elegant French and spoke directly to the concerns of men engaged in foreign policy.[344] Vattel's treatment of the balance of

341 Tribe, *Governing Economy*, 35–54. For a full, critical survey of German cameralism, see Andre Wakefield, *The Disordered Police State. German Cameralism as Science and Practice* (The University of Chicago Press 2009). The very negative image of cameralists in Wakefield's study has been challenged by Ere Nokkala, *From Natural Law to Political Economy. J. H. G. von Justi on State, Commerce and the International Order* (Vienna, LIT Verlag 2019), 14–16.

342 Vollhardt, 'Die Grundregel des Naturrechts', 137–47.

343 See especially Jan Schröder, 'Politische Aspekte', 19–34. Even Pufendorf and Thomasius argued that positive laws modified, formulated and implemented natural law and thus had precedence over it. See further Jan Schröder, '"Naturrecht bricht positives Recht" in der Rechtstheorie des 18. Jahrhunderts', in D. Schwab, D. Giesen, J. Listl and H-W. Strätz (eds), *Staat, Kirche, Wissenschaft in einer pluralistischen Gesellschaft* (Berlin, Duncker & Humblot 1989), 419–33.

344 For brief recent biographies, see Walter Rech, *Enemies of Mankind. Vattel's Theory of Collective Security* (Leiden, Nijhoff 2013), 19–24; Stéphane Béaulac, 'Emer Vattel and the Externalization of Sovereignty', 5 *Journal of the History of International Law* (2003), 242–7; Jennifer Pitts, *Boundaries of the International. Law and Empire* (Princeton University Press 2018), 68–70. See also André Bandelier, 'De Berlin à Neuchâtel. La genèse du *Droit des gens* d'Emer de Vattel', in M. Fontius and H. Holzey (eds), *Schweizer im Berlin des 18. Jahrhundersts* (Berlin, Akademie 1996), 45–56.

power was inspired by the War of the Austrian Succession in 1740, which had demonstrated the weakness of the empire's collective security system.[345] Many passages also reflect the recent experience from the Seven Years' War, though not really its global scope. Hardly inclined to spend much time with Wolff's cascading truisms, Vattel's readers found the work a much more accessible guide to justify and systematise what they already knew about European affairs.[346] It situated an old topos – the *ius gentium* – within the novel concern of efficient government, projecting Europe as a political system in a wider world for which it was assumed to provide a model.[347] The constructive ambiguity of the work made it seem variably cosmopolitan and sovereignty-centred.[348] Once it is situated in the stream of German eighteenth-century works on natural law, however, its ambivalence is tempered and its ambition becomes visible. Vattel put some of Wolff's technical notions to work to provide a realistic description of modern European politics.[349] It was true that human beings everywhere shared similar passions and had a duty to assist each other. Vattel wrote confidently of a single society of the human race.[350] But this society had no formal political expression. By contrast, what did exist was a community of European diplomats

[345] In a remarkable phrase, Vattel accused his formal sovereign, Frederick II, of having "published his manifesto in Silesia, at the head of sixty thousand men" and although he may have acted without a formal breach, "given all nations cause to hate and suspect him", Emer de Vattel, *The Law of Nations* (B. Kapossy & R. Whatmore ed. & intro., Indianapolis, Liberty Fund 2008), II 18 § 355 (457).

[346] For the enormous success of the work in Europe and the United States, see Francis S. Ruddy, 'The Acceptance of Vattel', *Grotian Society Papers* (1972), 177–96; Peter Haggenmacher, 'Introduction – Le modèle de Vattel', in Vincent Chetail & Peter Haggenmacher (eds), *Vattel's International Law in XXIst Century Perspective* (Geneva, Nijhoff 2011), 4–8. For the reception of Vattel in the United States, see David Armitage, *The Declaration of Independence. A Global History* (Harvard University Press 2008), 38–41 But see now especially Elisebetta Fiocci Malaspina, *L'eterno ritorno del Droit des Gens di Emer de Vattel (secc. XVIII–XIX). L'impatto sulla cultura giuridica in prospettiva globale* (Frankfurt am Main, Max Planck Institute for European Legal History 2017).

[347] Vattel, *Law of Nations*, III III § 47 (496).

[348] For the former assessment, see Emmanuelle Jouannet, *Le droit international libéral-providence. Une histoire de droit international* (Brussels, Bruylant 2011), and for the latter, Philip Allott, *The Health of Nations. Society and Law Beyond the State* (Cambridge University Press 2002). See also comments on this ambiguity by Pitts, *Boundaries*, 81–90.

[349] The question of the relationship between Vattel's Eurocentrism and his universalism is usefully discussed in Pitts, *Boundaries*, 77–81 where she contrasts her view against the strongly Eurocentric one in Ian Hunter, 'Vattel's Law of Nations. Diplomatic Casuistry for the Protestant Nation', 31 *Grotiana* (2010), 108–40.

[350] Vattel, *Law of Nations*, Préliminaires, § 21 (12).

and politicians, advisors and sovereigns, representing nations that did form a "political system, an integral body closely connected by the[ir] relations and different interests".[351] That the society of the human race was managed by the political system of states is the real meaning of Vattel's domestic analogy. It reproduced the civil society/state distinction at the level of the international world. It is not that states were "like" individuals. Instead, the relation of the European state-system to the society of humankind was analogous to that of government to civil society.[352]

To grasp the operation of the two levels of the international world in Vattel's treatise, it is useful to begin by noticing the clarity with which Vattel distinguished between the political laws that govern the state-machine and the civil laws "that regulate the rights and conduct of the citizens among themselves".[353] The separation of the two realms was somewhat blurred by the slippery way in which the notions of "nation" and "state" were used in the treatise.[354] In some passages Vattel made no distinction between them at all, for example when referring to both as "body politic, or a society of men united together for the purpose of their mutual safety and advantage".[355] At other times, Vattel breaks the corporate entity into two distinct parts, using the locution "nation" to refer only to the civil society in contrast to the "public authority" set up to manage its affairs that may be at different times "placed in different hands".[356] In this way, individuals in the state of nature form a nation that only later organises itself into the political state.[357]

Indeed, Vattel suggests that originally sovereignty belonged to the body of the society that eventually entrusted it to the ruler.[358] Public authority became the servant of the nation and the guardian of *salus populi*: "A nation becomes incorporated into a society, to labour for the common welfare as it shall think proper… [and] … with this view it

351 Ibid., III, III, § 47 (496).

352 Or as suggested by Stéphane Béaulac, in Vattel, sovereign states become the administrators of the international world, in 'Emer de Vattel and the Externalization of Sovereignty', 5 *Journal of the History of International Law* (2003), 237–92.

353 Vattel, *Law of Nations*, I 3 § 29 (92).

354 On Vattel's concept of statehood, see further, F. G. Whelan, 'Vattel's Doctrine of the State', 9 *History of Political Thought* (1988), 59–90; Ben Holland, 'The Moral Person of the State. Emer de Vattel and the Foundation of the International Legal Order', 37 *History of European Ideas* (2011), 442–5. See also R. Remec, *The Position of the Individual in International Law according to Grotius and Vattel* (The Hague, Nijhoff 1960), 172.

355 Vattel, *Law of Nations*, I 1 § 1 (81).

356 Ibid., I 1 § 3 (81–2).

357 Ibid., Preliminaries § 4 (68).

358 Ibid., I 4 § 38 (97).

establishes a public authority."[359] For this reason, public authority may not alienate sovereignty and there is no business for foreign powers to interfere with affairs of "solely national concern".[360] It also followed that although the nation may not usually resist its ruler, this was not so when the ruler turned against it, becoming "no better than a public enemy, against whom the nation may and ought to defend itself".[361] All of this was perfectly conventional. Frederick II constantly stressed that he was the "first servant of the state".[362] Vattel also had no difficulty to follow Frederick in making the sovereign the sole depositary of the nation's rights and duties.[363] The sovereign had full powers to determine how to act for the nation, including how private properties were to be used and when to take action because "public welfare and the safety of the state are concerned".[364] The argument is both authoritarian and liberal – the king decides, but he decides in view of my welfare.

However, there is a wider world out there. Even as members of nations, individuals "still remain bound to the performance of their duties towards the rest of mankind".[365] But this world-wide human solidarity had no political form. For such to exist, it would be "essential that each member have resigned a part of his right to the body of the society, and that there exist in it an authority capable of commanding all the members. . . . Nothing of this kind can be conceived or supposed to subsist between nations."[366] *Droit des gens* moved imperceptibly from the universal society of humankind to the system of European states that was Vattel's principal concern. The book's intricate distinctions reflect this two-level structure in many ways. "The first general law", we read, "is that each individual nation is bound to contribute everything in her power to the happiness and perfection of all the others."[367] But solidarity was not to get in the way of the principal task: "a nation owes to herself in the first instance, and in preference to all other nations, to do everything she can to promote her own happiness and perfection".[368] Moreover, no nation could impose its moral sentiments on another by punishing it for violations of the law of nature if it had suffered no harm. Such a moral war

[359] Ibid., I 5 § 69 (123). [360] Ibid., I 3 § 37 (96). [361] Ibid., I 4 § 51 (105).

[362] See e.g. T. C. W. Blanning, *The Culture of Power and the Power of Culture. Old Régime Europe 1660–1789* (Cambridge University Press 2002), 194–6 and passim.

[363] Vattel, *Law of Nations*, I 4 § 41 (99). [364] Ibid., I XXI § 255 (236).

[365] Ibid., Preliminaries § 10–11 (72–3). [366] Ibid., Preface (14).

[367] Ibid., Preliminaries, § 13 (73). [368] Ibid., Preliminaries § 11 (73).

would merely occasion "ravages of enthusiasm and fanaticism".[369] Our obligations of humanity only bind in conscience. The rights they produce are only imperfect, amounting to a mere "right to ask" in contrast to external duties that involve "the right of compelling"; these would be provided by what Vattel would call "voluntary law".[370]

Vattel received the all-important concept of voluntary law from Wolff who contrasted it with necessary natural law. It was true that free and independent states could only be governed by natural law.[371] However, necessary natural law was originally meant to apply to individuals and not to corporate bodies. To make it " suitable to the subject", necessary natural law needed to give way to voluntary law that permitted acts that "though in their own nature unjust and condemnable" were still allowed because they corresponded to the character of the law of nations that regulated the relations of free and independent entities.[372] By moving from necessary to voluntary law Vattel left the world of ethics and virtue without, however, collapsing into arbitrary law, "the will and consent of nations".[373] For despite its confusing name, voluntary law was likewise established by nature; it would ensure the proper operation of the states-society without deferring to anybody's private morality or what individual states might want at any point. It was close to customary law but, unlike the latter, not limited to Europe. It was what was necessary in the world of state power.[374] Situated between the perfectionist morality of necessary natural law and the fully consent-based arbitrary law, voluntary law produced a double feat: it took realistic account of the nature and needs of the states-society while still not having to defer to the consent of each and every state. Between the utopia of necessary natural law and the apology of arbitrary law, it offered a reasonably stable basis for allowing each state to pursue its policies relatively undisturbed by others.[375]

369 Ibid., II I § 7 (265). 370 Ibid., Preliminaries, § 17 (75).

371 Ibid., Preliminaries § 7–8 (70). 372 Ibid., Preliminaries § 22 (76–7).

373 Ibid., Preface (17).

374 Peter Haggenmacher, rightly, calls voluntary law "*élément porteur de tout le système*". 'Le modèle Vattel et la discipline de droit internatioinal', in Vincent Chetail and Peter Haggenmacher (eds), *Vattel's International Law in a XXIst Century Perspective* (Geneva, Nijhoff 2011), 22. See further Heinhard Steiger, 'Völkerrecht und Naturrecht zwischen Christian Wolff und Adolf Lasson', in Diethelm Klippel (ed.), *Naturrecht im 19. Jahrhundert* (Goldbach, Keip 1997), 48–50. Koselleck read Vattel as a key writer of the period precisely because he accepted that "to be law at all, the law of nations must of necessity be and remain morally imperfect", Reinhart Koselleck, *Critique and Crisis. Enlightenment and the Pathogenesis of Modern Society* (MIT Press, 1988), 47.

375 The tendency of natural law to collapse into *raison d'état* has often been remarked upon. See e.g. Hunter, 'Vattel's Law of Nations', 122–40 and Richard Devetak,

The most important aspect of voluntary law was that it allowed bracketing the question of a war's justice. Treating both sides equally was necessary "if people wish to introduce any order, any regularity, into so violent an operation as that or arms".[376] Avoiding the fanaticism of a moral war, it directed the combatants to do only what was needed for victory. Non-combatants ought to be left in peace and prisoners of war should not be killed.[377] No nation could arrogate the right to punish violations of natural law unless one was oneself a victim. Assistance or good offices may of course be offered. But nobody was entitled to act on behalf of some imaginary "great republic".[378] The Spaniards' claim to be reacting against Atahualpa's alleged violations of natural law had been nothing but self-serving justifications of aggression. Vattel's careful distinctions between what was internal and what external, what was imperfect and what perfect, allowed expressions of sympathy or solidarity, efforts to diminish the ills of war. That the nation's primary duties were to itself was another way of putting the point that the jurisdiction of public authorities was limited to communities of which they were the representatives and to which they were responsible. Intervention would only be allowed when public authority collapsed in civil war or turned against its people, where the justification of state authorities' original jurisdictional claim had lapsed.[379]

## A Law of Security and Welfare

*Droit des gens* was an elaboration of developments in German natural law no longer limited to the German context. It was unabashedly utilitarian. As Vattel wrote in an early essay, we obey public authorities because this is in our self-interest: we "sacrifice an immediate advantage to the greater good".[380] Part One of the book opened into a thoroughly

'Law of Nations as Reason of States. Diplomacy and the Balance of Power in Vattel's *Law of Nations*', 28 *Parergon* (2011), 106–14. I have discussed Vattel's legacy in modern international law in *From Apology to Utopia*, 112–22.

376 Vattel, *Law of Nations*, III XII § 190 (501).

377 See further, Stephen Neff, 'Vattel and the Laws of War. A Tale of Three Circles', in Vincent Chetail and Peter Haggenmacher (eds), *Vattel's International Law in a XXIst Century Perspective* (Geneva, Nijhoff 2011), 317–34.

378 Vattel, *Law of Nations*, II I § 7 (265).

379 This had justified William of Orange's military intervention in England. Ibid., II IV § 56 (290–1).

380 Vattel made his utilitarianism express in an earlier text, 'Essay on the Foundation of Natural Law and on the First Principle of Obligation Men Find Themselves Under

Wolffian overview of the ways in which public authorities were to produce "a happy plenty of all necessaries of life with its conveniences, and innocent and laudable enjoyments".[381] Their duties included the provision of necessities (chapters 6–10), seeing to education, arts, sciences and a well-functioning justice mechanism (11–13) as well as security (14–17), followed up by provisions on the government of territory and the establishment and protection of property (18–23). International lawyers have often wondered about those opening chapters: why pay such regard to matters that do not seem to deal with anything international?[382] But German natural law encompassed both international and domestic action to search for security and welfare. Its ambition was to produce a total view of how the state-machine was to be operated; the Holy Roman Empire, after all, had been both domestic and international. To speak of the "nation's duties to itself" was a way of speaking about the internal dimension while simultaneously supposing the presence of a wider normative world from which such duties could emerge.[383]

To carry out their duties, public authorities needed a good sense of the economic and political situation of the nation – "what advantages it possesses, and what deficits it labours under".[384] A principal aspect of public wealth was a growing and a healthy population, a "sufficient number of able workmen" to be educated in the virtues of labour and encouraged to live by their own work.[385] A flourishing agriculture was much more important than luxury trades.[386] But commerce, too, was a source of wealth and plenty.[387] All nations had the right to buy and

to Observe Laws', published as an annex to Vattel, *Law of Nations*, 753. The essay was written in 1740 and published in 1757. The quote is from that essay at 755.

381 Vattel, *Law of Nations*, I VI § 72 (126).

382 The complaints began early with Dietrich Heinrich von Ompteda, *Litteratur des gesammten sowohl natürlichen als positiven Völkerrechts, Erster Theil* (Regensburg, Montags 1785), 7.

383 See also Béaulac, 'Externalization', 256–9. This "two-tier construction" is also identified in Pablo Kalmanovitz, 'Sovereignty, Pluralism, and Regular War. Wolff and Vattel's Enlightenment Critique of Just War', 46 *Political Theory* (2017), 218–41.

384 Vattel, *Law of Nations*, I II § 25 (91).

385 Ibid., I VI § 73, 76 (126–7).

386 He was therefore ready to delete them from lists of neutral goods in wartime. See further, Koen Stapelbroek, 'Universal Society, Commerce and the Right of Neutral Trade', in Petter Korkman and Virpi Mäkinen (eds), *Universalism in International Law and Political Philosophy* (Helsinki, Helsinki Collegium 2008), 76–8.

387 Vattel, *Law of Nations*, I VIII § 86–7 (132); II II § 21 (273).

sell their products though that right became enforceable only on a treaty basis.[388] The economic situation often required all kinds of import and export restrictions and, even as monopolies were generally harmful, exclusive trading companies. Because wealth had become such an important part of state power, commerce was not only about procuring goods but an instrument of policy. By skilful management of its exports and imports, a state could administer the balance of power to its advantage.[389] In short essays written soon after the publication of the *Droit des gens* Vattel warned of the way the commerce of luxury contributed to a culture of laxity that might undermine patriotic commitment. Agriculture was the backbone of state power: "One thousand more ploughmen strengthen it more than two thousand workers who produce luxury goods."[390] The ruler was to pay much attention to education, public support to arts and sciences, *libertas philosophandi* and a well-functioning justice system. A good domestic order depended on wise regulations that

> will prescribe whatever will best contribute to the public safety, utility and convenience. . . . By a wise police, the sovereign accustoms the people to order and obedience, and preserves peace, tranquillity, and concord among the citizens.[391]

A nation could only be perfect if its ruler understood the political system of which it was a dependant part. Such an understanding could not be received from abstract theory (there was no such theory) but from having a good sense of the contingencies of the political and diplomatic environment. Parts Two and Three of *Droit des gens* developed into an almost endless

> array of "cases", "circumstances", and "occasions", in relation to which an open-ended series of "exemptions to [. . .] and moderations of the rigour of the necessary law" will be determined in accordance with national judgment and national interest.[392]

388 Ibid., II II § 26 (275–6).
389 Ibid., I XIV § 182 (201–3); II I § 16 (270). See further Isaac Nakhimovsky, 'Vattel's Theory of the International Order. Commerce and the Balance of Power in the *Law of Nations*', 33 *History of European Ideas* (2007), 157–73.
390 Vattel, 'General Considerations on Economic Policy', in Béla Kapossy and Richard Whatmore, 'Emer de Vattel's *Mélanges de literature, de morale et de politique* (1760)', 34 *History of European Ideas* (2008), 91.
391 Vattel, *Law of Nations*, I XIII § 174, 176 (193, 194).
392 Hunter, 'Vattel's Law of Nations', 125.

That European diplomats found Vattel useful must have related to his appreciation of the difficulty of their task, realisation that "such and such regulation, such or such practice, though salutary to one state, is often pernicious to another".[393] Instead of laying out substantive rights and obligations *Droit des gens* turned to how they were to be created and managed. Treaties were needed because of "the little dependence that is to be placed on the natural obligations of bodies politics, and on the reciprocal duties imposed on them by humanity".[394] Nothing prevented concluding agreements with non-Christians as well: "The law of nature alone regulates thc treaties of nations: the difference of religion is a thing absolutely foreign to them."[395] But treaties were flexible instruments. If a treaty became "pernicious", or had been concluded for an "unjust or dishonest purpose" then the state was released from it.[396] *Salus populi* would always override the formal instrument.

All this diplomatic detail provided a robust description of the transformations of eighteenth-century Europe. The turn away from the moral war of Grotius into a world of peaceful rivalry supported the position of the new bourgeois elites at the helm of the European polities.[397] For them, it was important that increasing attention was given to welfare, and welfare pushed nations to trade with each other. Vattel admired England. The English had understood that commerce was both an instrument of welfare and a pacifying vehicle. To emulate England the nations should seek to create a flourishing domestic industry and intense commerce with their neighbours. Because England (and perhaps a commercial nation in general) had such a free constitution, it had been superbly placed to act as a balancer between potentially hostile nations.[398] What had been done by Frederick II was in striking antithesis to all this. The Silesian campaign had been utterly egoistic, the motive of glory impossible to fit in any rational system of managing European policy. It had also been directed immediately against the interests of Vattel's employer, the king of Saxony. But it was not a type of action unheard of in Europe. On the contrary, as Gundling and others would argue, it was quite typical of European potentates. It was not something that could be wished away by moral exhortations. But it

[393] Vattel, *Law of Nations*, I III § 25 (91). [394] Ibid., II XII § 152 (338).
[395] Ibid., II XII § 162 (342). [396] Ibid., II XII § 160–1 (341).
[397] For this argument, see especially Koselleck, *Critique and Crisis*, 47–50.
[398] See e.g. Vattel, *Law of Nations*, I IV § 39 (97–8); I VI § 76 (127–8); I VIII § 85, 87 (131, 132); III III § 50 (500) and Richard Whatmore, 'Vattel, Britain and Europe', 31 *Grotiana* (2010), 85–107.

might be controlled and its effects limited if situated in a realistic portrayal of the European system.

## Monsters and Hypocrites: Understanding Europe

*Droit des gens* was the first large work to describe Europe as a politico-diplomatic system with intricate, historically developed rules to govern it. Violence was a principal concern. It was not only impossible but inadvisable to prevent it. After all, "*we prosecute our rights by force*".[399] But it could and should be hedged in such a way that it did not become a threat to the system itself. Much of what Vattel had to say about just war in Europe remained perfectly conventional. War was a great evil, only to be undertaken for the most cogent reasons.[400] Although war could not be just on both sides, voluntary law allowed bracketing the question of justice and invited the treatment of both belligerents as lawful.[401] This was the system of formal war that only sovereigns were entitled to wage for self-defence or the preservation of rights.[402]

Vattel's treatment of preventive war, likewise, exercised familiar themes. One was certainly entitled to act if there were verifiable military preparations, such as concentration of troops on the frontier. Increased power did not in itself justify prevention action, but history showed that the growth of power did often give indication of aggressive intent. It was impossible to formulate a general rule and "men are under a necessity of regulating their conduct in most cases by probability".[403] A state may require guarantees and, failing to receive such, may have to take measures. But even a guarantee might not always suffice, especially if a ruler or a nation had "already given proofs of imperious pride and insatiable ambition".[404] The coalition decision to go to war against Louis XIV in the case of the Spanish succession had certainly been right.[405]

A more interesting case was where no single ruler was aiming for universal monarchy but the systemic requirements of European order still required concerted action.[406] It is usual to assume that Vattel was here thinking precisely about the belligerent policy of Frederick II.

399 Vattel, *Law of Nations*, III I § 1 (469).
400 Ibid., III III § 24 (482).
401 Ibid., III III § 39–40 (489–90).
402 Ibid., III I § 4 (470). Defence included anticipation, obtaining reparation and guarantees for future security, II IV § 50–2 (288–9).
403 Ibid., III III § 44 (493).
404 Ibid., III III § 44 (494).
405 Ibid., III III § 44 (494).
406 See further, Rech, *Enemies of Mankind*, 171–92.

Frederick was not looking for global hegemony. Yet he was prone to using military force if he felt this useful and could get away with it. He also had little respect towards the institutions of the Reich.[407] Although Vattel did not mention Frederick specifically – for reasons of prudence no doubt, as his native Neuchâtel was ruled under Prussia and he himself had once tried to enter Frederick's service – he regarded Europe's political system as a legitimate object for defence by military force.[408] In a famous passage Vattel described the close relations between European nations, the continuous attention they paid to each others' doings, "the constant residence of ministers, and the perpetual negotiations".

> Hence arose that famous scheme of the political balance, of the equilibrium of power; by which is understood such a disposition of things, as that no potentate be able absolutely to predominate, and prescribe laws to the others.[409]

Here the balance was not an alternative to law but its necessary adjunct. The defensive or offensive nature of the operation was not essential for its legal characterisation; the simple objective to prevent the disturbance of the equilibrium made the action just and lawful.[410] Any state, even one that was not itself immediately threatened, was entitled to take action to defend the "system".[411]

But the most striking passages in Vattel were those that made the legality of the war rely on a formal show of respect to the rules. Vattel made it clear that a sovereign who did not keep an eye on the justice of the cause and the expediency of furthering it by arms was failing his people.[412] Waging war for hatred, revenge or glory was always an

[407] But see the nuanced discussion in Peter H. Wilson, 'Prussia's Relations with the Holy Roman Empire 1740–1786', 51 *The Historical Journal* (2008), 337–71. The relative independence of imperial institutions during 1756–63 is stressed in Duchhardt, *Gleichgewicht der Kräfte*, 96–101.

[408] The extent to which this part of the work – perhaps its most famous part – was also inspired by Vattel's Swiss perspective on the international world may be conjectured. A loose federation of independent entities, Switzerland worried over the rise of commercial empires, France and England. On Vattel's "Swiss" perspective, see Kapossy and Whatmore, '*Mélanges de litterature*', 79.

[409] Vattel, *Law of Nations*, III III § 47 (496).

[410] For a useful dissection of the various scenarios covered by Vattel's discussion of the balance, see Bruno Arcidiacono, 'De la balance politique et de ses rapports avec le droit des gens. Vattel, la "guerre pour l'équilibre" et le système européen', in Vincent Chetail and Peter Haggenmacher (eds), *Vattel's International Law in a XXIst Century Perspective* (Geneva, Nijhoff, 2011), 90–100.

[411] Vattel, *Law of Nations*, III III § 46 & 48 (495, 497).

[412] Ibid., III III § 24, 29 (483, 484–5).

abuse and "tarnishes the lustre of [the nation's] arms". In such case, justifying reasons were only pretexts. Nevertheless, giving pretexts did at least show deference to the formal rules of the system – "homage which unjust men pay to justice".[413] It made public the claims of the belligerent and allowed judging their well-foundedness. That is why a declaration was necessary. While only a formality, the declaration made possible a last-ditch effort to engage between the parties and avoid bloodshed. True, the justifications may well be hypocritical. But making them publicly expressed deference to and reinforced the validity of the system that required them.[414]

Vattel made an altogether dramatic distinction between the hypocrite who goes to war for whatever motives but paying lip-service to the rules – giving "pretexts" – and the one who gives no public justifications at all. The latter were simply "monsters, unworthy of the name of men ... enemies of the human race". They included a "government that authorizes its citizens indiscriminately to plunder or maltreat foreigners, to make inroads into neighbouring countries &c".[415] Non-Europeans such as "Turks and other Tartars" were included, as well as men such as Genghis Khan, Timur-Bec, Tamerlane or Attila.[416] The Uzbeks and the pirates of the Barbary States were likewise covered, not because they had engaged in immoral action (after all, Europeans were often immoral as well), but because they gave no justifications and therefore become a threat to the system itself. "All nations ha[d] the right to join in a confederacy for the purpose of punishing and even exterminating those savage nations."[417] Even Europeans fell into this category when they acted without lawful authority, as armies of banditti, buccaneers or pirates, "without a cause and without a declaration of war".[418]

The distinction between hypocrites and monsters helped Vattel contrast violence at home with much-feared non-European enemies and

413 Ibid., III III § 32 (486) ("un hommage, que les injustes rendent à la Justice").

414 "We owe this farther regard to humanity," Vattel wrote in *Law of Nations*, III IV § 51 (501). For the "doctrine of pretext" in Vattel, see also Gabriella Silvestrini, 'Vattel, Rousseau et la question de la "justice" de la guerre', in Vincent Chetail and Peter Haggenmacher (eds), *Vattel's International Law in a XXIst Century Perspective* (Geneva, Nijhoff 2011), 109–10 and James Q. Whitman, *The Verdict of Battle. The Law of Victory and the Making of Modern War* (Harvard University Press 2014), 127–30.

415 Vattel, *Law of Nations*, II VII § 78 (301). See also II 15 § 222 (388).

416 Ibid., III III § 34 (487).

417 Ibid., III III § 34 (487). See further, Rech, *Enemies of Mankind*.

418 His example were the Savoyards who were hanged after their failed attack in Geneva in 1602, Vattel, *Law of Nations*, III IV § 68 (508).

others who refused to play by the rules of the system. Like the German professors writing on *ius naturae et gentium*, Vattel was fully conscious that the search for glory had always been a common motive among European rulers, whatever formal reason they may have invoked. This was not acceptable, of course, for it put in danger soldiers and subjects, as Frederick II had himself acknowledged. But what placed Frederick beyond the pale (even as Vattel did not say this expressly) was that there had been no justification, no declaration, no regard for formalities. That is why the Silesian campaign associated Frederick with Attila. For most European rulers were still somehow limited and "civilised" because they at least paid lip service to shared rules, thereby reaffirming their validity. They still "retain[ed] some sense of shame".[419] One could hardly expect more of them.

[419] Ibid., III III § 32 (486). The hypocrite at least "tacitly acknowledges that a flagrant injustice merits the indignation of all mankind", 487.

# 12

# The End of Natural Law

## *German Freedom 1734–1821*

*Droit des gens* was the last important work of its kind. Neither the brief *Discourse* by Mackintosh of 1796 nor Rayneval's *Institutions* of 1803 came anywhere close to the fame it enjoyed; its spread among the diplomatic chancelleries up to the mid-nineteenth century has become legendary.[1] Many reasons may explain its success. It had enough of a philosophical background to appeal to a readership looking for a general view, but not too much to deter politicians needing a handbook on diplomacy. It was respectful of natural law but recognised and justified the power of domestic sovereignty. It embodied a moderately republican worldview that posed no danger to the foreign policy thinking of the old regime. It expounded an overall attitude to the world of policy and law that many people had come to regard as "realistic". And it was an easy read. Nevertheless, in 1795 Kant indicted Vattel among the "sorry comforters" who are "still dutifully quoted in *justification* of military aggression, although their philosophically or diplomatically formulated codes do not and cannot have the slightest *legal* force".[2] What might Kant have meant?

Kant was a critical observer of the dynastic politics, wars and colonial appropriations of the old regime. Early in life he had supported the rationalising efforts of the Prussian king, but like many others, was soon disillusioned by the foreign policy of Frederick and his successor.

[1] For a recent discussion, see Elisabetta Fiocchi Malaspina, *L'eterno ritorno del Droit des gens di Emer de Vattel (secc. XVIII–XIX)* (Max Planck Institute for European Legal History 2017).

[2] Immanuel Kant, 'Perpetual Peace. A Philosophical Sketch' [hereinafter PP], in Immanuel Kant, *Political Writings* (Hans Reiss ed., Cambridge University Press 1991), 103.

Although he had to be careful about the formulation of his critiques, he used the preliminary articles of *Perpetual Peace* to attack such contemporary practices as territorial changes following dynastic succession, standing armies, war debts (particularly important in the prolongation of the Seven Years' War) as well as interferences in other countries' constitutions – a thinly veiled attack on the recent peace of Basel that had organised the final partition of Poland.[3] Kant had no faith in the European peace system. The balance of power was "pure illusion".[4]

Kant attacked Vattel and the natural lawyers because, however ironically or in the name of political *Klugheit*, they nevertheless succumbed to justifying the world as it was. They had no vision of a tomorrow that would be different, and better from today. They had no sense of progress. This was, for Kant, both a moral and an intellectual failure. The problem had to do with the very realism of natural law writings in which "the depravity of human nature [was] displayed without disguise".[5] These texts depicted society as a species of nature where people acted mechanically in response to their desires. Law for them was a tool to manipulate those desires so as to attain what they called happiness. But happiness, Kant pointed out in several of his essays, could mean anything; in practice, it would justify paternalistic forms of rule under which nothing is left of freedom.[6] By contrast, Kant proposed to view freedom as the world's inner meaning, valuable in itself and not owing to any other good, such as happiness.[7] By "freedom" Kant meant two things: autonomy among humans, namely "independence from being constrained by another's choice",[8] as well as rational self-rule, independent from the powers of desire. When Kant then inserted freedom in society, he found that it opened into a future

[3] Ibid., 96. Poland's alleged "anarchical" condition had been the object of intense debate through the latter half of the eighteenth century. The reference is made clear by Kant's express denial of the right of external interference in such a situation. For the context, see Oliver Eberl and Peter Niesen, *Immanuel Kant, Zum ewigen Frieden. Kommentar von Oliver Eberl und Peter Nielsen* (Frankfurt, Suhrkamp 2011), 192–5.

[4] Kant, 'On the Common Saying: "This May be True in Theory but it does not Apply in Practice"' [hereinafter TP], Kant, *Political Writings*, 92.

[5] Kant, PP, 103.

[6] Kant, 'Idea for a Universal History with a Cosmopolitan Purpose' [hereinafter IUH], in *Political Writings*, 74, 80.

[7] Kantian "freedom" is a complex notion. It is best understood as providing the ultimate standard of evaluation of normative arrangements, as the "inner value of the world" that can no longer be instrumentally validated, as suggested in Paul Guyer, *Kant on Freedom, Law, and Happiness* (Cambridge University Press 2000), 96–117.

[8] Immanuel Kant, *The Metaphysics of Morals* [hereinafter MM] (Mary Gregor ed., Cambridge University Press 1996), 30 [6: 237].

that was *different* from the present. History was not something unchanging, dictated by nature but the outcome of the free choices people made. This grounded Kant's legalism. To channel those choices while respecting the equal freedom of everyone, a constitution was needed. As he stated it at the outset of his legal theory: "Right [*Recht*] is . . . the sum of the conditions under which the choice of one can be united with the choice of another in accordance with the universal law of freedom."[9]

But freedom at home could not be established independently of what took place abroad: "the problem of establishing a perfect civil constitution is subordinate to the problem of a law-governed external relationship with other states, and cannot be solved unless the latter is also solved".[10] Owing to the interdependence of the modern world, no state was able to set up a law-governed republic at home without some such process taking place in the international level as well. The intellectual problem with Vattel and the whole of the natural law idiom was that it compelled accepting the present organisation of humanity as natural or inevitable. But it was not. Having observed the enthusiasm with which onlookers had greeted the French Revolution, Kant had concluded that there was a moral tendency in humanity towards progress through which every people would eventually "give itself a constitution".[11] This did not necessarily mean democracy. The key point was that for freedom to become a reality, the citizens united in a nation were to be entitled to give laws to themselves and those laws were to be impartially applied under a constitution.[12] Kant did not believe that this could take place immediately. A revolution was morally and politically inadmissible.[13] For this reason he sketched a gradualist programme from the present world to a federation of free states. Because the present organisation of the world was one of "lawless freedom", there was a legal duty

[9] Ibid., 24 [6: 230]. [10] Kant, IUH, 47.

[11] An early formulation of Kant's view that rational reflection of the present and the past necessitates thinking that "the human race is constantly progressing" is in PP, 88, 87–92 and is linked to what Kant, emboldened by the experience of the French Revolution, identified as a moral tendency in 'The Contest of the Faculties', in *Political Writings*, 182–5.

[12] Although Kant believed that legislative power should belong to the people, he also thought that only those who had economic independence should have the right to vote. Kant, MM, 91–2 [6: 314–15].

[13] Kant limited his optimism to the reaction of the "spectators" and while he admired the determination of the French and predicted that their example might be followed elsewhere, his legalism still made it impossible to accept that a people might have a *right* to revolution. Kant, 'Contest of Faculties', 184n. See further, Kant, TP, 81–3; MM, 95–8 [6: 318–23].

to leave it. Kant was optimistic about this. For the natural lawyers, progress meant simply understanding nature's requirements and learning to comply with them. With Kant, however, progress opened the way to something that was completely new, and better: "[M]an was not meant to be guided by instinct or equipped and instructed by innate knowledge; on the contrary, he was meant to produce everything out of himself."[14] The progressive nature of history was not something that could be proven, although much in the past tended to support it – the experiences of wars and the spirit of commerce would prompt even a "nation of devils", as Kant famously put it, to understand the rational interest in peace and lawfulness.[15] Whatever would happen with the French Revolution, it was one of those events that would not be forgotten and would support renewed attempts towards a constitutional order at home and in the world "until a cosmopolitan society is created".[16]

Kant's critical philosophy and his political theory, including the ideas of freedom and the historicity of human experience, had an immediate and massive effect in German debates about the law of nature and of nations.[17] After the 1790s, one could no longer write like Vattel without sounding, as Rayneval did, like an apologist for the old regime. The spread of Vattel's text in foreign offices around the world speaks volumes about the assumptions and worldviews of foreign policy elites in a post-revolutionary time. But as a form of intellectual imagining, this type of natural law was over. Instead, one could respect it by conducting "positivist" elaborations of the treaties and customs, the instruments and techniques of European diplomacy, along the lines of the professor of the law of nature and of nations at the University of Göttingen, Georg

[14] Kant, IUH, 43.

[15] Kant, PP, 114, 112–13. The most elaborate discussion of the way nature "supported" freedom towards the creation of universal lawfulness was Kant, IUH, 41–53.

[16] Kant, 'Contest of Faculties', 188.

[17] Measuring Kant-reception among German jurists is complicated by the breadth of Kant's writings and the interpretative difficulties it occasioned: a "Kantian" could be a natural lawyer and a "positivist", legal philosopher or specialised in private or public law, draw inspiration from Kant's methodological or his political or legal writings. Reception appears to have been massive until the 1820s and more limited as attention turned to the historical school in the 1840s and 1850s. Nevertheless, both as rationalist legal philosophy and within special fields (such as constitutionalism), its influence remained great. Joachim Rückert, 'Kant-Rezeption in juristischer und politisher Theorie (Naturrecht, Rechtsphilosophie, Staatslehre, Politik) des 19. Jahrhunderts', in M. Thompson, *John Locke and Immanuel Kant. Historical Reception and Contemporary Relevance* (Berlin, Duncker & Humblot 1991), 144–215.

Friedrich von Martens (1756–1821). Imagining the law of nations as Martens did, as the external public law of European states, was quite compatible with the frame offered to legal thought by the natural lawyers. But focus would now move from the frame to the details. The revolution was over. One needed to be realistic. "It is nothing but empty play of words when phrases about a morality of nations are written into a Declaration of the rights of nations," Martens commented on Abbé Grégoire's 1795 draft to the French Convention.[18] But while the old world could be restored as a political and diplomatic practice, it was dead for the life of the imagination. It was dead until Georg Wilhelm Friedrich Hegel (1770–1831) gave new life to the Restoration concept of external public law in a philosophy of history that shared Kant's progressive concern for freedom but rejected the view that a cosmopolitan world was needed to make it a reality. Instead, "the state is the more specific object of world history in general, in which freedom attains its objectivity and enjoys the fruits of its objectivity".[19] Kant, Hegel wrote elsewhere, had proposed that monarchs set up a dispute settlement system and that the Holy Alliance "was meant to be an institution of much the same kind". But states were individuals and individuality implied negation. And so, "the fact remains that wars occur when the nature of the case requires. The seeds burgeon once more, and talk is silenced by the solemn recurrences of history."[20]

This chapter traces the transformation of natural law into four languages that would take its place in the nineteenth century and beyond: the languages of empirical political science, economics, critical philosophy and modern law of nations. Natural law's status had been based on its ability to justify the existence of monarchic states as independent polities. But once it had provided those justifications, something more was needed to help governments to fulfil their objectives, the *Staatszweck*. Ambitious men in Germany would turn their attention to policy science (*Polizeiwissenschaft*) or *Staats*- and *Nationalökonomie*. Some would engage in philosophical contemplation about the nature of modernity while others would follow courses on the management of the European diplomatic system. In these contexts the law of nations expressed a historical view

18 Georg Friedrich von Martens, *Einleitung in das Positive Europäische Völkerrecht* (Göttingen, Dieterich 1796), Vorbericht, ix.

19 Georg Wilhelm Friedrich Hegel, *Lectures on the Philosophy of History. Introduction* (H. B. Nisbet trans., D. Forbes intro., Cambridge University Press 1975), 97.

20 G. W. F. Hegel, *Outlines of the Philosophy of Right* (T. M. Knox trans. & S. Houlgate intro., Oxford University Press 1952/2008 [1821]), § 324 (308).

about the universal realisation of freedom in the structures of the modern state. The chapter will end with the apotheosis of that view among German lawyers around the mid-nineteenth century. That was also the time when its utter insufficiency to respond to the dynamic pressures of civil society began to become clear. How to organise the productive forces within the modern state? How to channel their expansive ambitions outside the state? In opting for the language of civilisation, as briefly referenced in the Epilogue, the law of nations would finally become the conservative–liberal project that took it to the twentieth century.

## The Göttingen Project

That it was universities and professors who carried the enlightenment forward in Germany contrasts quite strikingly with France, Spain or England. Consolidating the rule of territorial princes and providing a sense of community to their towns had inspired already the establishment of the universities of Helmstedt (1575–6) and Giessen (1607).[21] After the Thirty Years' War, however, theology would lose its leading role in the academy. With the help of Thomasius and his followers, Protestant rulers would direct their universities towards pragmatic reforms of the *Fürstenstaat.* And in the universities, "[i]t was jurisprudence, and the topics subordinate to it in the philosophy faculty, that began the renewal".[22] This had much to do with the juridification of social and religious conflict in post-Westphalian Germany.[23] The empirical–historical orientation of Thomasian *Rechtsgelahrheit* redefined the old objective of the common good from the perspective of an instrumental science of the state (*Staatswissenschaft*), intensely focused on maintaining existing social relations and political hierarchies.[24] Thomasian natural lawyers believed this was best achieved by freedom

[21] See especially Helga Robinson-Hammerstein, 'The Common Good and the University in the Age of Confessional Conflict', in Ciaran Brady and Jane Ohlmeyer (eds), *British Interventions in Early Modern Ireland* (Cambridge University Press 2004), 75–84.

[22] Notker Hammerstein, 'Zur Geschichte und Bedeutung der Universitäten', 241 *Historische Zeitschrift* (1985), 314.

[23] See Patrick Milton, 'The Early Eighteenth-Century German Confessional Crisis. The Juridification of Religious Conflict in the Reconfessionalized Politics of the Holy Roman Empire', 49 *Central European History* (2016), 39–68.

[24] Hammerstein, 'Zur Geschichte und Bedeutung', 319; Notker Hammerstein, 'Die Deutschen Universitäten im Zeitalter der Aufklärung', 10 *Zeitschrift für Historische Forschung* (1983), 76; Axel Rüdiger, *Staatslehre und Staatsbildung. Die Staatswissenschaft an der Universität Halle im 18. Jahrhundert* (Tübingen, Niemeyer 2005), 8–11.

of research and scientific debate. The business of the church was to be limited to the care of the soul. In Germany, "State sovereignty and scientific freedom entered in a reciprocal relationship".[25]

Three decades after its establishment Halle would receive a competitor from the Georgia Augusta University in Göttingen (1734/37). This was not because England's George II would have shown much interest in his small German principality; it was rather his Halle-educated Minister Gerlach Adolf von Münchhausen (1680–1770) who became "the de facto 'founder' and until the end of his life in the truest sense the 'curator' of the University".[26] In Göttingen, law and philosophy became the leading faculties, with over half of the students enrolled in the former.[27] Like Halle, Göttingen was financed from public funds and operated under state supervision. Intolerance and sectarianism were prohibited; professors had high salaries and far-reaching freedom to lecture and publish. Focusing on matters of practical concern within the university was strengthened by the general mid-century expansion of public debates – *Öffentlichkeit* – and interest in English liberties.[28] By the end of the Seven Years' War, the university had become the preeminent academic institution in Germany, perhaps in the whole of Europe. As its leading light, the law faculty offered courses not only in public law but in the many related disciplines deemed useful for the needs of territorial and imperial offices:

The internationally recognised high level of teaching in Göttingen covered alongside the law of the territorial estate (*Landesrecht*) also imperial law, and alongside the history of the estate also imperial history, universal history,

[25] Rüdiger, *Staatslehre*, 42. Of course, for men like Thomasius, "*libertas*" meant spiritual, not political freedom, though it was not without political consequences. Werner Schneiders, 'Vernunft und Freiheit. Christian Thomasius als Aufklärer', 11 *Studia Leibnitiana* (1979), 15.

[26] Rudolf Vierhaus, 'Göttingen Die modernste Universität im Zeitalter der Aufklärung', in Alexander Demandt (ed.), *Stätten des Geistes. Große Universitäten Europas von der Antike bis zur Gegenwart* (Klön, Bohlau Verlag 1999), 247.

[27] But 10 percent of the students entered the philosophy faculty – a much larger number than usual, where they now could study alongside the old logico-metaphysical subjects history, natural history, physics and empirical psychology as well as dance, music and fencing. See e.g. Anne Saada, 'Les universités dans l'empire au siècle des lumières. L'exemple de Göttingen. Une réussite inédite', in Frédéric Attal et al. (eds), *Les universités en Europe du XIIIe siècle à nos jours* (Paris, Publications de la Sorbonne 2005), 259–63.

[28] Hammerstein, 'Zur Geschichte und Bedeutung', 303–8. On Göttingen's rise to leading enlightenment university in Germany, see also Michael Stolleis, *Geschichte des öffentlichen Rechts in Deutschland*, I (München, Beck 1988), 309–17.

history of the European states-system, as well as history of international trade and colonies. This is where emerged the theory of public law (*Staatswissenschaften*), that included empirical state-theory (*Statistik*), policy-science (*Polizeiwissenschaft*), economy and politics.[29]

The close connection between *doctor* and *princeps* meant in practice that professors were used in all kinds of counselling tasks, the preparation of legislation and policy ordinances as well as despatched on missions to neighbouring countries.[30] The fame of the Göttingen scholars lay in their ability to connect a historical understanding of civil society with an increasingly instrumental–technical, pragmatically oriented concept of public law. These directions were eventually taken into account and partially copied at other Protestant and some Catholic universities. Halle and Göttingen now provided the standard for academic excellence everywhere, proposing "tighter centralization of the state, a more humane juristic practice and the implementation of better 'economies'".[31]

## Transformation of Natural Law 1: Into Empirical Political Science: Schmauss

Among the first professors recruited for the new university was Johann Jacob Schmauss (1690–1757), Gundling's student, court counsellor at Baden-Durlach, advisor, diplomat and representative of the bishop of Strasbourg in the imperial Diet.[32] Schmauss was to teach the law of nature and of nations though he had had little to do with the subject earlier. Hence he had no difficulty in appearing as a reformer, writing freely on the "true concept" or "new system" of natural law.[33] He followed Pufendorf and Thomasius in separating natural law from theology but went further than his predecessors in providing an

29 Vierhaus, 'Göttingen', 250.

30 Hammerstein, 'Zur Geschichte und Bedeutung', 299–300.

31 Hammerstein, 'Die Deutschen Universitäten im Zeitalter der Aufklärung', 88.

32 On Schmauss' life, see Wolfgang Sellert, 'Johann Jacob Schmauss – ein Göttinger Jurist', 11 *Juristische Schulung* (1985), 843–4. For the recruitment of Schmauss, see also Gottfried Zieger, 'Die erste hundert Jahren Völkerrecht an der Georg-August-Universität Göttingen. Vom ius naturae et gentium zum positiven Völkerrecht', in Fritz Loos (ed.), *Rechtswissenschaft in Göttingen. Göttinger Juristen aus 250 Jahren* (Göttingen, Vandenhoeck & Ruprecht 1987), 39–40. Another good treatment is Ere Nokkala, *From Natural Law to Political Economy. J. H. G. von Justi on State, Commerce and International Order* (Vienna, Lit 2019), 53–66.

33 Johann Jacob Schmauss, *Vorstellung des wahren Begriffs von einem Recht der Natur* (Göttingen, Vandenhoeck 1748).

anthropological grounding for the field.[34] His main work, *New System of the Law of Nature*, published shortly after his death in 1757, was a brisk attack on Wolffian rationalism. It highlighted the importance of human drives for a proper concept of natural law of which the most important was that of self-preservation. Reason was a secondary pendant of culture and calculation. Drives gave rise to fear and hope, and it was the latter that directed the will to choose well – "like the traveller chooses the safe road through a forest with wild animals".[35] This provided a purely factual, rather than normative, basis for natural law. The drives were accompanied by corresponding rights and freedoms: the instinct of self-preservation came with a right of self-preservation, including a subjective right to everything that contributed to that purpose. At one point Schmauss even suggested that as large fish have the natural drive of eating small ones it followed that they "undoubtedly" had the right to this, too.[36]

The *New System* offered an extensive list of innate freedoms and rights (*iura connata*) that included, in addition to self-preservation, the rights to freedom and equality, equal respect, self-defence and to occupy ownerless things.[37] Yet people also possessed a natural sense of justice and equity that made them perfectly capable of settling their rights-conflicts by applying the natural law precept "do not do to others what you do not wish to be done to yourself".[38] All the rest of natural law followed from this; its great advantage was that it was followed spontaneously. No mediating institutions were needed, or they were needed only to clarify the direction that drives were to take.[39] This system produced virtually no law at all outside statehood. Almost everywhere a bargain had been struck to replace the state of nature by states for the realisation

[34] E.g. ibid., 25–7. See further Johann Jacob Schmauss, 'Neues Systema der Rechts der Natur', published as the Third Part of the *Neues Systema der Rechts der Natur* (Göttingen, Vandenhoeck 1754), 503–6, 526–9. The first part is a history of natural law and the second a review of some classical dilemmas ("dubia") of natural law. For Schmauss' critique of Pufendorf, see *Vorstellung*, 12–15.

[35] Schmauss, *Neues Systema*, 512–13. [36] Ibid., 472. [37] Ibid., 471–503.

[38] Ibid., 506, 508, 508–11, 517–18. See also Johann Jacob Schmauss, *Kurze Erläuterung und Vertheidigung seines Systema juris naturae* (Göttingen, Vandenhoeck 1755), 21.

[39] Schmauss, *Neues Systema*, 531. It is striking that with his anthropological approach, Schmauss left much of the period's moral code outside *iustum*. He could thus espouse a liberal sexual morality and even endorse a natural right to suicide – as this created no harm to others. See further Frank Grunert, 'Das Recht der Natur als Recht des Gefühls. Zur Naturrechtslehre von Johann Jacob Schmauss', 12 *Annual Review of Law and Ethics* (2004), 142–3.

of long-term interests.[40] Not much would remain of those original rights, at most they might be used as interpretative guides or gap-filling devices behind positive laws.[41]

Schmauss was a radical whose anthropological empiricism was precisely contrary to Wolffian rationalism; he even made the risky choice of citing long passages by Spinoza throughout his *oeuvre*.[42] Where most naturalists based the state's wide-ranging powers on the need to suppress human drives, Schmauss stressed their positive and constructive role. The study of public law should not limit itself to ideal forms of statehood. Instead, it should describe the way public institutions had learned to accommodate and balance the interests of the estates. The objectives of good law and good history coincided in the usefulness of their outcomes.[43] To put the teaching of the law of nations, too, on an empirical footing Schmauss published a large compilation of diplomatic documents. Together with the earlier collections by Leibniz, Amelot and le Clerc, these would help elucidate dispute-settlement among European states in practice.[44] But Schmauss did not think that treaties would ground a positive law of nations; such could only emerge in a formal superior–inferior relationship absent from the international world.[45] Instead, treaties were important for what in another work he termed the science of state-interest. This was neither the law of nature or of nations nor *ius publicum universale* but instead "a science that would only regard the question of 'interest', without attention to the rights and wrongs of the matter".[46] This was crucial. European states were to be studied in view of

[40] Schmauss, *Neues Systema*, 500–2.

[41] Jan Schröder, '"Naturrecht bricht positives Recht" in der Rechtstheorie des 18. Jahrhunderts', in Dieter Schwab et al. (eds), *Staat, Kirche, Wissenschaft in einer pluralistischen Gesellschaft* (Berlin, Duncker & Humblot 1989), 430–3; Diethelm Klippel, 'Der politische Freiheitsbegriff im modernen Naturrecht', in Otto Brunner et al. (eds), *Geschichtliche Grundbegriffe. Historisches Lexikon zur politisch-sozialen Sprache in Deutschland* (8 vols., Stuttgart, Klett-Cotta 1976), II, 86.

[42] For Schmauss' relations to Spinoza, Hobbes and Thomasius, see further Grunert, 'Das Recht der Natur', 146–9.

[43] Notker Hammerstein, *Jus und Historie. Ein Beitrag zur Geschichte des historischen Denkens an deutschen Universitäten im späten 17. und im 18. Jahrhundert* (Göttingen, Vandenhoeck & Ruprecht 1972), 347.

[44] Johann Jacob Schmauss, *Corpus Juris Gentium Academicum, enthaltenden die vornähmsten Staats-Gesetze Friedens- und Commercien-tractate, Bündnisse und andere Pacta. Erster Theil. Die Historie der Balance von Europa* (Leipzig, Gleditsch 1730), Vorrede.

[45] Zieger, 'Die Erste Hundert Jahren', 41–2.

[46] Johann Jacob Schmauss, *Einleitung zu der Staats-wissenschaft, und Erleuterung des von ihm herausgebenen Corpus Juris Gentium Academici und aller andern seit mehr als zweyen Seculis her geschlossenen Bündnisse, Friedens- und Commercien- Tractaten* (Leipzig, Gleditsch 1747), Vorrede.

the types of interests they had pursued without trying to translate those into a juridical system. The student of this empirical state-science was to lay out the strengths and weaknesses of every state, with special attention to distinguishing merely superficial interests from those with a solid empirical grounding.[47]

Schmauss commenced the production of a many-volumed treatise to explain in detail the operation of this new science. It would build upon his voluntarist anthropology and form a kind of preliminary for all state-sciences, including public and international law.[48] Only the first and second volumes came out, however. The former was a 600-page manual for politicians and diplomats on the operation of the European balance of power and the latter a history of the states of northern Europe. In the preface of the manual Schmauss explained that he had collected documents from all over the continent so as to enable the student to grasp how the balance realised the state-interest of each European state. He had included materials from the East and West Indies too, because colonies and questions of trade and commerce had now come to form an important *casus belli*, he stressed.[49]

The practical exercises conducted by Schmauss became exemplary of the pedagogical reforms that would contribute to Göttingen's Europe-wide fame. Having followed Schmauss' courses, a young man, it was said, "would not need a new education once he moved from the free air of the academy to the world of practical affairs".[50] Like his long discussion of the history of the balance of power, his teaching focused intensely on the political and economic interests of European states. Lamenting in 1740 what he assumed was future French supremacy on the continent, Schmauss did not with one word discuss the legal aspects of such a development.[51] History and empirical state-science had made *ius gentium* pointless. When Schmauss wrote that he wanted to contribute to a renewed study of the *ius publicum Europaeum*, he meant thereby a science of political skill, based on the empirical study and technical mastery of state-interests.[52]

47 Ibid., Vorrede. 48 Rüdiger, *Staatslehre*, 262.
49 Schmauss, *Einleitung*, Vorrede.
50 Zieger, 'Die Erste Hundert Jahren', 43. See also Sellert, 'Schmauss', 846–7.
51 Schmauss, *Einleitung*, 625–32.
52 Schmauss, *Corpus juris gentium*, Vorrede. Schmauss identified Gundling as the founder of this science.

## The Many Ways of State-Wisdom: Achenwall

The Göttingen scholars viewed the university as a place for thinking about how to meet the needs of the surrounding world. For Münchhausen, a lawyer by training, this effort should be led by law instead of the philosophy faculty whose teaching still bore traces of old-fashioned Aristotelianism. Among the most influential of the legal scholars he was able to recruit were Johann Stephan Pütter (1725–1807) and Gottfried Achenwall (1719–72), friends and collaborators in their joint authorship of the *Elementa juris naturae*, a widely used textbook from mid-century onwards.[53] Pütter was the century's most famous German public lawyer. High bureaucrats across the empire took pride in having been taught in his *Teutsches Staatsrecht*.[54] His contribution was limited to the public law sections of the *Elementa*, perhaps one-sixth of the whole, while Achenwall composed the parts of "pure" natural law and the law of nations, situating them in the overall frame of his political thought.

From his first years in the philosophy faculty, and having received appointment as *Ordinarius* in the law faculty in 1761, Achenwall struggled to develop an appropriate teaching curriculum that would contain an orderly arrangement of all the disciplines, both general and particular, normative and descriptive, that might be needed in the government of the modern state. His *Staatslehre* would consist of a philosophical and a historical part. The former would include public and civil law (*Staatsrecht, Civil-Recht,* sometimes simply *das natürliche Recht*) as well as state-wisdom (*Staatsklugheit*), which would combine the legal and utilitarian aspects of government.[55] Historical *Staatslehre*, again, would embody alongside *Staatsgeschichte* the empirical sciences of statehood (*Statistik, Staatsbeschreibung,* cameralism and economics), supposed to produce descriptions of particular states in order

[53] Eight editions were published between the 1750s and 1780s. The last ones came under Achenwall's name only. I have used the German translation of the first edition, Gottfried Achenwall and Johann Stephan Pütter, *Anfangsgründe des Naturrechts* (Jan Schröder ed., Frankfurt, Insel 1995). Data about the work is to be found in the essay by Schröder at the end, 333–51.

[54] On him, see Stolleis, *Geschichte*, I, 312–16; Paul Streidl, *Naturrecht, Staatswissenschaften und Politisierung bei Gottfried Achenwall (1719–1772). Studien zur Gelehrtengeschichte Göttingens in der Aufklärung* (Munich, Utz 2000), 30–60.

[55] Gottfried Achenwall, *Die Staatsklugheit nach ihren ersten Grundsätzen* (Göttingen, Vandenhoeck 1761), § 4 (2–3).

to assist in the conduct of their internal and external policies.[56] The relations between these many disciplines were complex. In his private correspondence Achenwall appears to have regarded natural law as the foundation for all "state-wisdom", which, in his view, and in contrast to Schmauss, should always operate within the limits of legal justice.[57] In the published work on *Staatsklugheit*, he was quite clear that a "rule of politics" that did not respect the boundaries of the legal was "not a rule of politics but an error".[58] But the natural law works remained abstract and general, and in *Staatsklugheit*, utilitarian considerations predominated.

Achenwall's work was situated at the forefront of the early German enlightenment. He wanted to renew legal science by situating it with other bodies of thought that would later be summarised as *Staatswissenschaften*, disciplines committed to the happiness and perfection of the state. He admired early comparative legal researches and wanted to replace old practical philosophy with an empirical, historically situated type of politico-legal knowledge.[59] This meant a knowledge of the state in its general features but above all in its specificity:

> The State is not just an abstract concept . . . Instead, it is a concept with much narrower boundaries in which I will include . . . for example its Christian religion, the gold and silver it uses for money, the state of its present army, trade and how to achieve stable relations with other States. Briefly, I regard the State as our States are in reality.[60]

56 In his theoretical treatise on politics, *Die Staatsklugheit* 'Ordnung und Inhalt', Achenwall divided practical state-wisdom into three parts: knowledge of the state's constitution, and of its internal and its external affairs. For overviews, see Muhammed H. Rassem & Guido Wölky, 'Zur Göttinger Schule der Staatswissenschaften bis zu der Freiheitskriegen', in Wilhelm Bleek & Hans J. Lietzmann (eds), *Schulen in der deutschen Politikwissenschaft* (Leske, Opladen 1999), 93–4 and Hans Erich Bödeker, 'Das staatswissenschaftliche Fächersystem im 18. Jahrhundert', in Rudolf Vierhaus, *Wissenschaften im Zeitalter der Aufklärung. Ans Anlaß des 250jährigen Bestehens des Verlages* (Göttingen, Vanderhoeck & Ruprecht 1985), 153–5. For a useful description of Achewall's work as a mediator between Conring's seventeenth-century *Staatenbeschreibung* and the Politics (*Politice*) developed by his successors in Göttingen, see Pasquale Pasquino, 'Politisches und historisches Interesse. Statistik und historische Staatslehre bei Gottfied Achenwall (1719–1772)', in Hans Erich Bödeker et al. (eds), *Aufklärung und Geschichte. Studien zur Deutschen Geschichtswissenschaft im 18. Jahrhundert* (Göttingen, Vandenhoeck & Ruprecht 1986), 144–68.

57 This is the main argument in Streidl, *Naturrecht*. That "Klugheit" operates within what is legally allowed, is also stated in Achenwall, *Die Staatsklugheit*, § 4 (2).

58 Achenwall, *Staatsklugheit*, § 8 (4).

59 Streidl, *Naturrecht*, 230.

60 Achenwall, *Staatsklugheit*, Vorrede § 4.

That was the starting-point of state-wisdom in its empirical mode. In its philosophical mode, *Elementa* turned into a kind of update to Grotius. Its four parts dealt with "pure" natural law applicable outside organised political society; the law of small communities (families above all) in the state of nature; a combination of universal public law (*ius publicum universale*, later to be addressed as *Allgemeine Staatsrecht*) and principles of private law (including property and persons as well as criminal law, not yet separated from public law); and it would contain the law of nations (*ius gentium universale*).

*Elementa* provided a total view of the government of states in their internal and external relations.[61] The normative foundation was received from the Wolffian principle of perfection, interpreted empirically in the sense of pleasure or pain that perfection or its lack brings.[62] The highest moral law said: perfect yourself (*perfice te*, *vervollkommene dich*), and it extended to the right to gain the objects of perfection/pleasure lawfully available.[63] But Achenwall did not share Wolff's rationalism: perfection was not a matter of logical inference but a product of historically determined state action.[64] This is why history, especially modern history, was so important. It would show each state what had been useful and what harmful in its past. The most important of Achenwall's works on international history, preparatory to the study of the law of nations, was his *History of the General Relations of European States in the Prior and Present Century* (first edition 1756).[65] The many-sided interdependence between European nations, he wrote there, had made it impossible to know and govern them on the basis of purely national studies. It was imperative to view them through their varied relationships with each other, paying especial regard to how those relations had

[61] In *Staatsklugheit*, Achenwall clearly laid out the "*doppeltes Ziel*" of ruling a polity: security of the state and its inhabitants as well as the growth of their "perfection" ("*Zuwachs an [ihre] Vollkommenheiten*"), II I § 6 (61).

[62] Achenwall, *Anfangsgründe*, *Vorkänntnisse* § 33–4, 40 (26/27, 28/29).

[63] Ibid., I IV § 176 (60/61).

[64] See Streidl, *Naturrecht*, 98–101.

[65] Gottfried Achenwall, *Geschichte der allgemeineren europäischen Staatshändel des vorigen und jetzigen Jahrhunderts im Grundrisse* (4th edn, Göttingen, Vandenhoeck 1779). See also *Anzeige seiner neuen Vorlesungen über die grosse europäische Staatenhändel des XVII–XVIII Jahrhundert, das ist über die Geschichte des europäischen Staaten-Systems seit 1600. Teil II der Europäischen Geschichte* (Göttingen, 1755). Achenwall used the term "constitution" in a "wide" sense as denoting all special features of a state ("*die würklichen Merkwürdigkeiten eines Staats*") and in a narrower sense (as "*Grundverfassung*") where it concerned the basic elements of its public law ("*Staatsrecht*"); see Gottfried Achenwall, *Staatsverfassung der heutigen vornehmsten europäischen Reiche im Grundrisse* (Göttingen, Vandenhoeck 1762), § 5 (3) and § 21 (12).

changed in time.[66] The objective was a historical understanding of the European states-system (*Europäische Staastssystem*) in its different moments of transformation and consolidation.[67] Particularly interesting was the way in which Achenwall used the term "constitution of Europe" to refer to the constellation of the principal powers at each moment, bringing the historical–empirical and the legal standpoints together into a comprehensive science of government.

Achenwall and Pütter read the basic principles of enlightened absolutism into their *ius publicum universale*. The original community of absolute rights could not survive the loss of life's simplicity. People wanted more and better goods and this necessitated setting up rights of exclusive ownership.[68] In due course, individuals would occupy territory and begin contracting on movable and immovable property as well as exercising other economic activities. They would also begin to unite for better security of their possessions and increased welfare (*ad vitae sufficientiam*). The state would emerge gradually as a "community of several families that has been set up for the common good under a unified system of power".[69] Achenwall was also keen to follow up the way subjects developed increasingly specialised institutions and integrated forms of collaboration. Industrially manufactured goods were being produced and advanced forms of exchange and division of labour emerged.[70] England's economic vitality was altogether admirable. An ideal constitution, he felt, was one that juxtaposed the ruler with a population of equals engaged in production and commerce and where nobility played no important role.[71]

All this supported extensive governmental tasks. The provision of security alone required a large police and military force, an extensive

[66] Like other Göttingen scholars, Achenwall wanted to focus on the "transformations" in the system (*Veränderungen*, *Revolutionen*), as the most important pedagogical moments. Achenwall, *Geschichte der allgemeineren europäischen Staatshändel*, Vorrede.

[67] The period from 1600 was divided into four moments, beginning from the opposition of every state against Spain and ending in the Peace of Aachen (1748), every moment described in terms of its "constitution". Because the work was meant to assist in Achenwall's lectures, it gave brief paragraphs marking the dates and principal provisions of the most relevant multilateral treaties. The point was not, Achenwall observed, just to help students remember individual facts – wars, treaties, peace agreements – but to put them in a continuum so as to make visible the causal relations between them. The work also included brief sketches of the economic situation, particularly the indebtedness of the countries as a key element explaining their rise or fall. Achenwall, *Geschichte der allgemeineren europäischen Staatshändel*, Vorrede.

[68] Achenwall, *Anfangsgründe*, I I § 260, 276 (89, 92/93).

[69] Ibid., III I § 653, 657 (210/211).

[70] Ibid., I II Title 1 (90/91–4/95).

[71] Streidl, *Naturrecht*, 232, 239–44.

system of taxation and a well-organised financial administration. The objective of welfare prompted regulation of the most varied economic activities – forestry, agriculture, mining, manufacture etc. – as well as governmental services for education, health and poverty-alleviation. No place was reserved for an independent civil society; the state was to regulate everything.[72] The ideal ruler was "a patriotic and perfect Prince and a real *Landesvater* in whose governmental activities goodness, justice, equity and honesty would constantly combine with constant care for the common good".[73]

The world of European diplomacy was one where the nations ruled by such princes possessed absolute rights of equality, freedom and respect and the associated rights to preserve and perfect themselves.[74] These were followed by hypothetical rights – those of property (i.e. territory), occupation and contract – as well as the authority to wage just war. But Achenwall was sceptical of the presence of any positive law of nations in Europe. He had once rejected the proposition to write a treatise on the customary law of nations because, as he wrote down in his notes, the general principles were already too familiar to need restatement and the Seven Years' War had demonstrated that anything could be justified by the citation of a practice that was hopelessly contradictory.[75] Besides, a specification of the customary law could not really add much to what he had already written in his history of the relations of European states; the facts, the causal relations and the momentary "constitutions" he had sketched there were what governed the European system.

Achenwall's works gave close descriptions of the history and laws of government of the most important European states, their natural resources and principal forms of livelihood, their industries, their activities in commerce and colonisation, their financial and monetary policies and the spirit of their people. They peaked in an explication of the state-interest, the most important policy considerations that would inform their government.[76] Such state-interest may be permanent or temporary.

72 Achenwall, *Staatsklugheit*, II I § 6 & 13 (61, 63).

73 "*ein patriotischer, ein vollkommener Furst, und ein wahrer Landesvater, in dessen Regierungs-Handlungen sich Gute, Gerechtigkeit, Billigkeit, Redlichkeit, und Sorgfalt für das gemeine Besten beständig äußern*". Ibid., Vorrede § 25.

74 See further Achenwall, *Anfangsgründe*, IV § 907, 910 (301/302–3/304).

75 Streidl, *Naturrecht*, 71.

76 The fourth, revised edition of *Staatsverfassung* (1762, first edition 1749), for example, included long discussions of Spain, Portugal, France, Great Britain, the United Provinces, Russia and Sweden. As these descriptions were updated and expanded, the materials would by 1785 spread over two large volumes.

It may have to do either with security or with growth and well-being. It also varied in the state's relationship to others.[77] In taking action, the ruler needed a clear view of the interest of other states, their history, constitution and other factors that might affect their attitudes.[78] Consistency was important and this required following state-maxims that would be specific for each state. Small states, for example, had interest in forming alliances while middle-size states had an interest in playing the powers against each other.[79] Depending on its power, a state could choose between a maintenance-system or a growth-system, a peaceful system or a war-system. Knowing all this was especially important for those who travelled in foreign countries, dealt with trade or "cameral-things" or prepared for negotiations with foreign powers.[80]

The objectives of foreign policy did not differ from those of domestic policy.[81] In considering whether to follow a treaty it should be borne in mind that it was in the interests of a state to be regarded as a trust-worthy ally.[82] But nothing was worse than being trapped in a harmful alliance.[83] There was, however, no natural enmity between states and it was in every state's interests to participate in the European diplomatic network. Under the law of nations, war could be resorted to only when there had been an injury and no reparation or guarantee for future security had been received.[84] But war was dangerous and unpredict-able, not to be employed lightly. Prevention, for example, was lawful only against a concrete and historically foreseeable threat. It was better first to try peaceful means.[85] In such case, mediation was preferable to arbitration that took the settlement out of the hands of the parties. But the fact could not be overlooked that sometimes the most efficient way to attain a goal was to despatch a warship to a foreign port.[86]

Towards the end of his career, Achenwall began to show interest in developing a view of civil society by scrutinising reports that were pouring into Europe from the colonies. In a short essay on North America dating

77 Achenwall, *Staatsklugheit*, II I § 10, 12 (276). 78 Ibid., II I § 15 (277).
79 Ibid., II I § 21–5 (279–80).
80 Gottfried Achenwall, *Staatsverfassung des heutigen europäischen Staaten im Grundrisse* (4th edn, Göttingen, Vandenhoeck 1762), Vorbereitung § 56 (33).
81 As expressly stated in *Staatsklugheit*, II I § 2 (273) Achenwall used the standard works by De Callières and Wiqcuefort to discuss the techniques of negotiation and the qualities of good diplomats, ibid., II III (295–305).
82 Ibid., II II § 3 (287). 83 Ibid., II II § 16–29 (291–3).
84 Achenwall, *Anfangsgründe*, II 3 § 477, 486 (154/155, 158/159).
85 Ibid., II 3 § 523–8 (168/169); IV 4 § 955 (316/317).
86 Achenwall, *Staatsklugheit*, II VI (306–25).

from 1767, which he wrote after a visit by Benjamin Franklin to Göttingen, he discussed the politics, economy and the constitutional status of the colonies as well as the way of life of the original inhabitants.[87] Achenwall admired the colonists, including what he believed were their relatively "liberal" slave laws, and assumed that their relations with Indian tribes were conducted under generally accepted natural law principles. He appreciated the spontaneity and peacefulness of the natives and lamented the tragedy, as he called it, that once they had been touched by civilisation they could no longer continue as before and, still not quite civilised themselves, fell in an uneasy limbo.[88] He did not believe in stories about the greatness of the Aztec empire: they had neither agriculture nor arts – how could they possibly have constructed such great cities?[89]

To create the kind of empirical state-science they were after, the Göttingen jurists proposed a reorganisation of the whole university education. The old Aristotelian triad of ethics, politics and oeconomy, with its emphasis on ethics, had to be changed. Ethics was to be about the production of internal happiness, a task to be delegated outside state institutions (not wholly, however, for although the state could not guarantee internal perfection it was nonetheless called upon to create conditions, such as the establishment of schools and universities).[90] In order to sort out the relations between law and the remaining two terms – politics and oeconomy – these were to be understood technically and instrumentally in contrast to the normative substance of natural law, now reconceived as a background justification of princely sovereignty instead of a source of substantive rules. Politics and economy took an increasingly central role in theoretical *Staatsklugheit* as well as in the more descriptive *Statistik*, alongside principles of *Policey* and the administration of taxation and public finances (cameralism).[91] Achenwall's fame is largely due to the way he united these empirical disciplines and mercantilist techniques under a single conception of politics, accompanied by historical illustrations of good and bad government.[92]

87 Gottfried Achenwall, *Herrn Gottfried Achenwalls Anmerkungen über Nordamerika und über dasige Grossbritannische Colonien* (from the oral account of Dr Franklin, Frankfurt und Leipzig 1769).

88 See Streidl, *Naturrecht*, 112–23.

89 Achenwall, *Anmerkungen*, 8, 25.

90 Achenwall, *Anfangsgründe*, III 2 I § 719–20 (234/235).

91 Achenwall, *Staatsklugheit*, Vorrede.

92 Achenwall's historical studies were in a way extended versions of his *Statistik*. See his *Geschichte der heutigen vornehmsten europäischen Staaten im Grundrisse* (5th edn, Göttingen, Vandenhoeck 1779). For an assessment, see e.g. Jutta Brückner, *Staatswissenschaften*,

But Achenwall still imagined his work on state-science as a jurist would: a study of constitutions, within which he read not only the laws governing the functioning of state organs but also the particular features of every nation from the administration of its *fiscus* to the orientations of its people. He never separated the "economy" into an autonomous element of *Staatsklugheit* and civil society played no independent role for him. The production of livelihood, industry and commerce, as well as monetary and fiscal affairs, were all important parts in his *Staatsklugheit.*[93] Such "economic" matters took up more space than all the rest of Achenwall's domestic government put together. But they were treated as much as parts of state-wisdom as justice, education, religion or military affairs.

## Transformation of Natural Law 2: Into Economics: Justi

If Achenwall was one of Göttingen's pioneering luminaries, Johann Heinrich Gottlob Justi (1717–71) travelled restlessly between Austrian and German courts, spending two important years in the Hanoverian university from where he adopted Schmauss' views about the leading role of drives in human behaviour.[94] Alongside providing more or less welcome administrative advice to German princes he published a huge number of books and pamphlets (comprising altogether sixty-nine volumes) extending from instructions on the management of the royal *Kammer* and good order (*Policey*) to treatises on metallurgy, statehood and the balance of power. Justi admired Montesquieu, agreed with the published views of Frederick II and supported the reforms carried out by the king's formidable counsel, Samuel von Cocceji (1679–1755).[95] Justi had received his legal training in Wittenberg in the 1740s and later spent short periods teaching cameral sciences and *Policey* in Göttingen and in the Theresian academy in Vienna. Most of his later life was taken up in advising the courts of Saxony-Eisenach, Vienna, Hannover,

*Kameralismus und Naturrecht. Ein Beitrag zur Geschichte der politischen Wissenschaft im Deutschland des späten 17. und frühen 18. Jahrhunderts* (München, Beck 1977), 257–65.

93 Achenwall, *Staatsklugheit*, Vorrede, § 11.

94 Schmauss' role in Justi's intellectual development has been highlighted in Nokkala, *From Natural Law to Political Economy*, 53–66.

95 However, his attacks on the balance of power supported Frederick and might have been inspired by his life-long ambition to enter Prussian service. Ere Nokkala, 'Just and Unjust Neutrality. J. H. G. von Justi's Defence of Prussian Maritime Neutrality (1740–1763)', in Koen Stapelbroek (ed.), *Trade and War. The Neutrality of Commerce in the Inter-State System* (Helsinki, Helsinki Collegium for Advanced Studies 2011), 43–5.

Denmark and finally Prussia (after 1758), but he ended his life in prison suspected (perhaps unjustly) of fraud in state service.[96]

Justi was a complex figure with a tendency to burn bridges to hosts and colleagues at his various places of employment. He dealt with constant financial problems by plagiarising himself, and at times others and by self-publishing endless revisions of his massive works. He was a well-known user of the state-machine metaphor, which in his texts oscillated between the old image of a human organism that highlighted the interdependency between ruler and subjects and the newer one of the clock that focused on the technical qualities of state administration.[97] The objective of statehood was happiness, which Justi divided initially in the conventional way into security and welfare, to be attained, respectively, by *Staatskunst* (a "politics" that also included law), and by a combination of cameralism plus *Policey*.[98] Justi was aware that welfare could not be separated from security in a competitive foreign policy environment. In his later writings, he began to include freedom as a third objective of statehood, meaning both the freedom of the state in its relations to other states and the freedom of citizens to follow their drives consistently with the law. Happiness could only be realised in an independent state where the will of the *Volk* was united with that of the ruler.[99] It was important to fit freedom within a comprehensive system of government in order to contribute towards

[96] For biographies, see Ulrich Adam, *The Political Economy of J. H. G. Justi* (Frankfurt am Main, Peter Lang 2006), 23–54; Marcus Obert, *Die naturrechtliche "politische Metaphysik" des Johann Heinrich Gottlob von Justi (1717–1771)* (Frankfurt, Peter Lang 1992), 7–23; Keith Tribe, *Governing Economy. The Reformation of German Economic Discourse 1750–1840* (Cambridge University Press 1988), 56–61.

[97] Johann Gottlob Justi, *Natur und Wesen der Staaten als die Quelle aller Regierungswissenschaften und Gesezze* (Mitau, Steidel 1771 [1760]), 3 §§ 30–44 (61–95). See also commentary in Barbara Stollberg-Rilinger, *Der Staat als Maschine. Zur politischen Metaphorik des absoluten Fürstenstaats* (Berlin, Duncker & Humblot 1986), 109–16 and Ere Nokkala, 'The Machine of State in Germany – The Case of Johann Heinrich Gottlob von Justi (1717–1771)', 5 *Contributions to the History of Concepts* (2009), 71–93.

[98] Tribe, *Governing Economy*, 61. See further Hans Maier, *Die ältere deutsche Staats- und Verwaltungslehre* (Munich, C. H. Beck Verlag 2009), 183–5. *Policey* would thus contrast with the much more narrowly conceived (though older) cameralism and *oeconomie*. "Politics", again, would contrast with "*Policey*" by focusing on sovereign decision-making and the implementation of the constitutional order, that is, the relations of the ruler and subjects.

[99] "Die Glückseeligkeit als die Richtsnur aller Gesetze des Staats, kommt aus Freiheit, innerliche Stärke und Sicherheit an", Johann Heinrich Gottlob Justi, *Der Grundriss einer guten Regierung in fünf Büchern* (Frankfurt & Leipzig, Garve 1759), § 77 (63–4) and § 81, 198 (71–2, 244–5). See further *Einleitung* and § 32, 34 (20–2, population as key to the strength of the state), § 85 (78, freedom within the limits of law).

an active economic life. This had an immediate consequence on his views on the international world. A wise government would understand the importance of enlisting the *Volk* in building up its industries and commerce.[100] Such government would realise that it was in the nature of commerce to be free; there was no rational basis to subordinate trade to politics. This would only raise artificial obstacles to commercial dealings.[101] In the end, the rise and fall of nations reflected the ability of governments to engage the skill and industriousness of their subjects, preferably under comprehensive plans.[102]

Justi's prolific writings used the idiom of natural law whose focus moved from the justification of state power to strengthening it by enlisting the forces of an economically active *Volk*. Over and again Justi explained the origin of states in the unification of many families into one *Volk* anxious to protect themselves and their properties against internal disorder and war. Social contract theories were utter fiction; no such transactions had ever been concluded. Instead, what had transpired was that families had emerged from wildness into freedom and, eventually through war, to political statehood. The result was an organic whole in which any damage to a single part would immediately concern the whole state body.[103] Already early on in the natural state, economic activities such as hunting and fishing had organised families in small, competitive societies. But eternal schisms and disorder persuaded heads of families to subordinate themselves under a single constitution (*Grundfverfassung*, *Grundgesetze*).[104] Sociability was nothing innate, as Justi agreed with Pufendorf and Adam Smith, but was a conclusion reasonable persons drew from experience and from advantages of cooperation.[105] Constitutional government would allow limiting the powers of the ruler and help guarantee the freedoms and properties of the subjects. At one point Justi stressed that it was best if the difference of wealth between families was not too great. The riches of one family did not compensate for the poverty of five. But elsewhere he wrote that the

[100] Johann Heinrich Gottlob Justi, *Die Chimäre des Gleichgewichts der Europa* (Altona, Iversen 1758), 39, 39–58.

[101] Ibid., 58, 71–2. [102] Justi, *Grundriss*, § 212–23 (263–78).

[103] Justi, *Natur und Wesen*, 2 § 27–9 (54–60), 3 § 30–44 (61–95). See also commentary in Stollberg-Rilinger, *Staat als Maschine*, 109–16. On the notion of das *Volk* and its relation to the "family" in Justi, see Obert, *Die naturrechtliche "politische Metaphysik"*, 118–20.

[104] Justi, *Natur und Wesen*, 1 § 3–18 (8–40), 2 § 27–9 (54–60); Obert, *Die naturrechtliche "politische Metaphysik"*, 86–90.

[105] Justi, *Natur und Wesen*, 8 § 211 (474).

state had no right to intervene in property rights, apart from cases of necessity, and then against a fair compensation. It was not entitled to engage in distributive policies, inequality was a natural phenomenon and the right of property of subjects was sacred.[106] Overall, however, Justi appreciated a reasonable distribution of wealth as an important objective of state policy. Although there was in this respect no great difference between constitutional forms, the nobility ought not to have too great a role and in practice monarchy tended to work best.[107] Because the foundation of state power lay in the people, only the people were empowered to change constitutional laws. They could also resist an unconstitutional ruler and, if necessary, take state power into their hands.[108]

Justi regarded the growth of state power as a normal outcome of the wisdom of their governments. War in itself was a legitimate tool of statecraft as long as it was used rationally for the good of the nation.[109] Justi regarded the Prussian capture of Silesia (1740), the attack on Saxony (1756) and even the first partition of Poland (1772) as ultimately successful and thus justified.[110] By the time Frederick ascended the throne some three-quarters of Prussia's revenues were allocated to the upkeep of the army and the conduct of its military

106 Ibid., 1 § 29 (60); *Grundriss*, § 40 (25), § 194 & 199 (239–41, 245–7). Justi held that the state had a feudal type of superior right (*Obereigenthum*) over its territory (he did not have the concept of jurisdiction); but this did not entitle it to intervene in private properties, § 199 (246–7). For general commentary, see Horst Dreitzel, 'Justis Beitrag zur Politisierung der deutschen Aufklärung', in Hans Erich Bödeker and Ulrich Herrmann (eds), *Aufklärung als Politisierung – Politisierung der Aufklärung* (Studien zum Achtzehnten Jahrhundert, Bd. 8) (Hamburg, Felix Meiner 1987), 167–8.

107 Aristocracy, Justi held, was unjust and destructive for rational government, an "animal with a thousand legs", each running in a different direction. *Natur und Wesen*, 5 § 74–5 (168–72), 6 § 109 (251) and Adam, *Political Economy of J. H. G. Justi*, 118–30.

108 Justi, *Natur und Wesen*, 4 § 46 (100–2). On the quite complex notion of "constitution" in Justi, see further Obert, *Die naturrechtliche "politische Metaphysik"*, 90–2. See also Adam, *Political Economy of J. H. G. Justi*, 143–7. On the right of resistance, see *Natur und Wesen*, 11 § 131 (299–302) and Obert, *Die naturrechtliche "politische Metaphysik"*, 147–50.

109 This, he argued, had seldom been the case. Charles V, Louis XIV or Sweden's Charles XII, for example, had wasted the resources of their countries by needless wars. Adam, *Political Economy of J. H. G. Justi*, 65–9.

110 Justi supported Prussia's occupation of Saxony by publishing a satirical biography of Saxony's powerful minister, Count von Brühl, accusing him of despotism. See ibid., 158–63. It is hard to fit this with Justi's stress on the need to respect the independence of peoples, however. Was this merely opportunistic rationalisation in order to please Frederick?

operations.[111] Somewhat oddly, Justi did not seem to have a problem with this. Perhaps as a contrarian reflex against more conventional writers, Justi even came to support the idea of universal monarchy (though not the Wolffian construction of *Civitas Maxima*). Of course, rival princes were critical of such claims, jealous of their power and looking to defeat their neighbours. But in fact, the welfare of private families would expand even outside Europe.[112] In his other texts, however, Justi resignedly accepted that nations did their utmost to avoid subordination to foreign power. Nor was there any European republic: European peoples had joined in states and vested them with supreme power precisely to avoid anything of the kind.[113] Their relations had sometimes degenerated to altogether barbarian levels. It was only the more enlightened rulers who understood the value of peace and cooperation, and Justi briefly speculated about whether it might be possible to use economic coercion to compel reluctant rulers to see justice.[114]

Justi rejected the wisdom of the balance of power. The Göttingen scholars had speculated on the balance in terms of the relative wealth of states – the size of their population, their resources and their ability to purchase goods from abroad. This had led them to support the use of military force against a state that had increased its power inordinately. In the *Chimera of the Balance of Power* (1758) Justi took a contrary view. The very foundations of balance-thinking were mistaken. It had become impossible to calculate the relative power of states reliably. Neither extensive territory, large population, massive military force nor the ruler's wealth provided an adequate criterion. Because state power coincided with the wisdom of its government, operating in a fluctuating world of economic success and decline, organising the security of European nations by the policy of the balance was pure chimera. How could wisdom be measured?[115] The suggestion to fix

[111] Perry Anderson, *Lineages of the Absolutist State* (New York, Verso 2013), 213; John Galigardo, *Germany under the Old Regime, 1600–1790* (London, Longman 1991), 308.

[112] Justi viewed wars and the destruction they wrought as aspects of the world's evil that God had created for reasons unknown to us. Nevertheless, even when divided into separate states, Europe was the best of communities and there was no reason to believe that eradication of evil and progress towards a universal monarchy (in Europe) would remain forever impossible. Johann Gottlob Justi, 'Beweis dass die Universalmonarchie vor die Wohlfahrt von Europa und überhaupt des menschlichen Geschlechts die größte Glückseligkeit wirken würde', in Justi, *Politische und Finanzschriften über wichtige Gegenstände*, vol. II (Copenhagen, Roth n/d), 235–300.

[113] Justi, *Natur und Wesen*, 8 § 211 (473).

[114] Ibid., 8 § 212 (477–9); 8 § 215 (485–6).

[115] Justi, *Die Chimäre des Gleichgewichts der Europa*, 27–39.

the powers of states was frankly nonsensical because it implied that skilful and well-ordered governments should refrain from optimising the use of their resources. The very idea had been born out of envy that some princes felt towards their more successful neighbours. It was an offshoot of the dangerous policy of the *raison d'état* that, instead of restraining violence, provided only an excuse for endless "bloodshed, despair and unhappiness".[116]

During the Seven Years' War Justi restated these points in an attack on the French effort to rally European states against British commercial hegemony. After the famous *Renversement des alliances*, Prussia had found itself allied with England while France had joined with its old arch-enemy, Habsburg Austria. In the course of the war, England used its maritime superiority to unsettle French colonial trade, and it was to this that the French Minister Maubert de Gouvest reacted by proposing that alongside the balance of power, there ought also be what he called a "balance of trade". In the *Chimera of the Balance of Power in Commerce and Shipping* (1759), Justi emphasised the utter irrationality and injustice of such a suggestion. The argument from balance of trade accepted that state power was above all commercial power. But commercial power could not be limited in the way suggested by the French. It was the nature of commerce to be free. Every nation tried to export as much of its excess product as it could and to buy what it needed from whomsoever was willing to sell at the lowest price.[117] Success in such dealings depended on the industry and skilfulness (*Arbeitsamkeit und Geschicklihckeit*) of the population, and power increased naturally as economic contacts expanded.[118] The proposal did not only strike at the commercially successful nation but also the (presumably "innocent") nation that traded with it. The French proposal, Justi concluded, was merely a hypocritical effort to dress France's military interests in the form of a principle of European public law.

This argument drew a sharp divide between politics and economy, describing the latter in terms of a global market where all nations competed freely to the best of their capacities. To set limits to this would arbitrarily curtail the expansion of the most resourceful and

[116] Ibid., 3. Justi regarded the balance as utterly incompatible with justice and the rules of good *Staatskunst*, 59–84. See further Adam, *Political Economy of J. H. G. Justi*, 70–82.

[117] Johann Gottlob Justi, *Die Chimäre des Gleichgewichts der Handlung und Schiffahrt*, (Altona, Iversen 1759), 11–21.

[118] Ibid., 27, 49. See further Adam, *Political Economy of J. H. G. Justi*, 82–92; Nokkala, *From Natural Law to Political Economy*, 195–203.

industrious countries. It also failed to have regard to the fact that there was a natural balancing aspect in trade itself. The more successful a nation was, the more there would be money circulating in it, and the more salaries would rise and the more expensive its goods would become.[119] With such arguments Justi separated the operation of international economy from the policies of European states precisely as he was joining the period's political thinkers in regarding economic strength as the most vital aspects of a state's power.

## The Rise of the "Economy"

In Justi's naturalist metaphysic, legislation was an important technical aspect of government, subordinated to concerns of welfare and security-production. Attention at law schools was to be directed from the study of positive law to comprehensive legislative plans that would involve a division of labour between the governmental branches in view of the functions of each. This was sketched in Justi's widely read works on economy (*Staatswirtschaft*, 1755) and the principles of cameralism and *Policey*-science (*Grundsätze der Policey-Wissenschaft*, 1756). Here Justi suggested that empirical *Staatskunst* should be accompanied by a science of good government (*gute Policey*) whose object would be "the review, control, and management of the human resources available to the state".[120] In later texts he further elaborated the details of these disciplines, highlighting the independence of welfare-production from other governmental functions. Among its special features was cooperation with private actors. Everything did not need to be carried out by the state itself. "It is a general observation", he wrote, "that a wise government need in many things relating to trade and industry undertake no especial supportive action whatsoever other than to remove the obstacles from their way."[121]

Pragmatically oriented policy ordinances had been part of local government in Germany since the late fifteenth century. In the early eighteenth century *Policey-wissenschaft* had turned into an instrument for the Wolffian search for social perfection with a potentially unlimited sphere:

[119] Justi, *Die Chimäre des Gleichgewichts der Handlung und Schiffahrt*, 35–6. These arguments went directly against those made by Hume and others in Britain in the "jealousy of trade" debate.

[120] Tribe, *Governing Economy*, 63.

[121] Justi, *Gesammelte politische und Finanzschrifte*, quoted in Dreitzel, 'Justis Beitrag zur Politisierung der deutschen Aufklärung', 169.

the state would operate not only to produce security but everything contributing to welfare.[122] Under Wolffian influence, a specific *Policeyrecht* was developed whose content was assumed to be derivable logically from the ends of statehood.[123] However, with the realisation that state power was dependent on the productive and commercial activities taking place in the *bürgerliche Gesellschaft*, it began to seem necessary to obtain new types of expert advice. How to learn to compete with neighbours in wealth-creation and management? At the beginning of the eighteenth century the "economy" did not possess identity as a university discipline beyond the Aristotelian ethics of household management.[124] After a fitful start with older *Hausvaterlitteratur*, tracts began to appear that linked *Oeconomie* with state management, fiscal policy and social discipline, opening the door for *Policey* and cameralism to take the place of the already rather marginal Aristotelian "chresmatic".[125] Ambitious students were now guided from constitutional debates (Gundling's "architectonic") towards more practically oriented tasks ("administration").[126] Complemented by an empirical *Staatskunst* that situated the legal system within a narrative about the history and objectives of statehood, *Policey*-science promised a much more concrete governmental agenda than could ever have been developed by formal–legal study. Natural law would still provide the philosophical basis of state power. But for the purposes of public service, it would be accompanied by the practical sciences of government, *Staatskunst* and cameralism.[127]

[122] See especially the detailed study on the effects of the expansion of the *Staatszweck* doctrine in Wolff and the Wolffians by Peter Preu, *Polizeibegriff und Staatszwecklehre. Die Entwicklung der Polizeibegriff durch die Rechts- und Staatswissenschaften des 18. Jahrhunderts* (Göttingen, Schwarz 1983), 107–25.

[123] Ibid., 131–3; Maier, *Die ältere deutsche Staats- und Verwaltungslehre*, 200–7; Stolleis, *Geschichte*, I, 386–93.

[124] See Keith Tribe, 'Cameralism and the Science of Government', in Keith Tribe, *Strategies of Economic Order. German Economic Discourse 1750–1850* (Cambridge University Press 1995), 263–84; Maier, *Die ältere deutsche Staats- und Verwaltungslehre*, 168–81.

[125] See Tribe, *Governing Economy*, 55–90.

[126] Johann Christian Pauly, *Die Entstehung des Polizeirechts als wissenschaftliche Disziplin. Ein Beitrag zur Wissenschaftsgeschichte des öffentlichen Rechts* (Frankfurt am Main, Klostermann 2000), 55. See also on the later discussion of the need of a separate "law of policy", 77–80.

[127] See Dreitzel, 'Justis Beitrag zur Politisierung der deutschen Aufklärung', 165–6; Hans Erich Bödeker, 'Das Staatswissenschaftliche Fächersystem im 18. Jahrhundert', in Rudolf Vierhaus, *Wissenschaften im Zeitalter der Aufklärung. Ans Anlaß des 250 jährigen Bestehens des Verlages* (Göttingen, Vanderhoeck & Ruprecht 1985), 147–8; Stolleis, *Geschichte*, I, 322–3.

The first university chairs in cameralism were established in the Halle law faculty and the philosophy faculty of Frankfurt an der Oder in 1727. The appointed professors, a jurist and a historian, were to focus on agricultural economy and public finances.[128] Additional positions were soon set up in other universities and special training institutions outside Prussia, with the field of teaching expanding gradually over the whole field of economic activity.[129]

In the 1750s and 1760s, policy-science and cameralism arose as rivals to the old legal disciplines. In Justi's view, it was no longer possible to rule the state only by lawyers – one needed "universal cameralists", men who would be knowledgeable about the different aspects of the economy and the uses of the state's resources.[130] Because the substance of cameral and policy-science was not clearly delineated, they could expand into an undifferentiated pursuit of scientific and technical vocabularies in the hands of ambitious *politici*.[131] Rivalry for the prince's ear contributed to strategic accommodations between disciplines that ended up transforming the way public law and the chairs of *ius naturae et gentium* were conceived.[132] As a result, cameralism soon began to seem overly narrow in its focus on the operations of the state. To bring about the desired welfare gains, attention was to be directed to the economy as a whole. Justi had already defined the wealth of a state as a combination

[128] Hans Maier, 'Die Lehre der Politik an den älteren deutschen Universitäten, vornehmlich vom 16. bis 18. Jahrhundert', in Dieter Oberndörfer (ed.), *Wissenschaftliche Politik. Eine Einführung in Grundfragen ihrer Tradition und Theorie* (Freiburg, Verlag Rombach 1962), 96–7, 177–9; Tribe, *Governing the Economy*, 42–4; Stollberg-Rilinger, *Staat als Maschine*, 77–85. The first professor of cameralism in Halle, Simon Peter Gasser (1667–1745) readily complied when his monarch, Frederick William I – no friend of jurists – wished to coordinate teaching in the new discipline as closely as possible with the needs of Prussian financial administration. Although his follower, Johann Friedrich Stiebritz (1707–1772), expanded the discipline to cover industrial production and manufacture, the new monarch Frederick II ended the study of cameral sciences as unsuitable for the university in 1772. Rüdiger, *Staatslehre*, 205–13.

[129] The most important new institution was the "High School of Cameralism" originally established in Lautern in 1763 but transferred to the University of Heidelberg in the late 1770s. On this and on the expanding content of textbooks in cameral science in the 1760s and 1770s, see Tribe, *Governing Economy*, 91–118.

[130] Ibid., 67; Stollberg-Rilinger, *Staat als Maschine*, 78.

[131] The disciplines became, Bödeker writes, "akademischen und literarischen Sammelplatz verschiedener technisch-rechtswissenschaftliche und wirtschaftlich-sozialwissenschaftliche Kenntnisse", 'Staatswissenschaftliche Fächerssystem im 18. Jahrhundert', 149.

[132] For this competition in the political field, see Maier, 'Die Lehre der Politik', 97–102.

of the wealth of private families and wise statecraft, suggesting that private exchanges frequently worked best without excessive public interference.[133] In his later writings, Justi made many proposals towards an open market. Commerce in luxury was welcome as it would contribute to the rise of a wealthy merchant class that would then be emulated by the rest of the population. Indeed, it was one of the objectives of the state "to have rich and powerful merchants".[134] The prohibition of noble commerce was an utter anachronism. There was no reason at all to maintain the military ethos of the noble estate and to avoid applying the economic rationale to it.[135] Monopolies might be needed at the outset of large investment projects. But the objective of a flourishing economy necessitated their removal, together with guilds and other restrictive provisions.[136]

"To be free", Justi explained in a 1759 work, had to do with the subject's ability to realise their will unhindered. But as subjects had joined the state to realise their happiness though it, they could be really free (*wahrhaftig frey*) only when they obey the laws.[137] Having handed their natural freedoms over to the state, they had obviously done this only to the extent that was necessary to enable the state to carry out its tasks.[138] A good ruler was never to invade their "wise freedom" unnecessarily. Taxes, for instance, were never to be raised without good reason; the ruler was to regard the property of his subjects as their "holiest and the most inviolable" good.[139]In his late works, Justi wrote increasingly about civil freedom, the ability of subjects to operate freely in the economy. Political freedom, the right to participate in government, was no more part of his scheme than it was of the writings of most

[133] Adam, *Political Economy of J. H. G. Justi*, 194–9.

[134] Justi, *Abhandlung von denen Manufakturen und Fabriken, I–II* (1758/61), cited in Adam, *Political Economy of J. H. G. Justi*, 199.

[135] Justi had also translated into German the pamphlet by Abbé Coyer, *La noblesse commerçante* (1756). See further Barbara Stollberg-Rilinger, 'Handelsgeist und Adelsethos', 15 *Zeitschrift für historische Forschung* (1988), 298–306.

[136] Justi, *Staatswirtschaft*, § 194 (209).

[137] "Der Bürger aber ist frey, wenn er seinen Willen ungehindert erfüllen kann." Justi, *Grundriss*, Einleitung § 32 (21). As Justi also elaborated at length, an unlimited government could *never* be a good government. One who looks for happiness needs to have "power over themselves" ("Herrschaft über sich selbst"), § 170, 172 (210, 212–13). See further Torsten Moos, *Staatszweck und Staatsaufgaben in den protestantischen Ethiken des 19. Jahrhunderts* (Münster, Lit 2005), 48–50.

[138] Justi, *Grundriss*, § 85, 87 (78, 80).

[139] "die allerheiligste und unverletzlichste Sache", ibid., Einleitung, § 40 (25), § 199 (245–7).

other jurists.[140] He simply suggested that the state ought to allow fathers to govern their families freely, pleading occasionally "for freedom of conscience, freedom of the press and of the domestic 'private sphere'", mostly because he understood these freedoms as preconditions for a properly functioning economy.[141] To obtain an abundance of goods and conveniences available to the population demanded an active economic life, including a flourishing foreign trade.[142] Justi had much to say about how to train merchants and stressed that an active life in production and exchange among subjects was the ultimate source of state power.[143] But he was no Adam Smith. Good policy ordinances were needed to see to the orderly conduct of economic actors. The objective of trade was to meet the needs of the people – but the objective of merchants was profit. The state was needed to align these objectives by well-planned regulatory policies. Earlier on, he wrote, rulers believed that they were to keep their subjects poor and needy. "Nowadays" everyone agreed that "a poor land leads to the poverty and weakness of the prince". But the wealth of the subjects was still just a subordinate objective for state action. More important was the happiness of the people and the wealth of the state, and this would require, among other measures, provision to prevent harmful concentrations of wealth and to see to the broad equality of the subjects.[144]

Everything that Justi wrote about good government assumed a supervisory role for the ruler, preferably under a comprehensive plan that would cover all things necessary for "happiness". But he was also critical of excessive regulations and increasingly in the course of his career sought to fit the regulatory ambitions of good government with the freedoms of the subjects. That objective gave a new set of tasks to natural law.

## Transformation of Natural Law 3: Into Philosophy: Kant

By the 1790s, Prussian autocracy had come to be challenged both in theory and practice. Wolffian natural law had undergone a spectacular fall as the official philosophy of the state. The vocabularies of perfection and happiness turned out empty of criteria for distributive choice and

[140] Klippel, 'Der politische Freiheitsbegriff', 479–82.
[141] Nokkala, *From Natural Law to Political Economy*, 109.
[142] Justi, *Grundriss*, § 235 (300–1).
[143] Ibid., Einleitung § 32 (21) and § 77 (66); § 93–5 (87–90).
[144] Ibid., § 193–4 (238–41). Justi, *Staatswirtschaft*, § 179, 197 (184–5, 211–12).

gave no reality to individual rights. Physiocrat readings and translations of Adam Smith brought into question cameralist doctrines of welfare-creation, and the convocation of the French National Assembly turned German intellectuals towards republican and constitutionalist ideals.[145] The Göttingen historian August Ludwig Schlözer (1735–1809) wrote in 1793 that a system of government was like a fire that provided warmth for the community but needed to be watched closely so that it did not burn and destroy everything.[146] The language of political freedom penetrated an emerging public sphere. When Immanuel Kant's *Critique of Pure Reason* (1781) descended upon German intellectual life, philosophical support for older natural law collapsed. When Kant then came to publish his critical moral philosophy in 1785 and 1788, "the categorical imperative was immediately taken as providing a new foundation of natural law theory".[147]

During the decade leading up to the Revolution, Kant had not yet written anything specifically legal or political. But it was obvious that his writings on the inner freedom of individuals, the universal power of the transcendental imperative and his legalism posed all kinds of demands for political life as well.[148] The perspective laid out in the *Groundwork of the Metaphysic of Morals* (1785) and *Critique of Practical Reason* (1788) presumed that people were not just creatures of instinct and that their moral objectives could not be circumscribed by the search for happiness. A human being was "*more than a machine*".[149] Like Grotius, Kant believed that social life was to be constructed around the human ability to commit to life by rules. Also like Grotius, he began with the individual subject entering a social world through private arrangements whose enforcement was to be guaranteed by the public power of the state. But unlike Grotius, he understood freedom as the underlying objective of all

145 For a good summary, see Diethelm Klippel, 'Kant im Kontext. Der naturrechtliche Diskurs um 1800', in R. Oldenbourg (ed.), *Jahrbuch des historischen Kollegs* (Munich, Verlag 2001), 85–97.

146 August Ludwig Schlözer, *Allgemeine Statsrecht und Statsverfassungslere* (Göttingen, Vandenhoeck & Ruprecht 1793), 111. Schlözer's book followed Rousseau's writings on the social contract, extending natural rights into the life of the state and depicting the ruler as the servant of his subjects.

147 Knud Haakonssen, 'German Natural Law', in Mark Goldie and Robert Wokler (eds), *The Cambridge History of Eighteenth-Century Political Philosophy* (Cambridge University Press 2006), 279.

148 See further, Reidar Maliks, *Kant's Politics in Context* (Oxford University Press 2014), 16–38.

149 Immanuel Kant, 'What is Enlightenment?', in *Political Writings*, 60.

those social and legal rules and institutions.[150] This was not just about the legal order, however. The idea bore a larger cultural and political meaning that pointed to a new way of thinking about history and the role of human beings in it. If freedom was the inner meaning of the world, then there was a need to depart from the world as it was. As Kant wrote in 1784:

> The greatest problem for the human species, the solution of which nature compels him to seek, is that of attaining a civil society which can administer justice universally.[151]

Of course, past speculations about universal justice had always been struck down by the realist retort that in view of what we knew of human nature and history, they could never become reality. But Kant now seemed to have a response to show that it was the realists whose views were based on indemonstrable dogmas; there was nothing in human nature or history that prevented this objective from being realised. Not only did humans have a duty to look for it, they also had good reason, including empirical reason, to hope for its fulfilment.[152] No surprise, then, that revolutionaries such as Sieyès received Kant's writings enthusiastically, despite their author's eventual condemnation of revolution. Although he was accused of idealism, Kant was actually extremely careful to stress the gradual and provisional nature of his proposals. In his first clearly political essay on 'Theory and Practice' (1792), Kant situated natural rights firmly within the polity. He rejected Achenwall's limited authorisation for the subjects to resist their sovereign. If the right of resistance were made into what Kant called a "maxim" of rightful behaviour, it would "make all lawful constitutions insecure".[153] But he softened this conclusion by stressing the inalienable nature of the rights that all humans carried also within the state and that involved the authority to make public grievances about public measures that appeared to violate them.[154]

150 The complexity of Kantian freedom is, however, visible in his denial that it necessitated equality either in rights of participation, in public institutions or in the possession of resources (see e.g. TP 75 and MM § 46, 91–2).

151 Kant, IUH, 45.

152 For the original form of the argument, see Kant, TP 88–92. The empirical reasons had to do with the unsocial sociability that Kant propounded in the IUH 53 as well as in PP First Supplement (112–13).

153 Kant, TP, 81–7.

154 Kant invited his readers to presume that rulers would consider such claims in good faith and reform themselves in case they provided correct, ibid., 84–5.

In *Perpetual Peace* (1795) and in his *Rechtslehre* (1797) Kant devoted much attention to the present situation of sovereign states remaining in a state of nature between each other, a situation he condemned as unlawful but was still ready to discuss in the broadly Hobbesian terms that have puzzled commentators. Nor did he advocate a world state, at least not immediately.[155] But he thought it obvious that states had a duty to leave their "savage" freedom and to set up a global federation. The inner freedom of individuals can only be realised, their natural capacities and talents only developed, in a "*law-governed social order*" and this cannot take place within a single state but only once there also emerged a "*law-governed external relations with other states*".[156] Because all of this, he believed, would be the work of freedom, it could never be just inferences from what had gone before. What was groundbreaking in Kant in relation to Vattel and the natural lawyers in Halle and Göttingen was that he did not think of enlightenment in terms of developing a better empirical or historical understanding of the state-system. Nor was he in the business of proposing a new type of policy to realise the happiness of subjects. With Kant, and the revolutionary period in which he was writing, a gap had opened between experience and expectation. The future would not be what people had learned or could learn from the past. Whether or not Kant was the originator of the German term for "progress" (*Fortschritt*), what he suggested was that among free people, the horizon of future would remain open for something that would be "genuinely new".[157]

## The Laws of Freedom

To say that Kant is a complex thinker is a platitude but needs to be said in view of some of the commentary on his views on international law

[155] Kant expressed his views about the desirable international order in different writings differently, and his final views have been subject to much debate. The best view is, perhaps, that he advocated a federation of free states that might gradually develop into a "state of peoples" (*Völkerstaat*) that would realise the conditions of constitutionalism at a global scale. See Eberl and Nielsen, *Kommentar*, 347–57; Otfried Höffe, 'Fédération de peuples ou république universelle?', in Pierre Laberge et al. (eds), *L'année 1795. Kant. Essai sur la paix* (Paris, Vrin 1997), 140–59.

[156] Kant, IUH, 44, 47 (italics in the original).

[157] I have employed here the felicitous terminology of experience/expectation introduced by Reinhart Koselleck who used it so as to underline the transformation of the understanding of history and historicity in the West during what he called the "saddle time" (*Sattelzeit*). See e.g. Koselleck, '"Space of Experience" and "Horizon of Expectation". Two Historical Categories', in *Futures Past. On the Semantics of Historical Time* (trans. & intro. K. Tribe, Columbia University Press 1979), 255–75.

having suggested that they are exempt from the vicissitudes of his thought in general. In fact, Kant's political writings, including his writings on international and cosmopolitan law, become understandable only against the bulk of his *oeuvre.* This is especially important owing to the close relationship between his critique of the epistemology of naturalism and the consequent morality of freedom, his metaphysical defence of private property, his concept of republican statehood, and his view of history as an open-ended "horizon".[158] In the middle of the discussion of the "antinomies of pure reason" in the *Critique of Pure Reason* (1781) Kant made the following point:

> Unfortunately for speculation – but perhaps fortunately for the practical interests of humanity – reason, in the midst of its highest anticipations, finds itself jostled by claims and counterclaims, from which neither its honour nor its safety will permit it to draw back.[159]

"[P]erhaps fortunately for the practical interests of humanity": with that enigmatic expression Kant referred to the way the limits of abstract reason constituted a hopeful opening towards freedom, which he viewed as the basic principle around which morality and politics in an enlightened period would turn. The critique of pure reason was targeted against two kinds of paternalistic adversaries. One was the philosophies of abstract reason that failed to grasp their own situatedness in the world and thus left their axioms either hanging in the air or defensible only in a circular manner. The happiness touted by these philosophies first dissolved itself into the many desires that people happened to have and then empowered the ruler to determine with binding force against everyone what it

[158] The relationship between Kant's moral theory and his views on law and politics have been subject to intense, sometimes hair-splitting commentary. The view that Kant's political–legal thought is a development of the categorical imperative as the "supreme principle of morality" that enables us to know and to limit our freedom with respect to the freedoms of others is well expressed in Paul Guyer, 'Kant's Deductions of the Principles of Right', in Mark Timmons (ed.), *Kant's Metaphysics of Morals. Interpretative Essays* (Oxford University Press 2002), 23–64. The opposite position, namely that "his opinions neither are nor can be justified and elucidated by using the principles to which his moral philosophy commits him", is defended in Arthur Ripstein, *Force and Freedom. Kant's Political and Legal Philosophy* (Harvard University Press 2009), 2. That there is a close *connection* between the two cannot, I think, be denied, and in the text above I have assumed that the abstraction of moral theory is fundamental for understanding Kant's views on law and politics.

[159] Immanuel Kant, *Critique of Pure Reason* (Vassilis Politis ed., London, Everyman 1991 [1781]), 342 [A463/B491].

might mean.[160] These abstract systems produced nothing that was not put into them from the outside – yet they had no way of dealing with that outside to which they therefore had a profoundly uncritical attitude. Wolff's *Civitas Maxima* was a perfect illustration of this kind of *Weltfremd* reasoning, an incident of the hubris of pure reason with which the world's problems cannot be resolved. Any attempt to do this would only produce "a soulless despotism [that], after crushing the germs of goodness, will finally lapse into anarchy".[161]

The other adversary was the empirical jurists and civil philosophers for whom the task of reason was only to explicate the empirical conditions of human existence and demonstrate how they could be operated to produce happiness. With this Kant meant the Pufendorf school, Vattel and the Göttingen scholars, especially Achenwall whose natural law texts Kant used in his teaching during his pre-critical period. As we have seen, these jurists constructed public law and the law of nations law by extrapolating from the historical operation of human drives. When Kant boldly claimed that their "philosophically or diplomatically formulated codes do not and cannot have the slightest *legal* force", this not only meant that they could produce no way of *lawfully* constraining states.[162] The very idea of drawing norms out of empirical facts – whether the sociability of the Grotians drives or the interests of Gundling or Schmaus – was fundamentally misconceived. The principles of *Staatsklugheit* were indeed received from close scrutiny of history and action.[163] But the resulting idioms of "self-love", "human animal", "will" and "happiness" were *too firmly* embedded in the view of human beings responding mechanistically to natural inclinations and external stimuli. The question for Kant was not at all empirical, not "how to be happy but how we should become worthy of happiness" – a distinction people may not always honour but that they routinely made.[164] In

[160] For the indeterminacy of happiness making it unable to yield a law, see Kant, TP, 80 and Immanuel Kant, *Critique of Practical Reason* (Mary Gregor ed., Cambridge University Press, 1997), 23 [5: 25].

[161] Kant, PP, First Supplement, 113. This is Kant's most extreme characterisation of a world state. In other places, he shows much more sympathy for it. For example, in the 'Second Definitive Article', he regards it as a thesis necessitated by the same reason that compels humans to join in a state – but unrealisable owing to this being "not the will of nations", 105.

[162] Ibid., 103.

[163] Samuel Pufendorf, *On the Duty of Man and Citizen* (James Tully ed., Cambridge University Press 1991), I 3 (33).

[164] Kant, TP, 64, 68–72.

assimilating human beings as parts of (passive) nature, the technicians of empirical state-wisdom and *Policey* left no room for freedom.

Kant's critique of Wolffian rationalism emphasised the necessity of anchoring theoretical understanding – reason – in the world of experience. The Göttingen jurists achieved this but only at the cost of subordinating subjects to the choices of their rulers. Empiricism had its own dogmatism that was parallel – though opposite – to that of rationalism. It was unable to explain how the mass of representations on our senses, and the intuitions we form of them, could be organised into "knowledge".[165] Consciousness was unable to receive the things in themselves: "all our intuition is nothing but the representation of appearances . . . and . . . appearances cannot exist out of themselves but only in us".[166] Theory was thus necessarily prior to practice and knowledge was an *internal* relationship between the representations received from the external world and the cognitive "understanding" of the knowing subject. Though the quest for knowledge remained internal to the subject, it was not arbitrary. This was so owing to the universal character of those *a priori* principles ("elements of knowledge") that organised sensible intuitions into inter-subjectively communicable knowledge.[167] We could still *reason* about them.

This turn to the subject made the pretensions of all prior natural law appear untenable. If we cannot know the external world, we also cannot know the laws of nature. References to historical examples were useful but insufficient. What were needed were metaphysical principles that would allow judging those examples.[168] Here now was the basis of Kant's transcendental doctrine of law – law as not something that exists already but "an end to pursue, a task to accomplish".[169] The legislative aspects of reason began to seem foundational; they were the heart of freedom, understood as independence or autonomy on the one hand, self-legislation on the other.[170]

165 Then there was the problem of how such historical or empirical knowledge could be translated into normative projects. "Happiness", for example, as Kant repeated in many places, was simply whatever anyone wanted it to mean. See e.g. Immanuel Kant, *The Groundwork of the Metaphysics of Morals* (Mary Gregor ed., Cambridge University Press 1997), 27–9 [4: 417–18].

166 Kant, *Critique of Pure Reason*, 61 [A41/B59].

167 Ibid., 78–90, 117–19 [A66/B91–B114]; [B165–B169].

168 Kant, MM, 124 [6: 355].

169 Simone Goyard-Fabre, *Kant et le problème du droit* (Paris, Vrin 1975), 96.

170 See e.g. Susan Shell, *The Rights of Reason. A Study of Kant's Philosophy and Politics* (University of Toronto Press 1980), 23–5, 41–3.

The question about a universal law would be not where we can "find" it, but how we should go about constructing it.

Where the *Critique of Pure Reason* demonstrated the limits of the laws of reason and causality, the *Critique of Practical Reason* (1788) laid out the laws of freedom. Initially, it may seem odd to associate freedom with lawfulness. However, from a Kantian perspective it was precisely the ability of human beings to act under a (self-legislated) moral law that embodied their freedom. Pufendorf, Thomasius and the Göttingen scholars had conceived freedom in terms of the management of human desires, including the desire for freedom. If, as Pufendorf had taught the natural lawyers, things did not have moral value in themselves, then value attached to them through human imposition, especially imposition through will. And if human beings willed things they desired – such as happiness – then happiness was the subject of morality. However, construing morality on empirical desires brought humans back into nature, turning politics into the manipulation of what they wanted. This was inadmissible for Kant. People were free not if they followed desires but to the extent they obeyed laws set by themselves. This was hardly the reality of late eighteenth-century Prussia. The association of will with desire gave the sovereign an impeccable technical legitimacy, based on his knowing best what his subjects desired. But Kant rejected such paternalism. It went directly against freedom and prevented the development of an enlightened public sphere in which – as revolution was prohibited – a critical spirit could be cultivated that would make possible approaching the objective of a law-governed republic.[171] To reopen the possibility of freedom, "will" had to be conceived as autonomous both from desire and external command (heteronomy). It had to emancipate itself from dogmatic rationalism and direct itself not to "happiness" but to "duty". For this purpose, will must imagine itself not as particular but as *universal will*, a will to act in accordance with principles that every free person would have reason to follow; its dictates must have the form of law.[172]

[171] Kant, TP, 73–4, 83. Kant's "gradualist" politics and the role of the public sphere as central to Kant's political theory is highlighted in Elisabeth Ellis, *Kant's Politics. Provisional Theory for an Uncertain World* (Yale University Press 2005), 11–40, 155–80 and Maliks, *Kant's Politics*, 41–8.

[172] Kant, *Groundwork*, 33 [4: 424]. Or, as Kant formulated that law in the categorical imperative supposedly valid universally, "*act only in accordance with that maxim through which you can at the same time will that it become universal law*", 31 [4: 421].

## Between Freedom and Nature

The demonstration of the limits of theoretical reason established the primacy of practical reason in Kant's mature philosophy. The most important questions would no longer concern what we can know but what we should do. The peculiarly legalistic bent in Kant followed from the way the search for a universal morality turned into the search for rules having the form of law. But law's importance was not merely theoretical. It was also that aspect of human activity where freedom would become practical reality. Although law was an aspect of morals, Kant was wholly in agreement with the later Thomasius and his followers that it was distinct from virtue that remained internal and inaccessible to others. Law had only to do with the "external and indeed practical relation of one person to another".[173] It was precisely law's externality that was the key to its function as part of the famous "passages" between theory and practice and as a foundation of the philosophy of history within an overall humanistic worldview.[174]

The passage first led from nature to freedom. In Kant's version of the natural state everyone had an innate right to freedom. This was the only right that everyone had merely on the basis of their humanity.[175] That freedom enabled you to choose freely and prohibited anyone from choosing on your behalf. But because humans lived in societies with limited resources where their freedoms clashed, they needed to make arrangements about those resources in such a way that, as Kant put it, "the choice of one can be united with the choice of another in accordance with a universal law of freedom".[176] The private law part of the *Rechtslehre* (Doctrine of Law), greatly influenced by the writings of Achenwall, discussed three sets of rights – possession, contractual arrangements and status – all of them now assumed valid universally as parts of natural law.[177] For, Kant believed, freedom cannot be reality unless I can use things, make contracts and command (some) people in

[173] Kant, MM, 24–5 [6: 230]. No doubt, witnessing the use of virtue made by the Montagnard party in Paris, Kant felt he had good additional reason to limit the activity of the legislature to enforceable external duties.

[174] This passage is elaborated especially in Immanuel Kant, *Critique of the Power of Judgment* (Paul Guyer ed., Cambridge University Press 2000), 61–6 [5: 174–9]. For useful commentary on the role of history in the passage, see Alain Renaut, *Kant aujourd'hui* (Paris, Flammarion 1997), 336–7.

[175] Kant, MM, 30–1 [6: 237–8].

[176] Ibid., 24 [6: 230].

[177] See the very useful discussion in Ripstein, *Force and Freedom*, 19–22. Also Peter Haggenmacher, 'Kant et la tradition du droit des gens', in Pierre Laberge et al. (eds), *L'année 1795. Kant. Essai sur la paix* (Paris, Vrin 1997), 133–4.

the pursuit of my freely chosen ends. Kant's (natural) right of property emerged neither from some hypothesised initial contract nor from labour, as with Locke, but from possession. Property was what it was rational, not useful to have.[178]

Kant shared the methodological individualism of the natural lawyers. The freedom of the state of nature belonged to individuals and it was accompanied by the right of property, and the unflagging duty on everyone else to respect them. Property, he held, followed from freedom itself, understood as the equal right of humans to pursue aims they had set to themselves, and to employ external objects that were instrumental for reaching them.[179] While this conclusion was valid provisionally already in the state of nature, it could only become enforceable in the lawful condition of the state.[180] Although Kant rejected the social contract construction as a historical fact, he accepted it as a rational necessity without which a lawful condition could not exist.[181] Progress meant the increasing security of private rights and scrupulous implementation of contracts within constitutional republics that were open to trade and "hospitality" to strangers.

Like earlier natural lawyers, Kant assumed that to make a reality of their *iura connata* individuals had to set up public institutions to define, delimit and to enforce their rights under a constitution. Unlike his German predecessors, Kant assumed that they had a moral duty to do this, based on the principle that only a lawful condition would preserve those rights equally.[182] Again, the argument was not empirical but *a priori*. If property was needed to give reality to freedom, then

[178] That is to say, if you had a right to something, it was rational to presume that you also had the right to the means whereby you could attain that something. Ripstein, *Force and Freedom*, 66–9.

[179] Kant's views on acquired rights and property are extremely complex and build upon the duty of everyone to respect the choice of others, including their wish to acquire things not (yet) in anybody's possession. If "inner freedom" involved the right to acquire external objects, denying that choice would become an arbitrary limit of freedom and endow all external things the status of *res nullius*: "it is a duty of right to act towards others so that what is external (usable) could also be someone's", Kant, MM, 42 [6: 252]. See further, Ripstein, *Force and Freedom*, 62–3, 86–106; Maliks, *Kant's Politics*, 70–4.

[180] Kant, MM, 51–2 [6: 264–5].

[181] Kant, TP, 79.

[182] Ibid., 290–1 [8: 290]; MM, 89 [6: 311]. See also 'Conjectures on the Beginning of Human History', in Immanuel Kant, *Political Writings* (Hans Reiss ed., Cambridge University Press 1991), where Kant discussed the stages through which humankind arrived at the realisation of the need of a lawful order under a constitution and where he also contemplated on the dual role of war as an evil and an "indispensable means of advancing" human culture, 221–34, 232.

government was needed to give reality to property.[183] There could be no other basis for government among a free people.[184] This provided Kant with the basis for a critique of a number of actual institutions – privileges of nobility, serfdom, slavery, despotism, state religion and colonialism, for instance.[185] On the other hand, because Kant did not think happiness or welfare the objectives of law, tampering with existing property arrangement by coercive redistribution was prohibited, though taxation was allowed.[186] The unconditional duty on the ruler to enact only such laws that give effect to freedom was accompanied by the equally unconditional duty on the citizens to obey.[187]

The progressive passage from nature to freedom took place at home by the adoption of a republican constitution and internationally by the establishment of a federation of free states. The further passage – from freedom to nature – was opened by the historical teleology whereby law and republican statehood would contribute to changing the world itself. It cannot be emphasised too much that Kant was not in the business of institutional reform: "no policy prescription, regime or political institution may be deemed conclusive under his theory".[188] He was aware of the dogmatism in believing that such models might capture the real nature of something like international relations, for example.[189] It was to be left for political judgment and moral statesmanship to decide what kinds of institutions would best realise lawfulness.[190] Kant's institutional proposals are products of what he calls reflecting judgment, a type of reasoning that does not operate with pre-existing, objective criteria but only suggests more or less persuasive ways for dealing with practical problems.[191] Two such problems were despotism and war.

[183] See e.g. Kant, MM, 89–90 [6: 312–13]. [184] Ibid., 93 [6: 315].

[185] Ibid., 66 [6: 283]; 91–2 [6: 314–15]; 102–4 [6: 328–30] and 121–2 [6: 353].

[186] Ibid., 100–1 [6: 326]. [187] Ibid., 95–8 [6: 318–23].

[188] Ellis, *Kant's Politics*, 71.

[189] This point is usefully highlighted in Mark Franke, *Global Limits. Immanuel Kant, International Relations, and Critique of World Politics* (State University of New York Press 2001), 105–10 and passim.

[190] See especially Simone Goyard-Fabre, *Philosophie critique et raison juridique* (Presses Universitaires de France 2004), 65–70.

[191] "Reflecting judgment" is one Kant's most complex and contested notions. It contrasts with "determining judgment" and is not conclusive like the latter. For its use in teleological reflection on the object of progress, see Kant, *Critique of Judgment*, 266–71 [5: 395] and comments in Gérard Raulet, *Kant, histoire et citoyenneté* (Presses Universitaires de France 1998), 18–19; Katerina Deligiorgi, *Kant and the Culture of Enlightenment* (State University of New York Press 2005), 112–18.

With respect to the problem of despotism, reflecting judgment was to guide political action towards a "perfectly rightful constitution" in which "all natural capacities of mankind can be developed completely".[192] According to Kant, we cannot think about the history of humanity, together with the developments of industry, commerce, culture, science and arts without adopting the hypothesis of a future of a constitutionally organised peaceful international system.[193] While having a constitution was mandatory, its contents were left for political judgment – not wholly, however. As is well known, Kant regarded democracy as despotic owing to the arbitrary nature of the decisions of the majorities that would rule therein. In addition, he believed it necessary to limit political rights, the rights of citizenship and voting to men with independent means. In the final formulation of Kant's rule, inspired by Sieyès' distinction between active and passive citizens, the right to vote presupposed economic independence, thus removing "all women, and in general, anyone whose preservation in existence ... depends not on his management of his own business but by arrangements made by another".[194]

The second problem – war – was to be dealt with by understanding that peace was not just another political objective or a pragmatic compromise. It was an "idea" that reason commands as an aspect of a lawful condition.[195] This did not mean that there would be no right to go to war in self-defence, for example. States may defend their rights by war in case that is necessary. But peace was binding as an *a priori* principle, and authorities were legally bound to struggle towards it, even when the chances of its realisation might seem small.[196] In the end, of course, Kant believed that reason would attain this objective, supported by the ability of individuals and societies to learn from their

[192] Kant, MM, 137 [6: 371]. In IUH Kant wrote that a constitution was the "thing in itself", 50. By this he meant that it was not an instrument for some other goal, such as happiness. It was the embodiment of a rightful condition (that condition, again the pragmatic realisation of freedom), valuable in its own right.

[193] Kant, TP, 92.

[194] Kant, MM, 92 [6: 314–15]. Needless to say, these exclusions have been the object of much debate among Kantians at the time and later. See e.g. Maliks, *Kant's Politics*, 90–111.

[195] Simone Goyard-Fabre, *La construction de la paix. Ou le travail de Sisyphe* (Paris, Vrin 1994), 188–91.

[196] At the end of the *Doctrine of Law*, Kant speculated that perpetual peace might coincide the ultimate purpose of the theory of law inasmuch as property can be secure only under peaceful conditions that we are duty-bound to seek to create, Kant, MM, 123, 124 [6: 355].

mistakes and gradually realise as actually achievable that which reason dictated as their duty, namely that only a "law-governed social order" was able to provide freedom.[197]

Kant's suggestion that nature would "help" in making a reality of freedom has sometimes been condemned as "fundamentally incompatible" with his stress on autonomy and self-legislation.[198] But Kant's teleological history was not intended a statement of a law of nature, a rational or empirical prognosis. Instead, it operated as an "idea" that reason used to interpret the past so as to give it a meaning that was compatible both with empirical history (as far as it could be known) and the freedom of every individual. Far from being predetermined in its course, history consisted of contradictory tendencies, movements back and forth. In the maelstrom of events it remained for free individuals to choose, and they would learn from choosing wrongly:

> [H]ow wide must the chasm [be] which must necessarily exist between the idea and its realization are problems no one can or ought to determine – and for this reason, [. . .] it is the destination of freedom to overstep all assigned limits.[199]

These two passages – from nature to freedom and from freedom back to nature – gave Kant's legal writings a powerful feel of movement. The present is viewed with its coming transgression in mind: despotism and war will be replaced by republican order and peace. But Kant did not assume that the way to this result would already have been found by either in theology or science. It had to be achieved by human beings themselves. As Kant put it in the Preface to the *Doctrine of Law*: "the concept of right [law] is a pure concept that still looks to practice (application to cases that come up in experience)".[200]

197 Kant, IUH, 44; TP, 90–1. The assistance that unsocial sociability would give in this process was famously formulated in this way: "Wars, tense and unremitting military preparations, and the resultant distress which every state must eventually feel with itself, even in the midst of peace – these are the means by which nature drives nations to make initially imperfect attempts, but finally, after many devastations, upheavals and even complete inner exhaustion of their powers, to take the step which reason could have suggested to them even without so many sad experiences – that of abandoning a lawless state of savagery and entering a federation of peoples [*Völkerbund*] in which every state, even the smallest, could expect its security and rights not from its own power or from its own legal judgment, but solely from this great federation (*foedus Amphictyonum*), from a united power and the law-governed decisions of a united will." IUH, 47.

198 Ellis, *Kant's Politics*, 67; Alain Renaut, 'Garantir la paix', in Pierre Laberge et al. (eds), *L'année 1795. Kant. Essai sur la paix* (Paris, Vrin 1997), 287–305.

199 Kant, *Critique of Pure Reason*, 246 [A316/B372].

200 Kant, MM, 3 [6: 205].

Kant left the future form of the constitutional order at home and in the world open to deliberation between "free" individuals and thus, perhaps surprisingly, appeared to fall into the position of Thomasius, Gundling and his Göttingen predecessors who had dealt with that problem it by inaugurating an empirically or historically oriented *Staatsklugheit*, political prudence.

Kant was aware of this danger. To address it, he adopted the distinction between "political moralist" and "moral politician" in the unappreciated Appendix to *Perpetual Peace*.[201] Political realists had commonly denied that the moral principles valid at home would be applicable in the international world.[202] In his response Kant focused on the subject-position from which moral and political decisions, including foreign policy decisions, are made. A "political moralist", he wrote, was one who "fashions his morality to suit his own advantage as a statesman". The moralist's attitude to political choice is *purely* instrumental to the chosen objective (typically some version of happiness); the idea of legality has no independent sense. By contrast, the moral politician has a commitment not only to their "client" or some purpose outside the law but to the legal form itself – "the mere idea of the law's authority".[203] While political moralists make cost–benefit calculations in the single case, moral politicians, for Kant, believed legal rules had independent value as carriers of freedom and aimed to follow them irrespective of whom they might favour in the single instance. While the moral politician tries to make the best case one in view of the point and purpose of the law, the political moralist engages in what Kant called

201 See Kant, PP, Appendix, 116–25. I have debated this contrast previously in my 'Constitutionalism as Mindset. Reflections on Kantian Themes about International Law and Globalization', 8 *Theoretical Inquiries in Law* (2007), especially at 23–37.

202 Kant's discussion was propounded by the "popular philosopher" Christian Garve (1742–1798) who had argued that as states lived in a state of nature, it followed that everyone not only had to see to their security themselves, they also had to judge for themselves whether their security was implicated, and to do this by thinking about the national interest. In the state of nature, there was no difference between right and power. Whether to commence war had nothing to with judicial decision. It all depended on the courage and perception of the decision-maker. Christian Garve, *Abhandlung über die Verbindung der Moral mit dem Politik oder einige Betrachtungen über die Frage in wiefern es möglich sei die Moral des Privatlebens bei der Regierung der Staaten zu beobachten* (Breslau, Korn 1788), 7, 11, 14–17.

203 Kant, PP, 118. One could possibly say that Kant's "moral politicians" would decide by understanding political institutions in view of the progressive teleology of peace and freedom that they adopted as their "maxim". I abbreviate and paraphrase violently from Kant, *Critique of the Power of Judgment*, especially from the critique of taste and teleological judgment, 111–24, 235–55 [5: 226–40 and 5: 362–83].

chicanery, giving no regard to alternative preferences. Kant rejected as meaningful Vattel's distinction between monsters and hypocrites. Both were equally condemnable. Hypocrisy obstructed the teleology of genuine lawfulness.[204]

## World-Wide Freedom

*Perpetual Peace* (1795) was neither a prediction nor a blueprint. It was the result of reflecting judgment that aimed to tie what we know of empirical history with the conditions of freedom that people have a duty to advance. The essay had four parts: six preliminary articles addressing the political situation at the time, three definitive articles canvassing three types of law that were needed for peace to become a reality, two supplements and an Appendix, the whole designed to lay out a complete, though sketchy, recipe for getting from illegitimate constraint to peace and freedom. The essay was followed up two years later by the *Rechtslehre* whose Hobbesian outlook contrasted sharply with the earlier text.[205] But both texts argue that humanity has a moral duty to leave its present unlawful condition by joining in a constitutional arrangement that Kant called a federation of free states (*Föderalism freier Staaten*) in the earlier and a permanent congress of states (*permanenten Staatenkongress*) in the latter text.[206]

Kant's view of the present law of nations was sombre. The "savage" freedom of states was "a condition of constant war".[207] Unlike most jurists, Kant did not believe that rulers were entitled to compel war on their countrymen. Citizens were not their property and war could be

[204] The character of political decision-making was not discussed in detail by Kant. But many have suggested that what Kant wrote on the nature of "reflecting judgment" in his aesthetic theory opens a way to think about political and legal work as well. In both situations, judgment aims not at "truth" but is still not just irrational expression of feeling, either. It called upon, and often received, the rational assent of others. On "reflecting judgment" that does not involve subsumption under a rule but still connects with purposiveness, see Kant, *Critique of the Power of Judgment*, 17–21 [20: 213–18], 66–8 [5: 179–81] and especially (on judgments about beauty), 97–8 [5: 212–13]. The most famous use of Kant's aesthetic theory in the analysis of political judgment is in Hannah Arendt, *Lectures on Kant's Political Philosophy* (R. Beiner ed., The University of Chicago Press 1992).

[205] The many apparent contradictions between the texts (such as the condemnation of war in the former and the elaboration of lawful war in the latter) underline their different purposes: the bright future to be created from the description of a dark present. Eberl and Nielsen, *Kommentar*, 125–8.

[206] Kant, PP, 105, Kant, MM, § 61 (119) [6: 350].

[207] Kant, MM, 114–15 [6: 344].

launched only by a decision by the legislature.[208] There were still rightful grounds for war: self-defence was allowed against an immediately threatening injury, and quite strikingly, by small powers against larger ones even pre-emptively.[209] This was wider than even Grotius or Achenwall had suggested; no concrete or manifest threat was required. In his earlier writings Kant had critiqued the peace-making qualities of the balance as "pure illusion".[210] Now he allowed it as part of the provisional present that the states were called upon to leave as soon as possible. Perhaps Kant's view of the wide extent of the right to use force was only intended to sharpen the sense of urgency of the latter task. There were also a number of rules of warfare: punitive wars and war for subjugation or extermination were prohibited. Any means of defence could be used "except those that would make [the defenders] unfit to be citizens". Plundering a country or robbing its citizens were prohibited.[211] This corresponded to contemporaneous humanitarian sentiments but was only provisional, subject to the need to move to permanent peace where rights would be guaranteed. Kant believed neither in a world state nor, somewhat differently from what he had written two years earlier, in perpetual peace – though he did think that their continual approximation "can certainly be achieved".[212]

The sketch for *Perpetual Peace* of two years before had a very different tenor. Its preliminary articles laid out the necessary, though not sufficient, conditions for perpetual peace and contained a critique of practices current in eighteenth-century diplomacy – treacherous treaties, standing armies, war debts and the use of assassins, poison and treason in warfare.[213] Alongside the critique of the partition of Poland, Kant also attacked the allied efforts to influence the course of the French Revolution.[214] The integrity and inviolability of existing states was to be guaranteed so as to create conditions of confidence and common purpose on which the future international legal system would be based.

208 Ibid., 116 [6: 346].
209 Ibid., 116 [6: 346]. This was the manner in which Kant allowed even war to uphold a balance of power. See also Eberl and Nielsen, *Kommentar*, 152–5; Georg Cavallar, *Kant and the Theory and Practice of International Right* (University of Wales Press 1999), 100–2.
210 Kant, TP, 92.
211 Kant, MM, 117 [6: 347]. See also Eberl and Nielsen, *Kommentar*, 155–60.
212 Kant, MM, 119 [6: 350].
213 For a discussion, see Ellis, *Kant's Politics*, 79–86; Eberl & Niesen, *Kommentar*, 179–207.
214 See further Cavallar, *Theory and Practice*, 51–2, 83–93.

The definitive articles address each of the three types of public law that Kant believed necessary to the establishment of perpetual peace: state law, international law and cosmopolitan law. The first article committed states to adopting a republican constitution, i.e. a representative (non-despotic) form of government.[215] What later would be called the democratic peace thesis expressed Kant's extraordinary optimism; representative government would have a natural predilection against war.[216] Kant's views on the form of the universal lawfulness, dealt with in the second article, changed over the course of the years. In 1784 he was still thinking in terms of a cosmopolitan state – though he suspected not much more could be achieved in the foreseeable future than a kind of collective security pact.[217] In 1792 he rejected the idea owing to the danger that it would lead into the "most fearful despotism".[218] In *Perpetual Peace*, finally, Kant supported a "pacific federation" to "preserve and secure the freedom of each state in itself, along with that of other confederated states".[219] The absence of clear institutional design was not an oversight. None could be proposed without foreclosing the nature of history as the surface over which the moral–political task of global lawfulness remained to be accomplished. While it might operate under a perfect, republican constitution as a regulative idea informing the moral and political choices at each moment, a federation of free states – perhaps little more than a collective security arrangement – may be received from the exercise of the faculty of judgment in view of any present circumstances.[220]

Instead of a world state, Kant's third article offered cosmopolitan law that was strictly separate from both present law of nations as well as the proposed federation. All individuals were to have the right to travel and to engage in commerce and lawful colonisation. But because it was a simply a reflective judgment deduced from reason, no mechanism existed to compel states to realise it. Its content was also quite modest. The stranger simply had the right not to be treated with hostility when he or she arrives in someone else's territory.[221]

[215] This does not necessarily mean democracy. The basic idea is that government acts under the rule of law and is responsible to the citizenry. For a discussion of Kant's uses of the term "republic", see Otfried Höffe, *Kant's Cosmopolitan Theory of Law and Peace* (Cambridge University Press 2006), 178–81.

[216] Kant, PP, 100. [217] Kant, IUH, 49. [218] Kant, TP, 90.

[219] Kant, PP, 104–5.

[220] A useful discussion is Francis Cheneval, *La cité des peuples. Mémoire de cosmopolitismes* (Paris, Cerf 2005), 214-233.

[221] Kant, PP, 105.

This did not mean a right to any particular type of treatment, merely to allow the foreigners to conduct their affairs peaceably. The text was an attack on colonial expansion, a commonplace in the writings of the *Aufklärers*. It is hard to say what meaning should be attached to the claim that the increasing international contacts would accomplish that a "violation of rights in *one* part of the world is felt *everywhere*".[222] This was not a justification of humanitarian intervention. Perhaps Kant meant something similar to the "enthusiasm" he had detected in the European spectators of the French Revolution. For it was clear to Kant that Europe stood for progress, perhaps not as the fact of European law and policy in the present but as the "idea" that Kant sketched in his reflections on universal history.[223]

That Kant wrote the essay on *Perpetual Peace* as a commentary on the ironic sign of a Dutch innkeeper shows that he did not see himself participating in a diplomatic exchange of institutional proposals but as an intellectual, suggesting a certain way for his readers to think about the world that was undergoing what most people felt as massive transformations.[224] With this, he contributed to the end of natural law as a concrete political force – it would now be an aspect of philosophical debates and treatises in jurisprudence, important for moulding the consciousness of part of the intellectual classes, but no longer a wellspring for government or policy. Its principles could carry the German legal heritage beyond the caesura of 1803 and 1806.[225] But its instantiation in a concrete constitution or a view on Europe and its laws had to wait for a new notion of statehood to emerge within the German realm.

[222] Ibid., 107–8.

[223] Examining history from Greeks to the present, Kant assumed that "we shall discover a regular process of improvement in the political constitutions of our continent (which will probably legislate eventually to all other continents)", IUH Ninth Proposition, 52. This was less meant as assumption about present Europe's imperial growth than about an idea that would gradually expand. "Europe" was, in a sense, an *interpretative category*. "I call 'European' a nation that accepts being constrained by the law, and in consequence being limited in its liberties by universally valid rules." A reflection from 1795, reproduced in Jean Ferrari, 'L'abbé Saint-Pierre, Rousseau et Kant', in Pierre Laberge et al. (eds), *L'année 1795. Kant. Essai sur la paix* (Paris, Vrin 1997), 33.

[224] For the view that Kant should not be read as an institutional blueprint-proponent but as a philosopher using a particular stylistic device, see Simone Goyard-Fabre, 'Les articles préliminaires', in Pierre Laberge et al. (eds), *L'année 1795. Kant. Essai sur la paix* (Paris, Vrin 1997), 42–3.

[225] See Michael Stolleis, *Geschichte des öffentlichen Rechts in Deutschland. Zweiter Band 1800–1914* (Munich, Beck 1992), 48–57.

## Freedom and Human Rights

From the mid-eighteenth century onwards, many Germans had begun to believe that natural law allowed the ruler to interfere unnecessarily or even harmfully in the most minuscule aspects of subjects' lives.[226] The vocabulary of German freedom had a long pedigree; now it would be resorted to by a new generation of lawyers and political commentators who often supplemented it with new emphasis on subjective rights.[227] There had of course been earlier opposition to absolutism but it had taken the form of the defence by the estates of their freedoms and privileges. This could not be fitted with liberal attitudes and individual rights.[228] With the spread of French physiocratic theories and Adam Smith's writings in Germany in the 1770s and 1780s, interest arose in civil liberty (*bürgerliche Freiheit*), which was imagined as a part of a private realm left over from legal regulation. At the same time, the vocabulary of civil society (*societas civilis, bürgerliche Gesellschaft*) began to depart from its old association with the state and to connote a sphere separate from and occasionally even opposed to the state. As Schlözer pointed out, all people live in civil societies, while most have formed states in which they live under public authority (*Obrigkeit*).[229] These manoeuvres inspired new kinds of cosmopolitan thinking as well, sometimes with a moral, sometimes a commercial tone.[230]

Like Kant, most intellectuals followed excitedly the events in France. Eventually, the notion of civil freedom as a merely negative quality reflecting the absence of legislation was supplemented by a

[226] See e.g. Justi, *Grundriss*, III III § 259 (335).

[227] Diethelm Klippel suggests that at this time natural law began to be understood as a "science of human rights", 'Der Diskussion der Menschenrechte am Ende des 18. Jahrhunderts in Deutschland', 23 *Giessener Universitätsblätter* (1990), 29 and 33–6; Klippel, 'Politische Theorien im Deutschland des 18. Jahrhunderts', 2 *Aufklärung* (1987), 59–60. See also Stolleis, *Geschichte*, I, 322–5.

[228] Klippel, 'Der politische Freiheitsbegriff', II, 485–8.

[229] Schlözer, *Allgemeines Statsrecht*, Einleitung (4).

[230] See Manfred Riedel, 'Gesellschaft, bürgerliche', in Otto Brunner, Werner Conze & Reinhart Koselleck (eds), *Geschichtliche Grundbegriffe. historisches Lexikon zur politisch-sozialen Sprache in Deutschland* (8 vols., Stuttgart, Klett-Cotta 1976), vol. 2, 753–6. See further Frederick Beiser, *Enlightenment, Revolution and Romanticism. The Genesis of German Political Thought 1790–1800* (Cambridge University Press 1992), 21–2. Klippel, 'Der politische Freiheitsbegriff'', 475–7. For German interest in physiocracy, see Klippel, 'Politische Theorien im Deutschland', 74–7. A list of types of German cosmopolitanism is produced in Pauline Kleingeld, 'Six Varieties of Cosmopolitanism in Late-Eighteenth-Century Germany', 60 *Journal of the History of Ideas* (1999), 505–24.

more positive sense, alive also in the monarchic state. In 1793 Schlözer wrote about *Metapolitik*: "The person is free who knows his natural rights and feels his natural powers (*Kräfte*) and is able to use both without internal or external disturbance."[231] Notwithstanding the limitations arising from state law, subjects preserved their natural rights even within the state: "*They are not the ones to serve . . . it is the ruler who serves them.*"[232] Or as the Kantian public lawyer Johann Wilhelm Petersen wrote a few years later: "The security of human rights or, what amounts to the same, as large a freedom as possible, is the first and the original purpose of the state."[233]

Already Justi had included subjects' freedoms into the *Staatszweck*, but writers who identified themselves as Kantians rejected the paternalism lurking behind such language. If freedom was subordinated under the *Staatszweck* and its realisation given to the ruler, then very little had been gained. In the 1790s, German Jacobins in particular began to take up the theme of political freedom and stress its persistence within political society as human rights, *Menschenrechte.*[234] These would not be something granted by a well-disposed ruler but existed on their own and limited the ruler's powers.[235] In 1795 the young Gottlieb Hufeland (1760–1817), professor of law at Jena, a well-known Kantian, wrote of the natural (coercive) rights that all humans preserved also in the state. Alongside the right to life, these included the freedom of religion as well as the right to educate oneself. The state's regulatory powers were based on and limited by the social contract.[236] But Hufeland did not envision that his subjects would also possess rights of political participation, and although he claimed that neither perfection nor happiness were lawful purposes of the state, it was still up to the monarch to implement the

231 Schlözer, 'Metapolitik', in *Allgemeines Statsrecht*, § 7 (34).

232 Ibid., III § 9 (107), emphasis in original. The rights of the citizens were, however, listed after their duties, which included those of obedience, payment of taxes, thankfulness and reverence, 103–5.

233 Quoted in Horst Dreitzel, 'Universal-Kameral Wissenschaft als politische Theorie. Johann Friedrich von Pfeiffer (1718–1787)', in Frank Grunert and Friedrich Bolhardt (eds), *Aufklärung als praktische Philosophie. Werner Schneiders zum 65. Geburtstag* (Tübingen, Max Niemeyer 1998), 149.

234 Oliver Lamprecht, *Das Streben nach Demokratie, Volkssouveränität und Menschenrechte in Deutschland am Ende des 18. Jahrhunderts* (Berlin, Duncker & Humblot 2001), 128–40.

235 Against the paternalist habit of rulers constantly claiming that they are working for the rights of the people, Kant asserted his formal principle of freedom that required "nothing short of a government in which people are co-legislators", 'Contest of Faculties', 184n. See further, Klippel, 'Der politische Freiheitsbegriff', 479–82.

236 Gottlieb Hufeland, *Lehrsätze des Naturrechts* (Jena Cuno's 1795), § 562–8 (301–4).

subjects' rights as he saw best.[237] This made those rights scarcely any more opposable to state policy than the old *iura connata* had been, as Kant himself had occasion to point out.[238] The further step that *Menschenrechte* might sometimes invalidate contrary legislation was suggested by the Kant-inspired Erlangen philosopher Johann Heinrich Abicht (1762–1816). Human rights, he explained, could never be received from history; they derived from the character of the human person as an end for themselves. Nobody was born subordinate to another. The absolute rights of freedom were valid everywhere and formed the foundation of all public power. Even social order arose from *Selbstverpflichtung* – voluntary submission to laws designed to make social life among free persons possible.[239] Subjects had the freedom to express their political opinions in the public realm and challenge the way public officials acted.[240] But it still remained for the ruler and the public administration to translate the absolute rights into hypothetical ones, written into positive laws, and even to limit individual rights against their postulated social purpose.[241]

Neither Hufeland's nor Abicht's view of the law of nations differed greatly from Vattel's. In particular, no room was provided for cosmopolitan law or progress towards a federal order. Their *Völkerrecht* was based on the "general rights of each people" where Abicht defined a "people" as any community – state or not – united by virtue of language, common territory or social objective.[242] Like individuals, nations were free, bound only by *Selbstverpflichtung* through treaty or custom.[243] But their absolute rights could also be limited by what Abicht called humanity's purpose

237 Ibid., § 425 34 (225–30) He called the state purpose "security", claiming that it could equally well be called "freedom" in the Kantian sense.

238 See Maliks, *Kant's Politics*, 34–5.

239 Johann Heinrich Abicht, *Neues System eines aus der Menschheit entwickelten Naturrechts* (Bayreuth, Erben 1792), 31–3.

240 Ibid., 514–19. Abicht speculated on the three Aristotelian constitutional forms (including democracy), but laid extraordinary weight on the public administration's task in fulfilling the *Staatszweck*, 500–14.

241 Ibid., 355–6.

242 Ibid., 525. Hufeland's international law was derived in part from the notion of a "free and independent nation", in part from the treaties and customs that such peoples had adopted. *Lehrsätze*, § 670–1 (354–5). The law between nations was identical with the basic laws of natural law. The first among them was that "Every nation has the right to coercively implement its and others' perfect rights", § 674 (356). Like Abicht, Hufeland understood the "nation" first of all as the aggregate of its individual members, and secondarily as the collective construct of a "moral person", § 664 (350–1).

243 Abicht, *Neues System*, 527.

(*Menschheitszweck*)[244] The result sounded like Vattel, and was certainly much less radical than Abbé Grégoire's draft *Declaration of the Rights and Duties of Nations.* The most notable institutional proposal was for a permanent court of nations "to develop the law of nations further" and to decide claims and disputes on the basis of criteria derived from the rights of humanity (*aus den Rechten der Menschheit erwiesen*).[245]

Prominent among the rights propounded in lists of *Menschenrechte* was commercial liberty and the languages of competition and market began to be heard, though still within existing political structures.[246] Kant himself wrote that civil freedom and the growth of commerce were intrinsically linked so one could not be tampered with without having a negative effect on the other. The spirit of commerce was an essentially progressive historical force.[247] The extension of the debate from state policy to the whole field of economic activity began to bring into question the relevance of the perspectives offered by *Policey* and the *Kammer.* German readers of the physiocrats started to speculate about a natural economic order operating outside the state-machine.[248] And further:

> the principles that [Adam] Smith advanced were integrated with the redefinition of social order that arose from the reform of Natural Law, a reform which also implicated a separation of the State and civil society.[249]

244 Ibid., 526–7. 245 Ibid., 550.

246 Hellmuth Eckhart, *Naturrechtsphilosophie und bürokratischer Werthorizont. Studien zur preussischen Geistes- und Sozialgeschichte des 18. Jahrhunderts* (Göttingen, Vandenhoeck & Ruprecht 1985), 122–40; Christopher Dipper, 'Naturrecht und Wissenschaftliche Reformen', in Otto Dann and Diethelm Klippel (eds), *Naturrecht – Spätaufklärung – Revolution. Das europäische Naturrecht im ausgehenden 18. Jahrhundert* (Hamburg, Felix Meiner 1995), 165–73. See also Stolleis, *Geschichte*, I, 383–5.

247 Kant, IUH, 50; Kant, PP, 114.

248 See Diethelm Klippel, 'The True Concept of Liberty. Political Theory in Germany in the Second Half of the Eighteenth Century', in Eckar Hellmuth (ed.), *The Transformation of Political Culture. England and Germany in the Late Eighteenth Century* (Oxford University Press 1990), 456–60 and Klippel, 'Naturrecht als politische Theorie. Zur politischen Bedeutung des deutschen Naturrechts im. 18 und 19. Jahrhundert', in Hans Erich Bödeker & Ulrich Herrmann (eds), *Aufklärung als Politisierung – Politisierung der Aufklärung* (Studien zum Achtzehnten Jahrhundert, Bd. 8) (Hamburg, Felix Meiner 1987), 273–7. For the various Smith translations and the debate on "Smithianimus" in Germany, see Tribe, *Governing Economy*, 130–48 and Liah Greenfeld, *The Spirit of Capitalism. Nationalism and Economic Growth* (Harvard University Press 2003), 180–8.

249 Tribe, *Governing Economy*, 175. Tribe suggests, however, that the one never replaced the other but that the view of the economy as a self-propelling national system and one that was managed by the state co-existed at least until the 1820s, 175–82. See also his 'Cameralism and the Science of Government', in *Strategies of Economic Order. German Economic Discourse 1750–1850* (Cambridge University Press 2009), 25–31.

As a result, demand arose for novel kinds of governmental expertise – a call met by the creation of the first faculty of public economy at the University of Tübingen in 1817.[250] Jurists had great difficulty following suit. When Wilhelm von Humboldt in the 1790s suggested limiting the state's role to that of guardian of "security", this threatened to undermine the role of the legal class that had since Pufendorf committed itself to expanding the workings of the state-machine.[251] Nevertheless, with the inclusion of basic studies in economics, policy and financial sciences into the legal curriculum, German jurists in the nineteenth century were able to recuperate those (admittedly few) positions earlier briefly held by cameralists.[252] The ideology of the *Rechtsstaat* exorcised economic management into the private realm.

However, it was one thing to support "civil freedom" as autonomous citizen activity at home and in the world of economic exchange, another to allow citizen control of or participation in government. Conservative jurists looked back into the Revolution and argued that "true freedom" lay not with taking part in the highest public power but in the "undisturbed enjoyment of personal rights and freedoms, the security of property".[253] Moreover, it was pointed out that freedoms collided and had to be limited in some way. Who else could draw those lines than the government?[254] Making the distinction between "real" and merely "imagined" freedoms or "responsible" and "anarchical" freedoms opened the field for conservative arguments that highlighted the integration of rights within communities of tradition. Friedrich Gentz's 1793 translation of and commentary on Burke's *Reflections* made a powerful impact. The endless abstraction of rights was meaningless as a standard for governing actual societies, and in practice a receipt for mob rule: "What justifies a revolution is not what its claims but what results it produces."[255]

250 Tribe, *Governing Economy*, 177–9.

251 Wilhelm von Humboldt, 'Über die Sorgfalt der Staaten für die Sicherheit gegen auswärtige Feinde', 20 *Berlinische Monatsschrift* (1797), 346–54.

252 Stolleis, *Geschichte*, II, 230–7.

253 I. Iselin (1772), quoted in Stolleis, *Geschichte*, I, 325. See further Hans Erich Bödeker, 'The Concept of the Republic in Eighteenth-Century German Thought', in Jürgen Heideking & James A. Henretta (eds), *Republicanism and Liberalism in America and the German States, 1750–1850* (Cambridge University Press 2002), 35–52. All "liberals" did not share republican ideas and if they did, they could fit them with varying constitutional forms. Beiser, *Enlightenment, Revolution and Romanticism*, 13–26.

254 Hellmuth, *Naturrechtsphilosophie*, 200–11.

255 Friedrich Gentz, 'Anmerkungn des Übersetzers', in Edmund Burke, *Betrachtungen über die französische Revolution nach dem englischen des herrn Burke* (2 vols, Hohenzollern 1794), II, 341, 145 ff.

Few jurists believed that natural rights could operate as governmental directives. They might assist in interpretation or gap-filling but not override positive law.[256] For the rest, the law of nature retreated to the world of morality and jurisprudence. As idealist philosophy it would continue to exist as a respectable aspect of legal education without, however, opening young jurists an automatic way to administrative positions.[257]

## The Rights of the "Nation"

A principal claim emerging from Paris was to recapture the sovereignty of the nation from kings and privileged elites. "The nation," Sieyès wrote, "exists prior to everything; it is the origin of everything. Its will is always legal. It is the law itself."[258] The Declaration of the Rights of Man and Citizen in 1789 reaffirmed that "*[l]e principe de toute souveraineté réside essentiellement dans la nation*" and the Constitution of 1791 provided that "*[l]a Souveraineté est une, indivisible, inaliénable et imprescriptible. Elle appartient à la Nation ; aucune section du peuple, ni aucun individu, ne peut s'en attribuer l'exercice.*" As the revolutionary troops left the *Hexagone* in 1792, their declared purpose was to assist fellow nations to begin to rule themselves after the French model.

The old language of German nationhood had been occasionally referenced by academic jurists and historians, too, though usually without a revolutionary intent. Schlözer, for example, wrote that political power, *GrundGewalt*, lay originally with nations (*beim Volke*) that had donated it to the states because they were incapable themselves of exercising it. Expressly suspicious of the notion of national sovereignty, he refrained from deriving republican conclusions from that notion.[259] The end of the empire in 1806, however, offered a handful of intellectuals the opportunity to seek to resuscitate the notion of German nationhood from the realm of the imaginary where it had been relegated by Napoleon's troops.[260] Johann Gottlob

[256] Jan Schröder, '"Naturrecht bricht positives Recht"', 430–3.

[257] Klippel, 'Naturrecht als politische Theorie', 277–82; Stolleis, *Geschichte*, I, 296.

[258] Emmanuel Sieyès, 'What Is the Third Estate?', in *Political Writings* (Michael Sonenscher ed., Indianapolis, Hackett 2003), 136.

[259] Schlözer, *Allgemeines Statsrecht*, I § 3 (98).

[260] Reinhart Koselleck, 'Volk, Nation', in Otto Brunner, Werner Conze and Reinhart Koselleck (eds), *Geschichtliche Grundbegriffe. Historisches Lexikon zur politisch-sozialen Sprache in Deutschland* (8 vols., Stuttgart, Klett-Cotta 1976), vol. 7, 330–5. Napoleon had actually assisted German unification by abolishing most of the Reich's over 300 small principalities. That still left 39 entities regarding themselves

Fichte's (1762–1814) *Addresses to the German Nation* of 1808 brought together many of the relevant themes. He lamented the "dead" spirit of foreignness that had descended upon Germany. He attacked the view of the state as a mere "mechanism" and of social life as "a huge, artificial pressure engine and wheelwork, in which each individual part is always compelled by the whole to serve the whole".[261] He contrasted such a utilitarianism with a "genuinely German statecraft" that persisted "perpetually in motion".[262] For the German spirit, he suggested, the state was a "means for a higher end", namely the flourishing of the nation.[263] To achieve this was no simple task but a gradual achievement that in Germany was to be attained through carefully organised state-led *Bildung*. Fichte also spoke against the violence of international relations, against trades in luxury, against empire and the balance of power.[264] Although he was a liberal who wanted to see all nations flourish, he still felt that a special role belonged to the Germans. There were nations that were restless and self-absorbed and wanted to "annihilate" everything. But other nations only wished for their particularity to be respected and recognised, "grant[ing] and permit[ting] other peoples their own particularity also". "To these the Germans undoubtedly belong."[265]

Nationalist propaganda fell on fertile soil as young Germans found themselves enlisted as conscripts to Napoleon's *Grande armée*. As the Austrians pushed back against the French in 1809 in occupied Bavaria, they addressed the population as part of the "German nation" to be assisted by Austria to freedom and happiness. A similar rhetoric accompanied the Prussian "Wars of Liberation" in 1813, though without a clear political or legal programme:

> The sense of national solidarity felt by the masses – and the same might be said of all Central and Western Europe in the early nineteenth century – was still diffuse, not related to any positive political programme, governed merely by the image of a common foe.[266]

But Fichte's addresses had touched an important nerve. Even though relatively marginal at the time, they gave expression to the wish to

as "sovereign" (37 members of Napoleon's Confederation of the Rhine plus Austria and Prussia). Fragmentation and the authoritarianism of most remaining "sovereigns" made coordinated national action impossible.

261 Johann Gottlieb Fichte, *Addresses to the German Nation* (G. Moore ed., Cambridge University Press 2008), 88.

262 Ibid., 90. 263 Ibid., 111. 264 Ibid., 169–72. 265 Ibid., 175.

266 Hagen Schulze, *States, Nations and Nationalism* (London, Blackwell 1996), 188.

overcome in Germany the kind of rationalistic individualism that had spread with Kantian and other liberal influences. Romanticism and conservative pathos provided allegedly more genuinely German ways to think about the nation and European politics. The French Revolution's turn to violence had spread further doubts about the kind of freedom offered by foreigners that was aligned with anarchy and rule by the rabble that was to have no room in Germany.[267] Fichte himself argued against the commercial ethos in his 1800 advocacy of a closed commercial state, viewing unchecked rivalry among trading nations as a principal cause of international war, massive global inequality as well as corruption back home.[268] But the *Addresses to the German Nation* in 1808 put forward a progressive history that situated mature nations in a cosmopolitan frame in which they would flourish by interacting peacefully with each other.[269]

## Transformation of Natural Law 4: Restoration Diplomacy As Modern Law of Nations: Martens

When he looked around in Europe at the end of his career in 1821, Hanover's representative at the Congress of Vienna in 1814–15, former professor of natural law and the law of nations in Göttingen, Georg Friedrich von Martens, expressed his satisfaction that the years of revolution, war and occupation were over:

> It is excellent to see that having shed the yoke weighing over it, Europe has returned to the principles anterior to this period without refusing the modifications that the progress of the Enlightenment have made to seem desirable.[270]

From the publication of the first editions of this work – *Introduction to the Modern Law of Nations of Europe based on Treaties and Practice* – in the 1780s Martens had expressed his conviction that Europeans were related by their habits, religion and treaties into a kind of society so that although there was no single instrument uniting them, one could

[267] Klippel, 'Der politische Freiheitsbegriff', 482–3; Koselleck, 'Volk, Nation', 327.

[268] See now in detail, Isaac Nakhimovsky, *The Closed Commercial State. Perpetual Peace and Commercial Society from Rousseau to Fichte* (Princeton University Press 2011).

[269] Koselleck, 'Volk, Nation', 331–2.

[270] "Il est donc fort heureux de voir que l'Europe, après avoir secoué le joug que l'opprimait, soit retournée aux principes antérieures de cette époque, sans se refuser à des modifications que les progrès des lumières ont pu faire paraitre désirable", Georg Friedrich von Martens, *Précis du droit des gens moderne de l'Europe fondé sur les traités et l'usage* (Gottingue, Dieterich 1821), 17 §10.

generalise positive rules from their treaties and practices.[271] In a new preface for the German edition of 1796, composed just after the Peace of Basel, as Hanover had been declared neutral in the Franco-Prussian conflict, he still believed it possible to understand Europe as a whole despite the differences of ambition and constitutional principle that had become so obvious. He could therefore preserve the basic structure of his work throughout the years of the Revolution.[272] In later editions up to and including the one from 1821 (still in print in the 1864 French edition) Martens decided to publish that part of the 1796 preface that attacked the revolutionary proposal for a *Déclaration du droit des gens*. This was the closest Martens ever came to a statement of principles underlying his work.

As we saw in Chapter 6, the proposal by the Abbé Grégoire had sought to do to the world what the 1789 *Declaration on the Rights of Man and Citizen* had done to the old regime at home. The new order would be based on the equal right of independence and sovereignty of every European nation. Every nation was to treat every other nation as it would wish itself to be treated. They would have an obligation to peace, and if at war, to harm their adversaries as little as possible. There would be no distinction between representatives of nations and ambassadors would enjoy immunity only inasmuch as that would be necessary for the accomplishment of their mission.[273] Martens had little sympathy for such proposals. True, there was no lack of aspects of international law where agreement between European powers would be desirable. But the idea of a general code was devoid of any realism. It was in fact only a warmed-up version of projects for eternal peace that must, in the world of human beings as they were, to remain a pure chimera (*eine blosse Chimaire bleiben*).[274] To declare principles of morality was pointless: they can be realised only under conditions that, if they were present, would make their declaration unnecessary.[275] The principles of the Declaration were self-evident

[271] Ibid., 1821 § 7 (10–11). Actually, the first English translation was entitled, *A Compendium of the Law of Nations founded on the Treaties and Customs of the Modern Nations of Europe* (W. Cobbett trans., London, Cobbett 1802).

[272] Georg Friedrich von Martens, *Einleitung in das positive europäische Völkerrecht auf Verträge und Herkommen gegründet* (Göttingen, Dieterich 1796), *Vorbericht*, III–IV.

[273] For the proposal, originally presented in 1793, see Boris Mirkine-Guetzewitch, 'L'influence de la révolution française sur le développement du droit international dans l'Europe orientale', 22 *Recueil des Cours* (1928), 309–16; Marc Belissa, *Fraternité universelle et intérêt national (1713–1795)* (Paris, Kimé 1998), 365–6, 419–20.

[274] Martens, *Einleitung* (1796), *Vorbericht*, vii. [275] Ibid., *Vorbericht*, viii–ix.

but empty as practical directives. Some of them were undoubtedly part of "pure natural law" (e.g. the equality of state representatives) that would not stand a chance of being adopted as attested by the ridiculous but recurrent disputes over ambassadorial precedence. The representative of San Marino will never be equal to the French ambassador. The national interest should naturally yield to the general interest of humanity. But where is the nation that would be ready to follow such principle? Many of the principles were dangerous. The claim that only constitutions founded on equality and liberty conform with the rights of peoples and the prohibition of alliances that may violate the interest of a nation would only open the door for endless interventions.[276] From utopian ideals, abstract principles turn into deadly weapons in the hands of enemies; their dark side was either revolutionary terror or counter-revolutionary dictatorship.

It did not take long for such doubts to receive confirmation. In the year following the first publication of the foreword, Martens, by now head of famous programme of teaching diplomats in Göttingen, was appointed counsel for the German imperial delegation at the Conference of Rastatt (1797–9) that ended up allotting the left bank of the Rhine to Napoleon. As part of the Electorate of Hanover, Göttingen was in personal union with Britain and therefore an enemy of France.[277] On the other hand, Prussia had long coveted the Electorate, which became, in the course of the wars, a frequent pawn in the negotiations between the two powers, being eventually occupied by both sides as war fortunes fluctuated. Returning from Rastatt, Martens was appointed dean of the law faculty (1799–1800 and 1803–4) as well as pro-rector of the university (1803–5), no doubt owing to his Europe-wide fame as a teacher of diplomacy and the law of nations – qualities badly needed as the university tried to negotiate its relations with the belligerent parties. It did remain a "heaven of peace and economic prosperity" until May 1803 as war broke out anew.[278] Resistance was pointless. As pro-rector, Martens wrote to Napoleon to spare the university from requisitioning and quartering of French

[276] Ibid., *Vorbericht*, xiv–xv.

[277] The legal characterisation of the British–Hanoverian link as personal union derives from Pütter himself. Nicholas Hardin, 'Hanover and British Republicanism', in Brendan Simms & Torsten Riotte (eds), *The Hanoverian Dimension in British History 1714–1837* (Cambridge University Press 2007), 301–2.

[278] Thomas Biskup, 'The University of Göttingen and the Personal Union', in Brendan Simms & Torsten Riotte (eds), *The Hanoverian Dimension in British History 1714–1837* (Cambridge University Press 2007), 142.

soldiers. Though Hanover was occupied, Göttingen was first spared and the university accorded protection. But as war fortunes changed, first the university and then even the professors were finally required to quarter French officers. A Prussian occupation in 1806 almost did away with the autonomy of the university. After the battle of Jena, Göttingen was joined to the newly established Kingdom of Westphalia with Napoleon's brother Jérome as its head. In September 1807 Martens was granted audience by Napoleon in Paris, only to learn that the ties to England had been permanently broken. The university would henceforth be French.[279]

The changing occupations, both French and Prussian, the restorationist diplomacy of the Congress and the rearrangement of the German territories by Diktat all seemed to confirm Martens' political realism. Abstract idealism was not only ineffectual, it was actually dangerous. The second French edition of the *Précis* of 1801, published in the short period of peace before Napoleon's push into Russia, highlighted the betrayal by the Revolution of its own principles: "it is no longer to plant the trees of liberty that conquests are being made ... it is nothing new that the right of the stronger overrides other considerations".[280] The third French edition of 1821 took stock of the changes in Europe after the Congress of Vienna, highlighting the role of the great powers in the creation of conforming behaviour. The "concert" that had existed before the Napoleonic wars had now been restored. The future would tell, Martens wrote, "whether the more intimate relationship that had been formed between some of the European Great Powers, that had continued after the war and had extended also to other states by the more general treaties and the Holy Alliance will become permanent".[281]

[279] The university suffered from the new order. Opportunities for research and publication became scarce and the number of students fell. Martens resigned and took up a position in Kassel as a member of the Council (*Staatsrat*) of the kingdom. As the kingdom fell in 1813, Martens reintegrated himself in the administration of Hanover. He assisted Count Münster, representing Hanover at the Congress of Vienna in 1814–15, after which he was assigned the task of representing Hanover in the Frankfurt parliament in which he was one of its most active members until his death in 1821. For these events, see Walter Habenicht, *Georg Friedrich von Martens. Eine Biografische und völkerrechtliche Studie* (Göttingen, Vandenhoeck & Ruprecht 1934), 35–47.

[280] "ce n'est plus au moins pour planter des arbres de la liberté qu'on a continué à faire des conquêtes ... ce n'est pas de nos jours que le droit du plus fort a commencé à l'emporter sur d'autres considérations", Martens, *Précis*, 1801, xvi.

[281] Ibid., § 17 (50–1).

To dismiss Martens only as an apologist of the Restoration would be simplistic. He was a conservative, a representative of the tradition of realism and prudence, with suspicion of abstract principles and large theories, and a fixation on the evil of human nature.[282] His positivism was an inclination towards avoidance of harm. It was a conservative disposition, but one that was also respectful of cultural difference. Natural law, wrote Martens, did not entitle Christian princes to take territory occupied by savages – "even if practice," he wrote, "offers only too many examples of such usurpations".[283] That he was not a dogmatic supporter of the old regime can be seen from his occasional, though rare, use of tropes from eighteenth-century enlightenment rhetoric. Where the 1789 edition began with a careful typology of laws and rights, the later editions began, astonishingly, with these sentences:

L'homme considéré dans le rapport avec son semblable est né libre. Cette liberté, apanage égal de tous, offre à la fois et le *principe* et les *bornes* de la légitimité externe et naturelle de ses actions, indépendamment de leurs motifs; ou le principe et les bornes du droit naturel absolu et proprement dit.[284]

To write this at the outset of a work that acknowledges that the only legality among nations is one they have created by treaties or by custom, and that the law among nations emerges from their will, shows the essential compatibility of the rhetoric of freedom with positivism and state power. By now, natural law had ended as a living force, a platform for imagining other futures. As with Martens, the only role left to it was to inaugurate the state as the highest sphere of human interaction.

## "External Public Law"

Martens was neither a philosopher nor a nationalist. He was a professor of the law of nature and of nations at one of Europe's leading

[282] This is the basis on which Martens' French commentator de Lapradelle condemns his "dryness", his scepticism and what he calls the latter's lack of imagination. De Lapradelle credits Martens' "modernity" to the demise of the influence of humanism in post-Revolution Europe and ends his review by a cryptic sentence – "Le droit des gens est en danger." Albert de Lapradelle, *Maitres et doctrines du droit des gens* (2nd edn, Paris, Editions Inter-nationales 1950), 181. A much better appreciation is in Arthur Nussbaum, *A Concise History of International Law of Nations* (New York, Macmillan Co. 1947), 179–85. Yet it is hard to associate Martens with the humanistic tradition too, see Ingo Hueck, 'Peace, Security and International Organisation. The German International Lawyers and the Hague Conference', in Randall Lesaffer (ed.), *Peace Treaties and International Law in European History. From the Late Middle Ages to World War One* (Cambridge University Press 2004), 260.

[283] Martens, *Précis*, 1801, § 36 (66).

[284] Ibid., § 1 (1).

universities, known for its research in theology, in universal history and anthropology, as well as the multi-disciplined orientation of its public law. A humanist and a cosmopolitan spirit reigned at the University of Göttingen where Martens had inscribed himself in 1775 in the footsteps of his brother who had already embarked upon a diplomatic career.[285] His doctoral dissertation from 1780 concerned the jurisdiction of imperial courts, making points on general and imperial public law, as well as European and German practice. But no international law issues were discussed.[286] Martens became *Ordinarius* on 18 August 1784, and received the title of *Professor des Natur- und Völkerrechts* three years later. He had given courses in German public law but gave it up perhaps because Pütter was teaching it simultaneously and the subject had become of rather ephemeral interest.[287] Like Achenwall, Martens also taught foreign public law of the most important European states, doing this because, as he himself recounts, knowing something about such matters had become increasingly important for enlightened persons across Europe.[288] In 1786 Martens became the teacher of Britain's crown princes as George III sent them to study at Göttingen. This contributed greatly to the fame of his courses and led Martens to become the head of something like a diplomatic academy. During his 25 years in Göttingen, Martens had compiled the basic legal sources that lawyers could use to work with international law as a specialist field. His best-known work, without a doubt, is the *Recueil de Traités* – the single most important collection of treaties, declarations and other international acts until the League of Nations' Treaty Series.[289]

[285] Habenicht, *Georg Friedrich von Martens*, 11. Robert Figge, *Georg Friedrich von Martens. Sein Leben und seine Werke. Ein Beitrag zur Geschichte der Völkerrechtswissenschaft* (Gleiwitz, Hill 1914) gives the year as 1776, but he had already enrolled in the university in the previous fall.

[286] Figge, *Georg Friedrich von Martens. Sein Leben und seine Werke*, 25–6; Habenicht, *Georg Friedrich von Martens*, 12–14.

[287] Habenicht, *Georg Friedrich von Martens*, 23.

[288] Only one volume was published.

[289] *Recueil des principaux traités d'Alliance, de Paix, de Trêve, de neutralité, de commerce, de limites, d'éxchange etc. conclus par les puissances de l'Europe tant entre elles qu'avec les Puissances et États dans d'autres parties du monde depuis 1761 jusqu'à présent. Tiré des copies publiées par autorité, des meilleurs collections particulières de traités, et des auteurs les plus estimés* (Gottingue 1791). The title is very informative and shows nicely the "inductive" method at work. The first three volumes came out in 1791 and covered the years from 1761 onwards. In 1801 the *Recueil* was extended to seven volumes with another four to succeed the following year. In 1817, already well into retirement, Martens began his *Nouveau Recueil* with yet another four volumes. After his death, the *Recueil* was edited by several German lawyers so that the third series covered the years 1908–44 and consisted of 41 volumes. The total number of volumes in five series rose to 126. See

By the 1780s it was widely assumed that the law of nations covered the forms of interaction between European states that, despite their independence, had a rational need to cooperate. That Martens limited this science to a study of *European* states resulted simply, he assumed, from the fact that the *moeurs* of other nations – even other *civilised* nations – differed too much from those of Europeans.[290] He was interested in contributing to the increasingly professionalised system of negotiation and treaty-making in Europe. The management of this system needed a well-educated political class. For his first lectures in international law in Göttingen Martens prepared his own text, the *Primae lineae iuris gentium Europaearum Practici in usum auditorum adumbratae*, thereafter reproduced in one German and three French editions during his lifetime.[291] After his death two additional French versions of the by then well-known *Précis de droit des gens de l'Europe* came out and the book was translated into several other languages, including English at the request of the United States government in 1802.[292] The most important aspect of this work is external to its substance, namely the fact it was written as a handbook on the practices of European diplomacy, to be used in teaching future state officials on the workings of European public law. Its notion of law was that of a technical craft that the more advanced students were expected to learn during the practical exercises that Martens held twice a week, once in French and once in German. From the date of his appointment in 1783 until his retirement from the university in 1808 his teaching was always accompanied by practical lessons.[293]

further Habenicht, *Georg Friedrich von Martens*, 62–6 and Ferdinand Martiz, 'Der Recueil Martens', 40 *Archiv des öffentlichen Rechts* (1921), 22–72.

290 Martens, *Précis*, 1821, § 9 (14). He also noted the "vagueness" of the notion of "civilization" and refrained from using it in his 1821 treatise. Nevertheless, he suggested that commerce and colonisation in Asia and Africa had given birth to a "*double droit des gens*" – one applied in Europe and another to European overseas possessions, § 141 (260).

291 Georg Friedrich von Martens, *Primae lineae iuris gentium Europaearum Practici in usum auditorum adumbratae* (Gottingae, Dieterich 1785). The German version came out in 1796 as *Einleitung in das positive europäische Völkerrecht auf Verträge und Herkommen gegründet* (Göttingen, Dieterich 1796). The French versions appeared as *Précis du droit des gens moderne de l'Europe fondé sur les traités et l'usage* (Gottingue, Dieterich 1789, 1801 and 1821).

292 G. F. von Martens, *A Compendium of the Law of Nations founded on the Treaties and Customs of the Modern Nations of Europe* (Cobbett, London 1802). For detail on Martens' publications, see Habenicht, *Georg Friedrich von Martens*, 58–9.

293 On his appointment, Martens was also nominated to the *Spruchkollegium*, a kind of informal court that also gave advisory opinions – a rather typical practical

All principal works by Martens were explorations of the laws applicable in European diplomacy. These include the *Erzählungen merkwurdiger Fälle des neueren europäischen Völkerrechts*, two volumes of over 1,300 pages intended as a case-book for the use of students and diplomats.[294] His *Cours diplomatique ou tableau des relations des puissances de l'Europe* came out in three volumes and was meant for assisting the teaching of "particular international law" – that is to say, the law concerning the relations between particular states – on which Martens concentrated his practical exercises.[295] In later years, he chose to expand Achenwall's history of the relations of European states to assist in his teaching of the more recent European peace treaties – a work where he expressly acknowledged his debt to the Göttingen historical school.[296] The point of all this prolific publication was to imagine and present the practices of European diplomacy as aspects of an actually operating legal system. The reality of the empire had once lain on the shoulders of the jurists who had been able to see a system in its near-chaotic set of institutions and practices. The empire was no longer – so they could turn their imaginative efforts to Europe. With the materials produced by Martens, it was possible for legal minds to imagine how European diplomacy unfolded in the creation and application of legal rules. True, no single treaty worked as a European constitution – and as Martens presciently noted, there will probably never be one. But the practices of European nations still converged so that it was possible to speak of a practical and a positive European international law.[297] Three points characterise his science.

First, it was a work of empirical jurisprudence, opening with a discussion and even enumeration of European states.[298] This was the *a priori* from which the rest of the chapters emerged, prefaced by just one paragraph of the history of the law of nations plus a somewhat longer, though still cursory, literary history. No other explanation was

assignment for a law professor at the time. See Habenicht, *Georg Friedrich von Martens*, 21; Figge, *Georg Friedrich von Martens. Sein Leben und seine Werke*, 28.

294 Georg Friedrich von Martens, *Erzählungen merkwurdiger Fälle des neueren europäischen Völkerrechts* (Göttingen, 1800–2).

295 Georg Friedrich von Martens, *Cours diplomatique ou tableau des relations extérieures des puissances de l'Europe*, 3 vols (Berlin, Mylius 1801).

296 Georg Friedrich von Martens, *Grundriss einer diplomatischen Geschichte der Europäischen Staatshändel und Friedensschlüsse* (Berlin, Mylius 1807). Martens noted his friendship with Johann Gottfried Eichhorn and his appreciation of universal histories, refraining from using them owing to his wish to concentrate only on the more recent periods, *Vorerinnerung*, v.

297 Martens, *Précis*, 1821 § 6, 7 (7, 9–11).

298 Ibid., § 16 (42).

given than that it had "appeared natural to examine more closely what are the proper… and the common relations under which the powers of Europe may be considered as a whole".[299] Seeing himself as a continuator of Achenwall's work Martens viewed Europe as a system of formally equal states with different degrees of power and a tendency to ally themselves for the attainment of balance of power. It was the product of a history whose moments were separated by large wars and peace treaties. Martens appreciated the effort to separate the empirical description of particular states (*Statistik*) from the more speculative general theory of statehood, an effort that led Martens (as it had led Achenwall) to some rather painful discussion about which facts to choose as the basis of one's history.[300] And if such an approach did not allow fully certain conclusions for all cases (for example, concerning relations between Turkey and Europe), Martens noted, this was true of all empirical reasoning. Outside the sphere of inductive reference – that is, outside Europe – the principles no longer applied.[301]

The second noteworthy aspect has to do with how Martens' discussion of the law proceeded by an endless series of static classifications, divisions and subdivisions of each subject-matter to its component parts. The law was divided into natural and positive, public and civil. Public law, again, was subdivided into universal and particular, necessary and voluntary. With these, a series of combinations could be attained to grasp the entire European legal landscape: states with full and with less than full sovereignty; unitary and composed states; maritime powers and continental powers; states classified by reference to geographical location, size and rank and differing by way of type of constitution: monarchy, aristocracy and democracy, each subdivided further into species.[302] This same technique was followed throughout. Negotiations were classified by method, official envoys by rank and function. The law of territory was divided into rules on land and sea,

299 Ibid. [repeated from 1788], Préface, viii.

300 In describing his choice of relevant facts Martens wrote that he tried to find a midway between overly "synchronistic" and excessively separate recounting. The point was to collect events and treaties from different parts of Europe and to arrange them around the policies of the leading states, tracing the shifts of power as the transformation (or revolutions) of the system, Martens, *Grundriss einer diplomatischen Geschichte, Vorerinnerung*, viii–x.

301 Martens, *Précis*, 1821, *Introduction*, 13–15. For a brief discussion of the position of Martens with respect to Kant and the idea of world state in the Göttingen context, see Luigi Marino, *Praeceptores Germaniae. Göttingen 1770–1820* (Göttingen, Vandenhoeck & Ruprecht 1995), 239–45.

302 Martens, *Précis*, 1821 § 18–22 (52–60).

rivers and lakes, treaties into private and public, conditional and unconditional, with a long list of their objects, effects and conditions of validity.[303] This was an eighteenth-century science: analysis and composition of things as they appear to the senses. Teleology and derivations from principle were excluded.[304] The law itself was a historical product, an outcome of wars and peacemaking. Only studying that history will help to understand the system.[305] And once that understanding was in place, elaborating its content was a purely empirical–analytical exercise to be pursued by classifying the elements by their observable properties, as in natural sciences: this insect has eight legs, that political community is ruled by aristocracy; the leaves of this flower are round, the competence of that envoy ranks him as a minister of the third class. The legal world did not open its secrets by examining its moral or political value, but by the synchronic arrangement of its parts.[306]

Martens regarded all debate about international morality and justice as unfruitful and pointless. War had no intrinsic legal status, it was a fact and a process, on a par with and defined by its opposition to peace.[307] The task of the law was to describe and systematise, not to prophesy or dictate. This was a natural history paradigm, indeed justified by a naturalist notion of statehood. One had just to collect the raw data – the flower from the forest, the native from the Orient, the treaty from that conference. And one had to publish it.[308] Publicity was part and parcel of an enlightened civilisation.

Third, why would this be binding as law? No normative teleology underwrote Martens' texts, and of Kant's idea of cosmopolitan law he

303 Ibid., § 34–45 (77–92).

304 See the discussion in Michel Foucault, *The Order of Things. An Archaeology of the Human Sciences* (London, Tavistock Publications 1970), 132–62, 355–87.

305 Martens, *Grundriss einer diplomatischen Geschichte*, *Vorerinnerung*.

306 This type of arrangement of empirical elements into a "system" was precisely the technique of the empirical state-science that Achenwall and other Göttingen scholars were pursuing by their *Statistik*. See André de Melo Araújo, *Weltgeschichte in Göttingen. Eine Studie über das spätaufklärische universalhistorische Denken 1756–1815* (Bielefeld, Transcript 2012), 201–2.

307 Although war was endemic in the post-Utrecht period (1713), it was low in destructiveness and normally did not involve civilians. It "was not considered a serious problem requiring systematic diagnosis or prescription . . . in most spheres of life commercial and other contacts between societies continued much as in peacetime." Kalevi J. Holsti, *Peace and War. Armed Conflicts and International Order 1648–1989* (Cambridge University Press 1991), 102–3.

308 This is why the compilations by Leibniz and Moser had taken "le vrai chemin", Martens, *Précis*, 1821, § 13 (25).

only wrote that it belonged to philosophy rather than law.[309] But he appreciated the way Kant had separated morality from law and had suggested the necessity of supplementing natural with positive law.[310] What he wished to do was to present the "positive law of nations" that he claimed had been so far largely neglected.[311] But he was not in the least ideologically *opposed* to natural law. Indeed, he was a professor of "the law of nature and of nations" and had taught *Staatsrecht* "*nach dem Pütter*".[312] He opened his most famous work by contrasting between two types of law – natural and positive – and reserving the former to the kinds of rules that may be derived from the concept of the "state" and the nature of the relations between states.[313] He followed the natural lawyers by describing the state as a moral person established by individuals escaping the precariousness of the state of nature.[314] And, for example, when he explained that a state's rights on its territory were based on occupation, he noted that this resulted from natural law.[315] Martens had no quarrel whatsoever with the natural law basis of the states-system. And like his predecessors, he noted that because natural law had originally dealt with individuals, it had to be modified in order to apply to the relations between states. These modifications were the treaties and customs that Martens then defined as the "modern European law of nations".

Martens felt no need to develop or challenge older natural law. He was perfectly happy with the world they created and justified, and indeed rejected outright the revolutionary challenge they had been faced with. Instead of seeing natural and positive law as somehow mutually exclusive, they were perfectly compatible.[316] If natural law provided a basic framework of the world, explaining its elements and their relationships, positivism laboured with its details. Martens took for granted the existence of a Europe of separate states, sovereign, but also interdependent. The details of the science of "general, positive, modern

309 Ibid., § 9 (15). 310 Ibid., § 12 (19). 311 Ibid., § 6–7 (7–11).
312 Habenicht, *Georg Friedrich von Martens*, 12.
313 Martens, *Europäische Völkerrecht*, § 1 (1–2).
314 This was different from Hegel who denied that the state could be justified by anything about its origin. It was a rational principle, not a historical accident, G. W. F. Hegel, *Outlines of the Philosophy of Right* [hereinafter "PR"] (S. Houlgate rev. ed., Oxford University Press 1952/2008), § 258 (229–30).
315 Martens, *Précis*, 1821 § 34 (77).
316 Martti Koskenniemi, 'Transformations of Natural Law. Germany 1648–1815", in A. Orford and F. Hoffmann (eds), *The Oxford Handbook of International Legal Theory* (Oxford University Press 2016), 59–81.

and practical European law of nations" would then emerge from that frame, from materials produced above all by "the Great Powers of Europe either in the form of particular treaties, express or tacit, uniform or resembling one another, or by usages of a conforming type".[317] This science arose from an eighteenth-century view of the international world, as an offshoot of old-regime *Staatskunst,* alongside the "vast and important science" of *Statistik* that he referenced in the *Cours diplomatique* given to his students. International law was, he wrote, like a tree in the garden of state-sciences that would undoubtedly "cure political illnesses" and advance the course of peace and intellectual progress much better than "*toutes les rêveries pour une paix perpetuelle*".[318]

Martens followed natural lawyers such as Achenwall or Justi in his derivation of the substance of the law of nations from state policy. But he did not integrate larger aspects of what others had begun to think of as the *bürgerliche Gesellschaft* in his work. International law was to let private rights, property and contract lead their life undisturbed. "War", he wrote, "does not suspend the effects of property in the relations between the belligerent powers or their private individuals; [in particular] states are not entitled to regard property relations as extinguished."[319] Like most eighteenth-century writers, Martens believed that commerce had become "one of the most important objects of the law of nations". It had enormous influence on the welfare of citizens and "the riches, respect and power of the state".[320] Nevertheless, "*[l]a liberté naturelle du commerce*" entailed only the "vague and imperfect" obligation on states not to refuse commerce with each other. In practice, many rules had been set to limit it.[321] It remained part of the nation's foreign policy that outsiders or private individuals were not entitled to challenge; freedom of commerce did not constitute a legal limit to the state's regulatory powers.[322] In his 1820 handbook on trade law Martens focused on the law of promissory notes (*Wechselrecht*) and maritime law (*Seerecht*). Guilds and privileges continued to play a dominant role in a work that was, again, mostly concerned with classifying

317 Martens, *Précis*, 1821, § 8 (13). 318 Martens, *Cours diplomatique*, ix.
319 Martens, *Précis*, 1821 § 279, 281 (477, 485). 320 Ibid., § 139 (256).
321 Though they were entitled to limit such trade as their interests required this, ibid., § 140 (257-8).
322 ibid., § 142 (261). Perhaps oddly, he made no distinction between private property and the power of the state over its territory, noting especially that the state had the right to distribute (but perhaps not redistribute?) property rights in its territory, § 72 (136–7).

types of contract and commercial operator.[323] But the heart of the treatise were states; the content of commercial law reflected state will and policy. Everything in the world of international activity reflected the foreign policies of states. If *Staatsklugheit*, as Achenwall had postulated, needed to be based on empirical *Statistik*, it was equally true that modern *Völkerrecht* could only be external public law of European nations, *das auswärtige Staatsrecht, droit public externe*.[324]

Among German jurists writing on international matters at the beginning of the nineteenth century Martens was the brightest star. Theodore von Schmalz, conservative Kantian and first rector of the newly established University of Berlin, commended the "excellent handbooks" in which Martens had presented European public law "for the first time as a full system".[325] Julius Schmelzing's three-part volume made frequent reference to Martens' work and the author aligned himself completely with the foreword of the 1796 edition where Martens attacked the international application of the revolutionary principles.[326] And Friedrich Saalfeld, Martens' successor in Göttingen, attributed the turn to interest to international legal science predominantly to Martens. He had found a way between Wolff and Moser, between naturalist abstraction and the description of state policy.[327] Even the more liberally minded Heidelberg professor Johann Ludwig Klüber referenced Martens as someone whose many publications and lectures in Göttingen provided a great service to international law. Like Martens, Klüber also defined the subject-matter as part of the external public law of the nation, translated as aspects of European diplomacy.[328]

This was not a German idiosyncrasy. Oke Manning in Britain regarded Martens as "perhaps the most valuable modern writer on the law of nations" whose *Précis* was "the most complete treatise that exists on the law of nations, as recognised by the states of Europe [and] of more frequent reference than any other treatise".[329] In a prior chapter I noted Reddie's reference to Germany as the "great and

[323] Georg Friedrich von Martens, *Grundriss des Handelsrechts* (Göttingen, Dieterich 1820).

[324] Martens, *Einleitung*, § 2 (3); *Précis*, 1821 § 4 (5).

[325] Theodor Schmalz, *Das europäische Völcker-Recht in Acht Büchern* (Berlin, Duncker & Humblot 1817), 29.

[326] Julius Schmelzing, *Systematischer Grundriss des praktischen Europäischen Völker-Rechts* (3 vols, Rudolfstadt, Hof-Buch- und Kunsthandlung 1818), I, 16.

[327] Friedrich Saalfeld, *Handbuch des positiven Völkerrechts* (Tübingen, Osiander 1833), 11.

[328] Jean-Louis [Johann Ludwig] Klüber, *Droit des gens moderne de l'Europe* (Paris, Aillaud 1831), § 2, 6 & 16 (5, 10 & 26).

[329] Oke Manning, *Commentaries on the Law of Nations* (London, Sweet 1839), 39.

parental cultivatrix of the science of international law". It was Martens that he identified as its "head".[330] Wheaton's *History of the Law of Nations* from 1842 included a critical appreciation of Martens as someone who had concluded that "there were as many special international laws in Europe as there were special relations between particular nations".[331] No general understanding or theory could be received from that work. Everything was reduced to individual state-to-state relations. As Wheaton noticed, others had ventured further. Towards the end of his *History*, Wheaton came to the passages in Hegel's *Outlines of the Philosophy of Right* that in Wheaton's telling projected the international world as a state of nature where all treaties were precarious and war a type of education in moral strength.[332] In those passages Hegel employed Martens' language of external public law, *das äussere Staatsrecht*. But Wheaton ignored the historical frame within which the German philosopher had situated those "external" laws of individual states. He was reading Hegel with an eighteenth-century mind. Kant had already pushed his readers towards a view of modernity where freedom would be realised by the open horizon of history. It was Hegel who had the more powerful sense of what that might mean.

## Into the Modern World: Hegel

Up to this point there has been practically no discussion about property in the German context. *Ius naturae et gentium* at Halle and Göttingen focused on public law and statehood as carriers of universal history, with economic considerations pushed into the state-operated science of *Policey* or cameralism. Property was understood as an aspect of freedom, derived from the state of nature as one of the aspects of the civil law that Achenwall and Pütter classed under *ius civile privatum universale*. But it would be up to domestic law to determine the conditions of how property is acquired, used and extinguished. Its role in the creation of public welfare might be discussed as part of *Staatskunst* or develop into *Staatsökonomie*. Kantians such as Hufeland or Schlözer would see it as an aspect of the *bürgerliche Gesellschaft*, separate from though not in sharp contrast with statehood, and with no tangible international dimension.[333] Law of nations was understood to cover commercial relations, perhaps

330 James Reddie, *Inquiries in International Law* (London, Blackwood 1842), 96, 97.

331 Henry Wheaton, *Histoire des progrès du droit des gens en Europe* (Leipzig, Brockhaus 1842), 248.

332 Ibid., 431–4.

333 See Riedel, 'Gesellschaft, bürgerliche', 753–6.

even to endorse free trade, but substantive discussion of property rights in the international sphere was limited to explaining the provisions of commercial treaties, the special character of colonial monopolies, the functions of consuls and commercial arbitration.[334] There was no sense of an international world of growing commerce and even less any reflection of a world government as a rational necessity of the kind found in the works of the Göttingen private lawyer Gustav Hugo (1764–1844), the founder of the German historical school of law.[335] The view of cosmopolitan legality (*rechtliche Zustand*) as a rational necessity for the realisation of private rights was absent from the imagination of German jurists professionally oriented towards the law of nations.[336]

A much better grasp of the conditions of the modern world came from the most advanced reader of the Scottish political economists, namely Hegel.[337] Political economy, he wrote, was "one of the sciences which have arisen out of the conditions of the modern world".[338] Its modernity lay in the manner it focused on the "system of needs" where individuals arose from their mere particularity as members of families to their universal role as partners in economic transactions, buyers and sellers, consumers and producers. Social interaction in modernity took place within what Hegel called the ethical life (*Sittlichkeit*), which contained three "moments" – family, civil society and the state. Where the life led by individuals in the family was that of immediate particularity, in civil society they took on universal roles as legal subjects, parties to economic transactions, members of classes and corporations. Both moments expressed aspects of modern life that were necessary but also encroached on freedom. They were ultimately included in but also transgressed by the state, which was "in and for itself the ethical whole, the actualization of freedom".[339]

Unlike his predecessors, Hegel understood that modern life revolved around the economic transactions that created a "system of complete interdependence".[340] Its core lay in work, accomplished through the division of labour where the universal character of the humanness of

[334] See e.g. Schmalz, *Das europäische Völcker-Recht*, 193–201.

[335] Hugo was expressly looking for something more than Kant's *Völkerbund* or *Staaten Congress*, Gustav Hugo, *Lehrbuch des Naturrechts* (4th edn, Berlin, Mylius 1819), § 85 (103–4).

[336] See e.g. the discussion of the right of a state to legislate on properties in its territory in Martens, *Précis* (1821), § 72 (136–7).

[337] For a useful discussion of this aspect of Hegel, see Pierre Rosanvallon, *Le capitalisme utopique, Histoire de l'idée de marché* (Paris, Seuil 1979), 162–78.

[338] Hegel, PR, § 189 (187). [339] Ibid., § 258 (232). [340] Ibid., § 183 (181).

labourers becomes visible in their infinite replaceability.[341] The division of labour also achieved Hegel's equivalent of Smith's invisible hand, namely the cunning of reason; while everyone has their eye on private interest, also others will become better off.[342] But while division of labour provides people with a livelihood, it also becomes the origin of serious problems: "[T]he abstraction of production makes work more and more mechanical, until finally the human being is able to step aside and let a machine take his place."[343] The automatisation of work leads into "dependence and distress of the class tied to work of that sort, and these again entail the inability to feel and enjoy the broader freedoms and especially the spiritual benefits of civil society".[344] Great riches are produced for some, while others are impoverished.[345] The pauperisation of the masses, Hegel believed, can only in part be dealt with by civil society itself. The involvement of the state is needed, not as another realm of private needs but as the realisation of the ethical idea "in which freedom comes to its supreme right".[346]

For our purposes, the most important aspect of Hegel's analysis of modernity lies in its restless dynamism of production and consumption that drives it "to push beyond its own limits and seek markets, and so its necessary means of subsistence, in other lands which are either deficient in the goods it has overproduced, or else generally backward in creative industry etc."[347] In agrarian societies, production was geared towards limited markets. With the industrial production of goods not intended only for subsistence, a different development steps in:

> [T]he natural element for industry, animating its outwards movement, is the *sea.* In pursuit of gain, by exposing such gain to danger industry at the same time rises above it, instead of remaining rooted to the soil and the limited circles of civil life with its pleasures and desire, it embraces the elements of fluidity, danger, and destruction.[348]

Here now was the epitome of modern civil society, understood as the pursuit of private interests through trade at an ever-expanding

[341] Ibid., § 209 (198).

[342] Ibid., § 199 (192). The phrase "cunning of reason" is from G. W. F. Hegel, *Lectures on the Philosophy of World History. Introduction* [hereinafter WH] (Cambridge University Press 1975), 89.

[343] Hegel, PR, § 198 (191).

[344] Ibid., § 243 (221).

[345] "[I]t leaves them more or less deprived of all the advantages of society, the opportunity of acquiring skill or education of any kind, as well as administration of justice, health-care, and often even the consolation of religion", ibid. § 241 (220).

[346] Ibid., § 258 (228).

[347] Ibid., § 246 (222).

[348] Ibid., § 247 (222).

geographic scale: "[T]rade by sea creates commercial connections between distant countries and so relations involving contractual rights . . . trade acquires world-historical significance."[349] The process would not stop at commercial nations. Colonies were also needed. The expanding economy created a surplus population that needed work; and overproduction at home necessitated finding new markets.[350]

The constant expansion of civil society in the domestic and the international sphere gave rise to all kinds of social problems and "in general distress of every kind".[351] The differing interests of social groups, especially of producers and consumers, collided, raising the danger of rebellion or even revolution. Such disturbances called for a system for the administration of justice, positive laws, courts and the police for the protection of property, though when public authorities exercised their "oversight and care", they were to do this without seeking to "provide for everything and define everyone's labour".[352] The state was not to overwhelm or subordinate the family or the economy but instead offer a platform where social conflict would be included, mitigated and eventually overcome. The universal nature of these conflicts made the state itself universal.[353]

## The State As Freedom

In seeking to find a new frame to encompass the experience of modern life, including the Revolution, Hegel presented his state as a concrete manifestation of reason in history. It was, Hegel wrote in his typically elusive style, "the march of God in the world; its ground or cause is the power of reason realizing itself as will".[354] In his early work on German statehood, composed during the turmoil of the War of the Second Coalition (1798–1802) as the estates of the Reich had collapsed one after another to the revolutionary armies, Hegel had attacked both jurists who had quarrelled over the normative details of the constitution as well as those who had studied the state "empirically without

[349] Ibid., § 247 (222). [350] Ibid., § 248 (223). [351] Ibid., § 242 (220).

[352] Ibid., § 208, 209, 236, 245 (197–8, 217–18, 221–2).

[353] Hegel makes this point for example in contrasting between state and the church (or religion) – it was no accident for him that "it was *in the state that freedom of thought and science* had their origin. It was the Church, on the other hand, which burnt Giordano Bruno, forced Galileo to recant on his knees . . . and so forth", ibid., § 270 (251).

[354] Ibid., § 258 (228).

conforming to a rational Idea".[355] As the sphere of concrete freedom, the state was more than constitutional form or an instrument for particular purposes. Hegel agreed with many Kantian ideas about the meaning of freedom as autonomy, self-sufficiency and self-legislation. But he shared neither the rationalistic individualism of the Kantians, nor the romantic nationalism of many others. Freedom involved transgressing the pure subjectivity of will and desire as well as the abstract categories of personhood, property, contract and legal responsibility. This was to take place in the state where "the interest of the whole is realised in and through particular ends", where the universal and the particular coincide in the historically appropriate way.[356] By this he meant that the state provided the context in which individual freedom and the system of needs in civil society could best accommodate each other. This view of statehood would become the heart of European politics in the nineteenth century and preserve itself into the twentieth and beyond. It would be defined in its juxtaposition to those two other aspects of modern life, the family and the economy, containing yet not being reducible to them.

Although Hegel changed many of his views between his early years in Jena (1798–1806) when he contemplated the collapse of the Reich and the publication of his main political–legal work *Philosophy of Right* (1821), the analysis of the elements of the modern state and the critique of natural law's failure to appreciate them remained. Two of those elements he shared with Kant. First was a total rejection of the instrumental notion of statehood. The modern state *did* protect property rights, individual freedom and a well-functioning economy. But these were not its *telos*, it was the other way around. For Kant the objective of statehood was to create a constitutional order in which each person's freedom could coincide with the equal freedom of everyone else while for Hegel ownership and exchange of things were to support the state as the sphere of what he called absolute ethical life (*absolute Sittlichkeit*).[357]

355 G. W. F. Hegel, 'German Constitution', in L. Dickey & H. B. Nisbet (eds), *Hegel, Political Writings* (Cambridge University Press 1999), 6.

356 The unity of the particular and the universal in the state is an example of what Hegel call's the "actuality" of the state, namely the accommodation of contrasting freedoms in a fashion that fits the historical moment in the life of the state, Hegel, PR, § 270, *Addition* (253).

357 "If the state is confused with civil society, and if its specific end is laid down as the security and protection of property and personal freedom, then *the interest of individuals as such* becomes the ultimate end of their association, and it follows that membership of the state is something optional. But the state's relation to the

A second element was the qualified endorsement of the egoism in modern commercial society. Kant's unsocial sociability and Hegel's cunning of reason performed both the work of Smith's invisible hand in joining the principle of freedom with the production of general welfare.[358] But both also critiqued the privatised life of an individual *bourgeois* within the confines of the economy.[359] In Kant, the search for material interests was to remain trapped in a world of desire; Hegel demonstrated the path it opened into alienation and inequality. Both accepted that the state was to alleviate the conflicts in civil society by taxation, organising poor relief and health care, carrying out infrastructure works and administering justice.[360] But it was to keep itself from intruding unnecessarily in the subjects' freedoms. Hegel once attacked the French state where "everything is regulated from above, and where nothing of universal significance is entrusted to the management and execution of interested sections of the people".[361]

Hegel's freedom was different from the individual freedom of Locke, Smith or the Kantians. Abstract individuals could link to each other through the pursuit of wish-fulfilment, property, exchange and production. They could even believe that a cosmopolitan morality linked them to a world community. But they would fail to realise that individuality itself was possible only if the system of needs were connected with institutions of public-mindedness and the ethical life. This, Hegel suggested, could appear only when the modern state "actualiz[ed] itself as will".[362] Of course, individuals led their emotional lives in their families and satisfied their wants in civil society. But in the state they entered a different kind of life where, "for one thing, they also pass over of their own accord into the interest of the universal, and for another thing, they know and will the universal; they even

individual is quite different from this. Since the state is objective spirit, it is only as one of its members that the individual himself has objectivity, truth, and ethical life", ibid., § 258 (228–9).

358 On the cunning of reason, see ibid., § 199 (191) and WH, 89.

359 Hegel first described this aspect of modernity in 'On the Scientific Ways of Treating Natural Law', in L. Dickey & H. B. Nisbet (eds), *Hegel, Political Writings* (Cambridge University Press 1999), 149–51, linking Gibbon's description of Roman history to what he saw around himself in Germany. The private life of wants and their fulfilment was described but in much more detail and less critically in PR, §182–256 (180–228). See further, Shlomo Avineri, *Hegel's Theory of the Modern State* (Cambridge University Press 1972), 84–5, 91–8.

360 Kant, MM, 100–2 [6: 326–8); Hegel, PR, § 241 (220).

361 Hegel, 'German Constitution', 25.

362 Hegel, PR, § 258 (234).

recognise it as their own substantial spirit; they take it as their end and aim and are active in its pursuit".[363]

In Hegelian jargon, "the system of right is the realm of freedom made actual".[364] To say that freedom was made actual invoked Hegel's famous *Doppelsatz*, "*What is rational is actual and what is actual is rational*".[365] Here "actuality" meant the historical truth of a moment. Hegel distinguished between existence and actuality (*Existenz/Wirklichkeit*), where the former stood for a truth as it appeared at the moment and the latter for truth as it revealed its historical orientation. As a historical category, freedom would mean different things at different times. This was not to endorse relativism, however, as the succession of different periods followed, in Hegel's world-historical view, an order of specific stages.[366] In contrast to the Kantian idea of freedom as the autonomy of the rational individual, Hegel's "concrete freedom" was framed in the historical conditions of family, society and the state. To write that the state was "actual", as Hegel did, was to claim that it represented the historically appropriate coincidence of the particular and universal standpoints, and, as he insisted, their transcendence.[367]

Hegel believed that the experience of the French Revolution had demonstrated the unsatisfactory character of absolute freedom. This invoked a homogeneity that it was impossible to realise in modern conditions. People led different lives, they thought different thoughts and their participation in a diversified economy provided them different amounts of wealth and influence. To push for *volonté générale* was a receipt for terror.[368] Freedom could not be realised suddenly, by a single transformation. It could only come about by a historical process. Greek city-states, imperial Rome and old-regime Europe had each had their specific reason. The post-revolutionary moment, likewise, would have its own reason that its political institutions were to reflect. As its present-day manifestation, the modern state invited its members to become more than family members or commercial actors so as to share "the spiritual Idea externalised in the human will and its freedom".[369]

[363] Ibid., § 260 (235). [364] Ibid., § 4 (26).

[365] Ibid., Preface, 14. See further e.g. Robert Stern, 'Hegel's *Doppelsatz*. A Neutral Reading', 44 *Journal of the History of Philosophy* (2006), 235–66.

[366] Frederick Beiser, *Hegel* (Abingdon, Routledge 2005), 209–13.

[367] Hegel, PR, § 6–8, 259, 270 (30–4, 234, 253).

[368] For these arguments, see the excellent Charles Taylor, *Hegel* (Cambridge University Press 1975), 406–19.

[369] Hegel, WH, 120.

In a world split between collapsing utopias and pure selfishness, it offered the only firm centre.

## Law and Universal History

Hegel's discussion of law sought to transcend the familiar oppositions between rationalism and voluntarism, or natural law and positivism, aiming to meet them on the "higher plane" of an historically adequate willing. His point was to try to give a sense of freedom as something that would be equally distant from arbitrary choice and pure determination and that would arise from the ethical life of a community, aware of its own historicity. A particular moment in world history brought forth its particular type of reason within an overall progressive frame. Because Hegel's view of history was teleological, this meant that the right natural law for a moment was that which was adequately poised for the realisation of its proper end.[370]

As the modern state transcended the contradictions of civil society, it expressed the historical truth of the present and, joining abstract right with the will of the humans who worked and lived in it, could actualise their freedom.[371] This is what it meant to say that the state, instead of the monarch or the people, was sovereign.[372] It followed that Hegel did not believe in any cosmopolitan law or a substantial world federation.

[370] Ibid., 69. "The aim of world history, therefore, is that the spirit should attain knowledge of its own true nature, that it should objectivise this knowledge and transform it into a real world, and give itself an objective existence," WH, 64.

[371] As property-holders and legal subjects, individuals possess "abstract" freedom, interacting with each other through the categories of person, property, contract and wrong. But this pays no regard to the *concrete* situation where e.g. property emerges, changes hands and where it and the autonomy of the subject is (or is not) protected. "Abstract right" (i.e. property, contract and legal responsibility), Hegel wrote, "involved [] only a *possibility*". Hegel, PR, § 38 (55). It needed to be transcended by being made concrete, which is what "morality" did for Hegel, in which the will becomes "for itself" and "actual", § 104 (107). In a typical *Aufhebung*, the dialectic of "abstract right" and pure subjectivity of "morality" is transcended in the ethical life (*Sittlichkeit*) that contains, for example, the existing economic system, as discussed above.

[372] Ibid., § 278–9 (265–71). No doubt, this was a conservative (though not reactionary) view; Hegel's state had nothing to do with nationalism, although he admitted that one of the irrational aspects of existing states was their tendency to justify their boundaries by ethnic or nationalist myths. A "people" (*Volk*) had no identity outside statehood: it is "wild" and a "formless mass" that is constituted by the state, not the other way around, § 279 (269). Organised in a *democratic* way, the state might, as had happened during the Revolution, become an instrument to nationalist myth and terror. Taylor, *Hegel*, 414–15.

He regarded such speculation as contrary to the stage that the historical spirit had attained – the operations of the economy, technology and the prevalent myths of religion and community. It was a merely formal idea, distant from modernity's substance. By contrast, what was substantive was the state that "in its actuality [is] essentially an individual state, and beyond that a particular state".[373] The state was an individual and "individuality essentially implies negation"; not only did this exclude the possibility of a harmonious global federation but it made real the constant possibility of war.[374] Hegel had no faith in the pacific implications of expanding commerce. In fact, the conflicts between labour and production that were endemic to civil society were a constant source of friction in international relations as well. Hegel had many controversial things to say about war. War was not to be regarded as an absolute evil. It showed the vanity of external things and preserved the "ethical health of peoples".[375] The ideality of statehood, he wrote, was shown in the way war had in the past consolidated states and prevented domestic unrest. Long periods of peace bring about stagnation and ossification in the people while war strengthens it.[376]

These were classical republican points about warrior virtues and patriotic vigour. They aimed probably more at the illusions of liberal pacifism than to defend the benefits of war as a political instrument. Anyway, Hegel believed that war would be limited in a way that the Napoleonic campaigns had already tended to disprove.[377] But he did not think that the danger of war undermined the possibility of a lawful international order. To the contrary, just as individual freedom in civil society depended on the recognition of the abstract right of personhood and property by others, the individuality of the state presupposed its acceptance in a community of states. The view of mutual recognition was absolutely central to the Hegelian view of individuality, strengthened and made concrete in his analysis of the interdependent conditions of the modern economy. State sovereignty was created and sustained precisely by such recognition that, Hegel wrote, "*remains even in war*".[378] Hegel's understanding of international law was ultimately very similar to the one presented by Martens. The concreteness of

[373] Hegel, PR, § 259 (234).
[374] Ibid., § 324 (307–8). Hegel expressly rejected Kant's proposal of perpetual peace that he saw having been attempted in the Holy Alliance.
[375] Ibid., § 324 (306–7). [376] Ibid., § 324 (307).
[377] Paul Franco, *Hegel's Philosophy of Freedom* (Yale University Press 2002), 334.
[378] Hegel, PR, § 328, 338 (309, 314).

sovereignty was manifested to the external world as the will of the state, made visible in treaties, customs and all the rest of its external public law (*das äussere Staatsrecht*).[379] Because under conditions of modernity, each state was not only factually dependent on each other, but also received identity by its being recognised by others, this meant that the state was reason-bound to respect this law in the same way it was expected to respect its constitution – not owning to fear of external judgment but because that was the rational thing to do. It then respected its own identity, including the many private rights it had guaranteed, as forged in the system of reciprocal recognitions.[380]

It was not impossible to have an international law that would bind the state. But it could exist only as the external public law of states-as-individuals, engaged in diplomacy, trade, colonisation and occasional, but limited, war. The state was no less dependent on the community around it than human beings were: "Whether a state in fact has being in and for itself depends on its condition . . . and recognition, implying as it does an identity of both form and content, is conditional on the neighbouring state's perception and will."[381] This tied each modern – European – state tightly in the community of other such states and, indeed, limited statehood and international law to Europe. But the liberal lament about Hegelian "particularism" and the merely coordinative character of his external public law never grasped the point that although individual states had their interests and policies, the rationality of modern statehood was a concrete actualisation of the universal that was already historically present.[382] Words such as "federation", "perpetual peace" or "world state" added nothing by way of universality to statehood as it existed, even as they may challenge its specific instantiations. All they did was, as Hegel argued in his late lectures, support "the pretence [*Lüge*] of Empire [that] ha[d now] broken into sovereign states". This, he added, was "the point which consciousness ha[d] now

379 Ibid., § 330(311). 380 Ibid., § 323 (305). 381 Ibid., § 331 (311).

382 This failure of understanding runs through the history of Western commentary on Hegel's international law writings. For a rather well-informed and serious late version, see Sergio Dellavalle, 'The Plurality of States and the World Order of Reason. On Hegel's Understanding of International Law and Relations', in Stefan Kadelbach et al. (eds), *System, Order, and International Law* (Oxford University Press 2017), 352–78. Hegel was not thinking of particular states; what he had in mind was the idea of the state that for him had universal validity. To attack states for what some states have done was like attacking the notion of human person, he wrote, because some persons have committed crimes, PR, § 258 (234).

reached, and these are the chief formal moments in which the principle of freedom has been actualised".[383]

## The Legacy of German Imagination

The effort to imagine a law that would be applicable everywhere is as old as legal thinking itself. In Roman times, it peaked in Stoic ideas about the universality of human nature. Alongside that philosophically inspired idea, Romans also developed the law of nations – *ius gentium* – in part to address institutions that, even as they could not be said to be natural in that sense, were nevertheless applicable to those who were not citizens.[384] The idea of natural law was in due course Christianised to address the immutable effects of creation. But its high level of abstraction suggested to theologians that there was need for more practical law that would address actually existing human institutions, for example the "buyings and selling" of Aquinas. The Salamanca scholars read into it the institutions of sovereignty and property from which they would derive justification for the contemporary practices of diplomacy, commerce and warfare. These, it was assumed, were part of human nature, not in an absolute way, but as adaptations to meet the needs of present social life. Even positive law was natural inasmuch as it came about as a response to challenges of government given by the world as it was.

German natural lawyers operated the idiom of *ius naturae et gentium* to articulate laws that would be universally applicable. They were encouraged to do so by the spectacular advances of the natural sciences. If only one were able to turn law into a technique of government like operating a machine, then it could become a real science of social life. But this search was undermined by a doubt about what it meant for a law to be "natural". Was it that which worked empirically – or that which philosophy suggested corresponded to perfection of human communities? Would it be what Europeans had been accustomed to doing – or the principles through which they viewed what they were doing? What was the role of non-European "barbarians"? Did they represent an earlier phase of civilisation, or

[383] G. W. F. Hegel, 'Lectures on the Philosophy of History (1827–1831), Part IV, Section 3: The New Age', in L. Dickey & H. B. Nisbet (eds), *Hegel, Political Writings* (Cambridge University Press 1999), 223.

[384] The best account of pre-Grotian ideas of *ius gentium* is in Peter Haggenmacher *Grotius et la doctrine de la guerre juste* (Presses Universitaires de France 1983), 311–58.

were they a degenerate form of the present? The search for a natural law meant different things to different people. Something could be regarded as natural because one countered it everywhere, the search for happiness, for example. But was happiness to be reached in the instinctual world as suggested by Schmauss, or in the world of reason and deliberation as purported by the Wolffians? And why should one necessarily look for the universal – something could equally well be termed natural if it was specific as, for example, in "it is natural for Europeans".[385] How, indeed, did nature and history relate to each other? In their search for a truly scientific concept of law, German academic jurists of the eighteenth century were, as Kant noted, engaged in a contest of the faculties that ended up dividing the law faculty itself, sending splinters flying off in all directions. Achenwall's systematic of the human sciences, divided between more or less abstract philosophical and more or less empirical and historical branches was an impressive effort to control that fragmentation.

The search for natural law would be transcended in Göttingen by expanding interest in state-history, universal history and ultimately the history of humanity. Schlözer's *Vorstellung seiner Universalhistorie* (1772) suggested that it was not nature but history that joined humankind. The world was not always like it was now; humankind had experienced several "revolutions".[386] In order to understand it, one needed to know it in its mutations, and not only in Europe but everywhere.[387] While it is true that men like Schlözer (and such other Göttingen universal historians as Johann Christop Gatterer and Johann Gottfried Eicchorn) were path-breaking as academic scholars, supporting the rise of anthropological and ethnographic studies, it was still not clear how their efforts could be turned to practical use in the German chancelleries. One direction was provided by the modernisation of *Policey*-science and cameralism that led into empirical political science (*Statistik*) and *Nationalökonomie*. Another was the "modern law of nations" that Martens and his colleagues derived from the historical

[385] On the conflict between universal nature and specific natures, see L. Daston *The Morality of Natural Orders. The Tanner Lectures on Human Values* (2002) 380–92, available at: tannerlectures.utah.edu/_documents/a-to-z/d/daston_2002.pdf.

[386] August Ludwig Schlözer, *Vorstellung seiner Universalhistorie* (Göttingen, Dieterich 1772), I § 4 (8). "A human being is nothing naturally, but may through experience become everything; indeterminacy constitutes the other part of his being", § 3 (6).

[387] As with Achenwall and Martens, such study would have to proceed by classifying nations into those that lead and those that follow, ibid., IV § 44–6 (106–10).

relations of European nations – a system that could only be realistically studied in its specificity.[388]

The four transformations surveyed in this chapter have to do with what has been conventionally called the "crisis of natural law". But it may be better to think of them as four ways in which natural law renewed itself so as to continue exercising authority within a world whose consciousness of itself had become profoundly historical. The legacy of the contest of the faculties extends to this day. Should we be ruled by economics or philosophy? Should we be governed in the way we have always been governed, or might some new knowledge help us govern ourselves better? It is surely no accident that nineteenth- and twentieth-century legal imagination remained saturated by ideas that crystallised in the course of the European enlightenment, and that international lawyers' debt to German academy from the period 1648–1821 is so great. As long as the field shares the ambitions of Western science, whether in its rationalist or historicist, formalist or voluntarist versions, the temptation has been to think about the most urgent problems of human society in terms of jurisdictional delimitation between vocabularies competing in their projection of what might seem natural for us – natural, and therefore in no need of further justification. The space of human nature however, as Schlözer himself noted in his *Universal History* is utterly indeterminate – *Unbestimmt.*[389] Which means it may be filled with whatever qualities we are inclined to feel as normal and decent. Whenever the legal imagination moves in the sphere of the universal, it will be accompanied by the now-familiar eighteenth-century languages, means of measurement, standards and criteria that we associate with science and enlightenment and for which the human appears as the ambivalent figure of that which is both free to live by the laws it has chosen and thoroughly enchanted by the technical tools that it has convinced itself are nothing but the instruments of its self-expression. Yet it is not easy to shed the suspicion voiced by one of the most perceptive commentators of the era: "In this context the proposition that tools are prolongations of human organs can be inverted to state that the organs are also prolongations of the tools."[390]

[388] For the discussion by early nineteenth-century Göttingen historians and jurist–historians such as Spittler, Eichhorn, Gatterer, Schlözer and Heeren of topics such as *Staatengeschichte*, *Universalgeschichte*, *Weltgeschichte* and *Geschichte der Menschheit*, see Marino, *Praeceptores Germaniae*; Araújo, *Weltgeschichte in Göttingen*; Bödeker et al., *Aufklärung und Geschichte*.

[389] Schlözer, *Universalhistorie*, I § 3 (6).

[390] Max Horkheimer, 'Traditional and Critical Theory', in Max Horkheimer, *Critical Theory. Selected Essays* (New York, Herder & Herder 1972), 201.

# Conclusion and Epilogue

## I

"... the organs are also prolongations of the tools". According to one view, language works as an instrument for human intentions, including the imagining in which we engage in our lives. In this book I have taken the opposite to that perhaps commonsensical view, namely that the language we have determines for us the experience we have of the world, and in particular what alternatives for action we perceive. I have not adopted this view as a philosophical dictum. Like most such large dicta, I find it in the end too strong to be fully believable, even paradoxical. But in my life as an international lawyer, I have learned to rely on it as a very good rule of thumb when trying to understand the complexities of the governance of the international world. Why do well-educated professional women and men think and act the way they do? The technical or scientific languages we have learned to master – law, development, human rights, security, environment, and so on – provide us both with an interpretation of the world as well as a recipe for dealing with its problems. Indeed, it outlines for us what those "problems" are in the first place. Having learned those languages, we attain positions of authority from which to tell people whom we address what they ought to believe or do. Professional languages have authority, and employing them we ourselves become authoritative, we become their *prolongation.* That is both an appealing and a problematic position in which to be. To exercise authority, we must adopt an authoritative language. But in immersing ourselves in that language, we lose critical distance from it.

One of the ways in which I find the thesis about the primacy of language to thought and action to be too strong is that it exaggerates the passivity of imagination. What I have in this book and elsewhere addressed as imagination is a critical capacity, one that enables shifting between professional languages, and between professional and ordinary languages. It implies the ability to step outside the position of authority to examine it critically, and perhaps to redirect its use. This effort touches on a large philosophical theme which I have not pursued here. Instead, I have wanted to account not only for how the idiom of *ius gentium* and its many cognates have been employed as part of different professional vocabularies in the context of intellectual and political struggle but also to transform what can be achieved by it by shifting between vocabularies, finding new uses for old idioms, creating hybrids or using the languages against themselves. As I wrote at the beginning, this is not a history of international law, it is a history of the legal imagination.

The chapters above have looked backwards to the intellectual spaces from which, during half a millennium, ambitious men tried to imagine a law between nations. That effort turned out to be an intervention in what Kant labelled the contest of the faculties, the struggle for a voice to speak authoritatively about and for the whole humanity. Kant himself was not an impartial analyst of this contest. Unsurprisingly, he discovered that it was his own discipline, philosophy, that understood the reasons behind the laws, and was therefore in a position to propose a law to rule over the entire world. Kant did not think much of the lawyers. All they saw was the code, he believed, and had nothing interesting to say about how it ought to be used or developed.[1] That view had specific targets in the eighteenth-century German legal academy. And it aimed to consolidate the final relegation of theology into the private world where it would not bother the mundane business of governing people. In a sense, it was a response, from the distance of two centuries and a half, to Francisco de Vitoria who, speaking as a theologian, found that precisely because so many things in the world had a bearing upon matters of conscience, it was up to the theologians to prescribe about them. One can understand the anxious reactions to such a proposition in the years between by Protestant legal writers such as Alberico Gentili and Hugo Grotius. Would it not be much better to organise human relations by reference to what could be learned from human nature or the nature of society, as communicated by observation and experience? Was that not what the best theologians were anyway

[1] Immanuel Kant, *The Conflict of the Faculties* (M. Gregor ed. & intro., New York, Abris 1979), 37–9, 161–5.

doing, though pretending divine inspiration? Besides, if there was to be a law of nations, why seek its content from anywhere but from law itself?

Kant, Vitoria, Gentili and Grotius used the languages available to them – philosophy, theology, Roman and natural law – to speak imaginatively about a new world about which they felt some anxiety and in which they hoped to exercise some influence. For that purpose they employed idioms that were familiar enough to be understood and impress but in a new way that would illuminate some novel problem and perhaps propose a way ahead. The operations were intellectual and linguistic, but their point was to influence the exercise of power in their cultural neighbourhood – especially power in its two most conspicuous forms, sovereignty and property. To the extent that these men succeeded in sounding persuasive, they themselves came to be regarded as authorities, or as we might now say, turned into prolongations of new, powerful languages. Three large stories were woven in foregoing chapters to throw light on this process of imaginative persuading. One had to do with how such languages rise, flourish and are then pushed aside as new ones take their place. Another examined the process of imagining itself as it moves from close to home to ever-expanding spaces and materials in order eventually to speak about humanity as a whole. And the third links these two by calling attention to what lay at the centre of all this imagining, namely the effort to justify, consolidate and critique the uses of power outside the realm that is conventionally and flexibly imagined as the domestic. This book is about legal imagination in its relationship to power abroad.

The first story was about the "contest of the faculties", the way in which imagination operated in a dynamic context of conflict – conflict about territorial government at home and abroad, about the distribution of resources, about the determination of the conditions of life of domestic or alien communities. Sometimes the conflict took the form of physical violence, war and conquest, occupation or rebellion where the opposite sides used clashing idioms to address the justice of their cause and the injustice of their opponents'. More often, the conflict took place among the prince's counsellors, among courtiers, judges, legal polemicists, ministers or professors, among a reading public or the relative security of the academy. Opposite ideas about just government took the form of clashing idioms – idioms such as divine providence, *raison d'état*, *dominium*, fundamental rights, sovereignty, customary law, human nature, jurisdiction and so on. Only imagination set limits to how such idioms could be combined in wide languages representing ideological systems and specific ways to justify, consolidate or critique power. One large theme was the migration of authority between theology, law, politics and economics but also their intermixture at particular moments. The writings of Grotius on the sociability that all humans shared were hard to distinguish from his Christian ecumenism. The *Code noir* was a piece of French domestic legislation, designed for application outside metropolitan France to non-citizens with the stated intention to "baptize and instruct [the slaves] in the Catholic religion" (Art II). Ideas about improvement that underlay legal claims of British colonial expansion engaged divine providence with assumptions about economic efficiency. The mutation of the language of natural law at German universities in the seventeenth and eighteenth centuries offered a complex spectacle on the rise and fall of religious, moral, political and economic ideas about good government through which relations between federal units and eventually the nations of the world were to be organised.

A second narrative in the foregoing chapters addressed what some might treat as a philosophical problem about the ambivalence of the particular and the universal standpoints but which I have here turned into a question about the place from which legal imagination starts. My intuition was – and this is how I have structured this book – that this type of imagining could only emerge from the legal education and the local experience of those who engaged in it. If a thirteenth-century Frenchman, trained at the law school in Bologna or Orleans, is called upon to justify the authority of his ruler towards the church, a foreign banker or a potentate, it is surely not surprising that he would begin with the language found in the *Corpus iuris*, expressly claiming validity over the whole world and handily available in domestic law. It seems equally unsurprising that a Spanish theologian would start from fragments of the civil law available in Dominican religious tradition as well as in the *Siete partidas* as he begins to contemplate the colonial violence of his countrymen or the global expansion of a commercial ethic. Then again, if a French lawyer in the seventeenth and eighteenth century spends no energy at all to develop a legal view of French rule in the Caribbean, that seems quite logical for someone with a domestic experience of subordination under a system of flexible accommodation between ruling families called "absolutism". Eighteenth-century English jurists, we have seen, will have the alternative vocabularies of the royal prerogative and the common law to fight out the division of the spoils from imperial expansion, and while the German jurist will mostly stay at home contemplating the Holy Roman Empire, that will finally produce the most complex thinking for squaring the circle about how to fit claims about sovereignty with imperial pre-eminence.

Imagining starts at home, and a persuasive language is one that is understood by those to whom one speaks or writes. There is no global Esperanto for lawyers to justify rights or duties purported to have a universal scope. To think about activities or interests outside conventional jurisdictional limits may require reading of old materials in a new way or imagining altogether new materials as legally pertinent. Eventually, a civil lawyer needs to reach beyond civil law – for example, the customary law of a neighbouring country, a passage from Aristotle or text from a historian of Italy – to sound persuasive to the humanist courtiers that compose his audience. An English preacher may join the words of Jesus to a passage from Roman law and a French legal publicist may cite travel stories from China or Persia to contemplate the justice or domestic government or the rights and wrongs of colonial expansion. A whole line of professors of *ius naturae et gentium* at German enlightenment universities celebrated an "eclectic" approach that would aim to master as many scientific languages as possible to learn to operate the state-machine in its internal and external relationships. The fragments available for legal *bricolage* may be those close at hand, but there is no limit to using them to think across conventional boundaries. Theology, Roman law, *raison d'état*, politics – even natural science, physics and biology – were used as novel frames to imagine and argue differently. In due course, the frame of *bricolage* itself expands. Knowledge travels, languages are translated, the foreign becomes familiar. Legal imagining is both specific to the time and place where it takes places and continuous with imagining that has taken place and will occur in different places and at different times.

But there is a limit to the context-transgressing ability of legal work. To paraphrase Marx, the imagination of all past generations "weighs like a nightmare on the brains of the living". The most obvious and yet somehow most depressing limit in the imagination of the men in the above pages, apart from the fact that that they are all species of *male* imagination, is their hopeless Eurocentrism. That feature penetrates their every work, every chapter, every sentence. It does so to the extent that the question may justifiably be posed about the point of rehearsing these texts once again. Why not just forget about them? One response is that doing so would deprive our own collective imagining of resources enabling us to have a well-informed, instead of prejudiced, view of the kinds of thinking and doing that have created today's world. Depending on what we think of this world, it may then invite us to do our own imagining better. Another way to put this is to underline the sense that historical work on law is interesting and important to the extent that it is a history of power.

The third and last major theme of this book, perhaps its main theme, is that of power or authority. Language is power, we have learned to think, and I have here tried to demonstrate how legal imagination in these five centuries has sought to elaborate forms of language with which to justify, stabilise and critique power at home and abroad. It was perfectly comprehensible that when the protagonists of this book first began to imagine how to think about power, what they grasped was the language of the Bible that pointed them back to the first moments after creation when God had said, "Let us make mankind in our image, in our likeness, so that they may rule over the fish in the sea and the birds in the sky, over the livestock and all the wild animals, and over all the creatures that move along the ground" (Genesis 1:26). From this passage, the notion of "ruling over" in its Latin form *dominium* was then integrated with the *Corpus iuris* to be eventually divided into two major forms, *dominium iurisdictionis* and *dominium proprietatis*, the ruler's power over the ruled and the owner's power over everyone else. These are the two principal forms of power addressed by the legal idioms of which this book is about. In their different idioms, what all of these theologians, lawyers, political pamphleteers, professors and courtiers attempted to do was to justify, consolidate or critique claims about sovereign power or about the power to exclude others from the thing that one supposedly owns.

This is a book about the legal imagination but it is also an intervention in debates about critical legal history. One of the burdens weighing on historical analysis has been the conventional distinction between public and private power, loosely associated with sovereignty and property. That distinction has underlain critical analyses of European imperialism, capitalism, militarism, nationalism and so on. Focus has been on formal empires – the Spanish, the French, the British, the American – and their military and colonial exploits, their treaties and their diplomacy. Global power has been associated with the extension of European sovereignty. Alternatively, critical histories have focused on the gradual creation of a wholly global network of commercial relations, a system of trade and investment, the exploitation of and depletion of the world's resources by powerful private actors, transnational corporations, banks, investors, rogue capitalists and so on. Here, the essence of European predominance would appear as capitalism, the global power of ownership.

In this work I have tried to show that neither of these optics alone captures the role of law in the consolidation of Europe's global hegemony. It is possible, of course, to focus on the European sovereign: *l'état c'est moi*. In this famous apocryphal statement attributed to Luis XIV, supposedly at the height of his power after 1660, we are inclined to see sovereignty at its peak. And yet, at that very moment, it would be possible to respond truthfully to the question "what is France?" by referring to the over 50,000 venal officeholders, men who bought their way to office that they held as private property that was also inheritable by their eldest sons. Britain would never have become a great power had there not been enterprising merchants in London and Manchester and noble landholders across the country and in the colonies whose relationship to the crown was organised by an essentially feudal system. This made it lucrative for private actors to engage in the king's wars and to carry out trade and expansion as part of the crown's blue-water strategy and the informal empire of later years. Vitoria was worried over what his sovereign was doing in the Indies and with his endless wars against France. But he was equally if not more anxious about the global spread of the silver from the mines of South America, administered by *cambistas* at trade fairs across Europe, which created the kinds of wealth in which traditions of Christian ethic, such as the prohibition of usury, could no longer survive. And yet it is unlikely that all of this private wealth-creation could have taken place without there being a crown, a colonial administration, a legislative body and a military force as well as a people ready to make the kinds of sacrifices for their nation that underlay the creation of the colonial world. This is also a history of the power of the state, and the language of statehood, and all that belongs to it.

So in a nutshell, the legal imagining treated in this book is not about public or private law, the power of sovereignty or the power of property. It is instead about law as *bricolage* – about the imaginative use of both of these two idioms to create structures of legal argument that are respectful of local tradition but also sensitive to novel circumstances and the needs of change. This is what legal work *is* – the combination of materials lying around in order to persuade those whose opinions and words matter. Approaching a moment in political and legal history, we tend to see first either its public or its private face, with the obverse face hidden. What may be visible is the war offensive or the peace conference, the king or the diplomat signing a treaty – in that case, it is best to scratch the surface of that image, so that what will become visible are the exchanges of property that provide the resources on which the king sits, the war is waged and that guarantee the success or failure of the peace. Or the other way around. One may perceive a trade pattern or an investment in a foreign country as what makes the world turn. But it would not spin the way it does were there not a king, a military force, an administration and a whole legal system that endows the capitalist their property, limits it and secures its passage across the world. My ambition in this book has been to show that European power is neither the power of sovereignty nor of property but always a particular, locally specific combination of the two. *Sovereignty and property are the yin and yang of European power.*

## II

When the old-liberal Heidelberg professor Robert von Mohl (1799–1875) glanced backwards half a century from 1860, he could find little international law of scientific worth. The law itself had expanded into new lands and even new parts of the world, but the science had undergone "a long period of silence during which it had fallen wholly behind comparative disciplines".[2] Among German international law works of the past century he could find just one jurist with significant achievements in the field, Georg Friedrich von Martens. In the stream of famous Göttingen jurists, Martens had produced a valuable collection of legal materials to which he had also provided systematic order. His work had been useful not only for scholars but to diplomats and holders of public office across Europe. In all the years since Martens' retirement, Mohl noted, nobody in Germany or elsewhere had provided a comparable level of knowledge on the foreign relations of European states.[3]

But Martens was a scholar of an old world, his work looking back to pre-revolutionary diplomacy and limited to an external aspect of state law, *äusseres Staatsrecht*. Even before Mohl, other lawyers had expressed

[2] "einen langen Stillstand gemacht und war entschieden hinter verwandten Disciplinen weit zurückgeblieben". Robert von Mohl, *Staatsrecht, Völkerrecht und Politik. Erster Band* (Tübingen, Laupp 1860), 580.

[3] Robert von Mohl, *Die Geschichte und Litteratur der Staatswissenschaften. Zweiter Band* (Erlangen, Encke 1856), 472, 461–72.

their dissatisfaction with the state of the field. Philosophically oriented jurists such as Christoph Gagern, Karl Theodor Pütter and Carl Kaltenborn had vented their frustration about the failure of scholarship to give systematic expression to the new, post-revolutionary law of nations. They lamented the absence of a good legal history that would, as Kaltenborn put it, provide the field with a foundational idea (*Völkerrechtsidee*).[4] All that was now visible were disparate facts "raw and incomplete, apparently unconnected and confused". A more profound scholarship was needed to look beyond single facts and describe international law at a "higher, world-economical plane striving for fullness".[5] This required a philosophical perspective, they suggested. But there was no timeless philosophy, every thinking was a product of its time (*Zeitalter*). There was no view of humanity as such, merely particular views that reflected the periods in which they were formed:

> Just like no nation in its totality is ever able to rise above the boundaries of the particular and the local, or overall its positive, concrete definiteness . . . so also is the philosopher called upon to suffer this limitedness.[6]

Together with the other philosophical jurists, Kaltenborn rejected the chimera of a single universal law; a properly historical view would seek to give an account of the way the individuality and sovereignty of states ("subjective principle") could be accommodated with a public order ("objective principle") – the old problem of the Roman–German Empire. Kaltenborn was imagining a philosophy that would be true to the moment and "show the way from the present to a future of a better legal life (*eines besseren Rechtslebens*)".[7]

Kaltenborn's view of progress was limited by his assumption that it was possible only among Christian nations; only they could fit religious and political freedoms with a robust public order at home and bring this mediation to their external relations.[8] Others shared Kaltenborn's historicism but neither his Christian conservatism nor his belief that it was philosophy that would solve the law's problems. In a long review of

[4] Carl Baron Kaltenborn von Stachau, *Kritik des Völkrerrechts nach dem jetzigen Standpunkt der Wissenschaft* (Leipzig, Meyer 1847), 238–9, 270–2. See also Karl Theodor Pütter, *Beiträge zur Völkerrechts-Geschichte und Wissenschaft* (Leipzig, Wienbrack 1843), 13–14.

[5] Kaltenborn, *Kritik*, 239.

[6] "Wie keine Nation, in ihrer Totalität nicht einmal, keine Zeit über die Schranken der partikulären und localen, überhaupt der positiven, concreten Bestimmtheit sich zu erheben vermag . . . so wird auch der Philosoph an dieser Bornirtheit zu leiden haben." Ibid., 251.

[7] Ibid., 253. [8] Ibid., 270–1.

Heffter's *Völkerrecht* of 1845 the young Lorenz von Stein (1815–1890) observed that of all the parts of the law, there was least public attention on international law. Stein confessed himself surprised to find out that lectures were given on the subject at all, and that new books, such as Heffter's, were being published; anyway, he noted, they dealt more with the *science* of the field than international law itself. Stein made a note of the predominance of Martens, but also of the way his law of nations was reduced to hardly more than the listing of the number, title and rank of states.[9] It gave no expression to the "richness of our contemporary life". People had begun to travel and across the world the shadow of war had retreated; trade and industries had expanded, giving rise to common interests expressed in divergent social formations (*weiterzweigte Gesellschaftungen*) extending around the world. The emergence of customs unions, the German Confederation and the Monroe Doctrine manifested new types of international life far beyond eighteenth-century diplomacy and the balance of power. We are at a "point of transition to a new period", Stein suggested.[10]

For Stein, like many other German liberals, the Napoleonic wars constituted a sharp caesura in European history; there was the old regime, here an industrial, progressive modernity; there the old theories of self-sufficient statehood, here the internationalisation of the most varied aspects of social life. Stein lamented the conventional reduction of all human relations into statehood and the absence of analyses of society (*Gesellschaft*) – an expression that would become a fighting word in the run-up to 1848 and the object of intense analyses about the nature of the bourgeois class society.[11] Stein wanted to employ the expression to analyse the conflicts between interest groups and classes within more conventional types of historical, legal and economic scholarship, exemplified in his own studies of French social movements.[12] Mohl shared his interest in *Gesellschaft* and sought to employ the categories of the *Rechtsstaat* to analyse and mediate the conflicts that the revolution had brought to surface. In his 1859 encyclopaedia

[9] Lorenz von Stein, 'Review of Aug. Wilh. Heffter, *Das europäische Völkerrecht der Gegenwart*', *Allgemeine Literatur-Zeitung* 1845 (nos 16–18), 121, 129, 139.

[10] "auf dem Punkte des Überganges zu einer neuen Zeit", ibid., 143, 140–3.

[11] See the excellent studies by Manfried Riedel, 'Gesellschaft, bürgerliche', and 'Gesellschaft und Gemeinschaft', in Otto Brunner et al., *Geschichtliche Grundbegriffe. Historisches Lexikon zur politisch-sozialen Sprache* in *Deutschland* (8 vols, Stuttgart, Klett-Cotta 1972), II, 719–800 and 801–62.

[12] Lorenz von Stein, *Geschichte der sozialen Bewegung in Frankreich von 1789 bis auf unsere Tage* (3 vols, Leipzig, Wiegand 1850).

of state-sciences he defined "society" as the totality of spontaneous types of interaction crystallising around a specific interest shared by a group of people that organises their willing and acting towards a common objective.[13] Such social formations (*gesellschaftliche Kreise*) were not the product of a formal will but arose spontaneously to occupy larger or smaller part of the lives of their members. They may be more or less important and more or less extensive, ranging from a social circle in a village to a class (*Klasse*) of people with an analogous situation in life (*Lebensstellung*), such as shared profession or education, common religion or membership in an economic class or a governmental hierarchy.[14] What was common to social formations was that they were neither created by states nor confined in their activities within the formal structures of statehood. They could have their own rule-systems as well as internal and external hierarchies that it would be a mistake to reduce to the relationships within the states where they operate.[15]

According to Stein and Mohl, old public law was incapable of articulating the thinking and acting of such communities, reducing them either into actions by individuals or then as types of state activity. But there was more in modern life than individuals and the state. The nature of the uprisings in Europe in the past decades could not be understood without seeing them in relation to the social question.[16] Both also suggested that the development had immediate relevance in the international sphere. In his 1860 work Mohl suggested that it was now time for international law to develop a doctrine of "international society" – *Lehre von der*

[13] Robert von Mohl, *Encyclopädie der Staatswissenschaften* (2nd edn, Tübingen, Mohr 1872), 27.

[14] Ibid., 27–34, 48–53.

[15] Ibid., 34. In his various texts, von Mohl tried to sketch the relations between political science (*Staatswissenschaften*) and what he now called social sciences (*Gesellschaftswissenschaften*), including the proper placement of public and international law among them. See especially Robert von Mohl, "Theorie der Staatswissenschaften', in *Politische Schriften* (Wiesbaden, Fachmedien 1966), 1–12. To the extent that law regulated the internal or external relations of such social formations, all law, including state law, was social law (*Gesellschaftsrecht*), designed to advance their purposes and fulfil their needs.

[16] A more limited rival understanding of "society" had emerged in the Scottish enlightenment with a predominantly commercial connotation (adopted also by Hegel, as we have seen). See also Peter Wagner, *A History and Theory of the Social Sciences* (London, Sage 2001), 131. Stein was an acute analyst of the bourgeois social state, including its class conflicts, but commentary is divided whether he was a social conservative or a radical reformer. An assessment of various interpretations is Karl Hermann Kästner, 'From the Social Question to the Social State', 10 *Economy and Society* (1981), 7–26.

*internationalen Gemeinschaft.*[17] This was one of the spontaneous formations to have emerged in recent times through the actions of groups of individuals, corporations, social classes, associations of states and other transnational types of activity. Mohl believed that the workings of international society would need to be studied in the same way as other social formations, by reference to its ordering function and its success in fulfilling the needs of its elements – in the case of international society, those elements being states, subsidiary associations and individuals. How does international society organise its legislation, adjudication, preventive policing and implementation? How does it carry out its need-fulfilment functions (*polizeilischen Fürsorge*), such as organising trade and communication, control of emigration and epidemics, securing the availability of foodstuffs?[18]

Stein and Mohl imagined what they called international society as not only a platform for cooperation between states, but for various "private" associations and communities to fulfil their objectives and advance their interests (these would include professional associations, churches, companies, guilds and noble societies for example). Increasing civilisation would lead to expanding activity across international borders independently of the state. It was important that the international society recognise the right for companies and professional, religious and other societies to operate internationally as long as they complied with local laws.[19] There were thousands of ways people moved about in foreign countries to which they had all kinds of obligations and from which they could expect protection. By providing a structured order for these relations, international law could become the law of an international society, functioning by treaties and customs but also through the intermediary of state laws, local ordinances and customs. Mohl agreed with the philosophical jurists that the law of nations was a product of European history and culture. From a social

[17] Robert von Mohl, 'Die Pflege der internationalen Gemeinschaft als Aufgabe des Völkerrechts', in *Staatsrecht, Völkerrecht und Politik* (Tübingen, Laupp 1860), Erster Band, 580.

[18] Ibid., 613–20. Mohl recognised that states operated in the international society in order to fulfil their purposes, as derived from the civilisational level (*Gestattungsstufe*) of their people. To do this, they could neither isolate themselves nor give themselves up to others. But the more civilised a state was, the more it would seek cooperation. Also smaller social formations sought to fulfil their purposes internationally. There was thus no reason for why international law would not take those purposes as well into account. There is no doubt, he claimed, that such cooperation could best be organised through international conferences with the widest possible attendance, 593–8.

[19] Ibid., 620–6.

perspective, it could hardly seem otherwise. In order to fulfil its ordering function, however, it was quite possible that it would be developing in a federal direction as well as perhaps, with increasing civilisation, into a common organisation of humanity itself.[20]

Like Stein, Mohl used the *Rechtsstaat* idea to mediate the social conflicts of the mid-century, most famously by transforming *Policey*-science gradually into administrative law. Although he was admirer of judicial review and American constitutional law, he was not a democrat but a supporter of constitutional monarchy and a "small-German" solution for unification.[21] He was critical of overly individualistic notions of freedom and believed that it was a principal task of the state, alongside with other societies, to advance the common good.[22] Mohl had been elected one of Baden's representatives in the Frankfurt Parliament in 1848 where he was active in the constitutional committee until being appointed minister of justice of the ultimately short-lived German republic. After the failure of the 1848 revolution he returned to teach at Heidelberg. Not all of his Paulskirche colleagues were equally lucky. Many had taken refuge in foreign countries where they opposed extradition requests by German authorities to stand trial in Germany. Perhaps for that reason, Mohl's only extensive study of international law's substance was a work on the right of asylum.[23] He also preserved his seat in the First Chamber of Baden's *Landtag* where he would eventually cooperate with his successor at the university, Johann Caspar Bluntschli (1808–1881).

Bluntschli had arrived in Munich in 1848 from his native Zurich where he had become the target of radical and Catholic activism. In conservative Munich Bluntschli devoted himself to scholarship in public law, but in the more liberal world of Heidelberg he began to take active part in Baden's internal and constitutional debates and in the wider discussions over the reform of the German Confederation. He was also

[20] This would be very far in the future, if at all, and it would require a number of intermediary steps and a higher level and more integrated spiritual life among the people. Mohl, *Encyclopädie der Staatswissenschaften*, 41–7, 418–23.

[21] Stolleis *Geschichte*, II, 174–5.

[22] Monica Cioli, *Pragmatismus und Ideologie. Organisationsformen des deutschen Liberalismus zur Zeit der zweiten Reichgründung (1878–1884)* (Berlin, Duncker & Humblot 2000), 23–4.

[23] Robert von Mohl, 'Die völkerrechtliche Lehre vom Asyle', in *Staatsrecht, Völkerrecht*, 637–764. Here Mohl came to support a "modified cosmopolitan" position with a distinction between extradition requests on the basis of breaches of foreign private and public law. The latter should in principle operate only among "decent states" (*gesittige Staaten*) and never in such a manner as to sacrifice humanitarian principles, 711–20.

active in many liberal societies and took initiatives in the establishment of the German *Protestantenverein* (1863) and became eventually one of the founding members of the *Institut de droit international* (1873). Bluntschli appreciated his predecessor's works in public law but was in utter opposition to Mohl's advocacy of the conceptual frame of "society" and the idea of a social law (*Gesellschaftsrecht*).[24] He associated these notions with Saint-Simonianism, socialism and communism and an effort needlessly to situate a sphere of human action between the family and the state. To do this, Bluntschli argued, Mohl and others had separated the private and public realms too sharply, failing to see them in a continuum, penetrating each other in a way that allowed covering the context of modern life. The relations of political parties, nations, races and economic classes did exceed boundaries; thousands of commercial and monetary contacts bound humans across the world. But none of this had put into question the importance of states. No new realm of society was needed to capture such activities.[25]

Despite such criticisms, Bluntschli appreciated Mohl's not joining the socialists and the communists in an effort, as he saw it, to collapse the prevailing legal system but to give legal articulation to the real relations (*reale Verhältnisse*) of the modern world.[26] In his *Modern International Law of the Civilised World* (1868), Bluntschli sought to do the same by coming over again to the way international law was both a law between states, an aspect of their external public law, as well as the law of the human community (*menschliche Rechtsgenossenschaft*).[27] It did not emerge from state will but from an informal legal consciousness of humanity

[24] For Bluntschli's brief assessment of Mohl as a great scholar and a warm-hearted and friendly colleague, though somewhat lacking in statesmanlike qualities, see Johann Caspar Bluntschli, *Denkwürdiges aus meinem Leben* (3 vols., Nördlingen, Beck 1884), III, 26. For his part, Mohl regarded Bluntschli as a justly famous scholar and a skilful politician who, nevertheless, had many conflicting traits and engaged in too many disparate political activities to the cost of his ability to concentrate and produce in later years research of the same quality as earlier. Like many others, Mohl critiqued Bluntschli's dependence on the eccentric theories of the psychologist–philosopher, Friedrich Röhmer, including the latter's "insane" (*verrückt*) analogy between the state and the human body with its organs. Mohl regarded him nevertheless as the most efficient member of the *Landtag* during the period 1861–70. Robert von Mohl, *Lebenserinnerungen* (D. Kerle ed., Stuttgart, Deutsche Verlags-Anstalt 1902), 153–4.

[25] Johann Caspar Bluntschli, 'Über die neuen Begründungen der Gesellschaft und des Gesellschaftsrecht', 3 *Kritische Überschau der deutschen Gesetzgebung und Rechtswissenschaft* (1856), 256–61.

[26] Ibid., 247–8.

[27] Johann Caspar Bluntschli, *Das moderne Völkerrecht als Rechtbuch gestellt* (Nördlingen, Beck 1868), I § 1 (53).

(*Gemeinbewusstsein der Menschheit*).[28] Whereas Mohl tried to capture the novel forms of informal interaction by the vocabulary of "society", Bluntschli employed the idealist and psychologically tainted language of a "collective consciousness". While Mohl's *Gesellschaft* was a horizontal sphere of interaction between separate types of interest-formation and collective pursuit, Bluntschli's *Bewusstsein* projected a vertical hierarchy where from the totality of humanity a part emerged – the civilised part – to rule over the rest.[29] If Mohl's proposal was for a law emerging more or less spontaneously from the operations of international society, Blunstchli's international law was a product of what he called civilisation, authoritatively represented by the Christian nations.[30]

The contrast between Mohl and Bluntschli was a divergence between two ways of reacting to what was understood as an increasingly international modernity. They illustrated two types of legal *bricolage.* Both used materials that had been "lying around" in their political and intellectual milieu for some time and with which it might be possible to advance beyond an ahistorical, antimodern natural law. Mohl believed that it was possible to capture the spontaneous transformations of the present by a vocabulary of society, an inheritance of the attitudes that had led him to the Frankfurt Parliament in 1848. Bluntschli saw no reason to imagine society as the proper language for the analysis of modern law. Instead, he believed it was important to follow what he called the legal consciousness (*Rechtsbewusstsein*) of human communities. This was equally fluid as society but instead of focusing on the relations between human groups would highlight their inner lives, attitudes and ideologies. Bluntschli would be the more successful of the two.

The years of the mid-century had been those of great domestic and international upheaval. The Franco-Prussian War had suggested to Bluntschli that even civilised countries would occasionally descend to meaningless violence. There was therefore reason to guide them back to the right path, to highlight their common Christian heritage and to take seriously the humanitarian values they kept promoting officially. Blunstchli was a man of action (even excessively so, Mohl recounts in his memoirs) and interested in professional cooperation for shared causes.

28 Ibid., I § 3–4 (54–5).

29 "Die civilisierten Nationen sind . . . die Ordner und Vertreter des Völkerrechts", ibid., I § 5 (55).

30 This did not mean that international law would have a religious content, Bluntschli stressed. Its basis was "human nature" and its objective a human world order, to be brought about by the work of states, science and practice. Ibid., I § 6 (55).

It was therefore with great pleasure, as he put it, that he could write to the Grand Duke of Baden on 3 March 1873 about an initiative raised among a group of lawyers from Germany, Belgium, Italy, France, the Netherlands, United States and Switzerland to set up an international academy of international law: "Science alone may not have the power to influence the excited passions of peoples and governments and to direct them to the obedience of international law. However, scientifically grounded and clearly expressed legal conscience may have a positive influence on the peaceful relations of nations."[31] A few days later Bluntschli corresponded with a younger acquaintance, the Belgian advocate, Gustave Rolin-Jaequemyns, proposing the establishment of two institutions: an international academy as well as a society of international law. A meeting was then held in Heidelberg in May 1873 where Bluntschli, Rolin and a British colleague, John Westlake, decided that it would be task of such a body to serve as an "organ of the legal consciousness of the civilized world".[32]

[31] Bluntschli to Great Duke William, 3 March 1873, in *Denkwürdiges* III, 329.
[32] Ibid., 331.

# *Bibliography*

## Documents and Cases


'A justification for Planting in Virginia', in S. M. Kingsbury (ed.), *Records of the Virginia Company of London* (4 vols, Washington, US Government Printing Office 1933), III, 1–3

'Act for the Continuing in the East India Company for a Further Term, the Possession of the Territories in India, 53 Geo III c. 155, (East India Act 1813)', in *The Law Relating to India and the East India Company* (2nd edn, London, Allen 1847), 167–8

'Act to Regulate Trade in China and India, 28 August 1833', in *The Law Relating to India and the East India Company* (2nd ed., London, Allen 1847), 439–42

'Acte de l'Establissement de la Compagnie des Indes Occidentales (22 May 1664)', in *Édits, Ordonnances royaux, déclarations et arrêts du Conseil d'État du roi concernant le Canada* (Québec, Desbarats 1803), 29–39

'Acte pour l'établissement de la Compagnie des cent Associés pour le commerce du Canada (29 April 1627)', in *Édits, Ordonnances royaux, déclaration et arrêts du Conseil d'État du roi concernant le Canada* (Québec, Desbarats 1803), 1–16

'Allegacio domini pape Bonifacii pro confirmando rege Romanorum Alberto', *Monumenta Germaniae Historica* (MGH), *Constitutiones*, IV (Hanover, Hahn 1906), No. 173, 139–40

'An Act to Remove Doubts as to the Exercise of Power and Jurisdiction by Her Majesty within Diverse Countries and Places out of Her Majesty's Dominion (Foreign Jurisdiction Act)', 6 & 7 Vict., c. 94 (1843)

'Année 1731', in Charles-Irénée Castel de Saint-Pierre, *Annales Politiques de feu monsieur Charles Irenée Castel, abbé de St. Pierre*, tome II (2 tomes, London 1758), 286–94

'Articles d'association', in Jean-Baptiste Du Tertre, *Histoire générale des antilles habitées par les françois*, tome I (4 tomes, Paris 1667–71), 8–11

'Attorney General 29 February 1704', State Papers Colonial Series 1704, www.british-history.ac.uk/cal-state-papers/colonial/america-west-indies/vol22/pp41-62

*Blankard* v. *Galdy* in William Salkeld (ed.), *Reports of Cases Adjudicated in the Court of King's Bench* (3 vols., London, Strahan 1795), II 411–12 and 90 ER 1089 (1693)

'Body of Liberties (1641)', history.hanover.edu/texts/masslib.html

*Campbell v. Hall* 98 ER 1045 (1774)

'*Case of Impositions* (Bates' case 1606)', *Cobbett's Complete Collection of State Trials*, II (33 vols., T. B. Howell ed., London, Hansard 1816), 371–533

'*Case of the King's Prerogative in Saltpetre* (1607)', *The Reports of Sir Edward Coke in Thirteen Parts. A New Edition in Six Volumes*, VI (London, Butterworths 1826), Part XII, 206–10

'*Case of Monopolies* (*Darcy* v. *Allein*)', *The Reports of Sir Edward Coke in Thirteen Parts. A New Edition in Six Volumes*, VI (London, Butterworths 1826), Part XI, 159–210

'*Case of Ship Money*' (*Proceedings in the Case of Ship-Money, between the King and Mr John Hampden Esq*), *Cobbett's Complete Collection of State Trials*, III (33 vols., T. B. Howell, ed., London, Hansard 1809), 826–1314

'*Case of the Postnati*' (Calvin's case, 1607)', *Cobbett's Complete Collection of State Trials*, II (33 vols. T. B. Howell ed., London, Hansard 1816), 559–697

Charter for the Province of Pennsylvania; 20 February 1681', avalon.law.yale.edu/17th_century/pa01.asp

'Charter Granted by Queen Elizabeth, 31 December 1600', in John Shaw (ed.), *Charters Relating to the East India Company from 1600 to 1761; reprinted from a former collection with some additions and a preface for the Government of Madras* (Madras, Hill 1887), 1–14

'Charter Granted to the EIC by Charles II on 9 August 1683', in John Shaw (ed.), *Charters Relating to the East India Company from 1600 to 1761; reprinted from a former collection with some additions and a preface for the Government of Madras* (Madras, Hill 1887), 69–73

'Charter Granted to the EIC by James II on 12 April 1686', in John Shaw (ed.), *Charters Relating to the East India Company from 1600 to 1761; reprinted from a former collection with some additions and a preface for the Government of Madras* (Madras, Hill 1887), 74–83

'Charter Granted to the EIC relating to the Island of Bombay, 27 March 1669', in John Shaw (ed.), *Charters Relating to the East India Company from 1600 to 1761; reprinted from a former collection with some additions and a preface for the Government of Madras* (Madras, Hill 1887), 47–56

'Charter in Favor of Sir William Alexander, 1621', in Edmund Slafter et al., *Sir William Alexander and American Colonization* (Boston, Wilson 1873), 127–48

'Charter of 12 April 1686 by James II', in John Shaw (ed.), *Charters Relating to the East India Company from 1600 to 1761; reprinted from a former collection with some additions and a preface for the Government of Madras* (Madras, Hill 1887), 74–83

'Charter of 31 May 1609', in John Shaw (ed.), *Charters Relating to the East India Company from 1600 to 1761; reprinted from a former collection with some additions and a preface for the Government of Madras* (Madras, Hill 1887), 16–31

'Charter of Maryland; 20 June 1632', avalon.law.yale.edu/17th_century/ma01.asp

'Charter of New England, 3 November 1620', avalon.law.yale.edu/17th_century/mass01.asp

'Charter of Rhode Island and Providence Plantations; 15 July 1663', avalon.law.yale.edu/17th_century/ri04.asp

'Charter of Virginia; April 10, 1606', avalon.law.yale.edu/17th_century/va01.asp

*Cobbett's Complete Collection of State Trials* (T. B. Howell ed., 33 vols, London, Hansard 1816–28)

'Commission 31 October 1626', in Baptiste Du Tertre, *Histoire générale des antilles habitées par les françois*, tome I (4 tomes, Paris 1667–71), 11–14

'Commission du Roy au sieur de Monts, 8 November 1603', in Marc Lescarbot, *Histoire de la nouvelle France* (2 vols, continuous pagination Paris, Peier 1617), II, 416–24

'Constitution of 22 August 1795 (accepted in a plebiscite of 23 September 1795)', www.conseil-constitutionnel.fr/les-constitutions-dans-l-histoire/constitution-du-5-fructidor-an-iii

'Constitution of the Year VIII (13 December 1799)', www.conseil-constitutionnel.fr/les-constitutions-dans-l-histoire/constitution-du-22-frimaire-an-viii

'Contrat du retablissment du Compagnie des Isles d'Amérique avec les Articles accordez par sa Majesté aux Seigneurs Associéz', in Jean-Baptiste Du Tertre, *Histoire générale des antilles habitées par les françois*, tome I (4 tomes, Paris 1667–71), 46–50

'Contrat pour l'etablissment des français à l'île Sant-Cristophe', in Pierre Margry, *Belain d'Estambuc et les normans aux Antilles* (3 tomes, Paris, Faure 1863), I, 99

'Déclaration de l'assemblée nationale', 29 décembre 1792, in Condorcet, *Oeuvres de Condorcet*, tôme 10 (Paris, Firmin 1847), 253

'Déclaration du roi, 8 February 1605', in Marc Lescarbot, *Histoire de la nouvelle France* (Paris, Perier 1617), 427–31

'Declaration of Independence, 4 July 1776', www.archives.gov/founding-docs/declaration-transcript.

'Declaration of Rights' 1689, avalon.law.yale.edu/17th.century/england.asp

'Déclaration sur affranchissements, 24 octobre 1713', in M. Petit, *Traité sur le gouvernement des esclaves* (2 tomes, Paris, Knapen 1777), I, 61–4

'Declaratory Act of 18 March 1766', www.stamp-act-history.com/documents/1766-declaratory-act-original-text/

'Decree of 21 November 1806 (published 5 December)', 46 *Le Moniteur universel* No. 339 (1809)

'Décret de Déclaration de paix au monde. Article 4', *Archives parlementaires de 1787 à 1860* (Première série 1787–1799, Paris, Dupont 1885), XV, 661–2, fr.wikipedia.org/wiki/Décret_de_Déclaration_de_paix_au_monde.

'Decretal of Gregorius IX', Title XXIII, in Aemelius Friedberg (ed.), *Corpus Iuris Canonici II* (Graz, Academische Druck- und Verlagsanstalt 1959), 353–9

'Definitive Treaty of Paris, 30 May 1814', www.napoleon-series.org/research/government/diplomatic/c_paris1.html

'Draft Declaration of Rights and Duties to the Constitution of 1793', in M. Bouloiseau et al. (eds), *Oeuvres de Maximilien Robespierre*, tome IX (Presses Universitaires de France 1958), 469

'East India Company Act, 1784 (24 Geo III, c. 25)', in *A Collection of Charters and Statutes Relating to the East India Company* (London, Eyre & Strahan 1817), 211–37

'East India Company Act, 1773 (13 Geo III c. 63)', in *A Collection of Charters and Statutes Relating to the East India Company* (London, Eyre & Strahan 1817), 144–55

East India Company Act, 1813 (53 Geo III c. 155), in *The Law Relating to India and the East India Company* (2nd ed., London, Allen 1741), 167–99

*East India Company* v. *Sandys* (Sandys case), *Cobbett's Complete Collection of State Trials, 1680–1685*, vol. X (London, Hansard 1811), 371–555

'Ecclesiastical Appeals Act 1532, 24 Hen. 8 c. 12 (Eng.)'

'Edict du Roy en faveur de la Compagnie des îles de l'Amérique, March 1642', in Jean-Baptiste Du Tertre, *Histoire générale des antilles habitées par les françois*, tome I (4 tomes, Paris 1667–71), 209–15

'Édit de Création du Conseil Supérieur du Québec' in *Édits, Ordonannces royaux, déclarations et arrêts du Conseil d'Etat du Roi concernant le Canada* (3 tomes, Québec, Desbarats 1803), I, 21–3

'Edit du Roy contenant le pouvoir et Commission donné par sa majesté au Marquise de Cottenmeal ed de la Roche, 12 January 1598' in Marc Lescarbot, *Histoire de la nouvelle France* (3 tomes, nouvelle édition, Paris, Tross 1866), II, 398–405

'Édit en forme des Lettres-Patentes pour l'Etablissment de la Compagnie Royale de Saint-Domingue (Septembre 1698)', in Médéric Louis Elie Moreau de Saint-Méry, *Loix et constitutions des colonies françoises de l'Amérique sous le vent*, tome 1 (6 tomes, Paris, Quillau 1784), 610–18

'Edit portant l'Etablissment d'une Compagnie des Isles Occidentales (28 May and 31 July 1664)', Art XXI, in Médéric Louis Elie Moreau de Saint-Méry, *Loix et constitutions des colonies françoises de l'Amérique sous le vent*, tome 1 (6 tomes, Paris, Quillau 1784), 100–14

'Encyclica in Forma Maiori, 29 June 1312', in *Monumenta Germaniae Historica* (MGH), *Legum Sectio* IV, Part IV/2 (Hanover, 1909–11), No. 801, 322–6

'First Letters Patent Granted to John Cabot and his Sons, 5 March 1496', in James A. Williamson (ed.), *The Cabot Voyages and Bristol Discovery under Henry VII* (Cambridge University Press 1962), 204–5

'Frédéric II, Considérations sur l'état présent du corps politique de l'Europe', in *Oeuvres posthumes de Frédéric II, Roi de Prusse*, tome VI (Amsterdam 1789), 61–102

Government of India Act 1833 (4 Will IV c. 85), in *The Law Relating to India and the East India Company* (2nd ed., London, Allen 1841), 439–42

'Grant of the Province of Maine, 1639', in Francis Newton Thorpe (ed.), *The Federal and State Constitutions, Colonial Charters, and Other Organic Laws of the States, Territories, and Colonies Now or Heretofore Forming the United States of America* (7 vols, Washington, Government Printing Office 1909), III, 1625–37, avalon.law.yale.edu/17th_century/me02.asp

'Great Case of Monopolies' (Sandys case, 1683), in *Cobbett's Complete Collection of State Trials*, vol. X (33 vols., T.B. Howell ed., London, Hansard 1811), 371–554

'L'Ordonnance du roi, qui défend le commerce étranger aux isles (10 juin 1670)', in Médéric Louis Elie Moreau de Saint-Méry, *Loix et constitutions des colonies françoises de l'Amérique sous le vent*, tome 1 (6 tomes, Paris, Quillau 1784), 195–7

'Lawes Divine, Morall and Martiall' (Laws of 1612), www.encyclopediavirginia.org/Lawes_Divine_Morall_and_Martiall

'Letter of Lord Palmerston to Sir Henry Pottinger', in Hosea B. Morse, *The International Relations of the Chinese Empire* (3 vols, London 1910), I, Appendix K (656)

'Letters of Patent by Philip V on 5 November 1712', in J. Almon, *A Collection of All the Treaties of Peace, Alliance and Commerce between Great-Britain and Other Powers*, vol. I *(1688–1727)* (2 vols, London, Almon 1772), 110–31

'Letters Patent 8 March 1635', in Jean-Baptiste Du Tertre, *Histoire générale des antilles habitées par les françois*, tome I (4 tomes, Paris 1667–71), 57–9

'Letters Patent Granted to Richard Warde et al. 19 March 1501', in James A. Williamson (ed.), *The Cabot Voyages and Bristol Discovery under Henry VII* (Cambridge University Press 1962), 235

'Letters Patent Granted to the EIC relating to the Island of St. Helena, 16 December 1673', in John Shaw (ed.), *Charters Relating to the East India Company from 1600 to 1761; reprinted from a former collection with some additions and a preface for the Government of Madras* (Madras, Hill 1887), 59–61

'Letters Patent to Sir Humphrey Gilbert, 1578,' in Francis Newton Thorpe (ed.), *The Federal and State Constitutions, Colonial Charters, and Other Organic Laws of the States, Territories, and Colonies Now or Heretofore Forming the United States of America*, vol. 1 (Washington, Government Printing Office 1909), 49–52

'Letters Patents Granted on 3 April 1661 by Charles II, in John Shaw (ed.), *Charters Relating to the East India Company from 1600 to 1761; reprinted from a former collection with some additions and a preface for the Government of Madras* (Madras, Hill 1887), 32–46

'Lettres Patentes du Roy, en forme d'Edit concernant le commerce étrangère aus Isles & Colonies d'Amérique, Octobre 1727 (Paris, impremie royale 1727)', in Médéric Louis Elie Moreau de Saint-Méry, *Loix et constitutions des colonies françoises de l'Amérique sous le vent*, tome 1 (6 tomes, Paris, Quillau 1784), 225–36, eco.canadiana.ca/view/oocihm.43974/3?r=0&s=1

'Lettres-Patentes accordant au sieur Crozat, privilege pour le commerce au Louisiane', Isambert, *Recueil général des Anciennes loix françaises*, tome XX *(1687–1715)* (Paris, Bélin 1830), 576–82

'Lettres-Patentes portant règlement pour le commerce des Colonies Françoises, du mois d'Avril 1717', in Médéric Louis Elie Moreau de Saint-Méry, *Loix et constitutions des colonies françoises de l'Amérique sous le vent*, tome 1 (6 tomes, Paris, Quillau 1784), 557–65

'Lettres-Patentes sur l'Etablissement d'une Compagnie pour le Commerce Exclusif aux Côtes d'Afrique (Compagnie de Guinée), January 1685, Art XVI', in Médéric Louis Elie Moreau de Saint-Méry, *Loix et constitutions des colonies françoises de l'Amérique sous le vent*, tome 1 (6 tomes, Paris, Quillau 1784), 409–14

'Lettres-Patentes, portant établissement d'une nouvelle Compagnie Royale du Sénégal (Mars 1696)', in Médéric Louis Elie Moreau de Saint-Méry, *Loix et constitutions des colonies françoises de l'Amérique sous le vent*, tome 1 (6 tomes, Paris, Quillau 1784), 546–52

'Loi relative à la traite des noirs et au régime des colonies', 30 *Floréal An X* (20 May 1802), mjp.univ-perp.fr/france/1802/esclavage.htm

'Lord Aberdeen to Sir Henry Pottinger 4 November 1841', in Hosea B. Morse, *The International Relations of the Chinese Empire* (3 vols, London 1910), I, Appendix M

'Lord Palmerston to Plenipotentiaries in China, 9 January 1841', in Hosea B. Morse, *The International Relations of the Chinese Empire* (3 vols, London 1910), I, Appendix E

'Lord Palmerston to the Minister of the Emperor of China, 20 February 1840', in Hosea B. Morse, *The International Relations of the Chinese Empire* (3 vols, London 1910), I, Appendix A

'Mémoire sur le commerce de Jean-Baptiste Colbert (ministre d'état) à Louis XIV (roi de France), du 03 août 1664', in *Lettres, instructions et mémoires de Colbert, publiées par Pierre Clément*, II: 1 partie (Paris, Imprimerie impériale 1863), 263–72

Merlin de Douai, Philippe-Antoine. 'Rapport sur les droits seigneuriaux des princes d'Allemagne en Alsace, 28 octobre 1790', *Archives Parlementaires de 1787 à 1860 – Première série* (1787–1799, Paris, Dupont 1885), XX, 75–84

'New Scotland Charter, 1621', gutenberg.ca/ebooks/frasera-novascotiaroyal charter/frasera-novascotiaroyalcharter-00-h-dir/frasera-novascotiaroyal charter-00-h.html

*Miller* v. *Race*, in *Notes of Cases Argued, and Adjudged, in the Court of King's Bench, and of Some Determined in the Other High Courts [1753–1759]* (2 vols., London, Clarke 1825), II 189–202

'Notes on Colonisation by Richard Hakluyt, Lawyer, 1578', in E. G. R. Taylor (ed.), *The Original Writings & Correspondence of the two Richard Hakluyts* (2 vols. London, Hakluyt Society 1935), I Document 18

'Opening Address of Hugo Grotius held before King James I/VI at the Maritime and Colonial Conference in London on 6 April 1613', in Peter Borschberg, *Hugo Grotius, The Portuguese and Free Trade in the East Indies* (National University of Singapore Press 2011), 259–67

'Ordonnance sur la passage des Esclaves en France, 15 décembre 1738', in M. Petit, *Traité sur le gouvernement des esclaves* (2 tomes, Paris, Knapen 1777), I, 130–7

*Pillans* v. *Van Mierop*, 97 ER 1035 (1765)

'Report by Merlin de Douai 7 September 1793', in *Le Moniteur universel*, XXVI No. 11 & 13 (85–8, 111)

'Report on Legal Education', 7 *Law Magazine and Review: A Quarterly Review of Jurisprudence* (1847), 31–45

'Responsio Philippi Regis Franciae', *Monumenta Germaniae Historica* (MGH), *Legum Sectio* IV, IV/2 (Hanover 1909–11), No. 811 (812)

Salkeld, William, *Reports of Cases Adjudged in the Court of King's Bench* (3 vols, London, Strahan 1795)

*Somerset* v. *Stewart*, 98 ER 499 (1772)

"The Letters Patents, or Privileges Granted by her Majestie to Sir Edward Osborne…', in Richard Hakluyt, *Principall Navigations, Voyages, Traffiques and Discoveries of the English Nation*, vol. 13 (University of Adelaide ebooks), 192–202

'The Second Letters Patent… (7 January 1592)', in Richard Hakluyt, *Principall Navigations, Voyages, Traffiques and Discoveries of the English Nation*, vol. 13 (University of Adelaide ebooks), 296–303

'Tract by Sir Thomas Smith on the Colonisation of Ards in County of Down' ["A Letter sent by T. B. Gentleman…"], printed as Appendix to George Hill, *An Historical Account of the Macdonnells of Antrim* (Belfast, Archer 1873)

'Traité d'Amitié, de Confédération, de Commerce & de Navigation, 27 avril 1662', in Jean Dumont, *Corps universel diplomatique du droit des gens*, VI/2 (Amsterdam, Brunel 1728), 412–16

'Treaty between France and Great Britain, 31 March 1713, Articles X–XIII', in J. Almon, *A Collection of All the Treaties of Peace, Alliance and Commerce between Great Britain and Other Powers*, vol. I *(1688–1727)* (2 vols, London, Almon 1772), 136–8

'Treaty between China and Britain, 29 August 1842' (Treaty of Nanking), *Consolidated Treaty Series*, vol. 93, 465–74

'Treaty of Amity Commerce and Navigation, between His Britannic Majesty; and The United States of America, 19 November 1794', *Consolidated Treaty Series*, vol. 52, 243–72

'Treaty of Amity, Commerce and Navigation between Great Britain and Rio de la Plata (2 February 1825)', in *Consolidated Treaty Series*, vol. 75, 75–84

'Treaty of Osnabrück', in Wilhelm G. Grewe (ed.), *Fontes Historiae Iuris Gentium. Sources Relating to the History of the Law of Nations* (4 vols, Berlin, New York, Walter de Gruyter 1988–92), 2, 188–201

'Treaty of Peace, Friendship and Commerce, Between Great Brian and China (Treaty of Tientsin), 26 June 1858', in *Consolidated Treaty Series*, vol. 119, 163–87

'Treaty on Amity, Commerce and Navigation between Colombia and Great Britain of 18 April 1825', in *Consolidated Treaty Series*, vol. 75, 195–206

*Triquet* v. *Bath*, 97 ER 936 (1764)

*Unam sanctam* (18 November 1302), translation in Internet Medieval Sourcebook, www.fordham.edu/halsall/source/b8-unam.html

Williams, William Peere, *Reports of Cases Argued and Determined in the High Court of Chancery* (3 vols, London, Gray's Inn 1740–9)

## Literary Sources

Abicht, Johann Heinrich. *Neues System eines aus der Menschheit entwickelten Naturrechts* (Bayreuth, Erben 1792)

Abulafia, David. *The Discovery of Mankind. Atlantic Encounters in the Age of Columbus* (Yale University Press 2008)

Achenwall, Gottfried. *Anzeige seiner neuen Vorlesungen über die grosse europäische Staatenhändel des XVII–XVIII Jahrhundert, das ist über die Geschichte des europäischen Staaten-Systems seit 1600. Teil II der Europäischen Geschichte* (Göttingen 1755)

*Die Staatsklugheit nach ihren ersten Grundsätzen* (Göttingen, Vandenhoeck 1761)

*Geschichte der allgemeineren europäischen Staatshändel des vorigen und jetzigen Jahrhunderts im Grundrisse* (4th edn, Göttingen, Vandenhoeck 1779)

*Geschichte der heutigen vornehmsten europäischen Staaten im Grundrisse* (5th edn, Göttingen, Vandenhoeck 1779)

*Herrn Gottfried Achenwalls Anmerkungen über Nordamerika und über dasige Grosbritannische Colonien* (from the oral account of Dr Franklin, Frankfurt und Leipzig 1769)

*Staatsverfassung des heutigen europeischen Staaten im Grundrisse* (4th edn, Göttingen, Vandenhoeck 1762)

*Staatsverfassung der heutigen vornehmsten europäischen Reiche im Grundrisse* (4th ed., Göttingen, Vandenhoeck 1762)

Acher, Jean. 'Notes sur le droit savant au moyen age', 30 *Nouvelle Revue Historique de Droit Français & Etranger* (1906), 125–214

Acosta, José de. *Natural and Moral History of the Indies* (J. E. Mangan ed., W. D. Mignolo intro., F. M. López-Morillas trans., Duke University Press 2002 [1590])

Adair, E. R. 'The Law of Nations and the Common Law of England. A Study of 7 Anne Cap 12', 2 *Cambridge Historical Journal* (1928), 290–7

Adam, Ulrich. *The Political Economy of J. H. G. Justi* (Frankfurt am Main, Peter Lang 2006)

Adorno, Francesco Paolo. *Le discipline de l'amour. Pascal, Port-Royal et la politique* (Paris, Kimé 2010)

Agamben, Giorgio. *Le règne et la gloire. Homo Sacer II, 2* (Paris, Seuil 2008)

Ahn, Doohwan. 'The Anglo-French Treaty of Commerce of 1713. Tory Trade Politics and the Question of Dutch Decline', 36 *History of European Ideas* (2010), 167–80

Alimento, Antonella. 'Competition, True Patriotism and Colonial Interest. Forbonnais' Vision of Neutrality and Trade', www.helsinki.fi/collegium/e-series/volumes/volume_10/010_05_Alimento_2011.pdf

Allais, Lucy. 'Kant's Racism', 45 *Philosophical Papers* (2016), 1–36

Allott, Philip. *The Health of Nations. Society and Law Beyond the State* (Cambridge University Press 2002)

Alonso Getino, Luis G. *El maestro Francisco de Vitoria. Su vida, su doctrina e influencia* (Madrid, Imprenta católica 1930)

Althusius, Johannes. *Politica* (Frederick S. Carney ed. & trans., Indianapolis, Liberty Fund 1996 [1603])

Althusser, Louis. *Montesquieu. La politique et l'histoire* (Paris, Presses Universitaires de France 1959)

Ambrosetti, Giovanni. *Il diritto naturale della riforma catolica* (Milano, Giuffre 1951)

Ammirato, Scipione. *Discorsi sopra Cornelio Tacito nuovamente posti in luce* (Florence, Giunti 1594)

Anderson, Adam. *An Historical and Chronological Deduction of the Origin of Commerce* (London, Walton 1778)

Anderson, M. S. *The Origins of the Modern European State System 1494–1618* (London, Longman 1998)

Anderson, Perry. *Lineages of the Absolutist State* (London, Verso 1974)

Andrews, Charles M. *British Committees, Commissions, and Councils of Trade and Plantations, 1622–1675* (Baltimore, Johns Hopkins Press 1908)

Andrews, Kenneth R. *English Privateering Voyages to the West Indies 1588–1595* (Cambridge University Press 1959)

*Trade, Plunder and Settlement. Maritime Enterprise and the Genesis of the British Empire, 1480–1630* (Cambridge University Press 1984)

Anghie, Antony. 'Vattel and Colonialism. Some Preliminary Observations', in Peter Haggenmacher & Vincent Chetail (eds), *Vattel's International Law in a 21st Century Perspective* (Geneva, Nijhoff 2011), 237–53

*Imperialism, Sovereignty, and the Making of International Law* (Cambridge University Press 2005)

[Anynomous] 'Before There Were Clerics', in R. W. Dyson (ed.), *Three Royalist Tracts 1296–1302* (Bristol, Thoemmes 1999), 2–11

[Anynomous] "A Debate between a Cleric and a Knight", in R.W. Dyson (ed.), *Three Royalist Tracts 1296–1302* (Bristol, Thoemmes 1999), 12–45

[Anonymous] 'International Law, No. 1', 9 *Law Review and Quarterly Journal of British and Foreign Jurisprudence* (1849), 22–49; No. 2 ibid. (1849), 260–87; No. 3, 10 ibid. (1849), 261–83; No. 4, 11 ibid. (1850), 26–41; No. 5 ibid (1850), 272–91

Anton, A. E. 'The Introduction into English Practice of the Continental Theories of Conflict of Laws', 4 *International & Comparative Law Quarterly* (1956), 534–41

Antonetti, Guy. 'Traditionalistes et novateurs à la faculté des droits de Paris au XVIIIe siècle', 2 *Annales d'histoire des facultés de droit* (1985), 37–50

Appleby, Joyce. *Economic Thought and Ideology in Seventeenth-Century England* (Princeton University Press 1978)

Aquinas, Thomas. *Political Writings* (R. W. Dyson ed., Cambridge University Press 2002)

Araújo, André de Melo. *Weltgeschichte in Göttingen. Eine Studie über das spätaufklärische universalhistorische Denken 1756–1815* (Bielefeld, Transcript 2012)

Arcidiacono, Bruno. 'De la balance politique et de ses rapports avec le droit des gens. Vattel, la "guerre pour l'équilibre" et le système européen', in Vincent Chetail & Peter Haggenmacher (eds), *Vattel's International Law in a XXIst Century Perspective* (Geneva, Nijhoff 2011), 77–100

Arendt, Hannah. *Lectures on Kant's Political Philosophy* (R. Beiner ed., The University of Chicago Press 1992)

Arici, Fausto. 'Il principe tra mediazione e supplenza', in Fausto Arici & Franco Todescan (eds), *Iustus ordo e ordine della natura. Sacra doctrina e saperi politici fra XVI e XVIII secolo* (Padova, CEDAM 2007), 217–44

Aristotle. 'The Politics', in *The Politics and The Constitution of Athens* (S. Everton, ed., Cambridge University Press 1996), 9–208

*The Nicomachean Ethics* (D. Ross ed., Oxford University Press 1980)

Armitage, David. 'John Locke, Carolina and the *Two Treatises of Government*', in David Armitage, *Foundations of Modern International Thought* (Cambridge University Press 2013), 90–113

'John Locke's International Thought', in David Armitage, *Foundations of Modern International Thought* (Cambridge University Press 2013), 75–89

*The Declaration of Independence. A Global History* (Harvard University Press 2008)

*The Ideological Origins of the British Empire* (Cambridge University Press 2000)

Arneil, Barbara. *John Locke and America. The Defence of English Colonialism* (Oxford University Press 1996)

Arnisaeus, Henning. *Doctrina politica in genuinam methodum qua est Aristotelis reducta* (editio nova, Amsterdam, Elsevier 1651)

Arrighi, Giovanni. *The Long Twentieth-Century. Money, Power, and the Origins of Our Times* (London, Verso 1994)

Arroy, Besian. *Questions decidées sur la Justice des armes de Roi de France* (Paris, Loyson 1634)

Artonne, André. *Le mouvement de 1314 et les Chartes provincials du 1315* (Paris, Alcan 1912)

Asbach, Olaf. 'L'abbé de Saint-Pierre et les transformations de la république des lettres au XVIIIe siècle', in Carole Dornier & Claudine Poulouin Dornier et al. (eds), *Les Projets de l'abbé Castel de Saint-Pierre (1658–1743)* (Presses Universitaires de Caen 2011), 51–62

*Staat und Politik zwischen Absolutismus und Aufklärung* (Hildesheim, Olms 2005)

Aubert, Jean-Marie. *Le droit Romain dans l'oeuvre de Saint Thomas* (Paris, Vrin 1955)

Aubery, Antoine. *Des justes pretensions du Roi sur l'Empire* (Paris, Bertier 1667)

Austin, John. *Lectures on Jurisprudence, of the Philosophy of Positive Law* (4th edn, R. Campbell ed., London, Murray 1873 [1869])

*The Province of Jurisprudence Determined* (H. L. A. Hart intro., Indianapolis, Hackett 1998 [1832])

Avenel, G. *Richelieu et la monarchie absolue* (Paris, Plon 1895)

Avineri, Shlomo. *Hegel's Theory of the Modern State* (Cambridge University Press 1972)

Avramescu, Catalin. *An Intellectual History of Cannibalism* (A. I. Blyth trans., Princeton University Press 2009)

Ayala de, Balthasar. *De jure et officiis bellicis et disciplina militarii libri tres* (Oxford University Press 1912 [1582])

Azo, *Ad singulas leges XII librorum Codicis Iustinianei commentarius et magnus apparatus nunquam* (Paris 1577)

Azpilcueta Navarro, Martín de. 'Notabile III in Relectio Cap. Novit. De Iudic', in Martín de Azpilcueta Navarro, *Commentarius utilis in rubricam de iudiciis* (Rome, Tornerii & Bericchia 1585), 105–66

*Commentaria in septem distinctiones de paenitentia* (Rome, Tornentia 1586)

'Commentary on the Resolution of Money', in Stephen J Grabill (ed.), *Sourcebook in Late Scholastic Monetary Theory* (New York, Lexington 2007), 21–107

*Manual de confessores y penitentes* (Toledo, Ferrer 1554)

Bachelard, Gaston. *The Formation of the Scientific Mind* (M. Macallester Jones intro. & trans., Manchester, Clinamen 2002)

Bachofen, Blaise. 'Les raisons de la guerre. La raison dans la guerre. Une lecture des Principes du droit de la guerre', in Bruno Bernardi & Gabriella Silvestrini (eds), *Jean-Jacques Rousseau. Principes du droit de la guerre. Ecrits sur la paix perpetuelle* (Paris, Vrin 2008), 131–92

Backhouse, Roger E. *The Ordinary Business of Life. A History of Economics from the Ancient World to the Twenty-First century* (Princeton University Press 2002)

Bacon, Francis. 'Considerations touching a War with Spain', in *Works of Francis Bacon, Baron of Verulam in Ten Volumes* (London, Baynes and Son 1824), III, 499–534

'Of Empire', in John Pitcher (ed.), *The Essays* (Harmondsworth, Penguin 1985), 115–20

'Advertisment touching a Holy War', in *Works of Francis Bacon, Baron of Verulam in Ten Volumes* (London, Baynes and Son 1824), III 467–92

Baeck, Louis. 'Monetarismo y teorías del desarrollo en la Península Ibérica en los siglos XVI–XVII, in S. J. Gómez Camacho & Ricardo Robledo (eds), *El pensamiento económico en la escuela de Salamanca*, (Ediciones Universidad de Salamanca 1998), 165–204

Bailyn, Bernard. *The Barbarous Years. The Conflict of Civilizations 1600–1675* (New York, Vintage 2012)

Bain, William. 'Saving the Innocent, Then and Now. Vitoria, Dominion and World Order', 34 *History of Political Thought* (2013), 588–613

Baker, J. H. 'The Law Merchant and the Common Law before 1700', 38 *Cambridge Law Journal* (1979), 295–322

Baker, Keith M. 'Enlightenment Idioms, Old Regime Discourses, and Revolutionary Improvisation', in Thomas E. Kaiser & Dale K. van Kley (eds), *From Deficit to Deluge. The Origins of the French Revolution* (Stanford University Press 2011), 165–97

'Political Languages of the French Revolution', in Mark Goldie & Robert Wokler (eds), *The Cambridge History of Eighteenth-Century Political Thought* (Cambridge University Press 2006), 626–59

*Inventing the French Revolution* (Cambridge University Press 1990)

Bandelier, André. 'De Berlin à Neuchâtel. La genèse du *Droit des gens* d'Emer de Vattel', in M. Fontius & H. Holzey (eds), *Schweizer im Berlin des 18. Jahrhunderts* (Berlin, Akademie 1996), 45–56

Banks, Kenneth J. 'Financiers, Factors, and French Proprietary Companies in West Africa 1664–1713', in R. H. Roper & B. van Ruymbeke (eds), *Constructing Early Modern Empires. Proprietary Ventures in the Atlantic World 1500–1750* (Leiden, Brill 2007), 79–116

Banner, Stuart. *How the Indians Lost Their Land. Law and Power on the Frontier* (Harvard University Press 2005)

Banu, Roxana. *Nineteenth-Century Perspectives on Private International Law* (Oxford University Press 2018)

Barber, Malcolm. *The Trial of the Templars* (2nd edn, Cambridge University Press 2006)

Barbiche, Bernard. *Les institutions de la monarchie française* (Presses Universitaires de France 2012)

Barbon, Nicholas. *A Discourse of Trade* (London, Milbourn 1690)

Barcia Trelles, Camilo. 'Fernando Vázquez de Menchaca (1512–1569). L'école éspagnole de Droit International du XVIe siècle', 67 *Recueil des Cours* (1939), 429–534

Barducci, Marco. 'The Anglo-Dutch Context for the Writing and Reception of *De imperio summarum potestatum circa sacra*', 34 *Grotiana* (2013), 138–61

Barrientos García, José. 'El pensamiento económico en la perspectiva filosófico-teológica', in S. J. Gómez Camacho & Ricardo Robledo (eds), *El pensamiento económico en la escuela de Salamanca*, (Ediciones Universidad de Salamanca 1998), 93–122

Barthélemy, Dominique. *L'ordre seigneurial* (Paris, Seuil 1990)

Basdevant-Gaudement, Brigitte. *Aux origines de l'Etat moderne. Charles Loyseau (1564–1627), Théoricien de la puissance publique* (Paris, Economica 1977)

Bates, David W. *States of War. Enlightenment Origins of the Political* (Columbia University Press, 2012)

Baumanns, Markus. *Die publizistischen Werk des Kaiserlichen Diplomaten Franz Paul Freiherr von Lisola (1613–1674)* (Baden-Baden, Humblot 1994)

Bayly, C. A. *The Imperial Meridian. The British Empire and the World 1780–1830* (London, Routledge 1989)

Beauchamp, Tom. 'Introduction', in David Hume, *An Enquiry Concerning Human Understanding* (Oxford University Press 1999), xi–civ

Béaulac, Stéphane. 'Emer de Vattel and the Externalization of Sovereignty', 5 *Journal of the History of International Law* (2003), 237–92

Beaulieu, Alain. 'The Acquisition of Aboriginal Land in Canada. The Genealogy of an Ambivalent System', in Saliha Belmessous (ed.), *Empire by Treaty* (Oxford University Press 2015), 101–31

Beaumanoir, Philippe de. *Les coutumes de Beauvaisis* (A. Salmon ed., Paris 1899)

Becker, Anna. *Gendering the Renaissance Commonwealth* (Cambridge University Press 2020)

Becker, Carl. *The Heavenly City of the Eighteenth-Century Philosophers* (2nd edn, Yale University Press 2003 [1932])

Beik, William. *Absolutism and Society in Seventeenth-Century France* (Princeton University Press 1985)

Beiser, Frederick. *Enlightenment, Revolution and Romanticism. The Genesis of German Political Thought 1790–1800* (Cambridge University Press 1992)

*Hegel* (Abingdon, Routledge 2005)

Belda Plans, Juan. *La escuela de Salamanca y la renovación de la teología en el siglo XVI* (Madrid, Biblioteca de autores cristianos 2000)

Belissa, Marc. 'La déclaration du droit des gens de l'abbé Grégoire (june 1793, 4 Floréal an III)', in revolution-francaise.net/2010/10/06/399-declaration-droit-des-gens-abbe-gregoire-juin-1793

*Fraternité universelle et intérêt national (1713–1795). Les cosmopolitiques du droit des gens* (Paris, Kimé 1998)

*Repenser l'ordre européen (1795–1802). De la société des rois aux droits des nations* (Paris, Kimé 2006)

Belissa, Marc & Bosc, Yannick. *Le Directoire. La République sans la démocratie* (Paris, La fabrique 2018)

Bell, David A. *Lawyers and Citizens. The Making of Political Elite in Early Modern France* (Oxford University Press 1994)

*The Cult of the Nation in France. Inventing Nationalism 1680–1800* (Harvard University Press 2001)

Belli, Pierino. *A Treatise on Military Matters and Warfare* (Herbert C. Nutting trans., Oxford University Press 1936 [1563])

Bély, Lucien. 'Behind the Stage. The Global Dimension of the Negotiation', in R. E. de Brion et al. (eds), *Performances of Peace. Utrecht 1713* (Leiden, Brill 2015), 40–52

'Objectifs et la conduite de la politique extérieure', in Jean-Christian Petitfils (ed.), *Le siècle de Louis XIV* (Paris, Perrin 2017), 351–73

*L'art de la paix en Europe. Naissance de la diplomatie moderne XVIe–XVIII siècle* (Presses Universitaires de France 2007)

*Les sécrets de Louis XIV. Mystères d'État et pouvoir absolu* (Paris, Tallandier 2013)

Benot, Yves. 'Le procès Sonthonax ou les débats entre les accusateurs et les accusés dans l'affaire des colonies', in Marcel Dorigny (ed.), *Léger-Félicité Sonthonax. La première abolition de l'esclavage. La Révolution française et la Révolution de Saint-Domingue* (Paris, Société française d'histoire d'outre-mer 2005), 55–63

*La modernité de l'esclavage. Essai sur la servitude au cœur du capitalisme* (Paris, Découverte 2003)

*La Révolution française et la fin des colonies 1789–1794* (Paris, Découverte 2004)

*Les lumières, l'esclavage, la colonization* (Paris, Découverte 2005)

Benot, Yves & Dorigny, Marcel. *Rétablissement de l'esclavage dans les colonies françaises 1802* (Paris, Maisonneuve & Larose 2003)

Bentham, Jeremy. 'A Plan for Universal and Perpetual Peace', in John Bowring (ed.), *The Works of Jeremy Bentham* (11 vols, Edinburgh, William Tait 1838–43), II, 547–60

'Anarchical Fallacies', in John Bowring (ed.), *The Works of Jeremy Bentham* (11 vols, Edinburgh, William Tait 1838–43), II, 489–534

'General View of a Complete Code of Laws', in John Bowring (ed.), *The Works of Jeremy Bentham* (11 vols, Edinburgh, William Tait 1838–43), III, 155–210

'Letters of Anti-Machiavel', in John Bowring (ed.), *The Works of Jeremy Bentham* (11 vols, Edinburgh, William Tait 1838–43), X, 210–12

'Manual of Political Economy', in John Bowring (ed.), *The Works of Jeremy Bentham* (11 vols, Edinburgh, William Tait 1838–43), III, 31–85

'Principles of International Law', in John Bowring (ed.), *The Works of Jeremy Bentham* (11 vols, Edinburgh, William Tait 1838–43), II, 535–60

*A Fragment on Government* (J. H. Burns & H. L. A. Hart eds, Cambridge University Press 1988)

*Emancipate your Colonies!* (London, Heyward 1830)

*Introduction to Principles of Morals and Legislation* (New York, Prometheus 1988 [1781])

*Of Laws in General* (H. L. A. Hart ed., London, Athlone 1970)

Benton, Lauren. *Law and Colonial Cultures. Legal Regimes in World History, 1400–1900* (Cambridge University Press 2002)

Benton, Lauren & Ford, Lisa. *Rage for Order. The British Empire and the Origins of International Law 1800–1850* (Harvard University Press 2016)

Benton, Lauren & Ross, Richard J. 'Empires and Legal Pluralism. Jurisdiction, Sovereignty and Political Imagination in the Early Modern World', in Lauren Benton & Richard J. Ross (eds), *Legal Pluralism and Empires 1500–1850* (New York University Press 2013), 1–17

Benton, Lauren & Straumann, Benjamin. 'Acquiring Empire by Law. From Roman Doctrine to Early Modern European Practice', 28 *Law & History Review* (2010), 1–38

Bercé, Yves-Marie. 'Ordre et désordres dans la France de Louis XIV', in Jean-Christian Petitfils (ed.), *Le siècle de Louis XIV* (Paris, Perrin 2017), 207–21

Bergin, Joseph. *Pouvoir et fortune de Richelieu* (Paris, Pluriel 1988)

Berkowitz, Roger. *The Gift of Science. Leibniz and the Modern Legal Tradition* (Harvard University Press 2005)

Berman, Harold J. 'The Origins of Historical Jurisprudence. Coke, Selden, Hale', 103 *Yale Law Journal* (1993–4), 1651–1738

*Law and Revolution. The Formation of the Western Legal Tradition* (Harvard University Press 1983)

Bernal, Antonio-Miguel. *Monarquía e imperio.* Volumen 3: *Historia de España* (Barcelona, Marcial Pons, Critica 2007)

Bernardi, Bruno. 'L'idée de l'équilibre européen dans le jus gentium des modernes. Esquisse d'histoire conceptuelle', 4 *Assecuratio Pacis. Les conceptions françaises de la sûreté et de la garantie de la paix de 1648 à 1815* (2010). www.perspectivia.net/content/publikationen/discussions/4-2010/bernardi_idee

'Rousseau et l'Europe. Sur l'idée de société civile européenne', in *Jean-Jacques Rousseau. Principes du droit de la guerre. Ecrits sur la paix perpetuelle* (Bruno Bernardi & Gabriella Silvestrini eds, Paris, Vrin 2008), 295–330

Berns, Thomas. *Souveraineté, droit et gouvernementalité. Lectures du politique moderne à partir de Bodin* (Clamecy, Léo Scheer 2005)

Besson, Maurice. *Histoire des colonies françaises* (Paris, Boivin 1931)

Beyme, Klaus von. *Geschichte der politischen Theorien in Deutschland 1300–2000* (Wiesbaden, VS Verlag 2009)

Bezemer, Kees. 'Jacques de Révigny's Contribution to the Concept of Subjective Rights and the Origin of the Maxim "Ex facto ius oritur"', 81 *The Legal History Review* (2013), 199–217

'The Law School of Orleans as a School of Public Administration', 66 *Tijdschrift voor Rechtsgeschiedenis* (1998), 247–77

*Pierre de Belleperche. Portrait of a Legal Puritan* (Frankfurt, Klostermann 2005)

*What Jacques Saw. Thirteenth Century France through the Eyes of Jacques de Révigny, professor of law at Orléans* (Frankfurt, Klostermann 1997)

Bhandar, Brenna. *Colonial Lives of Property. Law, Land, and Racial Regimes of Ownership* (Duke University Press 2018)

Biancardini, Baptiste. 'L'opinion coloniale et la question de la relance de Saint-Domingue 1795–1802', 382 *Annales historiques de la Révolution française* (2015), 63–80

Biggar, S. H. P. *The Early Trading Companies of New France* (University of Toronto Library 1901)

Bilder, Mary Sarah. *The Transatlantic Constitution. Legal Culture and the Empire* (Harvard University Press 2004)

Binns, J. W. 'Alberico Gentili in Defence of Poetry and Acting', 19 *Studies in the Renaissance* (1972), 224–72

Biondi, Carminella (ed.). *1789. Les colonies ont la parole. Anthologie*, tome 1 (Paris, L'Harmattan 2016)

Bireley, Robert. *The Counter-Reformation Prince. Anti-Machiavellianism or Catholic Statecraft in Early Modern Europe* (University of North Carolina Press 1990)

*The Refashioning of Catholicism 1450–1700* (London, Macmillan 1999)

Birocchi, Italo. 'Il de iure belli e "l'invenzione" del diritto internationale', in Luigi Lacchè (ed.), *"Ius gentium, ius communicationis, ius belli". Alberico Gentili e gli orizzonti della modernità: atti del convegno di Macerata in occasione delle celebrazioni del quarto centenario della morte di Alberico Gentili (1552–1608)* (Milan, Giuffrè 2009), 101–38

Biskup, Thomas. 'The University of Göttingen and the Personal Union', in Brendan Simms & Torsten Riotte (eds), *The Hanoverian Dimension in British History 1714–1837* (Cambridge University Press 2007), 128–60

Bisson, Thomas. 'Medieval Lordship', 70 *Speculum* (1995), 744–59

*The Crisis of the Twelfth Century. Power, Lordship and the Origins of European Government* (Princeton University Press 2012)

Black, Anthony. *Political Thought in Europe 1250–1450* (Cambridge University Press 1992)

Black, Jane. *Absolutism in Renaissance Milan. Plenitude of Power under the Visconti and the Sforza 1329–1535* (Oxford University Press 2009)

Black, Jeremy. *British Diplomats and Diplomacy 1688–1800* (University of Exeter Press 2001)

Blackburn, Robin. *The American Crucible. Slavery, Emancipation and Human Rights* (London, Verso 2013)

*The Making of New World Slavery. From the Baroque to the Modern 1492–1800* (London, Verso 1997)

*The Overthrow of Colonial Slavery, 1776–1848* (London, Verso 1988)

Blackstone, William. *Commentaries on the Laws of England in Four Books* (2 vols., Philadelphia, Lippincott 1893)

Blanchard, Blanche. *Reason and Belief* (1974), www.giffordlectures.org/books/reason-and-belief

Blancpain, François. 'Notes sur les "dettes" d'esclavage. Le cas d'indemnité payée par Haïti (1825–1883)', in Marcel Dorigny (ed.), *Haiti. Première république noire* (Paris, Société française d'histoire d'outre-mer 2004), 241–5

Blanning, T. C. W. *The Culture of Power and the Power of Culture. Old Regime Europe 1660–1789* (Cambridge University Press 2002)

*Frederick the Great. King of Prussia* (London, Penguin Random House 2015)

Blaufarb, Rafe. *The Great Demarcation. The French Revolution and the Invention of Modern Property* (Oxford University Press 2016)

Bloch, Marc. *Feudal Society*, vol. I: *The Growth of Ties of Dependence* (2nd edn, London, Routledge 1962)

Blom, Hans W. 'Sociability and Hugo Grotius', 41 *History of European Ideas* (2015), 589–604

'The Meaning of Trust. *Fides* between Self-Interest and *Appetitus Societatis*', in Pierre-Marie Dupuy & Vincent Chetail (eds), *The Roots of International Law* (Leiden, Brill 2014), 39–58

Blom, Hans W. & van Dam, Harm-Jan. 'Dossier. *Ordinum pietas* (1613), Its Context and Seventeenth-Century Reception', 34 *Grotiana* (2013), 7–10

Bluntschli, Johann Caspar. 'Über die neuen Begründungen der Gesellschaft und des Gesellschaftsrecht', 3 *Kritische Überschau der deutschen Gesetzgebung und Rechtswissenschaft* (1856), 229–66

*Das moderne Völkerrecht als Rechtbuch gestellt* (Nördlingen, Beck 1868)

*Denkwürdiges aus meinem Leben* (3 vols, Nördlingen, Beck 1884)

Bock, Annelise. 'Nicolaus Hieronymus Gundling (1671–1729) und sein "Entwurf einer Teutschen Reichs-Historie"', PhD diss. (Düsseldorf 2005)

Bödeker, Hans Erich. 'Das Staatswissenschaftliche Fächersystem im 18. Jahrhundert', in Rudolf Vierhaus (ed.), *Wissenschaften im Zeitalter der Aufklärung. Aus Anlaß des 250 jährigen Bestehens des Verlages* (Göttingen, Vandenhoeck & Ruprecht 1985), 143–62

'The Concept of the Republic in Eighteenth-Century German Thought', in Jürgen Heideking & James A. Henretta (eds), *Republicanism and Liberalism in America and the German States, 1750–1850* (Cambridge University Press 2002), 35–52

Bödeker, Hans Erich & Hont, István. 'Naturrecht, Politische Ökonomie und Geschichte der Menschheit. Der Diskurs über die Gesellschaft in frühen Neuzeit', in Otto Dann & Diethelm Klippel (eds), *Naturrecht – Frühaufklärung – Revolution* (Hamburg, Meiner 1995), 80–9

Bodin, Jean. *Exposé du droit universel. Juris universi distributio* (Presses Universitaires de France 1985 [1578])

*Les six livres de la république* (Lyon, Tournes 1579)

*Method for the Easy Comprehension of History* (B. Reynolds trans., New York, Norton 1969 [1567])

*On Sovereignty* (Julian H. Franklin ed., Cambridge University Press 1992)

Bois, Jean-Pierre. *L'Europe à l'époque modern. Origines, utopies et réalités de l'idée d'Europe* (Paris, Armand Colin 1999)

Boisguilbert, Pierre Le Pesant. *Le detail de France* (no publisher, 1695)

Boiteux, Lucas Alexandre. *Richelieu, "grand maître de la navigation et du commerce de France"* (Paris, CNRS 1955)

Bompaire, Marc. 'La question monétaire. Avis et consultations à l'époque de Philippe le Bel et de ses fils', in Jean Kerhervé & Albert Rigaudière (eds), *Monnaie, fiscalité et finances au temps du Philippe le Bel* (Paris, Comité pour l'histoire économique et financière de la France 2007), 105–40

Bonassieux, Pierre. *Les grandes compagnies de commerce* (Paris, Plon 1892)

Bonnet, Stephane. *Droit et raison d'état* (Paris, Garnier 2012)
Bonney, Richard. 'Absolutism. What's in a Name?', 1 *French History* (1987), 93–117
*The Limits of Absolutism in ancien régime France* (Norfolk, Variorum 1996)
Boone, Rebecca Ard. *War, Domination and the Monarchy of France. Claude de Seyssel and the Language of Politics in the Renaissance* (Leiden, Brill 2007)
Borah, Woodrow. *Justice by Insurance. The General Indian Court of Colonial Mexico and the Legal Aides of the Half-Real* (University of California Press 1983)
Borges, Pedro. 'Proceso a las guerras de conquista', in Juan de la Peña, *De bello contra insulanos. Intervención de España en America. Escuela Española de la Paz – Segunda generación. Posición de la Corona.* CHP vol. X (Madrid, Consejo Superior de Investigaciones Científicas 1982), 17–66
Borobio García, Dionisio. *El sacramento de la penitencia en la escuela de Salamanca. Francisco de Vitoria, Melchior Cano, Domingo Soto* (Publicaciones Universidad Pontifica Salamanca 2006)
Borschberg, Peter. *Hugo Grotius 'Commentarius in Theses XI'. An Early Treatise on Sovereignty, the Just War and the Legitimacy of the Dutch Revolt* (Berne, Peter Lang 1994)
Bosbach, Franz. 'The European Debate on Universal Monarchy', in David Armitage (ed.), *Theories of Empire 1450–1800* (Aldershot, Ashgate 1998), 81–98
Bosher, J. F. 'Government and Private Interests in New France', 10 *Canadian Public Administration* (1967), 244–57
Botero, Giovanni. *De la raison d'état (1589–1598)* (R. Descendre ed., Paris, Gallimard 2014)
*The Reason of State* (P. J. & D. P. Wale trans., London, Routledge 1956)
*The Reason of State* (R. Bireley ed., Cambridge University Press 2007)
Boucher, Philip C. 'A Colonial Company at the Time of the Fronde. The Compagnie de Terre ferme de l'Amérique ou France equinoxiale', 11 *Terrae incognitae* (1979), 43–58
'Comment se forme un ministère colonial. L'initiation de Colbert 1661–1664', 37 *Revue d'histoire de l'Amérique française* (1983), 431–52
'French Proprietary Colonies in the Greater Caribbean', in L. H. Roper & B. van Ruymbeke (eds), *Constructing Early Modern Empires. Proprietary Ventures in the Atlantic World, 1500–1700* (Leiden, Brill 2007), 163–88
Boulet-Sautel, Marguerite. 'Jean de Blanot et la conception du pouvoir royal au temps de Louis IX', *Septième centenaire de la mort de saint Louis (1970)* (Paris, Belles Lettres 1976), 57–68
'Le princeps de Guillaume Durand', in *Études d'histoire du droit canonique dédiées à Gabriel le Bras, doyen honoraire de la Faculté de droit et de sciences économiques de Paris, membre de l'Institut*, tome II (Paris, Sirey 1965), 803–13
Boureau, Alain. 'L'invention doctrinale de le souveraineté monarchique sur les biens à l époque de Philippe le Bel', in Jean Kerhervé &

Albert Rigaudière (eds), *Monnaie, fiscalité et finances au temps du Philippe le Bel* (Paris, Comité pour l'histoire économique et financière de la France 2007), 1–18

*La religion de l'Etat. La construction de la République étatique dans le discours théologique d'Occident médiéval* (Paris, Belles Lettres 2008)

Bourin-Derruau, Monique. *Temps d'équilibres, temps de ruptures* (Paris, Seuil 1990)

Bourguignon, Henry J. *Sir William Scott, Lord Stowell. Judge of the High Court of Admiralty 1798–1828* (Cambridge University Press 1987)

Bournazel, Eric. 'La royauté féodale en France et en Angleterre Xe–XIIIe siècles', in Eric Bournazel & Jean-Pierre Poly, *Les féodalités* (Presses Universitaires de France 1998), 389–510

Bourne, Kenneth. *Palmerston. The Early Years 1784–1841* (London, Allen Lane 1982)

Bove, Boris. *La guerre de cent ans* (Paris, Belin 2015)

Bowen, H. V. 'British India 1765–1813. The Metropolitan Context', in P. J. Marshall & Alaine Low (eds), *The Oxford History of the British Empire*, vol. II: *The Eighteenth Century* (Oxford University Press 1998), 530–51

'Investment and Empire in the Later Eighteenth Century. East India Stockholding, 1765–1791', XLII *The Economic History Review* (1989), 186–206

*Revenue and Reform. The India Problem in British Politics 1757–1773* (Cambridge University Press 1991)

Boyer, Allen D. *Sir Edward Coke and the Elizabethan Age* (Stanford University Press 2003)

Braddick, Michael J. 'Civility and Authority', in David Armitage & Michael J. Braddick (eds), *The British Atlantic World 1500–1800* (London, Macmillan 2002), 93–112

'The English Government, War, Trade, and Settlement, 1625–1688', in Nicholas Canny (ed.), *The Oxford History of the British Empire*, vol. I: *The Origins of Empire* (Oxford University Press 1998), 286–308

*State Formation in Early Modern England c. 1550–1700* (Cambridge University Press 2000)

Brady, Thomas A. 'The Rise of Merchant Empires, 1400–1700. A European Counterpoint', in James D. Tracy (ed.), *The Political Economy of Merchant Empires* (Cambridge University Press 1991), 117–60

Braudel, Fernand. *Civilization & Capitalism, 15th–18th Century*, vol. II: *The Wheels of Commerce* (University of California Press: 1992)

*Civilization & Capitalism, 15th–18th Century*, vol. III: *The Perspective of the World* (University of California Press 1992)

Braun, Guido. 'La diplomatie française à Munster et le problème des la sûreté et de garantie des traits de Westphalie', 4 *Perspectivia.net* (2010). www.perspectivia.net/content/publikationen/discussions/4-2010/braun_diplomatie

Breen, Michael P. 'Patronage, Politics and the "Rule of Law" in Early Modern France', 33 *Proceedings for the Western Society of French History* (2005), 95–113

Brenner, Robert. *Merchants and Revolution. Commercial Change, Political Conflict, and London's Overseas Traders 1550–1653* (London, Verso 2003)

Brett, Annabel. 'Liberty and Absolutism. The Roman Heritage and the International Order in Alberico Gentili', in *Alberico Gentili. Giustizia, Guerra, Impero. Atti del convegno XIV Giornata Gentiliana* (San Ginesio 2010), 181–214

'Natural Right and Civil Community. The Civil Philosophy of Hugo Grotius', 45 *The Historical Journal* (2002), 31–52

'The Space of Politics and the Space of War in Hugo Grotius's *De iure belli ac pacis*', 1 *Global Intellectual History* (2016), 33–60

'The Subject of Sovereignty. Law, Politics and Moral Reasoning in Hugo Grotius', 17 *Modern Intellectual History* (2020), 619–45

*Changes of State. Nature and the Limits of the City in Early Modern Natural Law* (Princeton University Press 2010)

*Liberty, Right and Nature. Individual Rights in Later Scholastic Thought* (Cambridge University Press 1997)

Brewer, John. 'The Eighteenth-Century British State. Contexts and Issues', in Lawrence Stone (ed.), *An Imperial State at War. Britain from 1689 to 1815* (London, Routledge 1994), 52–71

*The Sinews of Power. War, Money and the English State 1688–1783* (Harvard University Press 1988)

Briggs, Charles F. & Yardley, Peter S. *A Companion to Giles of Rome* (Leiden, Brill 2016)

Brissaud, Jean. *A History of French Public Law* (New York, Kelley 1969)

Brodhead, John R. *Documents Relative to the Colonial History of the State of New-York. Procured in Holland, England, and France* (15 vols, Albany, Weed, Parsons 1853–87)

Bromley, John Selwyn. 'The French Privateering War 1702–1713', in John Selwyn Bromley, *Corsairs and Navies 1660–1760* (London, Hambledon 1987), 213–42

'The Loan of French Naval Vessels to Privateering Enterprises 1688–1713', in John Selwyn Bromley, *Corsairs and Navies 1660–1760* (London, Hambledon 1987), 187–212

Brooke, Christopher. *Philosophic Pride. Stoicism in Political Thought from Lipsius to Rousseau* (Princeton University Press 2012)

Brooks, Christopher W. *Law, Politics and Society in Early Modern England* (Cambridge University Press 2008)

Brouwer, René. 'On the Ancient Background of Grotius' Notion of Natural Law', 29 *Grotiana* (2009), 1–24

Brown, Christopher L. 'The Politics of Slavery', in David Armitage & Michael J. Braddick (eds), *The British Atlantic World 1500–1800* (London, Macmillan 2002), 214–32

Brown, Elizabeth. '*Persona et gesta*. The Image and Deeds of the Thirteenth-Century Capetians. The Case of Philip the Fair', 19 *Viator* (1988), 219–46

Brown, Gordon S. *Toussaint's Clause. The Founding Fathers and the Haitian Revolution* (University Press of Mississippi 2005)

Brown, Harold E. *Juan de Mariana and Early Modern Spanish Political Thought* (Aldershot, Ashgate 2007)

Brückner, Jutta. *Staatswissenschaften, Kameralismus und Naturrecht. Ein Beitrag zur Geschichte des politischen Wissenschaft im Deutschland des späten 17. und frühen 18. Jahrhunderts* (Munich, Beck 1977)

Brufau Prats, Jaime. *El pensamiento político de Domingo de Soto y su concepción del poder* (Salamanca, Ediciones Universidad 1960)

Brundage, James. *Medieval Canon Law* (London, Longman 1995)

Buchan, James. *The Authentic Adam Smith. His Life and Ideas* (New York, Norton 2006)

Buckle, Stephen. *Natural Law and the Theory of Property. Grotius to Hume* (Oxford, Clarendon 1991)

Buck-Morss, Susan. *Hegel, Haiti and Universal History* (University of Pittsburgh Press 2009)

Bühler, Christoph. *Die Naturrechtslehre und Christian Thomasius (1655–1728)* (Regensburg, Roderer 1991)

Burge, William. *Commentaries on Colonial and Foreign Laws Generally in their Conflict with each other and with the Laws of England* (4 vols, London, Saunders 1838)

Burgess, Glen. *Absolute Monarchy and the Stuart Constitution* (Yale University Press 1996)

*The Politics of the Ancient Constitution. An Introduction to English Political Thought 1603–1642* (London, Macmillan 1992)

Burgin, Joseph. *Cardinal Richelieu. Power and the Pursuit of Wealth* (Yale University Press 1985)

Burke, Edmund. 'Reflections on the Revolution in France', in Edmund Burke, *Revolutionary Writings* (Ian Hampshire-Monk ed., Cambridge University Press 2014), 1–256

'Speech in reply', 30 May 1794, in P. J. Marshall (ed.), *The Writings and Speeches of Edmund Burke*, vol. VII: *India. The Hastings Trial 1789–1794* (9 vols., Oxford, Clarendon 2000), 281–335

Burns, J. H. 'Fortescue and the Political Theory of *Dominium*', 28 *The Historical Journal* (1985), 777–97

Bush, Jonathan A. 'Free to Enslave. The Foundations of Colonial American Slave Law', 5 *Yale Journal of Law and the Humanities* (1993), 417–70

Buzzi, Franco. 'Il tema de *iure belli* nella seconda scolastica', in Fausto Arici & Franco Todescan (eds), *Iustus ordo e ordine della natura. Sacra doctrina e saperi politici fra XVI e XVIII secolo* (Padova, CEDAM 2007), 63–72

Cabanis, Voir P. *Quelques considérations sur l'organisation sociale* (Paris, Imprimerie nationale l'An VIII)

Cain, P. J. 'Economics and Empire. The Metropolitan Context', in Andrew Porter (ed.), *The Oxford History of the British Empire*, vol. III: *The Nineteenth Century* (Oxford University Press 2001), 31–52

*Economic Foundations of British Overseas Expansion 1815–1915* (London, Macmillan 1980)

Cain, P. J. & Hopkins, A. G. 'Gentlemanly Capitalism and British Expansion Overseas. I: The Old Colonial System, 1688–1850', XXXIX *The Economic History Review* (1986), 501–25

*British Imperialism. 1688–2000* (London, Routledge 2001)

Calasso, Francesco. *I glossatori e la teoria della sovranità* (3rd edn, Milano, Giuffrè 1957 [1945])

Callières de, François. *L'art de négocier sous Louis XIV* (Paris, Nouveau Monde 2006 [1716])

Calloway, Colin. *Pen and Ink Witchcraft. Treaties and Treaty Making in American Indian History* (Oxford University Press 2013)

Camerlingo, Rosanna. 'Machiavelli a Oxford. Guerra e teatro da Gentili a Shakespeare', 56 (II) *Rinascimento* (2016), 123–38

Canning, J. P. 'Italian Juristic Thought and the Realities of Power in the Fourteenth Century', in Joseph Canning & Otto Gerhard Oxle (eds), *Political Thought and Realities of Power in the Middle Ages* (Göttingen, Vandenhoeck & Ruprecht 1998), 229–39

'Law, Sovereignty and Corporation Theory, 1300–1450', in J. H. Burns (ed.), *The Cambridge History of Medieval Political Thought c. 350–c. 1450* (Cambridge University Press 1988), 454–76

*The Political Thought of Baldus de Ubaldis* (Cambridge University Press 1987)

Canny, Nicholas. *Making Ireland British, 1580–1650* (Oxford University Press 2001)

Cano, Melchior. 'Quaestio 40 De bello', in Luciano Pereña et al. (eds), *Francisco de Vitoria. Relectio de iure belli o paz dinámica. Escuela española de la Paz* (Madrid 1981), 323–42

Cantù, Francesca. 'Alberico Gentili e lo ius legationis', in Stephano Andretta, Stéphane Péquignot & Jean-Claude Wacquet (eds), *De l'ambassadeur. Les écrits relatifs à l'ambassadeur et à l'art de négocier du Moyen Âge au début du xixe siècle* (l'École française de Rome 2015). books.openedition.org/efr/2914#

Capdevila, Nestor. 'Impérialisme, empire et destruction', in Bartolomé de Las Casas, *La controverse entre Las Casas et Sepúlveda* (Paris, Vrin 2007), 7–202

Carbasse, Jean-Marie & Leyte, Guillaume. *L'état royal XIIe–XVIIIe siècles. Une anthologie* (Presses Universitaires de France 2004)

Carbasse, Jean-Marie, Leyte, Guillaume & Soleil, Sylvain. *La monarchie française du milieu du XVIe siècle à 1715. L'Esprit des institutions* (Paris, CDU SEDES 2001)

Carmichael, Gershom. 'Natural Rights', in J. Moore & M. Silverthorne (eds), *Natural Rights on the Threshold of the Scottish Enlightenment. The Writings of Gershom Carmichael* (Indianapolis, Liberty Fund 2002 [1724]), 77–90

Carpin, Gervais. 'Migrations to New France in Champlain's Time', in R. Litalien (ed.), *Champlain. The Birth of French America* (McGill–Queen's University Press 2014), 163–79

Carranza, Bartolomé de. 'Ratione fidei potest Caesar debellare et tenere Indios novi orbis?', in Vicente Pereña (ed.), *Misión de España en América* (Madrid, Consejo Superior de Investigaciones Científicas 1956), 38–57

Carro, Venancio D. *Domingo de Soto y el derecho de gentes* (Madrid, Del Amo 1930)

Carta, Paolo. 'Dalle guerre d'Italia del Guicciardini al diritto di Guerra di Alberico Gentili', 10 *Laboratoire italien. Politique et société* (2010), 85–102

Carty, Anthony. 'Cardinal Richelieu between Vattel and Machiavelli', in Anthony Carty & Janne Nijman (eds), *Morality and Responsibility of Rulers. European and Chinese Origins of a Rule of Law as Justice of World Order* (Oxford University Press 2018), 149–66

Cassi, Aldo Andrea. 'Conquista. *Dallo* ius communicationis *allo* ius belli *nel pensiero di Alberico Gentili*', in Luigi Lacchè (ed.), *"Ius gentium, ius communicationis, ius belli". Alberico Gentili e gli orizzonti della modernità: atti del convegno di Macerata in occasione delle celebrazioni del quarto centenario della morte di Alberico Gentili (1552–1608)* (Milan, Giuffrè 2009), 139–64

Cassirer, Ernst. *The Philosophy of the Enlightenment* (Princeton University Press, 1979 [1951])

Castagnos, Pierre. *Richelieu face à la mer (De mémoire d'homme. L'histoire)* (Rennes, Éditions Ouest-France 1989)

Castilla Urbano, Francisco. *El pensamiento de Francisco de Vitoria. Filosofía, política e indio americano* (Barcelona, Anthropos 1992)

Catteeuw, Laurie. *Censures et raisons d'État. Une histoire de la modernité politique (XVIe–XVIIe siècles)* (Paris, Albin Michel 2013)

Cauna, Jacques de. 'Polverel et Sonthonax, deux voies pour l'abolition de l'esclavage', in Marcel Dorigny (ed.), *Léger-Félicité Sonthonax. La première abolition de l'esclavage. La Révolution française et la Révolution de Saint-Domingue* (Paris, Société française d'histoire d'outre-mer 2005), 47–65

Cavallar, Georg. *Kant and the Theory and Practice of International Right* (University of Wales Press 1999)

Cavanagh, Edward. 'Possession and Dispossession in Corporate New France, 1600–1663. Debunking a "Juridical History" and Revisiting *Terra Nullius*', 32 *Law and History Review* (2014), 97–125

Cederlöf, Gunnel. *Founding an Empire on India's North-Eastern Frontiers, 1790–1840* (Oxford University Press 2013)

Chafuen, Alejandro A. *Faith and Liberty. The Economic Thought of the Late Scholastics* (Lanham, Lexington Books 2003)

Chailley-Bert, Joseph. *Les compagnies de colonisation sous l'ancien régime* (Paris, Armand Colin 1898)

Chalk, Alfred M. 'Natural Law and the Rise of Economic Individualism in England', 59 *Journal of Political Economy* (1951), 332–47

Chalmers, George (ed.). *Opinions of Eminent Lawyers on various Points of English Jurisprudence*, vol. I (2 vols., London, Reed & Hunter 1814)

Chaplais, Pierre. 'La souveraineté du Roi de France et le pouvoir legislatif en Guyenne au début du XIVe siècle', LXIX *Le Moyen Age* (1963), 449–69

Chappey, Jean-Luc. 'Héritages républicains et résistances à l'organisation impériale des savoirs', 346 *Annales historiques de la Révolution française* (2006), 97–120

'Les idéologues face du Coup d'État du 18 Brumaire an VIII', 14 *Politix* (2001), 55–75

*La Société des Observateurs de l'Homme (1799–1804). Des anthropologues au temps de Bonaparte* (Paris, Société des études robespierristes 2002)

Charbit, Yves. 'L'échec politique d'une théorie économique. La physiocratie', 57 *Cairn* (2002), 849–78

'Les colonies françaises au XVIIe siècle. Mercantilisme et enjeux impérialistes européens', 22 *Revue européenne des migrations internationales* (2006), 183–99

*Charte aux normandes* (Caen, Le Roy 1788)

Chatterjee, Partha. *The Black Hole of Empire. History of a Global Practice of Power* (Princeton University Press 2012)

Chazan, Mireille. *L'empire et l'histoire universelle de Sigebert de Gembloux à Jean de Saint Victor* (Paris, Honoré Champion 1999)

Chen, Song-Chuan. *Merchants of War and Peace. British Knowledge of China in the Making of the Opium War* (Hong Kong University Press 2019)

Cheneval, Francis. *La cité des peuples. Mémoire de cosmopolitismes* (Paris, Cerf 2005)

Cheney, Paul. *Revolutionary Commerce. Globalization and the French Monarchy* (Harvard University Press 2010)

Cheyfitz, Eric. *The Poetics of Imperialism. Translation and Colonization from Tempest to Tarzan* (Oxford University Press 1991)

Child, Josiah. *A New Discourse about Trade* (5th edn, Glasgow, Foulis 1751 [1668])

Childs, Nick. *A Political Academy in Paris, 1724–1731. The Entresol and its Members* (Oxford, Voltaire Foundation 2000)

Chitty, Joseph. *Treatise on the Law of Commerce and Manufactures and Contracts Relating Thereto*, (4 vols. London, Stratham 1824)

Choquette, Leslie. 'Proprietorships in French North America', in L. H. Roper & B. van Ruymbeke (eds), *Constructing Early Modern Empires. Proprietary Ventures in the Atlantic World 1500–1750* (Leiden, Brill 2007), 117–32

Christin, Olivier. *La paix de religion. L'Autonomisation de la raison politique au XVIe siècle* (Paris, Seuil 1997)

Church, William F. 'The Decline of the French Jurists as Political Theorists, 1660–1789', 5 *French Historical Studies* (1967), 1–40

*Constitutional Thought in Sixteenth-Century France. A Study in the Evolution of Ideas* (Harvard University Press 1941)

*Richelieu and the Reason of State* (Princeton University Press 1972)

Cicero, *On the Commonwealth and On the Laws* (James E. G. Zetzel ed., Cambridge University Press 1999)

Cioli, Monica. *Pragmatismus und Ideologie. Organisationsformen des deutschen Liberalismus zur Zeit der zweiten Reichsgründung (1878–1884)* (Berlin, Duncker & Humblot 2000)

Clapmar, Arnold. *De arcanis rerum publicarum libri sex* (Amsterdam, Elzevirium 1644)

Clark, Charles. *A Summary of Colonial Law* (London, Sweet & Maxwell 1834)

Clark, Grover. 'The English Practice with Regard to Reprisals by Private Persons', 27 *American Journal of International Law* (1933), 694–723

Clark, Henry C. *Compass of Society. Commerce and Absolutism in Old-Regime France* (Lanham, Lexington Books 2007)

Claydon, Tony. *Europe and the Making of England 1660–1760* (Cambridge University Press 2007)

Coativy, Yves. 'Les monnaies de Philippe le Bel et leurs avatars', in Jean Kerhérvé & Albert Rigaudière (eds), *Monnaie, fidelité et finances au temps du Philippe le Bel* (Paris, Comité pour l'histoire économique et financière de la France 2007), 141–56

Codrington, Robert. *His Majesties Propriety and Dominion on the British Sea Asserted* (London, Thomas 1672 [1665])

Coke, Edward. *Selected Writings of Sir Edward Coke*, vol. I (The Online Library of Liberty)

*The Reports of Sir Edward Coke in Thirteen Parts. A New Edition in Six Volumes.* (London, Butterworths 1821)

*The First Part of the Institutes of the Laws of England* (2 vols, 18th & 19th eds., London, Clarke 1823 & 1832)

*The Fourth Part of the Institutes of the Laws of England* (5th ed., London, Flesher 1671)

Colavecchia, Stefano. 'Alberico Gentili oltre le ius belli. Tra Guerra giusta e repubblicanesimo. Proposte per l'Europa tra Cinque e Seicento', PhD tesis, Università degli studi del Molise (2013–14)

Cole, Charles W. *French Mercantilism 1683–1700* (New York, Octagon 1971)

Coleman, Janet. '*Dominium* in Thirteenth and Fourteenth-Century Political Thought and Its Seventeenth-Century Heirs. John of Paris and Locke', 33 *Political Studies* (1985), 73–100

'Property and Poverty', in J. H. Burns (ed.), *The Cambridge History of Medieval Political Thought c. 350–c. 1450* (Cambridge University Press 1988), 607–48

'The Intellectual Milieu of John of Paris OP', in J. Miethke & A. Bühler (eds), *Das Publikum politischer Theorie im 14. Jahrhundert* (Munich, Oldenbourg 1992), 173–206

*A History of Political Thought from the Middle Ages to the Renaissance* (Oxford, Blackwell 2000)

Colley, Linda. *Britons. Forging the Nation 1707–1837* (2nd edn, London, Pimlico 2003)

Collins, James B. 'State-Building in Early-Modern Europe. The Case of France', 31 *Modern Asian Studies* (1997), 603–33

*The State in Early Modern France* (Cambridge University Press 2012)

Collins, Stephen L. *From Divine Cosmos to the Sovereign State. An Intellectual History of Consciousness and the Idea of Order in Renaissance England* (Oxford University Press 1989)

*Complement des ordinances et jugements des gouverneurs et intendants du Canada* (Quebec, Fréchette 1856)

Condorcet, Marie-Jean-Antoine Nicolas. 'De l'influence de la Révolution d'Amérique sur l'Europe', in Arthur Condorcet O'Connor & M. F. Arago (eds), *Oeuvres de Condorcet*, tome 8e (Paris, Didot 1847), 11–21

*Esquisse d'un tableau historique des progrès de l'esprit humain* (Paris, Flammarion 1988 [1795])

*Réflexions sur l'esclavage des nègres* (Paris, Flammarion 2009 [1781])

Conring, Hermann. *Dissertatio de ratione status* (Helmstedt, Müller 1651)

*New Discourse on the Roman–German Emperor* (C. Fasolt ed. & trans., Tempe, AZ, Center for Medieval and Renaissance Studies 2005 [1641])

Constant, Benjamin. 'De M. Dunoyer et quelques-uns de ses Ouvrages', in *Mélanges de litterature et de politique* (Paris, Didier 1829), 654–78

'The Spirit of Conquest and Usurpation and Their Relation to European Civilization', in B. Fontana (ed.), *Constant. Political Writings* (Cambridge University Press 1988), 43–167

Conte, Emanuele. 'Framing the Feudal Bond. A Chapter in the History of the *ius commune* in Medieval Europe', 80 *The Legal History Review* (2012), 481–95

'Public Law before the State. Evidence from the Age of the Glossators of the Roman Law', 2 *Yale Law School Legal Scholarship Reporting* (2006)

Conway, Stephen. 'Bentham versus Pitt. Jeremy Bentham and British Foreign Policy 1789', 30 *The Historical Journal* (1987), 791–809

'Britain and the Revolutionary Crisis, 1763–1791', in P. J. Marshall & Alaine Low (eds), *The Oxford History of the British Empire*, vol. II: *The Eighteenth Century* (Oxford University Press 1998), 325–46

Coquillette, Daniel R. 'Radical Lawmakers in Colonial Massachusetts. The "Countenance of Authoritie" and the Lawes and Libertyes', 67 *New England Quarterly* (1994), 179–206

*The Civilian Writers of Doctors' Commons, London. Three Centuries of Innovation in Comparative, Commercial and International Law* (Berlin, Duncker & Humblot 1988)

Cordier, L. *Les compagnies à charte et le politique coloniale sous le ministère de Colbert* (Paris, Rousseau 1906)

Cornette, Joël. 'Fiction et réalité de l'état baroque (1610–1652)', in Henry Méchoulan (ed.), *L'État baroque. Regards sur la pensée politique de la France du premier XVIIe siècle (1610–1652)* (Paris, Vrin 1985), 7–87

'La tente de Darius', in Henry Mechoulan & Joël Cornette (eds), *L'état Classique. Regards sur la pensée politique de la France dans le second XVIIe siècle* (Paris, Vrin 1996), 9–42

*Absolutisme et lumières 1652–1783* (8th edn, Paris, Hachette 2016)

*La mort de Louis XVI. Apogée et crepuscule de la royauté 1er septembre 1715* (Paris, Gallimard 2015)

*Le roi de guerre. Essai sur la souveraineté dans la France du Grand Siècle* (Paris, Payot 1993)

Corriente Córdoba, José Antonio. 'El derecho de gentes en la obra de Martín de Azpilcueta, "el Doctor Navarro"', in Fernando M. Mariño Menéndez (ed.), *El derecho internacional en los albores del siglo XXI. Homenaje al profesor Juan Manuel Castro-Rial Canosa* (La Rioja, Dialnet 2002), 159–74

Cosandey, Fanny & Descimon, Robert. *L'absolutisme en France. Histoire et historiographie* (Paris, Seuil 2002)

Coste, Jean (ed.). *Boniface VIII en procès. Articles d'accusation et dépositions des témoins (1303–1311)* (Rome, "L'Erma" di Bretschneider 1995)

Costello, *The Political Philosophy of Luis de Molina (1535–1600)* (Roma Institute Historium 1974)

Cotter, William R. 'The Somerset Case and the Abolition of Slavery in England', 79 *History* (1994), 31–56

Cottrell, Philip L. 'London's First "Big Bang"? Institutional Change in the City 1855–83', in Yussef Cassis et al. (eds), *The World of Private Banking* (London, Routledge 2009), 61–98

Courcelles, Dominique de. 'Pensée théologique et événement. Droit de conquête et droit des gens de l'Empire espagnole du XVIe siècle', in Carmen Val Julian, *La conquête de l'Amérique espagnole et la question du droit* (Lyon, ENS-LSH Editions 2002), 15–31

Courtine, Jean-Francois. 'Vitoria, Suarez et la naissance du droit de nature moderne', in Alain Renaut (ed.), *Naissances de modernité*. 2: *Histoire de la philosophie politique* (Paris, Calmann-Lévy 1999), 127–81

Couzinet, Dominique. *Histoire et méthode à la renaissance. Une lecture de la Methodus de Jean Bodin* (Paris, Vrin 1996)

Covarrubias y Leyva, Diego. *Regulae peccatum. Iur. Lib. VI* ( Leyden, Honoratum 1560)

*Textos Juridico-Politicos* (Madrid, Institut de estudios politicos 1957)

Coyer, Abbé. *La noblesse commerçante* (Paris, Duchêne 1761)

Cremean, Damien J. 'The Early History of Admiralty Jurisdiction', 28 *Australia & New Zealand Maritime Law Journal* (2014), 16–24

Crespo, Ricardo F. 'La posibilidad y justicia del intercambio. De Aristoteles a Marx, pasando por Tómas de Aquino y Francisco de Vitoria', in Juan Cruz Cruz (ed.), *Ley y Dominio en Francisco de Vitoria* (Pamplona, Eunsa 2008), 267–76

Cromartie, Allan. *Sir Matthew Hale, 1609–1676. Law, Religion and Natural Philosophy* (Cambridge University Press 1995)

Cronon, William. *Changes in the Land. Indians, Colonists, and the Ecology of New England* (New York, Hill & Wang 1983)

Cropsey, Joseph. *Polity and Economy. With Further Thoughts on the Principles of Adam Smith* (South Bend, St Augustine's Press 2001)

Crucé, Émeric. *Le nouveau Cynée ou discours d'État representant les occasions et moyens d'établir une paix générale et liberté du commerce par tout le monde* (A. Fenet & A. Guillaume eds, Presses Universitaires de Rennes 2004)

Cruz Cruz, Juan. '*Ius gentium* bei Vitoria. Ein eindeutig internationalistischer Ansatz', in Alexander Fidora, Matthias Lutz-Bachmann & Andreas Wagner (eds), *Law and ius. Essays on the Foundation of Law in Medieval and Early Modern Philosophy* (Stuttgart, Fromman-Holzbook 2010), 301–32

'La soportable fragilidad de la ley natural. Consignación transitiva del *ius gentium* en Vitoria', in Juan Cruz Cruz, *Ley y dominio en Francisco de Vitoria* (Pamplona, Eunsa 2008), 13–40

*La ley natural como fundamento moral y jurídico en Domingo de Soto* (Pamplona, Eunsa 2007)

Curran, Andrew S. *The Anatomy of Blackness. Science & Slavery in the Age of Enlightenment* (Johns Hopkins University Press 2011)

Curzon, Alfred de. 'L'Enseignement du Droit Français les Universités de France', 43 *Nouvelle revue historique droit français et étranger* (1919), 209–356

Cuttler, S. H. *The Law of Treason and Treason Trials in Medieval France* (Cambridge University Press 1981)

D'Aguesseau, Henri François. 'Essai d'un institution au droit public', in M. Pardessus (ed.), *Oeuvres complètes du Chancelier D'Aguesseau*, tome XV (nouvelle édition, Paris, Fantin 1819), 164–272

'Méditations métaphysiques sur les vraies ou les fausses idées de la justice', in M. Pardessus (ed.), *Oeuvres complètes du Chancelier D'Aguesseau*, tome XIV (nouvelle édition, Paris, Fantin 1819)

d'Alembert, Jean Le Rond. *Preliminary Discourse to the Encyclopedia of Diderot* (The University of Chicago Press 1995 [1751])

d'Anglas, Boissy. 'Discours préliminaire au projet de constitution', Primidi, 11 Messidor l'An 3 (29/6/1795), in *Réimpression de l'ancien Moniteur*, tome 25 (Paris, Bureau central 1842), 81–4, 90–5, 98–101, 106–10, 113–15

*Discours prononcé à la Convention nationale de France sur la situation politique de l'Europe* (Paris, Imprimerie nationale l'An III)

d'Argis, Boucher. 'Droit des Gens' and 'Droit de la Nature ou Droit naturel', in Denis Diderot & Jean le Rond d'Alembert (eds), *Encyclopédie, ou dictionnaire raisonné des arts et des métiers etc.* (University of Chicago ARTFL Encyclopedia Project, Robert Morissey ed., encyclopedie.unchicago.edu)

D'Holbach, Baron. *La morale universelle, ou les devoirs de l'homme, fondés sur la nature* (Paris, Masson 1820)

*Système social ou principes naturels de la morale et de la politique* (Paris, Niogret 1822)

Dam, Harm-Jan van. 'De imperio potestatum circa sacra', in Henk M. Nellen & Edwin Rabbie (eds), *Hugo Grotius Theologian. Essays in Honour of G. H. M. Posthumus Meyjes* (Leiden, Brill 1994), 19–39

Dapper, Olfert. *Description de l'Afrique* (Amsterdam, Wolfgang et al. 1686)

Darwin, John. *The Empire Project. The Rise and Fall of the British World System* (Cambridge University Press 2009)

Daston, L. *The Morality of Natural Orders. The Tanner Lectures on Human Values* (2002), 380–92. tannerlectures.utah.edu/_documents/a-to-z/d/daston_2002.pdf

Dauchy, Serge. 'Le conseil souverain de Québec. Une institution de l'ancienne France pour le Nouveau Monde', 3 *Revue du Nord* (2015), 513–26

Davenant, Charles, *An Essay on the East India Trade* (London, 1696)

'An Essay upon Universal Monarchy', in C. Whitworth (ed.), *The Political and Commercial Works of Charles D'Avenant* (5 vols, London, Horsefield 1771), IV, 1–43

'Discourse on the Public Revenue and on Trade of England', in C. Whitworth (ed.), *The Political and Commercial Works of Charles D'Avenant* (5 vols, London, Horsefield 1771), I, 127–458

'Reflections upon the Constitution and Management of the Trade to Africa', in C. Whitworth (ed.), *The Political and Commercial Works of Charles D'Avenant* (5 vols, London, Horsefield 1771), V 77–346

Davenport, Frances Gardiner. *European Treaties Bearing upon the History of the United States and Its Dependencies to 1648* (4 vols., Washington, Carnegie 1917–37)

Davies, Sir John. *The Question concerning Impositions, Tonnage, Poundage, Prizage, Custom &c.* (London, Twyford 1656)

Davis, John P. *Corporations. A Study of the Origin and Development of Great Business Combinations and of their Relation to the Authority of the State* (New York, Franklin 1970 [1905])

Davis, K. C. *The Royal African Company* (London, Longman 1957)

Davis, Kathleen. 'Sovereign Subjects, Feudal Law, and the Writing of History', 36 *Journal of Medieval and Early Modern Studies* (2006), 223–61

*Periodization and Sovereignty. How Ideas of Feudalism and Secularization Govern the Politics of Time* (University of Pennsylvania Press 2008)

Davis, Ralph. 'England and the Mediterranean', in F. J. Fisher (ed.), *Essays in the Economic and Social History of Tudor and Stuart England* (Cambridge University Press 1961), 117–37

Dawson, Frank G. *The First Latin American Debt Crisis. The City of London and the 1822–1825 Loan Bubble* (Yale University Press 1990)

Déak, Francis & Jessup, Philip C. 'Early Prize Court Procedure', 82 *University of Pennsylvania Law Review* (1934), 677–94

Deckers, Daniel. *Gerechtigkeit und Recht. Eine Historisch-kritische Untersuchung der Gerechtigkeitslehre des Francisco de Vitoria* (Freiburg, Universitätsverlag 1991)

*Déclarations du Roy, Portant sur l'établissement d'une Compagnie pour le Commerce des Indes Orientales* (Paris, 1664)

Decock, Wim. *Theologians and Contract Law. The Moral Transformation of the* Ius Commune *(ca. 1500–1650)* (Leiden, Nijhoff 2013)

Decoster, Caroline. 'La Fiscalisation des aides féodales', in Jean Kerhervé & Albert Rigaudière (eds), *Monnaie, fiscalité et finances au temps du Philippe le Bel* (Paris, Comité pour l'histoire économique et financière de la France 2007), 173–97

Dedieu, Jean-Pierre. *L'administration de la foi. L'inquisition de Tolède XVIe–XVIIIe siècle* (Madrid, Velázquez 1989)

Dee, John. *The Limits of the British Empire* (K. MacMillan & J. Abeles eds, Westport, Praeger 2004)

del Vigo, Abelardo. *Cambistas, mercaderes y banqueros en el siglo de oro español* (Madrid, Biblioteca de autores cristianos 1997)

Delgado, Mariano. 'Die Zustimmung des Volkes', in Frank Grunert & Kurt Seelmann (eds), *Die Ordnung der Praxis. Neue Studien zur spanischen Spätscholastik* (Tübingen, Niemeyer 2001), 157–81

Deligiorgi, Katerina. *Kant and the Culture of Enlightenment* (State University of New York Press 2005)

Dellavalle, Sergio. 'The Plurality of States and the World Order of Reason. On Hegel's Understanding of International Law and Relations', in Stefan Kadelbach et al. (eds), *System, Order, and International Law* (Oxford University Press 2017), 352–78

Demurger, Alain. *Vie et mort de l'ordre du Temple 1118–1314* (Paris, Seuil 1985)

Denis, Henri. *Histoire de la pensée économique* (Presses Universitaires de France 1966)

Denzer, Horst. *Absolutismus und ständische Verfassung. Ein Beitrag zu Kontinuität und Diskontinuität der politischen Theorie in der frühen Neuzeit* (Mainz, Zabern 1992)

*Moralphilosophie und Naturrecht bei Samuel Pufendorf* (Munich, Beck 1972)

Derry, John. 'Government Policy and the American Crisis 1760–1776', in H. T. Dickinson (ed.), *Britain and the American Revolution* (London, Longman 1998), 44–63

Desan, Suzanne. 'Foreigners, Cosmopolitanism and French Revolutionary Universalism', in Suzanne Desan, Lynn Hunt & William Max Nelson (eds), *The French Revolution in Global Perspective* (Cornell University Press 2013), 86–100

Descendre, Romain. 'Raison d'État, puissance et économie. Le mercantilisme de Giovanni Botero', 39 *Revue de métaphysique et morale* (2003), 311–21

*L'État du monde. Giovanni Botero entre raison d'État et géopolitique* (Genève, Droz 2009)

Deslandres, Dominique. '"Et loing de France, en l'une & l'autre mer, Les Fleurs de Liz, tu as fait renommer". Quelques hypotheses touchant la religion, le genre et l'expansion de la souveraineté française en Amérique aux XVIe & XVIIIe siècles', 64 *Revue d'histoire de l'Amérique française* (2011), 93–117

Deslozières, Baudry. *Les Egarements du nigrophilisime* (Paris, Migneret 1802)

Dessert, Daniel. 'Finances et société au XVIIe siècle. À propos de la chambre de justice de 1661', 29 *Annales. Économies, sociétés, civilisations* (1974), 847–81

Devetak, Richard. 'Law of Nations as Reason of States. Diplomacy and the Balance of Power in Vattel's *Law of Nations*', 28 *Parergon* (2011), 105–28

Dewar, Helen. 'Souveraineté dans les colonies, souveraineté en métropole. Le rôle de la Nouvelle France dans la consolidation de l'autorité maritime en France, 1620–1628', 64 *Revue d'histoire de l'Amérique française* (2011), 86–91

' "Y establir nostre auctorité". Assertions of Imperial Sovereignty through Proprietorships and Chartered Companies in New France, 1598–1663' (PhD thesis, University of Toronto 2012)

Dewar, Mary. 'The Authorship of the "Discourse of the Commonweal"', XIX *The Economic History Review* (1966), 388–400

*Sir Thomas Smith. A Tudor Intellectual in Office* (London, Athlone 1964)

Dickinson, John. *Essay on the Constitutional Power of Great Britain over the Colonies in America (With the Resolves of the Committee for the Province of Pennsylvania)* (Philadelphia 1744)

Dickmann, Fritz. 'Das Problem der Gleichberechtigung der Konfessionen im Reich im 16. und 17. Jahrhundert', in Fritz Dickmann, *Friedensrecht und Friedenssicherung. Studien zum Friedensproblem in der neueren Geschichte* (Göttingen, Vandenhoeck & Ruprecht 1971), 7–35

'Rechtsgedanke und Machtpolitik bei Richelieu', in Fritz Dickmann, *Friedensrecht und Friedenssicherung. Studien zum Friedensproblem in der neueren Geschichte* (Göttingen, Vandenhoeck & Ruprecht 1971), 36–78

*Der Westfälische Frieden* (Münster, Aschendorff 1959)

Dipper, Christopher. 'Naturrecht und Wissenschaftliche Reformen', in Otto Dann and Diethelm Klippel (eds), *Naturrecht – Spätaufklärung – Revolution. Das europäische Naturrecht im ausgehenden 18. Jahrhundert* (Hamburg, Felix Meiner 1995), 165–73

Doguet, Jean-Paul. 'Présentation', in Condorcet, *Réflexions sur l'esclavage des nègres* (Paris, Flammarion 2009), 7–20

Domat, Jean. *Quatre livres du droit public. 1697* (Université de Caen, Bibliothèque de philosophie politique et juridique. Textes et Documents 1989)

*Traité des lois* (Université de Caen, Centre de philosophie politique et juridique 1989 [1689])

Donaldson, Peter S. *Machiavelli and Mystery of State* (Cambridge University Press 1988)

Donne, John. 'A Sermon upon the Eighth verse of the First Chapter of the Acts of the Apostles', in H. Alford (ed.), *Works of John Donne* (6 vols, London, Parker 1839), VI, 225–43

Dorigny, Marcel. 'The Abbé Grégoire and the Société des Amis des Noirs', in J. Popkin & R. Popkin (eds), *The Abbé Grégoire and His World* (Dordrecht, Springer 2000), 27–39

Dorigny, Marcel & Gainot, Bertrand. *La société des Amis des Noirs 1788–1799. Contribution à l'histoire de l'abolition de l'esclavage* (Paris, UNESCO 1998)

Döring, Detlef. 'Biographisches über Samuel von Pufendorf', in Bodo Geyer and Helmut Goerlich (eds), *Samuel Pufendorf und seine Wirkungen auf die heutige Zeit* (Baden-Baden, Nomos 1996), 23–37

'Samuel von Pufendorfs Berufung nach Brandenburg-Preussen', in Fiammetta Palladini & Gerald Hartung (eds), *Samuel Pufendorf und die europäische Frühaufklärung* (Berlin, Akademie 1996), 131–54

Doyle, John P. 'Vitoria on Choosing to Replace a King', in Kevin White (ed.), *Hispanic Philosophy in the Age of Discovery* (The Catholic University of America Press 1997), 45–58

Doyle, William. *France and the Age of Revolution. Regimes Old and New from Louis XIV to Napoleon Bonaparte* (London, Tauris 2013)

Drayton, Richard. *Nature's Government. Science, Imperial Britain and the 'Improvement' of the World* (Yale University Press 2000)

Dreitzel, Horst. 'Justis Beitrag zur Politisierung der deutschen Aufklärung', in Hans Erich Bödeker and Ulrich Herrmann (eds), *Aufklärung als Politisierung – Politisierung der Aufklärung.* Studien zum Achtzehnten Jahrhundert, Bd. 8 (Hamburg, Felix Meiner 1987), 158–77

'Reason of State and the Crisis of Political Aristotelianism. An Essay on the Development of 17th Century Political Philosophy, XXVIII *History of European Ideas* (2002), 163–87

'The Reception of Hobbes in the Political Philosophy of the Early German Enlightenment', XXIX *History of European Ideas* (2003), 255–89

'Universal-Kameral Wissenschaft als politische Theorie. Johann Friedrich von Pfeiffer (1718–1787)', in Frank Grunert and Friedrich Bolhardt (eds), *Aufklärung als praktische Philosophie. Werner Schneiders zum 65. Geburtstag* (Tübingen, Max Niemeyer 1998), 149–71

*Protestantisher Aristotelismus und absoluter Staat. Die 'Politica' des Henning Arnisaeus (ca. 1575–1636)* (Wiesbaden, Steiner 1970)

Drelichman, Mauricio & Voth, Hans-Joachim. *Lending to the Borrower from Hell. Debt, Taxes, and Default in the Age of Philip II* (Princeton University Press 2016)

Du Tertre, Jean-Baptiste. *Histoire générale des antilles habitées par les françois*, (4 tomes, Paris 1667–71)

Dubois, Laurent. *Avengers of the New World. The Story of the Haitian Revolution* (Harvard University Press 2005)

*A Colony of Citizens. Revolution and Slave Emancipation in the French Caribbean 1787–1804* (University of North Carolina Press 2004)

Dubois, Pierre. *The Recovery of the Holy Land* (Columbia University Press 1956)

Dubuisson, Paul-Ulrich. *Lettres critiques et politiques sur les colonies & la commerce* (Genève & Paris 1786)

Duchhardt, Heinz. *Gleichgewicht der Kräfte, Convenance, Europäische Konzert* (Darmstadt, Wissenschaftliche Buchgesellschaft 1976)

Dufour, Alfred. 'Les "Magni hispani" dans l'oeuvre de Grotius', in Frank Grunert & Kurt Seelmann (eds), *Die Ordnung der Praxis. Neue Studies zur Spanishen Spätscholastik* (Tübingen, Niemeyer 2001), 351–80

'Pufendorf', in J. H. Burns & Mark Goldie (eds), *The Cambridge History of Political Thought 1450–1700* (Cambridge University Press 1991), 561–80

Dummer, Jeremiah. *The Defence of the New England Charters* (London, Wilkins 1721)

Dumont, Louis. *Homo aequalis. Genèse et épanouissement de l'idéologie économique* (Paris, Gallimard 1977)

Dupont de Nemours, Pierre Samuel. *De l'origine et des progrès d'une science nouvelle* (London, Desaint 1768)

Dupuy, Pierre. *Histoire du différend d'entre pape Boniface VIII et Philippe le Bel, Roi de France* (Paris, Cramoisy 1655)

*Traitez touchant les droits du Roy Très-Chrétien sur plusieurs Estats et Seigneuries possedés par divers princes voisins* (nouvelle édition, Rouen, Maurry 1670)

Durand, Guillaume. *Speculum Iuris. Pars Tertia & Quarta* (Lyon 1577)

Duve, Thomas. 'La teoria de la restitución en Domingo de Soto. Su significación para la historia del derecho privado moderno', in Juan Cruz Cruz, *La ley natural como fundamento moral y jurídico en Domingo de Soto* (Pamplona, Eunsa 2007), 181–98

Dzembowski, Edmond. *Un nouveau patriotisme français 1750–1770. La France face à la puissance Anglaise à l'époque de la guerre de sept ans* (Oxford, Voltaire Foundation 1998)

Eberl, Oliver & Niesen, Peter. *Immanuel Kant, Zum ewigen Frieden. Kommentar von Oliver Eberl und Peter Niesen* (Frankfurt, Suhrkamp 2011)

Eccles, W. J. *French America* (University of Michigan Press 1990)

Eccleshall, Robert. *Order and Reason in Politics. Theories of Absolute and Limited Monarchy in Early Modern England* (Oxford University Press 1978)

Eckhart, Hellmuth. *Naturrechtsphilosophie und bürokratischer Werthorizont. Studien zur preussischen Geistes- und Sozialgeschichte des 18. Jahrhunderts* (Göttingen, Vandenhoeck & Ruprecht 1985)

Edelstein, Dan. 'Enlightenment Rights Talk', 86 *Journal of Modern History* (2014), 530–65

*The Enlightenment. A Genealogy* (The University of Chicago Press 2011)

*The Terror of Natural Right. Republicanism, the Cult of Nature & the French Revolution* (The University of Chicago Press 2009)

Edmundson, George. *Anglo-Dutch Rivalry during the First Half of the Seventeenth Century* (Oxford, Clarendon 1911)

Edwards, Jess. 'Between "Plain Wilderness" and "Goodly Corn Fields". Representing Land Use in Early Virginia', in Robert Appelbaum &

John Sweet (eds), *Envisioning an English Empire. Jamestown and the Making of a North Atlantic World* (University of Pennsylvania Press 2005), 217–35

Ehrard, Jean. *Lumières et esclavage. L'Esclavage colonial et l'opinion publique en France au XVIIIe siècle* (Paris, Versailles 2008)

Elliott, J. H. *Richelieu and Olivares* (Cambridge University Press 1984)

*Spain, Europe & the Wider World 1500–1800* (Yale University Press 2009)

Ellis, Elisabeth. *Kant's Politics. Provisional Theory for an Uncertain World* (Yale University Press 2005)

Eon, Jean. *Le commerce honorable* (Nantes, Monnier 1646)

Epstein, James. *Scandal of Colonial Rule. Power and Subversion in the British Atlantic during the Age of Revolution* (Cambridge University Press 2012)

Epstein, M. *The Early History of the Levant Company* (London, Routledge 1908)

Epstein, Steven A. *An Economic and Social History of Later Medieval Europe, 1000–1500* (Cambridge University Press 2009)

Ertman, Thomas. *Birth of the Leviathan. Building States and Regimes in Medieval and Early Modern Europe* (Cambridge University Press 1997)

Escamilla-Colin, Michèle. 'La question des justes titres. Repères juridiques. Des bulles Alexandrines aux Lois de Burgos', in Carmen Val Julian (ed.), *La conquète de l'Amérique espagnole et la question du droit* (Fontenay-aux-Roses, ENS 1996), 81–103

Eschassériaux, Joseph. 'Des droits des peuples. Des principes qui doivent diriger un peuple républicain dans ses relations étrangères', 49 *Le Moniteur universel*, 19 brumaire l'An 3 (9 Novembre 1794), 445–51

Esmein, A. 'Le maxime *Princeps legibus solutus* est dans l'ancien droit public français', in Paul Vinogradoff (ed.), *Essays in Legal History read before the International Congress of Historical Studies, London 1913* (Oxford University Press 1913), 201–14

Eugène, Itazienne. 'La normalisation des relations franco-haïtiennes (1825–1838)', in Marcel Dorigny (ed.), *Haiti. Première république noire* (Paris, Société française d'histoire d'outre-mer 2004), 139–54

Evensky, Jerry. *Adam Smith's Moral Philosophy. A Historical and Contemporary Perspective on Markets, Law, Ethics, and Culture* (Cambridge University Press 2005)

Eyffinger, Arthur. '*De Republica Emendanda.* A Juvenile Tract by Hugo Grotius on the Emendation of the Dutch Polity', 5 *Grotiana* (1984), 1–135

'In Quest of Synthesis. An Attempted Synopsis of Grotius' Works in Accordance with Their Genesis and Objective', 4 *Grotiana* (1983), 76–88

Ezran, Maurice. *L'abbé Grégoire. Défenseur des juifs et des noirs* (Paris, l'Harmattan 1992)

Faccarello, Gilbert. *The Foundations of* Laissez-faire. *The Economics of Pierre de Boisguilbert* (London, Routledge 1999)

Faivre-Faucompré, Rémi. 'Aux origines du concept moderne de propriété. *Dominium et proprietas* dans le droit romano-canonique, XIIe–XVe siècle', in N. Laurent-Bonne, N. Posé & V. Simon (eds), *Les Piliers du droit civil. Famille, propriété, contrat* (Paris, Mare & Martin 2014), 103–17

Farewell Slafter, Edmund et al., *Sir William Alexander and American Colonization* (Boston, Wilson 1873)

Farr, James. 'Locke, Natural Law, and New World Slavery', 36 *Political Theory* (2008), 495–522

Fasolt, Constant. *The Limits of History* (The University of Chicago Press 2004)

Fauchon, Pierre. *L'abbé Grégoire. Le prêtre-citoyen* (Paris, Nouvelle-République 1989)

Faure, Edgar. 'Chancelier D'Aguesseau', *Revue des deux mondes* (1952), 577–87

Favier, Jean. 'Les légistes et le gouvernement de Philippe le Bel', 2 *Journal des Savants* (1969), 92–108

*Philippe le Bel* (édition revue, Paris, Fayard 1998)

Fawtier, Robert. 'Nogaret and the Crime of Anagni', in Charles T. Wood (ed.), *Philip the Fair and Boniface VIII* (2nd edn, New York, Holt, Rinehart & Winston 1971), 72–80

*The Capetian Kings of France. Monarchy & Nation (987–1328)* (L. Butler & R. J. Adam trans., London, Macmillan 1960)

Fay, Peter Ward. *The Opium War 1840–1842. Barbarians in the Celestial Empire in the Early Part of the Nineteenth Century and the War by Which They Forced Her Gates Ajar* (University of North Carolina Press 1975)

Feenstra, Robert. 'Jean de Blanot et la formule "Rex Franciae in regno suo princeps est"', in *Études d'histoire du droit canonique dédiées à Gabriel le Bras, doyen honoraire de la Faculté de droit et de sciences économiques de Paris, membre de l'Institut,* tome II (Paris, Sirey 1965), 885–95

'L'enseignement du droit à Orléans. Etat des recherches menées depuis Meijers', in *Le droit savant au moyen âge et sa vulgarisation* (London, Variorum 1986), 12–29

'"Quaestiones de materia feudorum" de Jacques de Révigny', in Robert Feenstra, *Fata iuris romani* (Leiden 1972) , 379–401

Felden, J. von. *Annotata ad H. Grotium de iure pacis et belli* (Jena, Birchner 1653)

Fénelon, François de Salignac de la Mothe-. 'Examen de conscience sur les devoirs de royauté. Mémoire pour le duc de Bourgogne', in François de Salignac de la Mothe-Fénelon, *Directions pour la conscience d'un roi* (Paris, Benovard 1825)

'Les aventures de Télémaque, fils d'Ulysses', in Louis Vives (ed.), *Oeuvres de Fénelon, Archevêque de Cambrai,* (22 tomes, Paris, Lefevre 1835 [1699]) III 1–154

'Lettre à Louis XIV', in François de Salignac de la Mothe-Fénelon, *Lettre à Louis XIV et autres écrits politiques* (Paris, Bartillat 2011 [1693])

'Sur la necessité des former des alliances, tant offensives que defensives contre une puissance étrangère qui aspire manifestement à la monarchie universelle', in Louis Vives (ed.), *Oeuvres de Fénelon, Archevêque de Cambrai*, (22 tomes, Paris, Lefevre 1835), III 360–3

Fenge, Terry & Aldridge, Jim. *Keeping Promises. The Royal Proclamation to 1763, Aboriginal Rights and Treaties in Canada* (McGill–Queen's University Press 2015)

Fernández-Bollo, Eduardo. 'Conciencia y valor en Martín de Azpilcueta. ¿un agustinismo práctico en la España del siglo XVI?', 118 *Criticón* (2013), 57–69

Fernández-Santamaría, J. A. *Natural Law, Constitutionalism, Reason of State, and War. Counter-Reformation Spanish Political Thought*, 2 vols (New York, Peter Lang 2006)

*The State, War and Peace. Spanish Political Thought in the Renaissance 1516–1559* (Cambridge University Press 1977)

Ferrari, Jean. 'L'abbé Saint-Pierre, Rousseau et Kant', in Pierre Laberge et al. (eds), *L'année 1795. Kant. Essai sur la paix* (Paris, Vrin 1997), 25–40

Ferro, Marc. *Colonization. A Global History* (London, Routledge 1994)

Fichte, Johann Gottlieb. *Addresses to the German Nation* (G. Moore ed., Cambridge University Press 2008)

Figge, Robert. *Georg Friedrich von Martens. Sein Leben und seine Werke. Ein Beitrag zur Geschichte der Völkerrechtswissenschaft* (Gleiwitz, Hill 1914)

Finkelstein, Andrea. *Harmony and the Balance. An Intellectual History of Seventeenth-Century English Economic Thought* (University of Michigan Press 2000)

Finnis, John. *Aquinas. Moral, Political, and Legal Theory* (Oxford University Press 1998)

Fiocchi Malaspina, Elisebetta. *L'eterno ritorno del Droit des gens de Vattel (secc. XVIII–XIX). L'impatto sulla cultura giuridica in prospettiva globale* (Frankfurt am Main, Max Planck Institute for European Legal History 2017)

Fisch, Jörg. *Die europäische Expansion und das Völkerrecht. Die Auseinandersetzungen um den Status der überseeischen Gebiete vom 15. Jahrhundert bis zur Gegenwart* (Stuttgart, Steiner 1984)

Fischer, Daniela. 'Nicolaus Hieronymus Gundling, 1671–1729. Der Blick einer frühen Aufklärers auf die Obrigkeit, die Gesellschaft und die gebildeten seiner Zeit' (PhD diss., Trier 2002)

Fischer, David Hackett. *Champlain's Dream* (New York, Simon & Schuster 2008)

Fitzgibbons, Athol. *Adam Smith's System of Liberty, Wealth and Virtue. The Moral and Political Foundations of the Wealth of Nations* (Oxford University Press 1995)

Fitzmaurice, Andrew. 'Powhatan Legal Claims', in Saliha Belmessous (ed.), *Native Claims. Indigenous Law against Empire 1500–1920* (Oxford University Press 2012), 85–106

'The Justification of King Leopold II's Congo Enterprise by Sir Travers Twiss', in Shaunnagh Dorsett & Ian Hunter (eds), *Law and Politics in British Colonial Thought* (New York, Palgrave Macmillan 2010), 109–26

*Humanism and America. An Intellectual History of English Colonisation 1500–1625* (Cambridge University Press 2003)

*Sovereignty, Property and Empire 1500–2000* (Cambridge University Press 2015)

Fitzsimmons, Michael. *The Night the Old Regime Ended. August 4, 1789 and the French Revolution* (Penn State University Press 2002)

Flynn, Dennis O. & Giraldez, Arturo. 'Born with a "Silver Spoon". The Origin of World Trade in 1571', 6 *Journal of World History* (1995), 201–21

Foisneau, Luc. 'Bodin ou l'affirmation des droits de la souveraineté', in Alain Renaut (ed.), *Histoire de la philosophie politique.* Tome III: *Naissance de la modernité* (Paris, Calmann-Lévy 1999), 237–50

'Sovereignty and Reason of State. Bodin, Botero, Richelieu and Hobbes', in Howell A. Lloyd (ed.), *The Reception of Bodin* (Leiden, Brill 2013), 323–42

Fontana, Biancamaria. *Montaigne's Politics. Authority and Governance in the* Essais (Princeton University Press 2008)

Forbes, Duncan. *Hume's Philosophical Politics* (Cambridge University Press 1975)

Forbonnais, François Veron de. *Elemens du commerce. Première partie* (2nd edn, Leiden, Briasson 1754)

*Essai sur l'admission des navires neutres dans nos colonies* (Paris 1756 – original has neither author nor time or place of publication)

*Principes et observations économiques* (tome première, Amsterdam, Michel Rey 1767)

Force, Pierre. *Self-Interest before Adam Smith. A Genealogy of Economic Science* (Cambridge University Press 2003)

Ford, Lisa. *Settler Sovereignty. Jurisdiction and Indigenous People 1788–1836* (Harvard University Press 2010)

Fortescue, Sir John. 'Extracts from the Nature of the Law of Nature', in *The Works of Sir John Fortescue* vol I (2 vols, London 1869), 187–337

'In Praise of the Laws of England', in S. Lockwood (ed.), *On the Laws and Governance of England* (Cambridge University Press 1997), 1–80

'The Governance of England', in S. Lockwood (ed.), *On the Laws and Governance of England* (Cambridge University Press 1997), 81–126

Foster, Stephen & Haefeli, Evan. 'British North America in the Empire. An Overview', in Stephen Foster (ed.), *British North America in the Seventeenth and Eighteenth Centuries* (Oxford University Press 2013), 18–66

Foucault, Michel. *'Il faut défendre la société'. Cours au Collège de France 1976* (Paris, Gallimard 1997)

*Naissance de la biopolitique. Cours au Collège de France 1978–1979* (Paris, Gallimard 2004)

*Sécurité, territore, population. Cours au Collège de France 1977–1978* (Paris, Gallimard 2004)

*The Order of Things. An Archaeology of the Human Sciences* (London, Tavistock Publications 1970)

Fraga Iribarne, Manuel. 'Presentación', in Diego Covarrubias y Leyva, *Textos Jurídico-Políticos* (Madrid, Instituto de estudios políticos 1957), i–xxxvii

Franco, Paul. *Hegel's Philosophy of Freedom* (Yale University Press 2002)

Franke, Mark. *Global Limits. Immanuel Kant, International Relations, and Critique of World Politics* (State University of New York Press 2001)

Franklin, Julian H. *Jean Bodin et la naissance de la théorie absolutiste* (Presses Universitaires de France 1993 [1973])

'Sovereignty and the Mixed Constitution. Bodin and His Critics', in J. H. Burns & Mark Goldie (eds), *The Cambridge History of Political Thought 1450–1700* (Cambridge University Press 1991), 298–328

Fraser Terjanian, Anoush. *Commerce and Its Discontents in Eighteenth-Century French Political Thought* (Cambridge University Press 2013)

Frayle Urbano, Luis. *El pensamiento humanista de Francisco Vitoria* (Salamanca, San Esteban 2004)

Frederick the Great. *Anti Machiavel ou Essai de critique sur le Prince de Machiavel* (La Haey, Paupie 1740)

Frey, Linda & Frey, Marsha. 'Grégoire and the Breath of Reason. The French Revolutionaries and the *Droit des gens*', 38 *Journal for the Western Society of French History* (2010), 163–77

Friedeburg, Robert von. 'Persona and Office. Althusius on the Formation of Magistrates and Councillors', in Conal Condren et al. (eds), *The Philosopher in Early Modern Europe. The Nature of a Contested Identity* (Cambridge University Press 2006), 160–80

Fulbeck, William. *A Parallele or Conference of the Civil Law, Canon Law, and the Common Law of this Realme of England* (London, Company of Stationers 1618)

*The Pandectes of the Law of Nations, containing Several Discourses of the Questions, Points and Matters of Law wherein the Nations of the World do Consent and Accord* (London, Wight 1602)

Fulton, T. W. *The Sovereignty of the Sea. An Historical Account of the Claims of England to the Dominion of the British Seas, and of the Evolution of Territorial Waters* (Edinburgh & London 1911)

Funck-Brentano, Franck. *Philippe le Bel en Flandre* (Paris, Champion 1896)

Furet, François. 'Ancien régime', in François Furet & Mona Ozouf, *Dictionnaire critique de la Révolution française* (Paris, Flammarion 1992), 25–43

'Féodalité', in François Furet & Mona Ozouf, *Dictionnaire critique de la Révolution française* (Paris, Flammarion 1992), 181–97

*La Révolution 1770–1814* (Paris, Fayard 2010)

Gainot, Bernard. 'Métropole/Colonies. Projets constitutionnels et rapport des forces 1798–1802', in Yves Benot & Marcel Dorigny (eds), *Rétablissement de l'esclavage dans les colonies françaises 1802* (Paris, Maisonneuve & Larose 2003), 13–28

*L'empire colonial français – De Richelieu à Napoléon* (Paris, Armand Colin 2015)

et al. 'Lumières et esclavage', 380 *Annales historiques de la Révolution française* (Juin 2015), 149–69

Galigardo, John. *Germany under the Old Regime, 1600–1790* (London, Longman 1991)

Gallagher, John & Robinson, Ronald. 'The Imperialism of Free Trade', VI *The Economic History Review* (1953), 1–15

(with Alice Denny). *Africa and the Victorians. The Official Mind of Imperialism* (London, Macmillan 1981)

Ganshof, François L. *Qu'est-ce que la féodalité?* (5th edn, Paris, Texto 1982 [1944])

García, Jorge E. 'Hispanic Philosophy. Its Beginning and Golden Age', in Kevin White (ed.), *Hispanic Philosophy in the Age of Discovery* (Catholic University of America Press 1997), 3–27

García García, Antonio & Alonso Rodríguez, Bernardo. 'El pensamiento económico y el mundo del derecho hasta el siglo XVI', in S. J. Gómez Camacho & Ricardo (eds), *El pensamiento económico en la escuela de Salamanca* (Ediciones Universidad Salamanca 1998), 65–92

Gardot, Jean. 'Jean Bodin. Sa place parmi les fondateurs du droit international', 50 *Recueil des Cours* (1934/IV), 545–747

Garnett, George (ed.). *Vindiciae, contra Tyrannos* (Cambridge University Press 1994 [1579])

Garnsey, Peter. *Thinking about Property. From Antiquity to the Age of Revolution* (Cambridge University Press 2009)

Garrett, Mitchell B. *The French Colonial Question 1789–1791* (Cornell University 1918)

Garve, Christian. *Abhandlung über die Verbindung der Moral mit dem Politik oder einige Betrachtungen über die Frage in wiefern es möglich sei die Moral des Privatlebens bei der Regierung der Staaten zu beobachten* (Breslau, Korn 1788)

Gauchet, Marcel. 'L'État au miroir de la raison d'État', in Yves Charles Zarka (ed.), *Raison et déraison d'État. Théoriciens et théories de la raison d'état aux XVIe et XVIIe siècles* (Presses Universitaires de France 1994), 193–244

*La révolution des droits de l'homme* (Paris, Gallimard 1989)

*La révolution des pouvoirs. La souveraineté, le peuple et la représentation 1789–1799* (Paris, Gallimard 1995)

*La révolution moderne. L'avénement de la démocratie*, I (Paris, Gallimard 2007)

*Le désenchantement du monde. Une histoire politique de la religion* (Paris, Gallimard 1985)

Gaukroger, Stephen. *The Natural and the Human. Science and the Shaping of Modernity 1739–1842* (Oxford University Press 2016)

Gauthier, Florence. 'Le Mercier de la Rivière et les colonies de l'Amérique', 20 *Revue française d'histoire des idées politiques* (2004), 37–59

*Triomphe et mort du droit naturel en Révolution 1789–1795–1802* (Presses universitaires de France 1992)

Gauvard, Claude. 'Ordonnance de reforme et pouvoir législatif en France au XIVe siècle (1303–1413)', in A. Gouron & A. Rigaudière (eds), *Renaissance du pouvoir législatif et genèse de l'état* (Montpellier, Publications de la société d'histoire de droit 1988), 89–98

(ed.). *Penseurs de Code Civil* (Paris, Collection de Histoire de Justice 2009)

Gay, Peter. *The Party of Humanity. Essays in the French Enlightenment* (New York, Norton 1959)

*Voltaire's Politics. The Poet as Realist* (Princeton University Press 1959)

Gazier, Michèle & Gazier, Bernard. *Or et monnaie chez Martín de Azpilcueta Navarro* (Paris, Economica 1978)

Geddert, Jeremy Seth. 'Beyond Strict Justice. Hugo Grotius on Punishment and Natural Rights', 76 *The Review of Politics* (2014), 559–88

Geggus, David P. 'Racial Equality, Slavery, and Colonial Secession during the Constituent Assembly', 94 *American Historical Review* (1989), 1290–1308

'The Caribbean in the Age of Revolution', in David Armitage & Sanjay Subrahmanyam (eds), *The Age of Revolution in Global Context c.1760–1840* (London, Palgrave 2010), 83–100

*Haitian Revolutionary Studies* (Indiana University Press 2002)

Gelderen, Martin van. '"So meerly humane". Theories of Resistance in Early-Modern Europe', in Annabel Brett & James Tully, with Holly Hamilton-Bleakeley, *Rethinking the Foundations of Modern Political Thought* (Cambridge University Press 2006), 149–70

'The State and Its Rivals in Early-Modern Europe', in Quentin Skinner and Bo Stråth (eds), *States and Citizens. History, Theory, Prospects* (Cambridge University Press 2003), 79–97

Gentili , Alberico. *De iure belli libri tres. Volume II, The Translation of the Edition of 1612* (John Rolfe trans., Coleman Phillipson ed., Oxford, Clarendon 1933)

*De legationibus Libri tres. Volume II, The Translation* (G J Lain transl., Oxford University Press 1924)

*De papatu Romano Anthichristo* (Giovanni Minnucci ed. & intro., Siena, Monducci 2018)

'De potestate regis absoluta', in *Regales disputationes* (London, Vautrolles 1605), 5–38

'De vi civium in regem semper iniusta', in *Regales disputationes* (London, Vautrolles 1605), 99–132

*Disputationes duae. I. De actoribus et spectatoribus fabularum non notandis. II De abusu mendacii* (Hanau, Antonium 1599)

*Hispanicae advocationis. Libri duo.* The Translation (F F Abbott transl., Oxford University Press 1921)

'Utrum possit princeps de regno suo, suorumque subditorum pro arbitratu statuere', in *Disputationum Dicas Prima* (London, Wolf 1587), 27–51

*The Wars of the Romans. A Critical Edition and Translation of* De armis Romanis (Benedict Kingsbury & Benjamin Straumann eds, Oxford University Press 2010)

Gentz, Friedrich. 'Anmerkungn des Übersetzers', in Edmund Burke, *Betrachtungen über die französische Revolution nach dem englischen des herrn Burke*, II (Hohenzollern 1794), 145–57

Getino, Alonso. 'Domincos españoles confesores de los reyes', 14 *Ciencía Tomista* (1916), 374–451

Ghachem, Malik W. 'Prosecuting Torture. The Strategic Ethics of Slavery in Pre-Revolutionary Saint-Domingue (Haiti)', 29 *Law and History Review* (2011), 985–1029

*The Old Regime and the Haitian Revolution* (Cambridge University Press 2012)

Gierke, Otto von. *Political Theories of the Middle Ages* (F. W. Maitland trans., Cambridge University Press 1900 [1881])

*Community in Historical Perspective* (Mary Fischer trans. & Anthony Black ed., Cambridge University Press 1990 [1868])

Giesey, Ralph. E. *Rulership in France. 15th–17th Centuries* (Burlington, VT 2004)

Giles of Rome (Aegidus Romanus). *De regimine principum libri III. Ad francorum regem Philip IIII cognomento pulchrum* (Rome 1556)

Giles of Rome (Aegidus Romanus). *On Ecclesiastical Power. A Medieval Theory of World Government* (R. W. Dyson trans. & ed., Columbia University Press 2004)

Gilles, David. 'Jean Domat et les fondements du droit public', 25–26 *Revue d'histoire des facultés de droit* (2006), 93–119

'Les acteurs de la norme coloniale face au droit métropolitain. De l'adaptation à l'appropriation (Canada XVIIe–XVIIIe s.)', 4 *Clio@Thémis* (2011), 1–45

Giordanengo, Gérard. 'De l'usage du droit privé et du droit public au Moyen Âge', 7 *Cahiers de recherches médiévales et humanistes* (2000), 1–21

'La difficile interprétation des données négatives. Les ordonnances royales sur le droit féodal', in A. Gouron & A. Rigaudière (eds), *Renaissance du pouvoir législatif et genèse de l'état* (Montpellier, Publications de la société d'histoire de droit 1988), 99–116

*Le droit feudal dans les pays de droit écrit. L'exemple de la Provence et du Dauphiné XII–début XIV siècle* (École française de Rome 1988)

Girard, Philippe R. '*Liberté, Égalité, Esclavage.* French Revolutionary Ideas and the Failure of the Leclerc Expedition to Saint-Domingue', 6 *French Colonial History* (2005), 55–77

Giraudeau, Martin. 'Performing Physiocracy. Pierre Samuel Dupont de Nemours and the Limits of Political Engineering', 3 *Journal of Cultural Economy* (2008), 225–42

Glafey, Adam Friedrich. *Vernunfft- und Völker-Recht* (Frankfurt 1723 [1722])

*Geschichte des Rechts der Vernunfft-* (Leipzig, Riegel 1739)

Glete, Jan. *War and the State in Early Modern Europe. Spain, the Dutch Republic and Sweden as Fiscal-Military States, 1500–1660* (London, Routledge 2002)

Godechot, Jacques. *La Grande Nation. L'expansion révolutionnaire de la France dans le monde du 1789 à 1799* (2ème éd., Paris, Aubier 1983)

Goebel, Julius. *The Struggle for the Falkland Islands. A Study in Legal and Diplomatic History* (Yale University Press 1927)

Gojosso, Eric. *Le concept de république en France (xvie–xviiie siècle)* (Presses Universitaires d'Aix-Marseille 1998)

Goldie, Mark. 'Edmund Bohun and *jus gentium* in the Revolutionary Debate 1689–1693', 20 *The Historical Journal* (1977), 569–86

Goldsmith, James Lowth. *Lordship in France 500–1500* (London, Peter Lang 2003)

Goldstein Sepinwall, Alyssa. *The Abbé Grégoire and the French Revolution. The Making of Modern Universalism* (University of California Press 2005)

Goldzink, Jean. *La solitude de Montesquieu. Le chef-oeuvre introuvable du libéralisme* (Paris, Fayard 2011)

Gómez Camacho, S. J. & Robledo, Ricardo (eds). *El pensamiento económico en la escuela de Salamanca* (Ediciones Universidad Salamanca 1998)

Gonner, R. C. K. *Common Land and Inclosure* (London, Macmillan 1912)

Goodell, William. *The American Slave Code in Theory and Practice* (London, Clarke etc. 1854)

Gordon, Robert W. 'Paradoxical Property', in John Brewer & Susan Staves (eds), *Early Modern Conceptions of Property* (London, Routledge 1995), 95–110

Gould, Eliga H. *Among the Powers of the Earth. The American Revolution and the Making of a New World Empire* (Harvard University Press 2012)

Goyard-Fabre, Simone. 'Commentaire philosophique de l'exposé du droit universel', in Jean Bodin, *Exposé du droit universel. Juris universi distributio* (Presses Universitaires de France 1985), 85–170

'Je ne suis que l'apothécaire de l'Europe', in Carole Dornier & Claudine Poulouin et al. (eds), *Les Projets de l'âbbé Castel de Saint Pierre (1658–1743)* (Presses Universitaires de Caen 2011), 19–37

'Les articles préliminaires', in Pierre Laberge et al. (eds), *L'année 1795. Kant. Essai sur la paix* (Paris, Vrin 1997), 41–59

*Kant et le problème du droit* (Paris, Vrijn 1975)

*La construction de la paix ou le travail de Sisyphe* (Paris, Vrin 1994)

*Philosophie critique et raison juridique* (Presses Universitaires de France 2004)

*Pufendorf et le droit naturel* (Presses Universitaires de France 1994)

Grabill, Stephen J. *Sourcebook in Late-Scholastic Monetary Theory. The Contributions of Martín de Azpilcueta Navarro, Luis de Molina, S.J., and Juan de Mariana, S.J.* (New York, Lexington 2007)

Grace, Richard J. *Opium and Empire. Lives and Careers of William Jardine and James Matheson* (McGill–Queen's University Press 2014)

Grafton, Anthony. *What Was History? The Art of History in Early Modern Europe* (Cambridge University Press 2007)

Grant, Daragh. 'Francisco de Vitoria and Alberico Gentili on the Juridical Status of Native American Polities', 72 *Renaissance Studies* (2019), 910–52

Gratian, *The Treatise on Laws (Decretum DD 1–20)* (A. Thompson trans., Catholic University of America Press 1993)

Gray, Robert. *A Good Speed to Virginia* (London, Kyngston 1609)

Greenberger, Gerald A. 'Lawyers Confront Centralized Government. Political Thought of Lawyers During the Reign of Louis XIV', 23 *American Journal of Legal History* (1979), 144–81

Greene, Jack P. 'Empire and Identity. From the Glorious Revolution to the American Revolution', in P. J. Marshall & Alaine Low (eds), *The Oxford History of the British Empire*, vol. II: *The Eighteenth Century* (Oxford University Press 1998), 208–30

*Evaluating Empire and Confronting Colonialism in Eighteenth-Century Britain* (Cambridge University Press 2013)

*Negotiated Authorities. Essays in Colonial Political and Constitutional History* (University Press of Virginia 1994)

*Peripheries and Center. Constitutional Development in the Extended Polities of the British Empire and the United States, 1607–1788* (New York, Norton 1986)

Greenfeld, Liah. *The Spirit of Capitalism. Nationalism and Economic Growth* (Harvard University Press 2003)

Grégoire, Abbé. 'De la littérature des nègres ou recherches sur leurs facultés intellectuelles, leurs qualités morales et leur littérature', in Abbé Grégoire, *Écrits sur les noirs*, tome 1 1789–1808 (Paris, Harmattan 2012). 103–226

'Lettre aux citoyens de couleur et nègres libres de Saint-Domingue, et des autres isles françaises de l'Amérique', in Abbé Grégoire, *Écrits sur les noirs*, tome 1: *1789–1808* (Paris, L'Harmattan 2012), 47–54

'Mémoire en faveur des gens de couleur au sang-melés de St Domingue, et des autres iles françaises de l'Amérique adressée 'à l'Assemblée Nationale', in Abbé Grégoire, *Écrits sur les noirs*, tome 1: *1789–1808* (Paris, L'Harmattan 2012), 3–46

Grégoire, Henri. *Convention nationale. Rapport sur la réunion de la Savoie à la France* (Paris, Imprimerie national 1792)

Grewe, Wilhelm. *The Epochs of International Law* (Berlin, Gruyter 2000) *Fontes historiae iuris gentium.* 2 vols (Berlin, De Gruyter 1988)

*Fontes historiae iuris gentium* (2 vols., Berlin, De Gruyter 1988)

Grice-Hutchinson, Marjorie. *Early Economic Thought in Spain 1177–1740* (London, Allen & Unwin 1978)

Griffiths, Percival. *A Licence to Trade. A History of the English Chartered Companies* (London, Benn 1974)

Grillon, Pierre (ed.). *Les papiers de Richelieu*, tome I: *1624–1626* (Paris, Pedone 1975)

Gross, Hanns. *Empire and Sovereignty. A History of the Public Law Literature in the Holy Roman Empire, 1599–1804* (The University of Chicago Press 1973)

Grotius, Hugo. *Commentary on the Law of Prize and Booty* (*De iure praedae Commentarius*, Martine Julia van Ittersum ed. & intro., Indianapolis, Liberty Fund 2006 [1604–6])

*De imperio summarum potestatum circa sacra* (Harm-Jan van Dam, intro., trans., comm., Leiden, Brill 2001 [1647])

*De jure praedae commentarius* (Ger. Hamaker ed., Paris, Thorin 1869)

*Defensio fidei catholicae de satisfactione Christi adversus Faustum Socinum Senensem* (Edwin Rabbie ed. & intro., H. Mulder trans., Assen, Van Gorcum 1990)

*Introduction to Dutch Jurisprudence* (C Herbert transl., London, Voorst 1845 [1631])

*Meletius sive de iis quae inter Christianos coneveniunt Epistola* (Guillaume Posthumus Meyjes ed., Leiden, Brill 1988)

*Ordinum Hollandiae ac Westfrisiae pietas* (Edwin Rabbie, trans., comm., Leiden, Brill 1995 [1613])

*The Antiquity of the Batavian Republic* (Jan Waszink ed. & trans., Assen, Van Gorcum 2000)

*The Free Sea* (D. Armitage intro. & ed., R. Hakluyt trans., Indianapolis, Liberty Fund 2011 [1609])

*The Rights of War and Peace* (*De iure belli ac pacis*, Richard Tuck ed. & intro., Indianapolis, Liberty Fund 2005 [1625/1631])

Grunert, Frank. 'Absolutism(s). Necessary Ambivalences in the Political Theory of Christian Wolff', 73 *Legal History Journal* (2005), 141–51

'Das Recht der Natur als Recht des Gefühls. Zur Naturrechtslehre von Johann Jacob Schmauss', 12 *Annual Review of Law and Ethics* (2004), 139–53

'The Reception of Hugo Grotius'. *De jure belli ac pacis* in Early German Enlightenment', in Tim Hochstrasser & Peter Schröder (eds), *Early Modern Natural Law Theories* (Dordrecht, Kluwer 2003), 89–105

*Normbegründung und politische Legitimation. Zur Rechts- und Staatsphilosophie der deutschen Frühaufklärung* (Tübingen, Niemeyer 2000)

Guenée, Bernard. 'Review of Joseph Canning, *The Political Thought of Baldus de Ubaldis*', 45 *Annales. Économies, sociétés, civilisations* (1990), 1097–9

Guessard, Francis. 'Pierre de Mornay, Chancellier de France', 5 *Bibliothèque de l'école des chartes* (1844), 143–70

Guetata, Jouda. 'Le refus d'application de la constitution de l'An III à Saint-Domingue 1795–1797', in Florence Gauthier (ed.), *Périssent les colonies plutôt qu'un principe!* (Paris, Société des études robespierristes 2002), 81–90

Guillot, Olivier, Albert Rigaudière & Yves Sassier, *Pouvoirs et institutions dans la France Médiévale. 1: Des origines à l'époque féodale* (3è éd,. Paris, Armand Colin 2014)

Guggenheim, Paul. 'Jus gentium, jus naturae, jus civile et la communauté internationale issue de la divisio regnorum intervenue au cours des 12e et 13e siècles', 7 *Comunicazione e studi* (1955), 3–15

Guicciardini, Francesco. *Dialogue on the Government of Florence* (Alison Brown ed., Cambridge University Press 1994 [1521])

*Maxims and Reflections (Ricordi)* (University of Pennsylvania Press 1965 [1530])

*The History of Italy* (Princeton University Press 1984 [1561])

Guizot, M. (ed.). *Chronique de Guillaume de Nangis* (Paris, Brière 1825)

Gundling, Nicholaus Hieronymus. *Ausführlicher Discours über den jetzigen Zustand Der Europäischen Staaten*, vol. I: *Von dem Nutzen und Noth-wendigkeiten der Staaten-Notiz überhaupt* (Frankfurt & Leipzig 1733)

*Ausführlicher Discours über die Natur- und Völcker-Recht* (2nd edn, Frankfurt & Leipzig, Springs 1734)

*Collegium Historico-Literarium oder ausführliche. Discourse über die Vornehmsten Wissenschaften und besonderes der Rechtsgelahrheit* (Bremen, Saurmann 1738)

*Einleitung zu wahren Staatsklugheit, aus desselben mündlichen Vortrag* (Frankfurt und Leipzig, Springs 1751)

*Erörterung der Frage. Ob wegen der anwachsenden Macht der Nachbarn man Degen entblößen könne?* (Frankfurt & Leipzig 1757)

*Ius naturae ac gentium* (2nd edn, Halle 1728)

Gutarra, Dannelle. 'The Discourses of Sonthonax's Mission in Saint-Domingue. The Coda to the Abolition of Slavery', 17 *French Colonial History* (2017), 81–102

Guy, J. A. 'The Origins of the Petition of Rights Reconsidered', 25 *The Historical Journal* (1982), 455–61

Guyer, Paul. 'Kant's Deductions of the Principles of Right', in Mark Timmons (ed.), *Kant's Metaphysics of Morals. Interpretative Essays* (Oxford University Press 2002), 23–64

*Kant on Freedom, Law, and Happiness* (Cambridge University Press 2000)

Guyot-Bachy, Isabelle. *Le memoriale historiarum de Jean de Saint-Victor. Une historien et sa communauté au début du XIVe siècle* (Turnhout, Brepols 2000)

Haakonssen, Knud. 'German Natural Law', in Mark Goldie & Robert Wokler (eds), *The Cambridge History of Eighteenth-Century Political Thought* (Cambridge University Press 2006), 249–90

*Natural Law and Moral Philosophy. From Grotius to the Scottish Enlightenment* (Cambridge University Press 1996)

*The Science of a Legislator. David Hume & Adam Smith* (Cambridge University Press 1981)

Haar, Edwin van. *Classical Liberalism and International Relations Theory. Hume, Smith, Mises and Hayek* (London, Palgrave 2009)

Habenicht, Walter. *Georg Friedrich von Martens. Eine Biografische und völkerrechtliche Studie* (Göttingen, Vandenhoeck & Ruprecht 1934)

Hadden, Sally E. 'The Fragmented Laws of Slavery in the Colonial and Revolutionary Eras', in Michael Grossberg and Christopher Tomlins (eds), *The Cambridge History of Law in America* (Cambridge University Press 2008), 253–87

Haggenmacher, Peter. 'Droits subjectifs et système juridique chez Grotius', in Luc Foisneau (ed.), *Politique, Droit et Théologie chez Bodin, Grotius et Hobbes* (Paris, Kimé 1997), 73–130

'Grotius and Gentili. A Reassessment of Thomas E. Holland's Inaugural Lecture', in Hedley Bull, Benedict Kingsbury & Adam Roberts (eds), *Hugo Grotius and International Relations* (Oxford University Press 1992), 133–76

'Just War and Regular War in Sixteenth Century Spanish Doctrine', 32 *International Review of the Red Cross* (1992), 434–45

'Kant et la tradition du droit des gens', in Pierre Laberge et al. (eds), *L'année 1795. Kant. Essai sur la paix* (Paris, Vrin 1997), 122–39

'Le modèle Vattel et la discipline de droit international', in Vincent Chetail & Peter Haggenmacher (eds), *Vattel's International Law in a XXIst Century Perspective* (Geneva, Nijhoff 2011), 3–48

*Grotius et la doctrine de la guerre juste* (Presses Universitaires de France 1986)

Haifry, Ofir. *John Selden and the Western Political Tradition* (Cambridge University Press 2017)

Hakluyt, Richard. 'Discourse of Western Planting', in E. G. R. Taylor (ed.), *The Original Writings & Correspondence of the Two Richard Hakluyts* (2 vols., London, Hakluyt Society 1935), II 211–326

'Pamphlet for the Virginia Enterprise, 1585', in E. G. R. Taylor (ed.), *The Original Writings & Correspondence of the Two Richard Hakluyts* (2 vols., London, Hakluyt Society 1935), II 327–38

*The Principal Navigations Voyages, Traffiques and Discoveries of the English Nation* (16 vols., Edinburgh, Goldsmith 1887 [1599])

Hale, Sir Matthew. *The Prerogatives of the King* (Yale, D. E. C. ed., London, Selden Society 1976)

Halpern, Jean-Claude. 'Entre esclavage et liberté. Les variations d'un éthnotype dans la France de la fin du XVIIIe siècle', in Marcel Dorigny (ed.), *Esclavage. Résistance et abolitions* (Paris, CTHS 1999), 129–38

Hammerstein, Notker. 'Die Deutschen Universitäten im Zeitalter der Aufklärung', 10 *Zeitschrift für Historische Forschung* (1983), 73–89

'Innovation und Tradition. Akademien und Universitäten im Heiligen Römischen Reich deutscher Nation', 278 *Historische Zeitschrift* (2004), 591–624

'Samuel Pufendorf', in Michael Stolleis (ed.), *Staatsdenker in der frühen Neuzeit* (Munich, Beck 1995), 172–96

'Zur Geschichte und Bedeutung der Universitäten im Heiligen Römischen Reich Deutschen Nation', 241 *Historische Zeitschrift* (1985), 287–328

*Geschichte als Arsenal. Ausgewählte Aufsätze zu Recht, Hof und Universitäten der Frühen Neuzeit* (Göttingen, Wellstein 2010)

*Ius und Historie. Ein Beitrag zur Geschichte des historischen Denkens an deutschen Universitäten im späten 17. und im 18. Jahrhundert* (Göttingen, Vandenhoeck & Ruprecht 1972)

Hancock, David. *Citizens of the World. London Merchants and the British Atlantic Community 1735–1785* (Cambridge University Press 1995)

Hanke, Lewis. *The Spanish Struggle for Justice in the Conquest of America* (S. Scafidi & Beter Bakewell intro., Southern Methodist University Press 2002 [1949])

Harcourt, William. *Letters by Historicus on Some Questions of International Law* (London, Macmillan 1863)

Hardin, Nicholas. 'Hanover and British Republicanism', in Brendan Simms & Torsten Riotte (eds), *The Hanoverian Dimension in British History 1714–1837* (Cambridge University Press 2007), 301–23

Hardinge, George. *Speech of Mr Hardinge, Counsel of the Directors of the East India Company at the Bar of the House of Lords, on Tuesday the 16th of December, 1783* (London, Stockdale 1784)

Haring, C. H. *The Spanish Empire in America* (New York, Harcourt Brace 1947)

Harouel, Jean-Louis. 'L'expropriation dans l'histoire de droit français', in Jean-Louis Harouel, *Histoire de l'expropriation* (Presses Universitaires de France 2000), 39–77

Harper, L. A. *The English Navigation Laws. A Seventeenth Century Experiment in Social Engineering* (Columbia University Press 1939)

Harrington, Matthew P. 'The Legacy of the Colonial Vice-Admiralty Courts, Part II', 26 *Journal of Maritime Law & Commerce* (1996), 581–606

Harrison, Peter. 'The Natural Philosopher and the Virtues', in Conal Condren et al. (eds), *The Philosopher in Early Modern Europe. The Nature of a Contested Identity* (Cambridge University Press 2006), 202–28

Harrisse, H. *Notes pour servir à l'histoire, à la bibliographie et à la cartographie de la Nouvelle-France et des pays adjacents 1545–1700* (Paris, Tross 1872)

Hart, H. L. A. *Essays on Bentham. Jurisprudence and Political Theory* (Oxford University Press 1982)

Hartung, Gerald. *Die Naturrechtsdebatte. Geschichte der Obligatio vom 17. bis 20. Jahrhundert* (Freiburg, Alber 1998)

Haudrère, Philippe & Le Bouëdec, Gérard. *Les compagnies des Indes. XVIIe–XVIIIe siècles* (Rennes, Ouest-France 2011)

Hauser, Henri. *La pensée et l'action économiques du Cardinal de Richelieu* (Presses Universitaires de France 1944)

*Richelieu. L'argent et le pouvoir* (Paris, Nouveau Monde 2018 [1949])

Hauterive, Alexandre-Maurice Blanc de Lanautte. *Conseils à un élève du ministère des relations extérieures* (Épreuves pour le seul usage du service des archives no date)

*État de la France en l'An VIII* (Paris, Henrics, An 9 1799)

Hazard, Paul. *Le crise de la conscience européenne 1680–1715* (Paris, Fayard 1961)

Headlam, Cecil (ed.). *Calendar of State Papers. Colonial Series. America and West Indies*, 1574–1739 45 vols. (London 1933), available at British History Online: www.british-history.ac.uk/col-state-papers/colonial/america-west-indies

Hebié, Mamadou. *Souveraineté territoriale par traité. Une étude des accords entre puissances coloniales et entités politiques locales* (Presses Universitaires de France 2015)

Héctor, Michael & Hurbon, Laënnec (eds.), *Genèse de l'État haitien* (Paris, Éditions de la maison des sciences de l'homme, 2010)

Heering, J. P. 'Hugo Grotius' *De veritate religionis christianae*', in Henk M. Nellen & Edwin Rabbie (eds), *Hugo Grotius Theologian. Essays in Honour of G. H. M. Posthumus Meyjes* (Leiden, Brill 1994), 41–52

*Hugo Grotius as an Apologist for the Christian Religion. A Study of His Work* De veritate religionis christianae (Leiden, Brill 2004)

Heers, Jacques. *La naissance du capitalisme au Moyen Age* (Paris, Perrin 2012)

Hegel, G. W. F. 'German Constitution', in L. Dickey & H. B. Nisbet (eds), *Hegel. Political Writings* (Cambridge University Press 1999), 6–101

'Lectures on the Philosophy of History (1827–1831), Part IV, Section 3: The New Age', in L. Dickey & H. B. Nisbet (eds), *Hegel. Political Writings* (Cambridge University Press 1999), 249–76

'On the Scientific Ways of Treating Natural Law', in L. Dickey & H. B. Nisbet (eds), *Hegel. Political Writings* (Cambridge University Press 1999), 102–80

*Lectures on the Philosophy of World History. Introduction* (H. B. Nisbet trans., D. Forbes intro., Cambridge University Press 1975)

*Outlines of the Philosophy of Right* (T. M. Knox trans., S. Houlgate intro., Oxford University Press 1952/2008 [1821])

Heilbron, John. *The Rise of Social Theory* (Cambridge, Polity 1995)

Helfman, Tara. 'Commerce on Trial. Neutral Rights and Private Warfare in the Seven Years' War', in Koen Stapelbroek (ed.), *Trade and War. The Neutrality of Commerce in the Inter-State System* (Helsinki Collegium for Advanced Studies 2011), 14–41

'Neutrality, the Law of Nations, and the Natural Law Tradition. A Study of the Seven Years' War', 30 *Yale Journal of International Law* (2005), 549–86

Helmholz, R. H. 'Natural Law and Human Rights in English Law. From Bracton to Blackstone', 3 *Ave Maria Law Review* (2005), 1–22

Henderson, W. O. 'The Anglo-French Commercial Treaty of 1786', X *The Economic History Review* (1957), 104–12

Henry, John F. 'John Locke, Property Rights, and Economic Theory', 32 *Journal of Economic Issues* (1999), 609–24

Herde, Peter. *Bonifaz VIII* (Erster Halbband, 43.1 Päpste und Papsttum, Stuttgart, Hiersemann 2015)

Hernández Martín, Ramón. *Francisco de Vitoria. Vida y pensamiento internacionalista* (Madrid, Biblioteca de autores cristianos 1995)

Herrera Ortíz, Margarita. 'La encomienda Indiana y sus repercusiones', in *Derechos contemporáneos de los pueblos indios. Justicia y derechos étnicos en México* (Universidad Nacional Autónoma de México 1992), 131–42

Hertslet, Edward (ed.), *The Map of Europe by Treaty*, 4 vols (London, Butterworths 1875–91).

Hertslet, Lewis (ed.), *Hertslet's Commercial Treaties*, 30 vols (London, Whitehall/ Butterworths 1840–1925)

Hildesheimer, Françoise. *Du siècle d'or au Grand Siècle* (Paris, Flammarion 2000)

*Relectures de Richelieu* (Condé-sur-Noireau 2000)

Hill, Christopher. *A Century of Revolution 1603–1714* (2nd edn, London, Routledge 1981)

Hinshelwood, Brad. 'Punishment and Sovereignty in *De indis* and *De iure belli ac pacis*', 38 *Grotiana* (2017), 71–105

Hinsley, F. H. *Power and the Pursuit of Peace. Theory and Practice in the History of Relations between States* (Cambridge University Press 1963)

Hirschman, Albert O. *The Passions and the Interests. Political Arguments for Capitalism before Its Triumph* (Princeton University Press 1997 [1977])

Hobbes, Thomas. *'De cive' in Man and Citizen (De Homine and De cive)* (B. Gert ed., Indianapolis, Hackett 1991 [1642]), 87–386

*A Dialogue between a Philosopher and a Student of the Common Laws of England* (J. Cropsey ed., The University of Chicago Press 1971 [1681])

*Leviathan* (C. B. Macpherson, ed. & intro., Harmondsworth, Penguin 1982 [1651])

*The Elements of Law. Human Nature and De Corpore Politico* (J. G. A. Gaskin ed., Oxford University Press 2008 [1640])

Hobsbawm, E. J. *Nations and Nationalism since 1780* (Cambridge University Press 1990)

*The Age of Revolution 1789–1848* (London, Abacus 1997 [1962])

Hochstrasser, T. J. *Natural Law Theories in the Early Enlightenment* (Cambridge University Press 2000)

Höffe, Otfried. 'Fédération de peuples ou république universelle?', in Pierre Laberge et al. (eds), *L'année 1795. Kant. Essai sur la paix* (Paris, Vrin 1997), 140–59

*Kant's Cosmopolitan Theory of Law and Peace* (Cambridge University Press 2006)

Hoffmann, Hasso. 'Hugo Grotius', in Michael Stolleis (ed.), *Staatsdenker in der frühen Neuzeit* (Munich, Beck 1995), 52–77

Hoffmann, Philip T. 'Early Modern France 1450–1700', in Philip T. Hoffmann & Kathryn Norberg (eds), *Fiscal Crises, Liberty & Representative Government 1450–1789* (Stanford University Press 1994), 226–52

Hoffmann-Loertzer, Günter. 'Studien zu Hugo Grotius' (diss., Munich 1971)

Hoke, Rudolf. 'Hippolitus à Lapide', in Michael Stolleis (ed.), *Staatsdenker in der frühen Neuzeit* (Munich, Beck 1995), 100–17

Holborn, Hajo. *A History of Modern Germany. The Reformation* (Princeton University Press 1959)

Holdsworth, Sir William Searle. 'The Prerogative in the Sixteenth Century', 21 *Columbia Law Review* (1921), 554–71

'The Relation of English Law to International Law', 26 *Minnesota Law Review* (1941–2), 141–52

*A History of English Law*, 17 vols (London, Methuen 1903–66)

Holland, Ben. 'The Moral Person of the State. Emer de Vattel and the Foundation of the International Legal Order', 37 *History of European Ideas* (2011), 438–45

Holsti, Kalevi J. *Peace and War. Armed Conflicts and International Order 1648–1989* (Cambridge University Press 1991)

Holtzmann, Robert. *Wilhelm von Nogaret. Rat und Grossiegelbewahrer Philippes des Schönen von Frankreich* (Tübingen, Mohr 1898)

Hont, István. *Jealousy of Trade. International Competition and the Nation-State in Historical Perspective* (Harvard University Press 2005)

Hoogensen, Gunhild. *International Relations, Security and Jeremy Bentham* (Oxford, Routledge 2005)

Höpfl, Harro. 'Orthodoxy and the Reason of State', XXIII *History of Political Thought* (2002), 211–37

*Jesuit Political Thought. The Society of Jesus and the State c. 1540–1630* (Cambridge University Press 2004)

Hopkins, Anthony G. 'Property Rights and Empire-Building. Britain's Annexation of Lagos, 1861', 40 *Journal of Economic History* (1980), 777–98

Horkheimer, Max. 'Traditional and Critical Theory', in Max Horkheimer, *Critical Theory. Selected Essays* (New York, Herder & Herder 1972), 188–243

Horn, Jeff. *Economic Development of Early Modern France. The Privilege of Liberty 1650–1820* (Cambridge University Press 2015)

Hotman, François. *La Gaule française* (Paris, Fayard 1993 [1574])

Hourdin, Georges. *L'abbé Grégoire. Évêque et démocrate* (Paris, Desclée de Brouwer 1989)

Howe, Anthony. 'Restoring Free Trade, 1776–1873', in Donald Winch & Patrick O'Brien (eds), *The Political Economy of British Historical Experience 1688–1914* (Oxford University Press 2002), 193–213

Hueck, Ingo. 'Peace, Security and International Organisation. The German International Lawyers and The Hague Conference', in Randall Lesaffer (ed.), *Peace Treaties and International Law in European History. From the Late Middle Ages to World War One* (Cambridge University Press 2004), 254–69

Hufeland, Gottlieb. *Lehrsätze des Naturrechts* (Jena, Cuno's 1795)

Hughes, Michael. *Law and Politics in 18th-Century Germany. The Imperial Aulic Council in the Reign of Charles VI* (London, Royal Historical Society 1988)

Hugo, Gustav. *Lehrbuch des Naturrechts* (4th edn, Berlin, Mylius 1819 [1798])

Hulsebosch, Daniel J. 'Nothing but Liberty. *Somerset's Case* and the British Empire', 24 *Law and History Review* (2006), 647–57

'*Somerset's Case* at the Bar. Securing the "Pure Air" of English Jurisdiction within the British Empire', 13 *Texas Wesleyan Law Review* (2006–7), 699–710

'The Ancient Constitution and the Expanding Empire. Sir Edward Coke's British Jurisprudence', 21 *The Law and History Review* (2003), 439–82

'The Origin and Nature of Colonial Grievances', in Stephen Foster (ed.), *British North America in the Seventeenth and Eighteenth Centuries* (Oxford University Press 2013), 289–317

Humboldt, Wilhelm von. 'Über die Sorgfalt der Staaten für die Sicherheit gegen auswärtige Feinde', 20 *Berlinische Monatsschrift* (1797), 346–54

Hume, David. 'Of the Balance of Trade', in *Political Essays* (Knud Haakonssen ed., Cambridge University Press 1994), 136–49

'Of Commerce', in *Political Essays* (Knud Haakonssen ed., Cambridge University Press 1994), 93–104

'Of Interest', in *Political Essays* (Knud Haakonssen ed., Cambridge University Press 1994), 126–35

'Of the Jealousy of Trade', in *Political Essays* (Knud Haakonssen ed., Cambridge University Press 1994), 150–3

'Of the Refinement of the Arts', in *Political Essays* (Knud Haakonssen ed., Cambridge University Press 1994), 105–14

*A Treatise of Human Nature* (E. C. Mossner ed., Harmondsworth, Penguin 1969 [1739–40])

Hunter, Ian. 'Global Justice and Regional Metaphysics. On the Critical History of the Law of Nature and of Nations', in Shaunnagh Dorsett & Ian Hunter (eds), *Law and Politics in British Colonial Thought. Transpositions of Empire* (London, Palgrave Macmillan 2010), 11–29

'Vattel's Law of Nations. Diplomatic Casuistry for the Protestant Nation', 31 *Grotiana* (2010), 108–40

*Rival Enlightenments. Civil and Metaphysical Philosophy in Early Modern Germany* (Cambridge University Press 2001)

*The Secularisation of the Confessional State. The Political Thought of Christian Thomasius* (Cambridge University Press 2007)

Huppé, Luc. 'L'établissement de la souveraineté européenne au Canada', 50 *Les Cahiers de droit* (2009), 153–206

Hutchinson, Allan C. *The Province of Jurisprudence Democratized* (Oxford University Press 2009)

Hyam, Ronald. *Britain's Imperial Century, 1815–1914. A Study of Empire and Expansion* (Boston, Barnes & Noble Books 1976)

Irwin, Terence. *The Development of Ethics. A Historical and Critical Study*, vol. II: *From Suárez to Rousseau* (Oxford University Press 2008)

Isidore of Seville. *Etymologies* (Ernest Brehaut trans. & ed., Columbia University 1912 [c. 615–630]. digital edition 2003, bestiary.ca/etexts/brehaut1912/brehaut%20-%20encyclopedist%20of%20the%20dark%20ages.pdf

Israel, Jonathan I. *Dutch Primacy in World Trade, 1585–1740* (Oxford, Clarendon Press 1990)

Ittersum, Martine van. 'The Long Goodbye. Hugo Grotius' Justification of Dutch Expansion Overseas 1613–1645', 36 *History of European Ideas* (2010), 386–411

*Profit and Principle. Hugo Grotius, Natural Rights Theories and the Rise of Dutch Power in the East Indies (1595–1615)* (Leiden, Brill 2006)

Iurlaro, Francesca. 'Il testo poetica della giustizia. Alberico e Scipione Gentili leggono la *Repubblica* di Platone', 2 *Fons* (2017), 177–96

'The Burden of Reason. *Ratio probabilis, consensio omnium* and the Impact of *humanitas* on Alberico Gentili's Theory of Customary International Law', 38 *History of Political Thought* (2017), 409–38

Jacquaret, Jean. 'Colbert', in Henry Méchoulan & Joël Cornette (eds), *L'état Classique. Regards sur la pensée politique de la France dans le second XVIIe siècle* (Paris, Vrin 1996), 181–200

Jainchill, Andrew J. S. *Reimagining Politics after the Terror. The Republican Origins of French Liberalism* (Cornell University Press 2008)

Jalabert, Laurent. 'La politique territoriale française sur la rive gauche du Rhin (1679–1697). Des "réunions" à la Province de Sarre', *Revue historique* (2011), 61–91

James, Alan. 'The Development of French Naval Policy in the Seventeenth Century. Richelieu's Early Aims and Ambitions', 12 *French History* (1998), 384–402

*The Navy and Government of Early Modern France 1572–1661* (Royal Historical Society, Boydell Press 2004)

*The Origins of French Absolutism 1589–1661* (London, Taylor & Francis 2006)

James of Viterbo. *De regimine christiano* (R. W. Dyson ed., Leiden, Brill 2009 [1302])

Janssen, Dieter. 'Die Theorie der gerechten Krieges im Denken des Francisco de Vitoria', in Frank Grunert & Kurt Seelmann (eds), *Die Ordnung der Praxis. Neue Studien zur spanischen Spätscholastik* (Tübingen, Niemeyer 2001), 205–43

Jaucourt, Louis de. 'Esclavage', in Denis Diderot & Jean le Rond D'Alembert (eds), *Encyclopédie, ou dictionnaire raisonné des sciences, des arts et des métiers, etc.* (University of Chicago, ARTFL Encyclopédie Project Spring 2011), Robert Morrissey ed.), encyclopedie.uchicago.edu/ (vol. 5: 937)

'Traite des Nègres', in Denis Diderot & Jean le Rond D'Alembert (eds), *Encyclopédie, ou dictionnaire raisonné des sciences, des arts et des métiers, etc.* (University of Chicago, ARTFL Encyclopédie Project Spring 2011), Robert Morrissey ed.), encyclopedie.uchicago.edu/ (vol. 16: 532–3)

Jaume, Lucien. 'Raison publique et raison métaphysique chez D'Aguesseau. La place des Méditations', in Claude Gauvard (ed.), *Penseurs de Code Civil* (Paris, Collection de Histoire de Justice 2009), 41–8

Jelsma, Auke. *Frontiers of Reformation. Dissidence and Orthodoxy in Sixteenth-Century Europe* (Farnham, Ashgate 1998)

Jenkinson, Charles. *Discourse on the Conduct of the Government of Great Britain in Respect of Neutral Nations* (London, Debrett 1801)

Jenkyns, Sir Henry. *British Rule and Jurisdiction beyond the Seas* (Oxford, Clarendon 1902)

John of Paris, *On Royal and Papal Power* (A.P. Monahan ed., Columbia University Press 1974 [1302])

Johnson, Richard R. 'Growth and Mastery. British North America, 1690–1748', in P. J. Marshall & Alaine Low (eds), *The Oxford History of the British Empire*, vol. II: *The Eighteenth Century* (Oxford University Press 1998), 277–99

Johnson, Robert. *Nova Britannia. Offering Most Excellent Fruites by Planting in Virginia. Exciting All Such as be Well Affected to Further the Same* (Samuel Macham, and are to be sold at his shop in Pauls Church-yard, at the signe of the Bul-head 1609)

Johnston, W. Ross. *Sovereignty and Protection. A Study of British Jurisdictional Imperialism in the Late Nineteenth Century* (Duke University Press 1973)

Jones, Chris. 'Understanding Political Conceptions in the Later Middle Ages. The French Imperial Candidatures and the Idea of the Nation-State', 42 *Viator* (2011), 83–114

*Eclipse of Empire? Perceptions of the Western Empire and Its Rulers in Late-Medieval France* (Turnhout, Brepols 2007)

Jones, Colin. *The Great Nation. France from Louis XV to Napoleon* (Harmondsworth, Penguin 2002)

Jones, J. R. *The Anglo-Dutch Wars of the Seventeenth Century* (London, Longman 1996)

Jonge, Henk de. 'Grotius' View of the Gospels and the Evangelists', in Henk M. Nellen & Edwin Rabbie (eds), *Hugo Grotius Theologian. Essays in Honour of G. H. M. Posthumus Meyjes* (Leiden, Brill 1994), 65–75

Jonsen, Albert R. and Stephen Toulmin. *The Abuse of Casuistry. A History of Moral Reasoning* (University of Califronia Press 1988)

Jouanna, Arlette. *Le devoir de révolte. La noblesse française et la gestation de l'État moderne 1559–1661* (Paris, Fayard 1989)

*Le pouvoir absolu. Naissance de l'imaginaire politique de la royauté* (Paris, Gallimard 2013)

*Le prince absolu. Apogée et déclin de l'imaginaire monarchique* (Paris, Gallimard 2014)

Jouannet, Emmanuelle. 'Les dualismes du *Droit des gens*', in Vincent Chetail & Peter Haggenmacher (eds), *Vattel's International Law in a XXIst Century Perspective* (Geneva, Nijhoff 2011), 133–50

*Emer de Vattel et l'émergence doctrinale du droit international classique* (Paris, Pedone 1998)

*Le droit international libéral-providence. Une histoire de droit international* (Brussels, Bruylant 2011)

Justenhoven, Heinz-Gerhard. *Francisco de Vitoria zu Krieg und Frieden* (Cologne, Bachem 1991)

Justi, Johann Gottlob von. *Der Grundriss einer guten Regierung in fünf Büchern* (Frankfurt & Leipzig, Garve 1759)

*Die Chimäre des Gleichgewichts der Europa* (Altona, Iversen 1758)

*Die Chimäre des Gleichgewichts der Handlung und Schiffahrt* (Altona, Iversen 1759)

*Natur und Wesen der Staaten als die Quelle aller Regierungswissenschaften und Gesezze* (Mitau, Steidel 1771 [1760])

*Politische und Finanzschriften über wichtige Gegenstände*, vol. II (Copenhagen, Roth n/d)

*Justinian's Institutes* (Peter Birks & Grant McLeod trans. & intro., Cornell University Press 1987)

Kadlec, Lauriane. 'Le "code Michau". La réformation selon le garde des Sceaux Michel de Marillac', in Les Dossiers du Grihl (ed.), *La Vie de Michel de Marillac et les expériences politiques du garde des Sceaux* (2012). journals.openedition.org/dossiersgrihl/5317

Kaeuper, Richard. *War, Justice and Public Order* (Oxford University Press 1988)

Kahle, Ludewig. *Commentatio juris publici de trutina Europeae* (Göttingen, Schmidt 1740)

Kaiser, Thomas E. 'The Abbé de Saint-Pierre, Public Opinion and the Reconstitution of the French Monarchy', 55 *The Journal of Modern History* (1983), 618–43

Kalmanovitz, Pablo. 'Sovereignty, Pluralism and Regular War. Wolff and Vattel's Enlightenment Critique of Just War', 46 *Political Theory* (2017), 218–41

Kaltenborn von Stachau, Carl. *Kritik des Völkerrechts nach dem jetzigen Standpunkte der Wissenschaft* (Leipzig, Meyer 1847)

*Die Vorläufer des Hugo Grotius auf dem Gebiete der Ius naturae et gentium*, (2 vols., Leipzig, Mayer 1848)

Kamen, Henry. *Spain 1469–1714. A Society of Conflict* (2nd edn, London, Longman 1991)

*Spain's Road to Empire. The Making of a World Power 1492–1763* (Harmondsworth, Penguin 2002)

*The Spanish Inquisition. An Historical Revision* (London, Phoenix 2000)

Kant, Immanuel. 'Conjectures on the Beginning of Human History', in *Political Writings* (Hans Reiss ed., Cambridge University Press 1991), 221–34

'Idea for a Universal History with a Cosmopolitan Purpose', in *Political Writings* (Hans Reiss ed., Cambridge University Press 1991), 41–53

'On the Common Saying "This May be True in Theory, but it does not Apply in Practice"', in *Political Writings* (Hans Reiss ed., Cambridge University Press 1991), 61–92

'Perpetual Peace. A Philosophical Sketch', in *Political Writings* (Hans Reiss ed., Cambridge University Press 1991), 93–130

'The Contest of the Faculties', in *Political Writings* (Hans Reiss ed., Cambridge University Press 1991), 176–90

*Critique of the Power of Judgment* (Paul Guyer ed., Cambridge University Press 2000)

*Critique of Practical Reason* (Mary Gregor ed., Cambridge University Press, 1997)

*Critique of Pure Reason* (P. Vassilis ed., London, Everyman 1991)

*The Groundwork of the Metaphysics of Morals* (Mary Gregor ed., Cambridge University Press 1997)

*The Metaphysics of Morals* (Mary Gregor ed., Cambridge University Press 1996)

Kantorowicz, Ernst H. *The King's Two Bodies. A Study in Medieval Political Theology* (Princeton University Press 1981 [1957])

Kapossy, Béla & Whatmore, Richard. 'Emer de Vattel's *Mélanges de litterature, de morale et de politique* (1760)', 34 *History of European Ideas* (2008), 77–103

Kästner, Karl Hermann. 'From the Social Question to the Social State', 10 *Economy and Society* (1981), 1–26

Kayaoglu, Turan. *Legal Imperialism. Sovereignty and Extraterritoriality in Japan, the Ottoman Empire, and China* (Cambridge University Press 2014)

Kaye, Joel. *A History of Balance, 1250–1375. The Emergence of a New Model of Equilibrium and its Impact on Thought* (Cambridge University Press 2014)

*Economy and Nature in the Fourteenth Century. Money, Market Exchange, and the Emergence of Scientific Thought* (Cambridge University Press 1998)

Keay, John. *The Honourable Company. A History of the East India Company* (London, HarperCollins 1993)

Keenan, James F. 'The Casuistry of John Mair, Nominalist Professor of Paris', in James F. Keenan & Thomas A. Shannon (eds), *The Context of Casuistry* (Georgetown University Press 1995), 85–102

Keene, Edward. *Beyond the Anarchical Society. Grotius, Colonialism and Order in World Politics* (Cambridge University Press 2002)

Keir, D. L. 'The Case of Ship-Money', 52 *Law Quarterly Review* (1936), 546–74

Keith, A. Berridale. *Constitutional History of the First British Empire* (Oxford, Clarendon 1930)

Kelley, Donald. 'Civil Science in the Renaissance. The Problem of Interpretation', in Donald Kelley, *The Writing of History and the Study of Law* (London, Routledge 1997), 57–78

*Foundations of Modern Historical Scholarship. Language, Law and History in the French Renaissance* (Columbia University Press 1970)

Kempshall, Matthew. *The Common Good in Late Medieval Political Thought* (Oxford University Press 1999)

Kent, Eddy. *Corporate Character. Representing British Power in Imperial India 1786–1901* (University of Toronto Press 2014)

Kent Wright, Johnson. *A Classical Republican in Eighteenth-Century France. The Political Thought of Mably* (Stanford University Press 1997)

Keohane, Nannerl. *Philosophy and the State in France. The Renaissance to the Enlightenment* (Princeton University Press 2017 [1980])

Kingdon, Robert M. 'Calvinism and Resistance Theory 1550–1580', in J. H. Burns and Mark Goldie (eds), *The Cambridge History of Political Thought 1450–1700* (Cambridge University Press 1991), 193–218

Kipp, Heinrich. *Völkerordnung und Völkerrecht im Mittelalter* (Cologne, Verlag Deutsche Glocke 1950)

Kishlansky, Mark. *A Monarchy Transformed. Britain 1603–1714* (London, Penguin 1996)

Klein, Herbert S. *The Atlantic Slave Trade* (Cambridge University Press 2010)

Kleingeld, Pauline. 'Six Varieties of Cosmopolitanism in Late-Eighteenth-Century Germany', 60 *Journal of the History of Ideas* (1999), 505–24

Kleinschmidt, Harald. *Charles V. The World Emperor* (Sutton, Stroud 2004)

*Geschichte der internationalen Beziehungen* (Stuttgart, Reklam 1998)

Klippel, Diethelm. 'Der Diskussion der Menschenrechte am Ende des 18. Jahrhunderts in Deutschland', 23 *Giessener Universitätsblätter* (1990), 29–40

'Der politische Freiheitsbegriff im modernen Naturrecht', in Otto Brunner, Werner Conze & Reinhart Koselleck (eds), *Geschichtliche Grundbegriffe. Historisches Lexikon zur politisch-sozialen Sprache in Deutschland*, 8 vols (Stuttgart, Klett-Cotta 1976), II, 469–88

'Kant im Kontext. Der naturrechtliche Diskurs um 1800', in R. Oldenbourg (ed.), *Jahrbuch des historischen Kollegs* (Munich, Verlag 2001), 77–107

'Naturrecht als politische Theorie. Zur politischen Bedeutung des deutschen Naturrechts im 18. und 19. Jahrhundert', in Hans Erich Bödeker & Ulrich Herrmann (eds), *Aufklärung als Politisierung – Politisierung der Aufklärung*. Studien zum Achtzehnten Jahrhundert, Bd. 8 (Hamburg, Felix Meiner 1987), 267–93

'Politische Theorien im Deutschland des 18. Jahrhunderts', 2 *Aufklärung* (1987), 57–88

'The True Concept of Liberty. Political Theory in Germany in the Second Half of the Eighteenth Century', in Eckar Hellmuth (ed.), *The Transformation of Political Culture. England and Germany in the Late Eighteenth Century* (Oxford University Press 1990), 447–66

*Politische Freiheit und Freiheitsrechten im deutschen Naturrecht des 18. Jahrhunderts* (Paderborn, Schönigh 1976)

Klüber, Jean-Louis [Johann Ludwig]. *Droit des gens moderne de l'Europe* (Paris, Aillaud 1831)

Knafla, Louis A. *Law and Politics in Jacobean England. The Tracts of Lord Chancellor Ellesmere* (Cambridge University Press 1977)

Knecht, Robert J. *French Renaissance Monarchy* (New York, Longman 1996)

Kniepel, Barbara. *Die Naturrechtslehre des Hugo Grotius als Einigungsprinzip der Christenheit, dargestellt an seiner Stellung zum Calvinism* (Kessel, Bladitsch 1971)

Knight, Alan. 'Britain and Latin America', in Andrew Porter (ed.), *The Oxford History of the British Empire*, vol. III: *The Nineteenth Century* (Oxford University Press 2001), 122–45

Kobusch, Theo. 'Pufendorf's Lehre vom moralischen Sein', in Fiammetta Palladini & Gerald Hartung (eds), *Samuel Pufendorf und die europäische Frühaufklärung* (Berlin, Akademie 1996), 63–73

Koehn, Nancy. *The Power of Commerce. Economy and Governance in the First British Empire* (Cornell University Press 1994)

Kolla, Edward James. *Sovereignty, International Law and the French Revolution* (Cambridge University Press 2017)

Konig, David Tomas. 'Regionalism in Early American Law', in Michael Grossberg & Christopher Tomlins (eds), *The Cambridge History of Law in America* (Cambridge University Press 2008), 144–77

Koselleck, Reinhart. '"Space of Experience" and "Horizon of Expectation". Two Historical Categories', in *Futures Past. On the Semantics of Historical Time* (K. Tribe trans. & intro., Columbia University Press 1979), 267–88

'Volk, Nation', in Otto Brunner, Werner Conze & Reinhart Koselleck (eds), *Geschichtliche Grundbegriffe. Historisches Lexikon zur politisch-sozialen Sprache in Deutschland*, 8 vols (Stuttgart, Klett-Cotta 1976), VII (with several authors)

*Critique and Crisis. Enlightenment and the Pathogenesis of Modern Society* (MIT Press 1988)

Koskenniemi, Martti. 'Between Coordination and Constitution. International Law As a German Discipline', 15 *Redescriptions. Yearbook of Political Thought, Conceptual History and Feminist Theory* (2011), 45–70

'Constitutionalism as Mindset. Reflections on Kantian Themes about International Law and Globalization', 8 *Theoretical Inquiries in Law* (2007), 9–36

'Transformations of Natural Law. Germany 1648–1815', in A. Orford & F. Hoffmann (eds), *The Oxford Handbook of International Legal Theory* (Oxford University Press 2016), 59–81

*From Apology to Utopia. The Structure of International Legal Argument* (Reissue with a New Epilogue, Cambridge University Press 2005)

*The Gentle Civilizer of Nations. The Rise and Fall of International Law 1870–1960* (Cambridge University Press 2002)

Kostal, R. W. *A Jurisprudence of Power. Victorian Empire and the Rule of Law* (Oxford University Press 2005)

Kremer, Bernd Mathias. 'Die Interpretation des Westfälischen Friedens durch den "Schulen" des IusPublicum', in Heinz Duchhardt (ed.), *Der Westfälische Friede* (Munich, Oldenbourg 1998), 757–78

Krever, Tor. 'The Ideological Origins of Piracy in International Legal Thought' (PhD thesis, The London School of Economics and Political Science 2018)

Krieger, Leonard. *The Politics of Discretion. Pufendorf and the Acceptance of Natural Law* (The University of Chicago Press 1965)

Krynen, Jacques. *L'empire du roi. Idées et croyances politiques en France, XIIIe–XVe siécle* (Paris, Gallimard 1993)

Kubben, Raymond. *Regeneration and Hegemony. Franco-Batavian Relations in the Revolutionary Era, 1795–1803* (The Hague, Nijhoff 2011)

Kuin, Roger. 'Querre-Muhau. Sir Philip Sidney and the New World', 51 *Renaissance Quarterly* (1998), 549–85

Labaree, Leonard. *Royal Government in America. A Study of the British Colonial System before 1783* (New York, Ungar 1930)

Ladurie, Emmanuel Le Roy. *L'ancien Régime* (Paris, Pluriel 1994)

Lagarde, Georges. *La naissance de l'esprit laïque*, tome I: *Bilan du XIIIe siècle* (Presses Universitaires de France 1934)

Laing, Lionel H. 'Historic Origins of Admiralty Jurisdiction in England', 45 *Michigan Law Review* (1946–7), 163–82

Lalou, Élisabeth. 'Les légistes dans l'entourage de Philippe le Bel', in F. Attal, J. Garrigues, T. Kouamé & J-P. Vittu (eds), *Les universités en Europe du XIIIe siècle à nos jours* (Publications de la Sorbonne 2005), 99–111

Lambertini, Roberto. 'Political Thought', in Charles Briggs & Peter Eardley (eds), *A Companion to Giles of Rome* (Leiden, Brill 2016), 255–74

Lamprecht, Oliver. *Das Streben nach Demokratie, Volkssouveränität und Menschenrechte in Deutschland am Ende des 18. Jahrhunderts* (Berlin, Duncker & Humblot 2001)

Landesberg, Ernst (ed.). *Die Questiones des Azo* (Freiburg, Mohr 1888)

Langer, Ulrich. 'Le "frein" du roi est-il une vertu? Éthique et langage symbolique chez Seyssel', in Patricia Eichel-Lojkine (ed.), *Claude de Seyssel. Écrire l'histoire, penser le politique en France, à l'aube des temps modernes* (Presses Universitaires de Rennes 2010), 25–41

Langholm, Odd. *Economics in the Medieval Schools. Wealth, Exchange, Value, Money and Usury According to the Paris Theological Tradition, 1200–1350* (Leiden, Brill 1992)

Langlois, Charles-Victor. 'Le mouvement de 1314 et les chartes provinciales de 1315', 10 *Journal des savants* (1912), 167–75

'The Power Politics of France', in Charles T. Wood (ed.), *Philip the Fair and Boniface VIII* (2nd edn, New York, Holt, Rinehart & Winston 1971), 26–32

Lapide, Hippolithi A. *Abriss der Staats-Verfassung, Staats-Verhältnis und Bedürfniss des Römischen Reichs Deutscher Nation* (Mainz 1761)

Lapradelle, Albert de. *Maitres et doctrines du droit des gens* (2nd edn, Paris, Editions Inter-nationales 1950)

Larrère, Catherine. *L'invention de l'économie au XVIIIe siècle* (Presses Universitaires de France 1992)

Las Casas, Bartolomé de. 'De regia potestate', in Paulino Castañeda Delgado (ed.), *Obras Completas* (14 vols. Madrid, Alianza 1990), XII

*La controverse entre Las Casas et Sepúlveda* (Paris, Vrin 2007 [1552])

Laslett, Peter. 'John Locke, the Great Recoinage, and the Origins of the Board of Trade, 1695–1698', 14 *William and Mary Quarterly* (1957), 370–402

Lauranson-Rosaz, Christian. 'La débat sur la "mutation féodale". État de la question', in Przemyslaw Urbanczyk (ed.), *Europe Around the Year 1000* (Warsaw, Polish Academy of Sciences 2001), 11–40

Laurent, Pierre. *Pufendorf et la loi naturelle* (Paris, Vrijn 1982)

Laurière de, E.-J., *Ordonnances des roys de France de la troisième race,* vol. I (Paris 1723)

Lauterpacht, Hersch. *International Law and Human Rights* (London, Praeger 1950)

Laval, Christian. *L'homme économique. Essai sur les racines du néolibéralisme* (Paris, Gallimard 2007)

Lavenia, Vincenzo. 'Alberico Gentili. I processi, le fedi, la guerra', in *Alberico Gentili e gli orizzonti della modernità. Atti del convegno di Macerata (2007)* (Milan, Giuffrè 2009), 165–96

'Giudici, eretici, infedeli. Per una storia dell'Inquisizione nella Marca nella prima età moderna', www.giornaledihistoria.net

'"Mendacium officiosum". Alberico Gentili's Ways of Lying', in Miriam Eliav-Feldon (ed.), *Dissimulation and Deceit in Early Modern Europe* (Berlin, Springer 2015), 27–44

Lavoie, Michel. *Le domaine du roi 1652–1859. Souveraineté, contrôle, mainmise, propriété, possession, exploitation* (Québec, Septentrion 2010)

Lazzeri, Christian. 'Introduction', in Henri de Rohan, *De l'intérêt des princes et des Etats de la Chrétienté* (C. Lazzeri ed., Presses Universitaires de France 1995 [1638]), 1–156

Le Blant, R. & Baudry, R. (eds). *Nouveaux documents sur Champlain et son époque,* vol. I: *1560–1622* (Ottawa, Archives publiques du Canada 1967)

Le Bret, Cardin. *De la souveraineté du Roy* (Paris, Du Bray 1643)

*Le Dictionnaire des cases de conscience décidés suivant les principes de la morale les usages de la discipline ecclesiastique, l'autorité des conciles et des canonistes, et la jurisprudence du Royaume,* tome 1 (Paris, Coignard 1733)

Le Goff, Jacques. 'Aspect religieux et sacre de la monarchie française du Xe au XIIIe siècle', in Elisabeth Magnou-Nortier (ed.), *Pouvoirs et libertés au temps des premiers capétiens* (Paris, Hérault 1992), 309–22

*La civilisation de l'occident médiéval* (Paris, Flammarion 2008)

*Le moyen age et l'argent* (Paris, Perrin 2000)

*Marchands et banquiers du Moyen âge* (Presses Universitaires de France 2001)

*Your Money or Your Life. Economy and Religion in the Middle Ages* (New York, Zone Books 1990)

Le Mercier de la Rivière, Paul-Pierre. *L'intérêt général de l'Etat ou la liberté du commerce des blés* (Amsterdam, Desaint 1770)

*L'Ordre naturel et essentiel des sociétés politiques* (London, Nourse 1767)

Leclerc, Jean. 'The Legitimacy of Boniface VIII', in Charles T. Wood (ed.), *Philip the Fair and Boniface VIII* (2nd edn, New York, Holt, Rinehart & Winston 1971), 35–9

Lee, Daniel. *Popular Sovereignty in Early Modern Constitutional Thought* (Oxford University Press 2016)

Lefebvre, Georges. *La France sous le Directoire (1795–1799)* (Paris, Editions sociales 1977)

*Napoléon* (Paris, Alcan 1935)

Leibniz, Gottfried Wilhelm. 'Caesarinus Fürstenerius', in *Political Writings* (Patrick Riley ed., Cambridge University Press 1988), 111–20

'Codex Juris gentium' (Praefatio), in *Political Writings* (Patrick Riley ed., Cambridge University Press 1988), 165–76

'Mars Christianissimus', in *Political Writings* (Patrick Riley ed., Cambridge University Press 1988), 121–45

'Opinion on the Principles of Pufendorf', in *Political Writings* (Patrick Riley ed., Cambridge University Press 1988), 64–76

Lemaître, Alain J. 'Le conseil souverain d'Alsace. Les limites de la souveraineté', 3 *Revue du Nord* (2015), 479–96

Leng, Thomas. 'Commercial Conflict and Regulation in the Discourse of Trade in Seventeenth-Century England', 48 *The Historical Journal* (2005), 933–54

'Epistemology. Expertise and Knowledge in the World of Commerce', in Philip J. Stern & Carl Wennerlind (eds), *Mercantilism Reimagined. Political Economy in Early Modern Britain and Its Empire* (Oxford University Press 2014), 97–116

Lentz, Thierry. 'Bonaparte, Haïti et l'échec colonial du régime consulaire', in Marcel Dorigny (ed.), *Haïti. Première république noire* (Paris, Société française d'histoire d'outre-mer 2004), 41–60

'De l'expansionnisme révolutionnaire au système continental (1789–1815)', in Françoise Autrand, Lucien Bély, Philippe Contamine & Thierry Lentz, *Histoire de la diplomatie française*, 1: *Du Moyen Age à l'Empire* (Paris, Perron 2005), 405–505

*Le grand consulat 1799–1804* (Paris, Fayard 1999)

Léonard, Rose-Mie. 'L'indépendence d'Haïti. Perceptions aux États-Unis, 1804–1864', in Marcel Dorigny (ed.), *Haiti. Première république noire* (Paris, Société française d'histoire d'outre-mer 2004), 207–25

Lesaffer, Randall. 'Alberico Gentili's *ius post bellum* and Early Modern Peace Treaties', in Benedict Kingsbury & Benjamin Straumann (eds), *The Roman Foundations of the Law of Nations. Alberico Gentili and the Justice of Empire* (Oxford University Press 2010), 210–40

'Argument from Roman Law in Current International Law. Occupation and Acquisitive Prescription', 16 *European Journal of International Law* (2005), 25–58

'Defensive Warfare, Prevention and Hegemony. The Justifications of the Franco-Spanish War of 1635' (Part I), 8 *Journal of the History of International Law* (2006) 91–123

Lescarbot, Marc. *Histoire de la nouvelle France* (Paris, Peier 1618, nouvelle édition, 3 vols, Paris, Tross 1866)

Lesné-Ferret, Maïté. 'Guillaume de Nogaret dans les Olim et l'école juridique languedocienne', in Bernard Moreau (ed.), *Guillaume de Nogaret. Un languedocien au service de la monarchie capétienne* (Nimes, Lucie 2012), 71–97

Leuwers, Hervé. 'République et relations entre les peuples. Quelques éléments de l'idéal républicain autour de Brumaire an VII', 318 *Annales historiques de la Révolution française* (1999), 977–93

'Révolution et guerre de conquête. Les origines de nouvelle raison d'état (1789–1795)', *Revue de Nord* (1993), 21–40

*Un juriste en politique. Merlin de Douai (1758–1838)* (Artois Presses Université 1996)

Levack, Brian. 'Law and Ideology. The Civil Law and Theories of Legal Absolutism in Elizabethan and Jacobean England', in Heather Dubrow & Richard Strier (eds), *The Historical Renaissance. New Essays on Tudor and Stuart Literature and Culture* (The University of Chicago Press 1988), 220–41

*The Civil Lawyers in England. A Political Study* (Oxford University Press 1973)

Levi-Strauss, Claude. *The Savage Mind* (The University of Chicago Press 1966)

Levy, Jean-Philippe. *Histoire de la propriété* (Presses Universitaires de France 1972)

Leyte, Guillaume. *Domaine et domanialité publique dans la France médiévale. XIIe–Xe siècle* (Presses Universitaires de Strasbourg 1996)

Lindsay, H. Hamilton. *Is the War with China a Just One?* (London, Ridgway 1840)

Linebaugh, Peter & Rediker, Marcus. *The Many-Headed Hydra. The Hidden History of the Revolutionary Atlantic* (London, Verso 2012)

Link, Christoph. 'Dietrich Reinkingk', in Michael Stolleis (ed.), *Staatsdenker in der frühen Neuzeit* (Munich, Beck 1995), 78–99

'Herrschaftsbegründung und Kirchenhoheit bei Hugo Grotius', in Christoph Strohm & Heinrich de Wall (eds), *Konfessionalität und Jurisprudenz in der frühen Neuzeit* (Berlin, Duncker & Humblot 2009), 347–64

'Rechtswissenschaft', in Rudold Vierhaus (ed.), *Wissenschaften im Zeitalter der Aufklärung* (Göttingen, Vandenhoeck & Ruprecht 1985), 120–42

*Hugo Grotius als Staatsdenker* (Tübingen, Mohr 1983)

Linklater, Ando. *Owning the Earth. The Transforming History of Land Ownership* (London, Bloomsbury 2013)

Lisola, Baron de. *Bouclier d'Estat et de Justice contre le dessein manifestement découvert de la Monarchie Universelle sous le vain prétexte des prétentions de la Reyne de France* (no publisher, 1667)

Lloyd, Howell A. *The State, France, and the Sixteenth Century* (London, Allen & Unwin 1983)

Lobban, Michael. 'Custom, Common Law Reasoning and the Law of Nations in the Nineteenth Century', in A. Perreau-Saussine & J. Murphy (eds),

*The Nature of Customary Law. Philosophical, Historical and Legal Perspectives* (Cambridge University Press 2006), 256–78

'English Approaches to International Law in the Nineteenth Century', in Matthew Craven et al. (eds), *Time, History and International Law* (Leiden, Brill 2006), 65–90

*The Common Law and English Jurisprudence 1760–1850* (Oxford University Press 1991)

Locke, John. 'Essays on the Law of Nature', in *Locke. Political Essays* (M. Goldie ed., Cambridge University Press 1997), 79–133

'Some Considerations of the Consequences of the Lowering of Interest and Raising the Value of Money', in *The Works of John Locke in Nine Volumes* (London, Rivington 1824), IV, 1–116

*Two Treatises of Government* (William S. Carpenter ed., London Everyman's 1984 [1690])

*Two Treatises on Government* (6th edn., London, Miller 1764), available at http://oll.libertyfund.org

Lockey, Brian. *Law and Empire in English Renaissance Literature* (Cambridge University Press 2009)

Logan, Rayford W. *The Diplomatic Relations of the United States with Haiti (1776–1881)* (University of North Carolina Press 1941)

López de Palacios Rubios, Juan. *De las Islas del mar Océano* (México, Fondo de cultura económica 1954)

Lot, Ferdinand & Fawtier, Robert. *Histoire des institutions françaises au moyen age*, II: *Institutions royales* (Presses Universitaires de France 1958)

Loughlin, Martin. 'Droit politique', 17 *Jus politicum. Revue de droit politique* (2017), juspoliticum.com/article/Droit-politique-1129.html

*Foundations of Public Law* (Oxford University Press 2010)

Lovell, Julia. *The Opium War. Drugs, Dreams and the Making of China* (London, Picador 2011)

Lowry, S. Todd. 'Lord Mansfield and the Law Merchant. Law and Economics in the Eighteenth Century', 7 *Journal of Economic Issues* (1973), 605–22

Loyseau, Charles. *A Treatise of Orders and Plain Dignities* (Howell A. Lloyd ed. & trans., Cambridge University Press 1994 [1610])

*Cinque livres du droicts des offices* (Paris, Sommaville 1620 [1610])

*Traité des seigneuries* (Paris, L'Angelier 1608)

Luig, Klaus. 'Christian Thomasius', in Michael Stolleis (ed.), *Staatsdenker in der frühen Neuzeit* (Munich, Beck 1995), 227–56

Lupher, David A. 'The *De armis Romanis* and the Exemplum of Roman Imperialism', in Benedict Kingsbury & Benjamin Straumann (eds), *The Roman Foundations of the Law of Nations. Alberico Gentili and the Justice of Empire* (Oxford University Press 2010), 85–100

*Romans in a New World. Classical Models in Sixteenth-Century Spanish America* (University of Michigan Press 2016)

Luther, 'On Secular Authority. How Far Does the Obedience Owed to it Extend?', in Harro Höpfl (ed.), *Luther and Calvin. On Secular Authority* (Cambridge University Press 1991), 3–43

Ly, Abdoulaye. *La Compagnie du Sénégal* (Paris, Karthala 2000)

Lynn, John A. *The Wars of Louis XIV 1667–1714* (London, Longman 1999)

Lynn, Martin. 'Policy, Trade and Informal Empire', in Andrew Porter (ed.), *The Oxford History of the British Empire*, vol. III: *The Nineteenth Century* (Oxford University Press 1999), 101–21

Mably, Gabriel Bonnot de. *Des droits et des devoirs du citoyen* (Paris, Lacombe 1789)

*Le droit public de l'Europe fondé sur les traitez*, (2 tomes, nouvelle édition, M. Rousset, Amsterdam, Uytwere 1748)

*Le droit public de l'Europe fondé sur les traitez*, (2 tomes troisième éd., Genève, Compagnie des Librairies 1764)

*Le droit public de l'Europe. Fondé sur les traitez conclus jusqu'en l'année 1740*, (2 tomes, The Hague, Duren 1746)

*Principes des négociations pour servir d'introduction au droit public de l'Europe (1757)* (Paris, Kimé 2001)

Macaulay, Thomas Babington. 'Speech in Parliament on the Government of India Bill, 10 July 1833', in G. M. Young (ed.), *Macaulay, Prose and Poetry* (Harvard University Press 1957), 717–18

MacCormic, Ted 'Population. Modes of Seventeenth-Century Demographic Thought', in Philip J. Stern & Carl Wennerlind (eds), *Mercantilism Reimagined. Political Economy in Early Modern Britain and Its Empire* (Oxford University Press 2014), 25–45

Macé, Mayeul & Gainot, Bernard. 'Fin de campagne à Saint-Domingue, novembre 1802–novembre 1803', in Marcel Dorigny (ed.), *Haïti. Premier république noire* (Paris, Société française d'histoire d'outre-mer 2004), 15–40

MacGilvray, Eric. *The Invention of Market Freedom* (Cambridge University Press 2011)

Machiavelli, Niccolò. *The Prince* (G. Bull trans., London, Penguin 1999 [1532])

Mackenthun, Gesa. *Metaphors of Dispossession. American Beginnings and the Translation of Empire, 1492–1637* (University of Oklahoma Press 1997)

Mackintosh, James. *A Discourse on the Study of the Law of Nature and Nations* (London, Goode 1799)

(ed.). *Memoirs of the Right Honourable Sir James Mackintosh*, vol. 1 (Boston, Little & Brown 1853)

MacMillan, Ken. 'Imperial Constitutions. Sovereignty and Law in the British Atlantic', in H.V. Bowen, Elizabeth Mancke & John G. Reid (eds), *Britain's Oceanic Empire. Atlantic and the Indian Ocean World c.1550–1850* (Cambridge University Press 2012), 69–97

*Sovereignty and Possession in the English New World. The Legal Foundations of Empire, 1576–1640* (Cambridge University Press 2006)

*The Atlantic Imperial Constitution. Center and Periphery in the English Atlantic World* (New York, Palgrave Macmillan 2011)

Macpherson, C. B. *The Political Theory of Possessive Individualism. Hobbes to Locke* (Oxford University Press 2011 [1962])

Magnusson, Lars. *Mercantilism. The Shaping of an Economic Language* (London, Routledge 1994)

Maier, Hans. 'Die Lehre der Politik an den älteren deutschen Universitäten, vornehmlich vom 16. bis 18. Jahrhundert', in Dieter Oberndörfer (ed.), *Wissenschaftliche Politik. Eine Einführung in Grundfragen ihrer Tradition und Theorie* (Freiburg, Rossbach 1962), 59–116

*Die ältere deutsche Staats- und Verwaltungslehre* (Munich, Beck 2009)

Maitland, F. W. 'The Corporation Sole', 16 *Law Quarterly Review* (1900), 335–54

Mäkinen, Virpi. *Property Rights in the Late Medieval Discussion on Franciscan Poverty* (Leuven, Peeters 2001)

Malcolm, Noel. 'Alberico Gentili and the Ottomans', in Benedict Kingsbury & Benjamin Straumann (eds), *The Roman Foundations of the Law of Nations. Alberico Gentili and the Justice of Empire* (Oxford University Press 2010), 127–45

'Hobbes, Sandys and the Virginia Company', in Noel Malcom, *Aspects of Hobbes* (Oxford University Press 2002), 297–321

*Reason of State, Propaganda, and the Thirty Years' War. An Unknown Translation by Thomas Hobbes* (Oxford, Clarendon 2007)

Malettke, Klaus. *Les relations entre la France et le Saint-Empire au XVIIe siècle* (Paris, Champion 2001)

Maliks, Reidar. *Kant's Politics in Context* (Oxford University Press 2014)

Malynes, Gerard. *Consuetudo, Vel Lex mercatoria or The Ancient Law-Merchant* (London, Bourne 1622)

*Treatise of the Canker of Englands Commonwealth* (London, Field 1601)

Manckall, Peter C. *Hakluyt's Promise. An Elizabethan's Obsession for an English America* (Yale University Press 2007)

Mancke, Elizabeth. 'Chartered Enterprises and the Evolution of the British Atlantic World', in H. V. Bowen, Elizabeth Mancke & John G. Reid (eds), *Britain's Oceanic Empire. Atlantic and the Indian Ocean World c.1550–1850* (Cambridge University Press 2012), 237–62

Mancke, Elizabeth & Reid, John. 'Elites, States and the Imperial Contest for Acadia', in J. Reid & E. Mancke, *The 'Conquest' of Acadia 1710. Imperial, Colonial and Aboriginal Constitutions* (Toronto University Press 2003), 25–47

Mandelblatt, Bertie. 'How Feeding Slaves Shaped the French Atlantic. Mercantilism and the Crisis of Food Provisioning in the Franco-Caribbean in the Seventeenth and Eighteenth Centuries', in Sophus Reinert & Pernille Rœge (eds), *The Political Economy of Empire in the Early Modern World* (London, Palgrave 2013), 192–220

Manning, Oke. *Commentaries on the Law of Nations* (London, Sweet 1839)

Mantena, Karuna. *Alibis of Empire. Henry Maine and the Ends of Liberal Imperialism* (Princeton University Press 2010)

Marchetto, Giuliano. 'Alberico Gentili e la tradizione. La letteratura consulente come fonte dello ius belli', in *Alberico Gentili (San Ginesio 1552–Londra 1608). Atti dei convegni nel quarto centenario della morte* (San Ginesio, 11–12–13 settembre 2008, Oxford e Londra, 5–6 giugno 2008, Napoli 'L'Orientale', 6 novembre 2007), 73–94

'Une Guerra giusta per una giusta pace. Il diritto dei trattati nel *De iure belli*, III (1598) di Alberico Gentili', 10 *Laboratoire italien* (2010). journals.openedition.org/laboratoireitalien/527

Mariana, Juan de. 'A Treatise on the Alteration of Money (1609)', in Stephen J. Grabill (ed.), *Sourcebook in Late-Scholastic Monetary Theory. The Contributions of Martín de Azpilcueta Navarro, Luis de Molina, S.J., and Juan de Mariana, S.J.* (New York, Lexington 2007), 241–304

*The King and the Education of the King (De Rege et Regis Institutione)* (G. A. Moore trans. & intro., Georgetown University 1947 [1598])

Marino, Luigi. *Praeceptores Germaniae. Göttingen 1770–1820* (Göttingen, Vandenhoeck & Ruprecht 1995)

Marion, Melville. 'Guillaume de Nogaret et Philippe le Bel', 127 *Revue de l'histoire de l'église de France* (1950), 56–66

Markus, R. A. 'The Latin Fathers', in J. H. Burns (ed.), *The Cambridge History of Medieval Political Thought* (Cambridge University Press 1988), 92–120

Marnier, A. J. (ed.). *Le conseil de Pierre de Fontaines ou Traité de l'ancienne jurisprudence française* (Paris, Durand 1846)

Marquer, Éric. *Léviathan et la loi des marchands. Commerce et civilité dans l'oeuvre de Thomas Hobbes* (Paris, Garnier 2012)

Marriott, James. *The Case of the Dutch Ships Considered* (London, Dodsley 1758)

Marshall, P. J. 'Britain Without America – A Second Empire?', in P. J. Marshall & Alaine Low (eds), *The Oxford History of the British Empire*, vol. II: *The Eighteenth Century* (Oxford University Press 1998), 576–95

'Parliament and Property Rights in the Late Eighteenth Century British Experience' in John Brewer & Susan Staves (eds), *Early Modern Conceptions of Property* (London, Routledge 1995), 530–44

*The Making and Unmaking of Empires. Britain, India and America c. 1750–1783* (Oxford University Press 2005)

Martens, G. F. von. *Compendium of the Law of Nations, founded on the Treaties and Customs of the Modern Nations of Europe* (William Cobbett ed. & trans., London, Cobbett & Morgan 1802)

*Cours diplomatique ou tableau des relations extérieures des puissances de l'Europe*, 3 vols (Berlin, Mylius 1801)

*Einleitung in das positive europäische Völkerrecht auf Verträge und Herkommen gegründet* (Göttingen, Dieterich 1796)

*Erzählungen merkwürdiger Fälle des neueren europäischen Völkerrechts* (Göttingen, 1800–2)

*Grundriss des Handelsrechts* (Göttingen, Dieterich 1820)

*Grundriss einer diplomatischen Geschichte der Europäischen Staatshändel und Friedensschlüsse* (Berlin, Mylius 1807)

*Précis du droit des gens moderne de l'Europe fondé sur les traités et l'usage* (2e éd. Gottingue, Dieterich 1801 & 3ème éd. Gottingue, Dieterich 1821)

*Primae lineae iuris gentium Europaearum Practici in usum auditorum adumbratae* (Gottingae, Dieterich 1785)

Martineau, Anne-Charlotte. 'A Forgotten Chapter in the History of International Commercial Arbitration. The Slave Trade's Dispute Settlement System', 31 *Leiden Journal of International Law* (2018), 1–23

Martínez, Albert J. 'The Palatinate Clause in the Maryland Charter 1632–1776. From Independent Jurisdiction to Independence', 50 *American Journal of Legal History* (2008–10), 305–25

Martínez Peñas, Leandro. *El confesor del rey en el antiquo régimen* (Madrid, Editorial Complutense 2007)

Martínez Tapia, Ramón. *Filosofía política y derecho en el pensamiento español del s. XVI. El canonista Martín de Azpilcueta* (Notarial de Granada 1997)

Martiz, Ferdinand 'Der Recueil Martens', 40 *Archiv des öffentlichen Rechts* (1921), 22–72

Marzagalli, Silvia. 'The French Atlantic and the Dutch. Late Seventeenth–Late Eighteenth Century', in Gert Oostindie & Jessica V. Roitman (eds), *Dutch Atlantic Connections 1680–1800* (Leiden, Brill 2014), 103–18

Mason, Keith 'Britain and the Administration of the American Colonies', in H. T. Dickinson (ed.), *Britain and the American Revolution* (London, Longman 1998), 21–43

Masson, Frédéric. *Le département des affaires étrangères pendant la Révolution 1787–1804* (Paris, Plon 1911)

Matheson, James. *Present Position and Prospects of the British Trade with China* (London, Smith 1836)

May, Louis Philippe. *Le Mercier de la Rivière. Aux origines de la science économique* (Paris, CNRS 1975)

McAleer, Graham. 'Giles of Rome on Political Authority', 60 *Journal of the History of Ideas* (1999), 21–36

McBride, Keally. *Mr. Mothercountry. The Man who Made the Rule of Law* (Oxford University Press 2017)

McCluskey, Philip. *Absolute Monarchy on the Frontiers. Louis XIV's Military Occupations of Lorraine and Savoy* (Manchester University Press 2016)

McCulloch, J. R. *A Discourse on the Rise, Progress, Peculiar Objects and Importance of Political Economy* (Edinburgh, Constable 1824)

McDonald, Ronald St John. 'An Historical Introduction to the Teaching of International Law in Canada', 14 *Canadian Yearbook of International Law* (1975), 255–80

McHugh, Paul. *Aboriginal Societies and the Common Law. A History of Sovereignty, Status and Self-Determination* (Oxford University Press 2004)

*Aboriginal Title. The Modern Jurisprudence of Tribal Land Rights* (Oxford University Press 2011)

McIlwain, C. H. *Constitutionalism Ancient and Modern* (Indianapolis, Liberty Fund 2007 [1947])

McLane, John. *Land and Local Kingship in Eighteenth-Century Bengal* (Cambridge University Press 2009)

'The Uses of the Rule of Law in British Colonial Societies in the Nineteenth Century', in Shaunnagh Dorsett & Ian Hunter (eds), *Law and Politics in British Colonial Thought. Transpositions of Empire* (London, Palgrave 2010), 71–90

McNally, David. *Political Economy and the Rise of Capitalism. A Reinterpretation* (University of California Press 1988)

McNamara, Jo Ann. *Gilles Aycelin. The Servant of Two Masters* (Syracuse University Press 1971)

McPherson, B. H. 'Revisiting the Manor of East Greenwich', 42 *American Journal of Legal History* (1999), 35–56

Meccarelli, Massimo. 'Ein Rechtsformat für die Moderne. *Lex* und *iurisdictio* in der spanishen Spätscholastik', in Christoph Strohm & Heinrich de Wall (eds), *Konfessionalität und Jurisprudenz in der frühen Neuzeit* (Berlin, Duncker & Humblot 2009), 285–311

'La nuova dimensione geopolitica e gli strumenti giuridici della tradizione. Approcci alla tema del ius belli e del ius communicationis nella seconda scolastica', in Luigi Lacché (ed.), *'Ius gentium, ius communicationis, ius belli'. Alberico Gentili e gli orizzonti della modernità* (Milano, Giuffrè 2009), 53–72

Mechoulan, Stéphane. 'L'expulsion des Juifs de France en 1306. Proposition d'analyse contemporaine sous l'angle fiscal', in Jean Kerhervé & Albert Rigaudière (eds), *Monnaie, fiscalité et finances au temps du Philippe le Bel* (Paris, Comité pour l'histoire économique et financière de la France 2007), 119–28

Medick, Hans. *Naturzustand und Naturgeschiche der bürgerlichen Gesellschaft* (Göttingen, Vandenhoeck & Ruprecht 1973)

*Medieval Sourcebook*, www.fordham.edu/halsall/source/b8-unam.html (2/3/09)

Medina, Bartolomé de. *Breve instrucción de como se ha de administrar el Sacramento de la Penitencia* (Barcelona, Graels & Dotil 1604)

Meijers, E. M. 'L'université d'Orléans au XIIIe siècle', in E. M. Meijers, *Etudes d'histoire de droit* (3 vols, Universitaire Pers, Leiden 1959), III, 3–148

'Les glossateurs et le droit féodal', in E. M. Meijers, *Etudes d'histoire de droit* (3 vols, Universitaire Press, Leiden 1959), III, 261–77

Meillassoux, Claude. 'Préface. De classe et de couleur', in Florence Gauthier (ed.), *Périssent les colonies plutôt qu'un principe!* (Paris, Société des études robespierristes 2002), preface

Melé, Domenec. 'Early Business Ethics in Spain. The Salamanca School (1526–1614)', 22 *Journal of Business Ethics* (1999), 175–89

Melon, Jean-François. *Essai politique sur le commerce* (Presses Universitaires de Caen 2014 [1735])

Menard, Pierre. *Le français qui possédait l'Amérique. La vie extraordinaire d'Antoine Crozat, escroc millionnaire sous Louis XIV* (Paris, Le Cherche Midi 2017)

Mendle, Michael. 'The Ship Money Case. *The Case of Shipmony*, and the Development of Henry Parker's Parliamentary Absolutism', 32 *The Historical Journal* (1989), 513–36

Mercado, Tomás de. *Suma de tratos y contratos* (Madrid, Editorial nacional 1975 [1568])

Miethke, Jürgen. *De potestate papae* (Mohr, Siebeck 2000)

Mildmay, William. *The Laws and Policy of England Relating to Trade* (London, Harrison 1765)

Mill, James. 'Law of Nations', *Supplement to the Encyclopaedia Britannica* (London, Innes 1825)

Mills, Alex. 'The Private History of International Law', 55 *International & Comparative Law Quarterly* (2006), 1–50

Milton, Patrick. 'The Early Eighteenth-Century German Confessional Crisis. The Juridification of Religious Conflict in the Reconfessionalized Politics of the Holy Roman Empire', 49 *Central European History* (2016), 39–68

Minnucci, Giovanni. '"Bella religionis causa movenda non sunt". La libertas religionis nel pensiero di Alberico Gentili', 102 *Nuova Rivista Storica* (2018), 993–1018

'Giuristi, teologi, libertas religionis nel pensiero di Alberico Gentili', 3 *Teoria e História do Direito* (2017), 13–36

'Un discorso inedito de Alberico Gentili in difesa della *iurisprudentia*', 44 *Quaderni fiorentini* (2015), 211–51

*Alberico Gentili tra mos italicus e mos gallicus. L'inedito Commentario ad legem Iuliam de adulteriis* (Milan, Monduzzi 2002)

*'Silete theologi in munere alieno'. Alberico Gentili tra diritto, teologia e religione* (Milan, Monduzzi 2016)

Minois, Georges. *Histoire du moyen age* (Paris, Perrin 2016)

Miquelon, Dale. 'Envisioning the French Empire. Utrecht 1711–1713', 24 *French Historical Studies* (2001), 253–77

Mirabeau, Marquis de. *L'ami des hommes, ou traité de la population* (3 vols, Avignon 1756; nouvelle édition 3 vols, no place of publication, 1759)

*Philosophie rurale, ou Économie générale et politique de l'agriculture* (Amsterdam, Les librairies associées 1763)

*La science, ou les droits et devoirs de l'homme* (Lausanne, Grasset 1774)

Mirkine-Guetzévitch, Boris. 'L'influence de la Révolution française sur le développement du droit international dans l'Europe orientale', 22 *Recueil des Cours* (1928), 295–458

Misra, B. B. *The Central Administration of the East India Company, 1773–1834* (Oxford University Press 1959)

Misselden, Edward. *Free Trade or the Means to Make Trade Flourish* (London, Legatt 1622)

*The Circle of Commerce, or the Ballance of Trade, in defence of Free Trade* (London, Bourne 1623)

Mohl, Robert von. 'Die Pflege der internationalen Gemeinschaft als Aufgabe des Völkerrechts', in *Staatsrecht, Völkerrecht und Politik*, 3 vols (Tübingen, Laupp 1860), Erster Band, 579–636

'Die völkerrechtliche Lehre vom Asyle', in *Staatsrecht, Völkerrecht und Politik*, 3 vols (Tübingen, Laupp 1860), Erster Band, 637–764

*Die Geschichte und Litteratur der Staatswissenschaften*, 2 vols (Erlangen, Encke 1856)

*Encyclopädie der Staatswissenschaften* (2nd edn, Tübingen, Mohr 1872)

*Lebenserinnerungen*, 2 vols (D. Kerle ed., Stuttgart, Deutsche Verlags-Anstalt 1902)

*Staatsrecht, Völkerrecht und Politik*, 3 vols (Tübingen, Laupp 1860)

Moïse, Claude. 'Création de l'État haïtien – continuités, continuités, ruptures', in Michel Hector & Laënnec Hurbon (eds), *Genèse de l'État haïtien (1804–1859)* (Paris, Éditions de la Maison des sciences de l'homme 2010)

Molen, Gesina H. J. van der. *Alberico Gentili and the Development of International Law. His Life and Times* (Leiden, Sijthoff 1968)

Molina, Luis de. 'Treatise on Money (1597)', in Stephen J. Grabill (ed.), *Sourcebook in Late-Scholastic Monetary Theory. The Contributions of Martín de Azpilcueta Navarro, Luis de Molina, S.J., and Juan de Mariana, S.J.* (New York, Lexington 2007), 139–237

'Utrum infideles sint compellendi ad fidem', in Luciano Pereña et al. (eds), *Juan de la Peña. De bello contra insulanos. Intervención de Espanña en América. Escuela espanola de la paz. Segunda generación. 1560–1585.* CHP vol. IX (Madrid, Consejo Superior de Investigaciones Científicas 1982), 351–72

Molinae, Ludovici. *De iustitia et iure. Tomi sex* (Antverpiae, Keerberginum 1615)

Molloy, Charles. *De Iure Maritimo et Navali. Or a Treatise of the Affairs Maritime and of Commerce in Three Books* (7th edn, London, Walthoe 1722 [1676])

Montaigne, Michel de. *The Complete Essays* (Harmondsworth, Penguin 1993 [1595])

Montchrétien, Antoyne de. *Traicté de l'économie politique* (Paris, Plon 1889 [1615])

Montesquieu, Charles-Louis de Secondat, Baron de la Brède et de Montesquieu. *Considérations sur la grandeur des Romains et de leur décadence* (Paris, Hachette 1907 [1734])

*Réflexions sur la Monarchie universelle en Europe* (Genève, Droz 2000 [1734])

*The Spirit of the Laws* (T. Nugent trans., New York, Hafner 1949 [1748])

Montoro Ballesteros, Alberto. 'El "Tractado de República" de Alonso de Castrillo (1521)', 188 *Revista de estudios políticos* (1973), 107–52

Moore, John Bassett. *A Digest of International Law* (8 vols, Washington, Government Printing Office 1906)

Moos, Torsten. *Staatszweck und Staatsaufgaben in den protestantischen Ethiken des 19. Jahrhunderts* (Münster, Lit 2005)

Morales Padrón, Francisco. *Teoría y leyes de la conquista* (Madrid, Ediciones cultura hispánica 1979)

Morange, Jean. *La déclaration des droits de l'homme et du citoyen* (Presses Universitaires de France 2004)

More, Thomas. *Utopia* (P. Turner trans., London, Penguin 1965 [1516])

Moreau, Bernard (ed.). *Guillaume de Nogaret. Un languedocien au service de la monarchie capétienne* (Nimes, Lucie 2012)

Moreau-Reibel, Jean. *Jean Bodin, et le droit public comparé dans ses rapports avec la philosophie de l'histoire* (Paris, Vrin 1933)

Morellet, Abbé. *Examen de la réponse de M. N. au mémoire de M. l'abbé Morellet* (Paris, Desaint 1769)

*Mémoire sur la situation actuelle de la Compagnie des Indes* (Paris, Desaint 1769)

Morgan, Edmund. *American Slavery, American Freedom* (New York, Norton 1975)

Morgan, Hiram. 'The Colonial Venture of Sir Thomas Smith in Ulster, 1571–1575', 28 *The Historical Journal* (1985), 261–78

Morgan, Philip D. '"To Get Quit of Negroes". George Washington and Slavery', 39 *Journal of American Studies* (2005), 403–29

Morison, W. L. *John Austin* (Stanford University Press 1982)

Moritz, Isenmann. 'Égalité, réciprocité, souveraineté. The Role of Commercial Treaties in Colbert's Economic Policy', in Antonella Alimento & Koen Stapelbroek (eds), *The Politics of Commercial Treaties in the Eighteenth Century* (New York, Palgrave Macmillan 2017), 77–103

Morris, Thomas D. *Southern Slavery and the Law 1619–1860* (University of North Carolina Press 1996)

Morrison, James Ashley. 'Before Hegemony. Adam Smith, American Independence, and the Origins of the First Era of Globalization', 66 *International Organization* (2012), 395–428

Morse, Hosea B. *The International Relations of the Chinese Empire* (3 vols, London, Longman 1910–18)

Moser, Johann Jakob. *Grund-Sätze des jetzt-üblichen Europäischen Völker-Rechts in Friedens-Zeiten* (Hanau 1750)

*Versuch des neuesten europäischen Völcker-Rechts in Friedens- und Krieg-Zeiten* (10 vols, Frankfurt 1777–80)

Mousnier, Roland. 'D'Aguesseau et le tournant des ordres aux classes sociales', 4 *Revue d'histoire économique et sociale* (1971), 449–64

*L'homme rouge ou la vie du Cardinal Richelieu* (Paris, Laffont 1992)

*Les institutions de la France sous la monarchie absolue* (2 tomes, Presses Universitaires de France 1980)

Mühlegger, Florian. *Hugo Grotius. Ein christlicher Humanist in politischen Verantwortung* (Berlin, De Gruyter, 2007)

Mukherjee, Ramkrishna. *The Rise and Fall of the East India Company* (Berlin, VEB 1955)

Muldoon, James. *Empire and Order. The Concept of Empire 800–1800* (London, St Martin's 1999)

Mun, Thomas. 'England's Treasure by Forraign Trade', in J. R. McCulloh (ed.), *A Select Collection of Early English Tracts on Commerce from the Originals of Mun, Roberts, North, and Others, with a Preface and Index* (London, Political Economy Club 1856 [1664]), 115–210

Muñoz de Juana, Rodrigo. *Moral y economía en la obra de Martín de Azplicueta* (Pamplona, Eunsa 1998)

Munro, W. B. *The Seigneurs of Old Canada. A Chronicle of Old World Feudalism* (Toronto, Brood 1915)

Muthu, Sankar. *Enlightenment against Empire* (Princeton University Press 2003)

Nakhimovsky, Isaac. *The Closed Commercial State. Perpetual Peace and Commercial Society from Rousseau to Fichte* (Princeton University Press 2011)

'Vattel's Theory of the International Order. Commerce and the Balance of Power in the *Law of Nations*', 33 *History of European Ideas* (2007), 157–73

Naudé, Gabriel. *Considérations politiques sur les coups d'État* (Louis Marin ed., Paris, Éditions de Paris 1988)

Nederman, Cary J. 'Conciliarism and Constitutionalism. Jean Gerson and Medieval Political Thought', 12 *History of European Ideas* (1990), 189–209

'Confronting Market Freedom. Economic Foundations of Liberty at the End of the Middle Ages', in Robert Bast & Andrew Gow (eds), *Continuity and Change. The Harvest of Late Medieval and Reformation History* (Leiden, Brill 2000), 3–19

Neff, Stephen. 'Vattel and the Laws of War. A Tale of Three Circles', in Vincent Chetail & Peter Haggenmacher (eds), *Vattel's International Law in a XXIst Century Perspective* (Geneva, Nijhoff 2011), 317–33

(ed.). *Hugo Grotius On the Law of War and Peace. A Student Edition* (Cambridge University Press 2012)

*War and the Law of Nations. A General History* (Cambridge University Press 2005)

Nellen, Henk. *Hugo Grotius. A Lifelong Struggle for Peace in Church and State 1583–1645* (Leiden, Brill 2014)

Nicholas, Barry. *Roman Law* (Oxford, Clarendon 1962)

Nicholas, David. *Medieval Flanders* (New York, Routledge 1992)

Nicholson, Bradley J. 'Legal Borrowing and the Origins of Slave Law in the British Colonies', 38 *American Journal of Legal History* (1994), 38–54

Nicolini, Ugo. *La proprietà, il principe e l'espropriazione per pubblica utilità* (Milano, Giuffrè 1952)

Nifterik, Gustaaf van. 'Hugo Grotius on Slavery', 22 *Grotiana* (2001), 197–242

Nijman, Janne E. 'Grotius' *Imago Dei* Anthropology. Grounding *Jus Naturae et Gentium*', in Martti Koskenniemi, Mónica García-Salmones Rovira & Paolo Amorosa (eds), *International Law and Religion. Historical and Contemporary Perspectives* (Oxford University Press 2017), 87–110

Nimako, Kwame & Willemsen, Glenn. *The Dutch Atlantic. Slavery, Abolition and Emancipation* (London, Pluto Press 2011)

Nokkala, Ere. 'Just and Unjust Neutrality. J. H. G. von Justi's Defence of Prussian Maritime Neutrality (1740–1763)', in Koen Stapelbroek (ed.), *Trade and War. The Neutrality of Commerce in the Inter-State System* (Helsinki, Helsinki Collegium for Advance Studies 2011), 42–60

'The Machine of the State in Germany – The Case of Johann Heinrich Gottlob von Justi (1717–1771)', 5 *Contributions to the History of Concepts* (2009), 71–93

*From Natural Law to Political Economy. J. H. G. von Justi on State, Commerce and the International Order* (Vienna, LIT Verlag 2019)

North, Douglass C. & Thomas, Robert Paul. *The Rise of the Western World. A New Economic History* (Cambridge University Press 1973)

Nussbaum, Arthur. *A Concise History of the Law of Nations* (2nd rev. edn, New York, Macmillan 1954 [1947])

Nys, Ernst. *Le droit international. Les principes, les théories, les faits* (3 tomes, Bruxelles, Castaigne 1904–6)

O'Banion, Patrick J. '"A Priest Who Appears Good". Manuals of Confession and the Construction of Clerical Identity in Early Modern Spain', 85 *Dutch Church History* (2005), 333–48

*Sacrament of Penance and Religious Life in Golden Age Spain* (The Pennsylvania State University Press 2012)

O'Brian, Patrick. 'Inseparable Connections. Trade, Economy, the Fiscal State and the Expansion of Empire 1688–1815', in P. J. Marshall & Alaine Low (eds), *The Oxford History of the British Empire*, vol. II: *The Eighteenth Century* (Oxford University Press 1998), 53–77

O'Keefe, Roger. 'The Doctrine of Incorporation Revisited', 79 *British Year Book of International Law* (2008), 7–85

Oakley, Francis. 'Jacobean Political Theology. The Absolute and Ordinary Powers of the King', 29 *Journal of the History of Ideas* (1968), 323–46

'The Absolute and Ordained Power of God in Sixteenth- and Seventeenth-Century Theology', 59 *Journal of the History of Ideas* (1998), 437–61

Obert, Marcus. *Die naturrechtliche "politische Metaphysik" des Johann Heinrich Gottlob von Justi (1717–1771)* (Frankfurt, Peter Lang 1992)

Obregón, Liliana. 'Empire, Racial Capitalism and International Law. The Case of Manumitted Haiti and the Recognition Debt', 31 *Leiden Journal of International Law* (2018), 597–615

Ogg, David (ed.). *Sully's Design of Henry IV* (London, Sweet & Maxwell, Grotius Society Publications 1923)

Ohlmayer, Jane H. '"Civilizing of these Rude Parts". Colonization within Britain and Ireland 1580s–1640s', in Nicholas Canny (ed.), *The Oxford History of the British Empire*, vol. I: *The Origins of Empire* (Oxford University Press 1998), 124–47

Oldendorp, Johannes. *Iuris naturalis gentium et civilis* (Cologne 1539)

Ompteda, Dietrich Heinrich von. *Litteratur des gesammten sowohl natürlichen als positiven Völkerrechts, Erster Theil* (Regensburg, Montags 1785)

Orbell, John. 'Private Banks and International Finance in the Light of the Archives of Baring Brothers', in Yussef Cassis et al. (eds), *The World of Private Banking* (London, Routledge 2009) 141–58

Orford, Anne. 'Food Security, Free Trade and the Battle for the State', 11 *Journal of International Law and International Relations* (2015), 1–67

'Theorizing Free Trade', in Anne Orford & Florian Hoffmann (eds), *The Oxford Handbook of the Theory of International Law* (Oxford University Press 2016), 701–37

Ormond, David. *The Rise of Commercial Empires. England and the Netherlands in the Age of Mercantilism, 1650–1770* (Cambridge University Press 2003)

Osiander, Andreas. *Before the State. Systemic Political Change in the West from the Greeks to the French Revolution* (Oxford University Press 2007)

Ourliac, Paul & Malafosse, Jehan de. *Histoire du droit privé*, vol. II (2nd edn, Presses Universitaires de France 1971)

Overstall, Richard. 'Encountering the Spirit in the Land. "Property" in a Kinship-Based Legal order', in John McLaren, A. R. Buck & Nancy E. Wright (eds), *Despotic Dominion. Property Rights in British Settler Societies* (University of British Columbia Press 2005), 22–49

Ozouf, Mona. 'Régénération', in François Furet & Mona Ozouf, *Dictionnaire critique de la revolution française: Idées* (Paris, Flammarion 1992), 373–89

Pagden, Anthony. 'Dispossessing the Barbarian. The Language of Spanish Thomism and the Debate over the Property Rights of the American Indians', in Anthony Pagden (ed.), *The Languages of Political Theory in Early-Modern Europe* (Cambridge University Press 1987), 79–98

'"The Struggle for Legitimacy" and the Language of Empire in the Atlantic c.1700', in Nicholas Canny (ed.), *The Oxford History of the British Empire*, vol. I: *The Origins of Empire* (Oxford University Press 1998), 34–54

*The Burdens of Empire. 1539 to the Present* (Cambridge University Press 2015)

*The Fall of Natural Man. The American Indian and the Origins of Comparative Ethnology* (Cambridge University Press 1982)

*The Lords of All the World. Ideologies of Empire in Spain, Britain and France c.1500–c. 1800* (Yale University Press 1995)

Palmerston, Henry John Temple. *The Speech of Viscount Palmerston in Reply to the Motion by Lord George Bentinck M.P.* (London, Royal Exchange 1848)

Panizza, Diego. 'Alberico Gentili's *De Armis Romanis*. The Roman Model of Just Empire', in Benedict Kingsbury & Benjamin Straumann (eds), *The Roman Foundations of the Law of Nations. Alberico Gentili and the Justice of Empire* (Oxford University Press 2010), 53-84

'Alberico Gentili's *De Iure Belli*. The Humanist Foundations of a Project of International Order', in *Alberico Gentili. Atti dei convegni nel quarto centenario della morte*, vol. II (Milan, Giuffrè 2010), 557–86

'I valori fondanti della *respublica magna* nel *De Iure Belli* di Alberico Gentili', in *Alberico Gentili. Atti dei convegni nel quarto centenario della norte*, vol. II (Milan, Giuffrè 2010), 491–513

'Il pensiero politico di Alberico Genili. Religione, virtù e ragion di stato', in Diego Panizza (ed.), *Alberico Gentili. Politica e religione nell'età delle guerre di religioni* (Milan, Giuffrè 2002), 57–213

'The "Freedom of the Sea" and the "Modern Cosmopolis", in Alberico Gentili's *De Iure Belli*', 30 *Grotiana* (2009), 88–106

'Theory and Jurisprudence in Gentili's *De iure belli*. The Great Debate between ""Theological" and "Humanist" Perspectives from Vitoria to Grotius', in Pierre-Marie Dupuy & Vicent Chetail (eds), *The Roots of International Law – Liber Amicorum Peter Haggenmacher* (Leiden, Brill 2014), 211–47

*Alberico Gentili, giurista ideologo nell'Inghilterra elisabettiana* (Padova 1981)

*Genesi di una ideologia. Il conservatismo moderno in Robert Ward* (Milan, CEDAM 1997)

Paradisi, Bruno. *Studi sul medievo giuridico* (2 vols., Rome, Instituto Palazzo Borromini 1987)

Paraguirre, Demetrio. *Francisco de Vitoria. Una teoria social del valor económico* (Bilbao 1957)

Pares, Richard. *Colonial Blockade and Neutral Rights 1739–1763* (Oxford, Clarendon 1938)

Parker, David. 'Absolutism, Feudalism and Property Rights in the France of Louis XIV', 179 *Past & Present* (2003), 60–96

'Sovereignty, Absolutism and the Function of Law in Seventeenth-Century France', 122 *Past & Present* (1989), 36–74

*Class and State in Ancien Régime France. The Road to Modernity?* (London, Taylor & Francis 2003)

Parker, H. C. *The Inconstant Savage. England and the North American Indian 1500–1660* (London, Duckworth 1979)

Parry, John & Keith, Robert (eds), *New Iberian World. A Documentary History of the Discovery and Settlement of Latin America to the Early 17th Century*, vol. 1: *The Conquerors and the Conquered* (5 vols, New York, Times Books 1984)

Pasquier, Étienne. 'Les lettres de Pasquier', Liv. XIX in *Les Oeuvres d'Estienne Pasquier*, (2 vols., Amsterdam 1723), II 1100–1441

Pasquino, Pasquale. 'Politisches und historisches Interesse. Statistik und historische Staatslehre bei Gottfried Achenwall (1719–1772)', in Hans Erich Bödeker et al. (eds), *Aufklärung und Geschichte. Studien zur Deutschen Geschichtswissenschaft im 18. Jahrhundert* (Göttingen, Vandenhoeck & Ruprecht 1986), 144–68

Patault, Anne-Marie. *Introduction historique au droit des biens* (Presses Universitaires de France 1989)

Paul, Joel. 'The Isolation of Private International Law', 7 *Wisconsin International Law Journal* (1988–9), 149–78

Pauly, Johann Christian. *Die Entstehung des Polizeirechts als wissenschaftliche Disziplin. Ein Beitrag zur Wissenschaftsgeschichte des öffentlichen Rechts* (Frankfurt am Main, Klostermann 2000)

Peabody, Sue. *"There Are No Slaves in France". The Political Culture of Race and Slavery in the Ancien Régime* (Oxford University Press 1996)

Pearson, M. N. 'Merchants and States', in James D. Tracy (ed.), *The Political Economy of Merchant Empires* (Cambridge University Press 1991), 41–116

Peckham, Sir George. 'True Report of the Late Discoveries', in Richard Hakluyt, *Principall Navigations, Voyages, Traffiques and Discoveries of the English Nation*, vol. 13 (University of Adelaide ebooks), 2–35

Pegues, Franklin J. *Lawyers of the Last Capetians* (Princeton University Press 1961)

Peña, Juan de la. 'Quaestio 40 De Bello', in Luciano Pereña et al. (eds), *Juan de la Peña. De bello contra insulanos. Intervención de España en América. Escuela española de la paz. Segunda generación. 1560–1585.* CHP vol. IX (Madrid, Consejo Superior de Investigaciones Científicas 1982), 397–498

*De bello contra insulanos. Intervención de España en América* (Luciano Pereña et al. (eds), Madrid, Consejo Superior de Investigaciones Científicas 1982)

Pennell, J. R. 'The Origins of the Foreign Jurisdiction Act and the Extension of British Sovereignty', 83 *Historical Research* (2009), 465–85

Pennington, Kenneth. *The Prince and the Law 1200–1600* (University of California Press 1993)

Pereña, Luciano. 'Estudio preliminaria. La tesis de la paz dinámica', in Luciano Pereña (ed.), *Francisco de Vitoria, Relectio de jure belli o paz dinámica. Escuela Española de la paz. Primera generación 1526–1560* (Madrid, Corpus Hispanorum de Pace 1981), 29–96

'La intervención de España en América', in Juan de la Peña, *De bello contra insulanos. Intervención de España en América* (Madrid, Consejo Superior de Investigaciones Científicas 1982), 23–135

*Diego de Covarrubias y Leyva. Maestro de derecho internacional* (Madrid, Asociación Francisco de Vitoria 1957)

*La escuela de Salamanca. Proceso a la conquista de América* (Salamanca, Caja de Ahorros y Monte de Piedad 1986)

*La idea de justicia en la conquista de América* (Madrid, Mapfre 1992)

*Misión de España en América 1540–1560* (Madrid, Instituto 'Francisco de Vitoria' 1956)

Pérez, Joseph. *La leyenda negra* (Madrid, Gadir 2009)

Perkins, Merle. 'Civil Theology in the Writings of the Abbé de Saint-Pierre', 18 *Journal of the History of Ideas* (1957), 242–53

*The Moral and Political Philosophy of the Abbé de Saint-Pierre* (Geneva, Droz 1959)

Petersson, Niels P. 'The Promise and Threat of Free Trade in a Globalizing Economy. A European Perspective', in Thomas Hippler & Milos Vec (eds), *Paradoxes of Peace in Nineteenth Century Europe* (Oxford University Press 2015), 92–110

Petit, M. *Traité sur le gouvernement des esclaves* (2 tomes, Paris, Knape 1777)

Petit-Renaud, Sophie. *'Faire loy', au royaume de France. De Philippe VI à Charles V (1328–1380)* (Paris, De Boccard 2001)

Petrina, Alessandra. 'Machiavelli's *Principe* and Its Early Appearance in the British Isles', in Alessandra Petrina, *Machiavelli in the British Isles* (London, Routledge 2009), 1–13

'Reginald Pole and the Reception of *Il Principe* in Henrician England', in Alessandro Arienzo & Alessandra Petrina (eds), *Machiavellian Encounters in Tudor and Stuart England. Literary and Political Influences from the Reformation to the Restoration* (London, Routledge 2013), 13–27

*Machiavelli in the British Isles. Two Early Modern Translations of* The Prince (London, Routledge 2009)

Pettigrew, William. *Freedom's Debt. The Royal African Company and the Politics of the Atlantic Slave Trade 1672–1752* (University of North Carolina Press 2013)

Petty, William. *Political Arithmetic* (London, Clavel 1690)

Peytraud, Lucien. *L'esclavage aux Antilles françaises avant 1780* (Paris, Hachette 1897)

Philips, C. H. *The East India Company 1784–1834* (Manchester University Press 1961)

Phillimore, Robert. *Commentaries upon International Law*, 4 vols (Philadelphia, Johnson 1854–61)

Phillipson, Nicholas. *Adam Smith. An Enlightened Life* (Yale University Press 2010)

Piirimäe, Pärtel. 'Alberico Gentili's Doctrine of Defensive War and Its Impact on Seventeenth-Century Normative Views', in Benedict Kingsbury & Benjamin Straumann (eds), *The Roman Foundations of the Law of Nations. Alberico Gentili and the Justice of Empire* (Oxford University Press 2010), 187–209

Pincus, Steve. *1688. The First Modern Revolution* (Yale University Press 2009)

*Protestantism and Patriotism. Ideologies and the Making of English Foreign Policy 1650–1668* (Cambridge University Press 1996)

Pirillo, Diego. 'Republicanism and Religious Dissent. Machiavelli and the Italian Protestant Reformers', in Allessandro Arienzo & Alessandra Petrina. (eds), *Machiavellian Encounters in Tudor and Stuart England. Literary and Political Influences from the Reformation to the Restoration* (London, Routledge 2013), 121–40

'Tra obbedianza e resistenza. Alberico Gentili e George Buchanan', in Luigi Lacchè (ed.), *"Ius gentium, ius communicationis, ius belli". Alberico Gentili e gli orizzonti della modernità: atti del convegno di Macerata in occasione delle celebrazioni del quarto centenario della morte di Alberico Gentili (1552–1608)* (Milan, Giuffrè 2009), 209–27

Pisanus, Huguccio. *Summa Decretorum*, tom I: *Distinctiones I–XX* (Biblioteca Apostolica Vaticana 2006)

Pitts, Jennifer. *A Turn to Empire. The Rise of Imperial Liberalism in Britain and France* (Princeton University Press 2005)

*Boundaries of the International. Law and Empire* (Princeton University Press 2018)

Plongeron, Bernard. *L'abbé Grégoire ou l'Arché de la Fraternité* (Paris, Letouzey & Ané 1989)

Pluchon, Pierre. *Histoire de la colonisation française. Le premier empire colonial, des origines à la Restauration* (Paris, Fayard 1991)

Pocock, J. G. A. 'Authority and Property. The Question of Liberal Origins', in J. G. A. Pocock, *Virtue, Commerce, and History. Essays on Political Thought and History, Chiefly in the Eighteenth Century* (Cambridge University Press 1985), 51–72

'The Mobility of Property and the Rise of Eighteenth-Century Sociology', in J. G. A. Pocock, *Virtue, Commerce, and History. Essays on Political Thought and History, Chiefly in the Eighteenth Century* (Cambridge University Press 1985), 103–24

'Political Thought in the English-Speaking Atlantic 1760–1790. Part I: The Imperial Crisis', in John Pocock (ed.), *The Varieties of British Political Thought 1500–1800* (Cambridge University Press 1993), 246–82

*The Ancient Constitution and the Common Law* (Cambridge University Press 1957)

Poirel, Dominique. *Philippe le bel* (Paris, Perrin 1991)

Pomfret, John E. & Shumway, Floyd M. *Founding the American Colonies 1583–1660* (New York, Harper 1971)

Poole, Thomas. *Reason of State. Law, Prerogative & Empire* (Cambridge University Press 2015)

Popkin, Jeremy D. 'Thermidor, Slavery, and the "Affaire des Colonies"', 38 *French Historical Studies* (2015), 61–82

*You Are All Free. The Haitian Revolution and the Abolition of Slavery* (Cambridge University Press 2010)

Porras, Ileana. 'Constructing International Law in The East Indian Seas. Property, Sovereignty, Commerce and War in Hugo Grotius' *De Iure Praedae* –The Law of Prize and Booty, or "On How to Distinguish Merchants from Pirates"', 31 *Brooklyn Journal of International Law* (2006), 741–804

Poser, Norman S. *Lord Mansfield. Justice in the Age of Reason* (McGill–Queen's University Press 2013)

Post, Gaines. *Studies in Medieval Legal Thought. Public Law and the State 1100–1322* (Princeton University Press 1964)

Postma, Johannes. *The Dutch in the Atlantic Slave Trade 1600–1815* (Cambridge University Press 1990)

Pownall, Thomas. *A Memorial most Humbly Addressed to the Sovereigns of Europe on the Present State of Affairs between the Old and New World* (2nd edn, London, Almon 1780)

*The Administration of the British Colonies*, 2 vols (London, Walter 1774)

*The Right, Interest and Duty of the Government, as Concerned in the Affair of the East Indies* (London, Almon 1781)

Preu, Peter. *Polizeibegriff und Staatszwecklehre. Die Entwicklung des Polizeibegriffs durch die Rechts- und Staatswissenschaften des 18. Jahrhunderts* (Göttingen, Schwartz 1983)

Priest, Claire. 'Law and Commerce 1580–1815', in Michael Grossberg & Christopher Tomlins (eds), *The Cambridge History of Law in America* (Cambridge University Press 2008), 400–46

Pritchard, James. *In Search of Empire. The French in the Americas, 1670–1730* (Cambridge University Press 2004)

Pronier, Thomas. 'L'implicite et l'explicite dans la politique de Napoléon', in Marcel Dorigny (ed.), *Rétablissement de l'esclavage dans les colonies françaises, 1802* (Paris, Maisonneuve & Larose 2003), 51–67

Pufendorf, Samuel. 'De systematibus civitatum', in Samuel Pufendorf, *Dissertationes Academicae Selectiores* (London, Junghans 1675), 264–330

'Severinus de Monzambano Veronese de Statu Imperii germanici ad Laelium Fratrem, Dominum Trezolani', *Liber unus – Über die Verfassung des Deutschen Reiches* (Berlin, Hobbing 1922 [1703])

*Commentarii de rebus Suecicis libri XXVI ab expeditione Gustavi-Adolfi ad abdicationem usque Christinae* (Utrecht, Ribbium 1686)

*De jure naturae et gentium, libri octo*, trans. as *On the Law of Nature and Nations. Eight Books*, 2 vols (W. Oldfather trans., Oxford, Clarendon 1934)

*De rebus gestis Friderici-Wilhelmi Magni Electoris* Brandenburgii, 2 vols (Berlin, Schrey 1695)

*Einleitung zu die Historie der vornähmsten Reiche und Staaten von Europa, vorinnen des KönigReichs Schweden* (Frankfurt, Knoch 1709)

*Introduction to the History of the Principal Kingdoms and States of Europe* (Jodocus Cull trans., Michael J. Seidler intro. & ed., Indianapolis, Liberty Fund 2013 [1682])

*On the Duty of Man and Citizen According to Natural Law* (James Tully ed., Michael Silverthorne trans., Cambridge University Press 1991 [1673])

*On the Nature and Qualification of Religion in Reference to Society* (S. Zurbruchen ed., Indianapolis, Liberty Fund 2002 [1687])

*The Present State of Germany* (M. J. Seidl ed. & intro., Indianapolis, Liberty Fund 2007 [1667])

*Two Books of the Elements of Universal Jurisprudence* (Thomas Behme ed. & intro., Indianapolis, Liberty Fund 2009 [1660])

Pütter, Karl Theodor. *Beiträge zur Völkerrechts-Geschichte und Wissenschaft* (Leipzig, Wienbrack 1843)

Quaglioni, Diego. 'Il "De papatu Romano Antichristo" del Gentili', in Luigi Lacchè (ed.), *"Ius gentium, ius communicationis, ius belli". Alberico Gentili e gli orizzonti della modernità: atti del convegno di Macerata in occasione delle celebrazioni del quarto centenario della morte di Alberico Gentili (1552–1608)* (Milan, Giuffrè 2009), 197–207

'Pour une histoire de droit de guerre au début de l'âge moderne. Bodin, Gentili, Grotius', 10 *Laboratoire italien* (2010), 27–43

'The Italian "Readers" of Bodin, 17th–18th Centuries. The Italian "Readers" out of Italy – Alberico Gentili', in Howell A. Lloyd (ed.), *The Reception of Bodin* (Leiden, Brill 2014), 371–86

Quaritsch, Helmut. 'Staatsräson in Bodin's "Republique"', in Roman Schnur (ed.), *Staatsräson. Studien zur Geschichte eines politischen Begriffs* (Berlin, De Gruyter 1975), 43–63

Quesnay, François. 'Le droit naturel', in M. Eugène Daire (ed.) *Collection des principaux économistes*. Tome 2: *Physiocrates* (Osnabruck, Zeller 1966 [1846]) 41–55

Rabb, Theodore K. *Jacobean Gentleman. Sir Edwin Sandys 1561–1629* (Princeton University Press 1998)

Rademacher, Ingrid. 'La science sociale républicaine de Pierre-Louis Roederer', 13 *Revue française d'histoire des idées politiques* (2001), 25–55

Randelzhofer, Albrecht. *Völkerrechtliche Aspekte des Heiligen Römischen Reiches nach 1648* (Berlin, Duncker & Humblot 1966)

Ranusack, Barbara. *Indian Princes and Their States* (Cambridge University Press 2003)

Rasilla del Moral, Ignacio de la. *In the Shadow of Vitoria. A History of International Law in Spain (1770–1953)* (Leiden, Brill 2017)

Rassem, Mohammed H. & Wölky, Guido. 'Zur Göttinger Schule der Staatswissenschaften bis zu der Freiheitskriegen', in Wilhelm Bleek & Hans J. Lietzmann (eds), *Schulen in der deutschen Politikwissenschaft* (Leske, Opladen 1999), 79–104

Raulet, Gérard. *Kant, histoire et citoyenneté* (Presses Universitaires de France 1998)

Raynal, Guillaume-Thomas. *Histoire philosophique et politique des Etablissements et du Commerce des Européens dans les deux Indes*, tome VI (Genève, Pellet 1781)

Rayneval, Joseph-Mathias Gérard de. *Institutions du droit de la nature et des gens* (nouvelle édition, Paris, Gravier 1832 [1803])

*The Last Waltz of the Law of Nations. A Translation of the 1803 Edition of the Institutions of Natural Law and the Law of Nations by Joseph-Mathias Gérard de Rayneval* (Jean Allain trans., Oxford University Press 2020)

Razilly, Isaac de. 'Mémoire du chevalier de Razilly', in Léon Deschamps (ed.), *Isaac de Razilly. Un colonisateur du temps de Richelieu* (Paris, Delagrave 1887), 374–86

Rech, Walter. *Enemies of Mankind. Vattel's Theory of Collective Security* (Leiden, Nijhoff 2013)

Reddie, James *Inquiries in International Law* (London, Blackwood 1842)

*Inquiries in the Science of Law* (London, Stevens & Norton 1847)

Reibstein, Ernst. *Die Anfänge des neueren Natur- und Völkerrechts. Studien zu den "Contrioversiae illustres" des Fernandus Vasquius (1559)* (Bern, Haupt 1949)

*Johannes Althusius als Fortsätzer der Schule von Salamanca* (Karlsruhe, Müller 1955)

Reinert, Sophus A. 'Rivalry. Greatness in Early Modern Political Economy', in Philip J. Stern & Carl Wennerlind (eds), *Mercantilism Reimagined. Political Economy in Early Modern Britain and Its Empire* (Oxford University Press 2013), 348–70

Reinhardt, Nicole. *Voices of Conscience. Royal Confessors and Political Counsel in Seventeenth-Century Spain and France* (Oxford University Press 2016)

Reinkingk, Theodor [Dietrich]. *Biblische Policey* (Frankfurt, Spörlin 1653)

Remec, R. *The Position of the Individual in International Law according to Grotius and Vattel* (The Hague, Nijhoff 1960)

Renaut, Alain. 'Garantir la paix', in Pierre Laberge et al. (eds), *L'année 1795. Kant. Essai sur la paix* (Paris, Vrin 1997), 287–305

*Kant aujourd'hui* (Paris, Flammarion 1997)

Renoux-Zagamé, Marie-France. *Du droit de dieu au droit de l'homme* (Presses Universitaires de France 2003)

*Origines théologiques du concept moderne de propriété* (Geneva, Droz 1987)

*Representation of the Lords Commissioners for Trade and Plantations to the King, On the state of the British Colonies in North America* (Board of Trade 1721)

Reynolds, Susan. *Before Eminent Domain. Towards a History of Expropriation of Land for the Common Good* (University of North Carolina Press 2003)

*Fiefs and Vassals. The Medieval Evidence Reinterpreted* (Oxford, Clarendon 2001)

Richelieu, *Testament politique* (A. Teyssier ed., Paris, Perrin 2011 [1688])

Richet, Denis. *La France moderne. L'esprit des institutions* (Paris, Flammarion 1973)

Richter, Melvin. 'The Comparative Study of Regimes and Societies', in Mark Goldie & Robert Wokler (eds), *The Cambridge History of Eighteenth-Century Political Thought* (Cambridge University Press 2006), 145–71

Ridley, Sir Thomas. *A View of Civil and Ecclesiastical Law* (Oxford 1676)

Riedel, Manfred 'Gesellschaft, bürgerliche', and 'Gesellschaft und Gemeinschaft', in Otto Brunner et al. (eds), *Geschichtliche Grundbegriffe. Historisches Lexikon zur politisch-sozialen Sprache in Deutschland*, (8 vols, Stuttgart, Klett-Cotta 2004), II, 719–800 and 801–62

Rigaudière, Albert. *Introduction historique à l'étude du droit et des institutions* (Paris, Economica 2001)

*Penser et construire l'Etat dans la France du Moyen Âge (XIIIe–XVe siècle)* (Paris, Comité pour l'histoire économique et financière de la France 2003)

Riley, Patrick. 'The Abbé de St Pierre and Voltaire on Perpetual Peace in Europe', 137 *World Affairs* (1974), 186–94

Rimner, Steffen. *Opium's Long Shadow* (Harvard University Press 2018)

Ripstein, Arthur. *Force and Freedom. Kant's Political and Legal Philosophy* (Harvard University Press 2009)

Rivière, Jean. 'Sur l'origine de la formule "Rex imperator in regno suo"', 4 *Revue des sciences religieuses* (1924), 580–6

*Le problème de l'église et de l'État au temps de Philippe le Bel* (Paris, Champion 1926)

Robert Scott, William. *The Constitution and Finance of English, Scottish and Irish Joint-Stock Companies to 1720*, vol. II (Cambridge University Press 1912)

Robespierre, Maximilien. *Oeuvres* (10 tomes, M Boiloiseau et al. eds., Presses Universitaires de France 1958)

Robins, Nick. *The Corporation That Changed the World. How the East India Company Shaped the Modern Multinational* (London, Pluto 2006)

Robinson, Jonathan William. *William of Ockham's Early Theory of Property Rights in Context* (Leiden, Brill 2012)

Robinson-Hammerstein, Helga. 'The Common Good and the University in the Age of Confessional Conflict', in Ciaran Brady and Jane Ohlmeyer (eds), *British Interventions in Early Modern Ireland* (Cambridge University Press 2004), 75–96

Rodgers, James Steven. *The Early History of Bills and Notes. A Study of the Origins of Anglo-American Commercial Law* (Cambridge University Press 1995)

Roeck, Berd. *Reichssystem und Reichsherkommen. Die Diskussion über die Staatlichkeit des Reiches in der politischen Publizistik des 17. und 18. Jahrhunderts* (Stuttgart, Steiner 1984)

Rœge, Pernille. 'A Natural Order of Empire. The Physiocratic Vision of Colonial France after the Seven Years' War', in Sophus Reinert & Pernilla Rœge (eds), *The Political Economy of Empire in the Early Modern World* (London, Palgrave 2013), 32–52

Roelofsen, C. G. 'Grotius and the Development of International Relations Theory. The "Long Seventeenth Century" and the Elaboration of a European States System', 17 *Quinnipiac Law Review* (1997–8), 97–120

Roger, Dominique. 'De l'origine du préjugé du couleur en Haiti', in Marcel Dorigny (ed.), *Haiti. Première république noire* (Paris, Société française d'histoire d'outre-mer 2007), 83–101

Rohou, Jean. *Le XVIIe siècle, une révolution de la condition humaine* (Paris, Seuil 2002)

Rommelse, Gijs. *The Second Anglo-Dutch War (1665–1667)* (Hilversum, Verloren 2006)

Roncaglia, Alessandro. *The Wealth of Ideas. A History of Economic Thought* (Cambridge University Press 2001)

Root, Hilton L. *The Fountain of Privilege. Political Foundations of Markets in Old Regime France and England* (University of California Press 1994)

Roover, Raymond de. *La pensée économique des scolastiques* (Montréal, Institute d'études médiévales 1971)

Roper, L. H. 'The 1701 'Act for the better ordering of Slaves'. Reconsidering the History of Slavery in Proprietary South Carolina', 64 *William and Mary Quarterly* (2007), 396–408

Ropes, A. R. 'Frederick the Great's Invasion of Saxony and the *Mémoire Raisonné*, 5 *Transactions of the Royal Historical Society* (1891), 157–75

Rosanvallon, Pierre. *Le capitalisme utopique. Histoire de l'idée de marché* (Paris, Seuil 1979)

Rothkrug, Lionel. *Opposition to Louis XIV. The Political and Social Origins of the French Enlightenment* (Princeton University Press 1965)

Rothschild, Emma. 'Global Commerce and the Question of Sovereignty in the Eighteenth-Century Provinces', 1 *Modern Intellectual History* (2004), 3–25

*Economic Sentiments. Adam Smith, Condorcet and the Enlightenment* (Harvard University Press 2001)

Roulet, Eric. *La Compagnie des îles de l'Amérique 1635–1651. Une entreprise coloniale au XVIIe siècle* (Presses Universitaires de Rennes 2017)

Roumy, Franck. 'L'origine et la diffusion de l'adage canonique *Necessitas non habet legem* (VIIIe–XIIIe s.)', in W. P. Müller& M. E. Sommar (eds), *Medieval Church Law and the Origins of the Western Legal Tradition: A Tribute to Kenneth Pennington* (Catholic University of America Press 2012), 301–19

Rousseau, Jean-Jacques. 'The First Discourse – Discourse on the Science and the Arts', in Susan Dunn (ed.), *The Social Contract and the First and the Second Discourses* (Yale University Press 2002 [1762]), 43–68

*A Discourse on Inequality* (M. Cranston trans. & intro., Harmondworth, Penguin 1984 [1755])

*Discours sur l'économie politique* (B. Bernardi dir., Paris, Vrin 2002 [1758])

*Émile, ou l'éducation* (4 tomes, Francfort 1762)

*Julie ou la Nouvelle Héloïse* (Amsterdam, Marc-Michel Rey 1761)

*Principes du droit de la guerre. Écrits sur la paix pérpetuelle* (Bruno Bernardi & Gabriella Silvestrini eds., Paris Vrin 2008)

*The Social Contract* (M. Cranston trans. & intro., Harmondsworth, Penguin 1958)

Rowen, Herbert H. *The King's State. Proprietory Dynasticism in Early Modern France* (Rutgers University Press 1980)

Rowlands, Guy. *The Dynastic State and the Army under Louis XIV. Royal Service and Private Interest* (Cambridge University Press 2002)

Rückert, Joachim. 'Kant-Rezeption in juristischer und politischer Theorie (Naturrecht, Rechtsphilosophie, Staatslehre, Politik) des 19. Jahrhunderts', in M. Thompson, *John Locke and Immanuel Kant. Historical Reception and Contemporary Relevance* (Berlin, Duncker & Humblot 1991), 144–215

Ruddy, Francis S. 'The Acceptance of Vattel', in Charles H. Alexandrowicz (ed.), *Grotian Society Papers. Studies in the History of the Law of Nations* (The Hague, Nijhoff 1972), 177–96

Rüdiger, Axel. *Staatslehre und Staatsbildung. Die Staatswissenschaft an der Universität Halle im 18. Jahrhundert* (Tübingen, Niemeyer 2005)

Rufinus, *Summa Decretorum* (H. Singer ed., Paderborn, Schöningh 1902 [c. 1159])

Rugemer, Edward B. *Slave Law and the Politics of Resistance in the Early Atlantic World* (Harvard University Press 2018)

Ruggiu, François-Joseph. 'Colonies, Monarchies, Empire and the French Old Regime', in Robert Aldrich & Cindy McCreery (eds), *Crowns and Colonies. European Monarchies and Overseas Empires* (Manchester University Press 2016), 194–210

Ruiz, Teofilo E. *Spanish Society 1400–1600* (London, Longman 2001)

Rumble, Wilfried E. *Doing Austin Justice. The Reception of John Austin's Philosophy of Law in Nineteenth-Century England* (London, Bloomsbury 2004)

Russell, Frederick H. *The Just War in the Middle Ages* (Cambridge University Press 1975)

Ruysscher, Dave de. 'La *lex mercatoria* contextualisée: tracer son parcours intellectuel', *Revue historique de droit français et étranger* (2012), 499–515

Ryan, Magnus. 'Bartolus of Sassoferrato and Free Cities. The Alexander Prize Lecture', 10 *Transactions of the Royal Historical Society* (1999), 65–89

Rymer, Thomas (ed.). *Foedera, Conventiones, Litterae*, I-2 (20 vols, London, no publisher 1816 [1726–35])

Saada, Anne. 'Les universités dans l'empire au siècle des lumières. L'exemple de Göttingen: Une réussite inédite', in Frédéric Attal et al. (eds), *Les universités en Europe du XIIIe siècle à nos jours* (Paris, Publications de la Sorbonne 2005), 257–68

Saalfeld, Friedrich. *Handbuch des positiven Völkerrechts* (Tübingen, Osiander 1833)

Saether, Arild. *Natural Law and the Origin of Political Economy. Samuel Pufendorf and the History of Economics* (London, Routledge 2017)

Sahlins, Peter. 'Natural Frontiers Revisited. France's Boundaries since the Seventeenth Century', 95 *American Historical Review* (1990), 1423–51

Saint-Louis, Vertus. 'Commerce exterieur et concept de l'indépendence', in Michel Hector & Laënnec Hurbon (eds), *Genèse de l'État haïtien (1804–1859)* (Paris, Éditions de la Maison des sciences de l'homme 2010), 275–96

'Relations internationales et la classe politique en Haiti (1789–1814)', in Marcel Dorigny (ed.), *Haiti. Première république noire* (Paris, Société française d'histoire d'outre-mer 2007), 155–75

Saint-Just, Louis Antoine Léon de. *L'esprit de la révolution suivi de fragments sur les institutions républicaines* (Paris, Éditions 10/18, 2003 [1791])

Saint-Méry, Médéric Louis Elie Moreau de. *Description topographique, physique, civile, politique et historique de partie française de Saint-Domingue* (Paris, Dupont 1797)

*Loix et constitutions des colonies françoises de l'Amérique sous le vent*, 6 tomes (Paris, Quillau 1784–91)

Saint-Pierre, Charles-Irénée Castel de. 'Projet pour perfectionner le Gouvernement des Estats', in Charles-Irénée Castel de Saint-Pierre, *Ouvrages de politique*, tome 3 (Rotterdam, Briasson 1733), 223–8

*Abregé du projet de paix perpetuelle* (Rotterdam, Beman 1729)
*Discours sur la polysynodie* (Londres, Tonsson 1718)
*Mémoires pour rendre la paix pérpetuelle en Europe* (pour le ministre M. de Torcy, 1 septembre 1712)
*Nouveau plan de gouvernement* (Beman, Rotterdam 1762)
*Projet de traité pour rendre la paix perpétuelle entre les souverains chrétiens* (Utrecht, Schouten 1717)

Saint-Victor, Jean de. *Traité de la division des royaumes. Introduction à une histoire universelle* (Turnhout, Brepols 2002)

Sainte-Marie, Alice Bairoch de. 'Les colonies françaises et le droit. Une approche globale, 1600–1750', 82 *Études canadiennes* (2017), 87–119

Sala-Molins, Louis. *Le Code Noir ou le calvaire de Canaan* (Presses Universitaires de France 2002)

Salkeld, William (ed.), *Reports of Case Adjudged in the Court of the King's Bench*, 3 vols (London, Strahan 1795)

Salter, John. 'Hugo Grotius. Property and Consent', 29 *Political Theory* (2001), 537–55

Sampson, Margaret. 'Laxity and Liberty in Seventeenth-Century English Political Thought', in Edmund Leites (ed.), *Conscience and Casuistry in Early Modern Europe* (Cambridge University Press 1988), 72–118

Santiano, Benoît. *La monnaie, le prince et le marchand. Une analyse économique des phénomènes monétaires au Moyen Age* (Paris, Classiques Garnier 2010)

Sass, Stephen L. 'Research in Roman Law. A Guide to Sources and Their English Translations', 56 *Law Library Journal* (1963), 210–33

Satow, Ernst. *The Silesian Loan and Frederick the Great* (Oxford, Clarendon 1915)

Scammell, G. V. *The First Imperial Age. European Overseas Expansion c. 1400–1715* (London, Unwin 1989)

Scattola, Merio. 'Jean Bodin and International Law', in Stefan Kadelbach, Thomas Kleinlein & David Roth-Isigkeit (eds), *System, Order and International Law* (Oxford University Press 2017), 78–91
'Naturrecht als Rechtstheorie. Die Systematisierung der "res scolastica" in der Naturrechtslehre des Domingo Soto', in Frank Grunert & Kurt Seelmann (eds), *Die Ordnung der Praxis. Neue Studien zur spanischen Spätscholastik* (Tübingen, Niemeyer 2001), 21–48
*Das Naturrecht vor dem Naturrecht. Zur Geschichte des 'ius naturae' im 16. Jahrhundert* (Tübingen, Niemeyer 1999)

Scelle, Georges. 'The Slave-Trade in the Spanish Colonies of America. The Assiento', 4 *American Journal of International Law* (1910), 357–97

Schabas, Margaret. *The Natural Origins of Economics* (The University of Chicago Press 2005)

Schermaier, M. J. '*Res Communes Omnium.* The History of an Idea from Greek Philosophy to Grotian Jurisprudence', 30 *Grotiana* (2009), 20–48

Schlözer, August Wilhelm. *Allgemeines Statsrecht und Statsverfassungslere* (Göttingen, Vandenhoeck & Ruprecht 1793)

*Vorstellung seiner Universalhistorie* (Göttingen, Dieterich 1772)

Schlüssler, Rudolf. 'Hadrian VI und das Recht auf Verweigerung zweifelhaft rechtmässige Befehle', in Norbert Brieskorn & Markus Riedenauer (eds), *Suche nach Frieden. Politische Ethik in der Frühen Neuzeit 3* (Theologie und Frieden) (Stuttgart, Kohlhammer 2003), 41–62

Schmalz, Theodor. *Das europäische Völcker-Recht in Acht Büchern* (Berlin, Duncker & Humblot 1817)

Schmauss, Johann Jacob. 'Neues Systema der Rechts der Natur', in *Neues Systema der Rechts der Natur* (Göttingen, Vandenhoeck 1754), 449–595

*Corpus Juris Gentium Academicum. Enthaltenden die vornähmsten Staats-Gesetze Friedens- und Commercien-tractate, Bündnisse und andere Pacta. Erster Theil: Die Historie der Balance von Europa* (Leipzig, Gleditsch 1730)

*Einleitung zu der Staats-wissenschaft, und Erleuterung des von ihm herausgebenen Corpus Juris Gentium Academici und aller andern seit mehr als zweyen Seculis her geschlossenen Bündnisse, Friedens- und Commercien- Tractaten* (Leipzig, J. F. Gleditsch 1747)

*Kurze Erläuterung und Vertheidigung seines Systema juris naturae* (Göttingen, Vandenhoeck 1755)

*Vorstellung des wahren Begriffs von einem Recht der Natur* (Göttingen, Vandenhoeck 1748)

Schmelzing, Julius. *Systematischer Grundriss des praktischen Europäischen Völker-Rechts* (3 vols, Rudolfstadt, Hof-Buch- und Kunsthandlung 1818)

Schmidt, Frank-Steffen. *Praktisches Naturrecht zwischen Thomasius und Wolff. Der Völkerrechtler Adam Friedrich Glafey (1692–1753)* (Baden-Baden, Nomos 2007)

Schmidt, Georg. *Geschichte des alten Reiches. Staat und Nation in der frühen Neuzeit 1495–1806* (Munich, Beck 1999)

Schmidt-Biggemann, Wilhelm. 'New Structures of Knowledge', in Hilde de Ridder-Symons (ed.), *A History of the University in Europe*, vol. VII (Cambridge University Press 1996), 489–528

Schmitt, Carl. *Der Nomos der Erde im Völkerrecht des Jus Publicum Europaeum* (Berlin, Duncker & Humblot 1988)

*The Leviathan in the State Theory of Thomas Hobbes. Meaning and Failure of a Political Symbol* (London& Westport, Greenwood 1996 [1938])

Schneewind, J. B. *The Invention of Autonomy. A History of Modern Moral Philosophy* (Cambridge University Press 1998)

Schneidemüller, Bernd. *Nomen patriae. Die Entstehung Frankreichs in der politisch-geographischen Terminologie (10.–13. Jahrhundert)* (Sigmaringen, Thorbecker 1987)

Schneiders, Werner. 'Die Philosophie der aufgeklärten Absolutismus. Zum Verhältnis von Philosophie und Politik, Nicht nur im 18. Jahrhundert', in Hans Erich Bödeker (ed.), *Aufklärung als Politisierung – Politiserung der Aufklärung* (Hamburg, Meiner 1987), 383–406

'Vernunft und Freiheit. Christian Thomasius als Aufklärer', 11 *Studia Leibnitiana* (1979), 3–21

*Naturrecht und Liebesethik. Zur Geschichte der praktischen Philosophie im Hinblick auf Christian Thomasius* (Hildesheim, Olms 1971)

Schnerb-Lièvre, Marion. *Le Songe du Vergier* (2 vols., Marion Schnerb-Lièvre ed., Paris, CNRS 1982)

Schöfer, Christian. *La France moderne et le problème colonial* (Paris, Alcan 1907)

Schofield, Philip. *Utility & Democracy. The Political Thought of Jeremy Bentham* (Oxford University Press 2006)

"Scholasticon", Index by Jacob Schmutz, www.scholasticon.fr/Database/Scholastiques

Scholz, Richard. *Die Publizistik zur Zeit Philipps des Schönen und Bonifaz VIII* (Stuttgart, Enke 1903)

Schrader, Wilhelm. *Geschichte der Friedrichs-Universität zu Halle. Erster Teil* (Berlin, Dümmler 1894)

Schröder, Jan. '"Naturrecht bricht positives Recht" in der Rechtstheorie des 18. Jahrhunderts', in Dieter Schwab et al. (eds), *Staat, Kirche, Wissenschaft in einer pluralistischen Gesellschaft* (Berlin, Duncker & Humblot 1989), 419–33

'Politische Aspekte des Naturrechts in der zweiten Hälfte des 17. Jahrhunderts', in Diethelm Klippel (ed.), *Naturrecht und Staat. Politische Funktionen des europäischen Naturrechts* (Munich, Oldenburg 2006), 19–34

Schröder, Jan & Pielemeyer, Ines. 'Naturrecht als Lehrfach aus den deutschen Universitäten', in Otto Dann & Diethelm Klippel (eds), *Naturrecht – Spätaufklärung – Revolution* (Hamburg, Meiner 1995), 255–69

Schröder, Peter. 'The Concepts of Universal Monarchy and Balance of Power in the First Half of the Seventeenth Century', in Martti Koskenniemi et al. (eds), *International Law and Empire. Historical Explorations* (Oxford University Press 2017), 83–100

'The Constitution of the Holy Roman Empire after 1648. Samuel Pufendorf's Assessment in His *Monzambano*', 42 *The Historical Journal* (1999), 961–83

'Vitoria, Gentili, Bodin'. Sovereignty and the Law of Nations', in Benedict Kingsbury & Benjamin Straumann (eds), *The Roman Foundations of the Law of Nations. Alberico Gentili and the Justice of Empire* (Oxford University Press 2010), 163–86

*Trust in Early Modern International Political Thought, 1598–1713* (Cambridge University Press 2017)

Schroeder, Paul W. *The Transformation of European Politics 1763–1848* (Oxford, Clarendon 1994)

Schulte, F. von (ed.). *Die Summa des Stephanus Tornacensis über das Decretum Gratiani* (Giessen, Roth 1891)

Schulze, Hagen. *States, Nations and Nationalism* (London, Blackwell 1996)

Schuman, Frederik L. 'The Ethics and Politics of International Peace', 42 *International Journal of Ethics* (1932), 148–62

Schumpeter, Joseph. *Histoire de l'analyse économique*, I: *L'age des fondateurs* (Paris, Gallimard 1983)

Schwartz, Daniel. 'Grotius on the Moral Standing of the Society of Nations', 14 *Journal of the History of International Law* (2012), 123–46

Scordia, Lydwine. 'Les autorités cités lors des débats sur l'impôt par les théologiens à la fin du XIIIe siècle', in Jean Kerhervé & Albert Rigaudière (eds), *Monnaie, fiscalité et finances au temps de Philippe le Bel* (Paris, Comité pour l'histoire économique et financière de la France 2007), 19–50

Scott, David. *Leviathan. The Rise of Britain as a World Power* (London, Collins 2013)

Scott, James Hope. 'British Jurisdiction in Foreign States', in Sir Henry Jenkyns, *British Rule and Jurisdiction beyond the Seas* (Oxford, Clarendon 1902), 5–39

Scott, Samuel Parsons & Burns, Robert J. (eds). *Las Siete Partidas*, 5 vols (University of Pennsylvania Press 2012)

Scott, William Robert. *The Constitution and Finance of English, Scottish and Irish Joint Stock Companies* (3 vols. Cambridge University Press 1912)

Seckendorff, Veit Ludwig von. *Christen-Staat* (Leipzig, Fritschen 1716)

Seed, Patricia. *Ceremonies of Possession in Europe's Conquest of the New World 1492–1640* (Cambridge University Press 1995)

Seelmann, Kurt. *Die Lehre des Fernando Vázquez de Menchaca vom Dominium* (Cologne, Heymanns 1979)

*Theologie und Jurisprudenz an der Schwelle zur Moderne* (Baden-Baden, Nomos 1997)

Seidl, Michael. '"Turkish Judgment" and the English Revolution. Pufendorf and the Right of Resistance', in Fiammetta Palladini & Gerald Hartung (eds), *Samuel Pufendorf und die europäische Frühaufklärung* (Berlin, Akademie 1996), 83–104

Selden, John. *Of the Dominion or Ownership of the Sea in Two Books* (London, Du Gard with the appointment of the Council of State 1652)

Sellert, Wolfgang. 'Johann Jacob Schmauss – ein Göttinger Jurist', 11 *Juristische Schulung* (1985), 843–7

Semmel, Bernard. *The Rise of Free Trade Imperialism. Classical Political Economy and the Empire of Free Trade and Imperialism 1750–1850* (Cambridge University Press 2009 [1970])

Sen, Sudipta. *Distant Sovereignty. National Imperialism and the Origins of British India* (New York, Routledge 2002)

Senellart, Michel. 'Y à-t-il une théorie allemande de la raison d'état au XVII siècle?', in Yves Zarka (ed.), *Raison et déraison d'Etat* (Presses Universitaires de France 1994), 265–93

*Les arts de gouverner. De régimen médiéval au concept de gouvernement* (Paris, Seuil 1995)

*Machiavélisme et raison d'état. XIIe–XVIIIe siècle* (Presses Universitaires de France 1988)

Serna, Pierre. 'The Sister Republics, or the Ephemeral Invention of a French Republican Commonwealth', in Alan Forrest & Matthias Middell (eds), *The Routledge Companion to the French Revolution in World History* (London, Routledge 2016), 39–60

Sève, René. 'Le discours juridique dans la première moitié du XVIIème siècle', in A. Robinet (ed.), *L'état baroque. Regards sur la pensée politique de la France du premier XVIIe siècle* (Paris, Vrin 1985), 119–46

*Leibniz et l'école moderne de droit naturel* (Presses Universitaires de France 1989)

Seyssel, Claude de. *The Monarchy of France* (Yale University Press 1981[1515])

Shapiro, Ian. *The Evolution of Rights in Liberal Theory* (Cambridge University Press 1986)

Sheehan, Michael. *The Balance of Power. History & Theory* (London, Routledge 1996)

Shell, Susan. *The Rights of Reason. A Study of Kant's Philosophy and Politics* (University of Toronto Press 1980)

Shepherd, Robert. *Turgot and the Six Edicts* (Columbia University Press 1903)

Sheppard, S. (ed.). *The Selected Writings and Speeches of Sir Edward Coke*, vol. I (3 vols, Indianapolis, Liberty Fund 2003)

Shovlin, John. *The Political Economy of Virtue. Luxury, Patriotism, and the Origins of the French Revolution* (Cornell University Press 2006)

Sievernich, Michael. 'Toleranz und Kommunikation. Das Recht auf Mission bei Francisco de Vitoria', in Frank Grunert & Kurt Seelmann (eds), *Die Ordnung der Praxis. Neue Studien zur spanischen Spätscholastik* (Tübingen, Niemeyer 2001), 183–204

Sieyès, Emmanuel. 'An Essay on Privileges', in *Sieyès. Political Writings* (M. Sonenscher ed., Indianapolis, Hackett 2003), 68–91

'Views of the Executive Means Available to the Representatives of France in 1789', in *Sieyès. Political Writings* (M. Sonenscher ed., Indianapolis, Hackett 2003), 1–67

'What Is the Third Estate?', in *Sieyès. Political Writings* (M. Sonenscher ed., Indianapolis, Hackett 2003), 92–162

*Préliminaire de la constitution française & Reconnaissance et exposition raisonnée des droits de l'homme et du citoyen* (Paris, Baudoin 1789)

Silvestrini, Gabriella. 'Vattel, Rousseau et la question de la "justice" de la guerre', in Vincent Chetail & Peter Haggenmacher (eds), *Vattel's International Law in a XXIst Century Perspective* (Geneva, Nijhoff 2011), 101–30

Simon, Paul E. 'Law and Politics', in Norman Kretzmann & Eleonore Stump (eds), *The Cambridge Companion to Aquinas* (Cambridge University Press 1993), 217–31

Simon, Thomas. *"Gute Policey". Ordnungsleitbilder und Zielverstellungen politischen Handelns in der Frühen Neuzeit* (Frankfurt, Klostermann 2004)

Simpson, A. W. B. *A History of the Land Law* (2nd edn, Oxford University Press 1986)

Simpson, Lesley Byrd. *The Encomienda in New Spain. The Beginning of Spanish Mexico* (University of California Press 1982)

Sivéry, Gérard. 'La notion économique de l'usure selon saint Thomas d'Aquin', 3–4 *Revue du Nord* (2004), 697–708

Skinner, Quentin. 'A Genealogy of the Modern State', 162 *Proceedings of the British Academy* (2008), 325–70

'From the State of Princes to the Person of the State', in Quentin Skinner, *Visions of Politics*, vol. 2: *Renaissance Virtues* (Cambridge University Press 2002), 368–413

*The Foundations of Modern Political Thought*, 2 vols (Cambridge University Press 1977)

Skirke, Christian. 'Cum sensu imbellicitatis. Grotius und die Wiederstandrecht', 62 *Zeitschrift für philosophische Forschung* (2008), 562–83

Skornicki, Arnault. *L'économiste, la cour et la patrie* (Paris, CNRS Éditions 2011)

Slack, Paul. *Invention of Improvement. Information and Material Progress in Seventeenth-Century England* (Oxford University Press 2014)

Slattery, Brian. 'French Claims in North America, 1500–59', 59 *Canadian Historical Review* (1978), 139–69

Smith, Adam. *An Inquiry into the Nature and Causes of the Wealth of Nations* (Harmondsworth, Penguin Classics 1982 [1776])

*Lectures on Jurisprudence* (R. L. Meek, D. D. Raphael & P. L. Stein eds, Indianapolis, Liberty Fund 1982 [1763])

*The Theory of Moral Sentiments* (P. Moloney ed., New York, Barnes & Noble Books 2004 [1759/1790])

Smith, David Chan. *Sir Edward Coke and the Reformation of the Laws* (Cambridge University Press 2014)

Smith, Thomas. *De republica anglorum* (L. Alston ed., Cambridge University Press 1906 [1583])

*Discourse of the Common Weal of this Realm of England* (Elizabeth Lamond ed., Cambridge University Press 1929 [1581])

Smith, William. *History of Canada from Its First Discovery to the Peace of 1763* (Quebec, Neilson 1815)

Sommerville, J. P. 'John Selden, The Law of Nature, and the Origins of Government', 27 *The Historical Journal* (1984), 437–47

'Selden, Grotius and the Seventeenth-Century Intellectual Revolution in Moral and Political Theory', in Victoria Kahn & Lorna Hutson (eds), *Rhetoric and Law in Early Modern Europe* (Yale University Press 2001), 318–44

*Royalists and Patriots. Politics and Ideology in England 1603–1640* (2nd edn, London, Longman 1999)

Somos, Mark. 'Selden's *Mare Clausum.* The Secularisation of International Law and the Rise of Soft Imperialism', 14 *Journal of the History of International Law* (2012), 287–330

*Secularization and the Leiden Circle* (Leiden, Brill 2011)

Sonenscher, Michael. 'Ideology, Social Science and General Facts in Late Eighteenth-Century French Political Thought', 35 *History of European Ideas* (2009), 24–37

*Before the Deluge. Public Debt, Inequality, and the Intellectual Origins of the French Revolution* (Princeton University Press 2007)

Sordi, Bernardo. 'Public Law before "Public Law"', in Heikki Pihlajamäki, Markus D. Dubber & Mark Godfrey (eds), *The Oxford Handbook of European Legal History* (Oxford University Press 2018), 706–28

Sosin, Jack M. *Whitehall and the Wilderness. The Middle West in British Colonial Policy 1760–1775* (University of Nebraska Press 1991)

Soto, Domingo de. *De iustitia et iure Libri decem / De la justicia y el derecho en diez Libros* (P. V. Diego Carro intro., P. M. Gonzalez Spanish trans., Madrid, Ordoñez 1967 [1559])

'Quaestio 40 De bello, A 1', in Luciano Pereña et al. (eds), *Francisco de Vitoria, Relectio de iure bello o paz dinámica. Escuela Española de la paz. Primera generación 1526–1560* (Madrid, Consejo Superior de Investigaciones Científicas 1981), 304–9

*Releccion 'De dominio'. Edición crítica y Traducción, con Introducción, Apéndices e Índices, por Jaime Prufau Prats* (Universidad de Granada 1964 [1534])

Souleyman, Elizabeth V. *The Vision of World Peace in Seventeenth and Eighteenth Century France* (Washington, Kennikat 1941)

Sousa, Nasim. *The Capitulatory Régime of Turkey. Its History, Origin and Nature* (Baltimore, Johns Hopkins Press 1933)

Specht, Rainer. 'Die Spanische Spätscholastik im Kontext ihrer Zeit', in Frank Grunert & Kurt Seelmann (eds), *Die Ordnung der Praxis. Neue Studien zur spanischen Spätscholastik* (Tuebingen, Niemeyer 2001), 3–17

Spector, Céline. 'L'Europe de l'Abbé de Saint-Pierre', in Carole Dornier & Claudine Poulouin Dornier et al. (eds), *Les Projets de l'abbé Castel de Saint-Pierre (1658–1743)* (Presses Universitaires de Caen 2011), 39–49

'Le Projet de paix perpétuelle. De Saint-Pierre à Rousseau', in Jean-Jacques Rousseau, *Principes du droit de la guerre. Ecrits sur la paix perpétuelle* (B. Bernardi & G. Silvestrini eds, Paris, Vrin 2008), 229–94

'Sujet de droit et sujet d'intérêt. Montesquieu lu par Foucault', 5 *Astérion* (2007), journals.openedition.org/asterion/766

*Montesquieu. Pouvoirs, richesses et sociétés* (Presses Universitaires de France 2004)

Spieler, Miranda Frances. 'The Legal Structure of Colonial Rule during the French Revolution', 66 *William and Mary Quarterly* (2009), 365–408

Spitz, Jean-Fabien. *Bodin et la souverainété* (Presses Universitaires de France 1998)

Stanley, George F. 'The First Indian "Reserves" in Canada', 4 *Revue d'histoire d'Amérique français* (1950), 178–210

Stapelbroek, Koen. 'Universal Society, Commerce and the Right of Neutral Trade', in Petter Korkman & Virpi Mäkinen (eds), *Universalism in*

*International Law and Political Philosophy* (Helsinki, Helsinki Collegium 2008), 63–89

Staum, Martin S. *Minerva's Message. Stabilizing the French Revolution* (McGill–Queen's University Press 1996)

Steele, E. D. *Palmerston and Liberalism, 1855–1865* (Cambridge University Press 1991)

Steiger, Heinhard. 'Der Westfälische Friede – Grundgesetz für Europa?', in Heinz Duchhardt (ed.), *Der Westfälische Friede* (Munich, Oldenbourg 1998), 33–80

'Rechtliche Strukturen der europäischen Staatsordnung 1648–1792', 59 *Die Zeitschrift für ausländisches öffentliches Recht und Völkerrecht* (1999), 609–48

'Völkerrecht und Naturrecht zwischen Christian Wolff und Adolf Lasson', in Diethelm Klippel (ed.), *Naturrecht im 19. Jahrhundert* (Goldbach, Keip 1997), 45–74

Stein, Lorenz von. Review of Aug. Wilh. Heffter, *Das europäische Völkerrecht der Gegenwart*, 16–18 *Allgemeine Literatur-Zeitung* (1845), 121–5, 129–36, 137–44

*Geschichte der sozialen Bewegung in Frankreich von 1789 bis auf unsere Tage*, 3 vols (Leipzig, Wiegand 1850)

Stein, Peter. *Roman Law in European History* (Cambridge University Press 1999)

Stein, Robert Louis. *Léger-Félicité Sonthonax. The Lost Sentinel of the Republic* (London, Associated University Presses 1985)

Stern, Philip J. '"Bundles of Hyphens." Corporations as Legal Communities in the Early Modern British Empire', in Lauren Benton & Richard J. Ross (eds), *Legal Pluralism and Empires 1500–1850* (New York University Press 2013), 21–48

*The Company-State. Corporate Sovereignty and the Early Modern Foundations of British Rule in India* (Oxford University Press 2011)

Stern, Robert. 'Hegel's *Doppelsatz*. A Neutral Reading', 44 *Journal of the History of Philosophy* (2006), 235–66

Stoebuck, William E. 'Reception of English Common Law in the American Colonies', 10 *William and Mary Law Review* (1968), 393–426

Stollberg-Rilinger, Barbara. 'Handelsgeist und Adelsethos', 15 *Zeitschrift für historische Forschung* (1988), 273–309

'Vom Volk übertragene Recht?', in Diethelm Klippel (ed.), *Naturrecht und Staat. Politische Funktionen des europäischen Naturrechts* (Munich, Oldenburg 2006), 103–18

*Der Staat als Maschine. Zur politischen Metaphorik des absoluten Fürstenstaats* (Berlin, Duncker & Humblot 1986)

Stolleis, Michael. 'Arcana imperii und Ratio Status. Bemerkungen zur politischen Theories des frühen 17. Jahrhunderts', in Michael Stolleis, *Staat und Staatsräson in der frühen Neuzeit. Studien zur Geschichte des öffentlichen Rechts* (Frankfurt, Suhrkamp 1990), 37–72

'Lipsius-Recepzion in der politisch-juristischen Literatur 17. Jahrhunderts in Deutschland', 26 *Der Staat* (1987), 1–30

'"Löwe und Fuchs". Eine politische Maxime im Frühabsolutismus', in Michael Stolleis, *Staatsrecht – Völkerrecht – Europarecht. Festschrift für Hans-Jürgen Schlochauer zum 75. Geburtstag am 28. März 1981* (Berlin, Walter de Gruyter 1981), 151–61

'Machiavellismus und Staatsräson. Ein Beitrag zu Conrings politischem Denken', in Michael Stolleis, *Hermann Conring (1606–1681). Beiträge zu Leben und Werk* (Berlin, Duncker & Humblot 1983), 173–200

'Textor und Pufendorf über die Ratio Status Imperii im Jahre 1667', in Michael Stolleis (ed.), *Staat und Staatsräson in der frühen Neuzeit. Studien zur Geschichte des öffentlichen Rechts* (Frankfurt, Suhrkamp 1990), 106–33

*Geschichte des öffentlichen Rechts in Deutschland. Erster band, 1600–1800* (Munich, Beck 1988)

*Geschichte des öffentlichen Rechts in Deutschland. Zweiter Band, 1800–1914* (Munich, Beck 1992)

*Staatsdenker in der frühen Neuzeit* (ed.) (Munich, Beck 1995 [earlier edition *Staatsdenker im 17. und 18. Jahrhundert*, Frankfurt, Metzner 1987])

Stone, Bailey. *The Genesis of the French Revolution* (Cambridge University Press 1994)

Stone, M. W. F. 'Scrupulosity and Conscience. Probabilism in Early Modern Societies', in Harald E. Braun & Edward Vallance (eds), *Contexts of Conscience in Early Modern Europe 1500–1700* (London, Palgrave Macmillan 2004), 507–50

Storez, Isabelle. 'La philosophie politique du chancelier D'Aguesseau', 266 *Revue historique* (1981), 381–400

Story, Joseph. *Commentaries on the Conflict of Laws* (Boston, Hilliard 1834)

Strachey, William. *The Historie of Travaile into Virginia Britannia* (London, Hakluyt Society 1849 [1612])

Stråth, Bo. *Europe's Utopias for Peace* (London, Bloomsbury 2016)

Straumann, Benjamin. 'The *Corpus iuris* as a Source of Law Between Sovereigns in Alberico Gentili's Thought', in Benedict Kingsbury & Benjamin Straumann (eds), *The Roman Foundations of the Law of Nations. Alberico Gentili and the Justice of Empire* (Oxford University Press 2010), 101–23

*Hugo Grotius und die Antike* (Baden-Baden, Nomos 2007)

*Roman Law in the State of Nature* (Cambridge University Press 2015)

Strayer, Joseph R. 'The Development of Feudal Institutions', in Joseph Strayer, *Medieval Statecraft and the Perspectives of History* (Princeton University Press 1971), 98–110

'Defense of the Realm and Royal Power in France', in Joseph Strayer, *Medieval Statecraft and the Perspectives of History* (Princeton University Press 1971), 312–20

*Les gens de justice du Languedoc sous Philippe le Bel* (Toulouse, Association Marc Bloch 1970)

*Medieval Statecraft and Perspectives of History* (Princeton University Press 1971)
*The Reign of Philip the Fair* (Princeton Legacy Library 2019)

Streidl, Paul. *Naturrecht, Staatswissenschaften und Politisierung bei Gottfried Achenwall (1719–1772). Studien zur Gelehrtengeschichte Göttingens in der Aufklärung* (Munich, Utz 2000)

Strype, John. *The Life of the Learned Sir Thomas Smith* (Oxford, Clarendon 1820)

Study, David J. *Richelieu and Mazarin. A Study of Statesmanship* (London, Macmillan 2004)

Sueur, Philippe. *Histoire du droit public français. XVe–XVIIIe siècle*, tome II: *Affirmation et crise de l'État sous l'Ancien Régime* (4th edn, Presses Universitaires de France 2009)

Sugarman, David & Warrington, Ronnie. 'Land Law, Citizenship and the Invention of "Englishness". The Strange Case of the Equity of Redemption', in John Brewer & Susan Staves (eds), *Early Modern Conceptions of Property* (London, Routledge 1995), 111–43

Suin, Davide. 'Principi supremi e societas hominium. Il problema del potere nella riflessione di Alberico Gentili', XXIV *Scienza e politica* (2017), 107–24

Sullivan, Robert E. *Macaulay. The Tragedy of Power* (Harvard University Press 2009)

Suprinyak, Carlos Eduardo. 'Merchants and Councilors. Intellectual Divergences in Early 17th Century British Economic Thought', 21 *Nova Economia* (2011), 459–82

Sylvest, Caspar. "The Foundations of Victorian International Law", in Duncan Bell (ed.), *Victorian Visions of Global Order. Empire and International Relations in Nineteenth-Century Political Thought* (Cambridge University Press 2007), 47–66

Symcox, Geoffrey. *The Crisis of French Sea Power 1688–1697. From the* Guerre d'Escade *to the* Guerre de Course (The Hague, Nijhoff 1974)

Talleyrand-Périgord, Charles-Maurice de. *Essai sur les avantages à retirer de colonies nouvelles dans les circonstances présentes* (Lu à la science publique de l'Institut national le 15 messidor an V 1797)

Tarrade, Jean. *Le commerce colonial de la France à la fin de l'ancien régime. L'évolution du régime de l'Exclusif de 1763 à 1789* (Université de Paris 1972)

Taylor, Charles. *Hegel* (Cambridge University Press 1975)

Telliez, Romain. *Les institutions de France médiévale XIe–Xve siècles* (Paris, Armand Colin 2009)

Tentler, Thomas N. *Sin and Confession on the Eve of the Reformation* (Princeton University Press 1977)

Terrel, Jean. *Les théories du pacte social* (Paris, Seuil 2001)

Tertre, Jean Baptiste du. *Histoire générale des Antilles habités par les françois* (4 tomes, Paris 1667)

Teschke, Benno. *The Myth of 1648. Class, Geopolitics and the Making of Modern International Relations* (London, Verso 2003)

Teyssier, Armand. *Richelieu. La puissance de gouverner* (Paris, Michalon 2007)

Théry, Julien. 'Le pionnier de la théocratie royale. Guillaume de Nogaret et les conflits de Philippe le Bel avec la papauté', in Bernard Moreau (ed.),

*Guillaume de Nogaret. Un Languedocien au service de la monarchie capétienne* (Nimes, Lucie 2012), 101–27

'Philippe le Bel, le pape en son royaume', 289 *Revue L'histoire (Dieu et la politique. Le défi laïque)* (2004), 14–17

'Une hérésie d'État. Philippe le Bel, le procès des "perfides templiers" et la pontificalisation de la royauté française', 60 *Médiévales* (2011), 157–85

Thier, Andreas. 'Heilsgeschichte und naturrechtliche Ordnung. Naturrecht vor und nach dem Sündenfall', in Matthias Armgardt & Tilman Repgen (eds), *Naturrecht im Antike und früher Neuzeit* (Tübingen, Mohr Siebeck 2014), 151–72

'Historische Semantiken von ius gentium und "Völkerrecht"', in Tilmann Altwickel et al. (eds), *Völkerrechtsphilosophie der Frühaufklärung* (Tübingen, Mohr Siebeck 2016), 29–47

Thierry, Eric. *La France de Henri IV en Amérique du Nord. De la création d'Acadie à la fondation de Québec* (Paris, Champion 2008)

Thieulloy, Guillaume de. *Le pape et le roi. 7 septembre 1303* (Paris, Gallimard 2010)

Thomas, Hugh. *The Golden Empire. Spain, Charles V and the Creation of America* (New York, Random House 2010)

Thomasius, Christian. 'The Right of Protestant Princes in Regard to Indifferent Matters or Adiaphora', in I. Hunter, T. Ahnert & F. Grunert (eds), *Essays on Church, State and Politics* (Indianapolis, Liberty Fund 2007 [1695]), 49–127

*Grundlehren des Natur- und Völkerrechts* (F. Grunert ed., Hildesheim, Olms 2003 [1709])

*Institutionum iuris prudentiae Divinae Libri tres* (Halle, Saalfeld 1702)

*Kurzer Entwurff der politischen Klugheit* (Frankfurt & Leipzig 1705)

Thompson, M. P. 'The Idea of Conquest in the Controversies over the 1688 Revolution', 38 *Journal of the History of Ideas* (1977), 33–46

Thomson, Erik. 'France's Grotian Moment? Hugo Grotius and Cardinal Richelieu's Commercial Statecraft', 21 *French History* (2007), 377–94

Thornton, Helen. 'John Selden's Response to Hugo Grotius. The Argument for Closed Seas', 18 *International Journal for Maritime History* (2006), 105–28

Thornton, Tim. 'The Palatinate of Durham and the Maryland Charter', 45 *American Journal of Legal History* (2001), 305–25

Thuau, Etienne. *Raison d'état et pensée politique à l'époque de Richelieu* (Paris, Albin Michel 2000 [1966])

Thuillier, Guy. *La première école d'administration. L'académie politique de Louis XIV* (Genève, Droz 1996)

Thumfart, Johannes. 'Freihandel als Religion. Zur Ökonomischen Theologie in den völkerrechtlichen Entwürfen Hugo Grotius' und Francisco de Vitorias', 46 *Archiv des Völkerrechts* (2008), 259–71

Tierney, Brian. 'Dominion of Self and Natural Rights Before Locke and After', in Virpi Mäkinen & Petter Korkman (eds), *Transformations in Medieval and Early Modern Rights Discourse* (Berlin, Springer 2006), 173–203

'Natura Id Est Deus. A Case of Juristic Pantheism?', 24 *Journal of the History of Ideas* (1963), 307–22

'Permissive Natural Law and Property. Gratian to Kant', 62 *Journal of the History of Ideas* (2001), 381–99

*Liberty & Law. The Idea of Permissive Natural Law, 1100–1800* (Catholic University of America Press 2014)

*The Crisis of Church and State 1050–1300* (University of Toronto Press 1988)

*The Idea of Natural Rights. Studies on Natural Rights, Natural Law, and Church Law 1150–1625* (Michigan, Eerdmans 1997)

Tilly, Charles. *Coercion, Capital and European States AD 990–1992* (Cambridge, MA, Basil Blackwell 1992)

Todd, David. 'Beneath Sovereignty. Extraterritoriality and Imperial Internationalism in Nineteenth-Century Egypt', 36 *Law and History Review* (2018), 595–619

Todescan, Franco. *Lex, natura, beatitudo. Il problema della legge nella scolastica spagnola del sec. XVI* (Padova, CEDAM 1973)

Toledo, Francisco de. 'Utrum ritus insularum sint tolerandi', in Luciano Pereña et al. (eds), *Juan de la Peña. De bello contra insulanos. Intervención de España en América. Escuela Espanola de la Paz. Segunda generación. 1560–1585.* CHP vol. IX (2 vols, Madrid, Consejo Superior de Investigaciones Científicas 1982), II, 377–83

Tomlins, Christopher. *Freedom Bound. Law, Labour and Civic Identity in Colonizing English America 1480–1865* (Cambridge University Press 2010)

Toulmin, Stephen & Jonse, Albert R. *The Abuse of Casuistry* (University of California Press 1988)

Toyoda, Tetsuya. *Theory and Politics of the Law of Nations. Political Bias in International Law Discourse of Seven German Court Councilors in the Seventeenth and Eighteenth Centuries* (Leiden, Nijhoff 2011)

Traboulay, David M. *Columbus and Las Casas. The Conquest and Christianization of America 1492–1566* (Lanham, University Press of America 1994)

Tracy, Antoine Destutt de. *Commentaire sur l'Esprit des lois de Montesquieu* (Université de Caen 1992 [1808])

Trapman, Johannes. 'Grotius and Erasmus', in Henk M. Nellen & Edwin Rabbie (eds), *Hugo Grotius Theologian. Essays in Honour of G. H. M. Posthumus Meyjes* (Leiden, Brill 1994), 77–98

Travers, Robert. *Ideology and Empire in Eighteenth-Century India* (Cambridge University Press 2007)

*Treaties, Conventions, Etc., between China and Foreign States. With a Chronological List of Treaties and of Regulations Based on Treaty Provisions, 1689–1886* (Shanghai 1887)

Tribe, Keith. 'Cameralism and the Science of Government', in Keith Tribe, *Strategies of Economic Order. German Economic Discourse 1750–1850* (Cambridge University Press 1995), 8–31

*Governing Economy. The Reformation of German Economic Discourse 1750–1840* (Cambridge University Press 1988)

*Land, Labour and Economic Discourse* (London, Routledge 1977)

Trudel, Marcel. *Histoire de la Nouvelle-France*, vol. III: *La seigneurie des Cent-Associés 1. Les événements* (Montréal, Fides 1979)

Tuck, Richard. 'Grotius and Selden', in J. H. Burns (ed.), *The Cambridge History of Political Thought 1450–1700* (Cambridge University Press 1991), 499–529

*Natural Rights Theories. Their Origin and Development* (Cambridge University Press 1979)

*Philosophy and Government. 1572–1651* (Cambridge University Press 1993)

*The Rights of War and Peace. Political Thought and the International Order from Grotius to Kant* (Oxford University Press 2001)

*The Sleeping Sovereign. The Invention of Modern Democracy* (Cambridge University Press 2016)

Tully, James. 'An Introduction to Locke's Political Philosophy', in James Tully, *An Approach to Political Philosophy. Locke in Contexts* (Cambridge University Press 1993), 9–68

'Rediscovering America. *The Two Treatises* and Aboriginal Rights', in James Tully, *An Approach to Political Philosophy. Locke in Contexts* (Cambridge University Press 1993), 137–76

*A Discourse of Property. John Locke and His Adversaries* (Cambridge University Press 1980)

Turgot, Anne-Robert-Jacques. *Reflections on the Formation and the Distribution of Riches* (New York, Macmillan [Liberty Fund] 1891 [1770])

Turner, Henry S. 'Corporations. Humanism and Elizabethan Political Economy', in Philip J. Stern & Carl Wennerlind (eds), *Mercantilism Reimagined. Political Economy in Early Modern Britain and Its Empire* (Oxford University Press 2014), 153–76

Twining, William. 'Reading Bentham', 75 *Proceedings of the British Academy* (1989), 97–141

Ubl, Karl. 'Genese der Bulle Unam sanctam. Anlass, Vorlagen, Intention', in Martin Kaufhold (ed.), *Politischer Reflektion in der Welt des Späten Mittelalters / Political Thought in the Age of Scholasticism. Essays in Honour of Jürgen Miethke* (Leiden, Brill 2004), 129–49

'Johannes Quidorts weg zur Sozialphilosophie', 30 *Francia* (2003), 43–72

Ullmann, Walter. 'The Development of the Medieval Idea of Sovereignty', CCL *The English Historical Review* (1949), 1–33

'This Realm of England Is An Empire', 30 *Journal of Ecclesiastical History* (1979), 175–203

*A History of Political Thought. The Middle Ages* (London, Penguin 1970)

*Law and Politics in the Middle Ages. An Introduction to the Sources of Medieval Political Ideas* (London, Sources of History 1975)

Valier, Jacques. *Brève histoire de la pensée économique d'Aristote à nos jours* (Paris, Flammarion 2005)

Vattel, Emer de. 'Essay on the Foundation of Natural Law and on the First Principle of Obligation Men Find Themselves Under to Observe Laws', in Emer de Vattel, *The Law of Nations, or Principles of the Law of Nature, Applied to the Conduct and Affairs of Nations and Sovereigns* (Indianapolis, Liberty Fund 2008 [1758]), 747–71

*The Law of Nations, or Principles of the Law of Nature, Applied to the Conduct and Affairs of Nations and Sovereigns* (B. Kapossy & R. Whatmore ed. & intro., Indianapolis, Liberty Fund 2008 [1758])

Vauban, Sébastien Le Prestre, Marquis de. 'Mémoire concernant la caprerie. La course et les priviléges dont elle a besoin pour se pouvoir établir', in Sébastien Le Prestre, Marquis de Vauban & Gabriel-Henri Gaillard, *Oisivetés de M. Vauban*, tome IV (Paris, Corréard 1842), 157–67

Vázquez de Menchaca, Fernando. *Controversiarum illustrium aliarumque usu frequentium libri tres* (2 vols, Fidel Rodríguez Alcade trans., Valladolid 1931–2 [1564])

*Illustrium Controversiarum aliarumque usu frequentium libri sex in duas partes divisi* (Francofurti, Schönwetterei 1668)

Velkley, Richard. *Being after Rousseau. Philosophy and Culture in Question* (The University of Chicago Press 2002)

Veracruz, Alonso de. *De iusto bello contra indios* (Edición crítica bilingüe, Madrid, Consejo Superior de Investigaciones Científicas 1997)

Vergerio, Claire. 'Alberico Gentili's *De iure belli*. An Absolutist's Attempt to Reconcile the *jus gentium* and the Reason of State Tradition', 19 *Journal of the History of International Law* (2017), 429–66

Vidal, Cécile. 'French Louisiana in the Age of the Companies', in L. H. Roper & B. van Ruymbeke (eds), *Constructing Early Modern Empires. Proprietary Ventures in the Atlantic World 1500–1750* (Leiden, Brill 2007), 133–61

Vierhaus, Rudolf. 'Göttingen Die modernste Universität im Zeitalter der Aufklärung', in Alexander Demandt (ed.), *Stätter des Geistes. Große Universitäten Europas von der Antike bis zur Gegenwart* (Köln, Bohlau Verlag 1999), 245–56

Villey, Michel. *La formation de la pensée juridique moderne* (Presses Universitaires de France 2003)

Viner, Jacob. *The Role of Providence in the Social Order. An Essay in Intellectual History* (Princeton University Press 1972)

Viroli, Mauricio. *From Politics to Reason of State. The Acquisition and Transformation of the Language of Politics 1250–1600* (Cambridge University Press 2010)

Vitoria, Francisco de. 'On Civil Power', in Anthony Pagden and Jeremy Lawrance (eds), *Vitoria. Political Writings* (Cambridge University Press 1991), 1–44

'On Dietary Laws, or Self-Restraint', in Anthony Pagden and Jeremy Lawrance (eds), *Vitoria. Political Writings* (Cambridge University Press 1991), 207–30

'On Law', in Anthony Pagden and Jeremy Lawrance (eds), *Vitoria. Political Writings* (Cambridge University Press 1991), 90–105

'On the American Indians', in Anthony Pagden and Jeremy Lawrance (eds), *Vitoria. Political Writings* (Cambridge University Press 1991), 231–92

'On the Law of War', in Anthony Pagden and Jeremy Lawrance (eds), *Vitoria. Political Writings* (Cambridge University Press 1991), 293–327

*Comentarios a la Secunda secundae de Santo Tomás* (Edición preparada por Vicente Beltrán de Heredia, Salamanca 1934/1952)

*Confessionario muy util y provechoso* (Antwerp, Tylenio 1570)

*Contratos y usura* (Idoya Zorroza ed., Pamplona, EUNSA 2006)

Voegelin, Eric. *History of Political Ideas*, vol. III: *The Later Middle Ages* (David Walsh ed., Missouri University Press 1998)

Vollhardt, Friedrich. 'Die Grundregel der Naturrecht', in Frank Grunert & Siegfried Wollhardt (eds), *Aufklärung als praktische Philosophie* (Tübingen, Niemeyer 1998), 129–48

Voltaire. *Candide ou l'optimisme* (Paris, Presses Pocket 1989 [1759])

Vyverberg, Henry. *Human Nature, Cultural Diversity, and the French Enlightenment* (Oxford University Press 1989)

Waddell, D. 'Charles Davenant (1656–1714) – a Biographical Sketch', XI *The Economic History Review* (1955), 279–88

Wagner, Andreas. 'Francisco de Vitoria and Alberico Gentili on the Legal Character of the Global Commonwealth', 31 *Oxford Journal of Legal Studies* (2011), 565–82

Wagner, Donald O. 'Coke and the Rise of Economic Liberalism', VI *The Economic History Review* (1953), 30–44

Wagner, Peter. *A History and Theory of the Social Sciences* (London, Sage 2001)

Wakefield, Andre. *The Disordered Police State. German Cameralism As Science and Practice* (The University of Chicago Press 2009)

Waley, Arthur. *The Opium War Through Chinese Eyes* (London, Routledge 2005 [1958])

Walter, Ryan. 'Governmentality Accounts of the Economy. A Liberal Bias?', 37 *Economy and Society* (2008), 94–114

Ward, Robert. *An Enquiry into the Foundation and History of the Law of Nations in Europe from the Time of the Greeks and Romans to the Age of Grotius*, 2 vols (London, Butterworth 1795)

*Treatise of the Relative Rights and Duties of Belligerent and Neutral Powers in Maritime Affairs* (London, Butterworth 1801)

Warren, Christopher. 'Gentili, the Poets and the Laws of War', in Benedict Kingsbury & Benjamin Straumann (eds), *The Roman Foundations of the Law of Nations. Alberico Gentili and the Justice of Empire* (Oxford University Press 2010), 146–62

*Literature and the Law of Nations 1580–1650* (Oxford University Press 2015)

Washbrook, D. A. 'India, 1818–1860. The Two Faces of Colonialism', in Andrew Porter (ed.), *The Oxford History of the British Empire*, vol. III: *The Nineteenth Century* (Oxford University Press 1999), 395–421

Washburne, George Adrian. *Imperial Control of the Administration of Justice in the Thirteen American Colonies, 1684–1776* (New York, Columbia University 1923)

Waszinck, Jan. 'Lipsius and Grotius. Tacitism', 39 *History of European Ideas* (2013), 151–68

Watson, Alan. *Slave Law in the Americas* (University of Georgia Press 1989)

Watt, J. A. 'Introduction', in John of Paris, *On Royal and Papal Power* (Columbia University Press 1974 [c. 1302]), 9–63

'Spiritual and Temporal Power', in J. H. Burns (ed.), *The Cambridge History of Medieval Political Thought* (Cambridge University Press 1988), 367–423

*The Theory of Papal Monarchy in the Thirteenth Century. The Contribution of the Canonists* (London, Burns & Oates 1965)

Weaver, John C. 'Concepts of Economic Improvement and the Social Construction of Property Rights. Highlights from the English-Speaking World', in John McLaren, A. R. Buck & Nancy E. Wright (eds), *Despotic Dominion. Property Rights in Settler Societies* (University of British Columbia Press 2005), 79–102

Weber, Hermann. 'Dieu, le roi et la Chrétieneté. Aspects de la politique du cardinal Richelieu', 13 *Francia* (1985), 233–46

Webster, Anthony. *The Twilight of the East India Company. The Evolution of Anglo-Asian Commerce and Politics, 1790–1860* (Woodbridge, Boydell Press 2009)

Weigand, Rudolf. *Die Naturrechtslehre der Legisten und Dekretisten von Irnerius bis Accursius und von Gratian bis Johannes Teutonicus* (München, Münchener Theologische Studien 1967)

Welwod, William. 'Of the Community and Propriety of the Seas', in Hugo Grotius, *The Free Sea* (David Armitage ed., Indianapolis, Liberty Fund 2004), 63–74

Welzel, Hans. *Naturrecht und materiale Gerechigkeit* (Göttingen, Vandenhoeck & Ruprecht 1990)

Westerman, Pauline. *The Disintegration of Natural Law Theory. Aquinas to Finnis* (Leiden, Brill 1998)

Whatmore, Richard. 'Vattel, Britain and Peace in Europe', 31 *Grotiana* (2010), 85–107

Wheaton, Henry. *Histoire des progrès du droit des gens en Europe* (Leipzig, Brockhaus 1842)

Wheeler, John. *A Treatise of Commerce* (London, Harison 1601)

Whelan, F. G. 'Vattel's Doctrine of the State', 9 *History of Political Thought* (1988), 59–90

Whitman, James Q. 'The Moral Menace of Roman Law and the Making of Commerce. Some Dutch Evidence', *Yale Law School Legal Scholarship Repository* (1996), 1841–89

*The Legacy of Roman Law in the German Romantic Era. Historical Visions and Legal Change* (Princeton University Press 2014)

*The Verdict of Battle. The Law of Victory and the Making of Modern War* (Harvard University Press 2014)

Widow, Antonio. 'Economic Teachings of Spanish Scholastics', in Kevin White (ed.), *Hispanic Philosophy in the Age of Discovery* (Catholic University of America Press 1997), 130–44

Wieacker, Franz. *History of Private Law in Europe* (T Weir transl., Oxford University Press 1996 [1952/67])

Wieruszowski, Helene. *Vom Imperium zum nationalen Königtum* (München, Oldenbourg 1933)

Wijffels, Alain. 'Alberico Gentili e il rinnovamento del diritto pubblico nella tradizione dello *ius commune*', in *Alberico Gentili. Atti dei convegni nel quarto centenario della morte*, vol. II (Milan, Giuffrè 2010), 519–56

'Antiqui et Recentiores. Alberico Gentili – Beyond Mos Italicus and Legal Humanism', in Paul J. du Plessis & John W. Cairns (eds), *Reassessing Legal Humanism and Its Claims*. Petere Fontes? (Edinburgh University Press 2017), 11–40

'Une disputation d'Alberico Gentili sur le droit du souverain de disposer de son royaume et des biens de ses sujets (1587)', in Jacques Krynen & Michael Stolleis (eds), *Science politique et droit public dans les facultés de droit européennes (XIIIe–XVIIIe siècle)* (Frankfurt, Klostermann 2008), 469–84

Wilbur, Margaret Eyer. *The East India Company and the British Empire in the Far East* (New York, Russell & Russell 1945)

Wildman, Richard. *Institutes of International Law*, 2 vols (London, Benning 1849)

Wilks, Michael. *The Problem of Sovereignty in the Middle Ages* (Cambridge University Press 1963)

Williams, Eric. 'The Golden Age of the Slave System for Britain', 25 *The Journal of Negro History* (1940), 60–106

Williams Jr., Robert A. *The American Indian in Western Legal Thought. The Discourses of Conquest* (Oxford University Press 1990)

Williams, William Peere. *Reports of Cases Argued and Determined in the High Court of Chancery* (3 vols, Dublin, Moore 1790)

Williamson, James A. *The Caribbee Islands under the Proprietary Patents* (Oxford University Press 1926)

Willoweit, Dietmar. 'Hermann Conring', in Michael Stolleis (ed.), *Staatsdenker in der frühen Neuzeit* (Munich, Beck 1995), 129–47

Wilson, Charles. *England's Apprenticeship 1603–1763* (London, Longman 1965)

Wilson, Jon E. *The Domination of Strangers. Modern Governance in Eastern India, 1780–1835* (New York, Palgrave 2008)

Wilson, Peter H. 'Prussia's Relations with the Holy Roman Empire 1740–1786', 51 *The Historical Journal* (2008), 337–71

*The Holy Roman Empire 1495–1806* (2nd edn, London, Palgrave 2011)

Wincek, Henry. *An Imperfect God. George Washington, His Slaves, and the Creation of America* (Baltimore, Farrar, Straus & Giroux 2003)

Winch, Donald. *Riches and Poverty. An Intellectual History of Political Economy in Britain, 1750–1834* (Cambridge University Press 1996)

Winters, Peter Jochen. 'Johannes Althusius', in Michael Stolleis (ed.), *Staatsdenker in der frühen Neuzeit* (Munich, Beck 1995), 29–50

Winthrop, John et al. 'Reasons for the Plantation in New England', c. 1628 (The Winthrop Society), available at winthropsociety.com/doc_reasons .php

Wippel, John F. 'Metaphysics', in Norman Kretzmann & Eleonore Stump (eds), *The Cambridge Companion to Aquinas* (Cambridge University Press 1993), 85–127

Wiseman, Sir Robert. *The Law of Laws, or the Excellency of the Civil Law above all other Humane Laws Whatsoever* (London, Royston 1686)

Witte Jr., John. 'Canon Law in Lutheran Germany. A Surprising Case of Legal Transplantation', in Michael Hoeflitch (ed.), *Lex et Romanitas. Essays for Alan Watson* (University of California, The Robbins Collection 2000), 181–224

*Law and Protestantism. The Legal Teachings of the Lutheran Reformation* (Cambridge University Press 2002)

Wokler, Robert. 'Ideology and the Origins of Social Science', in Mark Goldie & Robert Wokler (eds), *The Cambridge History of Eighteenth-Century Political Thought* (Cambridge University Press 2006), 699–709

'Saint-Simon as the Passage from Political to Social Science', in Anthony Pagden (ed.), *The Languages of Political Theory in Early-Modern Europe* (Cambridge University Press 1987), 325–38

Wolff, Christian. *Grundsätze der Natur- und Völkerrechts* (Halle, Renger 1769)

*Jus gentium methodo scientifica pertractatum* (J. H. Drake trans., Oxford, Clarendon 1934)

*Vernünfftige Gedancken von den gesellschaftlichen Leben der Menschen und in sonderheit dem gemeinen Wesen* (6th edn, Frankfurt 1747 [1721])

Wollgast, Siegfried 'Die deutsche Frühaufklärung und Samuel Pufendorf', in Fiammetta Palladini & Gerald Hartung (eds), *Samuel Pufendorf und die europäische Frühaufklärung* (Berlin, Akademie 1996), 40–60

Wood, Alfred C. *A History of the Levant Company* (London, Cass 1964)

Wood, Diane. *Medieval Economic Thought* (Cambridge University Press 2002)

Wood, Ellen Meiksins. *Citizens to Lords. A Social History of Western Political Thought from Antiquity to the Middle Ages* (London, Verso 2008)

*Liberty and Property. A Social History of Western Political Thought from Renaissance to Enlightenment* (London, Verso 2012)

Wood, Neal. *Foundations of Political Economy. Some Early Tudor Views on State and Society* (The University of Chicago Press 1994)

*The Politics of Locke's Philosophy* (University of California Press 1983)

Woolf, Cecil N. Sidney. *Bartolus of Sassoferrato. His Position in the History of Medieval Political Thought* (Cambridge University Press 1913)

Worden, Blair. *The Sound of Virtue. Philip Sidney's Arcadia and Elizabethan Politics* (Yale University Press 1996)

Wyatt, Michael. *The Italian Encounter with Tudor England. A Cultural Politics of Translation* (Cambridge University Press 2009)

Xifaras, Mikhail. *La propriété. Etude de philosophie de droit* (Presses Universitaires de France 2004)

Yirush, Craig. *Settlers, Liberty and Empire. The Roots of Early American Political Theory, 1675–1775* (Cambridge University Press 2011)

Zagorin, Perez. *Ways of Lying. Dissimulation, Persecution, and Conformity in Early Modern Europe* (Harvard University Press 1990)

Zahedieh, Nuala. 'Economy', in David Armitage & Michael Braddick (eds), *The British Atlantic World 1500–1800* (London, Palgrave 2002), 51–68

Zarka, Yves Charles. 'Raison d'État, maximes d'État et coups d'État chez Gabriel Naudé', in Yves Charles Zarka, *Raison et déraison d'État. Théoriciens et théories de la raison d'état aux XVIe et XVIIe siècles* (Presses Universitaires de France 1994), 101-20

*Philosophie et politique à l'âge classique* (Presses Universitaires de France 1998)

Zavala, Silvio. 'La encomienda indiana', 2 *El trimestre económico* (1935), 423–51

Zieger, Gottfried 'Die erste hundert Jahren Völkerrecht an der Georg-August-Universität Göttingen. Vom ius naturae et gentium zum positiven Völkerrecht', in Fritz Loos (ed.), *Rechtswissenschaft in Göttingen. Göttinger Juristen aus 250 Jahren* (Göttingen, Vandenhoeck & Ruprecht 1987), 32–74

Ziegler, Karl-Heinz. 'Die Bedeutung des Westfälischen Friedens für das europäische Völkerrecht', in Karl-Heinz Ziegler, *Fata Iuris Gentium. Kleine Schriften zur Geschichte des europäischen Völkerrechts* (Baden-Baden, Nomos 2008), 129–51

Zouche, Richard. *An Exposition of Fecial Law and Procedure or of Law between Nations and Questions Concerning the Same* (translation of *Juris et judicii fecialis sive, iuris inter gentes et questionum de eodem explixation*, by J. L. Brierly, Washington 1911 [1659])

*The Jurisdiction of the Admiralty in England Asserted* (London, Basset 1686)

# Index